# DOMINIC SANDBROOK

# Who Dares Wins

*Britain, 1979–1982*

PENGUIN BOOKS

PENGUIN BOOKS

UK | USA | Canada | Ireland | Australia
India | New Zealand | South Africa

Penguin Books is part of the Penguin Random House group of companies
whose addresses can be found at global.penguinrandomhouse.com.

First published by Allen Lane 2019
Published in Penguin Books 2020

001

Copyright © Dominic Sandbrook, 2019

The moral rights of the author has been asserted

Set in 8.87/11.75 pt Sabon LT Std
Typeset by Jouve (UK), Milton Keynes
Printed and bound in Great Britain by Clays Ltd, Elcograf S.p.A.

A CIP catalogue record for this book is available from the British Library

ISBN: 978–0–141–97528–3

www.greenpenguin.co.uk

*To my father, Rhys Sandbrook,*
*and to Catherine and Arthur, with love.*

'The fifth volume of Dominic Sandbrook's superb history of
Britain . . . Like its predecessors, *Who Dares Wins* is a rich mixture of
political narrative and social reportage. It is scholarly, accessible, well
written, witty and incisive. It fizzes with character and anecdote. And it
presents an unrivalled portrait of the age of Austin Metros, Sinclair
home computers, Lymeswold cheese, McDonald's, Greenham Common
anti-nuclear demonstrators, IRA hunger strikers, Sloane Rangers and
sporting heroes such as Daley Thompson, Sebastian Coe, Steve Davis
and Ian Botham' Piers Brendon, *Sunday Times*

'An excellent account of an action-packed three
years . . . Magisterial . . . If anyone wants to know what has been
happening to Britain since the 1950s, it is difficult to imagine a
more informative, or better-humoured guide . . . a Thucydidean
coolness, balance and wisdom that is superb . . . absolutely
breathtaking' A. N. Wilson, *The Times*

'This is vividly panoramic history, ranging from high affairs of
state to the tiniest textural details of everyday life: the 'Falklands
factor' and the F-plan diet, monetary targets and the 'mania
for home improvement', steel strikes and Sloane Rangers . . . His
sources are joyously eclectic . . . We wait impatiently for the
next course of this richly satisfying historical
feast' Francis Wheen, *Literary Review*

'Painstaking, enjoyable, even-handed . . . you may feel a nice
balance of piquancy and poignancy in having those years
brought to life by the historian's magic wand. ranging over
the sights, sounds and smells of an era that looks almost
quaint 40 years on' Anthony Quinn, *Observer*

'Dominic Sandbrook's great chronicle of Britain locates
the big political narrative always in a wider social context than
just by-election swings and Westminster roundabouts . . . It all
comes flooding back' Charles Moore, *Spectator*

'Masterful, mammoth ... rich and rewarding ... One of the book's great strengths is that although we know how the story will end we are still kept in suspense – not because of doubts over the outcome, but because Sandbrook situates the reader firmly back in those crucial years' John McTernan, *Financial Times*

Dominic Sandbrook's exemplary series on post-war Britain, its scope more demotic than Hennessy's, continues with *Who Dares Wins: Britain 1979–82*. Breathtakingly broad and beautifully written, it covers the triumph of the Conservatives under Mrs Thatcher in 1979, the teetering of the economy after her drastic restructuring of it, and the paving of her path to a second term by victory in the Falklands' *Daily Telegraph*, Books of the Year

'More than 800 pages to cover three years may seem disproportionate, but Sandbrook has packed them with so much enjoyable detail and so many revealing quotes and anecdotes that it's hard to argue the book is too long. Sandbrook covers everything ... the good, the bad and the ugly from three colourful, controversial years in a richly entertaining history' Nick Rennison, *Daily Mail*, Books of the Year

'Margaret Thatcher, the Falklands War, Northern Ireland, civil unrest, Duran Duran, snooker and a truly revolutionary act: Marks & Spencer's invention of the pre-packaged sandwich' *Mail on Sunday*, Books of the Year

ABOUT THE AUTHOR

DOMINIC SANDBROOK is one of Britain's best-known historians. Born in Shropshire in 1974 and educated at Oxford, St Andrews and Cambridge, he taught at the University of Sheffield before becoming a full-time writer. He is the author of seven other books, most notably his bestselling histories of Britain since the 1950s. He has presented numerous BBC radio and television documentaries, among them histories of science fiction, the Post Office and the German car industry, as well as his widely acclaimed series on Britain in the 1970s and 1980s. He writes regularly for the *Daily Mail* and *Sunday Times* and is a visiting professor at King's College London. A former Gold Run-winning contestant on the cult quiz show *Blockbusters*, he lives in Oxfordshire.

*In reality, there are many little Circumstances too often omitted by injudicious Historians, from which Events of the utmost Importance arise. The World may indeed be considered as a vast Machine, in which the great Wheels are originally set in Motion by those which are very minute, and almost imperceptible to any but the strongest Eyes.*

Henry Fielding, *The History of Tom Jones,*
*A Foundling* (1749)

*The tales and descriptions of that time without exception speak only of the self-sacrifice, patriotic devotion, despair, grief, and the heroism of the Russians. But it was not really so . . .*

*Most of the people at that time paid no attention to the general progress of events but were guided only by their private interests, and they were the very people whose activities at that period were most useful.*

Leo Tolstoy, *War and Peace* (1869), trans.
Louise and Aylmer Maude

*Nobody dances like the British. They deserved the Falklands!*
Darius Jedbergh (Joe Don Baker) in
*Edge of Darkness* (1985)

# Contents

PART FOUR
The British Are Back!

# List of Illustrations

Every effort has been made to contact all copyright holders. The publishers will be pleased to amend in future editions any errors or omissions brought to their attention.

## Cartoons

## Plates

# Preface: We're Still a Super Power

*I don't think I've had a chance to put pen to paper since the SAS dust-up at Prince's Gate. Best thing since the Coronation. High time a few wogs bit the dust and thank God there was a British finger on the trigger.*

'Denis Thatcher', in Richard Ingrams and John Wells, *The Other Half: Further Letters of Denis Thatcher* (1981)

It was just before 7.30 on the evening of Monday 5 May 1980, and across the United Kingdom millions of people were enjoying their favourite hobby: watching television. On BBC1 John Wayne was fighting off outlaws in the American West. On ITV *Coronation Street*'s Brian Tilsey was trying to raise £1,000 for a deposit on a new house. And on BBC2, with Cliff Thorburn and Alex Higgins neck-and-neck and only a few frames to go, the Embassy World Snooker Championship was approaching a nail-biting conclusion.

As the camera tracked across the baize, as Higgins mopped his brow and Thorburn inched closer to glory, the tension was almost intolerable – and then, quite suddenly, the picture was gone. Instead, a BBC announcer was explaining that they were going live to South Kensington, where the elite Special Air Service had just launched an operation to storm the Iranian Embassy. A few moments later, as *Coronation Street*'s credits were beginning to roll, ITV followed suit. The picture cut to a long terrace of tall white stucco houses. A masked black figure peered out from behind a first-floor balcony. There was a bang; then another bang; then gunshots; then screams. More masked figures emerged. Then came the explosion, a colossal burst of smoke ripping out a window at the front of the building. More shots; a woman's screams; sirens, alarms and barking dogs; then bang after bang after bang, hammering through the smoke. There were small fires now at the front of the building. A man clambered out of a window, scrambled across a balcony and disappeared into the building next door. Inside, unseen by the cameras, the SAS were going about their deadly work. And all the time, millions at home were staring at their screens, gripped by one of the most extraordinary spectacles in television history.

The high drama of the Iranian Embassy siege had begun five days earlier. Just before midday on Wednesday 30 April, six armed Iranian Arabs, demanding autonomy for the province of Khuzestan, had burst into the embassy in Prince's Gate. Within minutes, they had taken twenty-six people hostage, most of them Iranian staff, but also a handful of visitors, a police constable, two BBC crewmen and the building manager. More police arrived within moments, but it was too late. By the afternoon the pattern was set. Inside, the terrified hostages huddled together, surrounded by six men with grenades and sub-machine guns. Outside, in Prince's Gate, the police closed off the area opposite the embassy, while just 200 yards away reporters, cameramen and curious onlookers jostled for position. In Downing Street, ministers and officials pored over their options. And by the small hours of the following morning, two SAS teams had moved into the buildings either side of the embassy. They had been practising for this moment for years. As one told the BBC's Peter Taylor, 'we didn't want them to surrender. We wanted them to stay there so we could go in and hit them. That was what we lived for and trained for . . . We wanted to go in there and do the job.'[1]

For the last decade, the United Kingdom had lived in the shadow of terrorism. In Northern Ireland, almost every day had seen some new outrage: a young man shot in a pub, a shopping street devastated by a car bomb, a warning that came too late, a family torn apart by tragedy. But in Britain, too, these had been terrible years, with bombs going off at Aldershot Barracks, the Old Bailey, pubs in Birmingham and Guildford, a coach on the M62 and the Houses of Parliament. In the last year alone, the war hero and Conservative MP Airey Neave had been killed by a car bomb at the Palace of Westminster; the last Viceroy of India, Louis Mountbatten, had been killed by a bomb while fishing in Ireland; and eighteen British soldiers had been killed in an ambush at Warrenpoint, County Down. Like her predecessors, the new Prime Minister insisted that the terrorists would never prevail. 'The people of the United Kingdom', Margaret Thatcher had said after Warrenpoint, 'will wage the war against terrorism with relentless determination until it is won.' Yet still the killing went on. So what happened at Prince's Gate was hardly a shock; it was just more of the same.[2]

For the next four days, as the world's media looked on, the tension steadily rose. On Friday afternoon, Mrs Thatcher and her Home Secretary, Willie Whitelaw, discussed the consequences of a 'planned shoot-out'. If the SAS struck now, they reckoned 'they had a 60% chance of getting the hostages out alive'. But 'even with the best planning and the best intelligence', Whitelaw told his boss, 'there was bound to be a risk that an assault would end with casualties'.[3]

Another day passed. Inside the embassy, the hostages waited, ever more exhausted, ever more frightened, their captors increasingly angry at the lack of progress. Just before midnight, Whitelaw rang Mrs Thatcher. Everything was 'organised and ready', he said, and 'we are now in a much better position for obvious reasons than we were before'. 'Willie, I think that's absolutely first-class,' Mrs Thatcher said. 'I'm sorry you're all having to be there over the weekend.'[4]

Sunday went by, another long, anxious day. It was a Bank Holiday weekend, but the weather was unseasonably cool and the roads were quiet; most people seemed to be watching television. Although the gunmen had now released five hostages, they showed no sign of surrendering. Monday came, and the kidnappers' patience ran out. At one that afternoon, their leader told the police that unless they let him speak to a sympathetic diplomat within the next forty-five minutes, he would start killing the hostages. Exactly forty-five minutes later, the gunmen shot the Iranian press attaché, later throwing his body out of the front door.

At that moment, Whitelaw was sitting down to lunch at his official country residence, Dorneywood, in Buckinghamshire. When he heard there had been shots at the embassy, he left immediately for London. At about 6.30 the gunmen's leader announced that he would shoot one hostage every half-hour. More shots rang out; in fact, they were just for show, but there was no way the police could know that. Shortly after seven Whitelaw told the SAS to go in. At exactly 7.23 the first team broke through the roof and the back of the building, while moments later the second team blasted through a window at the front. With the embassy wreathed in smoke and millions transfixed to their televisions, Operation Nimrod took just seventeen minutes. By the time it was over, all but one of the remaining hostages were out, five of the six gunmen were lying dead and the SAS had seized the imagination of the world.[5]

Operation Nimrod came a year and a day after Margaret Thatcher had become Britain's first woman Prime Minister. From her perspective, the timing was perfect. The economic picture was darkening by the hour, with inflation heading towards 22 per cent and unemployment racing towards 2 million. But now, at last, the lion had roused himself from his slumbers. The fact that the world had been watching made success all the sweeter. Among the telegrams flooding into Downing Street, one came from the former American President Richard Nixon, who told Mrs Thatcher that 'the superb demonstration of British guts and British efficiency by your commando operation is an inspiring example to free people throughout the world'. Another came from the Commonwealth Secretary General, Sir Sonny Ramphal, who thought Britain had 'won the admiration of the international community', while the premier of Ontario told her that 'the free world owes Britain a debt of gratitude for demonstrating such brave resolve'. Even the *New York Times*, which loved to portray post-imperial Britain as an object lesson in shabbiness and failure, changed its tune. 'Americans' first reaction to the remarkable hostage rescue in London is admiration,' an editorial admitted. 'The audacity and precision of the Special Air Service's commandos reaffirms the intrepid British image of a Winston Churchill, a Francis Chichester, or even James Bond. "Who Dares Wins" is the commandos' motto; they dared, and they saved real lives in 14 electric minutes.'[6]

At home, the operation was greeted as a modern-day equivalent of the relief of Mafeking. The headlines in the *Daily Express* – 'VICTORY!', 'The Decision and the Triumph', 'So Proud to Be British', 'Our Country at Its Best' – captured the mood. To most papers, the SAS were heroes, real-life versions of James Bond who had restored the nation's pride in the eyes of the world. For Jean Rook, the 'First Lady of Fleet Street', they had proved that the British lion could still roar like no other:

> Fearful and bloody pity it is that we had to go through hell-smoke and gunfire to prove it, at least we know that Britain is still a great nation – and so does the rest of the world.
>
> They sniped that we were a second class power, going bust – until we blasted open the Iranian Embassy siege, saving 19 lives (16 of them not our own), and showing America, and open-eyed millions watching the show-down live on TV, how it should be done.
>
> In 45 minutes flat we proved to a gaping world that we're still a Super Power – and a super people . . .
>
> It was the British at our best . . . our finest three-quarters of an hour in years.
>
> All our greatness was there, and all the old discipline . . . We produced the fastest and best in the SAS – that shadowy, space-age, masked and medal-less crack force of unknown warriors. Their motto: 'Who Dares, Wins.'

And this, she said proudly, was 'not Dunkirk or the Battle of Britain'. It was Britain here and now, in 1980. 'This wasn't the way we were. It's the way we are.'[7]

Not everybody rejoiced at the Battle of Prince's Gate. In *The Times*, Fred Emery thought the celebrations 'made it seem as if we had won a war' and betrayed a neurotic 'lack of self-confidence'. And in the

*Guardian*, the newsletter of liberal Britain, some readers were beside themselves with horror. What had happened in London, wrote Rosemary Sales, was a chilling reminder of 'the SAS's activities in Ireland', which she considered so heinous that she did not need to describe them. From the University of Aston, Michael Townson advised the 'thinking public' to reject Mrs Thatcher's 'jingoistic self-congratulation', as well as the bloodthirsty methods of the SAS. Another academic, F. M. Chambers of Keele, was similarly appalled by the 'jingoistic congratulations of politicians and the media on the ability of the British to shoot (and kill) terrorists'.

But even many *Guardian* readers thought these complaints outrageous. One dismissed the academics as 'tendentious and gratuitous'; another wondered whether Dr Townson would have preferred 'cold-blooded death . . . to rescue by the SAS and their methods'. The controversy even drew a letter from a Mr Duckett, who had once served in the SAS. It was, he wrote sadly, only 'to be expected that in our typically British fashion after any good piece of news . . . there has to be the knockers who try to denigrate any successful operation'. It was not surprising, he thought, that both letters came from academics. Britain's universities had 'more than their fair share of political activists who are prepared to knock law and order at every opportunity and to tear down a democratic system without any suitable alternative'.[8]

The Prime Minister never wavered in her admiration for the SAS. Only hours after the siege had ended, she and her husband Denis had visited their Regent's Park barracks. As one of her officials recalled, 'the air was thick with testosterone', the men kicking back with bottles of beer to celebrate a job well done. According to one account, Denis jokingly complained: 'You let one of the bastards live.' But the SAS did not mind. Together they watched the coverage on the evening news, the men giving Mrs Thatcher a raucous running commentary. At one point, one of them remarked: 'We never thought you'd let us do it,' a tribute she never forgot. 'Wherever I went in the next few days,' she wrote in her memoirs, 'I sensed a great wave of pride at the outcome.' Afterwards, their brigadier rang Number 10 to let Mrs Thatcher know that the regiment had been 'thrilled to bits' by her visit. 'Her smile', one soldier said afterwards, 'would have lightened up the darkest room.'[9]

From that moment, the romance between Mrs Thatcher and the SAS was sealed. For all her patriotic rhetoric, she had come to power as an earnest economic reformer, promising to sort out the nation's household budget. In the spring of 1980, few people imagined she would ever take Britain into battle. But now, at a time when everything seemed to be going wrong, she had enjoyed her first taste of a promising new role: the warrior queen, the British St Joan, Britannia incarnate. Looking back, one of her officials recalled that in the days after the operation, she had become 'the nearest thing to Queen Elizabeth at Tilbury'. And in December, with the economy deep in recession, she found time to visit the SAS regimental headquarters in Herefordshire. They were, she declared, 'a marvellous example of leadership, purpose and resolve'.[10]

Even after another dramatic military operation had transformed her worldwide image and ensured her place in history, Mrs Thatcher maintained a soft spot for the SAS. In January 1983 she accepted an invitation to dine with the regiment at the Royal Hospital, Chelsea, the guests including almost all the majors and captains who had served in the Falklands. Afterwards, she received a gushing letter of thanks from Colonel David Stirling, who had founded the SAS during the Second World War. In the mid-1970s Stirling had returned to the headlines as the founder of GB75, a group of 'apprehensive patriots' who would 'intervene' in the event of a general strike. He was still a patriot, but he was no longer apprehensive. Like his fellow SAS veterans, he told Mrs Thatcher, he had been 'exhilarated' by the opportunity 'to pay tribute to your leadership'.[11]

Many years earlier, Stirling had coined the regiment's motto, 'Who Dares Wins'. Though hardly afraid of patriotic rhetoric, Mrs Thatcher never used it. Perhaps she thought it too unsubtle. But amid a flood of cash-in books, the phrase began to seep into popular culture. In November 1980 the Confederation of British Industry's director general, Sir Terence Beckett, told business leaders that in making their case to the government, they should remember 'the SAS rescue at the Iranian Embassy. Their motto, as you know, is "Who Dares, Wins". They knew exactly what they had to do, and with a practised and punctilious professionalism, they did it.' In the sitcom *Only Fools and Horses*, which began in September 1981, the would-be entrepreneur Derek Trotter is always telling his brother: 'Remember, Rodney: he who dares, wins!' And a year later, *The Times*'s political correspondent David Watt suggested that Mrs Thatcher might already be 'suffering from a form of hubris that is the commonest disease of successful politicians . . . "Who dares, wins", you may say; and up to a point that is true. But Nemesis awaits the politician who confuses good fortune with good management and good management with the righteousness of his or her cause.'[12]

One man who took the SAS's motto seriously was the film producer Euan Lloyd. Best known for *The Wild Geese* (1978), which starred Richard Burton, Roger Moore and Richard Harris as mercenaries in southern Africa, Lloyd was a man of firmly conservative opinions. 'I watched in awe at what these SAS men did and truly I felt very proud,' he said later. On the evening of the operation, he called his lawyer in New York and told him to register the title *Who Dares Wins* with the Motion Picture Association of America. Then he commissioned *The Prisoner*'s scriptwriter George Markstein to write a story and hired Lewis Collins to play the lead. He could hardly have made a more apt choice. Not only was Collins already playing an ex-SAS hard man in ITV's *The Professionals* (1977–83), but he was fascinated by the armed forces. Having joined the Parachute Regiment as a reservist in 1979, he applied to join the SAS after the film came out, passed the brutally demanding selection tests and was only rejected because his fame made him a security risk.[13]

The plot of *Who Dares Wins* is obviously modelled on the Iranian Embassy siege, but this time the terrorists are the hard left, who are using the nuclear disarmament movement as a Trojan horse. When they seize the American Embassy, their chief demand is that the Americans detonate a nuclear bomb in Scotland, so as to discredit the nuclear deterrent and pave the way for unilateral disarmament. This storyline did not go down well with the Campaign for Nuclear Disarmament. At the premiere in London in August 1982, demonstrators stood in pouring rain for three hours to make a silent protest in Leicester Square. And in a revealing footnote, the veteran actor Kenneth Griffith, who plays the pacifist Bishop of Camden ('Jesus Christ was a militant radical!'), paid the price for taking the producers' shilling. Having won great acclaim for his iconoclastic historical documentaries, Griffith had been asked to introduce a programme of progressive films at a festival organized by Islington North Labour Party to mark the borough's birth as a self-styled 'socialist republic'. But when the organizers heard that he was in *Who Dares Wins*, they withdrew the invitation. As it happened, the guiding force in the North Islington party, already adopted as its candidate for the next general election, was a young man called Jeremy Corbyn.[14]

Lloyd had imagined *Who Dares Wins* as a riposte to the negativity of British popular culture, symptomatic, he thought, of an age of national decline. But by the time it came out, the mood had changed completely. The Falklands War was over; the flag flew proudly again. Isolated and beleaguered at the time of the Iranian Embassy siege, Mrs Thatcher now dominated the political landscape like no Prime Minister for decades. So instead of standing against the tide, *Who Dares Wins* felt like propaganda for the winning side, less a bracing restatement of unfashionable values than a reheated helping of tabloid jingoism. In any case, who cared about the embassy siege now, when the Falklands heroes were splashed all over the papers? And to make matters worse, the reviews were awful. *The*

*Times* considered it 'so antiquated in technique that it might have escaped from a cobwebbed Pinewood vault', and thought one scene so boring it deserved the 'reverse of an Oscar'. It was, lamented the *Guardian*, a 'truly dreadful' film.[15]

Yet some people clearly liked it, since *Who Dares Wins* was the tenth most popular film of the year. And at least one Hollywood veteran adored it. According to the *Los Angeles Times*, President Reagan requested a special screening for 'friends and cabinet members', and gave it a 'rave review'. His Secretary of State, Alexander Haig, told the paper that they thought it a 'terribly exciting drama' and a 'realistic portrayal of the world in which we live'. Almost incredibly, the producers had been asked to arrange special screenings for the Los Angeles Police Department, the FBI and the US Army, who were hoping for anti-terrorist tips before the Los Angeles Olympics. Once again, then, the Americans were learning from the mother country. The natural order had been restored; all was right with the world. It was just a shame it was such a terrible film.[16]

This book tells the story of Britain during the most exciting and contro-versial years in our post-war history, from the spring of 1979 to the summer of 1982. It begins with Margaret Thatcher walking into Number 10 as Britain's first woman Prime Minister. It ends with the high drama of the Falklands War, a ten-week conflict that could easily have smashed her premiership into fragments. If it had, then Britain today might be very different. If nothing else, defeat in the Falklands would surely have con-firmed Britain's self-image as a country trapped in an inexorable cycle of post-imperial decline. But the war was, of course, a triumph. The Task Force returned to a carnival of pomp and patriotism. The Union Jacks waved, and after the economic agonies of her first three years, Mrs Thatcher seemed the mistress of all she surveyed. From then on, the national narrative became very different.

In some ways this period looks like the final chapter of a long 1970s. The headlines were dominated by inflation, strikes and unemployment, street violence, football hooliganism and terrorist bombings. Commenta-tors wrung their hands at Britain's wretched economic performance, bemoaned the collapse of the political centre and argued about the nation's relationship with Europe. The Irish republican hunger strikes horrified the world, vast crowds marched against Cruise missiles and tensions between the police and black communities exploded into shocking vio-lence. The two major parties seemed fatally divided, manufacturing industry was lurching towards oblivion and an entire generation of school-leavers seemed doomed to life on the scrapheap.

But the early 1980s were not quite like the 1970s. When television documentaries recreate the era, bright young things with elaborate eye make-up always seem to be listening to Ultravox's 'Vienna' while Brixton smoulders in the distance. And although this is obviously a caricature, this short period did have an intense flavour of its own. Cultural moods are tricky to pin down, but by the turn of the decade there was an indefinable vibrancy, a sense of colour and confidence, that had not quite been there in the mid-1970s. These were the years of Joy Division, the Specials and Spandau Ballet, of *Juliet Bravo*, *Minder* and *To the Manor Born*. They were the years of *Brideshead Revisited* and *Chariots of Fire*, Salman Rushdie's *Midnight's Children* and Jeffrey Archer's *Kane and Abel*, the Austin Metro, *Not the Nine O'Clock News* and the New Romantics. In Moscow, Steve Ovett and Sebastian Coe battled for gold. At the Crucible, Steve Davis became a symbol of Thatcherite efficiency. At Headingley, Ian Botham became the greatest patriotic icon of the age. And for perhaps the first time since the early 1960s there was a palpable sense of the future rushing to meet the present, embodied in everything from Gary Numan's synthesizers and Clive Sinclair's computers to the microwave ovens and video recorders of the middle classes. In many parts of the country, the Victorian Britain of factories, pubs and chapels was collapsing amid dreadful hardship. But in shiny new shopping centres and suburban living rooms, the next century was at hand.

Even four decades later, the story of these years is bitterly contested. There is no consensus about the 1980s, and there never will be. No single narrative can do justice to the complexity of the national experience: the steelworker who lost his job, the computer enthusiast who set up his own business, the couple who bought their council house – and even these examples, while real enough, teeter on the brink of caricature. And because these years were so divisive, not even the most judicious account can capture every nuance. So it is probably worth saying at the outset that this is absolutely not a partisan book. I have no desire to waste the reader's time, or indeed my own, by picking sides. And though there is no such thing as a truly objective history, I set out from the start to get the facts right, to dig beneath some of the myths and, above all, to be fair.

My previous books about post-war Britain – *Never Had It So Good*, *White Heat*, *State of Emergency* and *Seasons in the Sun* – covered a period when I was not yet born or too young to remember anything. But I was 4½ when Margaret Thatcher became Prime Minister and almost 8 by the time of the Falklands. I cannot honestly say, though, that the great events of the day made any impression. My memories are entirely dominated by school and family, toys, books and films. I played a lot of *Space Invaders*, was obsessed by *Star Wars* and watched what now seems an enormous amount of television. But I found *Doctor Who* much too frightening, at least until Peter Davison took over, and was not allowed to watch *Grange Hill*. I went to McDonald's for the first time for my friend's birthday party, and regarded it as the finest restaurant in the world. I went on my first foreign holiday, staying in a concrete monolith on Malta, which I barely remember at all. I conducted a long campaign to blackmail my parents into buying a home computer on the entirely fraudulent basis that I would use it for 'education'. But although I had probably heard Tony Benn, Sir Geoffrey Howe and General Galtieri mentioned on television, I knew little about them and cared even less. I had heard of Mrs Thatcher, of course. But I never gave her the slightest thought.

In the popular imagination, the first woman Prime Minister dominates the story of the 1980s. Whatever divides her admirers from her critics, both agree that she was uniquely transformative. With one wave of her magic nation-saving wand, a new shopping centre materializes in Peterborough. At one touch of her special working-class-destroying button, a factory explodes in South Wales. She destroys Britain; she saves it. But were the changes that swept over Britain during the 1980s really attributable to just one woman? Was she really as transformative as both her enthusiasts and her detractors claim?

Even before Mrs Thatcher came into office, Britain was becoming a much more private, domestic, individualistic society. Full employment was dead. The heyday of heavy industry had peaked; the transition to services was underway. The old world of working-class masculinity was breaking up; more women were working than ever before. Globalization was already altering people's daily lives and working habits. Mines and factories were already closing; the City was already opening its doors to the world. In Cambridge, Sinclair's engineers were already working on Britain's first mass-market computer; in Liverpool, thousands of school-leavers were already contemplating life on the dole. These were aspects of a wider global story, not an exclusively British one; a story driven, however unconsciously, by the choices of millions of people. Similar things were happening all over the world, in American car factories, French coal mines, German shopping centres and Italian boardrooms. Life would certainly have been different if Labour's Michael Foot had been Prime Minister. But not, perhaps, as different as people think.

As a person, Mrs Thatcher remains a uniquely divisive figure: the woman who rescued Britain for some, the woman who broke it for others. Both of these views are perfectly understandable, though both are exaggerated. No fair-minded observer can deny that she could be strident, ungenerous, blinkered and immensely annoying. But no fair-minded observer can deny, either, that she showed extraordinary courage, resilience and moral commitment, and there are too many anecdotes about her personal tolerance and kindness for them all to be invented. This book treats her as a historical actor like any other: neither a saint nor a sinner, but a human being, by turns anxious, domineering, frustrating and sympathetic, a professional career woman trying to cope with the colossal changes of the day.

What this book shows is that many of the things people believe about Mrs Thatcher and the early 1980s are just not true. It is not true, for example, that she rigorously followed an economic blueprint. In fact, there was a considerable element of making it up as she went along. It is not true that she deliberately set out to destroy British manufacturing; in fact, she always believed she was saving it. It is not true that the lady was 'not for turning'; in fact, she was far more flexible than either her admirers or her critics pretended. It is not true that she cared only for market values; in fact, she had an intensely romantic sense of Britain's history. It is not true that she was exceptionally anti-European; in fact, she was probably more pro-European than most ordinary voters. It is not true that she cut spending, since spending kept on rising, and it is not true that she turned off the tap to industry, since she kept handing out multi-million-pound subsidies. It is simply not true that she took Britain to war in the Falklands merely to secure her re-election, just as it is not true that she sank the *Belgrano* to destroy any chance of peace negotiations. Finally, it is not true that she only won re-election in 1983 because of the schism in the Labour Party. Even if Labour had remained unhappily united, she would almost certainly have won the next election.

There is more to the story, though, than Westminster politics. By and large, history is driven, not by one or two individuals, but by countless everyday decisions by people who rarely feature in the history books, the anonymous masses about whom Tolstoy famously wrote in *War and Peace*. So *Who Dares Wins* goes into the factories, homes and high streets of Britain in the 1980s. We visit a vegetarian restaurant in Barnstaple, a snooker hall in Romford, a peace rally in Glasgow and a holiday camp in Minehead. In rural Derbyshire, a village school bans its female staff from wearing trousers. In Sussex, a man builds his own nuclear bunker. In Oldham, rioting hooligans reduce Jack Charlton to tears; on Majorca, irate pensioners tell a horrified Polly Toynbee how much they hate the Germans. It is often said that the early 1980s were uniquely conflicted years, which saw the nation divided against itself as never before. But most ordinary people did not see themselves as combatants in an ideological civil war. They were too busy getting on with their lives. When *Private Eye*'s Denis Thatcher comes across the former Labour Prime Minister Harold Wilson in the House of Lords bar and asks what happened in the 1980 Budget, Wilson says that 'he didn't know and didn't give a bugger'. In this respect, yesterday's man spoke for millions.[17]

Finally, why the title?

What was really distinctive about the early 1980s, it seems to me, was not the shock of mass unemployment, the triumph of individualism or even the novelty of a woman Prime Minister. It was something more primal: the rebirth of a patriotic populism that would have seemed very familiar to the eighteenth-century mob or to the readers of Edwardian newspapers. When the *Express* gloried in 'OUR COUNTRY AT ITS BEST', when the *Sun* told Argentina to 'STICK IT UP YOUR JUNTA', when the *Mail* roared 'THE BRITISH ARE BACK!' they were not saying anything that would have shocked or surprised earlier generations. But these were not, by and large, things people had said in the 1960s and 1970s, when the Union Jack was being hauled down across the world and the only chance of a prosperous future seemed to lie within the European Community. There is no doubt that Harold Wilson and his Labour successor Jim Callaghan were deeply patriotic men, often to the point of parochialism. But in their world-weary way, they seemed to embody a kind of national defeatism, a sense that Britain's best days were behind her. Perhaps this is unfair. But when Callaghan told his colleagues that, as he shaved every morning, 'I say to myself that if I were a young man I would emigrate,' he was only half joking.[18]

This was what changed in the first few years of the 1980s. What underpinned everything Mrs Thatcher believed in, the premise for her entire project, was her passionate belief that Britain had been great, was trapped in a spiral of decline and could be great once again. To some of her own colleagues, this seemed a simplistic and reactionary way of looking at the world. But for millions of her fellow Britons it struck a very powerful chord. She never doubted that the people were with her. 'Deep in their instincts,' she told the *Sunday Times* three months after the Iranian Embassy crisis, 'they find what I am saying and doing right, and I know it is, because that is the way I was brought up.'

And although millions never liked her, she was probably right. When the political controversies of the 1980s are forgotten, the role that will define her is surely the Iron Lady, the victor of the Falklands, a patriotic populist who dreamed of standing alongside Churchill, Nelson and Elizabeth I. 'I have always voted Labour,' a Birmingham shop steward said in the autumn of 1982. But 'I am an admirer of Margaret Thatcher as a leader. She impressed me over the Falklands. She said it was ours and we were going to defend it . . . I have never seen my way clear to voting Conservative. It is only what Maggie has done over the last three years that has made me waver.' He was not, of course, alone.[19]

When Mrs Thatcher talked of reviving British greatness, when she paid homage to 'our boys' in the South Atlantic, when she spoke of Britain leading the world into a bright new tomorrow, she was consciously rekindling a patriotic tradition, a faith in Britain's unique past and glorious future, that had seemed close to extinction a few years earlier. Whatever their politics, this was something many people loved to hear. This was why the words 'Who Dares Wins' struck such a chord. This was why people remembered the adverts for the Austin Metro, 'a British car to beat the world'. This was why they cheered the SAS, adored Ian Botham and wept at the return of their Falklands heroes. Not everybody, of course; there were always doubters, dissenters, citizens of the world, just as there had been radicals and pacifists in the Victorian age. But it is only a slight stretch to suggest that, had it not been for the revival of their patriotic self-image, the British might not have remained so doggedly suspicious of the European project. Perhaps, if they had still seen themselves as a nation in decline, reeling from the loss of Empire and the collapse of industry, they would have become more like their neighbours, and would never have thought of breaking away. Perhaps it was here, then, that the road to Brexit began.

But this is a book about the past, not the present. It opens, as promised, in the spring of 1979. And before we get to Margaret Thatcher, we begin, as all books should, with *Fawlty Towers*.

# Author's Note

Most readers should just ignore this and crack on. But for those who enjoy such things, a bit of housekeeping.

Since the history of the 1980s is so contested, it may be worth saying something about my sources. I read every edition of *The Times*, the *Guardian*, the *Mirror* and the *Express* from the early 1980s, and dipped into countless other newspapers and magazines, from the *Sun* to *Smash Hits*. There is already a vast academic literature about Thatcherism, as well as books on every conceivable aspect of life in the 1980s. But by far the most valuable resource is the Thatcher Foundation's colossal archive, brilliantly curated by Christopher Collins at https://www.margaretthatcher.org. Not only does this contain every word Mrs Thatcher said in public, it also has thousands upon thousands of pages of her private papers and declassified documents from the National Archives. If it did not exist, this book would look very different. The benefit is that I was able to see everything that Mrs Thatcher read, wrote and said, day by day, as Prime Minister. The downside is that I spent years scrolling through documents, trapped inside Margaret Thatcher's head.

Because the Thatcher website is so user-friendly, I have usually given the citation TFW (Thatcher Foundation website) rather than the more complicated National Archives reference. Sometimes, though, I have cited National Archives files directly, usually when the documents were not on the Thatcher website. The other major online archives I used were the Hansard website at https://api.parliament.uk/historic-hansard/index.html and Ulster University's collection of digitized government documents from the Public Record Office of Northern Ireland, at http://cain.ulst.ac.uk/proni/index.html.

Perhaps my favourite source, though, was the Mass Observation Project, which was not running during the period covered by my previous books. Inspired by the Mass Observation movement of the 1930s, this was launched in 1981 as a 'national life writing project' and continues to this day. In 2012 a selection covering the 1980s was published online as part of a University of Sussex project, 'Observing the 80s', at http://blogs.sussex.ac.uk/observingthe80s/. For this book, I picked eleven people whose accounts struck me as particularly vivid. Under Mass Observation guidelines their real names are hidden, but you are allowed to give brief biographical details and to invent pseudonyms. I naturally decided to name them after the members of Wolverhampton Wanderers' League Cup-winning side of 1980. For their first names, I used the census to find the most popular names when they were born. That gave me the following XI:

- Margaret Bradshaw, a 45-year-old former journalist from Lambeth, south London, married to a policeman.
- Jenny Palmer, a 40-year-old *Guardian*-reading mature student from Lancaster, married, who later founded her own business.
- Sheila Parkin, a 40-year-old assistant manageress of a camping and leisure shop from Brentwood, Essex, who bought her own council house.
- Carol Daniel, a 29-year-old shelf-stacker at a Tesco in Romford, Essex, married with children.
- Lesley Hughes, a 36-year-old cleaner and single mother from Stowmarket, Suffolk.
- Stephen Berry, a 48-year-old architectural technician from Chelmsford, Essex.
- Peter Hibbitt, a 47-year-old lorry driver turned depot supervisor from Basildon, Essex, a great fan of Tony Benn.
- Jean Carr, a 44-year-old part-time cleaner in a library near Chelmsford, Essex, married with children.
- Susan Gray, a 39-year-old journalist on a Darlington paper, married with a daughter.
- Mary Richards, a 54-year-old woman from Newton Abbot, Devon, who collected eggs on a battery farm.
- Anne Eves, a 40-year-old clerk, married, who bought her own council flat.

As volunteers, they were obviously self-selected. Still, they give a surprising insight into what self-consciously 'ordinary' people made of life in the early 1980s.

Two other quick points. First, although this book is absurdly long as it is, some things inevitably had to be left out. Readers looking for *Space Invaders*, Greenham Common, gay rights, *Grange Hill*, Martin Amis or video nasties will have to wait until the next book in this series, which will cover the period from the end of the Falklands War to the end of the miners' strike in the spring of 1985.

Finally, some readers may wonder why I call the woman who became Prime Minister in 1979 'Mrs Thatcher' rather than 'Thatcher'. There are really three reasons. The first is that her biographers all call her 'Mrs Thatcher'. The second is that 'Mrs Thatcher' reinforces the most unusual thing about her: the fact that she was a woman. Whenever newspapers or broadcasters referred to her in the 1980s, they called her 'Mrs Thatcher'. Even a passing mention, therefore, hammered home the fact that she was different from almost every other politician in the land. 'Thatcher' might have been a man. '*Mrs* Thatcher', though, was a woman.

The most important thing, though, is that it just sounds right. As a child, I was used to hearing her described as 'Mrs Thatcher' on television. Sometimes people called her 'Maggie' or 'Mrs T', which usually implied approval. But whenever I heard people talking about 'Thatcher', it was almost always during some withering denunciation. Even now the word 'Thatcher' often carries an electric charge, as if the speaker is gearing up to tell you about her thirst for slaughter and hatred of the poor. A BBC documentary producer once told me that he went through his directors' scripts changing 'Thatcher' to 'Mrs Thatcher' because it made them sound more considered. I knew exactly what he meant.

All the same, in my earlier books I never called Barbara Castle 'Mrs Castle'. So I don't claim to have been consistent.

# PART ONE

# What the Hell's Wrong with This Country?

# I

# Whatever Happened to Britain?

*Wasn't the Seventies a drag, you know? Here we are: well, let's*
*try to make the Eighties good, you know? 'Cos it's still up to us*
*to make what we can of it.*

John Lennon's last radio interview, 8 December 1980

*In a quiet way the British were hopeful, and because in the cycle*
*of ruin and renewal there had been so much ruin, they were glad*
*to be still holding on – that was the national mood – but they were*
*hard put to explain their survival.*

Paul Theroux, *The Kingdom by the Sea:*
*A Journey around the Coast of Great Britain* (1983)

A miserable, rainy evening in March 1979, and after hours ploughing
through the spray of the M5, Mr and Mrs Hamilton have finally pulled
up at their hotel, a handsome white building on the English Riviera. 'Everything on the wrong side of the road,' Mr Hamilton mutters grimly, 'and
the weather, what do you get for living in a climate like this?' They deserve
a stiff drink, he says: then something nice for dinner. Unfortunately, the
Hamiltons are in for a shock. As the hotel's owner explains, the kitchen
has just closed for the evening. 'The chef does actually stop at nine,' he
says awkwardly. Perhaps they would like a sandwich instead. 'Ham?
Cheese?' Mr Hamilton, who lives in California, can barely believe his
ears. 'What the hell's wrong with this country?' he snaps. 'You can't get
a drink after three, you can't eat after nine, is the war still on?'

Eventually Mr Hamilton hands over £20 – 'Mickey Mouse money', he
calls it – to persuade the chef to stay for an extra half-hour. But his ordeal
has only just begun. He orders a screwdriver, but nobody knows what it
is. His English-born wife explains that it is vodka and orange juice, but
when it arrives he spits it out in horror. He was expecting freshly squeezed
juice, not 'freshly unscrewed'. He orders a Waldorf salad, but his host

claims to be 'just out of Waldorfs'. 'What the hell's going on here?' Mr
Hamilton demands. 'You know something, fella? If this was back in the
States I wouldn't board my dog here.' And then, at last, matters come to
a head. Discovering that the hotelier pocketed his money, let the chef go
and is trying to cook the meal himself, Mr Hamilton loses his temper.
'This place', he roars, 'is the crummiest, shoddiest, worst-run hotel in the
whole of Western Europe!' At that, one of the hotel's most faithful residents, a former major, feels bound to intervene: 'No! No! I won't have
that! There's a place in Eastbourne!'[1]

Mr Hamilton, who appears in a memorable episode of the second series
of *Fawlty Towers*, never existed. But he might have done. For if the turn
of the 1980s brought terrible devastation to Britain's steel, coal and car
industries, it also brought an unprecedented influx of foreign visitors. In
1980, a year after Mr Hamilton's supposed visit, almost 13 million tourists, many of them Americans, landed on British shores. They brought an
estimated £4 billion into the national economy; but as so often, success
bred discontents of its own. That summer, *The Times* complained that
crowds in London meant 'lengthening queues at underground stations',
exorbitant prices for 'souvenirs, soft drinks and ice cream' and shouting
mobs in Westminster Abbey. There were so many visitors that the capital's
hotels were booked solid, forcing some holidaymakers to sleep in dormi-
tories. 'A groaning system is already overloaded,' lamented the archdeacon
of Westminster. 'Visitors to London by sheer force of numbers are destroying what they come to see.'[2]

What *had* all these millions of visitors come to see? Most of them probably dreamed of a historic, unchanging Britain that seemed utterly remote
from the messy realities of most people's daily lives: Buckingham Palace
and the Tower of London, the West End, Westminster Abbey and Windsor
Castle, the Royal Crescent and the Royal Mile. Yet modern Britain could
not be shut out entirely, even on a flying visit. Indeed, if the guidebooks
were to be believed, the state of the nation was grim indeed. Here, for
example, is the *Let's Go* guide for 1982, written by Harvard students and
aimed at young American backpackers:

> Imagine a country with the proudest democratic traditions, where freedom
> is apparently accepted almost as a law of nature. Imagine that all has gone
> well for a century or two – more than well. Two world wars have been fought
> and won (with a little help from friends) and everything ought to be rosy.
>
> So consider what happens when, quite unexpectedly, for twenty years
> in succession everything goes wrong. Rapid economic decline, massive loss
> of prestige in world politics, unemployment, inflation, the insoluble

problems of Northern Ireland, riots in the inner cities and growing confusion are faced on every side. Such is Britain's position today, every turn for the worse compounded by a very British disbelief that things could really have become so bad here of all places.

The same year's *Fodor's Guide*, written for older American visitors, was scarcely more reassuring. 'For all its increasing air of shabbiness, its strikes, its unpredictable weather, its rapidly rising hotel and restaurant costs,' began the foreword, 'Britain is still a highly desirable destination to the visitor with a sense of tradition and a love of those things which matter in life.' Chief among them were the countryside, the art galleries and the 'lovely and luxuriant' gardens. But in the 1982 edition, the authors had made a special effort to include as many stately homes as possible, because they were so clearly doomed by economic decline and crippling taxes. The last lines of the foreword struck an ominous note. 'You would be wise, during your visit, to see as many of the great houses as you can,' it warned, 'while they are still cared for by those who have a close personal attachment to them. The chill winds of change can he heard rustling the leaves of their ancient oaks.'[3]

Both guidebooks agreed that American visitors would be foolish to expect the basic competence they were used to at home. Anyone with 'a lot of urgent telephone calls to make, or domestic appliances needing installation or repair', warned *Fodor's Guide*, would soon weary of Britain's endemic inefficiency. Even getting around, agreed *Let's Go*, could be an ordeal. Rail fares had 'skyrocketed, largely because of wage settlements won by the unions and the rising cost of fuel', while bus fares were 'exorbitant', the vehicles 'slow' and night services 'very limited'. As for driving, petrol was very expensive and few petrol stations opened late, 'so if you travel by night, be sure to stock up on petrol before 6pm'. And because of Britain's economic difficulties, even planning the holiday budget was fraught with difficulty. 'Current monetary problems make it impossible to budget accurately long in advance,' began a *Fodor's* section carrying the ominous title 'Devaluation – Inflation'. 'We suggest that you keep a weather eye open for fluctuations in exchange rates, both while planning your trip – and while on it.'[4]

Then, of course, there were the hotels. In *Fawlty Towers*, Basil's infamous establishment is a metaphor for the nation itself, its guests a cross-section of society, its owner a Frankenstein's monster of middle-class anxieties. But if hotels really were windows into the national soul, then Britain was in trouble. In the spring of 1982, the American travel writer Paul Theroux, who had lived in London for the previous decade, set off around the British coastline. Every large hotel, he wrote afterwards, was 'run down or badly managed, overpriced, understaffed and dirty, the staff overworked and slow'. The problem was that while the British were very friendly in personal relations, 'anonymity made them lazy, dishonest and aggressive'. Even over the phone Theroux found them 'unhelpful and frequently rude'. For all the talk of British collectivism, they were terrible team players, since 'they disliked working for others and they seemed to resent taking orders'. As a result, their hotels were indistinguishable from 'prisons or hospitals', being 'run with the same indifference or cruelty'.[5]

Whenever Americans wrote about travelling in Britain, the same two words came up. The first was 'shabby'. The *Fodor's* foreword talked of Britain's 'increasing air of shabbiness', while *Let's Go* warned that accommodation in London was 'frequently impersonal, ill-equipped and shabby'. Indeed, the capital emerged remarkably badly from the two guidebooks. 'London has changed,' began the *Fodor's* entry, deploring the 'sad prevalence of garbage in the streets', while *Let's Go* thought visitors would find London 'perplexed and saddened', a study in 'urban fatigue'. It was particularly unimpressed by Piccadilly Circus, where 'after dark, the tone of the place is set by Boots the Chemist, where London's registered heroin addicts can fill their prescriptions'. For *Fodor's*, though, the real tragedy was Oxford Street, 'nondescript and drab', one of the 'least appealing' streets imaginable. All in all, most American observers agreed that the capital was sunk in a kind of terminal seediness, sliding inescapably towards dereliction. As Paul Theroux's train pulled out of London that spring, he felt relieved to leave behind 'the crowds and the scribbled-on walls, the dirty old buildings and the ugly new ones'.[6]

The second word was 'rude'. Both *Let's Go* and *Fodor's* thought the British could be spectacularly unfriendly. Many hoteliers, warned *Let's Go*, were 'rather gruff'. Some were downright 'surly', and if they found out that prospective guests were foreign, 'they won't abuse you, they'll just tell you that the house is full'. *Fodor's*, meanwhile, was shocked by the 'aggressive rudeness' that had seeped into the nation's service culture, 'a mean-minded expectation of payment for services which the British once performed gratuitously, out of good nature'. The guidebook thought this had 'something to do, perhaps, with Britain's decline from top-nation status and a feeling that everyone who comes to London nowadays is a rich Arab'. Perhaps the authors were trying too hard to find a political explanation for what was sometimes just plain bad manners. Still, the travel writer Jonathan Raban, who had been brought up in Norfolk but now lived in Seattle, was similarly horrified by the Basil Fawlty-style surliness he encountered in the summer of 1982. On the South Coast people 'carried rudeness to the point of open challenge', taking 'revenge on the tourists by marking up their bills and serving them with a dismissive I'm-as-good-as-you-are slamming down of plates on tables'. 'Can I have the bill please?' Raban would ask. 'When I'm ready,' came the inevitable reply.

That summer, Raban took a coach tour of London with a group of foreign tourists. All of them had a 'fund of sad stories about their reception in England. Urgent messages for them had been casually mislaid by the staff of their hotels, they'd found inexplicable charges on their bills, "Service" had been rudely demanded on top of a 15 per cent standard service charge, their queries had been met with shrugging discourtesy.' When Raban apologized for his former compatriots' rudeness, the tourists insisted that everything was fine and that they had enjoyed themselves anyway. The coach crawled on towards St Paul's. A few moments later, with exquisite timing, it got stuck in traffic outside a council tower block. The sign, Raban noticed, read 'Camelot Tower'. Underneath, somebody with a spray can had added the words: 'IS SHIT'. For the next few minutes, as the coach just sat there, they all stared silently at the damning message.[7]

Perhaps it was not surprising that outsiders took such a dim view of Britain at the turn of the 1980s. Seen from abroad, the British experience since the end of the Second World War often looked like a long nightmare of imperial retreat, economic indiscipline and industrial decline, played out against a surprisingly catchy soundtrack. The last illusions of Empire had been blown away at Suez, while the short-lived bubble of Swinging London had been punctured by recurrent sterling crises and terrible trade deficits. Having initially sneered at the fledgling European Community, the British had suffered the humiliation of seeing Charles de Gaulle blackball their first applications. And by the time their neighbours agreed to let them in, the United Kingdom itself seemed in danger of breaking up. In the course of the 1970s, sectarian violence in Northern Ireland had claimed more than 2,000 lives, the vast majority of them civilians. During the worst of the Troubles, bombs went off in Belfast every day, while in 1974 a general strike brought down Northern Ireland's power-sharing executive, forcing the government to impose direct rule from Westminster. Here, said some commentators, was a preview of the coming ideological showdown in Britain itself. Viewed from abroad, there could hardly have been a more damning reflection of a governing elite that had lost its authority and a disunited kingdom on the verge of disintegration.

And then there was the economy. On the face of it, the United Kingdom's 56 million people were richer, healthier, better fed, better educated and better housed than ever. As recently as 1957 Harold Macmillan had boasted, with considerable justification, that most people had never had it so good. But even as homes filled with the fruits of affluence, commentators were fretting that, in everything from profits and productivity to investment and industrial relations, Britain was falling behind its European competitors. By the turn of the 1960s, they were already asking, 'What's wrong with Britain?' and they never stopped. Nothing was right: the country was too old, too elitist, too complacent, too class-ridden; too slow to invest, too conservative to innovate, too lazy to compete.

So out went the tweedy Tory politicians of the Macmillan years, and in came the meritocratic modernizers. First was Labour's Harold Wilson, promising a new Britain fired by the white heat of the technological revolution and the gleam from his Gannex raincoats. But strikes and sterling crises blew him off course, and in 1967 he was forced to devalue the pound. Next came the Conservatives' Edward Heath, another thrusting technocrat with plans to reform everything from the trade union laws to the names of Britain's counties. Although Heath managed to secure admission to the European Community, his premiership lasted less than four years, ending in the chaos of two miners' strikes, rampant inflation, power cuts and a three-day week. So back came an increasingly hangdog Wilson, who bought off the unions with a series of pay deals that pushed inflation towards a record 26 per cent. Weary, demoralized and ill, Wilson hung up his raincoat after barely two years, but by then international confidence in Britain's economy had reached rock bottom. With the pound under unrelenting pressure, the new Labour Prime Minister, Jim Callaghan, was immediately plunged into the worst sterling crisis yet, ending with the humiliation of a $3.9 billion (£2.3 billion) bailout from the International Monetary Fund. 'Goodbye, Great Britain,' concluded a famously scathing editorial in the *Wall Street Journal*, 'it was nice knowing you.'[8]

For a time, Callaghan seemed to have steadied the ship. Then, at the end of 1978, the unions rebelled against his pay policy, which had been squeezing living standards to bring inflation down. So began the Winter of Discontent, immortalized by the images of rat-infested rubbish piled up in Leicester Square, picketing nurses outside hospitals, bodies unburied in Liverpool and the *Sun*'s mordant headline 'Crisis? What Crisis?' After everything that had come before – the sterling crises, the strikes, the power cuts, the bombs – it felt like the final straw. Even the *Guardian*, one of the Labour government's few defenders on Fleet Street, thought things had gone seriously wrong. The overflowing bin-bags and padlocked cemeteries, wrote its political columnist Peter Jenkins, were merely symptoms of a 'chronic British condition', rooted in 'falling production, eroding competitiveness and deteriorated productivity'. It was all very well to argue that the press were blowing things out of proportion. But 'wages in Britain *are* low, living standards *are* becoming inadequate . . . We are living in an expensive and increasingly poor country.' What Britain needed, he thought, was 'a bold government' and a 'psychological break' from the 'dreary cycle of failure'.[9]

At the end of March 1979, three weeks after Mr Hamilton's disastrous expedition to the English Riviera, Callaghan lost a vote of confidence and was forced to call a general election. With the Winter of Discontent so fresh in voters' minds, few Labour insiders seriously expected to win. By now the thirst for change was almost palpable, and as the party leaders addressed crowds across the country, the issue of national decline hung in the air. A week before polling day, a leader in the *Daily Express* captured the mood:

> Underlying all the other issues in this General Election campaign is the need to do something to halt the economic decline of Britain.
>
> Whoever takes office at the weekend will have this as the main, central task. For without a sustained improvement in our economic performance none of our collective and individual hopes will be realised.
>
> After the war Britain was in the top five countries in the world in terms of living standards. By the early 1970s we were out of the top 10. Now we are at No. 22 in the world.
>
> The American Hudson Institute has predicted that on current trends – if nothing is done – by the end of the century our world position will be much like that of Portugal now. What a prospect for our children!

Nobody hammered this home more relentlessly than the woman hoping to displace Callaghan as Prime Minister. 'Unless we change our ways and our direction,' the Conservative leader told supporters in Bolton, 'our greatness as a nation will soon be a footnote in the history books.' Not everybody liked her, of course. But by now there was little doubt that millions agreed with her.[10]

In the meantime, Britain's friends looked on in disbelieving horror. For the best part of a decade, foreign commentators had routinely presented Britain as the 'Sick Man of Europe', trapped in headlong and irreversible decline. Even in the corridors of power, among people who liked and did business with their British counterparts, such views were very common. In January 1975 the US Secretary of State, Henry Kissinger, told President Gerald Ford that Britain was a 'tragedy . . . begging, borrowing, stealing until North Sea oil comes in . . . That Britain has become such a scrounger is a disgrace.' Eight months later, West Germany's Chancellor Helmut Schmidt, a Social Democrat, told the *Guardian* that although 'a very anglophile person', he thought Britain's 'social set-up', 'industrial set-up' and even 'political set-up' had fallen behind, and that the British people 'for too long a number of years [have] taken too many things for granted'. And on the first page of his book *Britain Against Itself* (1982), the Harvard political scientist Samuel Beer recounted a recent conversation with one of his students. When Beer asked why she had chosen his class, she explained that her father had suggested it. 'Study England, a country on its knees,' he told her. 'That is where America is going.'[11]

To see just how deeply the idea of Britain's irreversible decline had taken root, you need only turn to the most influential of all overseas papers, the *New York Times*. As it explained in 1976, Britain was 'an admirable country: the mother of modern democracy and modern industry, a peaceful country of backyard rose gardeners and unarmed cops that has produced more than its fair share of scientists, statesmen, poets and even eminent economists'. (That 'even' was a gratuitously cruel touch.) Then came the sting. Unfortunately, 'Britain swirls in economic chaos. As inflation persists and the pound falls, Britons have been getting poorer for two years straight, and they are likely to keep getting poorer for years to come.'

To American observers, Britain at the turn of the 1980s was a country in terminal decline. In this damning cartoon by the *Washington Star*'s Pat Oliphant (6 July 1981), it is not clear whether the lion is merely exhausted or already dead.

The author listed the usual culprits: complacent politicians, inept managers, stroppy trade unionists and, of course, the British class system. Above all, he identified a specifically 'British disease', characterized by 'boredom, lethargy and a good-humored I'm-all-right-Jack acceptance of irredeemable decline'. Professor Ralf Dahrendorf, head of the London School of Economics, told him that British people were instinctively opposed to 'individual effort'. Another expert, disinterred from the conservative Hudson Institute, claimed that Britain's 'habits of mind and outlook' were 'mired in the medieval and agrarian habits of preindustrial society'. 'Britain is fundamentally less able to develop than other countries,' explained a Dutch EEC official, perhaps a little too gleefully. 'It is a country that simply doesn't work very well.'[12]

Every few months the *New York Times* published some fresh diagnosis of Britain's backwardness, dilapidation and general incompetence. In December 1977 the paper ran a piece about Savile Row tailors exasperated by their countrymen's 'shabby, old-fashioned clothes'. 'You see these shabby men everywhere,' one tailor said. 'I saw a party of them getting off a plane at Hamburg and I was embarrassed to be British.' The following July, the paper returned to the much-loved subject of 'Britain's economic malaise', blaming 'sluggish domestic entrepreneurship', 'top-heavy elitist structures' and 'peculiarly intractable labor relations'. And in December 1978, the books section ran a long essay by Paul Theroux, who was already turning his experiences in London into a cottage industry. It was an 'indisputable fact', wrote Theroux, 'that Britain has a relatively low standard of living, a poor choice of consumer goods, bungling and slowness at all levels and a *mañana* attitude that infuriates even Spaniards'. Ambition was 'seen to be a vice', muddling through had become a 'way of life' and rudeness was a national pastime. True, the British were good at some things: running schools and libraries, maintaining parks, brewing beer and – ironically, given the coming Winter of Discontent – emptying bins. But none of them made any money. The typical Briton, Theroux claimed, set out to 'make amateurism and uncompetitiveness the goals of nearly every endeavor'.[13]

Surely this was an exaggeration? Not according to Theroux's compatriot, the historian Martin J. Wiener. 'The leading problem of modern British history is the explanation of economic decline,' read the first sentence of his book *English Culture and the Decline of the Industrial Spirit*, published in 1981. In Wiener's view, the fundamental problem was that the British elite had never reconciled themselves to industrial life. To put it simply, they thought themselves above making money and looked down on people who did. Even people who did make money had reinvented themselves as country gentlemen, losing touch with the entrepreneurial values that had once made them successful. Instead of celebrating the factory, they made a fetish of the country house; instead of prizing professional expertise, they idolized the gentleman amateur. Even now, said Wiener, the British shrank from the modern world. While their cities crumbled around them, they consoled themselves with their Betjeman poems and Morris wallpaper. For a government hoping to change course, overturning this anti-entrepreneurial frame of mind would be by far the 'most fundamental challenge'.[14]

In Britain, some historians considered Wiener's thesis wildly exaggerated. But it won plenty of influential admirers: the new Secretary of State for Industry, Sir Keith Joseph, found it so persuasive that he sent copies to his Cabinet colleagues. And his enthusiasm told its own story. For all the clichés about the bulldog spirit, visitors were often struck by the unflagging pessimism with which the British talked about their own country. A different people might have been infuriated to hear the relentless abuse of their hotels, their trains, their towns and their factories. Yet, far from being mortally offended, the British were only too keen to put the boot in themselves. Even Theroux, who made a good living from being rude about Britain's shabby seafronts and dilapidated hotels, was amazed that people could be such 'wet blankets' about their own country. 'We're awful,' they would tell him. 'This country is hopeless. We're never prepared for anything. Nothing works properly.' This was not just comic self-mockery, he thought, but a 'tactic for remaining ineffectual. It was surrender.'[15]

Talk of national failure was nothing new. It had been an obsession for Britain's elites since the late nineteenth century, when the shock of German and American economic competition and the army's poor performance in the Boer War had inaugurated a national fondness for morbid self-flagellation. And even though a supposedly failing nation had somehow contrived to win two world wars, weather the Great Depression, build the welfare state and survive the loss of Empire, the idea that Britain was doomed to decline was more entrenched than ever. 'In the last ten years Britain has had no companion in failure. She stands alone,' wrote the Cambridge economist John Eatwell in *Whatever Happened to Britain?* (1982), which accompanied an eight-part series on BBC2. That might have sounded harsh – but not to the economic historian Sidney Pollard, whose book *The Wasting of the British Economy* was published in the same year. Looking at recent figures for gross domestic product (GDP) per head, Pollard found that since the Second World War Britain had been overtaken by, in turn, Norway, Iceland, Finland, Denmark, the Netherlands,

Belgium, West Germany, France, Luxembourg, Austria, Australia, New Zealand and Japan. Only Italy was keeping Britain off the bottom of the table of the world's industrialized nations. This, said Pollard, was a 'staggering relative decline, such as would have been considered utterly unbelievable only a little over thirty years ago ... After having led the world for two hundred years, Britain is no longer counted among the economically most advanced nations of the world.' Indeed, the gap between Britain and West Germany was 'now as wide as the difference between Britain and the continent of Africa. One short generation has squandered the inheritance of centuries.'[16]

On the right, talk of national decline was sometimes coloured with nostalgia for Empire. After dinner one night in May 1980, the maverick Conservative MP Alan Clark and his son James pored over an old atlas of Britain's colonial possessions. 'All gone, in 40 years, all of it,' Clark lamented. But this sort of talk came from all sides, not just from the reactionary right. It is, in fact, almost impossible to think of *any* major political figure at the turn of the 1980s who seriously disputed that the last few decades had been characterized by precipitous national decline. Even Tony Benn, the irrepressibly cheerful evangelist of the left, thought so. Catching a train from Bristol in February 1981, he found himself sharing a first-class compartment with his ideological arch-enemy, Sir Keith Joseph. They got on famously, chatting about 'crippled capitalism', the likely 'breakdown of the social fabric', the problem of unemployment and even the prospect of a Soviet invasion. And although they disagreed about almost everything, there was one moment of perfect harmony. 'At least we agree on this, Keith,' Benn said happily, 'that the last thirty-five years have been a disaster!'[17]

In the dying weeks of the Callaghan government, the deputy editor of *The Times*, Louis Heren, began writing a book about the state of the nation, with the cheery title *Alas, Alas for England*. Britain, he believed, had palpably 'failed to adjust to a changing world ... We are not a society at peace with ourselves. Most of us are no longer proud of being British.' Whenever Heren talked to the great and the good, they all sounded the same notes: regret at wasted opportunities, laments for lost ambitions, gloom about the prospects ahead. In Whitehall, one Permanent Secretary told him that 'the spirit and pride as well as the power and influence of Britain had been diminished ... He did not believe that Britain would go down the drain, but it would if we did not pull ourselves together within the next ten years.' Even Labour's veteran general secretary Ron Hayward, who had served in the RAF, agreed that the country had lost its self-belief. Forty years earlier, he said sadly, people had had a 'sense of companionship'. But now that had gone. 'Britain had lost its sense of direction. It seemed that nobody thought of Jerusalem, or wanted to make a contribution; but of course many remembered and wanted to do something but there was no real leadership. Labour was as bad as the Tories.'

Later, Heren went to see Lord Carrington, a hereditary peer, Old Etonian and former Guardsman who had won the Military Cross in the battle for Nijmegen in 1944. In almost every particular, Carrington was the embodiment of the old order, stamped by his experiences during the Second World War. But he could hardly have been more fatalistic about Britain's fortunes. 'We had had it easy too long,' he explained. 'We had been basically sheltered from economic reality by the captive markets of empire, and we had not yet learned to live in a harsh world.' What Carrington said next, however, was even bleaker:

> This was why he supported Maggie Thatcher. Every other course had been tried, and if hers failed we could expect some sharp crises. If she had got it wrong we would get to the bottom quicker than by other means, but it was worth a try. The alternatives would only hasten our genteel decline, and it would become progressively less genteel, more shabby and eventually rather nasty.

'Sharp crises . . . get to the bottom . . . genteel decline . . . shabby . . . nasty.' Such were the words of a man respected across the political spectrum for his experience and judgement, the embodiment of patrician wisdom, the personification of the post-war consensus.[18]

Talk of national decline seemed to be everywhere that summer. On 2 June 1979, a few weeks after the general election, *The Economist* published a leaked diplomatic despatch from Sir Nicholas Henderson, Britain's outgoing ambassador to France. Henderson had meant it as a parting shot: at 60, he had assumed that Paris would be his last posting, and wanted to use his traditional valedictory despatch to deliver some home truths about Britain's fall from grace. But after the election, Carrington, an old friend, had asked him to serve as ambassador to the United States. That, said *The Economist*, made his leaked despatch 'unusually forthright and timely'. For instead of being a parting shot from our last man in Paris, these were now the unvarnished thoughts of our new man in Washington.[19]

Henderson's despatch bore the stark title 'Britain's Decline: Its Causes and Consequences'. In the mid-1950s, he wrote, Britain had been the 'strongest European power'. Since then, it had been downhill all the way.

Today we are not only no longer a world power, but we are not in the first
rank even as a European one. Income per head in Britain is now, for the
first time for over 300 years, below that in France. We are scarcely in the
same economic league as the Germans or French. We talk of ourselves
without shame as being one of the less prosperous countries of Europe . . .

You only have to move about Western Europe nowadays to realise how
poor and unproud the British have become in relation to their neighbours.
It shows in the look of our towns, in our airports, in our hospitals and in
local amenities; it is painfully apparent in much of our railway system.

In foreign policy, Henderson thought, this had dire consequences. Britain
was so weak economically that 'we can no longer play our historic role'
and 'are unable to influence events in the way we want because we do not
have the power or will to do so'. Most painfully of all, his French friends
now talked about Britain 'as a model not to follow if economic disaster is
to be avoided'.

What had gone wrong? Like many commentators, Henderson blamed
the 'lack of professionalism in British management', as well as the
fragmentation and short-sightedness of the unions. But as was also common, he thought the deeper problems were psychological, rooted in a
combination of arrogance, complacency and sheer ignorance. Viewed
from abroad, he wrote, 'the British people do not give the impression that
they are fully aware of how far Britain's economy has fallen behind that
of our European neighbours'. They needed a government with the courage
to 'enlighten' them about the extent of their decline, as well as the humility
to copy the Germans and the French. 'It may be our turn to learn from
others,' he thought, 'having been teachers for so long.'[20]

The irony, barely remarked on at the time, was that a less plausible critic
of Britain's patrician complacency could scarcely have been imagined. The
son of the Warden of All Souls, 'Nico' Henderson had been educated at
Stowe, was a former president of the Oxford Union and had spent almost
his entire career in the Diplomatic Service. Despite his strictures about
Britain's economic weaknesses, he himself had no direct experience of
business or industry. Even an admiring profile in the *Guardian* conceded
that his time in Paris had been notable for his 'knack of staging marvellous
parties'. Indeed, since Henderson was just about the last person anybody
could picture on the British Leyland shop floor, readers might have been
forgiven for dismissing his despatch as a cry for help from a demoralized
upper-class elite, itself embattled by social and political change.[21]

Yet after an election campaign in which the issue of national decline
had featured so prominently, *The Economist*'s coup was perfectly timed.

'Envoy Hits at "Poor" Britain', read the *Mirror*'s headline, above a summary of Henderson's 'shock verdict' that 'Britain is all washed up'. Even the *Guardian* thought his analysis was spot on, though it doubted whether Britain would ever be able to emulate France and Germany. 'They started from a position of defeat and humiliation. There was every goad to restore greatness. There were ruins to repair. That psychological imperative does not make itself felt in Britain. We have not been defeated, only overtaken.' And many ordinary readers thought Henderson was right. Two weeks later, one *Economist* reader wrote to offer 'congratulations on your courage and devotion to England'. It had been a 'masterly' diagnosis, agreed a reader from South Africa, though he feared its effect would be to 'demoralise John Bull' rather than to 'make Britain great again'. The only solution, wrote an American reader, was for Britain to be kicked out of the G7* until it got its act together: 'Britain is not worthy of admission into "the club", nor can it afford the price either economically or politically.'[22]

Much of what Henderson wrote was fair enough. Although the image of the 1970s as a decade of unparalleled misery is a bit of a caricature, there is no doubt that Britain had some very serious problems. Other countries might have had more strikes, but nowhere else had industrial relations become such a bitter trial of strength between government ministers and local union representatives, the much-mythologized shop stewards. As for the economic woes diagnosed by foreign commentators, they were all too real. The flight from the pound in the summer of 1976, which forced Britain to take its begging bowl to the IMF, was not the result of some perverted malice on the part of the world's investors: it was a withering verdict on Britain's inability to keep inflation down. Indeed, almost every indicator showed Britain performing much worse than its European rivals, let alone the industrial behemoths of the United States and Japan. Britain's inflation rate for the 1970s had been 13 per cent. West Germany's was just 5 per cent. Britain's unemployment rate was 4 per cent; Germany's was 2 per cent. Britain's productivity growth rate was barely 1 per cent; the German rate was more than 3 per cent.

As a result, British manufacturing was in headlong retreat. In fifteen years since the mid-1960s, its share of the world car market had fallen from 11 per cent to 5 per cent. In shipbuilding its share had fallen from 8 per cent to 4 per cent, in steel from 6 per cent to 3 per cent, in electrical machinery from 14 per cent to 8 per cent, in transport equipment from 16 per cent to 6 per cent. These might look like tediously dry figures. But

---

* The talking shop of the seven richest Western nations, namely Britain, Canada, France, Germany, Italy, Japan and the United States, which had been set up after the 1973 oil crisis.

falling sales meant closing factories, disappearing jobs, empty cupboards and broken communities. As the *Guardian*'s Peter Jenkins melodramatically wrote in the autumn of 1978, 'no country has yet made the journey from developed to underdeveloped. Britain could become the first to embark on that route.'[23]

What underlay much of this was something that was only gradually becoming apparent: the colossal, very painful transformation from an industrial economy to one based largely on services. Today it is often thought, quite wrongly, that this began in the 1980s, as a result of something called 'neoliberalism'. In reality, it had already been going on for a quarter of a century. Industrial employment had peaked in the mid-1950s, at the high point of the post-war consensus. Then it began to fall, slowly at first but with steadily gathering speed. By 1979 the coal and steel industries had been haemorrhaging jobs for decades. The docks had fallen silent; shipbuilding was already almost extinct. In part this explains the growing militancy of so many trade unionists: not only were their living standards being squeezed by inflation, but foreign competition and technological change were remorselessly eroding the industrial landscape they took for granted. We know now that this was not just a British phenomenon. But because it happened earlier in Britain than anywhere else – industrial employment in West Germany, France and Italy did not peak until the 1970s – people at the time assumed that Britain had gone uniquely and spectacularly wrong. Hence all the talk of national decline; hence the 'British disease'; hence the 'Sick Man of Europe'.[24]

But 'decline' was not the whole story. Not all *Economist* readers agreed with everything Henderson had said; indeed, some thought him hysterically pessimistic. One American reader suggested that Britain's problems were very similar to those of major nations everywhere, adding that it should be proud of its 'open and free society, its sense of justice and decency, its calm outlook and even its complacency'. Another reader, G. G. Anthony of Cambridge, struck a rousingly patriotic note. 'We have salmon breeding again in the Thames, our real ale is the best in the world and we continue to change governments with good humour and dignity,' he wrote. 'When the chips are down, we will still stand up to be counted. Success is more than stodgy figures and shining airports.' And for the academic and essayist Lincoln Allison, all this business about national decline was the kind of thing you heard from 'retired, middle-class people who live in nice suburbs and hold dinner parties for nice people'. Over their Elizabeth David meals, they liked to tell each other that 'the country is in a state of moral and material collapse, that no work is done in English factories and that urban areas are a seething and perpetually revolutionary riot organized by social workers'. But this, Allison thought, was rubbish. As he saw it, pessimistic diagnoses such as Henderson's despatch had become a kind of national tic, 'formal, ritualized', but bearing little relation to reality.[25]

As Allison pointed out, talk of irreversible decline completely missed the simple, inarguable fact that most people's lives were longer, healthier, more comfortable and more colourful than ever before. One of the common misconceptions about the state of the nation, for example, was that Britain was getting poorer. It was not just foreigners who said so. People often said so themselves. 'We're not a rich country any more. We're poor,' they told Paul Theroux when he travelled the country in 1982. On the South Coast, Theroux asked a retired wing commander why Britain had not yet followed through on its long-discussed plans for a Channel Tunnel. 'No money,' the man said curtly. 'This isn't a rich country. We can't do things like that any more. The Japanese have all the money now, and the Germans, and these Arabs . . . We've got to learn how to tighten our belts.'[26]

In what meaningful sense, though, was Britain poor? By historical standards, the United Kingdom in 1979 was a very rich country indeed. In terms of its GDP, it was the sixth richest country in the world, a position it maintained for at least the next four decades. And although people loved to grumble about the woes of the nation's manufacturing industries, the state of the pound and the alleged laziness of the British worker, the reality was that, in their own day-to-day lives, most had never been better off. Allison reported a typical conversation in a Midlands pub:

'I see the country's in a diabolical state, economically speaking.'

'Dead right, mate. They should all be shot.'

'Who should?'

'Doesn't matter. All of 'em. How's the new Capri going?'

'I like it. We was even thinking of taking it to Spain this year, but's it not worth it by the time you get there, with the price of petrol in France. Where are you going?'

'We've booked for Rimini again.'

The new Capri, the drive to Spain and the holiday in Rimini were as much part of the national experience as the plunging pound and double-digit inflation. Indeed, even Louis Heren conceded that the 'average working-class family' in 1980 enjoyed what people in 1940 would have defined as an affluent middle-class lifestyle, from bank accounts, foreign holidays and household appliances to a new car and a colour television.[27]

One telling sign of all this was the kind of books people read. As

Theroux observed, bookshops at the turn of the 1980s seemed to be full of titles such as *Britain: What Went Wrong?* or *Is Britain Dying?* But none of them made the slightest impression on the bestseller lists. Instead – and despite the political controversies of the next few years – the lists reflected the relative contentment of an affluent, aspirational society. Even if all the books analysing Britain's national decline were counted together, they never came close to challenging the popularity of Geoffrey Smith's *Indoor Garden* (1980) or Alan Titchmarsh's *Avant Gardening: A Guide to One-Upmanship in the Garden* (1984). Nor did they come remotely close to matching Madhur Jaffrey's *Indian Cookery* (1982), let alone the all-conquering publishing phenomenon that was St Delia Smith, whose *Complete Cookery Course* (1978–80) was still topping the hardback lists in 1983. Even if people were worried about the state of the nation, they were clearly much more concerned about their waistlines: the single best-selling book of 1982 was Audrey Eyton's diet book *The F-Plan*, which shifted a whopping 1.2 million copies in just seven months. And were the British really as lazy, unambitious and anti-materialistic as their critics claimed? If so, what explained their enthusiasm for Jeffrey Archer's *Kane and Abel* (1979) and *The Prodigal Daughter* (1982), which sold hundreds of thousands of copies – and which unashamedly revelled in people getting ahead and making no apology for it?[28]

Far from bearing out the diagnosis of a nation sunk in terminal misery, then, Britain's bookshelves hinted at a rather more optimistic story. This was a nation spending more money on more books than ever before, self-confident enough to laugh at its failings, curious enough to explore foreign cookery and leisured enough to cultivate its gardens. Indeed, although the newspapers warned that the increasingly demanding culture of the work-place was taking a heavy toll in stress, illness and family breakdown, most people had more free time, and more things to do with it, than ever before. They not only read more books, they listened to the radio more and watched more television. They got out more, too: the Pony Club, the Cyclists' Touring Club, the British Field Sport Society and the British Sub-Aqua Club had all seen their memberships more than double between 1970 and 1981.[29]

In the summer of 1983, the Mass Observation Project asked its corre-spondents to describe how they filled their spare time. What was striking was the sheer length and variety of the responses. 'Reading, knitting, listening to radio, watching TV, writing poetry,' began Peter Hibbitt, a Basildon depot supervisor in his late forties. He was a tenants' representa-tive to the district council and secretary of his local Transport and General Workers' Union branch. He brewed his own beer, grew cactuses and did all his own DIY; he enjoyed tinkering with his car and cooking the Sunday dinner, and liked to 'hold profound discussions with my daughter and occasionally doze off in the armchair'. Another correspondent, Stephen Berry, an architectural technician from Chelmsford, sent in an even longer list, which began with shopping, washing up, hoovering and gardening, before moving on to eating out, 'having a weekly bath', reading, writing letters, 'seeing a good film', planning holidays, going to the library, walking on the Sussex Downs, going to art galleries, 'drinking wine with friends', making excursions by train, picking fruit, listening to live jazz and 'chatting things over with my wife'.

To some eyes, perhaps, all this might seem mundane. Yet just a few decades earlier, much of it would probably have struck many people as gloriously opulent, not least the meals out, the rail trips, the art galleries and the wine. To people in the 1950s, let alone the 1930s or the 1900s, the idea of these lists being compiled during an age of national decline would have seemed so outlandish as to be laughable. Even amid the unprecedented prosperity of the early 1980s, though, one thing stood out. The greatest pleasure of all, Stephen wrote, was 'watching my children grow up and playing and reading with them'. In that respect, at least, life had not changed at all.[30]

If there was one thing that embodied the new wealth of the age, it was the home. Every morning the British people read about the woes of the industrial economy, the scourge of strikes, the horrors of terrorism, the latest political disasters and national humiliations. But when they put down their papers and looked around, the evidence of their own homes told a different story.

In the early 1920s, when the new Prime Minister had been born, fewer than one in four British households had owned their own home. In 1961, shortly after she entered Parliament, the proportion was still less than half. But by the time she moved into her new home at 10 Downing Street, it was 55 per cent and rising fast. Even at this stage, home ownership had already become one of the great watchwords of the age. To many observers, it was the defining feature of Britain's newly affluent society, the cornerstone of a new landscape of consumerism, domesticity and individualism. And although intellectuals loved to sneer at the suburbs, with their privet hedges, garden gnomes, sundials and rockeries, almost nine out of ten people told researchers that a suburban house represented 'the ideal home'.

Home ownership was a marker of status, but it was more than that. In an age when so many people could remember damp, dingy housing, with paper-thin walls, outside toilets and indifferent landlords, owning your own home meant not just success but freedom. In the sitcom *Whatever Happened to the Likely Lads?* (1973–4), nothing better captures the difference between traditional, backward-looking Terry and aspirational, proto-Thatcherite Bob, both from working-class backgrounds in Newcastle, than their attitudes to their homes. Terry lives with his parents in their red brick terrace. But Bob, to his friend's scorn, has splashed out on a house on a brand-new suburban estate. 'Oh Bob! The damp course!' says his fiancée, Thelma, as they gaze lovingly at slides of the new house being built. 'My house! You know, I can't get used to saying that,' he muses. '*Our* house,' she says gently. And that two-word phrase was one of the keys to the age. When Madness used it in their jaunty Top Ten hit in the autumn of 1982, they meant it as a nostalgic paean to the heyday of the working-class terrace, when 'our house was our castle and our keep'. But in its unapologetically rose-tinted evocation of place and belonging, privacy and domesticity, 'Our House' was the perfect anthem for an increasingly suburban, home-centred people.[31]

When Mass Observation asked its correspondents to describe their homes, the answers spoke volumes about the comforts and clutter of modern living. Indeed, several correspondents admitted that they really ought to have a clear-out. Carol Daniel, for example, was a 29-year-old Tesco shelf-stacker, living at the end of a terrace in Havering, Essex, with her husband and children. Their living room had an armchair, an orange three-section sofa, a birdcage, a fish tank and a wooden room-divider. There was a large television above a rack stuffed with newspapers, comics and holiday brochures; there were three pot plants, boxes of toys, another box of cassettes and a typewriter. It is worth emphasizing that by no standards were they rich: they had no central heating, even though Carol was always nagging her husband about it. Yet even a few decades earlier, the sheer volume of stuff would have seemed astonishing.

It was the same picture in Darlington, where the 39-year-old Susan Gray, a journalist, lived with her husband and daughter. The Grays' living room boasted not just a television, a stereo, a typewriter and a computer, but china plates, musical instruments, toys, board games, a biscuit barrel, a bowl of nuts and countless ornaments. And in Lancaster, where the mature student Jenny Palmer and her husband owned a mock-Georgian 'executive-type' house, built in 1975, there was even more clutter: not just the inevitable television, record player and typewriter, but piles of unread copies of the *Guardian*, half-read books by Iris Murdoch and Simone de Beauvoir, the 'latest Habitat catalogue' and a truly spectacular array of ornaments, including tankards, rice bowls, vases and candlesticks.[32]

It was easy, of course, to sneer at the materialism of the suburban lower-middle classes. Just think of Mike Leigh's savage portrait of Beverly and Laurence Moss in *Abigail's Party* (1977), with their leather-bound copies of Shakespeare, their olives and Beaujolais, their Demis Roussos records, their Van Gogh and Lowry prints. Similarly, in her state-of-the-nation novel *The Middle Ground* (1980), Margaret Drabble lists the contents of a typical lower-middle-class home:

> flowered carpets, best tea-sets, an ingenious variety of draped lace curtains, Spanish-style vinyl tiles, wall clocks rayed like the sun in never-dying Deco, china Siamese cats and pigs and dogs, Toby jugs, glass fish, plastic rabbits, rubbery trolls, outsize turquoise teddies, plastic daffodils, plastic palm trees, fake fur rugs bristling with spidery white acrylic electric light, all the wonderful eclectic bad taste of the English.

Not even that word 'wonderful' can hide the condescension.[33]

To many people, though, these were the signs of status, the proofs of progress. Since even homeowners in their thirties could remember the thin gruel and narrow horizons of the 1940s, it was no wonder their homes were such temples to abundance, their mantelpieces and coffee tables creaking under the rewards of affluence. And it was this eagerness to show off how far they had come that explains why they made so much of their holiday souvenirs. Just as the eighteenth century's Grand Tourists had shown off their classical booty, so middle-class homeowners gave pride of place to things they had brought back from their package holidays. Among Susan Gray's ornaments, for example, was a 'carved wooden plate from Yugoslavia', while Jenny Palmer's vast haul included a pottery lady on a mule from Corfu, two museum prints from Cyprus, a jug and vase set from Kos and a woven Cypriot wall hanging. On the coffee table there was even some Turkish delight, yet another reminder of a recent holiday. Who, forty years earlier, would have dreamed of such a collection?

The other striking thing was how colourful all this was. Indeed, judging by the Mass Observation responses, many people had deliberately chosen colour schemes that were not so much violent as downright sadistic. In Stowmarket, Suffolk, the 36-year-old Lesley Hughes, a single parent and part-time industrial cleaner, lived in a semi-detached council house decorated with pictures of daffodils and of the Custom's House at King's Lynn, as well as a picture of the Queen with the infant Prince Andrew and a corgi. Her curtains were green. Her paintwork was green with 'darker green' over the fireplace. Her sofa was 'black leather with orange seats'. At its foot was an orange rug, while the carpet was brown 'with orange and mustard circles'. The ceilings and doors, she added, were 'mustard shade'.[34]

Even at the time, some people would probably have considered all this unforgivably tasteless. But to Lesley, as to so many others in the early 1980s, the contrasting colours probably seemed vivid and modern, so unlike the dreary greys of her childhood. The journalist Jeremy Seabrook encountered a similar picture when, on a trip to Bolton in 1981, he visited a post-war council estate. The streets could hardly have been bleaker, but whenever a door opened, he found 'bright curtains', 'brindled green and yellow or crimson' carpets and pictures of flamenco dancers and Chinese girls. Middle-class homes were often just as colourful: in Darlington, Susan Gray's living-room walls were lined with beige wallpaper decorated with pink and brown roses, while the paintwork was 'warm mushroom' and the carpet a swirling mixture of 'golds and browns'. But this was positively restrained compared with the scene in Lancaster. There Jenny Palmer's living room boasted a carpet with a 'geometric design in green with black, fawn and white'. As even she admitted, it clashed with her wallpaper, a 'large splodgy design of pale green and beige flowers'. So to 'try and balance this', she had put in 'dark chestnut brown velvet curtains'. The tentative tone suggests that she had not quite pulled it off.[35]

Reading people's descriptions of their homes in the early 1980s, one word comes up again and again: 'electric'. It is easy to forget that millions of people could remember a time without 'our one source of energy / The ultimate discovery', to borrow the words of Orchestral Manoeuvres in the Dark's splendid single 'Electricity', released in May 1979. Half a century earlier, just one in five homes had been connected to the grid, and as late as the 1960s some isolated villages were still without power. Yet in a matter of decades, electricity had utterly transformed the life of the home. By 1979 some 96 per cent of households owned a television, with seven out of ten being colour models. More than nine out of ten households had a fridge; half had a freezer; two-thirds had a telephone.[36]

When Mass Observation asked its correspondents to list their household gadgets, they often filled an entire page. In Basildon, Peter Hibbitt had two deep fat fryers, a coffee percolator, a toaster, a food mixer, a radio, a washing machine, a fridge, a microwave oven, a television, a stereo and two vacuum cleaners. In Darlington, Susan Gray had two cassette recorders, a television, a sewing machine, a computer, a fridge, a freezer, a washing machine, a slide projector, two hairdryers, a toaster, various blenders and mixers, a coffee percolator, a filter coffee maker and no fewer than four cameras and four radios. Even Mary Richards, a 54-year-old woman who worked collecting eggs on a battery farm in Newton Abbot, Devon, owned a television, a vacuum cleaner, a fridge freezer, a sandwich toaster and a Yamaha organ.[37]

But perhaps the most impressive thing about homes in the early 1980s was something future generations would take completely for granted. They were *warm*. For people who could remember the bone-chilling cold of a winter morning, the advent of central heating seemed an extraordinary blessing. Indeed, banal as it may sound, the take-up of central heating says a great deal about the unprecedented comfort of so many people's lives in the 1970s and 1980s. Even as the newspapers were wringing their hands about national decline, the proportion of homes with central heating surged from just 37 per cent in 1972 to 55 per cent in 1979, and continued to grow thereafter. But since it was expensive, people were understandably keen to keep their costs down, providing the perfect opportunity for that great villain of the age, the double-glazing salesman. By the autumn of 1981, despite the recession, demand for double-glazing was greater than ever, and by the following spring British homeowners were spending some £400 million a year, behind only the West Germans in the European double-glazing championship. One exception, however, was the Daniel household. As Carol told Mass Observation, a salesman had visited Romford and quoted £2,000 to do their windows. 'His sales pitch was very good and a lesser mortal would have been talked into signing for them,' she wrote, 'but my husband's will is very strong'.[38]

The mania for home improvement did not end there. A decade or two earlier, many people would have regarded showers, fitted carpets and built-in wardrobes – let alone patio doors, conservatories and double garages – as the luxuries of the professional classes. Not now, though. In 1981, reported *The Times*, the 'home improvement business' was already worth some £5 billion a year; by 1983 it had reached £8 billion, 'and the end is nowhere in sight'. Loft conversions were increasingly popular, but the supreme status symbol of the age was the conservatory. A new conservatory was very expensive: the largest firms typically quoted at least £7,000, including installation, the equivalent of well over £20,000 today. Still, by the spring of 1983 the country's top three firms were putting up some 600 conservatories a year, a figure inconceivable even a decade earlier.

For *The Times*, Britain was going through a 'great conservatory revival', driven partly by a wider interest in all things Victorian, but also by a desire to maximize light and unite house and garden. 'Conservatories are enjoying something of a renaissance,' agreed the *Guardian*, which preferred a rather more cynical explanation: a conservatory was 'cheaper and less drastic than divorce when she wants to extend the living room and he wants a bigger garden'. Both papers thought the garden was more important than ever, with Britain becoming a patchwork of 'vegetable plots, hen runs, goldfish ponds, billiard-table lawns, swimpools, pigeon lofts and patios'. Indeed, it is a safe bet that millions of people would have nodded at the *Guardian*'s definition of the good life in the spring of 1982: 'a patio on which to relax with a drink among sweet-scented flowers on rare summer evenings'.[39]

There were, of course, millions of people for whom the dream of a flower-decked patio was never remotely close to becoming a reality. Yet although poverty and unemployment were never far from the headlines, the fundamental fact about life in the 1980s is that most people were better off than they had ever been. It is easy to forget that in the first half of the decade, households' total disposable income rose, in real terms, by more than a tenth. Often they spent the extra money on going out: cars and caravans, restaurant meals and shopping expeditions, day-trips and package holidays. But as the sales figures for televisions, microwaves, central heating and conservatories show, they were increasingly spending it on staying in. Even as the dole queues lengthened, spending on appliances went through the roof. Every year, sales of washing machines, tumble dryers, fridge freezers, even toasters and coffee machines, reached new heights. In twelve months, reported the *Guardian* in October 1983, sales of microwaves had gone up by 70 per cent, colour televisions by 31 per cent, even deep fat fryers by 30 per cent – and this when Britain was limping out of the worst downturn since the Depression. Even sales of takeaway food and cans of beer had recorded similar increases: a sign, wrote the columnist Victor Keegan, that 'the average Briton's response to the first microchip recession is to retreat into his home and make that the centre of his entertainment and an escape from the outside world'.[40]

To see this merely as an escape from the recession, though, misses the point. For decades, social scientists had argued that Britain was becoming a more private, home-centred society. Under pressure from television, collective institutions of all kinds – pubs, churches, even football clubs – were losing members. A BBC survey in the summer of 1983 found that on weekdays, seven out of ten people spent the evening at home, while six out of ten spent Sundays at home, too. And of course this helps to explain the appeal of that irresistible symbol of individual choice, the video recorder. Take-up was simply extraordinary. In 1978 there were only 100,000 households with video recorders, yet by 1982 there were already more than 2 million. No other country in the world, not even the United States or Japan, had such a high rate of video-recorder ownership.

As cinema owners, restaurateurs and football-club chairmen looked on in horror, therefore, the suburban living room was becoming Britain's chief cultural marketplace. It was at home that people encountered new

ideas; it was at home that they made sense of their country and their place
within it; it was at home, tucked up on the sofa with a microwaved lasagne,
that they listened to the politicians of the day. And although some critics
deplored what they saw as the turn away from public citizenship to private
self-indulgence, from the collective 'we' to the individualistic 'I', most
recognized that there was no going back. Soon, predicted *The Times*, every
home would have a 'high definition television, a video recorder . . . and a
home computer controlling everything'. This, it thought, would make it
'even more difficult to persuade people to venture away from the home
for entertainment. They might even not have to leave home to work.'[41]

For some commentators, all this meant the death of community. To
Jonathan Raban, England seemed 'withdrawn, preoccupied and inward – a
gloomy house, its shutters drawn, its eaves dripping, its fringe of garden
posted against trespassers'. But this is easily exaggerated. Instead of reducing people to atomized individuals, social change actually gave rise to new
kinds of communities, from computer clubs and caravan parks to Neighbourhood Watch schemes and *Dungeons & Dragons* clubs. This was not
just the age of the rented video and the ready meal: it was the age of ice
rinks and bowling alleys, of shopping centres, multiplex cinemas and
amusement parks. Far from barricading themselves into their homes, people
seem to have been just as neighbourly as they had been beforehand. A survey in 1984 found that an impressive 84 per cent of people thought their
neighbours were 'mainly pleasant'. In 1948, at the supposed high point of
collectivism, the corresponding figure had been just 68 per cent. Perhaps
the cynical explanation is that in Clement Attlee's day, people had known
their neighbours much better, and therefore liked them much less.[42]

One of the strangest examples of the way technological change fostered
a new kind of community was the craze for citizens' band radio. Having
originated across the Atlantic, CB allowed users to talk to each other on
the 27-MHz short-wave radio frequency. In May 1980 there were an
estimated 70,000 British users, most of them using rigs fitted under their
car dashboards. By the autumn of 1981, *The Times* even claimed that CB
jargon was 'the fastest-growing foreign language in Britain'. The paper's
reporter, David Hewson, was clearly a bit baffled by it: after driving
around London with one enthusiast, he thought the real problem was that
'after the standard exchange of CB jargon, the British have very little to
say over it'. The transmission range was so limited that even the safest
topic, the weather, was a waste of time, because 'if it is raining on your
communicant then it is almost certainly raining on you'. The result was
endless 'gaps and uncomfortable pauses', as if at some disastrous dinner
party. If the weather was off limits, what else was there to say?[43]

For a time, however, CB radio seemed the technology of the future, a 'people's radio' in which, freed from the tyranny of the broadcasters, users would not just make their own content but would find like-minded friends and soulmates. Since a basic set cost just £60 and a car aerial £15, there seemed no reason why the entire population might not become part of a giant social network. Indeed, by November 1981 the newspapers were recording a 'flood of CB books and magazines', with some experts predicting as many as 5 million users. But then the bubble burst. By January 1982 *The Times* was already printing an obituary for the 'boom that never was'. CB radio, it turned out, appealed to people on long journeys, farmers and the disabled, but most other users soon lost interest. According to a survey for *Which?*, many found other users more 'annoying' than they had expected, while parents were put off by the 'bad language'.

By the end of 1983, with licence numbers in free-fall, CB already seemed like yesterday's embarrassing fad. It was, said one report, used by too many 'irresponsible people, mainly in urban areas, who use bad language, play music and use Channel 9, the emergency only channel, for ordinary conversation'. Not even cutting-edge technology, it turned out, could alter the reality of human nature. Nor, apparently, could it change the national character. 'I don't think the British like the idea of matey chats with all and sundry on the air as happened in the United States,' said one disappointed retailer. 'People here are more reserved.'[44]

So what was next? CB might have come to nothing, but the pace of technological change, especially in the home, meant another hi-tech fad was bound to be along soon. In May 1981 an exhibition of 'homes of the future', held in Milton Keynes, imagined pyramid-shaped houses, solar panels and an enormous amount of glass. A year later, Milton Keynes hosted an even more impressive vision of the future, with an 'IT House' to celebrate the government's Information Technology Year. The kitchen boasted a computer to organize the household accounts and control the freezer, linked to a bedroom camera for 'remote' babysitting. A second computer controlled the temperature and ran the bath, while the lounge had a fax machine and a third home computer with 'the promise of electronic mail'. There was even a 'try-it area in the garage', with electronic instruments and a voice synthesizer. Very soon, predicted the journalist Michael Tracey, 'homes will themselves become "smart", monitoring everything that is happening within them and, where necessary, communicating with their owner'. Cities, too, would 'become "smart", seeing, understanding and regulating everything that happens within their boundaries, from traffic accidents, to crime, to pollution, to voting'. All this, apparently, by 2001.[45]

Yet most people's fantasies were more mundane. Mary Richards probably came close to capturing the national ideal in a letter to Mass
Observation in the spring of 1982. What, they had asked, was her dream
home?

> I don't like bungalows. The house I would like would be detached with a
> small garden in front and a little veg garden at the back it would have three
> bedrooms with fitted cupboards and a tiled bathroom with a shower and
> a separate WC upstairs.
> *Downstairs*
> A tiled fitted kitchen (like lady Diana) come diner.
> A lounge and a utility room downstairs, gas central heating, double
> glazing and a garage. And a swimming pool.

Although the swimming pool was an unusually exotic touch, Mary's
vision was widely shared. One man who undoubtedly understood it was
Lawrie Barratt, who had been born in 1927 to a Newcastle power station
engineer. After leaving school at 14, Barratt had trained as an accountant.
In the early 1950s, married with two young children, he wanted to buy a
house, but could not afford the mortgage. So he built his own, using his
savings to buy a plot of land, digging at evenings and weekends, and
bringing in craftsmen where necessary. The result, a four-bedroom
detached cottage, cost him just £1,750 to build (perhaps £114,000 today).
But even before he had moved in, it was worth £3,000. Britain had its first
Barratt home. By the end of the century there would be at least 200,000
more.[46]

Decried by his critics as a salesman of cheap nostalgia, Barratt had a
good claim to be the man who built modern Britain – the Britain people
actually lived in, rather than the one written about by architecture critics.
By the end of the 1970s he was the country's biggest house-builder, completing 10,000 houses a year, many of them for first-time buyers. In just
ten years, his annual turnover had soared from less than £3 million to a
whopping £285 million. Famed for his punishing work ethic, Barratt was
virtually a national celebrity: travelling in his celebrated helicopter, he
visited two sites a day and aimed to visit each of his 500 sites every month.
Yet the 'Lawrie Barratt' people thought they were seeing in his ITV
adverts was not really Lawrie Barratt at all. For all his success, Barratt
was a shy man who avoided the camera. The rugged man in the helicopter
was actually the veteran actor Patrick Allen, whose other credits included
*Dial M for Murder*, *Where Eagles Dare* and – as luck would have it – *Who
Dares Wins*. Allen was also the voice of the government's *Protect and
Survive* films, designed to be broadcast in the event of a Third World War.

So if the bomb had dropped, people might have been reassured to find that the man telling them how to build their fallout refuge was the same man who had sold them their 95 per cent mortgage.[47]

In the summer of 1983, Barratt set an all-time national record, completing some 16,500 new homes in almost every corner of the country. Already a backlash was underway: when *World in Action* attacked his timber-frame construction system, the applause from architecture critics echoed across the land. But there were good reasons for Barratt's success. For one thing, his business model – cheap mass production, close attention to social surveys and extremely aggressive marketing – clearly worked. He was a brilliant salesman, using gleaming show-homes and glossy brochures to reel customers in, and offering to sort out their fees and mortgages. If necessary, he would even buy your old home and sell it for you. And once he had you, he meant to keep you. After a cheap starter home, a young couple might move up to a three-bedroom semi. Then, as their children grew up, they might aspire to a detached house with a double garage and large garden. There was a Barratt home for everybody. The only exception, ironically, was Barratt himself. He had long since moved into an eighteenth-century mansion in rural Northumberland.[48]

By the early 1980s the look of Barratt's houses had become a national cliché. Most of his developments were unashamedly suburban, in quiet cul-de-sacs on the fringes of thriving towns, with bright flags to lure the punters. Critics winced at the pantiled roofs, the mock-Georgian doors and the 'Tudorbethan' façades. In reality, this was merely the mass production of a suburban style that had been popular for at least sixty years. But the familiarity of the style was all part of the appeal. To lower-middle-class first-time buyers, Barratt's houses were precisely what houses ought to look like. They were new, but they were old. They were recognizably modern, but they were reassuringly nostalgic. They were satisfyingly cheap, but they had a touch of gentility. They were houses for people who were moving up and getting on. They were homes for people who thought the country was in a bit of a mess, but were themselves doing better than ever; people who were worried about schools, crime, inflation and debt, but were planning their annual foreign holiday, saving up for their first video recorders and eagerly devouring the latest Jeffrey Archer. They were, in a word, aspirational.[49]

While admirers saw Barratt's homes as the embodiment of the new opportunities of the age, his critics saw them in a very different light. After inspecting an executive house at the Dulwich Park development in south London, the *Observer*'s architecture writer, Stephen Gardiner, could scarcely contain his horror. If Barratt's mock-Georgian houses caught on, he wrote, they would 'turn the clock right back' and mark the 'dead-end of the line for British architecture'. But they did catch on, because Barratt's vision chimed perfectly with the values of hundreds of thousands of home-buyers. A very good example was one married couple, not far from retirement, who were looking to move out of central London and fancied a home near the Dulwich and Sydenham golf course. They had previously looked at a more expensive house in Regent's Park, but were worried about taking on so much debt. Visiting Dulwich one day at Easter 1985, they went to look at Barratt's new gated development. By the summer, they had spent £350,000 on a five-bedroom executive house.

'For the first time in my life, I've got the kitchen I always wanted,' Margaret Thatcher said happily. It was going to be a 'country kitchen', she explained, in keeping with the fashionable style of the day. As it turned out, though, Lawrie Barratt's political heroine never spent more than a night or two there. A workaholic to the last, she could never tear herself away from her office. But with its blend of nostalgic pastiche and suburban populism, the reassurance of tradition and the comforts of modernity, 11 Hambledon Place could hardly have been a more fitting symbol of her new Britain.[50]

# 2

# The Line of Duty

*I am a very emotional person. I am a romantic, you know, at heart, and believe wholeheartedly in love. Anyone who doesn't must be terribly unhappy.*

Margaret Thatcher, interviewed in
*Woman's World*, October 1978

*Sometimes I think Mrs Thatcher is a nice kind sort of woman. Then the next day I see her on television and she frightens me rigid. She has got eyes like a psychotic killer, but a voice like a gentle person. It is a bit confusing.*

Sue Townsend, *The Secret Diary of
Adrian Mole Aged 13¾* (1982)

It had just gone four in the afternoon of Friday 4 May 1979 when, to cheers and boos from the waiting crowd, a black Rover turned off White-hall and into Downing Street. 'Good afternoon, Prime Minister,' shouted a BBC reporter, as the first woman to follow in the footsteps of Sir Robert Walpole climbed out of the car and waved to the crowd. As Margaret Thatcher stepped towards the waiting journalists, a group of burly police-men moved protectively around her. Not for the last time, however, she seemed almost oblivious of her surroundings, her attention fixed on the cameras.

'How do you feel at this moment?' asked the man from the BBC. 'Very excited, very aware of the responsibilities,' she said softly, almost humbly:

Her Majesty the Queen has asked me to form a new administration and I have accepted.

It is, of course, the greatest honour that can come to any citizen in a democracy. I know full well the responsibilities that await me as I enter the door of Number 10 and I'll strive unceasingly to try to fulfil the trust and

confidence that the British people have placed in me and the things in which
I believe.

And I would just like to remember some words of St Francis of Assisi,
which I think are really just particularly apt at the moment:

'Where there is discord, may we bring harmony.

Where there is error, may we bring truth.

Where there is doubt, may we bring faith.

And where there is despair, may we bring hope.'

By now she was looking right into the camera, her voice gentler than ever,
her gaze almost imploring:

And to all the British people – howsoever they voted – may I say this. Now
that the election is over, may we get together and strive to serve and
strengthen the country of which we're so proud to be a part.

And finally, finally, one last thing: in the words of Airey Neave, whom
we had hoped to bring here with us, 'There is now work to be done.'[1]

Never had any Prime Minister made such a dramatic entrance. It was
pure political theatre, meticulously scripted by Mrs Thatcher's speechwriter, the playwright Ronald Millar. Not wanting to tempt fate, Millar
had kept the draft of her speech to himself until the small hours of the
morning, when the result was certain. 'The lady rarely showed her deep
feelings,' he later recalled, 'but this, on a night of high tension and the
constant switchback of emotion, proved too much. Her eyes swam. She
blew her nose.' Yet as a much more cautious politician than many people
realized, Mrs Thatcher hesitated. A few hours later, she told Millar that
she was considering ditching the prayer. It might be controversial, she said.
'What's wrong with that?' Millar asked. 'Churchill spent half his life being
controversial and much of what he said is remembered whether people
agreed with it at the time or not.' At that, 'she brightened visibly'. As Millar knew, even the slightest mention of Churchill was usually enough to
carry the day.[2]

Not everybody appreciated Mrs Thatcher's words on the threshold of
Number 10. Behind the heavy black door, her adviser Michael Dobbs was
waiting with the civil servants to applaud her into the building. Now,
listening from inside, he thought she had 'gone mad'. Indeed, even at the
time there were plenty of people who found her pious promises almost
comically insincere. But her theatrical delivery betrayed none of the doubts
she had entertained only hours earlier. And when she stepped through the
doorway, accompanied by the loyal Denis, she seemed supremely collected, the picture of serene self-confidence. When the introductions were

over, her new Principal Private Secretary, Ken Stowe, showed her into the Cabinet Room, where a huge stack of briefing documents awaited her. And only then did she show a hint of uncertainty. 'Ken,' the new Prime Minister asked, 'what do I do now?'[3]

One of the first things people noticed about Margaret Thatcher was her voice. Politicians' voices are central to their public image, from Harold Macmillan's languid drawl and Harold Wilson's Yorkshire vowels to Edward Heath's artificial drone and Jim Callaghan's reassuring burr. Mrs Thatcher's voice, like Heath's, was a testament to ambition and self-improvement. When she won the Conservative leadership in February 1975 it was widely considered high-pitched and condescending, the cut-glass voice of a moneyed Home Counties housewife. Her public relations guru, Gordon Reece, famously advised her to drop a semitone, even hiring a voice coach from the National Theatre to help her sound 'sexy, confidential and reasonable'. But although she managed to lower it and slow it down, she never pleased everyone.

'When she talks to you on the telly you feel about five years old,' one Huddersfield woman remarked during the election campaign. 'She talks to me,' said the *Mirror*'s Keith Waterhouse, 'as if my dog has just died.' Indeed, before the election the wet-fish merchant Henry Root was even motivated to send her a word of advice. 'In the coming campaign, *don't worry about your voice*,' he wrote. 'Don't listen to people who say you sound like a suburban estate agent's wife. What's wrong with suburban estate agents? They have a vote!'*[4]

For some of her critics, Mrs Thatcher's efforts to modulate her voice were a sign of her fundamental inauthenticity. Even during the 1979 campaign, the BBC's Michael Cockerell told viewers that there had been two Margaret Thatchers on show: '"Our Maggie", the housewife's friend' and 'the crusading Iron Maiden, promising a radical blend of free enterprise politics'. When he put this to her, she smiled. 'Oh, three at least,' she said. What were the three? She laughed, and then thought for a moment. 'There is a very logical one,' she said, 'there's an instinctive one, and there's just one at home.'[5]

So who was she, really? The Grantham schoolgirl, the dutiful Methodist, the Oxford chemist or the businessman's consort? A working mother, a populist crusader, a patriotic warrior or a radical reformer? The truth,

---

* For younger readers, I suppose I should point out that Henry Root did not exist, but was a hoax created by the satirist William Donaldson. Contrary to what is often thought, this was a golden age of political humour, from the letters of *Private Eye*'s Denis Thatcher to the diaries of fictional creations such as Adrian Mole and Tony Benn.

of course, is that she was all of them, though not always at the same time. As Ronnie Millar remarked, politics is a 'form of theatre', and Mrs Thatcher was a performer to her fingertips. Like any true diva, she worked hard at her art, honing her speeches so that, in Millar's telling phrase, she could 'command' her audience. She was a quick learner: shrill and hectoring in 1975, she had become huskier, almost confiding four years later. It helped that, unlike Heath, she enjoyed the show-business element of politics, which brought out what her biographer, Charles Moore, calls her 'actressy' side. She was very good at walkabouts and stunts, and even her fiercest opponents conceded that she had star quality. As Moore writes, 'she always had a sense of occasion and of fun. She injected drama into these visits, and made the members of the public caught up in them amused and excited to be there.' In the years to come, that sense of drama would become one of her defining characteristics.[6]

What about the woman off-stage? One of the most acute accounts was written years later by the journalist Ferdinand Mount, who ran her Policy Unit after the Falklands War. Mount admired Mrs Thatcher enormously, but he was very conscious of her comic aspects. He first encountered her in the mid-1960s, when she struck him as 'a little cross and unmistakably pretty', as well as 'entirely calm'. He found her voice painfully sharp, but she had lowered it by the time he came to work for her. One thing she never changed, though, was her 'eager, waddling walk . . . like a hen who hasn't the slightest desire to leave the coop'. Another astute observer, the novelist Alan Hollinghurst, seized on her walk in his book *The Line of Beauty* (2004). Making her long-awaited entrance at a party, she comes in with 'her gracious scuttle, with its hint of long-suppressed embarrassment, of clumsiness transmuted into power'. Every word is perfectly chosen. The novelist Sebastian Faulks told Charles Moore that he had once met the elderly Lady Thatcher at a lunch party and advised her to read Hollinghurst's novel. She had never heard of it, but as she left she said intently: '*The Line of Duty*. I shall remember that.' As slips go, it could hardly have been more revealing.[7]

One of the things that made Mrs Thatcher such a satisfying comic figure was that she had very little sense of the ridiculous. It is not true that she had no sense of humour: when one of her secretaries reported that a Tory MP had made a 'massive lunge' at her in a taxi, shambolically scattering her handbag all over the floor, Mrs Thatcher 'cried with laughter'. Yet even her greatest admirers admitted that her sense of the absurd was underdeveloped, to say the least. Working for her, wrote Mount, was a 'holiday from irony'. In particular, she was completely blind to double entendres, which were all the funnier because she was so painfully earnest. Introduced to a young man in Putney carrying a gigantic wrench, for example, she said seriously: 'Goodness! I've never seen a tool as big as that!' On another celebrated occasion, she walked into the Conservative Research Department holding a copy of the *Sun*, open at page two, where she had been impressed by the paper's leader columns. 'There!' she triumphantly told her male aides, completely oblivious to the spectacle on page three. 'What do you think of those two, eh?' Even this, however, pales by comparison with the story of her tour of the Falklands in January 1983, perhaps the most emotionally satisfying moment of her political life. She was inspecting a huge field gun when a soldier asked if she would like to fire a round. At that she looked worried: 'But mightn't it jerk me off?'[8]

Mrs Thatcher's former aide Matthew Parris once remarked, quite rightly, that she was a bit like the Wizard of Oz. To Dorothy and her friends, the wizard seems an almost supernatural figure, but he turns out to be just an ordinary old man from Omaha, Nebraska. And in some ways, despite everything, Margaret Thatcher was an ordinary middle-aged, middle-class woman from Grantham, Lincolnshire. When the journalist Louis Heren first met her in 1975, he thought her a 'stereotypical middle-class competent Mum with a loving husband and a minimum of worries'. Her favourite colour was turquoise; her favourite food was Dover sole; her favourite childhood book was *A Tale of Two Cities*; her family teddy bear was called Humphrey. She bought her clothes from Marks & Spencer; she liked chocolates and whisky and soda; she loved *Yes Minister*. She was fond of classical music: her favourite composers, she told the *Observer*, were Chopin, Beethoven and Bach. Contrary to what is often thought, she liked reading. Her correspondence shows that during the mid-1970s she read Fyodor Dostoyevsky's *The Possessed** and Arthur Koestler's *Darkness at Noon*, while she often talked about her enthusiasm for John le Carré. She enjoyed poetry, spending the summer of 1976 ploughing through Rudyard Kipling's collected poems, and she was able to quote – or rather, slightly misquote – Philip Larkin's poem 'Deceptions' to him when they met in 1980. And despite her reputation as the enemy of tradition, she liked collecting antiques. She took a keen interest in paintings for Number 10, specifically requesting pictures of Nelson and Wellington, and was baffled that her predecessors had been 'satisfied with inferior pictures'. At a reception in 1982 she gave the journalist Hugo Young a tour of the new paintings, proudly pointing out Walpole, Nelson and Pitt the Younger. 'She knew them all,' Young recorded; 'the provenance of the pictures and of every item of silver.'[9]

---

* Better known today as *Demons*.

# 36

# WHO DARES WINS

Most people would have recognized these as the tastes of a conventional middle-class Englishwoman in her mid-fifties. To Mrs Thatcher's critics, however, they were evidence of her irredeemable unsophistication. She was, claimed the writer Jonathan Raban, a complete philistine, who knew nothing of 'doubleness, contradictions, paradox, irony, ambiguity', and who regarded books, art and ideas as 'just so much Black Forest gateau'.* Her government, agreed another writer, Hanif Kureishi, was run by 'vicious, suburban-minded materialistic philistines'. Even on the right there were plenty of people who shuddered at her alleged intellectual limitations. She was a woman of 'common views but uncommon abilities', said the backbencher Julian Critchley. She had 'absolutely no interest in ideas for their own sake', said Oliver Letwin, a young member of her Policy Unit in the mid-1980s. 'She has no ideas, not even views I think,' Sir Ian Gilmour, her most waspish Conservative critic, told Hugo Young. All she had were 'some strong prejudices'.[10]

Even readers unsympathetic to Mrs Thatcher might think this a bit unfair. By these standards, how many of modern Britain's political titans would pass muster? Did Jim Callaghan spend his free time relishing paradox, irony and ambiguity? The irony is that in some respects she was *unusually* keen on political and economic ideas. She certainly loved getting advice from intellectuals: as the Conservative Research Department's Chris Patten recalled, she was always 'seeing a crazed Swiss professor'. And although not an intellectual herself, she did have one familiar intellectual quality: she could not stop arguing. It was 'her favourite recreation', explained the Conservative treasurer Alistair McAlpine. 'If she was truthful, this is what she would put in a biographical entry. She has a genuine and insatiable love of good argument. Of course, she is terrifically good at it. Her capacity to absorb detail makes her almost impossible to beat. She is so well informed.'[11]

What is undoubtedly true, though, is that Mrs Thatcher was not blessed with much imagination. In some ways this was a strength, because she never wandered from her narrow certitudes, but it also meant she could be painfully short of empathy. If people thought differently from her, they were not just different; they were *wrong*. It was as if she could not imagine what it was like to be poor, to be insecure, to be frightened of change, to be daunted by opportunities, to be intimidated by ambition. Even her allies were troubled by what Douglas Hurd privately called her 'narrow

---

* This is a very odd comparison. A half-decent Black Forest gateau is much more socially useful than lots of paradoxical books.

horizons', her 'inability – not unlike Ted [Heath]'s – to put herself in others' shoes'.[12]

A glorious example came after she had left office, when she met Matthew Parris at a dinner party. She asked what he was up to: 'You always have some grand plan, some wild and woolly expedition.' He said he was planning a trip to the Desolation Islands, in the Indian Ocean. Before he could elaborate, she cut him off. She knew why he wanted to go, she said:

> You want to go thousands of miles to some remote and dangerous place, and climb to the top of a mountain, and look up at the moon and the stars, and say, 'Here I am in a wild and dangerous place, miles from anywhere, looking at the moon and the stars.'
>
> You'll go all that way. And you'll succeed – oh yes, you always do. You'll see the moon and the stars. And it will be worth one newspaper article, or at the most two. And then you'll have to come all the way back again.
>
> Now take my advice, dear: don't bother. You can see the moon and the stars from Spalding.

Thousands of pages have been written about Mrs Thatcher, but none of them captures her better than that last line.[13]

For Mrs Thatcher's critics, one of the first items on the charge sheet was that she ushered in an age of unprecedented materialism. For Labour's Denis Healey, she had inaugurated the rule of 'fear and greed'. For the *Observer*'s Robert Chesshyre, she had persuaded people that 'there was nothing wrong in being greedy', and presided over a generation 'raised in a materialistic ambience, devoid almost entirely of spiritual or cultural values'.[14]

Yet Mrs Thatcher herself was neither materialistic nor greedy. Thanks to her Methodist upbringing, she was positively parsimonious. When, a month after she had she moved into Number 10, her aides forwarded the refurbishing bill for her approval, she went through it with a fine-toothed comb. She was horrified by the costs of the new linen (£464) and crockery (£209), and insisted on paying for the new ironing board herself. Contrary to what was often thought, the Downing Street flat was not free: she and her husband had to pay £3,000 a year in rent. When it was redecorated, Mrs Thatcher paid the bill herself. When her first-floor office was redecorated, she paid for that too. Uniquely among major world leaders, she organized her own cleaner. And even when she was not personally liable, she was obsessed with keeping costs down, getting rid of some of the photocopiers and prowling around to switch off the office lights. When her Welsh Secretary, Nicholas Edwards, sought permission to renovate his Cardiff office to provide a small one-bedroom flat for visiting ministers, she rejected the first quotation ('I just don't believe that a one-room + bathroom + kitchenette can cost £26,000') and only gave the go-ahead after the Welsh Office found a cheaper solution.[15]

Mrs Thatcher always thought of herself as house-proud. Talking to *Living* magazine, she claimed to love 'turning out the airing cupboard' or 'straightening out' the kitchen. In reality, though, she was only interested in one thing: work. Macmillan had famously gone to bed with a Trollope, but Mrs Thatcher just could not switch off. The idea of relaxing for its own sake struck her as deranged. She could not see the point of holidays, had no friends outside politics and spent little time with her family. As her Private Secretary for Foreign Affairs, Sir John Coles, recalled, 'her main form of relaxation was political or economic discussion; she was often at her happiest with a whisky and soda in her hand and surrounded by half a dozen politicians, businessmen, bankers or economists engaged in a lively argument.' Everything was political. Whenever the conversation moved away from politics, she could not wait to steer it back. She was always performing, always working, always *on*.[16]

For her advisers, this could be wearying beyond belief. When her policy chief, John Hoskyns, first met her in 1976, he found her 'a limited, pedantic bore', relentlessly lecturing her listeners about 'things we were quite well aware of'. Ferdinand Mount, too, was astounded by her total dearth of small talk. She would go on and on and on, in the same 'one-paced assertive style', no matter whom she was talking to. When her guests had left Number 10, she and Mount would have a glass of Scotch, she would kick off her shoes, and 'she would resume the harangue, as though we had never met before, as though I had not heard the same spiel half-a-dozen times already that day'. Later, he recalled one evening at Chequers when, after her ministers had gone home, she asked another aide to play the piano. She sat 'upright at the end of the sofa', he remembered, 'like a schoolgirl on her first trip to the Wigmore Hall', and Mount wondered what was going through her head. 'Is her mind drifting away to all the things she never speaks to us about, childhood, Oxford, her first kiss? Or is she making a mental note to call Alan Walters* about the inconsistencies in the latest money supply figures?' It is pretty obvious which he thought more likely.[17]

In Whitehall, Mrs Thatcher's work ethic became the stuff of legend. As her civil servants recalled, she was always exceptionally well prepared and virtually never made a factual error. They may have found her

---

* A monetarist economist who became her chief economic adviser at the beginning of 1981.

annoying, hectoring or plain wrong, but they very rarely questioned her intelligence or hard work. John Coles thought her tireless application was 'the habit of a lifetime', since she 'had been brought up to regard hard work as a virtue'. Another mandarin, Robin Butler, thought it was born of anxiety: because Mrs Thatcher was always the outsider, the lone middle-class woman surrounded by patrician men, she was determined to prove she was better than they were. Either way, no other post-war Prime Minister won so many plaudits for being so well informed. She was 'really amazing' in her 'mastery of briefs', her Attorney General, Sir Michael Havers, told Hugo Young.* He might 'spend most of a night getting into some big brief'. Yet at the next day's Cabinet she would stroll in and prove herself 'completely on top of it'.[18]

But all this came at a cost. Even before she became Prime Minister, Mrs Thatcher was famous for her lack of sleep. At five in the morning she often listened to the BBC World Service news, and by seven she was already at work. In the evenings, wrote John Coles, she commonly worked until 'midnight or beyond', curled up on the sofa with a glass of watered-down whisky, while 'if there was a major speech in the offing it was not uncommon to work till 2.00 or 3.00 a.m.' This was, by any standards, a punishing routine, especially since she worked at weekends. Perhaps she felt that, as a woman, she could not afford to show weakness. But even her stamina had its limits, and her intimates could tell when she was flagging because she would talk more than ever. In the archives there are three very telling letters, all dated 31 July 1980, written by government whips who had been round for dinner the night before. All express the same sentiment in slightly different words: 'I do hope that you do get a chance of a rest', 'I do hope that you get a proper break', 'I do hope that you have a good rest'. Clearly they were trying to tell her something.[19]

All this is a useful reminder that Margaret Thatcher was not just a political icon but a human being. Of course some people found this impossible to believe. Among her critics it was widely thought that she had no human feelings at all, which was something no sane person would have said about Churchill or Macmillan. Raymond Briggs drew her as the 'Old Iron Woman', while the Comic Strip parodied her as the 'Ice Maiden'. 'Do you weep, Mrs Thatcher, do you weep?' wrote Adrian Mole in a poem for the *New Statesman*. 'Do you wake, Mrs Thatcher, in your sleep?'[20]

* Havers was no fool. Having served in the Royal Navy during the Second World War, he was made Queen's Counsel in 1964. He was the father of the professional charmer Nigel Havers.

She did, and she never denied it. Contrary to her public image, Mrs Thatcher was an anxious and not always immensely confident person, a surprisingly common trait in successful politicians. Matthew Parris thought her apparently serene command was 'tinged with a panic' that she was always 'managing not quite to betray'. Robin Butler, who worked with her first as Principal Private Secretary and then Cabinet Secretary, thought her lack of confidence was 'the key to her style . . . That was why she was so assertive. She had to pump herself up with adrenaline before any big occasion.' Even her long-serving bodyguard, Barry Strevens, noticed that things sometimes seemed to get her down. There would, he recalled, be a 'slight crack to her voice and if she was upset, her shoulders drooped and she somehow seemed smaller than usual'. Rather sweetly, he would offer her a mint to cheer her up.[21]

None of this was a secret. 'Do you get nervous sometimes?' asked an interviewer from the *News of the World* in 1980. 'Oh yes,' said Mrs Thatcher. 'Of course you do, you never get rid of it.' Then the reporter asked the question that bothered Adrian Mole: 'Do you ever wake up in the night and worry about some problem?' Yes, she said: she had spent a 'very uneasy night' before the last European summit. As for the crying, she never hid it. 'There are times when I get home at night and everything has got on top of me when I shed a few tears, silently, alone,' she told *Woman's World*. Nobody liked hearing 'things which are wounding and hurtful . . . and I am no exception'. While she was Leader of the Opposition, the rakish Tory backbencher Jonathan Aitken, then going out with her daughter Carol, once found Mrs Thatcher in the sitting room, 'red-eyed, visibly upset'. When he asked what was wrong, she sniffed that one of her own MPs had been 'unbelievably unpleasant' to her in the Commons and 'said I was wrecking the party'. 'He was probably pissed,' Aitken said. 'Don't let it get to you.' 'I hurt too, you know,' she said sharply, getting up and walking out. It was then, Aitken wrote, that he realized 'the Iron Lady had a soft centre'.[22]

Like many sensitive people, Mrs Thatcher found it hard to forgive and forget. 'She's a hater, you know,' Edward Heath once told Aitken. 'She can't always separate the political from the personal, you see . . . She bears grudges.' Aitken thought this was a bit rich coming from somebody himself making an attempt on the world grudge-holding record, but it was accurate enough. What was to Mrs Thatcher's credit, though, was that she was unusually kind to her staff. On Barry Strevens's first day as her bodyguard, one of her secretaries was giving him a lift when they had a minor car accident. When Mrs Thatcher heard about it, Strevens recalled, 'she sat me down and fussed over me, fetching me a drink. I was taken aback by how motherly she was and her genuine concern.' On another occasion, when he and a police sergeant were on patrol, the latter trod in dog excrement and managed to smear it all over Mrs Thatcher's carpet. The sergeant panicked, but the Prime Minister said: 'Never mind!' Before they knew it, Strevens reported, 'she'd got soap and water and was on her hands and knees scrubbing away'.[23]

Strevens clearly idolized her, but there were many such stories. One of the Downing Street messengers, a lifelong Labour voter, told John Hoskyns that 'he had never known Number Ten to be such a happy place as it was under Mrs Thatcher'. 'She takes so much trouble over us all,' he explained. If they had personal problems, she was all ears. If she suspected somebody had not eaten, she would bring food down from the flat. If one of their children was ill, she would be 'talking about it for some days afterwards'. When the scandal of her minister Cecil Parkinson's affair with his secretary broke in 1983, she was remarkably sympathetic. When the Lord Chancellor Lord Hailsham's dog Mini died, she wrote him a personal condolence letter. And she could be much more tolerant of ordinary human failings than outsiders realized. One private secretary told Charles Moore about an incident when he was having an argument on the phone with the Treasury. When he put the phone down, he exploded: 'Shit! Fuck!' – and then realized, to his horror, that Mrs Thatcher was only a few feet away. But her eyes were 'shining with pleasure'. 'Temper! Temper!' she said happily.[24]

The most famous and revealing story, though, concerns a meeting at Chequers in the early days of her premiership, when she was having lunch with her senior ministers. As was traditional, they were being served by Wrens,* one of whom was very nervous. Carrying roast lamb, the Wren stumbled and spilled it all over Sir Geoffrey Howe, who was covered in 'bits of meat and drops of gravy'. Mrs Thatcher immediately jumped to her feet – not to look after Sir Geoffrey, but to comfort the mortified Wren. 'Don't worry, my dear!' she said. 'It could happen to anyone!' What the Chancellor of the Exchequer made of this can easily be imagined. Still, he got his revenge eventually.[25]

There is, of course, a danger of substituting one caricature for another, of replacing the uncaring hammer of the working classes with the saintly dispenser of drinks and medicines. Even her admirers admitted that Mrs Thatcher could be staggeringly overbearing. In meetings she was notorious for talking too much, not listening to alternative views and refusing to admit defeat even when she was obviously wrong. Many of her ministers

* Members of the Women's Royal Naval Service.

saw this as the insecurity of the anxious schoolgirl, desperate to prove that she knew better than anyone. But even her natural allies often found her insufferable. In arguments, wrote Ferdinand Mount, she became steadily 'ruder and more dismissive, scarcely troubling to listen any more but merely repeating what she had said half-a-dozen times already'. Cecil Parkinson wrote of her 'rudeness' to her colleagues. Nigel Lawson deplored her 'authoritarian' and 'irritating' way of running meetings. Jonathan Aitken lamented her 'unpleasant streak' and 'bullying manner', while John Biffen found her 'bossy and intemperate'. Even off duty she could be intolerable. In May 1980 she invited all the Permanent Secretaries, the most senior civil servants, to Number 10 for dinner. As her voice rose and the atmosphere became increasingly acrimonious, Sir Frank Cooper, who ran the Ministry of Defence, quietly slipped away. 'Where has he gone?' whispered one of the guests. 'To tell the SAS to come and get us,' muttered his neighbour.[26]

Yet this was only part of the picture. The older mandarins, with a healthy sense of their own importance, were often furious to find themselves browbeaten by a woman. But plenty of younger officials found her style refreshingly direct and loved working for her. The future MP George Walden, then an official at the Foreign Office, was struck by her 'plain speaking' and 'can-do style', and thought it was a myth that she would not listen. What she could not stand were waffle and weakness, but 'if you made your point with conviction and could prove you were right, she would take the argument, while avoiding any appearance of doing so'. Some people wilted under the 'electric blue eyes'. Others loved it. The economist Terry Burns, a Durham coal miner's son who became chief adviser to the Treasury, was just 36 when she summoned him for their first one-to-one meeting. It was, Burns recalled, 'the most frightening experience of my life at that point. I was drained by her directness and the intensity of her questioning.' It was, he said, 'without doubt the most exhausting yet also the most exhilarating meeting I ever had'.[27]

Above all, her officials were always struck by her sense of duty. Matthew Parris thought 'one of the nicest things' about his former boss was that she 'never grumbled' when asked to 'take some small trouble to help a nobody'. When letters came, she was 'unstinting with her own time where personal replies were called for'. And the evidence of her papers bears this out. Given the pressure of life as Prime Minister, it is remarkable how often she took the time to write personal replies: a letter to a little boy who had offered her one of his hamsters, for example, or a letter to another boy who was worried that his parents were going to get divorced. 'Perhaps the best advice I can give', she told the latter, 'is that you and your brother should talk to your mother and father. I am sure they will listen.' Underneath she added a scribbled PS:

> And perhaps you would tell them that you have written to me, and show them this letter. I should so much like to know what happens. My own children had a happy time and I should like you to have the same.
>
> Perhaps you would let me know if you ever come to London and I could arrange for someone to take you to see Parliament, and I could speak to you myself.[28]

Perhaps the most extraordinary exchange, though, came in the spring of 1980, when she received a letter from a boy called David Liddelow, aged 9. The son of a vicar in Borehamwood, Hertfordshire, David wanted her to settle a theological dispute. 'Last night when we were saying prayers my Daddy said everyone has done wrong things excep [*sic*] Jesus,' he wrote. 'I said I don't think you have done bad things because you are the Prime Minister. Am I right or is my Daddy?'

On 1 April, a day packed with meetings and Commons questions, Mrs Thatcher dashed off two handwritten pages in reply:

> Dear David,
>
> What a difficult question you ask, but I will try to answer it.
>
> However good we try to be, we can never be as kind, gentle and wise as Jesus. There will be times when we say or do something we wish we hadn't done and we shall be sorry and try not to do it again. We do our best, but our best is not as good as his daily life. If you and I were to paint a picture it wouldn't be as good as the picture of great artists. So our lives can't be as good as the life of Jesus.
>
> As Prime Minister, I try very hard to do things right and because Jesus gave us a perfect example I try even harder. But your father is right in saying that we can never be as perfect as He was.
>
> Yours sincerely,
> Margaret Thatcher

It is hard to imagine many other modern Prime Ministers writing those words.[29]

Even before Mrs Thatcher walked into Number 10, she had achieved something beyond any other post-war premier. She had been credited with her very own 'ism': Thatcherism. The irony, though, is that it had been coined by her opponents as a term of abuse. They invented the word

'Thatcherism' to describe what they saw as her right-wing fanaticism, which was supposedly out of step with the broad traditions of British political life. Not surprisingly, therefore, she tried to discourage it. In her first major speech after becoming Tory leader, she observed that 'to stand up for liberty is now called a Thatcherism', but dismissed it as one of Labour's 'tired and silly slogans'. And on the *Today* programme two years later, she again dismissed the idea of Thatcherism as an 'ogre', a 'ridiculous' idea invented by her opponents.[30]

The idea caught on, of course. Yet although some aspects are obvious – low taxes, free markets, a smaller state, strong defence – historians have never really agreed what Thatcherism was. The most influential interpretation, still enormously popular in the academic world, appeared in January 1979 in, of all places, *Marxism Today*. According to the cultural theorist Stuart Hall, Thatcherism was a kind of 'authoritarian populism – an exceptional form of the capitalist state', arousing public support by exploiting issues such as crime, race and education.* Soon other commentators weighed in with their own interpretations. Some saw it as a transatlantic import, with Mrs Thatcher heading a British subsidiary of the American New Right. Others looked across the Channel for parallels. The former Labour MP David Marquand thought it was a 'sort of British Gaullism', with Mrs Thatcher as the nation's self-appointed saviour after years of retreat. His erstwhile colleague Austin Mitchell, however, likened her to a rather different French politician, the anti-tax populist Pierre Poujade. Thatcherism, he wrote, was simply 'scrimping, saving and the politics of the *Daily Express*, the *Daily Mail* and Hayek under the bedclothes'.[31]

As the years passed, the arguments went on. Some saw Thatcherism as an inevitable result of the decay of social democracy, others as a middle-class backlash against egalitarianism, still others as an unexpected product of the anti-Establishment radicalism of the 1960s. Was it a revolutionary attack on the institutions that had underpinned the post-war consensus? Or was she actually *defending* that consensus against the militant left? Did it reflect a new stage in the evolution of industrial capitalism, or a new phase in the Cold War? Or was it was the realization of the free-market ideas of Friedrich Hayek and Milton Friedman? Was it a defence

* Why Hall's interpretation is *still* so influential is mystifying. It is not as though it was especially revelatory, since almost all Conservative governments have had some element of 'authoritarian populism'. What is more, his essay was published in January 1979, so it says nothing about what she actually did. For example, he devotes pages to crime and education, which were pretty tangential during her three administrations. Yet he barely mentions the trade unions, has little to say about economics and does not mention inflation once.

of big business after years of falling profits, or was it an uprising of the self-employed and small businessmen? Was it about making the central government stronger? Or was it about weakening it? Was it, perhaps, all of these things at once? And if it was, does it really make sense to talk of 'Thatcherism' at all?[32]

Among Mrs Thatcher's allies, many did believe there was such a thing as Thatcherism. The most articulate, the future Chancellor Nigel Lawson, famously described it as 'a mixture of free markets, financial discipline, firm control over public expenditure, tax cuts, nationalism, "Victorian values" (of the Samuel Smiles self-help variety), privatization and a dash of populism'. And even Mrs Thatcher, having resisted the label for so long, eventually conceded that there was something to it. 'Sir Robin, it is not a name that I created in the sense of calling it an "ism",' she told *Panorama*'s interrogator Sir Robin Day in 1987. But then she went on:

Let me tell you what it stands for. It stands for sound finance and Govern-ment running the affairs of the nation in a sound financial way. It stands for honest money – not inflation. It stands for living within your means. It stands for incentives because we know full well that the growth, the eco-nomic strength of the nation comes from the efforts of its people . . .

It stands for something else. It stands for the wider and wider spread of ownership of property, of houses, of shares, of savings. It stands for being strong in defence – a reliable ally and a trusted friend.

People call those things Thatcherism; they are, in fact, fundamental common sense and having faith in the enterprise and abilities of the people. It was my task to try to release those. They were always there; they have always been there in the British people, but they couldn't flourish under Socialism. They have now been released. That's all that Thatcherism is.

It is a wonderfully revealing passage, but also a surprising one. Almost everything Mrs Thatcher said – honest money, living within your means, incentives, ownership, strong defence – could have been said by any Con-servative leader since the dawn of time. But what is most striking about her definition is its simplicity. The most important words come near the end: Thatcherism, she says, is just 'fundamental common sense'.[33]

Of course not everybody saw it that way. To Sir Ian Gilmour, who served in Mrs Thatcher's Cabinet from 1979 to 1981, Thatcherism was merely 'nineteenth-century individualism dressed up in twentieth-century clothes', the bastard offspring of 'Manchester Liberalism'. As he saw it, Mrs Thatcher was an interloper, a ghastly Gladstone-in-drag act who had somehow fooled his colleagues into giving her the reins of their party. Even some of her allies agreed with him. Her friend Woodrow Wyatt, a former Labour MP who had swung well to the right, claimed that she was 'not a Conservative', but a 'radical making a revolution which horrifies many Conservatives'. The economist Friedrich Hayek, whose book *The Road to Serfdom* (1944) is often seen as a central influence on Thatcherite thought, described himself as a liberal and even wrote an essay entitled 'Why I Am Not a Conservative'. And the other great idol of the free-market right, the American economist Milton Friedman, sounded a similar note. 'The thing that people do not recognize is that Margaret Thatcher is not in terms of belief a Tory,' he explained. 'She is a nineteenth-century Liberal.'[34]

· It is true that, with her Methodist middle-class roots, free-market rhetoric and open distrust of the party establishment, Mrs Thatcher sometimes sounded like a Victorian Liberal. In 1983 she joked that 'if Mr Gladstone were alive today he would apply to join the Conservative Party'. But if she was really a Liberal, what had she been doing in the Conservative Party since 1943? Why did nobody notice? Why did they make her leader of their party? The obvious answer is that she was saying nothing that most Conservatives did not themselves believe. Free-market liberalism had been part of their repertoire since Sir Robert Peel's day, while cutting taxes, rolling back the state and encouraging private enterprise had been Tory themes for decades. And if a true-blue Conservative leader such as Andrew Bonar Law or Stanley Baldwin had read Mrs Thatcher's party conference speeches, he would surely have agreed with almost every syllable.[35]

Of course this contradicts the common view that Thatcherism was a revolution in British political economy, marking a great break between one era and another. Yet it is telling that Mrs Thatcher never sought to dissociate herself from her party's history. 'All my predecessors – yes, I agree, Disraeli; yes, Harold Macmillan,' she told Robin Day, 'I would say I am right in their tradition.' Nigel Lawson said much the same. Was Thatcherism really 'some alien creed masquerading as Conservatism', he wondered in 1980, before answering his own question: 'I can only say that, as a Conservative, it feels pretty Conservative to me.' Yes, the government sometimes invoked 'new sages – such as Hayek and Friedman'. But that was simply because these writers were 'reinterpreting the traditional political and economic wisdom of Hume, Burke and Adam Smith'. So what was so new about Thatcherism? 'In economic terms,' Lawson concluded, 'very little.'[36]

In many ways Lawson was right. Thatcherism *was* nothing new. Almost all its common themes – dissatisfaction with the welfare state, distrust of the trade unions, anxiety about the advance of socialism – had been

Conservative grass-roots sentiments for decades. When the young Margaret Roberts got involved with national politics in the late 1940s, her supposedly radical ideas were already very common among the kind of people who stuffed envelopes and knocked on doors for the party. No wonder, then, the activists fell so hard for her after she secured the leadership. Not since the 1930s had a Conservative leader been so obviously in touch with the rank and file. As Lawson observed, her predecessors had treated the ordinary party members as little more than cannon fodder. 'Harold Macmillan had a contempt for the party, Alec Home tolerated it, Ted Heath loathed it,' he wrote. 'Margaret genuinely liked it. She felt a communion with it, one which later expanded to embrace the silent majority of the British people as a whole.' This was one of the secrets of her appeal. She was one of them.[37]

One of the common misconceptions about Thatcherism, especially on the left, was that it was a fixed, coherent, 'neoliberal' creed with clearly defined methods and principles. But this is nonsense. Thatcherism was not a rigid, monolithic project. It was always fluid, always changing. In 1976 Mrs Thatcher had talked about standing up to the Soviet Union; in 1979 she emphasized taming the unions; by the end of 1984 her focus had already shifted to privatizing the public utilities, which she had not even mentioned five years earlier. Some historians even think there was no one 'Thatcherism' but 'several different Thatcherite projects' competing for attention. What is certain is that there was no blueprint, not even Hayek's *Road to Serfdom*, because Mrs Thatcher did not believe in blueprints. 'Vision, not blueprint; values and principles, not doctrines,' she told a Conservative audience in 1977. Even the word 'monetarism' rarely passed her lips. Instead she preferred to talk about 'sound money' and, of course, 'good housekeeping'.[38]

This was not just spin. Mrs Thatcher was a practical politician, not a political philosopher. As she herself told Michael Cockerell in 1979, she was guided by 'instincts and feelings', not doctrines or textbooks. This does not mean, of course, that she was a mere opportunist. Her principles were clear and unchanging: free markets, low taxes, law and order, strong defence, a horror of inflation and so on. But like any successful politician, she was flexible about how she interpreted them. She liked winning elections; if that meant downplaying some elements or compromising on others, she was perfectly happy to do so. She usually hid this pragmatic side from the public, because she was worried it would make her look like Ted Heath in a dress. But her civil servants saw how she really worked. 'More often than not,' thought John Coles, 'her approach to a new problem was hesitant and cautious.' Her longest-serving Cabinet Secretary,

Robert Armstrong, even remarked that he had never met a politician who was more skilful 'in combining rhetoric which was faithful to her principles with policies that were totally pragmatic'.[39]

The best way to think of Thatcherism, then, is not as a philosophical dogma but as a loose mixture of themes, instincts and attitudes, rooted in the soil of Middle England and the long history of the Conservative Party. As her political adviser Alfred Sherman remarked, it had originated 'less as a doctrine than as a mood', defined by 'beliefs and values' rather than policies and pledges. But it was also a product of a very particular historical moment, the late 1970s. And one principle, more than almost any other, underpinned everything Mrs Thatcher did: her belief that Britain was in deep national decline.[40]

Mrs Thatcher was not, of course, the first party leader to argue that Britain was going backwards. But none of her predecessors, with the possible exception of Joseph Chamberlain, had been so passionate or so apocalyptic. As she saw it, everything began with decline. Her first election broadcast, on 16 April 1979, put it centre stage:

> We can go on as we are. In a way that is the easy option. But we could not do that for long. Year after year we have been falling further behind friends and neighbours. And the British people will not indefinitely tolerate our country becoming the poor relation of Western Europe. If we go on declining, we shall sooner or later fall; and we shall become a quite different kind of country . . .
>
> But we needn't go on as we are. There is nothing inevitable about our continued decline. Britain was once a great country. She still is a great country, though few would have known it from the way we have behaved this winter. Yet our greatness will soon disappear altogether unless we change our ways.

She sounded the same note at her set-piece rallies, warning audiences that without change, 'our glories as a nation will soon be a footnote in the history books'. And when she talked to the BBC's Michael Cockerell a week before polling day, her voice almost cracked as she contemplated the nation's fortunes. 'I can't *bear* Britain in decline. I just can't,' she said earnestly. 'We who either defeated or rescued half Europe, who kept half Europe free, when otherwise it would be in chains! And look at us now!'[41]

Almost all Mrs Thatcher's allies shared her belief that the nation was in near-terminal crisis. Her future press secretary, Bernard Ingham, formerly a keen Labour activist, said he had 'had enough of us being laughed at as a country'. Many of her colleagues saw things in even bleaker terms. Britain was charting 'a unique course', declared Sir Keith Joseph, 'as it slides from the affluent Western world towards the threadbare economies of the Communist bloc'. Even in private they were often astonishingly pessimistic. 'We in the Western world have learned to live for today not tomorrow,' Sir Geoffrey Howe told Hugo Young. 'We are heading for a really terrible time unless we can reverse this trend . . . a kind of Romanian or other East European economy.' The next election, Nigel Lawson remarked in February 1979, was 'our last chance to rescue the British economy from the depressing spiral of decline'. Not all of Mrs Thatcher's admirers were convinced that she could do it. But she was in no doubt. In her memoirs she quoted Pitt the Elder in 1756: 'I know that I can save this country and that no one else can.' It was, she admitted, a 'presumptuous' comparison. 'But if I am honest, I must admit that my exhilaration came from a similar inner conviction.'[42]

What makes Mrs Thatcher's invocation of Pitt the Elder so revealing is that she is often thought to have been indifferent to the value of history. All she cared about, her opponents said, was the market. But this is just not true. As Charles Moore's biography shows, she had an intensely romantic sense of history, which is why she took so much trouble getting pictures of Nelson and Wellington for Number 10. In this respect, she was nothing if not conservative. When the South African writer Laurens van der Post interviewed her at the end of 1982, she took great delight in showing off not only Robert Clive's Chippendale table, Pitt the Younger's desk and Churchill's chair but also a 'little scientific gallery' she had built up in the dining room, with pictures and busts of Humphry Davy, Joseph Priestley and Isaac Newton. Warming to the historical theme, van der Post asked if she would have been a Roundhead or a Cavalier. 'I'd have been a Cavalier, a Royalist,' she said instantly. As the conversation wore on she became positively lyrical, delivering misty-eyed tributes to Magna Carta, Lord Salisbury, the Duke of Wellington and 'our great early judges – the Blackstones, the Cokes'. Even the British people's preternatural love of liberty got a look in. 'If one were to go into a pub at a time of national crisis,' she said earnestly, 'possibly the phrase you'd hear on everyone's lips as they discuss things would be: "We're a free country." Everyone takes it for granted – we're a free country.'[43]

She meant every word. At heart, thought her policy chief, John Hoskyns, she was driven by 'a patriotic impulse and a sense of shame about what had happened to our country'. Nobody who cared only for market values would have chosen 'I Vow to Thee, My Country' as her favourite hymn. No Roundhead revolutionary would have treated the Queen with such exaggerated deference, or been so fond of pomp and pageantry. And what people often miss about Thatcherism is just how much she was inspired by her faith in Britain's exceptional history and unique destiny. 'Britain is not just another country; it has never been just another country,' she told Robin Day. 'We would not have grown into an Empire if we were just another European country with the size and strength that we were. It was Britain that stood when everyone else surrendered.'

That last line is very telling. At the outbreak of the Second World War, she had been an impressionable 14-year-old. Even decades later, her voice thickened with emotion whenever she mentioned 'Winston'. Not even someone with her sense of destiny, however, could have guessed that General Galtieri would grant her a finest hour of her own.[44]

So was there *anything* distinctive about Thatcherism? There was, but it was a question of tone as much as content. When Ferdinand Mount went to see Mrs Thatcher about working in Number 10, he was taken aback by her unapologetic moral earnestness:

> Education is only part of it. What we really have to address are the values of society. This is my real task, to restore standards of conduct and respon-sibility. Otherwise we shall simply be employing more and more policemen on an increasingly hopeless task. Everyone has to be involved. At one time, women's magazines played quite a constructive role. Now they've just caved in. Personal responsibility is the key. That was what destroyed Greece and Rome – bread and circuses. It has to stop, Ferdy, it has to stop.

Mount found all this 'both startling and thrilling'. After years of 'weary, professional cynicism', nothing had prepared him for 'the naked zeal, the direct, unabashed appeal to morality, the sheer seriousness' of her vision. Not since Gladstone, he thought, had there been a Prime Minister whose politics were so firmly anchored in what she called the 'real and absolute difference between right and wrong'.[45]

With all politicians, there is always a suspicion that they may not mean what they say. But Mrs Thatcher's moralism was absolutely genuine. The proof lies in the handwritten notes for her conference speeches, before her speechwriters had polished them into something more conventional. The case for 'economic freedom', she scribbled in October 1979, was not that it made people richer, but that it was consistent with 'certain fundamental moral principles of life itself. Each soul [and] person matters. Man is imper-fect. He is a responsible being. He has freedom to choose. He has obligations to his fellow men.' In a foreshadowing of her much-misunderstood remark that there was no such thing as society, she added: 'Morality is personal. There is no such thing as a collective conscience . . . To talk of social justice, social responsibility, a new world order may be easy . . . but it does not absolve each of us from personal responsibility.'[46]

Not surprisingly, none of this made the final draft. But two years later, she was at it again. 'Virtue of a nation is only as great as the virtue of the individuals who compose it,' she began. 'Concept of the *nation* – at the heart of the Old Testament & one which those who wrote the New Testament accepted. Idea of *personal* moral responsibility . . . Can't rid ourselves of our own responsibilities by handing them over to the community.' It is almost impossible to imagine Ted Heath or Harold Wilson writing something like this. But her notes show that she relished the chance to set out her moral vision. 'All the great religions teach us that life is a struggle between good and evil,' she scribbled. 'Life without struggle is no life at all. Each human being carries the potentiality of choice between good and bad. That choice must be examined alone, and in the small family unit. A collectivity cannot choose to be good.' On and on she went, for twelve pages. Her speechwriters cut the lot.[47]

Yet the public were left in no doubt about Mrs Thatcher's moralistic outlook. In her adoption speech at Finchley in 1979, she claimed that Britain's economic ills were merely a reflection of a wider 'decline of manners, of morals, of shared beliefs'. Indeed, there was almost no subject that she did not see in religious terms. Inflation, she told a church service in 1981, was a 'moral issue, not just an economic one'. Even wage restraint was a 'moral responsibility'. This was just not the kind of thing senior politicians said. Would Heath have claimed that throughout Britain's history 'God was the source of our strength'? Would Wilson have told his audience that 'the teachings of Christ applied to our national as well as our personal life'? Yet Mrs Thatcher insisted that Britain's decline was rooted in the fact that 'only a minority acknowledge the authority of God in their lives'. And although her speeches were not always so explicitly Christian, they almost always had a religious dimension. Again and again she reached for the language of the Sunday school. 'I am in politics because of the conflict between good and evil,' she told one interviewer, 'and I believe that in the end good will triumph.'[48]

Where all this came from is no mystery. As a child, Margaret Roberts had been brought up to say grace before every meal and to go to chapel four times on Sundays. Her father was a lay preacher, whose sermons insisted on the importance of hard work, clean living and individual salvation. And although she later moved away from Methodism to join the Church of England, she always drew inspiration from what she had heard on the hard wooden pews of Grantham. Indeed, it was the hard wooden pews of Grantham that gave Thatcherism its distinctive character. No modern party leader had ever talked so openly about virtue and vice, salvation and responsibility, freedom and servitude. Some of her ministers found this embarrassing, but her admirers found it invigorating. For years they had been listening to left-wing speakers arguing that conservatism was merely a front for selfishness and wickedness. Now the boot was on the other foot. And this surely helps to explain the virulence of her critics' hatred. They were used to occupying the moral high ground; yet now they were facing somebody who said, entirely sincerely, that they were the agents of wickedness.[49]

Yet Thatcherism was more than just political Methodism. Indeed, although Mrs Thatcher relished talking about her faith, she was never more effective than when she took politics out of the chapel and into the home. Whenever she turned to the economy, for example, she instinctively talked in terms of good housekeeping and the family budget. To her critics, this was proof of her fundamental shallowness, but because it came from a working mother it was immensely effective. 'I too know what it's like running a house and running a career. I know what it's like having to live within a budget. I know what it's like having to *cope*,' she told a studio audience in April 1979. And whenever her opponents accused her of ideological extremism, she had the perfect answer. 'My politics are based not on some economic theory,' she told the *News of the World*, 'but on things I and millions like me were brought up with: an honest day's work for an honest day's pay; live within your means; put by a nest-egg for a rainy day; pay your bills on time; support the police.' Who could disagree with that?[50]

The fact that those words appeared in the *News of the World* is very revealing. Mrs Thatcher was not the first Prime Minister to flirt with populism, but none had ever done it so vigorously. Her critics sneered that she had turned the party of estate owners into the party of estate agents; one historian has written that 'Thatcherism owed more to the *Sun* than the *Spectator*'. But there were millions more *Sun* readers than *Spectator* readers, and an awful lot more estate agents than estate owners. As Gordon Reece told her, their goal was to reach the kind of people, especially women, who watched *Coronation Street* and *Top of the Pops*, who listened to Jimmy Young and *Woman's Hour*. And since this meant reaching across class lines, she talked not of working-class or middle-class people, but of 'ordinary people', the 'quiet majority' or 'ordinary working families'. Today these are staples of our political life, but it was Mrs Thatcher who turned them into clichés. Historians have calculated that between 1975 and 1990, she used the phrases 'ordinary people' or 'ordinary working people' at 175 different events.[51]

The idea of 'ordinariness' played a central part in the political culture of the 1980s. If nothing else, it was a clever way of appealing, in the same word, to middle-class and working-class voters alike. In Mrs Thatcher's moral universe, both groups were natural Conservatives. As ordinary people, they were decent, patriotic and respectable: they worked hard, owned their own homes (or wanted to), cherished their families and obeyed the law. As she told a conference of Conservative trade unionists in 1978, there was nothing remarkable about being a Tory. They were simply 'a party of ordinary, commonsense, hardworking freedom loving people'. Against them, though, was pitted a stuck-up, self-satisfied establishment of socialist politicians, trade union barons, left-wing teachers, militant students and rent-a-mob rabble-rousers. They did not understand good housekeeping. They did not love British history. They did not care about the nation's moral and economic decline. And they were not, of course, ordinary.[52]

It was here that Grantham came in so handy. For Grantham was the quintessence of ordinariness. The *Sun* even called it 'the most boring town in Britain'. Not only was it literally in the middle of England, it was Middle England in microcosm. The young Margaret Roberts had been in no hurry to stay: after she left at the age of 18, she spent the rest of her life in the richer and more glamorous South, and never returned for more than a day or two. But once she became Conservative leader, boring old Grantham became very useful. Every time she invoked the grocer's shop, the grammar school and the Methodist chapel, she reinforced the message that she was, in her own words, a 'plain straightforward provincial', just like the voters she was trying to reach. As one of her allies explained a week before the 1979 election, she was 'Grantham writ large'.

No wonder, then, that she always insisted that she had learned her ideas in the Grantham grocer's shop. In her telling, the Lincolnshire market town in the 1930s was Eden before the Fall, a united, contented community where ordinary people worked hard, raised their families and went to church without worrying about inflation or strikes or students or subversives. This was the Britain she wanted to build, Grantham wreathed in glory. And so on the steps of Number 10, at the moment of supreme triumph, she did not forget the obligatory nod to her home town – or to her father, the self-made grocer and Methodist preacher from whom she had got all her ideas. 'Well, of course, I just owe almost everything to my own father. I really do,' she said seriously. 'He brought me up to believe all the things that I do believe and they're just the values on which I've fought the election. And it's passionately interesting for me that the things that I learned in a small town, in a very modest home, are just the things which I believe have won the election.' It was the last thing she said before she stepped through the black door.[53]

It would be easy to leave her there, the applause of her admirers ringing round the little street. But even as Mrs Thatcher was speaking, there were boos among the cheers. Despite the efforts of her strategists, she had never been popular. To many observers, including some loyal Conservatives, she was too narrow, too bossy, too strident and too unsympathetic. As Leader of the Opposition she had never come close to challenging Callaghan's popularity, and the election campaign had actually made things worse. The more people saw of her, the less they liked her. In just a month, Callaghan's personal lead over her had widened from 7 per cent to almost 20 per cent, and even four out of ten Conservatives thought he would be the better Prime Minister. Of course victory changes everything. But with less than 44 per cent of the vote, she had secured a smaller mandate than Heath in 1970, let alone Wilson in 1966 or Macmillan in 1959. Her aspirational rhetoric had been rewarded with big swings in the South and the Midlands, yet in the industrial North, Scotland and Wales, the Conservatives had made no progress at all. And among the 37 per cent who supported Labour and the 14 per cent who voted Liberal, there were millions who already shuddered at the very sound of her voice.[54]

Against this background, a different leader, anxious to win over what the *Guardian* called the 'have-nots, the have-littles and the have-problems', might have hesitated. But although she was a pragmatist, Mrs Thatcher was not one for wavering. She did not care if her policies were unpopular: as she saw it, being unpopular usually showed you were right. 'Her distinguishing feature', a senior civil servant told Hugo Young, less than six months into her premiership, was that 'no other PM of modern times has been more prepared to live with short-term political unpopularity'. To her admirers, this was what set her apart: she had backbone. Ferdinand Mount often wearied of her 'insistent, harsh concentration', but thought that she 'remained heroic, intolerable often, vindictive, even poisonous sometimes, but always heroic'. He conceded that a different Prime Minister might have adopted a kinder tone and a more gradual approach. But 'there are times', he wrote, 'when what is needed is not a beacon but a blowtorch'.[55]

But there was a downside. A Prime Minister sometimes needs to play the national figurehead, transcending partisan differences and appealing to people in every corner of the land. As Mrs Thatcher said on the steps of Number 10, the occupant has to speak 'to all the British people – howsoever they voted'. But this was the one role she could never bring herself to play. In February 1975 the *Daily Express*'s cartoonist Michael

From an early stage, Mrs Thatcher's bullish patriotism, need for enemies and enthusiasm for battle were central to her image, as in this Kal cartoon for *The Economist* (20 June 1981).

Cummings had drawn her as 'St Joan Margaret de Finchley, Saviour of the Middle Classes, Scourge of the Lower Orders and the Left'. The image was perfectly chosen: the holy warrior riding into battle. There were 'our people', and then there were the enemy. Socialism was not just wrong: it was 'immoral', 'poisonous', the 'political organisation of hatred'. Life was struggle; generosity was appeasement; consensus was surrender. As a result, wrote Ludovic Kennedy in the *Spectator*, Mrs Thatcher was 'too partisan, too narrow in her outlook to heal the schisms in the country'. She might speak for the middle classes, but 'she can never speak for the country as a whole'. Even her allies talked of her deafness, her utter inability to understand the anxieties of others. Mount, for instance, thought that over time she 'became blind to the fears and interests of the untalented, the unlucky and the mildly slothful'. But the signs had always been there. She had never offered much for the unlucky.[56]

As St Joan went from 'underdog to top dog', the watching Matthew Parris felt increasingly uneasy. Once a loyal backroom boy, now a Tory MP, he was well aware that their opponents were 'neither evil nor, any longer, particularly formidable'. He still thought Mrs Thatcher's policies were right, but recognized that they were 'hurting many people, most of them small people'. So why could she not express regret? Why could she not admit that some people were poor or unemployed because of inheritance, illness or sheer bad luck? Why was she so crowing, so combative in victory? Why could she not be more gracious? But when Parris raised all this with her Parliamentary Private Secretary, Ian Gow, the latter just laughed. 'As the Lady would put it,' Gow explained, 'if you're crocodile hunting and after a hell of a struggle you finally drive your croc into the shallow where he's floundering in the mud, do you help him back into the deep? No. Hah! You stick the knife in.'[57]

Mrs Thatcher spent her first hours in Downing Street as she planned to go on. Instead of going up to see her new flat, she remained cloistered in the study, poring over the briefs prepared by her civil servants and sifting through names for her first administration. Having slept for only two hours the night before, she ought to have been exhausted. But she kept working till eleven, running on pure adrenaline. Because she stayed so late, the girls on the switchboard had to stay late, too, phoning around to organize her appointments for the next day. Before she went home to Chelsea, she made a point of going in to thank them personally.[58]

In the next few days, as she and her ministers got down to business, messages of congratulation poured in. There were more than 13,000 letters in the first ten days, reflecting her novelty value as the first woman to hold the highest office in the land. They came from rich and poor alike: from the *Sun*'s editor, Larry Lamb; from Lulu, Barbara Cartland and Petula Clark; from the Davis Cup tennis team; from fellow politicians and from ordinary voters. There was a telegram from Peter Sellers, who was delighted by her 'marvellous victory'. There was a letter from the anti-permissiveness campaigner Mary Whitehouse, who had been thrilled to hear 'the marvellous words of St Francis' and already sensed a nationwide 'lifting of the spirit'. Another came from Friedrich Hayek, who thanked her for the 'best present on my eightieth birthday anyone could have given me'. And there was a message from Milton Friedman, who hoped that Britain could lead the world to a 'rebirth of freedom'. Mrs Thatcher's reply perfectly captured her style. 'The battle has now begun,' she wrote. 'We must win by implementing the things in which we believe.'[59]

But the most heartfelt exchange was one she began herself, on her first morning as Prime Minister. Amid the blizzard of meetings, she found time to write to Ronnie Millar, the man who had provided the prayer for her entrance to Number 10. An experienced West End playwright, educated at Charterhouse and Cambridge, he brought a touch of greasepaint to life at Number 10. 'Humorous, camp, silk-dressing-gowned, slightly seedy', in Charles Moore's words, Millar treated her like a diva. 'Come on, darling,' he would say, 'they want you to show you really feel it.' Sometimes Mrs Thatcher found him a bit much, but he appealed to her love of the limelight, her flair for the dramatic. Now, like an Oscar-winning actress, she made sure to thank her scriptwriter, assuring him that she 'could not have done it without you'. A few days later, Millar replied, clearly moved. It had been 'an honour and a privilege', he wrote, 'to "be there on St Crispin's Day" ... The whole country walks with a lighter step today because of you. Do you sense it? I'm sure you must.' There was, he added, more than enough work to be getting on with. 'At least three Parliaments' worth, I think, don't you?'[60]

Perhaps better than anybody, Millar understood how Margaret Thatcher saw her place in history. Only nine months earlier, he had taken her to see a new West End musical, which told the story of a young woman from a humble provincial background who finds herself catapulted to political stardom. Afterwards, she had sent him another note:

My dear Ronnie,

It was a strangely wondrous evening yesterday leaving so much to think about. I still find myself rather disturbed by it. But if they can do that *without* any ideals, then if we apply the same perfection and creativeness to *our* message, we should provide good historic material for an opera called Margaret in thirty years' time!

Love
Margaret

The fact that she could contemplate an opera about herself, even in jest, says a great deal about her sense of destiny. In her own mind she was always the star of the show. And in a sublime irony, which nobody could possibly have appreciated at the time, the musical she had seen that night was *Evita*.[61]

# 3

# You'd Look Super in Slacks

*For seven years now I have been warning readers of* Private Eye
*that English women are growing more masculine, their waists and
wrists are thickening, their breasts are getting smaller, their voices
harsher, their opinions sillier, their behaviour more aggressive and
unstable.*

Auberon Waugh's *Private Eye* diary, 7 October 1979

*My mother has gone to a woman's workshop on assertiveness
training. Men aren't allowed. I asked my father what 'assertiveness
training' is. He said, 'God knows, but whatever it is, it's bad news
for me.'*

Sue Townsend, *The Secret Diary of
Adrian Mole Aged 13¾* (1982)

In the village of Chedworth in Gloucestershire, one man watched Mrs
Thatcher's arrival in Downing Street with grim resignation. Formerly a
pilot in the RAF, David Stayt worked as a planning officer in nearby
Cheltenham. A man of distinctly firm opinions, he might have been
expected to cheer the arrival of a new Conservative Prime Minister. But
as the founder of the Campaign for the Feminine Woman, Mr Stayt knew
that there could be no rest in the struggle against the 'dangerous cancer
and perversion' of feminism. 'The ideal woman', he once said, 'is one who
naturally wants to submit, obey and please the male: to bear his children
and to create the happy home.' Yet here was one of the best-known women
in the country – a wife and mother who had abandoned her domestic
responsibilities to enter the workforce – walking into the most important
office of all! There could have been no more powerful symbol of everything that was wrong with modern Britain.[1]

A year later, the *Daily Express* sent a reporter to Mr Stayt's 'rambling
stone mansion'. She found him on uncompromising form. Appropriately

enough, he was joined by his Dutch-born wife, Yvonne; but it was Yvonne, ironically, who did most of the talking. 'Funny term, "Women's Lib",' she mused. 'What are we supposed to be liberated from? What's wrong with being a homemaker?' Yvonne was sick of people claiming that 'fathers and mothers can do the same thing both inside and outside the home', which was obviously nonsense. 'A husband should be responsible and a wife submissive. Both our daughters want to marry after university and they want to marry a *real* man, someone who cares for them.' But the real villains in all this, David said, were the government. As part of their 'near-conspiracy to pervert men's roles as providers', they had altered the tax laws to push women, against their will, into the workforce. Disappointingly, however, the reporter never pressed him on the obvious question. Was Mrs Thatcher part of the conspiracy? Or was she one of the many women working against their will?[2]

Among the consequences of the feminist revolution that bothered David Stayt, one loomed particularly large: the terrible sight of women in trousers. 'They really shouldn't wear trousers,' he told the *Express*. 'I mean, they look so much nicer in skirts.' This was not a new complaint. For at least a decade, as thousands of vulnerable young women fell into the arms of Britain's trouser salesmen, Fleet Street's letters pages had simmered with controversy. But despite a campaign by the feminist magazine *Spare Rib*, which produced a 'GIRLS CAN wear trousers' badge and offered advice on 'how to organise an effective trousers protest', the struggle was far from over. Indeed, at the turn of the 1980s plenty of people still shared Mr Stayt's view that trousers were undermining family values. Even the *Guardian*, running a feature on the dazzling variety of trousers available in 1980 – jeans, dungarees, breeches, trouser suits, flying suits, 'colonial-style long shorts' – conceded that while 'the trousered European female may no longer be regarded as a threat to the very fabric of civilisation . . . a little of the old subversive flavour lingers on'.

Some commentators thought trousers were still so controversial that women would be safest to avoid them altogether. In his book *Women, Dress for Success* (1981), John T. Molloy, an 'authority on career woman dressing', claimed that the trouser suit was a 'failure outfit. Testing showed it to be extremely ineffective when dealing with men . . . If you have to deal with men, even as subordinates, you're putting on trouble. I advise against wearing them.' And some older women, in particular, were appalled to see their younger sisters dressing like men. 'I've never seen a woman who looked good in trousers because they've got the wrong-shaped behind,' Barbara Cartland declared in 1983. 'If women looked at themselves behind then they wouldn't wear trousers.' All this, she said sadly,

was merely part of a bigger story. For thanks to the advent of a 'new breed
of sexually strident amazons, wearing ugly, ill-fitting clothes, men's hats
and dinner suits', many men were taking their pleasures with other men
instead. In other words, it was feminism that was driving the newfound
acceptance of homosexuality. Sometimes, Dame Barbara would wag her
finger at her young female secretary: 'It's all your fault!'[3]

Perhaps the most dramatic of all trouser-themed confrontations took
place less than a year before Margaret Thatcher came to office. The
battleground was Maiden Erlegh School, a large comprehensive on the outskirts of Reading. The headmaster, James Dunkley, had long been an
opponent of trousers, insisting that 'lady members of staff should wear
dresses'. In June 1978, however, nine teachers turned up wearing trousers
and had to be corralled in a classroom, presumably for the safety of their
impressionable charges. Soon four more teachers joined them, prompting
mediation attempts from both the National Union of Teachers and the local
council. As the union saw it, women teachers should wear what they liked.
'Trousers', explained a union official, Ray Fox, 'are a perfectly respectable
form of dress and are probably more suitable for schools than mini-skirts.'
What was more, 'some of the women look very smart in them'. That, of
course, implied that some didn't. Fortunately he was too polite to name
names.[4]

For the press, the Battle of Maiden Erlegh was a gift. The *Express*
thought that the headmaster had shown 'no more strategic sense than
Edward Heath', and warned that the women, 'like the miners, are invincible and the best policy is one of surrender on as favourable terms as can
be got'. The 'right to wear trousers', it declared, was 'good, just and
proper'. But the *Express* urged Britain's women to accept, 'for everybody's
sakes, that ladies measuring more than 38in round the hips should show
restraint'. This did not go down well. A few days later, a group of office
workers from Andover signed a letter steaming with outrage. 'Yes, some
women do look dreadful in trousers,' they conceded, 'but so do many men,
especially those with paunches.' It was time, they suggested, that men with
waists of more than 33 inches stopped wearing trousers. A reader from
Sidmouth in Devon agreed that men, not women, should seek alternative
forms of clothing, gleefully picturing 'all those plump, pompous executives
and beery labourers being forced to wear kilts'. But some readers maintained that women's trousers were just wrong. 'I am heartily sick of
all those women who insist on kicking up a fuss,' wrote Irene Smith
of Leicester. 'If half the women in trousers could see themselves they
would think twice about wearing them.'[5]

In the end, it was the headmaster who blinked first, conceding that the women could wear trousers after all. 'Principles are always worth fighting for,' said their leader, Norma Bird, 'but we are very pleased it is at an end. We will carry on as normal – and wear trousers.' But although Maiden Erlegh had fallen, the war continued. Every few months some new trouser controversy appeared in the newspapers. In August 1981, for example, a Derbyshire woman complained to the *Guardian* that her daughter's headmaster 'considers trousers detrimental to her education'. Amazingly, the primary school in question did not even have a uniform, but the head-master had nevertheless banned women teachers and dinner ladies, as well as the girls, from wearing trousers. This time, perhaps because the school was so small, the forces of reaction won the day.[6]

An even more flagrant example came in the spring of 1983, when Gold-ers Green Crematorium in north London sacked a memorial counsellor, the 40-year-old Jeanne Turnock, who had ignored her boss's warnings not to wear trousers. As Mrs Turnock told an industrial tribunal, she had started wearing the offending garment, described as a 'lady's business trouser suit', during a cold snap. The crematorium's managing director – a man, obviously – explained that he regarded trousers on women as akin to 'mini-skirts, see-through blouses, plunging necklines, teeshirts with slogans and men wearing sweaters or earrings'. 'We are dealing with elderly people recently bereaved', he said sternly, 'and a large number may find some offence in a lady in trousers coming to deal with them.' The tribunal unanimously agreed with him.[7]

As Britain's first woman Prime Minister, Margaret Thatcher could hardly have been a more striking symbol of social change. When her car pulled up outside Number 10 that May morning, the spectacle of the lone woman in her trim blue suit, surrounded by men – policemen, photographers, her husband – brought home her novelty. But, perhaps with one eye on her constituents in Golders Green, she drew the line at appearing in trousers. 'Do you wear slacks?' asked the *News of the World*'s Rosalie Shann in April 1980. 'Only if I have to go and inspect a submarine, or something,' Mrs Thatcher said, laughing. What about jeans? 'No, I will just wear a tweed skirt and top.' Why not? 'I haven't got the figure for it.' 'I think you'd look super in slacks,' Shann said encouragingly. But Mrs Thatcher muttered some-thing about not knowing 'if my colleagues will like it', and they moved on.[8]

As the first woman to lead a major political party, Mrs Thatcher gave a lot of thought to her appearance. She had always enjoyed fashion, and took immense care to get things right. She knew that as a woman she would face unsparing scrutiny: it was all right for Ted Heath to put on weight, for Harold Wilson to look puffy and shabby, for Jim Callaghan to make his grand entrance at Number 10 with his tie tucked into his trousers, but she could not have one hair out of place. When *The Times*'s Brian Connell was granted a long interview to mark Mrs Thatcher's first year as Prime Minister, he began by describing her as 'trim and comely', before lavishing praise on her 'meticulously coiffed hair' and 'fine-boned features'. Oddly, no journalist had ever noticed Harold Wilson's fine-boned features, but there were different standards for women. 'Nobody complains about the cut of Mr Callaghan's trousers. Nobody tears him to pieces if he sounds like a pompous policeman. *Yet who would want a dowdy female fatty for Prime Minister?*' asked the *Sun* in 1979. 'After all, if a person can't control her weight, doesn't it occur to everybody that she may not be able to control other, more important things?'[9]

Mrs Thatcher was not the only woman who felt immense pressure to control her weight. In an age saturated with images of athletic beauty, from fashion magazines to pop videos, dieting had become big business. According to a survey in 1980, three out of ten women had been on a diet in the previous twelve months, compared with just one in ten men. Diet books were proven money-spinners, with Audrey Eyton's million-selling *The F-Plan* in the vanguard. At the newsagents, readers could choose not only from *Slimming*, *Successful Slimming*, *Slimmer* and *What Diet*, but *Health*, *Health Now* and *Healthy Living*, as well as *Work Out*, *New Health* and *Fitness*. Health spas, exercise bikes, early-morning jogs and lurid sportswear were becoming familiar features of the national landscape. 'In summer,' said the *Financial Times*, 'the British look as if they have just completed a jogging circuit and in winter, with their anoraks, as if they had just finished skiing.' No wonder, then, that when Chris Brasher launched the London Marathon in March 1981 it proved a smashing success, attracting some 6,700 runners. The winner of the women's race was the 43-year-old Joyce Smith, a veteran cross-country runner. In good Thatcherite style, she described herself as an ordinary 'housewife and mother'. Another of the first female finishers, one Mrs Barry, told the BBC that she had four children. 'Women use children as an excuse,' she said firmly. 'If they really wanted to, they could easily find ten minutes a day to train.'[10]

Mrs Thatcher herself was about as likely to train for the London Marathon as she was to invest in a new pair of Levi's. But like many women, she thought a lot about her waistline. 'Your clothes tell you. You don't need to weigh yourself,' she told Rosalie Shann. She had to be careful, because 'if you come in late, you know, and you pick something up the chances are that you pick something up starchy'. Before the election, she had spent two weeks on a strict diet of grapefruit, eggs and meat, ticking off each meal against a list that included the stern warning 'NO EATING BETWEEN MEALS'. Later, she switched to a different diet, about which she gave a hilariously incongruous interview to the *Sun* ('My Face, My Figure, My Diet'). She was not a fan of lettuce, she said, and hated oysters. But her real weakness was for anything sweet. 'Lovely toast and marmalade. I can never eat that,' she said sadly. 'Now and then I eat chocolates, but I find it hard to stop at one. It's often best, you know: to do without completely. You can't indulge. It will sit on your hips.'[11]

Mrs Thatcher also gave considerable thought to her clothes. Like many professional women, she experimented with various looks before hitting on one that suited her. As she told the *Observer*, her role models, in fashion as in so much else, were her parents, who had 'always looked neat, well-tailored, but never flamboyant'. In later years, she adopted a more obviously American style, all hairspray and shoulders, like an extra from *Dynasty*. But in the first years of the 1980s she was keen not to appear too expensively groomed. After all, as a self-described 'plain straightforward provincial', the Prime Minister could hardly splash out *à la* Nancy Reagan. So her look was more understated: plain, sensible, tweedy and professional, with leather shoes and an omnipresent handbag. And when Rosalie Shann asked where she got her clothes, she immediately cited the national favourite. 'Marks and Spencer's always sends one down for me to look at, they know what I like,' she mused. 'Lots of blouses. And they do some excellent suits and I have one overcoat from there. And, of course, everything.' Shann pounced: 'What, all your undies are Marks?' Mrs Thatcher detected danger: she did not want her knickers splashed all over the *News of the World*. 'Yes, yes, I'm sorry, please don't put it like that,' she said hastily, 'but you know, yes we all do.'[12]

It would be easy to dismiss all this as trivial. But as all working women knew, clothes were more than mere fripperies. To give an obvious example, Shirley Williams, Mrs Thatcher's only rival as the leading female politician of the 1980s, was widely seen as a clever, decent and good-humoured woman, which is why she was often mentioned as a possible Prime Minister. But she was hobbled by the perception that she was 'scruffy', which supposedly showed how disorganized she was. In her case, the personal really was political. In a spectacularly rude profile, the *Express*'s Geoffrey Levy suggested that while Mrs Thatcher 'exudes precision, as befits a research chemist', Mrs Williams ('a lover of chips') was notable for her 'legendary untidiness' and a 'brown thatch as uncontrollable as the Marxists in the Labour Party'. Some of Mrs Williams's worst critics, though, were other women. 'Her clothes look like they might come from jumble sales,' wrote Lucy Abelson in the *Sunday Express*, who again drew a contrast with the 'neat and tidy' Mrs Thatcher: 'Being well dressed is a sign of efficiency and such people are usually far better able to help than messy people precisely because they are better organised.' Even ordinary readers agreed. 'What a scruffy lot the Labour Party leaders are – especially Shirley Williams,' Mrs Constance of Bexleyheath, southeast London, wrote to the *Daily Mirror*. 'I dress smarter than her, even on my pension.'[13]

The problem for women like Margaret Thatcher and Shirley Williams was that there was no universally accepted office uniform. As *The Times*'s fashion writer Suzy Menkes pointed out in 1981, women were damned whatever they wore:

> How can a man, who is forever perfectly dressed in a decent business suit, understand the effort and the anxiety his female colleagues go through to be appropriately dressed for the same executive role?
>
> To be taken seriously in a high-flying job, a woman must not dress provocatively or untidily. She should look cool, business-like and unrumpled, wear sober colours and a simple unfussy cut. Yet . . . these are not the kind of clothes that are fashionable in any other part of a woman's life. Flamboyant and casual clothes, and especially trousers, are the staple of most women's out-of-work wardrobes. To suppress all personality and personal taste when behind a desk is most frustrating. And we cannot even show our colours by choice of tie.

For card-carrying feminists, this posed real difficulties. During the 1970s, admitted the *Guardian*, there had been a prevailing view that 'a flattering frock and a smear of lipstick are defeatist concessions to the traditional male view of women as sex objects and domestics'. But many women had got stuck in a wardrobe of 'jeans and T-shirts, jeans and shirts, jeans and sweaters', and were unable to break out. In an entertaining experiment in the summer of 1979, the paper persuaded the feminist academic Joni Lovenduski to submit to a makeover, ditching the sweaters and trying out some Clinique make-up, smart shirts and a Burberry rainjacket. The result was a triumph: proof, the *Guardian* said, that even an 'academic, socialist feminist' could 'end up looking right in clothes that, on another body and under another face, would have looked almost county'.[14]

This little experiment reflected a wider trend. A decade after women's lib had hit the headlines, fashion had moved on from the self-conscious informality of the early 1970s. Instead of defying convention, younger women were keen to show that they could be just as smart and efficient as their male counterparts. That meant dressing up, not down. 'Pride in one's appearance', said the *Guardian*, 'equals pride in one's personality and pleasure in expressing it.' Indeed, in 1981 a marketing consultant told the paper that overtly feminist fashion was on the way out. 'Women are setting out to abandon their jeans, boots and bra-less image and are adopting a very frilly feminine style,' explained Anthony Edwards. 'In the seventies female clothes shops were very casual – chromium-plated poles, denim and canvas. Now there's going to be a move towards highly feminine boudoirs.'

A few years earlier, talk of a frilly feminine style would have sent most self-respecting feminists reaching for their copies of *The Female Eunuch*. But fashion was 'newly fashionable on the Left', said the *Guardian*, which credited the emergence of a generation of feminists who were perfectly happy 'to compromise with high heels, make up and tight waists'. Even the paper's feminist-in-chief, Jill Tweedie, thought it high time women stopped feeling guilty about looking good. 'You don't have to signal a social conscience by looking like a frump,' she told her readers in October 1983:

> Lace knickers won't hasten the holocaust, you can ban the bomb in a feather boa just as well as without, and a mild interest in the length of hemlines doesn't necessarily disqualify you from reading Das Kapital and agreeing with every word. Stick up two sequinned fingers at the Puritans, kick up two silver heels, come up with all frills flying and remember – the art of exterior decoration is light years older than Paris.[15]

On the high street, the big winner from the rise of the professional working woman was Next, which opened in February 1982, specifically targeting the aspirational '25-plus younger career girl'. But even high fashion, which often seemed dizzyingly remote from the kind of women who shopped at places like Next, reflected the same trend. The important thing, explained one of the best-known designers of the early 1980s, Katharine Hamnett, was to use 'the alphabet of the workman while emphasizing erogenous zones'. She herself had 'benefited from the emancipation of women which has been taking place and I believe my clothes are designed to match the strength and confidence more and more women are gaining'. At the same time, Hamnett was keen to include a 'sexual element', since clothes were about 'allowable fantasies'.

This was not exactly ground-breaking stuff: for decades designers had boasted that their clothes were all about confidence and sexuality. But some of Hamnett's themes were new. 'Clothes should enable a woman to be exciting, sexy, efficient, functional,' she explained. 'She should be able to play the Las Vegas tart, conduct a business meeting and fry fish fingers in the same garment. Clothes need to perform for the way women live now.' These were clothes, agreed *The Times*, for women who wanted to be 'substantial, active, sexually assertive, glamorous, businesslike, equal'. Efficient, functional, glamorous, business meetings, *businesslike*: here was the new language of the 1980s.[16]

The date is June 1979, the place California, and in the futuristic head-quarters of Drax Industries, the United Kingdom's most celebrated lover of women is in for a shock. Resplendent in his smart new blazer, James Bond has come to investigate the disappearance of the *Moonraker* space shuttle, and the firm's boss, the peculiar Hugo Drax, has asked one of his astronauts to show him around. At the entrance, a pretty young woman with a clipboard comes to greet him. 'My name is Bond, James Bond,' Roger Moore says, flashing his most dazzling smile, 'and I'm looking for Dr Goodhead.' The woman smiles: 'You just found her' – and for a frac-tion of a second Moore's eyes widen in surprise. And then, coolly, almost flatly, with just the slightest hint of amusement, he says what everybody is thinking: '*A woman.*'

Dr Goodhead bristles. 'Your powers of observation do you credit, Mr Bond,' she says icily. No doubt she has been through this many times before. Despite her unfortunate surname, she is clearly a woman of great intellect: when, later in the film, Bond runs into her in Venice, she tells him that she is 'addressing the European Space Commission'.* 'Heady stuff!' Bond says. 'There again, I keep forgetting you are more than just a beautiful woman.' 'If you're trying to be ingratiating, don't bother,' she says wearily. But this is James Bond, so we all know how it will end: 'I think he's attempting re-entry, sir!'

By the time James Bond and Holly Goodhead found themselves hurtling into outer space, the strong, self-willed, independent woman, asserting herself against the prejudices of her colleagues, had become a familiar feature of British popular culture. In *Doctor Who*, Tom Baker's compan-ions in the late 1970s and early 1980s included a knife-wielding warrior from an alien planet (Leela), a Time Lady who always knows best (Romana) and an Australian air hostess for whom he can do no right (Tegan). In December 1980, just before Baker hung up his scarf, *Grange Hill* acquired its first headmistress, the formidable Mrs Bridget McClusky, for whom the words 'firm but fair' might have been invented. The actress who played her, Gwyneth Powell, said later that she had been written as

---

* Actually, she is an undercover agent for the CIA. But of course that only makes her all the more impressive.

a 'twin set and pearls' part, but she wanted her to be more assertive. 'I think Mrs McClusky became memorable', she remarked, 'because we had a prime minister like that.' And almost a year later, the BBC began showing a drama series dominated entirely by female faces, *Tenko*, which follows a group of women imprisoned by the Japanese during the Second World War. The *Guardian* complained that its characters were merely a parade of female stereotypes ('the spoilt beauty . . . the battleaxe . . . the flirt') but *Tenko* proved enormously popular. The *Mirror*, in a glorious misunderstanding, thought it was 'the saga of women imprisoned in a supermarket'.[17]

Perhaps the most striking examples of change, though, were two series exploring the lives of women police officers in a male-dominated world, both of which began in mid-1980. The first was ITV's *The Gentle Touch*, which was first shown in April and starred Jill Gascoine as a widowed single parent, Maggie Forbes, who is an inspector with the Metropolitan Police. Maggie is far more than a cardboard heroine: even as she engages with some remarkably hard-hitting social issues, from rape and homosexuality to racism and child abuse, she is struggling to cope with her teenage son and elderly father. By contrast, the heroine of the BBC's *Juliet Bravo*, launched four months later, has life a little easier. Jean Darblay (Stephanie Turner) is a police inspector in Lancashire, and although her husband has been made redundant, at least he is still alive. Like Maggie, though, Jean has to fight for every inch against her colleagues' prejudices. Even her superintendent warns her that 'there are quite a few around who'd be pleased to see you fail'.[18]

*Juliet Bravo* was written by Ian Kennedy Martin, the man behind *The Sweeney*. He based its central character on a real officer, Inspector Wynn Darwin, who ran the police station in Great Harwood, Lancashire. 'When she'd arrived in her new post, it'd taken months to stop her men opening squad car doors for her,' Kennedy Martin recalled. 'She was always in the hairdressers under a dryer when news of a major incident came through, and if she was in civvies she would then have to tear back home, put on her uniform, and then go to the incident because without the uniform she'd be ignored.' Turning her experience into a drama, however, had its complications. Kennedy Martin had to persuade the BBC not to call the series *A Fair Cop*, while some of his writers had never put a woman centre stage before. But the show was a tremendous hit, although the best thing about it was the theme tune. Talking to the *Express*, Stephanie Turner hoped Jean would inspire real women to join the police. 'I'm sure most policewomen feel, as she does, that they have to be twice as good as a chap to get ahead in the force,' she remarked. Alas, the *Mirror* rather let the side down. 'It was girls, girls, girls yesterday as BBC bosses unwrapped their autumn TV package,' began its story announcing the new show. The headline was 'Watch the Birds'.[19]

Behind shows like *Juliet Bravo* was a seismic shift in the experience and aspirations of millions of women. For young women who, like Jean Darblay, had come of age since the 1960s, modern Britain offered unprecedented educational and economic opportunities. By 1980 four out of ten university applications were from women, with the total rising every year. Even at Oxford and Cambridge, three out of ten students were women. As women were better educated, so they were likely to have loftier career goals; as contraception freed them from the routine of childbearing, so they tailored their family lives to suit their ambitions. Perhaps the most important thing, though, was the transition from labour-intensive heavy industry, which suited men, to white-collar clerical and service work, which women could do equally well, if not better. In other words, not only were there more women who wanted to work, there were more jobs for them to do. By the time Mrs Thatcher took office, almost six out of ten women were working in some capacity, a higher proportion than in any other Western European country outside Scandinavia. As the *Guardian* remarked in 1981, this was 'one of the biggest social revolutions since the war. Neither the tax system, nor the social security system nor many personnel directors nor the trade unions nor many husbands have even begun to adjust to these changes.'[20]

In many ways the outlook for Britain's women at the turn of the 1980s was rosier than ever. Only a few years earlier, many professions had been virtually all-male. In the City, women were not even allowed on to the floor of the Stock Exchange until March 1973. But as female recruits flooded into the professions, it became more common to see a female doctor, a female lawyer or a female bank manager. Even more tellingly, ambitious young women were very quick to react to the boom in self-employment. Between 1979 and 1992, the number of self-employed women rose by a staggering 109 per cent, while the number employing staff went up by 49 per cent, compared with just 14 per cent for men. Evidently many women preferred working for themselves to enduring the patronizing jokes of the male-dominated office. Researching the subject for the *Guardian*, the economics writer Frances Cairncross came across 'women with children who cook for boardroom lunches, who decorate Moses baskets for Liberty's, who teach English to foreign students and foreign languages to English students, who do typing or editing or translation', as well as a woman who had opened her own toy shop and a woman who sold dried flowers. She even met a woman with two small children, who, working from home, handled public relations for the Chicago Pizza Pie Factory chain. She made very little money, but did it 'because it gives me a tremendous sense of achievement. I'm not creative enough to paint the house or do patchwork. This keeps me in touch with the real world.'[21]

Of all Britain's female entrepreneurs, the best known was Anita Roddick, who opened her first Body Shop in 1976 and had forty-three outlets by the spring of 1984, exploiting young women's newfound fascination with 'ethical consumerism'. But a more surprising example was Stephanie ('Steve') Shirley, who had founded F International, one of Britain's biggest software companies, as far back as 1962. As Britain's first female computer entrepreneur, she became one of the faces of the computer boom, turning over some £7 million and employing 1,000 people by 1984. Remarkably, more than nine out of ten of her staff were women, reflecting Shirley's determination to support mothers juggling children and careers. In her own words, she had 'never considered myself an entrepreneur', but had wanted to show that she was as good as any man. 'I also used to wear grey suits so that I could hide amongst them,' she told Polly Toynbee. 'But I've grown out of that now. No more grey suits.' She still called herself 'Steve', though, having adopted the name because 'Stephanie' would have deterred investors. Mrs Thatcher, as a woman, a scientist and a champion of entrepreneurship, looked very kindly upon her, awarding her an OBE in 1980 and inviting her to join various public bodies. Shirley herself, though, was not a very political animal. At her first Downing Street reception, she went up to a man on his own, introduced herself and asked who he was. 'The name's Thatcher,' he said.[22]

What women like Anita Roddick and Steve Shirley represented was not just success but *empowerment*. Born of the individualistic culture of the 1960s and 1970s, empowerment became a central theme of political and social life under Mrs Thatcher. While the Prime Minister talked of 'returning power to the people' through privatization, feminists insisted that women needed to be 'empowered' to become equal citizens in a non-patriarchal democracy. It is not hard to see why. Touring the industrial North in the mid-1980s, the radical writer Beatrix Campbell met more than a few older women who had no money, no work experience, few friends, no opportunities and no *power*. In Wigan, she met an 85-year-old woman who would have liked to have worked, but had been forbidden by her husband. She had no money of her own, relied on her daughter for help and subsisted on crisps and cottage cheese. In Sheffield, Campbell met another elderly woman who occasionally went out to play dominoes in a community centre. This lady, too, had no money. In fact, she had *never* had any money. As a treat, her husband bought her an ice cream on

Fridays and paid for her to have her hair permed once a year. 'He says I should be thankful,' the woman explained, and her dominoes-playing friends gave a hollow laugh. 'Aye,' one said quietly, 'that's how it is.'[23]

This was an older Britain, settled and secure but also narrow and stifling, reassuring but also repressive; a world in which men worked and women cooked, men earned and women cleaned. By the early 1980s, though, it was passing into history. Younger women, in particular, were very conscious of their rights to equal pay, equal opportunities, financial independence, legal equality, sexual freedom and reproductive choice. Few people still believed that women should be chained to the kitchen sink: a poll for the *Mail on Sunday* in 1983 found that 86 per cent agreed that women should be able to work if they wanted to, and more than half thought that women could combine a full-time job with having a family.

Indeed, the idea of equal opportunities had acquired an institutional momentum of its own, thanks to the Sex Discrimination Act of 1975 and the creation of an Equal Opportunities Commission. But the most controversial example was the Greater London Council's women's committee, which was established after Ken Livingstone became leader of the council in 1981 and spent some £7 million annually on 'women's interests'. The tabloids howled with laughter, especially when the committee handed money to such groups as Babies Against the Bomb, the Black Women's Radio Group and the Southall Black Sisters. But where London led, other Labour-run cities – Birmingham, Leeds, Nottingham, Edinburgh – followed. 'In future,' the chair of the GLC's women's committee, Valerie Wise, promised in 1982, 'every committee report will have a paragraph stating its implications for women.' At the time, her critics thought she was deranged. But then they laughed at the word 'chair', too.[24]

For obvious reasons, empowerment is often seen in terms of having sex and not having children. Thanks to the Pill, women were not only having fewer children but having them later, after beginning a career. Among women born in 1960, whose twenties coincided almost exactly with the Thatcher years, one in three reached the age of 30 without having children. But although sexual freedom got a lot of attention, the new financial freedoms were just as important. In 1974 only one in eight British women had a building society account and one in three had a bank account. Yet by 1983, almost half had building society accounts, while two-thirds had bank accounts. Women could now get mortgages, too: half of all women under the age of 34 either owned or co-owned their own homes. In the same year, Sonia Copeland, a Conservative member of the GLC, told the magazine *City Limits* that 'the chequebook and the Pill have been very liberating and that's probably among the reasons women can break from marriage and cope on their own'. The Pill gets most attention. For many women, though, what really mattered was the chequebook.[25]

Women's liberation had its limits. More women might be working than ever, but most were not prosecuting cases at the Old Bailey, running the Dudley branch of the Midland Bank or setting up their own publishing empire. The vast majority were cleaners, dinner ladies, shop assistants, secretaries, social workers, nurses and teachers. They still earned much less than men, and in the recession of the early 1980s their pay actually fell back from almost 76 per cent to about 70 per cent of men's. Even in the unions, where women accounted for almost a third of the total membership, they typically held subordinate roles. When Beatrix Campbell interviewed trade unionists in the early 1980s, she found that a great gulf separated the women, who wanted to talk about childcare, maternity leave and equal pay, from their male representatives, who were more interested in pay rises and job losses. One woman, who worked in a Midlands engineering factory, asked the men when they had their branch meetings. 'Why do you want to know?' they asked suspiciously. It turned out the meetings were in another town. 'How could I go?' she said bitterly. 'I didn't have a car and I had kids.'[26]

In more conservative quarters, opposition to working mothers died hard. Indeed, some senior figures in Mrs Thatcher's own party seemed to forget that she was a working mother. 'Quite frankly I don't think mothers have the same right to work as fathers do,' her social services spokesman, Patrick Jenkin, declared in 1977. 'If the good Lord had intended us to have equal rights to go out to work he wouldn't have created men and women.' Even in 1981, after his boss had been Prime Minister for almost two years, Jenkin told a Conservative women's conference that the government should not 'give an unreserved welcome to the mothers of young children going out to work'. The best way to bring up children, he said, was 'at their mother's knee'. What small children really wanted was 'the love, care and attention of a mother for most of their waking and sleeping day'.[27]

Jenkin was not the only senior Conservative who seemed not to notice that his own boss was a wife and mother. In October 1981 Mrs Thatcher's ideological soulmate Sir Keith Joseph told a teachers' conference that he was a great believer in 'young mothers being with their children'. It was not the government's job, he said, to provide childcare for toddlers. Perhaps it is a shame that Sir Keith had not been on hand in Leicester a few months earlier. For that January, the teenage Adrian Mole was hit by a bombshell: his mother was going out to work. 'I could end up a delinquent roaming the streets and all that,' writes Sue Townsend's disgusted diarist. 'And what will I do during the holidays? ... I will be a latchkey kid, whatever that is.' A year later, having been sucked into a nightmarish world of feminism, consciousness-raising and Greenham Common-visiting, Mrs Mole invites her women's group to use their house for meetings ('No men or boys allowed in our front room'). At that, Adrian's father mutters that 'women ought to be at home cooking'. But he says it in a whisper, 'so that he wouldn't be karate-chopped to death'.[28]

Not surprisingly, many women were outraged by what they saw as men's attempts to put them back in their box. In the *Daily Express*, hardly a hotbed of feminist subversion, Helen Franks gave Sir Keith Joseph a blistering telling-off. Mothers worked, she wrote, not because they were careerist harridans, but 'to provide cash that is needed to pay off the mortgage, keep growing children in clothes, or add a few luxuries to the weekly shopping basket'. When 'the teachers, the secretaries, the shop assistants [and] the nurses' left their children at home, they did so 'with the strong sense of guilt that has been laid on them through generations of a totally male orientated society'. Clearly Joseph was too dim to understand why many women craved independence and stimulation, rather than 'depression and isolation'. Many Tory activists would have agreed with every word. As Beatrix Campbell found when she interviewed Conservative women in the mid-1980s, many party activists were themselves working women, while Mrs Thatcher's younger ministers were often married to professional women. Indeed, the Conservative women's organization constantly pressed for policies such as equal pay, new rights for part-timers and better provisions for women juggling work and home.[29]

For many women, the working day did not end when they walked back through the front door. In 1979 a survey found that British men were keener on housework than anybody else in Europe, with 85 per cent saying that they were happy to wash up, 30 per cent to change their babies' nappies and even 29 per cent to do the ironing. (By contrast, just 21 per cent of Italian men were prepared to wash up, 13 per cent to change the nappies and a pitiful 6 per cent to do the ironing.) Yet in every country surveyed, women insisted that their husbands actually did far less than they claimed. Indeed, another study five years later found that nine out of ten British women did all the washing and ironing, seven out of ten did all the household cleaning and five out of ten did all the shopping. In Romford, Carol Daniel spent her evenings stacking shelves at Tesco. But her days were not her own: far from it. 'Up at 6.30, make breakfast for Doug (my husband),' began a housework log she complied for Mass Observation. 'Dress children ... Take children to school ... Wash up, put on washing, make beds . . . Tidy kitchen . . . Prepare tea . . . Wash up . . .' It was a wonder that she found the time to write it all down.[30]

Not all husbands were equally useless. By and large, the younger and better educated the husband, the more likely he was to help. 'My own husband is a gem,' reported Susan Gray from Darlington. 'When we both worked full time the housework was divided equally.' When their daughter was very young, 'he probably did more housework and baby-care than most husbands', and he always did his share of the shopping. 'This sort of attitude seems general among friends and acquaintances,' Susan wrote, 'and even the most Andy Capp-like man we knew became a changed character after his wife slipped two discs in her spine.' Even the 56-year-old Mary Richards said that although she generally hated social change, she heartily approved of the new 'relationship between men and women'. 'They do seem to be better partners than when I was young,' she wrote. 'The interest my son and son-in-law take in their children amazes me. They change babies' nappies, feed babies, take them walkies. My husband would not be seen pushing a pram and never changed a nappy in his life. "That was woman's work." '[31]

Already struggling to juggle childcare and housework, many women found full-time jobs effectively impossible. By 1981 more than eight out of ten of Britain's part-time workers were women, most of them married women who worked as cleaners, dinner ladies and so on. Not only were these jobs very poorly paid, they were very insecure. As the journalist Frances Williams noted, women were often 'first in line for redundancy' because many firms had 'last in, first out' rules, under which maternity leave counted against them. Firms were also keener to get rid of part-time workers, even though it was technically against the law. On top of all that, Mrs Thatcher's spending cuts fell disproportionately on women because the services slashed by local authorities – 'school meals, home helps, nurseries' – relied so heavily on female staff, which left wives and mothers stepping in to fill the gaps.[32]

It is remarkable, then, how rarely women appeared in the images of unemployment that defined the early 1980s. The official figures showed that women made up about a third of the jobless total, but since many unemployed women simply gave up looking for work, they were not counted. Photographers sent to capture the plight of working-class Britain typically took pictures of men, not women. Journalists talked to husbands, not wives. There are virtually no women's voices in the protest songs of the era, while not one of the seven central characters in ITV's *Auf Wiedersehen, Pet* (1983–4) is a woman. Even in Alan Bleasdale's *Boys from the Blackstuff* (1982), the vast majority of the characters are men. It is true

that there are some strong female roles, above all Julie Walters's spirited
Angie Todd, the only character who genuinely wants to fight back against
the economic forces holding them down. For Walters, Angie was her great
screen breakthrough. But it is Bernard Hill's searing portrayal of Yosser
Hughes, the embodiment of collapsing working-class masculinity, that
has entered television legend. By contrast, Angie Todd, a woman surrounded by men, is almost entirely forgotten.[33]

What about all those women who *didn't* go out to work? Half of all mothers
in 1980 remained at home, yet their stories never make it into the history
books. A quarter of a century earlier, the housewife had been the mistress
of the home, the cornerstone of the family, the ideal consumer, the 'kitchen
goddess'. But now portraits of housewives tended to be much more
negative.

On television, housewives were often lonely, repressed and frustrated,
like Wendy Craig's Ria in Carla Lane's sitcom *Butterflies*, which ran from
1978 to 1983. Married to a reserved, unromantic dentist, with two feckless
grown-up sons, Ria is the embodiment of suburban frustration. She is not
a feminist, and still loves her husband. But she is bored. Daydreaming of
another life, she falls into a platonic semi-affair with her friend Leonard.
Her story clearly struck a chord with millions of viewers. 'Most women
are comforted to see that "Butterflies" is exactly like their own homes,'
Craig told the *Express*. 'I share the same weaknesses, shout at my children,
get upset by the monotony of life and the constant demands of a family,
and I have a husband who comes back tired from work and unable to
communicate.' Later, she recalled getting letters from housewives who
told her that *Butterflies* was 'the story of my life', and wondered if she
was 'looking in through my letter-box'.[34]

For some observers, the fact that housewives still existed at all was a
sad reflection of the limits of feminism. In 1980 the former editor of the
*Guardian*'s women's page, Suzanne Lowry – who described her own page,
only half-jokingly, as the home of 'pre-menstrual tension and post-natal
depression, plus grim, humourless tracts on equality and man-hating' –
published *The Guilt Cage*, lamenting the 'dreary and demeaning' plight
of Britain's housewives. Why, Lowry wondered, was it 'so difficult, even
for women who recognise the restrictions of the housewife's lot, to give
it all up and strive, as the feminists so cogently urge, for a more independent life'?

As she recognized, there was no simple answer. 'Fear, lack of money
and loss of confidence' all played their part. But so did 'male dominance',
as well as women's reluctance to lose their 'domestic power base'. Lowry

barely considered the possibility that some housewives, at least, might find their lives genuinely enjoyable and fulfilling. But she was surely right to suggest that television commercials – the Persil and Fairy Liquid campaigns, for example, or the famous Oxo family – still pushed a conservative image of the 'woman in the kitchen, serving her family as the perfect all-weather provider, addicted to washing-up liquid and obsessed by clean surfaces'. Even among working women, she wrote, 'Mum in the kitchen is still at the centre of our dreams and nightmares, if not about ourselves, then about others.'[35]

Yet many women who had chosen to stay at home bridled at being told that their existence was 'dreary and demeaning', and hated being written off as brainwashed slaves. When Mass Observation sent its correspondents a questionnaire about their health and well-being, they got a moving reply from a 29-year-old single mother who lived with her parents and her two children, aged 7 and 8. She had never had a permanent job and was not looking for one. In answer after answer, she denied that she felt frustrated and insisted that she found life happy and meaningful. But beside the statement 'I sometimes feel that people are looking down on me', she ticked 'Completely agree'. And at the end, she let rip:

> I think success is graded to a large extent by how much you earn, have you a degree in sciences, have you been abroad?
>
> A person staying at home, in my opinion, to look after children should be considered just as powerful as a director in a company. Don't they influence future workers? Aren't they keeping the world from halting birth altogether? Life on earth would come to a standstill if women refused to have babies for the next twenty years.
>
> The point is, of course, nobody sees it that way. The housewife is seen, virtually, as a non-person – doesn't get paid enough, if anything. She's the world's biggest doormat and yet she's the most important cog in the machine.

In almost every line, her frustration and bitterness – not with her lot as a housewife, but with her declining status in a society that seemed to care only about work, earnings and individual achievement – were etched on to the page.[36]

There was, however, one very prominent career woman who respected the work of Britain's housewives – or claimed to. In the summer of 1982, Mrs Thatcher was invited to give a lecture in honour of the Liberal suffragist Dame Margery Corbett Ashby, who had died a year earlier. Yet to her audience's visible displeasure, the Prime Minister went out of her way to present herself, not as the handmaiden of social change, but as the guardian of domesticity. 'Women know that society is founded on dignity, reticence and discipline,' she declared, adding that for Britain's children, 'much depends upon the family unit remaining secure and respected'. This meant that 'the home should be the centre but not the boundary of a woman's life'. Indeed, it was women's experience in the home that gave them the 'special talents' they brought to public life. They had different skills from men, she explained, because 'we women bear the children and create and run the home'.

This might have been calculated to infuriate many of her listeners, who included several veteran Liberal feminists. But Mrs Thatcher was merely warming up. 'When children are young,' she went on, 'however busy we may be with practical duties inside or outside the home, the most important thing of all is to devote enough time and care to the children's needs and problems.' This would have come as news to her own children, whose mother had relied on a nanny to handle the childcare. Then Mrs Thatcher turned to women's rights, for which Dame Margery had campaigned so vigorously. 'The battle for women's rights', she declared, 'has been largely won. The days when they were demanded and discussed in strident tones should be gone for ever. And I hope they are. I hated those strident tones that you still hear from some Women's Libbers.'[37]

After all that, none of the audience would have mistaken Mrs Thatcher for a feminist. Yet her position was more nuanced than is often remembered. She had, after all, spent her career as a working mother in a man's world. And although she liked to lay into 'women's libbers', she never failed to beat the drum for working women. In an interview with *Living* magazine, reflecting on her experience as a female Prime Minister, she said she was annoyed that people always referred to her that way: 'People don't evaluate the contribution *men* have made to life – so why do they do it with us?' But she recognized that women in politics faced particular difficulties, and that she had been unusually fortunate. 'If my husband's work had been in Cornwall or Cardiff I couldn't have left my children to be an MP,' she admitted. 'And my husband is supportive. Denis said, "It's absurd for you not to use your talents."' In other words, if Mr Thatcher had not been so encouraging, the world might never have heard of Mrs Thatcher. As she herself put it: 'I'm just lucky that things have bounced right for me.'

As in her lecture, Mrs Thatcher maintained that women's domestic experience actually worked in their favour – an argument that never failed to annoy her feminist critics. 'Women are natural decision-makers,' she explained. 'We're very practical and we don't moan about things – we get on with life ... Being a housewife is a managerial job – you're used to taking responsibility and living within a budget, and we need those qualities in government, and everywhere else.' In other words, it was precisely because women were so good at running the home that a woman – preferably one from Grantham, perhaps with experience in a grocer's shop – ought to run the country. Indeed, women's domestic backgrounds even meant they were better suited to winning wars. When, a few weeks after the end of the Falklands campaign, the *Express*'s George Gale asked about the pressures of the war, Mrs Thatcher reached, as so often, for the domestic analogy. 'Many, many women make naturally good managers,' she explained. 'You might not think of it that way, George, but each woman who runs a house is a manager and an organizer. We thought forward each day, and we did it in a routine way, and we were on the job 24 hours a day.' She made it sound a bit like organizing her children's laundry; and that, of course, was the point.[38]

The paradox of all this is that Mrs Thatcher completely failed to promote other women. Year after year, photographs of her Cabinet showed one woman surrounded by men in suits. To be fair, the Conservatives were hardly unusual in remaining overwhelmingly male. Although Labour claimed that Mrs Thatcher was letting other women down, its own senior ranks were almost entirely populated by men, too. In Michael Foot's Shadow Cabinet there was just one woman MP, Gwyneth Dunwoody, who was given the traditionally female-friendly health portfolio. Yet many Conservative women were disappointed that Mrs Thatcher, who had an unprecedented opportunity to promote their interests, showed no interest in doing so. In the *Guardian*, Polly Toynbee argued that a male Prime Minister would have done more for women, because he would have felt guilty. But Mrs Thatcher felt 'no guilt about women, because she is one. She is that all too familiar creature, the Queen Bee. The one who makes it herself, and pulls up the ladder behind her.'[39]

Queen Bees were common targets in liberal newspapers in the 1980s, often getting a kicking from feminist writers such as Jill Tweedie and Katharine Whitehorn. 'Queen Bees are women who have fought to succeed and made it, and now fear competition ... or simply don't see why others should have it any easier,' explained the *Observer* in 1980. And given the near-total absence of women from her Cabinet, it is easy to see why so many people saw Mrs Thatcher as a particular offender. The truth is that she visibly enjoyed being the only woman in the Cabinet Room, and had no desire to share the limelight. As Charles Moore notes, not only did she make very little effort to ingratiate herself with her ministers' wives, she could not even be relied upon to support women's equality measures.* At first she was even against the ordination of women priests, before she was persuaded to change her mind.[40]

To her critics, this left Mrs Thatcher's crown as the first woman Prime Minister tarnished beyond repair. But was she even a woman at all? When Mrs Thatcher won the Tory leadership, the admiring Barbara Castle had called her 'the best man among them'. Castle meant it as a joke. But it was not long before the idea of Mrs Thatcher as a woman pretending to be a man – or simply as a man in drag – caught on. The psychiatrist Anthony Clare, for example, wrote that she 'looked like a woman, talked and walked like a woman but behaved with the ruthlessness and confidence which had hitherto been assumed to be the prerogative of men'. On the satirical puppet show *Spitting Image* (1984) she was typically shown in a suit and tie, using the men's urinals and speaking in an unnaturally deep voice. The owner of the voice in question, the comedian Steve Nallon, made a decent living out of Mrs Thatcher, although it was hard to tell if he was a man impersonating a woman impersonating a man, or a man impersonating a man impersonating a woman. Even some Cabinet ministers – perhaps *especially* some Cabinet ministers – enjoyed his act. The only person who disliked it was Nallon's grandmother. A former seamstress from Leeds and a staunch working-class Conservative, she was outraged to see him mocking the Prime Minister. 'We don't watch *Spitting Image* in this house,' she once told him. 'We watch *That's Life*.'[41]

On the left, there were always those who questioned whether Mrs Thatcher deserved her status as the nation's first woman Prime Minister. 'She may be a woman but she isn't a sister, she may be a sister but she isn't a comrade,' explained the playwright Caryl Churchill, adding that there was 'no such thing as right-wing feminism'. So in Churchill's play *Top Girls* (1982), Mrs Thatcher is represented by the ruthless Marlene, who has sacrificed her femininity and abandoned her child to compete with men and get to the top. Marlene is naturally a great fan of the Iron Lady. 'She's a tough lady, Maggie. I'd give her a job,' she says admiringly. 'First woman prime minister. Terrifico . . . I believe in the individual . . . I don't believe in class. Anyone can do anything if they've got what it takes.' *Top Girls* has a tremendous reputation in some circles (academics, basically), but it has to be said that its analysis of Thatcherism falls well short of the height of sophistication. 'I hate the working class,' says Marlene, who thinks the term just means 'lazy and stupid'. This, of course, was exactly

---

* But there were exceptions: Nigel Lawson records that whenever his wife was ill, Mrs Thatcher sent her a handwritten note, sometimes with flowers.

the kind of Cruella de Vil-style thing that Mrs Thatcher's critics believed she said. But she never did.

Among radical feminists, *Top Girls*'s basic argument – that women like Mrs Thatcher only got on by surrendering their femininity and betraying their sisters – was very popular. There was an 'air of unreality' about her, thought Sheila Rowbotham. 'Not only the voice is contrived; her whole body can be seen in permanent tension, shifting across the borders of femininity and masculinity.' Mrs Thatcher had completely failed to develop a 'critique of the patriarchal family', agreed Beatrix Campbell. 'Femininity is what she wears, masculinity is what she admires. She wants to be a woman who does what men do.' And in some quarters this view proved remarkably enduring. 'The first Prime Minister of female gender, OK. But a woman? Not on my terms,' thundered the Oscar-winning Labour MP Glenda Jackson after Mrs Thatcher's death. 'She set back the cause of women in public life,' agreed the novelist Hilary Mantel. 'She imitated masculine qualities to the extent that she had to get herself a good war . . . The idea that women must imitate men to succeed is anti-feminist. She was not of woman born. She was a psychological transvestite.'[42]

But she *was* a woman. All Margaret Thatcher's biographers agree that her femininity was absolutely fundamental to her sense of herself, her political experience, her relations with her colleagues and her public image. Even her public nickname, 'Maggie', identified her as a woman. And because she was a woman in a man's world, she felt she always had to prove herself. Few people recognized this more clearly than her Private Secretary for Foreign Affairs, John Coles, who wrote a fascinating memoir of his time at her side in the summer of 1984. As Coles observed, most of her colleagues could draw on 'the shared experience of a few public schools, university, the services and the major Pall Mall clubs. They draw on a reserve of accepted thought and behaviour, of male humour, argument and sign-language from which a woman is excluded.' By contrast, Mrs Thatcher was the eternal outsider, a 'woman among men', who knew that there were 'many ready and waiting to criticise the choice of a woman to lead the Conservative party just as soon as she could be shown to be given to unreasonable feminine behaviour'.

Coles thought few people realized the 'emotional cost' to Mrs Thatcher of sustaining her leadership under such pressure, or 'the steps to which she had to resort to defy the conventions'. Perhaps she did not even realize it herself. For instance, Coles thought her hatred of compromise derived in part from the fact that it seemed to have a 'male quality, the civilised talk of clubland'. If she was 'upset or offended by a particular line of argument', he recalled, 'the resentment could bubble on for days. Not for her the political clash followed by the reconciliation over a drink in the club. She didn't have a club; she distrusted appeals to the team spirit.' It was this isolation that explained her 'abusive, rude and unpleasant' style, as well as her denigration of dissenters as 'soft', 'wet' or 'backsliding'. It was because she was a woman, Coles thought, that she could never back down, pushing disagreements 'to the point of extreme embarrassment to other listeners'. But for some of her ministers, who had not had to endure such treatment since the days of their boarding-school matrons, this seemed almost unbearable. As her colleague and frequent critic Jim Prior admitted, she brought out their 'male chauvinism'. Prior had been perfectly happy to tolerate rudeness from Ted Heath. But it seemed much worse 'when the challenger is a woman and the challenged is a man'.[43]

Mrs Thatcher was never allowed to forget that she was a woman. Because she seemed so different from her predecessors, people often compared her with other strident women who had come to prominence in the 1970s. The most obvious was Penelope Keith's magnificent Margo Leadbetter in *The Good Life* (1975–8), a staunch Home Counties Conservative, but also a bully and a snob with no sense of humour. But when the *Guardian* invited people to write in with unflattering nicknames for the Prime Minister in 1980, one of the most popular choices was 'Servalan'. As discerning readers will know, this refers to the Supreme Commander of the Terran Federation in the BBC1 science-fiction series *Blake's 7* (1978–81). Played with scenery-chewing relish by Jacqueline Pearce, Servalan is at once immensely glamorous and thoroughly evil. One *Blake's 7* character calls her 'the sexiest officer I have ever known'; another calls her 'spoilt, idle, vicious'; a third calls her 'a tasteless megalomaniac'. That was pretty much what *Guardian* readers said about the Prime Minister.[44]

Like Servalan, Mrs Thatcher was perfectly happy to exploit her femininity. Her biographers often describe her as an actress working her way through the female repertoire – the housewife, the mother, the nanny, the nurse, the diva – with her handbag as the essential prop. When Ludovic Kennedy visited Downing Street to make a programme about her murdered friend Airey Neave, she played the 'charming and considerate hostess', showing the crew around and telling them about the portraits. But when Kennedy saw her on television, he might have been watching a different person, giving a theatrical performance of 'extreme femininity', 'assumed intimacy' and 'mild flirtatiousness'. The BBC's John Simpson was similarly struck by her love of performing. In 1980 he was covering a press conference in Venice when she launched a ferocious attack on the BBC for calling the Afghan mujahedeen 'guerrillas'. Approaching her afterwards, Simpson tried to explain why they did it. She put her hand on his arm and looked at him 'coquettishly'. 'My dear,' she said softly, 'you are sensitive.' It was, he recalled, 'like flirting with Queen Victoria'.[45]

She was no less ruthless about using her femininity in private. Matthew Parris felt she sometimes teetered on the verge of self-parody, running her fingers disapprovingly over dusty paintings and telling her colleagues that only 'a *woman* knows whether a room's been cleaned *properly*'. But the best example comes in Alan Clark's diaries. In June 1981 she hosted the Defence and Foreign Affairs Committees at Number 10. Various back-benchers came in first, then the ministers, led by Lord Carrington, 'very bronzed and la-di-dah'. But then:

> The Lady came in and sat down on the yellow silk sofa on which Carrington had perched himself. There took place one of those curious, almost petty, but completely feminine, scenes which remind me of my mother. We all had drinks in our hands. Carrington had put his on a minute coffee table beside the right arm of the yellow silk sofa. The Lady had nowhere to put hers but an empty chair immediately on her left. Just as we were about to begin she called to Ian [Gow], who was at the far end of the room, and asked him to bring her a table for her glass. Ian was fussed by this, there was no table in sight or accessible. As he looked round Carrington got the message and got up. Against a background of 'no, no Peter,' etc., he removed his glass, put it on the mantelpiece, picked up the small table and stooping carried it round the sofa and put it down by the Prime Minister's left hand. I enjoyed this, not least because I could see that he did not. *What* a bore for all those men in the Cabinet to have as their leader not only a woman, but a woman who, whether subtly or overtly, insists on being treated as such.

She knew exactly what she was doing, of course.[46]

Clark himself found Mrs Thatcher downright attractive: '*so* beautiful . . . quite bewitching, as Eva Peron must have been'. In this instance, though, his swashbuckling reputation was slightly misleading. As he told Charles Moore, 'I don't want actual penetration – just a massive snog.' Astounding as it might seem, his enthusiasm was widely shared. The United Biscuits chairman Sir Hector Laing was so smitten that he would send notes to be placed underneath her pillow. Even François Mitterrand's famous quip about her having the eyes of Caligula and the mouth of Marilyn Monroe was a kind of compliment. Power had something to do with it, of course, but it was not the whole story. The novelist Kingsley Amis thought that Mrs Thatcher was 'one of the best-looking women I had ever met'. It was not, he conceded, a 'sensual or sexy beauty', but that did not make it a 'less sexual beauty', which he thought a much 'under-rated factor in her appeal (or repellence)'. Not even her parliamentary

adversaries were immune to her charms. Across the aisle, the future Social
Democrat leader David Owen was evidently beside himself with excitement. 'The whiff of that perfume, the sweet smell of whisky,' he mused
to his friend Brian Walden. 'By God, Brian, she's appealing beyond belief.'

Some of Mrs Thatcher's own ministers agreed with him. When John
Nott retired as Defence Secretary in January 1983, he wrote her a farewell
letter. In the press, Nott was generally seen as a superhumanly dull and
gloomy figure, yet his note surely ranks among the most extraordinary
letters ever sent by a minister to a Prime Minister:

My dear Margaret . . .

Our friendship has been sustained for me – through years of happy coop-
eration and occasional fierce disagreement (tinged with moments of positive
dislike on both sides, I suspect!) – by your wonderful personality.

   Your greatest triumph as a PM, if I may say so, is that your colleagues
(with very few exceptions) actually like you as a person. Some of them even
love you, just a little!

   It is inexcusable to say so nowadays but I actually admire you as a
woman – your good looks, charm and bearing have always attracted me,
as a man. I'm sorry, but what's wrong with that! . . .

Love
John

As the Thatcher Foundation's archivist Christopher Collins notes, Mrs
Thatcher scribbled on almost every document she ever read, but not this
one. Maybe she was embarrassed by it. Maybe she was flattered; she
always enjoyed compliments. After she appeared on the radio with a heavy
cold, Jim Prior, hardly her greatest fan, teased her about her 'sexy voice'.
She had the perfect comeback: 'What makes you think I wasn't sexy
before?'[47]

Of course there were millions of people who would have shuddered at
the thought of Mrs Thatcher being sexy. For every voter who saw her as
a modern-day Boadicea or a reincarnated Elizabeth I, there was another
who saw her as a battleaxe, a witch or a wicked queen. In this respect, at
least, the feminist revolution was far from complete. For the angrier Mrs
Thatcher's critics became, the more they turned to what now looks like
remarkably sexist, even misogynistic abuse. Almost without exception,
the nicknames coined by her fellow MPs emphasized the fact that she was
a woman, from 'the Great She-Elephant' and 'Attila the Hen' to 'the
Catherine the Great of Finchley', 'the Maggietollah' and, of course, 'That

Woman'. For Denis Healey, her most colourful critic, she was 'virago intacta', the 'Pasionara of middle-class privilege', 'Florence Nightingale with a blowtorch', 'a mixture of a matron at a minor public school and a guard in a concentration camp'. Even the nickname 'She Who Must be Obeyed', as her biographer John Campbell points out, refers to the diabolical African queen in H. Rider Haggard's *She* (1887).

The irony, of course, is that Mrs Thatcher's critics typically saw themselves as right-on champions of women's rights. But just as her admirers saw her as Britannia incarnate, so her critics returned again and again to the affront of her femininity. It is often suggested that their vehemence reflected the astringency of her economic policies. Yet when Ted Heath had presided over a ferocious confrontation with the unions, two miners' strikes and the three-day week, the antagonism had never been so personal or so bitter. Heath had been *wrong*. But Mrs Thatcher was cruel, mad, *evil*. In parodies and satires she was Mary Poppins's twisted twin, the Wicked Witch of Westminster, the Nurse Ratched of Greater Grantham. In newspaper cartoons there was an edge that had never been there in pictures of men. In the pop music of the 1980s the contrast was even stronger. Morrissey imagined her on the guillotine. Elvis Costello urged listeners to 'tramp the dirt down'.

No wonder, then, that even some feminists, who generally hated Mrs Thatcher, felt uneasy. The left-wing writer Clare Ramsaran, then in her late teens, thought that Mrs Thatcher was simply 'a whole new excuse for men on the left to stop feeling guilty about sexism'. But 'if you didn't laugh,' she wrote, 'you weren't just a humourless feminist, but – horror of horrors – a TORY'. Times changed, of course, but the hint of misogyny never went away. When Mrs Thatcher died in 2013, the song adopted by hard-left activists to mark her demise came from *The Wizard of Oz*. The title said it all: 'Ding-Dong! The Witch Is Dead'.[48]

# 4

# No Money, Margaret Thatcher!

*Happily for us, Margaret Thatcher – a strong man like yourself – is*
*about to come to power. As she stomps the country, invoking*
*the glorious example of such great Englishmen from our island*
*story as Sir Francis Drake and Sir Walter Pidgeon,\* the streets*
*ring with the sound of do-gooders breaking wind and taking to*
*the boats.*

> Henry Root to the President of Pakistan,
> General Zia, 26 April 1979, in Henry Root,
> *The Henry Root Letters* (1980)

*Mrs Thatcher has set her course. There can be no going back now.*
*EITHER SHE SUCCEEDS – OR WE BUST.*

> *Daily Mirror*, 13 June 1979

On the evening of Sunday 30 September 1979, the most popular sitcom
of the age made its debut on BBC1. *To the Manor Born* is the story of
Audrey fforbes-Hamilton, whose family has owned Grantleigh Manor,
in the heart of rural Somerset, for the last 400 years. But when her husband
dies leaving crippling debts, Audrey discovers that blue blood is no defence
against bankruptcy. In desperation, she sells up and moves into the lodge
at the end of the drive. But to her horror, Grantleigh is snapped up by
Richard DeVere, the self-made owner of a supermarket chain. To make
matters worse, Audrey discovers that not only is DeVere *nouveau riche*,
he is not even English, having arrived as a refugee from Czechoslovakia
in 1939. In just a few days her world has been turned upside down. 'To
think that Grantleigh is in the hands of a man who has no interest in
farming, doesn't go to church and now, it turns out, hasn't even heard of

---

\* In reality, a Canadian actor probably best known for *Mrs Miniver* (1942) and *Forbidden*
*Planet* (1956).

Winnie the Pooh,' she snaps at her suavely unruffled successor. 'You think A. A. Milne is a motoring organisation, I suppose.'

Despite glorious performances from Penelope Keith and Peter Bowles, some critics were very sniffy about *To the Manor Born*. 'Here we are in the midst of a recession,' wrote *The Times*'s Stanley Reynolds in December 1979, 'with starvation in Cambodia, boat people in Vietnam and the Mullahs on the warpath . . . and there is Penelope Keith as Mrs fforbes-Hamilton, the gentry widow, about to burst her tweed seams because a Jew has moved into the manor and is acting like the squire.' It was, he thought, all too 'safe and secure and snug'. But the public loved it. Thanks to an ITV strike, the initial viewing figures were tremendous, and once people started watching, they never stopped. The finale of the first series, which went out on 29 November, commanded 24 million viewers, the highest dramatic audience of the 1970s. A poll in the *Mirror*, meanwhile, found that the Christmas special had been the most popular programme of the season.[1]

'What has Audrey fforbes-Hamilton got to say that is so special to the people of Britain?' the veteran anatomist of Britain, Anthony Sampson, wondered in the *Observer*. A lot of it, he thought, was down to a yearning for the lost certainties of hierarchy and order – but not all of it.

> The spell of Audrey fforbes-Hamilton is surely more, much more, than the spirit of nostalgia. There she sits, all too terribly contemporary, fingering her invitation to the hunt ball and fending off the bank manager, watching with her binoculars the comings and goings of the upstart foreigner De Vere at the Manor, and preposterously trying to keep up appearances with her old Rolls-Royce, her bogus visits to Spain, and her botched-up Christmas crib for the local church, which is hopelessly outdone by the electronic crib provided by De Vere.
>
> The more we see of her, the more we realise that she sees herself as the very spirit of Britain, preserving her dignity and status while leaving it to the foreigner to dirty his fingers with trade, confident that her values will win out in the end.

And that, of course, was the attitude that Margaret Thatcher had come into office to overturn.[2]

Although *To the Manor Born* had been written before Mrs Thatcher took office, it was to become indelibly associated with the mood of her first term. A few years earlier, critics had remarked on her resemblance to *The Good Life*'s aspirational super-snob Margo Leadbetter. It was equally tempting to see her reflected in Audrey's cut-glass accent, withering putdowns and unashamed jingoism. Yet, as Sampson pointed out, *To the Manor Born*'s politics are a bit more complicated. As the tweedy representative of the old elite, Audrey is actually much closer to paternalist patricians such as Sir Ian Gilmour. It is DeVere, the self-made millionaire, who is the show's genuinely Thatcherite figure. To Audrey, he is merely 'trade'; at one point she even calls him a 'grocer'. That was precisely the kind of snobbery that the Grantham grocer's daughter had come to expect from her colleagues. Of course the series has a happy ending. Watched by more than 21 million people in 1981, the wedding of Audrey and Richard represents the union of the old aristocracy and the new entrepreneurs, the estate owners and the estate agents. But restoring peace to Grantleigh was easier than bringing unity to Westminster. Audrey fforbes-Hamilton might have vanquished her prejudices. But hell would have frozen over before Margaret Thatcher tied the knot with Sir Ian Gilmour.

No sooner had Downing Street's new chatelaine picked up the keys to her home than she was thinking about her staff. And among the letters that poured into Number 10 in the first weeks of May 1979 was one from an admirer with strong views about the people she needed. It was vital, wrote the fictional wet-fish merchant Henry Root, to 'form a Cabinet of hard-nosed men to prosecute our number 1 priority: the crackdown on the unions, the work-shy, law-breakers and homosexuals'. He advised her against appointing 'too many Oxbridge men', who had trouble 'discovering what day of the week it is'. Among various eclectic suggestions, Root recommended the Southampton football manager Lawrie McMenemy as Defence Secretary, on the grounds that the Saints had recently played in Europe, 'so he's had invaluable experience of "kicking the foreigners into the stands"'.* For Home Secretary, he suggested Mary Whitehouse, 'a mother like yourself'. He had been impressed by a *Sun* report that Mrs Whitehouse had visited Mrs Thatcher in the Commons, 'and how you showed each other pornographic pictures and knelt on the floor and prayed together. That was moving.' But he ended with a word of warning: 'I don't think we should have any bachelors in our Cabinet unless it's entirely necessary.'[3]

If Mrs Thatcher had had the sense to follow Henry Root's advice, history might have been very different. Bafflingly, however, there was no place for Whitehouse or McMenemy, although she did find room for bachelors and Oxbridge men. The truth was that although she had won

---

* Root copied this letter to McMenemy, who wrote back a few days later. He was 'very flattered', he said. 'Seriously, I think she might have chosen her Cabinet by now and, like yourself, I do hope she does a good job.'

the election, she was not secure enough to appoint the 'hard-nosed' Cabinet Root wanted. As she told the Canadian premier Joe Clark, her priority was to form 'what I call a "well-balanced Government" . . . to give a certain confidence that one is determined to take the middle ground'.[4]

When the names were announced, therefore, the striking thing was just how 'well-balanced' her Cabinet was. Almost all of Edward Heath's lieutenants had senior jobs, most obviously Lord Carrington, who was Foreign Secretary, and Willie Whitelaw, who was Home Secretary. Whitelaw, in particular, was a figure of colossal importance. As runner-up in the leadership contest four years earlier, he could probably have roused the Cabinet against her at any point in the first few years. Instead, this big, shambling former tank commander served her with what one writer calls 'an almost military sense of subordination'. There were also places for Heath loyalists such as Jim Prior (Employment), Francis Pym (Defence), Peter Walker (Agriculture), Michael Heseltine (Environment), Sir Ian Gilmour (Lord Privy Seal), Christopher Soames (Lord President of the Council) and Lord Hailsham (Lord Chancellor). There was no room, though, for thrusting young Thatcherites such as Nigel Lawson, Norman Tebbit, Cecil Parkinson or Nicholas Ridley, who had to be content with junior roles. Had Heath still been in charge, he would probably have picked much the same crew.[5]

To the doubters, this was a sign that Mrs Thatcher was, after all, going to govern from the centre ground. One of the most prominent sceptics, for example, was Jim Prior, the new Employment Secretary. It was no secret that Prior considered her economic policies 'dogmatic' and 'simplistic', to use his own words. But when he looked around the Cabinet table, he felt reassured that her radical ambitions would be 'moderated by the realities of Government'. What he had overlooked, though, was that the crucial economic ministries were all in Thatcherite hands. The new Chancellor was Sir Geoffrey Howe, supported by fellow monetarists, John Biffen and Nigel Lawson, as Chief Secretary and Financial Secretary. The conscience of the right, Sir Keith Joseph, took the Department of Industry, while the impeccably loyal John Nott went to the Department of Trade. What was more, Mrs Thatcher had no intention of having economic debates in Cabinet, where her inner circle might be outvoted. Instead, policy was decided at the Cabinet's E Committee, to which few sceptics were invited, or at weekly breakfast meetings with trusted allies. Later, Sir Ian Gilmour complained that the dissenters had been frozen out by a 'secretive monetarist clique'. But this was clever political management, the hallmark of a Prime Minister playing her hand with meticulous care.[6]

Even so, Mrs Thatcher's reputation for pitiless cunning can be a bit overstated. She had surrounded herself with Heath's old fan club because she had to, not because she wanted to. The result was a Cabinet that looked decidedly old-fashioned, not to say old-school. Of its twenty-two members, all but one were male, all but three had been to public schools, and only one – in flagrant contravention of Henry Root's advice – had gone to a university other than Oxford or Cambridge. Six had been to Eton and three to Winchester; five were barristers; five had served in the Guards and two in the cavalry; several owned landed estates; three were baronets and three more were hereditary peers. On top of all that, nine had fought in the Second World War, three of whom – Whitelaw and Pym, as well as Carrington – had won the Military Cross. When the journalist Louis Heren saw them at a Westminster drinks party, he thought they seemed the embodiment of privileged complacency, beaming with 'self-confidence and well-being'. In this company Mrs Thatcher was the outsider. She had not just gone to the wrong school: she had done the wrong subject at Oxford, had never served in the war and did not belong to the right clubs. She was not even a man.[7]

Among Mrs Thatcher's allies, her isolation was cause for serious concern. In November 1979 her Parliamentary Private Secretary, Ian Gow, told Alan Clark that she was 'out-numbered three to one in the cabinet', with most of her ministers 'mutely or vociferously hostile'. The Tory backbencher Anthony Royle said the same a few days later. 'Look at the people round her,' he told Clark. 'Carrington – hates her; Prior – hates her; Gilmour – hates her; Heseltine – hates her; Walker – loathes her, makes no secret of it; Willie – completely even-handed, would never support her against the old gang; Geoffrey Howe – no personal loyalties – durable politburo man, will serve under anyone.'

Clark thought this was about right. Few people, he mused, realized 'how precarious' her position was, or how easily a revolt of the 'old guard heavies' would open the way for the 'ageing, sulky, shapeless but still expectant Edward Heath'. Of course *we* know that Heath would never return to front-line politics, but nobody knew that then. After all, it was barely five years since he had been running the ship. Still in his early sixties, he made no secret of his belief that his old crew would soon come to their senses and recall him to the bridge. And throughout Mrs Thatcher's first term, he was the Trotsky to her Stalin: a focus for opposition, a reminder of her insecurity, a shadow from which she could never fully escape.[8]

Outnumbered in her own Cabinet, Mrs Thatcher relied on a little court of advisers, friends and hangers-on, much like Harold Wilson's inner circle in the 1960s. The former Conservative researcher John Ranelagh called them 'Thatcher's people'. Self-made, competitive, impatient, chafing at what they saw as the defeatism of the Establishment, they were 'driven by an intellectual and programmatic dislike of their own country'. A striking number came from Jewish backgrounds: not just the former Communist Alfred Sherman, who ran the Centre for Policy Studies, or even advisers and officials such as Norman Strauss, David Wolfson and Stephen Sherbourne, but ministers such as Sir Keith Joseph, Leon Brittan and Nigel Lawson. Why? Strauss thought that because Jews were outsiders, they were often personally loyal to her, not the party. Others thought it was because Jews tended to be 'entrepreneurial' and to believe in 'thrift and savings and doing things by your own efforts', as she did. As John Biffen put it, she saw in the Jewish community another version of the 'Methodist values of Grantham'.[9]

The two most influential figures, though, were not Jewish. The first was her press secretary, Bernard Ingham, who joined in November 1979 from the Department of Energy. Born in 1932, Ingham was a former Hebden Bridge Grammar boy who played up to his image as a curmudgeonly Yorkshireman. At the time, contemporaries were struck by his extraordinary aggressiveness in his mistress's defence, as well as his enthusiasm for knifing her ministers in off-the-record briefings. But what was really interesting about him was not his manner but his background. As the Tory MP Julian Critchley put it, Ingham came from 'solid Labour, Nonconformist stock', all chapel, cricket and the *Daily Herald*. A former Labour candidate for Leeds City Council, Ingham was one of several people who supported her because he felt that 'for far too long the British decision-making process had been in the hands of an effete, spoiled, silver-tongued, privileged minority out of touch with most men in the street'. 'One of the things you and I have in common, Bernard,' Mrs Thatcher once said, 'is that neither of us is a *smooth* person.'[10]

The other key figure was the head of her Policy Unit, John Hoskyns. Born into an army family in 1927, Hoskyns lost his father during the fall of France, served for more than a decade in the Rifle Brigade and worked for IBM before setting up his own systems consultancy in 1964. Like Ingham, he was far from being an instinctive Tory, but he was fervently patriotic. By the mid-1970s, convinced that Britain was in deep decline, he had begun work on a series of elaborate charts, which showed what was wrong and how it could be fixed. These caught the attention of Sir Keith Joseph, who introduced him to Mrs Thatcher, and by the election Hoskyns had become an important part of her backroom team.

In some ways Hoskyns and Mrs Thatcher were a very odd fit. Despite his officer's charm and his apparently unshakeable belief that a total economic meltdown was only moments away, Hoskyns was basically a systems man, a technocrat for whom the best way to stave off the apocalypse was a flow chart and a 27-point action plan. To Mrs Thatcher, his 'over-numerical, over-analytical, computerised approach' often seemed wildly over-ambitious and politically naive. 'If I asked for a joke for a speech,' she once remarked, 'I got back twenty pages of strategic analysis.' But she admired his radicalism and intellectual integrity. For his part, Hoskyns believed she was the only person who could avert disaster, although he chafed at her caution. Indeed, even in victory he could not shake the feeling that it might all be for nothing. He spent election night watching the results at Conservative Central Office. But in the small hours, as Mrs Thatcher was on her way to celebrate victory, he slipped away to bed. He 'could not get excited about the victory celebrations', he recalled, because he knew that 'the chances of the government achieving anything where so many had failed were small'.[11]

On Saturday 5 May Mrs Thatcher's ministers trooped into Buckingham Palace to kiss hands with the Queen. Later, Sir Geoffrey Howe remembered that they were 'all much more excited and nervous than we tried to appear', like 'new boys at school'. But excitability was not a quality usually associated with Mrs Thatcher's new Chancellor. Born to a Port Talbot solicitor in 1926, Howe was a scholarship boy, educated at Winchester and Cambridge. After National Service in East Africa, he had been called to the Bar, became a modernizing Tory MP and served as Heath's Solicitor General. While socially liberal, he was clearly on the free-market right, which is why Mrs Thatcher had made him Shadow Chancellor. At the time, he was generally seen as a safe, earnest, even dull choice. But Howe's soft-spoken style masked what his friend Nigel Lawson called his 'fine mind, intellectual conviction, courage, integrity, tenacity, resilience [and] great courtesy, allied to almost ruthless ambition'. Probably no modern politician was so consistently underrated, not least by his own boss. Behind the owlish appearance there was a core of steel.[12]

Odd as it may sound, Howe's world-class boringness was one of his greatest assets. Listening to what Hugo Young called his 'defensive, narcoleptic monotone', it was impossible to believe that this methodical, lawyerly figure, blinking behind his thick glasses, could be up to anything radical. He was 'perfectly cast', thought *The Times*'s sketchwriter Frank Johnson. 'There is nothing meretricious or demagogic about him. He is openly the bearer of bad news ... [He] just stands there at the Dispatch Box, announces his [tax] increases, and courteously replies to the Labour baying and general accusations of brutality.' Yet in terms of practical policy, it was arguably Howe, even more than Mrs Thatcher, who was the real author of the changes in British economic life in the 1980s. He was not just the 'inexorable tortoise' of his political generation, wrote Young. He was 'Thatcherism's chief mechanic, the indispensable overseer of the machine'. It was Mrs Thatcher who chose the destination, shouted out the directions and posed for photographs behind the wheel. But it was Howe who did much of the driving.[13]

A few moments after Howe's appointment had been announced, he had a call from his Labour predecessor, Denis Healey, who wanted to pass on some tips about the 11 Downing Street kitchen and to wish him 'the best of luck on the bed of nails'. Having guided the British economy through the chaos of the mid-1970s, Healey knew better than anybody how sharp those nails were. And when the new Chancellor arrived at the Treasury, his new officials handed him a document that made extremely depressing reading.

To put it bluntly, the outlook was terrible. Thanks partly to the revolution that had broken out in Iran at the end of 1978, the world economy was tipping into recession. On top of that, Britain had serious problems of its own. Driven by people's anxiety that their earnings were being eroded by inflation, pay settlements were running at about 14 per cent a year, with prices rising at 11 per cent. With growth trickling to a halt, unemployment was certain to rise. Company profits were very poor, productivity was awful and international competitiveness was deteriorating all the time. 'Lying behind these trends', the Treasury briefing said sadly, 'is a long history of industrial inertia, inefficiency and lack of innovation'. And with the exception of North Sea oil, 'the prospects for the rest of the economy, particularly manufacturing, are extremely worrying'.[14]

As Howe settled into life at Number 11, the bad news poured in. One particular concern was inflation. Having peaked at almost 27 per cent in August 1975, it had fallen during the Callaghan years but was now rising again, thanks largely to the explosion in public pay after the Winter of Discontent. As for public spending, the Cabinet Secretary, Sir John Hunt, reported that the new government had a 'dreadful inheritance'. The Callaghan government had planned on the basis that the economy would continue to grow and inflation would continue to fall. But now both assumptions looked wildly over-optimistic, leaving Howe staring at a hole in the public finances before he had even started. Originally, Labour had forecast a budget deficit – then known as 'the public sector borrowing requirement', or PSBR – of about £8½ billion in the next financial year. But with pay settlements running out of control, the Treasury now expected it to be more than £10 billion. So if Howe wanted to reduce taxes, as he had promised in the campaign, he would have to make deep spending cuts.[15]

These were merely the most immediate issues. Underpinning everything else, from the dire inflation figures to the woes of Britain's exporters, was a pervasive crisis of confidence. In Whitehall, there was a sense that, with Britain doomed to decline, no government could do anything but stagger from crisis to crisis. The last ten years, wrote *The Times*'s economics editor, David Blake, in December 1979, had 'produced a fundamental change in the attitude of most ordinary people and policy-makers', which meant that 'belief in the inevitability of prosperity [had] disappeared from Britain'. This was what Mrs Thatcher had been elected to fix. Yet when John Hoskyns listed the various problems – 'trade union obstruction, inflationary expectations, the tendency of the best talent to keep away from manufacturing industry, fiscal distortions, high interest rates, an overvalued pound, stop-go economic management, the low status of engineers, poor industrial design, the anti-enterprise culture' – he wondered whether economic decline was 'like the weather, simply beyond human intervention'. The biggest problem of all, he wrote, was that 'sense of futility, the feeling that nothing in Britain was ever going to change'.[16]

As if all this were not bad enough, Howe's job was complicated by two things over which he had no control. The first was a commission on public sector pay, chaired by the industrial relations expert Professor Hugh Clegg, which was due to report in August. In reality, Clegg had been handed a blank cheque by the Callaghan government to buy off public sector workers after the Winter of Discontent. Since their pay had been squeezed for the last three years, everybody knew Clegg was bound to recommend hefty rises. In her heart of hearts, Mrs Thatcher hated everything about it; but with the election looming, she had reluctantly promised to honour Clegg's recommendations. This was great news for the public sector workers, but far from ideal for the new Chancellor. On 1 August, Clegg filled in the cheque with all the munificence Howe had feared, with some workers getting as much as 26 per cent. In just twelve months the government's wage bill went up by almost a quarter. For a Chancellor desperate to show his mettle against inflation it was a dreadful start.[17]

The more serious issue, though, was the much-discussed black gold in the North Sea. Since the discovery of the Ekofisk field in 1969, the oil companies had spent a fortune on platforms, pipelines and shipyards, transforming the economy of north-eastern Scotland. By the time Mrs Thatcher came to power, some 20,000 men were already working on twenty platforms in unimaginably cold, grim and dangerous conditions. The rewards were enormous. By 1980 Britain was practically self-sufficient in oil. A year later, it became the first major Western oil exporter. As luck would have it, this happened at the very moment when the price was surging, because of the revolution in Iran. So by the middle of 1983, with the North Sea platforms pumping out 2 million barrels a day, the Treasury was banking almost £8 billion annually in oil revenue. By 1985 it was making £12 billion, which was just under a tenth of Britain's total tax revenue. So, by a fluke of timing, Mrs Thatcher was the political equivalent of a lottery millionaire. As one of Callaghan's old aides put it, she and Howe were 'inheriting a bonanza'.[18]

Yet as every lottery winner invariably finds, there is always a downside. Yes, Britain was now shielded from balance of payments crises and the prospect of another oil shock. The problem, though, was that the pound had become a petro-currency, which made it immensely desirable. Indeed, on Howe's first day as Chancellor, the Governor of the Bank of England, Gordon Richardson, greeted him with a grimly prescient warning. Ever since the IMF bailout, Richardson wrote, sterling had been under 'upward pressure' on the exchange markets. To put it simply, North Sea oil made the pound an excellent investment. Until the last months of 1977 the Bank had held sterling below $1.77, but by the time Howe took office it had reached $2.07, and further rises seemed inevitable.

The good news was that a strong pound helped to get inflation down. The bad news was that a strong pound was terrible for British manufacturers, because it made their products very expensive abroad. With every fraction of a cent that the pound rose in value, Britain's exporters lost more customers. So why not intervene in the markets to reduce the value of the pound? Alas, Richardson explained, it was not that simple. Experience had shown that when the Bank tried to intervene, investors worked out what they were doing and reacted accordingly, so they found themselves 'encouraging rather than reducing pressure'. In short, there was 'very little scope' for action. They just had to hope that the pound stopped rising. For if it went as high as, say, $2.30, or even, God forbid, $2.40, then British manufacturers would be facing an economic holocaust.[19]

So what was the plan?

Although Mrs Thatcher's manifesto had been remarkably cautious, her basic approach was well established. A good starting point is a summary prepared by Howe's officials after the election, entitled 'The Government's Economic Strategy'. 'The facts of Britain's post-war economic decline,' it began, 'are well-known . . . We have slipped further and further behind our competitors in terms of living standards and the quality of public services.' The authors singled out inflation, 'which damages competitiveness, causes divisive social pressures, and creates uncertainty about the future'. But instead of adopting an incomes policy, 'which deals only with a symptom of the disease', Mrs Thatcher was committed to 'control of the money supply', using monetary targets to bring inflation down. Elsewhere, the government would encourage free enterprise by 'cutting back the role of the State' and 'promoting small businesses' – which meant reducing taxes as much as possible. Finally, they would not shrink from 'difficult decisions' on public spending. That meant cutting the Callaghan government's spending commitments, which had been based on an 'over-optimistic view' of the economy.[20]

The fact that this document gave so much attention to inflation was no accident. To many commentators at the turn of the 1980s, inflation was more than just another economic problem. It was a chronic condition, a cancer remorselessly eating away at salaries, savings and living standards, eroding individual ambition and social unity. As Mrs Thatcher explained, it was 'one of the greatest threats to liberty – to all our freedoms . . . the freedom to save, to find a job, to do better for our families'. And after she had won the election, her ministers took every opportunity to remind their listeners of the scale of the challenge. 'So long as it persists,' Howe told the Commons in 1980:

> economic stability and prosperity will continue to elude us. So long as it persists, social coherence will also elude us . . . The violence of the picket lines and last winter's examples of hospital patients denied supplies, and of the dead denied burial, would have been unthinkable 20 years ago. They reflect the social disintegration caused by inflation. That is one of the reasons why the conquest of inflation is so important.[21]

Nobody was under any illusions, though, that beating inflation would be easy. For decades, successive governments had promised to stop the surge in prices, yet with every fresh offensive the rate of increase seemed to quicken. Under Churchill, Eden and Macmillan inflation had been 3½ per cent. Under Wilson in the 1960s it had been 4½ per cent. Under Heath it had been 9 per cent, and after 1974 it had been 15½ per cent. And quite apart from its impact on ordinary people – especially pensioners, people dependent on their savings and those not represented by a union – inflation seemed to demolish the economic wisdom of the post-war years.

For a quarter of a century, governments had worshipped at the altar of the economist John Maynard Keynes, whose disciples argued that the priority must be to fight unemployment by borrowing and spending to maintain demand. But as inflation mounted, Keynesianism began to look like the gospel of a bygone age. In September 1976 Callaghan had explicitly told his party conference that the Keynesians' cosy world, 'where full employment would be guaranteed by a stroke of the Chancellor's pen', was gone forever. 'We used to think that you could spend your way out of a recession and increase employment by cutting taxes and boosting Government spending,' Callaghan said. 'I tell you in all candour that that option no longer exists.' The speech had been written by his son-in-law, *The Times*'s economics editor, Peter Jay. But the fact that it was delivered by a man nicknamed 'the Keeper of the Cloth Cap' made it all the more striking.[22]

So if Keynesianism was dead, by what lodestar would governments chart their course? The Conservatives' answer was an economic doctrine that had first become fashionable across the Atlantic, and had been taken up in the early 1970s by an eclectic assortment of free-market economists, think-tanks and columnists. This was monetarism, associated above all with the Chicago professor Milton Friedman. The basic outline was simple enough. As Friedman saw it, by borrowing and spending to keep unemployment down, Western governments had inadvertently sent inflation through the roof, throwing the economy off course and putting hundreds of thousands out of work. Instead of getting worked up about unemployment, they should focus on the one thing they could genuinely control, which was inflation. The government's job, Friedman argued, was to set clear monetary targets, which would stop the money supply from growing too quickly. If inflation did get out of hand, the only solution was to squeeze the money supply: for example, by slashing spending or raising interest rates. This would be very painful, of course, and people would lose their jobs. But, in the long run, it would be worth it.[23]

Monetarism has not, by and large, had a very good press. As early as 1977, the *Guardian*'s Peter Jenkins was pouring scorn on the 'false disciples' and 'ill-founded dogma' of the 'money religion', and this kind of language has endured ever since. Sir Ian Gilmour's book *Dancing with Dogma* (1992), for example, portrays monetarism as Mrs Thatcher's Marxism, a crackpot pseudo-science espoused by fools and fanatics. Even Howe admitted that his arrival in office was painted as 'the start of an era of uncoupled dogma and unprecedented lunacy'. But as he pointed out, it was actually *Labour* that introduced monetarism to British economic policy, not the Conservatives. The Bank of England had quietly adopted money supply targets as far back as 1973, while Harold Wilson's Policy Unit had urged 'a stricter monetarist approach to government finances' after his return to office a year later. Indeed, the first Chancellor to publish a money supply target was not Howe but Denis Healey, in the summer of 1976. It was Healey who first talked about controlling sterling. It was Healey who started cutting taxes and spending. It was even Healey who abandoned Keynesianism by concentrating on inflation rather than unemployment.[24]

It is true that there were differences. Healey's monetarism was driven by reluctant pragmatism rather than burning conviction. He was operating within a more rigid financial system, and he was still employing an informal incomes policy. Even so, the fact is that monetarism, in the words of the Labour MP Austin Mitchell, had been 'introduced and house-trained by Labour, ready for the Conservatives to turn it into the only instrument of policy'. But it suited neither side to admit it. The Conservatives preferred to portray their predecessors as feckless spendthrifts, while Labour painted Howe and his allies as fanatical ideologues. 'What one calls virtue,' remarked *The Times*'s David Wood in 1982, 'the other damns as sin.' But as the realists on both sides knew, there was more than enough sin to go around.[25]

The problem, though, was that like all economic theories, monetarism was less straightforward than it looked. As Howe's friend Nigel Lawson

As Nicholas Garland recognized, there was more continuity between Denis Healey and Sir Geoffrey Howe than either admitted – not least in the challenges they had to face (*Daily Telegraph*, 16 November 1979).

explained, it was based on two simple ideas: first, that changes in the money supply determined inflation; second, that governments could control the money supply. But both propositions were hotly disputed. Even if the money supply did determine inflation, monetarists did not agree how to measure it. (The government's preferred yardstick was sterling M3, 'broad money', which included cash, bank deposits and various funds and securities.) As for controlling it, some economists thought the government should manage the monetary base directly, setting targets for the banks' reserves at the Bank of England. Others thought the government should concentrate on its own budget, bringing inflation down by cutting public borrowing. And still others preferred the blunt instrument of interest rates, reducing the demand for money by making it punitively expensive to borrow.

By the turn of the 1980s, these arguments had reached theological heights of obscurity, comparable to the quarrels about the divine nature of Christ in the late Roman Empire. In the newspapers, columnists hammered out long essays about the nature and meaning of the money supply. In Whitehall seminars and think-tank briefings, politicians and civil servants contemplated the differences between M0, M1, M2 and M3, the virtues of Monetary Base Control and the problems of the Medium Term Financial Strategy. Given the sheer complexity of the issues, it is a safe bet that not all of them really knew what they were talking about. ('This is the bit I have never understood,' says *Private Eye*'s Denis Thatcher, 'and strictly between ourselves, Bill, I don't think Howe does either.'*) It is an equally safe bet that most ordinary people were bored and baffled by the entire business. In an episode of *Yes Minister*, there is a lovely exchange between Nigel Hawthorne's Sir Humphrey Appleby and the banking boss Sir Desmond Glazebrook, who confides that he buys the *Financial Times* but never reads it. 'Can't understand it. Full of economic theory,' Sir Desmond says. 'It took me thirty years to understand Keynes's economics. And when I just caught on, everyone started getting hooked on these monetarist ideas. You know, *I Want To Be Free* by Milton Shulman.'†[26]

For all the talk of doctrines and dogma, monetarism was less a blueprint than a never-ending argument. But in opposition, at least, it had some compelling attractions. It offered a clear, moralistic narrative about what had gone wrong. It chimed with a growing national feeling that the

---

* An inspired creation, the *Eye*'s Denis wrote a fortnightly letter to his friend Bill, filling him in on life at Number 10. Legend has it that after a while, the real Denis began deliberately playing up to the caricature.
† Milton Shulman was, in fact, a columnist and theatre critic for the *Evening Standard*.

government had lost its way, taxes were too heavy and inflation was too high. It allowed the Conservatives to push the union leaders into the shadows, because it eliminated any need for incomes policies. Above all, monetarism seemed to be something *new*, creating an impression of radical momentum and promising a clean break with the failures of the past.

And given monetarism's optimistic vision of a nation transformed, if only its leaders chose the path of righteousness, it is no wonder some observers saw it as a kind of religion. It is telling that in the weeks after the election, some of Mrs Thatcher's key ministers talked not of changing policies but of changing Britain's entire political culture. What was needed, wrote Lawson on 18 July, was 'a sustained campaign to educate the public about the economic facts of life'. Thirteen days later, the Treasury's summary of the government's economic strategy declared that 'the Government intend to change, and change radically, the framework of expectations that forms the key to individual behaviour'. In their own minds, Mrs Thatcher and her allies were missionaries, embarking on a crusade of national conversion. For as the Chief Missionary told the *Sunday Times* in May 1981: 'Economics are the method; the object is to change the heart and soul.'[27]

All too often, though, the path to redemption is lined with suffering. Few of Mrs Thatcher's allies doubted that life would be tough. Sir Keith Joseph, for example, had always maintained that to defeat inflation a successful government must be prepared to accept more unemployment. And in the early summer of 1979, most senior figures expected things to get worse before they got better. The Treasury's strategic summary, for example, could hardly have been more downbeat. 'It would be foolish – and counter-productive – to aim for overnight solutions,' it warned: 'the road to recovery will inevitably be long and gradual.' Recovery would take time, agreed John Hoskyns. The 'first two to three years' would be hellish, and they must harden their hearts: 'Ministers must say "No", and keep on saying "No", until their jaws ache.'[28]

Yet not all the architects of Mrs Thatcher's revolution were so pessimistic. Even months after the election, Howe was enthusing about the 'enormous fun' of working for someone whose openness, vigour and 'unwillingness to be cowed' made her so *'dramatically* exciting'. Lawson, too, recalled the 'excitement of those first few weeks in office', the 'thrill' of attempting 'something genuinely new'. And at the beginning of August, one of Howe's special advisers, Peter Cropper, sent a remarkable note to his colleagues. They should stop being so downbeat, he said. 'The world economy may be gloomy, but there is absolutely no need for *us* to be gloomy.' Indeed, when Cropper read the Treasury's summary of their economic strategy, he was shocked by how miserable it was:

> There is no hint of the reforming crusade that some of us think we are launched on, and no hint of the end goal of it all – joy, wealth, national power, two acres and a cow, a second car in every garage, interesting jobs, leisure, comfortable trains, channel tunnels, atomic power stations, gleaming new coal mines, everyone a bathroom, patios for all etc. etc.
>
>   We started out, quite rightly in my view, by displaying the bareness of the cupboard and emphasising the size of the job. But we must constantly remember that leadership, which is what we were elected to provide, consists largely in cheering people up, making them laugh, and keeping them that way.

Gleaming new coal mines, second cars, patios for all: these were noble ambitions. But if the British people really wanted somebody to cheer them up and make them laugh, they should have chosen a different leader.[29]

Howe's first task was to deliver a Budget, due on 12 June. Given the likelihood of a world recession, the obvious approach would have been to tread carefully. But both he and Lawson were convinced that they would never get a better chance for radical course-correction. If they hesitated, the government's energies would be dissipated in the everyday fire-fighting of parliamentary life, while their national popularity would probably never be higher than it was now, in the aftermath of victory. So, as Lawson put it, their instinct was 'to press ahead, because deferment can become a way of life'.[30]

   But the Budget presented Howe with a nasty dilemma. In effect, he was committed to doing various contradictory things at once. Chief among them was cutting income tax. Contrary to what is often thought, the tax burden in 1979, about a third of GDP, was not especially high by European standards. What *was* unusual, though, was that so much tax was levied on personal income, which, according to the Conservatives, stifled individual ambition and free enterprise. The basic rate of tax was 33 per cent, which was high compared with some of Britain's neighbours. But Howe's real target was the controversial 83 per cent top tax rate, paid by those earning more than £25,000 a year (perhaps £175,000 today), which had driven a motley collection of big names, from Rod Stewart and Michael Caine to David Bowie and Don Revie, to shelter their earnings abroad.

   As Mrs Thatcher had told an audience in 1978, she regarded this as 'sheer confiscation'. By scrapping this 'symbol of British socialism – the symbol of envy', the Conservatives would not only signal their enthusiasm for 'hard work, responsibility and success', they would also send a message that 'top people', such as Billy Butlin, Roger Moore and Engelbert Humperdinck, were free to return to their native land. Indeed, during the election she maintained that cutting income tax was the key to turning Britain around. 'We really do need far more incentive in the economy to make it worthwhile for people to work hard, to create new businesses and to expand them,' she explained. 'Unless someone does that . . . then I see no hope and I see no change from perpetual decline.'[31]

As soon as Howe moved into the Treasury, he told his officials to begin work on cutting the higher tax rate to 60 per cent and the basic rate from 33 per cent to 30 per cent. Although this is sometimes seen as the moment when Mrs Thatcher's Britain began to slide into right-wing extremism, the truth is that by European standards the new rates were utterly unremarkable. Under Howe, the richest taxpayers would hand over the same as in France, while they still paid more than their counterparts in West Germany or the United States. The real issue, from the Treasury's point of view, was how the new Chancellor proposed to pay for it. His tax cuts would leave a £4 billion hole in the government's finances. Yet Howe was *also* committed to reducing borrowing to about £8 billion a year, and this at a time when the Treasury was predicting a deficit of at least £10 billion. So how would he reconcile these apparently contradictory commitments?[32]

The obvious answer was to raise more money through VAT. Labour had bequeathed two different VAT rates: 12½ per cent on so-called 'luxuries' and 8 per cent on everything else. Howe's plan, therefore, was to bring in a single VAT rate of 15 per cent. But as he was often to find, every solution brought problems of its own. For one thing, the Conservatives had explicitly denied rumours during the election campaign that they were going to double VAT. Raising it from 8 to 15 per cent was not quite doubling it, but it came pretty close. Howe described this as 'the small change of election campaigning'. But at the very least it looked pretty cynical.[33]

The bigger problem was that, with inflation already in double figures, the higher VAT rate would mean big price increases. Howe also knew it would encourage the unions to demand bigger pay settlements. But it was worth the risk, he thought, to bring down income tax and show the government's determination to realize its radical aspirations. Unfortunately, Mrs Thatcher did not share his confidence. Just twelve days into her premiership, she summoned him to Number 10 and gave him a ferocious grilling. She was 'extremely perturbed', she said, by the thought of raising VAT to 15 per cent, which 'could be catastrophic for the next pay round'.

Instead, they ought to be making deep cuts in public spending, on which they were being 'not nearly tough enough'.[34]

Here was the first hint of what became a familiar pattern. In the public imagination, Mrs Thatcher was the Iron Lady, radical, dogmatic and unbending, the sworn enemy of appeasement and U-turns. In reality, she was acutely conscious of her own vulnerability and much more risk-averse than people imagined. Indeed, whenever Howe and Lawson presented her with genuinely daring or difficult ideas, her instinct was often to hesitate or even to say no. But for all his apparent mildness, Howe was a man who stuck doggedly to his guns. At a second meeting on 22 May, he told Mrs Thatcher that raising VAT to 15 per cent was the absolute minimum if she really wanted to cut income tax. Hang on, she said: what about inflation? And now she made what, given her reputation, seems an extraordinary suggestion. According to the minutes, she 'wondered whether it was necessary or wise to try to achieve all of the Government's objectives on the income tax front in the first year'. Why not focus on cutting spending, and leave their tax reforms till later? Why did they need to change everything at once? Why risk so much on a single throw of the dice?[35]

Today many historians would say that Mrs Thatcher was right, and that a more cautious approach might have avoided some of the agonies of the next two years. But Howe, supported by his Chief Secretary, John Biffen, had a plausible counter-argument. Cutting income tax had been one of their most eye-catching election promises, and the Budget would be seen as a crucial 'test of our resolution'. If they bottled out of it, who would believe that they were going to deliver on their other commitments? Yes, Howe said, 'it is true that the perceived rate of inflation will suffer an immediate shock, but this will not then be repeated month after month . . . In my judgement, this Budget provides our only opportunity to make a radical switch from direct to indirect taxation and thus honour the commitment on which our credibility depends.' This was Biffen's view, too. This was their only chance, he said. The next few years would be rough, and they could be 'facing industrial unrest in a couple of years such as would make a later hike unthinkable. We needed to do it now if at all.'[36]

In the end, Mrs Thatcher grudgingly gave way. But no sooner had they disposed of one bone of contention than another took its place. Since Howe had ruled out a return to incomes policies, he intended to use interest rates to keep inflation down. Having peaked at 15 per cent during the IMF crisis, rates had steadily fallen during the late 1970s, shot back up during the Winter of Discontent and settled at 12 per cent at the time of the election. But on 6 June, Howe told Mrs Thatcher that, thanks to the explosion in public sector pay, the money supply, measured in sterling M3, was already running out of control. He had talked to the Bank of England, and they agreed that rates should go up to 14 per cent as soon as possible – preferably the very next day.[37]

Mrs Thatcher was not at all happy. High interest rates penalized her most loyal supporters: young, aspirational, middle-class homeowners with limited means but sizeable mortgages. So when, later that evening, Howe and Gordon Richardson visited Number 10, she gave them a very hard time. (She hated Richardson anyway: charming, clever but almost comically grand, he was precisely the kind of patrician bigwig who had condescended to her all her life. In private, she called him 'that fool who runs the Bank of England'.) It would be madness, she said, to raise rates the next day, because that was the day of the European Parliament elections, and in any case a 2 per cent rise was much too drastic. In effect, then, she told them to go away and think about it. But as with VAT, Howe was not for turning. The day before the Budget, he reported that he and Richardson had indeed thought about it, but 'we remain convinced that it should be 2 per cent'. Entirely characteristically, Mrs Thatcher got her private secretary to write back and tell him they were still wrong. But she was 'willing to abide', she said grumpily, 'by the Chancellor's and the Governor's judgement in this matter'. So Howe got his rate rise, but she got the last word.[38]

At half-past three on Tuesday 12 June, a decanter of gin and tonic at his elbow, Howe rose to present his Budget. He began in mournful fashion, setting out the details of Britain's 'long decline':

> Only a quarter of a century ago – within the memory of almost every Member of this House – the people of the United Kingdom enjoyed higher living standards than the citizens of any of the larger countries of Europe. Amongst the free nations of the world, Britain was then second only to the United States in economic strength.
>
> It is not so today . . . The French people now produce half as much again as we do. The Germans produce more than twice as much, and they are moving further ahead all the time . . .
>
> In the last few years the hard facts of our relative decline have become increasingly plain, and the threat of absolute decline has gradually become very real. That is not a prospect that I am prepared to accept. Nor, I believe, are the British people. They realise that we cannot for ever go on avoiding difficult choices in the fatal, and increasingly futile, quest for easy solutions.

Howe promised no overnight revolution. Indeed, he thought it was time to admit that there was 'a definite limit to our capacity, as politicians, to influence these things for the better'. But he was determined to make a start anyway.

The theme of the Budget was cuts. In total, Howe trimmed £2½ billion from Callaghan's spending plans, partly through cash limits and civil service cuts, but also through tweaks such as higher NHS prescription charges. By selling the government's shares in BP, he also hoped to raise a further £1 billion. But the big story was his tax changes. As agreed, income taxes came down, the top rate from 83 per cent to 60 per cent, the basic rate from 33 per cent to 30 per cent, while VAT went up to 15 per cent. Yet at the same time, Howe tightened the money supply growth target for the next twelve months to between 7 and 11 per cent, a very optimistic ambition given the reality of rising borrowing and runaway pay. All this, he said, was merely the first step in his plan 'to reduce the role of Government. Government will spend less, Government will borrow less.'[39]

Perhaps never in living memory had a new government made such a daring start. In the *Mirror*'s words, 'Thatcher Keeps Her Promise . . . AND HOWE!' 'A change of direction we were promised, and a change of direction we surely have got,' said the *Express*, while even the *Guardian* applauded the government's 'refreshing' determination to deliver on its radical rhetoric. By contrast, the *Observer* thought the new government had sent Britain on to a 'race track without escape roads', and deplored its 'dogmatically anti-egalitarian' tax changes. And none of this was lost on the public. Many people thought the Budget 'divisive in terms of social class', reported Conservative Central Office, adding that 'it was widely seen (even amongst the rich themselves) to be favouring the rich and penalising various less well off groups'. Even so, 'it was seen by a substantial majority to involve a completely different approach to the country's problems, to be tough but necessary and to have reflected what the majority of electors who voted Conservative had voted for'.[40]

Labour, of course, hated it. But perhaps the most heartfelt opposition came from the government front bench, where Jim Prior, the most ebullient of the old Tory paternalists, found it an 'enormous shock'. The evening before, the Employment Secretary had given Moss Evans, leader of the Transport and General Workers' Union, dinner in his London flat, and had assured him there was no way they would raise VAT to 15 per cent. Now he felt like a fool. 'It was then', Prior wrote, 'that I realised that Margaret, Geoffrey and Keith really had got the bit between their teeth and were not going to pay attention to the rest of us at all if they could possibly help it. That first budget also brought it home to me that I was really on a hiding to nothing from the very beginning.'[41]

Later, Mrs Thatcher's critics portrayed the Budget as proof that she and

Howe had fallen victim to a crazed monetarist cult. It is more accurate to
see the Chancellor as a gambler, taking a calculated risk that he could
deliver his long-promised tax cuts while still keeping a lid on inflation. But
as the weeks passed, his courage began to look an awful lot like recklessness. He had assured Mrs Thatcher that, as people's expectations fell into
line with the government's targets, wage and price growth would return
to more manageable levels. Yet in the four months that followed his Budget,
retail price inflation surged from just over 10 per cent to more than 15 per
cent, while sterling M3 ballooned by 14 per cent. And as the unions pressed
for double-digit pay increases and oil prices surged, inflation roared on,
reaching a staggering 21 per cent by the spring of 1980. In an irony that
Mrs Thatcher did not enjoy, a government elected to banish the memories
of the Wilson years was now presiding over the worst inflation since 1975.[42]

By now even many monetarists thought Howe had paid a dangerously
high price for his political success. While they generally applauded his tax
cuts, economists such as Alan Walters argued that he should have never
have raised VAT so high, and should have cut spending instead, as Mrs
Thatcher had suggested. 'I asked for too little, didn't I?' she had muttered
to one of her officials after the Budget. Her opponents crowed that her
policies had been exposed as a counterproductive shambles. But her supporters countered that this only proved how hard it would be to cure the
'British disease', a condition more deep-seated than they had realized.
'Nothing', declared the *Daily Express* that August, 'can excuse the fact
that at the moment the British have become the Playboys of the Western
World, living way beyond our means. If any one of us kept on spending
borrowed money in the spendthrift way we as a nation have, he would
long ago have been declared bankrupt.'[43]

That summer, as the playboys of the Western world relaxed on the beaches
of Majorca, Marbella, Crete and Rhodes, Howe considered his next step.
Given the inflationary situation, the obvious course would be to raise interest rates again. But higher rates would make life very painful, not just for
ordinary homeowners but for Britain's increasingly hard-pressed manufacturers. What was worse, higher rates would have serious consequences for
the pound. Far from dampening the upward pressure on sterling, Howe's
Budget had intensified it. In the weeks after the Budget the pound rose and
rose, reaching the dreaded heights of the $2.30s at the end of July. Nobody
had expected such a surge; even Lawson thought it 'astonishing'.

Inside the bunker, Hoskyns was already telling people that sterling had
gone too high, stifling exports, strangling industry and making recession
inevitable. At the Bank of England, too, some officials thought it might

be better to cut interest rates and relieve the pressure. But that would undermine the government's commitment to sound money. In effect, then, Howe was damned whatever he did. He could cut rates to relieve the pressure on the pound and buy some breathing space for Britain's manufacturers, but that would send inflation even higher. Or he could raise rates to bring the money supply under control, but that could send the pound shooting past $2.40 and make Britain's exports punitively uncompetitive. Or he could do nothing and get the worst of all worlds. Never had a Chancellor more sorely needed a magic wand.[44]

Mrs Thatcher, meanwhile, was becoming increasingly agitated. She hated inflation, but she also hated high interest rates. So when, scouring the Sunday papers on 24 June, she read that Howe was planning to raise mortgage rates, she scribbled a note pronouncing herself 'very worried'. 'This *must not* happen,' she wrote, heavily underlining the word 'not'. In her note she suggested a 'temporary subsidy' to keep rates down, which seemed to fly in the face of all her free-market principles. Alarmed, Howe pointed out that such a subsidy would be very expensive and would 'seriously damage the Government's credibility'. Even so, on 4 July she convened a meeting where she announced that any rise in mortgage rates would be 'politically disastrous'. But Howe stood firm. The government's entire monetary policy would be 'fatally impaired', he said, if they were seen to 'hold down interest rates by artificial means'. Eventually Mrs Thatcher gave way. But it was a telling sign that, whenever free-market principle collided with the interests of the home-owning middle classes, her instinct was almost always to put 'our people' first.[45]

One of the odd things about Mrs Thatcher's first government is that she and her allies are often portrayed as slaves to a meticulously crafted ideological blueprint. In reality, they spent so much time arguing about the implications of their ideas that it is a wonder they managed to get anything else done. Here was a perfect example. In effect, Howe was implementing an old-fashioned monetary squeeze, using high interest rates to wring inflation out of the economy. But although Mrs Thatcher backed him publicly, she was not happy about it. Every time Howe gloomily announced that they needed to put interest rates up, she winced and looked for reasons not to do it. She is supposed to have gone around telling people: 'There is no alternative.' Yet, as Howe recalled, she was 'ever on the lookout' for an alternative. In essence, she liked the idea of getting inflation down, hated the thought of doing it with high rates, and was convinced that someone, somewhere, must have invented a less painful way. As Lawson sardonically put it, 'there was no more assiduous seeker for gimmicks which would supposedly give us tight money without high interest rates than Margaret Thatcher'.[46]

In the early years of her administration, the gimmick that caught her attention was Monetary Base Control. The gist of this was that instead of relying on interest rates, the government should seek to control the money supply directly, by setting strict targets for the banks' reserves with the Bank of England. Some of the most influential monetarist academics, notably the sainted Milton Friedman, were all for it, as was Mrs Thatcher's favourite City insider, the stockbroker Gordon Pepper. But Howe and Lawson were dead against it, while Gordon Richardson pointed out that there was no guarantee Monetary Base Control would 'make it any easier to avoid high interest rates'. For the time being, therefore, the Bank of England fobbed her off with a promise to look into it more closely. But she never gave up on Monetary Base Control. Whenever there was a bad set of inflation figures, or whenever Howe asked her to approve another interest-rate rise, it was not long before she brought out the dreaded three words.[47]

In the meantime, Howe had become convinced that he had no choice but to drive down inflation with the blunt instruments of high interest rates and deep spending cuts. On 6 July he circulated an exceedingly gloomy paper to his Cabinet colleagues. The economic position, he said, was awful, and unless Britain was to sink into terminal decline, 'there is an urgent need to bring about major improvements in inflation, productivity and competitiveness'. And since he could only hike up interest rates so high before stifling any chance of recovery, the only solution was to cut spending and slash the deficit. Ideally, he was looking for cuts of about £6½ billion, which would 'entail accepting a loss of output and employment in the short-term. How severe these losses will be, and how long they will last, will depend partly on how quickly our policies change the climate of expectations in which price and pay decisions are made.' But it would be 'unrealistic' to expect a real recovery before 1983, which meant they were in for a 'very difficult time'.[48]

Chancellors demanding spending cuts are never popular with their colleagues. In fact, Howe's proposed cuts were only cuts in the future programmes prepared by the Callaghan government, not existing programmes. In real terms, spending was still going up, as it did every year during the Thatcher premiership.* Even so, as early as 11 July the Cabinet Secretary, Sir John Hunt, warned Mrs Thatcher that some of her ministers were 'becoming alarmed' by her Chancellor's proposed tactics. Characteristically, she decided to attack them head-on, opening the next day's Cabinet meeting with a ringing declaration that they had to swallow Howe's cuts

---

* The obvious comparison is with Denis Healey, who *did* cut spending in real terms in 1976–7 and 1977–8.

whether they liked it or not. Going through 'this vale of tears', the Chancellor added, was the 'last chance of restoring sanity'. But his position did not go unchallenged. In a sign of things to come, Jim Prior spoke up for his fellow moderates, insisting that cuts on this scale would mean 'massive redundancies'. Britain, he said, was heading for a 'severe depression', and they were in danger of making it worse. But Howe dug in his heels. In what was to become a familiar Thatcherite formula, he and Biffen told their colleagues that this would be a 'crucial test of our determination to stick to our announced policies'. And in the end they got their way, the Cabinet eventually agreeing to £6 billion in cuts at the end of October 1979.[49]

By now some of the defining themes of the next few years had become apparent. Already there were hints of tension between Number 10 and the Treasury, though they were as nothing compared with the divide between hawks and doves in the Cabinet. Already key government figures were disagreeing about the right ways to measure and control the money supply. And already the upbeat tone of the Conservatives' election campaign – 'Don't just hope for a better life. Vote for one' – was giving way to a mood of relentless pessimism.

When Nigel Lawson got back from holiday at the end of August, he sent Howe a long note about the way they were selling their plan. 'There is no way in which we can avoid being attacked, whatever we do,' Lawson wrote, so 'we must be guided by the reflection that it is better to be attacked for the right policies than the wrong ones, and concentrate on getting our own message across.' For this he recommended using 'primitive' language, not the jargon of academic monetarism. They were right to talk about 'the absolute disaster that would follow any change of course'. But they should not forget why people had voted for them in the first place:

> The [other] note that really must be struck, along with the other two, is the note of confidence and above all of hope; the message that there is indeed light at the end of the tunnel. This is absolutely vital, not least if we are to maintain a reasonable degree of business confidence over the difficult 18 months that lie ahead. But it goes wider than that. Churchill may have told the British people that he had nothing to offer them but blood, sweat, toil and tears, but that wasn't strictly true. There was something else he offered them: the promise of victory – and that was why they followed him.

Mrs Thatcher would have loved the comparison.[50]

Summer faded into autumn, and the mood darkened by the day. On 12 October the Chancellor sent Mrs Thatcher his grimmest warning yet. The outlook was even 'more pessimistic' than he had foreseen a few months earlier. GDP was likely to fall faster than expected; price inflation was likely to be much worse; consumer spending was likely to be lower; and thanks to the high pound, Britain's trading prospects were bleaker than ever. Worse news followed. On 31 October the Confederation of British Industry (CBI) reported that business confidence was lower than at any point in the organization's history, with its 1,800 member companies blaming the high pound, rampant inflation and massive pay settlements. Five days later, Howe told Mrs Thatcher that the Treasury was now predicting unemployment of about 1.25 million in 1979–80 and 1.6 million in 1980–81. So much, then, for putting Britain back to work. And as events were to prove, even these figures were wildly optimistic.[51]

By now Howe had taken one of the most momentous decisions of his chancellorship: indeed, one of the most important decisions of the entire period. In the summer of 1979, Britain still had the strictest foreign exchange controls in the industrialized world. Imposed during the Second World War, they had been maintained by the Attlee government to stop capital flooding out of the country. For decades afterwards, they seemed to be set in stone, thanks to the anxiety about the balance of payments and state of the pound. To the left, exchange controls were a guarantee that firms would invest their money at home, providing British jobs for British workers. So even as other governments got rid of their controls, British firms still found it hard to invest money overseas, British tourists could take no more than £50 abroad and ordinary people were still not allowed to buy gold. Even in the City, the outlook remained resolutely parochial. Of almost £100 billion invested by British insurance firms, pension funds, investment trusts and unit trusts in 1979, less than £8 billion was invested abroad. London, one stockbroker told the City's historian David Kynaston, 'was still a little island'.[52]

By the turn of the decade, however, there was a growing sense that exchange controls had become an intolerable obstacle to competition and innovation. 'National borders', the head of the American firm Citibank told a conference in London in June 1979, 'are no longer defensible against the invasion of knowledge, ideas or financial data.' In its way, this was an excellent motto for the age of globalization. And the timing was perfect. Callaghan had considered abolishing exchange controls but thought it too risky. The Bank of England, however, thought there would never be a better time to do it, because North Sea oil and the high interest rates meant there was little danger of people taking their money out of London. So in his first Budget, Howe had relaxed some of the restrictions on firms investing abroad and people travelling overseas. But on 4 October, Lawson persuaded him to go further. They should get rid of the lot, Lawson said: not slowly, not gradually, but all at once. This would be the definitive signal that instead of sheltering behind protectionist borders, Britain 'would now live and die in the real world economy'.[53]

This was, by any standards, an astonishingly daring step. Despite backing abolition in principle, the Bank of England was wary of moving so quickly. Some of the Cabinet were nervous, too, though the only minister to speak against it was Michael Heseltine, who warned that people would 'buy villas in the south of France' instead of investing in British industry. Most strikingly, Mrs Thatcher, as was her wont, was very worried about such a radical departure. In one early discussion she declared that it would be a 'mistake to relax the controls further until the Government's market philosophy was being seen to work', because the uncertainty might send capital flooding out of the country. In the end, though, Howe's and Lawson's joint efforts did the trick. 'On your own head be it, Geoffrey, if anything goes wrong,' she said. He decided she was joking. Even so, he recalled, it was the 'only economic decision of my life that caused me to lose a night's sleep'.[54]

When, on 23 October, Howe announced his decision, it took the Commons completely unawares. The Labour left, who saw exchange controls as an essential step towards building socialism in one country, were appalled. The backbench firebrand Bob Cryer claimed that abolition represented a 'classic betrayal of the workers of this country by a Tory Government who are the lickspittles of the capitalist sector', while Tony Benn gloomily recorded that 'international capitalism has defeated democracy'. The *Observer*'s economics editor, William Keegan, even predicted that controls would be back by 1985. But the right were delighted, and most of the papers were pleased to see the government dismantling the barriers of the 1940s. Now at last, said that bible of rapacious capitalism, the *Guardian*, people were free to 'buy gold bars by the truckload; or to walk through the Customs clutching armfuls of pound notes; or to speculate to our heart's content on any currency or stock exchange which will let us'.[55]

Although it is rarely mentioned as one of the landmarks of the Thatcher years, the abolition of exchange controls was immensely important – and not just for the financial sector. Lawson thought that 'without it, the City would have been hard put to remain a world-class financial centre', and he was probably right. Now the City's outlook became genuinely global: with millions flowing in and out of London every day, it became increasingly integrated with markets abroad, especially New York, which brought new opportunities, new risks and new temptations. Even before the 'Big Bang' of 1986, the days of the City as a 'little island' were over. And the end of exchange controls also sent a potent symbolic message. Only three years earlier, some of Callaghan's ministers had seriously talked about adopting import controls and a siege economy. Even now the Labour left were committed to building the New Jerusalem behind a protectionist trade wall. But for all her patriotic rhetoric, Mrs Thatcher wanted to see Britain in the vanguard of liberal globalization, rather than skulking behind protectionist barricades.[56]

Later, the end of controls came to seem inevitable, part of a worldwide movement driven by financial innovation and information technology. But a different Prime Minister might have made different choices. In France, President François Mitterrand, desperate to stop capital fleeing the country, actually *tightened* exchange controls before abandoning his socialist experiment in the second half of the 1980s. But Mrs Thatcher thought Britain had shrunk from global change for too long. 'For forty years the commercial sector of our economy has operated from within the Bastille of exchange control,' she told the Lord Mayor's Banquet in November 1979. 'Now the prison doors have been thrown open. Once again Britain is prepared to face the world on the same terms as other major Western nations.'[57]

In the short term, though, there was an obvious problem. As in so many areas of economic policy in the early 1980s, it sometimes seemed that as soon as Howe fixed one part of the machine, steam burst out somewhere else. In this case, scrapping exchange controls made it much harder for the government to manage the money supply, because British firms were now able to borrow in other currencies. In very simple terms, the more freely capital could flow in and out of the country, the harder it was to control.[58]

On 5 November, just two weeks after his ground-breaking announcement, Howe warned Mrs Thatcher that the latest figures were 'worse than disappointing', with government borrowing up by £1 billion and bank lending at a record £1.2 billion. As a result, inflation was very unlikely to come down by the end of 1980. Mrs Thatcher was outraged, but there was worse. With the money supply out of control, investors were refusing to buy government debt, known as 'gilts'. Instead, they preferred to wait until interest rates went up, which the markets now considered inevitable. The only option, Howe said gloomily, was to give them what they wanted and raise rates by at least 2 per cent. Once again Mrs Thatcher was horrified. She had been looking forward to bringing interest rates down to relieve the pressure on her beloved middle-class homeowners – and here was her Chancellor wanting to put them up! No, she said. Two days later, Howe was back, pointing out that gilts were not moving at all. No again. Higher interest rates would cause her serious 'political problems'. What about trying Monetary Base Control? At this, Howe said patiently that 'he too was most unhappy . . . but he did not think there was any alternative'.[59]

In the end, Howe the tortoise wore her down. On the morning of

15 November, the Chancellor told the Cabinet that he was raising interest rates by 3 per cent to 17 per cent, the most punitive increase in history. He was trying to keep things as 'un-unpleasant' as possible, but this was the only way the government could end the orgy of borrowing and get investors to buy gilts again. Many of the faces around the table were white with horror. Speaking for the dissenters, Jim Prior said he was 'disappointed and shocked' by news that would wreak terrible damage on business confidence. But despite her doubts, Mrs Thatcher threw her weight behind her Chancellor. Interest rates were only so high, she said, because they had all been too slow to trim their budgets. 'It wouldn't be 17 per cent if we got our expenditure down.'[60]

The gentleman raised his eyes above his newspaper and looked curiously at Jemima— "Madam, have you lost your way?" said he...

(THE TALE OF JEMIMA PUDDLE-DUCK)

In this lovely Beatrix Potter-inspired cartoon (*Daily Telegraph*, 14 November 1979), Nicholas Garland captures the growing alarm among the Tory faithful at the state of the economy.

By now the glow of election victory had long since faded. It was lucky for Mrs Thatcher that the next day's front pages were dominated by the revelation that Sir Anthony Blunt, the former Surveyor of the Queen's Pictures, had been the Fourth Man in the Cambridge spy ring. Even so, the *Express* thought it 'the bleakest hour' since she had come to power, while the *Mirror* called it a 'vicious new credit squeeze' that would punish 'commuters, housewives, home-owners and council tenants, ratepayers and small businessmen' for the incompetence of the 'Scrooge Tories'.

Even on the Tory benches, the mood was very anxious. The spy revelations, thought Alan Clark, had been a 'lucky break for Geoffrey because the whole Blunt affair diverted attention from the really alarming manner in which our economy seems to be conducted'. A week later, *The Times* reported 'growing concern among some Conservative MPs' that the government was doing terrible damage to British industry. 'The picture', wrote the paper's economics editor, David Blake, on 23 November, 'is an appallingly stark one.'[61]

He was right. In Whitehall everything seemed to be going wrong at once. By mid-December, inflation had reached 17½ per cent, with most experts predicting that it would hit 20 per cent by the following summer. 'The difficulties we face are greater than we had any reason to expect,' Howe told his colleagues on 10 December. Not only was inflation rising more quickly than he had feared, but borrowing was currently projected to hit around £13 billion by 1982, which would be a colossal blow to international confidence. The only solution, he thought, was to slash £1 billion immediately and another £2 billion a year later. Ten days later, *The Times* declared that 'no Government since the war' had been confronted with such a 'dangerous and bleak' prospect so soon after taking office, and suggested that Mrs Thatcher 'appeal to the larger interest of the nation, for the sake of its survival, against the destructive self-interest of particular groups'. But Wilson, Heath and Callaghan had been banging that particular drum since the mid-1960s. It had not done them a blind bit of good.[62]

In any case, Mrs Thatcher's most urgent challenge now was to stave off a revolt by her own ministers. Listening to the Prime Minister and her Chancellor, Sir Ian Gilmour thought they were like First World War generals, marching their men towards certain annihilation. And that autumn, speaking off the record, Jim Prior told the journalist Hugo Young that he was 'appalled by the seriousness of the situation, sceptical about the Treasury's extremism, highly aware of the possibility of failure'. It was true, Prior said, that 'nothing has worked in the past, so we must try it our way'. But like a growing number of his colleagues, he seriously doubted that Thatcher and Howe could turn things around. 'We are sober people', he said grimly, 'who can see real collapse staring this country in the face.'[63]

Mrs Thatcher spent Christmas at Chequers. On Christmas Eve she visited the British troops in South Armagh, but she was back by the evening, which she spent with her family. In this, as in much else, her tastes could hardly have been more traditional. Her Christmas lunch, according to her press office, began with an 'avocado pear and grapefruit salad', followed by turkey and all the trimmings, Christmas pudding and mince pies. In a modern twist, both the BBC and ITV had sent video recordings of the year's best programmes. And as a John le Carré fan, she was particularly looking forward to seeing *Tinker Tailor Soldier Spy*, which had gone out earlier that autumn.

But she could never sit still. Her bodyguard, Barry Strevens, recalled that on Christmas Eve his Special Branch partner was summoned home because his child had fallen ill. Mrs Thatcher, just back from Northern Ireland, told Strevens to drive him home, because 'family must always come first'. When Strevens got back to the outbuilding they used as their Chequers base, he was astonished to find 'Christmas decorations up, a log fire blazing, a tin of biscuits on the table alongside a flask of coffee and a mini bottle of whisky'. On the mantelpiece was a Christmas card, with a handwritten message from Mrs Thatcher herself. 'I stood there incredibly touched by what this lady – the Prime Minister – had just done for me on Christmas Eve, knowing I was away from my wife and children because my job meant I had to be there for her instead,' he later told the *Sun*. 'It was at that moment I knew I would stand in the way of a bullet for Margaret Thatcher without hesitation. And that I would remain utterly loyal to her for the rest of my life.'[64]

A week later, Britain bade farewell to the 1970s. Almost without exception, Fleet Street's commentators were pleased to see them go. *The Times*'s Louis Heren thought they would be 'remembered as the decade when the decline of Britain, at home and abroad, accelerated at an alarming speed', while the *Observer*'s Peter Conrad could think of 'no apter farewell to the unlamented Seventies' than the spittle of Britain's punks, 'a wet and well-aimed discharge'. 'The Seventies were rougher than anyone thought they would be,' agreed the *Mirror*, lamenting that 'two thousand were killed in Ulster, 20,000 in Rhodesia, several hundred thousand in Uganda and millions in Vietnam and Cambodia'. As for the future, the *Mirror* was not optimistic. 'If the 1980s are as awful as they predict,' it thought, 'the only people working at the end of them will be the experts forecasting unemployment for everyone else.'[65]

For a more cheerful view of the decade ahead, newspaper readers were better off turning to the former deputy Labour leader George Brown, now a great Thatcher enthusiast. 'The great joy for me this coming week', he declared in the *Sunday Express*, 'is that we can say goodbye to one of the worst decades Britain has known. A decade of despair and disintegration.' For the first time in ages, Brown was looking forward with hope; for Mrs Thatcher had already brought a 'sense of purpose and determination to her office that No. 10 has not seen in many a year'. As a patriot, he was convinced that she would 'lead us to bury once and for all the Dean Acheson taunt . . . that "Britain had lost an empire and failed to find a role".' And he concluded on a stirring note: 'Ten years from now, we shall then look back on these dreadful seventies and wonder how we ever sank so low!'[66]

For readers who preferred to put their faith in *Old Moore's Almanack*, which had been forecasting the future since 1697, there was similarly cheery news. In the year ahead, Old Moore predicted, 'a powerful sense of initiative' would rouse 'the aspirations of the ordinary men to greater self-reliance and enterprise', which was precisely the sort of thing that the Prime Minister liked to hear. Perhaps Old Moore was really Old Margaret in disguise. But a book called *The 80s*, written by three Americans who claimed to be looking back from the future, made for humiliating reading. In 1982, with Britain's exports having dwindled to 'a chest of drawers and five dozen jars of marmalade', the country was going to be advertised for sale in the world's press: 'For Sale: One country: Quaint. Needs work. Best offer.' After being snapped up by Disney, Britain would become the United Magic Kingdom amusement park, admission 50p. To add insult to insult, its native employees would prove so 'work-shy and disruptive' that 45 million of them were going to be sacked and shipped to India.[67]

Perhaps the most revealing indication of the national mood was, of all things, an Ovaltine advert, which ran in the national press over the New Year. The malted-drink firm had commissioned a cartoon by the *Guardian*'s Les Gibbard, showing an ordinary family outside their semi-detached house. The family are gazing in horror at the black clouds overhead, which are labelled 'Recession', 'Inflation' and 'Strikes'. 'Hello everyone. Here is the weather forecast,' says the copy:

> A deep economic depression, centred over the entire country, will remain stationary, while associated troughs of despondency will be slow moving.
>
> Political visibility will be poor to moderate, due to thick fog in the Westminster area, and there will almost certainly be long outbreaks of industrial unrest with the possibility of heavy overnight recession.

Barometric pressure on the pound is still rising and causing widespread inflation which could cause a sharp freeze over low-lying assets.

Still it's an ill wind that blows nobody any good, and my wife always has a nice, warming mug of Ovaltine ready when I get home. Almost at once, the clouds roll back, and out comes the sun . . .

The slogan was perfectly judged. 'Ovaltine: In place of strife.'[68]

Even abroad, it seemed, not many people shared George Brown's confidence that the new decade would mark the start of a golden age. On the *Mirror*'s 'Old Codgers' letters page, Mr K. Davis of Bath reported that he and his family had just got back from a week's holiday in Tunisia. The fact that a *Mirror* reader had been to Tunisia at all told a fascinating story of change, but that was not the point. Mr Davis was writing with a story that 'made us both laugh and wonder what the rest of the world was thinking of the UK'. He and his family, he said, were strolling through the medina in the coastal resort of Hammamet when a 'young Tunisian girl, no more than eight years old', came up and tried to get them to buy some ostensibly local handicrafts. They declined, politely of course, but the girl did not seem surprised. She just shrugged. 'English,' she said knowingly. 'No money, Margaret Thatcher!'[69]

# 5

# The Word Is . . . Lymeswold!

*Our pleasure lies in returning from a day's work, transferring the evening meal from freezer to cooker, then sitting back over the first drink to watch Delia at work.*

Joan Bakewell, *The Times*, 15 March 1980

*I wonder what picture is conjured up by your mind's eye when I say the name 'Lymeswold'?*

*The World at One*, BBC Radio Four,
19 October 1981

On her first night in Downing Street, Mrs Thatcher took her evening meal in the State Dining Room, joined by her senior officials. Since there was no Number 10 canteen, her personal assistant had brought over some shepherd's pie, cooked in Chelsea beforehand. Denis made sure everybody had a glass of wine, and Mrs Thatcher herself played hostess, carefully spooning the pie on to her officials' plates. As it happened, Jim Callaghan's last meal in Number 10, only hours earlier, had been shepherd's pie, too. Some of the civil servants must have been sick of it. It was almost impossible, though, to imagine Callaghan doling it out, like a schoolmaster serving dinner to his pupils. But then his successor was hardly a typical Prime Minister.[1]

Ever since Mrs Thatcher had become leader of her party, interviewers had asked her about food. But the questions were rarely about eating it; they were about cooking it. Nobody had ever asked Harold Wilson if he liked preparing the family breakfast, or invited Edward Heath to suggest a recipe for spotted dick. But from the moment Mrs Thatcher stepped into the political limelight she had actively encouraged the misapprehension that she was, at heart, an ordinary suburban housewife. 'What people don't realise about me', she said piously, 'is that I am a very ordinary person who leads a very normal life. I enjoy it – seeing that the family have a good breakfast. And shopping keeps me in touch.'[2]

Although this was far from being the whole truth, Mrs Thatcher very obviously wanted to believe it. Even though she had *never* been merely an ordinary housewife, she remained a child of the 1920s and 1930s, convinced that it was a wife's responsibility to look after her husband and children. Not long after she became Conservative leader, a journalist made the mistake of asking whether she still made breakfast for Denis and Mark. Mrs Thatcher looked at him 'incredulously' and said firmly: 'Mum makes the breakfast. Fresh fruit and a cooked dish. Currently, they prefer scrambled eggs to fried.' She was not exaggerating. When the raffish Conservative MP Jonathan Aitken visited the Thatcher household in the mid-1970s, he discovered that his leader 'cooked breakfast every morning for Denis, who could get pernickety if his bacon was not grilled in a certain way'.

At other mealtimes, too, Mrs Thatcher bustled around the kitchen 'at high speed like a television chef on fast forward', specializing in traditional favourites such as roast beef and coronation chicken. She was, Aitken thought, 'an excellent if monomaniac hostess, insisting on doing all the wine pouring, cooking and washing up herself, interspersed with imperious commands to the onlookers such as, "Watch out!", "Move your elbows, dear!", "Look sharp!", "Out of the way!" and "Drink up!"' And she was no stranger to the labour-saving appliances on which so many professional women depended. 'She has the modern working wife's Godsend – a freezer,' reported the *Barnet Press* in September 1978. As always, though, Mrs Thatcher was keen to look as organized as possible. 'I try to cook two or three things at the same time', she explained, 'to have dishes to put in the fridge or freezer in reserve.'[3]

Amid the hurly-burly of the 1980s, Mrs Thatcher's critics often painted her as some fantastically cruel and decadent empress, swilling champagne as she cackled over the unemployment figures. In fact, the strict rules governing life in Downing Street meant all food and drink came out of her own pocket. 'We don't have a cook,' she told the *Sun*. 'I never wanted one. I like cooking but when I come back in late, if there's anything to be done . . . what we want is really something simple. I no longer cook anything very complicated.' What that meant was 'vegetable soup and inevitably something like poached eggs on toast or Marmite'. She still liked to think of herself as an organized housewife, though. Talking to *Living* magazine, she claimed that at weekends she liked to 'go through the freezer to see what we're running out of. I can't allow it to get low. I've got to have a certain number of shepherd's pies, lasagne, stews – yes,

I still do it, and I like it.' But whether this happened regularly is very dubious. In reality, she and Denis relied on Marks & Spencer's ready meals or frozen meals brought in by the Downing Street staff, which she had to pay for privately. All in all, it was hardly a luxurious picture; indeed, she probably lived more frugally than thousands of anonymous professional women.[4]

In the kitchen, as elsewhere, Mrs Thatcher's tastes were often very nostalgic. Her fondness for coronation chicken, for example, reflected her upbringing in a middle-class provincial household in the reign of George V.* Yet even here she was far from being a walking throwback. As a working wife who found little time to cook, relied on ready meals and became increasingly dependent on her freezer, she was very much a woman of the 1980s. In this respect, her experience was more like that of a much younger professional woman than that of a woman of her own age. Talking to the writer Beatrix Campbell later in the decade, one elderly Conservative activist – 'a tough Tory' who lived in the Borders and hated 'scroungers and vandals and communists' – spoke for many in deploring the laxness of the modern working mother. 'That film *E T* just proved how indifferent the modern mother is,' she explained. 'She just packed the fridge with food, there was no discipline and ET was there but she didn't know! Standards are going down. I'd never dreamt it would be like this. I don't know who's to blame – it's the mothers going out to work too early!' The irony, of course, is that she could easily have been talking about her leader.[5]

When the Mass Observation project was revived in 1981, one of its volunteers' first assignments was to describe their typical weekly diet. The answers offered a perfect snapshot of a country poised between the reassurance of heavy, traditional British meals on the one hand, and the allure of exotic, spicier foreign food on the other.

In the kitchen, as elsewhere, class mattered. Working-class families still called their evening meal 'tea', rarely 'dinner' and never 'supper', and were much less likely to try expensive novelties from abroad. They also drank a gargantuan amount of tea. Here, in her own words, is what Margaret Bradshaw, the 45-year-old wife of a retired policeman in Lambeth, south London, prepared for her family on a typical weekday in 1981:

* It is true, of course, that coronation chicken was not officially invented until 1953. But it was inspired by a very similar dish, jubilee chicken, created for George V's Silver Jubilee in 1935, when the young Margaret Roberts was 9.

9 Porridge and Tea.

11 Biscuit and Tea.

12.30 Egg and Tomato Sandwich, Tea.

3pm Ice cream or Tea & Cake or Shandy or Lemonade.

5pm Pork Chop, New Potatoes, Peas, Apple Sauce, Pineapple Rings, Custard. More Tea.

7pm Tea and Biscuit.

9.30pm Toast and Cheese. Tea or Milk.

For Jean Carr, a library cleaner from Chelmsford, the weekday menu seemed to have barely changed for decades, apart from the addition of spaghetti:

My husband always goes to work with a cooked breakfast inside him. I have bread and marg and marmalade.

4 days a wk we have tea at 5 o'clock and that is tea, bread and butter, paste, cheese spread and jam, also some home made cakes, sometimes shop bought if they are at a reduced price.

3 days a wk we have a hot tea or a salad which could be egg and chips, or mushrooms on toast, or egg on toast, spaghetti and sausages, any kind of hot meal like that.

For a salad, we would have lettuce, tomatoes, luncheon meat, hard boiled eggs or maybe a salad of beetroot, spring onions, pork and egg pie and hot potatoes and we could also have with the salads coleslaw and pickled onions, salad cream and pickle.

My sons usually have a cup of tea and cereal before going to school . . .

For dessert it could be a plain steam pudding, Golden Syrup and custard, or a crumble and custard, bananas and custard, rice or a macaroni pudding so long as it's hot and sweet.

Luncheon meat, pork pies, steamed puddings, crumble: this might have been a family menu from 1951.[6]

In more affluent households, food more obviously reflected cultural change. Jenny Palmer, the *Guardian*-reading mature student from Lancaster, gave two sample weekday meals: a 'casserole of sweet and sour chicken' with rice, followed by apple crumble; and 'grilled bacon, home-made burgers and mushrooms', followed by jelly and cream. Meanwhile, Susan Gray, the journalist on a weekly paper in Darlington, began her day with yoghurt and cereal, while her husband had cornflakes and scrambled eggs. Lunch was relatively austere – 'crispbread and cheese' for Susan and 'meat sandwiches with tomato' for her husband – but dinner was very old-fashioned: toad in the hole with onion gravy, cabbage and potatoes, followed by rhubarb and custard. In one respect, though, the Grays were unusual. As Susan proudly recorded, all their yoghurt, bread, cakes and biscuits had been homemade, while all their fruit and vegetables came from their garden or the local allotment. Clearly they had been great fans of *The Good Life*.[7]

But perhaps the most interesting case was that of Peter Hibbitt. As a former lorry driver who had recently become night supervisor at his Basildon depot, he might have been expected to subsist on a diet of egg and chips. In fact, his tastes were much broader. He too had cereal for breakfast, with 'boiled egg, beans on toast or individual pietza [*sic*]' for lunch, and 'anything from egg or cold meat and chips via spaghetti Bolognese, shepherd's pie, steak [and] kidney pie or pudding, kebab, sausages and onions [or] chops' for dinner. But on Sundays, he wrote, 'the evening meal is a bit more elaborate . . . lasagne or moussaka with the authentic ingredients', or perhaps a roast with vegetables, 'often some of the more unusual ones'. Like many other respondents, he placed great emphasis on the 'sweets' ('generally a choice of two'), followed by 'percolated coffee' and, terrifyingly, 'home made wine'. And like so many people at the turn of the 1980s, Peter put away 'vast quantities of tea with everything'. 'I drink about 12 *pints* a day from a pint mug', he wrote. Perhaps it was no coincidence that his political hero was Labour's Tony Benn, the only man in Britain who drank more tea than he did.[8]

To younger readers, all those pies and puddings, all those cold meats and pickled onions and cups of tea, probably sound like something from a gastronomic Stone Age. At the time, however, what was striking was the sheer pace of change, especially for older people who remembered the ration books of the Attlee years. According to the National Food Survey, people in 1981 ate far more margarine and cheese than they had in 1950, as well as twelve times as much pork, usually as bacon or sausages. But they ate less white bread, butter, mutton and lamb, fewer potatoes and much less pudding. According to a survey just before the 1979 election, only one in six housewives served as many puddings as they had three years before, and only half of all families finished off Sunday lunch with a pudding. The *Guardian* thought this was terrible news. 'A terrible future of pudding-less dinners and lunches is in store for Britain', it warned, 'unless the country's children take direct action.' But it was no good. Even the greatest pudding of the 1970s was about to enter an irreversible fall from grace. As Susan Gray reported to Mass Observation, the emblematic pudding of the age, Black Forest gateau, had now 'gone the way of scampi and chips, chicken Kiev and beef stroganoff . . . very non-U!'[9]

The biggest loser, though, was fresh fish, which was close to vanishing as a regular part of the national diet. In effect, it had been ousted by the single biggest winner of the post-war years, battery-farmed chicken. As the *Guardian* observed in 1978, almost a third of Britain's fish and chip shops had shut down in just twenty years. Indeed, for fishmongers these were dreadful years. 'For a while,' wrote one food writer a few years later, 'literally not a day passed without someone somewhere abandoning the fish trade.' He was not exaggerating. In Essex, Jean Carr bought her fish from a supermarket, lamenting that the fishmonger had simply 'disappeared from the high street'. Years earlier, she remembered, there had been two fish shops in her village, 'but now with frozen fish on sale, housewives do not or will not know how to fillet or gut a fish'. As a child she had always eaten fresh fish on Fridays. 'But now it is on the way out,' she wrote sadly, 'and most likely will be gone in a few years, to be replaced by frozen packets of fish.'[10]

All the time, the great engine of culinary innovation roared on. Mealtimes were less formal, dishes lighter and cooking times shorter. Younger people often shrank from their parents' beloved sauces, preferring simpler, cleaner flavours instead. Herbs and spices were more popular than ever: it was telling that when Mass Observation asked Susan Gray to list the 'new foods' that had transformed her family's diet, she turned first to her spice cupboard. Her mother had relied on just seven or eight spices. By contrast, Susan's cupboard contained everything from cumin and turmeric to garam masala, oregano, cardamom and chilli powder – and this not in Islington but in Darlington. 'Even in the North East tundra', she added, 'we can get kiwi fruit, pomeloes, mangoes, uglis, sweet potatoes, okra and so on, which were unheard of, say, ten years ago.' Not all families in north-eastern England, of course, were regularly stuffing themselves with mangoes and okra. Even so, the typical British family in the early 1980s enjoyed a diet that was more obviously globalized than ever before. In Basildon, reported Peter Hibbitt, Chinese takeaways, lychees and kiwi fruit were all taken for granted. As a child in the Second World War he had grown up with cheese that tasted 'akin to Sunlight soap'. Now he regularly bought Edam, Brie, Camembert and Danish Blue.[11]

One man who would not have been impressed by all this was the late George Orwell. With the return of mass unemployment reawakening memories of the Depression, Orwell's shadow loomed over the cultural landscape of the early 1980s. Almost no state-of-the-nation survey failed to pay homage to *The Road to Wigan Pier* (1937), and few literary travellers failed to spend a day or two in Wigan. But given his belief that fruit juice was an unmistakeable sign of bohemian perversion, Orwell would not have approved of the food and drink of the 1980s. Above all, he would have been deeply displeased by the rise of vegetarianism, about which he was extremely scathing. The mind boggles, for example, at what he would have made of the scene at Heavens Above in Barnstaple, Devon, which won high praise from Lesley Nelson's guidebook *Vegetarian Restaurants in England* (1982):

> The cafe is a casual meeting-place for Ecology Party supporters, anti-nuclear demonstrators, busted buskers, and, on Friday night, anyone who wants to play folk music. There's a regular menu of snacks like turmeric-flavoured pasties filled with black-eye bean mixture, baked potatoes with cheese, scotch eggs, salad-filled rolls, and carob brownies. And special dishes like stuffed marrow, bean chili, vegetable casserole, and baked apples are prepared on weekdays. The cafe seats 40 to 50 people, amiably grouped round communal tables, and when the food runs out the room is hired to ecology groups, mime artists, and writers.

Mime artists! You could almost believe it a spoof. But in the early 1980s vegetarianism was a serious business, picking up new adherents every week. 'By AD 2000', one vegetarian advocate claimed, 'Britain will be a vegetarian society'.[12]

As that Barnstaple review suggests, vegetarianism had not entirely thrown off its reputation as the gastronomic redoubt of pacifists, eccentrics and university lecturers. The country's most successful vegetarian chain, founded back in 1961, did not call itself Cranks for nothing. Yet vegetarianism was now far more mainstream than in Orwell's day, driven as much by anxieties about health and fitness as by philosophical or ethical concerns. Health food shops, which appealed at first to people with hippyish, lentil-fancying leanings, had mushroomed during the 1970s, and one estimate suggests that by the time Margaret Thatcher came to power, there were some 1,200 across the country. Often they tried to attract more conservative shoppers by selling coffee beans, wholemeal bread and cream cheese, which you could not get in the supermarkets and did not have to be a mime artist to enjoy. And so, almost by stealth, vegetarianism began to spread. Eating meat was becoming less automatic, and as many people found themselves eating meat-free meals almost without thinking about it, vegetarianism became casual rather than cranky.[13]

The biggest divide, though, was not between carnivores and herbivores, but between people who had money and people who did not. For if food was a potent symbol of middle-class ambition, it was an equally powerful symbol of working-class poverty. Even the vast differences in household budgets told a story of division. One family in twenty spent more than £100 a week on food. Yet at the same time, one in twenty spent less than £20. And for writers chronicling the lives of the low-paid, the unemployed, the sick and the old, their empty plates lent a dash of descriptive colour to the statistics. When Beatrix Campbell retraced Orwell's journey to Wigan, she wrote with scarcely suppressed fury of the gap between the food teenage mothers saw on television and the reality of their daily 'toast and tea, beans, bread and chips'. In Coventry, an unemployed couple told her that they only had cooked meals at weekends and lived on beans and toast the rest of the time. Another jobless family told her that good days meant spaghetti Bolognese, bad days meant beans on toast or biscuits, and 'some days we just don't eat'.[14]

To some extent, the gap was narrowing. Most people, if they were in work, lived more comfortably than ever. And with food prices dropping, tastes that had once been reserved for London's professional middle classes were now within the reach of millions. In Lancaster, Jenny Palmer was 'amazed to find working-class pensioners buying *steak* on a weekday' – and not from their local butcher, but from Marks & Spencer, where prices were famously high. 'Yes it is expensive', one pensioner told her, 'but you know it's good from here.' And in *The Times*, the food writer Christopher Driver suggested that the success of television cooks such as Delia Smith, the idealized middle-class housewife who taught millions of people how to pronounce the word 'lasagne', might lead to a culinary renaissance among the urban working classes. Legend had it that many people watched her programmes with a microwaved ready meal on their lap. But Driver remained optimistic. 'Gastronomy in Gateshead?' he mused. 'All things are possible.'[15]

Is it really true that people watched Delia Smith while eating microwaved ready meals? It certainly sounds plausible. In a country where six out of ten women went out to work, the days when the suburban housewife spent her afternoon assembling an elaborate three-course meal were a distant memory. What was more, most people spent longer at work than ever before in living memory. For although British productivity was notoriously dreadful, the average worker actually spent more hours at the factory or the office than his – or her – American, French and German counterparts, and took fewer holidays than almost anybody else in Europe.[16]

When Britain's workers got home, then, many had precious little appetite for slaving over the stove. But their rumbling stomachs were somebody else's opportunity. In the autumn of 1981, Penguin brought out a commuters' cookbook, billed as a 'cookery book for victims of the twentieth

century'. It was 'not an I-hate-cooking book,' explained the author, Beryl
Downing. 'It's an I-like-it-but-I-haven't-the-time . . . a daily recipe service
specially created for commuters who – married, single, old, young, men,
women – all travel at least half an hour a day to their offices.' The recipes,
she promised, would take no more than thirty minutes to prepare, a formula that would later be familiar to fans of Jamie Oliver. But as might
also be familiar, many of the recipes looked suspiciously complicated for
something that might be ready in half an hour. A typical example was
'fish thermidor', which boasted an absurdly rich sauce made from butter,
milk, mustard, Emmental and brandy, and required the cook to have been
simmering 'home-made fish stock' with bones from the local fishmonger.
That was not much good to the harassed commuter just off the 6.15 from
Waterloo.[17]

The obvious alternative was the chilled ready meal. People had been
eating 'TV dinners' since the late 1950s, but the real breakthrough came
with Marks & Spencer's chicken Kiev, which first appeared on the shelves,
with satisfyingly perfect timing, in October 1979. They were expensive:
£1.99 for a pack of two, the equivalent of about £10 today. But that was
part of their appeal, because they were marketed as high-end products for
professional women. The point, according to Marks & Spencer's product
developer, was that 'the British public was entitled to be able to buy
restaurant-quality food to enjoy in their own home'. Given the quality of
British restaurant food, this was not, perhaps, as enticing as it sounded.
But the chicken Kiev proved a tremendous success, and was soon followed
by lasagne, chilli con carne and chicken tikka masala. Other retailers
followed suit: by 1982 there were a host of firms making upmarket ready
meals for special occasions, such as the Gourmet Hostess Foods company,
based on a Lancashire farm, which promised that 'the filling for a freezer,
or ready-to-reheat dinner party, can be delivered to your nearest railway
station the day after you order it'.[18]

There was, of course, a cost to all this, even though few people remarked
on it at the time. Cheapness and convenience came with serious caveats:
thanks partly to the rise of the ready meal, people now consumed twice
as many additives as they had in 1955. In fact, almost all processed food
now contained artificial flavourings. 'Potato crisps no longer taste of
potato but of chicken,' lamented the *Observer*; 'chicken tastes of fishmeal;
and fish come not with fins but in battered bite-size fingers.' Some products
fell painfully short of the promise on the label. Tinned ham often contained 40 per cent water, and by the mid-1980s supermarkets were selling
'country-style' sausages with a meat content of just 10 per cent. The 'country' in question, presumably, was North Korea.[19]

The trend for convenience foods, however, was irresistible. As spokesmen for the food industry pointed out, ready meals were an inevitable consequence of the trend for women to work outside the home. Indeed, some food companies looked forward to a future in which, as in the Downing Street flat, old-fashioned home cooking had virtually died out completely. 'A fundamental change in British eating habits has begun,' exulted a report by Ross Foods, the nation's third biggest provider of frozen food, in April 1979. 'The typical household menu of the mid-1980s will be foreign in origin, fast and frozen. The kitchen will be a centre for the unwrapping of ready-made portions from the freezer and the take-away food shop . . . less of an everyday cooking workshop and more of a family distribution centre.'[20]

At the centre of this revolution was the freezer. Sales were soaring: in 1970, barely 4 per cent of British homes had one, rising to more than 40 per cent in 1978 and almost two-thirds by 1985. 'Today frozen goods are at the heart of every grocer's display,' declared *The Times* in 1980, in an article celebrating the twenty-fifth anniversary of the fish finger. Mocked on their introduction in 1955, fish fingers were now 'as British as teabags, instant mash and salad cream', although frozen pizzas were challenging their high standing in the hearts of the nation's children. Indeed, most people took frozen food for granted. When, in the winter of 1982, Mass Observation asked its volunteers about eating fruit and vegetables in season, the general response was complete bewilderment. Almost all replied that since the advent of the freezer, they no longer thought about it. One typical respondent was the battery-farm worker Mary Richards. Asked how her family's eating habits had changed, she immediately pointed to their freezer, which was full of 'fish fingers, beef burgers and frozen peas, chips, oven chips, chicken pieces . . . pizas [*sic*] sometimes, ice cream, fish cakes and frozen pies'. 'I go to work', she added, 'and don't have time to do the home cooking I used to do and my Mother used to do.'[21]

The appliance that really came to stand for the social changes of the early 1980s, though, was the microwave. Contrary to popular belief, microwaves had been available in Britain since 1959, but their size and cost, as well as popular fears of radiation poisoning, meant sightings were rare. But by the late 1970s sales were climbing. Indeed, some early adopters were positively evangelical about the delights of microwave cookery. When the *Guardian*'s Jenny Webb first bought a microwave, she viewed it with 'apprehension'. But after a few initial experiments – 'a jacket potato in five minutes, scrambled eggs in two, roast beef in under thirty and peas cooked from frozen in six' – she was converted.

Within one and a half hours I could be tucking into my chicken or in eight minutes enjoying a trout cooked to perfection and covered in melted butter and almonds . . .

I could hardly believe that in under 12 minutes I could cook any one of so many time consuming dishes such as soups, pates, beef stroganoff, peaches in gammon, suet pudding and others, all of which became part of my fast menu . . .

It sounds as if I am besotted with my microwave but it truly is a remarkable appliance . . . Imagine being able to soften rock hard butter in thirty seconds, to melt cheese on toast in the same time, to melt chocolate in a minute or to heat up a cold cup of coffee in about two. Some manufacturers even suggest that you can dry your rain sodden newspapers or curl your false eye lashes!

If curling false eyelashes were not enough – we should probably gloss over the 'peaches in gammon' – Webb had some other useful tips. To make a cup of tea, for instance, people should simply 'put the tea bag in a cup of water and microwave'. To improve the taste of their cream crackers, they should heat them 'for a few minutes' in the microwave. And to brighten up their vegetables, they should 'pop a slice of processed cheese on top . . . and melt in the microwave for a few seconds'.[22]

Amazingly enough, readers did not immediately rush to follow her advice. For one thing, microwaves were very expensive, and by the end of 1983, barely 1½ million microwaves had been sold. But at this point public enthusiasm reached a tipping point. In the next twelve months the manufacturers shifted a further million, and by the middle of the decade demand for microwave ovens was higher in Britain than in the rest of Europe put together, reflecting the much higher proportion of women who were going out to work. 'People are no longer frightened of the technology and are buying them as a main cooking aid,' thought *The Times*. Perhaps surprisingly, though, the Prime Minister was not among them. Her memoirs claim that when she was working late during the Falklands campaign, her microwave 'did sterling service when sudden meals were required'. But this seems to have been pure invention by her ghostwriters. A few years later, when Mrs Thatcher visited the headquarters of Asda, she told them that although she was impressed by the speed of the microwave, she did not own one herself.[23]

The real mark of success, of course, was not having to cook at all. Even before the Big Bang transformed the City, high-minded observers shuddered at the excesses of the capital's financiers. 'In the City and big companies all over the country,' wrote a disapproving Polly Toynbee in 1980, 'good eating is part of the rich fabric of everyday top management life.' Oddly, bankers' meals were tax-deductible if they ate in their wood-panelled dining rooms, but not if they went out to a restaurant. So the first years of the decade saw a boom, not just in specially built directors' dining rooms, but in agencies providing cooks for the City. Menus were unsurprisingly lavish: blinis with caviar, smoked salmon and sour cream, steak and oyster pie, and so on. Not even the boardroom, however, was immune from the winds of fashion. 'Avocado pears used to be smart,' Toynbee reported, 'but now that *hoi polloi* eat them in wine bars, king size prawns have taken their place. Quails are popular at the moment, but Chicken Kiev has become vulgar.' The latest trend in puddings, meanwhile, was 'exotic fruits, specially flown in . . . Chinese gooseberries, passion fruit and persimmons'. In this respect, at least, the Square Mile was already a global village.[24]

Yet even at this point, with American institutions moving into the City, the wine-fuelled three-course lunch was on its way out. The Americans arrived early and left late; even more disturbingly, they worked so hard that they only had time for lunch at their desks. The obvious solution would have been a sandwich. But not only were British sandwiches about as non-U as it was possible to imagine, they were generally agreed to be absolutely abysmal. During the Attlee years, the *Daily Mail* had run a celebrated story about a respectable commuter whose briefcase fell open on the train to reveal four jam sandwiches, the ultimate metaphor for what the *Mail* regarded as the enforced degradation of the middle classes. And thirty years on, the words that many people automatically associated with 'sandwich' were 'British Rail', conjuring up a terrifying image of a yellowing ham sandwich, its corners curling beneath the glass of a station buffet. Rehabilitating the sandwich, therefore, would be a herculean undertaking.[25]

According to City legend, the man who really rescued the British sandwich was a man called Robin Birley. Yet Birley was an intriguingly implausible candidate to become the saviour of the sandwich. His father had founded the upper-class nightclub Annabel's in 1963, for which Robin's mother, the eponymous Annabel, rewarded him by running off with Sir James Goldsmith. At the age of 11, Robin was mauled by a tiger owned by his parents' friend John Aspinall, the society bookmaker best known for his association with Lord Lucan and his unfortunate habit of losing zookeepers to animal attacks. He survived, though, and in September 1979, at the age of 21, he opened his first sandwich bar, Birley's, in Fenchurch Street. Soon he had two more, offering eighteen different fillings from prawn and avocado to curried turkey. At around £1.50, the equivalent of about £6 today, Birley's sandwiches were not cheap, and he also sold lager, Muscadet and Côtes du Rhône, which says something about his customers. But demand was booming, and by the turn of 1985 his runners were delivering some 600 orders a day to offices across the City.[26]

Birley was far from alone in spotting an opportunity in the capital's new office culture. In May 1980, the *Observer*'s Fiona Malcolm reported on the increasingly 'long queues inside and outside sandwich bars', as London's workers poured out of their buildings every lunchtime. Too many places, she lamented, specialized in 'the uniquely British combination of wet blotting paper smeared with yellow motor oil and filled with a slice of soapy cheddar or processed ham and a limp lettuce leaf', and there was a special place in hell for Olive's Pantry in Covent Garden, which packed its sandwiches with 'lumps of overcooked beef, fatty pork, tinned ham, pressed chicken and processed cheese'. But there were decent places, too. In Covent Garden, she recommended Neal's Yard, where for 50p the staff would fill a wholemeal sandwich with 'avocado, egg mayonnaise, peanut butter, banana and honey, cheddar, vegetable paté [and] hummus', though presumably not all at once. She was also a great fan of the 'scandalously expensive' sandwiches at the Danish Food Centre on Conduit Street, as well as the salt beef and pastrami sandwiches at Carroll's in Great Windmill Street, which was decorated, slightly oddly, with signed photographs of the glamour model Fiona Richmond, *The Good Life*'s Richard Briers and the one-eyed Israeli general Moshe Dayan.

One prediction Fiona Malcolm got completely wrong, though, was her belief that Londoners would prove easy pickings for sandwich-makers from the North, whose products were so much better. 'You wouldn't get many canny northerners paying the kind of prices you pay in London for pre-packed rubbish,' she insisted. 'I can't wait for cold roast pork and stuffing and saveloy and pease pudding sandwiches to come south at reasonable prices.' Yet the future lay not with the sandwich-makers of Harrogate and Hull, but with the giants of the high street. Once again Marks & Spencer led the way, selling four different flavours – salmon and cucumber, prawn and cream cheese, ham salad, and egg and tomato – in triangular containers in 1980. Boots soon followed suit, producing 'sand-wedges' of their own. What the workers of the 1980s wanted, it turned out, was not pease pudding, but prawn mayonnaise.[27]

The rise of the sandwich bar was part of a wider trend. Despite the economic downturn, these were boom years for eating out: as Christopher Driver remarked in the preface to the 1980 edition of the *Good Food Guide*, the 'visible popularity of restaurants, and the apparently affluent youth of their customers', suggested that the market was expanding every year. But he was honest enough to admit that visitors to Britain's restaurants faced some daunting challenges. Some owners seemed to regard *Fawlty Towers* as a model, such as the unnamed restaurateur 'who won a bet with his head waitress that he would not walk through the dining room without his trousers on'. Most establishments were immensely unfriendly to children, regarding smaller customers 'as an intrusion and their tastes an inconvenience'. Then there was the problem of smoking. 'There are plenty of places in this book', Driver admitted, 'whose atmosphere late on a Saturday night can only be compared with the residual smoking compartments on London tube trains, which even hardened smokers often try to avoid.'

Above all, though, there was the issue of quality. Driver thought the nation's restaurants had improved enormously in recent years; so too, hearteningly, did the authors of *Fodor's Guide*. The British no longer thought it 'shameful or sinful to enjoy good food', and American visitors would find that the days of 'stodgy, steamed puddings and over-boiled vegetables' were over. But the *Let's Go* guide for 1982 was more cautious, suggesting that young Americans stick to bangers and mash, cream teas and something the authors called 'Spotty Dick'. They should never order vegetables, which were 'often overcooked – ask for salads instead'. And when it came to hot drinks, *Let's Go* issued a stark warning. 'Always choose tea . . . British coffee is not well made.'[28]

What might a visitor in the early 1980s expect to eat? At the top end, the food was still French-inspired and, by modern standards, dementedly rich. At the Oven d'Or in Orpington in south-east London, customers might expect to find hot pâté in puff pastry with Madeira sauce, roast crab with herbs and cream sauce or *Crêpes Edouard VII*, 'stuffed with smoked salmon in a delicate curry sauce'. And even the 1980 *Good Food Guide* was horrified by the chaos at Walton's in Knightsbridge, which had been bombed five years earlier by the IRA's Balcombe Street Gang. Hazelnut omelette; mousseline of sea trout with saffron sauce; pan-fried collops with pickled walnuts; 'a concoction of banana, raspberries, mint ice-cream and chocolate sauce': here was a menu to bewilder even the most experienced gourmand. At least Walton's had the decency to provide a menu in English, which many upmarket establishments still refused to do. *Fodor's* claimed that London offered 'dozens of possibilities with exciting, adventurous cooking served in intriguing surroundings', which sounded a bit ominous. But the *Let's Go* guide advised young Americans to eat at pubs or wine bars, instead of wasting their money at supposedly high-end places. More than anything, it begged its readers to 'avoid at all costs' the steak houses in the West End – advice that generations of tourists have ignored at their peril.[29]

It would be cheering to report that outside the capital the food was better. *Fodor's* certainly thought so, claiming that standards improved 'the further north you go in England'. But the *Good Food Guide*'s survey of restaurants outside London, based on the testimony of ordinary customers, was the stuff of nightmares. One Huntingdon hotel came warmly recommended, 'if you don't mind eating and sleeping on an overgrown traffic island'. ('Vegetables dire and the beef tough,' reported another reader.) Shropshire was a 'gastronomic Arizona', a land not of blue remembered hills but of 'dreadful pub sandwiches'. Manchester's finest dining room, the Midland Hotel, boasted 'soft and leaden' pastry, obviously reheated tripe and 'inept service'. In 'the best restaurant in Newcastle', meanwhile, diners could look forward to 'disastrous vegetables', 'overcooked steak' and 'cheesecake with too much gelatine'. If this was the city's *best* restaurant, what were the others like?

In Edinburgh, one recommended restaurant specialized in 'very fatty goose' and a 'ratatouille overcooked and short of aubergines', while another offered 'appalling mushroom savoury and lasagne'. Nor did Wales offer much relief. Visiting the Red Lion in Llangynidr, Powys, one reviewer waited for an hour and finally 'settled for [a] meal abandoned by less patient people: beef not bad, but under-cooked potato, near-raw cabbage', as well as something called 'Black Death', a very brave order given the standards of the day. But another Powys establishment offered a warmer welcome. Some guests raised their eyebrows at the Lake Vyrnwy Hotel's signature 'kipper en croûte', but its 'tongue braised with raisin sauce' went down very well. As one reader observed, 'it was the sort of meal my late headmaster would have greatly enjoyed'.[30]

One thing that might have surprised his old headmaster, though, was what people were drinking. Twenty years earlier, wine ('a foreign drink', according to *The Times*) had been perceived as something for special occasions, yet by 1981 sales had increased by 250 per cent in just two decades. Drinking a bottle of wine was a way of looking stylish and sophisticated, a citizen of the world, but it was also becoming a common pleasure in parts of the country where it would once have been exceptionally rare. In Lambeth in 1981, Margaret Bradshaw and her family ate a traditional Sunday roast every weekend, just as her parents would have done. But now they liked to have a bottle of wine, too – something her parents would surely have considered unimaginable.[31]

But the really fashionable drink of the early 1980s was not wine, lager or even real ale, which had recently begun to make a comeback. It was water. Even a decade or two earlier, people would have laughed at the idea of paying for water in a bottle when you could have tap water for free, yet by 1981 some 500 million gallons of Perrier, Evian and Malvern Water were changing hands a year. Indeed, the craze for bottled water was such that in January 1982 the British Tourist Authority tried to market drinking water from Britain's fading spa towns. The *Guardian*'s reviewer liked Harrogate Sparkle ('freshly brisk, with a touch of stimulating impatience, though perhaps a little thin and nervous') but disapproved of Sparkling Ashbourne ('bland and assured . . . full-bodied and flat'). Surely, though, this was just a fad? Not a bit of it: in 1982 the British spent some £50 million on mineral water, and when water workers went on strike in early 1983, demand was such that many supermarkets ran out. As one observer put it, the strike had done for mineral water 'what television has done for darts and snooker'. The Consumers' Association objected that expensive bottled water was no better for you than tap water, but it was no good. Nobody ever looked like a citizen of the world by drinking water from the tap.[32]

The rise of so-called 'sparkling' water was nothing short of sensational. In the course of the 1980s, Perrier's annual sales rocketed from 12 million bottles to 152 million. Playing up their product's Continental *élan* ('Eau la la!') and supposed health benefits ('Neau calories'), their campaigns were aimed squarely at that emblematic consumer group of the early 1980s: young, socially ambitious, professional women. It was also this group who frequented that supremely symbolic institution of the Thatcher years, the wine bar. After all, the point of wine bars was not so much that they served wine, or even water, but that they served women. Pubs belonged to men, but as the *Guardian* explained in July 1982, the wine bar was 'providing a vast section of society with a freedom they never had before . . . that of sitting in a drinking place without being accosted, pinched, chatted up or loudly and anatomically commented upon'. Wine bars' popularity was a question of atmosphere rather than alcohol, agreed Derek Orme, who had opened an establishment in Balham. 'Women can go into them and be reasonably sure that they won't get hassled.'

The story of Derek Orme's bar, one of some 250 wine bars in London by 1982, nicely captured the social and economic forces transforming Britain in the first half of the decade. Previously a sales executive for Procter & Gamble, Derek had spent years 'moaning to friends at dinner parties about how you never make any money unless you work for yourself'. Now in his early thirties, he gave up his job and began renovating a dilapidated house in Clapham, which he had bought for £9,000. Four years later, he sold it for £38,000 and poured the profits into Orme's, a 'wine bar-cum-bistro' in south London. The location, a formerly run-down area now being gentrified by young middle-class couples, was perfect. So was the atmosphere, all plants, wood and 'subdued lighting'.

But while Derek Orme was a wine enthusiast, not all establishments were labours of love. The *Guardian* complained that most wine bars charged gigantic mark-ups on their wines and carried out 'sheer candle-light robbery' when it came to the food ('some terrible things are done in the name of smoked mackerel'). The following year's *Which? Wine Guide* was even more damning, attacking the 'overpricing, poor service and uninspired choice of wines' in most new establishments. Among other things, wrote the editor, they were too keen to exploit their customers' ignorance, with lists reading only 'Beaujolais £5' or 'Volnay £13'. 'It would be hard to find a bunch of people selling to the public who are as secretive about their wares', she remarked, 'as the average wine bar owner.'[33]

For diners who preferred to avoid anonymous Beaujolais and ancient mackerel, there was, at least, a good choice of exotic alternatives. After three decades of Commonwealth immigration, the British diet was more obviously globalized than ever before. By 1982 the *Good Food Guide*'s entries for London included eighteen Chinese restaurants, sixteen Italian, twelve Greek or Turkish Cypriot, four Spanish, three Japanese, two Portuguese and one each from Afghanistan, Germany, Hungary, Korea, Lebanon, Sweden and Thailand. Even people wanting fast food, said *The Times*, could choose 'spring rolls from China, samosas from India, kebabs of the Near East, Mexican tacos and Italian pizzas, as well as British breakfasts and good old baked potatoes'. No other city in Europe could claim to be such a melting pot.[34]

As Christopher Driver admitted, all this gastronomic larceny often came without much attention to authenticity. Many of the nominally Italian, Indian and Chinese restaurants that flourished in the 1980s were heavily adapted to save money and pander to the locals. 'The tandoori chicken is dyed, not marinated; the taramosalata is flavoured with smoked roe rather than made of it; the Pekin duck is not Pekin duck because it is deep-fried not roasted,' Driver wrote. When, in an ostensibly Italian restaurant, he asked for his spaghetti *al dente*, the waiter replied solemnly: 'It will take a little longer, sir.' Yet the novelty of foreign food had long since faded. Pasta, aubergines and coriander were no longer exotic; they were mainstream. Indeed, the largest pasta factory in Europe had just opened, not in Rome or Naples, but in St Albans. The academic Lincoln Allison, born in 1946, had grown up in Colne in Lancashire, 'a town with only one café'. Now he lived in Leamington Spa, where he could easily find 'restaurants and delicatessens in a dozen national styles . . . yams and

tortillas, cabanos and cracowska, grappa and pitta bread'. With five bis-
tros and five Indian restaurants, Leamington in 1981 felt like 'London
and New York rolled into one', with 'a level of luxury and extravagance
to tempt the fate of Sodom and Gomorrah'.[35]

There was, however, one culinary import that no sane person, even in
the early 1980s, would have associated with luxury and extravagance. This
was American fast food, spearheaded in Britain by Kentucky Fried Chicken.
Having opened its first branch in Preston in 1965, Colonel Sanders's chain
had some 250 British outlets by the mid-1970s, though their reputation
took a bit of a battering when health inspectors denounced their 'un-
hygienic conditions'. In 1976, therefore, KFC began to introduce open
kitchens, copying McDonald's, which had arrived in Britain two years
earlier. Yet at first there was some confusion about their target audience.
One of the first mentions of McDonald's in *The Times*, for example, came
in a survey of places offering pre-theatre dinners. The reviewer, who had
clearly never been to McDonald's before, was not impressed ('I would
regard a pre-theatre snack here as a really desperate measure'). And as late
as 1983 burger bars still had a surprisingly upmarket image. *The Times*'s
diarist spotted City workers having breakfast at McDonald's on King William Street, while at the Wimpy on Piccadilly Circus he was pleased to see
three people reading the Establishment's favourite paper. At the Burger
King on nearby Coventry Street, meanwhile, the customers were so upmarket that the manager played piped classical music at lunchtime.[36]

To some visitors, the ethos of the new fast-food restaurants seemed
almost offensively American. 'In the shiny shiny fast food stores where
every sales host and hostess smiles a fresh disposable smile, service is
smoother than even the Concorde lounge at Heathrow,' began a long
*Guardian* feature in May 1980. 'Your order is programmed to reach you
in 90 seconds. Here is sanitised scoffing such as the British have never
known.' Why, the writer, wondered, did it take Americans to sell fast food
in Britain? The obvious answer is that such places succeeded precisely
because they were American, trading on an image of slickness, speed and
modernity. Indeed, by the end of 1980 the competition among American
or faux-American burger bars was more intense than ever, with Wendy's
joining McDonald's, Burger King, Trumps, Huckleberry's Strikes, Wimpy,
Burgerland and Burger Master in an attempt to gain a foothold in the
British market.

With competition so intense, the right image was absolutely crucial.
KFC, for example, were thrown into a panic when market researchers
found that, during the recession of the early 1980s, they had become
identified with unemployed or very low-paid young men, who came in

after the pubs closed for a cheap chicken dinner to take home. By contrast, McDonald's relentlessly targeted families with young children. 'Britain seems full of middle-class parents protesting that they only go to McDonald's because the kids drag them there. Two-year-olds are seen climbing out of pushchairs to pull their mothers in,' wrote one observer in late 1983. But in a country notorious for treating families with cold contempt, McDonald's had identified the perfect market. As a boy, I went to McDonald's for the first time in about 1982 for my friend Robert Greenwood's birthday party. We all had cheeseburgers, a grinning Ronald McDonald handed out balloons and afterwards we were given a guided tour of the kitchen. I found the whole experience mind-bogglingly thrilling, and no sooner had I got home than I was pestering my parents to take me again. 'The chain practically eats children,' sighed *The Times*, and of course it was right.[37]

Despite her grocer's shop background, Mrs Thatcher had much better things to worry about than the remorseless advance of McDonald's. By an extraordinary coincidence, the man she asked to run the Ministry of Agriculture, Fisheries and Food (MAFF) had also grown up in a grocer's shop. Smooth, clever and ambitious, Peter Walker, the son of a greengrocer in Brentford, west London, had left school at 16 and made millions in the City before becoming one of Edward Heath's chief lieutenants. Although MAFF was hardly one of the great offices of state, Walker's energy and reforming ambition put even the most ardent Thatcherite to shame. The nation's farmers, he insisted a year after taking the job, must adjust to the changing tastes of the nation's families. It was time for British fruit juice, British yoghurt, British pizzas and British pâtés. And shoppers must do their bit, too. 'The time has come', Walker declared, 'for the British house-wife to see that when she brings home the bacon, she brings home British bacon.'[38]

But it was cheese, not bacon, that became the symbol of this bold new era. With milk and butter sales falling, the Milk Marketing Board was desperate to find something to do with its dairy surplus. Inside its processed-foods division, Dairy Crest, a 'special products group' contemplated ways of getting rid of it, from pre-grated cheese and flavoured butter to powdered yoghurt and, alarmingly, 'artificial meat' made from milk powder. What the Milk Marketing Board really wanted, though, was a 'luxury cheese', because under their arcane pricing system, Dairy Crest would have to pay them more for the milk. So Dairy Crest began work on a soft blue cheese to compete at home with Camembert and Brie and bite off a slice of the North American market. After testing it in Somerset, they enlisted an advertising agency, Butler Dennis Garland, to devise a name redolent of a 'lightly wooded region of rolling hills and ancient buildings'. The advertisers suggested 'Wymeswold', but somebody pointed out that since there was already a place called Wymeswold, they would be deceiving the shopper. So they changed the name to 'Lymeswold'.[39]

In September 1982 Peter Walker summoned the press to the Savoy Hotel in central London and unveiled Lymeswold to the world. The new cheese was 'mild and creamy', wrote one reporter, with a white rind that darkened with age. At more than £2 per pound it was expensive, but the whole point was that it was an upmarket product. What about the made-up name? 'The Americans are crazy for that sort of thing,' explained Dairy Crest's marketing director. And Walker himself was in no doubt. Lymeswold, he said, would go down as 'one of the great national success stories of the next twelve months'. It was 'very delicious and very tasty, and I've been privileged to have it for some months now . . . My children are fans, we are fans, and if he can ever get any, my dog is a hell of a fan . . . What a marvellous bargain it is!'[40]

After such an introduction, Lymeswold could hardly fail to be a disaster. But the problem was not the cheese itself, which generally got good reviews. Even the label, which described it as 'English, Blue and Mild', seemed to have something for everyone. Nor did people seem to mind that it was entirely inauthentic, a cheese devised by committee. The problem was that the launch had been too successful. By chance, Dairy Crest had chosen a day on which there was very little other news. Almost every paper carried a picture of Peter Walker tucking into a lump of Lymeswold, the BBC and ITV ran reports on the evening news, and everybody remembered the remark about Walker's dog. Perhaps there was a Falklands factor, too. With popular patriotism at extraordinary heights, news of 'the first new British cheese for centuries' went down even better than Dairy Crest had hoped. Quite apart from the news coverage, they had already spent £1 million on a television campaign promoting Lymeswold as the very acme of pastoral Englishness. The advertisement follows two French cheese enthusiasts, driving around Somerset in a Citroën 2CV. 'Among people who know about good food', a voiceover says, 'the word is abroad that we British have perfected a new cheese. The word is . . . Lymeswold!'

What followed was a public relations catastrophe. Popular demand was not just higher than Dairy Crest had anticipated; it was five times higher. Although they had spent millions on modernizing their Somerset dairy, production could not keep pace with demand. This was a familiar failing for British manufacturers in the 1980s, not least in the home computer industry. In any case, within two weeks of the launch Lymeswold had disappeared from the shelves. By early November, Sainsbury's had completely run out. Harrods, where the price had reached £2.80 a pound, claimed to be turning away customers 'in their thousands'. Even Fortnum & Mason, which had hiked up the price to an eye-watering £4, claimed to be experiencing 'severe shortages'.

Dairy Crest frantically ordered the creamery to step up production, though they privately admitted that 'they cannot hope to catch up until Christmas'. Almost incredibly, there were now reports of people hoarding Lymeswold. One man even tried to order a million cases, each containing six pounds of cheese, which was as much as the creamery could produce in a year. In the meantime, Dairy Crest commissioned an apologetic new advertising campaign, promising that people would get their Lymeswold eventually. 'We are going to ask the housewife to bear with us,' their marketing manager said limply. By a supreme irony, he was speaking on the same day that the British Agricultural Council handed out its annual award for marketing innovation. It went, of course, to Lymeswold.[41]

By the time Dairy Crest got their act together, Lymeswold's image was in ruins. It had been transformed from a symbol of national ambition into a badge of national incompetence. Dairy Crest might have conceived it as an 'aspirational cheese', but there was nothing aspirational about being a punchline. When *Private Eye* began using the name 'Lymeswold' as an all-purpose signifier of rural backwardness, the game was up. Even in the Commons, some of Walker's fellow Conservatives could not resist giving him a ribbing. 'Does my right hon. Friend agree that the development of Lymeswold cheese has been a significant marketing success?' wondered Skipton's MP John Watson. 'Is he aware that it is still not sufficiently available in some parts of the country? Could it be that his dog is eating too much?'[42]

The story of Lymeswold's rise and fall makes an irresistible metaphor, but for what? The revival of popular patriotism in the early 1980s? The romantic myth of the English countryside? The triumph of advertising over authenticity in a decade obsessed by image? Or, perhaps more simply, the incompetence of British management and the shoddiness of British food? Writing in the *Guardian*, the food critic Drew Smith thought the basic problem had been a deep national indifference to tradition. Cheeses like Lymeswold and Melbury – another Dairy Crest committee cheese – were 'jokes', insults to 'our national intelligence . . . about as British as bouillabaisse'. Yet was the problem really inauthenticity, or just bad luck and bad timing? After all, some other 'invented' cheeses, such as Shropshire Blue, proved extremely successful. Indeed, Dairy Crest proved that inauthenticity was no handicap when, a year later, they carved a much more successful product out of their vast butter mountain. A 'low-fat butter' with an equally pastoral name, Clover was carefully targeted at housewives worried about their health. In a decade saturated with images of beauty, fitness and success, you could make an awful lot of money from women's anxieties about their weight. Mrs Thatcher could have told them that.[43]

In the meantime, Peter Walker continued his crusade to drag the reputation of British food out of the gutter. In November 1982 his ministry sponsored a stand at the Paris food fair, where, on the first morning, President Mitterrand dropped in for some samples. 'But by late afternoon', *The Times* reported gloomily, 'there was only a trickle of visitors, gazing rather suspiciously at legs of lamb and at a sample of Lymeswold cheese.' Since they were in France, the Lymeswold had been rebranded as Westminster Blue. But not even the whiff of political prestige was enough to woo Gallic shoppers. Undeterred, an embassy official told the press that Britain's stand had been by far 'the best in the show and that that was agreed by everyone'. Nearby, a listening Frenchman shook his head and murmured sadly: '*Quelle cuisine extraordinaire!*'

A few weeks later, Walker launched a £20 million campaign with the imaginative title 'Food from Britain'. 'By the end of the decade,' he promised, 'British food will be leading the world.' The event was held at the Barbican's cavernous concert hall in the City, where more than 2,000 farmers, grocers, supermarket managers and food manufacturers gathered for instruction on 'the need for positive marketing'. Originally Mrs Thatcher was going to speak, but she dropped out at the last minute to attend a memorial service. Perhaps it was just as well. After three hours of extremely boring lectures, there was a break for a 'wholesome British cold lunch', to be washed down with the very finest English wine. Unfortunately, Walker's officials had forgotten to provide any chairs, so the delegates were forced to have their lunch 'in considerable discomfort, squatting on the floor or bending awkwardly over tables'. There was a metaphor there too, somewhere.

The next day, their cross-Channel rivals, Food and Wine from France, struck back with a magnificent spread of cheeses, followed by a lavish lunch in the banqueting hall of the Stationers' Company. The French, needless to say, had remembered to put out some chairs. One reporter asked the head of Food and Wine from France whether his compatriots might ever be tempted to buy British food. And if so, what would they choose? The Frenchman paused for a long time, as if lost in thought. Then, at last, he said: 'Biscuits?'[44]

# 6

# You Are Mad and We Hate You

*We can live without steel for quite a while. People will not die or starve.*

John Hoskyns to Mrs Thatcher, 9 January 1980

*The TUC meets in Brighton this week, but for all the effect its speeches will have upon the Government it might as well be in Timbuctoo . . .*

*The Government regards them with a coolness little short of contempt. They are not treated as beasts of the jungle any more. Only paper tigers. And there is little they can do about it.*

Daily Mirror, 1 September 1980

At the beginning of 1979, things were going well for Bob Simpson. He had been married to Morag for ten years, and they had a 4-year-old daughter, Sharon. Like his wife, Bob had been born in Scotland, but after a spell in the shipyards he had moved south to Northamptonshire to find a steadier job. Now he worked as a plater for British Steel, earning more than £100 a shift, while Morag worked as a part-time cleaner. They had lived in the same house since they were married, with a garage and a little garden. After renting from the council, they had bought it in 1973 and every year had made improvements, from new wallpaper to central heating. In the future, Morag hoped, they might put in new carpets and redo the lounge. And every year they had managed a holiday, often at home but sometimes in Spain. This year they had bought a caravan and were planning a trip to France. It was hardly the high life. But it was their life, and they were proud of it.

There was, however, a cloud overhead. Bob and Morag Simpson lived in Corby, a town dominated by the chimneys of the huge British Steel factory. And in the spring of 1979 Corby was in trouble. For years the steel factory had lived in the shadow of the axe, and at Bob's union branch there were rumours that the management were planning to close the doors. The dole queues were already longer in Corby than in the other towns of the East Midlands, and when Bob thought about the future, a chill ran down his spine. He was perfectly prepared to get on his bike and look for work. But the only jobs in nearby Northampton paid far less than he was getting already, and that was even before the cost of petrol. He had talked to Morag about moving to Australia. But how would they sell their house? Who would buy it? Who on earth would want to move to Corby now?

To outsiders, Corby seemed an extraordinary place, a Scottish enclave in the heart of the East Midlands. Half a century earlier, it had been a quiet village. But in the early 1930s the steel firm Stewarts & Lloyds chose Corby as the location for a massive new plant, and brought in thousands of workers, most of them from depressed areas in the west of Scotland. In 1979 seven out of ten people were still first- or second-generation immigrants from Glasgow, Clydebank, Paisley and Greenock. Every year Corby hosted its own Highland Games. Local children followed Rangers and Celtic, drank Irn-Bru and spoke with Scottish accents. Its neighbours treated it as an embarrassment, a black hole, even a disaster area. Visiting in early 1979, the *Guardian*'s Lesley Adamson was very conscious of its reputation as a 'one-class working-class place, a dirty industry town of "foreigners" in a county which has never known heavy industry . . . a rough place where the population is usually drunk and brawling, where you daren't park your car for fear of slashed tyres, where you must not walk alone because of muggers'. There was a fair amount of prejudice in this. But there was indeed more crime in Corby, more violence, more unemployment and more alcoholism. Even the heart disease and infant mortality figures were the highest in Britain. Still, Adamson thought it a 'warm and friendly place which welcomes strangers, because everyone in Corby is a stranger'. And for Bill and Morag Simpson, and thousands like them, it was home.

Even before Mrs Thatcher came to power, Corby was doomed. The town's iron ore was of relatively low quality, which made it very expensive to produce. In six years the Corby plant had lost £75 million. In August 1979 alone it lost £3 million, three times more than forecast. Since British Steel was already producing 5 million tons of unwanted steel a year, and had been ordered by the government to cut its losses, everybody knew that meant curtains for Corby. They also knew closure would be a social catastrophe. 'They are already calling Corby the ghost town of the eighties,' wrote Adamson.* In January 1979 Corby was already suffering double-digit unemployment. Visitors remarked on the 'derelict shops and decaying flats', the council houses 'boarded up with bits of wood and corrugated iron'. Social services reported record levels of vandalism and juvenile delinquency. And now, in a town where two out of three men worked for British Steel, they were going to close the steelworks.[1]

British Steel announced its long-dreaded decision on 1 November 1979. In Corby, where thousands of people demonstrated outside the local British Steel office, the mood seemed one of 'resigned desperation' rather than outright defiance. The town's industrial padre, Canon Frank Scuffham, 'an out-of-step cleric with longish grey hair and a copy of the *New Ecologist* under his arm', tried to see a silver lining. Corby without steel, he said brightly, 'could show us the future where there will be ways of living without work'. But few people shared his optimism. As a local policeman mordantly put it, 'they will be cutting them down from the rafters within a couple of years'.

On 22 April 1980, in front of a funereal little group of older workers, Corby cast its last steel. Afterwards, at the Strathclyde Hotel, the wake lasted until long past closing time. 'Coming to the Chinkie?' one man asked his friend when the last bottle was gone. 'I'm on the dole next week,' the other man said. 'Yeah, but with a few thou,' said the first man. 'Come on.' So they went.[2]

What happened to Corby was a symptom of a wider and grimmer story. In the nineteenth century, Britain had led the world in making steel. Even in 1950 it was still the world's third largest exporter, behind only the United States and France. But from then on it was all downhill. By the late 1960s exports were in steep decline, factories were antiquated and over-manned, firms were short of capital and investment had fallen off a cliff. So in 1967 the Wilson government took the steel companies into public ownership. Unfortunately, things got worse. Shielded from competition, British Steel became a symbol of everything that was wrong with British industry. Exports collapsed: overtaken by Japan and West Germany, Britain's share of the world market plummeted to just 5 per cent. Even domestic customers complained that British steel was poorly finished, and the Ford car giant started ordering steel from the Netherlands instead. And productivity was simply abysmal. In 1975 a British Steel worker

---

* When Tony Benn visited the town to join a steelworkers' demonstration against the threat of closure, he did not have the courage to tell them that 'the Labour Cabinet had decided in February this year to support the closure of Corby . . . I felt tremendously guilty.'

typically produced 122 tons of crude steel a year. By contrast, an American steelworker produced 280 tons, a West German 370 tons and a Japanese worker 520 tons. For British Steel to catch up with its rivals, advised a report by Sheffield Polytechnic, it should either sack half its workers, some 110,000 people, or double its total output. Neither seemed likely. But as *The Times* remarked in 1977, people were fooling themselves if they thought this could go on forever. 'Without higher productivity', it said bluntly, 'there is no future for Britain as a steelmaking nation.'[3]

Since the unions resisted any attempt to cut jobs, the government's initial answer, as so often, was to reach for the chequebook. Between 1975 and 1979, Britain spent £3 billion on steel subsidies, six times more than its French counterpart. In effect, the steel industry had become a sink into which politicians poured vast sums of public money. Yet still the losses continued. In the first half of 1979, British Steel lost £145 million. To Margaret Thatcher, there could scarcely have been a more flagrant example of political cowardice. British Steel simply had to 'run down the numbers of people they employ', she insisted during the election campaign. 'The lesson is that nationalisation does not and cannot save jobs when they are yesterday's jobs and you are not competing on the product . . . Steel is a classic example, and you cannot avoid redundancies.'[4]

In Mrs Thatcher's eyes, British Steel's problems were bound up with the fact that it was owned by the state. 'I think monopoly is bad,' she told *Weekend World*'s Brian Walden in January 1980. 'If steel hadn't been nationalised we should not have the problem we've got now.' To many people, of course, nationalized industries were a natural feature of the economic landscape, employing some 1½ million people and accounting for about 10 per cent of Britain's GDP. But the Conservatives had long been hostile to the idea of nationalized monopolies. And as British Steel, British Leyland and the National Coal Board haemorrhaged money, some of Mrs Thatcher's younger advisers began to contemplate a massive programme of industrial privatization. In the autumn of 1980, John Hoskyns suggested the 'liquidation' of British Steel as an example to 'managers and workers in the remaining nationalised industries'. But his boss was more cautious. She agreed that the nationalized industries were 'over-subsidised, uncompetitive and monopolistic', but thought radical change would alarm floating voters. In opposition she ruled out 'rushing into mass denationalisation', and her election manifesto did not mention privatization at all. As her aide Oliver Letwin put it, her real priority was not selling off the nationalized giants; it was 'getting the industries concerned to run properly and getting rid of their subsidy'.[5]

To sort out British industry, though, you needed to sort out the trade unions. So ran one of the core principles of Thatcherism, which cast the unions as the greatest obstacle to Britain's economic renewal. By later standards their prominence in the nation's political life was simply extraordinary. Every week the papers carried front-page stories about strikes, go-slows, overtime bans and work-to-rules. On the evening news, burly men with thick spectacles were forever trooping out of Number 10, shaking their heads at what their members would think of the government's latest offer. To the right, they were over-mighty barons, blind to the realities of economic life. But to the left, they were the defenders of working men and women, protecting the weak from inflation and unemployment. Membership was close to an all-time peak: by the end of the 1970s more than 13 million people, about 56 per cent of the workforce, belonged to a trade union. And since they were so effective at protecting their members' interests, there seemed no reason why membership would not keep rising. The unions, wrote *The Economist*'s labour correspondent Stephen Milligan in 1976, had 'more power and influence than [the] political parties'. All things considered, he thought them 'the major political force' in the land.[6]

Despite its reputation as the 'Sick Man of Europe', Britain was not alone in suffering from strikes. Nor were British workers unusually attached to the ideals of revolutionary socialism. In fact, polls found that most union members just wanted better pay and better conditions, while their leaders, despite the press caricatures, were generally thoughtful, cautious and thoroughly pragmatic. But Britain was unusual in having so many competing unions, some of them almost comically small and old-fashioned, which meant they were engaged in what seemed an endless competition to outflank one another on the left. Britain was unusual, too, in suffering from so many unofficial strikes, triggered by shop stewards who were often much more militant than their leaders.

Perhaps above all, because so many major industries were owned and run by the state, industrial action often pitted trade unionists against the government itself. That turned almost every major strike into a test of the state's authority. And when the unions won – as the miners did in 1972 and 1974, or the public sector unions in 1979 – it only added to the sense that Britain was becoming 'ungovernable'. Even before the Winter of Discontent, eight out of ten people thought the trade unions were too powerful. The irony, as the *Financial Times*'s labour correspondent Robert Taylor pointed out, was that their supposedly overweening leaders were 'uncertain, rather frightened, reactive and muddled men', desperately trying to keep up with their own members. Still, there was little doubt that something had gone badly wrong.[7]

Even after Mrs Thatcher's victory, the question of union power continued to dominate the front pages – with one notable exception. *The Times*
had nothing to say about it, because in November 1978 it had been shut
down after the print unions refused to accept new computer technology.
It was almost a year before the paper returned to the newsstands. In the
meantime, the ITV network was closed down in August 1979 after the
technicians' unions rejected a 15 per cent pay offer. They only returned
in October when the television companies gave in and offered them 45 per
cent. In the grand scheme of things this was a sideshow. But it made a
huge impression on public opinion, not least since fans of *Crossroads* and
*Coronation Street* were left staring at a darkened screen for three months.
And at the time there seemed no reason why this particular soap opera
might not continue indefinitely. 'An air of ominous inevitability is gathering already around the new Government's bid to escape from the pattern
of recent history,' wrote the *Guardian*'s Peter Jenkins that summer:

> No government has found an answer to the relentless momentum of
> competitive collective bargaining in Britain . . . The trade unions in effect
> have brought down the last three elected governments, not by unconstitu-
> tional confrontation, but by making it near-impossible for them to govern.
> The country is caught in a syndrome of decline and the industrial relations
> system is an important part of it.[8]

In private, many of Mrs Thatcher's allies agreed with him. In June 1977
a secret report on Britain's nationalized industries by Nicholas Ridley
warned that a Conservative government would inevitably face a challenge
from 'our enemies' in the unions, probably 'between 6 months and 18
months after the Election'. The most likely battlegrounds, Ridley thought,
were the coal mines, the electricity industry or the docks, and the government should 'take every precaution possible to strengthen our defences
against all out attack in a highly vulnerable industry'. Another report by
the moderate Lord Carrington was even bleaker, suggesting that there was
little a Conservative government could do if they were challenged by the
miners or the power workers. In fact, almost every member of the new
administration thought conflict with the unions inevitable. In Hoskyns's
words, they 'assumed from the outset that once the unions realised that
the Government meant what it said about anti-inflation policy and trade
union reform, they would try to break the Government's policies and
authority by direct strike action'.[9]

Hoskyns believed beating the unions was the key to everything. In 1976
he and his colleague Norman Strauss, an unorthodox Unilever systems
analyst, had prepared a blueprint to turn Britain around, entitled 'Stepping

Stones'. The greatest obstacle to 'national recovery', they wrote, was 'the negative role of the trades unions'. So they thought Mrs Thatcher should campaign against 'the dictatorship of unsackable union leaders' and win a mandate for sweeping reform. Presciently, they believed the key to success lay with union members themselves. The ordinary member, they wrote, 'is precisely the man we must get to vote Tory'. Mrs Thatcher agreed with every word, but thought their blueprint far too radical to be exposed to the public eye. During most of her time in opposition her attitude towards the unions was remarkably cautious. The Winter of Discontent allowed her to harden her rhetoric, telling Radio Two's Jimmy Young that 'the unions are confronting the British people; they are confronting the sick, they are confronting the old, they are confronting the children . . . If someone is confronting our essential liberties, if someone is inflicting injury, harm and damage on the sick, my God, I will confront them.' Yet still she hesitated to adopt Hoskyns's radical agenda. The only way to roll back union power, she told him in February 1979, was to do it 'incrementally . . . like grandmother's footsteps'.[10]

The most obvious sign of Mrs Thatcher's pragmatism was her choice of Employment Secretary. With his florid features and affable style, Jim Prior appeared the picture of a rural Tory squire. Behind the jolly banter and muddy wellies, however, was a canny political operator. The son of a successful solicitor, educated at Charterhouse and Cambridge, Prior had worked as a land agent before buying his own farm, which he ran on modern, mechanized lines, even supplying vegetables to Birds Eye. After serving as Ted Heath's factotum in the late 1960s, he had finished joint third in the leadership election, standing on an unrepentantly moderate One Nation platform. The union leaders liked him; so did most journalists, who praised his 'shrewdness and courage', his 'engaging honesty' and his 'earthy common sense'. Prior also had the distinction of having appeared, thinly disguised, in an entire series of novels. At Charterhouse he had struck up a close friendship with the future writer Simon Raven, who turned him into the character Peter Morrison in his 'Alms for Oblivion' sequence. For Prior this was clearly a bit embarrassing: later, he complained that it was 'not quite cricket' for the raffish Raven to involve him in 'exploits dredged up from the murk of his psyche', among them a liaison with an Indian prostitute. His old friend's novels, he once remarked, were 'James Bond books for poofs'.[11]

Given his old-school style and One Nation principles, Prior might have expected an unceremonious departure from Mrs Thatcher's court. Unlike some of his contemporaries, he refused to tailor his opinions to the new order, and treated her with a mixture of amused condescension and incredulous horror. As for Mrs Thatcher, she saw Prior as the classic example of a 'false squire'. 'They have all the outward show of a John Bull – ruddy face, white hair, bluff manner,' she wrote in her memoirs, 'but inwardly they are political calculators who see the task of Conservatives as one of retreating gracefully before the Left's inevitable advance.' 'All they're thinking about is how to plan the next retreat,' she told Ferdinand Mount. 'That's not why I came into politics.' Yet, for the time being, she thought it best to keep Ted Heath's old lieutenant inside the tent, rather than allowing him to roam around outside. In any case, she later admitted, keeping Prior was a good way of reassuring the union leaders: 'Jim was the badge of our reasonableness.'[12]

Even so, Mrs Thatcher was determined to stamp out the beer-and-sandwiches culture of the Wilson and Heath years once and for all. Instead of inviting the union leaders to settle the affairs of the nation inside Number 10, wrote Nigel Lawson in 1976, their aim must be to treat them with 'benign neglect'. There would be no incomes policies, no pay 'norms', no concordats, no deals. Unions and management must reach agreements on their own, without government interference. As Charles Moore remarks, the point was not to have a better working relationship with the unions. It was to create the conditions 'in which government had virtually no need for a relationship with the unions at all'. So when, on taking office, Prior recommended early talks with the Trades Union Congress to discuss their pay objectives, Mrs Thatcher wrote simply: 'No.'[13]

Prior's priority was to begin the painstaking work of reforming Britain's industrial relations without provoking the unions into rebellion. In this respect, it helped that he had been so close to Heath and had learned from his old boss's mistakes. As he told Mrs Thatcher on 14 May, it would be 'fatal to follow the 1970 pattern and rush things too much'. Instead of directly attacking the closed shop, for example, his Employment Bill simply required that new closed shops be approved by 80 per cent of the workers in a secret ballot.* Similarly, there was no insistence on compulsory ballots before strikes, although Prior offered public funds for unions that wanted to hold one. Finally, the strike laws were tightened, with a ban on secondary picketing, although not on broader secondary action. All in all, it was a remarkably careful package, especially by comparison with Heath's efforts in the early 1970s. There were no high-profile legal experiments, no new courts and no new powers to jail individual trade

---

* In a closed shop, all the workers in a given firm *had* to join the union, whether they wanted to or not. The Conservatives had long abhorred the closed shop, regarding it as an attack on individual freedom.

unionists. As Prior put it, the aim was to 'bring about a lasting change in attitude by changing the law gradually, with as little resistance, and there-fore as much by stealth, as was possible'.[14]

As might have been predicted, the unions condemned Prior's bill as a disgraceful attempt to roll back the hard-won rights of Britain's workers. But the greatest fury came from the right, where many Tory backbenchers, egged on by the *Telegraph*, the *Mail* and the *Express*, saw him as an appeaser. Even his Cabinet colleagues asked why he was not doing more to tackle violent picketing, to impose ballots before strikes or to eliminate the closed shop. From one perspective, all this worked in Prior's favour. With the Conservative press attacking his bill as far too weak, it was easier for him to dismiss the unions' complaints that it was too confrontational. The obvious downside, though, was that he was caught in the middle, with abuse raining down from both sides.

And it was at precisely this point, with Prior's critics sharpening their knives, that events took a dramatic turn. On 7 December, after weeks of arguments about pay, the steelworkers' leader, Bill Sirs, called for an all-out strike. Four days later, with terrible timing, British Steel announced 52,000 redundancies. On 21 December they made a fresh pay offer. Sirs rejected it outright. On the second day of 1980, the steel strike began.[15]

The origins of the steel strike, the first great confrontation between Mrs Thatcher and the trade unions, pre-dated her arrival in office. After years of heavy losses, British Steel's management had long recognized that they needed to save money. Callaghan had set them the target of breaking even by March 1980, but they were clearly going to miss it. So, in the autumn of 1979, the firm's chairman, Sir Charles Villiers, a former member of the Special Operations Executive in the Second World War, decided on drastic measures. The annual pay round was approaching, and with inflation at more than 17 per cent and rising, the miners and car workers had already secured handsome rises. But Villiers offered his steelworkers a nominal increase of just 2 per cent with local productivity bonuses.

To Bill Sirs, the leader of the Iron and Steel Trades Confederation (ISTC), Villiers's offer was outrageous. Sirs had grown up in County Durham in the 1920s as one of ten children who slept, five to a bed, on the ground floor of a terraced house, before becoming an errand boy, a crane driver and a union representative. He was not a militant. He just wanted a fair deal for his men. But even British Steel's revised offer, 5 per cent, would not come close to keeping his members' heads above water in an age of high inflation. As Sirs remarked, it was as if 'they were trying to make us look small'. He had no choice, he said, but to call his men out.[16]

Later, Mrs Thatcher's critics claimed that she had deliberately picked a fight with a moderate, weaker union to further her anti-union agenda. But the archives show that this is not true. Even the hawkish Hoskyns thought the steelworkers had been hard done by and hoped a strike could be avoided. The problem, though, was that British Steel was losing £7 million a week, and Mrs Thatcher had publicly said that any pay increase must be paid for by better productivity. So, just as Villiers was the prisoner of his balance sheet, and Sirs was the prisoner of his members' expectations, she was trapped by her own rhetoric. As Sir Keith Joseph told her on 21 December, they 'really had no choice', since giving in to the steelworkers would signal 'the abandonment of our general policy of firm financial discipline in the public and private sectors'. In Hoskyns's words, the strike was an 'opportunity to give the public a first lesson in economic reality', as well as 'a political stepping stone on the long road to a reformed trade union movement'. But he saw it as a fight that had been forced upon them, not one they had chosen themselves.[17]

The most important part of the lesson, as Mrs Thatcher saw it, was that the government would no longer intervene to settle disputes, but would respect the 'management's right to manage'. Her predecessors had never been able to stay out of industrial disputes, invariably summoning the warring parties to Number 10 before miraculously finding some extra cash so that everybody could go home happy. But she was determined to break the cycle. On 17 January, Joseph told the Commons that the strike was a classic example of the 'British disease', characterized by the government's inability to let managers fight to the finish. The public, he said, 'have come to see giving way as the decent and normal thing to do. The Government are called upon to "settle it" – meaning to give way – often with the taxpayers' money.' As a result, Britain had 'lost competitiveness, lost jobs and lost the better pay, better pensions and better public services that we could have had and that most of our neighbours have'. So this time the government would stay out.[18]

To Jim Prior, these words were profoundly shocking. It was 'inconceivable', he thought, that any other post-war government would have remained aloof from a dispute in one of the nation's key industries. But his own position now seemed increasingly fragile, because the strike handed so much ammunition to his critics inside the Tory Party. Indeed, it was a sign of the right's dread of the unions that their rhetoric became so strident so quickly. On 14 January the Centre for Policy Studies' director Alfred Sherman, never famed for his sense of proportion, sent Mrs Thatcher a long memo under the title 'The Blockade of Britain – Decisive for British Democracy'. The dispute, he wrote, was 'not a strike but an

insurrection ... a major threat to democracy and the chances of a
Conservative Government restoring the country to economic viability'.
Sherman blamed the Communists, which was paranoid even by his
standards. But his message was merely part of a chorus of anti-union
hysteria, partly incited by Mrs Thatcher's Parliamentary Private Secretary,
Ian Gow. An inveterate plotter, Gow welcomed the chance to discredit
one of his heroine's rivals. On 5 February he sidled up to Alan Clark and
asked if he was planning to ask anything at Prime Minister's Questions.
'Nothing special,' Clark said. 'Anything I can do for you?' Muttering 'out
of the corner of his mouth', Gow said: 'Ask when they are going to put
some teeth into the Employment Act.' 'Ian loathes Prior', Clark noted,
'and never ceases to complain about him.' He never got to ask his question,
though – because another Tory backbencher asked it instead.[19]

Among Mrs Thatcher's cheerleaders in the press, the clamour for
tougher reforms was accompanied by increasingly frenzied attacks on
Prior himself. 'WHAT THE HELL HAS CHANGED?' shrieked the front page
of the ever-understated *Daily Express* on 7 February. At the election, the
paper said, the Tories had 'vowed to end industrial chaos. And what have
we got? A pussyfooting Jim Prior and a wobbling Cabinet.' This was very
convenient, of course, for Mrs Thatcher, and some of the *Express*'s front
pages might almost have been dictated in her press office. 'PICKETS IN
CHARGE: Pussyfoot Prior's new law leaves unions' gate open,' ran another
front-page rant a week later. This time it claimed that thanks to the efforts
of 'Prior's "pussyfoot" section ... the country could face two more years
in the grip of the unions before the Government gets the law right'. That
line about the 'pussyfoot section' sounds uncannily like something Mrs
Thatcher might have said, even if she didn't.[20]

Inside Number 10, Mrs Thatcher's aides were itching for battle. At a
late-night meeting of anti-union hawks, the television interviewer Brian
Walden, a former Labour MP and the son of a trade unionist, told Hoskyns
that Mrs Thatcher should press for an immediate ban on secondary action
and the 'exposure of trade union funds'. The unions would 'take [the]
Tories apart', Walden said, 'unless we act now'. For good measure, Mrs
Thatcher ought to sack Prior, 'who was so disloyal behind Margaret's
back'. The next day, Hoskyns sent Mrs Thatcher and Sir Geoffrey Howe
a note suggesting an all-out assault on the unions' funds and immunities,
including giving employers the right to sack people who went on strike.
There would, he admitted, 'inevitably be some uproar', but it was better
to get 'it over now with solutions which are built to last'. Perhaps unwisely,
he nicknamed the likely reaction 'Havoc '80'.[21]

At this point Howe decided to get involved. Under Heath, he had been in charge of the Industrial Relations Act, which had collapsed in complete chaos in 1972. Yet Howe still seemed to believe that the best approach was to fix bayonets and charge into battle. On 4 February he sent Mrs Thatcher a long paper arguing that Prior must act against the unions' immunities straight away. They were going to face 'massive confrontation' anyway, Howe said, so they might as well go for it now. In any case, if they were not prepared to be radical, 'we might as well not have fought (and won) the last General Election'. This was the cue for ten days of heated squabbles between Howe and Prior about whether they should seize the chance to attack the unions once and for all. By the time the Cabinet met on the 14th, Prior had decided that unless his fellow ministers backed him, he would resign. Cleverly, however, he had squared enough of them to have a critical mass of supporters, and moderation eventually prevailed. Mrs Thatcher, who had been privately backing her Chancellor, was not pleased. A few hours later, she allowed herself a little jab in revenge, telling the Commons that strikers would have their benefits cut by some £12 a week if they were getting strike pay from their union. Howe was delighted. Prior, taken unawares, was furious.[22]

In the meantime, the temperature in Britain's steel towns, too, was rising. On 11 February, with his characteristic blend of physical courage and extreme foolhardiness, Sir Keith Joseph made a personal expedition to South Wales to explain to the steelworkers the error of their ways. It went as well as could have been predicted. In Swansea he was pelted with tomatoes and rotten eggs, in Port Talbot he was jostled and bombarded with unidentified 'missiles' and in Cwmbran, where he had a meeting with Gwent County Council, the police had to fight a pitched battle with pickets just to get him into the building. Among the demonstrators, interestingly, was a local steelworker and Labour councillor called Paul Flynn, armed with a placard that read: 'You are mad and we hate you.' Not inappropriately, he later served in Jeremy Corbyn's Shadow Cabinet.[23]

A week later, public attention switched from South Wales to South Yorkshire. For days tension had been mounting outside Sheffield's East Hecla factory, which was owned by a private steel firm, Hadfields. Since Hadfields was too small to sustain heavy losses, its men had voted to go back to work. By Wednesday 13th, however, the steelworkers' picket was several hundred strong. And when Hadfield's employees arrived for work on Thursday morning, more than a thousand pickets were waiting, among them hundreds of miners led, inevitably, by Arthur Scargill, the militant Yorkshireman who had masterminded the successful mass picket at Saltley Gate coke depot in 1972. For the next few hours, Hadfields followed the same script: pitched fighting between pickets and policemen, with twenty-two men arrested and dozens injured. In the end, the managers had to shut the factory. 'Intimidation and anarchy have won a total victory,' said the plant's boss, 'Big Dan' Norton. 'Before very long someone is going to get killed.'

To anyone who remembered the 1970s, all this was very familiar. Even Scargill's guest appearance strengthened the impression that, once again, sheer muscle had won the day. Yet by now many people, even on the left, had lost patience with the scenes of pushing and fighting. 'The lads were sickened when they saw Scargill on the bandwagon again,' one Hadfields convener told the *Express*. 'He has no right to poke his nose in. No one asked him to turn up here.'

The next day's papers were unanimous in their contempt for Scargill and their horror at the violence. *The Times*, for example, got hold of police statements written by Hadfields' female staff, who claimed that they had been 'spat upon, kicked, sworn at' and called 'scabs, bastards and whores'. Even the *Mirror*, which supported the strike, denounced the 'steel picket fury' as a 'mass demonstration of hate'. As for the *Express*, it worked itself into a tremendous frenzy even by its own standards. 'This is why you need to act, Pussyfoot Prior,' read the caption on a front-page photograph of fighting pickets:

### ANARCHY HAS WON!

This was Hadfields, Britain's biggest private steelworks, yesterday.

One thousand two hundred pickets, many led by Yorkshire miners' leader Arthur Scargill, frightened the workers back on strike . . .

One of Hadfields' convenors argued: 'Loss of life has nothing to do with the trade union movement. But after all we have been through today it became obvious lives may be lost . . . I would challenge anyone to go through that picket line and face what we went through today.'

His words, Pussyfoot Prior, are a cry for help. His experience, Pussyfoot Prior, is why the people of this country voted you and your party into office.

They want protection. They want a law to defend them against intimidation . . . from flying pickets like these. Now![24]

That weekend, Mrs Thatcher retreated to Chequers, where she too worked herself into a state of intense agitation. Sunday's papers were more apocalyptic than ever, with the *Sunday Express* claiming that the unions were planning to 'unleash an army of battling pickets across Britain' in 'the worst industrial anarchy yet seen'. 'Why is Mr Scargill not this weekend behind bars?' wondered the paper's editor, John Junor, while the former Labour deputy leader George Brown announced that this would be remembered as 'The Week British Democracy Died'. Having detected at Hadfields 'the stench of the rotten state of the pre-Hitler Weimar Republic', Brown was struck by the similarity between Jim Prior and Hitler's ally Franz von Papen. Soon, he predicted, Prior would depose Mrs Thatcher as Prime Minister, in order to 'make the physical handover of our democracy' to 'Scargill's stormtroopers'. In the accompanying cartoon, Michael Cummings obligingly drew the Yorkshireman in stormtrooper's regalia. 'Hitler's Blackshirts couldn't conquer Britain', reads a placard, 'but Scargill's Redshirts can!'[25]

Despite her reputation, Mrs Thatcher was no stranger to panic. And as she scoured the papers that morning, she feared the worst. She spent the rest of the day glued to the telephone. First Joseph rang to tell her that Hadfields was a 'massive breach of common law', then she called her Home Secretary, Willie Whitelaw, demanding an 'emergency one-clause bill' to ban secondary picketing. Joseph rang back to discuss charging Scargill; then she spoke to the Attorney General, Sir Michael Havers, who agreed that they could 'not simply stand by' in the face of mass unrest. By now she had whipped herself into a gigantic lather. Hadfields was 'mass intimidation', she told Whitelaw that evening. 'It was a public order situation. The Government needed to know where the pickets would turn up the next day and would have to stop pickets before they got there. It was not a civil law issue but one of criminal law.' Whitelaw pointed out that they could not treat the police like hired enforcers. But she returned to her theme: 'the need to stop pickets before they arrived at their destination'. She had decided to call an emergency meeting on Monday morning. 'The police must have guidance over their handling of the criminal offences.'[26]

Although Mrs Thatcher got her meeting, the result was not as she had hoped. In the cold light of day, her ministers decided against anything that might look like a vindictive attack on the striking steelworkers. But although the Prime Minister backed down, the episode had been very revealing. For one thing, it showed just how vividly she remembered Heath's defeat by the miners in 1972. For all her bullish rhetoric, her political nightmares were still dominated by 'barons' and 'bully-boys', supposedly poised to topple her at any moment. Even more remarkable is how uncannily all this anticipated the miners' strike four years later. Almost everything Mrs Thatcher mentioned on the phone that Sunday – the dangers of mass intimidation, the spectacle of street violence, the importance of stiffening chief constables' resolve, the need to find out where pickets were going and to stop them from getting there – would come up again in 1984. Even Scargill's cameo was a preview of what was coming.[27]

The irony is that for all the hysteria, the steel strike was actually going very well for the government. The timing was perfect: with the economy slowing, demand for steel was low. Stocks were high, imports were getting through and generally the economic life of the nation was continuing as normal. Far from presaging some colossal showdown, the Hadfields crisis soon petered out, and by the end of February the air was seeping out of the strike. Both sides wanted a way out; and, at the end of March, Bill Sirs decided to accept the verdict of a three-man court of inquiry. This recommended a deal worth 11 per cent, with another 4½ per cent dependent on productivity improvements. It fell well short of the union's demands, but Sirs took it anyway. Thirteen weeks into the strike, with victory nowhere in sight, he effectively had no choice. Afterwards, the Trotskyist filmmaker Ken Loach made a controversial ITV documentary, *A Question of Leadership* (1980), which argued that Sirs and his colleagues had betrayed their own members. Evidently Loach thought they should have stayed out indefinitely, but of course that was easy for him to say.[28]

The steel strike was extremely expensive. By the end of the 1979–80 financial year British Steel's losses had reached a staggering £1.8 billion, the worst figure in its history. In June, Villiers told the government that he would need another £400 million to keep going, on top of the £450 million they had already given him. But Mrs Thatcher thought the strike had been a battle 'for the economic well-being of the country as a whole', because the unions needed to realize that they could no longer 'ignore commercial reality and the need for higher productivity'. Even more importantly, it had demonstrated her determination to break the habits of her predecessors. From first to last, she had kept out of it, just as she had promised. Of course her supposed neutrality was a bit of an illusion, since everybody knew the government wanted British Steel to win. Even so, the fact that she had allowed the strike to drag on for thirteen weeks was a telling lesson in her new approach. It was a tragedy, Sir Geoffrey Howe wrote later, that 'so many different groups of workers apparently needed to learn by first-hand experience that the government would not change its mind'.[29]

For the steel industry, the strike was a watershed. With the union at bay, Villiers felt emboldened to abandon national bargaining for local deals on pay and conditions, with up to a fifth of a worker's earnings tied to his factory's productivity improvements. Closures continued apace: first Consett and Corby, then Scunthorpe, Shotton, Ebbw Vale, Cardiff and Rotherham. But even as the management were laying the foundations for recovery, the government was hunting for a new chairman to accelerate the pace of change. At a cost of almost £2 million, they found him: Ian MacGregor, an Edinburgh-trained metallurgist who had made a fortune in New York. One profile described him as a 'tough old Scots-American of sixty-seven with thin lips and a deadpan face like a block of granite'. And as chairman, MacGregor proved duly uncompromising. 'The world', he once said, 'goes to people with a sense of individual competition.' Mrs Thatcher thought he was wonderful: she once told Prior that 'he was the only man she knew who was her equal'. MacGregor had strong views about her, too. 'In some ways', he wrote later, 'she was like my mother – who always had a clear idea of what she wanted to do.'[30]

Under MacGregor, British Steel was transformed. The government still poured in subsidies: some £4½ billion over five years, more than Wilson and Callaghan had spent in the five years after 1974. But the difference was that as MacGregor slashed jobs, making some 90,000 people redundant by the middle of the 1980s, British Steel's productivity boomed. One analysis found that it now had lower costs, per ton, than any other major steelmaker in the world – a statistic that would have seemed incredible only a few years earlier. By 1988, when the steel industry was privatized, it was setting international records for profitability, quality and customer satisfaction. Pre-tax profits were now some £400 million, a stark contrast with the losses of the late 1970s, while productivity in man-hours per ton had improved threefold. The first line of a *Guardian* feature, just before the business was floated on the Stock Exchange, captured the changing mood: 'There was once a very ugly industrial frog called British Steel, which became a shining and profitable prince . . .'[31]

The steel strike was Mrs Thatcher's first real victory. Yet, when it was all over, there was little jubilation, just a sense of relief that things had not been worse. After the dust had settled, Hoskyns compiled a report on the strike and its lessons. His tone could scarcely have been more downbeat. It was 'far from an unqualified "victory"', he told his boss. 'We should be under no illusions about how badly the strike might have gone . . . We gained little, probably lost a good deal; but avoided losing everything.' An uninformed observer might never have guessed that they had won.[32]

The truth was that, despite the steelworkers' defeat, most Conservatives still feared the spectre of trade union power. And even as the steelworkers licked their wounds, the wider union movement seemed to be stirring. At the end of March, the general secretary of the Trades Union Congress (TUC), Len Murray, called for a National Day of Action to protest against Mrs Thatcher's economic and industrial policies. 'We want all the people out that day that the unions can get out,' he said: miners and nurses, printers and dockers, engineers, railwaymen, teachers and car workers. As the big day approached, the Conservative papers rolled out their most blood-curdling warnings. 'Lenin Murray and the Bully Boys of the TUC', said the *Express*, had called a 'strike for anarchy and against democracy'. It would be not merely a 'Day of Shame', warned the Conservative MP George Gardiner, but a 'dress rehearsal for something far bigger – a full General Strike'. 'Make no mistake,' the *Express* concluded, 'this is the road to dictatorship!'[33]

But when, on Wednesday 14 May, the Day of Action dawned, it quickly became obvious that it was not, after all, going to be the first step towards a Soviet Britain. Despite the dire warnings of cancelled trains and deserted hospitals, most people barely noticed it was happening. In Wolverhampton a survey of more than thirty firms found that all but a handful of staff had turned up for work; indeed, some employers said there were 'fewer absentees than on a normal Wednesday'. 'Shops, banks, cinemas, public houses, schools and hospitals were open as normal,' wrote a visiting reporter. 'Post, bread and milk was delivered and traffic wardens were on duty.' Indeed, in Wolverhampton the 'only tangible effect of the Day of Action' was a desultory rally in the town centre, attended by no more than 500 people. This was hardly the stuff of a workers' revolution: the 'most vociferous', apparently, 'were a group of punks holding aloft colour pictures of the tax exiled pop singer, Rod Stewart'.

As Wolverhampton went, so did the nation. A BBC poll beforehand found that 73 per cent of trade union members were dead against the Day of Action, while almost nine out of ten were planning to go to work. 'The day of action has been exactly that,' said a gleeful spokesman for the Confederation of British Industry. 'The action has been on the shop floor, exactly where it belongs.' 'Whatever victory the TUC may claim for the Day of Action,' agreed the usually supportive *Daily Mirror*, 'the unions will think twice before they order another one.'[34]

Barely a year earlier, all of the talk had been of union power, the images of overflowing bin-bags and deserted hospital wards seared into the national consciousness. So how could things have changed so quickly? Unemployment certainly had something to do with it: with the dole queues lengthening, many workers were acutely conscious of the danger of losing their jobs. But there had also been a palpable shift in the political temperature. The Winter of Discontent had dealt a shattering blow to trade unionists' morale. Even at the time, many ordinary members had been shocked by the hospital and gravediggers' disputes. In five years the proportion of *union members themselves* who felt the unions were too

"I hereby invest you with this decoration for outstanding courage beyond the call of duty in coming to the aid of the Conservative Party."

The failure of Len Murray's Day of Action was a gift to Mrs Thatcher. In the *Daily Express* (16 May 1980), Michael Cummings drew the inevitable contrast with the Winter of Discontent.

powerful had risen by 22 per cent. As for the public in general, more than eight out of ten told Gallup at the end of January 1979 that the unions were too powerful, while a poll in early February found that almost half believed the unions' very existence was a 'bad thing'. Among young and old, rich and poor, diehard Tories and traditional Labour voters, there had been a marked turn away from the unions.[35]

All of this meant that Mrs Thatcher was swimming with the tide of public opinion. As her strategists reported, polls showed that most union members themselves strongly supported reform, from compulsory strike ballots to a ban on secondary picketing. Indeed, more than four out of ten trade unionists thought their own unions were taking an 'unreasonable view of the Government's plans'. Many clearly agreed with Labour's Denis Healey, who thought the union leaders' 'cowardice and irresponsibility' had not only handed victory to the Tories, but 'left them with no grounds for complaining about her subsequent actions against them'. The really striking thing, though, is that even in late 1982, after unemployment had risen above 3 million, the public mood had not changed. Two out of three people still said they were unhappy with the trade unions, while almost half wanted to see even more stringent union reforms. 'To me they just represent different sections of working class people all trying to get the most possible for themselves. My female friends seem to think the same way,' Mary Richards, herself working-class, told Mass Observation a few months later. 'In the past Unions did a lot of good, they are still needed but not as they were in the Winter of Discontent. Something went wrong then.'[36]

None of this was lost on the union leaders themselves. As the *Guardian*'s Peter Jenkins had pointed out in January 1979, the lesson of the Winter of Discontent was 'their powerlessness to govern their own members. Their national leaders have lost control. I have never known them to be more alarmed.' Six months later, the CBI's chief, John Methven, told Hoskyns that the union leaders were 'on the defensive, well aware that they had lost a great deal of their authority and moral credibility'. And although Hoskyns remained obsessed with union power, some senior ministers drew different conclusions. After the failure of the Day of Action, Sir Geoffrey Howe told Mrs Thatcher that the so-called 'union barons' had never been weaker. 'Their influence with their own membership seems to have waned', he wrote, 'and disputes among themselves have weakened their authority further . . . There is a good deal of evidence of the unpopularity of the national trade union leadership amongst ordinary members.' Perhaps surprisingly, Howe wondered whether it might soon be time 'for the Government to show magnanimity and make a new move to establish better relations with the TUC'. But magnanimity never came naturally to Mrs Thatcher.[37]

At the top of the union movement, there was little appetite for a showdown. The nation's most senior trade unionist, Len Murray, disliked conflict and shunned the limelight. A Shropshire farm worker's son and Methodist lay preacher, he had been to grammar school, took part in the Normandy landings and got a first at Oxford before working his way up the TUC ranks to become general secretary in 1973. A palpably decent and serious man, he had suffered two stress-related heart attacks already, and interviewers found him increasingly withdrawn. 'His sad face', reported Louis Heren, 'suggested an infinite capacity for absorbing pain.' That was just as well, for there was a lot more pain to come. 'The Government has declared war on the unions. Mrs Thatcher really hates us, you know,' one of Murray's officials told the *Observer*. 'We know Prior believes in a consensus, in one nation,' another said despairingly. 'But what do you do when others don't want your advice, and you are continually insulted in public?'[38]

To critics on the left, Murray seemed unforgivably defeatist. Yet his resigned pragmatism chimed with the instincts of the new generation of leaders who had emerged in the last years of the Callaghan premiership. At the largest union in the country, the Transport and General Workers'

Union (TGWU), the autocratic Jack Jones, a former Communist, had been succeeded by the quieter, humbler Moss Evans. A miner's son from the Welsh valleys, Evans saw his job as representing his members rather than leading them. When, in September 1980, an interviewer asked him what he had achieved so far, he said that his officials now had 'access to video recorders and Ceefax'. 'Not', the interviewer thought, 'the kind of issues Mr Jones would have mentioned.'[39]

It was a similar story at the other leviathan of the labour movement, the Amalgamated Union of Engineering Workers. Until 1978 the AUEW had been run by another formidable Marxist, Hugh Scanlon. But he had given way to the Wolverhampton-born Terry Duffy, a pugnacious prag-matist with a strong appeal to the skilled workers of the West Midlands. In almost every particular, Duffy offended radical instincts. He vigorously supported the anti-Communist Solidarity campaign in Poland, happily accepted government funds for union ballots and even pledged to stop 'frittering away union funds in strikes'. His critics denounced him as a conservative sell-out. But when, in November 1980, Duffy stood for re-election on a platform of 'no confrontation' with Mrs Thatcher, he won on the first ballot.[40]

What lay behind this turn to the right? Unemployment made a differ-ence, certainly. It was hard to walk out on strike when benefits were being cut, factories were closing and there were hundreds of applicants for every vacancy. 'These days,' says one character in Alan Bleasdale's *Boys from the Blackstuff* (1982), 'y' go out on strike, before y' can get out of the gates, management are havin' sing songs and wearin' party hats.' Paradoxically, therefore, as the job losses mounted, the unions found themselves with less to do. Enthusiasm dried up; attendance declined; meetings were cancelled for lack of interest. When the journalist Beatrix Campbell visited union offices in the Midlands, people told her that they just sat around reading 'novels waiting for someone to call'. And though there were still occasional demonstrations, they never came close to matching the vast turnout of the early 1970s. 'I think that the unions stand indicted for what they've failed to do. The boilermakers, my union, don't cater for the unemployed,' one Bolton shop steward told the journalist Jeremy Seabrook. He had tried to fire his members up, but the older ones just laughed and said he was naive. 'OK, they had a march, Liverpool, Glasgow, the March for Jobs,' he said angrily. 'But what's come of it? In the future, people will look at the trade unions and say, "What the fuck did they do?"'[41]

But the jobless figures were not the whole story. What is often forgotten is that for most people in the early 1980s living standards steadily went up. Even during the recession real earnings actually went up by 8 per cent, a stark contrast with the stagnant wages of the late 1970s. And when a TGWU official told Anthony Sampson that his union was full of Tories ('and many of them aren't just Tories, they're Alf Garnett Tories'), he was not far wrong. One in three trade union members had voted for Mrs Thatcher in 1979; half thought she had the best tax policies, and more than a third preferred her approach to inflation and unemployment. To radical activists, these figures were genuinely shocking. But the unions had changed since the days of Ernest Bevin and Jack Jones. Despite the donkey-jacket clichés, almost half of all trade union members had white-collar jobs, and there were more immigrants, women and homeowners than ever. Younger members, in particular, had grown up in an increasingly individualistic and anti-deferential age. When their elders invoked the struggles of the past, many just shrugged.[42]

In Coventry, one shop steward reported that when he asked members to join the Right to Work campaign, 'the young chaps were saying they didn't want to because they had jobs. They'd have a collection and chuck a quid in, but they didn't want to strike and lose a day's pay.' And although left-wing activists liked to appeal to collective solidarity, many workers treated the idea with derision. 'People who don't work in industry don't understand what it's like,' said another Coventry man, a machine-tools engineer who had lost his job. 'Every time redundancies were declared in our firm's other plant, we all should've gone out to fight for them. But they cared about us as much as we did about them, which is nowt.'[43]

By the autumn of 1980, Prior's Employment Act had become law. After all the squabbling and plotting, after all the accusations of appeasement and surrender, he had got precisely what he wanted. In her memoirs, Mrs Thatcher grumbled that he ought to have been tougher. Yet his approach proved an unqualified success, and when Norman Tebbit became Employment Secretary in the autumn of 1981, he followed Prior's pragmatic formula to the letter.

Like Prior, Tebbit thought it best to be 'always just a little behind' public opinion. His own Employment Act, passed a year later, tightened the restrictions on closed shops, made it easier for firms to sack disruptive workers and made the unions liable for civil actions if they pursued an unlawful dispute. But he did not ban the closed shop outright, nor did he make it compulsory to have ballots before strike action – a decision that was to have immense consequences in the miners' strike two years later. As before, there was a lot of grumbling on the Tory right. The *Daily Express*, almost incredibly, branded him 'Tiptoe Tebbit' and laid into his 'anaemic' package as 'too little and too tentative'. But like Prior, he held

firm. 'I don't believe in miracles', Tebbit told a *Financial Times* conference
in April 1982, 'or that it is possible to transform industrial relations
overnight.'[44]

Later, Mrs Thatcher's critics suggested that it was the shock of unemployment, rather than the effect of her reforms, that really changed the
unions. Sir Ian Gilmour, for example, saw the new laws as a symptom,
not a cause, of their decline. There is a degree of truth in this. If unemployment had been lower and the union leadership more assertive, she would
surely have faced greater opposition. Even so, her strategy – or rather,
Prior's strategy – was impeccably judged. Both Wilson and Heath had
gone all-out for change and failed completely. By contrast, Mrs Thatcher's
government moved slowly but steadily, never allowing the union leaders
to arouse popular sympathy, never offering opportunities for martyrdom,
always slightly behind the national mood. All in all, it was an object lesson
in the merits of patience, timing and tactical caution.[45]

By the spring of 1982, it was obvious that the unions' glory days
belonged to history. In just twelve months the TUC had lost half a million members. The TGWU had lost 411,000 members in two years; the
AUEW had lost 200,000 and the General and Municipal Workers'
Union had lost a further 101,000. 'Ten years ago the unions were on the
peak of a wave,' wrote the *Observer*'s labour correspondent Robert
Taylor. 'Now it is hard to mobilise the rank and file for any major offensive, even on pay.' The political mood, too, had changed completely.
Now nobody talked about beer and sandwiches, 'barons' and 'concordats'. For the union leaders, there were no more late-night summits at
Number 10, no more cosy chats about the future of the economy over
smoked mackerel and Black Forest gateau. The worst thing was not that
Mrs Thatcher was rude about them. It was that she barely acknowledged
their existence at all.[46]

On the factory floor, shop stewards talked of a new insecurity, a terrible
dread of redundancies which tempered men's militancy and robbed them
of control over their own working lives. But managers told a different
story. When the *Guardian*'s industrial correspondent John Torode spoke
to a group of managers at a Manchester Business School seminar, they
said they had recovered the confidence they had lost in the 1970s. The
recession had sharpened their sense of urgency, while the unions' crisis of
confidence meant shop stewards were hesitating to call their men out.
With the threat of the dole queue never far away, swift single-figure pay
settlements had replaced the protracted wrangling of the past, and at the
infamously strike-plagued Ford and British Leyland factories the men
themselves had agreed to new working practices and gleaming new

technology.* Indeed, the managers told Torode that the details of the government's reforms had been much less important than the message. 'It helped boost morale,' they said. 'It was a psychological indication that the Government supported management's right to manage.'[47]

By this point, few people still talked of the 'British disease'. In 1979 some 1,270 working days had been lost to strikes for every 1,000 workers in Britain, at least five times more than in France or the United States. But in 1980 this fell to 520 and by 1981 it was down to just 190. And although it rose again during the miners' strike, it remained below 200 for the rest of the decade. The headlines were no longer full of strikes and go-slows; the front pages were no longer dominated by pictures of angry crowds at factory gates or bespectacled union leaders trooping into Downing Street. Even on the left there were those who marvelled at the transformation. Nobody, wrote the economist John Wells in *Marxism Today* in 1989, could deny that Mrs Thatcher had restored a sense of 'realism and responsibility' to the factory floor. Once ridiculed as stagnant and sclerotic, Britain had one of the most flexible labour markets in the world.[48]

There was another obvious benefit. For years commentators had wrung their hands at Britain's atrocious productivity, which had fallen so far behind its major competitors that, in 1979, hourly output was at least a third lower in Britain than in France and West Germany. But under Mrs Thatcher, for the first time in living memory, Britain began to close the gap. By the early twenty-first century it had drawn level, something un-imaginable in the days of Wilson and Heath. Nobody now called Britain the 'Sick Man of Europe'. Of course Mrs Thatcher had not done it single-handedly; it was countless managers who introduced the new technology and working habits that made such a difference to Britain's productivity. But would it have been possible without the new political climate of the early 1980s? Would so many Japanese firms have followed Nissan into Britain if the headlines had still been dominated by wildcat strikes, secondary picketing and the closed shop? It seems very unlikely. Many years later, the Oxford economics professor Simon Wren-Lewis, an adviser to Jeremy Corbyn, wrote that it had become 'taboo on the left' to admit that there had been anything wrong with industrial relations in the 1970s. But there had. And whatever else economists thought of Mrs Thatcher, most of them agreed that she had fixed it.[49]

None of this, though, came without a cost. In Corby, talk of an economic renaissance seemed like a black joke. The steel factory's closure in the

---

* On British Leyland, see chapter 13.

spring of 1980 had brought an even greater surge in alcoholism, vandalism and mental illness. The government declared the town an Enterprise Zone, with tax breaks for new businesses. Meanwhile, local councillors worked overtime to attract new jobs, luring Oxford University Press, Allied Mills, Golden Wonder and even, briefly, the computer giant Commodore. But by early 1981 unemployment was rocketing past 30 per cent. Visiting Corby that summer, one reporter was struck by the sight of so many 'shamefaced' men with Scottish accents helping their wives with the shopping. Three years later, Corby's plight inspired the Scottish group Big Country's number one album *Steeltown*, a paean to the town's lost factory, resounding to the 'call of the steel that would never stop'. And the scars never faded. Even in the early twenty-first century Corby still had some of Britain's highest levels of obesity, smoking, alcoholism and drug abuse. It was a proud place, and life went on. But a man from rural south Northamptonshire was likely to live more than five years longer than his neighbour from Corby.[50]

Yet in some ways Corby was relatively lucky. With its central location, between the M1 and A1, it had an obvious appeal to employers wanting cheap labour. Other steel towns were less fortunate. For decades, Consett, in County Durham, had been similarly dependent on its steelworks, which employed some 8,000 people, directly or indirectly. But in December 1979 British Steel announced that Consett, too, would have to close. As in Corby, Mrs Thatcher got the blame, and Consett became another symbol of her assault on the industrial working class. Once again, though, the rot went deeper. According to British Steel's figures, Consett had lost more than £13 million in 1978–9 and another £8 million in 1979–80. The archives show that the government tried to find a private buyer, but none was forthcoming. As the Department of Industry reported to Number 10, it was simply too far from raw materials or major markets. In public, the steelworkers' union made a fuss. In private, as the same report noted, they accepted that Consett was doomed.[51]

In Consett, as in Corby, closure seemed a total catastrophe. 'I just can't imagine it. I'm 60. All my life the works have loomed over this town,' said the chairman of the factory's shop stewards. 'My Dad worked there; his dad before him. As a kid I went to sleep with the sound of those mills running. I just can't imagine this town without a steel works.' In July 1980 hundreds of steelworkers marched through London to deliver a petition to Number 10. But it was no good. After more than a century, the last steel was cast on 12 September, each worker taking home a little ingot. That weekend, wrote one visitor, 'the pubs and clubs were bursting', the atmosphere heavy with nostalgia. Of the 2,900 men who had left the factory for the last time, just three had found jobs. That summer, there were just eight jobs for Consett's 1,400 school-leavers. Some estimates put the local jobless rate at more than 40 per cent.

Seven years later, as the government prepared to sell British Steel to private investors, one in four adults in Consett was out of work. Among young men and women under the age of 25, unemployment stood at almost 80 per cent. Faced with such a staggering waste of potential, such a colossal sacrifice of youth and energy, visiting journalists often searched for the positives, hailing the solidarity and spirit of 'the ghost town that held on to life'. 'Almost overnight', wrote the *Guardian*'s Anne McElvoy, Consett had been 'turned from a red-dust industrial town into a clean, windswept one.' But that was no consolation to the men and women who found themselves on the scrapheap, with little hope of ever finding a job or escaping the daily pangs of anxiety and hunger. 'We've paid a bloody high price', one of them said, 'for clean air.'[52]

# 7

# Who Needs Enemies?

*Britain has had the same foreign policy objective for at least the last five hundred years: to create a disunited Europe . . . We had to break the whole thing up, so we had to get inside. We tried to break it up from the outside, but that wouldn't work. Now that we're inside we can make a complete pig's breakfast of the whole thing.*

Sir Humphrey Appleby (Nigel Hawthorne), in *Yes Minister*, 'The Writing on the Wall', 24 March 1980

*Personally, I think the most effective wheeze would be to send the entire British [Olympic] team to Moscow with instructions to deliberately come last in every event.*

James Murray, *Daily Express*, 30 June 1980

The year is 1959, and we are in a holiday camp in Crimpton-on-Sea, Essex. The camp belongs to the all-conquering Maplin group, but its new entertainments manager is a Cambridge archaeologist, Jeffrey Fairbrother, who has packed in his old job because he was sick of academia. Among his new employees, the Yellowcoats, are the camp host, Ted Bovis, with a colourful line in Teddy Boy suits; the nervous young comedian Spike Dixon, whose routines typically end in disaster; and the hapless Lancastrian chalet maid Peggy, the butt of every joke. The dominant personality, though, is the chief Yellowcoat, Gladys Pugh, driven, humourless and exceptionally Welsh, a man-eater with a burning passion for her new boss. Yet despite the staff's tragicomic tribulations, life is good. The war has been won; austerity has been consigned to history. Class barriers are falling; rock and roll has crossed the Atlantic. And no matter how joylessly Gladys delivers her call to arms – 'Hello campers. Hi-de-hi!' – there is no mistaking the guests' contentment, as they roar back as one: 'Ho-de-ho!'

To the millions watching in January 1980, *Hi-de-Hi!* must have seemed

a poignant throwback to a kinder, gentler Britain, a lost summer of collective holidays, family entertainment and full employment. Written by
Jimmy Perry and David Croft, the team behind the similarly nostalgic
*Dad's Army*, the new sitcom was extremely successful. Many reviewers
dismissed it, yet by 1982 *Hi-de-Hi!* was firmly established in the BBC's
top ten. In all, it ran for fifty-eight episodes, attracting 17 million viewers
at its peak. Later, when cultural critics looked back at the comedies of the
decade, they always remembered *The Young Ones*, *The Comic Strip Presents* . . . and *Spitting Image*. They never remembered *Hi-de-Hi!* It was
too gentle, too conservative, too nostalgic to be fashionable. But with the
headlines dominated by dole queues and disasters, that was precisely why
tens of millions of viewers liked it.[1]

Although the world that *Hi-de-Hi!* celebrated so fondly was 20 years
old, it was not quite dead. In the spring of 1982, Paul Theroux paid a visit
to the Butlin's camp in Minehead, Somerset, which had been built to house
14,000 people. With its 'barracks-like buildings and forbidding fences', it
reminded him of a prison camp. The weather was terrible, yet the place
was packed. There was nobody on the boating lake or the crazy golf
course, in the chapel or the pool, but there were hundreds, even thousands
of people feeding money into fruit machines, eating fish and chips and
playing bingo. But Theroux detected little of the innocent enthusiasm of
*Hi-de-Hi!*, just the deadened unhappiness of a 'sleazy paradise, in which
people were treated more or less like animals in a zoo'. The whole experience was astonishingly cheap: just £178 per week (about £270 today) for
a family of four, including two meals a day. At one point Theroux asked
one of the Redcoats where all the guests came from. 'From all over,' the
man said. Theroux asked what sort of jobs they did, and the Redcoat
laughed. 'Are you joking, sunshine?' he said. 'Half the men here are unemployed. That's the beauty of Butlin's – you can pay for it with your dole
money.'[2]

For Theroux, as for other travellers, Butlin's seemed an irresistible
symbol of a working-class Britain abandoned to inexorable decay. Its
camps in Clacton and Filey closed in 1983, while Barry Island was sold
three years later. The British seaside now seemed seedy, downmarket and
irredeemably old-fashioned. Visiting Morecambe one sunny June day, a
reporter from *The Times* found the theatres empty, the sands deserted and
an elderly couple waltzing alone at the end of the pier. Further south,
among the 'rusting caravans' of Camber Sands, Theroux was reminded
of a 'Third World country' where people let effluent run into the sea and
rubbish pile up on the beaches. In his three-month odyssey around the
British coast, he never found a hotel or guesthouse that was full, 'though

I found many that were completely empty'. Many proprietors were embarrassed by their empty rooms. 'We'll be packed in June,' they said defensively in May. 'Things are quiet now, but it'll be a madhouse in July,' they said a month later. Only sometimes did they admit the truth. People had stopped coming.[3]

At the beginning of the 1980s, most people went on more exotic holidays than ever before. A decade earlier, British tourists had taken just over 4 million holidays abroad. In 1979 they took more than 10 million, rising, despite the recession, to 12 million a year later. As the dole queues lengthened, so did the lines at the check-in desks. In August 1981, tour operators reported that bookings were up by a third on the previous summer, while the four biggest firms, Thomson, Horizon, Intasun and Cosmos, had invested in bigger planes to cope with the demand. Polls found that more than half of British adults had been to France, while four out of ten had been to Spain. In the summer of 1981, Margaret Bradshaw, the ex-policeman's wife, compiled a list of her friends' holidays that year. One family had just spent three weeks in Cyprus and a fortnight in Hong Kong, another had been to Jersey for a week and Malta for a fortnight, and a third had spend two weeks in Miami, a week in Jersey and a week in Scotland. One couple had even come back from five weeks touring Africa.[4]

By now the holiday experience was already moving on from the smoke-filled planes, unfinished hotels and disastrous flamenco evenings of the recent past. The list of the most popular destinations in 1981 would have seemed almost crazily exotic to previous generations. Spain, Greece and Italy led the way, the United States had risen to fourth and Yugoslavia and Tunisia now made the top ten. Yugoslavia's appeal was particularly remarkable because it was still a one-party state, albeit one desperate to attract foreign currency. In 1979 the *Daily Express*, not usually keen on the Communist world, published a long feature on the 'dreamily beautiful' Balkan coastline, where packages cost less than £200 for a fortnight. Four years later, the same paper ran a gushing report on, of all things, a nudist cruise through the Dalmatian islands, where the British passengers included 'a fireman, a psychiatrist, a plumber, an actor and a female magistrate'. For less adventurous travellers, there was always the reassuringly British 'Pontinental' camp in Istria.[5]

In the first weeks of 1981, Polly Toynbee visited the Bahamas Hotel in Arenal, Majorca, which specialized in winter holidays for British pensioners. It is fair to say that she was not a fan: the town's 'unremitting concrete and tatty vulgarity', its mock-Tudor pubs and full English breakfasts, struck her as 'more horrible than any English seaside resort'. But the costs were astonishingly low – just £47 a week for the first month, falling to

£28 a week if people stayed longer – and many people found it much cheaper than staying at home to pay the fuel bills. Apart from the free sangria, not much was obviously Spanish about it. The cabaret was British, the tea dances were British and even the food was British ('meat or liver or kidneys or fish'). The dance organizers, Vivienne and Jim McFarland, came from Coventry. Having worked for Rolls-Royce and British Leyland, they now spent their winters abroad and their summers working in holiday camps, including Butlin's in Minehead.

As for the guests, most were the kind of people – an ex-foreman in a carpet-sweeper plant, say, or a man who had worked in a Christmas card factory – whose parents would never have dreamed of wintering in the Balearics. Lena Pow had worked in a Bristol laundry, while her husband had been a welder. They lived frugally, never drank or smoked, and put every spare penny towards their holidays. The previous winter they had spent nine weeks in Benidorm; other destinations included New York with a cruise up the Hudson ('we didn't like that'), Capri, Rome, Venice and, slightly surprisingly, Moscow. Next year, Lena said, they wanted to go to California. 'I worked my fingers to the bone in that laundry,' she explained, 'and now we're enjoying ourselves.'

For some British holidaymakers, however, there was a cloud in the otherwise perfect Mediterranean sky, a threat to their happiness that made cancelled flights, lascivious waiters and amoebic dysentery look like trifling irritants. It was, of course, the Germans. 'They're pigs, real pigs,' explained Anne Hebson from Accrington:

> I've never seen anyone eat the way they do. I'm a big eater, but I couldn't put away a fraction of what they do.
>
> And they're up to all the tricks. We watch them. One German this morning ate six boiled eggs, yes six! They need nose bags, not plates. And they steal. They take tea bags, sugar, rolls and packs of butter out of the dining-room. Just yesterday we saw one German woman ask the waiter for something and soon as his back was turned she emptied the fruit bowl into her bag. The waitress saw her and made her empty her bag out. It was full, choc-a-bloc, with food.

As Mrs Hebson's voice rose, more British holidaymakers joined the chorus. A particular target was somebody they called 'Mr Goatee', an elderly German gentleman whom they accused of stuffing his pockets with figs. The Germans! They hadn't changed![6]

Actually, popular antipathy to the Germans is easily overstated. When a survey in 1983 asked people to identify 'Britain's friends in Europe', West Germany topped the list, with the Dutch second and the French third. It is perhaps telling that in the BBC's French Resistance sitcom *'Allo 'Allo!*, which started in 1982, the German adversaries are comically inept rather than truly wicked. It is telling, too, that even ITV's *Auf Wiedersehen, Pet*, which follows seven unemployed British builders to West Germany, steers clear of the usual stereotypes. Only one of the builders, Jimmy Nail's Oz, is anti-German, and he gets a stern ticking-off from their leader, Dennis (Tim Healy). 'I've seen blokes like you come and go all the times I've worked in Germany,' Dennis says contemptuously:

> Never been out the UK before. Never eaten foreign food, never drank foreign beer. Fish out of water without the wife or the mother to lend a guiding hand. After a week they've lost their passports, they've got pissed, lost most of their money and become ridiculously nationalistic for the country that can't even bloody employ them in the first place.[7]

One of the most common myths about the 1980s is that, under Mrs Thatcher's guidance, Britain became markedly more nationalistic. True, the tabloids were pretty jingoistic, but they had *always* been jingoistic. There is no real evidence that their readers were more nationalistic, and no evidence that people were nostalgic for Empire. In 1981 Gallup found that only three out of ten thought Britain should 'try to be a leading world power', compared with six out of ten who preferred to emulate 'Sweden and Switzerland'. Even the Commonwealth barely featured in the public imagination. Two years later, another survey found that only 25 per cent thought the Commonwealth should be Britain's international priority, compared with 26 per cent who picked the United States and 39 per cent who named Europe. By contrast, in 1961 some 48 per cent had picked the Commonwealth, only 19 per cent the United States and just 18 per cent Europe. In that sense, most people were probably less imperialistic and more pro-European than they had ever been.[8]

What they were *not*, though, was enthusiastic about the European project. Decades later, when Britain voted to leave the EU, it was often said that Mrs Thatcher's premiership had been the turning point. Her biographer John Campbell, for example, argues that her 'most far-reaching legacy may be Brexit', since by bashing Brussels in the pursuit of 'cheap applause', she whipped up popular antipathy to the European project. But the British public were *already* exceptionally Eurosceptic, even before she walked into Downing Street. It is true, of course, that in 1975 they had voted by two to one to remain in the European Community. But that referendum was probably an anomaly, having taken place at the absolute nadir of a national crisis of confidence. With runaway inflation and the headlines full of doom and gloom, it was hardly surprising that so many people had wanted to stay in the European lifeboat. Very soon, however, public opinion reverted to its natural scepticism. By the middle of 1978, Gallup found that only 25 per cent were pleased with EEC membership, while fully 48 per cent thought it was bad for Britain – and this almost a year before Mrs Thatcher had come to power.[9]

Almost every poll in the late 1970s and early 1980s produced similar findings. In November 1979 ITN found that 53 per cent would like to leave the European Community. A year later, Gallup found that the likely Leave vote had risen to 59 per cent, and in September 1982 Mrs Thatcher's aides sent her a survey which found that, even after a budget rebate, 51 per cent would vote to leave the EEC and only 41 per cent to remain. At this stage, potential leavers tended to be Labour voters, and no fewer than seven out of ten Labour voters said they would prefer to come out. By contrast, only one in three Conservatives wanted to leave. Indeed, the really striking thing – given what happened thirty years later – is how consistent the picture was. Between May 1979 and July 1984, Gallup asked people on twenty occasions whether the EEC was good or bad for Britain. 'Good' came out on top just four times, usually by tiny margins. Yet sixteen times a majority said 'bad', sometimes by as much as 25 or 30 per cent.[10]

The truth is that most people could not care less about the European Community. And when they did think about it, they were, by Continental standards, exceptionally unenthusiastic. When the first European Parliament elections were held in June 1979, turnout was a risible 33 per cent, compared with 61 per cent in France, 66 per cent in West Germany and 86 per cent in Italy. Three years later, when Mass Observation asked its correspondents to identify Ivor Richard, who had recently become one of Britain's two European Commissioners, not a single person knew who he was. 'It is with real apathy that I approach this subject,' began Margaret Bradshaw's reply to a questionnaire about the EEC:

> When we joined the Common Market I thought it would be good for our children and the quality of their life. Mainly because of the threat of war diminishing in the light of a united Europe and the power of our solidarity. Since the Falklands conflict I am now unsure of this. It seems to me that our old allies from the extinct Commonwealth rallied round considerably better than our new ones to whom we had to plead.
>
> Economically I just don't know ... I don't know if it affects our unemployment figures ... There is a certain anti-French feeling about but I don't think this is particularly due to the Common Market; more due to our temperament.

Other correspondents were, if anything, even more bemused. 'Don't know . . . Don't know . . . Don't know,' wrote Mary Richards. 'Don't know who Ivor Richard is. Never heard of him in my life . . . Don't know the name of my Euro MP, in fact I didn't know I had one.' She asked her family and friends the same question. None of them knew either, though some thought Michael Foot and Jim Callaghan might be MEPs.

As for Carol Daniel, she was not a fan of the EEC at all. 'I wish we hadn't joined,' she wrote. 'We lost a lot of our tradition and have been forced to conform with everyone else.' Among other things, she blamed Britain's new partners for metric measures ('a mystery to me'), and was convinced that soon 'we will have to drive on the right hand side'. She had not, of course, heard of Ivor Richard, nor could she name a single MEP. 'I know it is one of the cabinet members,' she wrote. 'Could it be Mr Primm, I think I recall him at a meeting during the Falklands Crisis discussing the common market's veto of Argentinian exports.'* Like Margaret Bradshaw, she thought the Falklands had shown the Europeans in the worst possible light. 'I do know one thing,' she wrote, 'the EEC were *not* exactly a pillar of strength during our last little bit of trouble. With friends like these, who needs enemies?'[11]

Margaret Thatcher would, of course, have agreed with every word. Or would she? For when she came to power in 1979, there was no reason to doubt that she was a committed European. She had been happy to back Harold Macmillan's first bid to join the EEC in the early 1960s, and wholeheartedly supported Edward Heath's bid ten years later. It is true that during the referendum, just months after she became Tory leader, she played only a supporting role. But like many Conservatives, she still saw Europe, and in particular West Germany, as a model. Welcoming the West German Chancellor, Helmut Schmidt, to Downing Street a week after the 1979 election, she told him that his country offered 'an enviable example of economic and social progress combined with social and political stability'. She was 'committed', she said, to EEC membership: 'We believe it is not only right for Europe but right for this country.' And although she was already making ominous noises about the Community budget, she struck a similar note at her party conference. 'It is no use joining anything half-heartedly,' she told her activists in October 1979. 'Five months after taking office we have done much to restore the trust and confidence that the last Conservative Government enjoyed with our partners in Europe,

---

* 'Mr Primm' certainly sounds like a Thatcherite minister, but she was probably conflating Francis Pym and Jim Prior.

and which the Labour Government did not. We are a committed member of the Community.'[12]

It was no accident that she drew an explicit contrast with Labour. Wilson and Callaghan might have backed the EEC during the referendum, but Michael Foot, Barbara Castle and Tony Benn had been in the vanguard of the 'No' campaign, the Brexiteers of their day. After the election, Labour returned to its default position, portraying the EEC as an elitist project to undermine parliamentary sovereignty and frustrate the advance of democratic socialism. In October 1980 the Labour conference voted by a two-thirds margin to make withdrawal from the Community a priority, with tumultuous applause for the Shadow Foreign Secretary Peter Shore's verdict that European membership had been a 'rape of the British people and of their rights and constitution'. To the government, all this seemed a gift. Peter Walker declared that Labour's position 'would be warmly welcomed in the Kremlin', while Mrs Thatcher never failed to remind voters that she, unlike her opponents, was a good European. 'They are running out on Europe,' she warned during the next general election campaign. 'More than 2½ million British jobs depend on British membership of the Common Market.' If people voted Labour, 'every single one of those jobs would be at risk'.[13]

But Mrs Thatcher's enthusiasm had its limits. She hated talk of a 'United States of Europe', and almost physically shuddered when people talked about European federalism. 'They are paid much too much – from our taxpayers' money. It looks like a real gravy-train,' she scribbled on a note about Brussels salaries in February 1979. More fundamentally, she was just not one of life's Europeans. As her foreign policy adviser Sir Percy Cradock recalled, 'she did not like the Europeans; she did not speak their languages; she had little time for their traditions'. Her father had told the Grantham Rotary Club that he would 'sooner be a bootblack in England than a leading citizen in a good many of the other leading countries in the world today', and she almost certainly agreed with him. 'They are all a rotten lot,' she explained to the former Labour politician Roy Jenkins, who had become President of the European Commission. 'Schmidt and the Americans and we are the only ones who would do any standing up and fighting if necessary.' In particular, she was outraged that her European partners were not permanently grateful for Britain's help during the Second World War, a debt that could never be repaid. 'How on earth can Britain be treated in this way?' she asked her aides during one European squabble. 'After all, we saved their skins in the war.'[14]

At first foreign policy was very far down Mrs Thatcher's list of priorities. 'Must I do all this international stuff?' she had asked her aides before becoming Prime Minister. Her initial plan was to leave most of it to Lord Carrington, her patrician Foreign Secretary. Although their backgrounds could hardly have been more different, Carrington was the sort of aristocrat she liked: 'unfailingly civil, effortlessly charming, unexpectedly witty', as Hugo Young put it. In private, the Foreign Secretary's attitude to 'the Boss', as he called her, was a bit more complicated. Charles Moore reports that once, climbing the stairs to her study, Carrington told her Principal Private Secretary: 'Clive, if I have any more trouble from this fucking stupid, petit-bourgeois woman, I'm going to go.' Yet Carrington never betrayed a hint of this to Mrs Thatcher, treating her with faultless respect and a hint of flirtatious teasing. Even Denis, no fan of Carrington's liberal views about Africa, regarded him as a 'mighty man'. By contrast, Carrington's deputy, Sir Ian Gilmour, was not her kind of person at all. Clever, disdainful, a bit snobbish, Gilmour might have been hand-picked to play a languid patrician in some 1950s comedy about the amateurs running Britain's foreign policy.[15]

In some ways it is odd that Mrs Thatcher picked Carrington and Gilmour to run the Foreign Office, since they conformed absolutely to the stereotype of everything she distrusted about it. But although she always complained about the Foreign Office, she usually followed its advice. The prime example was Rhodesia, which had been an embarrassment ever since Ian Smith's white supremacist regime had declared independence in 1965. Like many on the right of her party, Mrs Thatcher instinctively sympathized with the Rhodesian whites, not least because Denis had business interests in South Africa and pretty intransigent views on the subject. When she became Prime Minister, many people expected her to back Smith's puppet regime. In fact, she allowed Carrington to orchestrate a deal ensuring a black majority government under Robert Mugabe. Even Gilmour thought she 'performed brilliantly' to secure the decisive agreement in December 1980, praising 'her restraint and her readiness to be persuaded'. This was a Margaret Thatcher rarely seen in public: cautious and open-minded, a pragmatist who knew how to give as well as take. But as her European partners were to discover, there was more than one Margaret Thatcher.[16]

On Mrs Thatcher's first day in Number 10, one of the documents awaiting her was a two-page briefing entitled 'European Issues'. By far the most pressing was the immensely complicated question of Britain's contribution to the EEC budget, which had been festering for the last couple of years. The basic problem was this. Every year, each country paid billions into the collective budget, based on a formula that penalized countries

importing a lot of goods from outside Europe. As a result, Britain was one
of the biggest contributors. Yet to the delight of hundreds of thousands of
French farmers, almost three-quarters of the budget was spent on the
infamous Common Agricultural Policy. And since Britain had a very small
agricultural sector, the British got less than anybody else. This had been
identified as a problem years earlier, and Harold Wilson's renegoti-
ation of the EEC terms was supposed to have sorted it out. But by 1979,
Britain was paying in almost £1 billion more than it got back. As Jim
Callaghan told his European partners, that was not on at all.[17]

In Brussels, the Conservative victory came as something of a relief.
Since the Tories were more pro-European, most insiders assumed they
would be easier to handle. But they had bargained without Mrs Thatcher.
Here was her perfect issue: an opportunity to swing her handbag at the
foreign foe, presenting herself as the champion of British thrift against the
byzantine wastefulness of the Continental bureaucrats. And no sooner
had she arrived in Downing Street than she began to limber up for battle.
'It has been suggested by some people in this country that I and my government will be a "soft touch" in the Community,' she told Helmut
Schmidt during his first visit. 'In case such a rumour may have reached
your ears . . . it is only fair that I should advise you frankly to dismiss
it . . . We shall judge what British interests are and we shall be resolute in
defending them.'[18]

In some ways the events of the next twelve months were a good preview
of Britain's relationship with its neighbours for the next three-and-a-half
decades. As even Gilmour admitted, the budget anomaly left Britain with
very good grounds for complaint. But far from recognizing that Mrs
Thatcher had a legitimate grievance, many European leaders were shocked
that she brought it up. As far as they were concerned, a good European
should simply hand over her contribution and trust Brussels to use it for
the greater good. Indeed, the French were outraged that she wanted to
publicize who got the most, because they knew the inevitable furore might
erode their share. Above all, they were appalled when she started talking
about 'our money', meaning Britain's money. No good European would
talk about 'our money'. '*Voilà parle la vraie fille d'épicier*,' an unnamed
European politician muttered during one of the many strained hours to
come.* He did not mean it kindly.[19]

To Mrs Thatcher's new partners, almost everything about her was a
shock. Some handled it better than others. The worldly Schmidt, a Social
Democrat, had previously warned American officials that she was a 'bitch'.

---

* 'There speaks the real grocer's daughter.'

But when he actually dealt with her he was impressed by her command of detail, while she was delighted to find that economically he was 'more right-wing than she was'. On the other hand, the French President Valéry Giscard d'Estaing, who *was* on the right, was completely unable to cope. A man of almost comical grandeur, who clearly fancied himself as the reincarnation of Louis XIV, he treated her with breathtaking condescension. When she made her first visit to Paris, Giscard insisted on being served first at lunch because he was a head of state, whereas she was a mere head of government. Later, in an immensely revealing anecdote, he recalled that as a boy he had had 'an English nanny . . . very correct, very tidy, with a very neat hairdo. She was efficient, religious, always opening the windows, especially when the children were ill; rather tiresome. When I met Mrs Thatcher, I thought, "She is exactly the same, *exactly* the same!"'[20]

Mrs Thatcher's first European summit, at Strasbourg in June 1979, set the tone. Not only did Giscard dismiss her attempts to bring up the budget issue, he conspicuously refused to sit next to her at the two formal dinners, even though he was the host and she was the new girl. Later, one European Commissioner, speaking anonymously, said that Giscard and Schmidt had been 'very rude, even patronising' to her throughout, clearly assuming that as a 'mere woman' she would soon give way. Even Roy Jenkins, who liked Giscard, was shocked by his 'extraordinary performance', though he was impressed that Mrs Thatcher 'showed no sign of reacting to the slight'.[21]

But she felt it. In the short term, she got her revenge by deliberately seating Giscard opposite two enormous portraits of Nelson and Wellington when he next came to Downing Street. More seriously, she now realized that she was in for a long struggle. 'I get more and more disillusioned with the EEC,' she told one of her officials that September. 'We are going to have a real fight over the budget and by one means or another we have to get our way. We need the money.' A month later, giving a lecture in Luxembourg, she took off the gloves. 'I must be absolutely clear about this,' she said ominously. 'Britain cannot accept the present situation on the Budget. It is demonstrably unjust. It is politically indefensible: I cannot play Sister Bountiful to the Community while my own electorate are being asked to forego improvements in the fields of health, education, welfare and the rest.' As usual, she ended with some fine words about her commitment to European friendship. But everybody knew what the real message was.[22]

The next round was scheduled for Dublin at the end of November. In a revealing sign of her anxieties, Mrs Thatcher packed a brand-new suit, of which she was very proud, but decided not to wear it because 'I didn't

"PIGS!"

Even by the standards of the day, Stanley Franklin's *Sun* cartoon (20 October 1979) is remarkably uncompromising. Still, the French and German pigs make very satisfying antagonists.

want to risk tainting it with unhappy memories'. This was just as well, since the mood was 'extremely and increasingly hostile'. Giscard and Schmidt had clearly decided to put her in her place, and told her that the best they could do was a refund of some £350 million: a 'third of a loaf', as she put it. 'They had decided to test whether I was able and willing to stand up to them,' she wrote. 'It was quite shameless: they were determined to keep as much of our money as they could.'

The following scene became part of her Iron Lady legend. As Jenkins recalled, Mrs Thatcher had been pretty 'shrill' that afternoon, but she was only 'tuning up'. When she arrived for their working dinner, she was in recklessly aggressive form. Almost as soon as she sat down, she started talking, and she never stopped. 'She kept us all round the dinner table for four interminable hours,' Jenkins wrote, during which she 'talked without pause, but not without repetition'. The tables were cleared; the clock ticked towards midnight. On and on she went, while her partners sat in silence.

Schmidt pretended to go to sleep. Giscard started reading a newspaper.*
Outside, on the French president's instructions, the official cars revved
their engines. But still Mrs Thatcher went on, until at last she ran out of
steam. Later, Gilmour joked that Schmidt and Giscard now realized what
her ministers had to put up with.[23]

What really captured the public imagination, though, was Mrs Thatcher's diatribe at the press conference the next morning. Even a long excerpt
does not really capture the extraordinarily hectoring effect, almost hypnotic in its intensity:

> We are not asking for a penny piece of Community money for Britain. What
> we are asking is for a very large amount of *our own money back* ... It is
> not asking the Community for money; it is asking the Community to have
> *our own money back* ...
>
> Some people think I am asking for other people's money. I am not ...
> We cannot go on putting money in the Community's coffers. We are giving
> notice of that and we want a very large proportion of *our own money
> back*, because we need it at home and we are having to cut expenditure
> at home.
>
> The first difficulty here – I do not disguise it from you – has been to get
> over that fundamental thing to the Community, that all we are doing is
> asking for *our own money back* because we cannot go on being Europe's
> biggest benefactor.

To devoted Europeans, this was the most outrageous performance of all.
As they saw it, that mantra – '*our own money back*' – made a mockery
of everything the Community stood for.† But the British press corps loved
it. The BBC's John Simpson recalled that when she finished, 'most of the
journalists stood up and applauded her: something I had never seen before,
and have never seen again'.[24]

Even decades later, the shock at Mrs Thatcher's performance had not
quite faded. To European enthusiasts, here was proof that British politicians would always play to their national audience instead of putting the
Community first. Roy Jenkins thought Dublin established the image of
Britain as a country always demanding special treatment, 'half in and half
out'. Yet most observers agreed that Giscard and Schmidt had treated the
Prime Minister with unforgivable condescension. Even the pro-European

---

* In fairness, when Charles Moore asked Giscard about it years later, he denied it. But it
sounds pretty plausible.
† It is often said that she asked for '*my* own money back', but this is an exaggeration. She
used the phrase 'our own money back' eight times, but 'my own money', which was probably
a slip of the tongue, only once.

Hugo Young thought they had been 'rude and derisive, and determined not to meet her anywhere near halfway'.

Indeed, Labour's spokesmen thought she had *not been strident enough*. In the Commons, Jim Callaghan warned that she was clearly preparing for a sell-out, while Tony Benn claimed that she had shown herself to be a 'paper tigress'. Extraordinarily, therefore, Mrs Thatcher actually ended up defending her European antagonists. At one point she told Benn that their £350 million offer, which had annoyed her so much, was 'not bad'. When he advised her to boycott European institutions, she snapped: 'What is the point of boycotting? It is far better to be there.' And when he asked if she would consider leaving the EEC altogether, she said firmly: 'No', adding that if Britain left, 'the only people who will cheer are those who are based [in] Moscow'.[25]

In private, though, she remained on the warpath, lashing the Foreign Office for not being 'tough enough or imaginative enough in arguing the British case'. When they suggested offering the Europeans access to North Sea oil, she scrawled angrily: 'That statement would be disastrous for Britain and I am not prepared to make it. The idea that we should have to sacrifice our main assets to secure some of our own money back is one that may appeal to the Foreign Office but it doesn't to me.' Indeed, by the spring of 1980 she was ready to contemplate very drastic measures. The 'only thing that would make Europe sit up', she told the backbencher Terence Higgins in March, 'would be to withhold' – in other words, to stop British money going into European accounts.[26]

But her adversaries' resistance was weakening. In April the European Council raised their offer to more than £700 million a year for two years, a striking advance on £350 million for just one. Mrs Thatcher turned it down. Schmidt apparently left the council chamber 'shaking with rage' and muttering: 'I can't stand this any longer. I can't deal with someone like that.' Even Giscard came close to losing his Olympian detachment. 'I will not allow such a contemptible spectacle to happen again,' he said coldly on his way out. But her intransigence was wearing them down. As Jenkins recorded, 'everybody except Mrs Thatcher had become bored to death'. Unfortunately, she was now getting such a kick out of the battle that she did not want it to end. When Carrington told her there was talk of a three-year-deal, she proclaimed herself 'horrified' and tried to squash it. Only reluctantly did she let Carrington and Gilmour discuss a deal with their opposite numbers at the end of May. In the meantime, she told the Treasury to prepare to cut off British funds from the Community's accounts.[27]

The denouement was pure Audrey fforbes-Hamilton. On 29 May,

Carrington and Gilmour stayed up all night to secure a rebate of more than £700 million a year for the next three years. By nine the next morning the deal was done, and as the two men flew back to RAF Northolt, they shared a bottle of champagne. When they reached Chequers, Mrs Thatcher was at the door to greet them. She was furious. 'Had we been bailiffs arriving to take possession of the furniture, or even Ted Heath paying a social call in company with Jacques Delors,' wrote Gilmour, 'we would probably have been more cordially received.'

She showed them into a sitting room, and told them at once that they had 'sold the country down the river'. She would have to resign. No, said Carrington, they would resign. No, she would resign. At this point a civil servant from the Treasury, Rachel Lomax, piped up and said that actually it was a pretty good deal. That took the wind out of Mrs Thatcher's sails. As Gilmour recalled, she offered objection after objection, only for Mrs Lomax, 'sweetly but a little wearily', to dismiss them one by one ('No, Prime Minister, you have not got that quite right . . . No, I think you must be looking at the wrong page'). At last, after hours of this, Carrington lost his temper. 'Prime Minister,' he burst out, 'we have been up all night, we have not had one moment's sleep, we have been here for hours. Could we please have a drink?'

It was now that Gilmour realized what was bothering Mrs Thatcher. There was nothing wrong with the deal. What annoyed her was the thought of losing such an excellent populist cause. Unlike everybody else, she had enjoyed every moment of the budget battle, and was sorry to say goodbye to it. In the end, though, Carrington and Gilmour outsmarted her. That evening, they briefed the press that the agreement had been a stunning vindication of her patriotic resistance to the Brussels bureaucrats. 'A great success for Mrs Thatcher', declared the next day's *Times*, while the *Sunday Express*'s cartoonist Michael Cummings, marking the fortieth anniversary of Dunkirk, drew Giscard and Schmidt standing forlornly on the French coast and clutching a piece of paper entitled 'Maggie's Common Market Fight'. 'There are times, Dr Schmidt,' says a miserable Giscard, 'when I wish the British had stayed away and not come back on D-Day.' So when Mrs Thatcher met her Cabinet the following Monday, she found them united behind the deal. 'We have no alternative but to accept,' said Lord Hailsham. 'We shan't get better. The press have treated it as a victory.' She was still cross. She had no choice, though, but to agree.[28]

The great budget battle, which recouped more than £700 million a year for Britain, the equivalent of at least £4 billion today, had been a gift to Mrs Thatcher. At a time when nothing else seemed to be going right, she

had won a significant victory. Her critics conceded that her intransigence
had paid off; even the bruised Carrington admitted that she had got a
better result by ranting and raving than she would if she had played the
good European. At home, the imbroglio established forever her image as
'battling Maggie swinging her handbag and standing up for Britain', as
her biographer John Campbell puts it. But in the capitals of Europe she
became something of a bogeywoman, striking dread into politicians and
officials alike. That, of course, was just as she liked it.[29]

But the battle of the budget was about more than just £700 million a
year. It was about Britain's national pride and its place in the world, its
patriotic self-image and its relationship with Europe. Mrs Thatcher knew
perfectly well that many people regarded entry to the Common Market
as a sad but inevitable result of national decline. She knew that few saw
themselves as Europeans, and that most wanted to see somebody standing
up for Britain. This was a role that, by instinct and temperament, she was
perfectly suited to play. Now that she had sampled the pleasures of the
anti-European grievance, she would never lose her taste for it. Her scribbled comments on government papers tell the story: 'No – the procedure
is ridiculous. Its whole purpose is to demean Britain . . . we must fight this
one . . . No . . . Woolly . . . Never . . . It is our water and, but for the Common Fisheries Policy, *our fish*. Don't give them away.'

Four years later, she returned to the fray, taking on Helmut Kohl and
François Mitterrand to win a permanent British rebate. This time, if anything, tempers became even more strained. In March 1984 Greece's Prime
Minister, Andreas Papandreou, declared that as far as most people were
concerned, 'it would be a great relief if Britain left the EEC'. But Mrs
Thatcher never wavered. 'There are nine of them being tiresome and only
one of me, and I can cope with nine of them, so they ought to be able to
stand one of me,' she told *Panorama*. 'And anyway, they could end the
tiresomeness and stubbornness by giving me what I want.' And in the end,
they did.[30]

The paradox was that Mrs Thatcher was also one of the most pro-
European Prime Ministers in British history. If Callaghan had still been
Prime Minister, or if Michael Foot had beaten her in 1983, it is hard to
believe that Britain would have been *more* pro-European. And even as
Labour promised to pull out, she never wavered in her commitment to the
Community. In January 1983 she published a statement to mark the tenth
anniversary of Britain's accession. 'It is a matter of profound regret to me',
she wrote, 'that much political energy in our country is still devoted to
the hoary question of whether we should be "In" or "Out".' As far as she
was concerned, that question had been settled for good. Her government

was devoted to 'the unity of Europe as a force for peace, freedom and democracy'. She just had a funny way of showing it, that was all.[31]

On the face of it, Mrs Thatcher's commitment to the European Community might seem a bit odd. But, as she saw it, the European project was merely part of the much greater project of Western resistance to international Communism. Not since the days of Churchill and Attlee had Britain had a Prime Minister who was so invested in the Cold War as a moral crusade against a genuinely evil enemy. When she first stood as the Conservative candidate for Dartford in 1951, her election address began like this: 'Every Conservative desires peace. The threat to peace comes from Communism, which has powerful forces ready to attack anywhere ..., Britain therefore must be strong, strong in arms, and strong in faith in her own way of life.' And almost three decades later, as Hugo Young remarked, her rhetoric had not changed at all. 'Communism never sleeps, never changes its objectives, nor must we,' she told a Youth for Europe rally in June 1979.* 'Our first duty to freedom is to defend our own. Then one day we might export a little to those peoples who have to live without it.'[32]

All Conservatives said they disliked Communism. Few, though, seemed to mean it as much as she did. In 1976 her hostility to the Soviet Union had earned her the 'Iron Lady' nickname, coined by the Red Army newspaper after she warned that 'the Russians are bent on world dominance, and they are rapidly acquiring the means to become the most powerful imperial nation the world has seen'. But this was merely one of a series of extraordinarily bleak warnings she delivered in the late 1970s. Many were written by the historian Robert Conquest, best known for exposing the scale of Stalin's Great Terror. Conquest undoubtedly encouraged Mrs Thatcher's belligerence, assuring her that the Kremlin was out to destroy Western democracy. He also encouraged her belief that the West was in headlong retreat, comparing champions of détente with the appeasers of the 1930s. 'We delude ourselves if we think that our ways, whether they be 200 or 1200 years old, are winning,' she told an American audience in 1975. 'At present they are not. We represent a diminishing band of brothers and sisters.'[33]

In December 1979 Mrs Thatcher paid her first prime ministerial visit to the headquarters of the Western alliance, Washington, DC. At this stage, the White House was occupied by the former Georgia peanut farmer Jimmy Carter, with whom she enjoyed a non-existent rapport. Mrs

---

* The fact that she came out with this stuff at a Youth for Europe rally says a great deal about what she thought Europe was for.

Thatcher liked her foreign counterparts to be charming and worldly, which is why she got on so well with Ronald Reagan and François Mitterrand. Carter, however, was a world-class killjoy who did not even serve alcohol to White House guests. He did not much care for her either, and it speaks volumes that his administration consistently referred to her as 'Margaret R. Thatcher', despite the fact that her middle name was Hilda. All the same, her trip was a great success, thanks not least to her sabre-rattling militancy. The Soviet Union, she declared, posed a direct 'military challenge . . . The time has come when the West – above all Europe and the United States – must begin to substitute action for introspection.' At a time when Carter was dithering between détente and confrontation, this was hard-hitting stuff, and many Americans were delighted to hear it. The Soviet leaders, she added, 'have labelled me "the Iron Lady". They're quite right – I am.'[34]

Mrs Thatcher had been back for less than a week when the Cold War took a dramatic twist. While she and Denis were enjoying their first Christmas Day at Chequers, Soviet paratroopers were landing in Afghanistan. Two days later, KGB commandos stormed Kabul's presidential palace, killing the president and installing a new leader under Soviet protection. On the face of it, there could hardly have been a more dramatic example of the Kremlin's thirst for expansion. Yet Afghanistan was already a Communist country with a significant Soviet presence, and for months the Kabul government, struggling to suppress a tribal insurgency, had been begging Moscow to send more troops. Far from being desperate to invade, the Kremlin had dithered until the last moment, intervening only when it became obvious that their Afghan clients were incapable of restoring order. And far from being a step towards world domination, therefore, the Soviet invasion was, if anything, a sign of weakness. Indeed, given that the Red Army remained bogged down for nine years, incurring tens of thousands of casualties, the leaders of the West should perhaps have treated it as an unexpected Christmas present.[35]

But that was not how it looked at the time. Three days after Christmas, Carter telephoned Mrs Thatcher and told her that the Soviet invasion was an 'extraordinarily grave development' with 'profound strategic consequences'. It was essential, he added, that they make it 'as politically costly as possible to the Soviet Union . . . I don't think we can afford to let them get away with this.' This was Mrs Thatcher's kind of talk. To her, the invasion vindicated everything she had been saying for years. When an adviser pointed out that the Kremlin had only invaded as an 'act of desperation', she brushed him aside. 'I knew the beast,' she wrote later. 'What had happened in Afghanistan was only part of a wider pattern.' Indeed, in many ways she was relieved, because now the gloves were off. After the invasion, she reflected, 'the whole tone of international affairs began to change, and for the better. Hard-headed realism and strong defence became the order of the day.'[36]

The problem, though, was that there was not much the West could do. Even before the invasion, the Americans had been sending aid to Afghanistan's Islamist rebels, the *mujahedeen*, but they were not going to beat the Red Army any time soon. So Carter and Thatcher had to fall back on symbolic gestures, and one gesture was more symbolic than any other. In July 1980 the Olympic Games would kick off in Moscow, and within days of the invasion Carter was contemplating an American boycott. Only if the world's athletes stayed away, he told Mrs Thatcher, would ordinary Russians realize 'the world's outrage at Soviet aggression'. She agreed. Two days later, she wrote to Sir Denis Follows, the chairman of the British Olympic Association (BOA), telling him that 'it would be wrong' to give the Kremlin such a propaganda opportunity, and urging him to press for an alternative venue. The implication was clear: if the Moscow Games went ahead, British athletes should not go.[37]

Mrs Thatcher's bid to frustrate the Moscow Olympics was a very long shot. As early as 3 January, Sir Denis Follows told the press that, as far as he was concerned, British athletes would go to Moscow. Meanwhile, Mrs Thatcher's officials advised her that, because of the long-standing tradition of sporting independence, the government could not simply 'impose its will' on the BOA. But as her European counterparts already knew, Mrs Thatcher did not give up easily. In the next few weeks she cranked up the pressure, reminding Follows that British athletes had 'the same responsibilities towards freedom and its maintenance as every citizen of the United Kingdom'. But Follows did not give up easily, either. A former secretary of the Football Association, he was about to turn 72 and had weathered plenty of storms before. When an American congressman asked Lord Carrington if there was going to be a British boycott, Carrington asked if he had met Sir Denis Follows. No, the American said. 'Well,' said Carrington, 'he's made of cement from the tips of his toes to the top of his head.'[38]

Mrs Thatcher was far from alone in believing that Britain's athletes should stay away from Moscow. One of the most fervent advocates of a boycott, for example, was the Labour MP Jim Wellbeloved. British participation, Wellbeloved told the Commons, would effectively 'condone the invasion and the occupation of Afghanistan, the suppression of the dissidents and the treatment of the Soviet Jews'. Both the future Archbishop of Canterbury, Robert Runcie, a former tank commander in Normandy, and the Bishop of Liverpool, David Sheppard, a former England batsman, agreed with him. It was an 'illusion', Runcie said, 'to suppose that you can separate politics from sport'.

And even before the boycott campaign had got going, the letters pages simmered with outrage. 'Given Russia's attitude to human rights, with countless thousands in labour camps,' wrote Alan Green of Woodford Green, Essex, it would be 'intolerable' to join in the 'flag-waving' in Moscow. Well before the 'rape of Afghanistan', he added, it had been obvious that Moscow would simply be a replay of the 'infamous Berlin Olympics of 1936'. Another Woodford Green resident, Robert Mitchell, had actually taken part in the Berlin Games, representing Britain at water polo, and remembered 'the enormous political benefit' for the Nazis. If the Moscow Games went ahead, he warned, 'Russian dissidents will be as evident as were German Jews in 1936.'[39]

Mitchell was not the only former Olympian who thought his successors should take a stand. In a letter to *The Times*, Stephen Marsh, who had competed in the luge at the 1972 Winter Olympics, conceded that it would be 'dreadfully hard' on the athletes to give up on their dreams, 'yet it is hard for the Afghanis and Cambodians who are being killed in their thousands by Russian-backed troops'. On the same day the paper printed a letter from the former runner Chris Chataway, who had competed in Helsinki in 1952 and had been Conservative MP for Chichester during the Heath years. Now Chataway claimed that the invasion of Afghanistan was 'the most deadly blow in 30 years to the ultimate survival of democracy'. If British athletes were 'prepared to assist in an enormous propaganda coup for the Soviet Union', he thought, 'the Kremlin, like the Nazi leaders before them, will conclude that there is no will to resist in the free world'.[40]

But not everybody agreed. *The Times*'s sports editor, for example, deplored the 'cynical and unfeeling posturings' of Britain's politicians and thought there was 'no reason why [athletes] alone should make sacrifices'. The *Mirror*, too, wondered why politicians were not talking about breaking other 'sporting and cultural links with the Russians', and pointed out that some of the fiercest champions of the Moscow boycott were those most firmly opposed to boycotting South Africa. Among the general public this argument clearly cut through. By March the *Mirror*'s sports pages had received hundreds of letters about the boycott, only three of them supporting it. 'I wish Maggie and her mob would keep their noses out of sport,' sighed Mrs C. Archbutt of Sydenham, south-east London, while A. W. James of Forest Gate in east London wondered if 'Mrs Thatcher is guilty of secondary picketing by joining a US boycott of the Moscow Olympics'.[41]

Even some of the Prime Minister's natural supporters were uneasy at the thought of 'bullying' athletes into abandoning their dreams. In a free country, wrote Enoch Powell in the *Sunday Express*, 'the citizen is perfectly free to do what the law does not forbid'. The *Daily Express*'s normally ferocious George Gale told his readers that it was 'not up to government to decide whether this man or that, or this team or that, competes here or there or anywhere'. And the *Daily Mail* was even more damning:

> Margaret Thatcher has blundered. Her attempt to deploy state power in order to prevent British athletes from going to Moscow is illiberal, alien and counter-productive ... This is a free country ... our sportsmen and women must make up their own minds ... It is intolerable that this Government, of all Governments – a Government that abhors Communist serfdom – should now seek to make British athletes jump to the Tories' bidding with what is no more or less than a crack of the totalitarian whip.

To cap it all, even the minister organizing the boycott, Douglas Hurd, thought it was a waste of time. It was, he later remarked, the most 'deeply foolish' thing he was ever asked to do as a minister.[42]

The fundamental flaw in the boycott campaign was that Mrs Thatcher simply did not have the power to make Britain's athletes stay away. The obvious solution was to apply overwhelming public pressure, but no such pressure materialized. In late January a *Newsnight* poll found that if the Moscow Games went ahead, only 35 per cent thought British athletes should stay at home, while 58 per cent thought they should go. Almost half agreed that it should be the athletes' own decision, while only 16 per cent thought it should be up to the government. Indeed, if anything Mrs Thatcher's campaign made matters worse. Amid allegations of 'bullying', a poll in mid-March found that support for the boycott had fallen to just 23 per cent, while 69 per cent thought the athletes should go to Moscow.[43]

By the spring it was obvious that Mrs Thatcher was flogging a dead horse. Having trained so hard for so long, most athletes were desperate to go to Moscow, and there was nothing the government could do to stop them. And when the BOA held its long-awaited vote on whether a British team should be sent to Moscow, the result was never seriously in doubt. Only four traditionally conservative, cut-glass sports – hockey, shooting, yachting and equestrianism – agreed to honour the boycott, but the others voted to go. 'Sir Denis Follows and his colleagues are, in effect, collaborating with the Soviet Imperial State,' shrieked the *Express*, but by this stage it was too late.[44]

Among athletes themselves, the episode left a bitter taste in the mouth. Later, the British rowing eight's cox, Colin Moynihan, a future Sports Minister, recalled his crewmates' fury at the unfairness of young men and women being asked to give up on the 'dream for which we had worked throughout our youth'. Moynihan was already a keen Conservative but vehemently opposed the boycott, even though he was sent 'veiled threats' that his political career would be finished. The British Weight Lifters' Association issued a statement deploring what it saw as a smear campaign, while the sprinter Allan Wells claimed that he had been sent 'six letters from No. 10'. The last, he recalled, included 'a picture of a young girl sprawled dead on the ground, with a doll lying six inches from the tips of her fingers. It made me so angry I became even more determined to compete.'

As for the British team's undisputed stars, they had no intention of skipping the Games. When Hurd organized a private meeting with the runner Sebastian Coe's father, Peter Coe, he was taken aback by the 'bitterness' with which Coe senior spoke of the pressure on his son. The supremely dedicated decathlete Daley Thompson, however, never gave Afghanistan the slightest thought. 'I didn't really care,' he said of the boycott. 'I didn't give a damn who was going.'[45]

The Moscow Olympics kicked off on 19 July 1980. With sixty-five nations staying away – including the United States, Canada and West Germany – and only eighty nations taking part, the atmosphere was very far from that of an innocent carnival of sport. The police had blocked major routes into the city, while foreign visitors were outnumbered by men in uniform. Plain-clothes policemen were everywhere: to get into their hotel for dinner, British journalists had to spend at least half an hour filling in forms. As the British Embassy reported, the build-up had been 'singularly joyless. The continuous rain has not helped. Nor has the fact that Moscow is still half-empty.' For as the Embassy observed, 'the oppressive feeling of the city is increased by the virtual absence of children', since thousands of families had been deported to the countryside for the duration of the Games.[46]

The athletes themselves had other things on their minds. In the end, Britain had sent 149 men and seventy women to Moscow, the largest of all the Western teams. Slightly oddly, the British athletes, like many Western European teams, competed under the Olympic flag to express their disapproval of the occupation of Afghanistan, while the Olympic anthem played during their gold medal ceremonies. Both the BBC and ITV scaled back their coverage, and the latter promised to increase its number of 'critical programmes about the Soviet bloc', which made no impact whatsoever. To Mrs Thatcher's discomfort, however, the Soviet media revelled in the presence of so many British athletes, one Moscow paper even claiming that the British had set an example by forcing 'a breach in the boycott wall'.[47]

Did British viewers really care? In the public imagination, the Olympics were memorable less for the fact they were in Moscow than for the triumphs of Britain's five gold medallists: the swimmer Duncan Goodhew, the sprinter Allan Wells, the middle-distance rivals Steve Ovett and Sebastian Coe, and the decathlete Daley Thompson. Given the absence of the Americans and West Germans, this was a pretty feeble haul, and despite the boycott, Great Britain still only finished ninth. The big new star was Thompson, still only 21 but already the best all-round athlete in the world. But not even Thompson's stroll to victory could match the excitement of the titanic battle between Steve Ovett and Sebastian Coe, the two most famous runners on the planet. First, to almost universal surprise, Ovett snatched victory in Coe's trademark event, the 800 metres. Then, with an estimated 15 million people watching back home, Coe took his revenge in the 1,500, crossing the line with a howl of triumph that became one of the most famous images in sporting history. For sheer drama, there was nothing to touch it.[48]

Britain's athletes flew back into Heathrow to a rapturous welcome from hundreds of fans. But there was no Downing Street reception, as there had been for previous winners. And although Fleet Street was only too happy to glory in their triumphs, the scars of the boycott row had not quite healed. The real heroes of Moscow, said the *Express*, were the 'equestrians, marksmen [and] yachtsmen' who had refused to go. 'They put liberty and justice before personal sporting ambitions. It was a hard thing to do, and we are proud of them for doing it.' *The Times* agreed. The athletes who had stayed away had 'sacrificed the chance of a lifetime but their consciences will be lighter . . . The moral achievement of those who did not go to Moscow, especially those who could have expected medals, must surely outshine the sporting achievement of those who did.' These were fine words. But it was Coe and Ovett that people remembered. Nobody ever remembered the missing equestrians.[49]

On the last day of the year, there came one last twist. When Buckingham Palace published the New Year's honours list, not one of Britain's medallists had been included. It was a calculated snub, and Mrs Thatcher did not bother to disguise it. 'I advised them strongly not to go,' she said. 'They chose to accept their democratic right to go to a country which has no democratic rights. I respected their view. I did not agree with it.'

Instead, she preferred to think about those 'people in Afghanistan who are genuinely fighting for the very freedom which our Olympic people take for granted'.

'Three cheers to Mrs Thatcher,' read a letter from John Vernon to the *Daily Express*. 'It is obvious to everyone who has the slightest belief in common dignity that they should never have gone to Moscow in the first place.' By contrast, the former Olympic steeplechase champion Chris Brasher wrote that he had 'yet to meet anyone who does not think that Mrs Thatcher is petty and schoolmarmish'. Indeed, even the *Express* found room for a letter simmering with outrage. 'What a mean, spiteful, petty attitude,' wrote H. Jacobs. 'They dared to disobey her – so what? Britain is supposed to be a democracy.' Of course it was only a trivial issue, and they did get their honours eventually. But as Mrs Thatcher's European counterparts had learned, she rarely forgave a slight and had a knack of provoking fierce passions. Not all the issues at stake would be so trivial.[50]

# 8

# Mrs Thatcher's Final Solution

*I've just been chatting to Bob [Conquest] on the telephone. She's had it according to him ... All the fucking wets in the Cabinet will stop her being tough enough and the effort will collapse.*
Kingsley Amis to Philip Larkin, 7 March 1980, in Zachary Leader (ed.), *The Letters of Kingsley Amis* (2000)

*Everyone in the Cabinet loathes the PM, is out to do her down.*
Alan Clark's diary, 12 April 1980

On 6 January 1980 Mrs Thatcher welcomed the cameras to Downing Street. In her first live interview since the general election, she had agreed to take questions from the former Labour MP Brian Walden, now presenting London Weekend Television's *Weekend World*. Walden's introduction set the tone:

> Britain enters the Eighties under the most radical leadership the country has known for a generation. Not since Clement Attlee arrived here in Number 10 thirty-five years ago have we seen a Prime Minister so determined to change things. Margaret Thatcher insists that prosperity must return to Britain and she believes that the way to ensure that this happens is to stamp out inflation and improve incentives ...
>
> There were those who thought Mrs Thatcher would be forced into a U-turn within the first six months, but she hasn't been. Instead she's made it clear that she intends to do whatever's necessary to make her plan work, and it's now apparent that this may mean a rougher ride for all of us than anybody expected.

In private, Walden, the grammar-school-educated son of a Black Country glass-worker, was a keen Thatcher fan. But as he relentlessly interrogated her about the impending steel strike, her union reforms and the next Budget, few viewers would have guessed. And moments before the credits rolled, he identified what many critics saw as a key weakness in her philosophy.

Even if her reforms succeeded, Walden said, she 'would still have created a society that was more unequal, riddled with avoidable injustices'. So was 'the price for our economic recovery and prosperity greater inequality in this country'? Mrs Thatcher leaned forward. 'I don't believe many people go for equality, except in equality before the law, equality in voting rights,' she said. 'No, you will get a more thriving society when people can rise to the limit of their talents, and out of the wealth they create, we shall all be better off.'

'But it does mean more inequality, does it not?' Walden insisted. And what she said next became part of her legend. 'Yes indeed,' she said earnestly. 'If opportunity and talent is unequally distributed, then allowing people to exercise that talent and opportunity means more inequality, but it means you drag up the poor people, because there are the resources to do so. No one would remember the Good Samaritan if he'd only had good intentions; he had money as well.'[1]

That a Methodist preacher's daughter would remember the parable of the Good Samaritan was hardly surprising. What shocked her critics, though, was how she interpreted it. For the *Mirror*, 'Maggie's Thought for the Day' was a highly revealing glimpse into her 'brutal' philosophy. She had completely missed the point that 'it is better to help those who fall by the wayside – through no fault of their own – than rush selfishly past them. The welfare state is based on THAT message. Not Mrs Thatcher's.' 'Could she complete the revelation', one *Guardian* reader asked scornfully, 'by telling us how much money Jesus Christ had?'[2]

How much money? That was the question. When the latest Treasury figures were published a few weeks later, they showed price inflation at 20 per cent, the pound on the brink of $2.30 and unemployment rising at record speed, with some 1.3 million people officially out of work in February 1980. By now Mrs Thatcher's ministers were no longer pretending that things were going to get better. Their own forecasts showed unemployment reaching 2 million before the end of the year, while at the end of February Sir Geoffrey Howe told the Engineering Employers' Federation that it could take a decade before the economy was 'really strong again'. In Downing Street, John Hoskyns agonized over the soaring exchange rate, which meant that imports – the proverbial German cars and Japanese video recorders – were rising ten times faster than exports. In the Treasury, Howe's special adviser Adam Ridley recorded the thoughts of sympathetic City economists, almost all of whom agreed that the high pound was 'gratuitously damaging to industry'. And all the time, Mrs

Thatcher seethed in frustration at her ministers' reluctance to cut their budgets. At the end of January, her aide Tim Lankester sent her a note about Howe's plans for higher prescription charges. On the back, she scribbled, with multiple underlinings: 'We have *got* to get *economies*.'[3]

On the left, Mrs Thatcher's extremism and folly were already articles of faith. On the right, there was a growing consensus that she had just not been tough enough. But even among her supporters there was no agreement about what they should do next. Hoskyns, for example, thought interest rates were far too high and wished they had made really radical spending cuts instead. By contrast, the free-market Institute of Economic Affairs organized an open letter by sympathetic economists, calling for the government to 'go further and faster' in raising interest rates to squeeze 'excess money and credit out of the economy'.

Perhaps most striking, though, were the prescriptions of the 80-year-old Friedrich Hayek, who told the right-wing Monday Club that the government could bring inflation down overnight by ordering the Bank of England to throttle the monetary base. Among other things, Hayek thought Mrs Thatcher should call a national referendum on abolishing trade union rights, and believed Howe should balance the budget straight away by slashing at least £10 billion in public spending. Even Mrs Thatcher blinked at that, telling him that it would cause 'too much social and economic disruption in the short run'. But Hayek did not give up. Two years later, he advised her to model herself on Chile's General Pinochet, whose government had brought inflation down to single figures from more than 500 per cent. But much as Mrs Thatcher might have disliked Ted Heath and Arthur Scargill, she had no immediate desire to see them electrocuted with cattle prods. The Pinochet regime certainly offered a 'striking example of economic reform', she wrote back. 'However, I am sure you will agree that, in Britain with our democratic institutions and the need for a high degree of consent, some of the measures adopted in Chile are quite unacceptable.'[4]

For some of Mrs Thatcher's ministers, the fact that she was not yet ready to call in the torturers was just as well. For inside her Cabinet the mood was becoming increasingly rebellious. On 7 February, in a calculated gesture of ideological independence, Sir Ian Gilmour went to Cambridge and poured scorn on almost every aspect of his leader's world-view. True Conservatives, he told a student audience, hated 'ideology and dogma' – code, many listeners thought, for monetarism. They rejected 'economic liberalism *à la* Professor Hayek', because its 'failure to create a sense of community' was a threat to political freedom. They believed in moderation, conciliation and consensus, virtues not understood by the 'leader writers of some of our right-wing newspapers'. They knew there was more to life than market forces, were strong supporters of the welfare state (a 'thoroughly conservative institution') and welcomed a 'mixed' economy, with a prominent role for the state. Above all, they believed, like Lord Salisbury, that 'political theory should never get in the way of sensible political action'. On her copy of Gilmour's speech, Mrs Thatcher underlined those words in black ink. The fact that one of her own ministers could so publicly rubbish her political philosophy, if only indirectly, spoke volumes about the insecurity of her position. Later, she would have wasted little time in showing Gilmour the door. But now she did nothing.[5]

It was at about this point, in the spring of 1980, that a new word entered the political lexicon. To the press, Gilmour and his friends were the 'Wets'. The term had originated a few years earlier, as a term of abuse for people Mrs Thatcher regarded as weak and woolly. To be a Wet, wrote Hugo Young, was to believe in 'moderation, caution and the middle-minded approach to politics'. It was 'to be paternalistic and speak the language of One Nation. It was also to be fearful of extreme measures, such as severe anti-union laws, and unfamiliar conditions, such as high unemployment.' And it was to be a particular kind of Conservative: seasoned and worldly, decent and reliable, a man of sense, a man of *bottom*, a man you could picture sitting back with a large brandy at the club. Gilmour was a Wet. Christopher Soames was a Wet. Jim Prior was the ultimate Wet. But Mrs Thatcher could never be a Wet. For one thing, she was a woman.[6]

As *The Times* remarked, it was tempting to see the story of the Wets as a morality tale, with the Thatcherites as the mean-spirited villains and the Wets as 'the good guys . . . sympathetic and interesting politicians who have a sense of the unity of Britain, and a consciousness of their descent from the moderate and progressive wing of the Conservative Party'. Yet there was more than a hint of snobbery in all this. Many of the Wets were Old Etonians, who seemed unable to shake their disbelief that the grocer's daughter had beaten them to the top job. At lobby briefings, Ferdinand Mount was struck by the 'patronising' way that the 'Soameses and Gilmours' talked about her, clearly 'regarding the propping up of this suburban little person as a temporary interruption'. When the former party chairman Edward du Cann described her and Denis sitting on his sofa 'like a housekeeper and a handyman applying for a job', or when Gilmour warned that she would corral the Tories 'behind a privet hedge into a world of narrow class interests and selfish concerns', it was hard to miss the condescension. As Matthew Parris recalled, looking down with a 'collective snigger' on Mrs Thatcher was 'a matter of good taste'. She was not one of us. She was staff. 'The trouble is', muttered Francis Pym, late of Eton, Cambridge and the 9th Lancers, 'we've got a corporal at the top, not a cavalry officer.'[7]

Why were the Wets so ineffective at restraining their leader? After all, the doubters included not just Gilmour, Pym, Soames, Prior, Walker, Norman St John-Stevas and Michael Heseltine, but the Home Secretary, Willie Whitelaw; the Foreign Secretary, Peter Carrington; and the Lord Chancellor, Quintin Hailsham. But the Wet label suggests a unity that never existed in reality. Gilmour thought there were only really four 'open and consistent' dissenters: himself, Walker, Prior and St John-Stevas. If Carrington and Whitelaw had rallied the others to join them, things might have been different. But Gilmour complained that Carrington was 'never wholly engaged' and 'did not understand economics', while Whitelaw, too, simply 'did not understand the economic question'. As the runner-up in the last leadership contest, with enormous appeal across the party, Whitelaw made a very plausible alternative leader. But he regarded himself as 'second-in-command of a battalion' and would 'absolutely never get in her way'. He was, Gilmour said contemptuously, 'the weakest man I have ever known'.[8]

This was very unfair. Since Carrington and Whitelaw had both won the Military Cross, they were hardly short of courage. But they saw themselves as men of honour, duty-bound to serve their commanding officer. They were well aware that they knew little about economic policy, and although Carrington had qualms about the costs of Mrs Thatcher's approach, he 'believed that there was, in fact, no alternative'. In any case, what was Gilmour asking them to *do*? At this stage, the Conservative Party had little history of open rebellion, which is why Heath had been able to ignore the right for so long. There was no modern precedent for a gang of Cabinet ministers forcing the Prime Minister and her Chancellor into a radical change of course, let alone driving them from office so soon after an election. And even if the Wets had launched a coup, Mrs Thatcher was never going to go down without a fight. As Whitelaw's biographers put it, the Wets were 'like an army that lacked any conventional forces: they had only a nuclear device, which could not be deployed without serious risk to themselves, to the party and (so they had reason to think) to the country'. Not surprisingly, they always found a reason not to use it.[9]

The other reason why the Wets failed to force the issue is that they had nothing to say. Looking back, Howe wondered why they had never raised their objections face-to-face, and concluded that they simply had 'no practical alternative policy'. They all hated mass unemployment; they all agreed that monetarism was not working. They were very good at diagnosing the contradictions of Howe's policies: the hasty tax cuts, the roaring inflation, the missed monetary targets, the lengthening dole queues. They were good, too, at wringing their hands at the effects of his medicine, adopting what Lawson dismissed as 'cold feet dressed up as high principle'. But not one of them developed a practical alternative. As Hugo Young remarked, they were 'moderate men' who simply wanted 'less of everything from monetarism to unemployment'. But they had no idea how to obtain it.[10]

Later, in his anti-Thatcher polemic *Dancing with Dogma*, Sir Ian Gilmour addressed this criticism head-on. It is not fair, he says, that people mocked the Wets for not having an alternative, since dissenters are 'entitled just to oppose what is being done, to point to its calamitous consequences and to urge its abandonment'.* In any case, Gilmour insists that they did have an alternative. What was it? It was 'never a single, simple unalterable blueprint', he adds hastily, but it did exist. The Wets would have used North Sea oil to 'finance a massive increase of investment in industry and in the infra-structure'. He never spells out which industries, nor how the investment would be used, nor how this would have been more successful than the industrial policies of the 1970s. Happily, 'the social repercussions of economic change could have been cushioned', industry would have been 'restructured and made more competitive' and the 'tax and benefit systems and the system of pay bargaining could been reformed'. But how would all this have come about? A Britain that reinvested in industry, modernized its infrastructure, reformed its tax system and sorted out its industrial relations, while cushioning its people from economic change, would have been the envy of the world. But no such country ever existed. This was not an alternative policy. It was the political equivalent of a Miss World contestant's hopes for world peace.[11]

The Wets had nothing to say because they were pining for a vanished age. 'They do not understand the difference between the 1950s and the 1980s, and they do not understand economics,' said *The Times*. 'They are historically out of phase and intellectually out of their depth.' That was harsh, but it was true. The Wets had come of age in the days of Anthony Eden and Harold Macmillan: paternalistic patricians, like themselves, who had presided over booming economies with full employment and low inflation. It was natural that they were nostalgic for the carefree policies of their youth. But the context had changed. Even if Macmillan had been in charge in the 1980s, he would have had to face the fact of high inflation and the need for unpopular measures to handle it. As *The Times* put it,

---

* This might be a tolerable argument from, say, a *Daily Mail* columnist, but surely not from a Cabinet minister, who ought to have something constructive to say.

'To attempt to apply the principles of the 1950s to the circumstances of the 1980s is not compassion; it is an invitation to catastrophe.'

For perfectly understandable reasons, Gilmour and his friends were shocked by the costs of Howe's drive to wring inflation out of the economy with high interest rates. But what would they have done instead? Gilmour implied that they wanted to spend their way out, driving up public borrowing to restart the motor of growth. But when Harold Wilson had tried that in the mid-1970s, it had ended with runaway inflation and a bailout from the IMF. This was why Jim Callaghan, like Heath and Wilson before him, had fallen back on an incomes policy to handle inflation. The Wets thought Mrs Thatcher should adopt an incomes policy, too. But only somebody who had been asleep during the 1970s could have seriously believed this would work. The unions had flatly refused to co-operate with the Tories' last attempt to regulate prices and incomes, and the lesson of the Winter of Discontent was that holding down workers' pay only led to more trouble in the long run. Did the Wets seriously think they could succeed where Callaghan, the unions' closest political ally, had just failed?[12]

It is not true, though, that there was no alternative. A second Callaghan government would probably have pursued a more cautious version of Mrs Thatcher's approach, but with some sort of concordat with the unions to bring down inflation more slowly – though the Winter of Discontent suggests this would have ended in tears eventually. A more radical government under, say, Tony Benn would have adopted the left's beloved Alternative Economic Strategy, borrowing heavily, subsidizing industrial jobs, accepting high inflation and imposing import controls. But whereas the Labour left brimmed with ideas, however lurid or far-fetched, the Wets preferred to moan about Mrs Thatcher. Later, they complained that she never allowed them to have a proper economic discussion. But since they had nothing constructive to say, that was probably just as well.

They could, of course, have resigned. But as the former Labour minister Edmund Dell scathingly remarks, 'their determination to whinge in the background, and in coded messages, was equalled only by their determination to cling on to their portfolios and their lack of confidence in their own alternative'. So they stayed where they were: muttering endlessly about mutiny, but apparently incapable of issuing an open challenge to their beleaguered captain.[13]

In the meantime, Mrs Thatcher steered grimly towards the storm. It was now almost a year since she had come to power, she told the nation on 12 March. The time had come 'to ask ourselves one or two important questions'. She urged people to remember that Britain had only recently emerged, 'scarred and shaken', from the 'appalling Winter of Discontent', and that the election had given her a mandate to 'stop the rot and change direction'. But as she admitted, this was not proving easy:

> You'll say to me the prices are still going up, unemployment is still rising. Haven't we been caught in another prolonged and damaging strike in which, whatever the outcome, there are no winners, only more problems for both sides – and for Britain?* All this is undeniable. Indeed we spoke about it many times when we asked for your vote last year. We didn't promise you instant sunshine. We pointed out over and over again that a nation can't accelerate downhill for years and then jam the brakes on and suddenly return to prosperity as though the past had never happened. We had to start by slowing down before turning round and beginning the long, slow climb back up the hill to recovery . . . We are paying the price for years and years of make believe and now all the problems of those years have come home to roost.

She knew some people would prefer a quiet life, 'but we must change and if Britain changes too slowly it won't recover'. And in an image that was to become very familiar, she likened herself to a doctor trying to save a long-neglected patient. 'I'm afraid some things will get worse before they get better,' she said. 'After almost any major operation you feel worse before you convalesce. But you don't refuse the operation when you know that without it you won't survive. Is this perhaps beginning to get through?'[14]

Two weeks later, Howe presented his second Budget to the Commons. As before, the Wets had been shut out of the planning, but this time the Budget seemed much less eye-catching. To the next day's papers, the most exciting elements were Howe's decisions to cut strikers' benefits, put 50p on a bottle of whisky and increase prescription charges by a pound. Like Mrs Thatcher, the Chancellor admitted that times would be tough, but insisted that this was the 'price to pay' for the 'long-run decline of our economy'. This provoked some rumbustious oratory from Denis Healey, who, embracing Mrs Thatcher's medical metaphor, damned the Budget as 'another enormous dose of a medicine that has already made the patient as sick as a dog'.[15]

But the Budget made little impression on the general public, and a poll for the *Sunday Times* found that 47 per cent approved of it, compared with 36 per cent who were unimpressed. *Private Eye*'s Denis Thatcher probably spoke for many when he told his friend Bill that Howe should simply have stood up and said, 'A quid on fags, couple of quid on petrol, etc.', and then sat down, instead of treating them to a 'ballsaching lecture

---

* That is, the steel strike of early 1980.

beforehand on the state of the nation'. In the *Eye*'s version of events, the fictional Denis escapes by sneaking away from the Commons gallery to the House of Lords bar, where he finds Harold Wilson, 'a bottle of brandy in one hand and a balloon glass in the other'. 'At about five o'clock', Denis reports, 'they started serving tea and cakes, and I asked him what had happened in the Budget, but he said he didn't know and didn't give a bugger. I know you'll find it hard to believe, Bill, but I think he's one of us.'[16]

If Denis and Harold had been paying attention, they would, in fact, have heard Howe announcing one of the most controversial experiments in British monetary history. This was the Medium Term Financial Strategy, usually referred to by the initials MTFS – which meant critics liked to call it 'Mrs Thatcher's Final Solution'. The tabloids largely ignored it, devoting more attention to the duty on cigarettes and brandy, and in fairness it hardly sounds very thrilling. Yet it mattered. For the first time, the government set out what Howe called 'a four-year path for monetary growth, public spending and tax policies'. There were two main elements. First, there would be gradually falling targets for money supply growth, measured in sterling M3. The rate in 1980–81, for example, would be between 7 and 11 per cent, but by 1983–4 it would come down to between 4 and 8 per cent. Second, public borrowing would also come down, with spending projected to dip below 40 per cent of GDP by the end of the cycle. This, Howe argued, would allow interest rates to fall, relieving pressure on the exchange rate and giving manufacturers a chance to breathe. Of course there was a political risk in all this: no government had ever tied itself so closely to specific targets, especially so far ahead, and it would be very embarrassing if they missed them. But Howe insisted that by looking ahead to 1984 the MTFS would bring some much-needed certainty to the chaotic world of British economic policy.[17]

The idea of the MTFS had been floating around academic circles since the mid-1970s. But its political godfather was Nigel Lawson, who had written an article in *The Times* in 1978 urging a 'long-term stabilisation plan to defeat inflation'. After a decade of economic uncertainty, Lawson thought businesses were crying out for the return of 'known rules', like the gold standard that had governed economic policy before the First World War, or the Bretton Woods system that had regulated the world's major currencies until 1971. Howe thought this was a great idea. Like Lawson, he yearned for some kind of anchor, some clear, practical framework that would banish the chaos and indiscipline of the 1970s. In the MTFS he found what he wanted. The targets would keep ministers in check, while publishing them so far in advance made a U-turn almost impossible. As long as they stuck to the plan, inflation would come down, the economy would recover and everybody would go home happy. And as Charles Moore remarks, it made sense politically, too. Suffering today, jam tomorrow: this was the Thatcherite message in a nutshell.[18]

Right from the start, the MTFS was intensely controversial. The Bank of England was very dubious about it. Only three weeks before the Budget, Gordon Richardson told Mrs Thatcher that he had 'serious misgivings about the whole exercise'. 'It was hard enough', he said, 'to set a monetary target for one year ahead: it was much harder for a four-year period.' Howe's deputy John Biffen, too, thought it madness to publish targets they might struggle to meet. Even many monetarists were very sceptical. The economist Alan Walters thought the government was using the wrong measure of inflation, since sterling M3 was so broad it would be impossible to control. And monetarism's Supreme Leader, Milton Friedman, thought it was a terrible idea, telling the Treasury Select Committee he 'could not believe [his] eyes' when he read that Howe and Lawson were proposing to use spending cuts and interest rates to force inflation down.

Ironically, given that the MTFS was supposedly such a key part of her economic strategy, Mrs Thatcher shared the sceptics' fears. As Howe recorded, she disliked the idea of being forced into a straitjacket, regarding it as a 'graph-paper strategy' that would give her no room for manoeuvre. But the Chancellor played on one of her favourite themes, arguing that the MTFS would help to bring interest rates down. So in the end, as with the rise in VAT and the end of exchange controls, she went for it.[19]

The obvious thing to say about the MTFS is that, having published their targets, boasted about their rigour and congratulated themselves on their sense of responsibility, Howe and Lawson proceeded to miss every single one of them. Indeed, not only did they miss them, they overshot so wildly that, had they been medieval archers, their bows would have been confiscated for the safety of the people in the next village. In this sense, the MTFS was an utter failure. To give merely the most flagrant example, M3 growth in 1980–81 was supposed to be between 7 and 11 per cent. In fact, it was more than 18 per cent. The following year, it was supposed to be between 6 and 10 per cent. It came in at almost 13 per cent. Even in 1982–3, when the target was between 5 and 9 per cent, M3 growth was still more than 11 per cent. By this time, as the relatively sympathetic economics writer David Smith put it, the MTFS had become a 'laughing stock'. Even Lawson, not renowned for his humility, admitted that his scheme was 'never fulfilled in any literal sense'. That was certainly one way of putting it.[20]

What went wrong? The obvious answer is that the MTFS was simply incompatible with the government's other commitments. The point of the MTFS was to exert tight control over the money supply. Yet not only had Howe scrapped exchange controls, he had chosen his second Budget as the moment to get rid of the corset, a Bank of England scheme introduced in 1973 to discourage banks from lending too much money. With exchange controls gone and people able to borrow from foreign banks, the corset was completely redundant. All this was in perfect accordance with the government's free-market principles. Unfortunately, Britain's banks celebrated their liberation by loosening their purse strings. In just two months, their lending spree added not 3 per cent to the money supply, as the Bank of England had forecast, but 8 per cent. In a matter of weeks, the government's liberalization strategy had blown a hole in its monetary strategy. And this set the tone for what was to follow. In just two years after 1980, mortgage lending alone doubled from £7 billion to £14 billion. As for lending in general, it ballooned by 22 per cent in 1982, 17 per cent in 1983 and 18 per cent in 1984, before growing even faster later in the decade.[21]

Yet when Lawson claimed that 'in terms of its fundamental aims, the MTFS succeeded', he was not being entirely ridiculous. After all, the MTFS was meant to get both public borrowing and inflation down, and both *did* come down, only more slowly than he had hoped. The budget deficit fell from almost 6 per cent of GDP in 1980–81 to 3 per cent by 1984–5, and by the late 1980s Britain was running annual surpluses. As for inflation, the annual rate fell remarkably quickly after 1980, down from 16 per cent to 11 per cent, 9 per cent and 5 per cent in successive years. Much of this was attributable to high interest rates and high unemployment, but falling world commodity prices – especially oil – also had a lot to do with it. All the same, there is no denying that the government had done what it promised. It said it would get inflation down, no matter how high the price. It had certainly paid a high price. But it did get it down.[22]

In political terms, though, the government's abject failure to meet its own targets was beside the point. What mattered was that the targets existed at all. As the historian Jim Tomlinson points out, by turning the money supply figures into the be-all and end-all, Howe and Lawson were effectively shrugging off responsibility for unemployment. To reuse the medical metaphor, they had turned the money supply figures into the only meaningful indicator of the patient's health, while relegating unemployment to an unfortunate side effect.

But what was even more important was the MTFS's role as a public relations exercise. The very thing that had, ironically, worried Mrs Thatcher – its inflexibility – became a sign of her determination to stick to her guns. For by publishing the targets with such fanfare, and by promising not to abandon them, she and Howe had made it impossible for themselves to change course. 'My colleagues and I will not be deflected,' she told the Press Association a few weeks after the Budget. 'There will be no U-turns along this road. Please be very sure of that. We have a goal in sight, and we mean to achieve it.' Yet even now, in the face of all the evidence, the Wets still believed she was bound to change course. The odd thing is that, at the same time, they were always complaining about how stubborn she was.[23]

At the beginning of May, Mrs Thatcher celebrated the first anniversary of her arrival in Downing Street. Interviewing her to mark the occasion, the journalist Brian Connell found her the picture of 'relaxed ease', a 'trim and comely lady . . . composed and smiling' in her first-floor study. How was she coping with the pressure? 'I don't feel any sign of physical strain at all,' she said. 'I like it. I have a tremendous amount of energy and for the first time in my life it is fully used.' She relaxed, she said, by reading 'the John le Carré kind of thing, which I love', as well as 'biography and some philosophy and anything in connexion with the home. I love going through the *House and Garden* magazines, seeing what other people are doing who have time and money to do it.'

But most of their conversation focused on the economy. Once again Mrs Thatcher cast herself as a doctor, prescribing bitter medicine for the patient's own good. 'We have taken all the necessary steps and they will work through,' she said firmly. 'There's a time when you are still suffering from the disease and you take the medicine, and there is a time when you are suffering from both the disease and the medicine. That doesn't mean you stop the medicine, you know you have to take the medicine if you are to be cured of the disease.' So, Dr Thatcher explained, they had started cutting spending and were now, apparently, 'controlling the money supply': 'The immediate effect of that, I am afraid, is increased interest rates, just as sometimes the immediate effect of an antibiotic can be rather damaging to your digestive system.'

Connell asked if it was true that she was taking Britain back to the 1930s. 'Absolute poppycock,' she said. 'There is absolutely no comparison between today and the 1930s, none whatsoever.' It was true, she admitted, that 'unemployment will rise . . . You have to slim down industries like shipbuilding and steel to make them efficient, to be able to conserve the industry for the future and to let it expand again.' But she knew that ordinary people, deep down, were on her side. 'There's a tremendous individualistic streak in the British people . . . I think it is far better they are off my apron strings. You feel far more self respect, pride and responsibility when you do things yourself.'[24]

On the right, the anniversary of Mrs Thatcher's arrival was a moment for rejoicing. 'In one short year of power,' said the *Sunday Express*, 'Mrs Margaret Thatcher has stamped her personality on the whole of Britain, and captured the political imagination of the world. Not since the wartime years of Winston Churchill has a leader displayed so much aggression, such determination or such confidence . . . Margaret Thatcher has already restored the pride of Britain.' But the *Mirror*, speaking for her critics, took a very different view. 'After one year of power – Inflation 19.8% – Mortgages 15% – Jobless 1½ m – The REAL Face of BRITAIN', roared its front page, beside before-and-after pictures of a serene, fresh-faced Mrs Thatcher, taken in 1979, and a haggard, anxious Prime Minister in 1980.

Inside, the *Mirror* ran a full-page interview with Donald and Christine Kirby, a young Stevenage couple who a year earlier had voted Tory 'for the first – and last – time'. Donald was a skilled plater-welder, while Christine helped out in her parents' electronic dealership. They came from Labour families, Christine said, but were 'fed up with all the strikes during the winter and it looked like the unions were taking over. We wanted a change and we were sure things couldn't get worse.' But that only showed 'how wrong you can be'. Prices had gone up, Donald was paying £3 a week more in tax and her parents' business had ground to a halt. 'It's a joke really,' Donald said bitterly. 'I feel a right Charlie falling for that woman's promises.'

If anything, Christine was even more self-critical. When she listened to housewives complaining about the prices in the Co-op, she felt ashamed of herself:

> I know it's people like me to blame. Voting for that woman is one of the biggest mistakes I've ever made – and God knows I'm paying for it . . .
>
> You'd think she wasn't a woman at all. The price of school dinners has doubled. The kids have to wait longer to get into nursery school, and she has cut back on education.
>
> The kids used to have jumble sales to pay for extras at the school. Now it's to foot the bill for necessities . . . like books . . .
>
> I hate making the kids miss out. I just have to say 'Mummy's got no pennies' when they ask why.
>
> To me it's like Mrs Thatcher is the wife and the nation is the henpecked husband. And like in most families, the wife gets the final say.

So quite apart from the woes of the economy, there were two problems with Mrs Thatcher. She was like a nagging wife, and she wasn't a woman at all. And this was another woman talking.[25]

When, on 5 May, the SAS stormed the Iranian Embassy, the Prime Minister's second year seemed to have got off to the perfect start. But within days the cold rain of reality was falling once again, the headlines dominated by surging prices and closing factories. On 16 May the official inflation figure reached 21.8 per cent, higher than in any other member of the EEC, while the collapse of exports meant Britain's trade gap had widened to £264 million. 'Another milestone of misery', said a spokesman for the Trades Union Congress. The government made the usual noises about hard but necessary decisions. But for most people, said *The Times*, the reality was 'higher rates and rents, electricity and gas price rises, dearer transport and food'.[26]

By now the mood in Whitehall was grimmer than ever. Addressing the Conservative women's conference on 21 May, Mrs Thatcher quoted Sir Francis Drake before singeing the King of Spain's beard at Cadiz: 'When we endeavour any great matter it is not the beginning but the continuing of the same until it be thoroughly finished which yieldeth the true glory.' She would 'not stop', she said, 'however hard the road'. But her defiance was rather undermined by the fact that, earlier that day, John Biffen had told the same audience that in the 'next year or so' they would face a 'protracted winter of discontent', when they would need 'all the friends we have got'. Behind the scenes, Biffen was seriously worried about the economy, urging Howe to put income tax back up as soon as possible. Within Hoskyns's Policy Unit, too, there was a sense of real anguish. On 28 May, his colleague David Wolfson told him he was 'v. despairing about Margaret at present. Reads papers superficially, treats colleagues very badly, still overexcited by being PM, will not sit down and think about key issues. Prior and Co. simply registering their reservations for the record, but biding their time for a forced U-turn when she will have to resign.'[27]

In public, Mrs Thatcher talked of standing firm and staying the course. But even her closest supporters were wobbling badly. As Hoskyns recalled, he and his team were 'convinced that the monetary stance was too tight, while the fiscal stance had always been too loose'. They were paying the price, he thought, for Howe's first Budget, too lax and 'too rushed'. And as *The Times*'s Ronald Butt reported on 22 May, there was a growing consensus in the Commons, too, that Howe's 'own policies of raising VAT and high interest rates' had set off a bonfire of price rises, wage settlements and bank lending. Even some Tory MPs now believed they would have to strike an informal deal with the unions to keep wages down, just as the Wets had been saying for months. But the problem, as Butt noted, was that 'the Government could not get an incomes policy agreed with the unions [even] if it wanted', because the union leaders would demand so many concessions 'that the Conservatives might as well have never taken office'. In effect, then, they were stuck with the current approach, whether they liked it or not.[28]

Dreadful news had now become a daily ritual. On 23 May *The Times*'s lead story fell like a hammer-blow on the government's remaining supporters. 'Britain on the brink of slide into recession', read the headline, above a report that industry sources were expecting the worst slump since the Second World War. The pound had just hit its highest level against the dollar for five years, the respected *Economist* Intelligence Unit was forecasting unemployment of 2 million by the end of the year, and companies as diverse as ICI, GKN and Cadbury Schweppes had all issued profits warnings. A few weeks later, the *Mirror* ran a blistering front-page editorial. 'Britain is now in the worst slump since the 1930s,' it began. 'And it's only the beginning . . . There are few rays of hope anywhere. Not even North Sea oil can get the Tories out of it this time.'[29]

It was at this point, despite the horrendous inflation figures and soaring exchange rate, that a third issue began to dominate the headlines. Fear of mass unemployment had been gathering strength since the early 1970s, with the jobless total passing 1 million under Heath, falling under Wilson and then surging back above a million under Callaghan. Most observers had been anticipating a further increase ever since Mrs Thatcher's arrival in Downing Street. But it was not until in the summer of 1980 that they glimpsed the scale of what would become one of the defining issues of the age.

The tipping point came on 24 June, when Jim Prior announced that unemployment had jumped by 49,400 in a month, the biggest rise for almost five years. With some 6 per cent of the workforce officially out of work, the jobless total had reached 1.47 million, a post-war record. In the Commons, the news sparked uproar, the Speaker having to eject Labour's perennially irascible Dennis Skinner when he 'roared to his feet and began shouting incomprehensible things at Mr Prior'. At Prime Minister's Questions Mrs Thatcher insisted that since her priority was 'to squeeze inflation out of the economy, it is, sadly, inevitable that in the short run we shall suffer some unemployment'. But this only provoked so much shouting from the Labour benches that she could scarcely be heard above the din. 'For how long does the right hon. Lady propose to bask in that complacent air of hers?' Jim Callaghan asked bitterly. 'For how long does she think we can go on suffering? How much industry will be left by the time she thinks that she has conquered inflation?' Across the chamber, Conservative backbenchers howled with fury. But on the government benches, there were more than a few who agreed with him.

Even at this stage, many observers could barely credit the scale of the calamity. When, under Heath, unemployment had reached 1 million, the newspapers had treated it as a national disaster. Yet as an editorial in *The Times* warned on 25 June, the downturn made it almost certain that unemployment would pass 2 million in the first half of 1981 and keep rising until 1982 or even 1983. 'By that time it will have reached levels, 2½ or 3 million, that are quite without precedent in postwar experience.

It is impossible to predict the economic, social and political consequences of entering into this entirely uncharted terrain.' What worried the paper most were the implications for Britain's youngsters, the boys and girls who would once have expected to walk into jobs in local factories. 'The potential damage to social attitudes and the social fabric of this situation', it said, 'cannot be over-estimated.' The government must direct resources to find jobs for Britain's teenagers, though what those might be *The Times* did not say. Otherwise, 'the nation will reap a bitter harvest of alienation, even violence, in the rising generation of adults'.[30]

A few weeks later, some 820,000 teenagers were due to leave school. But with 108,700 boys and girls under the age of 18 already out of work, their prospects were bleak. In interviews, they spoke again and again of the shock and demoralization at finding themselves on the scrapheap so young, as well as their fury at being dismissed as failures or scroungers. In Surrey, job vacancies had fallen by 60 per cent in a year, while youth unemployment was up by 40 per cent. In King's Lynn, the Gaywood Park comprehensive was teaching teenagers how to sign on – not unreasonably, given that the town already had 500 unemployed youngsters and just eleven vacancies. And when a new Sheffield boutique, Jeanery, advertised in the local paper for shop assistants, its owners were astonished to find almost 500 people waiting outside the next morning. Most were teenagers; some had degrees; such was their desperation that many had been waiting for two hours. 'It was a sad sight,' said one of the directors, 'but it was quite impossible for us to interview all of them . . . You could call it a queue of despair.'[31]

'Where there is despair, may we bring hope.' Such had been Mrs Thatcher's words, just over a year earlier. Yes, she had promised to take difficult but necessary decisions, but as the columnist David Wood pointed out, there had been no talk during the election of 'bitter medicine'. The British people had not been invited to vote for high inflation, collapsing exports and a catastrophic recession; 'they believed, and were encouraged to believe, that their life would be better'. Yet when the next set of unemployment figures were released on 22 July, they showed that a further 71,000 people had lost their jobs, taking the total to 1.6 million, the highest since records began in 1948. When school-leavers were included, the total jumped to 1.9 million, a level not seen since the 1930s.

On the front page of *The Times*, Mel Calman's cartoon showed three men waiting in line. 'Is this the queue for the Thirties?' one asks. In the Commons, Mrs Thatcher insisted that Britain was paying a tragically high price for the mistakes of the past. In Liverpool, the careers office had 6,907 registered job seekers and just five jobs. How did that campaign slogan go again? 'Don't just hope for a better life. Vote for one . . .'[32]

# PART TWO

# I Have Forgotten the Rest of the Trick

# 9

# Your Boys Took a Hell of a Beating

*When they go abroad they represent Britain and it is up to them to back up jolly good teams to show the best of Britain and not to show her in the worst light. It was a very dark day when that happened.*

Margaret Thatcher, speaking after the
European Council, 13 June 1980

*The deep blue, smoky, specifically November air resounds to a huge, joyous, rhythmic bark of 'You're-gonna-get-your-fuckin'-'eads kicked-in.'*

Lincoln Allison, *Condition of England:
Essays and Impressions* (1981)

On Thursday 5 June 1980, Mrs Thatcher's schedule was typically frenetic. Meetings all morning, Cabinet at eleven, Prime Minister's Questions in the Commons – and then the first of two unusual and memorable engagements. The finance minister of Argentina, José Alfredo Martínez de Hoz, was in town, and Mrs Thatcher was keen to hear his thoughts about the difficulties of implementing a monetarist economic strategy.

'The first year was quite easy, years two and three the most difficult, year four the first when really impressive results became apparent,' Martínez de Hoz told her, adding that it was 'vital not to change course or let up'. That, of course, was music to Mrs Thatcher's ears. But in his record of the conversation, her junior minister Nicholas Ridley noted three differences between Britain and Argentina. 'They started from an infinitely worse position,' he wrote. 'They had infinite difficulty in changing the expectations of people that inflation was going to continue.' Finally, and most importantly: 'We are a democracy, and they are not.'[1]

Just over an hour later, Mrs Thatcher welcomed a very different group of guests to Number 10. After ten years in the international wilderness, England's footballers had qualified for the finals of a major tournament, the European Championships in Italy, and Mrs Thatcher had invited the squad for drinks before they flew out. Some of the younger players were obviously overawed. 'I was very shy back then and a little tongue-tied,' the full-back Kenny Sansom recalled. 'On meeting the Prime Minister, what do you say?' But Southampton's burly central defender Dave Watson remembered the occasion more fondly. 'She seemed to take a liking to me for some reason, and came over and took hold of my hand,' he remembered. 'Suddenly we were off on this excursion. She showed me these paintings of the ex-Prime Ministers that were hanging on the walls and gave me their history. It was very enjoyable – we didn't talk football at all.'[2]

For the oldest player in the squad, the trip to Number 10 was a chance to rekindle an old friendship. Four years earlier, Mrs Thatcher had made a trip to Anfield, striking up an unlikely rapport with Liverpool's captain, the ebullient Emlyn Hughes. They got on so well that in February 1978 she sent him a handwritten letter congratulating him on victory over Manchester United in the FA Cup. Among tens of thousands of documents in her personal and political papers, this is surely the most unexpected:

Dear Mr Hughes,

A note to say how much I rejoiced with you in your victory last Saturday against Manchester United. I watched it on 'Match of the Day' but without knowing the result. At first it was agony seeing the near misses – almost as bad for me watching as for you playing! But at least I only had the tension for half an hour before getting the result I was longing for.

No reply – you will be far too busy preparing for the next round of the European Cup. Very good luck.

Yours sincerely,
Margaret Thatcher

It is worth repeating that this was written by hand, not typed by some football-loving adviser. Did Mrs Thatcher really sit through *Match of the Day*? Was she really 'longing' for a Liverpool victory? Of all the roles she played in her political career, that of the fervent Liverpool fan, mentally swaying on the Kop in her red-and-white scarf, is surely the most implausible of all.[3]

Yet as Hughes's England teammates sipped their drinks in Number 10, many were surprised by the Prime Minister's enthusiasm. According to some reports, she climbed on to a chair, as if channelling Elizabeth I, and told the players: 'We shall love you if you win, and we shall still love you if you lose.' Afterwards, as the players lined up for photographs, Hughes and the England captain, Kevin Keegan, persuaded Mrs Thatcher to pose with a football while they gave her a kiss, a gesture she would never have tolerated from the Argentine finance minister. In the next day's papers, she was pictured grinning self-consciously, while Hughes and Keegan doubled over with laughter. Years later, the photographer David Levenson remembered that as soon as the Prime Minister picked up the football, Hughes said: 'I bet you wish you could grab hold of Arthur Scargill's balls like that!' Levenson recalled her 'looking bemused', but the photos show her with a definite smile. There was an omen there, if only Scargill had known it.[4]

With the winds of recession whipping through the factories of industrial Britain, the prospect of victory in the Italian sunshine came as a welcome tonic. For ten years England's fans had endured a succession of disappointments. But now millions dared to hope that their heroes might rekindle the spirit of 1966 and return home decked with glory. Even the manager, Ron Greenwood, seemed a throwback to a vanished age, a decent, schoolmasterly man who had grown up wearing clogs in Burnley, left school at 14 and begun his working life as an apprentice sign-writer. And as Greenwood prepared to take on Europe's finest, the *Daily Express*'s David Miller joined many of his fellow writers in predicting that the manager's 'lonely crusade to change the face of English football' would end in triumph. 'By that achievement, with the style Greenwood has promoted,' he wrote, 'England would have done more for the world of football than any team other than Hungary, Brazil or Holland.' This was high praise indeed, given that their tournament had not even started.[5]

As England's opening game approached, optimism surged to new heights. Watching the players fly out from Luton 'in marvellously confident mood', the *Mirror*'s Frank McGhee thought they had 'all the calm authority of young executives departing for a sales conference', a slightly odd compliment, but a compliment nonetheless. And the *Sunday Express*'s James Mossop, too, foresaw that their courage, skill and patriotic enthusiasm would propel them to glory. 'The spirit and willingness of Greenwood's team is greater than I have ever known it,' he explained. 'No player in the tournament will work harder than Steve Coppell or Keegan. Few will display the vision, craft and authority of Ray Wilkins and Trevor Brooking . . . By Sunday evening, June 22, they could be standing in the Olympic Stadium in Rome as champions of Europe.'[6]

In the early evening of 12 June, with millions watching at home, Greenwood's men walked out into the sunshine in Turin for their opening game against the unfancied Belgians. When Ray Wilkins put them ahead with a lob of exquisite delicacy, it seemed as if the patriotic predictions might, for once, be realized. Three minutes later, however, Belgium equalized, and then grim reality came crashing down. On the crumbling terraces of the Stadio Comunale, where a paltry 15,186 fans had paid to see the game, the Belgian goal was the cue for bedlam. As Frank McGhee put it, 'the louts and drunks who defile the Union Jack they wrap around themselves immediately started hitting out at any neutral who happened to be handy'.

As bottles rained down from the terraces, the riot policemen waded in, first with batons and then with tear gas. On television, pictures showed hundreds of fans, including Italian women and children, wiping tears from their eyes. What was worse, as clouds of yellow smoke drifted on to the field, some of the England players were clearly affected, waving for help as tears streamed down their cheeks. Eventually the referee led both teams off the pitch, and although play restarted eight minutes later, any sense of innocent excitement had long since disappeared. At half-time, with running battles continuing in the stands, an official read a message from Greenwood over the public address system: 'You are doing the chances of the England team and the reputation of England no good at all. Please, please behave yourselves.'[7]

What happened in Turin that evening could hardly have been a more humiliating indictment of English football. On television, the former World Cup winner Bobby Charlton told viewers that he was 'certainly not proud to be British right now', while Kevin Keegan, interviewed after the match, said he was 'ashamed to be English'. Greenwood, too, said he felt ashamed of his own supporters. 'We have done everything to create the right impression here, then these bastards let you down,' he said bluntly. 'I wish they could all be put in a boat and dropped in the ocean . . . The Italians must think we are idiots.'

Plastered with pictures of the weeping England players and the chaos on the terraces, the next day's front pages made for excruciating reading. In the *Mirror*, an editorial drew attention to Charlton's words, adding that 'he spoke from the heart and he spoke for us all'. There was talk of kicking England out of the tournament, and the mayor of Turin warned that their next match, against Italy, would be cancelled if there was more trouble. One travel agent claimed that some England fans, frightened by the backlash, were holed up in their hotel rooms and refusing to come out, while a BBC team were turned away from a Turin restaurant when the owner found out where they were from. 'Life', the *Guardian*'s correspondent dolefully reported, 'has become something of an ordeal for other Britons in Turin.'[8]

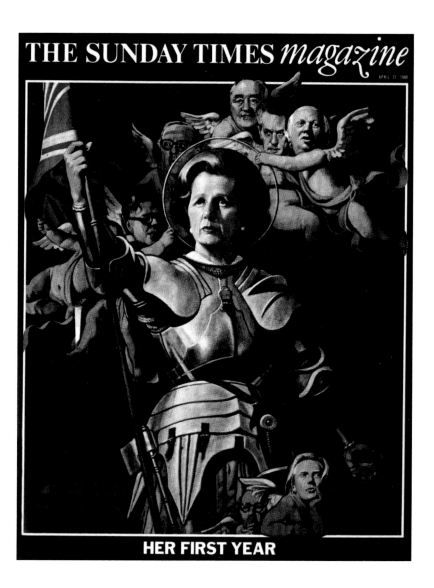

THE SUNDAY TIMES *magazine*

APRIL 27 1980

**HER FIRST YEAR**

1. To her admirers, Margaret Thatcher was Britain's warrior queen, leading the nation into a bold new era. Yet by the time the *Sunday Times Magazine* ran this extraordinary cover, Britain was in recession, the cherubs were in revolt and her armour looked distinctly rusty.

2. The new Britain. *Above*, the pleasures of *Asteroids*, 1982. *Below*, New Romantics model their exciting hairstyles.

3. The old Britain. *Above*, holidaymakers enjoy a summer's day in Skegness. *Below*, delegates at Labour's tumultuous Brighton conference, 1981.

4. By the autumn of 1980, Mrs Thatcher's brave new world looked like an unmitigated disaster. *Top*, Jim Prior keeps his distance at the Conservative party conference. *Above*, Sir Geoffrey Howe and Lord Carrington do their best to look supportive.

5. These were terrible years for British industry. *Top left*, British Leyland's Michael Edwardes polishes his Austin Metro; *top right*, Derek Robinson puts a brave face on his dismissal. *Above*, striking South Wales steelworkers give their verdict on the Thatcher experiment.

6. As the recession deepened, an entire generation seemed destined for the scrapheap. *Above*, unemployed youngsters outside a derelict factory in Billingham, Teesside. *Below*, the dole queue in a south London social security office.

7. The stuff of nightmares. Few people were reassured by the *Protect and Survive* booklet, *above left*, let alone by the mordant humour of the peace movement's *Gone with the Wind* parody, *above right*. Little wonder, then, that tens of thousands joined CND's march in London in October 1981, *below*.

8. Sport as a window into the national soul. Visiting Turin for the 1980 European Championships, England's football hooligans do their best to charm the locals, *top*. But snooker's Steve Davis strikes a rather more family-friendly pose on *Tiswas*, *above*.

For Mrs Thatcher, the banter on the steps of Number 10 now seemed a very painful memory. By a hideous mischance, she too had been in Italy that evening, attending a meeting of the European Council in Venice. And since she was still trying to win her famous budget rebate, her country-men's misbehaviour could hardly have been more embarrassing. When she met the press the next day, she was visibly angry. The fans' behaviour, she said, was 'disgraceful', not least because they had betrayed their own players. 'They are a splendid team and I think most of them stand for all that is best in Britain and I understand that it would have been extremely embarrassing for them – anything that fell below the best of British stand-ards. I can't speak too strongly about it.'[9]

During the 1970s and 1980s, when no weekend seemed complete with-out news of some railway-station riot, there were always those who claimed that hooliganism was blown out of all proportion by reactionary politicians and exploitative journalists. This view was not shared by the correspondents who had seen the fighting in Italy at first hand. As the *Observer*'s Hugh McIlvanney pointed out, the scenes in Turin were merely the latest in a long line of horrific incidents abroad, including the 'attempted sacking of Barcelona by a contingent of the Glasgow Rangers infantry' in 1972, the 'assault on Rotterdam by Tottenham fans' in 1974, the rioting by Leeds fans at the European Cup final in Paris in 1975 and an outbreak of hooliganism by England fans in Luxembourg in 1977. Of course other countries' fans were not perfect; still, McIlvanney thought Britain was unrivalled 'as the world's leading exporter of football hooligans', whose arrival overseas was 'only marginally more welcome than consignments of the Black Death'. Perhaps it was just as well, then, that the predictions of English glory turned out to be completely misguided, since Greenwood's side lost their next match and came home after the group stage. 'We'll Fight Back', promised the *Mirror*. Given what had happened in Turin, it was not the best choice of words.[10]

What had happened in Turin was not an unfortunate aberration; it was part of a depressing trend. Probably the best-known England match of this period came just over a year later, in September 1981, when they were humiliated 2–1 in Oslo in a World Cup qualifier. It was this result that inspired the local commentator, Bjørge Lillelien, to deliver one of the most famous tirades in sporting history, and certainly the only example of Norwegian television that most people in Britain have ever heard of:

*Vi har slått England! England, kjempers fødeland!* [We have beaten England! England, birthplace of giants!] Lord Nelson, Lord Beaverbrook, Sir Winston Churchill, Sir Anthony Eden, Clement Attlee, Henry Cooper,

Lady Diana, *vi har slått dem alle sammen, vi har slått dem alle sammen!*
[We have beaten them all, we have beaten them all!] Maggie Thatcher, can
you hear me? Maggie Thatcher! . . . Your boys took a hell of a beating!
Your boys took a hell of a beating!*

Amazingly, this outburst was later chosen by the Norwegian Arts Council
to represent their country's contribution to mankind's cultural heritage.
Still, Greenwood's men managed to scrape through the group, while Norway finished bottom. So, although nobody remembers it this way, Lord
Nelson and Lord Beaverbrook had the last laugh.[11]

In the public mind, the match in Oslo was that relative rarity, an England game that made the headlines for what happened on the pitch rather
than off it. Rather more typical was a trip to Basle three months earlier:
another 2–1 defeat, memorable this time for the reaction of the travelling
fans. The *Mirror*'s front page captured the mood:

### A STAB IN THE BACK FOR BRITAIN

In the Battle of Basle, a youth stabs a rival in the back and shames his
nation.

All around him hooligans wearing the colours of England and carrying
Union Jacks were punching and kicking anyone within reach.

The battle started after Switzerland scored twice against England in
Saturday's World Cup qualifying game. The mixture of drink and looming
defeat sent the thugs wild.

England's outraged soccer chiefs are now threatening to ban all fans –
good and bad – from following the team.

They fear this could be the only way to stop the Union Jack becoming
an emblem of shame in Europe.

Even allowing for exaggeration, the so-called 'Battle of Basle' was a genuinely shameful moment for English football. Only 2,000 fans had travelled
to Switzerland, yet they caused mayhem, looting a jeweller's shop and
ransacking a pub in the city centre before the game. During the match
they not only attacked dumbfounded Swiss supporters but battered a
security man with – of all things – a Union Jack flagpole. The Football
Association complained that their hosts should have made more stringent
preparations, yet this was the first match in Swiss history to which the

---

* It has to be said that this is quite an odd list. Nelson, Churchill and Diana were obvious
choices, and Eden and Attlee make some sort of sense. Even Henry Cooper was still quite
famous. But Lord Beaverbrook? Lillelien had once studied journalism. Perhaps he had specialized in the history of the *Daily Express*.

local police had brought tear gas and dogs. It was clear, though, that the long-serving FA secretary, Ted Croker, was tired of apologizing for his countrymen. 'Personally,' he said, 'I don't care if we have no more support away from home.'[12]

In the meantime, Fleet Street's leader writers wrung their hands with exquisite distress. 'The nation that gave football to the world can now only give it the football hooligan,' said the *Mirror*. 'We leave our mark in Europe not through the skill of our players but by the riots, wreckage, vandalism, arrests and deportations of those who follow them.' The Union Jack, agreed the *Express*, had become a 'flag of shame', while the *Guardian*'s Patrick Barclay thought that 'the events in Turin and Basle . . . verged on international incidents [which] went beyond football'. He blamed 'the emergence in recent years of a disagreeable, pseudo-patriotic strand in British society or, to be more precise, English society'.

There was a lot of truth in this. Nobody who had watched England play since 1966, or who had read the tabloids during the long years of strikes and stagflation, could have failed to notice that the disappointments of the age had given rise to a peculiarly joyless kind of patriotism, shot through with surly resentment. Visitors to Wembley invariably found that the atmosphere had become a cross between Hogarth's *Gin Lane* and a Bavarian beer hall in the early 1920s, the bleak concrete terraces lined with 'crop-headed, thick-necked men' who sang 'mind-bogglingly obscene' patriotic songs and gave 'drunken Nazi salutes' during the national anthem. As McIlvanney remarked, it was as if 'the Brits, having been swept into a corner economically and politically, are currently afflicted with a national sense of inadequacy that includes among its cruder manifestations a tendency to kick foreigners in the testicles'.[13]

But Barclay was right to identify this as a peculiarly English, rather than British, phenomenon. When the World Cup kicked off in Spain in 1982, no fewer than three teams from the United Kingdom had qualified. As was traditional, the Scots crashed out in the first round, while Northern Ireland performed splendidly to defeat the hosts. Yet among thousands of travelling fans from Scotland and Northern Ireland, a mere handful were arrested, usually after drink had been taken. Even in defeat, wrote one reporter, Scotland's fans 'danced, dived into ornamental fountains, performed highland flings and gathered around the pipers to sing themselves hoarse'. But 'there was no trouble', and in Malaga, where the Scots played their final game, they were so popular that 'thousands of men, women and children' came to see them off, 'waving tartan scarves and lion rampant flags'.[14]

The contrast with the Scots' southern counterparts was, from an

English perspective, painful to behold. Once again England arrived in Spain with genuine hopes of winning the competition. Once again optimism gave way to inevitable disappointment, as, after a promising start, Greenwood's men fizzled out with two goalless draws. And once again their fans made themselves thoroughly unpopular. With victory in the Falklands having been secured a few days earlier, many Englishmen arrived wearing T-shirts with the legend 'World Cup Task Force 82', and sang 'Argentina, Argentina, what's it like to lose a war?' The people of Bilbao, wrote the *Observer*'s Robert Low, had 'looked forward to welcoming the English because of their historic links with us'. But they would 'not be sorry to see the last of the massed gangs of yobs swathed in Union Jacks, after the familiar trail of broken bar windows, assaults, abuse and unpaid drink bills'.

The really depressing thing was that, by now, broken windows and late-night brawls had become so routine that most papers barely reported them. Even the relentlessly nationalistic songs provoked remarkably little comment back home. As Low mordantly put it, 'Jingoism rules OK.' By the time they left, sodden with drink and scorched by the sun, England's fans had made themselves no friends at all. And that, of course, was precisely how they liked it.[15]

'Football matters,' wrote Lincoln Allison in his book *Condition of England* (1981). 'It is part of the fabric of English life in many different ways. It affects the hopes, dreams and the sense of personal identity of the millions who follow it and gamble on it and the hundreds of thousands who play it or watch it "live".' There were millions, of course, who hated football, or were simply indifferent to it. Yet for those who loved the national game, it often provided a public narrative far more meaningful than anything that happened at Westminster. It was the supreme expression of the 'identity, the loyalty and solidarity' of countless working-class communities, from Aberdeen and Arbroath to Bolton and Blackburn. And in the eyes of the press, football acted as a mirror, reflecting society as it coped with political and cultural change. When a united Great Britain team thrashed the Rest of Europe in 1947, it was a reminder that British was best. When England won the World Cup in 1966, the celebrations became part of the rose-tinted legend of the Swinging Sixties. And so, when hooligans ran riot in Basle and Turin, it was hardly surprising that so many people saw it as a damning reflection of the state of the nation.[16]

Football, as Allison pointed out, was a living link with the Victorian past, dominated by teams playing 'in the same competition, to the same rules, on the same grounds and in the same colours as they did three generations ago'. So perhaps it was fitting that, with so many Victorian institutions crumbling beneath the juggernaut of economic change, the Victorian game was in such a wretched condition. In the late 1940s, the high point of the game's popularity as a national spectacle, the Football League had sold more than 40 million tickets a season. Yet, by 1982, the total had fallen below 20 million for the first time in living memory, reaching a nadir of just 16½ million four years later. Once, football had been the 'working man's ballet', but now the working man had better things to do on a Saturday. Affluence and mobility had eaten away at the old loyalties; as the *Guardian* remarked in April 1980, 'television provides rival attractions, and the private car gives people opportunities to pursue other interests which were undreamt of by our grandfathers'. Indeed, at the turn of the 1980s it was hard to open a newspaper without coming across an obituary for football as a national pastime. In the future, predicted the paper's David Lacey, 'soccer will inevitably become less of a mass entertainment and more of an occasional diversion'.[17]

Football was not alone in struggling to hold on to its traditional adherents. Rugby clubs, cricket counties, even pubs and churches faced similar challenges; for every football chairman agonizing over his empty stands, there were plenty of vicars contemplating rows of deserted pews. But what made football's decline so compelling was that it was accelerated by fears of hooliganism. Later, some fans, reacting against the alleged corporate corruption of the Premier League, tried to rehabilitate the 1970s and 1980s as a lost golden age of the industrial working-class game, with an honesty and vibrancy that have now been lost. But this is absolutely not how it appeared at the time.[18]

Take, for example, what happened on the first Saturday in September 1980, only a few weeks after England's disgrace in Turin. In many respects it was a typical Saturday in the football calendar. Even the disturbances at Chelsea's match against West Ham, where forty-two fans were arrested, were really just par for the course. Yet they were driven off the back pages by events at Second Division Oldham, who were hosting Sheffield Wednesday. Enraged by a contentious sending-off, the visiting fans 'tore lumps of concrete out of the terraces to use as ammunition', clambered over the fences and invaded the pitch, causing a half-hour delay until the police restored order. What was really shocking, though, was that when Wednesday's manager, the former World Cup winner Jack Charlton, went on to the pitch to remonstrate with his fans, they attacked him, too. When he walked off the field, he wept.

'The last time a Charlton eye shed a tear in public', observed David Lacey, 'was during England's moment of triumph at the end of the 1966

World Cup final'. That happy hour seemed so distant that it might as well have happened in the reign of Queen Victoria. Back in 1966, Charlton had been renowned as one of the hardest men in English football, yet now he had been reduced to tears by his own fans. 'All these rats make me sick,' he explained afterwards. 'When I cried at Oldham I did not cry just for football – I cried for all the innocent people who are not connected with the game. I cried for the mothers and fathers who took their children out of the ground. Supporters who will be lost to the game.'[19]

Eleven days later, West Ham were in Madrid to play in the European Cup Winners' Cup. The club had done its utmost to deter potential troublemakers from travelling. Members of the official supporters' club had been asked to submit photos and passport details when they applied for tickets, and the captain, Billy Bonds, had signed a letter to every ticket-holder begging them to behave. But it was the same old story: fighting on the terraces, baton charges by the police, 'waves of fleeing spectators . . . scrambling across the distant terraces'. The West Ham fans, as was traditional, insisted that they were completely blameless and had been provoked by the police. But the British press corps told a different story. 'It is beyond reason', thought *The Times*'s correspondent, 'that a human being can travel so far, supposedly in support of his club, and before the echo of the first whistle of a potentially memorable evening has died away start to urinate from a balcony on to the crowd below.' As punishment, West Ham were ordered to play the return leg behind closed doors. But as Bonds remarked, it was only a matter of time before the European football authorities decided, 'That's it, we've had enough,' and banned English clubs for good. As it turned out, it took them less than five years.[20]

Most fans were not hooligans. As the novelist Nick Hornby later recalled, football crowds in the early 1980s included 'actors and publicity girls and teachers and accountants and doctors and nurses, as well as salt-of-the-earth working-class men in caps and loud-mouthed thugs'. But as Hornby's book *Fever Pitch* (1992) makes very clear, hooliganism was a reality, not an invented panic. Violence was more common, he thinks, in the early 1970s ('that is to say, there was fighting more or less every week'), but by the 1980s it had become 'less predictable and much nastier', with police regularly confiscating 'knives and machetes and other weapons I did not recognise, things with spikes coming out of them'. It was too easy to dismiss hooliganism as a 'moral panic', agreed the historian James Walvin in *Football and the Decline of Britain* (1986), written after the Heysel disaster. 'The problem of hooliganism among fans is a real one; the behaviour of certain sections of fans has changed, has become more violent, more abusive (and more racist).'[21]

Anyone who thinks hooliganism was invented by the tabloids to frighten the middle classes ought to read the coverage in liberal newspapers such as the *Guardian* and the *Observer*. Here, for example, is the opening of a feature by the *Guardian*'s Robert Armstrong in December 1979:

> Violence threatens in many forms at a football match. Bricks, bottles, belts, darts, coins, combs, knives and boots are some of the better-known objects that can be transformed into a lethal weapon and used to maim or even kill. Serious injury can also befall the innocent bystander caught up in a police charge or swept against the crush barriers or trampled underfoot when the crowd surges forward to get a better view of the goal . . .
>
> Many supporters, especially those over 35, have drawn their own conclusion: avoid a broken head by staying at home and watching *Grandstand*. Others will only turn up if they can lay their hands on stand tickets. A few adopt the strategy of avoiding the terraces behind the goals – the time-honoured rendezvous of the young Turks the press love to hate. Violence can, of course, take place outside or well away from the ground on the day of a match and no one can be sure of avoiding the random incident.

As Armstrong observed, the clubs always denied that hooligans were 'true supporters'. But all the evidence showed that 'the aggressors are drawn from those hard-core supporters who never miss a match, home or away'. It was a myth, therefore, that violence was an alien intrusion that had inexplicably seeped into football's bloodstream. By the early 1980s violence was an indelible part of the game.

Armstrong thought football was suffering from the same disease that had blighted British industry since the Second World War: a catastrophic lack of capital investment, which had left many stadiums little better than overcrowded slums, their crumbling terraces left open to the elements, their fans fenced in like animals in a zoo. And in stark contrast to modern writers who romanticize the lost world of scarves, rattles and Inter-City football specials, he saw nothing romantic in the squalid surroundings and Stone Age violence of Saturday afternoons. Even the transport facilities, he pointed out, were often abysmal. Since supporters smashed up the carriages and tore out the toilets, British Rail had taken to corralling them in dilapidated trains without any facilities at all. 'The sight of overweight 16-year-olds tanking up on canned lager on a British Rail Away-day', he wrote, 'should convince club chairmen that there is nothing sacred about a day out at a game of football.'[22]

Few subjects provoked so much debate in the early 1980s as football hooliganism. If you went to watch Millwall, people joked, you were more

likely to find yourself standing next to a group of sociology lecturers on
a field trip than a mob of working-class hooligans on the rampage. Yet
there were as many competing explanations as there were hooligans. The
right often blamed permissive morality and progressive education: the
*Daily Express*, for instance, thought hooliganism merely 'an extension of
an ugly thread that runs through modern society, which so fashionably
spurns the virtues of restraint and self-discipline and glamorises aggression and selfishness'. *The Times*, too, thought 'society has created the
football hooligan', since 'football violence is only a part of the much wider
problem of growing juvenile crime'. And the game's authorities were often
quick to deflect blame on to society at large. The problem, explained the
new FA chairman Bert Millichip in the autumn of 1981, was that football
had been infiltrated by 'skinheads and bovver boys'. And when, after the
Heysel disaster four years later, Mrs Thatcher summoned football's top
brass and demanded to know what they were going to do about their
hooligans, the FA secretary Ted Croker immediately hit back. 'These
people are society's problems', he allegedly replied, 'and we don't want
*your* hooligans in *our* sport, Prime Minister.'[23]

The words '*your* hooligans' went down very well with Mrs Thatcher's
critics, many of whom saw football violence as a reaction to her supposedly
brutal assault on the working class. But if so, why did hooliganism first
become a serious problem in the mid-1960s, when wages were high and
unemployment was virtually unknown? If the young men who rampaged
across Europe in the 1980s were Mrs Thatcher's hooligans, does that mean
the Leeds fans who rioted at the 1975 European Cup final were Harold
Wilson's hooligans? As for the argument that hooliganism reflected sys-
temic poverty, this too was very dubious. When Thames Television
interviewed 140 members of West Ham's 'Inter City Firm' in the mid-
1980s, they found four chefs, three electricians, three clothes-makers, six
motor mechanics, two solicitors' clerks, a landscape gardener and an insurance underwriter. The idea that they were venting their anger at Thatcherite
economics is patently ridiculous. In any case, as Lincoln Allison wondered
in 1981, 'why didn't it happen in more deprived times? Why doesn't it happen in more deprived places? Anyway, how come the deprived masses show
up in places like Madrid and Turin, more belligerent than before when
faced with the sight of foreigners and inflamed by cheap booze?'[24]

Perhaps surprisingly, very few football writers associated hooliganism
with unemployment or economic deprivation. Even in the left-leaning
broadsheets, most thought ultimate responsibility lay with football itself,
not the government. The *Guardian*'s Patrick Barclay, for example, lambasted
the 'bleating chairmen who seek to opt out of their social responsibility',

and insisted that hooliganism was 'a problem for football to solve rather than "society"'.* Chairmen and officials, agreed the *Observer*'s Hugh McIlvanney, had spent far too long blaming football's ills on society in general instead of taking responsibility for their own game. They should be 'obliged to take direct responsibility for offenders attracted to their colours, and, if necessary, should be punished with closures until there is definite improvement'.[25]

The truth is that, as a spectator sport attracting tens of thousands of young men, football had always carried the germ of hooliganism. There had been hooligans as long as there had been crowds: as the historian Geoffrey Pearson wrote in 1983, the 'modern football rowdy' was simply 'a reincarnation of the unruly apprentice, or the late Victorian "Hooligan"'. Even in the supposedly law-abiding 1950s, as Arthur Hopcraft noted in his classic *The Football Man* (1968), 'trains, carrying rampaging young fans, would end their journeys with windows broken, upholstery smashed, lavatory fittings broken, the carriages running with beer and crunching underfoot with broken glass like gravel'. Back then, though, teenage vandals had been vastly outnumbered by older men. Later, fans remembered that if they stepped out of line, their fathers had given them 'a bloody good hiding'. But as working-class supporters began to share in the fruits of affluence, the crowds changed. Instead of taking the bus to watch their local team, married men stayed at home, took their wives shopping or went out for drives and day-trips. As crowds dwindled, the fans misbehaved and gate receipts fell, clubs stopped investing in their grounds. And so football violence became a self-fulfilling prophecy. The fans behaved badly; the authorities treated them badly. The authorities treated them like animals; they behaved like animals.[26]

But what did they get out of it? What demons, what resentments, drove them on? The most persuasive answers came from, of all people, an American student. One cold Saturday evening in 1982 a young man called Bill Buford was waiting for a train in a village station outside Cardiff. Buford had lived in England for almost five years, having moved from California after winning a postgraduate scholarship to King's College, Cambridge. He had never been to a football match. On the platform, he sipped his tea, while beside him a man leafed through his newspaper. It was a 'misty, sleepy, Welsh winter evening'. All was quiet. And then, suddenly, a train roared in.

---

* With those mocking quotation marks, we are perilously close to 'no such thing as society' territory here – and in the *Guardian*, of all places!

One moment, Buford had been lost in a melancholic reverie. The next, he was staring at a scene worthy of Hieronymus Bosch:

> The train was a football special, and it had been taken over by supporters. They were from Liverpool, and there were hundreds of them – I had never seen a train with so many people inside – and they were singing in unison: 'Liverpool, la-la-la, Liverpool, la-la-la' . . . pounded out with increasing ferocity, echoing off the walls of the station. A guard had been injured, and as the train stopped he was rushed off, holding his face. Someone inside was trying to smash a window with a table leg, but the window wouldn't break. A fat man with a red face stumbled out of one of the carriages, and six policemen rushed up to him, wrestled him to the ground and bent his arm violently behind his back . . .
>
> The train left. It was silent.*

At the time, Buford was convinced that 'the violence was a protest . . . a rebellion of some kind – social rebellion, class rebellion, something', which was what his Cambridge friends believed. To his surprise, though, none of them regarded his story as particularly shocking. 'It was one of the things you put up with,' he wrote: 'that every Saturday young males trashed your trains, broke the windows of your pubs, destroyed your cars, wreaked havoc on your town centres.' This, after all, was England.[27]

For Buford, whose experience of American sporting events was utterly different, all this seemed at first horrifying, then weirdly fascinating and at last exhilarating. He went to one match, then another. He joined a group of hard-core Manchester United fans and travelled to Turin for the European Cup Winners' Cup semi-final. He joined them in fighting fans from Chelsea, Tottenham and West Ham; he went away with England; he even went to the World Cup. As he wrote in his memoir *Among the Thugs* (1991), the experience of the terraces was like 'alcohol or tobacco: disgusting, at first; pleasurable, with effort; addictive, over time'. And because he was the last person you would expect to be interested in football violence, his account of life among the hooligans was all the more gripping.

The people he met were not the kind of people he had expected. His first real contact, for example, was a man called Mick, a Manchester United fan with a 'fat, flat bulldog face', his arms stained with tattoos of

---

* Buford gives no date for this incident. But the clues (a cold Saturday evening, after Liverpool had played in South Wales) suggest it was either 2 January 1982, when Swansea hosted them in the FA Cup, or 18 September 1982, when the two sides met in the First Division.

a Red Devil and the Union Jack. Here was a classic hooligan, steeped in alcohol and simmering with aggression. But to Buford's surprise, 'he was not unemployed or, it seemed, in any way disenfranchised'. Quite the reverse: Mick was a 'perfectly happy, skilled electrician from Blackpool', who paid for his drinks with a large wad of £20 notes. On a typical Saturday following Manchester United, he might spend around £60, more than most unskilled manual workers earned in a week. When Buford met him, he had just spent £155 on a package tour to follow United to Turin, the equivalent of at least £500 today. Whatever else he was, Mick was not a man protesting against social deprivation.[28]

In Buford's experience, Mick turned out to be pretty typical. Many hard-core supporters 'had their lives remarkably well sorted out – at least financially'. Travelling to Turin, Buford found himself alongside a lawyer and another electrician, this time from Cambridgeshire. Later, collecting articles about men convicted of football-related offences, he found himself reading about a successful self-employed decorator, a man who ran his own courier business, a solicitor's clerk, a chef, a builder and a former Royal Navy submariner. In a Yates's Wine Lodge, Buford met another electrician, Steve, who lived in the suburban south-east, was married to a hairdresser and was about to buy his first house. Steve owned a 'colour television, an expensive camera, a video player, a car, a van, CD and stereo equipment'. In many ways he was the self-reliant, entrepreneurial young man of Mrs Thatcher's dreams. Buford thought that 'if the *Daily Mail* had been asked to create a twenty-two-year-old working-class lad with his life sorted out, it could have presented Steve'. The only problem was that Steve was addicted to football violence. But whenever Buford asked him about it, he merely shrugged and said, 'It's human nature, I guess,' or 'I don't know, I've never really thought about it.'[29]

But Buford did think about it. One of the things people missed about football hooliganism, he thought, was that it was *fun*. Pounding through the streets of Turin, he felt 'an excitement that verged on being something greater, an emotion more transcendent – joy at the very least, but more like ecstasy. There was an intense energy about it; it was impossible not to feel some of the thrill.' Some of it was the pleasure of feeling part of 'something exclusive – a club, cult, firm, cultural phenomenon . . . whatever it might be called'. But it was also the violence itself. In Manchester a factory worker told him that he couldn't 'wait to get out on a Saturday afternoon', not because he felt disenfranchised, but because 'we've all got it in us. It just needs a cause . . . Everyone's got it in them.' Even Buford, the Cambridge postgraduate, had it in him. And in contrast to academics who were always looking for economic explanations, Buford thought there was sometimes 'no "reason" for it at all'. Most of the young men he met had jobs, money, even wives and girlfriends. Why did they do it? Because they enjoyed it.[30]

But it was not quite as simple as that. Football violence had not come out of nowhere, and Buford thought it was also part of a bigger story: the disintegration of the old working-class landscape, which was gathering momentum in the recession of the early 1980s. The hooligan subculture, he suggested, had emerged amid the ruins of a more authentic culture of masculinity, rooted in the rituals of work and place. In other words, it was a product as much of affluence as of deprivation, reflecting what Buford saw as the hollow decadence of suburban 'video players, computer games, portable telephones and electronic kitchens', as well as 'central "invisible" heating'. Deprived of community, he thought, young men had turned to 'a bloated code of maleness, an exaggerated embarrassing patriotism, a violent nationalism, an array of bankrupt antisocial habits'. Perhaps he was right, though there was something a bit predictable about a Cambridge postgraduate dismissing other people's lives as alienated and meaningless. Most working-class men coped with electronic kitchens without becoming football hooligans. Incredible as it may seem, there had even been plenty of boors and bruisers before the invention of invisible heating.[31]

What is true, though, is that the erosion of industrial Britain left at least some young men, who might once have followed their fathers to the factory on Saturday morning and the match on Saturday afternoon, bereft of allegiance. It was this sense of abandonment that fuelled groups like the skinheads, who wore ostentatiously nostalgic working-class clothes such as checked shirts, braces and Dr Martens boots. Skinhead culture had first originated in areas like the Isle of Dogs in east London in the late 1960s, and it became particularly associated with the hooligan firms following teams such as Millwall and West Ham – in other words, teams from declining areas going through wrenching social and economic change.

By and large, skinheads got a very bad press, since they were often dismissed as football hooligans with Nazi tattoos. There was some truth in this, though in a society awash with male eyeliner and mascara, the nostalgic celebration of working-class masculinity was never going to be the height of fashion. Most unfashionable of all was the aggressive punk offshoot known as Oi!, which was typically seen as the music of the far right. Yet its most prominent champion, the *Sounds* critic Garry Bushell, who described himself as 'a socialist, a trade unionist, and a patriot', insisted that it was not music for neo-Nazis but simply music for working-class men. Indeed, as the historian Matthew Worley points out, many Oi! bands came from traditional working-class, Labour-voting backgrounds, while their lyrics celebrated a vision of working-class culture – 'pubs, football, boxing, the bank holiday beano, Butlin's, the betting shop' – that seemed like something from the 1940s. Like skinheads, Oi! bands were effectively acting out a masculine working-class fantasy, a dream of paradise before middle-class hippies, suburban shopping centres, factory-closing account-ants, dark-skinned immigrants and hectoring Conservative women came along and ruined it. And in many ways that was what football hooliganism was, too.[32]

But there was a difference between football hooliganism and Oi! music. Football hooliganism travelled; indeed, some of the most notorious inci-dents happened abroad. Supporters had been travelling to Europe in large numbers since the early 1970s, and by the time Buford followed Manches-ter United to Italy, the rituals had become all too familiar. This was not just a proletarian performance; it was a self-consciously patriotic one. As soon as the fans touched foreign soil, something changed. They 'were no longer supporters of Manchester United; they were now defenders of the English cause'. Even as the plane was taxiing towards the terminal, they started putting on Union Jack T-shirts. Their songs were not just about Manchester United; they were about 'being English and what a fine thing that was'. Somebody even started singing 'Rule, Britannia'.

They hit the centre of Turin like a conquering army. Arriving in a cen-tral square, Buford found hundreds of Englishmen already there, 'singing and drinking and urinating into a fountain . . . an island race who, swel-tering under the warm Italian sun, had taken off their shirts, a great, fatty manifestation of the history of pub opening hours, of gallons and gallons of lager and incalculable quantities of bacon-flavoured crisps'. They looted shops with impunity, while the Italians looked on in horror. They urinated through the doors of cafés, while 'uncomprehending Italians jumped out of their seats to avoid getting wet'. After the match, they rampaged through the streets, attacking random passers-by, beating and kicking a man who was trying to get his children into his car, frenziedly attacking an 11-year-old boy who had fallen to the ground.

To Buford, all this made for an incomprehensible scene. No other people in Europe, he thought, would have conducted themselves in such a way:

> It was inconceivable that an Italian, visiting a foreign city, would spend hours in one of its principal squares, drinking and barking and peeing and shouting and sweating and slapping his belly. Could you imagine a busload from Milan parading round Trafalgar Square showing off their tattoos? 'Why do you English behave like this?' one Italian asked me, believing that

I was of the same nationality. 'Is it something to do with being an island race? Is it because you don't feel European?' He looked confused; he looked like he wanted to help. 'Is it because you lost the Empire?'

Buford did not know what to say. But one thought did strike him. It was natural, he thought, to assume that the supporters were 'performing for the benefit of the Italians', putting on 'the war dance of the invading barbarians' to terrify the locals. In reality, the visiting Englishmen were not interested in the locals: 'they were performing solely for themselves'. Most had brought cameras, to record what they saw as a holiday. But they did not take photos of the city, still less its inhabitants. They took pictures of themselves: the English abroad.[33]

As Buford observed, one of the defining characteristics of the English hooligans was that 'they did not like people'. He made a list of the things they did like, including lager, the Queen, the Falkland Islands, Margaret Thatcher, sausages, 'lots of money' and themselves. 'That was the most important item,' he thought: 'they liked themselves; them and their mates.' They hated the rest of the world and its 'essential inhabitant', the stranger; and above all they hated that strangest of all strangers, the foreigner. But in their eyes, foreigners were no longer safely confined to cities like Turin. They were wandering around the streets of England itself – and worse, they were actually playing for English teams.

In one of Buford's early expeditions, he took an American friend to watch Queen's Park Rangers. As soon as a black player touched the ball, a 'deep, low rumbling' went up from the crowd. 'It's because a black player has the ball,' Buford explained. 'They are making an ape sound because a black player has the ball.' As his friend stared in disbelieving horror, the grunting got louder, coming from 'everyone on the terraces – old, young, fathers, whole families'. Eventually the player passed the ball on to somebody else, and the grunting stopped. But then 'another black player got the ball and the grunt resumed'. Stricken with embarrassment, Buford struggled to explain it. 'It's England,' he said at last.[34]

Of all the stains on football's record in the early 1980s, racism was one of the worst. By this point, aggressive racial abuse had become so common that many fans simply took it for granted. Behind it, paradoxically, lay a story of assimilation: one reason so many fans roared abuse at 'wogs' and 'niggers' was that most opposing clubs now had prominent black players, from West Bromwich's Cyrille Regis and Nottingham Forest's Viv Anderson to Tottenham's Garth Crooks and Watford's Luther Blissett. Yet that did not make it any the less shocking. And like the violence itself, racism seeped from the terraces into the surrounding streets.

On the same day that Sheffield Wednesday's fans rioted at Oldham, a welder, Osborne Swaby, was walking down Leyton Road in Walthamstow in north-east London with his young daughter, Jennifer. A bus rumbled towards them, carrying Grimsby fans who had been watching their team play Leyton Orient, and as it passed, the fans 'dropped their trousers and bared their bottoms'. When Swaby yelled that there were small children watching, one man jumped off the bus and grabbed him. 'What's the matter with you, you wog?' he said. Then he hit him with a hammer. At that, Jennifer screamed: 'Don't hurt my daddy!' So the man from Grimsby hit her, too. This was a pretty dreadful tale in every respect. But the key word was surely that three-letter insult: 'Wog'.[35]

Against this background, it was hardly surprising that football had few defenders. 'It is impossible not to notice the racism and obscenities', wrote James Walvin, who loved football but hated the 'general atmosphere of menace and unpleasantness'. Indeed, by this point many sportswriters agreed that the game was doomed to a long, shabby decline. In the broadsheets, obituaries for the working man's ballet were very common. Most agreed that the game had completely failed to adjust to the loss of its massive post-war audience or to offer compelling reasons to keep coming. The *Guardian*'s Patrick Barclay was typical in drawing a damning contrast with American sports, with their futuristic stadiums and friendly crowds, where spectators were treated as valuable customers rather than as escapees from a maximum-security prison. Like many writers, he saw this as a reflection of Britain's class-ridden backwardness compared with its cousin's forward-thinking optimism. 'I cannot see', he wrote in 1979, 'why football should escape the general, apparently inexorable decline of Britain.'[36]

*The Times* thought so too. 'Football is sick', wrote its sports editor a year later, 'and the illness may be terminal.' The situation was 'desperate', agreed the *Guardian*'s David Lacey. The game was 'like an ageing car whose exterior bodywork has been washed and polished while the inside rust has been ignored'. It would take only one tap to bring complete disintegration. And although Hugh McIlvanney, the greatest of all British sportswriters, thought obituaries for football had become a cliché in their own right, he admitted that the game's woes were more ingrained than ever before. McIlvanney still thought football the best game ever invented. But it was time to admit that it had no 'God-given right to a special place in our society'.[37]

The most ominous vision of football's future came not at a glamorous club like all-conquering Liverpool or forward-thinking Tottenham, but

in a town that had once been synonymous with the game's industrial heritage, built on coal and steam, bricks and steel. For more than a century,
Wolverhampton Wanderers had dominated the imagination of the men
who toiled in the foundries and furnaces of the Black Country. 'In those
days', a local reporter remembered:

> no working man in Wolverhampton would go home when the Saturday
> lunchtime hooters went. They would all take their sandwiches and queue
> to get into the ground from 12.30 and wait happily two hours for kick-off.
> Local manufacturing was reliant on Wolves – no joke, if the team won you
> could guarantee production would be up the following week, and down if
> they lost.

Like many Victorian institutions, Wolves were rooted in the religious
culture of urban England. Formed as a church-school team in 1877, they
were one of the twelve original members of the Football League. For
much of the twentieth century the men in the old gold shirts had been
one of a handful of teams with a genuinely nationwide following. 'Wolverhampton Wanderers grew out of the very bedrock of the English
game', wrote the *Guardian*'s Frank Keating, 'and it is not too fanciful to
call them a national institution.' Even their grand old stadium, Molineux,
stood 'like some sort of medieval cathedral, four square and proud at the
very heart of the town, the very centre of the community'. Fittingly, their
golden age had come in the 1950s, the Indian summer of British manufacturing, when they had pioneered floodlit matches against the top
European sides. But what happened to Wolves in the early 1980s could
hardly have been a better metaphor for the fate of industrial working-
class Britain.[38]

Wolves had entered the new decade in a distinctly battered state. With
gate receipts falling, Molineux was in a dreadful condition, and new
safety legislation meant at least one stand was in danger of closure. In
a bid to break out of the cycle of failure, the board spent a record £3
million on a new stand with 9,500 seats and forty-two executive boxes,
gambling that this would radically transform their fortunes. It did, but
not in the way the directors hoped. As interest rates headed through the
roof, the club's debt became increasingly unsustainable, while the board
discovered that spending money off the pitch was no substitute for investment in the team. Visiting in May 1982, the journalist David Lacey wrote
that Molineux was:

> a monument to frustrated ambition and the inability to marry a glorious
> past to an uncertain future, with the present lost somewhere in between.

Approach the ground from the east and the new stand, all tinted glass and
executive suites, suggests lasting affluence. Arrive from the west and the
old main stand, with its grubby brickwork and dusty corners, pines for the
days of Mullen, Hancocks, Broadbent, Swinbourne and Wright.

He was talking about Wolves. He might have been talking about
Britain.[39]

In May 1982 Wolves slid into the Second Division with debts of £2.6
million. What followed was the most catastrophic decline in British football history, from which this great club took decades to recover. In July,
after Lloyds had run out of patience with the club's failure to meet its
£1,000-a-day interest payments, Wolves called in the receiver. With only
days until the deadline, it seemed likely that the club would simply cease to
exist. Even the local council declined an offer to buy the ground, pointing
out that, thanks to government cuts, they had no money to spend. Most
experts predicted that it would be turned into houses or a supermarket.
In a town already scarred by the collapse of manufacturing, it seemed the
cruellest blow imaginable.

At Molineux, the club advertised a 'survival fund', with a barometer
showing a £500,000 target. But when an *Observer* reporter visited the
West Midlands, she found it stuck on zero. No wonder, she thought. The
area seemed chronically depressed, while the infamous new stand, 'submerged behind vast new developments and ring roads', looked like 'a
cardboard box abandoned in a builders' skip'. Even Billy Wright, who had
captained Wolves and England in the 1950s and was now head of sport
at Central Television, seemed thoroughly pessimistic. 'It's heartbreaking,'
he said. 'Unemployment is already higher in the West Midlands than in
the rest of the country, so it's already a very sad area, and if Wolves goes
it'll be even sadder . . . The only club I had since I was a boy – it's part of
my life. Half my body will die if Wolves dies.'[40]

Three minutes from the deadline, a consortium led by the former
Wolves striker Derek Dougan stepped in to save the club. As one of television's most outspoken pundits, Dougan talked a good game, promising a
£21 million stadium redevelopment that would include 'a supermarket,
condominium, a trade centre, high technology units and a youth centre'.
But like one or two other grand redevelopment projects inaugurated in
the early 1980s, his castle was built on sand. In reality, he was merely the
front man for two reclusive Pakistani brothers, Mahmud and Mohammad
Akbar Bhatti, who were interested not in the club but in the supermarket.
That a working-class institution had fallen into the hands of foreign-born
investors was a sign of things to come, though nobody realized it at the

time. In any case, when the council turned down their application for planning permission, the brothers lost interest, and Wolves continued on a slide unprecedented in football history, plummeting from First to Fourth Divisions in successive seasons.[41]

By now Wolves had been transformed from a national institution into a national joke. By the spring of 1984, fewer than 7,000 people were turning up to watch, and this in a stadium that had welcomed more than 60,000 people before the Second World War. A year later, the club had no chairman, no chief executive, no manager, no money and vanishingly little hope. A year after that, attendances were down to barely 3,000, total debt had reached £1 million and annual interest payments had hit £100,000. At Molineux, only two of the four stands were open because the others had been declared unsafe. The local football writer Pat Murphy thought the story 'would interest a soap opera mogul', but it was more *Crossroads* than *Dallas*, and even that was being generous. In the end, salvation came from the unlikely combination of the Labour-run council and the supermarket giant, Asda, who agreed to cover Wolves's debts in return for a store behind the stadium. But the nadir came in the autumn of 1986, when the former champions of England were beaten 3–0 in the FA Cup by Chorley Town of the lowly Multipart League. Never before had any major club sunk so low. Indeed, even in an age when so many great Victorian institutions seemed under threat, it is hard to think of a more striking example of mismanagement and decline.[42]

'Dark days in the Black Country,' wrote the *Guardian*'s Frank Keating after the Chorley match:

> You wander round Molineux, famous home of a famous club, and all you get is the feeling of one of those ghostly deserted ranches which cowboys came across in the West. Signs creak wonkily on rusty hinges, shrubs grow out of gutterings, ancient graffiti mocks faded dreams, paint peels. It is the colour of sad, yellow ochre, self-scorning the celebrated old gold shirts made famous when Wolves were men and they blazed trails across the world a quarter of a century ago.

Rust, graffiti, sadness, ghosts: here was the language of countless articles in the 1980s, mourning the deserted buildings that had reverberated with so many working-class voices in the nation's industrial heyday. 'It's a desolation now,' remarked one local reporter, who had missed only two home games since the Second World War. And for Stan Cullis, who had captained the team in the 1930s and 1940s and led them to three league titles as manager in the 1950s, things were so bad that he no longer bothered going.* 'My Wolves was not only a football club, you see, it was the very integral part of its community,' he said sadly. 'We considered ourselves far more than footballers: we were carrying a banner for the town and its people . . . Quite frankly, when I go there now, it's like going to a foreign place.'[43]

In football, and in so much else, this was to become a familiar refrain.

* Cullis was an indubitably mighty man. Quite apart from his record at Wolves, he was the only Englishman who refused to give the Nazi salute when England played Germany in Berlin in 1938.

# 10

# A Bit of Freedom

*Thousands of people in council houses and new towns came out
to support us for the first time because they wanted a chance to
buy their own homes.*

Margaret Thatcher, 15 May 1979

*These council house buggers have obviously got jam on it . . . If
you seriously think a few quid on the rent is going to hurt these
spongeing sods you must all be mad.*

'Denis Thatcher', in Richard Ingrams and John Wells, *Dear Bill:
The Collected Letters of Denis Thatcher* (1980)

You could hardly find a more ordinary street than Amersham Road. Walk
past its mock-Georgian front doors and neat front gardens today, a dog
barking in the distance, a woman passing on the other side with her shopping, children playing in the little park up ahead, and you might be in any
suburban street in England. But like all streets, Amersham Road has a
history. A few minutes from the main road leading east from Romford
into Essex, Amersham Road was built as part of the gigantic Harold Hill
estate after the Second World War. With the capital bursting at the seams,
planners had earmarked the farmland north of Romford as the perfect
spot to house more than 25,000 people.

At first residents lived in prefabricated houses constructed by German
prisoners of war, but by 1958 the estate was finished. Here, in this planned
community of wide streets and neat brick council houses, was post-war
Britain in microcosm, a monument to the modernizing ambitions of the
age. For the next quarter of a century, everything changed, and nothing
changed. Families came and went. Children played in the streets, went to
school, got their first jobs and moved away. Infants became teenagers;
young parents became grandparents. The streets filled with cars, the living
rooms with televisions, the kitchens with fridges. Hemlines rose and fell,

hairstyles came and went. On Amersham Road, life went on as it had since the beginning. And then, on 11 August 1980, the Prime Minister came for tea at Number 39.[1]

When Mrs Thatcher's car pulled up outside the front door of Number 39, she was greeted by a gaggle of demonstrators clutching placards and shouting about unemployment. But when she made it inside, there was a warm welcome from the house's new owners, James and Maureen Patterson, their daughter, Leisa, and their twin boys, Martin and Vernon. The Pattersons had lived in Amersham Road since 1962, having rented Number 39 from the Greater London Council. But now, after eighteen years and a deposit of just £5, the house was theirs. They were the 12,000th tenants to buy their home from the GLC, and it had cost them just £8,315, the equivalent of about £50,000 today. And as Mrs Thatcher handed Mr Patterson the deeds, she seemed thoroughly delighted. Here was a household after her own heart, ambitious, hard-working and admirably independent-minded. 'Don't you think this is lovely?' she asked the cameras, indicating the Pattersons' shiny new kitchen units. Mr Patterson gave an embarrassed half-smile, while some of his children looked as though they wished the ground would swallow them up. But when Mrs Thatcher was in full flow, there was no stopping her. 'Now, Mr Patterson is a handyman, and he's put in all these. He's done the garden, and the shed outside . . .'[2]

Years later, long after the Pattersons had left Number 39, the Prime Minister's visit was seen as a symbol of her revolutionary commitment to the sale of council houses. Decades on, newspapers still sent reporters to Harold Hill to gauge opinion about the impact of her most celebrated policy, the Right to Buy. The irony, however, is that the Pattersons' newfound status as proud homeowners had nothing to do with Mrs Thatcher, since the GLC had been selling council houses since the late 1960s. In streets like Amersham Road, the signs of change were already abundantly clear: joiners fitting smart new doors, decorators with tins of brightly coloured paint, double-glazing vans parked in the drive, even new gates to keep strangers out. 'There was a ceremony everyone seemed to have, when they would go out and change their old council wooden gate for a wrought-iron one,' one resident later recalled. 'That was how they announced they'd bought.'[3]

Conceived as the embodiment of Clement Attlee's Britain, Amersham Road had now become a symbol of a very different political moment: an age of aspiration and self-improvement, in which hundreds of thousands of families broke free from the embrace of the state; but also an era of widening inequality, the headlines full of cuts, shortages, benefits and homelessness. Even at Number 39, the Pattersons' story was touched with sadness. A few years after Mrs Thatcher's visit, their marriage broke up, leaving Maureen to pay the mortgage on her own. 'If I'd foreseen the end of my marriage I'd never have bought. I got trapped there without enough cash to cover bills,' she told the *Telegraph*. 'I was desperate in a house I couldn't manage and wished I'd never bought. It broke my heart when I had to sell.'

But Maureen refused to blame the Prime Minister. 'I don't blame anyone,' she said. 'It was my decision to make that investment.' Indeed, she still had warm words for the woman who came to tea that day. 'She was an icon to me,' she said wistfully. 'She was a lovely guest.' What Maureen remembered especially fondly was that, after looking around the house, Mrs Thatcher had turned to her and said: 'This is not a house – it's a home.' Nothing could have pleased her hostess more. 'I was so proud,' Maureen said. 'She had Downing Street and Chequers, but Number 39 was just as special to me.'[4]

The Right to Buy did not begin with Margaret Thatcher. The place to start is 1923, when the Conservative MP Noel Skelton argued that the 'true answer to Socialism' was something he called the 'property-owning democracy'. The idea caught on. Only three years later, the leader of the Tory group on Leeds Council told his opponents that if people owned their own houses, 'they turn Tory directly. We shall go on making Tories and you will be wiped out.' And although the ideal of home ownership receded a little during the great council-house-building surge of the late 1940s, it never disappeared. By the end of the following decade the Macmillan government had given local authorities the freedom to sell houses to their tenants, and throughout the 1960s many Labour MPs, as well as Conservatives, talked of home ownership as the ultimate goal of housing policy. Indeed, Edward Heath presided over the sale of tens of thousands of council houses, with more than 34,000 changing hands in 1973 alone. There was no shortage of potential owners; the only problem was that many local councils were reluctant to sell. This was where the Right to Buy came in.[5]

The irony is that, although the Right to Buy is usually seen as Mrs Thatcher's personal project, aimed squarely at the skilled working-class voters of Middle England, she was initially very sceptical about it. As Heath's Shadow Environment Secretary after the first election of 1974, she had to be cajoled into offering discounts for council-house buyers, because she was worried about alienating middle-class Conservatives who had saved up to buy private homes on the open market. But she gave in.

That October, the Conservative manifesto promised a 'right to purchase' to any tenant who had been renting for at least three years, at a discounted price 'one-third below market value'. And in an article for the *Telegraph*, Mrs Thatcher offered a preview of some very familiar themes. 'The greatest ambition of many people is to own their home,' she explained. 'In the Conservative party we must have as our prime objective a big increase in home ownership. If some greater financial incentive is required we shall have to be prepared to give it. It is better to help people towards self-reliance than State-reliance.'[6]

Contrary to myth, the Tories were not alone in being interested in the Right to Buy. By the end of the 1970s, there were some 6½ million council houses in Britain, accounting for one in three households nationwide. That was an awful lot of potential voters, and after 1974 Harold Wilson's senior advisers urged him to steal the Tories' thunder by offering an alternative scheme. Wilson's policy chief, Bernard Donoughue, had grown up in a council house and was acutely conscious of the petty restrictions that governed many tenants' lives, from the council-mandated colour of their front doors to their inability to move at short notice. The Right to Buy, he argued, would give people 'the freedom to decorate their homes as they wished and, very important, to move in pursuit of employment'. For months Donoughue worked on a plan allowing tenants to buy their council houses, with properties reverting to the local authority on the deaths of the owners or their dependants. Labour's left-wing activists hated it, and Wilson allowed it to wither on the vine. Even so, it is tempting to wonder how different history would have been if Wilson or Callaghan had pursued it. At the very least, as the academic Peter King remarks, it would have strengthened their appeal to skilled working-class households in the so-called 'Labour aristocracy': precisely those voters, of course, who defected to Mrs Thatcher.[7]

As it was, however, the Right to Buy remained a Conservative issue. During the run-up to the 1979 election, some Tories even argued that long-term tenants should simply be handed the keys, free of charge. As before, though, this made Mrs Thatcher nervous, since it might infuriate homeowners who had saved for years to pay off their mortgages. Instead, she approved a scheme devised by her Shadow Environment Minister, Michael Heseltine, with a sliding scale of discounts depending on how long tenants had been in their homes. Crucially, it would be enshrined in law, so local councils could not block it. And after the election, Heseltine put the plan into operation with unflagging vigour, combativeness and flair for publicity. Introducing the legislation in January 1980, he claimed that it was 'far more than just another housing Bill', and would rank among the 'finest traditions and philosophies of the Conservative Party'. No act of Parliament, he insisted, had ever 'enabled the transfer of so much capital wealth from the State to the people'. Reversing 'the trend of ever-increasing dominance of the State over the life of the individual', here was 'the basis for perhaps as profound a social revolution as any in our history'.[8]

The Right to Buy came into effect on 3 October 1980. Already the government had frozen the price of more than 5 million council houses, allowing tenants to buy them without worrying about inflation. On television and in the papers, the government ran a £600,000 advertising campaign explaining the discounts, which began at 33 per cent for people who had rented for three years and rose to 50 per cent for those who had rented for twenty years. In the meantime, with rather less fanfare, Heseltine was moving against local authorities themselves. Two months later, he announced an indefinite halt to all council spending on housing, banning them from borrowing any more money, entering into contracts or beginning work on new developments. Only when councils had proved that they could live within the government's new cash limits would they be allowed to start building houses again. Labour promptly branded him a 'housing-wrecker', while the veteran left-winger Frank Allaun yelled across the Commons that Heseltine was 'not a man or a Minister but a monster'. But for the Tories' blond bombardier, as for Mrs Thatcher, abuse from the left merely proved that he was right.[9]

Opposition to the Right to Buy was by no means confined to the Labour Party. The National Tenants' Organization was dead against it, warning that it would 'inevitably lead to a worsening of the housing crisis and soaring rents for council tenants'. The charity Shelter was equally damning, arguing that selling so many council houses would wreak 'untold damage' on the prospects of the homeless. Meanwhile, a survey found that almost all Labour-controlled authorities were against it, as well as almost one in three Conservative-controlled councils. This might seem surprising, given that the vast majority of councils in England and Wales had already sold some houses to their tenants. But what horrified so many councils was the government's insistence that they *had* to sell their houses, whether they wanted to or not, which destroyed any semblance of local autonomy.

In this respect, as Simon Jenkins wrote a few years later, the Right to Buy was not just a gigantic privatization, transferring billions of pounds of assets to individual families from the state. It was a colossal usurpation of power, with the central government effectively seizing control of millions of council houses. Like schools, public housing had always been seen as one of the essential elements of local government. Council houses belonged not to the government, but to the community. 'They were symbols', Jenkins wrote, 'of the community's role in determining the character of its neighbourhood and the welfare of its citizens.' But now, thanks to Thatcher and Heseltine, that power had gone for good.[10]

Even before the Housing Bill became law, some councils were drawing up plans to resist. Cornwall's independent councils begged for exemption on the grounds that their houses would inevitably become 'summer lets or second homes', making it impossible for young Cornish people to buy locally. (The government took no notice, but the councillors were absolutely right.) Many Labour councils, notably Lambeth, Sheffield and Newcastle, simply refused to hand out application forms. 'We are not stopping tenants from buying their homes,' explained Swindon's housing committee chairman. 'The Act does not say that we have to hand out the forms. If the tenants manage to get the forms from elsewhere and fill them in correctly, then we will sell them their homes.'

Meanwhile, Sheffield's young council leader, David Blunkett, spent £6,500 recruiting two officials to 'describe to potential buyers the disadvantages of home ownership', much to the fury of his Conservative opponents. There were, he argued, 27,000 people on the waiting list for homes, including 'large numbers of elderly and handicapped people', and the council had no right to abandon them. His housing committee chairman, the future Labour MP Clive Betts, was particularly exercised by the case of John Bradshaw, a greengrocer with three shops, who had lived in a two-bedroom council house for the last three decades. The house was worth £10,500, but thanks to his government discount, Mr Bradshaw had just bought it for £5,150. To Sheffield's Labour councillors, this was just not fair. 'People like Mr Bradshaw', said Betts, 'can afford to go and buy a house on the private market. It is wrong that he is purchasing a community asset when there are people on the waiting list who cannot afford to buy their own home.' But it was also, Blunkett added, a question of principle, for what was at stake was the 'existence of local democracy itself'.[11]

The struggle between central and local government would become a key theme of Mrs Thatcher's years in office, but it was a battle she generally won. Heseltine's Housing Act gave him the right to send in 'commissioners' to sell the houses if councils refused to do it, and throughout 1980 the government periodically threatened Labour-run councils with intervention. Rochdale and Greenwich even invited the government to send a commissioner, since as Rochdale's leader put it, they did 'not want to be any part [sic] to selling our houses'. The decisive battle, though, came in Norwich, where the Labour council took the fight all the way to the High Court. As it happened, the judge, Lord Denning, agreed that the Housing Act was a 'most coercive power', allowing 'central government to interfere with a high hand over local authorities', and warned that it might easily be 'exceeded or misused'. But the law was the law, so Heseltine got his way.[12]

Among the general public, not everybody approved of the Right to Buy. Probably very few people would have agreed with Basildon's Peter Hibbitt, who told Mass Observation that 'the whole concept of house purchase is to me one of the biggest confidence tricks ever perpetrated'. But anecdotal evidence suggests that older people, who had grown up with the idea that council houses were provided for the benefit of working people, tended to be more suspicious. Talking to residents in a 'bleak 1960s high-rise block' on a hill overlooking Rochester, Kent, one reporter found that while younger people were very enthusiastic, and often said that the issue would persuade them to vote Conservative, their older neighbours were much warier. Council houses were meant 'for people like us who could not afford to buy', said 63-year-old Rosina Ramsden, a catering assistant. And when a *Guardian* reporter visited the suburban streets of Hodge Hill, Birmingham, she too met pensioners who thought the sales were unfair. Public housing was for the poor, agreed Harriet Emms and her neighbour Constance Jones. If people wanted to buy, they should 'move out' to the private estates and leave the council houses for somebody else.[13]

In general, though, the Right to Buy was immensely popular. In the Birmingham conurbation, where some 25,000 tenants bought their council houses by the end of 1982, even reliable Labour voters said they approved of it. One was Melissa Jones, described as a 'middle-aged immigrant from Jamaica', who was just about to hand in her application. The council, she complained, had never got round to painting her front door; and since it would only cost her '£1 or £2 more each week to buy' – well, why not? 'Everyone should have the chance to buy his council home if he can afford it,' agreed 59-year-old Cyril Wilson, who had lost his job and held Mrs Thatcher personally responsible. Indeed, it is striking how many people who voted Labour, had lost their jobs or simply could not stand Mrs Thatcher nevertheless heartily approved of the Right to Buy. 'If you are a sitting tenant and you have got the money,' said Albert Sutton, a 61-year-old Labour stalwart from Rochester, 'good luck to you.'[14]

When Mass Observation canvassed opinion in early 1982, the responses were no less illuminating. Here, for example, is Anne Eves: a middle-aged clerk, no fan of the Conservatives and sceptical about the principle of the Right to Buy, but nevertheless exasperated after decades of council tenancy:

It has really got up my nose to be a second-class citizen in council housing. When first married the request for a mortgage was laughed at as my husband was never even in regular employment. Even though we had the required deposit and were paying a similar amount for furnished accommodation as would have been required for mortgage repayments, no-one would consider granting a mortgage.

Now by kind permission of the lothesome [*sic*] Tories I am to be able to buy my council flat for the discounted price of £9,880 plus £25 per month service charge plus £25 per month Rates. The market value was put at £18,250 . . .

I shall go ahead with the scheme even though I disagree with the principle of anyone being able to buy council stock as it is my only chance of owning my own place. Had I been able to buy in 1960 I would own my own house now and it would have cost about £2,500 and today be worth £25,000.

For people like Anne, who had rented for so long with little hope of owning their own home, the Right to Buy seemed genuinely liberating. It did not mean that they became Conservatives overnight, or that they were blind to the risks of a mortgage, or that they forgot about the other economic problems of the day. Sheila Parkin and her husband, for example, had rented their council house in Brentwood, Essex, since 1955. It was now worth £29,000. Thanks to their discount, they had bought it for £10,760, while their monthly mortgage repayments were just £1 more than their old rent. Yet even as she recorded her pride at owning her own home, Sheila lamented that her son-in-law had been made redundant after eight years. In what seems a colossal irony, he had worked for the local council repairing their housing stock, but had lost his job thanks to 'government cut-backs'. As Sheila noted, he had just 'signed on the dole, a thing he has never done before, and is very bitter towards this government who do not seem to care'.[15]

The most revealing letter, though, came a year later from Mary Richards in Newton Abbot. Here was a working-class woman in late middle age, precisely the kind of woman to whom the Labour Party was dedicated, and very far from being an automatic admirer of Mrs Thatcher. Yet she was bewildered by Labour's reluctance to embrace the principle of home ownership:

I sometimes think that even the Labour Party do not seem to want to see working people get out of the rut in case they vote for another party, hence the dislike for selling council houses.

We don't want charity but we want the chance to better our lot when the opportunities arise and they don't come often in a lifetime.

> My son who hopes he can (if he lives very economically) buy his council
> house said, 'If Mrs Thatcher gets in I can buy my house but am likely to
> loose [*sic*] my job but if Labour gets in my job would be reasonably safe
> but I will not be able to buy my house.'

Perhaps not surprisingly, he split the difference and voted Liberal.[16]

The Right to Buy was an immediate hit. Beforehand, some critics had
poured scorn on the idea of popular demand. The journalist David
Walker, later Mr Polly Toynbee, assured readers of *The Times* that
demand would be 'very small' and that sales would involve 'no large
fraction of council housing'. Yet in the first twelve weeks alone, more
than 100,000 people submitted application forms, the total rising to more
than 250,000 by the following June and a whopping 380,000 by October.
Behind these figures were hundreds of thousands of families, eagerly
looking forward to seeing their names on the deeds of their home, putting
in new doors or windows, repainting the outside, perhaps even building
an extension. And as the forms flooded in, Mrs Thatcher could barely
contain her delight.

'Wherever we can we shall extend the opportunity for personal ownership and the self-respect that goes with it,' she told her party conference
in 1982:

> Half a million more people will now live and grow up as freeholders with
> a real stake in the country and with something to pass on to their children.
> There is no prouder word in our history than 'freeholder'.
>
> Mr President, this is the largest transfer of assets from the State to the
> family in British history and it was done by a Conservative Government.
> And this really will be an irreversible shift of power to the people.
>
> The Labour Party may huff and puff about putting a stop to the sale of
> council houses. They may go on making life unpleasant for those who try
> to take advantage of their legal rights, and what a wicked thing it is to do
> that. But they do not dare pledge themselves to take those houses back
> because they know we are right, because they know it is what the people
> want.

The people did want it. By the end of 1981 some 86,545 council houses
had changed hands, rising to 290,874 a year later and 438,082 by the end
of 1983. For the rest of the decade, more than 100,000 houses were sold
almost every year. Never before had the Conservative dream of a property-
owning democracy come closer to being a reality. 'Everyone – almost
everyone, the overwhelming majority – of people . . . will be able to

say: "Look, they have got something to inherit. They have got a basis to start on!"' Mrs Thatcher proudly remarked. 'That is tremendous. That is popular capitalism.'[17]

Yet more than almost any other policy of the 1980s, the Right to Buy reflected the sharp divisions in British society. Most of the early sales were in suburban southern England. In Scotland and many northern cities, sales were very slow, not least because councils practised what David Walker called a mixture of 'town hall delays, obscurantism . . . obstruction [and] outright intimidation'. Despite Mrs Thatcher's hopes, many of the biggest urban estates saw virtually no applications, while people who wanted to buy flats in post-war tower blocks were vanishingly rare. Yet, as so often, the North–South divide was a bit simplistic: while people might have expected Bromley in south-east London to be keen sellers, who would have predicted that Nottingham, York and Berwick-upon-Tweed would be so keen to get rid of their council houses? Even the political divide was often misleading. Some Conservative councils, particularly in rural areas, owned relatively few houses and had no desire to hand them over. But others went out of their way to encourage prospective buyers. Rochester, almost unbelievably, put on a quiz with 'questions on home ownership, with a tie breaker if necessary', judged by a panel of councillors and local estate agents. The prize was, of course, a free council house.[18]

As for the homeowners who benefited from Mrs Thatcher's revolution, they tended to be very particular kinds of people. Older tenants were naturally at an advantage, because they often qualified for the most hand-some discounts. And although the Right to Buy was aimed at young couples embarking on married life, surveys found that buyers were typic-ally middle-aged or older couples with children. In the early years, at least, they generally came from small towns and suburbs in the south and the Midlands, such as Maidstone, Bracknell and Hemel Hempstead. By and large, they lived on small, well-maintained estates of semi-detached or terraced cottages, usually with gardens. They were certainly not poor: the great majority of husbands and wives were in full-time work, most had skilled manual or white-collar jobs and they typically brought home twice as much money as people who continued to rent. These, in other words, were 'respectable' people living on 'good' estates, the kind of people who had been keen to climb on to the housing ladder for years, but had never been able to obtain a mortgage. They were also, incidentally, the kind of confident, aspirational working-class voters the Tories had been courting for at least a century.[19]

Many years later, the housing academic Peter King suggested that the reason the Right to Buy had been so popular was that, unusually for a government policy, it transferred assets 'permanently and unconditionally' from the state to the family. It appealed directly to people's desire for privacy and control; it addressed them as individuals rather than groups; 'it did not seek to tell households what they wanted and how they should live', but rewarded 'private interest and aspirations'. Above all, it appealed to what King calls '*mineness*': people's sense of place and belonging, rooted in the principle of ownership. No wonder, then, that new homeowners could not wait to repaint their front doors, to put in new windows, fences and porches, to install new fireplaces, bathrooms and kitchens. Home improvements demonstrated that their houses were *theirs*, and that they were free to put their mark on them. 'I stood and looked at that kitchen ceiling for a quarter of an hour last night after I finished it,' one man said. 'I know it's silly but it's the satisfaction you get. And I wouldn't feel like that if I didn't own the place.'[20]

When Denis and Sylvia Abbott bought their three-bedroom terraced house in Coulsdon, south London, the first thing they did was to put in a mock-Georgian front door instead of the 'regulation blue drab' ordained by Croydon Council. Then they set about remodelling the interiors. 'We might have done that anyway,' Sylvia Abbott said, 'only now we do not have to ask the council's permission.' No casting agency could have supplied more typical council-house buyers: Denis, 60, was a lathe-turner, while 47-year-old Sylvia was a filing clerk. They had working-age sons, had rented for almost seventeen years, and had bought their £27,000 house with a 46 per cent discount. On their quiet suburban street, the 'signs of ownership' were everywhere: new front doors, freshly creosoted fences, aspirational new names for the houses. The Abbotts had voted Conservative all their lives. At last, they felt, their loyalty had been rewarded. Buying had been a 'nerve-wracking business to start with', said Sylvia, but now 'we have something to show for our money. The boys will benefit.' It was also a question of principle, her husband added: 'What it has given us is a bit of freedom.'[21]

Whether they knew it or not, the Abbotts' new mock-Georgian front door was one of the great social signifiers of the age. 'Houses being bought by former tenants often stand out because the wood-work has been painted, a new front door fitted, fencing erected and the regulation municipal garden concreted over to make a hard-standing for the car,' reported *The Times* in late 1982. But of all those things, by far the most emblematic was the Georgian door. The style commentator Peter York, always teetering on the edge of some wild generalization, was on great form when it came to what he called 'Britain's favourite door, the door to the Thatcher future, to Princess Diana's fairy castle and, by now, to several million houses in the realm'. It was, he thought, 'the most *expressive* piece of everyday symbolism' in the country:

> You see this door everywhere, but everywhere. On my way to work – crossing North London – I pass this small low-rise block of Sixties council flats where everything was originally *uniform*, rectangular and the original design had glazed doors . . . But now half the block has Georgian doors – *the* door.
>
> The door is on owner-occupied houses all over the country; I've seen it in every big provincial city, including Liverpool and in Scotland.
>
> What is the thought exactly? Such a door does seem to say *privatisation*, or, on the council flats, a revisionist burst of bourgeois individualism. Georgian doors definitely say trading up.
>
> But above all it says *keep out, you*. Georgian doors are strong and safe and solid, the very opposite of the let-the-sunshine-in glazed 1960s numbers. Georgian doors reflect a very real preoccupation with *security* everywhere.

All this was surely bang on, although York recognized that there were other associations too: with heritage, continuity, a kind of assumed grandeur and glamour. But the Georgian door was more democratic than it seemed, or at least more meritocratic. For York, it suggested the competitive values of the 'successful bootstraps Tory councillor' rather than the inherited wealth of 'the Whitelaw house'. But it also captured, 'in a way most left-wing people *never* understand, the "legitimate aspirations of ordinary people" who want their own places to be nice'. People, in other words, like Denis and Sylvia Abbott, and millions like them.[22]

The delights of home ownership were a common cultural refrain even before Mrs Thatcher came to power. Even so, it is striking how often the themes of wanting a house, buying a house and even losing a house recurred in the most popular television series of the era. The first episode of Channel 4's soap opera *Brookside*, which went out in November 1982, begins with the experience of Bobby and Sheila Grant, played by Ricky Tomlinson and Sue Johnston, who have just moved from a run-down council estate to a smart brick house on a brand-new estate. Similarly, in *Only Fools and Horses*, which first appeared in September 1981, David Jason's Derek Trotter lives in a cramped south London council flat in Nelson Mandela House, Peckham, and is desperate to work his way up the ladder. In one early episode he discovers that his brother Rodney (Nicholas Lyndhurst) has become chairman of their tenants' association, and concocts an elaborate but unsuccessful scheme to trick him into moving them into a smarter bungalow. And in the first episode of *Auf*

*Wiedersehen, Pet*, Kevin Whateley's Neville leaves his wife and children in Newcastle to find work as a bricklayer in West Germany. He hates having to leave and is desperately homesick when he gets there. But the point, he says, is to 'get some cash and buy us a nice house on a nice estate'.

To Mrs Thatcher, home ownership was a central pillar of the new Britain she hoped to build. Perhaps this explains the power of her chosen slogan, the 'Right to Buy', with home ownership framed as a *right*, embedded at the heart of British life. Nothing, she thought, must be allowed to undermine the bond between people and property. Hence her enthusiasm for mortgage interest tax relief, which could be claimed on the first £25,000 you borrowed against your home. Even many of her most loyal ministers thought this was an inexcusable subsidy for middle-class homeowners. Geoffrey Howe, for example, believed it was a 'glaring anomaly … unjustly favouring the better off and the south rather than the north'. The archives show that he pestered her to get rid of it, not least because it cost the exchequer at least £2 billion a year. But she refused to budge, maintaining that mortgage tax relief was 'of special value to "our people"'. Far from scrapping it, she said, they should increase it. In this case, as Howe later lamented, he could make no headway against the Prime Minister's 'populist instincts'.[23]

To her critics, Mrs Thatcher's obsession with mortgage tax relief for the middle classes was all the more shocking because she was simultaneously slashing housing benefits for the poor. What was more, it coincided with an unprecedented boom in bank lending, encouraging people to run up debts they would never have contemplated a generation earlier. At the end of the 1970s, the mortgage market had been almost entirely dominated by a cartel of building societies. But once Howe scrapped the banking corset, the high-street banks moved into the mortgage market in earnest. Unlike building societies, they could borrow cheaply from the capital markets, which meant they could offer much more generous loans. Led by Abbey National, the building societies reacted by abandoning their old caution, and soon the great mortgage bazaar was on. By 1983 lending had hit a record £19 billion, with demand so high that many borrowers had to wait weeks for their money. Customers of the Leeds Building Society's 400 branches, for example, faced delays of up to three months. Yet it had never been easier to borrow, and as house prices soared, so the old taboos about debt evaporated. Britain was becoming a nation of debtors: in ten years after 1979, annual mortgage borrowing ballooned from £6 billion to £63 billion.[24]

Was Mrs Thatcher personally responsible for this orgy of debt? Although she certainly made it easier to borrow, she never forced anybody to borrow money, just as she never forced the banks to lend it to them. The British people were not mindless pawns; they made their own decisions. And although no Prime Minister had ever made such a fetish of home ownership, it is often forgotten that home ownership was already rising anyway. By the time she took office it had already doubled since the early 1950s, and it is almost impossible to imagine a scenario in which that trend would have stalled. As the property writer Baron Phillips remarked at the time, the concept of home ownership was always particularly strong in Britain, 'ingrained in the system through the long-established building society movement'. Indeed, in the summer of 1983, a survey by the Building Societies Association found that eight out of ten people – including nine out of ten between 25 and 34 – would like to buy their own home. A Thatcherphobe might see this as proof of the Prime Minister's supernatural ability to brainwash the masses. But since a similar survey in 1975 had produced a figure of seven out of ten, that interpretation does not really stand up.[25]

It is not true, then, that Mrs Thatcher 'created' a new demand, as some of her critics maintain. It would be more accurate to say that she recognized a latent demand and set out to satisfy it, no matter what the cost. And when the voters went to the polls in 1983, she reaped the inevitable reward. Council tenants voted Labour by a margin of more than two to one; homeowners voted Conservative by three to one. Mrs Thatcher's canvassers even joked that wherever they saw a mock-Georgian door, new windows or a freshly painted front gate, they knew they would find Tory voters. And there is no doubt that for some people even the chance of home ownership, however distant, was politically decisive.

In Rochester, 20-year-old Rosanne Rodney, married with two young children, rented a council flat on the fourth floor of a high-rise block. 'We want to get out of here,' she told *The Times*. 'I am against Labour because they are against buying council houses. We hope to get a council mortgage and are looking for council houses now. That has influenced me to vote for the Tories.' Nearby lived Sandra Wildish, another housewife, who had been in the block for seven years. She had always voted Labour because 'being a council tenant, the Tories are very hard and Labour really looks after you better'. But, she said, 'when we move out of here and buy a home of our own, I will probably swing to the Conservatives'. Here, framed by the doorway of her high-rise council flat, was the walking embodiment of the property-owning democracy.[26]

On the face of it, the Right to Buy was a stunning success. Its popularity is beyond doubt: few government policies have ever become so closely associated in the public imagination with freedom, independence and self-improvement. As a result, no government ever reversed it, and by the Housing Act's 25th anniversary, almost 2½ million households had been handed the deeds to homes of their own. What was more, it was a colossal money-spinner. By the middle of 1983 more than £4 billion in receipts had poured into the Treasury coffers; and by the end of the decade the government had recouped more than £17½ billion. No other privatization of the 1980s made so much money for the British state.[27]

But there was a catch. As Charles Moore points out, the Right to Buy was driven not just by a sense of ideological mission but by rather less elevated financial motives. As an internal memorandum explained in July 1979, the government had earmarked housing as an area that would 'produce proportionately greater savings than any other programme'. To put it bluntly, they were planning to slash the housing budget to the bone.* With this in mind, the Treasury had no intention of letting councils benefit from the enforced sale of their own property. Above all, it did not want to see local authorities blowing their windfall on new council houses; indeed, at first councils were banned from building any new houses at all. Eventually Heseltine persuaded his colleagues to allow councils to spend three-quarters of the money on new houses, but even that did not last long. When Nigel Lawson took over as Chancellor in 1983, he wasted little time in cutting councils' share, first to half and later to a fifth.[28]

The result was entirely predictable. Council-house building was already in steep decline, but under Mrs Thatcher it fell off a cliff. By 1981 Britain was building just 55,000 council houses a year – down from 130,000 in 1975 – and in later years the total plummeted even further. Given the rising demand, with the population growing and more people living alone, this might appear completely deranged. Mrs Thatcher's ministers argued that if they used the money to cut the deficit and stabilize the economy, the private sector would fill the gap, with construction firms competing to meet the demand. Unfortunately, although private house-building did pick up a bit, it was not remotely enough to make up the shortfall. With too many people chasing too few houses, prices surged by as much as 10 per cent a year. From the day Mrs Thatcher walked into Number 10 to the day she left, the average house price went up from just under £20,000 to almost £60,000. And as even Charles Moore admits,

---

* In office, they stuck to their guns: housing cuts accounted for 75 per cent of the government's spending reductions between 1980 and 1984.

this meant not just a housing shortage but a housing bubble – the consequences of which are still with us today.[29]

There was another obvious downside. For Britain's growing population without a home, worrying every night about where they were going to sleep, terrified of being kicked out into the sleet and the snow, Mrs Thatcher's boasts about the joys of home ownership must have sounded like something from a different planet. In fairness, homelessness had been rising even before she took office, with at least 50,000 people on the streets before she walked into Number 10. The rising tide of family breakdown and drug abuse undoubtedly played a crucial part. So did the backlash against psychiatric hospitals, which had been gathering pace for decades and saw thousands of vulnerable young people released from institutions into what *The Times* witheringly called 'the mercies of a community care which does not exist'.[30]

Yet it was no accident that the homeless figures increased so dramatically after 1979. The fact that so many homeless people had lost their jobs tells its own story, while the collapse of council-house building meant there were simply not enough decent houses to go around. And although Mrs Thatcher's ministers later blamed the inertia of the private sector, they could hardly claim that they had not been warned. As early as December 1981, the former director of Shelter, Des Wilson, argued that the decline in council-house building meant Britain faced a 'major crisis . . . without parallel in our lifetime'. A year later, the Church of England issued an apocalyptic report, *Housing and the Homeless*, warning that Britain was facing an 'appalling and monumental housing crisis'. The government, it said, should redistribute resources from middle-class homeowners to the very poorest in society, 'for whom the Judaeo-Christian tradition has always demonstrated a particular concern'. But in this case Mrs Thatcher's Christian compassion had its limits. She loved talking about homes and homeowners. But in the first half of her premiership she could barely bring herself to use the word 'homeless' at all.[31]

None of this diminished her faith in the Right to Buy. In the future, she once told *The Times*, 'there will be quite a lot of people, very ordinary folk, great grandchildren, who will be inheriting something, because for the first time we will have a whole generation of people who own their own homes and will be leaving them, so that they topple like a cascade down the line of the family'. But while this was true of those fortunate enough to buy their own homes at a handsome discount, it was not true of those who were not. From the very beginning, it was obvious that plenty of people would miss out on her housing revolution. For tenants who were very poor, very young or simply unemployed, who were in insecure jobs, were frightened of taking on a mortgage or simply hated their council accommodation and dreamed of something better, buying was not a serious option. Of course tenants rushed to snap up semi-detached houses in small towns and suburbs. Since the typical Right to Buy mortgage cost only 43p per week more than the average council rent, they would have been mad not to. But on estates crippled by crime, vandalism and high unemployment, sales were virtually non-existent. What sane family, after all, would want to buy a flat they hated on an estate where they felt lonely and frightened?[32]

Missing out, however, carried a heavy penalty. From the moment it took office, the government was determined to raise council rents, which it felt had been suppressed for far too long. To Labour, this was an outrage: when, in November 1980, Heseltine proposed increasing rents by up to £3 a week, the result was a mass Commons brawl, all 'pushing, kicking and shoving', in which Labour MPs accused their counterparts of 'behaving like the louts they are so quick to condemn at football matches'.

'Did you have to tell him, "One day, my boy, all this will be yours"?'

Not everybody wanted to buy their home from the council. In tower blocks, in particular, many people shuddered at the thought of taking on such a responsibility, just as Mac had predicted in the *Daily Mail* (14 May 1979).

Temporarily, Heseltine backed down; but this was only a tactical retreat. Starved of funds by government cuts, local authorities saw no alternative to squeezing their remaining tenants. As early as October 1981, rents were going up by some 32 per cent a year. And as thousands embraced the Right to Buy, tenants became more vulnerable. In the next ten years the government squeezed even tighter, sending the average council rent from less than 7 per cent of average earnings to more than 11 per cent. That may not sound like much. But for people at the very bottom of the ladder, for whom even a small rent increase might mean missing out on a hot meal or an evening's central heating, the discounts offered to their more affluent neighbours must have seemed cruelly unfair.[33]

Perhaps above all, the Right to Buy fundamentally transformed council housing's image, and not for the better. For years thousands of self-consciously respectable families had seen nothing wrong with renting council houses. But even before Mrs Thatcher came to office, things were changing. In 1977 the Labour government had introduced statutory homeless provision, directing local authorities to give priority to the very poorest rather than the 'respectable' working-class families they had previously favoured. Their intention was wholly benevolent. But the unintended result was not just to push working families towards the back of the queue, but to change the character of the estates themselves.

Then, three years later, came Mrs Thatcher's Housing Act. Very quickly there was a clear divide between the kind of people who *bought* council houses and those who *rented* them. As early as 1983, David Walker estimated that two-thirds of Britain's council houses were being rented by people who were 'too poor to afford their rents'. In Hartlepool in County Durham, four out of five tenants had their rents paid by the state; in comparatively prosperous Wisbech and March in Cambridgeshire, more than seven out of ten were on housing benefit. Within just a few years, council housing was seen as a last resort for the elderly, the handicapped, single mothers and the unemployed. 'The Socialist dream of people from all walks of life living together', remarked *The Times*, 'has given way to the nightmare of the ghetto.' In the 1940s Paul McCartney's father had seen nothing wrong with living in a council house. Forty years later, though, he might have thought differently. In the public imagination, these were no longer homes fit for heroes. They were homes for the poor.[34]

In January 1981 the writer Jeremy Seabrook went to Sunderland. His journey took him to the suburb of Southwick, on the northern bank of the Wear, where male unemployment was estimated to be about 45 per cent.

As Seabrook described it, the area's narrow brick houses sounded like something from an urban nightmare:

> The brick dulls to the shade of dried blood, the green is sparse and faded. The privet hedges spike out in all directions, a broken fence collapses in a fan of creosote planks into a front garden. The neglected grass rustles in the biting wind that comes off the North Sea; an Alsatian dog turns on his chain on a patch of worn earth; a child plays with the rubbish spilt from an overturned dustbin. One house, blackened by fire, had been boarded up, but the plywood at the windows is torn away: inside, the litter suggests kids' glue-sniffing parties, and there are empty bottles of Newcastle Brown and cheap wine. The roads glitter with splinters of broken glass. Many windows are smashed; rough pieces of cardboard cover the cobweb of shattered glass; newspaper to keep out the draught flutters in the rusting metal window-frames.

Even the interiors struck him as appallingly shabby. In one house, 'colder than the street', he found four children huddled around a gas-fire in their coats, one drinking from a bottle of cough syrup. The walls, painted 'chocolate brown', were 'damp and sticky'; the cheap 'council wallpaper' was 'marked and greasy'; the window frames were 'rusty with condensation'. The television, old and blackened, no longer worked. Even the children's comics had fallen apart. On the floor lay a tattered cover, 'a picture of a red and green ape-like figure with an eye gouged out'. As Seabrook watched, the girl with the cough syrup, engrossed by her comic, picked at the sofa's nylon threads with a 'half-bitten fingernail'.[35]

In the early 1980s, almost every visitor to Britain's council estates emphasized the same things: poverty, vandalism, crime; misery, bleakness, shabbiness. And although travellers like Seabrook often concentrated on estates in northern England, the equivalent estates in Glasgow, Edinburgh and London were no better. In the capital, the concrete estates in run-down Hackney and Haringey had become dumping grounds for the immigrant population, among whom unemployment and poverty were appallingly high. The most infamous was the spectacularly depressing Broadwater Farm in Tottenham, built to hold 3,000 people in 1973 but blighted from the start by vermin, leaks and break-ins. Within just three years, half of all prospective tenants were refusing to go there, while dozens of residents were begging to leave. By the early 1980s it was common knowledge that you accepted a flat on the Farm only if you were absolutely desperate.

Yet despite its national notoriety, Broadwater Farm was hardly exceptional. Five miles to the south in Hackney, the high-rise towers of Holly

Street had originally been a symbol of optimism and opportunity. But by the early 1980s Holly Street had become a byword for unemployment, prostitution, drug abuse and racial violence. In just one week in 1980, the estate suffered twenty-one separate break-ins. 'The corridor is a thieves' highway,' one visitor wrote. 'At the corners where blocks join are dark passages, blind alleys, gloomy staircases. It is easy to get lost in these labyrinths, and easy for robbers to lurk or to lose their pursuers. The fear of muggings is so widespread that people, if they have to venture out at night, stick to the lit areas and walk hurriedly.' This was not a place, in other words, where any sensible family would want to exercise its right to buy.[36]

To the writers exploring the dark side of Mrs Thatcher's Britain, the most compelling symbol of the failures of the recent past – a structure that not only stood for the hubris and naivety of planning and modernization, but seemed to house all the demons lurking at the fringes of the public imagination – was the tower block. Wandering through the decrepit streets of Balsall Heath, Birmingham, Jeremy Seabrook looked up to see 'the blocks of flats, symmetrical towers on their grassy ramparts . . . gleaming like marble and regular as tombstones' on the horizon. Here was the brave new world of post-war Britain, promising a cleaner, happier life for the city's workers and their families. But 'when you get close to them', Seabrook wrote, 'the concrete base is covered with ugly graffiti, the lifts stink, there is litter and debris everywhere'. The towers had been conceived as symbols of modernity, pointing towards a brighter future. But for Seabrook they were 'places of defeat', proclaiming 'that people have acquiesced in what has been done to them'.[37]

Not all estates were equally bad. On the surface, the sprawling Craigmillar estate, on the south side of Edinburgh, was one of the most deprived places in Scotland, a depressing concrete jungle with severe drug problems, an unsurpassed level of family breakdowns and an unemployment rate four times the national average. But for years the local Craigmillar Festival Society, founded by mothers from a local primary school, had worked hard to create a sense of community, most famously through an annual arts festival. By 1981 the society ran an information office and a job centre, as well as a community transport service, a second-hand shop, numerous playgroups, support groups for the disabled and a music group with '15 different bands, everything from punk to trad'.[38]

But Craigmillar was the exception, not the rule. More typical was Fort Beswick in Manchester, an estate of more than a thousand homes, built at a cost of some £5 million between 1969 and 1973. Like many such estates, Beswick was part of a massive concrete package bought from the construction giant Bison. The residents, who came from Manchester's dilapidated brick terraces, hated it from the very beginning. Almost from the day the first tenants moved in, the council had been deluged with complaints about cracks, leaks and damp. As early as 1974, the area's Labour MPs, Gerald Kaufman and Frank Hatton, publicly denounced the developments in the House of Commons. 'Ugly blots . . . monstrosities . . . insects and vermin . . . young children are trapped . . . litter and debris . . . fouled by people and disfigured by graffiti . . . victims of an architectural vogue': their litany of complaint could hardly have been more familiar. Indeed, by the early 1980s Manchester's housing committee was already planning to raze Fort Beswick to the ground and start again. To get the estate into 'some kind of reasonable condition', explained the chairman, would cost at least £10 million. Almost incredibly, it was cheaper to knock it down and build hundreds of old-fashioned council houses instead.[39]

Today it has become fashionable to stick up for the estates of the 1960s, to swoon at their concrete ambitions and dismiss their critics as narrow-minded reactionaries. But the plain fact is that most people loathed living in them. In estate after estate, residents complained that they felt lonely, frightened, abandoned and betrayed. The historian Peter Shapely, who has studied Manchester's public housing in the 1970s and 1980s, shows that the council was beset almost from the beginning by complaints about 'decay, dampness, vandalism, noise and condensation'. On Manchester's catastrophic Hulme Crescents estate ('Colditz'), the largest public housing project in Europe, more than nine out of ten residents said they wanted to be moved elsewhere, with many saying they preferred the old slums. And when, in November 1981, a reporter asked the residents of Fort Beswick about the plans to demolish it, he found them queuing up to complain about the 'boredom, loneliness, fleas, cockroaches, cold and damp'. 'There is no atmosphere here and the kids are always fighting,' explained 21-year-old Pamela Burke, pointing out the streams of water pouring down her walls and the mould growing on her ceiling. 'We have had our house fumigated three times to get rid of bugs. I hope they pull the lot down.' Her neighbour, 24-year-old Nuala Murphy, agreed with every word. 'The toilets are blocked and the lift never works,' she added. 'There is a horrible smell on all the landings. It is a horrible place to live, and I am delighted to hear the buildings might be pulled down.'[40]

The backlash against concrete modernism naturally played into the hands of the Conservatives. To oppose tower blocks was to champion smallness, privacy, individuality: precisely the values that Mrs Thatcher associated with home ownership and popular capitalism. Later, the Marxist sociologist Ruth Glass claimed that criticism of the tower blocks was 'part of a general scheme to turn social objectives upside down', with their detractors portraying them as 'the work of the devil; peopled by the zombies of the welfare state'. But this is just not true. The criticism of Fort Beswick was led by local Labour MPs, while Jeremy Seabrook was a Marxist who specialized in writing about some of the very poorest people in Britain. Writers and politicians who pointed out the dreadful conditions in Hulme Crescents and Broadwater Farm were not part of some Thatcherite plot; they were simply reporting the grim reality for thousands of ordinary people. Even Tony Benn, canvassing for his son Stephen in London's local elections in May 1981, was horrified by the 'awful' condition of one council block, where 'people were terrified of coming to the door'. The idea that Seabrook and Benn were reactionaries trying to cast poor tenants as 'zombies' is simply ridiculous. Quite the reverse: they saw them as victims, betrayed by the architects, planners and councillors of the post-war decades.[41]

Even though the tide of opinion had turned by the beginning of the 1980s, the time lag between design and completion was such that some housing projects were still being finished after Mrs Thatcher had taken office. Perhaps the most infamous was the vast barrier block along Coldharbour Lane in south London, officially called Southwyck House but known locally as 'Brixton Nick'. The block had been designed in 1970 to shield residents from a planned inner-city motorway, with a fortress-like wall and depressingly tiny windows. By the time the GLC scrapped the motorway, Lambeth Council had already set aside £20 million, so they went ahead and built it anyway.

The result, not surprisingly, was a disaster. When the journalist Polly Toynbee went along to have a look in November 1981, the block was still unoccupied. Squatters had already taken possession of some of the flats, and many people on the waiting list had made it clear they would do anything to avoid living there. Gazing in horror at its 'colossal and fearsome' dimensions, Toynbee could understand why. 'What wouldn't we give now', she wondered, 'for a bit of mock-Tudor or mock-Gothic to counter the visual deprivations of the slab-block era?' Buildings like Southwyck House were

> the worst kind of municipal housing, an example of the ghetto mentality of planners, grandiose and authoritarian. Driving past it on the road out of Brixton to Camberwell, one can only shudder and ask who built it? What kind of insensitive megalomaniac could have dreamed up such a scheme, even now, when we might have learned the lessons of such vast estates, desolate, impersonal and crime-prone?

Gazing on what the planners had wrought, Toynbee was so cross that she wanted to 'find the architect and challenge him with the suffering he would be imposing on generations of wretched council tenants'. To her surprise, the architect was not a him but a her: a young Polish architect called Magda Borowiecka, 'gentle and thoughtful', whose parents had come to Britain during the war. As an idealistic student, Borowiecka had taken a job with the Greater London Council before going on to work for Lambeth Council. The barrier block had been her first assignment. Now, as she stood on one of the parapets, looking down at her creation, she admitted that she had changed her mind. 'I was a lot more Left-wing', she said, 'when I started out.'

Borowiecka no longer designed gigantic Brutalist blocks. Her most recent project, the Dunbar-Dunelm estate in suburban West Norwood, had been much smaller and more nostalgic: two winding streets of 'little yellow brick houses with dormer windows and steep, sloping, black slate roofs, each with a garden . . . full of character, corners and surprises'. Walking around the Norwood estate, Toynbee thought that it felt like 'a bourgeois estate . . . private, not municipal. There are no communal areas, everything is partitioned into little separate lots'. But that, Borowiecka insisted, was what people wanted: 'They don't want to be council tenants at all.'

Indeed, Borowiecka now thought the state should get out of building houses altogether. 'We should be subsidising people, not houses,' she explained. 'Give them the money and let them go out and buy their own houses on the open market, choose what they want for themselves.' But what would she think, Toynbee asked, if the tenants chose to buy the little houses she had designed in Norwood? Wouldn't she be 'sad that they no longer belong to the council'? 'No,' Borowiecka said. 'I would be most flattered.' There spoke the spirit of the age.[42]

# 11

# She's Lost Control

*How will the economy climb out of a recession so deep? . . . Who can believe that a spontaneous industrial regeneration will result from the policy of squeeze, squeeze and squeeze again?*
Peter Jenkins, *Guardian*, 19 November 1980

*Alan Clark (Plymouth) felt . . . that the level of unemployment was what was holding the Party activists steadfastly together in many constituencies. For better or for worse it was seen as giving the Trades Unions their deserts.*
Minutes of the Conservative backbench
finance committee, 11 November 1980

In the early hours of Sunday 18 May 1980, a young man called Ian Curtis hanged himself in the kitchen of his terraced house in Barton Street, Macclesfield. An introspective, bookish character, the 23-year-old Curtis had until recently worked as a civil servant in Macclesfield's Employment Exchange. As a boy he had won a scholarship to the local King's School, and in 1979 he had voted for Mrs Thatcher's party. He had married young and had a 1-year-old daughter, but suffered from deep depression, exacerbated by his severe epilepsy, for which he was taking extremely strong tranquillizers. On top of all that, his marriage was breaking down, partly because he was by nature a solitary, brooding man, but also because he had started seeing another woman. In April, Curtis made a first attempt to kill himself, but failed. The second time, after sitting up all night watching television, drinking spirits and drafting a suicide note, he succeeded.[1]

For the previous three years, Curtis's chief interest had been his role as lead singer in a local band, called Joy Division after the Auschwitz sex-slaves in the pulp novel *House of Dolls* (1955). At the time, Nazi and Holocaust imagery was par for the course for aspiring punk bands. But

there was something about Joy Division that marked them out: a hint of
David Bowie in the music, a despairing fatalism in Curtis's lyrics. When
Joy Division released their first album, *Unknown Pleasures*, in June 1979,
admirers talked of its pain and beauty, its 'eerie spatiality', as if Curtis
were howling into a void of suffering. 'This band has tears in its eyes,'
wrote the *NME* 's reviewer, something nobody would have said about the
Sex Pistols. But it was not just a performance. To an extent that not even
his bandmates realized, Curtis was in the depths of an existential
crisis.[2]

A few weeks after Curtis's death, Joy Division released the single 'Love
Will Tear Us Apart'. With its 'raw and exposed' sound, and desperate,
self-lacerating lyrics, writes the critic Simon Reynolds, it was 'taken as
Curtis's suicide note to the public'. Yet within weeks it had reached number
thirteen. For an obscure post-punk group on an independent label, this
was success almost undreamed of. A month later, Joy Division released
their second album, *Closer*, which made it to number six and attracted
ecstatic reviews. The cover, a classically pure black-and-white image of
statues in a Genoa cemetery, had been chosen before Curtis's death; now
it seemed morbidly fitting. *Sounds* praised the record's production as 'the
aural equivalent of a rich marble slab', while the *NME* thought *Closer* 'as
magnificent a memorial as any post-Presley popular musician could have'.
To this day, Joy Division's admirers invariably use the same words to
describe it: glacial, claustrophobic, ethereal, narcotic, angular, chilling,
serene, hypnotic, ghostly . . . the language of death.[3]

Although Joy Division's obsessions with love, pain and suffering struck
a chord with listeners across the world, theirs was a music rooted in a
particular place and time. Even the band's keyboardist, Bernard Sumner,
thought that 'some of the darkness of Joy Division's music' reflected the
landscape in which they had been born. He had grown up in a terraced
street in Salford, with a chemical factory at one end and 'a strong sense
of community'. But then the council demolished the terraces and moved
his family into a concrete tower block across the river in Manchester. 'The
place where I had used to live, where I had my happiest memories, all that
had gone,' Sumner said. 'For me Joy Division was about the death of my
community and my childhood.' To thousands of working-class youngsters
in the 1970s and 1980s, it was a very familiar story.[4]

Sumner, Curtis and their bandmates had reached adulthood in a city
that seemed to be dying. They came from skilled working-class families
and had been to aspirational schools, two of them at Salford Grammar
School, the other two at King's School, Macclesfield, a former direct-grant
school that had been forced to go independent. But by the time they came

of age, Greater Manchester's economy was in deep trouble, factories were closing and youth unemployment was rising fast. This was not Liverpool in 1960, let alone Carnaby Street in 1966. The very air seemed charged with defeat and loss. And even at the time, some listeners thought Joy Division were reflecting a wider picture. In May 1979, just days after Mrs Thatcher's election victory, one *NME* critic wrote that they were producing 'withering grey abstractions of industrial malaise . . . Unfortunately, as anyone who has ever lived in the low-rent squalor of a Northern industrial city will know, their vision is deadly accurate'.[5]

Although there is a danger of being too reductive, it was surely no accident that Joy Division came from Manchester. At the end of the 1970s, the great old Victorian city, once seen as a symbol of Britain's industrial ingenuity and commercial might, was in wretched shape. The music journalist Jon Savage, who moved to Manchester from London in 1978, found it 'grim beyond belief', its canals murky and listless, its chimneys cracked and cold, its warehouses silent and empty. Having ripped down the terraced houses immortalized in *Coronation Street*, Manchester's planners had moved thousands of people into concrete towers and crescents, which soon became bywords for drugs, vandalism and violence. In the city centre hundreds of shops stood vacant, while the supposedly space-age Arndale shopping centre, completed in 1979, was dubbed 'the longest lavatory wall in Europe'. Culturally Manchester seemed a backwater, a dreary, drizzly sort of place, a city where nothing happened.[6]

When the journalist Godfrey Hodgson visited Manchester after many years away, he was struck by the total disappearance of the industrial landscape he had known in the 1960s. Then it had been a world of warehouses and workshops, a 'dirty, shabby world, but crowded and busy'. Now the warehouses were empty, the workshops had closed and almost one in three men was out of work. As a result, by the early 1980s Manchester had an estimated 20 million square feet of abandoned industrial floor space, much of it in the mills and factories that had fallen victim to technological change. It was grimly ironic, then, that Joy Division's record label was called Factory Records, a name coined after the label's co-founder had seen a gigantic neon sign reading 'Factory For Sale'. Even Factory's legendary nightclub, the Haçienda, which opened in 1982, embodied Manchester's industrial decline. Once it had been just another brick warehouse, belonging to a steel firm. In the long run it became a symbol of the city's cultural rebirth. But that was only half of the story.[7]

Manchester's plight was far from unusual. Its leading rival as industrial England's pre-eminent city, Birmingham, had entered the new decade in a similar agony of the spirit. In 1964, impressed by Birmingham's inner-city expressways, concrete new market and Bull Ring shopping centre, the travel writer Geoffrey Moorhouse had called it 'the most go-ahead city in Europe'. Nobody called it that now. As younger, more skilled and ambitious families moved out to the suburbs, poorer immigrant families were moving in, sending property prices into a spiral of decline. And as the factory gates clanged shut and unemployment headed towards 20 per cent, the fabric of the city visibly deteriorated. Now the flyovers and tower blocks were symbols, not of optimism and progress, but of modernization gone terribly wrong. The Second City was in a 'wretched state', said one report in 1980, citing the 'horribly dirty, dispiriting and sometimes dangerous underpasses', as well as the 'ever-present litter that is the despair of many and must make visitors shudder with disgust'. When the novelist Beryl Bainbridge visited Birmingham she found it 'frightening', a 'labyrinth of subterranean passages and overhead tunnels'. She was struck by the sight of an elderly couple, 'clinging to each other . . . marooned on the pavement beneath the massive bulk of a multi-storey car park'. Somehow that image seemed to sum Birmingham up.[8]

At the beginning of the 1980s, Britain's cities seemed in terminal crisis. In the previous decade, Manchester and Birmingham had lost at least 90,000 people each; inner London had seen its population fall by a whopping half a million; and perhaps most strikingly, Glasgow's population had fallen from 982,000 to just 763,000, a 22 per cent drop in just ten years. Across the country, inner-city neighbourhoods were becoming ghettos for the old, the poor, immigrants and the unemployed. Urban manufacturing, one of the most obvious physical legacies of the Victorian age, was becoming a thing of the past. It sometimes seemed, wrote the journalist David Walker, that 'planners, socialist city councillors and international capitalists' were 'working to the same end: killing inner city jobs'. And decline became self-perpetuating: as a study by the Department of the Environment concluded in 1982, it was not just the high rents that put businesses off; it was the perception of 'congestion, vandalism and crime'.[9]

At the end of August 1981, *The Times* began a week-long series on 'Crumbling Britain'. 'For the last 60 years', it said bleakly, 'Britain has been living off the Victorian engineering legacy of railways, bridges, canals, sewers and buildings. They have not been – and are not being – adequately maintained or replaced. That legacy is now crumbling at an accelerating rate.' What followed was a vision of abandoned factories, run-down schools and polluted canals; barbed wire, corrugated iron and broken windows; 'the burst water main in the high street at the height of a drought; the letter posted in one part of London which reaches its destination in another part weeks later; . . . the legion of fitters required to mend a broken gas main'. The supreme symbol of the state of the public realm, *The Times* thought, was 'the rotting school window frame, unpainted for a decade past because the local authority has chosen to spend on staff rather than on maintenance'. In the cities, one in four primary-school children was educated in a building built before Victoria's death, while a quarter of schools still had outdoor toilets. In Manchester, local officials measured the city's collapsed sewers in DDBs. A 'four-DDB hole' was 'one into which four double-decker buses would fit'.[10]

Over this cracked and crippled landscape the recession broke with the force of a tidal wave. On Tuesday 22 July 1980, the day the government officially confirmed that Britain was in recession, 630 stationery-firm employees lost their jobs at plants in London, Liverpool and Hemel Hempstead, while 230 furniture factory jobs disappeared in Wigan, 238 chicken factory jobs went in Cambuslang, fifty timber workers lost their jobs in Boston and a further thirty foundry workers were made redundant in Kettering. On Wednesday, GKN Fasteners closed a subsidiary in Birmingham with the loss of 830 jobs. On Thursday, Ford and British Leyland put almost 10,000 workers on short-time working. On Friday, the chemicals firm British Celanese laid off 226 people in Derby. And so it went on, *every single working day* that summer: 740 tractor makers in Doncaster, 125 engineers in Derby, 500 potters in Stoke-on-Trent, 600 diesel-engine makers in Darlington, 600 truck-factory workers in Cheshire, 300 gearbox makers in Port Talbot, 9,000 truck makers in Lancashire, 680 Massey-Ferguson employees in Coventry, 1,600 paper millers in Ellesmere Port, 430 Timex employees in Washington, 600 tyre makers in Wrexham . . . on and on and on, unwanted makers of this, unloved makers of that, a relentless drumbeat of disappointment and disaster.[11]

By the end of August the unemployment figures, including schoolleavers, had reached 2 million, the highest total since 1935. 'Our jobless are growing over twice as fast as those in any other EEC country; and yet we are still only at the start of a long road,' said an editorial in the *Guardian*. It was a long road indeed. The recession lasted for five quarters, from the beginning of 1980 until the spring of 1981. In the first year alone Britain's GDP fell by fully 2 per cent, dropping a further 1.2 per cent in 1981. Company liquidations, meanwhile, rose from some 4,500 in 1979 to almost 6,900 in 1980, 8,600 in 1981 and more than 12,000 in 1982. The total did not begin to fall until three years later, which says a great deal about the lasting damage of the downturn.

Perhaps the most telling indicator, though, was the collapse of manufacturing output, which fell by a staggering 8.7 per cent in 1980 and a further 6 per cent in 1981. Not since the Depression had British manufacturers taken such a battering. The difference, though, was that this time many never recovered. Even the greatest names were not safe. In eight years after 1979, the nation's most celebrated industrial manufacturer, ICI, cut its workforce from more than 89,000 people to just 56,000, while the Midlands engineering giant GKN saw its workforce fall from more than 60,000 to barely 19,000. In all, most estimates agree that during Mrs Thatcher's first term Britain lost as much as a quarter of its manufacturing capacity.[12]

By the time it was all over, Britain's manufacturing heartlands had been changed almost beyond recognition. Entire industries, from toy cars to machine tools, had been virtually annihilated. In areas like the West Midlands, the North, Scotland and Wales, manufacturing employment fell by at least a third in just eight years. The irony was that at the same time, imports were booming. With the pound so strong, foreign products were cheaper than ever: great news for Volkswagen, Zanussi, Samsung and Toshiba, but not for their British competitors. As late as 1980, Britain had run a £4 billion trade surplus in manufactured goods. Then the recession came. By 1982 the surplus was already down to just £1.3 billion. In 1983 it vanished completely, replaced by a deficit of some £2.6 billion. The surplus never returned; the deficit steadily widened. There could hardly have been a more powerful symbol of what had happened to the workshop of the world.[13]

One of the things people often forget about the Thatcher years is that there was always likely to be a recession in the early 1980s. Her government had taken over at the precise point that the aftershocks of the Iranian Revolution were rippling through the international economy, with world oil prices trebling in just two years. Even if Labour had won the 1979 election, Britain would have been exposed to the global slump. Even so, the fact that the recession was *so* much worse in Britain than anywhere else, with more losses, more bankruptcies and far more unemployment, demands an explanation. The real problem, despite what Conservative ministers claimed, was not the world downturn, the obstructiveness of the trade unions or the supposed backwardness of the British worker. The real problem was the punishingly high exchange rate.[14]

One factor in all this was obviously North Sea oil, which had turned the pound into a turbo-charged petro-currency. In November 1980 British Leyland's chairman, Michael Edwardes, won huge applause when he told the Confederation of British Industry that 'if the Cabinet do not have the wit and imagination to reconcile our industrial needs with the fact of North Sea oil, they would do better to leave the bloody stuff in the ground'.* In reality, Mrs Thatcher never had the option to leave it in the ground, because the previous Labour government had signed a deal with the oil companies ruling out major production curbs until 1982. Even so, plenty of people thought Edwardes had a point. The Treasury's own figures suggested that at least a third of the pound's punitive rise in 1979–80 was down to oil. 'Looking round at the industrial havoc caused by the steepest recession since the war,' wrote Frances Williams in *The Times* a year later, 'it is certainly hard to believe that the British people have benefited from oil.' It had, she thought, become 'a burden rather than a blessing on the British people. Sir Michael Edwardes was right. We should have left the "bloody stuff" beneath the waves.'[15]

The role of North Sea oil in Britain's recent history is still hotly debated. At the time, Mrs Thatcher's critics often suggested that instead of absorbing the oil money into the general budget, she should have invested it all in industry. The problem, as the former Labour minister Edmund Dell pointed out, was that Whitehall had a dire record of investing in industry, having already wasted billions on an entire flock of lame, dying or dead ducks. Even if ministers had successfully identified the hi-tech businesses of the future, it would have taken years to produce significant results, which would not have been much good to the millions on the dole in 1981. In reality, political pressures would probably have forced an interventionist government to blow the money on ailing behemoths like British Steel or the National Coal Board. But Mrs Thatcher's ministers shuddered at the thought of reviving the industrial interventionism of the mid-1970s. In Nigel Lawson's words, they preferred to use their oil winnings 'to reduce Government borrowing, to cut taxes where this could be done on a sustainable basis, and generally improve the climate for enterprise'.[16]

A more enticing argument is that Mrs Thatcher should have put the money into a sovereign wealth fund, as Norway did. To cut a very complicated story short, the Norwegians set up a gigantic pension fund, which was worth around £150,000 for every living Norwegian by mid-2019. Yet it was Jim Callaghan, not Mrs Thatcher, who decided against investing in a wealth fund. As he told the Commons, he wanted to use the oil money to cut personal taxes and 'increase take-home pay and work incentives', which is exactly how Mrs Thatcher justified her own approach. The only difference was that Callaghan promised to put some of it into industrial

---

* But as Edmund Dell remarked, if they had left it in the ground, 'where would the government [have got] the revenue from which to subsidize British Leyland?'

retraining and social services too. But even if Callaghan or Thatcher had chosen to put the money into a fund, Britain's population is more than twelve times larger than Norway's. Even if a British fund had been just as big as the Norwegian one, it would be worth around £12,000 per head at the time of writing, and that is a very generous estimate. So it would hardly be a silver-bullet solution to the problem of an ageing population, as its advocates sometimes claim.

The other obvious point, as the historian Graham Stewart observes, is that if the oil money *had* been invested, this would have left a gaping hole in the national budget. By 1983 the Treasury was banking more than £8 billion a year from North Sea oil. To fill the gap, Mrs Thatcher would have probably cut spending even more aggressively, with the impact inevitably falling on the poorest, the oldest and the unemployed. For although it is often said that North Sea oil paid for her tax cuts, it *also* paid for millions of people's unemployment benefits, as well as a host of other services and benefits that otherwise would have been threatened. To put it very starkly, the pressures of globalization and technological change, which were making so many old industries redundant and piling pressure on the public finances, meant Britain could have *either* a reasonably generous welfare state *or* a sovereign wealth fund, but not both. As so often, there was no easy answer, and certainly no magic wand.[17]

Back, though, to the recession. Since leaving North Sea oil in the ground was not an option, sterling was always going to be higher in the early 1980s than it had been in the mid-1970s, when it had sunk to the depths of the $1.60s. That meant industry was *always* likely to face a tough time. Even so, the surge after Mrs Thatcher took office was simply colossal. On the day she walked into Number 10, the pound was just over $2.07, but by the summer of 1979 it had already reached the dizzy heights of the $2.30s. It then fell back again, but when Howe raised interest rates to 17 per cent after the autumn gilt strike, it once again began to climb, hitting $2.31 in February 1980. Then came another brief respite; and then the long, agonizing summer surge, sending the pound to a peak of $2.46 in late October 1980. As the former president of West Germany's Bundesbank told a Commons committee two years later, it had been 'by far the most excessive overvaluation which any major currency has experienced in recent monetary history'.[18]

Why did Mrs Thatcher's ministers do nothing about it? One answer is that the Bank of England strongly advised them to let the pound take care of itself. On Howe's first day, Gordon Richardson had explicitly told him that the Bank was dead against intervening in the currency markets 'because of the dangers of destabilising the exchange rate'. It was barely three years since the humiliation of 1976, when the Bank's mismanaged intervention had sent sterling into meltdown. With world exchange rates in chaos and Britain's international reputation still very shaky, Richardson could hardly be blamed for being jittery about a repeat performance.[19]

What was more, at least one of Howe's closest confidants thought a strong pound might be a blessing in disguise, because it would help to bring inflation down. As Nigel Lawson told the Chancellor in August 1979, 'the strong pound is the biggest thing we have going for us. Not only is it an integral part of our anti-inflation policy, but any attempt to weaken it would very quickly lead to a very serious loss of confidence in our resolve to stick to that policy.' Lawson conceded that things would be different if they were faced with a 'rapidly and inexorably rising pound', but he thought that was very unlikely. In this, though, he turned out to be completely wrong. As he later admitted, when inflation was taken into account, sterling actually rose by something between 30 and 50 per cent in the government's first eighteen months.[20]

Later, Lawson and Co. were at pains to present the rise of sterling as the economic equivalent of an act of God, a natural disaster over which they had little control. The cause, they argued, was North Sea oil. But was it? In January 1981 the ultra-Thatcherite Centre for Policy Studies commissioned a secret report by the Swiss monetarist Jürg Niehans, who found that the 'principal cause' was actually the excessive restrictiveness of their monetary policy. To put it in layman's terms, with every upward tick in interest rates, the government had sent the pound a little bit higher. In the end, obsessed with controlling the money supply, they had simply squeezed too tightly. Not surprisingly, Mrs Thatcher found Niehans's findings very inconvenient. When John Hoskyns advised her that 'we had had a tighter monetary policy than we realised, by accident', she warned him of 'the fatal error of saying such a thing – that it would come through in speeches and undermine Geoffrey's position. There were many in the Cabinet who would exploit that.' She said much the same to her new economic adviser, Alan Walters: 'NO-ONE must know about it – especially Bank of England.'[21]

There is little doubt, then, that Mrs Thatcher's policies made the recession worse. In an ideal world, Howe might not have rushed his inflationary tax changes through so quickly. Nor would he have abolished exchange controls and scrapped the corset at the very moment he was trying to get the money supply under control. He might have done better to cut public borrowing straight away, and he should have reacted more quickly to the mounting exchange rate, relaxing his monetary policy as soon as it became clear that the squeeze had been too tight. But politicians do not live in an ideal world. In an age characterized by high inflation, low growth and currency instability, the world's finance ministers were feeling their way through a thick fog. Howe certainly made mistakes, but so had Denis Healey and Anthony Barber before him. That was not because they were all idiots. It was because, in Howe's words, economic management in the post-oil-shock era had become a 'long trudge through a seemingly endless series of multiple-choice examination questions'. And although his critics rarely admitted it, none of the potential answers offered much comfort.[22]

Even today, Mrs Thatcher's most strident critics still cling to a very simplistic account of what went wrong. According to the hard left, she and Howe, driven by their maniacal devotion to a twisted creed, deliberately conspired to create a recession, destroy British manufacturing and throw millions of people out of work. But this is almost self-evidently nonsensical. Why would they want to destroy the industries in which millions of working-class Conservatives made a living? Why would they want to imperil their political survival by causing a recession? It is true that they knew beating inflation would involve a degree of economic pain, just as they knew their drive for better productivity would mean some people losing their jobs. But there is no evidence that they planned to eviscerate British manufacturing and crush the working class, or for any of the other sinister ambitions often attributed to them. Nor is there any evidence that they envisaged mass unemployment on the scale of the Great Depression. After all, Mrs Thatcher had spent the late 1970s promising to rebuild British manufacturing 'on the rock-hard and well-tested foundations of incentive and profit', an unlikely thing to say if she were planning to destroy it. Would she really have gone out of her way to point out that, under Labour, unemployment had 'risen by more than in almost any other major industrial country', if she had been planning to throw millions more on to the scrapheap a year later?[23]

Time and again in history, cock-up is a much better explanation than conspiracy. As some of Mrs Thatcher's ministers later admitted, they never expected the downturn to be so severe. They assumed that the pound would stop rising; they hoped their money supply targets would dampen inflationary expectations, job losses would be contained and recovery would not be long delayed. They were, of course, completely wrong. The historian Jim Tomlinson accuses them, not unreasonably, of '"adventurism" – a determination to pursue a radical policy shift with little serious analysis of what might follow'. Another way of putting it is that, faced with a series of extremely unpleasant options, they succumbed to wishful thinking and were shocked when reality failed to match their expectations.

But this was hardly unprecedented. After all, Reginald Maudling's dash for growth, Harold Wilson's reluctance to devalue, Anthony Barber's reckless boom and Denis Healey's refusal to deflate had not exactly been shining examples of tough-minded realism. In this respect, the Thatcher government was not so exceptional after all.[24]

In the popular imagination, the recession of the early 1980s is often seen as the moment when a lost paradise of booming factories, steady jobs and settled communities was unforgivably destroyed. But that world was already in deep decline. Deindustrialization had been underway since the 1960s, and while Mrs Thatcher accelerated it, she did not start it. The shift from manufacturing to services had deep roots, and almost without exception the major industries supposedly destroyed during her time in office, such as steel, coal and car making, had been in dire straits for years. The industrial landscape was blighted by years of poor investment, persistent strikes and declining market share: when Mrs Thatcher took office, Britain had *already* lost almost 1½ million manufacturing jobs since 1966. In fact, one reason she was able to survive the recession is that factory closures had been making the headlines for years already. To the Scottish shipbuilders who lost their jobs in the early 1970s or the Ebbw Vale steelworkers who saw their plant close in 1975, what happened in Mrs Thatcher's first term probably sounded depressingly familiar.[25]

No doubt Britain would have been better off if the recession had never happened, although the downside might have been a longer period of high inflation. It is also true that the exchange rate took a dreadful toll on smaller firms that might otherwise have survived for years. Even so, when Sir Geoffrey Howe insisted that manufacturing had written 'its own suicide note' years earlier, he was not necessarily wrong. Of course Howe was hardly unbiased. But Edmund Dell, who had been ICI's vice president of plastics before entering politics, agreed that much of the industrial capacity lost in the early 1980s was bound 'for the scrapheap in any case'. If the recession had never happened, would the factories and foundries built in the Victorian age really have survived into the twenty-first century? Would Britain seriously have escaped the deindustrialization that swept through other industrial nations, from the car plants of Detroit to the steel towns of Lorraine? The answer is only too obvious.[26]

One of the myths about Mrs Thatcher's first term is that by the time it was over, Britain was finished as a manufacturing nation. Actually, twenty-first-century Britain is still one of the world's top ten manufacturers, behind Germany but roughly level with France. And there are plenty of commentators who believe that the shock of the early-1980s recession actually *saved* British industry from even greater sclerosis. Lawson, for example, claimed that 'our industrial base emerged from the fire more productive, more efficient, more competitive in the best sense, and very much better managed'. In his definitive history of post-war industry, the former *Financial Times* editor Geoffrey Owen agrees that the trauma of the recession 'stimulated an urgent drive for lower costs and greater efficiency'. Perhaps most strikingly, *Marxism Today*, in a special issue to mark ten years under Mrs Thatcher, agreed that the recession had triggered a 'long overdue' clear-out of Britain's industrial 'dead wood'. The manufacturing 'rump' that survived the recession, explained the Cambridge economist John Wells, was 'leaner, fitter, employs a vastly reduced labour force more productively and is considerably more profitable'.

That word 'rump', though, is crucial. Despite the government's assurances that new factories would rise from the ashes of the old, British manufacturing never recovered its lost jobs and vanished capacity. Perhaps both were always doomed. Even so, this was hardly what most voters had imagined when they heard Mrs Thatcher promising to rebuild British industry on 'rock-hard and well-tested' foundations. Nor did they ever imagine that a fervently patriotic Prime Minister would preside over an economy that became so dependent on manufactured imports, which rose by a staggering 92 per cent in the ten years after 1979.[27]

And there was, of course, another dimension to all this. Every time a factory closed, the cost could be measured not just in vanished profits but in the sense of loss as an entire culture began to disintegrate. The future *Sunday Times* economics editor David Smith grew up in the 1950s and 1960s in the Black Country, not far from the seventy-five-acre Darlaston works of Rubery Owen. A long-established family engineering firm, Rubery Owen controlled twenty constituent companies, making nuts and bolts, wheels and ploughs, chains and tools, motor-industry components, aircraft landing gear and prefabricated houses. It owned entire streets, offering subsidized housing to its workers. The Darlaston factory had a day nursery for working mothers' children, as well as a Sons of Rest workshop for older men who did not want to retire. It organized cricket and football teams, theatre groups and coach tours. It even maintained a convalescent home in Barmouth, on the Welsh coast, for employees who had been ill or injured at work. It was more than a company; it was a community.

On 1 July 1981 Rubery Owen announced that the Darlaston factory was to close. Collapsing demand, exacerbated by the ordeal of the car giant British Leyland, had made the end inevitable. Two months later, the bullhorn sounded for the last time, and was forever silenced. The nursery, the cricket team, the convalescent home, the subsidized housing: all were gone. Once, wrote Smith, the factory had been a 'hubbub of noise and banter', ringing with 'human stories: stories of men and women who believed they had a job for life, people who often complained but for whom work, and taking home a pay packet at the end of the week, was their life'. Not any more. Now silence had descended where once all was clamour.

Two years later, one in five people in Darlaston was still out of work.[28]

As the hurricane roared through Britain's factories, Mrs Thatcher knew perfectly well what was happening. On 20 June 1980 the Treasury warned Number 10 that there was little prospect of *any* manufacturing recovery, since Britain's exceptionally weak competitiveness and productivity, coupled with the horrendous exchange rate, would almost certainly turn 'a modest recession for the world economy into a major decline for the UK'. Yet the Prime Minister showed few signs of self-doubt. A few weeks later, just before she left for her summer holiday, she gave an interview to the *Sunday Times*'s Hugo Young. More than ever, she believed she alone understood what the British people wanted. 'Deep in their instincts', she said,

> they find what I am saying and doing right, and I know it is, because that is the way I was brought up. I'm eternally grateful for the way I was brought up in a small town. We knew everyone, we knew what people felt. I sort of regard myself as a very normal, ordinary person with, all the right, instinctive antennae.

Most people, she said, knew there was a price to pay for the mistakes of the past, but they also knew recovery would come eventually. And then 'they will be able to look forward to a different kind of life to the one they were having at the end of socialism'. Could she really turn things around? 'Other people still believe we can do it,' she said earnestly. 'But, if I give up, we will lose. If I give that up I just think we will lose all that faith in the future.' And then, as if remembering herself: 'I hope that doesn't sound too . . . arrogant.'[29]

Mrs Thatcher spent her holiday in Switzerland, where she and Denis stayed with the former Tory backbencher Sir Donald Glover and his wife, a Swiss industrialist's widow, near the shore of Lake Zug. Since the Prime Minister was notoriously uninterested in relaxing, Lady Glover made sure to invite a series of interesting people for lunch. On 20 August her guests included the Swiss economist Karl Brunner, who was based in New York. Since Brunner was one of the founding fathers of monetarism, Mrs Thatcher was keen to hear his thoughts about her economic policy. But to her horror, he was not encouraging. Her strategy was fine, he said, but her tactics were terrible. By concentrating on sterling M3 instead of the wider monetary base, the Bank of England was badly letting her down. To cut a long story short, the money supply was completely out of control. And unless she took drastic action, the result would be disaster.[30]

By the time Mrs Thatcher returned to England three days later, she had worked herself into a blazing fury. She demanded to see the Governor of the Bank, Gordon Richardson, but he was on holiday. To inflame her further, the economic picture was even darker than at the beginning of the summer. Sterling was heading towards the eye-watering heights of the $2.40s. Company profits were tumbling; unemployment was mounting by the day. The borrowing figures were horrendous, thanks largely to a series of massive public sector pay increases and the desperate plight of the car, steel and coal industries, which needed regular injections of public money to keep going. And above all, the monetary position was simply abysmal. According to the MTFS, money supply growth for 1980–81 was supposed to be between 7 and 11 per cent. Yet in July and August alone, sterling M3 had increased by 8 per cent! As the Prime Minister's private secretary Tim Lankester wrote later, even the truest of true believers could not deny that they were now in 'a serious mess'.[31]

Oh, what a lovely monetary policy!

By the summer of 1980, it had become common to compare Mrs Thatcher's government to the British high command during the First World War. This is Leslie Gibbard in the *Guardian* (27 August 1980).

On 3 September, a few days after Mrs Thatcher had got back from holiday, the Treasury's chief economic adviser, Terry Burns, sent over their latest forecast. Unemployment was rising steeply, the money supply was growing much faster than the target, competitiveness was in free-fall and inflation in nationalized industry prices was running at 25 per cent. Mrs Thatcher covered her copy with outraged exclamation marks and ferocious underlinings. And when, later that day, the Treasury ministers and Bank of England officials finally trooped in to see her, she was seething. What followed, remembered Burns, was a 'bit of a rant'. She began by reporting Karl Brunner's view 'that British money supply was out of control, that her strategy was right, but that it was not being properly operated'. Now they had given her these disastrous figures. 'She was determined to see both money supply and public expenditure back under control.' What did they propose to do about it?

For Sir Geoffrey Howe and Gordon Richardson, the next hour was pure agony. Whenever they tried to explain why so much money was sloshing around, she broke in to argue with them. Much of her fury was directed at Richardson, who at one stage told her that she 'did not properly understand' what she was talking about. 'The centre-piece of Government strategy was being undermined by her own supporters,' she said bitterly. At that, the Bank's Charles Goodhart pointed out that banks could not just stop lending money to industry, 'or many more businesses would go bust'. That, she snapped back, 'confirmed comments from her Swiss friends that the Bank was simply unwilling to implement Government strategy'. At one point she even threatened to call in the heads of the major banks herself, which Howe hastily said would be a very bad idea. All in all, the atmosphere could scarcely have been worse. Afterwards, one of her private secretaries, Michael Pattison, advised his fellow officials that relations with Richardson were now 'appalling – at least in the PM's eye'. Even five days later, Pattison warned his colleagues that she was still on the warpath. She could not be dissuaded, he wrote, from 'what the Swiss bankers told her when she was on holiday . . . that the Bank of England is not interested in running her policy'.[32]

By this stage, Mrs Thatcher had been in Number 10 for less than one and a half years. But already she was showing signs of one of her worst qualities, her tendency to hector and bully her own ministers. Sitting through her 'tantrums' that autumn, Lawson was struck by her 'embarrassing tendency to abuse Geoffrey Howe in front of officials', while even Howe, apparently so imperturbable, was frequently 'angry with her often ceaseless and hectoring interruptions'.[33]

Her chief whipping boy, though, was Richardson. The atmosphere at their meetings, recalled Tim Lankester, was positively 'poisonous', and on 19 September Richardson actually rang Number 10 to complain about her behaviour. According to the official record, Lankester admitted that 'this sort of uncomfortable meeting has happened before both on the foreign and the domestic side and the Governor should not be alarmed about it. He noted that the Prime Minister had not done her homework having commanded that work be done at great speed.' 'Perhaps', Richardson said witheringly, 'the answer was not just to seize on the first weapon that came to hand', and Mrs Thatcher ought to know that 'the whole problem [should] be looked at coolly'. Since Richardson clearly did not enjoy being lectured by a woman, there may have been an element of hurt pride in all this. Even so, he was far from the last person to find Mrs Thatcher's behaviour pretty shocking.[34]

By now almost everybody agreed that the pound had to come down. From Howe's perspective, the obvious solution was to cut interest rates. But one reason rates were so high was that investors had refused to buy government debt during the gilt strike of late 1979. The Chancellor could ill afford a repeat performance. As his officials pointed out, the markets would only let him cut interest rates if he cut government spending at the same time. That, of course, would be immensely contentious, since it meant piling on misery during a recession. But the high pound was doing so much damage to industry that if cutting spending was the price for lower interest rates, they simply had to pay it.[35]

For his part, Howe knew perfectly well that cutting spending would provoke a furious reaction. Yet many people on the right, including many business leaders, were now saying he had made a terrible mistake not to cut more deeply in 1979, because borrowing had got completely out of hand. This tallied with the message from Hoskyns's Policy Unit, which was begging Mrs Thatcher to bring spending down. And on 10 October, as she was preparing to address the Conservatives' party conference, Howe sent her a 'warning of further serious problems'. Thanks to the atrocious finances of the car, coal and steel industries, borrowing was 'worse than ever'. The Treasury now expected a deficit of some £11 billion in 1981–2, which meant Howe would need cuts of at least £2 billion, particularly in health, defence and social security. He knew, of course, that this would be 'strongly resisted' by his Cabinet colleagues. 'But the overall arithmetic will persuade you, as it has persuaded me, that we have to think in this kind of way.'[36]

In the meantime, the industrial picture was worsening by the hour. Thanks to the high pound, the competitiveness of British industry had deteriorated by almost a third since 1978. With order books blank, manufacturing output had fallen to its lowest level since the late 1960s – and still it kept falling. It was clear, said *The Times* on the first day of September, that this was not just another recession. In the City, experts told the paper that 'the industries and factories that are closing down can never be replaced ... For the first time the basic fabric of British industry is being threatened.' And although other industrial nations were facing similar problems – in France, unemployment passed 1½ million in October – nowhere were they remotely as bad as in Britain.[37]

Almost every day brought a fresh reminder of the plight of the jobless. 'I'm afraid of answering the phone,' one union leader remarked: 'every time it rings there is news of even more redundancies.' On 14 October the chemical giant ICI announced 4,000 further job cuts, most of them in Scotland, Northern Ireland and northern England. On 17 October the *Mirror* reported that a group of teenage girls in the bleak New Town of Washington, Tyne and Wear, were so frustrated by the lack of opportunities that they were 'hiring themselves out to tackle any job', no matter how menial, for a pound a day. That evening, hecklers shouting about unemployment disrupted the BBC's *Any Questions?*, which was being recorded down the road at Newcastle Polytechnic. And three days later came the news that officials at the Department of Health and Social Security were on the hunt for some new computers. According to the latest projections, unemployment would reach 2.8 million by the end of 1981. But the DHSS's existing machines could only process 2.7 million claims. Like so many of the assumptions that had governed British political life, the old computers had been left behind by the tide of change.[38]

On Wednesday 8 October Mrs Thatcher left Number 10 for Brighton. The Conservatives were out in force for their party conference, and by the time Mrs Thatcher arrived on the Sussex coast, the streets were packed with demonstrators. 'The whole approach to the hotel and to the conference hall itself was filled with absolute hatred for all of us, with the police, on foot and mounted, barely protecting us from what appeared to be a lynch mob,' wrote John Hoskyns. It was just as well, then, that he was preoccupied by Mrs Thatcher's 'bloody speech', which he was writing with Ronnie Millar. It was not going well. Two days earlier, Mrs Thatcher had got herself into a panic about it, and the next day she and Millar had had a 'shouting match at dinner'. All this was par for the course in the run-up to a major speech. But perhaps it also said something about the mounting pressure.[39]

Heavy rain was falling when, on Friday morning, the Tory faithful began trooping into the Brighton Centre for their leader's speech. Outside the grey concrete fortress stood two long lines of policemen, with dozens

of mounted reinforcements stationed outside the Grand Hotel. The mood
was awful, the police dogs barking and baying above the chants of thousands of Right to Work demonstrators. 'Tory scum! Tory scum!' they
yelled, waving their sodden Socialist Workers' Party placards. 'Maggie,
Maggie, Maggie! Out, out, out!' The rain hammered down; the atmosphere
became ever grimmer. At one stage the demonstrators began throwing
flour-bombs, prompting the police to charge the crowd and make a handful
of arrests. 'They want a good wash and a good hiding,' said one Tory
activist, who had just emerged from a 'brief and unpleasant encounter with
a Socialist Worker'. And as the minutes ticked down to Mrs Thatcher's
entrance, the staff in the conference foyer began to build a huge pile of
blankets. 'They are to cover the bodies,' a steward explained grimly.

At 2.30, having been escorted through a back door to avoid the mob,
the Prime Minister took the stage. Even now there was no escape from
the tension. Only moments after she had got to her feet, two demonstrators started shouting: 'Tories out! Power to the workers!' The security
guards were on them in a flash, but on the platform Mrs Thatcher barely
missed a beat. 'Never mind, it's wet outside,' she said coolly, as the television pictures showed one of the men being dragged away. 'You can't blame
them. It's always better where the Tories are.'[40]

In its way, this brief outbreak of mayhem was entirely fitting, underlining what the *Guardian*'s Ian Aitken called 'the atmosphere of the Palace
of Versailles before the French Revolution'. Much of Mrs Thatcher's
speech was the familiar diagnosis of national decline and the usual defence
of her harsh medicine as the only way to save the patient. But this time
she went out of her way to sympathize with those who were suffering,
dramatically lowering her voice when she came to the crucial passage:

> The fact remains that the level of unemployment in our country today is a
> human tragedy. Let me make it clear beyond doubt. I am profoundly con-
> cerned about unemployment. Human dignity and self-respect are
> undermined when men and women are condemned to idleness. The waste
> of a country's most precious assets – the talent and energy of its people –
> makes it the bounden duty of Government to seek a real and lasting cure.
>
> If I could press a button and genuinely solve the unemployment problem,
> do you think that I would not press that button this instant? Does anyone
> imagine that there is the smallest political gain in letting this unemployment
> continue, or that there is some obscure economic religion which demands
> this unemployment as part of its ritual? This Government are pursuing the
> only policy which gives any hope of bringing our people back to real and
> lasting employment.

But nobody remembered this part of the speech. They remembered what came next, when she addressed the idea that she would have to change course eventually. No, she said. 'To those waiting with bated breath for that favourite media catchphrase, the "U" turn, I have only one thing to say.' She paused for effect. 'You turn if you want to.' The audience laughed, and a wave of applause rippled through the hall. On the platform, Mrs Thatcher stood motionless, imperious, utterly unsmiling. 'The lady's not for turning.'[41]

Despite its reputation, Mrs Thatcher's 'not for turning' line was nothing new. She had been saying something like it for months, and the reference to Christopher Fry's play *The Lady's Not for Burning* (1948) probably went completely over the heads of younger listeners. But it mattered. It mattered because the parable of a shameful retreat from radical commitments had become so deeply embedded in the Thatcherite version of history. Most of her supporters remembered Heath's screeching reversal in the early 1970s, when, as they saw it, he had surrendered to the unions and betrayed his promises. No wonder, then, that they cheered what Edmund Dell called 'the ultimate statement that she was different from Heath'.

And because the obstinate message so perfectly captured her public image, the tabloids loved it. The *Express*, for example, put it on the front page, while the *Mirror* devised a more damning version: 'The lady's not for learning.' For a woman who boasted of her hatred of compromise, it became an enduring mantra. The irony is that it had taken considerable effort to get her to understand the joke. As Ronnie Millar recalled, she simply 'could not grasp that the first "You" needed to be stressed, to echo the "U-turn" in the preceding sentence'. But since it became a defining part of her legend, his efforts were worth it. A couple of days later, she sent him twenty-five cigars to say thank you.[42]

Mrs Thatcher's catchphrase meant everything and nothing. In public, it became the supreme symbol of her determination to stay the course. Yet even as she boasted of her inflexibility, her officials were preparing an adjustment to the route. At the Treasury, Howe's special adviser Adam Ridley told his boss that their approach had been far 'too severe'. At Number 10, John Hoskyns, never knowingly understated, compared their efforts to 'someone pouring buckets of water on a fire, when the realist would have recognised that it was time to dial 999 for the fire engines'. And at the Bank of England, Gordon Richardson's deputy, Kit McMahon, wrote that the high pound was 'now clearly intolerable. There is no other country in the world who would permit – or has permitted – the rate of deterioration of competitiveness that we have suffered in the last year or so.' McMahon knew Mrs Thatcher treated the Bank's advice with utter contempt. But she needed to be 'rescued', he wrote, from the 'over-severity' of her own policies.[43]

On the Monday after the party conference, the principals reassembled at Number 10 to begin the laborious process of changing tack. It was Mrs Thatcher's fifty-fifth birthday, but instead of bringing a cake, Richardson presented her with another barrel-load of gloom. Looking forward, he was 'extremely pessimistic'. The recession was 'likely to intensify and continue into 1982', when unemployment would almost certainly hit 3 million. Worse, 'because of our loss of competitiveness, recovery in the UK looked far less certain than in other countries'. So far, Richardson said, 'industrial closures had largely taken place where, because of inefficiency, they should be happening anyway'. But now the recession was destroying 'well-managed' firms, which ought to have been able to weather the tempest, and on which Britain's recovery should have been based.

So what to do? Mrs Thatcher tried to revive her hobbyhorse of Monetary Base Control. But Richardson and Howe insisted that it was better to cut interest rates, which meant they also needed to cut government borrowing. That would mean a very tough Budget in 1981. And at this supremely inappropriate moment, recalled the Bank of England's Charles Goodhart, 'there was wheeled out into this room a cake, a large cake. I have to say it was one of the most hideous cakes I've ever seen in my whole life.' The birthday girl immediately began carving slices for her officials. Goodhart remembered that it 'had brown icing sugar on top of which was a picture of the House of Commons picked out in green icing sugar. It looked absolutely revolting.' His colleague Eddie George whispered: 'I just don't think I can eat this.'[44]

By early November the new direction was more or less settled. Ideally, the Treasury wanted to cut interest rates by 2 per cent. But as Howe told the Cabinet, he would only get away with slashing rates if he cut the budget deficit by at least £2½ billion, which would mean some 'very difficult and disagreeable decisions' on spending. Some of his colleagues were outraged: when the Cabinet discussed Howe's plans, they argued that cutting spending 'could force out of business . . . some of the best companies in the country on whom the prospects of recovery would depend'. 'It's really Geoffrey and me against the rest of them,' Mrs Thatcher told a sympathetic backbencher. But since she was the boss, her voice was crucial. And with the exception of defence, where Francis Pym fought like a tiger to protect his departmental budget, Howe got his way.[45]

All the time, clouds gathered over the Palace of Westminster. When the

Tory backbench finance committee met to discuss the government's strategy, the words 'failed' and 'failure' came up again and again, especially
when it came to controlling the money supply and cutting public borrowing. Yet even as many Conservative MPs sank into despair, one familiar
face took great pleasure in Mrs Thatcher's plight. On 27 October Alan
Clark sat down in the Commons chamber, only to find Ted Heath rumbling ominously beside him, like a long-dormant volcano beginning to
smoke. 'He swivelled massively in his seat,' Clark recorded, 'and said, "At
last you're beginning to learn something", then swivelled ponderously
back and stared ahead.' Clark knew what he meant: 'All of you idiots who
voted for The Lady are now beginning to realise the mess you are getting
yourselves into.'[46]

It was easy for Mrs Thatcher's supporters to ignore criticism from the
least gracious loser in modern political history. But it was more difficult
to dismiss complaints from their natural supporters. By the autumn of
1980, more and more businessmen were joining the chorus of protest. A
survey by the Confederation of British Industry found that most firms
were slashing investment, laying off workers and digging deep into their
reserves – that is, if they were managing to survive at all. In some areas –
chemicals, coal, textiles, clothing – the output figures were so bad they
were barely credible: in metal manufacturing, for example, production
fell by almost 20 per cent between August and October 1980. And
although ministers insisted that the recession would leave industry 'leaner,
fitter [and] more efficient', *The Times*'s Peter Hill thought most firms were
more likely to stagger into the daylight 'weak, emaciated and debilitated'.
Few people disputed that 'there was scope for industry to trim its fat'. But
this was not a trim. It was a massacre.[47]

On 17 October the boss of the house-building giant Taylor Woodrow,
Sir Frank Taylor, resigned from the Centre for Policy Studies with a blistering denunciation of the government's approach. 'Businesses are going
broke,' he wrote angrily: 'unemployment is growing, the monetary situation is out of hand and Government spending is astronomical.' Three days
later, ICI's chairman visited Number 10 to warn Mrs Thatcher that his
firm, the 'bellwether of British industry', was about to announce the first
quarterly losses in its history. And although not every industrialist was as
outspoken as Sir Frank Taylor, such criticisms were becoming increasingly
common. Businesses might be able to live with a 'deep world recession',
'severe government policies' and even 'high interest rates', said the chairman of the Yorkshire CBI. What they could not do, though, was 'survive
all these and a high exchange rate as well'.[48]

Where Yorkshire led, Britain followed. On 11 November the CBI's director general Sir Terence Beckett rose to address his annual conference in Brighton. Never, he said, had the economic outlook been bleaker. But the government was in danger of destroying so 'much of our industrial capacity' that Britain 'might win the battle against inflation but lose the war for prosperity'. Indeed, many CBI members had told him that 'if we are not careful a lot of industry won't be around when the revival comes'. Yet Mrs Thatcher's ministers refused to listen. 'How many of them in Parliament or the Cabinet', he asked, 'have actually run a business?' So unless business leaders wanted an 'inexorable and miserable decline into shabby gentility, if we are lucky, or, more probably, Bennery', they should 'take the gloves off and have a bare-knuckle fight' with the government. They should think of it as the political equivalent of 'the SAS rescue at the Iranian Embassy'.[49]

For the head of the CBI to attack any government in such stark terms was sensational enough. For him to attack a *Conservative* government was simply extraordinary. For some Tory MPs, Beckett's remarks were tantamount to treason, and a handful of firms resigned from the CBI in protest. The irony was that Beckett should have been a natural Thatcherite. A Black Country grammar-school boy, he had served in the army in India and Malaya before working his way up the ladder at Ford, ending up as chief executive and chairman. What was more, he agreed with Mrs Thatcher's diagnosis of decline, and had taken the job at the CBI precisely because he believed that 'our whole way of life' was at stake. What he had not expected was that the threat would come from the right.[50]

Not even the CBI's friendly fire, though, could shake Mrs Thatcher's resolve. When *Private Eye*'s Denis Thatcher mentions the plight of British manufacturing to his wife, recounting the woes of a chap called Sharples, 'who runs a biro factory near Chislehurst', the Boss says coldly that 'there were bound to be some innocent casualties in the war against inflation'. And although she was not quite so blunt in real life, she had no intention of giving ground. In an interview with Thames TV's Judith Chalmers, she came close to blaming industry itself. The basic reality, she said, was that 'British industry is not as competitive as some of our other countries, as Germany, as Japan, as Switzerland . . . we're over-manned, full of restrictive practices . . . The result has been, they've got the business and the jobs and we haven't.' She pointed out that more than half of all cars bought in Britain in 1980 had been made abroad. 'We in this country weren't producing either the models or the price, or the delivery that other people were, so we have to look at the state of our industry . . . If we're not going to buy our own goods, how can we expect other people to?'[51]

On 25 November Howe unveiled his Autumn Statement to the Commons. The main features were the much-discussed 2 per cent cut in interest rates, as well as a new petrol tax and a 1 per cent increase in employers' National Insurance contributions. Yet although cutting interest rates marked a striking departure from the government's previous approach, most commentators were preoccupied with the fact that, at a time of unprecedented economic misery, the Chancellor seemed to be piling on the pain. And when Howe met Tory backbenchers later that afternoon, the mood was astonishingly aggressive. The government was 'running out of time', said Terence Higgins. They had failed to 'get public spending under control', said Julian Amery. Cutting interest rates was 'totally unjustified by the present state of the money supply or public sector borrowing', fumed Alan Clark. 'It is perfectly plain that Government policy is now seriously off course – with consequences that can only be bad both for the Party and the country.'[52]

'Unemployment is now rising by one person every 30 seconds, around the clock, seven days a week,' began the lead story in *The Times* the next morning. After the biggest monthly increase since the war, the jobless total had now reached 2.16 million. Yet this was only the official figure. Most experts thought the real total, which included people who had not bothered to register, was already well over 3 million. Turning Mrs Thatcher's favourite metaphor against her, the TUC's Len Murray described the figures as a 'thermometer of misery, recording the nation's growing sickness', and compared her ministers to 'medieval physicians who thought blood letting was a cure for anaemia'. For the *Mirror*, meanwhile, the 'working heart of Britain' was 'being sacrificed to economic theories better confined to a madhouse . . . Last month's rise ALONE was equal to the population of Cambridge.' But as the *Mirror* admitted, the news was so bad that it provoked a kind of stunned apathy rather than national outrage. 'Who can visualise 2,163,000 unemployed? Who can imagine a dole queue stretching from here to Siberia?'[53]

The next day brought a mini-eruption from the reawakening Mount Heath, who chose a debate on the economic situation to make his first major attack on Mrs Thatcher's policies in the House of Commons. As if picking the ideal moment to infuriate his own party, he spoke directly after his old foe Jim Callaghan. He and Callaghan, he said, belonged to a political generation who had been 'determined to prevent what happened in the 1930s from occurring again'. For a quarter of a century, they had given people a 'better standard of living, bigger and better homes, better education, a better Health Service, better roads and better transport'. But thanks to Mrs Thatcher's mismanagement, their achievements were threatened, while the Conservatives would be tarred forever as the 'party of unemployment'. That went down about as well as could be expected.

'How many elections did you lose?' yelled the Tory monetarist Jock Bruce-Gardyne. When the former Prime Minister sat down, said *The Times*, there were 'roars of applause from the Labour benches and a grim silence from Conservatives'. Deep down, more than a few of Mrs Thatcher's MPs shared Heath's views. But they were never going to show it.[54]

Heath's attack left Mrs Thatcher seething. On the 28th she gave an interview to Independent Radio News's political editor, Peter Allen, who inevitably quoted the line about the 'party of unemployment'. At that, she opened up with both barrels. 'Unemployment rose very sharply in Ted's time as well,' she said bitterly.

> He tried to overcome it by pumping money into the economy. We got an artificial boom, and do you know where the money went? It did not go into investment or expansion; it went into the biggest property boom we've ever seen ... And in the meantime inflation rose and rose. And the moment inflation goes up you are much less competitive, and eventually unemployment *rose again*.

What about Heath's suggestion that she did not care about unemployment? At this, her temper flared again:

> I hope that he will admit that unemployment has gone on mounting for the last twenty years. What I will not accept is the policy of those who want to spend more money. We haven't got more money; we're already over-spending. If you were to say to a family that was over-spending and in difficulty, 'Never mind, go on spending, borrow it from where ever you can, let the future take care of itself,' the future will not take care of itself. That is the morality of a man who has his hand in someone else's pocket.

'Compassion seems to be the element missing from everything you've said,' Allen observed. 'Of course I'm thinking about the people involved!' Mrs Thatcher snapped, before reaching for her beloved medical metaphor:

> It's like a nurse looking after an ill patient. Which is the better nurse? The one who smothers the patient with sympathy and says, 'Never mind, dear, there there, you just lie back and I'll bring you all your meals. I'll bring you all your papers. Just lie back, I'll look after you'? Or the nurse who says, 'Now, come on. Shake out of it. I know you've had an operation yesterday. It's time you put your feet to the ground and took a few steps. That's right, dear, that's right. Now get back and take a few more tomorrow.' Which do you think is the better nurse?

'I know which one sounds more like you, Mrs Thatcher,' Allen said with a smile. But she was in deadly earnest. 'Which is the one most likely to

get results?' she demanded. 'The one who says: "Come on, you can do it."
That's me.'[55]

Yet although the Tory press remained loyal, the front pages made for
grim reading. Almost every day there were mutters about splits, rifts and
plots. With the Autumn Statement generally seen as a disaster, there were
widespread rumours that Howe's position was crumbling. On 10 December his deputy, John Biffen, told the Tory backbench finance committee
that the monetary strategy had completely failed and that even he struggled to understand the MTFS. 'It is all a foreign tongue to me,' Biffen said
gloomily, adding that their M3 target had 'lost its credibility' and 'there
is nothing we can do about it'. Unfortunately, his words were leaked to
The Times, which saw them as proof that the government had no idea
what it was doing. Mrs Thatcher's ministers, wrote the columnist Geoffrey
Smith, were 'contemplating a scene in which they do not know how to
control the money supply by means of their favoured instrument, in which
they have anyhow lost confidence; public sector borrowing is beyond their
grasp; public spending cannot be cut much more; and direct taxation may
have to be increased.' To put it another way, they were in a hole, their
spade was broken and they were probably digging in the wrong direction
anyway.[56]

Christmas came, and the headlines were awful. On Christmas Eve the
latest figures put the unemployment total at 2.24 million, almost a tenth
of the entire workforce. Never had any post-war recession destroyed so
many jobs so quickly. For fifteen months each new set of figures had been
worse than the last. Every thirty seconds a new claimant joined the dole
queue. And now not even the most bullish ministers pretended that unemployment would come down any time soon. In private, almost everybody
admitted that they could see no end to it. As The Times remarked, this
was an 'exceedingly bleak end to what has been a grim year for the
economy'.[57]

Across the country, the mood could hardly have been gloomier. When
Gallup asked people about their expectations for 1981, three-quarters
thought things would get worse. And even Mrs Thatcher was feeling the
pressure. Three days before Christmas, the economist Brian Griffiths went
to see her in Downing Street. On his way in, Howe took him aside and
asked him 'not to be too critical – "She's in a very odd mood."' Griffiths
was with her for an hour, during which she twice came 'near to tears'. She
was 'speechless' when Gordon Richardson's name came up, and made no
secret of her belief that Howe had 'lost grip'. Above all, though, she wanted
Griffiths to answer the question that was bothering most people in Britain:
'What had gone wrong?'[58]

Yet as the Prime Minister wobbled, two of her closest confidants were scribbling letters of encouragement. One came from Howe himself. They were, he wrote, '*not* off track: but we are less well on track – and less far down the track – than either of us would have wanted'. The problem was that so few people grasped the scale of the mess into which Britain had got itself. 'Industrially and economically we are a relatively backward nation, and becoming more so.' But they had one thing going for them, 'and that, basically, is the Thatcher factor'. For the first time in years, Britain had a Prime Minister who was trying to change the course of the national story, and who had made it plain that she would not be discouraged. That could make all the difference. 'We have made a start – but only a start,' Howe wrote. 'To carry things through to the next stage, we need a considered plan – and soon. The hopes of very many people are still with us.'[59]

The second message came from a man on whom Mrs Thatcher was becoming ever more reliant. On the last Sunday of the year, her press secretary, Bernard Ingham, spotted a story in the *Observer*, which he forwarded to his boss. The latest edition of *Old Moore's Almanack* was out, with the usual bizarre predictions about the year ahead, from 'crop failures in the Soviet Union and riots in Paris' to a 'boom in adventure holidays and a growth in Open University summer schools'. Old Moore had long been a fan of the Prime Minister, but now the almanac had outdone itself. Almost uniquely among economic forecasters, its soothsayers believed Mrs Thatcher's medicine was working. By 1983 inflation would be under control, interest rates would be coming down and 'the nation's prestige and reputation in the world' would be greatly improved. And Old Moore knew who would deserve the credit:

> There are rare moments in history when one man or woman can, almost alone, shape the future of a nation.
>
> Now is such a moment. Margaret Thatcher is such a woman.
>
> The compelling pattern of her fate is so intimately interwoven with the present destiny of the United Kingdom that it is impossible to imagine that she will pass from power before her mission to heal and regenerate Britain is complete.

This was stirring stuff. But as the bells rang in the New Year, not many people believed it.[60]

# 12

# Nice Video, Shame about the Song

*When you've opened the door of your council flat, when you go to a comprehensive school with 2,000 kids there, you don't want to merge into the background. You want to stand out from that background. You want to look good just individually, yourself.*

Spandau Ballet's Gary Kemp, interviewed on BBC1's
*Nationwide*, 6 March 1981

*None of us want to blow the money. We want to be – I don't know – substantially wealthy. I mean ridiculously wealthy, rolling in it.*

Duran Duran's Simon Le Bon,
interviewed in *Sounds*, 11 September 1982

At the turn of the 1980s, *Top of the Pops* was in its pomp. Every Thursday evening some 10 million people tuned in to BBC1, keen to see which of the nation's favourites had taken the coveted number one spot. But when, on the evening of 24 May 1979, David 'Kid' Jensen welcomed the audience to the latest edition, few could have guessed what was coming. The line-up was reassuringly familiar: Roxy Music, Donna Summer, David Bowie, the Electric Light Orchestra, Blondie . . . and of course the inevitable dance troupe, Legs & Co. But then, directly after Roxy Music, an unknown band took the stage. Their name was Tubeway Army, their front man called himself Gary Numan and their song was 'Are "Friends" Electric?'

As Gary Numan admitted, he was a very unlikely candidate for pop stardom. Born Gary Webb in 1958, the son of a Heathrow baggage handler, he had drifted through various jobs without really settling down. In 1977 he and his friends formed a punk-influenced band and secured a record deal, but failed to make the slightest impact. But then, by chance, Numan began experimenting with a Minimoog synthesizer he had literally found lying around in the recording studio. The result was something entirely different: an electronic blast of modernity, but modernity of an extraordinarily cold and claustrophobic kind.

Numan had always been a troubled boy. At school he had been sent to a child psychiatrist and prescribed anti-depressants, and later he was diagnosed with Asperger syndrome. 'All my early songs', he said later, 'were about being alone or misunderstood.' Like many lonely teenagers of his generation, he had become obsessed with Philip K. Dick and J. G. Ballard, with computers, cyborgs and cities of the future. His new album, *Replicas* (1979), was based on his vision of a dystopian London, thirty years into the future. 'These machines – "friends" – come to the door,' Numan explained. 'They supply services of various kinds, but your neighbours never know what they really are since they look human. The one in the song is a prostitute, hence the inverted commas.'[1]

In the summer of 1979, a song about a robot prostitute was not an easy sell. Nor was Numan, gawky, shy and acutely self-conscious, an obvious heartthrob. But as he and his friends stood there that Thursday evening, dressed entirely in black, sweating beneath the television lights, they looked extraordinary. They barely moved; even Numan remained fixed to the spot, pale, impassive, like an android himself. By his own account, he carried himself like a robot to hide his terror and had whitened his face to mask his acne. His make-up artist told a slightly different story. He was 'otherworldly', she remembered:

> I imagined him as someone who never saw the sun – not because of lots of partying, but because he seemed so disconnected from nature. I wanted his skin to look pallid, so used a very light base. To make him look weary, I put on lots of dark, heavy kohl. He had to seem like a very complicated character: dark and remote, but not sinister, just cut off from his emotions.[2]

Even today, 'Are "Friends" Electric?' sounds like something from the future. To most listeners in May 1979, the jolting electronic opening, mesmeric rhythm and inhuman vocals were absolutely extraordinary. And quite apart from what *Smash Hits* called its 'dark, threatening wall of synthesised sound', there were the lyrics: lonely, paranoid, utterly bleak. 'It's cold outside', intones Numan's remote, reedy voice, 'and the paint's peeling off of my walls.' The light fades. There is a knock on the door; the singer opens it to find the 'friend' he left in the hallway. He asks himself: are 'friends' electric? His model has broken, and now he is alone, with nobody to love. 'Gripping,' *Smash Hits* said breezily, 'but cheerful it ain't.'[3]

Numan's appearance on *Top of the Pops* changed his life. On 19 May 'Are "Friends" Electric?' had been at number seventy-one. By 30 June it had reached number one, where it remained for four weeks. Then Numan released his next song, 'Cars', a paranoid hymn to the sanctuary of the automobile, inspired by J. G. Ballard's novel *Crash* (1973).* It ought to have been a disaster. Within a month it had reached number one, too. Numan had now topped the singles chart twice in just three months. By mid-autumn he also had three records in the top twenty of the album chart. Only a few months earlier, nobody outside his friends and family had ever heard of him.[4]

On Fleet Street, Numan was that familiar story, the boy next door made good. 'The pasty-faced 21 year-old, who picked his new name from a Yellow Pages directory, has emerged in the last three months as THE face of 1979,' declared the *Mirror*. But to the paper's surprise, 'the pallid pop star, who still lives at home with Mum and Dad in the tiny village of Wraybury, Buckinghamshire', was not enjoying life at the top. 'I got into all this originally because I liked the idea of being rich and famous, and now I know what it's like, I don't think I like it that much,' Numan explained. 'I don't like a lot of the people I've met . . . A lot of my fans aren't that nice, either.' His interviewer thought that was a bit sad. 'Despite his apparent remoteness he's really quite a friendly chap at heart,' she wrote. 'And his show is pretty impressive – even if Gary doesn't seem to enjoy it as much as everyone else.'[5]

There was an obvious reason why Numan was not enjoying life at the top. He had always dreamed of stardom, yet the music press treated him like an interloper. In an industry that prized authenticity and masculinity, he seemed contrived, robotic, androgynous. He had not courted papers like *Melody Maker* and the *NME*; he was shy, difficult, a loner. He was not politically progressive; worse, he admitted to having voted for Margaret Thatcher. Above all, he made *electronic* music, 'sinister and frigid', the kind of music you might expect to hear on a space station in the twenty-second century, not the kind of music most critics valued in the summer of 1979.

Not everybody hated him. *Melody Maker*'s young writer Jon Savage, formerly a champion of punk, thought people should take Numan seriously as the 'aural equivalent of other late '79 obsessions: the ubiquitous computer game, *Space Invaders*, and the latest filmic sensation, *Alien*'. But his voice was drowned out by the chorus of contempt. The *Guardian*'s Robin Denselow dismissed Numan as a 'cheap and nasty gangster', producing music of 'numbing, pounding monotony'. The *NME*'s Danny

---

* By the time 'Cars' was released, Tubeway Army had been relegated to backing musicians, so the single went out under Numan's name.

Baker claimed he was 'just a ham with a synthesizer . . . making intelligent music for people who aren't intelligent'. But it was another old *NME* hand, Charles Shaar Murray, who plunged in the knife. 'Just what is it, I wonder, that makes Gary Numan so repulsive?' he began one review. 'Is it his whining voice, his tawdry little fantasies, his ridiculous appearance, his endless stream of clichés, or is it some other, previously unconsidered factor? . . . Numan still seems utterly corpselike . . . a man spiritually three-fourths dead and proud of it, too. What's soft and white and numb all over? Gary Numan!'[6]

In the end, the critics got what they wanted. Although Numan followed 'Cars' with three more Top Ten singles, his fortunes soon entered a deep, irreversible decline. As electronic music moved into the mainstream and the spotlight shifted to more media-friendly bands – Ultravox, the Human League, Spandau Ballet and Duran Duran – he rapidly faded from view. The irony was that Jon Savage had been absolutely right. In his electronic futurism, his pervasive paranoia, his love of dressing up and his androgynous persona, Numan had perfectly anticipated the cultural mood of the 1980s. But he paid a heavy price for being a pioneer. Few pop stars had ever risen so fast; few had experienced such a precipitous fall from grace. In the summer of 1979, Gary Numan had been the voice of the future. But within just three years he was yesterday's man.[7]

There was a good reason why Numan's music had struck a chord with millions of listeners. Three years after the Sex Pistols had exploded into the headlines, punk's diabolical energy had long since evaporated. As early as 1977, critics were complaining that it had become a formulaic self-parody, and when the Sex Pistols broke up the following February, the *Evening Standard* declared that 'punk is dead'. Even its supposedly shocking look – leather jacket, ripped T-shirt, dyed spiky hair – was now just another kind of dressing-up, memorably parodied by Adrian Edmondson in the BBC sitcom *The Young Ones*. These days, wrote the journalist Peter York in 1980, the typical punk was 'a nice little fifth former' from affluent, suburban Muswell Hill. 'It was always in the fine old provincial towns and county seats', thought Paul Theroux, 'that one saw the wildest-looking youths, the pink-haired boys and the girls in leopard-skin tights, the nose-jewels and tattooed earlobes.' Even Adrian Mole's spotty friend Nigel is a punk, though only at weekends. 'His mother lets him be one', records Adrian, 'providing he wears a string vest under his bondage T-shirt.'[8]

Most British youngsters never bought a punk record. Despite its impact on fashion and design, its presence in the charts was vanishingly small.

In fact, the general picture at the end of the 1970s seemed one of nostalgia to the point of total stagnation. The bestselling albums of 1978 were the soundtracks of *Saturday Night Fever* and *Grease*, with Nat King Cole and Buddy Holly not far behind. A year later, Blondie and the Electric Light Orchestra led the way, but the success of greatest hits albums by Leo Sayer, Barbra Streisand and Rod Stewart told its own story. Even in the singles charts, the bestselling songs of 1978 and 1979 came from Boney M, John Travolta and Olivia Newton-John, Art Garfunkel, and Cliff Richard. Meanwhile, the *NME*, *Melody Maker* and *Sounds* seemed to have sunk into terminally dreary, point-scoring earnestness. 'A lot of the articles', complained the young journalist Craig Brown, 'are hardly about pop stars at all, but full of discussion about how to change society'. Even the photos told the same story. Once pop groups had been photographed leaping about and having fun. Now they were pictured 'in very grainy black and white, looking miserable on a motorway or sad under a subway'.[9]

It was no wonder, then, that people were desperate for something new. Many teenagers at the turn of the 1980s could barely remember Johnny Rotten and Ziggy Stardust, let alone John Lennon and Paul McCartney. 'Teenagers who are picking up on pop for the first time should have a fresh, changing choice, not a stiff handed-down one,' lamented the pop writer Paul Morley. It was time, he wrote, to bring back 'colour, dance, excitement . . . intelligence, intrigue, a love of the little things in life, re-applying and reinforcing the essentials of the pop spirit for the new age . . . This doesn't mean escapism. But you can't moan all the time.'[10]

Almost unnoticed amid the furore about punk, there had been hints of a seismic change in the way people made music. Ever since the beginning of the 1970s, interest had been growing in electronic music, as popularized by Wendy Carlos's soundtrack for *A Clockwork Orange* (1971) and the first albums by the German synth-pop pioneers Kraftwerk. To its small band of admirers, electronic music was the future. To the general public, it was the music of high-rise blocks and windswept concrete estates, frigidity and fear. But in 1977 the Munich-based producer Giorgio Moroder put a synthesized backing track on to Donna Summer's 'I Feel Love', turning it into a massive worldwide hit. For the first time, electronic music was *fun*. In Berlin, Roxy Music's former synthesizer player Brian Eno burst into David Bowie's recording studio, waving a copy of Summer's hit and exclaiming that he had just heard the music of the future. 'If any one song can be pinpointed as where the 1980s began,' writes the critic Simon Reynolds, 'it's "I Feel Love".'[11]

In the past, making electronic music had required an arsenal of expensive synthesizers. But as synthesizers became smaller and lighter, the price of entry plunged. By the turn of the 1980s, the British firm EDP's Wasp synthesizer cost no more than £200 (just over £1,000 today). 'A small synthesiser now costs less than a good electric guitar, and it doesn't take years of practice to get something good out of it,' reported the *Observer* in August 1980. 'The synthesiser sets the musical imagination free very quickly. Not surprisingly, the new generation of musicians is taking to it in a big way.'[12]

The result was a new kind of skiffle, with synthesizers instead of guitars, but with the same spirit of do-it-yourself improvisation. In Sheffield, two computer operators, Martyn Ware and Ian Craig Marsh, formed a band called the Future, later renamed the Human League. In Liverpool, Andy McCluskey and Paul Humphreys formed Orchestral Manoeuvres in the Dark, using a cheap synthesizer bought from a mail-order catalogue. But at first these new synth-pop bands struggled for attention. Their sensibility was closer to progressive rock than to punk; they wrote songs inspired by J. G. Ballard, George Orwell and *Doctor Who*, not teenage ballads or shrieks of rage. As Reynolds puts it, they appealed to 'people who read *New Scientist* and watched *Tomorrow's World*', not people who read *Smash Hits* and watched *Starsky & Hutch*. David Bowie once said that watching the Human League was 'like watching 1980', a slightly barbed compliment given that he said it in 1979. But when 1980 arrived, most people had never heard of them.[13]

What the new generation needed was a story, something to seize the public imagination and capture the attention of the national press. The story eventually materialized, but it was not what many synth-pop pioneers were expecting. It was set, not in Sheffield or Liverpool, but in London, in a shabby Second World War-themed wine bar in a Covent Garden side street, with gingham tablecloths and framed pictures of Winston Churchill. The bar's name was the Blitz.

On 6 February 1979 the Blitz began running weekly 'Electro-Diskow' evenings, organized by a 19-year-old Welshman with thick make-up and very imaginative hair. This was Steve Strange, who had previously run a popular David Bowie-themed night at a Soho club called Billy's. Among London's young partygoers, Strange was already something of a cult figure, renowned for his outlandish costumes: 'leather jodhpurs and Nazi greatcoat' one week, 'clownish, white-face Pierrot' the next. At the Blitz, he said, he wanted only 'people who created unique identities'. Guarding the doorway on Great Queen Street every Tuesday, he would cast an unsparing eye over the queues waiting to get in. Sometimes he invited people to look in his little mirror: 'Would you let yourself in?' And while some of Strange's friends saw him as a bit of a joke, he was in deadly earnest. 'For me,' he said later, 'it wasn't just dressing up for the night.' It was Art.[14]

Music was an essential part of the Blitz's appeal. As the *Evening Standard*'s pop columnist David Johnson recalled, it pounded out a relentless soundtrack of Kraftwerk, Gina X and Giorgio Moroder: 'hard-edged European disco, synth-led but bass-heavy'. Yet what many of its regulars really remembered were the clothes. Inside, wrote Johnson, 'Hammer Horror met Rank starlet. Here was Lady Ample Eyeful, there Sir Gesting Sharpfellow, lads in breeches and frilly shirts, white stockings and ballet pumps, girls as Left Bank whores or stiletto-heeled vamps dressed for cocktails in a Berlin cabaret, wicked witches, kohl-eyed ghouls, futuristic man machines.' Another young regular recalled a 'costume box of a club', where on his first night he saw 'two boys, one in a shoulder cape and cummerbund, the other a military shirt with Sam Browne belt . . . two girls in black taffeta, glam with gothic trim . . . an androgynous thing with a shaved head, false eyelashes and a ruff . . . a red sash . . . Chinese slippers and winged collars'. On later visits he saw 'feathers and boas', a 'crushed stovepipe hat and Artful Dodger trousers', a 'silver-topped cane' or two. 'The neckerchief', he writes, 'was in evidence everywhere' – a line that would make a good epitaph for the entire period.[15]

The Blitz's appeal was very obvious. When it opened, the Winter of Discontent was in full swing: atrocious weather, industrial unrest, political paralysis, national gloom. Its first visitors had to pick their way past the heaps of sodden cardboard boxes and bursting black bin-liners, thanks to the public sector strikes that had turned the West End into a rubbish tip. 'The city was broken, it was a horrible place,' recalled one Blitz habitué, while another remembered that they 'badly wanted a new swinging London'. For youngsters alienated by punk, depressed about their prospects and desperate for a bit of excitement, the Blitz was pure escapism. As Strange put it, his customers were 'people who work nine to five and then go out and live their fantasies. They're glad to be dressed up and escaping work and all the greyness and depression.'[16]

Yet even at the time, the Blitz was invested with an extraordinary mystique. Its regulars, the so-called 'Blitz Kids', saw themselves as pioneers, striking out for a brave new world of individual self-expression. And for some of their supporters, their self-conscious flamboyance carried immense significance. One early visitor, the style journalist Peter York, wrote endless columns about the cultural symbolism of 'dressing up'. The *Standard*'s David Johnson claimed that 'dressing up at the Blitz became an act of affirmation', while the pop journalist Dave Rimmer even argued that, at the Blitz, 'each individual consumer choice [was] a creative act', leading

inevitably to 'the creative equality of consumption'. A cynic might think
this a very extravagant way of talking about a couple of hundred teenagers
in pink feather boas and copious amounts of eyeliner.[17]

Was the Blitz really so novel? Enthusiasts for the Blitz Kids often
claimed that they were different from, say, Mods, Rockers and Teddy Boys
because they chose their clothes for themselves, instead of wearing
a uniform. There were 'so many different styles on parade', writes Rimmer, that 'it looked more like a costume ball than a single, homogenous
scene'. But the people photographed in his book look almost exactly the
same: whitened faces, heavy eyeliner, white shirts, black capes, like people
queuing up to make a withdrawal from a Transylvanian blood bank. It is
hard to believe that dozens of 19-year-olds *independently* decided to invest
in an Elizabethan ruff, or that across Greater London hundreds of youngsters simultaneously realized that there was no such thing as too much eye
make-up. In any case, as one Blitz Kid remarked, 'Kids have always spent
what little they have on records and haircuts. They've never spent it on
books by Karl Marx.' 'They especially liked dressing up,' agreed Paul
Theroux in 1982. 'That seemed to be part of the English character – entering
into fantasy, putting on different clothes and setting the old dull personality aside.' As it happens, he was talking about steam-train enthusiasts. But
he could easily have been talking about the Blitz Kids.[18]

It was not long before people noticed the Blitz. After all, the whole
point of dressing up was to get people to look at you. In January 1980
David Johnson became the first journalist to write about the crowd at
Strange's Electro-Diskow, which he called 'the 80s Set'. The *Guardian*'s
Martin Walker goggled at 'two women in spangled leotards with shaven
hair . . . and between them a man in metallic robes, his face smeared away
in white mask, another face painted onto the back of his shaven head'.
Even *Newsnight* sent a film crew to see what all the fuss was about. One
of the most entertaining pieces, however, came in the *Mirror* that March.
'The Blitz Kids', the paper declared, were 'the chosen few [who] like to
think of themselves as a new kind of artificial aristocracy' – a line that
would have been familiar to anybody who remembered Swinging
London:

> Punk is past it. Mods are old hat. A new youth cult is, according to its
> bizarre disciples, all set to sweep Britain.
>
> They call themselves the Blitz Kids. Their idea of fun is sheer fantasy
> and almost anything goes . . .
>
> THEY DRESS in clothes ranging from crinolines to clown costumes.
> THEY LISTEN to loud, repetitive electronic music by cult bands.

THEY DANCE using a mesmeric mixture of mime and robot movements . . .

On my visit I saw a Marilyn Monroe lookalike . . . drinking . . . cuddling a clown.

And another young 'nun' being shot a line by a cowboy.

In fact, the *Mirror* admitted that most of the Blitz Kids were 'ordinary young people with everyday jobs', who simply liked to spend their money on 'their look of the moment'. The clown, for example, was actually Richard Wakefield, a 19-year-old telephonist from Putney in south-west London. He usually dressed less extravagantly, he said, although 'the ladies I work with say I cheer them up'. As for Marilyn, she was Jayne Sparkes, an 18-year-old secretary. She found the Blitz a nice change, because 'in pubs people usually ask you if you're going to a fancy dress party. When you say you're not, it's just the way you dress, they often get a bit rude or insulting.'[19]

Among the young men and women who flocked to Covent Garden on Tuesdays was an ambitious 19-year-old called Gary Kemp. Born into a working-class family in Islington, he had grown up in a world that seemed an eternity away from Swinging London. His father was a printer, his mother a part-time sewing machinist. They lived in a terraced house with no bathroom and a 'reeking, damp' outside toilet, infested with insects. Money was scarce: Gary remembered his mother bursting into tears when she realized his shoes were too small, because she could not afford a new pair. 'Everyone we knew owned very little,' he wrote: 'houses were rented, and everything we sat on, slept on, drove in and watched was on HP [hire purchase].'

Growing up in the 1970s, young Gary dreamed of clothes and parties, of making money, bettering himself and getting on. When, as a 12-year-old, he saw David Bowie on *Top of the Pops*, he fell in love with pop music, a 'theatre of glittering aspiration'. Later, he and his school friends were attracted to punk and formed their own band. But by the end of the decade they preferred soul music, cutting their hair in wedges and dressing in smart waistcoats. Even their band's name, the Gentry, was a sign of generational rebellion. Kemp called it an 'anti-punk statement'.[20]

Gary Kemp, his brother Martin and their schoolmates first discovered Steve Strange's club at the end of 1978, having heard that it was full of 'people in amazing gear'. It was 'very clothes orientated', he remembered. 'The music was irrelevant really.' There they befriended a student called Robert Elms, 'a cockney with the vocabulary of Nietzsche', who was similarly keen to break free from punk's dour grip and embrace the 'thrill

and flash of youth and style'. It was Elms who suggested they call themselves Spandau Ballet – a name that both recalled punk's obsession with
the Nazis and captured the growing fashion for German electronica. Yet
although people often think of Spandau Ballet as a synthesizer band, they
always saw themselves as a soul-influenced pop group. 'It's not weird
electronic music at all, it's dance music,' Kemp told *Sounds*. 'There's only
one synthesiser in it and it's not even dominant . . . The songs themselves
are very emotional, melody wise, not cold or clinical.'[21]

What set Spandau Ballet apart was their enthusiasm for dressing up.
Every appearance saw some fresh attack on conventional taste: billowing
shirts and ballooning breeches; capes, cravats and cummerbunds; tunics
and tabards; smoking jackets, waistcoats and monocles – as if they had
raided a Victorian fancy dress shop and wanted to wear everything at least
once. People mocked them for it, but they remained unrepentant. When
*Sounds* accused them of 'posing', Gary Kemp called it a 'terrible word'.
'Do you dress for functional reasons only?' he demanded. 'You dress to
attract and look good, don't you? . . . They rattle on about other people's
works of art when the real work of art should be you.' His friend and
manager, Steve Dagger, made the same point a few weeks later to the
*NME*. 'You can make a statement with the clothes you wear,' he explained.
'You can't express anything with the records you might buy but you can
express yourself with the clothes you choose – turn yourself into a piece
of art, if you want to see it in those terms.'[22]

Spandau Ballet made their first public appearance at the Blitz's Christmas party in December 1979, dressed in a surely unforgivable mixture of
wing collars, bow ties, 'tartan trousers and green velvet slippers'. They
went down very well, and soon the record companies began to circle. Being
so young, they were cocky: interviewed by London Weekend Television's
Janet Street-Porter, Kemp boasted that they were bound to 'sell thousands
of records'. By the summer, they had played a few more gigs, including
one on HMS *Belfast*, and soon afterwards they signed a reported £85,000
deal with Chrysalis. In a sign of the times, Chrysalis agreed to let them
manage their own merchandising rights and promised to produce a video
with every single they released. Spandau Ballet were 'not just a band with
an audience', Kemp told the record company; they were a 'multimedia
phenomenon'. At this stage, they had only played eight live dates, so that
was a very grand way of putting it. But it paid off.[23]

In the national press, Spandau Ballet were a story even before they had
released their first record. 'Coming up Poses' read the *Mirror*'s headline
on 22 October, hailing a band that was 'going to be one of the big sounds
of the Eighties'. And when, two weeks later, they released their first single,

'To Cut a Long Story Short', it duly reached number five, a strong debut for a band that only weeks before had been largely unknown. All the same, this was not quite the all-conquering performance they might have hoped for. Indeed, of their next eight singles only one made the top five, and it was not until the spring of 1983 that 'True' gave them their first number one. In pure sales terms, the likes of Adam and the Ants, the Human League and even Shakin' Stevens left them standing.[24]

But there was something about Spandau Ballet. One way of putting it is that, like the Beatles in the 1960s or the Sex Pistols in the 1970s, they were thought to embody the spirit of the age. When people said that about Spandau Ballet, however, they did not mean it kindly. 'Somehow, Spandau Ballet have managed to antagonise people who have only ever heard their name or seen a photograph,' observed the *NME* in November 1980. Most people thought they had got their deal 'just on the strength of their clothes and their photos'. And as the *NME* remarked, that made it 'one of the biggest snubs the long-suffering rock fan with his cherished notions of musical validity and paying one's dues has had since the Sex Pistols sent the whole thing spinning some three years back'.

The animosity between Spandau Ballet and the traditional rock music press is a very good example of the cultural fault lines running through the early 1980s. The people who wrote for papers like *Melody Maker* and the *NME* tended to be older, more middle-class and more politically committed. They saw themselves as guardians of the spirit of the 1960s, preserving the values of seriousness, authenticity and commitment. By contrast, Kemp and his friends had no time for rock music, bypassed the music press and presented themselves as youthful rebels against an ageing establishment. 'With what we're doing, there's no one over the age of 23 involved,' Kemp boasted. 'Everybody doing it – running the clubs, playing the records, dressing up, making the music, making the clothes – none of them are over 23.' It was ironic, he said, that the press 'don't mind some old shark like [the Sex Pistols' manager Malcolm] McLaren manufacturing something to make some money out of the kids, and yet they slag us off, us, the actual "kids". I just don't understand it.'[25]

Kemp talked of rock critics the way many young men of his age talked about their parents – or the way Mrs Thatcher's upwardly mobile supporters talked about the old patricians. 'A lot of the music papers have got their own archetypal view of the social system and order, and how it should be,' he told *Sounds*, 'and the thought of people like us actually spending their money on looking good and expensive and enjoying themselves, they just can't stand it.' Indeed, like a certain person who lived just off Whitehall, he saw himself as a champion of working-class ambition against a snobbish old guard. 'Middle-class journalists', he said scathingly, 'always connect style with being bourgeois and they spend their whole lives trying to escape it. I don't feel guilty because I've made enough money to own my own home. It's only the middle classes who feel that kind of guilt.'[26]

But Spandau Ballet did have their supporters. The early 1980s were years of great innovation for magazines and comics, with music and style publications in the vanguard. In 1978 the former *NME* editor Nick Logan had launched *Smash Hits*, a breezy, glossy publication that celebrated the music in the charts instead of debating whether some obscure punk band might be influenced by the Situationist International. By the summer of 1979, it was selling more than 166,000 copies every fortnight, more than *Melody Maker* and only 35,000 fewer than the *NME*. A few months later, Logan floated the idea of another glossy magazine, this time aimed at affluent music fans in their late teens and early twenties. He called it *The Face*, and the title could hardly have been more appropriate.[27]

As Logan explained to the publishers, *The Face* would be a magazine with photography front and centre, embracing the latest musical trends and devoted to the cult of the image. 'I'm looking for the kids who participate in the music scene,' he told the *Evening Standard*. 'The ones who have a good time rather than just sit at home listening to the hifi.' He made it sound remarkably similar to the magazines that had become synonymous with the pop-cultural explosion of the early 1960s, such as Jocelyn Stevens's *Queen* or the ground-breaking *Sunday Times Colour Section*. Indeed, his pitch explicitly envisaged it as an '"unofficial" monthly colour supplement' to 'weekly tabloids' such as the *NME*, *Melody Maker* and *Sounds*.[28]

The advent of *The Face* was very good news for bands like Spandau Ballet. Like them, the magazine saw pop culture as a visual phenomenon, devoting enormous amounts of time to its own image. In the late summer of 1980, Kemp's friend Robert Elms joined Logan's bandwagon, kicking off with three pages about – surprise, surprise – Spandau Ballet, 'openly poseur, stridently elitist', who were 'attracting the capital's pretty young things to an androgynous man'. Some people might have thought this a bit over the top given that they had yet to release a record. But since *The Face*'s early sales had not been as brisk as Logan had hoped, he decided to throw in his lot with the Blitz Kids. In the November issue he gave Elms his head, commissioning a long essay on 'The Cult with No Name'. Elms duly went back over the top, waxing lyrical about the 'immaculately if extraordinarily dressed young socialites' who had frequented the Blitz, a 'creative environment where individualism was stressed and change was vital'. That made the Blitz sound like a branch of the Young Conservatives. But it worked. For when Elms announced that he and his friends were setting 'the styles to be copied in terms of both look and sound', at least some of the readers believed him.[29]

*The Face* was not the only new magazine to profit from the new mood. In October 1980 the former art director of *Vogue* launched his own quarterly style magazine, *i-D*, which appealed to a similar market. Another fashion magazine, *Blitz* – the name apparently a complete coincidence – appeared in the same year, while *New Sounds New Styles*, with its truly terrible title, followed in 1981. None of them, it has to be said, was as much fun as *Smash Hits*. But they represented a marked turn against the political earnestness of the punk years, as well as an enthusiastic embrace of consumerism, hedonism, dressing up and showing off, wrapped up in the single word *style*. Even the look of the new magazines seemed more colourful, a 'bold, bracing geometry of hard angles and primary colour blocks'. Above all, though, they represented the triumph of aspiration. A few years later, after British pop had conquered the American charts, the broadsheets devoted long essays to the appeal of Britain's music videos, 'glossy brochures for fantasy lifestyles'. But their directors were merely putting on screen what magazines like *The Face*, and the colour supplements that inspired it, had been doing for years.[30]

By the middle of 1980, therefore, there had been a palpable shift in the cultural temperature. Punk was out; what Elms called 'the Cult with No Name' was in. Even David Bowie, the patron saint of silly outfits and clown costumes,* gave his seal of approval, visiting the Blitz in May 1980 to recruit performers for his 'Ashes to Ashes' video. They filmed the following morning on a beach near Hastings. Bowie, at his most grandiloquent, was dressed as a Pierrot, while Steve Strange and his friends were wearing long robes and otherworldly black hats, and looked like extras from *Blake's 7*. Later, the video was seen as a landmark in the popular culture of the 1980s, a riot of clashing images and computer graphics. But Bowie remembered it for another reason. Early in the morning, while they were filming on the beach, an old man walking his dog wandered into shot. Exasperated, the director pointed to Bowie and asked if the man knew who he was. The man looked him up and down. 'Of course I do,' he said. 'It's some cunt in a clown suit.'[31]

Whatever Bowie's friend on the beach might have thought, 'Ashes to Ashes' was an undisputed hit, topping the singles chart at the end of

---

* Sorry: that should read 'individual self-reinvention, self-expression and gender fluidity'.

August. The sound was Bowie's own, but the look was very much of the moment: flamboyant costumes, a white-faced clown and above all an atmosphere of doom-laden futurism, which Bowie called 'nostalgia for the future'. And where Bowie led, Steve Strange inevitably followed. Three months later, his band Visage released 'Fade to Grey', which became one of the defining hits of the early 1980s. Today it is probably best remembered for its video, all slow-motion close-ups of glassy-eyed models with elaborate hairstyles, robotically intoning lyrics to the camera. Much of this was obviously borrowed from Bowie, not least Strange's clownish get-up. If you thought about it, the song was completely meaningless, the non-story of a man with a suitcase sitting on a railway platform. But you were not supposed to think about it. You were supposed to enjoy the disco-influenced rhythms, to savour the portentous French lyrics, to yield to the atmosphere, at once fey, funereal and futuristic, as if Aubrey Beardsley had popped up in *Doctor Who*. It was ridiculous, of course. But it was fun.[32]

By the time 'Fade to Grey' reached the Top Ten, the emerging generation had a name. They were the New Romantics, a label coined by the *Sounds* journalist Betty Page in a Spandau Ballet profile on 13 September. Later, critics pointed out that it lumped together two slightly different trends. On the one hand were ambitious pop bands, often from London and associated with the Blitz and other dance clubs, such as Visage, Ultravox and Spandau Ballet. On the other were the electronic groups from industrial cities like Manchester and Sheffield, such as the Human League and Orchestral Manoeuvres in the Dark, who were more obviously indebted to Kraftwerk and Giorgio Moroder. But the name stuck. As Gary Kemp wrote, it 'seemed to sum up the anachronism of the fashions and the whimsical approach to clothes', as well as the 'mood-noise of the lyrics and music, with its conceit that it all somehow meant something grander'. Above all, Kemp thought 'it highlighted the cult of self, a powerful philosophy that would exemplify the coming decade'.[33]

If Visage popularized the New Romantic formula, Ultravox carried it to perfection. They shared some of the same personnel, not least the singer Midge Ure, who had produced 'Fade to Grey' while using Strange as a front man. That autumn Ultravox released perhaps *the* emblematic pop single of the early 1980s, the magnificently faux-decadent 'Vienna'. Like 'Ashes to Ashes' and 'Fade to Grey', it came with an immensely pretentious and hugely enjoyable video: misty black-and-white streets, gorgeous models in fur coats, decadent candle-lit parties, an opera house, men in sashes, a random horse – the works. 'It means nothing to me,' runs the chorus, and it probably meant nothing to anybody else either. *Melody Maker* thought it 'unbearably po-faced', which was a bit rich coming from *Melody Maker*. But the public loved it. Wreathed in industrial quantities of dry ice, 'Vienna' entered the singles chart in mid-January 1981 and remained there for an impressive fourteen weeks, four of them at number two. Famously, the song that denied it the top spot was Joe Dolce's mock-Italian 'Shaddap You Face'. That shows how foolish it is for historians to read anything into the singles charts.[34]

By now the New Romantic moment had definitively arrived. Like the beat groups of the early 1960s, synth-pop groups were riding a wave of popular enthusiasm. Youth culture, declared the *Observer* in March 1981, belonged to the 'electronic Futurists', with their 'bold and imaginative use of the latest in musical technology – synthesisers, computers, electronic gadgets in general'. And, as predicted, the summer of 1981 belonged to Spandau Ballet's 'Chant No. 1' and Duran Duran's 'Girls on Film', the Human League's 'The Sound of the Crowd' and 'Love Action', Orchestral Manoeuvres in the Dark's 'Souvenir' and 'Joan of Arc', Depeche Mode's 'New Life' and 'Just Can't Get Enough', even Adam and the Ants' 'Stand and Deliver' and 'Prince Charming'. As Simon Reynolds remarks, it was as if 'an invisible switch had been pulled and the floodgates opened to irrigate the charts with a rejuvenating gush of colour, exuberance and optimism'.[35]

Perhaps not since the mid-1960s had British pop seemed so catchy, so imaginative, so alive. The bestselling record of 1981 was Soft Cell's 'Tainted Love'; the coveted Christmas number one, meanwhile, was the Human League's splendid 'Don't You Want Me'. Even abroad the New Romantics seemed unstoppable. 'Tainted Love' spent a record-breaking forty-three weeks in the *Billboard* Hot 100 and topped the charts in Canada, Australia and West Germany. Amid growing fears of a second British Invasion, the *New York Times* launched a pre-emptive strike, denouncing the 'clichéd rhythms, clichéd arranging ideas and clichéd overall sound' of the 'British electro-pop bands'. But even the world's most pompous paper could see the writing on the wall. 'One suspects', it said sadly, 'that it's only a matter of time before a group like Soft Cell or the Human League scores a substantial pop hit here.'[36]

What did all these groups have in common? What made them distinctive? One common factor was the influence of David Bowie, whose song 'Starman' (1972) had inspired the young Gary Kemp. Steve Strange's first club nights had been billed as 'Bowie Nights', the tone set by his song 'Heroes' (1977), the extroverted atmosphere reminiscent of Ziggy Stardust in his pomp. But punk played a pivotal role, too. Many New Romantics had been punks at school. Their shock-and-awe approach to clothes came directly from punk; so did their cocky do-it-yourself spirit. The difference was that while punks had been reacting against the grandiose pretensions of the mid-1970s, Kemp's generation were rebelling against punk itself, the spiky hair and snarling aggression. 'Punk had become a parody of itself, an anti-Establishment uniform ... a joke, right down to the £80 Anarchy T-shirts,' recalled the future Boy George. 'Punk was safe, we were spinning forward in a whirl of eyeliner and ruffles.'[37]

None of this, perhaps, was very remarkable. What *was* remarkable was that when the New Romantics looked abroad for inspiration, they looked across the North Sea, not the Atlantic. Ever since the advent of rock and roll, the dominant influence on British music, from rhythm and blues to soul and disco, had been American. But the New Romantics were different. Uniquely among modern British youth subcultures, they looked to Europe, especially Germany. As before, Bowie had got there first, moving to West Berlin in 1976 and releasing two enormously influential albums, *Low* and *'Heroes'* a year later. As Dave Rimmer writes, Bowie inspired British bands to abandon the 'extraverted "American" idea of rock 'n' roll authenticity' for the 'introverted "European" artifice' of 'synthesizer pop and electronic landscapes'. To be European was to be 'withdrawn, passive, fatalistic', and so much worldlier than the earnest, unsophisticated Americans. The Blitz played lots of German dance music, but virtually nothing American. 'Fade to Grey' was partly in French; Ultravox wrote a song about Vienna; Orchestral Manoeuvres in the Dark wrote two songs about Joan of Arc. Even Spandau Ballet, whose hearts lay in American soul, were named after Berlin's infamous prison.[38]

What was also remarkable was that to be German, or at least German in spirit, was to belong to the future. Under the influence of Kraftwerk, pop music in the early 1980s had a sense of its own modernity, of reaching towards tomorrow, that had been almost completely missing for the previous decade. The Sex Pistols had proclaimed that there was 'no future', yet for Gary Numan, the Human League and Orchestral Manoeuvres in the Dark, there were, in Reynolds's words, 'still places to go . . . a whole new future to invent'. Hence the robotic dancing and dehumanized vocals, the lyrics about cyborg lovers and cities of the future; hence the nickname 'Futurists', which some of them preferred to 'New Romantics'.[39]

To the general public, though, what set the New Romantics apart was their extraordinary aesthetic. The photographers' darling was Adam Ant, formerly Stuart Goddard, who had started out as a punk before reinventing himself as an extra from *The Pirates of Penzance*. If songs like the chart-topping 'Stand and Deliver' and 'Prince Charming' were bombastic, his look was pure pantomime, described by the *NME* as 'half pirate, half

Red Indian . . . a strange blaze of gold and scarlet; a bizarre collage of feathers and braid . . . with vivid paint slashed across brown skin and teeth that flash startling white'. By tying a silk scarf around one arm, Ant said, he was acknowledging a 'debt to the Royalist/Cromwellian era', while his tricolour cummerbund paid homage to 'the idea of the French Revolution'. The overall impression, he hoped, evoked 'the early American settlers when they'd incorporated some of the Indian styles'.[40]

Although many people found Adam Ant ridiculous, his swashbuckling eclecticism, which took the foppishness of the Blitz Kids to its ultimate extreme, went down very well with the national media. It is probably no coincidence that his gold-braided heyday came at the very point when the recession was at its worst and the thirst for escapism was greater than ever. Indeed, by the beginning of 1981 the fashion pages were full of sashes, breeches and knickerbockers. When London's leading designers unveiled their latest collections that spring, the show opened with what one observer called 'a flurry of frills and a rustle of taffeta', all 'rich velvets', 'figured brocades', 'lace trimmings' and 'high-necked ruffs'.[41]

Even the *Mirror*, the voice of the Labour-voting working classes, ran a double-page spread on the 'outlandish fashion movement sweeping Britain', evoking a 'pantomime fantasy of the past'. The accompanying picture showed the 19-year-old George O'Dowd, wearing Chinese slippers, leg warmers, a 'black crepe Twenties dress', several tasselled belts, a long scarf, his mother's blouse and a black felt hat. The future Boy George was hardly typical, but the trend was undeniable. 'High camp Romance has now taken over from the cult of spit and sick,' wrote *The Times*'s fashion editor, Suzy Menkes, exulting that high-street stores were stocking up with 'ruffles and lace, brocade jackets and big-sleeved shirts'. This, she thought, 'must be a lighthearted relief for the jeans-and-sweatshirt generation who have had precious little chance to dress up . . . Long live Romance! Long live King Adam and his Ants!'[42]

The New Romantics were not, of course, the only game in town. Not everybody spent their Saturday evenings dressed as Long John Silver, and most teenagers in 1980 or 1981 looked as nondescript as ever. In any case, youth culture was far more fragmented than it had been twenty years earlier. These were not just the years of Ultravox, the Human League and Spandau Ballet; they were also the years of Kate Bush, 2-Tone and Joy Division, Madness, the Police and the Jam. When the *Sun* ran a feature on the 'seven tribes of Britain', the New Romantics were jostling for attention alongside punks, skins, mods, rockabillies, heavy metal fans and 'new psychedelics'. All the same, the New Romantics were the most novel, the most forward-looking and the most obviously fashionable. No other youth tribe attracted so much attention, or became so closely identified with the political and cultural currents of the day. And as a result, none inspired such hatred from its predecessors.[43]

From the start, most established critics loathed the Blitz and all its works. This 'narcissistic little scene', the former *Melody Maker* editor Richard Williams wrote at the end of 1980, consisted of 'young peacocks . . . in search of *paparazzi* to record them for the gossip columns'. As for their music, it was 'the ultimate and most depressingly sterile rerun of avant-garde pop's over-extended infatuation with the life-is-a-cabaret ethic. Fun for some, certainly, and cash for others, but it has no heart.' A year later, after the New Romantics had conquered the charts, the *NME*'s Ian Penman lamented that 1981 had been a year when 'dressing up became *de rigueur*' and when 'the narcissist's determined gaze could be found everywhere'. As prime examples, he pointed to the 'promo videos of Steve Strange, Spandau Ballet and Adam Ant', which represented the triumph of 'pure narcissism'.[44]

By this stage, the critics' minds were made up. The new generation were shallow, derivative, greedy and, above all, terminally self-absorbed. Their defenders pointed out that they were hardly the first pop musicians to enjoy dressing up and making money. But to critics who had come of age in the 1960s and 1970s, the New Romantics broke the rules that had supposedly governed rock music since its foundation. At a time when working-class life seemed to be disintegrating, they seemed to be on the side of change, rather than fighting for tradition. They gave too much thought to their clothes, and far too much to their videos. They were not overtly manly, wore eyeliner and lipstick, whitened their faces and even borrowed women's clothes. Instead of hurling themselves around the stage, strumming their giant phallic guitars, they stood almost motionless at their keyboards, tapping away like secretaries. Rock music was supposed to be authentic, primal and physical, but these newcomers were affected, prettified and pretentious. Where was the drummer, dripping with sweat? Where was the industry, the anger, the aggression?[45]

The fact that all this unfolded against the backdrop of the longest recession since the 1930s, with millions of men losing their jobs in manufacturing industries, women joining the labour force in record numbers and a woman assuming the most high-profile job in the land, was no coincidence. Even rock music had fallen victim to the twin horrors of feminization and computerization. 'There are some days when you turn on the radio and every record begins with a bleep or a bubble,' complained *Melody Maker*'s Penny Kiley, who had a 'nightmare vision of a world taken over by musicians in bleak industrial suits and robot haircuts, and punters with dyed red hair and baggy trousers'. To thousands of youngsters, of course, such a world probably sounded quite fun. But to *Melody Maker*, robots, computers, bleeps and bubbles were the work of the Devil. After Gary Numan moved to the United States in 1982, the paper suggested that, since 'almost single-handedly he made computer printouts designed as pop songs fashionable', Mrs Thatcher should consider 'remobilising the Task Force to prevent his re-entry to this country'.[46]

By this point, though, the critics had a new arch-enemy. This was Duran Duran, who had been formed in Birmingham in 1978 and broke through with 'Girls on Film' three years later. At first they looked like just another New Romantic band, all sashes and synthesizers. But when they spoke it was as though they had been primed by some evil genius to inflame the guardians of rock and roll. Talking to *The Face*, their keyboardist Nick Rhodes explained that they saw themselves as 'a cross between Kraftwerk and the Monkees'. And instead of paying the ritual homage to punk, Duran Duran virtually dismissed it. People were sick of punk, said their bass guitarist John Taylor. 'I'd like to see a return to the quality, and by that I mean critically acclaimed quality, of Rod Stewart and Queen, for example, in the Seventies.' Rod Stewart! Queen! It was almost as if he were doing it deliberately.

To make matters worse, Duran Duran clearly preferred talking about their famously well-favoured appearance to discussing their sound. Asked about their forthcoming tour, their guitarist Andy Taylor said brightly: 'It'll be strong visual entertainment and pure showmanship. We're going to use mood lights on the audience – subtle mauves and reds to create a happy atmosphere.' It is hard to imagine the Clash saying anything like that. But then Rhodes made it worse. 'Yeah, having a good time is what it's all about today,' he chipped in. 'We can't be bothered with all that political messaging. It's time entertainers got back to entertaining instead of preaching.'[47]

Right from the start, many critics saw Duran Duran, like their deadly rivals Spandau Ballet, as an embodiment of the materialism, selfishness and superficiality of the Thatcher era. For the *NME*'s Paul Morley, they were 'gummed up glammed over techno-rock twits', popular with people who were only interested in 'looking at the pictures'. For *Melody Maker*, they were 'candyfloss gods to a new generation of gullible adolescents with more money than sense'. The national press, too, gave them abysmal notices. *The Times* called them 'pop's lowest common denominator . . . homogenized and bland'. And even a relatively kind review in the *Guardian*, which recognized their huge appeal to teenage fans with 'frilled shirts' and 'floppy hair', found them insufferably 'narcissistic . . . less interested in entertaining than in displaying themselves'.[48]

None of this cut any ice with Duran Duran's fans. Nor did it bother the band, who consoled themselves with their colossal earnings and apparently inexhaustible line of female admirers. 'The sort of people we sell to do not question our relevance to society,' said John Taylor. 'I don't see why we should have to satisfy what I consider to be petty semi-graduate university thinking.' And while the semi-graduates sneered, Duran Duran reassured themselves that their forerunners had been similarly mocked and misunderstood. 'People have often said to me, "Why don't you write songs which are easier to understand?"' mused their lead singer Simon Le Bon. Yet as he pointed out, songs like 'Union of the Snake' and 'Hungry Like the Wolf' drew on a long literary tradition. 'I've always liked poets like T. S. Eliot who are a little bit obscure,' he explained, 'and that's definitely part of my style, lyrically.'[49]

For the New Romantics' critics, the really damning entry on the charge sheet was that they were so right-wing. As early as February 1981, *Melody Maker*'s Lynden Barber compared the sleeve notes on Spandau Ballet's *Journeys to Glory* ('Picture angular glimpses of sharp youth cutting strident shapes through the curling grey of 3 a.m . . . Follow the stirring vision and the rousing sound on the path towards journeys to glory') to the lyrics of a Nazi anthem. Under the New Romantics, Barber wrote, 'style is elevated to icon status and moral values and concerns are blown aside'. The 'ex-Blitz glitter clique' made 'superficial music for superficial people with superficial concerns', and were merely pop's answer to the 'upwardly mobile couples who join the Young Conservatives "for the social life"'. That reputation never went away. Almost thirty years later, the *Guardian*'s Michael Hann wrote that groups like Spandau Ballet embodied the 'aspiration to do nothing more than look good in a nightclub'. 'More than any other musical assembly with the possible exception of Stock Aitken and Waterman,' he wrote, 'they are Thatcherism on vinyl.'[50]

Some New Romantics were indeed Conservatives. Culture Club's drummer Jon Moss was a 'staunch Tory' who thought Mrs Thatcher 'bloody brilliant', while Spandau Ballet's Tony Hadley even considered standing as a Conservative MP. But there is no evidence that the pop stars of the early 1980s were any more likely to vote Conservative than their predecessors. Infuriated by the charge even in 1981, Gary Kemp told *The Face* that he had joined the Labour Party in his teens and was active in his school's 'socialist group'. 'However much money I get,' he added, 'I could never vote Conservative.' His brother Martin said much the same.

People accused them of being 'middle-class' because they liked drinking champagne, he said, 'but we're a very working-class band'. Even *The Face*, often seen as an advertisement for Thatcherite values, never hid its left-wing instincts. Among the 'dodgy concepts' of 1980, according to its end-of-year round-up, were 'Thatcher's independent deterrent', 'Keith Joseph's policies' and 'Recession, Depression, Unemployment'. And the broader atmosphere of early-1980s pop culture was very obviously anti-Thatcherite, from the Specials' 'Ghost Town' and UB40's 'One in Ten' to the Beat's 'Stand Down Margaret' and Heaven 17's '(We Don't Need This) Fascist Groove Thang'.[51]

Yet it is easy to see why so many critics thought the New Romantics were borrowing from the Grantham hymnbook. Ten years earlier, pop stars had talked about ending war and changing the world. Now they talked about moving up and getting on. 'We're saying, "make the best of yourself. Even if you can't write or play you can look good, and that's a form of expression,"' Gary Kemp explained to the *Guardian*. This, he said, was what set the Blitz Kids apart from their predecessors: they were 'people who want to develop, who want to achieve something, in any direction, whether it's art or whether it's money. It's ambition.' And while some readers might have seen this as the voice of a materialistic new generation rebelling against the collectivist values of their parents, Kemp did not see it that way at all. As he told *The Face*, his father had been just as interested in getting on and having fun. 'We were a working-class family, but we had a colour telly and a stereo,' he said. 'The difference between my dad and a more middle-class person is that if he won £10,000 tomorrow he'd go out and spend it, whereas a more middle-class person would invest it.'[52]

Of course pop stars had often talked about getting on. Even the supposedly anti-materialistic John Lennon had said repeatedly that his ambition was 'to be rich'. What was unusual about the cohort of the early 1980s, though, was how vocal they were about it. 'I want success,' Adam Ant told his early biographers, adding that the word 'cult' just meant 'loser'. 'With the punk thing, everyone was making impractical attacks on being rich or having money,' Boy George told the *NME*. But deep down, 'they all wanted to be rich. You have to be . . . I just want money so that I can be really irresponsible.' Duran Duran's ambition, agreed Simon Le Bon, was to become 'artistically satisfied and stinking rich'. (No doubt T. S. Eliot would have said exactly the same.) Even UB40, widely celebrated for their social conscience, were not ashamed of making money. 'Of course, we earn as much money as we can,' their saxophonist Brian Travers told *Sounds* in 1982. 'We tend to get slagged off for making a bit of money, being the type of band we are – but that's a totally middle-class idea.'[53]

Behind the caricatures, many of the pop stars of the early 1980s were more thoughtful than their critics recognized. Gary Kemp, for example, found it hard 'to justify the kind of money a pop star can make while his mother and father still live frugally in a council house'. He and his brother tried to help, 'but here I'd get it wrong too': for example, buying his parents a Wiener Werkstätte vase or a William Morris tile, which looked absurd on the mantelpiece and 'left me appearing like a snob'. After he and Martin parked their 'matching Porsches side by side outside our parents' home in a street full of rusting Fords', he worried that they might be rubbing salt into 'the wounds of a beleaguered working-class neighbourhood'. Even when Gary bought his first flat at the end of 1982, becoming the first person in his family to own his own home, he felt torn. 'As I placed art and books on the wall, church candles and interior magazines on the black enamelled coffee table,' he remembered, 'I felt a strong sense of denying everything my family was.' And as he sat on his William Morris chair, 'with a glass of claret in my hand and something light and choral on the stereo, I realised I'd become middle class'. Mrs Thatcher would have been proud of him. But he still felt guilty about it.[54]

To people who liked their idols to be suffering artists, Kemp's coffee table struck entirely the wrong note. But by the early 1980s suffering artists were no longer in vogue. Instead, the New Romantics liked to see themselves as successful businessmen. ABC's lead singer Martin Fry said they had changed their name from Vice Versa to give them a 'new brand name'. The Human League's Phil Oakey said there was 'only a point in putting out records if people are going to buy them', while Adam Ant boasted that he 'put a lot of thought into the product'. 'These days', reflected Smash Hits in 1982, 'your modern young musician wouldn't look out of place in the head office of Shell International. The corporate image – executive-style suits, ties and briefcases – is in!'

The most obvious example was Heaven 17, who had splintered from the Human League in 1980. Pop musicians were not 'tortured artists', the band's co-founder Martyn Ware told the NME, but people trying 'to make a living . . . The best and least hypocritical way of doing that is to act as a business.' So Heaven 17 was merely a 'subsidiary' of the British Electric Foundation (BEF), which Ware and his friend Ian Craig Marsh had set up after leaving the Human League. Its first album, Penthouse and Pavement (1981), carried the BEF logo with the corporate slogan 'The New Partnership – That's opening doors all over the world'. The cover showed the band with slicked-back hair and pinstriped suits, answering telephones and shaking hands against a background of Dallas-style office blocks. The point, Ware told Simon Reynolds, was to 'get rid of all this hypocrisy of "We're artists, we don't care about the money." Let's strip the façade bare and have a look at what's underneath – handshakes, signing contracts, *busy*-ness.' Ironically, Ware was on the left and had warm words for Tony Benn. But to the casual observer, *Penthouse and Pavement* looked less like a parody of busy-ness than an endorsement of business. And Ware and his colleagues did not look like radicals. They looked like yuppies.[55]

But it was Duran Duran who most aggressively seized the commercial possibilities of the 1980s. For their first global tour, which began in late 1983, Le Bon and his colleagues secured a sponsorship deal with Sony, which wanted to promote its new range of video cassettes. Not only were all their programmes, posters and tickets emblazoned with the Sony logo, but concert venues were dressed with Sony banners, while a 'girl merchandising force' handed out cassettes to anybody who bought a concert programme. And although abuse rained down, Duran Duran were not alone. Levi's had already sponsored Roxy Music and David Bowie, while two other video-cassette firms, TDK and Maxell, struck deals with the Rolling Stones and Japan (the band, not the country). 'This', said a spokesman for the 'music sponsorship consultants' West Nally, 'is just the tip of the iceberg.'[56]

The fact that three different groups were advertising video cassettes was no coincidence. Pop videos were not entirely new: many groups had recorded promotional clips in the 1960s, while Queen had made their ground-breaking 'Bohemian Rhapsody' video as far back as 1975. But with the success of the 'Ashes to Ashes' video, which cost a then-record £250,000, every New Romantic group wanted an expensive video of its own, preferably with a generous costume budget and a lot of dry ice. For all the talk of individualism, they often looked exactly the same, at once whimsical, bombastic and very obviously influenced by advertising. One celebrated example was Orchestral Manoeuvres in the Dark's 'Souvenir', filmed at Blenheim Palace, where Andy McCluskey drives around in a classic red sports car, and at Stowe School, where Paul Humphreys ponders the meaning of life on the Palladian Bridge. It looks like a parody of Jeremy Irons and Anthony Andrews in *Brideshead Revisited*, though it was actually made beforehand. But the video that really defined the age was Duran Duran's infamously luxurious 'Rio' (1982), the band resplendent in their baggy suits as their yacht cuts through the sun-kissed waters of the Caribbean. A casual viewer would hardly guess that they came from Birmingham. But perhaps it was because they came from Birmingham that they were so keen to do it.

To the New Romantics' critics, their videos proved beyond doubt that they had thrown in their lot with Mrs Thatcher's gospel of materialism. What did it say about pop music, lamented the *Guardian*, that with so many people unemployed, they were making 'expensive holiday films in exotic locations'? But making a glossy video made commercial sense, especially if you wanted to be successful across the Atlantic. Few American bands bothered making videos, so when the cable channel MTV was launched on 1 August 1981, it relied heavily on British acts, giving them a huge advantage in the battle for hearts and minds. Even MTV's very first video was British. Appropriately enough, it was the Buggles' 'Video Killed the Radio Star'.

It is a shame, though, that MTV never showed the greatest New Romantic video of all, first broadcast on BBC2 the following February. A man in a beret drives up to a country house; a Nazi goose-steps on the stairs; a bearded Cavalier brandishes his sword; a group of androgynous youngsters cavort in the grounds; a strange, vampiric figure wades through a burning lake. Every detail is impeccably judged, from the floppy hair and lurid make-up to the distorted graphics and impenetrable lyrics:

> Let's spend our honeymoon in East Berlin
> And though, like lemmings, we will never swim . . .
> By the river of blood, the children cry
> Their egos ruined by an alibi
> The cruel sea of a heartless earth, oh
> This must mean something to me . . .

The band's name, perfectly chosen, was Lufthansa Terminal. The song, meanwhile, was called 'Nice Video, Shame about the Song'. It was one of the best things the sketch show *Not the Nine O'Clock News* ever did. And actually, the song is not that bad.[57]


The story of the New Romantics was many things. It was a story about the aftershocks of punk, but it looked back to the founding spirit of pop. It was a story of working-class aspiration, but it was also one about entre-preneurship, consumerism and celebrity. It began in the back streets of Soho, but many of its most celebrated bands came from struggling indus-trial cities further north. It was dominated almost entirely by men, but men who wore mascara and eyeliner, frills and ruffs. It became identified with the spirit of Thatcherism, but many of its leading characters voted Labour. And although the outlandish costumes dominated the press cover-age, it was at heart a story about technological change. It was the cheap new synthesizers of the late 1970s that gave the music of the New Roman-tics its distinctive timbre. And like the voice of Margaret Thatcher, the hiss of the home video and the flicker of the computer screen, the sound of the synthesizer became an indelible part of the cultural texture of the 1980s.

It was another technological innovation, though, that really pointed to music's future. In May 1980 the *Daily Express* reported that Sony were about to launch a 'revolutionary new cassette player', which had been on sale in Japan since the previous summer. 'The Japanese call it the Walkman,' the paper explained, 'presumably because the gadget enables you to listen to your favourite music while walking, jogging, travelling on the tube – anywhere . . . Before long the streets will be full of wired-up fans!'[58]

Even in a market awash with new technology, the Walkman was a stunning success. In July 1981 the *Mirror* reported that Sony had already sold 100,000 sets in Britain and some 2 million worldwide. 'The demand is fantastic,' said a spokesman for the Laskys hi-fi chain. 'Our shops just can't get enough.' They were not cheap, with costs ranging from £50 to £125, the equivalent of perhaps £200 to £500 today. But already it was common to see people wandering the streets 'wired up to [their] earphones . . . They've been seen being worn by bicycling barristers and by art gallery and museum browsers. Some teenagers even take them to discos – preferring their own music to that of the DJ.'[59]

By the summer of 1982, the Walkman's place in British life was firmly established. Sony's total sales in Britain had now hit 750,000, while rival firms had sold at least 600,000 cheaper models. Cassette sales were surging, up from a fifth to a third of all record sales within just two years. Yet, as always, new technology brought new anxieties. In September a conference of environmental health officers heard that perhaps a thousand people a year were being deafened by their new gadgets, which produced sound levels 'well above the safety limits applied in factories'. Teachers, bus conductors and 'irate drivers' found them infuriating, while the British Cycling Federation warned that wearing headphones on a bike was 'terribly dangerous'. But there was no denying that the Walkman was cool: 'the first gadget', said the *Observer*, 'to combine hi-fi and high fashion'. Even Princess Diana had one. The *Daily Mail* claimed that while staying at Balmoral she had become 'so engrossed in the music that she failed to notice the Queen when they passed in the corridor'.

What did it all mean? Even at this early stage, the radio presenter Annie Nightingale thought the Walkman marked the onset of a 'musical revolution', which 'could mean the disappearance of the conventional long-playing disc by the end of the eighties'. And like so many cultural developments of the early 1980s, the Walkman struck some observers as a lamentable retreat from collective solidarity. The rock critic Tim de Lisle, who loved

his Walkman, recognized that its detractors saw it as 'something antisocial and sinister', a way of 'rejecting everyday life, dropping out', another
'unwanted invention of the Me Decade'. The radical magazine *City Limits*,
meanwhile, took a very dim view not just of the Walkman but of those
who had them. 'The Invasion of the Walkman People seems to have created a true post-punk blank generation, passing through without
contributing, escaping into an aural oblivion ominous in its alienation,'
wrote Cynthia Rose.

> Social disengagement isn't the same thing as fury or even resentment at the
> conditions of life around one. Are the Walkman People each marching to
> the individually-heard beat of Thoreau's different drum, or does this inva-
> sion just usher a new ME generation of narcissists into a world so abrasive
> and anarchic they no longer want to listen to it?[60]

In this, as in so many cultural debates, the final verdict fell to Roy Hattersley. In the spring of 1983, Labour's Shadow Home Secretary told
readers of the *Guardian* that he had just bought his first Walkman, an
'elegant silver Sony' with 'svelte ebony corners and space-age PVC belt
holster'. He had spent his Tube journeys listening to Stephen Sondheim's
*Follies*, and had been disturbed by a Labour aide while enjoying *Top Hat*
in his Commons office. But there were, Hattersley wrote, 'immense advantages in being able to shut out the world'. Now, whenever he was lunching
with a 'boringly beautiful girl', he could 'escape the tedium of her compliments' by switching on Radio Four's *The World at One*. Whenever he
strolled the streets of London, he felt part of 'a new electronic community,
bound together by the wires of our headsets'. And when people saw him,
they would, he hoped, 'think of me as being "into Walkman"'. So there
it was. Friends were electric, after all.[61]

# 13

# High Noon at Leyland

*At last Sir Michael Edwardes's appointment as the first dwarf to be chairman of British Leyland is explained. It was so that he could pose for photographs beside the new Mini Metro without giving away the fact that it was especially designed for childless dwarves.*

Auberon Waugh's *Private Eye* diary,
14 October 1980

*You've probably seen that the work-shy yobboes at BL are once again up to their seasonal pranks. I told the Boss that now surely we can come out of the closet and close the whole thing down once and for all.*

'Denis Thatcher', in Richard Ingrams and
John Wells, *One for the Road* (1982)

In the autumn of 1980, the vast Longbridge car plant, on the south-western edge of Birmingham, was buzzing with excitement. For years the car giant British Leyland (BL) had been planning a replacement for the Mini. Now, after apparently endless delays, the new car was almost ready. Everybody knew that this would be a decisive moment in the strike-plagued firm's desperate struggle for survival, a last chance to compete with foreign models such as the Ford Fiesta, Renault 5 and Volkswagen Polo. As British Leyland's South African-born chairman, Michael Edwardes, told the press, this would be the most advanced British car ever made, a 'child of information technology', built with the latest production-line techniques. But after years of terrible publicity, Edwardes knew that it was 'more than just a new car, it was the yardstick by which the whole company would be judged . . . Everything depended on its being right from day one. This time there would be no second chance.'[1]

Never had a British firm invested so much money, hope and political capital in a single product. By the middle of 1980 Edwardes had spent £285 million on the colossal New West Works at Longbridge, much of it coming from the taxpayer. By the standards of most British factories, the new plant was a technological cathedral, bright and airy with state-of-the-art assembly lines and more than fifty gleaming robots. Watching in awe as the machines clanked and clattered, one motoring journalist reported that on some lines just thirteen men were doing the work of eighty in an ordinary plant, while 'in another department, 38 do the work of 102'. Here was a vision to make Margaret Thatcher proud, a flexible team working at full throttle in one of the most advanced factories in Europe. The only downside was that it had been so extraordinarily expensive, with estimates suggesting British Leyland would need to sell 6,000 cars a week to make a profit. But early tests were extremely promising, and the first hatchbacks rolled off the production line without a hitch. All that remained was the name, chosen, in a clever bit of public relations, by Longbridge's workers. Some 20,000 men voted, and the winner, beating 'Maestro' by just 267 votes, was 'Metro'.[2]

It is hard to exaggerate the anticipation surrounding the Metro in the autumn of 1980. It was 'not just a car, more a symbol of national survival', declared the *Guardian*. 'On this car rests the hopes and possibly the life or death of a vast hunk of British industry.' If it flopped, that would mean disaster not only for 145,000 British Leyland employees, but tens of thousands whose jobs in engineering, components, steel and rail depended upon the car industry.

But all the signs were good. At the beginning of September, BL came up with an unusual way to introduce the car to its dealers, inviting them on a free cruise to the Isle of Man. This already rather dubious treat was almost scuppered by the weather, and Edwardes recalled a lot of 'rolling and pitching' as they ploughed through the waves. But when the Metro emerged 'amidst billowing mist from the centre of a globe', the dealers went berserk, clapping and stamping with delight. Some were so relieved by the new car's angular modernity that they burst into tears. And when, the next day, they got to drive it around the Isle of Man, their excitement turned into ecstasy. When they returned home, some arranged Metro-themed drinks parties for the launch day; others invited their customers to come for breakfast at the showroom on their way to work. 'Even by the extravagant standards of the car industry', wrote one reporter, there had never been hype like it.[3]

When Michael Edwardes awoke on 14 October, he looked out across the lake beside Birmingham's Metropole Hotel and thought of 'how great industries can be built up from small beginnings'. Even somebody with his immense self-confidence could have been forgiven for feeling nervous.

But he need not have worried. As his blue hatchback cruised into the cavernous National Exhibition Centre for the annual Motor Show, he could already hear the cheers. 'Metro Mike', said one paper, was the 'star model of this motor show'. He was the star of the Paris Motor Show, too. 'One has to raise one's hat a long way,' said *Le Figaro*, while *Le Matin* saw the Metro as 'the ideal small car, which many European constructors would have liked to have created'. The only real sceptic was *Private Eye*'s Denis Thatcher, who was not impressed by the sight of his wife test-driving a Metro at the Motor Show. 'The rather smarmy little South African johnny' might be 'cock-a-hoop about advance orders', Denis tells his friend Bill, but the 'bloody shop stewards' would soon ruin everything. 'I keep telling the Boss one of these days they're going to have to pull the plug on that lot, Metro or no, and concede victory to the Nips.'[4]

In the real world, the Metro was a triumph. Every newspaper was full of praise, and within days dealers were reporting thousands of orders. Cleverly, British Leyland marketed it not just as the most modern car in its class, but as a patriotic icon, the ultimate expression of the nation's thirst for renewal. The Metro's much-acclaimed television advert began with a doom-laden shot of military landing craft approaching the coast of southern England, preparing to unload their consignments of foreign cars. 'Some of you may have noticed', says a gravelly voice, 'that for the past few years Britain has been invaded by the Italians, the Germans, the Japanese and the French. Now we have the means to fight back.' As Metros roll off the Longbridge assembly line, the music switches to 'Rule, Britannia', while Union Jack-waving crowds rush to the motorway bridges to cheer them on. In a bucolic village, an old man, medals glittering on his chest, gives an emotional salute; his neighbour waves her handkerchief from her cottage window. At last, with the music reaching a patriotic crescendo, cars streaming on to the white chalk cliffs and the enemy retreating across the Channel, comes the tagline: 'The new Austin Metro. A British car to beat the world.'[5]

Made by the American firm Leo Burnett, the Metro advert was the best party political broadcast Mrs Thatcher never gave. Drenched in nostalgia for the Second World War, glorying in the potential of technological modernity, fired by the conviction that Britain was turning the corner after decades of decline, the advert perfectly captured her patriotic appeal. Even the print campaign hammered home the same message: 'Never before have so many gone so far on so little . . . Even Wellington never imagined a boot this big . . . Great space for Great Britain . . . Safe as the Crown Jewels . . . This could be your finest hour.'

There was a nice irony in the fact that, although British Leyland had designed the car with one eye on the European export market, it was relying on island-story imagery to sell it at home. But that too was pure Margaret Thatcher, the supporter of European integration who inveighed against a European super-state, the patriotic populist who threw open the doors to international capital, the champion of globalization whose voice throbbed with pride in Britain's unique history. In any case, the public loved it. By the end of 1980 the Metro was already the third most popular car of the year, and by 1983 annual sales had hit 130,000. Not since the Mini had any British car made such an impact.[6]

But British Leyland would not have been British Leyland if there had not been bad news, too. Almost every week in the autumn of 1980 brought reports of some squabble on the shop floor, but the worst came on 21 November, when a dispute about Metro seats escalated into open fighting. Ironically, this was a dispute born of the car's success. With demand surging, BL had been forced to buy in extra seats from outside. Outraged, the seat assembly team downed tools. The trim workers, however, wanted to carry on working, and their 'right to work' protest rapidly escalated into a saloon-style brawl. Fortunately the dispute fizzled out, but the publicity – 'Leyland Workers Run Riot at Metro Factory', 'Metro Jobs Rampage' – was awful. Even the *Guardian*, hardly an instinctive cheer-leader for BL's management, thought the dispute had been 'disgraceful'.[7]

When disputes interrupted production of the Metro, the press were predictably merciless. This is Jak in the *Evening Standard*, 18 April 1980.

To most people, though, reports of trouble at Longbridge were nothing new. There had been reports of trouble at Longbridge almost every month for the last ten years. And not even the Metro's brilliant campaign could reverse the irreparable, decades-long damage inflicted on the reputation of Britain's car industry. Two letters printed in the *Guardian* in December 1980 tell the story. In Amersham, Buckinghamshire, K. R. Sturley had been waiting more than a month for a new Ford Escort, but delays at the Halewood plant meant he had still not received it. 'Perhaps I had better cancel my order and change to a German, French or even Japanese car,' Mr Sturley wrote angrily. 'They have no waiting list.'

As for L. Barratt of Torquay, he had been driving British cars for almost thirty years, from the Humber Sceptre and the Singer Vogue to the Morris Marina and the Triumph Dolomite, 'all new, all expensive, all faulty'. Two weeks earlier, he had bought his first foreign car, a Datsun Bluebird, and was very pleased with it. He noted that representatives from Britain's car firms had recently been to Japan, hoping to 'persuade them to sell fewer cars in Europe and Britain'. The more sensible solution, Mr Barratt thought, would be to 'persuade Japanese car makers to turn out cars that are sloppy, out-dated, unreliable and very expensive', just like their British competitors. 'Then even we patriots wouldn't buy them.'[8]

At the turn of the 1980s, about 300,000 people worked for Britain's major car companies: British Leyland, Ford, Vauxhall and Talbot. Many people believed that buying a British-made car was the patriotic thing to do, while the newspapers treated the car industry as the supreme barometer of economic virility. But if that was the case, Britain badly needed medical intervention. Half a century earlier, it had produced more vehicles than any other country in Europe. But by the end of the 1970s the car industry was in deep trouble. Hamstrung by incompetent management, painfully slow to exploit the markets of Continental Europe, crippled by a culture of shop-floor militancy, it had become Exhibit A in every narrative of post-war decline. As Louis Heren reported in *Alas, Alas for England* (1981), it took ten British workers to build a Ford Escort at Halewood, but only four West Germans to make the same car at Saarlouis. For every 100 Cortina doors a British worker produced at Dagenham, his Belgian counterpart at Genk made 219.[9]

As a result, car exports were in steady decline, while foreign cars were roaring into Britain on a scale that horrified industry insiders. Extraordinary as it now seems, only 5 per cent of the new cars bought in 1965 had been imported. But by 1975 that figure had already leapt to 33 per cent, and every year it surged still higher. Once, brands such as Renault,

Peugeot, Fiat and Volkswagen had been exotic novelties. Now they were household names. Some of this, of course, was inevitable as soon as Britain joined the Common Market. Even so, the fact that no other major Western car market was so dominated by imports told its own story. In 1982 foreign-made cars commanded 27 per cent of the market in West Germany, 28 per cent in the United States and 31 per cent in France. In Britain their share was almost 60 per cent.[10]

At the centre of this sad story was British Leyland. Cobbled together by Tony Benn from the remains of Britain's motor industry in 1968, and encompassing household names such as Austin, Morris, Mini, Jaguar, Daimler, Triumph and Land Rover, the national car conglomerate was in a terrible condition. Only seven years later, it had become a ward of the state under the National Enterprise Board, with production spread across dozens of factories. But what followed was a shambles. By the end of the 1970s BL's output had fallen by more than half, annual exports had collapsed from 368,000 to 158,000 and domestic market share had tumbled from 38 per cent to barely 18 per cent, all in just ten years. Even the *Daily Mirror*, its biggest defender on Fleet Street, admitted that things had gone badly wrong. 'Since the 1960s,' lamented a blistering editorial in September 1979, 'Leyland has limped from one disastrous year to another, a car manufacturer with built-in suicidal tendencies.'[11]

A proper exploration of British Leyland's problems would take a book in itself. As Michael Edwardes recalled, they included 'ageing models', persistent strikes, an 'unachievable' strategy and a 'world image so damaging that the company craved only for silence, which it didn't get'. Fleet Street loved to blame the unions, but there was more to it than that. The management were at once criminally complacent and pathologically afraid of alienating the shop stewards, which meant many plants were ludicrously over-manned. Some observers claimed that in some factories there were 'two workforces who swapped over in mid-shift, playing cards the rest of the time'. Perhaps this was an exaggeration. Still, BL's non-executive director Ian MacGregor, later of steel and coal fame, was not alone in likening the firm's bosses to 'tribal chiefs of old, who measured their wealth in the number of slaves they had'. But what the firm was best known for was strikes. Every morning Edwardes was presented with a summary of the latest disputes, which usually came to at least four typewritten pages. In 1977 strikes cost the firm some 250,000 vehicles; in the next six months production was interrupted 346 times. Even in May 1979, Edwardes told his shareholders that strikes had cost them 110,000 vehicles and a staggering £200 million in the last year.[12]

Meanwhile, British Leyland was making vast demands on the public purse. In the decade after 1975 it swallowed a gargantuan £2.4 billion in public money: that is to say, more than *a million pounds every working day* for almost ten years.* If the cars had been any good, people might have thought it money well spent. But by the turn of the 1980s BL's cars were widely seen as rusty, old-fashioned and almost comically unreliable. When Edwardes joined the company, he asked the Two Ronnies to stop joking about its abysmal productivity, 'so that we heard less about workers clocking in by signing the visitors' book'. The wet fish salesman Henry Root, however, had a much better idea. 'I would remind you, Sir,' he wrote to Edwardes in 1979, 'that every time someone laughs at "British Leyland" they are laughing at Great Britain.' Root suggested changing the name to either 'Japanese Leyland' or 'Jamaican Leyland'. The words 'Japanese Leyland', he pointed out, would dramatically improve the company's image. 'And if jokes were made about "Jamaican Leyland", you could prosecute the offenders under the Race Discrimination Act.'[13]

That October, the *Daily Express*'s George Gale told his readers that for the first time in his life he was planning to buy a foreign car. 'I always thought, without thinking much, that British was best,' he wrote. 'I was brought up when "Made in England" was a sign of quality and "Foreign made" a sign of rubbish.' Deep down, Gale still wanted to buy a British car. He felt 'sick' when he pictured himself driving a car made in France, Germany, Italy or Japan. But after a decade of headlines about terrible productivity, strike-torn factories and unreliable models, he had had enough. Now, he admitted, 'I no longer think that British is best.'

To Gale's employers, this sort of talk was tantamount to surrender. 'If we will not buy our own goods how can we expect prospective customers overseas to have confidence in them?' the *Express* demanded in July 1980, launching a short-lived 'Buy British' campaign. Yet only a few years later, the columnist James McMillan lamented that nothing had changed: 'Jack, should we buy the Renault or the Fiat?' 'Well, Jill, I fancy the Volkswagen or possibly the Datsun.' This, McMillan wrote, was 'an everyday conversation that could be repeated hundreds of times a week – and probably is – up and down the country.' Like many commentators, he blamed 'slack managements' and 'short-sighted unions'. But he also recognized that the endless jokes about Longbridge tea breaks and Austin Allegros had done terrible damage to the domestic car industry. 'The perception "British is Best"', he wrote, 'has been transformed in the customer's mind to "British is Worst".'

This in turn reflected a wider picture. In the mid-1970s only a quarter

---

* Since this covers a decade of very high inflation, it is tricky to give a modern equivalent. Somewhere between £14 billion and £20 billion seems about right.

of the products sold on the high street had been made abroad. A decade later, half were imports. By the mid-1980s some 95 per cent of the cutlery, 85 per cent of the leather handbags, 84 per cent of the stereos, 83 per cent of the men's trousers, 81 per cent of the luggage and 74 per cent of the sports equipment sold in Britain, as well as almost half of the vacuum cleaners, fridges and colour televisions, had been imported, usually from Japan, South Korea or Taiwan. Given that Britain prided itself on being the workshop of the world, many people found these figures deeply embarrassing. Sometimes people said the British were work-shy, but this was not true. In fact, the typical working week at the turn of the 1980s was an hour longer in Britain than it was in France or West Germany. The real problems were much harder to sort out. When *The Times* compared thirty-six industrial groups across the Common Market, Britain came bottom of all but two. A Japanese steelworker made five and a half tons of steel for every ton produced by his British counterpart. Even a Pan Am employee handled three times the traffic of her British Airways equivalent. It was, the paper remarked, now a 'wearily familiar' story.[14]

Even in the 1970s the consequences were devastatingly clear: the collapse of textile jobs in Lancashire, the disappearance of shipbuilding on the Clyde, the slow death of steelmaking in South Wales. And this, of course, was what Mrs Thatcher had promised to fix. In a New Year message to the nation, published in the *News of the World* on the last Sunday in 1979, she addressed herself directly to the challenges facing British manufacturing:

> You are probably reading this sitting at home, maybe with your family around you. In the living room there is almost certainly a television set, probably a colour model.
>
> In the kitchen there is more than likely to be a washing machine and almost definitely a fridge. And there is about an even chance you will have a car outside.
>
> First: How many of these items were made in Britain?
>
> And second: How many of them or their equivalent did you or your parents have 20 years ago? . . .
>
> Once we were the best. We built well and sold well. We delivered on time, people bought British because British was best . . .
>
> Then we started to slip. In the last 15 years it became a disastrous slide. But now it is time to tackle the problems which have been neglected for years.

Few people would have disagreed with the diagnosis. But what Mrs Thatcher did not say, apart from a few anodyne remarks about ending strikes, was what she proposed to do about it. Even as she invited her readers to 'raise a glass to the eighties' and 'drink with me to the awakening of Britain', that question hung in the air.[15]

By the time Mrs Thatcher arrived in Downing Street, British Leyland had a new chairman. After leaving South Africa, Michael Edwardes had soared through the ranks of the battery-maker Chloride, winning the *Guardian*'s Young Businessman of the Year award. Living in a solar-heated house in Richmond, renowned for his competitiveness on the squash court, he seemed more like an American businessman than a British one. He made his colleagues take psychological tests and memorized their IQs; he wrote letters to *The Times* complaining that high taxes were driving the best people overseas; he told conferences that talk of industrial democracy was 'nonsense'. Short and combative, a man of great charisma and self-belief, Edwardes was often painted as Mrs Thatcher's hitman, the embodiment of the union-bashing climate of the 1980s. In fact, it was Harold Wilson who had appointed Edwardes to the National Enterprise Board and Jim Callaghan who had picked him to run British Leyland. When he got the call in the autumn of 1977, it had taken him just thirty seconds to say yes. He knew turning BL around would be an 'enormous, some might say impossible' task. But he was determined to try.[16]

Edwardes's arrival was like the coming of a tornado. Within six months he had purged all but two of the board, redeployed 200 managers and sacked ninety more. By the end of 1978 he had slashed 12,000 jobs and closed plants in Speke, Abingdon and Coventry. But he was more than just a hatchet man. He wanted more modern technology, more flexible workers and a calmer shop-floor culture. But he could have none of that if his men were always on strike. Contrary to myth, Edwardes was not automatically hostile to the trade unions, and was keen to 'win the hearts and minds' of BL's workers. But, like many union leaders, he believed the 1970s had seen a catastrophic breakdown in the unions' authority over their own members. It was the shop stewards who ruled at Longbridge and Cowley, not the national union leaders and certainly not BL's managers. 'Not to put too fine a point on it,' he wrote, 'we needed to take on the militants.'[17]

On paper, Edwardes seemed a natural ally for the new government. Before the 1979 election he had joined Sir Geoffrey Howe, Sir Keith Joseph and Nigel Lawson at an all-day seminar on 'turning Britain around'. But he was not partisan, and preferred Callaghan ('firm, friendly but personable') to Mrs Thatcher ('the exact opposite'). He first met her in January 1979, when she came for lunch at British Leyland's headquarters. In typically abrasive style, she opened with the words: 'Well, Michael Edwardes, and why should we pour further funds into British Leyland?' At that, he recalled, 'she glared stonily around the table at each of us in turn', while his colleagues gaped for 'a good ten seconds'. That set the tone for the next few years.

In public, Mrs Thatcher was never less than effusive about Edwardes's qualities. In private, she saw him as just another nationalized industry boss pestering her for money. 'I was told by those who knew her better that she admired what she saw as my persistence and courage in tackling BL's problems,' he wrote, 'but was not at all pleased when these qualities were applied to the task of extracting money from her Government.' Indeed, when her new economic adviser, Professor Alan Walters, visited BL for lunch in 1981 he was even less encouraging. The best thing, Walters told his hosts, would be to close the entire firm down straight away. The cost, he said blithely, would 'soon be offset . . . by the beneficial effect of the shock of closure on trades union and employee attitudes across the country', which would have a 'positive effect on the British economy within six months'. Edwardes later claimed that he admired Walters's 'audacity and intellectual integrity' in telling them that he wanted to close them down. But it seems unlikely that he thought that at the time.[18]

Edwardes's priority was to win over the new Industry Secretary, Sir Keith Joseph. On the face of it, Joseph was the least likely person imaginable to look kindly on British Leyland. The son of a Jewish construction tycoon, he was an immensely serious, gaunt and sickly man, crippled by 'an exaggerated feeling of underachievement and a vague sense of guilt'. After serving as Health and Social Services Secretary under Heath, he had undergone a spectacular conversion, becoming the chief advocate of radical surgery to slash the state and restore free-market values. Some people saw Joseph as a hero. According to the original treatment for the ITV series *Minder* (1979–94), the wheeler-dealer Arthur Daley (George Cole), who fancies himself as an entrepreneur, especially 'admires Sir Keith Joseph'. But unlike the irrepressible Arthur, who dodges and cadges his way across London without an atom of shame, Joseph cut an extraordinarily tortured figure. As the Conservatives headed for victory in 1979, he was seen smacking his own head in desperation. 'Oh God,' he groaned, 'what I'm worried about is all the mistakes we're going to make. I know we are going to make mistakes. I lie awake worrying about them.'

No sooner had Joseph arrived at the Department of Industry than Whitehall was buzzing about his eccentric behaviour. He began by giving his officials a reading list, which included nine books he had written himself. His admirers claimed this was a sign of his intellectual vision, but it was really a symptom of his childlike naivety. It is hard to think of any other minister who, on visiting an electrical factory in the early 1980s, would seriously ask his hosts if they thought television was 'here to stay'. Similarly, it is very difficult to think of any other minister who, having been interviewed live on television, refused to believe that he could not simply record the answers again.[19]

When the young Tory adviser Chris Patten nicknamed Joseph the 'Mad Monk', it seemed to capture an essential truth about the unworldly Industry Secretary. He appeared gripped by nervous tension, his brow shining with sweat, a vein at his temple throbbing ominously. Even his diet seemed to reflect his underlying oddness. Because of his terrible digestion, he subsisted on 'tea, chocolate, British Rail cake and hard-boiled eggs, preferably chopped'. The author of those words, Ferdinand Mount, recalled that Joseph was the only man he had ever met who could be seen genuinely slapping his brow in frustration or groaning with his head in his hands. At dinner he clutched a little black notebook in which 'he would without warning make notes'. Sometimes he jotted down a book title, but 'often something quite banal would appear to be completely new to him'. To Mount, the most unsettling thing was when Joseph just sat there, pen in hand, waiting for somebody to say something interesting.[20]

Four years earlier, the Department of Industry had laboured under the direction of Tony Benn. Now it found itself with another eccentric master inspired by a radical vision of Britain's political future. Like Benn, Joseph saw himself as a political evangelist, and, like Benn, he struggled with the stark realities of industrial life. It was all very well to condemn wasteful subsidies in opposition, but if Joseph turned off the tap, hundreds of thousands of people would find themselves on the dole overnight. So almost at once he found himself making choices – a stay of execution here, a subsidy there – that he would once have deplored. His critics loved to paint him as a lunatic slashing away at British industry. Yet, by the summer of 1980, he had not only persuaded Mrs Thatcher to support the British micro-electronics industry, but had handed out £66 million to the shipbuilder Harland and Wolff, £6 million to the tyre manufacturer Dunlop and even £14 million to the almost comically unsuccessful car maker John DeLorean. If Joseph really wanted to roll back the frontiers of the state, this was a strange way to start.[21]

The real test, though, was British Leyland. In July 1979 Joseph visited BL's Warwickshire research centre. There Edwardes told him that the surging pound had had 'traumatic consequences for BL', making 'our exports more expensive, and our competitors' imports a lot cheaper'. Without a huge cash injection, Edwardes said, 'the whole of our mid-car sector

programme over four years will have to go'. So the government faced a
stark choice: either give BL enough money to keep going, or close it down
now. And when, two months later, Edwardes sent Joseph his official corporate plan, the prognosis was even worse. Just to keep production going
for another year, Edwardes wanted a staggering £300 million. But if the
government preferred to close the doors, BL reckoned it would cost
the Treasury £4,000 a head in redundancy money for 160,000 workers in
the first year alone. And when BL calculated the impact of closure on the
West Midlands in general, the cost ballooned to some £1 billion.[22]

When Joseph showed these figures to Mrs Thatcher, she thought the
implications 'appalling'. Handing out so much money to a struggling
nationalized industry offended all her instincts. Most of her advisers
thought British Leyland was doomed anyway. On the other hand, she
knew that shutting it down would not only be extraordinarily expensive,
it would define her time in office. Even John Hoskyns, who thought BL
had 'virtually *no* chance of success', told her that 'public support for
Edwardes and what he is trying to do would make it extremely difficult
for Government to refuse to back him at this point'.

The only sensible course was to give Edwardes the money on the explicit
condition that 'BL as a whole will not be bailed out again'. The launch of
the Metro was still almost a year away; perhaps that would transform the
car giant's fortunes. At the same time, Hoskyns wrote, 'since we know
that BL is likely to fail in the long run, we must set the stage for that as
well'. They must tell the public that it was 'the result of years of appalling
labour relations, in which union militants have all but destroyed the company'. And when British Leyland collapsed, they must ensure the unions'
fingerprints were on the dagger.[23]

At that very moment, events on the edge of Birmingham seemed to be
playing into the government's hands. In September 1979 Edwardes had
unveiled his 'Recovery Plan', envisaging the loss of 25,000 jobs and the
closure or part-closure of thirteen more plants. Under normal circumstances, the chances of the unions accepting it would have been non-existent.
But Edwardes had decided to appeal to the workers over the heads of their
shop stewards, by holding a ballot organized by the Electoral Reform
Society. When the results were released on 1 November, almost nine out
of ten employees had voted in favour of his plan. The shop stewards
grumbled about 'blackmail', but Edwardes was delighted. 'If any manager,
shop steward or employee does not like the heat of the kitchen,' he declared,
'now is the time to get out.'[24]

Among Longbridge's radical shop stewards, however, discontent continued to fester. Within a couple of weeks Edwardes became aware that a little green pamphlet was circulating inside the Austin Morris factory, calling for strikes and occupations to bring the management to heel. What was more, the pamphlet bore a striking similarity to the record of a meeting between some shop stewards and officials of the local Communist Party, which had come into Edwardes's possession ('anonymously, through the mail', he claimed) at around the same time. He did not hesitate. By the third week in November, Austin Morris had decided to give formal warnings to three shop stewards and to dismiss a fourth, Derek Robinson, convener of Longbridge's combined shop stewards' committee.

On 19 November the Longbridge works director called Robinson into his office and ordered him to withdraw his name from the pamphlet. When Robinson refused, he was sacked. The news travelled fast. Within hours thousands of men were streaming out of Longbridge. By late afternoon, production was at a standstill. 'Nothing goes in or out,' one picket said ominously. 'The management won't get away with this,' added another. And in the hours after Robinson's dismissal, it seemed they were right. By the evening of the 20th, more than 30,000 men were on strike. At Longbridge all Mini and Allegro production had stopped; so had all Jaguar, Daimler and Triumph work at nearby Coventry, as well as Marina production at Cowley. 'OUT! OUT!' shrieked the front page of the *Mirror*. 'Red Derek's Fury', gasped the *Express*: 'Trouble-torn British Leyland was last night tottering on the brink of complete shutdown as it felt the full fury of the shopfloor . . .'[25]

All this, for just one man? But Derek Robinson was not your ordinary shop steward. In the autumn of 1979, the six-foot toolmaker was one of the best-known trade unionists in Britain, which meant he was more widely recognized than most government ministers. To millions watching the evening news, the sound of his Black Country accent was an unmistakeable sign that there was trouble at Longbridge again. To the press, he was 'Red Robbo', the Bolshevik bogeyman who could bring British Leyland to its knees with a click of his fingers. Four times Robinson had stood as the Communist candidate for Birmingham Northfield, never winning more than a thousand votes. But his self-confidence, physical presence and shop-floor credibility could not be ignored. His mantra was always the same: 'Not a job is to be lost, no work is to be transferred. Under no circumstances will the unions allow plant closures, part shutdowns or any redundancies.'

Michael Edwardes claimed that since Robinson had taken over as convener of the combined shop stewards' committee, he had been responsible for 523 stoppages and the loss of 62,000 cars and 113,000 engines, at a total cost of some £200 million. And to conservative columnists, Red Robbo embodied everything wrong with British trade unionism. The headline on George Gale's confession that he was planning to buy a foreign car, for example, read simply 'Damn You, Mr Robinson'. It was Red Robbo, Gale explained, who had made up his mind for him. 'Mr Robinson isn't interested in me buying a Leyland car. All he is interested in is keeping jobs at Leylands at the public's expense . . . Thank you, Mr Robinson. You have lifted a kind of patriotic burden off my back. I no longer feel obliged to buy British.'[26]

Although the press painted Red Robbo as a Stone Age bully, there was clearly more to him than that. Having left school at 14, the son and grandson of Black Country chain-makers, he had joined Austin as an apprentice toolmaker in 1941. As a young man he came under the influence of Dick Etheridge, an AUEW shop steward and a member of the Communist Party. Having introduced Robinson to Marxism, Etheridge watched with fatherly pride as his protégé rose up the union hierarchy. And at last, in 1974, Robinson succeeded his mentor as head of the unofficial shop stewards' combine, which covered workers across more than forty-two factories and insisted on handling all negotiations with the management.

Robinson's Communism was absolutely heartfelt: in an interview with *Marxism Today* in 1980, he talked enthusiastically about sharing Marxist ideas with his fellow car workers. But, as the same interview showed, he was an intelligent, often pragmatic man who was well aware of the challenges facing British Leyland. His solutions, though, were always the same: no job losses, no closures and, above all, more government money. That inevitably brought him into conflict with Michael Edwardes. The difficulty for Robinson, however, lay in judging his comrades' appetite for battle. For as one of his colleagues explained, Robinson's 800 shop stewards and 18,000 members followed him despite, not because of, his Communist politics. 'He just wants to get the maximum money he can for his car workers,' the shop steward said. 'His analysis is right; it is just that he sometimes picks the wrong fights.'[27]

Whether Robinson's analysis was right is very dubious. He told *Marxism Today* that both Labour and the Conservatives had 'conspired on every possible occasion' to undermine British Leyland, and claimed that Edwardes was openly colluding with the Thatcher government to 'run Leyland to an uncompetitive position'. This was not true. In fact, Labour had given BL hundreds of millions of pounds in public money, while the Conservatives were poised to follow suit. As for Edwardes, he was fighting like a tiger to get more money for the firm and restore its international competitiveness.

What is true, though, is that Edwardes was determined to break the power of the shop stewards, which meant bringing down Derek Robinson. Despite the furore over the inflammatory pamphlet, the sacking had been long prepared. In the run-up to the launch of the Metro, Edwardes was planning to make radical changes to BL's working practices, smashing the old demarcation lines and introducing more flexible arrangements to improve productivity. But that would be impossible with Robinson leading the opposition. 'We simply had to change all that in 1980,' Edwardes wrote, 'and the Communist challenge to the Recovery Plan could not therefore go unanswered.' He knew sacking Robinson would provoke a firestorm. But if he prevailed, he would prove that the days of 'weak management bowing to shop floor militancy' were over.[28]

There was another dimension to Robinson's dismissal. In his autobiography, Edwardes claimed that he had received the minutes of the meeting between the local Communist activists and BL shop stewards in the post. This was untrue. In a twist worthy of conspiracy thrillers such as Chris Mullin's novel *A Very British Coup* (1982), he had been given them by MI5. The minutes had been obtained by one of their agents, a senior official in the AUEW who knew Derek Robinson well and had the code-number 910. (As it happens, the agent's MI5 handler later told the journalist Peter Taylor that 910 had been very easy to run. All he wanted in return for his efforts was a couple of pints and some fish and chips on the way home.) MI5 gave the minutes to a new Cabinet Office unit, set up at Mrs Thatcher's behest to 'forestall industrial subversion' and run by John Deverell, a young MI5 high-flier. Deverell showed them to Mrs Thatcher, and she agreed that he could pass them to Edwardes, in a brown envelope with a Birmingham postmark. In turn, Edwardes showed them to the AUEW's general secretary, Terry Duffy, a moderate who was keen to bring his shop stewards to heel. And this explains what happened next.[29]

Despite all these machinations, Edwardes was taking a tremendous gamble. If Robinson's men walked out en masse, then Mrs Thatcher would almost certainly turn down his request for money. In that case, British Leyland would be finished. Indeed, on Wednesday 21 November, two days after Robinson had been dismissed, more than 30,000 men were still out at fifteen different plants. Robinson himself was in typically belligerent form, calling for a 'National Day of Action' and warning that his dismissal was merely the first shot in a 'determined attack on the whole trade union movement'. Yet by Thursday there were the first signs that his campaign was losing momentum. At more moderate plants, such as Solihull, thousands of men were working normally, while neither of BL's two major unions, the TGWU and the AUEW, had made the strike official. The *Mirror* tracked down Robinson's brother Ben, who worked night shifts at Longbridge and had ignored calls to join the strike. 'Derek obviously thinks what he is doing is right,' Ben Robinson said. 'But that doesn't mean I have to agree with him. Like a lot of other people at Longbridge I get fed up with strikes and disputes.'[30]

A few days later, Edwardes turned the screw. On Monday 26th he announced that if the unions made the strike official, BL's senior management would resign, which would almost certainly mean the firm's complete collapse. And as the union leaders hesitated, Robinson's support continued to evaporate. His much-trailed 'Day of Action' was a total non-event, while at Longbridge hundreds of men were drifting back to work. But everything depended on the AUEW leadership, who were due to meet Edwardes for make-or-break talks on Tuesday. 'High Noon at Leyland', began an apocalyptic editorial in that day's *Daily Express*, urging the union bosses not to 'let a company go down the drain because of a fanatic'. *The Times* even thought this was a showdown 'without parallel in our industrial history'. If the unions insisted on Robinson's reinstatement, there was no way the government could bail out British Leyland. Did the unions really want to 'risk the virtual extinction of BL? . . . Will they opt to save one job – or 100,000?'[31]

The answer came within hours. When the AUEW met Edwardes on Tuesday morning, they found him in uncompromising form. If their members refused to go back to work, he would terminate their contracts and find replacements. If that did not work, he would 'close the doors once and for all'. This was strong stuff, but since Edwardes had already shared MI5's brown envelope with Terry Duffy, he knew the odds were in his favour. And by mid-afternoon the AUEW had agreed to a compromise. Robinson was still sacked, pending a union inquiry, while Edwardes agreed to pay his wages until the union published its report. As Duffy told the press, the decisive factor had been Edwardes's warning that, if he lost, 'that would be the end for British Leyland'. There was no point, Duffy said, in fighting 'stark reality'. So for the time being, at least, Edwardes had won. 'SANITY!' rejoiced the *Express*. 'Everybody Back! (Except Red Derek.)'[32]

In Downing Street, Edwardes's gamble provoked very mixed feelings. On the one hand, Mrs Thatcher loved the thought of somebody standing up to the unions. On the other, it was now very hard for her to deny him the money he wanted. The irony was that Joseph's officials had already concluded that there was 'no hope for BL in its present form', and that 'continued run-down and break-up [were] inevitable'. But as Joseph gloomily told Mrs Thatcher, public opinion would not let them pull the plug 'without giving Sir Michael Edwardes a chance'. Edwardes, John Hosykns reluctantly agreed, had become a symbol of 'the possible renaissance of British management – straight, tough, determined, competent, etc . . . To reward [his] efforts and his work force backing with closure would seem to be a deliberate blow against everything the Government is trying to encourage.'[33]

On 20 December the Cabinet agreed to give Edwardes his £300 million. In private, Mrs Thatcher seethed with frustration. But Edwardes did not waste much time in celebrating. After all, Derek Robinson had not gone away. The AUEW still had to produce its report, while Robinson seemed certain he would be vindicated. Even as Mrs Thatcher's ministers were approving the bailout, he was addressing the National Union of Students. 'Of course I'm going to get my job back,' he told them. 'I hope the students will give us physical assistance on the picket lines . . . We intend Longbridge to come to a stop. Nothing will move in or out of any Leyland plant. We will seal the ports so that no Leyland product will leave the country.' A sceptic might have told him that anybody hoping to seal the ports with the 'physical assistance' of Britain's student population was on a hiding to nothing.

Even so, when the AUEW produced its report on 6 February 1980, Robinson had a glimmer of hope. Although it had stern words for his 'dominant and forceful' behaviour, the union thought he should get his job back. This was not, of course, what Edwardes wanted to hear, although he could hardly have been very surprised. So would British Leyland take Robinson back? The next day's headlines – 'No Surrender, Say Bosses: It's Him or Us!' – gave the answer. So BL's future was back in the balance. Now everything depended on Longbridge's 8,000 AUEW members, the men beside whom Robinson had worked for the previous four decades. If they voted to walk out, Austin Morris executives warned that it would mean the end of production at Longbridge and the immediate loss of some 20,000 jobs. It would also mean the end for Edwardes, although the stakes were now far bigger than the career of one chairman – or even one convener.[34]

But if anybody believed the British working classes were itching to throw off the yoke of Thatcherite capitalism, the mood at Longbridge would have come as a shock. When local television reporters conducted a straw poll of 250 men at the gates, they found that two-thirds were against a strike, while other journalists found plenty of men determined to carry on working. 'The men don't want him back,' remarked one maintenance worker. 'They have no trust in him now. Anyway, they are more worried about the pay deal than about his job.' 'People have made up their minds and 85 per cent are against Robbo,' an assembly worker told the *Mirror*. 'We don't want to lose any more money. I have got no intention of striking, even if there is an official stoppage.' 'There shouldn't be a strike and I won't come out if I can help it,' agreed a TGWU member. 'Nobody wants Robbo back.' Even in Robinson's old stamping ground, the toolroom, many men shook their heads. 'We've already made bloody fools of ourselves over him once,' one said. 'We're not daft enough to do it again.'[35]

Even so, the atmosphere as the men prepared to vote could scarcely have been more febrile. Outside Robinson's semi-detached house in suburban Rubery, a television crew camped on the pavement, while journalists rang every half-hour. The Birmingham newspapers kept up a drumbeat of invective: the *Evening Mail* told its readers, 'The choice is your job or Red Robbo', while one local columnist thought they should send him to Moscow, where he could spend the rest of his days exchanging 'Commie cant with his Marxist mates'. Yet although many men told the press that they did not want to strike, most said they would find it hard to cross a picket line. 'If we go in,' one said, 'we shall lose our union cards.'

As the decisive day, 20 February, dawned, not even Michael Edwardes felt entirely sure that that the vote would go his way. As it happened, he had a long-standing engagement to address the Birmingham Chamber of Commerce, just after the men had voted. As Edwardes was getting ready at his hotel, the men were gathering at Cofton Park, near Longbridge. In his hotel room, Edwardes laid out two speeches, one praising the men for their realism and good sense, the other announcing the death of Austin Morris as a national car maker. Then, moments before he went down to his chauffeur-driven car, a call came through. It was Longbridge. When Edwardes put down the phone, he tore one of the speeches into tiny pieces.[36]

Edwardes had won, and the margin was greater than he had dared to imagine. Despite the bitterly cold and misty weather, at least 12,000 men had turned up to vote, and from the start it was obvious Robinson was in trouble. Instead of being dispersed throughout the crowd, where they might have been shouted down, his critics were packed tightly together. Some carried placards – 'Out with Robbo', 'Knickers to Robbo', 'On Your Bike, Robbo' – while others had erected a gallows, from which an effigy of their old convener dangled in the breeze. And as soon as the first union representatives climbed up on the makeshift platform, urging their men to show solidarity and stand up to the bosses, the booing started. 'When Jesus Christ was condemned,' a speaker from the TGWU shouted, 'they threw him to the crowd and then they crucified him. Michael Edwardes has carried out a campaign to crucify Derek Robinson. He wants you to nail him to the cross!'

But it was no good; the jeering redoubled. At last, Robinson himself, a big, balding man in a tweed suit, took the microphone. At that point missiles began to rain down – mud, rotten fruit, even metal washers. 'Out! Out! Out!' yelled the crowd. The union men called for a vote on a strike, and the hands went up: a few hundred, some said, though others thought there might have been a thousand. Either way, it was a stunning humiliation. As a great roar went up from the crowd, Derek Robinson just sat there, a man alone, shaking his head in shock. For years he had revelled in his role in front of the cameras. Now, for perhaps the first time in his life, he had nothing to say. 'I never expected the vote to go this way,' he said quietly, his voice trembling. 'I don't know what I'm going to do.'[37]

To Robinson's foes, the result was a glorious victory, a sign that the British people had turned their backs on the militancy of the Winter of Discontent. In the Commons, Mrs Thatcher hailed a 'triumph for common sense'. In *The Times*, an editorial declared that Robinson had become 'an awful example of what happens to powerful shop stewards who abuse the interests and lose the mood of the people they represent'. 'Out You Go!' jeered the front page of the *Express*, which declared that 'the workers of Longbridge have struck a blow for common sense and genuine industrial democracy'. Only the *Mirror* had a crumb of sympathy for the beaten man, pointing out that Robinson had not been responsible for the outdated models that had done so much damage to British Leyland's reputation, nor for the 'managerial incompetence' that had pushed it to the brink of bankruptcy. He had become a scapegoat, the paper thought, a symbol of all the sins of the 'bloody-minded BL worker. And as a symbol he has been sacrificed. By the ex-bloody-minded BL workers.'[38]

A few days later, when the *Observer* caught up with Robinson at home in Rubery, he still seemed stunned by what had happened. What was he going to do next? He had no idea. 'I suppose I shall have to sign on in the next few days,' he said mournfully. He did not blame his old workmates; they had been tricked by the management and the media. But the scars took longer to heal than Robinson expected. A year later, he was still suffering from nightmares, had been diagnosed with depression and feared he was becoming addicted to tranquillizers. Yet not for a moment did he reconsider his politics, or the strategy he had pursued for so long. That autumn he tried to make a comeback, standing as a divisional organizer in the local AUEW. But he lost to Terry Duffy's brother Denis, who won more than twice as many votes. Robinson claimed he had been the victim of fraud, but nobody listened.[39]

By now with more than 2 million people out of work, the days when thousands cheered Robinson at the Longbridge gates were a very distant memory. In 1983 he even lost his place on the executive committee of the Communist Party, after a bitter struggle between his 'pro-Moscow' wing and a younger group of self-styled modernizers. What made it even worse was that, in reporting the story, *The Times* told its readers that he had once been known as 'Red Ronnie'. The fact that they had not even got his nickname right was the greatest indignity of all.[40]

Robinson was gone, then, and Edwardes had his money. The underlying picture, however, could scarcely have been bleaker. To many observers, the spectacle of British Leyland dicing with closure was a sign of the terminal sickness afflicting British manufacturing. And with the economy heading into recession, any prospect of recovery seemed vanishingly remote.

'British Leyland now promises to become the most serious industrial crisis facing this country since the war,' began an apocalyptic *Times* editorial on 14 February 1980. 'It will also be a test of fire for the industrial policies of the Government in general and of Sir Keith Joseph in particular.' Far from being addressed, all BL's weaknesses – 'thin management, poor labour relations, inadequate product range and the rest' – had been magnified by the economic downturn. Even Edwardes's much-vaunted 'Recovery Plan' was in tatters, superseded by the surge in the pound and the collapse of BL's market share. Against that background, remarked *The Times*, the 'problem with Mr Robinson' was only part of the story. The 'more fundamental issue' was 'whether British Leyland as the group we know today has any future at all'.[41]

Edwardes believed it did. By getting rid of Robinson, he had bought himself the freedom to push through his blueprint for radical reform. 'It calls for the most sweeping changes ever attempted in zealously guarded working practices,' wrote one reporter. 'It seeks to introduce full mobility of labour, the end of inter-union demarcation boundaries, free access for time and motion men and the creation of a new breed of worker retrained as an all-rounder.' As an inducement, Edwardes promised a 5 per cent increase in the basic wage, as well as an incentive scheme offering an additional £15 a week. And when, in April 1980, he put his blueprint into effect, there was barely a peep of protest. As Robinson's fate had demonstrated, the workforce's enthusiasm for conflict had evaporated, partly because so many people were frightened of losing their jobs, but also because, deep down, many agreed with Edwardes's diagnosis. And with the successful launch of the Metro, Longbridge's place in the public imagination was transformed. Once the embodiment of resistance to change, it now became a symbol of 'management's right to manage'.[42]

In public, Mrs Thatcher still claimed to be Edwardes's most fervent supporter. She even had warm words for the Metro, telling the BBC that it was a 'really super car. Super in design, super in petrol consumption.' But when the microphones were off, her views were very different. As she later recalled, she was 'increasingly unhappy' about BL's losses and infuriated by Edwardes's habit of blaming the exchange rate. Above all, she dreaded the thought of once again having to choose between letting the firm collapse, at the cost of at least 150,000 jobs, and pouring more money down the Longbridge plughole. As she told Joseph in April 1980, 'we couldn't risk hundreds of millions of taxpayers' money out of loyalty to Edwardes'. John Hoskyns even recorded that she had a 'paranoid obsession about Edwardes', whom she accused of having 'contractually undertaken to deliver BL success and then defaulted'.[43]

On 21 May 1980 Edwardes visited Downing Street for dinner. The food struck him as 'frugal', the atmosphere 'frosty' and Mrs Thatcher's conversational style 'somewhat reminiscent of the Spanish Inquisition'. Once again her opening words set the tone: 'Now, what's all this about? You're not going to ask us for more money?' In fact, this was precisely what Edwardes was going to do. With the surging pound destroying his firm's already feeble foreign sales, the government would need to pump 'more vast sums into BL to keep it going'. What was worse, he could not guarantee that the firm would *ever* make a profit. Mrs Thatcher asked why he could not just sell the entire business off, to which Edwardes replied that 'no company in the world' wanted to buy it. At best they might be able to sell bits of it, such as Land Rover, but that would leave the rest severely weakened. All of this went down very badly, and Mrs Thatcher's mood was not improved when an aide came in to whisper the latest currency figures, which showed the pound still moving upwards. That, of course, was more bad news for British Leyland.[44]

When, at the end of 1980, Edwardes submitted his latest plan, the figures were even worse than he had implied. Back in 1979 BL's forecasters had talked of needing £130 million to cover the next three years. But now they wanted a colossal £1.1 billion. Mrs Thatcher was aghast. There was 'no good reason', she thought, to throw so much money at a company that was still losing almost £600 for every car it made. But as Joseph gloomily reminded her, there was, in fact, a very good reason: the punitive cost of shutting it down. Her key economic ministers agreed that, despite the Metro, 'the prospect of BL returning to profitability was virtually zero'. But even Sir Geoffrey Howe, who was hardly disposed to throwing money around, thought closing BL was not a 'viable option'. 'Even if there were a case in principle for withdrawing support,' he explained on 12 January 1981, 'closures in the steel and shipbuilding industries should have higher priority; and it was not politically possible to achieve all at once.'[45]

There was, however, a twist. The day before the Cabinet was due to rubber-stamp the bailout, Joseph had an attack of conscience. As he told Mrs Thatcher, he had changed his mind and thought they should 'grasp the nettle now and accept the dissolution of BL' – despite the fact that his own officials had just spent the last few weeks sorting out the new funding. This was, by any standards, extraordinary behaviour. Not even Tony Benn had ever sold a difficult decision to his colleagues before changing his mind and swapping sides to argue against it. To Joseph's critics, it was definitive proof of his total unfitness to run a major department. In any case, he had left it too late. The next day, Mrs Thatcher's ministers gave the bailout the green light. On 26 January, physically writhing with unhappiness, Joseph broke the news to the Commons. A few days later, a relieved Edwardes had a letter from the comedian Spike Milligan, who had heard that he had come into possession of a billion pounds, and wondered if he could spare some change. Edwardes sent him a £5 note.[46]

For Joseph's critics, there was an exquisite irony in the fact that this passionate convert to economic liberalism, who had spent the last few years haranguing his former colleagues for their ideological apostasy, was now responsible for one of the biggest bailouts in British history. Yet contrary to political mythology, the government's generosity to British Leyland was the rule, not the exception. Under Wilson and Callaghan, Britain had spent 2.7 per cent of GDP on industrial subsidies, prompting howls of fury from the Conservatives. Yet in the first five years under Mrs Thatcher, Britain still spent 2.3 per cent, more than either the United States or Japan and almost exactly the European average.* Far from falling in the early 1980s, spending on trade and industry went up by almost a fifth, largely because, as the recession deepened, the government was forced to pour even more money into nationalized industries such as British Leyland, British Steel and the National Coal Board.

That it was Joseph, of all people, who signed the cheques made it all the more ironic. Later, he regretted that he 'didn't have the guts' to shut British Leyland down, blaming his own lack of 'conviction and moral courage'. But now even Mrs Thatcher had her doubts about her old friend's stability. In Cabinet she muttered caustic remarks when he was talking,

---

* In fairness, the level fell in the second half of the decade to just 1.7 per cent, so she did get there eventually.

and in January 1981 she asked her 'semi-house-trained polecat', Norman Tebbit, to become his deputy and political bodyguard. 'I want you to look after Keith – dear Keith, they are so unkind to him, and he needs someone to protect him,' she explained. But dear Keith was under no illusions. Once, when he and Tebbit were going to see her about British Leyland, one of their officials asked if there was anything they needed. 'No, thank you,' Joseph said wearily, and then corrected himself: 'Well, yes, ambulances for two at 3 o'clock.'[47]

By now Joseph's tenure at the Department of Industry had turned into a nightmare. To his colleagues, he seemed to have aged overnight, his face paler than ever, his behaviour ever more erratic. When he spoke at universities, he was jostled, punched and pelted with missiles. At meetings he seemed restless and distracted, and *Private Eye* claimed that during radio interviews he hesitated so long that listeners thought they had lost the signal. After the Commons debated British Leyland in May 1981, the *Sunday Times* reported that Joseph had sent out a 'formidable repertoire of distress signals', burying his face in his hands and kneading his own forehead 'until the veins turned purple'. 'Even his voice, deep, unnaturally calm,' the paper said, 'seemed to emanate from a spirit beyond the grave'.[48]

A few years earlier, Joseph had proclaimed that radical action to unleash the power of the free market would turn Britain around. Now he had become the embodiment of what the government's critics saw as a callous and catastrophic experiment. No wonder, then, that in one of the great parliamentary performances of the decade, Labour's deputy leader, Michael Foot, made him a prime target. The occasion was a debate on unemployment in the autumn of 1980, which had dragged on for hours. To guffaws from his colleagues, Foot remarked that whenever he saw the Industry Secretary 'walking around the country, looking puzzled, forlorn and wondering what has happened', he was reminded of an experience from his boyhood:

In my youth, quite a time ago, when I lived in Plymouth, every Saturday night I used to go to the Palace theatre. My favourite act was a magician-conjuror who used to have sitting at the back of the audience a man dressed as a prominent alderman. The magician-conjuror used to say that he wanted a beautiful watch from a member of the audience. He would go up to the alderman and eventually take from him a marvellous gold watch. He would bring it back to the stage, enfold it in a beautiful red handkerchief, place it on the table in front of us, take out his mallet, hit the watch and smash it to smithereens.

Then on his countenance would come exactly the puzzled look of the Secretary of State for Industry. He would step to the front of the stage and say, 'I am very sorry. I have forgotten the rest of the trick!'*

It was vintage Foot, a brilliant speaker at the top of his game. 'That is the situation of the Government!' he said gleefully. 'They have forgotten the rest of the trick!' And as Joseph sat there, listening to the laughter of his fellow MPs, there must have been a bit of him that feared Foot might be right.[49]

Michael Edwardes stepped down from British Leyland in the autumn of 1982. With characteristic perspicacity, he had accepted an offer to become chairman of Mercury Communications, the first real competitor to British Telecom. Like all good performers, the brusque South African left with applause ringing in his ears. At his last BL shareholders' meeting, two private investors made gushing speeches; another begged him to stay. A fourth said he had come to London just to gaze on the great man with his own eyes. 'I can see now that you are a man of little stature,' he said, perhaps a bit riskily. 'But I also know that in all other aspects you are a very big man indeed.'[50]

To his admirers, Edwardes was the most influential executive of the age, the hero who had restored the 'management's right to manage'. The *Guardian* described him as an undisputed '"Good Thing", the strong-man who stood up to the unions and bent a chaotic BL to his will'. And in some ways his record was extremely impressive. In five years he had trimmed some 90,000 jobs without provoking a major dispute, while the number of hours lost annually to strikes had fallen from 15 million to fewer than 4 million. Even Longbridge was unrecognizable from the ramshackle, strike-plagued monument he had inherited. Thanks to his workplace reforms, productivity had leapt from seven cars a man to more than twenty-five cars a man, and visitors now walked around in awe rather than in horror. Under Edwardes, said the *Sunday Times*, the vast factory had 'started to perform like its Japanese competitors', with state-of-the-art robots, a flexible workforce and a new culture of individual initiative. The performance records at Longbridge and Cowley, agreed *The Times*, were 'equal to the best in Europe', and a testament to the man who had 're-established management's right to run the company'.[51]

Yet by many standards British Leyland's record under Edwardes was absolutely atrocious. Between 1977 and 1982, annual car production fell

---

* A very similar thing once happened to Paddington Bear. In the story 'A Disappearing Trick' (1958), Paddington smashes Mr Curry's watch with a hammer. Paddington's excuse is that he 'forgot to say Abracadabra'.

from 651,000 to 405,000, while overseas sales collapsed from 170,000 to fewer than 80,000. Given the high hopes surrounding the launch of the Metro, the latter figure was particularly disappointing. Although BL sold hundreds of thousands of Metros, the vast majority never crossed the Channel. Even more seriously, BL had still not developed a mid-size competitor for the Escort or the Sierra, despite the fact that this was by far the most lucrative sector of the market. As a result, it found itself lagging far behind its foreign rivals. While BL sold 50,000 cars in the entire Common Market, West Germany's car makers were now selling 250,000 vehicles in Britain alone.

All of this left a hole in the balance sheet. In 1977, when Edwardes arrived at the firm, BL had lost £52 million. In 1979 it lost £145 million, in 1980 £536 million and in 1981 £497 million. In 1982, even after the triumph of the Metro, it still lost £293 million. Appearing before a Commons Select Committee, Edwardes insisted that BL was through the worst. But with its market share in free-fall, this seemed wildly over-optimistic. 'In the time it has taken you to read this paragraph', lamented a *Guardian* report on the firm's woes that March, 'Britain's state-backed car company will have lost another £1,000.'[52]

In fairness, little of this was Edwardes's fault. The truth is that British Leyland had always been a pantomime horse, not big or profitable enough to compete with giants such as Renault, Volkswagen and Ford, but not lean or productive enough to match upmarket firms like Volvo and BMW. In the circumstances, the South African had probably done as well as anybody could have expected, leaving behind a company that, for all its losses, was leaner, more confident and more productive, as well as far less prone to strikes. But British Leyland did not survive for long. By the end of the decade it had been broken up and sold off, just as Mrs Thatcher and her advisers had wanted. Some elements, notably Jaguar, Land Rover and Mini, thrived under foreign ownership. But names such as Austin and Morris disappeared completely.[53]

The future of British car making lay not at Longbridge, but hundreds of miles to the north. On 6 August 1980, as Edwardes's engineers were putting the final touches to the Metro, Sir Keith Joseph told Mrs Thatcher that he had received an approach from a Japanese car firm, Nissan, which was contemplating a European base for its growing business. If it worked out, it would be the biggest deal ever struck by a Japanese firm in Britain, as well as a spectacular demonstration of the government's openness to foreign investment. Of course it would mean encouraging a competitor to British Leyland, but Joseph thought this a price worth paying for a £300 million investment.

As Joseph knew, the spectacle of a Japanese car maker establishing a base in Britain would provoke 'strong feelings', so the government proceeded with caution. All the same, they relished the prospect of such a high-profile vote of confidence in the British economy. When Mrs Thatcher visited Tokyo in September 1982, she made a point of telling Nissan's chairman how pleased she would be to welcome his firm. And it worked. By March 1984 Nissan had selected a site just outside Sunderland. The choice was rich with symbolism: while Sunderland was a long way from the car-making heartlands of the West Midlands, it was a former ship-building and coal-mining town with one of the worst unemployment records in the country. When the plant opened two years later, Mrs Thatcher was the guest of honour. The choice, she said proudly, was 'confirmation from Nissan after a long and thorough appraisal, that within the whole of Europe, the United Kingdom was the most attractive country – politically and economically – for large scale investment and offered the greatest potential'.[54]

As British Leyland disintegrated, Nissan's Sunderland factory, supported by hundreds of millions of pounds in regional aid and tax breaks, went from strength to strength. Within five years the plant, with a work-force of just 3,500 men, was making a profit. By the twenty-first century it had become the most productive car factory in Europe, making more cars every year than all British Leyland's plants put together at the turn of the 1980s. There was no better example of Britain's newfound ability to attract foreign investment. To the general public, however, the plant was best known for having never lost a single minute to industrial action. 'Will the British worker be obedient enough for Nissan?' the *Guardian* had once asked. Now it had the answer.

Some observers credited the culture of the Japanese workplace; others pointed to Mrs Thatcher's union reforms. But Nissan's pioneering single-union deal, which made strikes impossible as long as both sides were still talking, had an awful lot to do with it. At the time, some trade unionists, as well as plenty of critics on the left, had been appalled. But there had been intense competition among the unions to get the contract to represent Nissan's British workers, and in the end it went to the Amalgamated Union of Engineering Workers. As it happened, that was Derek Robinson's old union. But by then Red Robbo was ancient history.[55]

# 14

# A Really Angry Brigade

*This area used to be really OK till my parents turned it into an urban village. I'm sick of lentils, old denim, Batik prints . . . my parents' obsession with sex & their endless rapping about the boring old Sixties when Dad joined student sit-ins & Mum was a Flower Child and Earth-Mother.*

Belinda Weber, in Posy Simmonds,
*Mrs Weber's Diary* (1979)

*Anthony Wedgwood Benn is no fool. He's a persecution maniac, and a dangerous aristocratic drop-out who'll publicly spit the silver spoon out of his mouth if it kills him. And ruins the country.*
Jean Rook, *Daily Express*, 7 November 1979

It was the afternoon of 8 December 1980, and across the Atlantic probably the best-known Englishman in the world was holding forth in his New York apartment. On the brink of middle age, John Lennon was no longer the iconoclastic rebel of the Beatles' heyday. Although he looked worn and gaunt after a decade of personal turbulence, he seemed calmer now, settled in his life with Yoko Ono, content with his lot as a husband and father. And when a team from a San Francisco radio station arrived to record an interview about his new album, *Double Fantasy*, they found him in reflective mood.

The record was not really meant for teenagers, Lennon said. It was made for people like himself, 'the Sixties group that has survived. Survived the war, the drugs, the politics, the violence on the street – the whole shebang – that we've survived it and we're here.' And as they talked, Lennon kept returning to the past and what it meant, all these years later. 'Maybe in the Sixties we were naïve, and like children everybody went back to their room and said, "Well, we didn't get a wonderful world of just flowers and peace and happy chocolate and . . . it wasn't just pretty and beautiful all the time,"' he said earnestly. 'And that's what everybody did . . . everybody went back to their rooms and sulked.' Still, although recent years had been full of disappointment, Lennon still held true to 'the possibility and the responsibility that we all had'. Perhaps, he said brightly, 'in the Eighties everybody'll say, "Well, OK, let's project the positive side of life again", you know?'[1]

When the interview was finished, Lennon and Ono went out to mix a song at a nearby recording studio, sharing a cab with the San Francisco radio crew. They did not get back to their apartment building until just before eleven. Lennon was looking forward to saying goodnight to his 5-year-old son, Sean. As he got out of the car, he noticed a man in the shadows by the archway, a copy of the new album under his arm. The man stepped forward. 'Mr Lennon,' he said softly, levelled a revolver, and fired.[2]

Lennon's murder by a twisted loner made front-page headlines in almost every country on earth. When Britain awoke to the terrible news, Radio One played Beatles records all day, while local phone-ins were deluged with callers choking back tears. Across the country, shops reported huge demand for all the Beatles' records, while both *Double Fantasy* and Lennon's latest single, '(Just Like) Starting Over', headed straight to the top of the charts. And in his home town of Liverpool, so badly scarred by deprivation and disappointment, there was a palpable sense of shock. In Mathew Street, where the Beatles had played at the Cavern Club, hundreds of people gathered in 'pathetic hushed groups', many in tears. When the council organized a peace vigil in his memory, some 20,000 people stood in silence for ten minutes, among them the Archbishop of Canterbury. Afterwards, several dozen people, mostly teenage girls, had to be treated for 'fainting and hysteria'. There could have been no more poignant reminder of the lost innocence of the 1960s.[3]

'He was just my John,' his devastated Aunt Mimi told the press. But the Beatles were 'more than just pop minstrels and Lennon was more than just their leader', said an editorial in the *Mirror*. 'They changed styles of dress and behaviour as well as music. They symbolised the end of dutiful respect for authority, whether of parents or of governments. They were classless and almost ageless.' Lennon was 'not just a nostalgic reminder of our lost times and selves', said the *Express*, 'but more, much more . . . With the Beatles, he uplifted a whole generation, helping them break through the low cloud barriers of their frustrations to a universe of limit-less possibilities.' Even *The Times* agreed that Lennon had personified the spirit of the 1960s, 'when England truly emerged from its postwar depression and became a country of joyful and envied excitement . . . His death, untimely and inappropriately violent, commits to history the decade that so utterly changed British society.'[4]

But not everybody was prepared to bury the hatchet. 'The eulogies bestowed on John Lennon were uncalled for,' Frederick Jackson wrote to the *Express*. 'Did he not insult the Queen by returning the MBE bestowed on the Beatles . . . and also was he not charged with the illegal use of drugs?' And while H. L. Hillman was sorry that Lennon had come to 'such a tragic end', he agreed that the 'current hysterical emotion' was over the top. 'The Beatles' social habits, including the taking of drugs, were not exactly the right examples to set', he wrote, 'and they lost a golden opportunity to give their fans the correct lead.' Nor had Mr Hillman forgiven Lennon for his notorious bed-in for peace, which he considered 'foolish'. 'If the Battle of Britain pilots stayed in bed during the Nazi bombings in the last war,' he pointed out, 'I am sure there would never have been The Beatles or anyone else left to enjoy our freedom today.' Some things never changed.[5]

By the time of Lennon's death, the excitement of the Beatles' heyday felt like a very distant memory. When the essayist Lincoln Allison visited Liverpool, he found that the original Cavern Club had gone, demolished during building work a few years earlier. A new incarnation, just down the street, stood 'closed and rather forlorn'. And when people rushed to buy the band's old records in the wake of Lennon's death, they did so out of sentimental nostalgia. This was the soundtrack from a lost golden age, not the sound of the 1980s. Guitars had given way to synthesizers, earnest optimism to knowing irony. Twenty years earlier, it had been possible to talk of British youth culture as a single phenomenon, millions of young-sters united by their enthusiasm for the Beatles. But now the audience had fractured beyond repair. 'Pop isn't IMPORTANT anymore,' wrote Jon Savage in *The Face* in April 1981. 'There's no consensus – that '60s ideal! – just markets: just good pop records that float to the surface and a few dedicated people doing what they can't do anywhere else.'[6]

This was not just a story about music. In the public imagination, Britain in the 1960s had been the land of James Bond and the Beatles, the Mini and the mini-skirt. The Beatles had been disbanded for ten years, mini-skirts had fallen out of fashion and the Mini had given way to the Austin Metro. As for James Bond, he had long since lost his thrilling modernity. When the National Film Theatre mounted a Bond retrospective at the beginning of 1980, *The Times* thought it showed just how much the series had declined, from the 'classless, liberated' Sean Connery films to the 'flabby and harmless' Roger Moore films, with their 'demented mechanic slapstick rendered impotent by its own lack of purpose and direction'. The sense of decline, of cynicism, of vanished optimism, was all too familiar. Even television comedy had turned its back on the impatient idealism of *That Was the Week That Was* (1962–3), preferring the scepticism of *Yes Minister* (1980–84) or *Not the Nine O'Clock News* (1979–82). As the latter's producer, John Lloyd, explained, his team no longer believed in the old 'optimistic assumptions' of 'satire as a force for change'. Instead, 'sad and cynical' as it might sound, their guiding assumption was that 'the world cannot be changed so we might as well go down laughing'.[7]

On the day John Lennon was shot, the *Guardian* had published the first in a series of essays about 'Punk, Pop and Politics'. The tone was unremittingly bleak. Twenty years earlier, wrote the journalist Martin Walker, Britain had been on the brink of 'the major cultural shift we call the Sixties'. Now, with the headlines full of 'dole queues and nuclear waste and racism on the terraces . . . another cultural shift seems to be underway'. 'A Culture at the End of Its Psychic Tether', read one headline. 'Nihilism Is the Message in Words and Music', declared another. 'We are into the age of the political illiterates,' explained the ubiquitous Peter York, warning that 'the old rationalist liberalism is being crushed to death'. The new decade, said the science-fiction writer Ian Watson, would be one of 'crusades . . . cults . . . a new wave of terrorism . . . a really angry brigade'. The 1980s, agreed the director Derek Jarman, would belong to 'massed dancing cults, mass suicide cults, new religions'. As Walker mordantly put it, 'the concept of Evil is back in our public life'.[8]

Some observers were glad to see the back of liberal utopianism. People had run 'out of faith in grand ideas', wrote Lincoln Allison, who felt relieved that concepts such as 'the "city of the future" and the "white heat of technology"' had 'receded over the horizon'. But to many people who had come of age in the 1960s, an era of full employment, economic growth and apparently endless opportunity, the new era came as a terrible shock. At a neighbourhood centre in Sparkhill, Birmingham, Jeremy Seabrook met a woman called Lynn, who worked as a volunteer on the reception desk. Dressed in a black anorak and jeans, she was a keen CND activist and admitted that she had been inspired 'by the 1960s'. Back then she had thought that work 'would always be there', allowing her to go travelling or to spend her time 'reading philosophy and studying Marx'. 'The whole feeling was different then,' she said sadly. 'It seemed as if life was going to become easier, more expansive.'[9]

This was a sadly familiar refrain. Life was harder; idealism had withered; dreams had turned to disappointments. Even the London listings magazine *Time Out*, launched in the summer of 1968, had abandoned its founding principles. For years it had been the last bastion of the alternative press, its articles blazing with radical passion. But in the spring of 1981 its founder, Tony Elliott, now 34, decided that its traditions of collective decision-making and equal pay for all, from the most senior journalist to the most junior secretary, could no longer be sustained. He wanted to introduce a trainee scheme, take on more senior executives and hire and fire like any other proprietor. In May dozens of journalists staged a sit-in; then they went on strike. Elliott was 'playing at being a big-time capitalist', one said. 'He's rich and very redundant.' But he got his way. The strikers decamped to set up a rival magazine, *City Limits*, which prided itself on its co-operative principles, hard-left politics and refusal to accept 'sexist' advertising. Some of the new publication's contributors went on to great things. But the mood in the office, recalled one of the editorial team, Deborah Orr, was one of 'victimhood, resentment, factionalism, incompetence and silliness'. It collapsed after little more than a decade.[10]

'It was easy to be a socialist when I was growin' up in the sixties,' says one character in Alan Bleasdale's *Boys from the Blackstuff*. 'Everyone was a friggin' socialist then. It was fashionable. But it's not now . . . Everythin's gone sour, everyone's lockin' the door, turnin' the other cheek, lookin' after number one.' Even in Britain's schools, people said the same. Ten or fifteen years earlier, with commentators wringing their hands about the supposed generation gap, the assumption had been that young people were far more radical than their elders. In reality, not only had Mrs Thatcher done extremely well among first-time voters in 1979, but their younger siblings hardly looked like fire-breathing Trotskyists. Polls found that most teenagers backed the monarchy, supported the police, wanted to restore the death penalty and thought the trade unions were too powerful. After talking to Bristol sixth-formers in late 1982, Tony Benn lamented that 'there are Thatcherites in every audience. She has armed a lot of bright young people with powerful right-wing arguments and, although I enjoy discussing them, I realise I am no longer dealing with the old consensus but with a new breed of right-wing concepts.' But were Bristol's teenagers really parroting Mrs Thatcher? Or was she merely saying what they already believed?[11]

Even at universities, stereotypically such radical hotbeds, the pendulum had swung away from protest. With youth unemployment so high, many 18-year-olds were relentlessly focused on their job prospects: hence the tremendous rise of business studies, offered by fewer than ten institutions a decade earlier, but now offered by almost seventy. Students were 'tired of politics', the new president of the National Union of Students (NUS), Trevor Phillips, admitted in 1979. A year later, the NUS announced that it would no longer devote so much attention to 'racialism and women's liberation', in order to focus on students' day-to-day concerns. 'We should no longer be regarded', it explained, 'as an all-purpose rent-a-mob for every cause.' In a sign of the times, Phillips' successor, David Aaronovitch, a Communist, agreed that the NUS should focus on 'bread and butter' issues, and accused more radical students of having 'science fiction attitudes' that would alienate ordinary people. Even at the London School of Economics, once famous for its sit-ins, the mood was 'remarkably quiet'. 'There is', said the *Guardian*, 'very little at the LSE these days of which the Establishment need be fearful.'[12]

When, in January 1981, BBC2 broadcast an adaptation of Malcolm Bradbury's campus novel *The History Man*, with Antony Sher putting in a splendidly horrible performance as the left-wing sociologist Howard Kirk, it already felt like a vision of the past – even though the novel was only 6 years old. The book was 'very dated now', admitted Bradbury, who taught English at the University of East Anglia. 'The Kirk figures – he was a composite of various radical academics I have known – have disappeared from the campuses. Or rather they've changed. They probably voted for Mrs Thatcher in the last election and now, instead of Left-wing politics, they are into jogging and tap-dancing.' What was more, 'student rebellion is also in the past. I'm impressed by the changing mood of my students today – it's a new mood of realism. They are much more motivated about their work and are working twice as hard.' Most of them, he thought, were 'conservatives with a small "c"'.[13]

Yet all this can be easily exaggerated. Not all students were small 'c' conservatives, not everybody had rejected the legacy of the 1960s, and not everybody was as apathetic as the students in *The Young Ones*. It is true that many universities had lively Tory enclaves, in which young men and women were free to put on their tweed jackets, indulge their hatred of Arthur Scargill and boast about their future in the City. But the general tone of student life was still pretty pinkish, from boycotting South African goods to marching against the bomb. When Sir Keith Joseph took the free-market message to universities, he was invariably bombarded with eggs. Most student unions were dominated by the left, and although the NUS was much less radical than in the 1970s, the presidency always went to a self-described socialist. 'Conversations revolved around what was "ideologically sound or unsound",' recalled one Northern Irish woman who studied at Sunderland Polytechnic: 'revolutionary communism, vegetarianism, feminism, ageism, racism, sexism. I was lost in all these "isms".'[14]

Among most of Malcolm Bradbury's colleagues, meanwhile, there was a real horror that Britain had shifted to the right. Even in the 1970s only about one in five academics had voted Conservative, the majority of them scientists. To make matters worse, Mrs Thatcher slashed the universities' budgets by 18 per cent over three years, which meant the disappearance of some 10,000 jobs. Such retrenchment was a challenge to academics' sense of status, even their sense of history. Most held the Prime Minister personally responsible: when the Royal Society elected her to a fellowship in 1983, no fewer than forty-four existing fellows, including six Nobel Prize winners, formally complained. And among literary intellectuals a passionate hatred of her alleged cruelty and philistinism was taken for granted, from Angela Carter ('loathsome . . . a twopenny halfpenny demagogue . . . meanness and cruelty') and Dennis Potter ('repellent . . . arrogant, divisive and dangerous') to Jonathan Miller ('loathsome, repulsive in almost every way') and Salman Rushdie ('thin-lipped . . . jingoist . . . dark goddesses rule; brightness falls from the air'). No Prime Minister had ever inspired such hatred around the dining tables of Britain's intellectuals. But when Mrs Thatcher talked of patriotism, private enterprise, aspiration and self-discipline, she was challenging everything they had believed for the last twenty years.[15]

The radical spirit was not dead, though. Indeed, the fact that Lennon's survivors felt so beleaguered made them more determined to keep the mood of the 1960s alive. It was there whenever two or three people gathered to lament the viciousness and folly of the capitalist establishment. It was there in the arts centres, women's groups, radical bookshops and vegetarian cafés that lined the leafy streets of Britain's gentrifying urban villages. It was there in the pot plants and crockery, the dog-eared copies of Angela Carter and half-read issues of *Marxism Today*, that were such familiar props of the Radio Four-listening, *Guardian*-reading, Labour-voting classes. It was there in places like east Oxford, described by one guidebook as a 'three-dimensional version of the *Whole Earth Handbook*, a fascinating clutter of alternative lifestyle places, Marxist bookstores, jumble shops, and scruffy natural restaurants'; it was there in Islington, where in early 1982 an impassioned young man called Jeremy Corbyn was selected as Labour's parliamentary candidate for the next election.[16]

As the *Observer*'s John Naughton noted, this was a landscape of once-handsome Victorian and Edwardian streets, dilapidated after years of decline, now being reinvigorated by young professional couples attracted by the low house prices. The pattern was always the same. First the 'For Sale' sign went up. Then:

A Renault 4, complete with Mothercare kiddie-seats, appears, soon to be followed by a rubbish skip. The front door of the house, hitherto a hideous sea-green, suddenly gleams with fresh pastel gloss and brass fittings. A new blue-and-white numberplate proclaims the address. The wall dividing front and back ground-floor rooms is demolished ... The formica-clad kitchen furniture is dumped unceremoniously in the skip, to be replaced with pine fittings. Tiny spotlights and huge paper globes abound, where previously centrally mounted bulbs battled unsuccessfully against the gloom. Book-shelves lined with Penguin books appear, accompanied by a hi-fi system. Floorboards are sanded, sealed with polyurethane, covered with straw matting. Large potted plants flourish where chrysanthemums once bloomed ...

The place has been transformed, nay *gentrified* ... First one house, then another.

Naughton called it the Muesli Belt, 'after the staple breakfast diet of the inhabitants'.[17]

As this might suggest, the earnestness of the muesli-eating classes made them irresistible targets for the less enlightened. Attending a women's rights festival in a school near London's King's Cross in 1981, *The Times*'s sketchwriter, Frank Johnson, struggled to keep a straight face, especially when offered a songbook that included such titles as 'Class Struggle Widow' and the 'hauntingly entitled' 'There's a Hole in the Condom', to be sung to the tune of 'There's a Hole in the Bucket'. The seminars and workshops, he reported, covered 'sexism in schools; El Salvador; nuclear weapons; rape; abortion; National Health Service cuts; rent strikes; South Africa; every conceivable form of racism and exploitation; more rape; a spot more abortion; women's health hazards at work; nursery closures; the need for women not to be browbeaten by capitalism into using deodor-ants'; and so on. Meanwhile, on the bookstalls 'all respectable political points of view were represented: Trotskyism, anarchism, Maoism, Sinn Fein, plus ordinary Communism for any passing moderates'.[18]

Since Johnson worked for *The Times*, he was obviously a fascist. But even non-fascists saw the potential for comedy in the high-minded left. There are few better portraits of the professional revolutionary than John Sullivan's BBC1 series *Citizen Smith* (1977–80), in which 'Wolfie' Smith (Robert Lindsay), the beret-wearing, fist-clenching leader of the Tooting Popular Front, is consistently exposed as a self-deluding fantasist. In the diaries of Adrian Mole, meanwhile, the radical classes are constantly sent up, from Adrian's adored Pandora, who lives in a handsome house with wooden blinds, house plants and towering piles of the *Guardian* and *New Society*, to the youth club leader Rick Lemon, who tells Adrian that choos-ing fruit is an 'overtly political act'. Rick rejects 'South African apples,

French golden delicious apples, Israeli oranges, Tunisian dates and American grapefruits', before settling on English rhubarb, even though 'the shape is phallic, possibly sexist'. In a nice detail, Rick's girlfriend, Tit, is 'cramming the trolley with pulses and rice', allowing Adrian to catch a 'glimpse of her hairy ankles'.[19]

Yet for all their comedy value, there was something admirable about the real-life Tits' commitment to social change. Whenever they moved into an inner-city neighbourhood, bringing with them their much-thumbed copies of *The Female Eunuch*, *Watership Down* and *The Making of the English Working Class*, they threw themselves into the life of the community. Not only did they typically work as teachers, lawyers, social workers and lecturers, they became involved with all kinds of local pressure groups, as 'conservationists, environmentalists, squatters, anti-nuclear campaigners, roads protesters, lobbyists for single mothers or playgroups, protesters against abortion or kerb-crawling'. No sooner had the muesli classes arrived, wrote John Naughton, than 'the area takes on a new identity. Babysitting circles, residents' associations, Encounter groups spring up. Sales of the *Guardian* improve. Local head teachers find themselves coping with a new influx of kids, backed up by articulate parents . . . The local council is bombarded with petitions – for better street lighting, Pelican crossings, no-go areas for through traffic, and so on.'[20]

An excellent example came in Bristol, where a young woman called Dawn Primarolo moved with her husband in the last years of the 1970s. The daughter of an engineer at Gatwick Airport, Dawn had been brought up in Croydon, south London. After school she took a secretarial course, married a teacher and ended up working in a law centre in east London. Not-for-profit law centres were classic radical breeding grounds. Established at the beginning of the 1970s, they attracted bright young lawyers, often specializing in areas such as housing and welfare. Dawn was inspired. After moving to Bristol she became a passionate local activist, a member of CND and a school governor. Her long-term dream was to become a lawyer. In the meantime, still only in her mid-20s, she threw herself into a well-known local organization that had seen better days. Run-down, tired and haemorrhaging members, it was crying out for a radical overhaul, and its most celebrated local figure enthusiastically welcomed her youth, energy and crusading passion. His name was Tony Benn. The organization was the local Labour Party.[21]

At the beginning of the 1980s, a casual observer might have thought the Labour Party had a lot going for it. The last general election had not been a complete disaster; with 11½ million votes, Labour had actually attracted more supporters than in October 1974. It had a well-liked leader in Jim Callaghan, rumbustiously supported by his former Chancellor Denis Healey. And as Britain slid into recession, Labour was perfectly placed to profit from Mrs Thatcher's misfortunes. In August 1979 it recaptured the lead in the opinion polls, and for more than a year it never looked like losing it. Since Labour had prevailed in four out of the last six general elections, many younger politicians assumed they would soon be back in office. After the election, Callaghan's former Secretary of State for Prices, Roy Hattersley, agreed to take on a sideline as a columnist: 'an interesting diversion', he thought, 'during my brief periods of enforced opposition'. He never held office again.[22]

In reality, Labour's apparent popularity masked some fearsome problems. Its share of the vote had fallen consistently since the mid-1960s, while its traditional heartlands, the industrial towns of northern England, Wales and Scotland, were in long-term economic and demographic decline. By appealing to first-time voters and skilled workers, Mrs Thatcher had made deep inroads into Labour's potential support. Equally worryingly, polls showed that many Labour voters approved of her position on issues such as tax cuts, trade union reforms and the Right to Buy. 'The people's flag', claimed the *Observer*, 'has turned deepest blue.' That was a bit of an exaggeration. But as the historian Eric Hobsbawm argued in *Marxism Today*, the spread of prosperity, the decline of class consciousness and the growing division between skilled and unskilled workers raised 'very serious questions' about the future of the Labour movement. The party's activists still believed history was on their side. But less impassioned observers drew a much less rosy conclusion.[23]

Labour's party machine, meanwhile, was in a desperate condition. 'Our membership was falling,' recalled the Staffordshire MP John Golding; 'there were fewer and fewer agents and Head Office organisation was a joke.' The best estimate of Labour's membership figures suggests that they had fallen to about 250,000 by 1979, down by at least two-thirds in thirty years. At most, just one in ten members bothered to attend meetings, fewer people than watched West Bromwich Albion on Saturday afternoons. In this respect, Labour was no different from countless other Victorian working-class institutions, from football clubs to working men's clubs. Indeed, its ethos – 'The Red Flag', the Durham Miners' Gala, all the talk of 'brothers' and 'comrades' – seemed like something from the days of Keir Hardie and Ramsay MacDonald. The former Labour MP David Marquand thought it a 'product of the age of steam, hobbling arthritically into the age of the computer'. When Frank Johnson went to see Labour's May Day concert at the Dominion Theatre, Tottenham Court Road, the musical fare was at least 40 years old. 'In the dreary 1940s,' Johnson wrote, 'so much of that big band music must have seemed touched by stardust. At a Labour Party gathering of today it is spangled with dandruff.'[24]

Later, looking back at Labour's woes in the early 1980s, commentators were often fascinated by the issue of infiltration ('entryism') from the Trotskyist fringe, above all the Militant Tendency. Militant certainly became a serious problem for the Labour leadership, winning control of the Young Socialists and, most famously, dominating Liverpool City Council for four years after 1983. In the public imagination, Labour's failure to deal with its puritanical, immensely disciplined cadres became the supreme symbol of the party's inability to govern. Even so, Militant's role in Labour's ordeal is probably exaggerated. In 1979 the party had no more than 1,500 active supporters nationwide. Even at its peak in the mid-1980s it still had, at a very generous estimate, only about 8,000 members. As the Conservative MP Matthew Parris, of all people, argued in *The Times*, its success was 'a consequence, not a cause, of the death of the old Labour Party. The infection spreads not because it is irresistible or uniquely virulent, but because the resistance of the host is low.'[25]

The broader issue, of which Militant was merely a symptom, was the enormous turnover of Labour members. With local membership figures plummeting, the tone was set not by the skilled manufacturing workers of old, who preferred to spend their evenings watching, say, *Open All Hours*; but by the teachers, lawyers, lecturers and social workers of the Muesli Belt. Columnists often mocked them as the detritus of Britain's polytechnics. But as Dawn Primarolo proved in Bristol, they were effective. Articulate, energetic, fired with ideological enthusiasm, they swept in and left nothing untouched. 'We used to have a lot of old people come to meetings,' explained one Islington councillor. 'The middle-class student types just laughed at them and mocked them, and so they stopped coming. In the old days we had meetings and then went off to the pub afterwards. These new people started coming in with sandwiches and flasks and the meetings went on until two or three in the morning.'[26]

For older Labour supporters, steeped in the values of the working men's club, this radical new left came as a shock. In Bristol, Tony Benn recorded that Primarolo and her husband had 'breathed vitality' into his constituency party, 'organizing surgeries, a city farm and so on'. But not everybody saw it that way. For the secretary of the Labour group on the city council, Primarolo and her friends were 'middle-class "trendies" . . . well educated, impatient, eloquent, inexperienced, and suffering from indigestion brought on by swallowing theories whole'. And for members who had been working behind the scenes for decades, the advent of an impassioned, ambitious young woman from London was not entirely welcome. In 1979 Primarolo stood against Benn's octogenarian constituency secretary, Herbert Rogers, who had been Sir Stafford Cripps's local agent and had held his post for sixty-one years. She won. 'People were shocked,' Benn wrote, 'though they had half expected the result.' Later, Rogers asked to see him. 'I've just come to tell you that I'll never come back again,' he said bitterly. But he was history now. Primarolo was the future.*[27]

The revolution that swept through the Labour Party was a victory for the radical spirit of the 1960s. Most of the new activists had gone to college or university, often studying politics or sociology, before taking jobs in the public sector. Hostile to authority, impatient with tradition, they saw themselves as an enlightened vanguard, appointed by history to lead the 'gormless battalions of voters brain-washed by the media', as *The Times* mockingly put it. In an increasingly irreligious age, their socialism had a markedly religious flavour, complete with messiahs, prophets, heretics and apostates. Like all millenarian groups, they believed fervently in a promised land: in this case, socialism. Indeed, many saw Mrs Thatcher as the equivalent of the Beast in the Book of Revelation, whose advent marks the beginning of the end. As the Labour MP Eric Heffer wrote in the *Daily Telegraph*, of all places, her 'right-wing, laissez-faire policies' would inevitably end in disaster. And then, Heffer said happily, 'it will not be too long before capitalism is swept aside'.[28]

As with many apocalyptic religions, the new socialism of the early 1980s was shot through with more than a hint of paranoia. In every meeting the stakes were sky-high, the emotional intensity at fever pitch, the mood swinging between wild euphoria and utter despair. Capitalism might be doomed, but it would not go down without a fight. 'There is an increasing awareness, even an alarm, at the way the State is clearly preparing to handle any unrest the 1980s might bring,' explained Peter Hain, formerly an earnest Liberal demonstrating against South African sporting tours, now an even more earnest fixture of the Labour left. As Hain saw it, the formation of the Metropolitan Police's Special Patrol Group (SPG), the aggressive policing of the Grunwick strike in 1977 and the Prevention of Terrorism Act in 1974 were clear signs that the government was about to introduce martial law. 'The State is prepared to become authoritarian,' he said darkly. 'It has taken the gloves off.' Some people might have thought this paranoid. But to the activist left it was common sense. Had

---

* After the inevitable journey back to the centre, she became a New Labour minister and ended up as a baroness.

not *Marxism Today* defined Thatcherism as 'authoritarian populism', determined to crush the power of labour once and for all?[29]

No wonder, then, that as the heirs of the 1960s contemplated Britain's future, they were seized with a sense of dread. 'We are in a fearful age, fear for one's job, fear of the Bomb,' explained Martin Crocker, a 'spare young man with a neat beard' who ran the Darlington Arts Centre in County Durham. 'A place like this . . . we feel it,' he said, gesturing at a 'group sitting quietly round a girl playing gentle guitar in one corner'. A more sanguine observer might have taken heart from the centre's enormous range of activities, 'chess clubs, canary fanciers, potters, silk screeners, water colourists, etchers and embroiderers, jazz and folk and pub theatre enthusiasts, songwriting groups', which reflected the underlying contentment of what was still a very prosperous and peaceful country. But Mr Crocker saw things differently. It might seem 'fanciful', he said, 'to talk of a new Dark Ages, with Arts Centres acting as sanctuaries, as repositories of a culture that thrived in civilised prosperity, like the monasteries were in the real Dark Ages'. Then he paused. 'Fanciful, but maybe not far-fetched.'[30]

One obvious problem with this kind of thinking was that it was very hard to rebut without outing yourself as a fascist. In right-on circles, it was not done to point out that there were no easy answers to issues such as inflation, deindustrialization or Northern Ireland, let alone to mock what Grimsby's Labour MP Austin Mitchell called 'Play School Marxism'. To doubt the bankruptcy of democracy, the corruption of the media or the sanctity of the trade unions, wrote the former chairman of London's St Pancras North constituency Labour party in 1981, was absolutely taboo. There was, he added, a 'growing appetite for conflict, demonstrated in violent rhetoric, street marches and the clenched fist salute; Parliament and the rule of law are frequently denigrated'. Under the influence of groups like Militant, even the left's vocabulary had become increasingly aggressive. Pamphlets were always calling for supporters to 'smash the system' or 'smash the Tories', who were, of course, 'scum'. And in the constituencies, moderate members often complained of being jeered and booed, 'being mobbed after meetings, receiving nasty telephone calls and being threated with physical violence'. It was no wonder, then, that many stayed away.[31]

Although the new activists loathed Margaret Thatcher, their favourite targets were closer to home. Chief among them were Harold Wilson and Jim Callaghan, the guilty men who had torn up their manifesto commitments, betrayed the working classes and sold Britain to the EEC, NATO and the IMF. Many Labour MPs considered these accusations outrageous. Roy Hattersley called them 'lies'. But *were* they lies? In fact, Wilson and Callaghan *had* ignored their manifesto commitments. In February 1974 the Labour manifesto had promised 'a fundamental and irreversible shift in the balance of power and wealth in favour of working people and their families', which had patently not materialized. There had been no wealth tax, no massive nationalization drive, no return to full employment; instead there had been spending cuts and incomes policies. Even Tony Benn's grandiose interventionist plans at the Department of Industry had been cut short when Wilson pulled the plug and exiled him to Energy.

It did not take a conspiracy theorist, therefore, to conclude that Labour had got into the habit of saying one thing in opposition and doing something different in power. Even Callaghan's former Trade Secretary, Edmund Dell, thought the activists had some justification in feeling betrayed. Successive leaders, he wrote, had not had the courage to tell their members that socialism in one country, insulated from economic change and international competition, was a 'mirage'. Instead, they had pandered to their activists, whipping them into a lather of anti-capitalist outrage. Then, in office, they miraculously discovered that 'circumstances had changed', or that 'not enough money was available', so they could not fulfil their promises after all.[32]

But the activists' patience was not inexhaustible. In the summer of 1973, a small group on the hard left had set up a Campaign for Labour Party Democracy (CLPD). As they saw it, Labour MPs should be spokesmen for a wider movement, reflecting what their activists thought. If the activists voted to nationalize Britain's twenty-five largest companies, scrap nuclear weapons and get out of the Common Market, then the MPs should make it happen. And the CLPD went further. It was outrageous, they argued, that the Labour leader could veto what was in the party's manifesto. In 1979 the National Executive had drawn up plans for the abolition of the House of Lords, only for Callaghan to strike them out at the last minute. Clearly he had let his role go to his head. He was the movement's chief servant, not its dictator. Still, this was what happened when the MPs alone chose the leader. The Labour leader should be elected by the whole movement. That way, they might get a socialist for a change.[33]

The CLPD's most incendiary idea was that Labour MPs should no longer have a job for life. Instead, they should be forced to submit themselves for reselection during each Parliament, enabling local supporters to replace them if necessary. This, the CLPD claimed, would make for much more lively local politics. And as even the sceptical Austin Mitchell admitted, it was not an automatically outlandish idea. Many European social democratic parties had some sort of mandatory reselection, just as many European parties gave members a say in electing the leader. Some Labour

MPs *were* corrupt, unresponsive or downright idle, just as some Tories were. And when the CLPD's critics accused them of being intolerant fanatics, they pointed to Reginald Prentice, Wilson's Education Secretary. After a long battle with his constituency party in Newham, east London, Prentice had been deselected in 1975, only to jump ship to the Conservatives. Here, said the CLPD, was proof that some Labour MPs really were just Tories in disguise. Would it not be better to get rid of them all, and have a genuinely socialist party?[34]

Most Labour MPs were terrified by talk of mandatory reselection. In effect, they were being told that they had to reapply for their own jobs every few years, a prospect people rarely greet with delight. Even Tony Benn conceded that the issue had created great 'fear in the minds of many MPs'. He had the security of inherited wealth, but most others depended entirely on their salaries. 'MPs are people. We've got wives, we've got kids, we've got mortgages, the same as you have,' the Nottinghamshire MP Joe Ashton told the party conference in 1979, begging them not to throw aside men who had 'given fifteen or twenty years to a constituency'.[35]

But it was also a question of principle. Moderate Labour MPs were horrified by the thought of being reduced, as Mitchell put it, to 'a team of denim-clad puppets'. Even the left-wing Michael Foot was appalled by talk of reselection, often quoting his hero Edmund Burke, who had argued that an MP should never be asked to sacrifice 'his unbiased opinion, his mature judgment, his enlightened conscience' to his electors. As Foot explained, MPs had to represent *all* their constituents, not merely their most impassioned activists, who were hardly typical of the ordinary man and woman in the street. In practice, the left's 'democracy' would mean that policy was decided by 'tiny groups of extreme left-wingers', passing endless resolutions about Palestine, Chile and Nicaragua, about which ordinary people could not care less. 'More people believe in flying saucers than attend constituency management committees,' wrote the *Sun*'s Jon Akass in 1980. 'To regard these good people as grass-roots democrats, representing the millions who vote Labour, is as daft as regarding every saucer spotter as an astronaut.'[36]

By now, though, the momentum was almost irresistible. To many young Labour supporters, the MPs looked like an elitist cabal, jealously refusing to share power with the rank and file. Perhaps more significantly, the left now commanded considerable support in the unions, which controlled nine out of ten votes at the party conference. They were particularly strong in white-collar public sector unions such as the National Union of Public Employees (NUPE) and the Association of Scientific, Technical and Managerial Staffs (ASTMS). And when NUPE or ASTMS activists looked at

Jim Callaghan, many did not see him as a working-class trade unionist who had done his best in terrible circumstances. They saw an arrogant grandee who had squeezed their wages and let them down.[37]

The CLPD were not household names: people like Vladimir Derer, a Czech socialist who had fled to Britain in 1939, or Jon Lansman, a young Cambridge graduate, could have walked down any high street in Britain without being noticed.* But they worked day and night to exploit Labour's arcane rulebook. They were 'superb "fixers"', thought John Golding, who loathed everything they stood for but marvelled at their ability to organize slates, draft resolutions and fix conferences. In particular, they persuaded dozens of local Labour parties to submit conference resolutions calling for mandatory reselection, creating an impression of irresistible energy. By 1979 no fewer than seventy-seven constituency Labour parties had signed up to the CLPD, up from just four in 1974. History really was on their side. Yet for all the CLPD's efforts, they would never have done so well without a fluent, charismatic and inspirational figurehead. They needed star quality. That was where Dawn Primarolo's friend Tony Benn came in.[38]

At the turn of the 1980s, Tony Benn was one of the best-known politicians in Britain. Appropriately enough, he had first come to public attention in the 1960s, first by fighting a long battle to disclaim his peerage, and then as Harold Wilson's modernizing Postmaster General and Minister of Technology. But after Labour's defeat by Edward Heath, Benn had undergone one of the most spectacular conversions in political history. Seized by the radical spirit of the age, he reinvented himself as the tribune of the plebs, carrying the gospel of socialism to every corner of the land. By the time he returned to office in 1974, he was the most reviled politician in the country, damned almost every week by the press as a 'Bolshevik', a 'commissar', a 'madman' and a 'maniac'. During the European referendum campaign in 1975, *The Times* seriously warned that he was a 'dangerous politician who stirs up and exploits political forces that will first bring Britain to economic ruin and then possibly use the rubble as the foundations for a collectivist regime'. And when the *Mirror* ran an interview giving Benn the chance to deny that he was a 'Dracula-like bogeyman', the front-page headline said it all: 'BENNMANIA'.[39]

In reality, Benn was neither a Bolshevik nor a maniac. Born in Westminster in 1925, the son of a Labour minister and a feminist theologian, he was the incarnation of high-minded progressivism. A teetotaller and a

---

* Lansman was later a key figure in Jeremy Corbyn's campaign for the Labour leadership, and founded the Corbyn fan club Momentum.

puritan, he adored gadgets, travelled with his own teabags and often asked for bread and cheese when he dined with colleagues. On the platform he was fluent and inspiring; behind the scenes, admitted *The Times*, he was 'an excellent mimic and a brilliant humourist'. Few politicians worked harder or thought more deeply about Britain's future in a world of economic change. None was so committed to politics as a public endeavour. At every demonstration, every meeting, he was always there, eloquent and evangelical. The Labour historian Kenneth Morgan called him 'the pied piper of every available left-wing cause', from workers' control and nuclear disarmament to feminism, environmentalism and gay rights. And through it all, Benn tried to live by John Wesley's apocryphal rule: 'Do all the good you can, in all the ways you can, to all the souls you can, in every place you can, at all the times you can, with all the zeal you can, as long as ever you can.'[40]

Yet for all Benn's qualities, many of his fellow Labour MPs absolutely despised him. Those who knew him well often said what a genuinely polite and friendly man he was, before going on to accuse him of being a sanctimonious, opportunistic, narcissistic hypocrite. Shirley Williams, who spent years alongside him in the Cabinet, recalled that 'personally he was the sweetest of men, concerned about his friends and colleagues, ready to help, funny and self-effacing'. But she also thought him a fanatic, drunk on his own charisma. Denis Healey thought he was a 'political ninny of the most superior quality'. Another Labour moderate, Bill Rodgers, thought him 'intellectually dishonest', using his fluency to peddle untruths to pliable audiences. Barbara Castle wrote of his 'unctuousness' and 'ambition'. Michael Foot, who came to loathe him, similarly thought he was 'obsessed by ambition'.[41]

Working-class MPs were often outraged by Benn's conversion, epitomized by his adoption of the proletarian-sounding 'Tony' instead of his old nickname 'Wedgie'. John Golding, a potter's son from Birmingham, 'could not stand him'. As a young MP Golding had been a great Benn fan. But in 1972 he took Benn to visit some striking miners and was appalled when, in the car, his hero said: 'John, what shall I tell them that will please them?' To Golding, Benn was a typical patrician do-gooder, pandering to his working-class audience instead of telling them the truth. Another centre-left MP remarked that the sight of Benn posing as the champion of the working classes reminded him of the German spies parachuted into England in 1940, who wore spats and monocles to pass themselves off as locals. A third MP remarked that Benn romanticized the working classes as 'virile and romantic' because he had spent his whole life in a patrician bubble, and was now suffering from 'Lady Chatterley syndrome'.[42]

Although Benn would have rejected the label, he was, in fact, a classic populist. The world was divided into heroes and villains. The heroes were 'the people': not people who went to garden centres and watched *Cagney & Lacey*, but real people, who became shop stewards, marched against Cruise missiles and came up to him on trains to tell him how wonderful he was. The villains were the City, the media, the Americans, the Europeans, the Conservatives, the Liberals and a large part of the Labour Party, including Harold Wilson, Jim Callaghan, Denis Healey and Michael Foot. Parliamentary democracy was a sham, an exercise in 'queuing up for the privilege of running a declining capitalist economy . . . under what is really basically a rotten establishment system'. Behind the façade, power was wielded 'by the military, by the Civil Service, by the multi-nationals, by the bankers', a 'narrow, secretive, undemocratic' elite.[43]

The fact that Benn had been educated at Westminster and Oxford, lived in a large house in Holland Park, west London, and had briefly been a viscount did not make him any less of a populist. History is littered with aristocratic champions of the people against the elite. Like all populists, Benn offered a simple programme that would, at a stroke, banish forever the evils of unemployment, poverty and inequality. Like many populists, he was at heart a nationalist, a little Englander who identified his enemies as the 'Common Market, NATO [and] the IMF' and dreamed of erecting import barriers to keep foreign goods out. And like all good populists, he always told his audiences what they wanted to hear. Unlike Sir Keith Joseph, who consciously tried to make converts, Benn preached only to the faithful and never told them anything that might discomfort them. As *The Times*'s Ronald Butt remarked in 1981, he used his remarkable eloquence 'to conjure up applause', never 'drawing attention to an inconvenient reality'. There would always be enough money; there would never be compromises, setbacks or disappointments. All that was needed was to dream of a better world, and then things would fall into place. Nothing to kill or die for, no need for greed or hunger: this was the politics of John Lennon's 'Imagine'.[44]

What made him tick? Some of Benn's colleagues saw him as a monster of self-aggrandizement, pandering to the activists to promote his ambitions. His diaries show that he was obsessed with the Labour leadership. Again and again he records people telling him that he will be leader one day, from senior union leaders to anonymous passers-by. In April 1979, with the general election in full swing, he asks his advisers 'whether I should stand against Callaghan immediately after the Election', only to be told he cannot win. But in the months that follow, the succession is never far from his mind. All the time he records encouragement from random members of the public, which he sees as a sign that the British people are on his side. In November, for instance, a man at Bristol station tells him that 'despite the attacks on you in the press I want you to know that everybody here supports you'. 'That sort of thing', Benn writes, 'is happening a lot at the moment.'[45]

It is unfair, though, to see Benn as nothing but an opportunist. If he had been, he would never have pursued a course that did such extraordinary damage to his own reputation. When he preached the gospel of the left, he believed every word. Brought up in an atmosphere of intense moral self-righteousness, he saw himself as a born-again socialist, a prophet chosen to bring the good news to the people. Becoming Labour leader was a crucial step towards that goal. 'I was always sure', wrote Golding, 'that what motivated Benn was a belief that he was the messiah and, with his small group of disciples and his chosen people, he would create a heaven on earth.' Unfortunately, Golding went on, 'many working-class British people knew that what he was offering was, in fact, hell on earth. They would never vote Labour until he was removed. He was God's greatest gift to Thatcher and had to be stopped if the Labour Party was to survive.'[46]

Golding was not alone in this view. Almost every week, more abuse came crashing down. 'Tony Benn is a liar,' declared the *Mirror* in the autumn of 1979: 'a cool, calculated, deliberate, with-malice-aforethought liar.' 'Though his tongue speaks with sweet reason,' said the *Express* the following summer, 'he has the mind of a ranter and the eyes of a fanatic.' Yet the criticism spurred him on. It was a sign that he was right, a badge of his martyrdom. There was a vast capitalist conspiracy to keep the masses down, and the media were a central part of it. And whenever things went wrong, it was obvious who was to blame. 'Quite a lot of people', Benn remarked sadly, 'believe the lies published in the papers.'[47]

The dust had barely settled after the general election when Benn launched his campaign. That weekend, Michael Foot invited him over for a post-election dinner. Benn turned him down. In Foot's words, 'he had his own plans and his own new body of close associates'. In fact, Benn had already decided to leave the front bench and stand in the next leadership election. A few days later, he told Callaghan that he intended to lead the campaign to curb the leader's power and hand the initiative to the activists. Callaghan snapped that reforming Labour's rules was a 'false issue'. But Benn's mind was made up. Changing the party, he wrote privately, was merely the first step in a wider campaign 'to educate the public not only about socialism but about the legitimacy of trade unions, the public services and full employment'.[48]

To a different Labour leader, this might have been the ideal chance to stamp his authority on his restive party. But, at 67, Callaghan was exhausted. Having held all four great offices of state, survived the IMF crisis and endured the Winter of Discontent, he had little appetite for a battle with his own activists. Left to himself, he would almost certainly have retired to his Sussex farm. But many of his closest supporters persuaded him that it was his duty to prepare the ground for a new regime under his former Chancellor, Denis Healey. So Callaghan told Healey that he would stay on for eighteen months to 'take the shine off the ball'. At the time, Healey was relieved, because he too was shattered and wanted to recharge his batteries before assuming the leadership. But as the Labour right-winger Bill Rodgers later put it, Callaghan's decision was a 'fatal error'.[49]

The recriminations began immediately. When Callaghan's old Cabinet met on 9 May, Benn suggested a major post-election inquest. 'I'll tell you what happened,' Callaghan said. 'We lost the Election because people didn't get their dustbins emptied, because commuters were angry about train disruption and because of too much union power. That's all there is to it.' Benn thought this disgraceful and told a public meeting that there must be a detailed inquiry into the party's failure. Five days later, the left-wing newspaper *Labour Activist* launched a savage attack on Callaghan for refusing to put out a radical manifesto. Then, on 16 May, Labour's MPs met for their first discussion since the election. For moderates like John Golding, Labour's problem was obvious: Mrs Thatcher had won over working-class voters by promising to bash the unions, restore law and order and let them buy their council houses. But the left saw things differently. 'We lost because of right-wing policies and a negative campaign,' insisted the Walsall MP David Winnick. 'We shouldn't blame the unions – the yellow press do that. We are a working-class party and activists are our best people.' It was less than two weeks since the election, and already civil war seemed inevitable.[50]

Over the summer the two camps prepared their forces, and in October they assembled in Brighton for the party conference. 'Stop feuding – start fighting the Tories,' begged an editorial in the *Mirror*. Yet even before the delegates had taken their seats, the air was laced with poison. In an extraordinary sign of the general mood, the organizers had arranged for the MPs to be clustered together on a kind of ramp to one side of the rostrum, like defendants in a show trial. One of Callaghan's former ministers compared the arrangement to a 'People's Court'; others likened it to a 'sin-bin', a 'ghetto' or a 'mass dock'. The tone was set by the chairman, the hard-left Frank Allaun, who kicked off by observing that there had not been a decent Labour government since the 1940s. There was only one reason Labour had lost the election, said Allaun, glaring at his fellow MPs: the 'Cabinet majority' had ignored the activists and pursued their own Tory policies. 'That is why Mrs Thatcher is in Downing Street.' The delegates roared with approval. On the platform, reported the *Mirror*, Callaghan 'sat grim and stony-faced'.[51]

But Allaun was just the warm-up act. Next came the former Birmingham MP Tom Litterick, who had lost his seat in May and was still seething. The general election, he said, had been a 'fiasco'. In his hand he brandished a sheaf of documents, each of them a left-wing policy on everything from women's rights to getting out of Europe. These, he said emotionally, should have been the basis for the election manifesto. 'Then, one day in April of this year, Jim Callaghan turned up, and that is what he did to your policies.' With that, Litterick hurled his papers in the air, from where they drifted down like confetti among his listeners. '"Jim'll fix it," they said,' he went on bitterly. 'Aye, he fixed it. He fixed all of us. He fixed me in particular.'

Litterick's attack brought loud cheers of approval. Even the party's veteran general secretary, Ron Hayward, could not resist having a dig at the last Labour government. The Winter of Discontent, Hayward said, had only happened because Callaghan's Cabinet had ignored their own activists. 'I wish our ministers or our Prime Minister', he added, 'would sometimes act in our interests like a Tory Prime Minister acts in their interests.' And although Michael Foot insisted that the charge of betrayal 'just isn't true', the mood was clearly against him. When Foot had finished, there were 'angry shouts' from the constituency section. It was 'contemptible', wrote Benn. 'There is no rebellion in Michael Foot any more; he is entirely an establishment figure.'[52]

The next day's papers were predictably dire, the *Guardian* lamenting 'an extraordinary day in the long and bloodstained history of Labour Party conferences'. But there was more to come. The next afternoon, the conference turned to the supremely contentious issue of mandatory reselection. The scene was set by Ron Hayward, who insisted that activists did not 'send an MP to the House of Commons to forget whence he came and whom he represents', and added that if any MPs thought they were indispensable, he had 'a queue a mile long that wants to go to the House of Commons'. Even Benn admitted that it was an 'angry' debate, with a 'lot of barracking from the floor'. But since the CLPD had laid the groundwork with supreme skill, the result was never in doubt. By a margin of some 2 million votes, mandatory reselection won the day.* 'The efforts

* In fact, the new rules had so many inconsistencies that the party's lawyers warned that they would not withstand a legal challenge. So mandatory reselection would have to wait for confirmation at the following year's conference.

of the right have failed,' wrote a jubilant Benn, who thought there were now '635 vacancies for candidates in the next Parliament'.[53]

All things considered, Benn thought, Brighton had been wonderful. 'The whole Conference has been really friendly', he wrote, 'and not only is it a turning point for the Party, but I felt I had been taken to its heart.' But almost nobody else saw it that way. Among Labour's natural supporters, the *Guardian* was reminded of an impeachment trial, while the *Mirror* was horrified to see Labour MPs 'corralled at one end of the hall', to be 'criticised, ridiculed and derided by the Bennites on the rostrum'. 'Even as a Tory', wrote the right-wing MP George Gardiner, 'I felt sick at the sight of Jim Callaghan being vilified by men who had rushed to lick his boots as Premier, while his party voted to make its MPs puppets on a string held by Anthony Wedgwood Benn.' And although Benn's supporters

"CHEER UP. JIM—YOU'RE STILL HEAD OF THE PARTY!"

Labour's woes were a gift to the newspapers. In this Stanley Franklin cartoon (*Sun*, 3 October 1979), Tony Benn appears in full Jacobin regalia, complete with hammer and sickle, while Eric Heffer knits at an upstairs window. Jim Callaghan makes a fine Louis XVI, while Michael Foot and Denis Healey are presumably next for the chop.

insisted that democracy had prevailed, most observers agreed that the real winner was sitting in Whitehall. 'No wonder Mrs Thatcher is so cheerful,' said the *Express*. 'With enemies like that, who needs friends?'[54]

The great irony of Benn's campaign was that he had been one of the very few people who had sat through every single moment of the Wilson and Callaghan Cabinets. Yet by the time the party left Brighton, he stood unchallenged as the chief critic of what he called 'twenty years of surrender'. His former colleagues could barely contain their outrage at being condemned by somebody who had worked alongside them for so long. Yet Benn never doubted that he was right, and by the end of 1979 he felt sure that history was running in his direction. Two days before Christmas, he began to make 'basic preparations' for a leadership election, photocopying the *Guide to the House of Commons*, cutting out all the Labour MPs' photos and dividing them into piles labelled 'for' and 'against'. After sleeping on it, though, he reflected that the MPs would never back him. The solution was to put pressure on them not to choose a new leader 'till Conference has endorsed an electoral college, then have a leadership election after that'. This, of course, would put him in pole position.[55]

In the meantime, the Labour right were in a state of shock. Some argued that they had no choice but to fight back: the former Foreign Secretary, David Owen, publicly urged them to 'challenge the authoritarianism, dogma and elitism of the activists'. But they needed a leader, and none was forthcoming. Callaghan, once renowned as a consummate bruiser, now seemed 'crumpled, beaten, isolated'. Even Healey seemed to have lost his fighting spirit. What was worse, the disappointments of the 1970s had almost visibly sapped the moderates' intellectual confidence, their cocksure certainty that they alone knew how to run the country. Like the Tory Wets, they knew what they were against. But what were they for? When pressed, they made the same old noises about incomes policies, higher spending and a more active role for the state, which sounded like a rerun of the Wilson years. As *The Times* remarked, at least the left had something to say, a sense of optimism and mission that kept their activists toiling into the early hours. By contrast, the right had run out of ideas.[56]

By the spring of 1980, therefore, everything seemed to be going Benn's way. Callaghan was on his last legs, the right were on the run and the future belonged to the left. If people could not 'accept Labour's socialist principles, aims and objectives', Benn's friend Eric Heffer declared on 3 February, 'then they really ought to join some other party which is more to their taste'. On 30 May Benn's allies formed the Rank and File Mobilising Committee, a hard-left coalition uniting the CLPD, the Labour

Co-ordinating Committee, the Militant Tendency, the Institute for Workers' Control, the Independent Labour Party and the Socialist Campaign for a Labour Victory behind the total victory of the left, or as he put it, the 'programme of Party democracy'. And that night, as he and his wife held a party for the Rank and File's leaders – among them Ken Livingstone, Chris Mullin, Peter Hain, Jon Lansman and Dawn Primarolo – he felt a rush of excitement. 'When the time comes,' he wrote, 'they will be the people who organise the Benn election campaign.'[57]

The new coalition's initial test came the very next day, at the first of a series of sensationally bitter party meetings. This opening bout had been arranged at the Wembley Conference Centre to approve a new policy statement, which had been drafted by Benn and his allies under the title *Peace, Jobs and Freedom*. In effect, it was a reheated version of the Alternative Economic Strategy of the mid-1970s, promising full employment, strict import and capital controls, massive nationalization, workers' control of businesses, nuclear disarmament and withdrawal from the EEC. It even dusted down the old pledge of a 'fundamental and irreversible shift in the balance of power and wealth in favour of working people and their families', which Wilson and Callaghan had treated with such derision. *The Times* considered it 'a vision of an East German proletarian state'. Most moderate Labour MPs regarded it simply as 'rubbish', a collection of airy fantasies with no details of how they would work. The whole thing, John Golding remarked, could be summed up as 'peace at any price, spend money you haven't got and deny freedom wherever possible'.[58]

Nobody doubted that the Wembley conference would approve *Peace, Jobs and Freedom*, not least because hundreds of moderate union delegates did not bother to turn up. Once again the atmosphere was venomous: Benn and Callaghan did not speak a word to each other all day. Some speakers, such as Benn's former special adviser Frances Morrell, openly talked of the Labour moderates as 'our opponents'. 'The democracy that is being pumped out in the capitalist press is their democracy, not ours,' insisted one delegate, the Militant member Terry Fields, who later became a Liverpool MP. 'We will found a new democracy when we have created a socialist state in this country . . . To the weak-hearted, the traitors and cowards, I say: "Get out of our movement. There is no place for you. Cross the House of Commons."' He had even warmer words for Margaret Thatcher. 'My kids sit and watch the television set,' he said. 'If they could get their hands on her, they would rip the throat out of her.'

The delegates liked Fields. They liked Benn, too, rewarding his appeals for nuclear disarmament, EEC withdrawal and the Alternative Economic Strategy with a standing ovation. But they did not like Callaghan, who issued a routine denunciation of the government without any mention of ripping Mrs Thatcher's throat out. One delegate told the former Prime Minister to 'retire to his farm', another called him 'mealy-mouthed' and 'shallow'. As Golding wrote, 'to have received star rating at this conference, he would have had to attack himself'. Denis Healey came in for equally rough treatment, his appearance at the rostrum being greeted with shouts of 'Out! Out!' To that, an unrepentant Healey shouted that he would never accept the 'clapped out dogmas' of the 'Toytown Trotskyists of the Militant group', which provoked more cacophonous booing.[59]

But it was a third scapegoat who attracted most ire that day. The former Foreign Secretary David Owen had not planned to speak at Wembley. But after sitting through the morning's speeches with his 'gorge rising', he could take no more. From the rostrum, Owen launched into a passionate attack on unilateral nuclear disarmament, which, he said, would leave Britain frozen out of negotiations between NATO and the Soviet Union. The delegates began to howl with rage, and then Owen made the fatal mistake of alluding to his own experience. 'I am telling you as someone who has dealt with these negotiations,' he said desperately – and the jeers resounded around the hall. He might as well have confessed to being a Tory. Afterwards, returning to his seat amid a torrent of abuse, Owen felt a pat on his shoulder. It was his old regional organizer, who murmured: 'In fifteen years you'll be very proud of that speech.' But for a man who had dreamed of becoming a Labour Prime Minister, it was a humiliating moment. 'David burns,' a friend told the politics professors Ivor Crewe and Anthony King. 'You don't quite know how he burns, but he burns away. Wembley was an extraordinarily deep shock to him.'[60]

If Wembley was bad, Bishop's Stortford was bizarre. This meeting, held two weeks later, was the final session of a 'commission of inquiry' set up to hammer out a deal on Labour's rules. The Hertfordshire setting could hardly have been more incongruous: Whitehall College on the edge of Bishop's Stortford, built at the turn of the century by the gin merchant Sir Walter Gilbey. This was now the pride and joy of ASTMS's general secretary Clive Jenkins, an unrepentant show-off who had not merely installed a swimming pool and a sauna, but had even bought new goldfish specifically to impress his Labour visitors. As Benn recorded, the rooms were equipped with drinks, ASTMS-themed mugs and ASTMS-branded penknives, presumably in case they needed to stab their leader in the back. 'The saunas, the swimming baths and champagne, everything laid on, is corrupting and you can't produce reform unless you withdraw from that, challenge it,' he lamented. Still, he steeled himself to go down to the pool, where he found Callaghan ploughing through the water. Benn promptly got out his camera and 'took some marvellous movie pictures'. Callaghan must have found that a bit unsettling. Fortunately they had left their penknives upstairs.

Despite the five-star surroundings, the meeting was predictably bloody. As was now the norm, the commission was heavily weighted towards the left, with the moderates commanding only two out of fourteen votes, namely Callaghan and the engineers' leader, Terry Duffy. After they voted on Saturday to approve mandatory reselection, Callaghan suddenly said: 'I can only tell you you have got a fight on your hands. The PLP will never accept this. I can't recommend this to the PLP.'* With that, wrote Benn, 'he picked up his papers and walked out', leaving the rest of them shell-shocked. Some of them assumed Callaghan had gone straight back to London. In fact, he had probably just gone back to the pool. For when they reconvened the next morning, there he was, as though nothing had happened.

It was Sunday's session that really confirmed the power of the left. The issue on the table was the leadership, and once again there was an over-whelming majority for change. All but three – Callaghan, Foot and Duffy – backed an electoral college; the only question was how the votes would be divided. With a canny eye on union support, the CLPD had recommended that the unions have 50 per cent, the MPs 25 per cent and the constituency parties 25 per cent. Callaghan said this would be a dis-aster: 'The country wouldn't accept it, it would give the impression the trade unions were running the country.' Michael Foot agreed: it would be 'daft' to give the unions so much clout. 'Be careful,' Foot said, 'because Mrs Thatcher will win the next Election if we go on like this.' These were prescient words, but Benn was not impressed. At lunch, he and Foot had a terrible row. 'For the last ten years your only answer to any question is "Don't rock the boat, you'll bring in Thatcher, lose power . . ."' shouted Benn. 'You haven't thought about anything for ten years, that's what's wrong with you.'[61]

After lunch, the commission agreed to recommend an electoral college that gave half the votes to the MPs and divided the rest between the unions and the activists. In other circumstances this might have been a workable compromise, though the final decision would be made by the party confer-ence in Blackpool. But the atmosphere was now so acrimonious that both sides went away disappointed. Even though Benn had secured mandatory

---

* Parliamentary Labour Party. Even by its own standards the Labour Party was then in the grip of initialism-mania: the PLP, the NEC, the CLPD, the LCC, the TULV, the RFMC . . .

reselection and control of the manifesto, he was seething that the MPs would still play a major part in choosing the leader. As for the Labour moderates, they were furious that Callaghan had swallowed an electoral college at all. When the Shadow Cabinet met a few days later, there was a blazing row. David Owen accused his leader of appeasing the left. Rodgers jumped in too, and, as one of them remembered, it all got 'very, very nasty'. When Owen left the meeting he felt utterly depressed. 'Waiting it out, hoping to turn things around, seemed pointless,' he remembered, 'for we had suffered a mortal blow at Bishop's Stortford.' For the first time, he contemplated leaving politics and going back to medicine. But then another idea struck him. Why should he leave politics? Why not set up a new party?[62]

To the press, Bishop's Stortford was the final nail in the coffin of Callaghan's reputation. The next day's front pages, which talked of a humiliating 'surrender to left-wing pressure', were awful. The editorial columns were worse. Expecting Callaghan to stand up to the activists, wrote *The Times*'s Bernard Levin, was like 'expecting a blancmange, left overnight on the dining room table, to rise from its plate and set about knocking down the burglars who have broken in and are busy stealing the spoons'. For the *Guardian*'s Peter Jenkins, meanwhile, Callaghan would go down in history as Labour's Neville Chamberlain, with Michael Foot as Lord Halifax and Bishop's Stortford as Munich. 'They have saved the party', he wrote bitterly, 'by offering to destroy its independence.'[63]

A week later, the *Daily Mirror*, for so long the party's greatest champion on Fleet Street, ran an impassioned front-page editorial. 'Message to the bickering, brawling Labour Party,' ran the headline: 'Don't you know there's a crisis on?' It was a disgrace, the paper said, that with Britain in the worst slump since the 1930s, the opposition was 'scrapping about how to pick its leader'. Labour should be the 'party of hope', but 'if it continued along its present road the millions who support it will have the same feeling about Labour as they do about the Thatcher Government. DESPAIR.'

Meanwhile, in the *Daily Express*, one habitual Labour voter wrote to express his horror:

> As a Labour supporter I am disgusted that the party that once stood for so much that was good and just in British politics has lost its will to fight the militant malcontents of the extreme Left and their Trotskyist pals who posture and spew out proposals for more nationalisation, disarmament and class warfare.
>
> This is a recipe for disaster at the next General Election, because I and hundreds of thousands like me will never vote to bring them to power.

We all know that nationalisation is futile and that a disarmament pro-gramme nearly lost us the last war.

I say to these people: In God's name go now – preferably to your beloved Russia.

In a coincidence too glorious for fiction, the writer, who came from east London, was a Mr D. Owen.[64]

# 15

# Another Day of Feud and Fury

*We had enough of you when you were here before, with your policy of turning this country into a* BLACK STATE, *after which you marched your arse off to Brussels . . . You are a useless money and glory-grabbing dolt . . . In fact you are hated by many people in this country.*

Letter from a Mrs Brown to Roy Jenkins,
*c.* November 1979, quoted in John Campbell,
*Roy Jenkins: A Well-Rounded Life* (2014)

HELMUT SCHMIDT: *Is there any possibility that Wedgwood Benn would become leader?*
MRS THATCHER: *None at all.*
HELMUT SCHMIDT: *That's good . . .*
MRS THATCHER: *No, you needn't worry about that, Helmut, we're not that badly off.*

Telephone conversation between Chancellor
Helmut Schmidt and Mrs Thatcher, 30 October 1980

It is the spring of 1981, and the Minister of Administrative Affairs, Jim Hacker, is worried about his future at the top of British politics. Unburdening himself at home with his wife Annie, he is interrupted by a telephone call. It is Brussels: would he be interested in becoming one of Britain's next European Commissioners? Hacker puts down the phone, deep in thought. It would be a 'great honour, in a way', he tells Annie, but it is an awful job really, 'terrible'. 'You're at the heart of that ghastly Brussels bureaucracy, and the whole thing's a gravy train,' he says, frowning darkly. 'Fifty thousand a year salary. Twenty thousand a year expenses. Champagne. Lobster. Foreign travel. Luxury hotel. Private limousines. Private aircraft. Siestas in the afternoon. Long weekends on the beach at Knokke-le-Zoute . . .' He pauses: 'I think we ought to go over and have a look, don't you?' 'Why not?' says Annie, clearly delighted. But there is a drawback. 'It's curtains as far as British politics is concerned,' Jim says thoughtfully. 'It's worse than a peerage. Absolute failure. Total failure. You're reduced to forming a new party if ever you want to get back.'[1]

As it happens, Jim Hacker never takes the Brussels job, which is just as well because it would have turned *Yes Minister* into something more like *Duty Free*. But as the studio audience laughed, they knew who the writers were really talking about. They were talking about the former Labour minister Roy Jenkins: a man who had served for four years as President of the European Commission, was no stranger to lobster and limousines, and really had formed his own party to get back into British politics.

Ten years earlier, everybody had expected Roy Jenkins to leave a deep imprint on the politics of the age. After spells as a reforming Home Secretary and successful Chancellor in the late 1960s, he was widely seen as the favourite to succeed Harold Wilson as Labour leader. But within just a few years his position in the party had begun to disintegrate. Passionately attached to the European cause, Jenkins led a rebellion to support British entry into the Common Market, and then resigned from the front bench when Wilson decided to back a referendum. Returning as Home Secretary in 1974, he cut an increasingly unhappy figure. When Wilson resigned, Jenkins threw his hat into the ring, but finished well behind Jim Callaghan and Michael Foot. He was disappointed, but not shocked. The truth was that he was tired of life in the Labour Party, sick of its aggressive partisanship and weary of the endless battles with the left. So when, at the turn of 1977, the chance arose to become the sixth President of the European Commission, he took it. To get out of British politics, he wrote, left him 'liberated and exhilarated', not least because he 'had come to believe that Britain was one of the worst governed countries in Western Europe'.[2]

To Jenkins's admirers, his eloquence and idealism put him far above the petty partisanship of most politicians. He was the champion of the 'civilized society', the standard-bearer of liberalism, the greatest Prime Minister Britain had never had. Alas, not everybody treated him with the respect his fans thought he deserved. The sketchwriter Frank Johnson could not resist mocking this 'grand, stupendously dignified and largely incomprehensible magnifico from another world', a 'gracious figure who is to the liberal classes what the Queen Mother is to the rest of us'. In some respects, this image of Jenkins as a claret-marinated grandee, 'a socialite, not a socialist', was a bit unfair. Despite the appearance of effortless superiority, he was a shy, bookish man who struggled with small talk, worried about his health and was given to bouts of gloom when things did not go his way. He was also much more industrious than most people realized. Shirley Williams, whom he later treated pretty badly, thought he was 'incredibly hard working', though he carefully disguised it.'[3]

But there was a lot of truth in the caricature, too. Few people who heard Jenkins's drawling accent would have imagined that he was the son of a Welsh miner. His tastes for long lunch parties, country-house weekends and patrician MPs' wives were real enough. And by going to the Babylon of Belgium, where Continental fat cats gorged themselves on the butter mountain before throwing British fishermen on to the dole, he had confirmed his critics' worst suspicions. In Brussels he was paid £50,000 a year, double the British Prime Minister's salary and the equivalent of £450,000 today. He also enjoyed a £20,000 annual expense account, three years' severance pay and a handsome pension. This allowed him to maintain a 'small art nouveau town house' in Brussels, from where he made regular sorties to the Belgian capital's finest dining places, as well as to the suburbs ('littered with Michelin two-stars') and to nearby cities such as Ghent, Bruges and Antwerp ('rich in restaurants'). What Tony Benn would have made of this can readily be imagined.[4]

Yet Jenkins was never entirely comfortable in exile. Part of him missed home: he spent one in four weekends in Oxfordshire, read the British papers avidly and kept up with his political friends and colleagues. In particular, he maintained a strong relationship with the young Liberal leader, David Steel. As Asquith's biographer, Jenkins was very well disposed to the Liberals, who had polled almost 20 per cent in the two elections of 1974. He had always been unusually non-tribal, and told friends that he was 'thoroughly fed up with the party system', which was 'a conspiracy against the people'. Working alongside Heath and Whitelaw in the European referendum, he had felt 'a considerable liberation of the spirit'. For a time, he hoped that the campaign might lead to a coalition of Tory Wets, Liberals and Labour moderates. But that never happened, so he went off to Brussels instead. It was telling, though, that in the 1979 general election he did not vote. His wife Jennifer voted Liberal.[5]

Not long after the general election, the BBC invited Jenkins to deliver the televised Dimbleby Lecture on 23 November. Here was an unrivalled opportunity to set out his credo, and one he seized with alacrity. Yet the result, entitled 'Home Thoughts from Abroad', was not exactly a ringing call to arms. The gist, dressed up in his typically florid prose, was that the current two-party system was not working. The Tories and Labour had drifted to the extremes, partisanship had reached unprecedented heights and the public were desperate for an alternative. It was time, he argued, for Britain to adopt proportional representation and coalition government. In particular, he called for a 'new grouping' committed to a mixed economy, 'co-operation and not conflict in industry' and a state that 'knows its place'. His ideal Britain, he said, would be classless, 'confident and outward-looking', without succumbing to an 'aggressive intolerant proletarianism' or to the 'brash and selfish values of a get-rich-quick society'. And he ended with what even he admitted was a hackneyed pay-off, a quotation from Yeats: 'The best lack all conviction, while the worst / Are full of passionate intensity . . . Things fall apart; the centre cannot hold.'[6]

Jenkins's lecture has entered political legend. Yet when his old friend Bill Rodgers told him that an early draft was 'rather dull', he was being generous. In fact, Jenkins said nothing that people had not heard a thousand times before. There were no specifics, just a succession of high-minded aspirations. And as *The Times*'s columnist David Wood observed, at least one of Jenkins's premises was plain wrong. Jenkins argued that British politics suffered from an excess of partisanship, with the country undergoing a succession of 'queasy rides on the ideological big dipper'. But as Wood pointed out, every administration since the war had actually ended up 'astride the point of balance on the see-saw', with incomes controls as the prime example. Far from being too extreme, the two parties had been 'too much alike', invariably abandoning their more daring commitments and governing from the centre. But after two decades of corporatist, social democratic underachievement, Wood thought the public wanted something new: a 'genuine choice of policies', as presented by Mrs Thatcher on the right and Tony Benn on the left. For all his talk of the 'radical centre', Jenkins was merely offering the same formulae that had failed before.[7]

This was, as it turned out, a very astute criticism. But with plenty of people shrinking from what they saw as the rival extremisms of the Bennite left and Thatcherite right, Jenkins's talk of civilized non-partisanship found a small but enthusiastic audience. 'Until now I believed that Roy Jenkins was the best Prime Minister we never had,' one admirer wrote to *The Times*. 'Now, I believe that he is the best Prime Minister we will have.' And for some of his admirers, the lecture was a welcome reminder that another world, or at least another political home, was possible. Bill Rodgers suddenly had a 'vision of himself sitting in the headquarters of the new party with his sleeves rolled up, actually organising things'. A week later, he told a meeting in Abertillery, South Wales, that Labour had only 'a year – not much longer – in which to save itself'. The next day, Rodgers had a long talk with Jenkins and Shirley Williams. A new centre-left party was not impossible, he said: it might win as many as sixty seats, with the Liberals taking another twenty-five.[8]

Yet for the next year nothing happened. There was no rush to the Old

Pretender's banners. As the definitive history of the Social Democratic Party points out, most Labour MPs saw their party as a 'cause, a way of life, a church – self-contained, comfortable and secure'. Even many moderates shuddered at the thought of giving it up to join an exiled political has-been. The day after Jenkins's lecture, David Owen told a Labour dinner that the moderates would 'not be tempted by siren voices from outside, from those who have given up the fight from within'. A new party, Owen told a friend, would be 'rootless, brought together out of frustration. It would soon split apart when faced with the real choices and could easily reflect the attitudes of a London-based liberalism that had neither a base in the provinces nor a bedrock of principles . . . My inclination is to go down with the ship – not search for a new boat.'[9]

Even Rodgers, on reflection, agreed with him. In January 1980 he told Jenkins that, for the time being, he would stay put. A centre party, he said, would sink without trace. To survive, a new party would have to supplant Labour, an almost impossible challenge by any standards. 'Otherwise it would split the left, to the benefit of the Tories.' And that, it seemed, was that. Rodgers went back to the front line inside the Labour Party. The moderates battled on, despairing but not yet entirely despondent. And Jenkins returned to Brussels and the pleasures of the table.[10]

Yet all the time other tectonic plates were shifting. First came Wembley, then Bishop's Stortford. Slowly but surely, the moderates were losing heart. Then, one day at the beginning of June, David Owen was walking through the tunnel from the underground station to the House of Commons when he bumped into a journalist from the *Financial Times*. The journalist wondered if he had heard that the Shadow Industry Secretary, John Silkin, had just unveiled a campaign to commit Labour to unconditional withdrawal from the Common Market. Owen had not, and was appalled. Further down the tunnel, he bumped into Rodgers and told him the news. They must do something, Owen said. Rodgers agreed, and suggested talking it over with Shirley Williams the next morning. In that moment the Social Democratic Party was born.[11]

Like Roy Jenkins, David Owen did not look like a Labour man. Born to Welsh parents in Plymouth in 1938, he had gone to public school and Cambridge, where he studied medicine. Only later, while he was training at St Thomas's Hospital, London, did he join the Labour Party, eventually becoming a junior minister. Then, in 1977, Callaghan catapulted him into the Cabinet as Foreign Secretary, the youngest in a generation. He was still only 38, and many of his colleagues never forgave him for it.

Owen had all the ingredients for political success: the brains, the looks, the charisma, the hair. Even a sceptical observer like the former Labour MP David Marquand was impressed by his 'gripping passion on the public platform, his relentless mastery of committee detail, his driving, sometimes self-lacerating energy, his personal magnetism and his unsleeping will'. Above all, Owen saw himself as a star, a quality he shared with Mrs Thatcher. Marquand wrote of the 'marvellous effrontery' with which he managed to be 'taken at his own valuation: as a heavyweight national politician whose sayings and doings were important simply because he said and did them'. Sometimes it was easy to forget that he had been in the Cabinet for barely two years.[12]

Yet few politicians of his generation had such a knack of falling out with their colleagues. Owen's memoirs reveal a man who was thoughtful, passionate and patriotic, and had, as a doctor, seen a different side of life from most of his fellow MPs. But perhaps because he seemed so well favoured, he had an unrivalled talent for alienating people. Again and again the same words come up: impatient, insouciant, brusque, arrogant. Austin Mitchell thought that Owen was a young man suffused with ambition, 'all bustle and shining ego'. Rodgers thought that, although 'vigorous and bold', he was a 'hollow man', who stood for nothing but himself. Jenkins compared him with the Upas tree, 'which destroys all life for miles around it'. Most memorably, Denis Healey remarked that although the good fairies had given Owen 'thick dark locks, matinee idol features, a lightning intelligence, unfortunately the bad fairy also made him a shit'.[13]

Yet perhaps because he was slightly detached from Labour's traditions and represented a working-class constituency on the South Coast, Owen understood, far better than many of his critics, the impatient, ambitious mood of the 1980s. It was telling that, like Mrs Thatcher, he was a passionate admirer of all things American. His wife was American; they held annual Fourth of July barbecues, with baseball games during which, Rodgers recalled, 'David usually made the highest score and was always determined to win'. Like Mrs Thatcher, too, Owen was fiercely patriotic. Having worked on a building site as a teenager during the Suez crisis, he never forgot his workmates' instinctive nationalism, and was determined to reflect their values rather than the 'sogginess' of the 'liberal establishment'. As Marquand put it, Owen combined a kind of 'southern English patriotism' with an aggressive anti-liberal populism, a 'yearning for hard, clear, simple solutions' and a 'contempt for compromise and compromisers'. And when he talked about his ideal Britain, 'thrusting', 'radical', 'dynamic', harnessing 'market forces' and 'promoting technological advance', it was easy to imagine the Prime Minister nodding in agreement.[14]

By the summer of 1980, Owen's patience with life in the Labour Party was stretched to breaking point. An intensely proud man, he had been shocked by his terrible reception at the Wembley conference. Although no shrinking violet, he had no desire to spend his political career being abused by his own members, nor did he want to spend it promoting policies he passionately opposed. So when, standing there in the Westminster tunnel, he heard about Silkin's plan to commit Labour to leaving the Common Market, he was furious. The next morning, he met Shirley Williams and Bill Rodgers, and together they drafted a statement for the Sunday papers, insisting that they would 'not accept a choice between socialism and Europe. We will choose them both.' Here, as Owen knew, was the first clear indication that they might consider a new 'socialist' party, should Labour turn its back on Europe.[15]

Until this point, few people had thought of Owen, Williams and Rodgers as a natural alliance. Rodgers, always the outsider in histories of the SDP, was the consummate backroom boy, the ultimate 'politicians' politician'. A child of Liverpool during the Depression, he had been Callaghan's Transport Secretary, but he was best known as the great organizer of the Labour right, toiling unceasingly behind the scenes to build support for the nuclear deterrent and the European cause. Perhaps more than any of his contemporaries, he remained faithful to the policies of the Wilson and Callaghan era: redistributive taxes, high spending and an incomes policy to restrain inflation, but no further nationalizations and no retreat from Britain's position in NATO and the EEC. By the turn of the 1980s, however, many grass-roots activists thought those views were tantamount to membership of the Conservative Party. After the general election, Callaghan had appointed him as Labour's defence spokesman. But Rodgers's support for nuclear weapons made him vulnerable: within a year the left were calling for his head.[16]

If Rodgers was little known outside Westminster, everybody knew Shirley Williams. The daughter of the political philosopher Sir George Catlin and the feminist writer Vera Brittain, she had risen quickly through the Labour ranks, becoming Wilson's Prices Secretary in 1974 and Callaghan's Education Secretary two years later. As an ardent advocate of comprehensive schools, she often infuriated the Tory papers, but few public figures enjoyed such widespread affection. Famously warm, earnest and articulate – and infamously scruffy and unpunctual – she was one of the only politicians whom ordinary people seemed genuinely pleased to see. *The Times*'s Louis Heren thought she was 'everybody's favourite aunt – albeit an aunt with a political science degree'. But she suffered from very bad luck. At the beginning of the 1970s, her husband, the philosopher Bernard Williams, had left her for another woman. As a single mother looking after a school-age daughter, which made her even more of an outsider in the masculine world of Westminster politics, Williams was constantly rushing to keep up – which puts a different complexion on all those taunts about her lateness.[17]

Williams's other slice of bad luck came in May 1979, when she lost her Stevenage seat. This was classic Thatcher territory, a successful New Town of ambitious skilled workers attracted by the Right to Buy. But by then Williams was already feeling miserable about her future inside the Labour Party. A keen pro-European, she had long despaired of Labour's 'ancient prejudices', and thought Wilson and Callaghan had 'conceded too much to the unions'. Above all, she was horrified by the growing 'intolerance and savagery' of the left, which was not a fashionable position when activists were always talking about crushing this and smashing that. She dreamed of a genuinely kinder, gentler Britain, not one that took its lead from the Militant Tendency. And although she found Tony Benn likeable enough, she could not stand the 'appalling insularity' and 'anti-parliamentarian' extremism of his politics. 'When he speaks about the primacy of the activists,' she told Hugo Young, 'he virtually parrots Lenin . . . He does not really know what he is saying.'[18]

Williams and Rodgers had been sharing thoughts about the party's future for years. And now, buoyed by Owen's impatient enthusiasm, they had the bit between their teeth. On 1 August 1980 the three of them published an open letter in the *Guardian*, intended as a last warning to Labour and a manifesto for a social democratic alternative. 'The Labour Party', read the first sentence, 'is facing the gravest crisis in its history – graver even than the crisis of 1931.' The priority, they argued, was to tackle Britain's enormous 'industrial, economic and social problems', which were 'far more intractable than they seemed in the comfortably optimistic 1960s'. Ironically, almost everything that followed could have been written in the 1960s, from a mixed economy and an incomes policy to European co-operation and the Atlantic alliance. The only difference was the last section, in which they warned that the hard left threatened democracy itself. The final lines read like an ultimatum. They were not prepared to 'abandon Britain to divisive and often cruel Tory policies' because people had no 'acceptable socialist alternative . . . If the Labour Party abandons its democratic and internationalist principles, the argument may grow for a new democratic socialist party to establish itself as a party of conscience and reform committed to those principles.'[19]

There was no mistaking what this meant. For the first time, three of Labour's most senior figures had publicly floated the idea of a 'new democratic socialist party'. The *Guardian*'s front page dubbed them the 'Gang of Three', borrowing a nickname coined by their left-wing critics. As for their open letter, Tony Benn thought it 'disgraceful'. But it is not clear what he expected the Gang of Three to do. He had fought for his principles for years; was it so illegitimate for them to do the same? If they stayed in the Labour Party, they were fifth columnists; if they got out, they were traitors. Presumably they should just have converted and joined the hard left. Alas, not everybody was as fortunate as Benn. He had been privileged to see the light. But they could have wandered up and down the road to Damascus for years without ever emerging from the fog of moderation.[20]

Yet the departure of the Gang of Three was by no means inevitable. Most commentators thought their threat was a political tactic, not a serious proposal. The day after their European statement was published, Roy Jenkins resurfaced with a speech to the parliamentary press gallery, suggesting that a new centre party would be like an 'experimental plane', which might 'soar in the sky . . . further and more quickly' than people imagined. But most observers thought it very implausible that the Gang of Three would ever board Jenkins's plane. After all, Shirley Williams had already said that a centre party would have 'no roots, no principles, no philosophy and no values'. If they stayed loyal to Labour, said *The Times*, then any new party would merely be 'Mr Jenkins's dining club going public'. Even harsher was the *Spectator*, which thought his plane would be better described as a 'fat, flabby and near-extinct bird endeavouring to fly but lacking the muscle and momentum to take flight'. To cap it all, a poll found that only three out of ten people would seriously consider voting for a centre party, with six out of ten considering it 'unlikely'.[21]

Jenkins spent the next few weeks sunk in gloom. If all else failed, he told friends, he could always join David Steel. And if things had unfolded differently inside the Labour Party, that is probably what would have happened. It is possible to imagine a scenario in which the major union leaders called for compromise and the party's warring factions reached an uneasy stalemate. In that case, Jim Callaghan might have been succeeded by Denis Healey, the Gang of Three might have stayed to fight for more moderate positions and Labour's internal divisions would probably have declined to a slow simmer. As for Jenkins, he would almost certainly have become a Liberal.[22]

But that, of course, is not what happened. The union leaders were in no shape to take on the left, the leadership had long since lost the will to fight and the activists were in no mood to compromise. So Labour went to Blackpool, and all hell broke loose.

*

On the last weekend in September, the Labour tribes assembled for what everybody knew would be an explosive showdown. The setting, at once gaudy and threadbare, a great Victorian resort abandoned by the tides of change, could hardly have been better chosen. Decades of decline, wrote Anthony Sampson, had left Blackpool 'more uncompromisingly working-class' than ever, the seafront lined with cheap bars and boarding houses, the 'elegant Victorian terraces and hotels' covered with 'hoardings and plastic façades'. The huge Metropole Hotel felt sad and shabby; the old Winter Gardens were hemmed in by amusement arcades. People still came to Blackpool in search of fun, but a council spokesman admitted that it was now 'regarded as the bargain basement of the holiday business'. Comedians joked that the council propped up dead bodies in the bus shelters, to make it look as if the town still had some life in it. That was the kind of thing they said about the Labour Party, too.[23]

From the moment the first delegates arrived, the party conference was charged with tension. The columnist Peter Jenkins thought it had the feel of a 'Chinese-style Cultural Revolution', the foyer of the Imperial Hotel 'like a Soviet permanently in session', the conference hall and sur-rounding corridors 'ankle-deep in leaflets and revolutionary newspapers'. And right from the start, the moderates knew the mood was against them. Bill Rodgers recalled the 'smell of almost revolutionary hysteria'. Shirley Williams remembered being jostled and heckled as she moved around. Some delegates even spat at her. The atmosphere was 'not only unpleasant', wrote Ivor Crewe and Anthony King; it was 'positively insane'.[24]

But of course the left did not see it that way. This was their hour, their moment in the sun after a decade of betrayals. And as Tony Benn moved from meeting to meeting, he radiated conviction, telling one audience that he saw himself as the heir to the Chartists, another that he was upholding the radical traditions of the Levellers and the Diggers. To his admirers, he had never been more charismatic, more eloquent, more obviously the man of the future. But to his critics he was literally mad, his 'staring eyes' a sign that he had lost his reason. He was 'at his apogee', remembered Williams. 'He seemed almost in a self-induced trance.'[25]

On the first full day, Monday 29th, Benn rose to speak on behalf of the National Executive during a debate on the economy. In a sign of the mood, Denis Healey had been hissed even before he had made it on to the rostrum. But when Benn stepped forward, nobody hissed. What was wrong with Britain, he said, was 'not just Mrs Thatcher'. It was capitalism. And 'if this woman and this Cabinet, who believe in capitalism, cannot make it work better than it does', then the next Labour government should tear it down once and for all. That meant scrapping defence spending, taxing wealth, halting imports, reintroducing capital controls, promoting workers' co-operatives and moving to a statutory thirty-five-hour working week. It also meant breaking the power of the City of London, defying the IMF and pulling out of Europe.

But all of this would only be possible, Benn said, if the next government passed three emergency bills within the first month. First, 'within a matter of days', they must push through an Industry Bill to 'extend common ownership, to control capital movement and to provide for industrial democracy'. Next, 'within a matter of weeks', they must pass a bill to take back all the powers ceded to Brussels, which would mean leaving the Common Market. Finally, because neither of those bills would get through the House of Lords, they must pass a third bill to abolish the second chamber. 'We shall have to do it', Benn said, 'by creating a thousand peers and then abolishing the peerage at the time that the Bill goes through.' The capitalist press would accuse them of setting up an elective dictatorship. But Labour could never govern 'if it only has control of half of Parliament'. 'Comrades,' he said grandly, 'this is the very least we must do!'[26]

In much of the hall the reaction to Benn's speech was unbridled ecstasy. When he reached the bit about abolishing the House of Lords, the 'roars of approval' were so loud that he struggled to be heard. But most of his fellow MPs simply gaped in horror. As Denis Healey mordantly remarked, Benn talked of restoring capital controls 'within a matter of days'; yet if he ever got the chance to put his plan into effect, capital would be gone within hours. 'Some said flatly – although not for attribution – that Mr Benn must have gone over the edge,' wrote the journalist Fred Emery. 'Others were unprintable, angry that through his demagogy he had nullified the party's earnest attempt to open proceedings by trying to get itself taken seriously.' The *Mirror* warned its readers that his programme would be 'physically, politically and democratically impossible WITHIN MONTHS, LET ALONE DAYS', while the *Express* thought 'he would be far more at home in a Polish Politburo than a British Government'. To Benn, though, the papers were being 'hysterical'. In his mind he had been positively 'prime ministerial'.[27]

That evening, the Gang of Three spoke at a meeting organized by the right-wing Campaign for Labour Victory. All three were in combative form, but none more so than Shirley Williams. Benn, she said, was living in a 'dream world'. Listing his three bills, she said witheringly: 'And all this would be done in a couple of weeks! I wonder why Tony was so unambitious. After all, it took God only six days to make the world.' There was some heckling at that, but she was no longer in the mood to pull her punches:

> There are too many good Labour members who are frightened to go to their local party meetings because they are frightened of being shouted at or abused or kept down . . . It is not easy if you are an elderly woman or a mother with young children or a man coming off the night shift to go along and be bawled down and abused and be told you are just a bloody Tory . . .
>
> I was brought up as a youngster to learn about fascism. My parents fought against fascism, and they were both on the Gestapo blacklist, so I know something about it. But there can be fascism of the left as well as fascism of the right . . .
>
> Too many good men and women in this party have remained silent. Well, the time has come when you had better stick your heads up and come over the parapet, because if you do not start to fight now, you will not have a party that is worth having.

Afterwards, in Williams's hotel room, the Gang of Three and their friends gathered to discuss the day's events. The evening news flickered in the corner: there was Benn, making his promises; there were the activists, cheering him to the rafters. As they watched, their mood darkened. By the time the meeting broke up, some were talking about leaving the party.[28]

The decisive day was Wednesday 1 October, which went down as one of the most extraordinary in the Labour Party's history. It began with a debate about Britain's future in Europe. The left's position was that a Labour government must get out immediately, without wasting time on a referendum. When Owen stepped up to make the case for remaining, some delegates hissed him. But he was not deterred. It would be a 'constitutional outrage', he said passionately, 'first to go to the British people and let them decide in 1975 and now not even to give the British people a chance to determine their own destiny'. As he stepped down there was a chorus of boos. Moments later, his front-bench colleague Peter Shore mounted the rostrum. His speech was much more to the activists' liking. 'At last', Shore said dramatically, 'the wraps have dropped from people's eyes.' There was no need for another referendum, since Britain's entry into the Common Market had been 'a rape of the British people, and of the British Parliament and the rights of our constitution'. A rape of the British people! That was the activists' kind of talk. And the result was even better than the left had hoped: 5 million votes for coming out, just 2 million against. Benn thought it 'a fantastic victory'.

Then the conference turned to mandatory reselection. From the rostrum,

Benn's former Parliamentary Private Secretary, Joe Ashton, made a last, desperate appeal, begging the activists not to drive their own MPs away. 'If Roy Jenkins wanted to form a party of twenty-five sacked MPs now, in this Parliament,' he said, 'they could be in business in six months.' 'No!' came the cries from the floor. Some delegates began a slow handclap: when Ashton finished, it was to a torrent of boos. Benn thought his old friend's speech 'disgraceful'. The delegates agreed. A few moments later, mandatory reselection passed. 'The Conference nearly went berserk,' Benn wrote happily.

Next on the agenda was control of the manifesto, a subject that had long been dear to Benn's heart. 'All the damned-up bitterness welled up,' wrote Fred Emery, who watched in disbelief as Benn launched into a long litany of Callaghan's alleged betrayals. 'Reflation of public sector service spending: ruled out! Substantial cut in arms expenditure: ruled out! The immediate introduction of a wealth tax: ruled out! The imposition of selective import controls: ruled out!' On the platform, Callaghan, visibly furious, shook his head and mouthed: 'It's not true. That's a lie.' Amid uproar on the floor, the conference voted on a motion to hand control to the National Executive. This time the moderates managed to eke out a victory, prevailing by 3.6 million votes to 3.5 million.

But Benn was not downhearted. Already he was looking forward to the next item on the agenda: the rules for electing the next Labour leader. After so many months of bickering, everybody knew this would be very close. It was, but after yet another nail-biting result – 3.6 million to 3.5 million once again – the delegates approved the principle of an electoral college. On television, the picture showed some punching the air, others jabbing their fingers at the MPs, one or two literally dancing with glee. Benn, not surprisingly, was thrilled. 'The left went crazy with delight,' wrote John Golding, but 'there was utter dismay on the faces of the moderates and most MPs'. He glanced at Healey, who looked completely 'shell-shocked'. Callaghan just sat there, grim-faced. It was, thought Owen, 'an awful day'. 'It is a day of total anarchy', said Rodgers afterwards, 'and assures 13 years of Tory rule.'[29]

But then came the twist. The party might have voted for an electoral college; but *which* electoral college? First the conference considered giving the MPs, the unions and the activists 33 per cent each. But the moderate unions voted no, so that failed. Then came a second motion, giving the unions 50 per cent and splitting the rest between the MPs and the constituencies. By the narrowest of margins – 3.55 million votes to 3.49 million – that failed, too. So the party was now in the bizarre position of having approved an electoral college in principle while rejecting two possible versions in practice. 'Constituency party representatives howled,' reported the *Mirror*.

'One man hurled his papers on the floor and jumped on them.' Meanwhile, 'Mr Callaghan gave a broad grin and an approving laugh.'

All was chaos, all was muddle. It could scarcely have been a worse advertisement for the Labour Party as a party of government. But more chaos followed overnight. At a hastily arranged evening meeting, Benn and his allies on the National Executive decided to back a formula that gave 40 per cent to the MPs and 30 per cent each to the activists and the unions. But after another meeting at midnight in the Imperial Hotel bar, the CLPD decided that this was a 'terrible sell-out' and sent Benn's old special adviser Frances Morrell to tell him that the unions should get 40 per cent, not the MPs. By his own account, she burst into his bedroom and harangued him while he sat there in his underpants, an odd scene by any standards. Unfortunately, when the National Executive met over breakfast the next morning, Callaghan was having none of it. If this was really what they wanted, he said, he would resign within weeks and let the MPs choose their own leader. Benn said that would be a disgrace. 'Well,' Callaghan snapped, 'I tell you that the Parliamentary Party will never accept a Leader foisted upon them. I'll tell you something else, they will never have Tony Benn foisted upon them.'[30]

On this cheerful note, Callaghan, Benn and their colleagues made their way into the hall for the last day. This time the delegates began by voting for unilateral nuclear disarmament and the closure of all American air bases on British soil. Then they returned to the question of the leadership, considering the National Executive's hastily revised plan for a 40–30–30 split in the unions' favour. Once again the activists and left-wing unions were largely in favour, the MPs and moderate unions largely against. But the unrivalled star of the debate, whose intervention became a staple of documentaries about the party's ordeal, was the maverick Staffordshire MP Andrew Faulds. An RSC-trained actor with a magnificent Victorian beard, he did not hold his own activists in high regard. 'I represent the true Labour Party in Smethwick,' he began, 'not the Workers' Revolutionary Party, nor the militant Trots, who have infiltrated so many constituency parties *as you know!*' At that, there were roars of protest from the floor. 'Madam Chairman, the baying of the beast betrays its presence!' Faulds roared. 'You can hear them!'

In the end, the chairman had to cut off Faulds's microphone, partly because he was clearly out to provoke the beast, but also because he launched into a personal attack on Tony Benn for 'welching' on his own government. But his intervention set the seal on what had been an extraordinary few days. In a ludicrously bathetic ending, the moderate unions again rejected the National Executive's electoral college, which meant muddle had given way to deadlock. At last, David Basnett of the General and Municipal Workers' Union (GMWU) suggested that they thrash it out at a special conference the following January. 'Another day of feud and fury,' sighed the *Mirror*. 'After the events of this week, the astonishing thing about the leadership of the Labour Party will not be the new method of election but that anyone should want the job.'[31]

Still, the left had good reason to celebrate as the conference came to an end. After so long in the wilderness, they had finally enjoyed a week of resplendent victory. After the traditional rendition of 'The Red Flag', some stayed behind to sing the 'Internationale', their clenched fists raised. For Tony Benn, too, it had been a week of pure ecstasy. It was a 'watershed', he wrote, that would change 'the future of British politics'. He was aware, of course, that the headlines had been appalling. But he knew why:

> The fact is that last week at Blackpool we really pulverised the Tories by the strength and force of our alternative policy. Nobody is going to tell me that Mrs Thatcher is frightened of Shirley Williams or Bill Rodgers or Jim Callaghan, of Denis Healey or Peter Shore. But they are transfixed by the thought that there might be a radical Labour Government.[32]

In reality, Mrs Thatcher's aides were delighted by what she called 'Labour's Orwellian nightmare of the Left'. And to the newspapers it seemed a debacle unprecedented in modern political history. 'LABOUR CHAOS', said the *Mirror*. 'LABOUR ANARCHY', said the *Express*. Both papers, despite their different perspectives, thought Labour had crossed a line. The *Express*, wiping away crocodile tears, declared that 'the Labour Party as we and our fathers have known it, the Party of MacDonald, Attlee, Gaitskell and Wilson; the moderate Party of social democracy as all, even its opponents, have respected it, was killed yesterday and consigned to the dustheap of history.' The *Mirror* was, if anything, even bleaker. The 'lunacy of the left', it said, had 'inflamed delegates into a mood of political madness', while Benn had made promises with a 'cynicism so blatant as to turn the stomachs of the mass of decent Labour supporters'. In the meantime, 'Mrs Thatcher might as well cancel her own conference at Brighton next week. Blackpool is doing the job for her.'[33]

In the broadsheets the mood was one of utter horror. For the *Guardian*'s Peter Jenkins, the conference marked the triumph of the 'lumpen polytechnic' – a phrase which brought a storm of letters from polytechnic lecturers over the next few days. 'Political liberty is now at threat in Britain,' he wrote gloomily, 'for I cannot feel confident that it would long survive the coming to power of the people who have taken hold of the Labour Party.' *The Times* was even more apocalyptic, printing an extraordinary editorial entitled 'The Dark Side of Britain'. Blackpool, it said, had been 'as remote from ordinary reality as a planet of lunatics', while Labour had succumbed to a blend of 'resentment, of phantasy, of paranoid suspicion, of hysteria, of hatred ... of hypocrisy and of an engulfing dark tide of preposterous zeal such as we have not seen in Britain since the seventeenth century'. If it ever gained power, it would turn Britain into a 'socialist state' closer to 'the countries of eastern Europe than to anything known among the advanced industrial countries of the West'. Yet *The Times* thought Labour's agony was merely a symptom of a deeper sickness: 'the damage that has already been done to Britain by a progressive social, political and economic decline. As a sign that is alarming; as a portent it is terrifying.'[34]

The Gang of Three left Blackpool in a state of near-total despair. No longer could they delude themselves that this was merely the darkest hour before the dawn; no dawn seemed remotely likely. For Rodgers and Williams, the thought of leaving a party they loved was almost physically painful. But Owen, always more impulsive, was ready to go. He was wary of any deal with Jenkins, but the more he thought about it, the more tempting a new party seemed. If he flinched now, he told a friend:

> all my life I will know there was a time in 1981 when perhaps had we had the courage, the vision; had we been prepared to break out, cut loose and accept being called traitors, things just might have been different. Britain just might have pulled itself up by its own collective will and common sense if it had just been given the chance. Who knows?[35]

But before Owen could make his decision public, there was a twist. When, on that last acrimonious morning, Callaghan had threatened to resign so that his fellow MPs could pick the next Labour leader, he had not been joking. As he remarked to John Golding at the end of the conference, 'there are better things to do'. Almost two weeks later, on the afternoon of Wednesday 15th, he announced that he was off. Nobody was particularly surprised. By now even his opposite number thought he had been hard done by. 'Jim looks a different man . . . so relieved,' Mrs Thatcher confided to Callaghan's old friend Helmut Schmidt a couple of weeks later. 'I feel a little sorry for Jim,' Schmidt said. 'Well so do I,' Mrs Thatcher agreed; 'he's such a nice man.' 'I don't know whether you know', Schmidt said, 'he is talking about you with a great amount of respect, if he talks to me anyway.' If Benn had been listening, it would have confirmed all his suspicions.[36]

Would Benn stand? Only two months earlier, he had drawn up a rough campaign strategy. But by resigning so suddenly, Callaghan had made things very difficult. Not only had Benn said many times that the old system was illegitimate, but he knew perfectly well that most of his colleagues

*The Three stood calm and silent,*
*And looked upon the foes;*
*And a great shout of laughter*
*From all the vanguard rose*

*And forth three chiefs came spurring*
*Before that deep array;*
*To earth they sprang, their swords they drew,*
*And lifted high their shields, and flew*
*To win the narrow way . . . (HORATIUS)*

After Blackpool, few people thought the Gang of Three could remain in the Labour Party. But in this splendidly literary cartoon for the *Daily Telegraph* (14 October 1980), Nicholas Garland pictures them as the 'dauntless Three' in Thomas Babington Macaulay's poem 'Horatius' (1842), defending the bridge into Rome against Tony Benn's invading horde.

detested him. Only a few days later, he got into a blazing row in the Commons tea room with a group of Labour MPs, some 'white with anger', others calling him a hypocrite to his face. 'They were having a collective nervous breakdown,' Benn wrote scornfully. 'They are in a state of panic, and the hatred was so strong that I became absolutely persuaded that this was not a Party I would ever be invited to lead, and nor could I lead it.'

Yet although Benn felt 'such an outcast' that he could barely face going into the Commons, he itched to throw his hat into the ring. Alas, his allies told him it was hopeless. The hard-left Audrey Wise thought Callaghan 'had no business to resign as leader', while Chris Mullin complained that Labour MPs were being 'very divisive' by going ahead with an election. But since the MPs were never going to back down, the Bennites knew the game was up. In a meeting at his Holland Park house, they advised him to stay out of the contest and wait for a 'real' election, fought on their new rules. Benn clearly found this hard to take, but he had no choice. 'Well, in that case, because I accept your judgement,' he said glumly, 'let me start with the real election campaign as soon as I can.'[37]

No Benn, then. So who would win? The overwhelming favourite was obviously Denis Healey. The Shadow Industry Secretary, John Silkin, rich and immensely ambitious, announced that he would stand, too. But Healey's only really heavyweight rival was the Shadow Foreign Secretary, Peter Shore. Angular and cerebral, with a relatively low profile outside Westminster, Shore was a brilliant speaker, particularly when savaging his great bogeyman, the Common Market. He was fervently attached to interventionist economic policies, which endeared him to the left, but he was also hawkish to the point of nationalism, which pleased the right. Most predictions had Healey and Shore as the final two. But few seriously doubted that the former would win comfortably.[38]

Among those who dreaded the prospect of a Healey victory were three of the most powerful union leaders in the land: the TGWU's Moss Evans, ASTMS's Clive Jenkins and the GMWU's David Basnett. All three bore the scars of Healey's intellectual contempt; none had forgiven him for his economic rigour during the late 1970s. The day after Callaghan's announcement they had a drink to discuss the situation. Shore, they agreed, could not win, so somebody else should stand instead. The somebody they had in mind was Michael Foot.[39]

For all the affection he inspired within the Labour family, the 67-year-old Michael Foot was few people's idea of a natural leader. With his scholarly style and white flowing hair, he looked more like a radical pamphleteer than a modern politician. Born into a family of West Country Nonconformists, he had grown up in a house crammed with 240 Bibles, 130 volumes by or about Montaigne and 300 by or about Milton, 3,000 tracts from the English Civil War and an entire room on the French Revolution. As a boy he had a diet of 'bacon for breakfast, Liberalism for lunch and Deuteronomy for dinner'. As a young man he had co-written a bestselling, if largely erroneous, attack on the 'guilty men' behind appeasement, while as an MP in the 1950s and 1960s he had become the chief guardian of the left-wing conscience. Very late in life, he had come in from the political cold, becoming Employment Secretary and then Leader of the House, largely as a sop to the left. Unlike Benn, he had proved a model of loyalty, working tirelessly to hold the party together. But it was entirely characteristic that when Labour lost the election, he devoted himself to writing a book of biographical essays on subjects such as Cervantes, Burke and Sarah, Duchess of Marlborough. Unlike Benn, he wrote every word himself.[40]

Foot never wanted to stand for the leadership. In his own mind he was too old: it was time to let Shore carry the banner for the left. But no sooner had Foot told the press that he would probably sit this one out, than he started getting letters, phone calls and even telegrams begging him to change his mind. In the Commons his young parliamentary neighbour Neil Kinnock, who adored him, rounded up potential supporters and reckoned that he would win at least 112 votes. So would he do it?

On Saturday 18th, Foot flew to Dublin to give a lecture about his hero Jonathan Swift. While he was away, the union leaders arranged a dinner at his house for Sunday night, when they planned to persuade him to stand. But, as it turned out, there was no need. By the time Foot returned from Dublin, his mind was made up, not least because his wife Jill, a documentary filmmaker, was adamant that he should do it. On Monday morning Foot broke the news to Shore, who was devastated. Then he gave a press conference to explain why he had changed his mind. He had been against it at first, he said unguardedly, but his wife had told him: 'You are letting down your friends.' He could not say no to his friends. 'Besides, if I did my wife might divorce me.'[41]

Even after Foot's volte-face, Healey remained the favourite. In public polls he led Foot by 71 per cent to 16 per cent among all voters and 68 per cent to 25 per cent among Labour supporters. Only among the hard-core activists was Foot in the lead. But for all his brains and experience, Healey suffered from some serious handicaps. As a loner who spent his free time with his family, he had no organized parliamentary faction. The left loathed him, partly because they were still outraged by his spending cuts as Chancellor. And even his friends admitted that, despite his much-advertised love of Milton, Turgenev and Dostoyevsky, Healey could be a terrible bully. The Labour MP Leo Abse, for example, never forgave him for mocking his teenage son about the books he was reading. The public saw him as a jovial old trouper, red-faced and down-to-earth. But to many of his fellow MPs he seemed arrogant, flippant and just plain rude.[42]

The other problem was that Healey was not a good campaigner. He could not be bothered, for example, to write a mini-manifesto in the *Guardian*, whereas Foot gladly poured out a torrent of anti-Tory gush. Indeed, instead of campaigning vigorously, Healey calculated that it was better to avoid doing anything controversial. Presumably hoping to woo left-wing MPs, he refused to repudiate mandatory reselection and the electoral college, played down his views on nuclear weapons and Europe and effectively said nothing of interest to anybody at all. The Labour right, who were thirsting for leadership, were horrified. The moderate Manifesto Group organized meetings with both Foot and Healey. 'Foot was friendly and polite,' one of them recalled. 'Healey was nonchalant to the point of rudeness.' When another Labour right-winger bluntly asked why they should vote for him, Healey simply shrugged and said: 'That's easy. Because you have nowhere else to go.'[43]

He was wrong about that. His campaign managers hoped for 120 votes on the first ballot. But when the result was announced on 4 November, Healey had only 112, with Foot on eighty-three, Silkin on thirty-eight and Shore on thirty-two. That made the second ballot impossible to call, since it depended entirely on where Silkin's and Shore's voters went next. 'Great depression,' Healey noted afterwards. Six days went by. Then, late on the afternoon of Monday 10 November, came the moment of truth. At five minutes to six, Healey was waiting in a Commons anteroom when a clerk came in and handed him a note. Healey read it, nodded calmly and handed it back. A minute later, grinning broadly, he strode down the corridor to the room where his fellow MPs waited. Michael Foot made his way in too, 'as white as a sheet', wrote Benn, while another supporter thought Foot looked 'as if he had suffered some awful shock'. He had. With 139 votes to Healey's 129, Foot had won.[44]

At first the reaction was complete astonishment. Foot's young apprentice, Neil Kinnock, hammered on the desk with his fist and let out an 'Indian war whoop', but most people just sat there in disbelief. Both Foot and Healey made emollient speeches. Then, for Benn, there was a nasty shock. Healey said it was time for Labour to unite and rebuild its popularity, adding that they had lost a lot of votes in the past thirty years, and 'not to extreme left-wing parties'. ('Odious,' Benn thought.) To that end, he would be delighted to serve as Foot's deputy. At that, almost everybody cheered; but only *almost* everybody. 'I glanced at Tony Benn,' Healey recalled. 'His face was ashen. So I knew I had done at least one thing right.'[45]

Then came a preview of the issues that would define Foot's leadership. At a press conference that evening, Foot announced that he would begin his tenure by leading a mass protest about unemployment in Liverpool, and went out of his way to emphasize his commitment to unilateral nuclear disarmament. After that, he went to a dinner organized by the union leaders at the St Ermin's Hotel, famously the place where Kim Philby and Guy Burgess had met their Soviet handlers.* 'We will beat the Tories,' Foot insisted. 'We'll fight them on jobs and on nuclear weapons.' His big

---

* Later, the Soviet defector Oleg Gordievsky told MI5 that in the 1960s Foot had been a KGB 'agent of influence'. Foot, he said, had dined regularly with a Russian contact and accepted donations worth a total of £37,000 today, which he probably handed on to the left-wing paper *Tribune*. When the story came out, Foot successfully sued the *Sunday Times* for reporting it. But Gordievsky had no reason to lie, and it sounds plausible enough. It does

night ended with drinks at his favourite restaurant, the Gay Hussar, where he and his friends sang 'The Red Flag' and the Italian socialist anthem 'Avanti Popolo'. But as two journalists reported, it seemed a 'slightly oddly muted occasion. People were pleased, but perhaps too tired to be ecstatic.' Perhaps they knew what was coming.[46]

By their standards, the next day's papers were not especially unkind to Labour's new leader. Foot was an 'outstanding Parliamentarian and orator', said the *Express*, though it noted that Labour now had a leader 'whose views scare half the country'. He was a 'kindly, friendly man' with a 'rather engaging' shabbiness, agreed the *Sun*, which claimed that if he rebuilt Labour as a 'respectable and responsible force in politics, then he will find the *Sun* in his corner'. But *The Times* was utterly scathing, calling his elevation an 'unmitigated folly' that would doom Labour to defeat in the next election. And *The Economist* thought Foot's victory must make the Gang of Three's position untenable. 'The question is no longer whether they should leave the Labour Party but when. The answer is now.'[47]

Given that the second ballot was so close, it is tempting to wonder if things could have been different. There is no doubt that many MPs voted for Foot because they saw him as the 'candidate of the quiet life', who might appease the activists and save them from deselection. But one or two, at least, had more cynical motives. Later, academics identified five future SDP defectors who deliberately voted for Foot because, as one put it, 'he would make the worst leader for Labour'. Had they acted differently, the result would have been a tie. And with just one more vote, Healey would have won.[48]

But if Healey *had* won, so what? Would Labour have been spared the agonies of the next few years? To begin with, he would undoubtedly have been challenged by Tony Benn under the new rules a few months later. Given how close their contest for the deputy leadership was, it is perfectly plausible that Benn would have won. And even if Healey had prevailed a second time, after what would have been the bloodiest leadership campaign in history, he would still have gone into the next election with a manifesto he opposed and with activists who hated him. There might still have been some sort of split, though perhaps from the left, not the right. At the very least, it is impossible to imagine Labour's wounds being stitched up overnight. And irrespective of Healey's qualities, it is hard to see him winning a general election as the captain of such an unhappy and divided ship.[49]

---

not, of course, mean that Foot was a traitor, or even a KGB agent in any meaningful way. It probably just means he was very naive.

In any case, Foot was the man. And since his leadership is usually regarded as an unmitigated disaster, it is worth pointing out that he began with some obvious assets. A passionate orator and brilliant writer, he was fondly regarded in almost every corner of the party, with the possible exception of the Benn household. Certainly no modern party leader was so well read: when Foot wrote for the *Observer* on 'My Kind of Party', he quoted or cited Oliver Goldsmith, R. H. Tawney, George Orwell, Arthur Koestler, Ignazio Silone, William Morris, Karl Marx, Alexander Herzen and William Hazlitt, all on the same page. There is something very endearing about the fact that he once sent his Shadow Home Secretary, Roy Hattersley, a handwritten letter demanding his resignation because he had been rude about the American writer Dorothy Parker. Hattersley was amused by Foot's erudition. But he was not prepared for the endless telephone calls from the leader's office, demanding a reply – and this 'when I was busy trying to be the Shadow Home Secretary and had other things to do'.[50]

The fact is that while Foot was the ideal person to deliver a lecture about Jonathan Swift, he was a risible person to elect as leader of a major party. He was completely out of his depth, and the public knew it. Before the leadership election, the overwhelming majority of ordinary voters had preferred Healey, and they never changed their minds. Kicking off with an already abysmal 38 per cent in November 1980, Foot's Gallup approval rating plummeted to 30 per cent in December, 26 per cent in January and 22 per cent in February, before a steady plunge to just 9 per cent by the end of his tenure. No other party leader since polling began had inspired such overwhelming disapproval. His friends blamed the press, but since Foot had been a well-known figure on radio and television for decades, the public did not need the *Sun* to tell them what to think. They knew him. Often they rather liked him. They just did not think he was any good.[51]

Foot's supporters often said that he was betrayed by modern Britain's obsession with image. But politics has *always* been about image, as his heroes Gladstone and Disraeli knew very well. In this respect, Michael Foot was ludicrously ill suited to leadership. For one thing, he actually looked older than his 67 years. A near-fatal car crash had left him with a permanent limp, while an attack of shingles had robbed him of the sight in his left eye. Two days after his election he fell downstairs and broke his ankle, which meant he had to have crutches and his right leg in plaster, never a very dynamic look. The cartoonists drew him as a wildly dishevelled old man peering through thick glasses. *Private Eye* mocked him as the talking scarecrow Worzel Gummidge. In *The Times*, Bernard Levin called him 'half blind and at least a quarter crippled', unable 'to blow his nose in public without his trousers falling down, lurching between disaster and calamity with all the skill and aplomb of a one-legged tightrope-walker'. It was cruel, but it reflected what millions of people thought.[52]

Foot was the personification of Labour as a party of opposition, an elderly, backward-looking leader for an elderly, backward-looking party. His books, his stick, his references to Beaverbook and Bevan, even his daily walks on the heath with his dog, identified him as a high-minded Hampstead intellectual, trapped in the late 1940s. His clothes, wrote the journalist Edward Pearce, 'looked socialist – corduroys, cardigans, dark shirts and woven ties which made even people who voted reliably Labour sense difference'. Mrs Thatcher might dress conservatively, but she was always impeccably turned out. Foot never looked anything other than a scatty mess. And every time he appeared on television, as Austin Mitchell mordantly remarked, he confirmed Labour's image as the 'party of permanent demonstration with unruly, chanting mobs, led by a limping figure with a walking stick'.[53]

In Brussels, Roy Jenkins thought Foot's victory was a 'sensational result', opening up a 'much greater prospect of political alignment'. For the Gang of Three, too, Foot's elevation made everything simpler. David Owen's mind was made up: in spirit he had left already. Shirley Williams was also effectively gone. She liked Foot personally, but regarded him as a Little Englander whose policies would be so 'disastrous for the country' that she could never support them at a general election. When, at the end of November, the Stevenage constituency party invited her to stand as their candidate again, she turned them down. But unlike the gung-ho Owen, she felt no exhilaration at the thought of breaking with the past. 'For me,' she wrote later, 'leaving the Labour Party was like pulling out my own teeth, one by one.'[54]

Bill Rodgers felt the pain of leaving more acutely than anybody. Part of him wanted to stay: unlike Owen, he still stood in the annual Shadow Cabinet election, finishing eighth. Since his teenage years in Liverpool, Labour had been his life. 'I had happy memories', Rodgers wrote, 'of Fabian days, the companionship of hard-fought elections, cheerful July evenings on the Terrace of the House of Commons when [his wife] Silvia came to join me, the exhilaration of battles won and the loyalty and kindness of men and women who owed me nothing. How could I break with this without weeping for ever?' Laid up after Christmas with a bad back, he consoled himself with Bernard Crick's new biography of George Orwell. He thought about Orwell, and about his own father, another man of awkward, earnest integrity. And eventually his path became clear. By leaving he would betray his party. By staying he would betray his principles. At last, he recalled, 'I just lay on my back and suddenly said, "What's the point – I'm going to do it." And I rang up Roy and Shirley and said, "Shirley, I've made up my mind. I'm coming."'[55]

It was not quite that simple, of course. Right from the start their project contained a subtle but explosive ambiguity. Was it a centre party, akin to the Liberals? Or a new left-wing party, hoping to replace Labour? Jenkins, lurking massively on the fringes, always favoured the former. But that made his potential partners very wary. Williams wanted a new party that was 'democratic but also socialist', committed to 'greater equality', comprehensive schools and redistributive taxation, and 'wasn't certain that Roy shared all those objectives'. Owen was even more suspicious, telling his colleagues that the new party must be 'different, young and fresh-looking'. Jenkins was none of these things.

When the two men had lunch at the end of November, Owen insisted that any new party must be on the left and that Williams should lead it. Jenkins agreed, or pretended to. But the issue of the Liberals did not go away. A few days later, Williams arranged for Ivor Crewe and Anthony King to brief them on the challenges facing a new party, and the issue came up straight away. Brandishing a huge flip chart, Crewe and King explained that, with the decline of the two-party system, the prospects for a new party had never been better. But – and it was a crucial but – they simply had to do a deal with the Liberals. In a first-past-the-post system, there were barely enough votes for three parties. There were definitely not enough for four.[56]

Even at this early stage, sympathetic observers could see storm clouds ahead. In a prescient article on 3 December, the *Guardian* columnist Peter Jenkins, who agreed with almost everything the Gang of Three stood for, warned that the prospects for their 'desperate venture' could not be 'rated good'. Yes, the conditions for an electoral realignment looked better than at any time since the 1920s. But a new party faced gigantic challenges. Almost by definition, they would be advancing policies that were widely thought to have failed in the 1970s. Like the Liberals, they could end up in 'the deep end of an ideological vacuum'. Jenkins agreed that change was needed. But the potential defectors, he thought, 'had better reckon with reality'. Any realignment on the centre-left might take the best part of two decades. 'Meanwhile, promising careers will be wasted in the wilderness, the Conservatives will probably be kept in power (although not necessarily Mrs Thatcher), and many failures may precede eventual success. Those who set out had better be prepared for a long haul into the unknown.'[57]

But the Gang of Three were not for turning. On 14 January 1981 they held their first proper meeting with Roy Jenkins, who had left Brussels for good a few days earlier. There were still tensions, but they were now definitively a Gang of Four. The trigger for their departure, they decided, would be Labour's special conference at Wembley on Saturday 24 January, when the question of the party's electoral college would be settled once and for all. Assuming the left prevailed, they would publish a detailed statement of principles the next day and launch a Council for Social Democracy, which Labour MPs could join as a prelude to the new party itself. In the week before the conference they began working on a draft, and by Wednesday it was almost ready. Everybody now expected them to go. The Labour Party, Rodgers told the *Today* programme on Friday morning, was 'near the end of its useful life as the alternative to Conservatism'. It was time for a 'shot in the dark'.[58]

On the morning of 24 January, Labour's delegates descended once again on Wembley's concrete conference centre. Even by the party's own standards, what followed was a byzantine mess. To cut a very long story short, the delegates had to choose between seven different formulae for electing a new leader. Only three of the options stood a serious chance of winning. One was the National Executive's latest plan, which gave the MPs, the unions and the activists 33 per cent of the vote each. The second, backed by Michael Foot, gave 50 per cent of the votes to the MPs and 25 per cent each to the unions and the activists. The third was a proposal backed by the moderate Union of Shop, Distributive and Allied Workers (USDAW), which gave 40 per cent to the unions and 30 per cent each to the MPs and the activists. Each formula would be put to the delegates in an exhaustive ballot. They would go on voting until there were only two left. The last one standing was the winner.[59]

As if all this were not convoluted enough, there were two complications. The CLPD had decided to rally the left behind USDAW's 40–30–30 formula, calculating that this would win support in the unions while weakening the MPs. By contrast, the moderates and trade union leaders were all over the place. The GMWU's David Basnett, for example, was pushing the formula that gave 50 per cent to the MPs. But the engineers' leader Terry Duffy thought the MPs should get 75 per cent and was determined to abstain on anything that gave them less than 51 per cent, which made it impossible for him to back Basnett's plan. For the left, this was a gift. The key thing was to get USDAW's proposal into the final two. And after a ferocious lobbying effort they managed it, squeaking past the National Executive's version by just 50,000 votes. That meant a final showdown against the Foot–Basnett formula, which had led from the beginning. And with the engineers abstaining, victory – by 3.4 million votes to 2.9 million – went to USDAW. The left had won.[60]

It was an extraordinary result, at once a tribute to the left's organizational skill and a staggering indictment of the moderates' divisions. The irony is that if the engineers had not been so stubborn, Basnett's formula would have won. Instead, Labour now had an electoral system opposed by its leader, its National Executive, most of its MPs and many of the major trade unions, which gave those same unions the biggest say in the choice of the next leader. And for Foot, who had cut a lonely and passive figure throughout, it was a dreadful public humiliation. 'He lost not only the vote but prestige and his reputation as a fighter,' said the *Mirror*. He had 'courageously faced the first test of his leadership', agreed Austin Mitchell, 'by giving no lead at all'. In a plaintive speech afterwards, Foot did his best to unite the delegates behind an attack on Mrs Thatcher. But even the *Guardian* thought he 'looked like someone who wished he had stuck to book reviewing'.[61]

On the left, all was jubilation. The CLPD had prevailed, boasted Jon Lansman, against 'the National Executive Committee, the Transport and General Workers' Union, the Parliamentary Party and Michael Foot. We won against all the establishment figures.' It was a 'historic day – the product of ten years of work', agreed Tony Benn. 'No praise is high enough for the enormous skill of the CLPD.' The power of the MPs, he exulted, had been broken for good. The 'movement' was now in charge: 'It will never be reversed, and nothing will be the same again.' He was much in demand, he noted happily, for television and radio interviews. He accepted only one, for the Soviet labour magazine, *Trud*.[62]

But many Labour MPs left Wembley in utter despondency. For the *Mirror*'s political correspondent Terence Lancaster, the biggest winner was Margaret Thatcher, who had been given a 'propaganda weapon that not all the resources of Saatchi and Saatchi could better'. At a time when the unions' national reputation was at its lowest ebb, Labour had adopted a system that might have been designed to prove that they were pulling the party's strings. And not surprisingly, the voters hated it. Six out of ten disliked the new system, almost a third said it made them less likely to vote Labour, and half thought the Gang of Three ought to break away. In less than two weeks Labour's popularity dropped by fully 11 per cent. It never recovered. In *The Times* an unknown wag placed a memorable entry in the announcements column. 'IN MEMORIAM . . . LABOUR. – Party on January 24, 1981, after a long illness at Wembley. Funeral Westminster. No flowers.'[63]

The next day, Roy Jenkins, David Owen, Shirley Williams and Bill Rodgers met in Limehouse, east London, and called for a new party.

# 16

# When the Wind Blows

*Where, I wonder, have I, and all those other thousands of CND members been all these years? Why did complacency descend on us like some heavy mushroom cloud?*

Polly Toynbee, *Guardian*, 23 June 1980

*The West is decadent and divided. It has no stomach to risk our atomic reprisals. Throughout Europe, daily demonstrations demand unilateral nuclear disarmament.*

General Orlov (Steven Berkoff), in *Octopussy* (1983)

Britain in the 1980s lived in the shadow of the bomb. For anybody under the age of 40, the threat of nuclear annihilation had always been there, an inevitable feature of the modern world. But with the Red Army's invasion of Afghanistan, the temperature of the Cold War had dipped below freezing. And not long after the Moscow Olympics, the international situation took a turn for the worse. Following years of stagnation, a Kremlin coup saw the ageing Leonid Brezhnev deposed by a junta of KGB hardliners. In February 1981, hoping to exploit the inexperience of the Reagan administration, Moscow's new masters began massing troops on the borders of Turkey and Yugoslavia. To demonstrate their resolve, the British and Americans moved reinforcements to West Germany. But instead of backing down, the Soviet hardliners stepped up their military preparations. And suddenly, almost out of nowhere, the world was heading for war.

By the second week of March, Mrs Thatcher's ministers were confronting the gravest international emergency for two decades. On the evening of Monday 9th, with reports of Warsaw Pact troops heading towards the Yugoslavian border, the Prime Minister addressed the nation, appealing for calm and emphasizing her determination to remain strong in the face of Soviet aggression. 'For Heaven's Sake Think', implored the next day's *Guardian*. The *Sun* was more bullish: 'Good On Ya Maggie!'

Every hour the skies grew darker. At home, the next few days brought reports of panic buying in supermarkets and 'growing shortages of canned foods, sugar and flour'. In the capital, petrol stations were running dry; in university towns, thousands of students marched for peace. Abroad, the situation moved closer to disaster. On Wednesday evening, with reports of intensified military preparations along the Turkish and Yugoslavian frontiers and thousands of people fleeing Britain's cities for the countryside, the Commons passed an Emergency Powers Act. Nobody doubted now that the world stood on the brink of disaster.

As ill luck would have it, the decisive day was Friday 13th. As the Red Army smashed across the border into Yugoslavia, there were reports of Iraqi troops moving into eastern Turkey. At home, all eyes were on what the Home Office called 'the deteriorating food situation'. Rural stores had run out of coal, oil, batteries and candles, while chemists were out of first aid supplies. The government declared a state of emergency, but it came too late to forestall outbreaks of looting in major cities. Sabotage was widespread: at Immingham, Lincolnshire, a terrorist bomb destroyed the entire oil refinery, while a bomb at the Devonport naval base killed four people. From across the Irish Sea came reports that Mrs Thatcher had offered a united Ireland in return for the provision of 'temporary evacuation camps for selected British subjects'. Meanwhile, the BBC, now running nightly 'Crisis Specials', ordered staff to emergency sites. But as the corporation reported, many were 'unwilling to leave their families' at a moment of national emergency.

By Saturday morning there was real panic. In the *Daily Mail* a poll found that almost half of the population believed war was inevitable. Some people tried to make light of it: the cartoonist Jak pictured Mrs Thatcher sheltering from a nuclear bomb beneath an umbrella, while the *Telegraph*'s Peterborough column debated the correct pronunciation of the word 'coupon'. But few people were in the mood for laughter. 'Civilian morale is not high,' reported the Home Office. 'Food rationing and lack of petrol have hit morale hardest.' Sixteen more people were killed in sabotage attacks, while at RAF Finningley, South Yorkshire, the station commander disappeared, presumed kidnapped. But the day's most eye-catching development came at Trafalgar Square, where a massive peace rally, led by 'prominent left-wing MPs, leading trade unionists and personalities from many walks of life including sport and showbiz', ended in clashes with the police. The next morning, every single paper ran the same picture on its front page: the Labour leader, Michael Foot, and the

Archbishop of Canterbury, Robert Runcie, arms linked as the police moved in to arrest them.

Sunday was a day of worrying and waiting. In Downing Street, Mrs Thatcher was holed up with her military advisers, who warned that an attack on the West was expected 'within hours rather than days'. Most of the papers ran 'Protect and Survive' adverts advising people how to react to a nuclear attack, while London's stations were overwhelmed by crowds trying to get out of the city. Some commentators called for the Queen to be evacuated to Balmoral, but Buckingham Palace was having none of it. 'The Queen', said a spokesman, 'has no intention of leaving the capital.'

Early the next morning, Monday 16 March 1981, came the moment Britain feared. While most people were still asleep, Soviet bombers struck at air defence and radar installations across the country. A few hours earlier, Warsaw Pact troops had launched a 'full scale assault' against NATO forces in West Germany. Now events were accelerating with devastating speed. All television and radio services were taken off the air, except for one BBC channel, controlled by the government. A few hours later, Whitehall was shaken by a colossal car bomb, followed by an explosion at Green Park Tube station that killed eight people and injured thirty-five. But there was no time to mourn, no time even to breathe. That afternoon, as enemy planes roared overhead, Mrs Thatcher declared war on the Soviet Union.

The next day, Tuesday, was one of the most dreadful days in Britain's history. Early that morning, reported the Ministry of Defence, the nation's air defences had been 'virtually eliminated'. Almost every hour brought more civilian casualties, with hundreds killed in Glasgow, Plymouth, Liverpool and Devonport, while dozens more died in sabotage attacks at Edinburgh Airport, Avonmouth docks in Bristol and London's Victoria station. In the streets, reported the Home Office, there were 'scenes reminiscent of Vietnam . . . as families with children push overladen supermarket trolleys along the roads out of cities'. In Wales, farmers were said to be using shotguns against 'marauding bands of youths'. And that night, as Mrs Thatcher addressed the Commons, the air was heavy with recrimination. In a conscious effort to emulate Winston Churchill, she invited Labour to join a National Government. But as reports later put it, the offer fell on 'stony ground'.

On Wednesday 18th, despite more raids overnight, the sun rose as normal. The newspapers agreed that Britain would soon face a terrible choice: surrender to Moscow, or fall back on the ultimate deterrent. 'Do or Die', thundered the *Telegraph*. 'Buy Time', begged the *Guardian*. At noon, the War Cabinet met at Number 10. Mrs Thatcher's intelligence

chiefs warned her that the Red Army would soon break through in northern Norway and central Germany. And now she was forced to contemplate
the most dreadful dilemma of all. When it came to it, would she press the
nuclear button?

No British Prime Minister had ever faced such a decision. Quite apart
from the human consequences, recorded the War Cabinet minutes, there
would be 'serious political repercussions . . . It would be imperative for
the Prime Minister to speak to the Leader of the Opposition and one of
his more reliable senior colleagues with a view to establishing a bipartisan
approach.' But there were 'grounds for believing . . . that the general public
would support resolute action by the Government'. And, in truth, the issue
was never in doubt. Long ago, Mrs Thatcher had cast herself as the Iron
Lady. Even if she had wanted to come to terms, she was the prisoner of
her own persona. By the time the War Cabinet broke up, they were agreed.
All that remained was to choose the target.

That night, the bombing continued, with hundreds killed at Gatwick
and Heathrow. Under the circumstances, the Home Office thought public
morale was pretty good, 'with a quiet calm and expectancy now prevailing'. But when the War Cabinet met on Thursday morning, the news from
the German front was worse than ever. Mrs Thatcher's ministers were
agreed: if the West's conventional forces were broken, 'the use of nuclear
weapons to restore political balance would be justified'. It was a terrible
gamble. The Ministry of Defence believed that Moscow would probably
hit back with at least '250–500' missiles of its own. On the other hand,
the Joint Intelligence Committee thought the Kremlin might only use
tactical nuclear weapons, which 'would not necessarily involve nuclear
strikes on targets in the United Kingdom'.

The way forward, then, seemed clear. Britain had no alternative but to
use its nuclear deterrent. But rather than striking at the heart of the Soviet
Union, it was safer to target Moscow's satellites in Eastern Europe.
Already NATO's Supreme Allied Commander Europe had suggested
between twenty and thirty targets. Was that a bit high? Perhaps, but the
strike could not be confined to 'a few targets in, say, Bulgaria' because
'the political signal would be weak'. In any case, Mrs Thatcher had already
discussed it with Michael Foot. Despite his commitment to nuclear disarmament, Foot was a patriot who recognized the darkness of the hour. 'He
raised no objections', she reported, 'to the use of nuclear weapons against
targets in Polish territory.'

At 9 a.m. on Friday 20 March, the War Cabinet met for the last time.
Overnight, Soviet bombers had levelled hundreds of homes in Liverpool,
Manchester and Carlisle. In West Germany, exhausted British and

American forces were falling back to the Rhine. France would be next, then the Channel. Mrs Thatcher had already received a formal request from the Supreme Allied Commander for a nuclear strike the following morning, with twenty-nine weapons aimed at military bases in East Germany, Czechoslovakia, Poland, Hungary and Bulgaria. It would be accompanied by a 'message of explicit warning coincident with or shortly after the strikes . . . to emphasize the restrained nature of our nuclear use and to warn of the grave risks of further escalation'.

This was it, the moment of decision. But Mrs Thatcher did not waver. If she lost her nerve now, all the sacrifices so far would have been for nothing. The West had done its best, she said, to 'bring the conflict to a halt without resorting to the use of nuclear weapons'. Indeed, 'never before had a Cabinet been faced with such a grim choice between capitulating to a powerful and malevolent aggressor, and embarking on a course of action which could end with the destruction of civilisation. But the choice had to be made, and it was the clear view of the Restricted War Cabinet that the consequences of bowing to aggression would be intolerable.'

And that was that. At dawn on Saturday 21 March 1981, as Britain slept, the missiles took off. By the time most people awoke, the apocalypse had begun.

There was, of course, no Third World War in March 1981. This was a secret 'transition to war exercise', codenamed WINTEX-CIMEX 81 and carried out in the Cabinet Office over two weeks. For some of the civil servants involved, it was clearly an opportunity to indulge a long-suppressed taste for fantasy, such as when they dreamed up tabloid headlines or imagined the police arresting the Archbishop of Canterbury. But there was more to it than bureaucratic role-playing. They spent days working out how Britain would cope during the drift into war, devoting almost 250 close-typed pages to petrol rationing, railway timetables, agricultural supplies and medical provision for injured servicemen. And the fact that the exercise ends with the decision to use nuclear weapons, taken at that last War Cabinet meeting on 20 March, speaks volumes about the unfathomable seriousness of such a moment. To go on would have been impossible: the consequences of a nuclear strike were simply too awful to contemplate.[1]

The early 1980s were a golden age for prophecies of Armageddon. A decade earlier, the prospect of nuclear war had seemed to be fading from view. But from about the middle of the 1970s the mood had begun to change. With the Western economy beset by inflation, the Soviet Union gaining ground in the Third World and the United States sunk in a gigantic post-Vietnam sulk, history seemed to be moving in Marxism's direction. And when revolution broke out in Iran at the end of 1978, it genuinely seemed that the world was spinning out of control. In many Western papers there was now talk of a worldwide Islamic fundamentalist upheaval, a global depression, an apocalyptic showdown for control of the Middle East. A year later, six out of ten people told Gallup that the Warsaw Pact was stronger than NATO, while almost nine out of ten agreed that the Soviet Union posed a threat to Britain. Almost two-thirds, meanwhile, thought there was a serious danger of military conflict. Few doubted that the Cold War was back on – or that the Communists were winning it.[2]

'Never has the Western world shown itself to worse effect than it does at the present,' wrote Lord Hailsham in the *Sunday Express* on 7 January 1979. The Soviet Union, he thought, boasted 'by far the most powerful navy that the world has ever seen', while 'their superiority in men under arms, tanks and aircraft is terrifying'. On the right, this was now the conventional wisdom. Only a few months earlier, the former commander-in-chief of the British Army in West Germany, Sir John Hackett, had published his unexpected bestseller *The Third World War* (1978), a vision of a world war in 1985, in which the Kremlin provokes a conflict by pushing into the Middle East and occupying Yugoslavia. Unlike the Cabinet Office's war game, Hackett's scenario envisaged the Soviet Union using nuclear weapons after their drive towards the Rhine grinds to a halt. In a bad blow for Jasper Carrott, UB40 and fans of Aston Villa, the book ends with Birmingham obliterated by a nuclear bomb. And although Hackett conceded that a genuine war might unfold differently, there was no mistaking his urgency. There was, he warned, 'a very high probability that, unless the West does a great deal within the next few years to improve its defences, a war with the Warsaw Pact could end in early disaster'.[3]

The woman whom the Red Army newspaper had nicknamed the Iron Lady would have agreed with every word. Yet Mrs Thatcher's reputation as the woman who laid the foundations for victory over Communism is a bit exaggerated. It is certainly true that no Prime Minister for years had spoken so fervently about the Cold War as a struggle between good and evil. But when it came to the nuts and bolts, there was more continuity between Mrs Thatcher and her predecessors than is often realized. It is a common fallacy, for example, that she loved spending money on defence. In fact, defence spending as a proportion of the total budget barely increased during her early years as Prime Minister, and actually declined in the second half of the 1980s. Her strategic priorities – Britain's position in West Germany and its nuclear deterrent – were exactly the same as those under Harold Wilson and Jim Callaghan. Even her decision to order the submarine-based Trident nuclear weapons system was inherited from Callaghan, who had first approached the Americans about it in January 1979. He had picked his moment carefully, sneaking across to Jimmy Carter's beach hut while they were at a summit in Guadeloupe. It is hard to imagine Mrs Thatcher doing that.

Like Callaghan, Mrs Thatcher kept nuclear decisions to a trusted group of senior colleagues. On 10 February 1981 her Defence Secretary, John Nott,* warned her that 'two-thirds of the Party and two-thirds of the Cabinet were opposed to the procurement of Trident' – almost certainly because, at a projected cost of £5 billion, it was so expensive. But Nott thought they should get it anyway. So did Lord Carrington, who added that 'failure to acquire Trident would have left the French as the only nuclear power in Europe'. As it happened, this was exactly what Carter had told Callaghan in Guadeloupe. And Mrs Thatcher herself was in no doubt. As she told the Commons a few months later, buying Trident 'makes it clear that we are resolved to defend our own freedom'.[4]

But there was now a bigger issue than Trident. At the end of 1976, the Soviet Union had started deploying its new SS-20 missiles. Each SS-20 had three nuclear warheads, which could be aimed at different targets. Because they were carried on the backs of trucks, they could be kept on the move, making them hard to track down. But from Britain's perspective the really frightening thing was that, because they were only 'intermediate' missiles with a range of about 3,500 miles, they posed little threat to the United States. In other words, the Kremlin could use the SS-20s to destroy a major European city without necessarily provoking an American response.

West Germany's Helmut Schmidt, who would be first in the firing line, was horrified. So was Mrs Thatcher. As her first Defence Secretary, Francis Pym, noted, this was a 'key test of NATO's collective will to ensure its security'. So on 12 December 1979, NATO agreed that West Germany would take delivery of 108 short-range nuclear-armed Pershing II missiles and ninety-six Cruise missiles. Britain would take 160 Cruise missiles, while the Italians would take 112 and the Dutch and Belgians forty-eight each. Since these missiles were not due to arrive until the end of 1983, the Kremlin still had a chance to withdraw the SS-20s. Realistically, though, that was not going to happen. Cruise was coming.[5]

To her critics, Mrs Thatcher's decision to accept the Cruise missiles was a reckless betrayal of Britain's interests. For the Marxist historian

* Nott was Mrs Thatcher's second Defence Secretary: he replaced Francis Pym in January 1981 and was at the helm, famously, during the Falklands War.

E. P. Thompson, a founder member of the Campaign for Nuclear Disarmament (CND), Cruise was a 'visible symbol of subjection', turning
Britain into a 'prime target' in the next world war. But even if this were
true, what was new about that? As *The Times* pointed out: 'For nearly 30
years, Britain has been a base for nuclear warheads on manned aircraft
and missiles operated either by British or American forces.' Indeed, in
some ways the explosion of anger following Mrs Thatcher's decision now
looks a bit odd. If Jim Callaghan or Denis Healey had faced the same
challenge, they would undoubtedly have made the same choice.* In the
early 1980s, anti-nuclear literature often pictured the nation caught in the
Soviet crosshairs, suggesting that Mrs Thatcher had turned it into a target.
But Britain had been a prime target for decades. Even in the Wilson years
it had already been the most heavily armed nuclear state in Western
Europe, with well over a hundred American facilities of various kinds. If
war had broken out at any time since the 1940s, Britain would have been
in the firing line. So in that respect Cruise made no difference at all.

As for Britain's supposed subjection to the Americans, the reality is
more complicated. Many CND activists invoked Orwell's Airstrip One,
while the feminist writer Angela Carter claimed that Britain was now 'a
moored aircraft carrier for instruments of destruction'. But it was not as
if the wicked Americans had forced their weapons on to their unwilling
colonial subjects. In reality, Mrs Thatcher and Helmut Schmidt had
begged for Cruise and Pershing, because, like Clement Attlee and Konrad
Adenauer before them, they were worried that a revival of American iso-
lationism might leave Western Europe defenceless. Indeed, for Mrs
Thatcher the problem with the Americans was not that they were so
domineering but that they were so flaky. 'I feel the real urgency to stiffen
up Washington,' the anti-Communist historian Robert Conquest told her
in August 1979. She underlined it in green ink.[6]

Cruise's critics did, however, make one unanswerable point. Because
Britain did not own the missiles and had not paid a penny towards them,
there was no 'dual key' system. In theory the Americans could launch a
nuclear strike without even bothering to tell Downing Street. So why
didn't Mrs Thatcher press for a dual key? After all, Washington had
offered it. The answer came down to money. If Britain wanted a dual key,
it would have to buy the missiles outright, for at least £1 billion. On top
of that, no other European country had asked for a dual key. If Britain

* According to Tony Benn's diary, Callaghan explicitly told his senior colleagues that he
and his Defence Secretary, Fred Mulley, had secretly 'prepared for Cruise missiles to be
introduced to this country'.

demanded one, then everybody else would want one, and the idea of a united deterrent would fall apart. For Mrs Thatcher, then, a dual key would create more problems than it solved. In any case, since 1952 there had been a vague agreement that Washington would never strike from British soil without a 'joint decision' by both governments. So perhaps she did not need a dual key anyway.[7]

To many people, though, these sounded like excuses, and at the end of 1982 John Nott urged Mrs Thatcher to think again. Without dual control, he wrote, they were 'very vulnerable politically to the charge of hazarding the UK for an American system'. Even Nott had doubts about their allies' reliability, remarking that if Britain had a dual key, 'I shall certainly then sleep more safely in my bed.' And evidently he was not the only Conservative who had trouble sleeping. At one point thirty-five MPs signed an early day motion in the Commons calling for a dual key system. So in early 1983 Mrs Thatcher's senior ministers returned to the issue. Once again, though, they decided against it, since it 'would be expensive, would delay the deployment of the missiles . . . and would be seen as evidence of distrust of American intentions'. In the Commons Mrs Thatcher insisted that it was irrelevant because 'no nuclear weapon would be fired or launched from British territory without the agreement of the British Prime Minister'. But the public unease never went away. When Mass Observation asked Carol Daniel if there was anything she disliked about Americans, one of her first thoughts – after 'the way they talk', naturally – was 'the fact that they have basses and nuclar bombs [sic] in this country and hold the key'.[8]

Francis Pym announced the details of the Cruise deployment on 17 June 1980. After a bit of haggling, the Americans had agreed to use the disused airfield at RAF Molesworth, in Cambridgeshire, and the US air base at RAF Greenham Common, near Newbury in Berkshire. In Newbury the local Labour Party immediately denounced the decision. The town, said its former parliamentary candidate, Joan Ruddock, was now 'in the front line', and when Pym addressed a public meeting at Newbury Racecourse, he was heckled with cries of 'Let's disarm!' and 'Get back to your bunker!' In general, though, the reaction was pretty muted. When a reporter from The Times tried to gauge the attitude on the streets, few people had strong views either way. Even the committee set up to protect Greenham Common said they were not in principle opposed to Cruise missiles, although a spokeswoman agreed that it was frightening to think of Newbury being a 'prime target for attack'.[9]

When The Times returned to Newbury nine months later, the mood had barely changed. In the interim, Joan Ruddock had been trying to drum up support for the Newbury Campaign Against Cruise Missiles, but it was hard going. By March 1981 her campaign had only eighty-two paid-up members and seventy-five 'interested supporters', and this in a town of more than 20,000 people. Newbury was a prosperous, contented sort of place, solidly Conservative since 1910, the worst possible place to recruit supporters. Most people recognized that it would have been a Soviet target anyway, because of the Atomic Weapons Research Establishment at nearby Aldermaston, the Royal Ordnance Factory at Burghfield and the American base at Welford. Not even the news that, in the latest NATO war game, Newbury had been destroyed by a nuclear warhead seemed to shake the town's complacency.

The government was not taking Newbury for granted, though. During Pym's most recent visit he had taken questions from residents anxious about the repercussions of Cruise. Two things particularly bothered them. Would flights to RAF Greenham interfere with the local racecourse? And would they affect farm animals? Horse racing and animals: the British never changed. Fortunately, Pym was able to calm their fears. Nothing, he said, would disturb the people of Newbury. Yes, the missiles were on their way. But life would go on as usual: quiet, peaceful and unchanging. After all, it was not as if hundreds of protesting women were going to descend on Greenham Common.[10]

By the time Mrs Thatcher became Prime Minister, the Campaign for Nuclear Disarmament had declined to the point of outright irrelevance. At its peak two decades earlier, CND had attracted tens of thousands of people to its annual marches. But détente had taken its toll. By 1979, with just four employees and barely 2,000 members, it was less a national movement than a pacifists' club. There were many more regular *Dungeons & Dragons* players than there were CND members – and most people had never heard of *Dungeons & Dragons*. When the organization's general secretary, the Catholic priest Bruce Kent, went to Rugby to address a meeting that summer, not a single person turned up.[11]

But as the international mood darkened, CND's fortunes picked up. By the beginning of 1980 peace groups were already on the march in Scandinavia, the Netherlands and West Germany. And although CND's rallies never matched the crowds who poured into the streets of Copenhagen, Amsterdam, Frankfurt and Bonn, it could hardly fail to profit from the changing mood. That spring, more than four out of ten people told a poll for Radio Four that they thought war was likely in the next ten years. And what if war did come? In a letter to *The Times*, the military historian Michael Howard warned that the government ought to be investing far more in civil defence, to show the Kremlin that Britain was not afraid of a fight. His letter struck a chord. The country's lack of readiness for war, agreed a *Times* editorial on 19 January, was a 'lethal failure of duty'. 'Other countries', it said sternly, 'persuade members of the public to enlighten themselves on the means of survival in the unlikely event of nuclear attack. In Britain, a Home Office booklet "Protect and Survive" remains unavailable.'[12]

At this point, most people had never heard of *Protect and Survive*. Later, it became the subject of countless paranoid myths, but the real story was pretty mundane. The government had been producing civil defence leaflets since before the Second World War, and *Protect and Survive* dated from the mid-1970s. Although it was never meant for general release, there was nothing sinister in that. As the Home Office minister Leon Brittan told the Commons in February 1980, it was 'not a secret pamphlet, and there is no mystery about it. It has been available to all local authorities and chief police and fire officers and to those who have attended courses at the Home Defence College at Easingwold'. The reason it had never been made public, Brittan explained, was that it had been commissioned specifically 'for distribution at a time of grave international crisis when war seemed imminent, and it was calculated that it would have the greatest impact if distributed then'.

By this stage, the Home Office was already besieged with demands to see the pamphlet. *The Times*, too, received dozens of letters from interested readers. Some people even went to the Stationery Office to ask for it; one was told that it was 'restricted', another that *The Times* had been 'naughty' in publicizing it. At last, the Home Office bowed to the pressure of the market. In May 1980 *Protect and Survive* went on sale, priced at a very reasonable 50p. In the Commons, Willie Whitelaw claimed that since 'most houses offer reasonable protection against radioactive fallout from nuclear explosions', which was patently untrue, the booklet showed that 'protection can be substantially improved by a series of quite simple do-it-yourself measures'. How strange, then, that so many people were still worried about the bomb![13]

At the heart of *Protect and Survive*'s terrifying reputation was the accompanying series of public information films, narrated by the actor Patrick Allen, which were released in March in a special edition of *Panorama*. On paper they sound almost boring: 'Nuclear Explosions Explained', 'Materials to Use for Your Fall-Out Room', 'Water and Food', 'Sanitation Care'. Even the advice, which was widely condemned as woefully inadequate, is not especially frightening. There is a lot about biscuits, mattresses and bin-bags of soil, and an awful lot of stuff about toilets. But the only really grim episode is the last, 'Casualties'. 'If anyone dies while you are kept in your fallout room, move the body to another room in the house,' Allen says sternly. 'Label the body with name and address, and cover it as tightly as possible in polythene, paper, sheets or blankets . . . The radio will advise you what to do about taking the body away for burial.' But if the radio goes dead and you have been staring at a corpse for five days, the best thing is to dump it outside. 'You should bury the body for the time being in a trench or cover it with earth', Allen says, 'and mark the spot of the burial.'

What made the *Protect and Survive* films so chilling was the incongruity of the style. Every episode opens with a childish animation of a mushroom cloud. Indeed, they feel strikingly similar to the children's programmes made at the same time, in the mid-1970s. Perhaps the producers did this deliberately because they were keen not to terrify people, but the overall effect is not unlike the toddlers' favourite *Bod* (1975): the slow pace, the simple animation, the bright colours, even the funereal narration. What is more, Allen often seems to have borrowed his voiceover from a *Blue Peter* presenter. 'First, choosing a fallout room,' he says slowly, as though speaking to an audience of 6-year-olds. 'And now a reminder about your inner refuge . . . Make a lean-to with wood . . . Here is a list of the most important things you will need.' You half-expect him to start talking about double-sided sticky tape.

*Protect and Survive* was a gift to CND. As one activist recalled, the furore 'pushed the concept of nuclear war into every living room and kitchen. Suddenly, the thing became very close, very menacing.' The historian E. P. Thompson, fast becoming the face of the new disarmament movement, rushed out a pamphlet of his own, *Protest and Survive*, which argued that the nuclear arms race had made 'the extinction of civilised life upon this island' a serious probability. Now CND rallies were attracting not dozens of people, but thousands. At the end of May 1980, a march in London drew 15,000 people, the largest turnout for years. There were skinheads, punks and Buddhist monks, a lone Scottish piper and the leader of the West German Green Party; 'women's lib and gay lib; and the Superior Brass Band'. 'For sheer variety', the *Guardian* said happily, 'it was hard to beat.'[14]

By now CND was working closely with the left of the Labour Party, which had long been sympathetic to unilateral disarmament. On 22 June 1980, five days after Pym had confirmed the details of the Cruise deal, Labour's National Executive Committee organized a march through central London. Despite horrendous rain, another 15,000 people turned up, and even sceptical observers were reminded of the Aldermaston marches. Tellingly, both Callaghan and Healey stayed away, but Michael Foot, Tony Benn and Neil Kinnock were much in evidence. The hard-left MP Jo Richardson made a speech in rather dubious taste, suggesting that the only cut worth making would be to 'Mrs Thatcher's throat'. Still, Benn thought it had been a 'jolly day', so that was all right.[15]

Two decades earlier, Labour's disagreements about unilateral disarmament had almost torn the party apart. But the left had never abandoned their opposition to nuclear weapons, and in the summer of 1980 they had the upper hand. When, in July, the National Executive discussed CND's next anti-Cruise march, Shirley Williams insisted that they 'shouldn't have anything to do with CND', while Callaghan 'supported her and said we were a world party'. But in a revealing sign of the mood, their colleagues voted to support the march. 'I will never agree to unilateralism, whatever the Party says,' Callaghan said defiantly. But his party no longer cared. By now at least a hundred Labour MPs were sympathetic to CND, and the anti-nuclear and anti-NATO votes at October's party conference set the tone for the next three years. In 1981 the conference again voted to scrap Cruise, Trident and Polaris, and in 1982 they voted to get rid of Cruise, close the American bases and adopt a 'non-nuclear defence' policy. By now the activists and the leader were singing from the same hymn sheet. Only hours after succeeding Callaghan in November 1980, Michael Foot had made his priorities clear. It was 'vital', he said, for Labour to embrace nuclear disarmament: 'The dismantling of those weapons is essential for the survival of our world.'[16]

Foot's elevation to the Labour leadership set the seal on an extraordinarily successful year for CND. It had already staged rallies in Oxford, Cambridge, Manchester and York, but the highlight was a massive 'Protest and Survive' march to Trafalgar Square on 26 October. Only a year earlier, CND had been delighted with crowds of a few hundred. Now it attracted an estimated 80,000 people, including yet more Buddhist monks, a delegation from Plaid Cymru, the Devizes branch of Friends of the Earth and a group called 'Pimlico School Kids Against the Bomb', as well as people wearing gas masks and 'bloodstained bandages'. 'It was a fantastic day,' wrote Tony Benn:

> I am not a descriptive writer but everything about it was thrilling. There were fourteen columns – the national column first, then Scotland and Wales, then East Anglia, and so on, right the way through. There was a huge balloon in the sky shaped like a hydrogen bomb with a mushroom cloud, and there was a children's puppet theatre. It had this element of gaiety and festivity about it, and there were tens of thousands of young people . . .
>
> It has been a really exciting day. The old CND is back, stronger, more determined, more united, with the Labour Party altering its view on nuclear disarmament.

As if that were not excitement enough, Benn also found time to speak at a CND festival at the Bristol Corn Exchange. Newbury's Joan Ruddock made what he thought a 'good speech', but the star attraction was the actress Julie Christie, who earned 'huge applause'. Afterwards, Benn travelled back to London with her, which was evidently a great treat. 'She likes farm life and is a dedicated sort of socialist,' he wrote enthusiastically. 'We talked about Vanessa Redgrave and Jane Fonda, and whether they suffered for their views.'[17]

Nine days after the march in London, the Americans handed CND its biggest gift of all. 'Reagan has beaten Carter in the American presidential election,' Benn wrote on 4 November, 'and it is a dark day for the western world.' The peace movement had long flirted with outright anti-Americanism, but Ronald Reagan made everything ten times worse. To many British observers, he seemed a walking parody, a Western gunslinger with his finger poised on the nuclear button. Reagan's hawkish policies, warned the *Guardian*, were 'misconceived to the point of peril', and could easily provoke a Soviet overreaction. It was dreadful, agreed the novelist Caroline Blackwood, to have an American president who genuinely believed that he was going to heaven and therefore viewed 'nuclear war with a certain nonchalance'. But it was a CND poster that put it best, advertising a new production of *Gone with the Wind* ('The Film to End All Films – The most EXPLOSIVE love story ever'). The picture shows a rugged Reagan sweeping Mrs Thatcher off her feet, while in the background a mushroom cloud rises into the sky. 'She promised to follow him to the end of the earth,' reads the tagline. 'He promised to organise it!'[18]

In reality, all this was based on a complete misapprehension. Despite his anti-Communist rhetoric, Reagan had a profound horror of nuclear weapons and dreamed that one day he would be able to get rid of them. The historian John Lewis Gaddis calls him 'the only nuclear abolitionist ever to have been president of the United States'. But very few people realized that at the time. As Reagan closed in on the presidency, a poll for *Panorama* found that 48 per cent of people believed a nuclear war was likely in their lifetime, while 70 per cent thought the threat had increased in the last twelve months. Two days after his victory, the *Mirror* ran what it called a 'shock issue': 'Britain and the Bomb! Will it keep the peace? Is YOUR home a target? What warning will we get? Would ANYONE survive?' Page after page hammered home the threat of disaster, from a spine-chilling profile of the Cambridgeshire village of Molesworth ('In Moscow's Sights: The Doomsday Village') to an unsettling picture of an entire family dressed in gas masks and radiation suits ('Enter the Nuclear Family'). 'Britain is Europe's number one target,' explained a cheerful

piece by CND's Bruce Kent. Unless the government immediately dis-
armed, it would find itself heading 'down the road to a national suicide
built on the willingness to commit mass murder'.[19]

By the autumn of 1980 this kind of talk was everywhere. In the next
few years publishers rushed out so many predictions of a Third World
War – *War Plan UK*, *Defended to Death*, *London After the Bomb*, *The
Fate of the Earth* – that a collector could have used them to build a fallout
refuge. Conservative novelists often imagined a future under Soviet occupation: in Kingsley Amis's *Russian Hide and Seek* (1980), the Russian
conquerors have become the aristocracy in a feudal Britain; while in Ted
Allbeury's *All Our Tomorrows* (1982), moral permissiveness, trade union
militancy and – of course! – French treachery have fatally undermined
Britain's defences. But many visions of the future were even bleaker, such
as Russell Hoban's brilliantly strange *Riddley Walker* (1980). Set in southern England, 2,000 years after a nuclear war, it depicts a neo-medieval
society where the language has decayed to the point of unintelligibility.
In the past, says the narrator, men and women lived in cities of magic and
machines. But then, one day, 'there come a flash of lite then bigger nor the
woal worl and it ternt the nite to day. Then every thing gone black. Nothing only nite for years on end. Playgs kilt people off and naminals nor
there wernt nothing growit in the groun.'[20]

If *Riddley Walker* was the most inventive version of a post-nuclear
Britain, the most unsettling was surely Raymond Briggs's *When the
Wind Blows*, published in 1982. A milkman's son who had studied at
art college, Briggs was one of the best-known children's writers in the
land, having won enormous acclaim for *Father Christmas* (1973) and *The
Snowman* (1978). His latest book used the same child-friendly style,
which is one of the things that makes it so moving. The characters, based
on Briggs's parents, are James and Hilda Bloggs, a gentle working-class
couple who build their own fallout shelter as war approaches. The book's
terrible power lies in the contrast between their naive optimism – their
nostalgia for the Second World War, their unquestioning faith in the
government – and the increasingly dreadful reality of their plight. In one
awful moment, they misunderstand the *Protect and Survive* instructions,
leave their shelter and go wandering about, exposing themselves to fallout. When they smell 'roast meat', they assume their neighbours are
cooking dinner; in fact, the smell comes from their neighbours' burning
bodies. In the book's final scene, they lie in their shelter, dying of radiation sickness, praying quietly together, before the story fades into
blankness. It is hard to think of any other book of the decade that packs
such a punch. But Briggs made no apology for being such a pessimist.

'How can you be anything else', he asked, 'when you're writing about a nuclear war?'[21]

Even in *When the Wind Blows*, there are moments of blackly comic humour, and on television some writers tried to squeeze every last laugh from the prospect of Armageddon. In the fourth episode of *The Young Ones* (November 1982), an unexploded atomic bomb falls into the students' house. 'I'm going to consult the incredibly helpful *Protect and Survive* manual!' says Nigel Planer's Neil, to the hilarity of the studio audience. And in one episode of *Only Fools and Horses*, 'The Russians are Coming!' (October 1981), Rodney Trotter persuades his brother Del to build their own fallout shelter. As Rodney explains, 'It only takes one little rumble in the Middle East, then missiles are gonna start flying.' After the brothers have put their shelter together, Del is heartened by the thought that they have a head start over their neighbours. 'When the alarm bells start ringing and the missiles start firing, and all the people are rushing about like mad mice trying to find somewhere to hide, we'll be tucked up in our own little nuclear shelter,' he says happily. 'If they started dropping the bomb on us now, we'd be as safe as houses, brother, safe as houses!' The camera pulls back to show where they have built it – on the roof of their Peckham tower block.

There were very few laughs, though, in the nuclear-themed pop music of the early 1980s, which was saturated in images of annihilation. No doubt this partly reflected the New Romantics' fascination with all things German. Nowhere was youth culture more overtly anti-nuclear than in West Germany, and British acts were hurrying to catch up. A good example was UB40's 'The Earth Dies Screaming', all abandoned highways and 'bodies hanging limp', released in the autumn of 1980. Another was Kate Bush's typically iconoclastic single 'Breathing', released a few months earlier. Here she imagines herself a foetus in the womb, breathing in fallout after a 'bright light' in the sky. The nuclear explosion in the second half of her video was considered too controversial for *Top of the Pops*. It did appear, though, on BBC1's early-evening magazine show *Nationwide*. As Bush earnestly told the programme's Hugh Scully, people should be 'very concerned about looking after each other [rather] than destroying each other' – a message with which no viewer could possibly have disagreed.[22]

The most memorable nuclear-themed song of the year, though, was Orchestral Manoeuvres in the Dark's sublime 'Enola Gay', one of the few hits of the decade to have been researched in the library. The band's creative force, Andy McCluskey, was fascinated by old aeroplanes and had long wanted to write something about the plane that dropped the first atom bomb on Hiroshima. Some of his bandmates were very dubious, and the BBC refused to play it on children's programmes such as *Multi-Coloured Swap Shop*. Even OMD's keyboardist Paul Humphreys felt 'uneasy' to have recorded a 'bright, perky pop song about a nuclear holocaust'. But it was, he admitted, 'insanely catchy'. In Britain it peaked at number eight; in Italy and Spain it reached number one, and it sold 5 million copies in all. As readers of a certain age will know, you merely have to hear the synthesizer hook, the musical equivalent of one of Proust's madeleines, to be catapulted back to the 1980s.[23]

By the beginning of 1981 CND had reached a level of popularity unimaginable only two or three years earlier. When, in mid-January, it arranged a torchlight procession in Newcastle, the organizers hoped for about 500 people. But despite the freezing weather more than 2,000 marched across the Tyne Bridge to hear speeches in the City Hall. Among them was Melvyn Bragg, who was struck by the ebullience of the crowd: the punks, the 'ghoulishly made-up quartet carrying a coffin with "Protest and Survive" daubed on its side', the children excitedly holding their torches, the 'solid core of people in their twenties and thirties, heavily wrapped up against the icy night'.

To Bragg, it appeared that few of the marchers had been to such an event before. One of the organizers told him that they had done 'very little evangelising. They come to us.' Among the speakers were feminists and clergymen, trade unionists and Labour MPs. One promised to sing a song about 'Maggie Thatcher and the wonders she's achieved', and then left the stage, never to return. Another, the *New Statesman* journalist Duncan Campbell, cheered the crowd with the news that in the event of a nuclear war, 'two out of three people on Tyneside would be killed instantly'. But although it went on for two hours, even the youngest stayed to the end, 'clearly glad to have been there'. Afterwards, somebody put on John Lennon's 'Imagine'. And then, wrote Bragg, 'the hundreds who were drifting away paused in the City Hall to listen, quietly, to what seemed an alternative anthem'.[24]

By now, with tens of thousands of people estimated to be signing up every month, CND had been transformed from a hobbyists' club to a nationwide movement. Even Sir Geoffrey Howe's 21-year-old son Alec, in his final year at the University of York, joined the crusade, becoming the press officer for his local CND branch. At one point there was a plan for Alec to lead a march through the streets of York, dressed as Ronald Reagan and leading a female student, dressed as Mrs Thatcher, by a leash around her neck. Fortunately for his father, who might have found this hard to explain to his next-door neighbour, this part of the proceedings was dropped, although Alec still went on the march.[25]

But CND's momentum survived unchecked. At Easter there were rallies everywhere from Newcastle to Plymouth. In June the largest peace rally in Scottish history brought more than 10,000 people to Glasgow's Kelvingrove Park. And then, at the end of the month, came an event that became part of pop-cultural legend, as CND joined forces with Hawkwind, New Order and Aswad at the Glastonbury Festival. In a special marquee, Peter Watkins's film *The War Game* (1965) played on a continuous loop, while from the Pyramid Stage, decorated with a huge CND logo, Bruce Kent and E. P. Thompson lectured the crowds. The festival was a triumph, attracting a then-record crowd of 24,000 people and making a £20,000 profit. At last, the unilateralist movement had broken free of the beard, the duffel coat and the folk revival. Nuclear disarmament was not merely popular; it was *cool*.[26]

In October, CND held another London rally, scheduled to coincide with similar events in Paris, Rome, Brussels and Helsinki. This time the crowds were bigger than the organizers' wildest dreams. 'The Embankment,' wrote one onlooker, 'was a mile long jam of multi-coloured hairstyles and banners'. The usual suspects were all in evidence: 'punks . . . anarchists . . . feminist poets . . . theatre groups . . . a boy with purple hair', as well as a lot of people 'wearing green anoraks and sensible shoes, huddled round thermos flasks and talking about Solidarnosc and "what I mean by Socialism"'. Not even Tony Benn, who gave a blistering speech urging the British people to 'stand up to the Pentagon as the Poles had to the Kremlin', had ever seen such enthusiasm. 'There must have been a quarter of a million people there,' he wrote afterwards. 'I have never seen such a crowd in any one place in Britain before.'[27]

When CND held its annual conference that November, the mood was a mixture of apocalyptic pessimism and ecstatic excitement. Even veteran activists thought it the most colourful meeting anybody could remember, complete with badges ('Morris Dancers Against the Bomb') and carols ('O Little Town of Newbury, How Still Your Ruins Lie'). In an ominous sign of things to come, it was also the most divided, thanks to the noisy participation of the Trotskyist left. But for the time being the moderates held sway, with Joan Ruddock prevailing in the election for a new chairman. From Fleet Street's perspective, CND could not have made a better choice. *The Times* admired her 'dimpled smile and soft Welsh voice', while the *Mirror* described her as a 'beautifully intact lady of 38, with model's legs and a great amount of femininity', her 'fine, dark eyebrows arched with passion'. 'She was an ideal choice for the leading role in CND: intelligent, smart and good-looking,' admitted her future antagonist, Michael Heseltine. 'If anyone was to articulate effectively the inherent fears which so many share of the menace of nuclear devastation, she was the person to do it.'[28]

Under Ruddock, CND reached its all-time peak. Because the organization was so decentralized, nobody ever knew exactly how many people joined in the early 1980s. National membership was around 50,000 in late 1982, but local membership may have reached half a million. The list of affiliated peace groups was endless, from Scientists Against Nuclear Arms to Babies Against the Bomb. There were women's groups and professional groups, Communists and Quakers, environmentalists and pacifists. The movement was 'now so diverse and widespread', remarked *The Times*, 'that it can scarcely be called by any single name such as "the peace movement"'. Even the Church of England was flirting with unilateralism. In the autumn of 1982, a working party produced a report, *The Church and the Bomb*, urging Britain to renounce nuclear weapons. The *Church Times* called it a 'first-class essay in moral theology'; the experts at the *Daily Express* considered it 'mushy theological waffle'. The General Synod sided with the *Express*, and rejected it by a clear majority.[29]

Although Cruise and Reagan were major factors in CND's success, there was a strong anti-Thatcher element, too. These were years of tremendous enthusiasm on the left, years of marching and joining, singing and protesting. Nuclear disarmament was the fashionable cause of the day, just as environmentalism had been the cause of the early 1970s. And, at first, support seemed so resilient that not even the Falklands War could dent it. When CND held its next London rally on 6 June 1982, British troops were fighting their way towards Port Stanley. Yet even the Conservatives' mole in the crowds, Peter Shipley, was impressed by the turnout, which he put at about 150,000 people. The crowd, he reported, was dominated by people who already belonged to peace groups, the 'extreme left', religious groups, environmentalists and 'miscellaneous gay, feminists and punks'. There was a 'rather folksy, relaxed atmosphere . . . the archetypal *Guardian* reading parents eating their nut cutlet picnics under the trees while the children watched a Punch (President Reagan) and Judy (Mrs Thatcher) sideshow.' But trade unionists and ethnic minorities seemed 'noticeably absent . . . CND still seems a very middle-class movement.'[30]

By now CND had drawn so close to the Labour left that, to the untrained eye, they had become practically indistinguishable. In particular, the unilateralist movement had the enthusiastic support of dozens of Labour-controlled local authorities, which had declared themselves 'nuclear-free zones'. The first, in November 1980, was Manchester, which asked the government not to position nuclear weapons inside the city boundaries, launched a public information campaign to spread the gospel of disarmament and refused to take part in civil defence exercises. By the following February there were forty-two nuclear-free zones nationwide, including Liverpool, Bristol and several London boroughs, and a year later the total had reached 150. Even very small councils got in on the act. In March 1982 the parish council in Coppull, a Lancashire village with a population of less than 8,000, declared itself a nuclear-free zone. 'There are no nuclear installations in Coppull', a spokesman said, 'and we don't want any.' If the Pentagon had secretly identified Coppull as the cornerstone of the West's nuclear defences, declared the *Guardian*, 'they had better think again'. They hadn't.[31]

Like many of the controversial initiatives sponsored by left-wing councils in the early 1980s, the nuclear-free zone policy was as much a roar of defiance at Whitehall as a serious attempt to change government policy. It was especially strong in Wales, where it became a totem of resistance to London, uniting the old Labour working classes and middle-class nationalists. When, on 23 February 1982, Clwyd followed seven other councils in declaring itself a nuclear-free zone, campaigners declared Wales the first 'nuclear-free country in Europe'. As the council deliberated, some 400 daffodil-waving demonstrators, including the poet R. S. Thomas and Plaid Cymru's figurehead Gwynfor Evans, were waiting outside. When the news came, they released a thousand daffodil-coloured balloons into the heavens. The former Archdruid of Wales read a proclamation to the crowd, while a team of runners set off with a 'peace torch' to RAF Sealand in the north. On the hilltops that night, giant CND emblems blazed in the darkness. It might have been an empty gesture, but it was terrific theatre.[32]

Were nuclear-free zones more than just a gimmick? As the *Guardian* admitted, there was nothing councils could do to stop the government moving nuclear materials through their areas, or from basing nuclear weapons wherever it liked. British Rail took no notice of nuclear-free zones whatsoever. Even Tyne and Wear's plan to put up signs telling motorists 'You are now entering a nuclear-free zone' was blocked by the Department for Transport. To the zones' supporters, this was beside the point: for the historian Dorothy Thompson, 'the nuclear-free movement is a ray of hope in a darkening situation because it signals a change of attitude'. And the nuclear-free zones did record one significant achievement. When the government arranged a civil defence exercise in the autumn of 1982, more than a hundred local authorities refused to take part, which meant it had to be cancelled. CND celebrated a great victory, but a year later the government introduced regulations compelling councils to update their civil defence plans and comply with any exercises ordered by Whitehall. There would be no repeat of the last fiasco.[33]

By this stage, with Labour having lost ground in May 1982's local elections, the rush to declare nuclear-free zones had abated. In December 1982, Bury's Conservative-controlled borough council became the first local authority in the country to declare itself a *nuclear* zone, because the council was so cross at being identified with Manchester's unilateralism. And the following April, Bradford, previously the first local authority to form a 'peace action group', became the first to reverse its nuclear-free status. A very close vote had been expected, with the Conservatives and Labour deadlocked and the Liberals likely to back the latter. But then a Labour councillor launched into what his own leader described as an 'appalling' attack on the British Army's record in Northern Ireland. The Liberals promptly changed their minds and voted with the Tories, and Bradford's nuclear-free zone was consigned to history.

Where the left held sway, however, the nuclear-free dream survived. In the capital, barely a month went by without some fresh row about the Greater London Council's refusal to support civil defence planning. And in David Blunkett's self-styled Socialist Republic of South Yorkshire, the city council advertised for an administrative officer to 'co-ordinate and develop the council's nuclear free zone policy', with a salary of £9,000 a year (roughly £40,000 today). The winning candidate was 32-year-old Jim Coleman, a former sociology teacher who was working at a centre for unemployed youngsters. By an astonishing coincidence, he was also the voluntary secretary of Sheffield CND and had been a member of the local Communist Party since 1975. To the Conservatives, it was a gift. The leader of the council's Conservative group, Irvine Patnick, claimed that Sheffield was practically a Soviet satellite, while one woman sarcastically told the local *Star* that 'she could sleep soundly now she knew that if missiles were targeted on the city, the council had a man with a big net to catch them'.

But when the press tracked down the man himself, he seemed disappointingly unthreatening. Coleman had spent his first months encouraging local schools to teach peace studies, setting up peace sections in local libraries and organizing a rent-free Peace Shop for an '18-member collective representing local peace groups'. To his evident unease, he had also been looking into the city's civil defence plans, as required under the government's new regulations. Yes, he admitted, there was a council bunker in the basement of the Town Hall. But in the event of a nuclear war, it was unlikely to hold out for long. 'It's a sort of broom cupboard with two Telex machines,' he explained. 'They keep the key over the door.'[34]

There were always people who laughed at CND. The conservative historian John Vincent claimed that with its 'mild religiosity, its belief in the end of the world, its sense of moral monopoly, its zeal in portraying the torments of the damned', the peace movement was basically a cult. It was telling, he thought, that its rallies were billed as 'carnivals', such as a forthcoming Bristol 'beano' that was advertising 'E. P. Thompson, floats, bands, exhibitions, food, discussions, theatre, films, videos, "and much much more"'. Another conservative columnist, Bernard Levin, agreed that CND campaigners seemed to be 'having the most *marvellous* time'. Whenever Bruce Kent came on screen ('sleek, plump, wonderfully self-satisfied'), Levin could almost hear him purring. As for E. P. Thompson, he had 'made an entire new life, clearly stimulating and enjoyable, out of urging military weakness upon the West'. If nuclear weapons vanished overnight, how would he fill his spare time?[35]

For some critics, however, CND was no laughing matter. For the *Express*'s George Gale, its supporters wanted to 'make war inevitable by making Soviet victory certain'. 'Each of those who wear the CND badge', he wrote, 'might as well put on the uniform of a soldier in the Red Army.' The CND emblem was a 'cross of shame', agreed the Conservative MP George Gardiner, for whom the campaign's rallies were an 'orgy of anti-Americanism' orchestrated by the 'tyrants and terrorists' in the Kremlin. 'A sick charade, masterminded from Moscow', agreed his colleague Winston Churchill, whose grandfather would surely have said much the same. Even *The Times* accused CND of being suffused with the 'spirit of appeasement of Soviet power and propitiation of any Marxist policy'. It was not some harmless association of well-meaning weirdos. It was a 'left-wing front . . . sprinkled with Communists and ex-Communists in key positions'.[36]

On the face of it, all this might sound paranoid. Yet when Bruce Kent described the Communist Party of Great Britain as CND's 'partners in peace', he was asking for trouble. And the official history of MI5 shows that the security service took allegations of Communist infiltration very seriously. A few years earlier, Communist Party members had occupied more than half of the seats on CND's national executive, and MI5 believed that plenty of Communists and Trotskyists had flooded into the organization in the early 1980s. Indeed, peace campaigners often complained that CND committees were 'packed with pro-Soviet members of the Communist Party', as one woman from the Greenham Common peace camp put it. But the Communists never had things all their own way. The Soviet defector Oleg Gordievsky reported that, although the KGB regarded the peace movement as 'natural allies', it never secured the influence it wanted. In particular, the KGB was very suspicious of Thompson and Ruddock, who were far too independent-minded for Moscow's taste, and they were frankly baffled by the women who camped outside the American base on Greenham Common.[37]

The East German secret police, though, had at least one agent on CND's national committee. Professor Vic Allen, a sociologist at Leeds and the official historian of the National Union of Mineworkers, was also an informant for the Stasi. Since he was an outspoken Communist, few of his colleagues were very surprised. What did surprise them, though, was the revelation many years later that his CND comrade Harry Newton, a lecturer in trade union law and former treasurer of the Institute for Workers' Control, was actually an agent for MI5. According to the whistle-blower Cathy Massiter, Newton had been working for the security service for decades. While appearing to be somewhere to the left of Pol Pot, he was secretly reporting on CND meetings and even warned his handlers that Bruce Kent was a 'crypto-communist'. But since Newton had seemed so devoted to the proletarian revolution, most of his friends refused to believe it. There could have been no greater tribute to his professional skill.[38]

For her part, Mrs Thatcher always suspected that the peace movement was a front for the Kremlin. After one seminar with a group of experts on the Communist bloc, she scribbled that the Soviet Union was 'genuinely concerned' about the deployment of Cruise and had launched a 'massive propaganda campaign' to stop it. The obvious problem was that 'peace' sounded much more attractive than 'deterrence', especially to younger audiences. In the summer of 1982, Conservative Central Office asked local activists to report on the state of public opinion. Many thought the government was losing the battle for hearts and minds, warning that 'membership of CND now included professionals, teachers and church activists as well as the more usual "long haired brigade"'. Local Tories were particularly worried that CND was infiltrating schools, complaining that in some areas 'teachers had been giving out badges to the children and discussions had been held on the subject during class'. In some schools, 'the "brainwashing" was so effective that when debates had been arranged, difficulty had been found in getting children to speak on behalf of multilateral disarmament'. And on top of that, every area reported that clergymen were very active in the local peace movement. The Church of England, they complained, was turning into CND at prayer.[39]

Yet CND never won over the silent majority. Many people were worried about a nuclear war, but they also wanted to be well defended. They were wary of *individual* weapons projects: a poll in November 1982 found that six out of ten people were opposed to both Cruise and Trident. Yet they were sceptical about unilateral disarmament and downright hostile to cutting defence spending. That autumn another poll found that just one in five people supported defence cuts, while almost a third thought defence spending should be higher. Only 31 per cent thought Britain should scrap all its nuclear weapons; by contrast, 78 per cent of Conservatives, 55 per cent of Labour voters and 64 per cent of SDP–Liberal Alliance voters thought Britain's deterrent should be maintained or even improved. And as time went on and the Third World War failed to materialize, the air leaked out of CND's balloon. As early as May 1983, another survey found that support for unilateral disarmament had collapsed to just 16 per cent, down by half since 1981. By now nine out of ten Tories, six out of ten Labour voters and eight out of ten Alliance voters were opposed to scrapping the deterrent.[40]

From CND's perspective, all this made for a very disappointing picture. Its cause could hardly have been more fashionable. Yet after all the rallies and the concerts, it had conspicuously failed to persuade the great majority of the British public. Perhaps it should have spent less time singing and more time trying to win over the conservative voters of Middle England, many of whom were sympathetic to the message but suspicious of the messenger. 'I believe that disarmament will never happen,' said Duran Duran's lead singer Simon Le Bon. 'I think there's a lot of other facets of CND which I wouldn't like to associate myself with. They're not just involved in getting rid of nuclear weapons, they bring party politics into the issues which they shouldn't do.' The former *Carry On* stalwart Kenneth Williams agreed completely. He was no fan of 'Atomic Bombs', which were 'useless'. But he had absolutely no time for the 'chanting weirdies of CND'. A successful social movement might have got away with losing one of Simon Le Bon and Kenneth Williams. But surely not both.[41]

What, then, did most people really think about the prospect of war? Did they lie awake at night, tormented by thoughts of life in a nuclear winter? Were they busy digging shelters and stockpiling bandages?

Although generalizations are risky, all the polls show that fears of nuclear war, particularly among people in their teens and early twenties, were far higher than they had been ten years earlier. Their parents, who had seen the world survive the crises over Berlin and Cuba, were more likely to be sanguine. But a survey of youngsters in Croydon and Newcastle in the autumn of 1981 found that anxieties about nuclear war had risen considerably. Two years earlier, only 8 per cent of under-25s had thought a nuclear war in their lifetime was 'very likely', and 21 per cent 'fairly likely'. Now those figures were 19 per cent and 32 per cent, which suggests that one in two British youngsters expected to see a nuclear exchange. Two years later, another survey of more than 400 teenagers for the *TV Times* found that at least half expected to see a Third World War before they died. And even if Doomsday did not come tomorrow, few doubted that it would come eventually: seven out of ten agreed that nuclear war was 'inevitable one day'.[42]

For one industry the prospect of Armageddon was very good news. By the summer of 1980, reported the *New Scientist*, there were already 300 small businesses selling fallout-shelter kits, radiation suits and Geiger counters. Customers could expect to pay £200 for a made-to-measure PVC suit and £50 for a child's version, as well as another £120 for a 'nuclear cot for babies'. CND's official historians saw their popularity as a sign that 'widespread apprehension' was much greater than it had been twenty years earlier. But perhaps preparing for Armageddon was just another kind of consumerism. In 1981 the *Daily Mail* even reported on the Ideal Nuclear Shelter Exhibition, held in North Yorkshire. The 'mini-prefabs' on display fell sadly short of the futuristic visions on show in the same paper's Ideal Home Exhibition; still, for people with £8,000 to burn, there were worse ways to spend your money. 'YOU CAN SURVIVE and it will be worth surviving,' read one brochure. 'Remember Hiroshima? It's now a bustling city.'[43]

In Balcombe, Sussex, one anxious homeowner built a seventy-man shelter in his back garden, complete with escape hatches, a decontamination chamber, two diesel engines, two toilets, a kitchen and a quadrophonic sound system. John Emin had thought of everything, even widening the stairs so that stretcher-bearers could pass. Initially he advertised places at £3,000 a head, but after 240 applications in the first few days he doubled the price. He picked candidates carefully: one advert in the *British Medical Journal* attracted two anaesthetists, several surgeons and a neurologist, and he also wanted people with 'mechanical, agricultural and horticultural skills'. The problem, though, was his neighbours, for whom Mr Emin had reserved only six places. One man openly told him that if war broke out, 'he would be prepared to get a gun and kill to gain entrance to the shelter'. There is perhaps a case that Mr Emin should have spent less time building up his defences against the Red Army and more time pursuing détente with the people of Balcombe. But he had no regrets. A reporter asked if he really thought he would need his shelter. 'Yes, no argument,' he said.[44]

But since most people showed no interest in building their own shelters,

how much did they *really* care about a Third World War? Clearly some
cared a lot, and genuinely lay awake at night thinking about it. But there
is no getting away from the fact that, when Gallup's monthly survey asked
people to name the most urgent problem facing the country, the total
choosing 'defence' or 'international affairs' was usually between 1 and 2
per cent. Writing in *The Times*, Bernard Levin had a lot of fun with the
idea that Britain was 'drowning in terror and despair'. If the peace campaigners were to be believed, he wrote:

> The shadow cast by the bomb is so dark and sinister that it disturbs the
> mind, paralyses the will, deadens the feelings and leads inevitably to
> aimlessness, social unrest and a constant increase in the incidence of crime,
> divorce, unemployment and *herpes*. The nation, obsessed by its impending
> fate, is mindful every time it puts its Sunday leg of lamb in the oven that it
> may shortly be badly overcooked itself. Conversation deals with nothing
> else, and the unbroken silence of an evening in every pub in the land, as
> unhappy patrons stare into their glasses and think upon their end, bears
> eloquent witness to the way in which thoughts of nuclear annihilation now
> occupy attention to the exclusion of all other subjects, from the ballet to
> the football pools.

In reality, Levin said, 'nobody actually spends time worrying, or even
thinking about it'. Having discussed the prospect of nuclear war with
people of 'every persuasion', he had never met anybody who showed any
sign that 'his or her life is actually affected by it, that any sleep is lost or
meal pushed away untouched'.

The women who had been camping outside the base at Greenham
Common since September 1981 might have had something to say about
that. Yet Levin was surely right to suggest that most people regarded a
Third World War as they regarded the possibility of a car accident: horrible, certainly, and best avoided, but not something that should distract
you from putting out the bins. Even the teenagers who claimed to be worried sick about nuclear war clearly had no problem getting on with the
rest of their lives. In this respect, as so often, Adrian Mole was typical. 'I
keep having nightmares about the bomb,' Sue Townsend's teenage diarist
writes on 6 January 1982. 'I hope it isn't dropped before I get my GCE
results . . . I wouldn't like to die an unqualified virgin.' The next day,
however, his mind turns to more urgent issues: 'Nigel came round to look
at my racing bike . . .' There, surely, spoke the voice of the nation.[45]

# PART THREE

# Onward! Onward!

# 17

# The Gang's on Its Way!

*It may seem ludicrous to imagine that hundreds of thousands –
even millions – of Conservative voters will flock to the drab little
banner offered by four tipsy-looking claret-guzzlers as they stand
giggling in the sun outside Dr Owen's irritating little house in
Limehouse, but I can see it happening.*

Auberon Waugh, *Spectator*, 7 February 1981

*[Rupert] Murdoch thinks their whole operation is a 'lot of crap'* . . .
*Says afterwards that his main impression was of four people who
hated each other's guts. He has got it quite wrong.*

The Gang of Four's lunch at *The Times*,
20 March 1981, in Ion Trewin (ed.),
*The Hugo Young Papers: Thirty Years of
British Politics* (2008)

The founding document of the Social Democratic Party was never meant
to be called the Limehouse Declaration. Originally, Shirley Williams, Bill
Rodgers and David Owen had planned to meet at Roy Jenkins's country
house in Oxfordshire after Labour's Wembley conference. There they
intended to put the finishing touches to a statement of principles and call
for recruits to a new party. But, in a hint of the tensions to come, the plan
went awry. A week earlier, the *Observer* had run a front-page report that
Jenkins was expecting the Gang of Three for a 'summit meeting at his
Oxfordshire home', with a picture of the great man standing imperiously
on his lawn, like a country squire waiting to receive a delegation from the
village. The infuriated Williams promptly refused to go, so they convened
at Bill Rodgers's house in Kentish Town, north London, instead. For their
meeting on Sunday 25th, they chose a new venue: David Owen's Georgian
terraced house in Narrow Street, Limehouse, overlooking the Thames in
east London.[1]

Limehouse was not a bad place to launch a breakaway from an ailing Victorian institution. For one thing, they were literally across the street from the Brightlingsea Buildings, where Clement Attlee had lived as an idealistic young man in 1912. Ten years later, Attlee had become the local MP, representing the area in Parliament until 1950. Since then, however, Limehouse had seen wrenching social and economic change. Attlee's Limehouse had been the bustling heart of the capital's docklands, a place associated with poverty, crime and disease, but also with industry, immigration and Empire. But by 1965, when Owen bought his house at 78 Narrow Street for some £3,000, Limehouse was in deep decline. At first he enjoyed gazing out across the Thames 'with the ships flashing past . . . activity and life everywhere'. But the docks closed, the ships disappeared and the life began to fade. In 1969 Limehouse Basin, far too small to handle the new container ships, closed to commercial traffic. The river rolled imperturbably on, the workers moved out, the warehouses fell silent. By the time Jenkins, Williams and Rodgers arrived in Narrow Street, Limehouse had become an object lesson in the costs of economic change.[2]

Now, as the press waited outside, the Gang of Four made the last additions to a document that would, they hoped, herald a national revival. At last, as the sun was beginning to dip, they emerged into the pale winter light. As they strolled self-consciously towards the river, the photographers snapping away, they cut oddly revealing figures, as if dressed by a costume designer with a keen eye for character. In the centre of the picture was Jenkins, round and sleek in his dark suit, as befitted a man who could never quite get over the fact that he was not already Prime Minister. On the right, sporting a lighter check suit and a slightly embarrassed grin, was the saturnine Owen. On the left was Rodgers, the perennial fourth man, who had declined to change out of his Marks & Spencer's jumper and looked as if he had just got back from the garden centre. And sandwiched between him and Jenkins was Shirley Williams, beaming delightedly for the cameras. She had borrowed a baggy shirt from Owen's wife Debbie, she wrote later, because 'my appearance at that moment was not compatible with a serious attempt to found a new political party'. What on earth had she been wearing?[3]

The next day's papers all led with their statement announcing the formation of a Council for Social Democracy, the decisive step towards a breakaway party. Yet to twenty-first-century eyes the Limehouse Declaration looks almost disappointingly uncontroversial. Like many political statements of the age, it began with the assumption of national decline, warning that 'the country cannot be saved without changing the sterile and rigid framework into which the British political system has increasingly fallen in the last two decades'. As Hugo Young noted, the Gang of Four clearly shared Mrs Thatcher's 'apocalyptic vision of the state of the country', but their prescriptions were much vaguer than hers. They were against extremism, poverty and inequality. They were for better services and a 'competitive economy with a fair distribution of rewards', which reminded some people of West Germany's Social Democrats. They liked the thought of 'radical change', but they also wanted 'greater stability of direction'. And they wanted a more 'self-confident' and 'outward-looking' Britain, committed to NATO and the European Community, not one that was 'isolationist, xenophobic or neutralist'.[4]

None of this was exactly radical. Scores of Labour and Conservative MPs, as well as millions of voters, would have agreed with almost every word. The Gang of Four did not spell out how they would handle inflation, nor how they would deal with mass unemployment. There were hints of the future, most obviously the pledge to 'create an open, classless and more equal society, one which rejects ugly prejudices based upon sex, race or religion'. But to many readers, the Declaration seemed a lament for the lost certainties of the 1960s: the mixed economy, the welfare state, the Atlantic alliance, the optimistic dream of European harmony. Tellingly, one early draft had talked of reviving 'the party of Attlee and Gaitskell'. But many young men and women who would cast their first votes at the next election had been born after Gaitskell's death, while it was thirty years since Attlee had sat in Number 10. No wonder the Social Democrats' critics joked that they wanted a 'better yesterday'.[5]

One other thing was very striking. The Limehouse Declaration mentioned the Labour Party several times, including in the very first sentence ('The calamitous outcome of the Labour Party Wembley conference demands a new start in British politics'). But the word 'Thatcher' never appeared at all. Not once did the Gang of Four mention her government, her policies or the need to beat her in an election. Owen later told Charles Moore that when they were devising their plans, she never even came up. To people like Jenkins and Williams, it was self-evident that, having been foolish enough to elect somebody so strident, aggressive and narrow-minded, the British people would not make the same mistake again. 'Roy and Shirley and Bill thought Mrs Thatcher was an aberration', Owen said, 'and they were looking ahead to the next bit. They assumed that they would come through the middle when Thatcherism failed.'[6]

Not everybody was carried away by the Limehouse Declaration. The *Spectator*'s Geoffrey Wheatcroft was struck by its 'unimaginative dreariness', and thought there was 'something irredeemably second-rate about the Gang'. But other people saw it differently. On Monday morning every paper put the Declaration on its front page, and within a week the Council for Social Democracy had attracted thousands of letters of support. Even the Conservative press were reasonably kind. 'THE GANG'S ON ITS WAY!' exulted the *Express*, which welcomed a 'decent, democratic alternative to the Tories' and claimed to wish the new party well.[7]

What did ordinary people think? *The Times* sent a reporter to Stevenage, which had rejected Shirley Williams in 1979. Now three out of every four people canvassed by the paper said they would consider voting for a new party. 'I would follow Shirley Williams to Timbuctoo,' said Wendy Skiggins, a 23-year-old housewife who had voted Labour in 1979, 'and I would probably vote for the social democrats even if she is not the leader. The party offers something new, away from the old extremes.' 'I could not vote for Michael Foot,' agreed Peter Thomas, a local businessman who had voted Conservative, 'but Roy Jenkins or Mrs Williams? Maybe, if the Tories do not stop cutting our throats.'

At a working men's club near Southampton docks, meanwhile, there was plenty of sympathy for the Gang of Four. The 74-year-old James Flannery, a retired van driver, had voted Labour all his life, but had already decided to switch to the Social Democrats. 'All the others are Marxists – Benn, Foot,' he said. 'The true Labour crowd are breaking away. The sooner they go in with [the Liberal leader David] Steel and form a good, solid party we will get rid of Maggie.' 'They could be for the working bloke,' agreed Brian Short, a 24-year-old lorry driver, while an older plant operator, who gave his name as Mr Newton, said he and his wife had already decided to vote for 'a new social democrat party, as they will have the new ideas, and we hope be more for the working class than Labour is'. Indeed, almost everybody in the club agreed that the old Labour Party had disappeared and that the Gang of Four were the only realistic alternatives to Mrs Thatcher. 'I have always voted Labour,' said Ray Hoskins, a scaffolder. 'But I am not interested in communism. And that is the way the Labour Party is going.'

Yet the picture was not entirely rosy. In Birmingham, bruised and battered by the crisis of manufacturing, there seemed much less enthusiasm for the new party. Workers at the engineering firm GKN told *The Times*'s future editor John Witherow that they were still loyal to Labour, 'the party for the working man'. The Social Democrats, one said, would be a 'nine day wonder, a protest vote'. But in Perry Barr, which had voted Labour in 1979, Witherow found one possible Social Democrat voter, a butcher who had opted for the Liberals in the last election. He would vote for the Gang of Four, he said – as long as they introduced 'conscription for the unemployed and the return of hanging'. He was not really Roy Jenkins's kind of person.[8]

While most of the Gang of Four's old comrades seethed at their breach of tribal loyalty, at least one welcomed the chance to draw a firm line between the elect and the fallen. On Monday afternoon, still buoyant after the left's victory at the shambolic Wembley conference, Tony Benn produced a motion for the party's National Executive, demanding that all Labour candidates swear an oath, 'wholeheartedly and without reservation', to the party and its left-wing manifesto. As almost anybody could have foreseen, most of Benn's fellow MPs were outraged, while the newspapers thought his proposed 'loyalty test' smacked of 'the Thought Police in Orwell's "1984"', as the *Express* put it. The Gang of Four could scarcely have wished for a better send-off.[9]

For Michael Foot, whose leadership was rapidly descending into chaos, it seemed scarcely credible that Benn had contrived to turn the Gang of Four's apostasy into yet another story about himself. But when he called Benn in for a dressing-down, the latter was utterly unapologetic. 'Why do we need it?' Foot asked, 'angry and red-faced'. 'Because the Social Democrats are saying they're going to leave,' Benn replied, before accusing his leader of being 'soft on the right'. The exchange soon degenerated into a row about whether Benn and his allies on the National Executive were running a secret 'left caucus'. Benn denied it. 'You're a bloody liar,' Foot said. 'So I just walked out,' Benn wrote. 'I am not being called a liar by anybody. I was pretty steamed up. So I went back to the left group . . . and told them what had happened.' Almost unbelievably, he seemed not to notice the irony.[10]

Meanwhile, the Gang of Four's bandwagon rolled on. On 5 February they took out a full-page advertisement in the *Guardian*, carrying the names of 100 vaguely prominent backers. The advert described them as a 'cross-section of people who have expressed their support', but as one observer remarked, it looked more like a list of their dinner-party guests. Almost half had previously been involved with the Labour Party, while thirteen had been Labour MPs, including the former deputy leader George Brown and the former Cabinet ministers Jack Diamond, Kenneth Robinson and Edmund Dell. Even more revealingly, a quarter were academics, including the historian Lord Bullock, the biographer Philip Williams, the chemist Sir Fred Dainton, the physicist Lord Flowers and the economists James Meade and Frank Hahn. Even the token celebrities – the rabbi Julia Neuberger, the opera singer Sir Geraint Evans, the presenter and musician Steve Race – were celebrities of a pretty highbrow kind.[11]

Benn thought the advert a roll call of 'middle-class' traitors and complained that the BBC ('the voice of Shirley Williams and Roy Jenkins') had given it far too much coverage. And some *Guardian* readers took it very badly. One pointed out that the list contained not one ordinary 'railway worker, bus driver, factory worker, electrician, plumber . . . or one out of the three million-plus unemployed'; another lamented that only fourteen were women; a third wondered if you had to be an 'actress, rabbi, historian, company director, ageing egotist, failed politician or biographer of Gaitskell' to join the Social Democrats. Yet as a public relations coup it was a triumph, creating the impression of a groundswell of support among the well educated and well connected. Within just a week, the Gang had received 8,000 letters, two-thirds of which contained money, and had a war chest of some £25,000. Within a month the mailbag had swollen to 80,000 letters and the bank balance to £175,000. Most of the money came from small individual donations; only thirty people gave more than £500 (the equivalent of almost £3,000 today), and only three gave more than £10,000. In this respect, the Social Democrats really could claim to be a grass-roots organization.[12]

In Westminster the new party was rapidly taking shape. Rodgers had already resigned from the Shadow Cabinet, but Williams did not leave Labour's National Executive until 9 February, declaring that 'the party I loved and worked for over so many years no longer exists'. The moderate John Golding told the press she was leaving because her 'gentle upbringing' had left her unable to 'stand the rough and tumble like those of us who are used to scrapping in working class organisations'. The next day's *Times*, meanwhile, called Williams a 'somewhat indecisive woman, of middling intellectual attainments, and mistaken views'. Yet the paper also thought she was 'often courageous, always human and always kind' and was 'quite likely' to become Prime Minister within a few years. At this stage, the formal launch of the new party was still weeks away. Yet already *The Times* thought that, in alliance with the Liberals, the Social Democrats could take power at the next election with 'about the same overall majority as the Labour Party had in 1945'.[13]

Events were now moving breathlessly fast. At midnight on 20 February the first four additional defectors, the MPs Ian Wrigglesworth, Tom Ellis, Richard Crawshaw and Tom Bradley, confirmed that they were leaving the Labour Party. Within a few weeks the total membership had risen to fourteen, who formed the first parliamentary committee of the Social Democratic Party. They did give some thought to alternative names: the Radicals, Progressive Labour, the Democrats, even the New Labour Party. But since the press had been calling them the Social Democrats for months, the label stuck. And for the founders, any nerves had been banished by an almost euphoric sense of relief. Jenkins remembered it as a period of 'great exhilaration', when they felt a 'mixture of heady excitement and slight apprehension that we were dicing with the unknown, sailing an uncharted sea'. Williams, meanwhile, likened it to the experience of rafting down the Colorado River. 'As I approached the rapids,' she wrote, 'I was gripped by a sense of excitement linked to an awareness of being no longer in control . . . I didn't know whether or not we were going to come through. It was too late to turn back, and therefore pointless to worry.'[14]

Yet it was not all sweetness and light. For many of those who jumped ship to the Social Democrats, the experience fell somewhere between an acrimonious divorce and an existential crisis. 'Being a member of a political party is not like being a member of a golf or tennis club,' wrote Owen. 'Membership carries with it tremendous emotional overtones, particularly in the Labour Party.' He knew he would attract flak from party workers back in Plymouth, for whom leaving Labour 'would be like amputating a limb'. Rodgers, too, did not escape without recriminations. At one point, three of his closest Commons associates visited his house to beg him to think again. He did not take it well, accusing his friend Giles Radice of being one of 'those tedious middle-class socialists who always feel guilty about the working classes'. 'It's all very well for you,' Rodgers said emotionally, 'you're a rich man and a public schoolboy.' At that, Ken Weetch, who had worked under Rodgers at the Department of Transport, buried his head in his hands. 'I can't believe this is happening,' he said desperately.[15]

Among the herbivorous classes who usually voted Labour, the defection of the Gang of Four felt like the beginning of a nightmarish family feud. The Fabian Society lost a thousand people within a year, almost a third of its entire membership. The *Guardian*'s columnist Polly Toynbee, then 34, was among the new party's first recruits and served on its steering committee. But even decades later she remembered the 'sheer vitriol' of the abuse from the left, and the 'venomous' rift within the newspaper's office. When she and her SDP-supporting husband, the columnist Peter Jenkins, came into the canteen, some colleagues literally picked up their plates and moved away, so as not to be contaminated. Even the world of Adrian Mole was not immune from the aftershocks. 'Pandora's parents have had a massive row,' he records in January 1982. 'They are sleeping in separate bedrooms. Pandora's mother has joined the SDP and Pandora's father is staying loyal to the Labour Party.' Fortunately, 'Pandora is a Liberal, so she gets on all right with them both.'[16]

The SDP's critics often accused them of being opportunists, even careerists. Roy Hattersley, for example, claimed they had left for the SDP

because 'they believed that they would do better in the new party and then
dressed up self-interest to look like principle'. But since they were joining
a party that stood far *less* chance of winning power, that was obviously
nonsense. Most had left reluctantly, after months of soul-searching. Years
later, some told the party's historians Ivor Crewe and Anthony King that
they had slept badly, drunk too much, quarrelled with their families and
even suffered from stress-related illness. 'I was tired of living a lie,' one
MP said. 'I couldn't go on week after week defending the indefensible.' 'I
just didn't want to go on seeming to stand for policies that I didn't believe
in,' said another. 'The choice in the end', said a third, 'was between ten
years in which I kept my head down and crept into the division lobbies
but didn't really respect myself and three glorious years – short, maybe,
but glorious.'[17]

In hindsight, the remarkable thing is how few Labour MPs followed
their example. Crewe and King estimate that in 1981 there were about 120
moderate Labour MPs in the House of Commons, most of whom were
deeply unhappy with the triumph of the activist left. Yet only twenty-eight
jumped ship, which means that more than three-quarters stayed put. What
was more, none of the Gang of Four's recruits was remotely close to being
a household name. How many people had heard of Ronald Brown, James
Dunn, David Ginsburg or Eric Ogden? If the SDP had managed to recruit
one or two former Cabinet heavyweights, such as Denis Healey or Roy
Hattersley, its history might have been different. But Healey and Hattersley
had too much to lose by leaving the Labour Party. With time, they told
themselves, the pendulum would swing back their way.

For lesser-known MPs, there was no single reason why they left. It is
not true that the split was all about Europe. Some of the most pro-
European MPs stayed in the Labour Party, while not all the defectors were
especially enthusiastic about Brussels. Nor was the split all about the
threat of deselection. Many of the defectors got on reasonably well with
their activists, although MPs with very supportive local parties were less
likely to break away. The SDP's recruiters thought working-class MPs,
terrified of losing their salaries, were less likely to defect. But Crewe and
King's research suggests that the really decisive factor was an individual
MP's relationship with the intensely tribal Labour movement: its community, its hymns and its history. An MP from a Labour family, who had
joined a trade union and served as a local councillor, was far less likely
to defect than one who had joined at university and spent years working
outside politics. For Owen, leaving was a wrench, but not the end of the
world. But for Hattersley, born and brought up in Sheffield's Labour Party,
it was literally unimaginable.[18]

One early disagreement was whether the defectors should resign their seats and force by-elections. Owen, buoyed by polls showing that he would annihilate the opposition in Plymouth Devonport, was all for it. A string of victories, he thought, would give them priceless legitimacy in the Commons and demonstrate their fighting spirit to the country. But Rodgers thought the practicalities were against them. It would, he pointed out, make it harder to attract defectors if they risked losing their seat in a by-election. What was more, the Labour whips would almost certainly schedule them in 'dribs and drabs' to puncture any momentum. As Rodgers recalled, 'we would be picked off one by one, probably starting with those MPs most vulnerable to defeat. I doubted whether even half of us would survive, and the morale of the party would be severely damaged.' But he was probably being too pessimistic. With the tide running so heavily in their favour, the defectors might well have retained most, if not all, of their seats. That would have given them a colossal morale boost, as well as much greater local traction two years later. As it was, they opened themselves up to Labour criticisms that they lacked the courage to face the voters. Of the fourteen original SDP MPs, just four survived the 1983 general election.[19]

The SDP's other obvious mistake was that it made no serious effort to attract Conservatives. On 16 March, during a debate on the Budget, Christopher Brocklebank-Fowler, the MP for North West Norfolk, suddenly announced that he was resigning the Conservative whip, crossed the floor and sat down with the Social Democrats. But where he led, nobody followed. Part of the problem was that Williams, Owen and Rodgers had always envisaged the SDP as a centre-left party, and never bothered to appeal to MPs from the other side of the aisle. Owen, for example, worried that an influx of Tory patricians would dilute their radicalism, though he later regretted not trying harder. By contrast, Roy Jenkins recalled that some Conservatives promised him that 'they were definitely coming. It was only a matter of choosing the time.' But the time never came. Most were in safe seats; if they walked away, they would lose careers and incomes as well as friends and status. If a relatively big name such as Sir Ian Gilmour had led the way, things might have been different. But the fact that somebody as semi-detached as Gilmour stayed put spoke volumes about the resilience of the old loyalties. Perhaps the fact that Jenkins was sleeping with Gilmour's wife had something to do with it.[20]

At 9 a.m. on Thursday 26 March, the Gang of Four took their places on the platform for the official launch of the Social Democratic Party. The venue was the Connaught Rooms on Great Queen Street: grandly old-fashioned, all cream and chandeliers. In an unlikely coincidence, it was just a few doors down from the Blitz club, where Spandau Ballet had made their first public appearance fifteen months earlier. An imaginative journalist could have had some fun with the fact that both organizations saw themselves as breaking with the pessimism of the 1970s, both sold themselves as a blast of fresh air, both placed a heavy emphasis on style and image, and both were decried by their critics as media-driven fantasies. But in the spring of 1981 few political commentators were connoisseurs of the latest pop music. As for the New Romantics, they had mixed feelings about their political counterparts. 'What kind of things annoy you?' an interviewer for *The Face* asked the Human League's Phil Oakey. 'People that vote for the SDP,' Oakey said, before correcting himself: 'But I don't know why that's so bad on reflection; if politics has got to be showbusiness you might as well give it to competent showbiz people like David Owen.'[21]

In good New Romantic style, the most memorable thing about the launch of the SDP was how it looked. 'We were out to show that we were a bright, modern, professional party,' remembered Owen, 'and proud of it.' The key figure was the pugnacious Newcastle MP Mike Thomas, who had a background in market research and had thought hard about how they should present themselves. It was Thomas who dreamed up their logo, based on the three letters SDP with a patriotic red-white-and-blue colour scheme. This, he explained, 'would touch on a national desire to pull Britain up by the bootstraps that people really do feel in the present economic mess'. The designer Dick Negus, best known for his work with British Airways, was credited with the finished product. But the final touch came from Rodgers's wife Silvia, who suggested putting a thick line under the three letters to make them stand out.

Purely as a spectacle, the launch could scarcely have been more successful. Nothing had been left to chance: even the publicity had been arranged by a City public relations firm, with a team of twenty working full time for a fortnight. Owen recalled an 'infectious mood of excitement and bustle', while Rodgers had never seen so many reporters and camera crews 'from most of Western Europe, the United States, the Commonwealth and the rest of the world, some 500 people in all'. On the ITN lunchtime news, all but two minutes were devoted to the SDP, while Mike Thomas estimated that they attracted at least £15 million worth of free coverage. And in a first for a British political party, people could join simply by ringing a helpline and handing over their credit card number, which seemed a breathtaking innovation. 'I lost my prejudice against plastic money', wrote Owen, 'and got my own credit card for the first time.'[22]

The day did not end there. As soon as the Gang of Four left the stage, they were whisked off by air, rail and road around the country, making individual appearances at Edinburgh, Cardiff, Birmingham, Leeds, Manchester, Southampton, Norwich and Plymouth. But not even they had envisaged how popular their appearances would be. In Norwich some sixty people were turned away from a Rodgers press conference, while Owen gave an impromptu speech on the steps of Southampton's Civic Hall to several dozen people who had failed to get in. Only once did he betray a hint of tiredness, when a woman berated him about the SDP's failure to publish a manifesto. It was up to the members to decide the new party's policies, he said. 'We are not going to spoon-feed them . . . Look, love, if you want a manifesto, go and join one of the other parties.'[23]

Even without a manifesto, the momentum was running in their favour. As the political scientist Ivor Crewe had argued just before the SDP's launch, the prospects for a third-party breakthrough were 'better than at any time since the present two-party system was formed in the 1920s'. The average of seven polls since the Limehouse Declaration gave Labour 31 per cent, the Tories 27 per cent, the SDP 26 per cent and the Liberals 14 per cent. Another survey for the *Observer* painted an even more sensational picture. This time it put an alliance on 46 per cent, which would mean an electoral landslide. Amazingly, even if the SDP stood on their own, they would *still* finish first, with 35 per cent to Labour's 29, the Tories' 27 and the Liberals' 7 per cent. Yet as the paper's commentator Anthony King noted, there was a potential time bomb in the small print. When Gallup asked people if they felt 'very close' to their preferred party, SDP supporters were the softest of all. Support was 'widespread, but far from solid. A lot of it could still evaporate.'[24]

In many respects the Social Democrats were always fighting an uphill struggle. Despite all the hype, they had no constitution, no leader, no policies and no voters. As one early account puts it, they 'had to run from the very start, just to keep up with events'. And although their critics painted them as the political equivalent of an advertising agency, all slick sound-bites and fancy logos, their hastily improvised machine often struggled to cope. Their policymaking got bogged down in endless sub-committees; hundreds of unopened letters piled up in mailbags; even their pioneering computer system, purchased from the Midland Bank, was incapable of sorting the list of party members into regions. Later, some writers saw their marketing efforts – balloons, T-shirts, tea towels, even a signed mock-antique copy of the Limehouse Declaration – as proof that they had sold out to the gospel of commercialism. What they really reflected, though, was how desperately the SDP missed Labour's union funding. In any case, the merchandising drive was a complete flop. Their chief marketing man left after just seven months, and the total profits came to just £14,509.[25]

Yet at first things went better than the Gang of Four had dreamed. Within ten days of the Connaught Rooms launch, they had 43,566 paid-up members and more than £500,000. More importantly, they had that most precious political commodity, momentum. With Tony Benn having challenged Denis Healey for the Labour deputy leadership, their old party was tearing itself apart, while the government appeared to be staggering from one economic calamity to the next. By contrast, in the words of the SDP's historians, the new party enjoyed an image of 'brightness, modernity and efficiency', offering a 'break with the past' and 'high hopes for the future'. And as a result, their polling remained spectacularly good. By the autumn of 1981, the combined SDP–Liberal average had reached 42 per cent, which would give them a crushing majority in the House of Commons. Never had any new party come so far, so fast.[26]

For the Gang of Four these felt like days of heaven. When, on 20 March, they had lunch at *The Times*, Hugo Young found them 'very buoyant', with the 'serenity of people who think they've done the right thing' as well as a palpable 'excitement at having got the show on the road so fast and well'. Every week seemed to bring another MP, a few more local councillors, more veteran activists, more fresh-faced members. For Rodgers, the sense of relief was 'altogether exhilarating'. A year ago they had been talking about winning a handful of seats. Now they were 'talking seriously amongst ourselves of forming the next government or, in more sober moments, of holding the balance of power'. Owen, too, felt 'free and unfettered' for the first time in months, revelling in the 'immense fun' of starting something new. And among their sympathizers there was a thrilling sense of expectation. After years of winter gloom, said an editorial in the *Observer*, 'the SDP's arrival coincides with the daffodils and the first bright days of spring'.[27]

To their admirers, one of the things that made the SDP stand out was their collective leadership. At first the Gang of Four met every week at the aptly named L'Amico, an Italian restaurant in Westminster, and it seemed to work well. Jenkins was in charge of policy, Williams handled publicity, Rodgers ran the party machine and Owen chaired their delegation in Parliament. Some of them thought they should keep it up indefinitely. Rodgers liked the idea of copying West Germany's Social Democrats, who effectively had two leaders in Willy Brandt and Helmut Schmidt. Williams, too, enjoyed their experiment with collective decision-making, which gave an impression of 'friendship and a common objective, by contrast to the civil war in the Labour Party and the growing strains in the Conservative government'.[28]

Yet even at this early stage, there were tensions. Owen's brusque ambition did not make him one of life's natural collaborators. The bigger problem, though, was Jenkins. He was older than the others, infinitely more experienced and far better known. In his own mind, he was an international statesman, who had issued a call to arms in his Dimbleby Lecture and had graciously allowed the others to fall in behind him. But to the Gang of Three, the SDP was *their* project, not his. They had been brave enough to break from the Labour Party; he had merely flown home from Brussels. They had brought the recruits, the energy, the enthusiasm; he was merely the fairy on the Christmas tree. They were naturally infuriated to find Jenkins's hangers-on treating them as vassals at the court of King Roy. As the SDP's historians put it, 'the Jenkinsites' snootiness and air of ineffable superiority, their pleasure in making cutting remarks about their rivals and opponents', even their fondness for 'a table laden with good food and wine', seemed intolerably offensive. Even when Jenkins invited Owen for lunch at the Athenaeum, the younger man felt insulted. 'He knew perfectly well', Owen wrote, 'that these all-male London clubs got up my nose.'[29]

On top of that, Jenkins seemed a very incongruous front man for a dynamic new political operation. When Owen talked of the SDP as young, different and 'fresh-looking', he was listing everything Jenkins – a former Home Secretary, Chancellor and President of the European Commission, with an intimate knowledge of Belgium's wine cellars and an accent from the mean streets of St James's – was not. In Rodgers's words, Owen always saw his former mentor as 'yesterday's man, a sybaritic and whiggish figure'. But Rodgers thought there was a fair degree of jealousy there, too: 'the resentment of an adolescent boy on discovering that his rejected father is dangerously attractive to his girlfriend and still a fast mover on the football field'.[30]

Williams's relationship with Jenkins was no less uneasy. She thought him grand to the point of pomposity; he considered her informal to the point of scattiness. And since they were by far the best-known members of the Gang of Four, there was an underlying personal rivalry, too. 'I readily conceded, publicly and privately, that Roy was a greater person than I was,' Williams wrote later, which was an odd thing to say given that she was far more popular. What she could not forgive, though, was that his admirers constantly told journalists that she was 'disorganised, indecisive and incapable of leadership'. If she had been less amiable, she might have reminded them that she was a single mother bringing up a teenage

Garland

TODAY
Lukewarm
Tory Tea
OR
Watered down
Socialist Beer

SDP WINE
Sparkling Rosé

**"PERHAPS M'SIEUR WOULD LIKE TO SEE THE WINE LIST?"**

This Nicholas Garland cartoon (*Sunday Telegraph*, 14 June 1981) perfectly
captures Roy Jenkins's image in the SDP's early days. The 'Sparkling Rosé'
is very nicely judged, but the teetotal Tony Benn would never have touched
'Socialist Beer'.

daughter, whereas he was a spoiled voluptuary who was literally incapable
of boiling an egg. But she said nothing, so his acolytes had it all their own
way. They even had fun with her name: an anagram, they pointed out, of
'I whirl aimlessly'.[31]

Behind these personal animosities lay a deeper issue. The SDP's founders agreed that things had gone wrong with Britain and that the country
needed something new. But what? To many commentators, the Limehouse
Declaration implied a return to the semi-mythical consensus of the 1950s,
uniting moderates of left and right in a non-ideological National Government. Yet at the launch on 26 March both Rodgers and Williams had gone
out of their way to describe the SDP as a new 'left-of-centre party', not a
centre party. And even that was ambiguous. It might mean a more moderate version of the Labour Party, appealing to a largely working-class,
socially conservative base. Or it might mean an updated version of the
Edwardian Liberal Party: classless, high-minded, open to new issues
like feminism, environmentalism and gay rights. So what was the SDP
really for?[32]

Each member of the Gang of Four would have answered this slightly differently. Rodgers was a Gaitskell tribute act, advocating incomes policies, high spending and high taxes, as well as the nuclear deterrent and the Atlantic alliance. Williams, too, saw the SDP as basically another Labour Party, shorn of the unions and the hard left. By contrast, Owen was more forward-looking, dreaming of an aggressively radical party that would emulate the 'vibrant, cocky . . . classless, market-orientated culture' of the United States, Canada and Australia. But the real anomaly was Jenkins. While his comrades still described themselves as socialists, he pointedly told the *Guardian* that he had not 'used the word socialist, or socialism, for some years'. In style he often struck a remarkably conservative figure, and many commentators treated him as a kind of Victorian Whig. And when he talked about policy, his prescriptions sounded identical to those of the Tory Wets. As the journalist Hugh Stephenson remarked in one of the first books about the SDP, Jenkins said absolutely nothing 'which could not have come from the lips of a radical Tory'.[33]

None of this was lost on Jenkins's partners. Owen even believed that Jenkins had never been serious about building the SDP as a separate entity with a political culture of its own, but was bent on a merger with the Liberals. From the start, he wrote, Jenkins 'subtly and systematically undermined the SDP's independence'. This might sound a bit paranoid, and Jenkins dismissed it in his memoirs. But there is a considerable amount of truth in it. As Jenkins's authorized biographer, John Campbell, points out, he had envisaged some sort of association with David Steel's party long before he joined the Gang of Three. In reality, he probably never saw the SDP as anything other than a bridge to the Liberals. Indeed, the reason he insisted on putting the word 'realignment' into the Limehouse Declaration, over Williams's objections, was precisely because he hoped to tilt British politics back towards his hero H. H. Asquith's old party.[34]

But the issue of the Liberals exposed the fault lines in the Gang of Four. They all knew there was no room in a first-past-the post system for four competing parties. But as Owen pointed out, liberalism and social democracy were not the same thing. Liberals tended to be individualistic to the point of outright eccentricity; they distrusted big government, disliked concentrated power and were famously hospitable to all kinds of mavericks and minorities. But the Social Democrats saw themselves as a natural party of government, wielding power to improve the lives of millions. People like Owen and Rodgers knew how the machine worked and were keen to use it, but many grass-roots Liberals saw the machine as the enemy.

The SDP, wrote Austin Mitchell, were 'smooth men'; the Liberals were 'hairy men'.[35]

The pace of events, however, left little time for debate. In April, Shirley Williams and Bill Rodgers met the Liberal leader, David Steel, at the annual Anglo-German Association meeting in Königswinter. They found enough common ground to issue a joint statement of principle when they got back, with Williams and Steel posing on the lawn outside the Palace of Westminster 'like two young lovers'. By the autumn the two parties had laid the foundations for a formal alliance, although that did not save them from months of squabbling about the division of seats. But while Jenkins, Williams and Rodgers were happy to do a deal with the Liberals, Owen was much less contented. He thought of the SDP as a thrusting, hard-nosed party, at once radical and patriotic. By contrast, he saw the Liberals as a 'miscellaneous collection of limp-wristed wets, frequently feeble as individuals, collectively incapable of action'. Why, he wondered, had they rushed into a deal with such a pack of losers?[36]

In hindsight, all this was merely a symptom of the SDP's fundamental problem. In a different electoral system there might have been room for both Liberals and Social Democrats. But under first-past-the-post, even an alliance of the two was always going to find it extraordinarily difficult to break the mould. Indeed, even before the SDP had fought a single by-election, some observers warned that once the economy recovered and Labour's civil war ground to a halt, they would end up being 'squeezed' as everybody's second choice. To succeed, the Social Democrats needed Labour to disintegrate, repeating the pattern of the Liberals' collapse in the 1920s. But if Labour steadied the ship, the SDP might end up as another version of the Liberals: a 'middle-class "cop out", "pious", a non-urgent protest vote', to use the words of their focus groups. They badly needed a social base, a demographic heartland to match the Tory shires and Labour cities. People thought them moderate, sensible, *nice*. But as the Liberals could have told them, niceness does not win elections.[37]

On the left, the launch of the SDP provoked all sorts of wailing and gnashing of teeth. It was a 'major media festival', complained Tony Benn, who thought it 'unreal and potentially dangerous . . . The attack on the two-party system, the attack on the democratic process, the attack on choice, the attack on debate, the attack on policy – all these have within them the ingredients of fascism.'

Even by Benn's standards, this was a truly ridiculous thing to say. But he was not alone in feeling an overwhelming sense of betrayal. John Golding described the SDP as a 'mixture of the posh set and a convalescent home for Labour MPs who have caved in to the rough and tumble of constituency politics'. Michael Foot claimed that the Gang of Four's new party had begun 'with an act of dishonour', and that they would 'never be able to wipe away the stain'. For good measure, Foot blanked them in the Commons corridors and even cancelled their invitations to a farewell dinner for Jim and Audrey Callaghan. The most spectacular abuse, though, came from Neil Kinnock. The Social Democrats, he said, were 'political lounge lizards' who had 'no moral or democratic right' to cling on to their Commons seats. Unless the Labour Party exposed the 'shallowness and dishonesty' of their leaders, they would become the 'Common Market loving, NATO worshipping, trade union bashing' puppets of every 'multinational boss, judge and general' in the land.[38]

Of all these complaints, the most common was that the new party was a media creation, promoted by the spoiled elite who wrote newspaper columns and edited the television news. Austin Mitchell, for example, blamed 'media Labour supporters' such as the *Guardian*'s Peter Jenkins and the *Observer*'s Adam Raphael, 'who used their positions to invent the new party' and then gave it 'disproportionate coverage . . . presenting it in the most favourable limelight, elevating it from opportunism and accident to a genuine contribution to political theory and new politics'. The left-wing paper *Tribune* claimed that the SDP was the political wing of the BBC. Benn, confusingly, argued that the BBC was merely an 'agency of the SDP'. And the hard-left activist and future peer Peter Hain went further, claiming that the Social Democrats were being promoted by a 'motley alliance' of media interests. By the next election, Hain predicted, their supporters would include not just *The Times* and the *Sun*, but 'the *Guardian*, BBC, ITV and perhaps even the *Daily Mirror*'.[39]

There was a minuscule grain of truth in all this. The SDP *did* benefit from extensive coverage, notably in the *Guardian* and the *Observer*. Four *Guardian* writers even stood as SDP parliamentary candidates, including the future saint, Polly Toynbee, and the future resident of HM Prison Leyhill, Chris Huhne. Even so, the claim that the party was 'invented' by the media is absurd. The press covered the birth of the SDP because it was an exciting and important story, not because they were biased. After the razzamatazz of its launch, however, the SDP never quite recaptured Fleet Street's interest. On the front page of *The Times* it was typically mentioned twice a week; on the front page of the *Mirror* it was mentioned twice a month. Above all, it never secured the unequivocal backing of a single newspaper. When the general election came around, not even the *Guardian* wholeheartedly endorsed the SDP.[40]

The other common criticism was that the SDP was less a party than a dinner party, a social club for people who had a new hatchback in the drive, a home computer in the sitting room and a prep-school prospectus on the kitchen table. The Social Democrats were 'people who run things rather than own them . . . the people who know what's good for the people', wrote the *Express*'s George Gale in October 1981. The Conservative backbencher Julian Critchley thought they were the kind of people who went to their party conference with a copy of the *Good Food Guide*; the journalist Peter York called them 'Volvo people', who helped 'with the washing up'. Listening to the speeches at their party conference, wrote *The Times*'s Frank Johnson, was like listening to the 'opinionated chatter about worthy subjects over the dinner party cassoulet or home-made taramasalata in one of the gentrified bits of North London'. The *Spectator*'s Ferdinand Mount thought their motto should be 'Keep the yobs away from the best claret', while the same magazine's Geoffrey Wheatcroft nicknamed them LAFITE, the 'League of Agreeable Fellows Incommoded by Tiresome Extweemism'. 'They are a posh lot,' agreed the *Sun*'s Jon Akass. 'They can argue that they are not posh at all, that they have impeccable working-class origins, but they are betrayed by the clothes they stand in and by their accents.'[41]

But were they really so posh? After studying various surveys of SDP members in the early 1980s, Ivor Crewe and Anthony King suggested that the typical recruit was a 'middle-class family man' in his late thirties or early forties, living in a suburb, commuter town or cathedral city in southern England. SDP Man (and he was a man) came from a relatively modest background, but had passed his 11-plus, gone to grammar school and studied at university before pursuing a professional or management career, probably in the public sector. He usually voted Labour and read the *Guardian*, but he was not very deeply rooted in his local community, and had probably moved at least once for work. He had fond memories of the 1950s and 1960s, when he had grown up and taken his first steps in the adult world. But he was worried about the future and exasperated by the two main parties, which seemed to have comprehensively failed. It was time, he thought, for something new.

'Posh', then, is not the right word. What made the party's members stand out was that they were *meritocrats*, conscious of 'having risen in the world'. They did not own businesses, were not self-employed and were not especially interested in making money. Instead, they worked as journalists, lecturers, teachers, social workers and local government employees. Their other defining characteristic was that they were exceptionally well educated. In Newcastle, for example, 31 per cent of SDP members had degrees, compared to 5 per cent of the electorate as a whole. The party's biggest branches tended to be in places where graduates lived: university and cathedral cities like Oxford, Cambridge and Winchester; gentrified inner-city enclaves like Battersea and Kensington; affluent London suburbs like Hampstead, Richmond and Twickenham; booming hi-tech towns like Bracknell and Wokingham. Perhaps most revealingly, the first 150 SDP parliamentary candidates in the 1983 election had published no fewer than fifty-two books between them, embracing everything from the future of socialism to the geology of the Malvern Hills.[42]

The problem with all this, of course, was that it was easy for the Social Democrats' critics to present them as sanctimonious prigs, more interested in their next trip to Tuscany than in the gritty realities of life at the bottom. Not all of the party's founders were blind to the danger. David Owen, for example, was desperate to reach the skilled working-class voters he had known in Plymouth: people who read the *Sun*, bought their own council houses and admired Mrs Thatcher's patriotic rhetoric. But his was often a lone voice, and SDP members like *Auf Wiedersehen, Pet*'s Barry (Timothy Spall), a Black Country electrician who tells his mates that they are the 'party of the future', were relatively thin on the ground. Perhaps the party should have thought harder about a throwaway remark by Bill Rodgers during the Crosby by-election, when he turned up with 'claret and chips' for the campaign volunteers. The key word was 'chips': even in the early 1980s there were a lot more chip eaters than claret drinkers. But the SDP always seemed more comfortable as the voice of the wine bar than as the party of the chip shop.[43]

Yet, in the spring of 1981, it was easy to overlook the SDP's weaknesses. The sun was shining, the polls were tremendous and the tide of history was running its way. Sir Geoffrey Howe's Budget on 10 March had been a public relations disaster, while Tony Benn's decision to challenge Denis Healey for Labour's deputy leadership had ignited the most vicious faction-fighting yet. Even the hunger strikes in Northern Ireland and the riots in the inner cities added to the picture of a broken political system and a nation crying out for a return to moderation. And then, in late May, came an unexpected stroke of luck. The Labour MP for Warrington, Sir Tom Williams, a working barrister, accepted a promotion to circuit judge, which meant he had to resign his seat. There would obviously be a by-election. If the Liberals agreed to stand aside, would the SDP put up a candidate? And if so, who?

On the face of it, Warrington was a singularly unpromising place for the SDP to make its first stand. A working-class manufacturing town between Manchester and Liverpool, it had returned Labour candidates in every election for decades and had given Sir Tom a whopping 62 per cent of the vote in 1979. But everybody knew the Social Democrats had to fight it. Since Owen and Rodgers were already in Parliament, the leading candidates were Shirley Williams and Roy Jenkins. Of the two, Williams was the more obvious choice. She herself thought that 'if ever a constituency was made for me, this was it – moderate Labour, Catholic, a cohesive community'. A poll in the *Sun* found that, if she stood, she would win a staggering 55 per cent, with Labour on 36 per cent and the Conservatives on a risible 9 per cent. 'You can do it, Shirl!' urged the headline.

But she blinked. As a single mother with a teenage daughter, she was anxious about conducting a long campaign so far from London. What was more, as a parent with few savings she worried that a second defeat would destroy her political career and leave her without a job. So she turned it down. It was, she wrote later, 'probably the single biggest mistake of my political life . . . My reputation for boldness, acquired in the long fight within the Labour Party, never wholly recovered.' The journalist Hugh Stephenson thought it a 'disastrous personal and political mistake', destroying her chances of ever becoming party leader. Owen, too, thought it 'the worst decision Shirley has ever made in politics'. Had she stood, he wrote, she would undoubtedly have won, setting her up to become the new party's leader. 'There would have been no question then', he added, 'but that it was a Social Democratic Party, standing in its own right as one of four parties in British politics. But it was sadly not to be.'[44]

To Owen's disappointment, Williams's decision opened the way for the man he least wanted to see as the SDP's chief standard-bearer. Warrington was hardly Roy Jenkins's natural stamping ground, even though he had represented the similarly working-class Birmingham Stechford for years. In a very Jenkins touch, he sent his wife Jennifer to inspect the terrain while he went off to 'an international bankers' convention in Switzerland'. On the night of 4 June, he recalled, 'I stayed in the Hôtel Beau-Rivage, Lausanne, and looked out from the balcony of my suite across a moonlit Lake of Geneva to the Savoy Alps.' Jennifer, on the other hand, 'stayed in the Patten Arms Hotel, Warrington, and looked out, without a balcony I think, over the railway station and the soap works'. Jennifer reported that although Warrington would be a 'very hard nut to crack', it had a 'fine church and a few good c. 1800 buildings'. She drew a veil over its restaurants, but Jenkins decided to go for it anyway.[45]

Warrington was the first in a series of extraordinarily dramatic by-elections, fought in the glare of the national spotlight, with memorably wry coverage by the BBC's Vincent Hanna. Nobody seriously thought the

SDP could win; the question was whether it could get close. It flooded the constituency with enthusiastic volunteers, while Jenkins and his comrades mounted a succession of cavalcades, driving around the town with speakers blaring out the theme from *Chariots of Fire* and Aaron Copland's *Fanfare for the Common Man*. Bill Rodgers remembered an 'atmosphere of infectious excitement', the local shopping centre packed with canvassers, the mood that 'of a festival'. 'Warrington has never seen anything like it,' wrote one visiting reporter. 'Never has it had such political attention.'[46]

To Jenkins's former colleagues, his appearance in Warrington seemed an intolerable affront. Labour's candidate, Doug Hoyle, a Bennite of such intemperance that the very mention of his opponent's name seemed likely to bring on an apoplexy, described him as a 'retired pensioner from the EEC', while a local trade unionist called him a 'pompous plutocrat, who is now showing his true anti-working class views'. Even Peter Shore, who had sat beside Jenkins in Cabinets since the late 1960s, got very overexcited, accusing him of succumbing to a 'sick, overriding passion for the Common Market' and a 'specious, dangerous dependence not on the support of individual men and women, but upon the good opinion of the media'.[47]

Yet the residents of this hitherto uncelebrated corner of the north-west seemed thrilled that such a statesmanlike figure had descended from his suite at the Hôtel Beau-Rivage to move among them. Jenkins's political manservant David Marquand never forgot seeing him discussing economic policy with an elderly working-class housewife, the latter 'looking up at him with an expression of bemused yet indulgent admiration, like an aged aunt applauding the exploits of a favourite nephew'. It was clear that she had not the faintest idea what Jenkins was talking about, but was 'delighted' that such a grand figure was soliciting her vote. The sketchwriter Frank Johnson, too, was struck by the enthusiasm for Jenkins's courtly manners and elevated accent, surmising that many people saw him as a 'figure above and outside politics, like the Queen'. At one point he interviewed a man called Mr Done, who just had been talking to Jenkins in the shopping centre. What did Mr Done think of Jenkins? 'A gentleman, and an educated man.' Why educated? 'Well, the Common Market.' Did Mr Done approve of the Common Market? 'No, detest it.' So why did it make him think better of Jenkins? 'Well, he got paid a lot of money by it, didn't he?'[48]

The result came late in the evening of Thursday 16 July. In private, Jenkins's campaign managers were hoping for about a third of the vote. In fact, he won a sensational 42.4 per cent, slashing Labour's majority to just 1,759 votes. Given that Jenkins's party had not existed four months earlier, it was a breathtaking performance. In his own words, it was his 'first defeat in thirty years in politics. And it is by far the greatest victory in which I have ever participated.' He was not exaggerating. The pro-Labour *Mirror* thought it the 'most dramatic by-election since the war'; the BBC's veteran pundit Robert McKenzie called it 'the most sensational by-election of the century'; the *Sun* proclaimed that a 'New Age of Politics Is Dawning in Britain'. If the Warrington result were repeated at a general election, wrote the *Mirror*'s veteran political editor Terence Lancaster, 'the Social Democrats would be swept to power in a landslide'. That, he conceded, was very unlikely. 'But one thing stands out. The Social Democrats are in with a chance of forming the next Government.'[49]

Warrington set the seal on a stunning six months for the Gang of Four. In January they had seemed friendless outsiders; now people were talking about them as a government in waiting. And the good news continued to roll in. When the *Daily Star* published the first nationwide poll after Warrington, it put Labour on 29 per cent, the Tories on 25 per cent and a putative SDP–Liberal Alliance on 43 per cent. Even the SDP's first party conference, held that autumn, was an eye-catching triumph. In a symbolic break from the norm, it was held at three different venues, Perth, Bradford and London, with a special train carrying delegates between them. 'On the train itself', write the party's historians, 'songs were sung, drinks drunk and stories told', the atmosphere one of 'tremendous good will'. Given the backstabbing at their rivals' conferences, the contrast could hardly have been more striking. Even Owen, despite his doubts about the Liberals, felt a sense of *'esprit de corps*, a mood of adventure and fun' that he had never known in the Labour Party.[50]

But if the mood at the SDP conference was upbeat, it was as nothing compared with the euphoria when their Liberal partners met in Llandudno. Almost overnight David Steel's party had been catapulted into the limelight, with a plausible chance of power for perhaps the first time since the early 1920s. A few Liberals, fearful of losing their independence, hesitated at the thought of a formal deal with the newcomers. But when Jenkins and Williams joined Steel and the former Liberal leader Jo Grimond to address 2,000 people in the Pier Pavilion, even experienced reporters were stunned by the delegates' fervour. As one speaker after another endorsed the alliance, the audience stamped and roared with approval. By the end, some were so overcome they had started crying.[51]

The following day, by a crushing margin, the delegates formally endorsed the alliance with the Social Democrats. As waves of applause rolled around the hall, some looked up to the gallery, where Jenkins, Williams and

Rodgers were beaming with approval. Only Owen was missing. But the day belonged to David Steel. The Alliance, he told his audience that afternoon, was the only way forward for Britain, the only chance of 'hope for the future'. And in his last words, the embodiment of Scottish Liberal sobriety yielded at last to the intoxication of enthusiasm. 'I have the good fortune', Steel told the hall, 'to be the first Liberal leader for over half a century to be able to say to you at the end of our annual assembly: "Go back to your constituencies and prepare for government!"'

Later, people laughed at that line. But nobody laughed at the time. Instead, they stood and cheered him for five minutes.[52]

# 18

# Up Yours from the Chancellor

*I said I hoped that the intimations of gloom were a double bluff and in fact there might be some 'good news' in the Budget. Jim Prior leant over my chair and said, 'Has it not occurred to you that the rumours of badness are simply to soften you up for something even worse?'*

Alan Clark's diary, 10 March 1981

*My verdict on that amazing attack on the Government by 364 economists: Insolent, conceited, cowardly, academic twaddle!*

George Gale, *Daily Express*, 31 March 1981

On the first Sunday of 1981, Mrs Thatcher welcomed one of her keenest admirers, the *Sun*'s owner Rupert Murdoch, to Chequers for lunch. With Murdoch putting together a bid for *The Times* and the *Sunday Times*, she was keen to wish him well, but she had an interview with Radio Four's *The World This Weekend* to get through first. For an hour she sparred earnestly with the presenter, Gordon Clough, about the dreadful state of the economy. Then, at the end, Clough threw in a googly. Her predecessor, he said, had 'got into the habit of giving the year ahead a sobriquet, a tag. One year I remember it was the year of the pendulum, another year was the year of decision.' If she had to choose a phrase to capture the spirit of 1981, what would it be?

For a second, Mrs Thatcher hesitated. And then, in true *Sun* spirit, she reached for the patriotic card. 'Well you know, in adversity,' she said. 'We've beaten most of the nations who are now our main competitors. If we stick at doing the right thing we shall win through. So we've got to do the right thing and we've got to stick at it and then we shall win through and we shall be a very formidable nation. And other nations know it.'[1]

Despite all the gossip about doubts and divisions, these were not the words of somebody who was giving up. Two days later, her speechwriter

Ronnie Millar wrote to congratulate her on a 'quite splendid' performance. It was a treat to hear her 'sane and balanced *optimism*', he wrote,
especially when compared with the 'eternal gloom and doom of the economic "forecasters"' . . . Oh, we *are* going to win through – I never felt it
so strongly . . . Up spirits!' A few hours after receiving his note, Mrs
Thatcher went on Thames Television's *Afternoon Plus* to be grilled by
Judith Chalmers. Again she struck a defiantly optimistic note. At one point
Chalmers asked if she ever dreaded the day ahead. Mrs Thatcher shook
her head. 'I look forward to every day, every day has new opportunities,'
she said earnestly. 'I like battling. I like battling . . . And if there's a row
I never mind it, because I can cope.'[2]

'I like battling' would have made a fitting epitaph for a leader who
defined herself through conflict. But since her officers seemed to be losing
heart, it was time for one of them to go, *pour encourager les autres*. On
5 January, in the first reshuffle of her premiership, Mrs Thatcher moved
John Biffen to Trade, replacing John Nott, who moved to Defence. The
Defence Secretary, Francis Pym, moved in turn to become Leader of the
Commons, replacing Norman St John-Stevas, who was sacked outright.
It was hardly butchery, but each step was highly revealing. Biffen was
paying the price for his doubts about their monetary policy. Pym lost
Defence because he had refused to make cuts, but got another senior job
as Leader of the House. Nott was a loyalist, methodical and economically
dry, who could, in Howe's words, 'be relied upon to get on top of the brass
hats'. But for the Wets, the most ominous change was the dismissal of St
John-Stevas. Flippant, gossipy and flamboyantly camp, Westminster's
answer to Larry Grayson had seen himself as Mrs Thatcher's court jester.*
But because so many people saw him as an essentially frivolous figure, he
was a soft target. When Mrs Thatcher booted him out, none of his fellow
Wets lifted a finger to save him.[3]

In the short term, the reshuffle changed nothing. On 19 January the
party chairman, Lord Thorneycroft, warned Number 10 that 'even among
our loyalest supporters' the government's message was failing to cut
through. The rationale for their economic policies, he wrote, was 'virtually
incomprehensible to any ordinary man or woman', and in the meantime
'the voters suffer and wonder why'. Six days later, the Gang of Four issued
the Limehouse Declaration. And although there was no immediate rush
of Tory MPs to join the new party, many of Mrs Thatcher's supporters

---

* According to his *Telegraph* obituary, St John-Stevas once 'asked to be excused from a
meeting because he had a reception to go to'. 'But I'm going to the same function,' Mrs
Thatcher said. 'Yes,' St John-Stevas replied, 'but it takes me so much longer to change.'

were seriously worried. Two days after Limehouse, Alan Clark went to a dinner of the Burke Club, where the conversation was '*exclusively* devoted to the Social Democratic Centre Party, Shirley Williams ad nauseam'. Clark maintained that 'the whole thing was balls, no one would vote for them, they would blow themselves out, quarrel, sub-divide, etc., long before the general election'. But his colleagues were less sanguine. Afterwards, when they went around the table discussing the government's 'achievements', Clark's answer was 'that we have really succeeded in putting a lot of people out of work'. There was grim laughter at that, but he was absolutely serious. The unions, he thought, had been 'disciplined by the fear of being put on the dole and this is a considerable, though brutal, achievement'. But apart from that, he could think of nothing else.[4]

At this point, the National Union of Mineworkers (NUM) entered the fray. Britain's coal mines were haemorrhaging money, and right from the start Mrs Thatcher had put the Coal Board under pressure to cut costs. But when, in early February 1981, it confirmed plans to close twenty-three pits, the union demanded a national strike. Given that less than a decade earlier the miners had won two strikes and destroyed the Heath government, this was clearly a moment of maximum danger. On 13 February, Bernard Ingham told Mrs Thatcher that the Coal Board was 'trying to achieve too much too quickly'. As 'the most cohesive industrial force in Britain', the miners would be very hard to beat, and the government was woefully unprepared. Three days later, her Energy Secretary, David Howell, told her that coal stocks were too low to sustain a protracted strike. So that was that. On 18 February the Coal Board backed down. Across the coalfields, jubilation reigned. 'The lady said she was not for turning', the leader of Nottinghamshire's 34,000 miners said gleefully, 'but now she has become an expert in doing double somersaults.'[5]

For Mrs Thatcher, the next day's front pages made awful reading. 'VICTORY TO THE MINERS!' exulted the *Mirror*, which thought that the NUM had 'achieved more than any other union or employer in forcing the Government to change its tune completely'. The *Express*, unsurprisingly, was less jubilant. 'SURRENDER TO OLD KING COAL', read the headline, above a front-page editorial lamenting a 'terrible industrial nightmare, all too familiar in Britain these days'. Mrs Thatcher's decision, it said, 'will be called a U-turn, will be branded as weakness and it will add spice to the arguments of the Left'. But even if she had wanted to fight, her government was completely unprepared. So although the surrender cost an estimated £500 million, it was worth it. As John Hoskyns put it, 'pragmatic withdrawal' was the only sensible option.[6]

Like Heath before her, Mrs Thatcher was in danger of being submerged by the sheer weight of events. On 5 February the Gang of Four published their advert in the *Guardian*. On 13 February the latest figures showed that manufacturing output had fallen to its lowest level since 1968. On 18 February the Coal Board surrendered to the miners. 'I am sorry to say there has been a noticeable deterioration in the morale of our backbenchers,' reported Ian Gow. He blamed not just the 'perceived defeat' in the pits but 'increasing concern about the extent of the recession and unemployment', and urged Mrs Thatcher to consider 'how we can restore the morale of our Party'. But had they already passed the point of no return? The party was 'much divided against itself', wrote Alan Clark on the 25th, noting that the rank and file were 'deeply gloomy about the absence of an industrial, or indeed any other kind of, strategy, and the way we seem to be reacting *ad hoc* and in panic to instant crises'. That afternoon, another MP, the experienced Michael McNair-Wilson, told him that the 'morale of the Party had never been lower'. As McNair-Wilson saw it, Mrs Thatcher was merely staggering from day to day, 'making decisions on impulse . . . just like Eden during the Suez Crisis'.[7]

As so often at Westminster, there was a considerable element of hysteria in all this. The key relationship, between Mrs Thatcher and her Chancellor, was just about intact. And while her inner circle despaired of her abrasive style, she had inspired a strong team spirit and even a kind of protectiveness among her closest advisers. But the same had been true of Ted Heath, too, and his own MPs had brought him down. Nobody could be sure that Mrs Thatcher would not suffer a similar fate. After a dinner on 5 March, Hoskyns recorded that, 'quite unprompted', two young ministers, Norman Lamont and Cecil Parkinson, had told him 'how appalled they were by the state of the Government, the miners surrender, the "all piss and wind" mood about MT – and they are really loyal supporters'. The worst thing, they said, was the growing indiscipline. In front of their officials, senior ministers were openly gossiping about 'how awful she was this morning'. To the loyalists, the fact that Mrs Thatcher's ministers no longer watched what they said was a very bad sign indeed.[8]

On Monday 5 January the *Mirror* welcomed Mrs Thatcher's latest recruit:

If first impressions are anything to go by, Professor Alan Walters will do for the British economy what Basil Fawlty did for the hotel trade.

As he packed his bags in Washington at the weekend, Mrs Thatcher's £1,000-a-week mastermind commented that Britain was 'not doing too badly'.

*With views like that, he will feel at home inside No. 10.*

> The characters there are straight out of The Wizard of Oz.
> They follow a yellow-brick road, paved with redundancies and bank-
> ruptcies, but always see gold at the end of the rainbow.

Walters was Mrs Thatcher's kind of person. Born in 1926, the son of a
Leicester greengrocer, he had never been part of the political establishment. Self-made and self-confident, 'with a shock of white hair and
somewhat cadaverous appearance', he had failed his 11-plus, left school
at 15 to work in a shoe factory, served in the army and then became an
academic economist. After teaching at the London School of Economics,
he had worked briefly for Ted Heath, but was sacked after accusing his
boss of being 'hooked on easy money'. That was typical Walters. Few
advisers derived greater pleasure from telling their masters that they had
gone disastrously wrong.[9]

Having been lured home from the United States to become Mrs Thatcher's chief economic adviser, Walters started as he meant to go on. On 6
January he began his first meeting by telling his new boss that her monetary policy 'had worked, if anything, too well', which was code for saying
she had squeezed too hard. To the press, he was even more outspoken.
When a *Financial Times* reporter asked what advice he would be giving
the Prime Minister, Walters said cheerfully: 'I'll tell her that the money
supply is far too tight.' 'But Alan, M3 is completely out of control,' the
journalist said. 'Oh, bugger M3!' Walters said. 'Sterling is obviously far
too high. That can only mean sterling is scarce.'[10]

To support his case, Walters brought in the Swiss economist Jürg Niehans, who briefed Mrs Thatcher's Policy Unit the next day. Niehans
vehemently agreed that 'monetary policy has been too tight'. It had, he
said, been the single biggest factor in the excruciating rise of the pound:
'If the Government goes on with its present monetary squeeze, you won't
just have a recession; you'll have a slump.' Indeed, Niehans argued that,
as a matter of urgency, they should intervene in the currency markets to
get the exchange rate down. 'Very risky – but better than ruining much
of the export industry,' scribbled Walters. For his part, John Hoskyns,
who was shocked by the diagnosis, thought the Swiss economist had been
'v. impressive'. And although Mrs Thatcher ordered her aides to keep
Niehans's analysis secret, she did not argue with it. In truth, it was exactly
what she wanted to hear. Monetary policy was too tight, so interest rates
should come down. And as she and her advisers saw it, the only way to
bring rates down without losing the trust of the markets was to cut
spending.[11]

By this point, Mrs Thatcher was already haggling with Sir Geoffrey

Howe over what they knew would be a make-or-break Budget on 10 March. The preparation of a Budget is rarely the stuff of thrilling melodrama. But this was different: not just an extraordinarily controversial moment in the life of her government, but one of the most contentious moments in Britain's modern economic history. Later, after the *dramatis personae* had discovered the joys of stabbing each other in the back, Mrs Thatcher tried to present herself as the Budget's true author, while Hoskyns presented his 'Downing Street irregulars' at the Policy Unit as the heroes of the hour. In fact, the archives show that responsibility always lay with the Treasury, and that despite their minor differences Thatcher and Howe were always singing from the same hymn sheet. Both wanted to see interest rates fall, both believed they had to cut borrowing, and both agreed there should be some combination of spending cuts and tax rises. In effect, their negotiations were an exercise in sorting out the details and reinforcing each other's resolve. 'The more ready she was to be tough,' writes Edmund Dell, 'the more readily he could be tough.'[12]

So what made it all so fraught? Part of the answer is simply the intense political pressure. The emergence of the SDP and the surrender to the miners had sent Tory backbenchers into a panic, while every day brought more headlines about closing factories and rising unemployment. The other obvious factor was the volatile tone of life at Number 10. Not only were Hoskyns and Walters unusually given to apocalyptic pessimism, but Mrs Thatcher's overtly emotional style never made for a quiet life. As her aide Tim Lankester recalled, she took bad news personally and 'found it hard to understand how and why, under her overall direction, things had gone so badly wrong'. When Hoskyns and Walters bombarded her with memos claiming that everything was falling apart and that the Budget was going to be a disaster, she was not best pleased. To cap it all, her confidence in Howe was fast evaporating: on one occasion her aides claimed to have overheard her telling him that if the Budget went wrong, 'you are for the chop'. This is surely an exaggeration, but there is little doubt that she thought it – and that her Chancellor knew it.[13]

By now Howe had perfected his performance as the lugubrious bearer of unwelcome news: the doctor who recommends an immensely painful operation, the accountant who spots a gaping hole in his client's finances, the vet who regrets that the family dog must immediately be put down. Briefing Mrs Thatcher's inner circle at Chequers on 17 January, he announced that, with tax receipts down and the unemployment bill soaring, and with Britain's nationalized industries still requiring huge injections of public money, the deficit was likely to be well over £11 billion, far more than the £8½ billion target in the last Budget. 'We should really have taken some of these measures a year ago,' Mrs Thatcher said bitterly. When Howe sent her a breakdown of the spending totals, she covered it with blue ink. 'Tim – I cannot just do nothing about this,' she scribbled to Lankester. 'We appear to have *no* control over expenditure . . .'[14]

Howe knew that with the economy in such a deep recession, even the slightest cuts would be immensely controversial. Yet even as his Cabinet colleagues badgered him for extra funds, he remained grimly focused. The deficit, he warned Mrs Thatcher on 5 February, was widening every day, which gave him no choice but to bring in a 'tough Budget', ideally slashing borrowing to no more than £10 billion. This would not, of course, be easy, since he had no desire to put VAT or income tax up. And with so many businesses struggling to stay alive, he could hardly squeeze more money out of corporation tax. But it tallied with the advice he was getting from the Bank of England, whose deficit forecast was even more pessimistic. High borrowing, Gordon Richardson told Howe the next day, would mean high interest rates, which would make it impossible to bring down the pound. So although it might seem perverse to cut spending in a recession, everybody thought they should do it. The only dissenters were the Wets, the opposition parties, most academic economists, much of the press and the overwhelming majority of the general public.[15]

On 10 February, Howe and Mrs Thatcher held the first of five fractious Budget meetings. Howe kicked off with the cheerful news that the deficit forecast had now risen to a whopping £13 billion. Since higher direct taxes were definitely out, his initial plan was to put a levy on bank deposits and freeze personal tax allowances, which were meant to increase in line with inflation. But to Hoskyns, Walters and the self-styled irregulars, this was not remotely enough. Whether from endemic pessimism, temperamental excitability or simply a bad case of institutional rivalry, they had become convinced that Howe was a dead loss, the Treasury was preparing to sell them all out and Britain was about to disappear down the plughole. So, later that day, Walters sent Mrs Thatcher a note warning that the deficit was really much worse than Howe had claimed, and that, without genuinely 'painful decisions', she would lose the next election. Then, very late that evening, Hoskyns, Walters and their colleague David Wolfson cornered her in Number 10. Treasury forecasts were always too optimistic, they told her, and the dangers of an 'underkill' Budget were too terrible to imagine. So, in Hoskyns's words, the Prime Minister 'must say she absolutely refuses to accept GH's forecast' and should insist on an 'overkill' Budget to slash the deficit.[16]

At the time, Mrs Thatcher appeared to agree with everything they were saying. But when Wolfson spoke to her the next morning, she 'seemed scarcely to remember what we'd discussed last night'. 'Oh dear!' recorded

Hoskyns. 'I think she'd had one or two drinks on an empty stomach and was v. tired as well – hence it had all seemed so easy.' This was a bit ungallant: the truth was probably that she was barely listening and just wanted them to go home. So the next day, the self-styled irregulars sent her another melodramatic note, repeating the prescription of a really painful 'overkill' Budget. This, they wrote, was 'like the choice about where to cut a firebreak to stop a forest fire ... You choose the strategy which makes the *worst* outcome *least* likely. WE HAVE NO CHOICE BUT TO GO FOR REALISM ... The 1981 Budget is absolutely the *last chance* for realism to take over from wishful thinking.' All this was good apocalyptic stuff. But when they went to see her the next day, they discovered she had not bothered to read it.[17]

After this rather tense build-up, the next performance was scheduled for 13 February. As Walters had predicted, the Treasury's deficit forecast had now risen to a staggering £13¾ billion. At this rate it was deteriorating at the rate of almost £1 billion a week. And after the cast had assembled in Number 10, Howe admitted that yes, ideally they would get the deficit down to below £11 billion, 'but he did not believe this was politically possible'. Raising income tax would be electorally disastrous, while 'he did not believe that colleagues would agree to a further round of public spending cuts'. Now Walters spoke up. A deficit of £11 billion, he said, would not satisfy the markets. It would mean a 'funding crisis either in the summer or the autumn', which would bring higher interest rates and throttle the economy beyond recovery. So they should have an immensely stringent Budget now, raising income tax by 1 or 2 per cent.

That was just not possible, Howe said. Given that they were already in 'the deepest recession since the 1930s', it would be political suicide to impose so much austerity. Mrs Thatcher agreed with him, and it was at about this point that things began to get very heated. Hoskyns remembered her advancing across the room towards them and saying: 'It's all very well for you, you don't have to stand up and sell this in the House.' Walters, meanwhile, remembered her 'screaming' at him: 'You are just an academic and you don't know what the political implications are.' Afterwards, when the two advisers retreated to Hoskyns's office, Walters said he was wondering 'whether he ought to leave, whether the whole thing wasn't a waste of time'.[18]

But the squabbling went on. When Mrs Thatcher used the excuse of the miners' dispute to cancel another late-night meeting with Hoskyns, Walters and Wolfson, the three irregulars spent the rest of the evening 'discussing how to bring her to her senses'. Their mood was bleak, and Hoskyns was now thinking of resigning. Given that the differences were actually pretty marginal, this speaks volumes about the hysterical urgency that had always prevailed in some corners of Mrs Thatcher's court. Indeed, on the 20th the prophets of doom sent her what Walters called a 'FACING DISASTER manuscript', warning that unless she insisted on a much tougher Budget, 'we shall be locked almost immediately into a vicious circle from which there will be no escape . . . IN SHORT, WE BELIEVE THAT THE BUDGET PRESENTED ON 10 MARCH WILL LARGELY DETERMINE WHETHER WE WIN OR LOSE THE NEXT ELECTION.' By now, though, she had clearly read enough apocalyptic memos in capital letters to last her a lifetime. In the margin she scribbled just two words: 'Hardly' and 'No'.[19]

Mrs Thatcher's patience with her own advisers was now exhausted. Before her next meeting with the Chancellor on 24 February, she expressly told Tim Lankester that neither Hoskyns nor Walters would be welcome, even though Howe was bringing his senior official, Sir Douglas Wass. 'All very secret,' scribbled the disgruntled Walters. But she had heard their arguments a hundred times and had no desire to hear them again. Howe said he could get the deficit down to just over £11 billion, but probably no further. She preferred £10½ billion, and suggested putting an extra penny on income tax. But Howe thought that would be 'extremely difficult politically and would be very bad for business morale'. She was still not entirely convinced. But as so often – and contrary to the stereotype – she was prepared to accede to Howe's judgement. She had pushed him as far as he would go, and by the time the meeting broke up they had settled on a deficit of about £11¼ billion.[20]

There was, however, a last twist. Having slept on it, Howe told his officials the next morning that he had changed his mind.* If they froze personal tax allowances, they would be able to get the deficit down to £10½ billion after all, which would allow them to cut interest rates by 2 per cent. A couple of hours later, he went into Number 10 to tell Mrs Thatcher. As it happened, she was due to fly to Washington that afternoon to meet President Reagan, and was already preoccupied with all things American. When Howe explained his change of heart, she simply nodded. To Lankester, 'it seemed she almost no longer wanted to know: it was now his Budget'. Lankester wondered if she was deliberately distancing herself from the final decision, 'in case it all went badly wrong'.[21]

That afternoon, Mrs Thatcher left for Heathrow. Before leaving, she had expressly ordered Lankester *not* to tell Hoskyns and Walters about the Budget agreement. Lankester thought this was 'ridiculous; it wasn't

---

* In her memoirs, Mrs Thatcher claims that she forced Howe into a change of heart. But the documents show that this is not true. In fact, she had already agreed to accept £11¼ billion. It was the Chancellor's own decision to settle on £10½ billion the next day.

the way they should be treated'. So he did tell them, and they took it just as badly as she had feared. Walters, in particular, flew off the handle. The decision to freeze tax allowances, he wrote in his diary, was 'stupid politically, indefensible morally and economically'. The next day, he told Sir Douglas Wass that the Budget was far too weak. They would soon be forced into 'crisis measures', and had given themselves no room to cut interest rates. Soon afterwards, he, Hoskyns and Wolfson drafted a joint resignation letter, to be delivered after the Budget. 'The opportunity to turn the UK economy round, presented by the May 1979 mandate, has passed,' they wrote. 'The best that can happen now is that the Tories win the next election on the back of Labour's disarray; and the UK decline continues in relative terms.' Fortunately for them, they never sent it.[22]

Mrs Thatcher's American trip was a perfectly timed break from the bickering about the Budget. When the British ambassador in Washington, Nicholas Henderson, discussed it with her beforehand, he initially found her 'a little worried'. 'She did not quite see how it would go,' he wrote. 'She admitted to being nervous about it. She looked drawn – pale and rather distinguished.' Yet, as they talked, 'the worries seemed to flow off her and she became less taut'. She seemed relieved, Henderson thought, at the prospect of visiting a country she loved, where she could briefly forget her domestic troubles. Indeed, as her departure for the United States approached, she seemed giddy with anticipation. She was 'intolerable', one of her Cabinet colleagues remarked. She was 'on a complete high', and 'tremendously worked up about seeing Reagan alone'.[23]

Mrs Thatcher had first met the new President in April 1975. In her own words, she was 'won over by his charm, directness and sense of humour', while Reagan was delighted to find that they were 'soul mates when it came to reducing government and expanding freedom'. And in some ways they were natural partners. They both hated Communism, they were both preoccupied with national decline, they both blamed the advance of social democracy and they were both committed to free-market capitalism. But there were deeper similarities, too. Both liked to talk in highly moralistic terms: as Hugo Young remarked, they shared a 'wonderful measure of certainty'. They were patriotic populists, seeing themselves as standing up for ordinary families against the intellectual elites, yet in office both proved more pragmatic than their critics often admitted. Above all, both drew on instinct rather than theory, taking inspiration from the axioms of their small-town childhoods. 'I am not a politician,' Reagan once said. 'I am an ordinary citizen with a deep-seated belief that much of what troubles us has been brought about by politicians; and it's high time that more ordinary citizens brought the fresh air of common-sense thinking to bear on these problems.' Common-sense thinking: that was Mrs Thatcher's kind of thinking.[24]

There were some striking differences, though. Mrs Thatcher was more abrasive, whereas Reagan always wanted people to like him. She rarely managed to rise above narrow partisanship; by contrast, Reagan, a former Democrat, loved playing the national statesman. And their economic tactics were quite different. When Howe and his officials met their American counterparts in September 1981, there was a palpable sense of mutual disapproval. Reagan's men kept asking why Howe had raised VAT, and seemed surprised when the Chancellor said he wanted to cut government borrowing. For while Mrs Thatcher and her allies believed in balanced budgets, Reagan had been converted to 'supply-side' theory, which held that if he cut taxes deeply enough, the economy would grow so quickly that he could throw around as much money as he liked. Not for nothing did *The Economist* call them 'Lord Wishful' and 'Lady Rigorous'. Reagan, the supreme optimist, promised jam today, tomorrow and always. By contrast, Mrs Thatcher offered cold porridge today with only the vague promise of jam tomorrow – as long as the voters were good.[25]

What this reflected was a difference that was as much temperamental as it was ideological. The Methodist grocer's daughter stayed up late with her red boxes before rising at dawn to crack on with the paperwork. But the Hollywood divorcee was so relaxed that, as President, he took Wednesdays off and ended early on Fridays. Of course this was partly an act, and Reagan was much more astute than many people imagined. Still, Mrs Thatcher was well aware of his limitations. Lord Carrington recalled their first meeting in the White House, where the President unburdened himself of his views on South Africa. 'Well of course, the South Africans are whites and they fought for us during the war,' Reagan said cheerfully. 'The blacks are black and they are Communists.' As Carrington put it, 'even Margaret thought this was rather a simplification'. As soon as they were out of the Oval Office, she turned to her Foreign Secretary and pointed at her head. 'Peter,' she whispered in horror, 'there's nothing there!'[26]

But Reagan had charisma, the most important political quality of all. At their first meeting, Mrs Thatcher had been struck by his 'warmth, charm and complete lack of affectation', which made for such a contrast with, say, Valéry Giscard d'Estaing. While Giscard embodied everything she disliked in a man, Reagan was the complete opposite, a 'buoyant, self-confident, good-natured American' who treated her with gallant respect. Later, François Mitterrand told friends of his disbelief that 'Mrs Thatcher, who can be so tough when she talks to her European partners, is like a little girl of eight when she talks to the President of the United States'. And, for his part, Reagan was secure enough not to feel irritated when she embarked on yet another lecture about the horrors of socialism. The story goes that once, when she had telephoned to harangue him about something, he put his hand over the receiver and beamed at his aides. 'Isn't she marvellous?' he said happily.[27]

On the morning of 26 February, Mrs Thatcher arrived at the White House to a spectacular welcome. Reagan had told his aides to 'make it special', and she was duly greeted by trumpeters, an honour guard, a Marine band and a nineteen-gun salute. Yet some of Reagan's advisers were nervous about associating themselves with somebody presiding over such a calamitous recession. According to a State Department briefing, Mrs Thatcher's team had 'failed to implement effectively' their economic goals, had 'failed to give due weight' to events outside their control, and had even 'implemented their strategy inefficiently'. Humiliatingly, the State Department thought Reagan should bring all this up with her, so that he could 'learn from British mistakes'. And on her first full day in Washington, the White House prepared another briefing on the differences between Reaganism and Thatcherism, criticizing her for increasing VAT and failing to cut spending. At lunchtime, Reagan's press secretary handed out copies to the media, clearly trying to disassociate his boss from a Prime Minister whose record seemed so unpromising.[28]

When Mrs Thatcher had settled into the Oval Office, Reagan duly asked about the economy. But she did not seem to mind. 'She is as firm as ever re the Soviets and for reduction of govt,' he recorded afterwards. 'Expressed regret that she tried to reduce govt spending a step at a time & was defeated in each attempt. Said she should have done it our way – an entire package – all or nothing.' Embarrassingly, however, that very morning the US Treasury Secretary, Don Regan, told a congressional committee that he had no intention of copying her policies, which had produced an 'explosive inflationary surge' and 'ruined their export trade'. By contrast, he said, 'our programme is much more sensible, much more comprehensive, and with a greater degree of chance of success than the British experience'. This could have been a disaster, but Mrs Thatcher made nothing of it. That speaks volumes about her eagerness to impress her hosts. Indeed, after she had visited Congress the next day, Reagan recorded that she 'was literally an advocate for our ec. program. Some of the Sen's. tried to give her a bad time. She put them down firmly & with typical British courtesy.'[29]

The high point came that evening at the British Embassy, where she was on extraordinarily effusive form. She and Reagan, she told the guests, shared 'the same way of looking at and doing things'. Addressing the new

President directly, she told him that there would be times 'when yours perhaps is the loneliest job in the world, times when you need what one of my great friends in politics once called "two o'clock in the morning courage"'. She knew very well 'what this two o'clock in the morning courage means, what a lonely job it is, and how in the end only one thing will sustain you, that you have total integrity and at the end of the day you have to live with the decision you have made'.

According to Charles Moore, she had written these lines herself. They were perfectly judged, since this was precisely the sort of melodramatic stuff that Reagan loved. His reply was pure Hollywood. 'The British people, who nourish the great civilized ideas, know the forces of good ultimately rally and triumph over evil,' he said. 'That, after all, is the legend of the Knights of the Round Table, the legend of the man who lived on Baker Street, the story of London in the Blitz, the meaning of the Union Jack snapping briskly in the wind.' *Private Eye*'s Denis Thatcher calls it a 'balls-aching encomium of the British Breed, apparently under the impression that Winston Churchill was still alive, and comparing the Boss with Boadicea standing up to the Trots'. But the real Denis probably enjoyed it, and Reagan meant every word. 'Truly a warm & beautiful occasion,' he wrote in his diary. Later, one of his aides told Henderson, 'without any prompting, that the President had been moved by Mrs T's embassy speech, especially the passage about two o'clock courage'.[30]

For Mrs Thatcher, it was an unforgettable evening. The Reagans left before the band got going, which was a shame because she had specifically asked to have dancing. At first nobody dared to invite her on to the floor, so Henderson stepped in. 'Prime Minister,' he said gallantly, 'would you like to dance?' She accepted, he wrote, 'without complication or inhibition, and, once we were well launched on the floor, confessed to me that that was what she had been wanting to do all the evening. She loved dancing, something, so I found out, that she did extremely well.' When they had finished, Denis materialized, presumably from the bar, and told her it was time to go to bed. Henderson suggested one more dance. 'Yes, come on,' she said eagerly. 'It was with some difficulty', Henderson recorded, 'that Denis eventually managed to extract her.' Even then she was clearly still buzzing with adrenaline, and said something about wanting to see Washington's monuments by night. 'But Denis put his foot down,' Henderson wrote, and said firmly: 'Bed.'[31]

The next morning, the Thatcher party flew on to New York. At the Waldorf Hotel she addressed an audience of old CIA hands, waxing lyrical about her admiration for Reagan, 'a man committed to . . . the virtues of plain speaking and less government – virtues in the defence of which I have myself earned some battle scars'. The two of them, she said, had embarked on a crusade 'to prevent aggression and to oppose tyranny'. Her audience loved it; so did Denis, who was spotted wiping away tears. Afterwards, Henderson recorded, they went up to her suite for a last drink before the flight home. But 'Mrs T was still in a state of euphoria from the applause she had received which was indeed very loud and genuine and she burst out: "You know we all ought to go dancing again."' Alas, Henderson pointed out that her plane was waiting on the tarmac at JFK, so she had to abandon her dancing plans for the time being.[32]

Everybody agreed that the trip had been a triumph, the perfect tonic at a time when Mrs Thatcher seemed so beleaguered. The American press called it a 'love-in' and a 'honeymoon', while Reagan's press secretary joked that it had been 'difficult to prise them apart'. 'I believe a real friendship exists between the P.M. her family & us – certainly we feel that way & I'm sure they do,' Reagan wrote in his diary. A week later, in her handwritten thank-you message to Henderson, Mrs Thatcher sounded a similar note. 'There will never be a happier party than the one you gave at the Embassy,' she wrote. 'I have great confidence in the President. I believe he will do things he wants to do – and he won't give up.' But not all of her ministers shared her enthusiasm. When a colleague asked Lord Carrington how the trip had gone, his reply was a masterpiece of its kind. 'Oh, very well,' he said. 'She liked the Reagan people very much. They're so vulgar.'[33]

And then it was back to Britain: the dreary skies, the downcast faces, the drab reality of recession. The news, as usual, was awful. According to the latest figures, manufacturing production had fallen by 15 per cent in the last year, and in some sectors one in six people had lost their jobs. There were, admittedly, two tiny shafts of sunlight. Inflation was down to 13 per cent, its lowest level since the summer of 1979, while the pound was falling at last. But as most commentators peered into the gloom they could see only darkness ahead. Some thought the Conservatives were doomed: in his Budget preview, *The Times*'s David Wood thought no government could win 'in circumstances of rising or abnormally high unemployment, factory closures, liquidations and bankruptcies, high interest rates, an over-valued pound, falling production, non-growth, and all the rest'. And with only two years until a likely election, Howe was running out of time to change the narrative.[34]

Budget Day was Tuesday 10 March. Late on Monday afternoon, Howe asked Jim Prior to come and see him. Only then did the Chancellor reveal his hand. 'I told him I thought it was awful and absolutely misjudged,' Prior wrote later. 'I couldn't say anything bad enough about it.' Later that evening, still in shock, Prior warned Sir Ian Gilmour that the Budget was 'appalling'. They agreed to meet for breakfast the next day, just before Cabinet. Should they threaten to resign? Gilmour was all for quitting there and then. No, Prior said. The Budget had been decided, so in this battle they were 'already beaten'. Far better, he thought, to stay and prepare for the next clash than to leave Thatcher and Howe in command of the field.[35]

At 9.30 a.m., the Wets joined their Cabinet colleagues to hear Howe go through the details. When the Chancellor had finished, there was a moment of silence. Then, Hoskyns recorded, Prior 'jumped in to attack, v. strong, red in the face, saying it was a disastrous budget'. Here was the Wets' last chance to rally their colleagues against the leadership. But they missed it. Instead of making a co-ordinated attack, the other dissenters confined themselves to grumbling and mumbling. 'We've been doing this for two years, and it doesn't seem to be working,' Carrington said gloomily. But then Howe's allies hit back. Would Prior prefer more borrowing, higher interest rates and a higher pound? At that, Hoskyns wrote, the Employment Secretary 'began to look isolated and foolish'. The battle was lost, and Prior knew it. In his memoirs he regretted that he had shrunk from the nuclear option of resignation, explaining that he felt he owed it to his supporters to stay on. Still, as Hoskyns noted, 'at least Jim had the courage to speak out'. The other Wets, living down to their nickname, had not even done that.[36]

Just after half-past three, Howe rose to present his Budget to the Commons. The deficit, he said, was now forecast to hit £13½ billion in 1980–81, which was 6 per cent of GDP, widening to £14 billion the following year. This was no good: he had decided to get it down to £10½ billion, which would 'enable us to achieve our monetary objectives without having to face intolerably high interest rates'. But it also meant 'some harsh decisions'. The nation's vices would be more expensive – the price of a pint of beer, for example, went up by 4p, a packet of cigarettes by 14p and a bottle of spirits by 60p – while there was a one-off tax on bank deposits over £10 million. Above all, Howe froze income tax allowances, instead of allowing them to rise by 15 per cent in line with inflation. 'This decision has not been lightly taken,' he said earnestly, 'and I share the disappointment that everyone will feel.' On the upside, he had decided to cut interest rates from 14 to 12 per cent. And then, after some optimistic noises about lower inflation and lower unemployment, he sat down. He had been speaking for an hour and a half; but the aftershocks would continue for years.[37]

No modern Budget has ever met a worse reception. Gallup found that it was comfortably 'the most unpopular Budget for 30 years', with seven out of ten people considering it 'unfair', while only one in four thought Howe was doing a decent job. 'The Budget is not well received,' began Bernard

Ingham's press summary – and that was virtually the best line in it. The *Guardian* called it a 'message of perverse destruction' from a government 'enslaved by a false and destructive dogma', while *The Times*'s economics editor, David Blake, predicted that Howe's measures would push up the value of sterling, put more people out of work and add millions to the annual welfare bill. Even Mrs Thatcher's most reliable cheerleaders were despondent. 'Howe It Hurts!' gasped the *Sun*, which thought 'the Chancellor, and indeed the whole Government, have failed to deliver the goods'. 'You Name It . . . He's Taxed It!' howled the *Express*. 'It is not good enough . . . True, inflation is being conquered – but by the time Sir Geoffrey has finished, what will be left of industry? How many people will be on the dole?' But the pithiest verdict came in the *Mirror*. 'If YOU Smoke, Drink or Drive,' said its front-page headline, 'UP YOURS from the Chancellor.'[38]

**"Here's a nice thing about you, Geoffrey!"**

Howe's 1981 Budget was the most widely reviled in modern history. His wife Elspeth would have needed an immensely powerful magnifying glass to find anything even vaguely complimentary. This is Jak in the *Evening Standard*, 13 March 1981.

Mrs Thatcher did not take all this lying down. At lunchtime the day
after the Budget she was due to present the *Guardian*'s Young Businessman of the Year award to John Gardiner, chief executive of the Laird
engineering conglomerate. Casting aside her text, she made a few dutiful
remarks about Gardiner's virtues and then reached for her shotgun. She
knew, she said, that the press had been critical of the Budget. But her critics were not just wrong, they were downright immoral:

> Now what really gets me is this, that it is very ironic that those who are
> most critical of the extra tax are those who were most vociferous in demand-
> ing the extra expenditure. And what gets me even more is that having
> demanded that extra expenditure they are not prepared to face the conse-
> quences of their own action and stand by the necessity to get some of the
> tax to pay for it. And I wish some of them had a bit more guts and courage
> than they have.
>
> Because I think one of the most immoral things you can do is to pose as
> the moral politician demanding more for health, for education, more for
> industry, more for housing, more for everything, and then when you see
> the bill say, 'No, no, I didn't mean you to pay tax to pay for it, I meant you
> to borrow more.'

But if the government had borrowed more, interest rates 'would have gone
up and then they would have stifled and strangled at birth any rebuilding
of stocks or any expansion of industry and investment'. Then she returned
to her critics:

> But what else do they mean? I tell you what they really mean, they mean,
> 'We don't like the expenditure we have agreed, we are unwilling to raise
> the tax to pay for it. Let us print the money instead.' The most immoral
> path of all. Because what that is saying is, 'Let us quietly steal a certain
> amount from every pound in circulation, let us steal a certain amount from
> every pound saved in building societies, in national savings, from every
> person who has been thrifty.'
>
> What they are saying is, 'Let's go and put a pair of bellows on to the rate
> of inflation we have now and make it a really big raging furnace.'

Even by her own standards, said a shocked *Guardian* the next day, this
was an 'astonishing' outburst. What was most remarkable, though, was
how starkly it exposed the divisions at the heart of her Cabinet. 'Those
who were most vociferous in demanding the extra expenditure . . . One
of the most immoral things you can do is to pose as the moral politician . . . We don't like the expenditure we have agreed . . . Let us print the

money instead . . .' She was not talking about the press. She was talking about her own ministers.[39]

Thursday's papers were more apocalyptic than ever. 'Chancellor under Savage Attack from All Quarters' ran the headline in *The Times*. Besieged by journalists at the Commons, Prior denied that he was going to resign, but pointedly added that he was 'going to fight my corner for the Government, and in the Government'. And Friday's headlines were, if anything, even worse. 'Cabinet Men Warn on Budget' read the *Sun*'s front page, reporting an 'open revolt' by Mrs Thatcher's ministers. 'In secret meetings, top Ministers have decided that they will never again allow Chancellor Sir Geoffrey Howe to spring such a shock on them at such short notice . . . Now the rebels insist that in future the entire Cabinet must discuss economic strategy before Sir Geoffrey is allowed on the rampage.' This, the *Sun* said, was not just 'a vote of no confidence in the Chancellor's judgement'; it was 'a political disaster that could threaten the stability of the Government'.

The paper had got its information from Francis Pym – whom Ingham had overheard briefing journalists in the Commons – but Whitelaw, Carrington, Prior, Gilmour, Walker and Soames were reportedly ready to join the 'mutiny'. The only good news was that the *Sun* sided with Mrs Thatcher, not the disgruntled grandees. These 'flat-footed Heathites', the paper said, were the 'real enemies' standing in the way of national reconstruction, and 'should be treated with contempt . . . If Mrs Thatcher and the Treasury cannot impose their will on their more timorous colleagues – some of whom are demanding a bigger say in what future Budgets should contain – the whole economic Battle of Britain will be lost. Forever.'[40]

If there was one place where the Budget provoked the greatest horror, it was not Liverpool, Birmingham or some other recession-plagued manufacturing town. It was not even on Mrs Thatcher's own front bench. It was Cambridge, the booming heart of 'Silicon Fen', a city that was actually doing very well in the early 1980s. Cambridge was the birthplace and *alma mater* of John Maynard Keynes, whose star still shone brightly at the university's economics faculty. So when, over coffee a few days after the Budget, two of Britain's most eminent Keynesian economists, Professors Robert Neild and Frank Hahn, decided to draft a broadside to *The Times*, they knew they would find plenty of horrified signatories among their Cambridge colleagues.

What they did not expect, though, was that they would get so many signatures that they exceeded the newspaper's limit. So Neild, the

Treasury's chief economic adviser during the 1960s, turned the letter into a statement and invited economists from other universities to sign:

> We, who are all present or retired members of the economic staffs of British universities, are convinced that:
>
> There is no basis in economic theory or supporting evidence for the Government's belief that by deflating demand they will bring inflation permanently under control and thereby induce an automatic recovery in output and employment;
>
> Present policies will deepen the depression, erode the industrial base of our economy and threaten its social and political stability;
>
> There are alternative policies; and
>
> The time has come to reject monetarist policies and consider urgently which alternative offers the best hope of sustained economic recovery.

By the time the statement was published, Neild and Hahn had collected 364 names, including fifty-four signatures from Cambridge, twenty-one from Warwick, thirteen from Oxford and forty-seven from various London institutions, including the London School of Economics. Among them were no fewer than five former government chief economic advisers: Professor James Meade, Lord Roberthall, Sir Alec Cairncross, Sir Bryan Hopkin and Sir Fred Atkinson. These were not student union philosophers or Marxist bomb-throwers. They were the great and the good, the Establishment incarnate, the post-war consensus in human form.[41]

When the 364 economists' statement appeared on 30 March, it was a sensation. 'Maggie Blasted by Egghead Rebellion', gasped the *Express*, while the *Mirror* thought it 'one of the most powerful indictments of any government'. Immediately, Mrs Thatcher's admirers raced to her defence. 'It should surprise no one that the lost generation of British economists who had succumbed to the teaching of Lord Keynes should form a panicky mob when a reversal of the policies they had inspired reveals the damage they have done,' Friedrich Hayek wrote scornfully to *The Times*. 'They significantly can only refer to, but cannot specify, the "other methods" by which their professed aim can be achieved.'

This was harsh, but not necessarily unfair, since the 364 had indeed failed to spell out what their 'alternative policies' would be. In fact, Neild and Hahn had deliberately avoided being too specific because they wanted to attract as many signatories as possible. But they should have known this was asking for trouble. 'The practical man is puzzled,' one Tory MEP, William Hopper, wrote mockingly. 'If workable policies are available, why did the distinguished former Chief Economic Advisers not apply them when they held sway? Or are we in trouble now because they did apply them? And why do they not disclose them now?'[42]

It is telling that both Hayek and Hopper turned the economists' eminence against them. For Mrs Thatcher's supporters, the men behind the statement were not disinterested experts; they were the 'guilty men' of the 1960s and 1970s. 'With a few honourable exceptions,' wrote Ralph Harris, director of the free-market Institute for Economic Affairs, 'the more prominent signatories read like a charge sheet of those responsible for Britain's relative economic decline since the war.' Given their record, agreed the *Spectator*'s Ferdinand Mount, how could they seriously expect 'simple folk' to grovel before their 'professional authority'? 'Governments crash, inflation whooshes up to annual rates of 20 and 30 per cent, unemployment steadily climbs. Yet still the 364 continue to argue that the sort of policies they espoused when in Whitehall are the best available . . . Surely, it is time for a tiny re-think, even if only for the look of the thing.' And in the *Express*, the reliably pungent George Gale went for the jugular:

> The economists profess that 'for the sake of the country – and the profession – it is time we all spoke up' . . . If they were really thinking of their profession's reputation instead of playing politics, they would not have come up with, promoted and signed a meretricious little document like this . . .
>
> Tendentious, disingenuous, impertinent, insolent and conceited, it represents nothing more than the poor and infertile patch of common ground on which these 364 could agree to stand.
>
> There they are, held together only by hostility to Thatcher, and a hankering after the good old spendthrift days when some of them were powers in the falling and declining land.

It takes little imagination to picture how that went down in Cambridge.[43]

What did the man and woman on the street make of all this? Most probably could not have cared less, but those who did tended to side with George Gale, at least if the letters pages are any guide. 'The fact that 364 of Britain's leading economists, including no fewer than five previous advisers to the Government of the day, have attacked the Government's economic policies has finally convinced me (and I suspect thousands of others) that Mrs Thatcher must be right,' wrote William Firth of Blackpool in *The Times*. 'I am relieved to see that, economically, Mrs Thatcher has got her sums right. She must have done if 364 economists claim she is wrong,' agreed Jack Braithwaite in the *Express*. And even in the Labour-supporting *Mirror*, J. Moffatt of Ealing thought 'the fact that 364 university economists condemn Mrs Thatcher's monetarist policy almost confirms

454                         WHO DARES WINS

that it is right. These voluble academics have been consistently wrong in
the past and I see no reason why they should be right over monetarism. I
would sooner put my trust in *Mirror* astrologer June Penn's predictions
than theirs.'[44]

Needless to say, this was not the reaction that the former chief economic
advisers had anticipated. But in an increasingly populist age, the weight
of their qualifications told against them. People who remembered the
economic disappointments of the last decade were hardly likely to be
persuaded by the very men who had been in charge, let alone by pronouncements from a Cambridge High Table. The irony, therefore, is that
in turning their guns on Sir Geoffrey Howe, the 364 economists probably
did him a favour. 'I can't quite put my finger on it,' one City broker wrote
a few weeks later:

> Somehow they don't seem to have brought off whatever it was they were
> trying to achieve. Rather like the Charge of the Light Brigade, they meant
> well but have ended up as slightly humorous subjects. They formed up in
> their cloistered courts, mounted on a motley collection of nags, clutching
> a variety of largely obsolete weapons, blunderbusses, spears and lances,
> and then weren't quite sure where they were going.

But the most memorable verdict came from Howe himself. 'An economist',
he remarked in his Mansion House speech that autumn, 'is a man who
knows 364 ways of making love – but who doesn't know any women.'[45]

The arguments about the 1981 Budget will never be settled. Perhaps the
most obvious point is that the 364 were guilty of what Lawson called
'exquisite' timing. In their statement they explicitly said that Howe's
measures would 'deepen the depression'. Yet the Budget marked the
moment when the economy began, very slowly, to turn the corner. In the
second quarter of 1981 growth inched into the black, and for the rest of
the decade the economy continued to grow. In this respect, then, Mrs
Thatcher and her allies were justified in declaring victory. Yes, they
admitted, the recovery was much weaker than they had hoped. But it was
still a recovery, which proved that their critics had been needlessly hysterical and that the strategy had been right all along. Hence, as Lawson
sardonically put it, 'the 1981 Budget came to be seen almost as a political
equivalent of the Battle of Britain: the Thatcher Government's finest hour;
its most widely acknowledged success and a turning point in its political
fortunes'.[46]

Unfortunately, this 'finest hour' narrative has some striking weaknesses. To take a small but revealing example, one of the chief justifications

for Howe's measures was that they would allow him to cut interest rates. On Budget Day he duly announced that they would fall from 14 to 12 per cent. Yet far from heralding a golden age of lower rates, this turned out to be a false start. The pound had started to fall at the turn of the year, and by the early autumn it had tumbled so low, down to just $1.75, that Howe had to put interest rates back *up* to 14 per cent. By October he was so worried about a run on the pound that he raised them still higher, to 16 per cent. So much, then, for the Budget allowing him to get rates down! Indeed, to the ever-stringent Edmund Dell, this suggests that Alan Walters was right all along: the Budget was too weak. Only when Howe raised interest rates in the autumn, Dell argues, were the markets persuaded that he meant what he said about tackling inflation.[47]

One other obvious point is that Howe would not have needed such a draconian Budget if he had made better choices in his first two years. Given the nightmarish combination of high inflation, a high pound and a chronically uncompetitive economy, probably no Chancellor could have navigated the tempest of the early 1980s without making mistakes. Even so, Howe would surely have done better to wait before cutting income tax and raising VAT. He might also have done better to tackle the budget deficit during the first year, which would have reassured the markets, dampened inflationary pressures and avoided the need for tax rises later. Finally, and most importantly, he should have relaxed his tight monetary policy much earlier, before sterling went through the roof. Many years later, when the free-market Institute for Economic Affairs (IEA) held a seminar to mark the Budget's twenty-fifth anniversary, every speaker agreed that the government had squeezed the money supply far too tightly, pushing up the exchange rate and putting British industry under intolerable pressure. This is not to say that another Chancellor would necessarily have done a better job. But even Howe must sometimes have wished that he had given himself more room for manoeuvre.[48]

As for the argument that the Budget coincided with Britain's triumphant emergence from recession, even this is not entirely straightforward. In some parts of the country there was barely any recovery at all. Unemployment carried on rising until the first quarter of 1984, while it took output no fewer than thirteen quarters to return to the level of late 1979. To some of the 364, this proved they were right after all. Decades later, the London School of Economics' Stephen Nickell maintained that Howe's Budget had been completely unnecessary, because with unemployment rising so fast inflation was bound to come down eventually. A more sensible course, Nickell argued, would have been to bring inflation down gradually, which would have ensured a stronger recovery. Instead, the

Chancellor piled on the misery, which 'did indeed deepen the depression just as predicted'. To borrow Howe's own analogy, he might well have known some women, but they might have had more fun if he had adopted a more patient technique.[49]

Even so, it is easier to identify what the government got wrong than to say what it should have done instead. It is untrue that there were no alternatives. The very fact that Howe, Mrs Thatcher and their officials spent so long arguing about the details suggests that they could have chosen differently. The problem, though, is that most of the obvious alternatives had been tried before. Indeed, the Labour economist Derek Scott, who had been Denis Healey's special adviser at the Treasury and worked for Callaghan after 1979, told the IEA seminar that it was 'complete nonsense' to imagine there was an easy alternative. In Scott's words, 'they'd all been tried, in one way or another . . . whether you go back to Heath or whether you go back to the Wilson and Callaghan government'.[50]

The Wets, for example, always argued that Howe should have changed course, reflated the economy and introduced an incomes policy to bring inflation down. Politically this would have been a suicidal U-turn, since both Howe and Mrs Thatcher had explicitly ruled it out. And there were other drawbacks. By keeping wage increases below inflation, incomes policies drove down people's living standards, which is why the trade unions hated them. As a result, Heath had faced two miners' strikes, while even Callaghan's informal pay restraint had provoked the Winter of Discontent. The chances of the trade unions meekly accepting another dose from Mrs Thatcher were non-existent. So when the Wets insisted that she could pour borrowed money into the economy and use incomes policies to handle inflation, they were living in a fantasy world.[51]

The other problem with the Wets' approach was that they never spelled out exactly how much money they were proposing to pump into the economy and to what end. In the summer of 1981, the *Economist* Intelligence Unit tried to predict the effects of the Wets' approach using the Treasury's own economic model. But when the forecasters reversed Howe's tax rises and factored in an extra £1 billion in annual spending, they found it would make virtually no difference at all. In fact, just to get unemployment down to 2 million, a Keynesian government would probably have had to spend an extra £40 billion over four years. Whether Prior, Gilmour and their friends were prepared to contemplate such a borrowing spree seems very unlikely. In any case, such a colossal figure was too big for the economy to absorb without triggering runaway inflation and the collapse of the pound – and then they would be back in the mid-1970s all over again.[52]

What about the left? Labour's senior figures were so evasive that it is virtually impossible to work out what their approach would have been. That leaves the Bennites' Alternative Economic Strategy, which held that, in an increasingly globalized world, Britain could only reboot its economy by retreating behind a protectionist trade wall. A Benn government would impose stringent controls on foreign imports and capital flows, while pumping borrowed money into jobs and manufacturing under the direction of a supercharged National Enterprise Board. On the right most people regarded this as utter lunacy, but when the *Economist* Intelligence Unit tested it using the Treasury's model, the results were striking. A Labour government spending an extra £6 billion would probably provide an extra 300,000 public sector jobs, while a 30 per cent tariff on imports might create another 300,000 jobs in manufacturing. So by 1984, the model found, a Benn government would be signing at least half a million fewer dole cheques than a Thatcher government.

But there were some compelling downsides. Perhaps the most obvious is that, contrary to his claims, Benn's approach would *not* bring back full employment, since about 3 million people would still be out of work. With foreign goods almost a third more expensive, inflation would rise sharply. Living standards would take a severe hit, and even after three years would be some 3½ per cent lower under Benn than under Mrs Thatcher. So although fewer people would be out of work, most people would be worse off. And that was not all. Protectionism on this scale was incompatible with membership of the Common Market, so Britain would have to pull out of Europe. Since the plan also involved massive public borrowing, it is difficult to see how a Bennite government would have survived for long without a collapse of international confidence and a catastrophic run on the pound. It is hard to believe that most voters would have seen this as a price worth paying.[53]

None of this means alternatives to Howe's approach were impossible. But they all came with heavy costs of their own, usually involving higher inflation and lower living standards. Indeed, if anybody doubted the scale of the challenge, they should have looked across the Channel. On 10 May 1981, two months after Howe's incendiary Budget, François Mitterrand won the French presidency after promising to build socialism in one country, financed by massive public borrowing. Not only did Mitterrand's new government pump almost £1 billion into extra welfare spending, it raised the minimum wage, offered subsidies for firms that took on more workers and nationalized a range of banks, industries and utilities – a programme to make Tony Benn weep with envy.

The results were a disaster. Inflation soared, while France's budget and balance of payments deficits went through the roof. Even worse, unemployment continued to rise, reaching 2 million in the spring of 1982. By this stage, collapsing market confidence had already forced Mitterrand to devalue the franc, and two further devaluations followed in the next twelve months. At last, after a series of humiliating political defeats, Mitterrand's finance minister, Jacques Delors, embarked on a colossal U-turn. In coal mines and car factories, shipyards and steelworks, the French government began laying people off. And so, by 1984, a president elected on a platform that could have been written by Tony Benn was presiding over an austerity programme that could have been written by Sir Geoffrey Howe. But, for Delors, austerity was simply the recognition of economic reality. 'The road to economic salvation', he said, 'can only follow a model which puts the accent on a drastic drop in inflation, maintenance of the buying power of our currency, and the ferocious search for competitiveness.' Howe would have agreed with every word.[54]

What happened in France was not unusual. In the Republic of Ireland, successive governments tried to spend their way out of recession and ended up crashing their own economy into the ditch, with inflation peaking at almost 25 per cent, youth unemployment reaching more than 20 per cent and total government debt soaring to some 65 per cent of national GDP. The basic truth is that, thanks to the rise of inflation and the decline of manufacturing, *every* Western government faced a choice of evils. It would be foolish to deny that Howe's approach came at a heavy cost: as *The Times* pointed out in March 1982, there had already been far more job losses and factory closures in Britain than in any other major economy. And even many of his supporters conceded that in the first two years monetary discipline was far too severe. If Howe had been given a chance to turn the clock back, it seems very unlikely that he would have squeezed so tightly a second time.[55]

But it would be equally foolish to deny that he had his successes. Even in the spring of 1982, it was obvious that Britain's productivity performance had turned a corner. Above all, when Howe left the Treasury a year later he had succeeded in the one thing that had eluded his predecessors, reducing inflation to its lowest level since the 1960s. Later, when the spectre of inflation had faded into history, it was easy to forget what an enormous achievement this was. It is true, of course, that it came at a heavy price in job losses. It is true, too, that success came partly by accident, since the government never anticipated that the recession would be so deep. But would Howe have conquered inflation if he had started more tentatively, or if he had followed the Wets' advice in 1981? Probably not. His friend Nigel Lawson freely acknowledged that in an ideal world they would have 'squeezed inflation out of the system without the high exchange rate'. But since no such alternative existed, Lawson argued, the only way to do it was with 'shock treatment'.

Of course Lawson was always going to say that. It is telling, though, that Denis Healey's former special adviser Derek Scott agreed with him. So did Healey's former Cabinet colleague Edmund Dell, who thought Howe's victory over inflation made him the most effective Chancellor since the war. There is no doubt that Howe made tactical mistakes. But he was surely right to ditch incomes policies, cut Britain's budget deficit, bring down direct taxes and lift the antiquated exchange barriers. Above all, he was right to recognize that the only way to end the cycle of chronic under-performance since the Second World War was to do whatever it took to beat inflation.* And although it was a tragedy that his victory came at the price of so many jobs, the fact is that no alternative strategy, not even Benn's siege economy, would have brought unemployment down below 2 million. That tells its own story.[56]

In Westminster, however, nobody cared about the long view. A Budget is nothing if not a political occasion, and in that respect Howe's measures seemed a complete disaster. No Budget had ever been more unpopular; no Chancellor had ever seen his approval ratings fall so low. The government's reputation was simply abysmal, with the Conservatives stuck in third place behind a putative SDP–Liberal Alliance and a very battered Labour. In the public mind, reported Bernard Ingham on 19 March, both the TUC and the CBI were 'ranged against the Government', while the bitter divisions within the Cabinet were 'manifest and sharply delineated'. Against this background, there was simply 'no basis for credible presentation of the Government's economic policies'.[57]

Perverse as it may sound, though, the chorus of condemnation actually played to Mrs Thatcher's strengths. As John Hoskyns remarked, the Budget was seen as 'such a courageous, almost foolhardy thing to do' that it left a lasting mark on public opinion. The more unpopular she became, the more she bolstered her image as a radical reformer. Not yet the all-conquering juggernaut of the mid-1980s, she was still something of an underdog, defying expectations, fighting the odds. Yet again she had demonstrated her willingness to endure public disapproval in pursuit of her aims. Yet again she had shown that the lady was not for turning. 'If you are going to achieve anything in life, you have to set your objectives and stick to them,' she told a Conservative rally at the end of March.

---

* Of course inflation did make a last lurching reappearance between 1988 and 1991, after the Lawson boom. But this was a one-off rather than a return to the old pattern.

'I do not greatly care what people say about me . . . This is the road I am resolved to follow. This is the path I must go.'[58]

But all this came at a price. After lunch in the Downing Street flat on 13 March, Ronnie Millar told Hosykns that 'he thought MT was pinched, thinner in the face and had obviously been under a lot of strain. She needed a boost to her morale.' But no boost came. Six days later, the *Observer*'s Adam Raphael warned Alan Clark 'that he felt conspiracies to displace the Prime Minister were now becoming quite flagrant; that she has made so many powerful enemies (the Governor of the Bank of England, Chairman of the CBI, etc.) and that he regarded her as being highly vulnerable'. The very next day, Hoskyns bumped into her old media guru Gordon Reece, who had just been to see her in Number 10. 'He had ¾ hr with her', Hoskyns wrote grimly, and 'warned her to be prepared, in June or July, for Macmillan, Thorneycroft and du Cann to come and visit her and tell her to stand down.'[59]

In public, Mrs Thatcher never betrayed the slightest hint of strain. But in private, every now and again, there were clues. A few weeks later, an admirer called Mr Fowler sent her a 'beautiful blue cashmere rug'. Despite all the pressures, she found the time to scribble a letter of thanks for such a 'very special gift':

> Not only is it exquisite in itself, and it is, but it came as a wonderful surprise and at a difficult time just when I needed a little thoughtfulness and kindliness. And you provided it.
>
> This task, to which I have set my hand, is the most absorbing and fascinating in the world. But sometimes it is lonely as one struggles to take the right decision.
>
> At such times, it is marvellous to know that one has good friends, constantly urging us on and wishing us well.

She was human, after all.[60]

# 19

# One in Ten

*My father had a letter that made his face go white: he has been made redundant from his job! He will be on the dole! How can we live on the pittance that the government will give us? The dog will have to go!*

Sue Townsend, *The Secret Diary of Adrian Mole Aged 13¾* (1982)

MRS MALONE: *Have you any idea what no shoes on your feet means?*

JOHN: *... It means the thirties, mam, and soup kitchens and hunger marches. You with your father marchin' from the North East and my dad with his. It means people standing together and fighting. And it means another time and age.*

Boys from the Blackstuff, 'George's Last Ride', 7 November 1982

At noon on 1 May 1981 the People's March for Jobs set off from Liverpool. At the Pier Head, bathed in spring sunlight as far as the eye could see, were hundreds of green anoraks, as well as thousands of well-wishers, roaring their encouragement as the marchers began the long journey south. Their destination was London, their mission to kindle national outrage at the plight of the unemployed. All 500 marchers had been provided with an anorak, backpack and sleeping bag by the Trades Union Congress, as well as a copy of the route, leading through Manchester, Stoke-on-Trent and Stafford to Wolverhampton, Birmingham and Coventry, then on through Northampton, Bedford and Luton to Watford, Wembley and Trafalgar Square. And although critics claimed the march was a 'political stunt', Liverpool's churchmen offered warm support. 'Those in the Home Counties and the capital have no real knowledge nor understanding of the extent and gravity of the plight facing the

jobless,' the city's Catholic Archbishop, Derek Worlock, told an ecumen-
ical service that morning. 'Our hope and prayer today is that the People's
March for Jobs will help to remind all parts of the country of this basic
principle.'

At first, as the marchers wound their way through the struggling towns
of the north-west, they encountered a warm reception. In Warrington, the
journalist Louis Heren found them 'in fine fettle, moving slightly faster
than an infantry company'. The night before, the local trades council had
given them a hearty dinner of Lancashire hotpot, apple pie and beer, and
they were in good voice. 'Maggie, Maggie, Maggie!' they chanted. 'Out,
out, out!' By now hundreds of sympathizers had joined the march: despite
a few CND badges and punk hairstyles, Heren thought most were
'middle-aged trade union stalwarts'. In Salford, the local Conservative mayor
offered some polite words of support, although he felt bound to tell them
that unemployment was a 'worldwide problem' with 'no simple solution'.
In Stockport, a 'quietly angry old man', disabled in the Second World War,
stood for more than an hour in the pouring rain to greet what he called
'the wounded. The lads and lasses of Britain. Bloody refugees.' In Tunstall,
they were cheered by local pottery workers; from Hanley to Stafford, they
were joined by hundreds of trade unionists. When Heren caught up with
them again a couple of days later, he found them in great spirits; they had
dined on roast pork, pudding and cheese, and one man had even gone
ballroom dancing.[1]

In Wolverhampton, the marchers stopped for a service in the splendid
red sandstone church of St Peter. There the Bishop of Wolverhampton –
joined, a bit incongruously, by Derek Robinson, the former Bishop of
British Leyland – told them they were making 'the dream of a community
come true'. The service ended with a passionate rendition of 'Jerusalem',
much to the delight of another visiting celebrity, Tony Benn. For Benn,
the obvious parallel was with the Jarrow Crusade of 1936, when hundreds
of jobless marchers had tried to capture the imagination of a society in
the grip of the Great Depression. And as the People's March wound its
way south, its supporters regularly invoked the spirit of 1936.

In Staffordshire, they were joined by 66-year-old Leslie Jones, a retired
teacher who had seen the Jarrow marchers as a schoolboy. The People's
March, he said, was 'Britain, the real Britain . . . a true community helping
each other'. Later, in Hemel Hempstead, they were greeted by 83-year-old
Mabel Jones, who remembered handing out soup to the Jarrow marchers
half a century earlier. Now she was on sandwich-dispensing duty in a
crowded parish hall, reminiscing with reporters as she patted a bemused
punk on the head and pressed an orange into his hand. 'I truly never

thought I'd see this happen again,' she said sadly. By a striking coincidence, it transpired that one of the unemployed marchers billeted in her hall, a 26-year-old man from Liverpool, was the grandson of a Jarrow Crusader. He knew little about his grandfather, but Mrs Jones claimed to remember him perfectly. 'He died on the march to London, you know,' she added. 'He'd be proud of you.'[2]

Yet the Jarrow parallel was not without controversy. When the People's March reached Stoke, the local paper thought it merely 'a shadow of its famous forerunner . . . a carnival with more razzmatazz than heart'. In a letter to the *Church Times*, a local vicar condemned it as 'trivial', 'pointless' and 'almost childishly meaningless', while the *Daily Express*'s reliably ferocious George Gale insisted that the marchers were a 'stage managed army' of 'Communists, Socialist Workers' Party revolutionaries, Militant Tendency, Trotskyists and the like'. They were 'not like the men who marched from Jarrow. They do not express the outrage of a nation; they will not stir the conscious [*sic*] of the country.'

In particular, Gale was displeased by their evening pleasures ('At night the marchers go to pubs and discos') and by their choice of anthems ('anti-war and anti-nuclear bomb and feminist slogans'). All this, he thought, reflected a wider picture: 'The eighties are not the thirties. There is no hunger now, no tattered clothes and barefoot children.' But to the *Mirror*, which vigorously supported the People's March, this kind of talk was a disgrace. 'Of course today's marchers are different from their grandfathers,' thundered an editorial. 'They are well-dressed, not tattered . . . But they are still out of work.'[3]

In the meantime, the marchers trudged on through the rain. As the Jarrow furore suggested, their reception was not always as positive as the organizers had hoped. In the mock-Tudor suburbs of one Lancashire town, a reporter saw people glaring from 'behind their net curtains', clearly displeased by their songs about 'jobs and Tories'. One man, 'manicuring his lawn', asked what it was all about. 'Oh yes,' he said, as the marchers explained. 'I've heard something about this. Well, it is not such a nice day for it.' Then he turned and went inside.

Yet at every stop from Warrington to Wembley, supporters waited with tea and sandwiches. In Birmingham, where the rain poured remorselessly down, Louis Heren saw Sikh elders with collecting boxes, men waving from the windows of a 'garishly painted West Indian hotel', church groups, social workers and brass bands. In Redbourn, Hertfordshire, the marchers were shocked to see a 'No Marchers' sign on the door of the Bull Inn, but delighted when they reached the village hall to find 'large sandwiches of crusty French bread and ham, daintily wrapped in paper napkins', as well as chocolate, mince pies and gallons of tea. In one corner, a local woman tended the marchers' blistered feet; in another, two old ladies comforted a young woman from Yorkshire, crying from tiredness after days on the road. 'Nonsense,' one of them said when she told them not to bother. 'I am going to take you home and put you to bed.' So much, Heren thought, for the stereotype of cold, unfeeling southerners.[4]

By the time the marchers reached London, having walked for more than 260 miles in dreadful weather, most were wet, footsore and utterly exhausted. Waiting for them was progressive Britain in all its pomp: punks and stilt-walkers, Liberals and Communists, families with young children and shop stewards with their banners, some 100,000 people united in their loathing of Mrs Thatcher. Once again the rain hammered down, but as the marchers approached Trafalgar Square the sun came out at last, and when the green anoraks came into view the crowd roared their support. To their sympathizers, the marchers' very presence was proof of their moral victory over the economic forces that sought to deny their humanity. Labour spokesmen even told the press that it had been 'their greatest propaganda success since Mrs Thatcher took office'. It was 'not a Jarrow crusade or a peasants' revolt', thought the *Mirror*, 'but it WAS a march into history'.[5]

On the next day, 1 June, a marchers' delegation visited Westminster to see the Employment Secretary, Jim Prior. Mass unemployment was terribly sad, he said, but the government was doing all it could to put the economy back on a solid footing and provide real jobs for Britain's people. The marchers, not surprisingly, described it as a 'dialogue of the deaf'. And then it was all over. By the time the sun dipped beneath the London skyline, the politicians had disappeared, the banners had been rolled up, the supporters had gone home, and the marchers were reluctantly turning their minds to the desolation of their working lives. Outside the Commons, some of them had told Tony Benn of their fear that 'when the march is over they will just be unemployed people again'. The tragedy, of course, was that they were right.[6]

The scene is a factory in Coventry, shortly after the turn of the 1980s. 'It was Thursday morning, and it's pay day, and everybody is excited,' the works convener later told the journalist Beatrix Campbell. He was a young man for a convener, still in his mid-thirties, but he had been there since leaving school, making lights for the car and electrical industries. At lunchtime, the wages clerk came to see him. 'There's something going on,' she said worriedly, 'they've just rung for six taxis.' 'Bloody hell!' the convener thought. Half an hour later, he felt a tap on his shoulder.

'In my office – now,' said the boss. I said, 'What for?' but they wouldn't tell me on the shop floor. In his office he said, 'Get all your members to switch off their machines and get them into the fitting bay. I've got something to tell them.' So he came out. 'I've got a statement to make and it's not very nice. We've just had a word with the bank, they've pulled the plug. You've got an hour's notice to get out.' It took him about thirty seconds. He said, 'Don't worry about the money, the government will pay.'

The convener was in shock. He tried to interest his comrades in occupying the plant, but 'everybody was running about all over the place to get their stuff out, all they wanted was out'. It was another two years before they got their redundancy money, but they had to go to an industrial tribunal first. They were awarded thirteen weeks' pay, which was immediately claimed by the Department of Health and Social Security against their interim social security payments. 'I got £1,324.96,' the convener said. 'Not much for eighteen years of your life, eh!'[7]

By the spring of 1981, stories like this had become so familiar that many people had stopped listening. Unemployment might be a 'human tragedy', to borrow Mrs Thatcher's words, but it had become part of the daily soundtrack, a constant low-level hum of job losses and factory closures. When the *Guardian*'s Peter Jenkins visited Coventry in February, he awoke to 'the news of the monthly unemployment figures':

> The familiar reassuring voice of Jim Prior tells us it's going to get worse before it gets better. For the United Kingdom the average is now 10 per cent. In the West Midlands it is 11.3, in Birmingham 12 and in Coventry 13 per cent. Coventry, the proverbial Klondike of the post-war affluent society – the idea of 13 per cent unemployment takes some getting used to.[8]

But people *were* getting used to it. They had no choice: it was on the front pages of the newspapers, day after day after day. Official figures showed that more than a million jobs had disappeared in 1980, the worst year since the war. Yet everyone knew this was a vast underestimate, because only two out of three workers who had lost their jobs bothered to register as unemployed. Even after seasonal adjustment, the jobless rate was almost exactly 10 per cent, a figure unimaginable only a few years before. In no other major Western economy were so many people on the dole. And never before in British history, not even during the slump of the 1930s, had so many people been out of work.[9]

As in the 1930s, though, the picture was more complicated than the headlines suggested. If you worked in a service industry in the affluent south-east, you were far less likely to lose your job than if you worked in a steel mill in the Black Country. In booming East Anglia, manufacturing employment did not drop *at all* between 1979 and 1987, yet in the West Midlands it fell by almost 30 per cent, in the North by 37 per cent, in Scotland by 35 per cent and in Wales by 34 per cent. The image of Mrs Thatcher's Britain as two nations, irreparably divided between North and South, is a bit of a cliché. Yet the fact remains that, during the worst months of the recession, seven out of ten redundancies came in the old industrial heartlands of the North, the Midlands, Scotland and Wales. 'You are insulated down there,' one man remarked when, during the People's March for Jobs, Louis Heren ducked into a Manchester pub. 'You don't know what life's like . . . You have no idea of what unemployment is like.' Heren explained that he had come to Manchester to find out. 'What's the use,' the man said wearily. 'You can't understand what it is like living in the North.'[10]

If there was one place that became synonymous with unemployment, it was Liverpool. Stranded at the edge of England, long over-reliant on its declining port, Liverpool was always likely to struggle when the downturn came. Even so, the sense of hopelessness was simply breathtaking. Liverpool was a 'time bomb', a 'disaster zone', a 'dying city', wrote an anguished Professor Fred Ridley, who taught politics at the local university, in January 1981. For although the picture was nowhere near as bad as it had been in Jarrow in the 1930s, it was bad enough. On some inner-city estates the unemployment rate was as high as 40 per cent, and this was only counting those who bothered to register. In Speke, formerly the home of the Bryant & May and Triumph factories, an estimated 45 per cent of the adult population had become dependent on the state. As Ridley wrote, there were large swathes of Merseyside where 'unemployment has become as normal as work'. In many of these areas, the atmosphere was 'depressing beyond belief', the shops boarded up, the houses vandalized, the people stripped of hope. 'We have survived two world wars, the blitz and the depression of the 1930s,' one local businessman told a Chamber of Commerce survey. 'I wonder whether we will last out the next twelve months?'[11]

Although Liverpool attracted most attention, it was far from alone. In Flint, North Wales, which was heavily dependent on two struggling firms – British Steel and the textile giant Courtaulds – adult male unemployment reached 32 per cent in the summer of 1980. Across the engineering heartland of the West Midlands, the jobless rate tripled in four years, reaching 18 per cent in Walsall, 17 per cent in Birmingham and 16 per cent in Coventry. And in the dying fishing ports and seaside towns, where few journalists came, the mood was perhaps saddest of all. Walking along Hull's Albert Dock in the spring of 1982, once alive with trawlers and fishermen, Jonathan Raban encountered only silence, the atmosphere bleak enough 'to make one sob for want of company'. The fishermen he had met on his last visit eighteen years earlier now worked in the oil business if they were lucky. If not, they were on the dole. Yet Hull, like Liverpool, was a reminder that the problem of unemployment went deeper than the policies of one government. 'History's not been very kind to Hull,' explained Jimmy Johnstone, who had been Hull West's Labour MP for almost twenty years. 'You can't blame it on Mrs Thatcher.'[12]

At the turn of the 1970s, Grimsby had boasted a deep-sea fishing fleet of some 122 ships. Now, thanks to Britain's capitulation in the Cod Wars with Iceland, there were just eleven. Among the casualties was 59-year-old John Keetley, a boatswain who by the autumn of 1980 had not been to sea for almost two years. He had started in the boats before the Second World War, and had survived being washed overboard three times. But now his working life seemed over. 'I am a skilled man but nobody wants my skill or my experience any more,' Mr Keetley told *The Times*. He was willing to 'go anywhere and do anything', he said. If somebody rang him at three in the morning asking him to put to sea as a deckhand, 'I would go like a shot.'

But they never did. He had used up his savings travelling the country looking for work at sea, but there was nothing. He hated the thought of social security; he did not understand the forms and found it humiliating to ask for help. Every morning he got up at 5.30: it was the 'habit of a lifetime' and to give it up 'would be like surrendering'. But he had nothing to do. Sometimes he took some local pensioners out for a drive, 'just for the company . . . anything is better than sitting at home'. So the time went by, one day after another, week after week. At last, swallowing his pride, he applied for a job as a road-sweeper. But he heard nothing back.[13]

For men like Mr Keetley, unemployment seemed a tunnel without end. Even when opportunities did surface, the competition was so intense that disappointment was far more likely than success. By the spring of 1981, there were ten jobless people for every vacancy in the country. In Liverpool, where 48,000 people were chasing just 1,000 jobs, there were typically hundreds or even thousands of applicants for a single post. Applications for visas to Australia, New Zealand, Canada and South Africa were all up; even army recruitment numbers were at their highest level for two decades. The *Guardian* offered some sensationally patronizing tips for long-term job seekers, who were assumed to be men. 'Cut your hair, wear a sporty-styled one-coloured shirt and tie, and trousers and a jacket,' advised the 'Workface' column. 'That will make them think you're full of energy and enthusiasm, willing to learn, a young man going places but knowing his place.'[14]

But what if you were an older man, ground down by chance and circumstance, your experience disregarded, your skills unwanted? Understandably enough, the press and the government talked endlessly about the plight of the young. 'Our first priority is centred on the young where the problem is at its worst,' Norman Tebbit told the Commons in November 1981. Indeed, the government spent more money on special measures to address youth unemployment – £400 million on the under-18s by the Manpower Services Commission alone in 1981 – than on any other demographic group. But of the million people who, by the second half of 1982, had been out of work for more than a year, many were far from young. For them there were virtually no special measures at all.

By now almost half of unemployment claimants over 60, and a third of those in their late fifties, had been out of work for more than a year. These were often men who had left school in their teens, had never been trained and had few obvious skills; often they were also men with children, living in homes where nobody worked. Not surprisingly, unemployment took a punishing toll. 'Many have reached a state of depression, apathy and acceptance of the state of unemployment,' concluded a leaked Manpower Services Commission report. It was all very well to imply that they should get on their bikes, but where would they live? What would happen to their families? Above all, where on earth should they go – and why should they imagine there would be jobs for them when they got there?[15]

Unemployment was extremely expensive. The Treasury estimated that one man out of work cost the government almost £3,500 a year in social security payments and lost tax revenues, the equivalent of at least £20,000 today. But this may have been an underestimate: later, the Institute for Fiscal Studies suggested that the true cost was more like £4,500 a year. As a result, the Treasury was desperate to keep costs down. So January 1980 brought the first cuts in state benefits since the Depression, with average cash benefits for the unemployed, the sick and pregnant mothers falling from £38.82 a week to just £34.65 a week, while married couples saw a reduction from £51.07 to £47.40.

That might not sound like much. But to people at the bottom, £4 a week was a lot of money. Indeed, by the end of 1981 Britain's army of unemployed were taking home less, in real terms, than at any time since 1971. Yet thanks to the recession, government spending on employment and training programmes actually went *up*, in real terms, by 50 per cent in the first half of the decade. Even more striking is the fact that social security spending, too, kept rising, up by 4 per cent as a proportion of the total and by a staggering 32 per cent in real terms. Given that Mrs Thatcher's critics loved to paint her as the hammer of the poor, there is a grim irony in the fact that no Prime Minister had ever spent so much money on social security. But as her critics argued, she was only doing so because of the consequences of her own policies.[16]

It was no fun being on benefits. At the time, newspapers like the *Daily Express* liked to go on about 'holidays on the dole', urging the government to clobber the 'loafers, shirkers, scroungers, fiddlers [and] cheats'. In reality, the British government was one of the least generous in Western Europe. If you were going to lose your job, you would be much better off in Copenhagen, Amsterdam, Paris or Munich than in London. Far from being a holiday, life on the dole meant being bored, empty, cold, hungry, frightened, lonely, even suicidal. For a single person in 1982, collecting barely £1,300 a year in unemployment benefit, every penny was precious. In Coventry, Beatrix Campbell met a family of three who spent just £15 a week on food, having toast and porridge for breakfast, nothing for lunch, and sandwiches or beans on toast for their tea. Only at weekends did they have a cooked meal, and the mother had no shoes but wore two pairs of socks with her sandals in winter. In the same city, a redundant car fitter, living alone in his mid-forties, received £61.02 in benefits every two weeks. He spent £38.08 on rent and utilities, leaving him less than £23 for everything else. He was too poor to pay his television licence, had to choose between washing powder, soap and toothpaste, kept his central heating to 60 degrees in winter and only used hot water twice a week.

Again and again, as she travelled around Britain, Campbell met people who lived on baked beans and biscuits, never switched their central heating on, never ate meat and struggled to afford clothes for their children. In Sunderland, almost one in five families on the run-down Southwick estate had had their gas cut off, rising to almost half of those with teenaged children. And as Campbell remarked, most unemployed families' budgets were so tight that things other people took for granted – 'a television licence, a holiday, a night out, trips to the swimming baths, roller skates, the *Radio Times*, a pound of plums' – were simply unthinkable. Fresh fruit, new clothes, newspapers and magazines, books and records, cinema tickets, even bus tickets: for some families, these things were no longer staples. They were luxuries they could ill afford.[17]

On 7 May 1981 two 19-year-old boys, Graeme Rathbone and Sean Grant, stole a car in Widnes. They drove it to the banks of the Mersey, attached a pipe to the exhaust and ran it through one of the windows, and then turned on the engine. In a note to their parents, they explained why they were killing themselves:

> What have we left to live for now there is no work for anyone? All teenagers have got to do is hang around street corners getting moved on by the police who think you're up to something.
>
> The way this country is going no one will be able to get jobs. That's why the young are turning to crime and violence. What is left?
>
> We've not got much to live for now. But whatever happens to us doesn't matter. It's the rest of you we feel sorry for. The earth is going to end with a very big bang.

Sean had also left a card for his parents, containing £21 and the message 'This is for mum, dad and the kids'. He was unemployed, having lost his job as a fork-lift truck driver three weeks earlier. Graeme had been out of work even longer, having lost his job in a storeroom in the autumn of 1980. His mother told the inquest that she sometimes found him crying in the kitchen. 'He always used to say there was nothing left. He had no job and there was no future.' The coroner thought the evidence was clear. Unless Mrs Thatcher's government found an answer to mass unemployment, he said, 'it looks to me as if we are going to get more cases like this where youngsters who have not got jobs feel the only way out is to take their own lives'.[18]

In reality, the story of the two boys may have been a bit more complicated, since they had earlier been charged with criminal damage and were due to face the magistrates. The press, however, played up the unemployment angle for all it was worth, and with good reason. For if unemployment was the scourge of the age, then *youth* unemployment was its most virulent manifestation. In Cleveland, 6,500 teenagers were registered as unemployed in the summer of 1981, almost a third of them having left school in 1979 or 1980. The Youth Opportunities Programme (YOP), established by the Callaghan government, was pitifully inadequate, with 700 applicants for every available place. Many teenagers were thrilled when they got on to the scheme, assuming that there would be a job at the end of it. But once they had completed their placements, four out of five went back on to the dole. One 18-year-old, Michael, thought that his stint at a local foundry had been a total waste of time. His take-home pay, he said, was £16, just £1 more than if he had been on supplementary benefit: 'Would you work an extra 40 hours a week for £1?'

In more prosperous Surrey, the prospects for unemployed school-leavers were little better. In Staines and Sunbury, there were almost 500 registered job seekers, most of them school-leavers, competing for just nine permanent jobs and seven YOP places. Paradoxically, the area's affluence made life harder for those who missed out. 'There is no tradition of unemployment here, and that makes it harder to come to terms with,' Surrey's careers officer explained. 'There is not the same family support. Parents say: "you could get a job if you really tried."' A reporter talked to one boy, 16-year-old Derek, whose story proved the point. Having left school with few qualifications, Derek had applied for job after job with no success. His father, exasperated by what he saw as his son's idleness, reacted by kicking him out. 'You feel like blowing your brains out,' Derek said. 'They say kids don't want to work, but that's a joke.'[19]

Even to most Conservatives, the ordeal of Britain's school-leavers seemed genuinely shocking. In a long leader, *The Times* thought it would be 'wholly understandable' for young people to feel 'rage' when ministers lectured them about working harder or 'pricing themselves out of work'. They were not feckless scroungers; they simply wanted 'to work and marry and earn a decent living for their future families'. It was Mrs Thatcher who should try harder, guaranteeing all school-leavers a job, a place at college or a place on a training scheme. In fact, this is pretty much what the government did. By 1983 the YOP scheme had become the Youth Training Scheme (YTS), with school-leavers effectively guaranteed places with local businesses, further education colleges or training courses, initially for a year. The problem, though, was that youth unemployment did not peak until the spring of 1984, when more than 1.2 million people under the age of 25 were officially out of work. Even if the government had poured twice as many resources into the YTS project, it would not have been enough.[20]

Yet for many writers who explored the impact of unemployment, the most compelling stories were those of older men who had lost their identities as breadwinners and providers. At a Sunderland community centre, the journalist Jeremy Seabrook saw the symptoms again and again: 'the bruised look beneath sleepless eyes, the pallor of the skin . . . bitten nails, nervous gestures, the air of defeat'. 'I never go out, never see any friends, only ever see a convener from another plant who sometimes calls me up,' one Coventry machine-tools engineer said. 'Sometimes I think my brain is dying. I get depressed – sometimes I shout and bawl. I'm not going mental, but I feel I might like to damage somebody.' Another machinist, who had been out of work for two years, said that being unemployed felt 'like you've committed a crime somewhere, but nobody tells you what you've done . . . Sometimes I think I'll go barmy. Of course you get depressed, you convince yourself it's you . . . You're a waste of time as a human being.'[21]

Beatrix Campbell thought that women, for all their tribulations, were better able to cope with unemployment because they could fall back on the traditional responsibilities of the housewife. But men were left without any obvious roles. Everywhere she went – Wigan, Sunderland, Coventry, Sheffield – she saw men sitting listlessly on 'public benches once occupied by pensioners and mothers', or self-consciously pushing buggies with small children, or cashing their giros 'in the same numbers as women cashing child benefit and old people collecting their pensions'. 'Men's tragedy', she wrote, 'is that unemployment makes them feel unmanned.'

Many men openly admitted that they felt emasculated. If their wives were also out of work, they were totally dependent on benefits. Yet if their wives were working, they felt the natural order had been turned on its head. 'All I hear is you are the breadwinner and we've got to be careful, we can't have this or that because we can't afford it,' one Wigan man snapped at his wife. 'If I wanted to go anywhere I had to scrounge from the wife. It was sickening,' said a Coventry car worker in his early sixties. 'The wife was the main one I had to depend on, which was disgraceful.' As he admitted, he found it impossible to do anything at home: 'I'm not the kind who does housework.'

*The Times* tracked down three couples who had effectively swapped roles, with the wives acting as breadwinners while their husbands cooked and cleaned. But two of the men admitted that they hated it. 'Housewives are not valued very highly in society,' said John Tanner, a former community relations officer from Scunthorpe, 'and at the moment I'm a housewife and I don't really like it.' As for Peter Smith, a former sales assistant from Poole, he woke every day with a headache and said he felt 'degraded'. He tried to keep a 'stiff upper lip', and would often encourage his wife to cheer up. Then he would look at her face, 'very miserable and white', and all his anxieties flooded back.

For many men, the idea of turning themselves into house-husbands was utterly unimaginable. Instead, they sank into a long torpor, not unlike Adrian Mole's father, who 'lies in bed until noon, then fries a mess in a pan, eats it, opens a can or bottle, then sits and watches *After Noon Plus*'. 'No, I never do any shopping, or housework, or washing, or cleaning,' one Coventry man, barely into his twenties, said glumly. 'The wife does it all . . . I get up about dinner time and just literally hang about. Then I watch telly. I get absolutely and totally absorbed in "Emmerdale Farm".' He had thought about suicide: 'I just generally have the feeling that I'm about to blow my brains out, thinking is this it?' In Sunderland, another young man, married with three small children, struck a similarly heart-breaking theme. 'My wife has known nothing but debt and poverty ever since we've been married,' he told Jeremy Seabrook. 'I just feel empty. I'm ashamed I can't provide them with everything they need. What kind of a father is that? . . . Some days I feel like topping myself. I'm not kidding. If there's no hope for me, what chance will they have? Life won't be worth living. I feel like topping myself and taking them with me.'[22]

Of all the stories of men struggling to come to terms with the shock of unemployment, one of the most affecting was that of Chrissie Todd, a Liverpool tarmac-layer, married with children. When we first meet him, in 1980, he is doing a job up in Middlesbrough. When we see him again, two years later, he has been out of work for months. Although he does a bit of building work on the quiet, he is desperate for a proper job. 'I know I'm losing money asking you this,' he says to the boss, 'but I'd rather be legit on a lot less. *I wanna be a working man again.* I wanna come home at night with dirt on me hands and not have to hide it from anybody.' The boss shakes his head. 'This is the building game, this is Britain in 1982,' he says. 'It's just not worth my while.'

So Chrissie's life spirals towards disaster. At home, his wife Angie is increasingly enraged by his failure to provide for their children. 'What are they going to be doing in ten years time? Are they still going to be wearing hand-me-downs at eighteen and twenty?' she yells. 'What are we bringing them up for – and what is the point of livin' our lives when – when y'get up in the mornin' and it's all downhill from then on?' She begs him to 'fight back': 'They're knockin' the shite and stuffin' out of you, Chrissie Todd, and if you haven't had enough, I have.' But the endless defeats have destroyed his confidence. 'What do you think it's like for me?' he shouts back. 'A second-class citizen. A second-rate man. With no money . . . and no job . . . and no . . . no place!'[23]

Chrissie's story was not real, though it often felt like it. Played with heartrending warmth by Michael Angelis, he is one of the central characters in Alan Bleasdale's *Boys from the Blackstuff*, the best-known cultural depiction of the impact of unemployment. Originally shown on BBC2 in the autumn of 1982, it was such a hit that it was repeated within months on BBC1, attracting some 4 million viewers, and won a BAFTA award as the best series of the year. Yet although it is commonly seen as a blistering indictment of Thatcherism, its origins are a little more complicated. The series was inspired by Bleasdale's one-off *Play for Today*, 'The Black Stuff', which went out on BBC1 in January 1980 but had been written and filmed two years earlier, when unemployment was Jim Callaghan's problem. Indeed, Bleasdale first pitched the idea of an extended series to the BBC well before Mrs Thatcher became Prime Minister. But it took

months for them to make up their minds, and there was another delay
before it went out. By then, unemployment was clearly Mrs Thatcher's
problem, and inevitably the series is remembered as a damning verdict on
her economic legacy.[24]

In his original proposal, Bleasdale had told the BBC that *Boys from
the Blackstuff* would be full of images of 'urban decay, spiritual deprivation and death' in order to suggest 'the hollowness and sense of
worthlessness that a lot of people feel when they're on the Dole'. That
makes it sound depressingly bleak, which it often is, but it is also remarkably funny. Bleasdale had no desire to produce a piece of agitprop, and
while the series never underplays the suffering of its working-class characters, they are not saints but rounded human beings. And although
Bleasdale captures the humiliation of claiming benefits, he never shows
the bureaucrats as caricatured villains, as Ken Loach would have done.
Indeed, he writes with considerable sympathy about the men and women
on the other side of the counters, such as the head of the fraud section,
Miss Sutcliffe, who is struggling to cope with her elderly mother's demen-
tia. Even the electrician who turns off unemployed families' power is
shown sympathetically. 'I hate this job,' he says sadly. 'I don't want to
disconnect people . . . I'm not that sort of person.'[25]

Above all, the series is remembered for Yosser Hughes, played by Bernard Hill with staring eyes, bristling moustache and thick Scouse accent.
Violent, inarticulate, a man on the brink of total mental collapse, Yosser
is one of the great fictional creations of the era, at once terrifyingly manic
and touchingly pitiable. Wherever he goes, we hear the same refrain: 'Gizza
job, go on, gizzit, gizza go, go on, I could do that,' most famously when
he trails disconsolately after a man marking the touchlines on a children's
football pitch. 'Look, here I am, a man,' Yosser tells Miss Sutcliffe. 'A man.
A man. With no job. Looking for one.' After attacking his estranged wife,
he takes his children home, but cannot make fish fingers and toast without
almost burning down his kitchen. Later, he sits alone in his overcoat in the
desolation of his living room, nursing a black eye, surrounded by an empty
tin of spam, two empty milk bottles, a tub of margarine and the remains
of a sliced loaf. 'Everything I've ever wanted, and all the things that I
thought I had, they've all been taken away,' he tells a policeman. Then he
tries to drown himself. Characteristically, he fails.[26]

If Britain in the 1980s had really been as self-centred as its critics
claimed, *Boys from the Blackstuff* would never have struck such a chord.
In fact, popular culture was suffused with images of unemployment. For
obvious reasons – the record market catered predominantly for people
under 25, who were most likely to be worried about unemployment – many

of the best-known examples were songs, such as the Specials' 'Ghost Town' (1981) or the Jam's 'Town Called Malice' (1982). The Birmingham reggae band UB40 took their name from a dole claim form, 'Unemployment Benefit Form 40', which they reproduced on the cover of their first album, *Signing Off* (1980). Their single 'One in Ten', which peaked at number seven a year later, explicitly refers to the unemployment rate in the West Midlands. Yet UB40's story is another reminder that history did not begin in May 1979, because they adopted their name months before Mrs Thatcher came to power. What she gave them was the perfect target: their song, 'Madam Medusa', for example, tells of the 'lady with the marble smile', who haunts 'the sick, the poor, the old' and revels in 'hate and greed and lies'.[27]

Television audiences in the early 1980s could hardly avoid the issue of unemployment. Channel 4's self-consciously gritty soap opera *Brookside*, for example, placed the issue at centre stage. The opening episode, which went out on the channel's first night in November 1982, shows Paul and Annabelle Collins moving into their new home in Brookside Close, Liverpool, having previously lived in the middle-class Wirral, after the fiercely conservative Paul has lost his job. Later episodes show him struggling with the humiliation of life on the dole, while next door young Damon Grant spends years looking for work after leaving school. And although *Brookside* was unusual in making so much of the disappointments of life on a brand-new estate, more established series did not ignore the issue. In *Coronation Street*, Bert Tilsley moves into the street in 1979, loses his job in a local foundry, spends years looking for work and is investigated by the DHSS for benefit fraud. Even *Doctor Who* touched on unemployment, if only obliquely. In Peter Davison's splendid send-off, 'The Caves of Androzani' (1984), set on a distant alien world, the corrupt tycoon Morgus laments that 'the stews of the city are full of such unemployed riff-raff'. 'Most of them unemployed, Trau Morgus,' the planet's president observes, 'because you have closed so many plants.'

Back on earth, many people's chief culprit was the woman in Number 10. 'Mrs Three Million', Labour's employment spokesman, Eric Varley, called her – and that was one of the more printable epithets. 'That woman! I detest her,' said an unemployed woman in Wigan. 'They've decimated our lot up here, the government. In the war we kept things going when the Germans tried to bomb our industry, but she's sorted it out in a couple of years. It's personal with me – I detest her.'[28]

Such an intense reaction was very common. When the Labour MP Ian Wrigglesworth compiled a dossier of letters from jobless families in his recession-scarred Yorkshire constituency of Thornaby-on-Tees, they made for blistering reading. Again and again people blamed the Prime Minister personally for their anxiety and hardship. 'Why doesn't Mrs Thatcher try living on the dole and see what it is like?' wrote one woman, who added that she could 'scream' whenever her children mentioned Christmas. Even if she turned Britain around, said another, 'people like myself will always remember the times and the cost of their marriages'. Indeed, to some critics the dole queues seemed definitive proof of her personal cruelty. 'The Cruel Summer of Mrs Thatcher', read a headline in the *Observer* in the summer of 1981. 'Our lives seem petty in your cold grey hands,' runs the Beat's 'Stand Down Margaret'. 'Would you ever give a second thought? / Would you ever give a damn?'[29]

Whether unemployment genuinely was Mrs Thatcher's fault is one of the fundamental questions of the entire decade. One obvious point is that it was already very high before she walked into Number 10. Under Jim Callaghan it had reached almost 1½ million, and by the end of the 1970s some four out of ten under-25s were already out of work. This was the context not just for the Conservatives' celebrated 'Labour Isn't Working' poster, but also for the explosion of punk rock ('dole queue rock'), as well as Alan Bleasdale's original play 'The Black Stuff'. Yet even on the centre-left there was already a fatalistic acceptance that mass unemployment was here to stay. It was Callaghan, not Thatcher, who told his party conference in 1976 that the 'cosy world' of full employment was gone, never to return. To the Bennites, these words were anathema, but many of Callaghan's own ministers agreed. 'We are seeing the increase of unemployment throughout the industrial world,' admitted Shirley Williams a few months later, 'and it is a problem for which we still have no real answer.'[30]

After May 1979 the political actors swapped scripts. Having previously deplored 'the tragedy of 1,500,000 people out of work', Mrs Thatcher now insisted that unemployment was an inevitable result of national decline and technological change. Meanwhile, the same Labour ministers who had found 'no real answer' to rising unemployment now claimed that the solution lay in Mrs Thatcher's hands, if only she had the sense to see it. Yet not everybody on the left pretended that everything was her fault. 'Too many union leaders and Labour Party leaders stand up at conferences and shout "Thatcher, Thatcher" as though Margaret Thatcher invented unemployment,' the President of the Bakers, Food and Allied Workers' Union, Terry O'Neill, told his annual conference in June 1981. Although O'Neill was on the left, he thought she had merely 'pressed the button that accelerated unemployment figures which were already too bad under Labour governments . . . It is too easy to go on television and use Thatcher as some kind of scapegoat.'[31]

Even so, there was an enormous difference between unemployment at almost 1½ million and unemployment at more than 3 million. Given the revolution in Iran and the resulting oil shock, some of this increase was probably inevitable. Britain was not alone in suffering double-digit inflation and a crippling recession: almost all its major competitors faced similar problems. All the same, there is no getting away from the fact that Britain's unemployment record was far, far worse than those of its neighbours. Between 1979 and 1981, British unemployment more than doubled. In no other major Western economy did it increase by more than half. So as the economists Gavyn Davies and David Piachaud wrote in *The Times*, 'all the facts point to our being, in terms of severity of unemployment, alone among the major nations. Our domestic recession bears one clear hall-mark: Made in Britain.'[32]

There is, admittedly, a case that Britain had entered the 1980s in a uniquely weak position, burdened by its recent history of amateurish management, dreadful labour relations and terrible productivity, which made it unusually vulnerable to a global downturn. As *The Times*'s economics editor, David Blake, observed, post-war Britain had an inglorious history of underperforming against its major competitors, exemplified by its abysmal inflation record. So even if someone else had been Prime Minister, it is hard to believe that unemployment would have remained below 2 million for long.

And yet, even on the right, most economic commentators thought Mrs Thatcher's approach had played a central part in pushing the jobless figures to such heights. At the London School of Economics, Richard Layard and Stephen Nickell calculated that about three-quarters of the unemployment increase was down to Mrs Thatcher's policies. And as Blake pointed out, even *without* the world recession the government's policies 'would have tightened the vice on the economy', pushing hundreds of thousands out of work. 'Some of the loss', Blake thought, 'simply consisted of the death of industries which had to go anyway. But some was the result of the loss of world competitiveness and tough domestic policies.'[33]

At one level, then, it seems reasonable to blame Mrs Thatcher for the mass unemployment of the early 1980s. Probably no alternative Prime Minister could have kept it below 2 million, but probably no other Prime Minister would have allowed it to rise above 3 million without changing course. It was not all her fault, but she had been perfectly happy to hammer Callaghan's unemployment record a few years earlier, so she could hardly complain when people did the same to her. Even so, any long-term verdict ought to be a bit more complicated. Britain's unemployment record under Mrs Thatcher was indeed truly terrible, especially by comparison with

France and West Germany. But it soon turned out that unemployment was *not* a uniquely British disease. In the two decades after 1990, it was France and Germany that suffered from unemployment rates of almost 12 per cent, whereas Britain enjoyed a long period with rates as low as 5 per cent.

The truth is that, as a result of global economic and technological change, *every* major industrial society went through a period of very high unemployment between the early 1980s and the early 2000s. The difference was that Britain, the first nation to industrialize, was also the first to experience the shock of deindustrialization. Only after a decade or two did it become clear that there had been nothing uniquely British, and indeed nothing uniquely Thatcherite, about it. In that context, what Mrs Thatcher did was effectively to speed up the process and get it over with. That made it all the more painful at the time, of course. The upside was that in Britain the shock lasted for about a decade, whereas in France it has lasted for three. But nobody knew that in the early 1980s. In any case, it would not have been much consolation.[34]

What was very unusual about Britain, though, was that the issue became so bitterly personalized. Whenever the French contemplated their painful unemployment figures, few of them seriously argued that Jacques Chirac or François Hollande had deliberately set out to inflict hardship on millions. But Mrs Thatcher was different. Her stridency, her certainty, her partisanship and her gender made her an obvious target. Every time she chose hectoring argument over emollient moderation, she cast herself as a scapegoat. 'Sometimes', Sir Geoffrey Howe admitted, 'we seemed almost to relish the intellectual certainty of telling people that their fate was unavoidable and that their activity was replaceable, if not expendable.' And by 'we', he almost certainly meant the Prime Minister.[35]

Mrs Thatcher's critics claimed that she never showed sympathy for those who had lost their jobs. But this is simply not true. 'I think it's terrible if a person who wants to work can't find a job,' she explained during a party political broadcast in 1977. 'You have no self-respect, you haven't got the respect of your family, if you somehow can't earn yourself a living and them a living too.' Of course it was easy to say this in opposition. It was much harder in office, when she bore personal responsibility for every new set of unemployment figures. Still, she never shied away from the topic completely. 'I feel deeply concerned when I have people who want jobs and can't get them,' she told a live audience on the BBC's *Nationwide* in May 1981. 'I do feel deeply about it. Of course I do. I wouldn't be human if we didn't.'[36]

Yet there was something missing. Whenever she talked about inflation – or indeed about working hard, bettering oneself, making money and getting on – everyone could tell that she meant it. Whenever she talked about unemployment, it was hard to banish the impression that she was doing it because she felt she had to. Exactly what was missing is hard to say. Conviction? Sincerity? Perhaps the answer is that whenever she talked about unemployment, there was never any sense of emotional investment. As the quintessential middle-class crusader, she cared passionately about inflation, which fell so heavily on Conservative voters in Middle England. By contrast, unemployment had always been a Labour issue, falling most heavily on the industrial working classes. It is easy to imagine her and Denis grumbling about surging inflation. It is impossible, though, to picture them talking so animatedly about unemployment.

Perhaps there was a generational factor, too. Her Conservative predecessors had been adults in the 1930s, and vividly remembered the days of the dole queues. But Margaret Roberts, born in 1925, had never been touched by the Depression. She had no recollection of the hunger marches, no memories of friends, neighbours or constituents crippled by unemployment. There is no reason to doubt that she was sorry to hear about people who had lost their jobs. But it never kept her awake at night. Her listeners knew it; and they remembered.[37]

For Mrs Thatcher's older critics, the prospect of a return to the 1930s seemed almost too much to bear. By now, however, references to the dole queues of the Depression or to George Orwell's book *The Road to Wigan Pier* had become clichés of the age.* 'We saw the Jarrow marches,' wrote the veteran political journalist David Wood, who had then been living in, of all places, Grantham. 'We saw the dole queues, and passed the labour exchanges where hundreds of men gathered daily to form the human scrapheap . . . I still see those awful dole queues of the 1930s, and remember interviewing the marchers as they made their way through Mrs Thatcher's home town towards Westminster.'

For years Wood had believed that people would never let this happen again. Yet now he knew he had been wrong. He talked to a man of his own vintage, a former Labour minister who had just come back from a trip to northern England. There the ex-minister had delivered a tub-thumping lecture about the evils of unemployment and the wickedness of Mrs Thatcher's government. Some of his audience were unemployed; others must have feared for their jobs. But they just sat there, showing

* Between 1980 and 1984, the *Guardian* and *Observer* invoked Orwell's legacy on no fewer than 435 occasions, once every four days. By contrast, they had mentioned him barely 300 times in the whole of the 1970s.

'polite interest at best and boredom with an old, old story at worst'. 'We are 1930s men,' Wood wrote sadly. 'We are economically out of date.'[38]

Why? One explanation is that the world of Orwell's Wigan was now so remote as to make parallels absurd. Mrs Thatcher insisted that there was 'absolutely no comparison between today and the 1930s, none whatsoever'. And, in fairness, she had a point. Unemployment had been far higher during the Depression, with some estimates suggesting a national peak of around 22 per cent, compared with 13 per cent in the 1980s. What was more, benefits were far more extensive fifty years later, even after the government's cuts. The flagrantly reactionary historian John Vincent, who claimed in *The Times* that unemployed people enjoyed 'gas central-heating' and 'wall-to-wall carpets', was deliberately exaggerating, but there was a grain of truth in his argument that the definition of poverty had changed enormously in half a century.

Indeed, when the *Guardian*'s Peter Jenkins mentioned the Depression to the former Labour minister Roy Mason in February 1981, the latter reacted with scornful incredulity. Born in 1924, Mason had been brought up in Barnsley and went down the mine at the age of 14 before becoming the local MP. He was no stranger to hardship, but he thought the parallel with the 1930s absurd. People now had so many comforts – including 'benefits legislated by Labour governments' – that 'nobody could tell him that things today compared with the thirties. He'd lived through the thirties and seen the soup kitchens in Barnsley and the mayor's boot fund. The only people who were making comparison with the thirties were left-wing intellectuals who weren't there.'[39]

The other obvious difference was that unemployment was no longer a public spectacle. As Jonathan Raban observed, the Depression had been a photographer's dream: 'hunger marches, dole queues, ragged men with their hands in their pockets loafing sadly at street corners . . . a magnificent subject, full of human colour and evocative squalor'. But fifty years later, 'English society had gone indoors'. People no longer stood about in the streets, no longer wore rags or walked barefoot, and no longer queued for soup in the freezing cold. Most spent their days at home, watching television. 'Unemployment', Raban wrote, 'had been a public event; it was now a private misery, to be borne alone, behind the curtains.' The real image of modern unemployment was 'a room, decently furnished in nylon upholstery, where a man and his wife sat in the middle of an afternoon watching one of last year's movies on the rented video machine'. Raban did not mean to dismiss their anguish. But he was surely right to suggest that, as people retreated indoors, they disappeared from the consciences of their neighbours. Meanwhile, those still in work pushed the plight of the less

9. 'Every record begins with a bleep.' Gary Numan wonders if 'friends' are electric, *above left*, while the similarly grim-faced Human League slap on the eye make-up, *above right*. But Duran Duran are clearly having a much more amusing time, *below*.

10. Electoral defeat triggered a civil war in the Labour Party. As leader, Michael Foot, *above*, found it impossible to impose his authority. *Below left*, David Owen is appalled by the 1981 Wembley conference; *below right*, a rather more cheerful Shirley Williams campaigns for the SDP.

11. On the left, Tony Benn, *above*, struck an ever more messianic figure, inspiring love and loathing in equal measure. His supporters included the Greater London Council's leader Ken Livingstone, *below*, pictured with Sinn Fein's Gerry Adams and an unidentified fellow enthusiast.

12. The Maze hunger strike marked a macabre new phase in Northern Ireland's history. *Top*, a masked republican poses beside graffiti supporting the strikers. *Above*, graffiti in one of Belfast's Protestant areas sends a less sympathetic message.

13. With Bobby Sands's death in May 1981, riots erupted across the province. *Top*, British soldiers and the Royal Ulster Constabulary try to restore order; *above*, masked Catholic youngsters on the streets of Belfast.

14. By the summer of 1981, Britain seemed to be tearing itself apart. *Top left*, an anti-racist leaflet denounces the police in Brixton. The greatest shock came after the riots in Toxteth, *above*. The *Sun*, in particular, was horrified by the 'fury in the ghetto', *top right*.

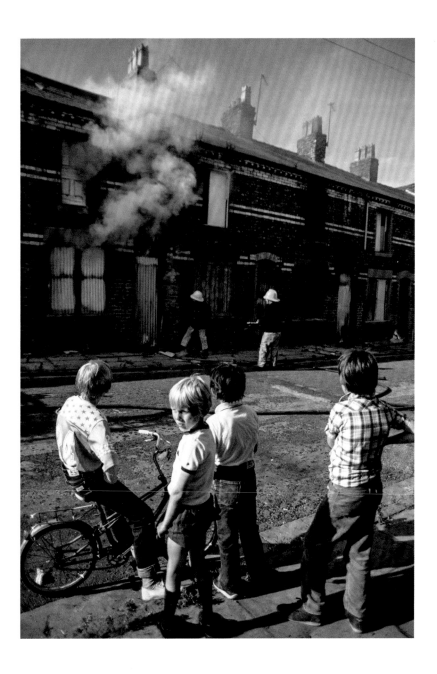

15. Toxteth: the morning after, July 1981.

16. 'We need heroes': Ian Botham on the fourth day of the Headingley Test, 20 July 1981.

fortunate to the backs of their minds. 'It's rather like death,' the Darlington journalist Susan Gray told Mass Observation: 'you don't talk about it very loudly.'[40]

For years one of the guiding assumptions of British politics had been that the public would never forgive a return to the dole queues of the 1930s. It seemed entirely natural, then, that as the dole queues lengthened, Mrs Thatcher's approval rating sank to the lowest levels since polling began. Unemployment was political poison: everybody said so. And the British people cared about it, or said they did. By the end of 1980, 68 per cent told Gallup it was the most urgent issue facing the country, rising to 74 per cent by the end of 1981 and 80 per cent by the end of 1982. For the next five years people consistently ranked unemployment as their single biggest concern, with no other issue getting remotely close. So, all other things being equal, Mrs Thatcher should have stood as much chance of retaining power as Boy George did of becoming Archbishop of Canterbury.[41]

Did people *really* care, though? Attitudes were more complicated than we remember. During the 1983 election campaign, Gallup found that only 50 per cent of the electorate thought unemployment an unquestionably 'bad thing', while 44 per cent thought it could be justified while the economy was going through a 'period of adjustment'. Asked about the unemployed, 43 per cent thought 'some' were on the dole 'through their own fault', while 47 per cent agreed that 'most' or 'some' could get jobs, 'if they tried'. As for possible solutions, only 29 per cent thought the onus lay with the government, while 68 per cent thought 'companies' held the answer. And even at the lowest point of the recession, despite the terrible figures and tragic stories, Mrs Thatcher could rely on the fact that *nine out of ten people were still in work*. Only one in ten people experienced unemployment directly, while only two out of ten experienced it in their family. Eight out of ten people, in other words, did not experience it at all.[42]

Even those who *did* lose their jobs did not always react as Tony Benn might have hoped. A few days before the Birmingham Northfield by-election in October 1982, one reporter talked to a 42-year-old legal secretary, Ineke Nesbitt. Her husband had lost his job just ten days earlier, yet both were planning to vote Conservative. 'There is no easy solution to the country's problems,' Ineke said calmly. 'It is no good borrowing more and more money and getting deeper and deeper into debt . . . It hurts, but I think we have got to swallow the medicine.' What about her husband's job? 'Redundancy did not scare us,' she said. 'Britain is a fabulous country . . . But it does need what Mrs Thatcher keeps on hammering again and again – and that is a change in attitude, more than anything else. It is just a shame that a lot of working class people have not got a lot of go and initiative.'

Many people would have found such sentiments shocking. But there were plenty who agreed with her. Visiting a working men's club in an industrial Midlands town, Jeremy Seabrook met an older man called Harry, who had just lost his job. Mrs Thatcher, Harry said, was the 'best thing that's happened to this country for years'. 'She put you out of a job,' somebody interjected. 'The world don't owe me a fucking living,' Harry said angrily. 'I don't need her to teach me that, like some of you silly fuckers. Eating seed-corn, that's what we've been doing for years. Eating seed-corn.'[43]

Even in the benefits office in Dudley, one of the most stricken areas in the country, a visiting reporter found ardent Thatcher supporters. Margaret Jones, 61, had been on the dole for more than three years, yet thought the Prime Minister was doing 'a great job'. Like many others, she blamed the worldwide recession, not the government, and thought local firms had 'not tried hard enough'. Another Dudley woman, 37-year-old Valerie Pugh, had been out of work for six months. She too was a great Thatcher fan, explaining that she had bought her own home and thought 'Conservatives were for that sort of thing'. Even Isabella Smith, a 19-year-old Wolverhampton shop assistant, out of work for almost eighteen months, living with an unemployed husband and a 10-month-old baby on just £50 a week, planned to vote for the Prime Minister next time. The reporter suggested that she might be voting against her own interests, but Isabella was not persuaded. 'Labour's worse, aren't they?' she said scornfully. 'When they were in last, what did they do? Just made it as bad.'[44]

Of course this can be exaggerated: the vast majority of the claimants in the Dudley benefits office said they were going to vote Labour. Yet despite Labour's attempts to pin the blame for unemployment on Mrs Thatcher, the wider public were never convinced. As early as the summer of 1980, Gallup found that only 23 per cent blamed the government for the rise in unemployment, while a further 23 per cent blamed 'people not wanting to work', 25 per cent blamed the unions and 35 per cent blamed 'world economic pressures'. Above all, many people clearly bought the line that unemployment was an inevitable result of economic and technological change. In Sheffield, a machine-tool engineer told Beatrix Campbell about a new machine that could do his job faster than he could. 'It was beautiful to watch it work,' he said. 'It was doing things that are impossible for us to do by hand.' And in Bristol, the women working in a tobacco factory, which would soon be completely automated, told Beryl Bainbridge that they had reconciled themselves to their own obsolescence: 'It couldn't be helped, could it?'[45]

On the Westminster front line, this kind of talk was unthinkable. Not only were Labour publicly committed to reducing 'unemployment to below a million within five years of taking office', a target no serious observer thought remotely plausible, but even Mrs Thatcher never admitted that full employment had gone for good. Yet few people were fooled. When Mass Observation asked correspondents about their expectations for the future, almost all thought mass unemployment was here to stay. 'I think it will still be 2½–3½ million in 1990,' wrote Chelmsford's Stephen Berry, an architectural technician. Higher unemployment was 'inevitable in this day of micro chip electronics', agreed Sheila Parkin, who worked in a camping shop. 'I hope that unemployment will decrease,' wrote Carol Daniel, a supermarket shelf-stacker, 'but to be honest the robot will put more out of work, because it is cheaper to run machines than pay men . . . The only thing that will reduce unemployment short of a mirical [sic] is another war, and if that is a nucular [sic] war then unemployment will be a luxury.'[46]

Even the Basildon depot supervisor Peter Hibbitt, a great admirer of Tony Benn, agreed that Britain was 'going to live with a steadily rising amount of unemployment', whether people liked it or not:

> There is no 'if' about large-scale, long-term unemployment. Structured unemployment will be as essential a part of the economy as jobs . . .
>
> The Empress of Westminster only wants 'real jobs', so that rules out a new set of Hell Fire Caves or a British Hoover Dam. The chances of retraining a shipyard plater, a coal miner or a foundryman into micro-electronics seem at best remote and the sort of brain which can accept eight hours a day on the assembly line is not ideal for a crash course in quantum mechanics or atomic physics: ergo structured unemployment . . .
>
> Before we can go any way along the road of providing for the unemployed, the politicians must admit that there is nothing they can, or want to, do about unemployment . . . Only then can we look at the workforce and find out who really wants to work and who would be prepared to be left to their own devices with adequate financial provision.

Intriguingly, Peter thought the government should arrange for the unemployed to do part-time jobs that 'make Britain unique for the foreign tourist . . . bell-ringing teams, Morris dancing sides, village bands, cottage gardeners, pub piano players, darts teams, singers, comedians'. This was, to say the least, an unconventional view, though no less realistic than many politicians' solutions. 'The future of Britain', Peter wrote, 'lies in the Tower of London, Stratford on Avon, Widecombe in the Moor, assorted cathedrals, Morris dancers and Ye Olde Worlde Tea Shoppes.' He was exaggerating, of course. But he was not entirely wrong.[47]

# 20

# Potting the Reds

*As soon as I got a cue in my hand, I knew I was the business at*
*something. And it changed my whole life . . . I went from being*
*an also-ran, you know, a clerical worker or something.*
Steve Davis, interviewed in the *Daily Mirror*, 26 June 1981

*We went to Bangkok with Steve Davis and they went mad there.*
*Mad. There was 40 foot high posters of Davis all over Bangkok.*
*It was like being in Romford High Street.*
Barry Hearn, interviewed in *The Times*, 29 April 1983

The date was Monday 20 April 1981, and at the Crucible Theatre in Sheffield a pale young man from south London was poised to seize his destiny.
On television sets across the country, the picture showed him sitting in
his starched white shirt, trim black waistcoat and wide bow tie, his thin
face apparently lost in thought, as the referee prepared the table for the
decisive frame. 'Steve Davis sits there,' said the BBC's Ted Lowe, 'waiting
for the most important frame of his young career.' Sixteen utterly hypnotic
minutes later, the stillness of the crowd almost suffocating in its intensity,
he was almost there. 'Can he slam this blue into the top pocket?' whispered
Lowe, and as the ball disappeared, the spectators let out a great roar of
relief and triumph. 'He's breathing heavily', said Lowe, with just a hint of
excitement, 'as he comes down to this final pink' – and then, almost casually, Davis swept it into the corner pocket. 'And that's it! The world
snooker champion 1981 – Steve Davis!'

On screen, the new champion just stood there, his eyes closed in private
contemplation, the cheers echoing around the Crucible. Then he caught
sight of someone coming from the crowd, and broke into a boyish grin
as the newcomer wrapped him in a bear hug and punched the air with
delight. 'Congratulations for the Embassy world champion from his
manager, Barry Hearn!' said Lowe. 'His friends, of course, climbing

around – Barry Hearn's wife gives him a big hug and a kiss. The young man, just 23 years of age, coming from Plumstead, London, is now, I believe, crying with joy at taking this title.' The television pictures showed Davis brushing away tears before taking a small sip of water. A moment later, when the BBC's David Vine asked, 'Has it sunk in yet?' he shook his head in shock, and murmured: 'Jesus Christ.' But even amid the heady rush of victory, Steve Davis never forgot where he came from. His first thanks went to the sponsors, the tobacco firm Embassy, and the event's promoter, Mike Watterson, and then there were warm words for 'all the people from Romford and from Plumstead' who had supported him. 'But most of all,' he said, 'I'd like to thank me mum and me dad, and Barry and Susan' – and it was then that his voice cracked, and emotion overcame him.[1]

Outside the snooker world, Steve Davis had been relatively unknown before the spring of 1981. But now all that changed. With the back pages full of the violent excesses of England's football supporters, here was the perfect antidote: a polite, good-humoured young man whose meteoric rise had been a monument to the virtues of hard work and self-improvement. As *The Times*'s snooker writer Sydney Friskin put it, Davis's 'boyish freshness and enjoyment' had already 'made him one of the more popular players in the world'. Even his astonishing self-control, which later encouraged people to mock him as boring, seemed excitingly novel. For the *Express*, he was 'the kid from Plumstead with a nerve as impenetrable as Don Bradman's'. Indeed, the papers in April 1981 regarded him as distinctly interesting, lapping up stories about his reassuringly ordinary fondness for bacon sandwiches or his addiction to playing *Space Invaders* in his hotel suite, 'in which he knocks down all the green mutants with the same accuracy as he applies to the snooker ball'.

Even Davis's biography became a kind of morality story, a parable in the virtues of hard work and filial duty. Born in Plumstead, south London, in 1957, the son of a London Transport depot worker, he had been given a toy snooker table as a Christmas present when he was 2. After Davis started school, his father bought him a half-size table, which they installed on top of the dining table. But even then, as one profile noted, 'Davis's father insisted that he cued properly and played by the rules, which probably accounts for his self-discipline and perfect cue action'. By Davis's teens he had become a regular at his father's working men's club, where he immediately stood out. There too, observed *The Times*, 'parental influence taught him to play the game in the right spirit'. It was no coincidence, the paper thought, that in his victory speech at Sheffield, 'he did not forget to thank his parents, as well as his manager, Barry Hearn'.[2]

Nobody doubted that Davis would become a superstar. He had piled up some £50,000 in prize money since the beginning of 1981, and the only question was whether he would ever stop. 'Now that he has won the title he's going to be very hard to beat in anything,' remarked his vanquished opponent, the gallant Welshman Doug Mountjoy, who thought Davis was 'at least a black ball better than any of us'. The snooker writer Clive Everton went even further. 'In his dedication, temperate habits, appetite for his chosen game, temperament and, in match play, his ability to reduce avoidable mistakes to a minimum, Davis resembles Bjorn Borg,' he told readers of the *Guardian*, explaining that his 'sharp brain' meant there was a 'sense of inevitability' before his matches had even started.

The only thing that could stop him, Everton thought, was the commercial pressure that came with his newfound prominence. After all, the young man was already the registered owner of three limited companies and had been deluged with inquiries 'regarding television commercials, sponsorship and other spin-offs'. Within hours of Davis's victory, Barry Hearn was openly boasting that he could make his client £200,000 in the next twelve months. 'We've got it geared up to the ceiling,' he said gleefully. 'Davis's manager does not want him merely to be the world champion,' explained *The Times*. 'He wants to turn him into a living legend.'[3]

A decade earlier, the notion of a snooker player as a 'living legend' would have seemed completely absurd. Footballers became legends. Cricketers, rugby players, tennis champions, racing drivers, even jockeys became legends. But snooker players? Snooker was an old man's game, the game of seedy back-street clubs, down-at-heel holiday camps and shabby smoke-filled halls. The senior professionals were like ghosts trapped in a world of Brylcreem and blazers, while the first truly modern snooker tournament, the 1972 world championship, was organized in conditions of almost laughable amateurishness. Even the final, which took place at a British Legion club in Birmingham, was played in risibly ramshackle conditions. Thanks to the miners' strike, there was no electricity, so the action took place under the gloomy light from a mobile generator. 'Beer supplies held up,' recalled Clive Everton, 'but toilet facilities proved sadly inadequate.'

Years later, the writer Gordon Burn remembered the scene: 'hundreds of men', clutching their pints in the near-darkness, 'hunched forward on hundreds of chairs stacked on beer crates', their 'boilersuits, haversacks, kit-bags and overalls' dumped in a huge pile in the corner. There were no cameras and no Fleet Street reporters, and to cap it all there was no serious sponsorship money either. The winner, the 22-year-old tearaway Alex

Higgins, walked away with a mere £480. One evening during the final, which was played over five days, Higgins introduced himself to West Bromwich Albion's star midfielder Asa Hartford in a local curry house. Hartford had never heard of him.[4]

What transformed snooker's fortunes was television. In July 1969 BBC2 had begun showing a single-frame tournament entitled *Pot Black*, designed to exhibit its new colour technology. The show's presiding genius was the commentator, 'Whispering' Ted Lowe, who made the players sign contracts obliging them to wear dinner jackets. 'That's where the clean-cut came from and where the old ladies came into it,' Lowe told Gordon Burn. '*I* brought the women and the children and all the other people who had never *thought* about watching a game of snooker, whatever your Barry Hearns and all the rest of them might claim today.' There was a lot of truth in this. Even at this early stage, the *Sunday Telegraph*'s Philip Purser thought the sight of snooker players in their dinner jackets made for a tremendous 'change from the hysterical pooves of the football field'.

But there was more to snooker's success than old-fashioned outfits. Crucially, it needed a television-friendly venue, and it was here that a Chesterfield car distributor called Mike Watterson came in. A former England amateur international who had since moved into snooker promotion, Watterson thought the game needed a more theatrical, upmarket image. If nothing else, he was sick of sitting on 'planks on beer crates'. All he needed was the right place, and when his wife returned one night from the theatre, she told him that she had found it.[5]

In April 1977 Watterson arranged to rent Sheffield's Crucible Theatre for two weeks for £6,600. He then persuaded the snooker authorities to let him promote the world championship, putting up £17,000 in prize money and striking a deal with Embassy, who had already dabbled with sponsoring the event the year before. But there was one more element before the picture was complete: proper lighting. In the first half of the 1970s, the gigantic lights required for *Pot Black*'s colour broadcasts had been so intense that the players were blinded by the glare from the balls and the sweat pouring down their faces. Some even burned their hands on the tables' Formica cushion rails. So when, in 1978, the BBC agreed to broadcast Watterson's tournament live from the Crucible, it devised a 'glare-free, shadowless canopy of lights', so that the players would feel as comfortable as if they were practising at home.

Showing so much snooker was a gamble; one writer joked that 'it could be a subversive experiment in mass hypnosis'. But on the first evening, 5 million people tuned in to BBC2, far more than anybody had expected.

'We opened the champagne when we got the first week's viewing figures,' the producer remarked. 'But we were premature. As the tournament went on, the audience simply kept growing.' Backstage, reported the *Guardian*, the players were thrilled that 'the game is at last being shown properly', and excited by the prospect of a 'whole new future'. Even the veteran Fred Davis, who had played in his first world championship in 1937, shared their excitement. One of the greatest players in the game's history, he had toiled in obscurity for decades. But now, he said, 'what the public are getting here is the feel of what it is like playing under that pressure, hour after hour, for days on end'.[6]

The BBC's experiment could hardly have been better timed. Snooker exploded into the public consciousness at precisely the moment when better-established sports were struggling, whether from falling attendances, crowd violence, boring play, abysmal sportsmanship or all of them at once. Only a few months before the BBC began its live coverage, England's football fans had rioted in Luxembourg, the first major hooligan incident involving the national team abroad. By the time Steve Davis won his first world title, football's terminal decline had become a staple of the sports pages. But Britain's other team sports seemed in poor shape, too. The major rugby story of 1980 was the savage Five Nations clash between England and Wales at Twickenham, disfigured almost from the first minute by brutal fighting. Amazingly, only one player – Wales's Paul Ringer – was sent off, but six more needed stitches for various wounds. 'It was like war on the field and like M\*A\*S\*H in the dressing room,' said the England doctor afterwards, a remark quoted in the *Mirror* under the sensitive headline 'SOMEONE WILL DIE'.[7]

For *The Times*, petulance and misbehaviour were becoming all too frequent, not just in rugby, but in 'tennis and even women's squash rackets', thanks to the influence of international superstars such as John McEnroe and Ilie Nastase. Even cricket, the paper lamented, had 'fallen prey to barbarism, with umpires defied and reviled'. As it happened, the summer of 1980 brought the perfect example: the 'bitter disappointment' of the much-anticipated Centenary Test between England and Australia at Lord's. That the game was blighted by driving rain was bad enough; the real story, though, was an extraordinary altercation on the third day, when frustrated MCC members, who had been drinking heavily during a rain delay, got into a fight with one of the umpires. *Wisden* called it a 'disgrace not only to English cricket but to the game in general', while *The Times* lamented that 'the language and behaviour of the football hooligan has at last invaded the home of English cricket'. The great W. G. Grace, the writer thought, 'would turn in his grave at the thought'.[8]

Against this background, snooker's administrators made great efforts to emphasize its courtesy and sportsmanship, symbolized by the players' smart dark waistcoats. Indeed, for such a modern product it seemed to offer a soothingly old-fashioned antidote to the contemporary world. Hour after hour, day after day, the camera's gaze was trained on a small rectangle of green baize, the silence broken only by the soft click of the balls or a rare burst of applause. Here, as the *Guardian* had predicted, was the stuff of mass hypnosis. Watching from his flat in Orkney, the writer George Mackay Brown waxed lyrical about snooker's gentle rhythms: 'the slight subtle touch of ball on ball; the wild foray that sets them in a scatter, helter-skelter'. You simply could not look away, he thought, from the shifting dots of colour on the bright green baize. 'Exciting and soothing at the same time', snooker had found the perfect television formula. Here was a sport built on stillness, an exercise in metronomic nothingness.

The contrast with football's restless histrionics could hardly have been more glaring. 'The atmosphere is quiet, there is a kind of gentlemanly approach which people like – no punch-ups or bad manners,' explained one BBC producer. Even Ted Lowe's hushed voice – 'by turns sonorous and sentimental, laced with malapropisms and ancient locutions, redolent of dog-baskets and antimacassars over uncut moquette . . . a voice which the Queen Mother would be pleased to entertain to tea', according to Gordon Burn – seemed a throwback to a slower, gentler age. Yet Lowe's real gift was his willingness to say nothing at all. When he was taken ill during a match in the mid-1980s, the BBC simply carried on broadcasting for the next eight minutes, and nobody noticed.[9]

What also made snooker a perfect fit for the 1980s was that it was a game of individuals. Even the way it was filmed – the novelist A. S. Byatt wrote of the 'suffering and exulting faces briefly picked out by the cameras' – emphasized the sense of personal confrontation. As *The Times* remarked, it was a producer's dream, with two central characters and a 'tight, intimate drama of competition', giving millions of viewers the sense of being 'grouped closely around the table, squinting at the angles over the players' shoulders'. And, as luck would have it, snooker at the turn of the decade was blessed with a cast of immediately recognizable characters, each with his own easily caricatured style and personality, and often even with his own nickname.[10]

One great favourite, for example, was Ray Reardon, a Welsh miner's son from Tredegar who followed his father down the pit, survived being buried alive in a rockfall for three hours, served as a Staffordshire policeman and turned professional at the age of 35. An immensely affable man,

Reardon cut a memorably vampiric figure: thanks to his trademark widow's peak, most people called him 'Dracula'. Yet not even he could
compete in the public imagination with the rebellious Alex 'Hurricane'
Higgins, a Belfast boy whose father had never learned to read and write,
and who had first sailed to England as a teenager in a doomed effort to
become a jockey. Higgins, said his first manager, had only three vices:
'drinking, gambling and women'. To the tabloids, he was the 'People's
Champion'. 'He gets sacks of fan mail,' remarked Mike Watterson in 1981,
rather ungallantly adding: 'God knows why women are attracted to him.
He's got a face like five miles of unmade road.' But despite his natural
talent, Higgins's record was pretty disappointing. By the spring of 1982,
struggling to kick his addiction to vodka, he was crying himself to sleep
in a private clinic in Lancashire. Yet he still found the energy to pour scorn
on Steve Davis's habit of sipping water during his matches. 'He'll be
haunted by me', Higgins said contemptuously, 'till I'm carried out in a
little brown box.'[11]

It was entirely typical of Higgins's story that, having apparently hit
rock bottom, he arose from his sickbed to defeat Reardon and win the
1982 world championship. Equally typical was the fact that he won it on
a diet of 'vitamin pills, milk and Mackeson's [stout]', surrounded himself
with 'sacred hearts, mementos and good-luck charms' and greeted his
victory by bursting into tears. In his own words, he was a 'bit like George
Best, only my fairy story has a happy ending'. The comparison with the
ill-fated Best was only too apposite. In the years that followed there were
so many lurid headlines that it was impossible to keep track. Higgins was
accused of lying, cheating and fighting; of snorting cocaine, punching and
head-butting tournament officials; and even of threatening to arrange the
murder of his fellow Northern Irishman Dennis Taylor. 'I come from
Shankill and you come from Coalisland,' he reportedly said, 'and the next
time you are in Northern Ireland I will have you shot.'

Yet none of this dented his popularity. Like Best before him, and like
Paul Gascoigne and Ronnie O'Sullivan afterwards, Higgins seemed all
the more human precisely because he was so flawed, an attention-seeking
man-child adrift in a multimillion-pound industry. Like other 'troubled'
sportsmen, he was a one-man soap opera, with more sex and violence
than *Crossroads*, *Coronation Street* and *Brookside* put together. 'I've been
waiting for Higgins to be destroyed for years. He's looking worse and
worse,' the promoter Barry Hearn remarked. 'But the fact is: people *like*
watching the process. This is what I think is one of the biggest things in
the game.'[12]

If snooker needed Higgins, it also needed his antithesis. That was where

Steve Davis came in. Right from the start, Fleet Street presented him as everything his rival was not. Higgins was the brilliantly talented but disastrously wayward Irishman, Davis the politely reserved but devastatingly effective Englishman. 'His potting is now remorselessly exact, his manner calm and reassuring,' declared *The Times* in December 1980. 'Like his play his dress is neat and tidy. His intellect is sharp but tempered with modesty.' At this stage, most readers had probably never seen him play, yet already his image was established. 'Immaculate and quite unmoved', the *Express* called him. It might have been talking about a Victorian officer facing down a native rebellion.[13]

To some extent, of course, this was a caricature. Despite Davis's reputation as the most boring man in Britain, he was, as Clive Everton recalled, a 'wry, self-deprecating and shrewd' man, as well as a future president of the British Chess Federation. Yet there was a kernel of truth in the caricature, too. What made Davis a household name was not just that he kept winning but that he did so in such ruthlessly methodical style, a metronomic champion for a metronomic game. Every sip of water, every chalking of his cue, every purse of his lips seemed perfectly calculated. Like other national sporting icons of the early 1980s, such as Sebastian Coe and Daley Thompson, Davis had an insatiable appetite for self-improvement. 'If I had to choose between sex and snooker, I'd choose snooker,' he once told *Woman* magazine. 'Snooker is my justification, my fulfilment.' Alex Higgins would never have said that.[14]

Davis was not, however, unbeatable. When he returned to the Crucible to defend his title in 1982, he crashed out in the first round, humiliated 10–1 by Tony Knowles. The snooker sages gave knowing nods. Just as they had feared, Davis had burned himself out on an exhausting commercial treadmill, which had reportedly earned him a staggering £600,000 in just twelve months. A year later, though, he thrashed Cliff Thorburn in the final to regain his crown, and in 1984 he secured a third title by narrowly defeating Jimmy White. Yet something had changed. It was the swashbuckling White – a man, in Simon Barnes's words, with 'the air of the second underfootman given to taking crafty swigs from the Madeira bottle' – who was the popular favourite now, not 'boring old Steve Davis . . . as inexorable as death'. As the *Express* reported, 'there is a belief in snooker that the sooner the 26-year-old millionaire loses his aura of invincibility the better it will be for the game'.[15]

There was, of course, another reason the public were turning against Steve Davis. Snooker had made him rich. Within a couple of years of winning the world title, Davis had graduated from an old Austin Maxi to a Porsche and a Cadillac, the latter fitted with 'colour TV, quadraphonic

stereo, refrigerator and dark tinted windows'. He was not merely an exceptional sportsman but an exceptional business, cashing in on the
transformation in snooker's image. Even before Davis's first world title,
Alex Higgins was making an estimated £5,000 a week and routinely
demanded £500 for newspaper interviews. By 1982 international firms
such as Yamaha and Lada had joined the rush to sponsor snooker, while
Davis had signed a £300,000 deal to promote Courage bitter. Three years
later, he was raking in three times as much from endorsements, an estimated £600,000 a year, than he was from tournament prize money. For
personal appearances he charged £4,000 a night; by contrast, the increasingly unreliable Higgins was stuck on £400. And to every engagement,
Barry Hearn sent an employee in the 'Stevemobile' to sell pens, posters,
key rings and videos. Nothing was left to chance; no opportunity was
turned down.[16]

Even in April 1981 almost every profile of Steve Davis mentioned his
manager. As journalists invariably pointed out, Hearn was a walking
advertisement for Thatcherite entrepreneurship. Born on a council estate
in Dagenham, Essex, in 1948, the son of a bus driver, he had started his
working life washing cars and selling vegetables before training as an
accountant and investing in a string of run-down billiard halls on the
north-eastern fringes of London. It was at his Romford hall that Hearn
first came across the teenage Davis, becoming his manager and mentor. It
was Hearn who persuaded Davis's parents that their young prodigy could
make a career in professional snooker. From that moment on, this competitive, ambitious, immensely ebullient man never looked back. When *The
Times* interviewed Hearn at the 1983 world championship, it found him
planning a move into the Far Eastern market, his face 'ruddy with costly
tan', his suit 'richly heavy' and his silk tie 'too new to make a tight knot'.
Why had he just accepted a huge bid for his London snooker halls? 'I got
greedy,' Hearn said, 'I couldn't resist.' Was he enjoying life on the road?
'It's fun,' he said. 'We have a fabulous time.' His clients, he said, were 'going
to gross a million quid this year. That's fabulous, isn't it?'[17]

Hearn's importance to Steve Davis, and indeed to British snooker, can
hardly be overstated. For although Davis's drive came from within, his
image was largely his manager's creation. As Davis remembered, Hearn
persuaded him that 'courtesy, politeness, smart presentation and always
being on time for an appointment would help me get to the top'. Under
Hearn's direction, he cut his hair, changed his car, ditched his prog-rock
T-shirts and even changed his handshake, previously 'very weak', but now
firm enough to 'let 'em know you're gonna be the guvnor'. It was Hearn
who persuaded him to dress in black away from the table and advised him

to 'work on his facial expressions' to show no emotion, even when under intense pressure. Some people, wrote Gordon Burn, saw Davis as a puppet, his every remark 'rehearsed and, if possible, scripted in advance'. But he always knew exactly what he was doing. In Burn's words, Davis and Hearn were 'equal partners in a business they have built up from scratch'. Given how much money they were making, the analogy was perfectly chosen.[18]

Snooker was not, of course, the only game to seize the public imagination at the turn of the 1980s. Darts had emerged from much the same working-class world of pubs and clubs, and was similarly rebranded as a clash of colourful personalities. The first world darts championship was held in Stoke-on-Trent in 1978 and sponsored, like the snooker championship, by Embassy. By 1980 some 10 million people were watching as Eric Bristow, the famously crafty Cockney, beat Bobby George to win his first world title. But darts remained firmly working-class; the players, who would have looked absurd in snooker's waistcoats, wore short-sleeved shirts and drank beer, not water, between throws. To some extent they never escaped from their caricature in *Not the Nine O'Clock News*, in which Mel Smith and Griff Rhys Jones play two darts players, Dai 'Fat Belly' Gutbucket and Tommy 'Even Fatter Belly' Belcher, who compete by downing pints and shots. ('That's a good start for Fat Belly,' says Rowan Atkinson's commentator: 'two doubles and a pint.') As a result, darts never came close to competing with snooker for sponsorship, endorsements or prize money. When Bristow won his final world title in 1986, the prize money had risen to £20,000. By this time, though, snooker's world champion, the unheralded Joe Johnson, was picking up £70,000, the equivalent of £250,000 today.[19]

As a working-class game that had supposedly sold its soul to television producers and advertising men, snooker made an obvious target for those who thought modern Britain knew the price of everything and the value of nothing. Even the entrepreneurs behind the snooker boom – Watterson, a former Vauxhall car distributor, and Hearn, an Essex-born accountant – might have been chosen specifically to infuriate the kind of people who lamented that the country was being run by a shopkeeper's daughter and a Cabinet of estate agents. Even so, it is astonishing how quickly critics began complaining that snooker had sold out, especially given how downbeat it had been before Watterson hired the Crucible. By 1983, wrote the journalist Neil Lyndon, 'middle-aged men in shabby suits could often be overheard . . . condoling with one another and saying, "All the pleasure's gone, hasn't it? It's all so serious now. There's too much money involved."' Many of them, Lyndon thought, were men who had fallen in love with the game back in the days of beer crates and mobile generators. They felt 'unhappy about the speeding changes' and pined for 'the vanished innocence in which they were more comfortable'.[20]

Among them, surprisingly, were some of the biggest names in the sport. 'All they want to do is make money. They don't want to enjoy their life or see anything,' the former miner Ray Reardon told Gordon Burn. The Welshman's glory days had come a little too early for him to profit from the boom, yet he seemed almost relieved to have missed out:

> If going round chemist shops autographing boxes of aftershave is what you want to do, then fine. You should sign with Barry Hearn. But I'm glad I did it when I did, before they turned the game from a game into a business. I wouldn't like to do it now. There's no fun in it now. It's too ruthless. It's a different phase of the game today. It's all money. But you can't stop, can you? You can't pick up where you left off something, and go back to something that was nice. Life isn't like that. Nothing goes backwards now. You've got to go forward. Onward! . . . Onward!

He was talking about snooker, but he might easily have been talking about so much more.

Even men who had more obviously gained from the snooker boom shared some of Reardon's fears. For his fellow Welshman Terry Griffiths, snooker had brought almost unimaginable riches. Born in Llanelli, Griffiths had been a miner, postman, bus conductor and insurance salesman before turning professional in 1978. The following year he won the world championship, and for the next decade he remained one of snooker's most popular personalities. Yet when Burn interviewed him during a tour of the Far East, Griffiths confided that money and fame had changed him. He used to be more open, he admitted, 'more of a giver . . . I don't really like the person I've changed into.' Partly this was because he was homesick. But the commentator Ted Lowe, one of the fathers of the snooker boom, diagnosed a deeper problem. The players might be 'richer than ever', he wrote in the *Daily Express*, but they were 'not as relaxed or happy as the old players who struggled to pay the rent'. Snooker was ruled by 'sheer greed', and even Lowe wondered if it had been worth it. 'The fun has gone out of the games', he thought, 'since it was taken over by big business.'[21]

Barry Hearn, however, made no apology for his pursuit of success. 'There's so many opportunities,' he told Gordon Burn, 'an' if you can take 'em, why not take 'em? 'Cause some other bugger's gonna do it.' In this, as in his designer watch and alligator shoes, he seemed the personification of Thatcherite materialism, the embodiment of entrepreneurial values, the ultimate Essex Man. Where, after all, had Hearn bought his first snooker hall? In Romford, where east London meets Essex, classic upwardly mobile working-class territory, home to thousands of 'East Enders who made good and moved out', as a contemporary profile put it. Here was snooker's heartland, a world of small businessmen and self-improvers, leather jackets and lock-up garages, working-class patriots and first-generation owner-occupiers.

This was Mrs Thatcher's heartland, too. In the 1960s it had been Harold Wilson country, but like neighbouring seats such as Norman Tebbit's Chingford, it was turning increasingly true-blue. From Hearn's club in Arcade Place it was just three miles to the huge post-war Harold Hill estate, where in August 1980 Mrs Thatcher handed over the keys to 39 Amersham Road. Those three miles were lined with suburban houses whose owners saw in her, and in Hearn, champions of hard work and self-improvement. And although Hearn sold his first club in 1989, the new owner was a man after his own heart: a self-made entrepreneur called Richard Willis, who later became vice chairman of the Romford Conservative Association. No wonder, then, that some people thought snooker had become a thoroughly Thatcherite game.[22]

In this context, not even the most accomplished casting agency could have found a more richly symbolic protagonist than Hearn's most famous client. As the son of a south London bus-depot worker, Steve Davis was the incarnation of the relentless self-discipline and restless social aspiration that Mrs Thatcher and her admirers talked about so often. With his sponsorship deals, his Porsche and his investments, Davis was no stranger to the new financial possibilities of the mid-1980s. And yet, even as he ploughed his winnings into land reclamation schemes in Scotland and property speculation in Mayfair, he never lost his populist instincts. He was still the same 'peasant from Plumstead', he said, though he would be happy to 'be regarded as a machine for the rest of my days if that is the price I have to pay for winning'. As for the fans, he was not concerned about those who hated him, or even those who loved him, but 'the floating voters in the middle. They are the ones who are going to be swayed by who wins and who loses. It is them I have to convince if I am to stay at the top.'

Those words might sound oddly political. But in the intensely politicized arena of the early 1980s, even snooker players looked like political figures. In a much-quoted piece in the *Evening Standard*, the television interviewer Brian Walden argued that the 'wholly disciplined, utterly determined' Davis personified the virtues that Britain needed to survive the economic blizzard of the 1980s. 'Though he has flamboyant elements in his character,' Walden wrote, 'he suppresses them in the interests of a successful performance . . . [He] behaves as the British must behave if they are to maintain any position in the world. Order, method, discipline, plus a stern control of eccentricity, is the passport to triumph in the modern world.' Yet to Walden's displeasure, the public only reluctantly applauded this 'marvellously proficient' performer. 'Does this not prove', he wondered, 'what an essentially frivolous people we are?'[23]

It was fitting, then, that when the Conservatives were seeking celebrity supporters to appear at Mrs Thatcher's infamous youth rally at Wembley in June 1983, they immediately thought of Steve Davis. His manager's answer, according to Gordon Burn, was 'an automatic and unqualified "yes"'. Later, Davis rather regretted accepting, because it alienated a large section of the snooker audience, such as the Yorkshire miners who glared at him when he walked into pubs and clubs. Even so, he had gained something from 'sitting up close to Margaret Thatcher and *watching* her perform . . . because she's in performance the same as everybody else is. I learned a lot from that.'

And at the time he certainly seemed to enjoy himself, sporting a large 'MAGGIE IN' badge and entertaining the crowd with a truly unforgivable joke. 'I started playing when I was 14', he told them, 'and I didn't realise how important it was potting reds then.' The crowd roared with laughter, or pretended to. And at least one person found it funny, since Mrs Thatcher later used it herself. 'Let me say how much I enjoy watching snooker,' she told a group of electronics manufacturers two years later. 'They spend so much time potting the reds!'[24]

For her part, Davis's political heroine claimed to be a great admirer of the green baize. 'Do you watch snooker? You know, this weekend it was absolutely fantastic!' Mrs Thatcher told her child interviewers on the show *CBTV*. Like so many commentators, she saw the game as an antidote to the violence and permissiveness that had seeped into Britain's sporting landscape. So when the *Sunday Mirror* asked about her cultural favourites, she mentioned not just the inevitable Agatha Christie, Frederick Forsyth and *Yes Minister* (and, surprisingly, *Cagney & Lacey*), but televised golf and snooker. 'I tell you something about both those sports,' she said firmly: 'the people who take part in them and the people who watch them have the highest possible standards . . . The highest possible standards. You know, there are no histrionics or anything like that. No histrionics . . . and that matters.'[25]

As a middle-aged, middle-class woman who did not generally like watching sport, Mrs Thatcher was precisely the sort of person for whom snooker had been redesigned. On television, its past in the smoke-filled working man's club was discreetly forgotten. As the journalist Hunter Davies remarked in 1982, snooker had become a 'feature of many family lives these days, that awkward table cluttering up suburban living rooms'. Thanks to television, he wrote, 'the game now crosses every social barrier and has made superstars out of young boys with nice manners and clean clothes'.

What was most striking, though, was its appeal to women. Indeed, snooker was reputedly the first televised sport watched by more women than men. 'Women,' Hearn said a year later, when asked if the boom could possibly continue. 'Women. They're only just coming into it. There's another 50 per cent of the market to go.' It was this insight that underpinned his decision to launch a range of toiletries with the Goya perfumery firm, based on the principle that wives and girlfriends tended to buy men's toiletries for them. The advertising campaign showed Steve Davis, Terry Griffiths and Tony Meo grinning in their dinner jackets above the inevitable snooker table. 'After Shave for Men Who Play to Win' read the slogan, which was true in Davis's case, at least.[26]

Yet although snooker embraced women as viewers and consumers, the idea of women as *players* was far from universally popular. Indeed, nothing better captures the tension between old-fashioned attitudes and newfound freedoms than the story of Sheila Capstick, a taxi driver from Wakefield, who found herself at the centre of a long-running saga involving the snooker table at the local working men's club. A mother of three, married to a local miner, Sheila was a paid-up member of the club, which, like many such clubs, had recently started admitting women. For three years she had been happily using the table, signing her name on the board and taking her turn. She did not claim to be especially good, but 'just played because I enjoyed it'.

But one day in 1979, another member complained that a mere woman should not have been using the table when he wanted to play. Under the Club and Institute Union's rules, women were only second-class members. They could join at cut-price rates, but could not serve on the committee, propose new members or use their membership cards to visit affiliated clubs – on the grounds, said an official from Birmingham, that they would 'want to go gallivanting'. Many clubs had rooms from which women were barred and even carpets on which they could not step. Above all, women were not allowed to play snooker. 'They said I might rip the cloth,' Sheila told Polly Toynbee. 'They say that in almost all clubs or pool halls, "women rip cloths". Bloody daft. No one ever rips the cloth, except in films, unless they do it on purpose.'

Sheila refused to give in. First she collected 2,000 signatures on a petition urging the management to let women become equal members. The
committee tore it up, but she proved an indomitable adversary. She had
T-shirts printed with the slogan 'Snooker for Women', organized a mass
picket outside the Wakefield club and even took her complaint to the Club
and Institute Union's Blackpool conference in June 1981. There, dressed
as a suffragette and supported by four coachloads of sympathizers, she
managed to sneak into the gallery, where she made such a racket that
stewards had to drag her out. In the months that followed she was hounded
by obscene phone calls, as well as letters accusing her of being a lesbian.
Surprisingly, though, she continued to drink at the Wakefield club, despite
the hostility of some male members. The campaign, she told Toynbee, had
'opened her eyes to a lot of things'. She even joined her local Workers'
Educational Association Women's Study Group. And in the end she won.
First the Wakefield club gave in; then, at last, the Club and Institute Union.
The only downside was that it took them almost thirty years.[27]

As snooker's defenders might reasonably point out, this was really a
story about working men's clubs rather than one about snooker. But
since professional snooker was so deeply rooted in this world, it inevitably shared its attitudes. Only days after Steve Davis's moment of glory
in April 1981, the *Daily Express* ran a long interview with the 'attractive,
brown-haired' Ann Johnson. A receptionist from Cheltenham, she was
one of the world's most accomplished female players. Now she was about
to partner Davis in the Guinness World Mixed Pairs, one of his first
engagements since becoming world champion. But although Ann was
keen to emphasize snooker's appeal to women players, the article inadvertently told a different story. The opening lines read like Jilly Cooper
on a bad day:

> They 'kissed' gently across the table, the white ball and the red ball.
>
> Then she smiled as the white delicately nudged the red into the pocket.
>
> She paused to rechalk the tip of her cue, the lightest of dustings, as if she
> were putting on face powder.
>
> Down at the table again, a click, a thunk, and I was hopelessly
> snookered.
>
> Ann Johnson, the world No. 3 woman snooker player, smiled charm-
> ingly at me and moved discreetly aside.

She was so good, the *Express* remarked admiringly, that she had 'been
refused entry to only two clubs in this country'. Even Ann thought it was
'easier for her to play in certain clubs because she was a "name"'.[28]

The truth is that although snooker was eager to embrace television, commercialism and even the Asian market, the notion of admitting women on equal terms with men was a step too far. As Barry Hearn put it, the 'aggressive male thing' was part of snooker's heritage. 'I'm a real traditional working-class lad,' he said. 'I believe in men in one role, women in another.' Most club managers agreed with him. The 1982 women's national champion, Vera Selby, a lecturer at Newcastle Polytechnic, complained that there was still 'tremendous resistance from clubs' to letting women play. She had taken up the game at the age of 37, purely because she 'fancied a go'. At the time, her first club told her that she had to come at six and be out by seven, because the men would not be happy. About a quarter of the clubs in the north-east would not even let her in, which meant that when her team (the rest of whom were men) played away fixtures, she had to drop out. And since private clubs were exempt from the Sex Discrimination Act, there was nothing she could do. It was a common story: across the country, no fewer than nineteen of the twenty-four main snooker leagues openly discriminated against women.[29]

As much as Mrs Thatcher enjoyed watching snooker, then, her chances of actually playing it were much smaller than if she had been a man. In the unlikely event that, inspired by Steve Davis's admiration for her politics, she had driven out to Essex for a few frames with one of the Downing Street secretaries, she might well have found the door closed politely in her face. Perhaps her best bet would have been to head down to what the *Express* called the 'luxurious Topspot Snooker Club' in Balham, south London, co-owned by Wally West, who also ran the Women's Billiards and Snooker Association. West was a great fan of female snooker players, although his explanation might not have won much admiration from ardent feminists. Men should welcome women, he thought, because 'in competition they are more ruthless than any man . . . What's more, they add grace and sophistication to snooker.'

Mrs Thatcher would surely have agreed with that, but she might not have liked what came next. For when the *Express* asked if the top women would ever rival their male counterparts, West shook his head. 'Never,' he said firmly. 'It's physically impossible. Without getting too personal or technical, boobs get in the way.'[30]

# 21

# To Think This Is England

POLICE OFFICER [*Rowan Atkinson*]: *Savage, in the space of one*
*month you have brought 117 ridiculous, trumped-up and*
*ludicrous charges . . . against the same man, Savage . . . a Mr*
*Winston Kodogo of 55 Mercer Road . . .*

*Savage, would I be correct in assuming that Mr Kodogo is*
*a coloured gentleman?*
CONSTABLE SAVAGE [*Griff Rhys Jones*]: *Well, I can't say I've ever*
*noticed, sir.*

Not the Nine O'Clock News,
3 November 1980

*Yesterday, in a feat of miraculous technology, man took a further*
*step in his conquest of space by launching the first reusable*
*spacecraft, the shuttle.*

*Surely, it cannot be beyond his ingenuity back here on earth,*
*in Britain, to create a society – black, brown, yellow, white – that*
*can live together in peace and harmony?*

Daily Express, 13 April 1981

On 2 March 1981 a demonstration set off from New Cross, south London.
It had been planned by black activists protesting against what they saw as
the cruelty of the Metropolitan Police, the indifference of the justice system
and the racism of Britain's politicians. And as the crowds assembled, even
the organizers were taken aback by the turnout. They had hoped for a
thousand people, yet by mid-morning some 4,000 had gathered in Ford-
ham Park, defying the forecasts of heavy rain. As far as the eye could see
there were banners and placards: 'Equal Rights and Justice Now', 'Ain't
No Stopping Us Now, We Are on the Move'. 'Masses of people, masses
and masses of people,' one marcher later recalled. 'It was real . . . It was
awesome, it was just amazing.' Another remembered 'waves and waves

and waves and waves and waves of black people coming down that hill. It was a Charge of the Light Brigade.'[1]

The march got underway just after eleven, bound for Hyde Park, the mood determined but buoyant. The rain fell, yet the crowd continued to grow, coachloads of supporters from Bristol, Birmingham and Manchester swelling the ranks. But when the first marchers reached Blackfriars Bridge, the mood changed. According to the next day's papers, several hundred young men broke away from the main group and charged ahead. When the police tried to hold them back, scuffles broke out, and stones were thrown. By the time the marchers reached Fleet Street the atmosphere had become downright ugly; by the time they reached Regent Street the fringes of the march had degenerated into a rolling battle between young black men and mounted white policemen. 'In Wigmore Street', claimed one report, 'a gang snatched shovels and bricks off a builder's lorry and started attacking police. One constable was felled, helmet flying. Car and taxi windows were smashed. A black policeman was taunted by the mob. A white one lay on the pavement, his face bloody.'

With seventeen policemen injured, six with head wounds, the next day's papers made bloodcurdling reading. 'RAMPAGE OF A MOB', shrieked the front page of the *Express*, which reported that 'hundreds of youths' had 'rampaged along pavements, kicking cars, knocking down people and smashing shop windows'. The *Daily Star* called it a 'terror riot'; the *Sun*, beneath the headline 'DAY THE BLACKS RAN RIOT IN LONDON', claimed that a 'frenzied mob' had indulged in a seven-hour 'orgy of looting and destruction in the West End'. Here was Middle England's worst nightmare: a savage horde loose on the streets of the capital, terrorizing 'home-going commuters' and 'mothers with children'. And to those who had long warned that Britain was nurturing an enemy within, it was a gift. 'Can my right hon. Friend think of anything more overtly racist and criminal, or a clearer demonstration of a breakdown in public order,' Alan Clark asked the Home Secretary, Willie Whitelaw, three days later, 'than the behaviour of the young blacks in the march through Southwark on Monday, when they broke into and damaged shops, terrorised the white population and shouted objectionable slogans about the monarchy to try to provoke the police?'[2]

There was, of course, another side to the story. What lay behind the march was widespread outrage at one of the most dreadful domestic tragedies of the decade. Late on Saturday 18 January, more than a hundred teenagers had gathered at a house in New Cross Road to celebrate Yvonne Ruddock's sixteenth birthday. The party went on all night, but shortly before six the following morning, a fire broke out. In the smoke and chaos, thirteen partygoers were killed, including Yvonne herself. The oldest victim was 22, the youngest just 14. After initially suspecting arson, the police concluded that the fire had started inside the house. But many local residents, including most of the victims' parents, saw things differently. Racial tensions were running high: the far-right National Front were on the march, while many New Cross residents saw the police as an army of occupation, who preferred harassing local teenagers to hunting for the racists who had started the fire. 'We have got our own Jack the Ripper', the activist Mike Phillips told a local meeting, 'wiping out a dozen black people at a time.' How could the police expect them to believe it had been an accident?

To make matters worse, the reaction to the fire suggested that black lives were cheap. As the New Cross activists pointed out, the Queen had sent a message of condolence after forty-eight youngsters were killed in a nightclub fire in Dublin, but she had sent no such message to her own people in south London. Even their protest march on 2 March, they claimed, had been grossly misrepresented. Yes, a few hundred youngsters had misbehaved. But the organizers maintained that the police had over-reacted and the violence had been enormously exaggerated, a view supported by *The Times* two days later. The tabloids were only too keen to report the fighting, but some did not even bother to report the marchers' refrain, 'Thirteen dead and nothing said.' As one protester remarked, she just wanted to say, 'We're here. Look at us. We're here. We're hurting, and you're not doing anything about it.' And yet still white Britain refused to look. Indeed, many protesters were shocked by the indifference or hostility of white passers-by. 'As we came up Fleet Street', the lawyer and future politician Paul Boateng recalled, 'the taunting and abuse that rained down upon us from the *Express* building in particular, I will never forget that.'[3]

The irony is that the police were almost certainly right. The New Cross fire was not a racist attack. Two decades later, a new forensic study concluded that the fire had indeed started inside the house, probably after a fight among the partygoers themselves. But the fact that so many black Londoners believed the allegations of a wider racist conspiracy could hardly have been more ominous. The Metropolitan Police Commissioner, Sir David McNee, told the press that the tragedy was being exploited by militant extremists, 'motivating and urging the black community to confront the police'. But as the weeks went by the anger intensified. When the inquest opened at County Hall in April, barely half an hour passed 'without some interruption from the public, whether . . . hissing the police, applauding the young black witnesses or yelling at the coroner'.

And when, on 13 May, the jury unanimously returned an open verdict, the court exploded with rage. When the coroner tried to express his sympathy, people shouted 'Shame!' and 'Murder!' Far from being deterred, the New Cross activists announced that they would redouble their efforts to expose the police cover-up. 'STAND UP AGAINST THE MASS MURDER OF BLACK PEOPLE,' read their leaflets. 'STAND UP AGAINST ATTACKS BY WHITE RACISTS ON BLACK PEOPLE. STAND UP AGAINST THE LIES AND CONFUSION SPREAD BY NEWSPAPERS, RADIO AND TELEVISION.' In the words of one man who wrote an angry letter to the *Guardian*, 'some black British have had enough'. As events were to prove, he was right.[4]

At the beginning of the 1980s, Britain was one of the most racially diverse countries in Europe. Although immigration had slowed since its peak twenty years earlier, just under 3½ million of the United Kingdom's 56 million people had been born abroad, almost three-quarters of them from the Caribbean and South Asia. Having been attracted by the plentiful jobs and cheap housing of the major conurbations, about half lived in Greater London, with a further quarter in the West Midlands. And by the time Mrs Thatcher became Prime Minister, many inner-city areas had long since acquired a distinctive multicultural character. When Beryl Bainbridge visited Sparkbrook, Birmingham, she found the high street full of 'men in turbans, women in saris and baggy muslin trousers, children dressed as fairies. Trinkets and rings and bangles in the windows of the shops, yams and roots of ginger and pomegranates laid out on the pavements.' But places like Sparkbrook were not exotic to the people who lived there, and least of all to the children for whom they were home. The writer Sathnam Sanghera, who grew up in the 1980s, later recalled the inevitable conversations with taxi drivers who asked where he was from. 'Wolverhampton,' he would say, to which the driver would invariably say: 'I mean, where are you from *originally*.' And invariably Sanghera gave the only accurate answer: 'I'm *originally* from Wolverhampton.'[5]

Although millions of people lived in areas with very few black and Asian Britons, anybody with a television could see that Britain was more racially diverse than ever before. As a boy, I grew up watching the Trinidad-born Floella Benjamin on *Play School*, as well as Lenny Henry, born to Jamaican parents, on *Tiswas*. Trevor McDonald, born in Trinidad, had been reporting for ITN since 1973, while in August 1981 Moira Stuart, whose parents had been born in Dominica and Barbados, became the first black woman to read the BBC news. The first black England footballer, Viv Anderson, made his international debut in November 1978; the first black England cricketer, Roland Butcher, made his Test debut in March 1981. And even people who hated immigration now accepted, very grudgingly, that British-born black and Asian children were not immigrants but natives. The disabled war hero Sir Douglas Bader had spent twenty years campaigning against immigration and in support of the white-dominated regime in Rhodesia. Yet when the *Express* invited him to issue a new broadside in 1978, even Bader conceded that there were 'many coloured British citizens who have been born and brought up in this country who are just as proud and patriotic as any of us'.[6]

Even so, Britain was a long way from being colour-blind. In the press, black and Asian Britons were almost completely invisible, except in stories about crime or racism. Partly this was a question of numbers. As the journalist Martin Kettle wrote in 1981, there was an obvious contrast with the situation across the Atlantic, where most major American cities had large black populations. No British city, not even London, was remotely comparable. As a result, the immigrant population's political clout was non-existent. There were no black and Asian MPs, judges, vice-chancellors, chairmen or chief executives. Even in youth clubs they struggled to be accepted. In September 1980 Birmingham's youth officer complained that community centres were barring black teenagers on the grounds of 'being too noisy' and 'liking too much reggae'. Effectively they remained outsiders, peering through a door that was at best only slightly ajar.

Twenty, even ten years earlier, many people would have considered this entirely unremarkable. But now they were beginning to notice that, in everything from housing to education, black Britons lagged far behind their white counterparts. On arrival, most had started out at the very bottom of the ladder. Yet thirty years on, most were still there, apparently stuck forever. Among the white male population, only 60 per cent of the workforce were in blue-collar, manual jobs. Among West Indians and Pakistanis, however, the figure was 92 per cent – and that was when they had jobs at all.[7]

While few places in the early 1980s were free from the shadow of unemployment, the outlook for black and Asian Britons was exceptionally bleak. In the capital, the unemployment rate for young black people was three times higher than the rate for whites. In many run-down inner-city areas, black jobless rates were at least 50 per cent. In Moss Side, Manchester, only three out of ten young black men were working, while in Handsworth, Birmingham, a survey of 500 homeless youngsters found that all but a dozen were black. 'West Indians feel, and have reason to feel, that the prospects of ever breaking out of this trap are worst for them,' explained the Very Reverend Basil Moss, who chaired Birmingham's Community Relations Council. Indeed, Moss was 'astonished that, the negative social factors being what they are, so many young unemployed blacks are cheerful, patient, responsible and law-abiding. I often wonder if I would behave as cheerfully and responsibly at that age under such circumstances.'[8]

The gap was not just economic. More than thirty years after the *Empire Windrush* had docked at Tilbury, old prejudices still died hard. An apparently trivial example was the Robertson's golliwog, which had appeared on the firm's marmalade and jam jars since 1930. Not surprisingly, many people found it offensive, and over time the firm had reacted by tweaking his eyes and adjusting his name to 'golly'. But when, in the spring of 1980, the firm launched a range of 'table mats, badges, pens, bags, pendants, aprons, oven mitts, egg cups, spoons and even thermometers' promoting 'Fifty Golden Years of Robertson's Golly', many black Britons were outraged. 'It is perpetuating an image, a caricature of black people which is counterproductive and distasteful, considering the multiracial nature of our society,' said Basil Manning, a Lewisham community worker and spokesman for the National Committee on Racism in Children's Books. Mr Manning already had one victory under his belt. After Boots had launched a range of golliwog bath sponges in December 1979, he had sent the managing director a parable in which children were given golliwogs for Christmas and grew into adults who marched through London shouting, 'Wogs out!' To their credit, Boots dropped the sponges. But Robertson's were less accommodating: not until the beginning of the next century did they ditch the golly.[9]

Would it be fair to describe Margaret Thatcher's Britain as a racist country? Perhaps not. Yet as Paul Theroux travelled the land in 1982, he regularly saw racist graffiti. 'NAZIS ARE THE MASTER RACE', read a scrawl in Margate, while graffiti in St Ives, Cornwall, proclaimed, 'Wogs ought to be hit about the head with the utmost severity', and 'Niggers run amok in London – St Ives next!' As an outsider, Theroux noticed that people's everyday language reflected their unconscious prejudices. If a black runner won a race against foreign opponents, he was English. But 'if he lost, he was "coloured". If he cheated, he was "West Indian".' And because Theroux was an outsider, people sometimes dropped their guard and said what they really thought. In Middlesbrough he was looking at the grim economic news in the local paper when a 'respectable-looking' man called Mr Strawby struck up a conversation with him. The reason things were so miserable, Mr Strawby explained, was 'the blacks . . . We whites are the original inhabitants of this coontry [*sic*], but they make all the laws in favour of the blacks. That's why it's all gone bad.'[10]

The truth is that, at the turn of the 1980s, you did not have to look far to find examples of racism: sometimes casual, almost unthinking, but sometimes charged with hatred and resentment. 'Everywhere you see these aimless wogs,' recorded the actor Kenneth Williams one stifling summer's day. 'In the park loads of 'em with scruffy families adding to an air of dereliction and desuetude. [Enoch] Powell was right, they should have stopped immigration years ago – all it's done has [*sic*] imported alien cultures and poverty.'

Born in 1926, Williams – who once blacked, or at least browned, up to play the Khasi of Khalabar – was famously misanthropic. Yet when *The Times* conducted a large survey of young people in 1981, many were just as prejudiced. 'I think they're over-protected,' said 17-year-old Linda from Newcastle. 'They shouldn't be allowed in, at least not to start businesses.' Local councils had been 'scared' into giving them jobs, agreed 19-year-old Steve from Croydon. 'You get a bunch of coons walking in, "We're unemployed, we want a job," and they say No, and then they say it's racial discrimination.' And most strikingly of all, 26 per cent wanted to see compulsory repatriation, with a further 18 per cent backing subsidies to encourage people to return home. So, in total, as *The Times* pointed out, almost half wanted to 'send them home'.[11]

'Yeah, we got coloured geezers, sambos and all that, but we all take the piss,' one working-class teenager, who had just joined the British Army, remarked in 1981. 'I mean last month we pretended to be the Ku Klux Klan. We put pillow-cases over our heads and went around the barracks at night moaning and wailing and telling them all that Maggie Thatcher was going to kick 'em all out. But everybody gets the piss taken out of them, they know it's only a joke like.' But sometimes there was not even the pretence of humour. It was the 'blackies' who really ran the country, teenagers on a Sunderland council estate told Jeremy Seabrook. 'They should all be shipped out, all the blackies, then there'd be jobs for our own people.' And when Seabrook talked to three unemployed Birmingham teenagers, they told him black people were poised 'to take over this country . . . There's more black people than there is white.' Britain, one said, was 'becoming the dustbin of the world, all the shit of Pakistan that's not wanted comes over here, sucking our life-blood, bringing the plague back and taking our jobs'.[12]

Of course people had always said prejudiced things. Yet over time the tone had changed. Racism had always been a legacy of Empire, fuelled by an unthinking sense of superiority. But by the 1980s it had a more obviously bitter, aggressive edge, sharpened by a sense of national decline, shot through with victimhood and resentment. And all the time the temperature was rising. In the summer of 1981, the anti-racist paper *Searchlight* reported an arson attack on a disabled Sikh woman in Leeds, the petrol bombing of an Asian shop in Ilford, arson attacks on two Asian shops in Bolton, the petrol bombing of a black family in Reading – and this is merely a sample. In Coventry, where Satnam Singh Gill was killed by skinheads in a shopping centre and Ami Dharry was murdered while buying fish and chips, the bishop's adviser on race relations warned that working-class white men were 'looking for scapegoats'. And in Oldham the community relations officer, Keith Bradford, warned that racial tensions were reaching pressure-cooker levels. In this deeply depressed industrial town, recent months had seen young Asians stoned in the streets, National Front slogans daubed on walls, garden gates set on fire and petrol bombs thrown at Bengali temples. Given the economic situation, Bradford told *The Times*, an explosion was inevitable. 'I can see piles of brick and rubble from here,' he said. 'Where there are broken bricks lying around you can be pretty sure that there will soon be people ready to pick them up and throw them at somebody.'[13]

In an ideal world, black and Asian Britons would have trusted the police to protect them from harassment. But this was not an ideal world. For one thing, the police were glaringly unrepresentative, especially in the inner cities. Of some 117,000 officers in England and Wales in 1981, just 286 were black or Asian. And when the filmmaker Roger Graef interviewed dozens of policemen and women, black and Asian officers told some hair-raising tales. 'An ethnic officer joining this job should anticipate a hard time,' said one, whose parents had come from India. 'Everybody calls us "wogs, coons, groids",' said a young Met WPC. A northern detective constable remembered hearing a colleague who was a Muslim ('I think he's Iranian. I'm not really sure') being told why he did not get any tea, like the others: 'You're a fucking nigger. Make your own tea.' And a young black constable said that, off duty, he had been stopped in his Ford Cortina 'many times' by white policemen, who only dropped their aggressive tone when he showed them his warrant card. 'The police force is ultra right wing,' he said sadly, 'no doubt about it.'[14]

Why were the police so racist? The obvious explanation is that because many officers came from the self-consciously respectable working classes they were keen to distinguish themselves from 'unrespectable' elements, with immigrants seen as the lowest of the low. A report by the Policy Studies Institute in 1983 found that the force's 'canteen culture' involved endless jokes about 'nignogs, spooks, sooties, spades, coons [and] monkeys'. Some officers did not bother to deny that they were prejudiced. 'You know why there aren't more black coppers?' asked a Home Counties detective sergeant. 'They're too fucking lazy, that's why . . . And I don't think they've got the brain power for it either.' A Met inspector told Roger

Graef that he often thought back to Enoch Powell's speeches in the late 1960s. 'The black population of this country do not want to be part of this country,' he said. 'What the hell do we do with people who can't read and write? They don't want a job, they don't want a house, they just want to wreck everything. We think being British is the greatest thing in the world. They think being British is shit.' And even young recruits were often intensely prejudiced. Most 'niggers', said one probationary constable, were 'just dirty, smelly backward people who will never change in a month of Sundays'. 'The country is being taken over slowly but surely by coloured immigrants,' said another: 'if we continue like this there will be no white people left.'[15]

Not unreasonably, then, many immigrant communities saw the police as the enemy. As early as 1972, black activists warned a Commons committee that there would be 'blood on the streets' unless the police cleaned up their act. In particular, black Londoners were convinced that the Met was abusing the so-called 'sus' ('suspected person') laws, which, under the Vagrancy Act of 1824, empowered officers to arrest people whom they believed to be loitering with 'intent to commit an arrestable offence'. Nationwide, about four out of ten people arrested on 'sus' were black, rising to almost eight out of ten in south London. For young black men growing up in the capital, recalled the brothers Mike and Trevor Phillips, 'the police were a natural hazard, like poisonous snakes, or attack dogs off the leash. You walked past them with care because you knew that if anything happened you would be questioned and searched or arrested.' The criminologist John Benyon recounted the story of Mark Bravo, who bought a motorbike after turning 16 in 1982. According to his mother's journal, in one two-week period Mark was stopped four times on 2 April, once on 4 April, twice on 5 April, seven times on 7 April, twice on 8 April, twice on 9 April and five times on 14 April. Not once had he done anything wrong.[16]

Slowly but steadily, frustration rose. In the *New Statesman*, Mike Phillips warned of a 'siege mentality in the inner cities, especially among the black community'. With young black men taking refuge in reggae and Rastafarianism, many observers detected a growing sense of separateness, of alienation, of anger. In 'Sonny's Lettah' (1979), the dub reggae poet Linton Kwesi Johnson imagines a boy writing to his mother from Brixton Prison, having been charged with murder after fighting back against the racist policemen who attacked his little brother. 'I can't take no more of that / No, I can't take no more of that,' sings the hero at the end of the low-budget, X-rated film *Babylon* (1980), as the police are smashing down the doors to break up his reggae gig. And in March 1980 the Commission for Racial Equality explicitly warned that, such was the tension between the police and young black men, 'we could well see an eruption such as we have seen in America in the past'.[17]

Two weeks later came the first explosion. The setting was St Paul's, Bristol, a typical inner-city mixture of dilapidated terraced streets, boarded-up shops and bleak council high-rises. St Paul's had a reputation as a hotbed of prostitution, drugs and petty crime: black residents themselves, who accounted for about half the area's population, called it 'the Jungle'. The trouble began on the afternoon of 2 April, when the police raided the Black and White Café, arresting the owner for cannabis possession and confiscating large quantities of illegal alcohol. The café was packed with young men drinking, playing cards and listening to reggae, who did not take well to the arrival of almost forty officers. A crowd gathered; a man claimed the police had ripped his trousers; a bottle was thrown, then a barrage of bricks and stones. The shadows lengthened, and the momentum built. Two police cars were turned over, and one was set on fire. The crowd attacked a breakdown van; then they set more cars on fire, broke into local shops and set light to a branch of Lloyds Bank. At last, just before 7.30, the Chief Constable arrived on the scene, realized his men were overrun and withdrew them for their own safety. For more than three hours, the mob looted and burned to their hearts' content. Only by about 11 p.m., when the police returned in force, did the chaos die down.[18]

Nobody died in the St Paul's riot. Even so, with twenty-two officers badly injured, twenty-one buildings burned and some £150,000 worth of goods stolen, it was clearly more than just a rowdy evening out in Bristol. The national papers played it up for all it was worth: 'MOB FURY!' roared the *Mirror*. 'MOB ON RAMPAGE', agreed the *Express*. And even at the time many observers saw St Paul's as a warning. The local Labour MP, Arthur Palmer, pointed out that Bristol was not the only city with an alienated black population packed into a 'narrow enclave of streets'. 'Time', he wrote sternly, 'is running short.' The causes, agreed the *Sun*, lay in the 'squalor and deprivation of decayed urban centres, in empty lives, and lack of work and opportunity. These same conditions exist on a far greater scale in other cities: Liverpool, Manchester, Newcastle and London itself.' Even the Police Federation's parliamentary spokesman, Eldon Griffiths, thought St Paul's might be 'the first of many' riots in the years ahead. 'WHICH CITY WILL BE NEXT AFTER BRISTOL?' asked the *Sunday Express*. Almost exactly a year later, it learned the answer.[19]

'In the benign April sunshine', began a long feature in the *Observer* in April 1981, 'Rattray Road is a pleasant street of substantial mid-Victorian terraced houses.' To the casual visitor, it looked like a street on the up, with plenty of new cars, middle-aged men setting off to work and elderly women passing the time of day. The birds sang, the builders drank their tea in their vans, the decorators and window-cleaners climbed their ladders. There was even, the paper said, a hint of gentrification: 'Rattray Road could be near the centre of any large English city, and a lot of people would be glad to live there.'

But Rattray Road was not just anywhere. 'Eight days ago', the paper went on, 'the roofs reflected the orange glow of flames, and the noise of riot and rage filled the smoke-tainted air. Youths with petrol bombs chased down side streets, and police armed with riot shields and snatched-up dustbin lids chased them back again.' Now, as children played on their bikes in the spring sunshine, it all seemed so hard to imagine. But then 'the harsh clatter of a helicopter's rotorblades broke the illusion . . . The front line was under observation.' The *Observer* made it sound like Belfast. In fact, this was Brixton.[20]

At the turn of the 1980s, few places better encapsulated the problems of the inner city than this scruffy corner of Lambeth, south London. About a quarter of Brixton's residents were black, rising to about half of those under 16. Housing conditions were awful, and the waiting list for council flats was some 18,000 names long. The jobs picture, meanwhile, was horrific. In the borough as a whole, careers offices had just one vacancy for every forty-four registered teenagers. But many young people were too demoralized even to register. Most observers reckoned that black unemployment, which had risen threefold since the beginning of the recession, was three times higher than for whites. Indeed, although an official report later suggested that at least half of Brixton's black male teenagers were out of work, the true figure was probably much higher.[21]

To outsiders, Brixton was associated with one thing above all: crime. The Metropolitan Police called it 'unique in terms of its violent street crime', while the great modern historian of London, Jerry White, describes it as 'the capital's capital of street robbery'. The Met's figures showed that in the last four years of the 1970s the figures for mugging and pickpocketing had gone up by 38 per cent in London as a whole, but by 66 per cent in Lambeth and by a staggering 138 per cent in Brixton. The epicentre was Railton Road, known locally as the 'Front Line', surrounded by abandoned and boarded-up houses. To white visitors, Railton Road often seemed a threatening place: a world of 'shebeens, gambling dens and cannabis dealing', where groups of young black men loitered 'for want of anything better to do'. Even locals admitted they felt unsafe there. With mounting unemployment, said a spokesman for the local youth centre, 'crime has become more commonplace and more acceptable. This is a vicious circle to which there is no present end in sight.'[22]

As many young black men told it, however, the real problem was the police. In March 1980 a poll of black residents found that seven out of ten had little or no confidence in the police and two-thirds feared there would soon be serious trouble. In Lambeth as a whole, one in three people stopped by the police in 1979 and 1980 was black. In Brixton, half of all arrests involved young black men. A particularly sore point was the Met's ultra-aggressive Special Patrol Group, which had been deployed four times in Brixton since 1978, making hundreds of arrests. And although resentment of the police was hardly unknown elsewhere, everybody agreed it was especially intense in Brixton. 'Everyone has a story which happened either to themselves or a relative or a friend,' wrote Mike Phillips. 'The police are the enemy.'[23]

It was against this background that on Monday 6 April 1981 the police launched a massive new operation, codenamed 'Swamp 81', designed to sweep Lambeth's muggers off the streets. The name, intended for internal use only, could hardly have been more unfortunate, reviving memories of Mrs Thatcher's controversial remark in 1978 about the fear of being 'rather swamped by people with a different culture'. In fact, it derived simply from the police tactic of 'swamping' the area with more than a hundred officers in plain clothes. Later, in his official report on the Brixton riots, Lord Scarman said that Swamp 81 had been a 'serious mistake'. At the time, though, the police considered it a great success, since in five days they stopped 943 people, half of them black, made 118 arrests and charged seventy-five people. But then, late on the afternoon of the fifth day, a lovely warm spring Friday, things suddenly went wrong.[24]

The spark came when a police constable spotted a 19-year-old black man, Michael Bailey, running across the road, pursued by two other men. The policeman cornered Bailey and wrestled him to the ground, only to find that his shirt was soaked in blood. It turned out that Bailey had a three-inch stab wound in his back, but he refused to tell the police what had happened. Eventually the constable, who had been joined by some colleagues, began to apply first aid and called for an ambulance. But by this stage a small crowd had gathered, most of them young black men who assumed, wrongly, that Bailey had been attacked by the police. Despite the fact that the police were trying to bandage his wound, the crowd bombarded them with bricks and bottles, dragged him from the car and spirited him away. By about 6.30 the mood had turned very ugly, with perhaps a hundred people hurling missiles at about forty policemen. After an hour or so the fighting subsided. But the police were jittery. That night, they decided to have twelve extra pairs of officers patrolling the streets the next day. They did not, however, cancel the Swamp operation.[25]

Saturday 11 April was another unseasonably warm day. With dozens of uniformed policemen patrolling the streets as well as almost fifty plain-clothes Swamp officers, the atmosphere felt swelteringly tense. 'Everyone knew that something was going to happen after the Friday night,' wrote Mike Phillips. 'There was an intense throbbing vibe in the air, like feeling the bass on some incredible sound system pounding into action.' Late that afternoon, near the top of Railton Road, two young plain-clothes detectives questioned a minicab driver, whom they suspected of dealing drugs. A small crowd gathered; the atmosphere became heated; a scuffle broke out between one of the detectives and a young black man. The detectives arrested the man, who was struggling ferociously, and threw him into the back of a police van. The crowd began to shout and shove, the police called for reinforcements, the first bricks began to fly – and suddenly the riot was on.[26]

A timeline published in the *Guardian* two days later captures the momentum of events:

> *5 pm*: An abandoned police car is set on fire in Atlantic Road. Jewellery and clothing stores are broken into in the road and several police officers are hurt by flying bricks.
>
> *5.30*: Fighting continues in Atlantic Road and spreads into Railton Road and Mayall Road. Police get out riot shields and form cordons at the east end of Railton Road.
>
> *6.30*: The first petrol bombs are thrown, setting fire to police and private cars in Railton and Leeson roads.
>
> *6.40*: Fire brigade summoned to the area to cope with petrol bomb attacks but are unable to get through because their vehicles are stoned . . .
>
> *7.40*: A fire engine turntable set alight in Railton Road. Minutes later, youths commandeered a fire engine which they then drove up and down Railton Road.
>
> *7.45*: A petrol bomb sets fire to the Windsor Castle pub in Leeson Road which is completely destroyed by 9.30pm. At the same time, the George public house in Railton Road is petrol bombed . . .
>
> A white couple with two young children living just off Railton Road in a mixed street have their door kicked in by a group of eight black youths armed with knives who threaten them for money. A black family across the road try to dissuade the youths but fail.
>
> Black crowds drive police down Railton Road towards Atlantic Road with missiles. Police group in Mayall Road and try to push the rioters back.

Then a lull occurs. Buildings, including the post office, a car spares business, a plumber's shop, an off-licence and a school in Effra Road all burn during this period. Serious looting begins.

9.30: The Windsor Castle pub collapses and electricity fails along Mayall Road.

10.0: Police begin to regain control of the area.

What this does not capture, though, is the shock of seeing barricades and petrol bombs on the streets of London, the terror of the police as missiles hailed down around them, the horror of the fire and ambulance crews as the mob turned its fury on them, the near-ecstasy of the crowd as they hijacked buses and fire engines, or the extraordinary, apocalyptic spectacle as black smoke billowed over the blazing cars and gutted pubs. 'Red-hot debris dripped from a series of burning buildings along both sides of the road,' wrote one reporter. 'Amid the roaring of the flames and the crashing of collapsing buildings, there were screams and shouts. Despite the furnace of heat, figures could be seen running through the smoke, hurling missiles at unseen police.' One policeman thought it 'looked like World War III. Cars blazing, people running everywhere'. The *Observer* thought the scenes of burning pubs and rubble-strewn streets reminiscent of 'the blitz or Belfast'. The *Express* called it 'the bloody blitz of Railton Road'. Another officer said it was 'like Beirut, not London. It was like another country.'[27]

The police did not regain control of Brixton until late on Monday evening, three days after the trouble had started. But by then the riots had already become the most violent and costly disturbances of the twentieth century, with more than 450 people injured, 207 vehicles damaged or destroyed, among them 118 police cars and four ambulances, 145 buildings burned or vandalized and 354 people arrested, at a total cost of more than £6 million. Afterwards, some residents talked of the 'festival atmosphere', the 'buzz' as the community united to fight the police. But the local residents who owned the plumbing store, the off-licence or the little shops in Brixton Market did not share their enthusiasm. And the Brixton riots were not victimless crimes, as the people kicked, robbed, beaten and stamped on would attest. One 25-year-old white woman, who had lived in the area for three years, opened her door late on Saturday night, thinking that the knock came from a neighbour who had offered to give her a lift. In fact, it came from a youth with a scarf tied around his face, who pushed her into the living room and raped her at knifepoint. After fleeing the scene, she returned to her flat the next day, and found that looters had stolen her jewellery and hi-fi.[28]

For the police, the weekend had been, as one put it, an 'absolutely copper-bottomed fucking nightmare'. In total, some 110 officers were hospitalized, sixteen of them with head injuries, as well as twelve firemen and three ambulance men. Many freely admitted that they had been terrified. 'I was as scared as hell,' one 21-year-old constable, who lived in Brixton, told the press. 'They were throwing everything at us. Lumps of concrete, iron bars and petrol bombs.' 'We tried to take cover,' said a traffic policeman, who had been among the reinforcements, 'but they were chanting and shouting and it seemed that the whole world had gone mad. It was a very frightening experience. It was terrible.' One WPC admitted that when it was all over and she had time to think, she just could not stop shaking. She suffered from 'nightmares long afterwards'.[29]

Even before the fighting had died down, people were looking for explanations. A spokesman for the Met, vigorously denying that its aggressive policing had anything to do with it, claimed that the riots had been orchestrated by outsiders: a 'lot of people, many of them white, with cameras, who were not press photographers'. This became a common theme in newspapers like the *Express* and the *Mail*, which were convinced that a hard-left cabal of 'political extremists' had directed the whole thing. But most shopkeepers and residents told a different story. Almost all blamed the police, both for flooding the streets on Saturday and for years of aggressive harassment. 'When you get a lot of people who are treated as badly as this, what can you expect?' remarked a local vicar. 'This has been coming for twenty-five years,' said a veteran black community worker. 'It's been coming a long time,' agreed the head of a local community centre. 'A lot of us have been saying this would happen for years and no one has been paying attention.'[30]

The Home Secretary, Willie Whitelaw, visited Brixton on Sunday. Jeered by local residents, he was visibly shocked by what he saw. Almost immediately he announced a public inquiry under the veteran judge Lord Scarman, but in the meantime he warned Mrs Thatcher that further 'severe disorder' was very likely. As a Home Office report put it, 'increased militancy and large numbers of bored, unemployed youths may spark off disturbances in almost any large town, with the police a main target'. This, the papers agreed, was the most chilling thing about Brixton: not that it had happened at all, but that it would happen again. Unless something drastically changed, said the *Express*, 'Bristol and Brixton will turn out to be but warnings of far worse to come. That is not an astrological prediction. It is an absolute certainty.' The front page of the *Mirror*, which carried a huge picture of policemen sheltering from the mob, made the same point in three words. Its banner headline read simply: 'THINGS TO COME.'[31]

It was twelve weeks, however, before the inevitable sequel arrived. The setting this time was Toxteth, Liverpool, one of the most deprived, depressed and dangerous areas in Britain. Even in a city scarred by unemployment and petty crime, Toxteth stood out. As skilled white working-class families left for the suburbs, it had become a ghetto for the poor, the old and the marginalized. Many of its terraced houses, wrote a local politics lecturer, had been 'vandalised beyond repair, boarded up or torn down, all adding to the atmosphere of decay'. As in Brixton, its black residents – who numbered 30,000 – felt abandoned and alienated. As in Brixton, the local unemployment figures were horrific, with at least eight out of ten black men out of work. And as in Brixton, relations with the local police were characterized by incomprehension, suspicion and outright hostility. When, in 1980, sociologists at the local university prepared a report for the Commons Home Affairs Committee, their verdict could hardly have been bleaker. 'Time is running out,' they concluded. 'A combination of one of Britain's bleakest unemployment areas with one of Britain's most disadvantaged black communities could be disastrous.'[32]

The detonation came on the night of Friday 3 July, and in many respects it was Brixton all over again. The trigger this time was an altercation with a young black man on a motorbike, which the pursuing police wrongly believed had been stolen. When the man fell off and the police tried to arrest him, an angry crowd gathered and pelted them with bricks and stones. In the confusion, the man got away, but for the next two hours the crowd bombarded the police cars with more missiles. Night fell and the fighting died down, but on Saturday afternoon, as police reinforcements poured into Toxteth's narrow terraced streets, battle resumed in earnest: barricades and bottles, petrol bombs and pickaxe handles, looting, burning and beating.

Sunday was even worse. By now the police were out in force, some 800 strong. But as a contemporary account records, they were totally overwhelmed:

> Rioters commandeered milk floats, a stolen fire engine and a cement mixer and drove them straight into police lines. They were armed with every conceivable weapon, including lengths of scaffolding which they thrust at the riot shields like medieval knights. One policeman was speared in the head by a spiked six-foot railing. As a blanket of smoke rose into the sky, the rioters pressed forward yelling 'stone the bastards' and parading their trophies – police helmets and riot shields. At one point they managed to seize a fire hose which the police had been using on them and turn it on the officers.

As in Brixton, the police seemed powerless, huddling behind their shields while rioters and looters ruled the streets. Witnesses reported seeing children as young as 5 crawling through broken windows, encouraged by their parents. 'They brought shopping carts to ship it out,' one said. 'Refrigerators, dryers, you name it. I even saw one lady hold up a piece of carpet and ask if anybody knew if it was 6ft by 4ft.' In the end, during a lull while patients were evacuated from a local hospital, the Chief Constable, Kenneth Oxford, ordered his men to fire tear-gas canisters. Never before had the police used tear gas in mainland Britain; indeed, Oxford was breaking Home Office rules, which stipulated that it could only be used against armed criminals. But the ferocity of the violence, he argued, had left him with no choice.[33]

By the time peace returned to Toxteth, the riots had caused £4.7 million worth of damage, while 244 people had been arrested and hundreds more injured. These figures did not capture the extraordinary intensity of the violence, which many observers thought even more vicious than in Brixton. The police were prepared to face bricks and stones; they were not prepared, however, to face rioters with axes and sledgehammers, trying to run them down with cars and fire engines, or dousing them with petrol and trying to set them alight. 'No amount of training can prepare you for that. I hope to God I never see anything like it again,' one said afterwards. 'I realised, standing there with a shield, that people out there wanted me dead.' Many complained that their strategy had been far too passive, leaving them trapped behind their shields while petrol bombs exploded around them. 'I don't know how you can describe the smoke and the flames and the terror, absolute terror,' another constable said. 'It went on for so long. I was dreaming about it. I had to see a psychiatrist.'[34]

What was really shocking, though, was the fact that the riots now seemed to be part of a national trend. On Friday 3 July, the night the disturbances broke out in Toxteth, several hundred skinheads were in Southall, west London, for a concert at a local pub. To Southall's large South Asian population, already alarmed by skinhead harassment and the rise of the National Front, this seemed an intolerable provocation. Outside the pub, hundreds of Asian men, most of them Sikhs, built barricades to lay siege to the skinheads, and as the night drew on the confrontation escalated into a pitched battle, the Asians pelting the police and the skinheads with bricks, milk bottles and Molotov cocktails. At one stage, while black smoke from burning buildings drifted overhead, the rioters even commandeered a police bus and tried to break through into the pub forecourt. Yet these were not, by and large, unemployed or alienated young men. Britain's Sikhs were famously law-abiding, while Southall was a relatively affluent, well-integrated suburb, with high levels of education and home ownership. When local Asian leaders were asked to describe their neighbourhood, the word they often used was 'friendly'. If this could happen in Southall, where would be next?[35]

The answer came four days later. Late on Tuesday 7 July, there were reports of clashes between police and black youths in the deprived, crime-blighted neighbourhood of Moss Side, Manchester. The following evening Moss Side saw more trouble, with about a thousand people laying siege to the local police station, smashing windows, hurling bricks and over-turning cars. It took three nights for the police to regain control, but by this stage the rioting seemed to be spreading uncontrollably. On Friday 10th there was trouble in Handsworth in Birmingham, as well as in Wol-verhampton, Nottingham, Sheffield, Hull, Preston, Slough, Ellesmere Port and Reading. Saturday was even worse. With rumours spreading and shopkeepers anxiously boarding up their windows, there were reports of rioting not just in Handsworth and Brixton, but in Southampton, Ports-mouth, Luton, Derby, Nottingham, Sheffield, Leeds, Bradford, Halifax, Huddersfield, Blackburn, Preston and Blackpool, as well as countless other cities and towns across the country.[36]

In retrospect, some of this was almost certainly exaggerated. Drunken rowdiness in High Wycombe, Gloucester and Aldershot was not in the same league as rioting in south London, while a single petrol bomb being thrown at a car in Cirencester was hardly the same as a hail of incendiaries on the streets of Liverpool. In most towns the trouble lasted only for a night or two, and a fortnight later the nation's attention switched to the coming wedding of Prince Charles and Lady Diana Spencer. Yet to most of the press, this felt like the End of Days. 'Looting, arson, riots – now we're reaping the progressive whirlwind,' shrieked a front-page editorial in the *Daily Express* on Tuesday 7 July:

How many riots in how many cities? How much pillaging, looting and arson in how many decayed streets and urban wastelands?

How many more weekends like the past one is this civilised country to suffer before authority reasserts itself?

How often are we to see our police forces attacked for the fun and the hell of it by teenage black, yellow and white skinheads, tinheads and yobs before the country's weight is put behind its police?

How long are we expected to endure mindless young hooligans and vicious young vandals terrorising housing estates, marauding buses and trains, bullying their way along the pavements before the powers that be stop feeling sorry for thugs and start making our cities safe again?

The headline, a scream of anguish, said it all: 'HOW MUCH MORE MUST WE TAKE?'[37]

For the Prime Minister, as for so many people, the summer's riots came as a terrible shock. 'Oh, those poor shopkeepers!' Mrs Thatcher exclaimed when she saw the pictures of the devastation in Toxteth. To her critics, her words perfectly captured her instinctive sympathy with the property-owning classes. And while a more emollient politician might have found the right words to heal the wounds, she seemed incapable of striking the right note. When she addressed the nation in a party political broadcast on 8 July, her banal pieties about the importance of obeying the law were widely mocked, even by her allies, as completely inadequate. 'Her tone is too strident and defensive to meet the needs of a fearful society,' said *The Times*. She seemed 'strained, tired and over-wrought', agreed the *Observer*. And a brief trip to Liverpool five days later was a public relations disaster, an angry crowd bombarding her car with toilet rolls and tomatoes. The symbolism was awful. This was not a commanding Prime Minister arriving to take charge. This was an uncertain, beleaguered woman, reeling from crisis to crisis, unable to get out of her car without people screaming abuse.[38]

In the meantime, Britain was struggling to come to terms with the legacy of destruction. Riots were supposed to happen in other countries, in Paris, Rome, Los Angeles or Detroit. They did not happen in Britain. So the chaos in Brixton, Toxteth, Southall and Moss Side seemed not just an attack on all the old assumptions, but a symptom of a dreadful sickness at the heart of modern British society. 'People are bound to ask what is happening to our country,' lamented the *Express*. 'Having been one of the most law-abiding countries in the world – a byword for stability, order, and decency – are we changing into something else?' And in *The Times*, David Watt agreed that 'we have lost, or at least mislaid, some of our collective sense of assured national identity', with society disintegrating into 'a collection of pressure groups, social classes, regional groupings, economic vested interests – and races'. 'What', he wondered, 'has become of our national pride?'[39]

Here, then, was more proof that Britain was trapped in a terrible spiral of national decline. But now it was clear that the disease was as much moral as it was economic, the symptoms bloodied policemen, burned-out cars and looted shops. 'WHERE ARE WE GOING?' asked a heartfelt *Times* leader on Monday 13th:

The riots of the past week are a severe blow to British self-esteem. They are a living testimony to a collapse of morale in one section of the community – and they have been damaging to the confidence of the country as a whole. One of the qualities upon which we have been accustomed to pride ourselves as British people has been the orderliness of our way of life. We may no longer have an Empire. We may no longer be the workshop of the world. We may even have difficulty in paying our way. But this is still one of the most pleasant countries in which to live, a comfortable society renowned for tolerance and gentleness. Now that too seems to have been exposed as a false dream.

A few weeks later, the paper ran a round-up of some of the incidents across Britain one Saturday in August. At a protest march in Toxteth, two police-men had been hospitalized with stab wounds; in Sheffield, three policemen had been injured in a city-centre brawl with '500 youths, mostly black'; in Llandudno, four policemen had been hurt after fighting as hundreds of youngsters left a disco. Violence, violence everywhere. No wonder Ken-neth Williams thought it was 'getting a more barbaric world in every way, compared with the world I knew in my youth'. And as Paul Theroux travelled along the coast in the spring of 1982, he was struck by the alien-ation, the graffiti, the sense of looming physical threat. 'England – perhaps the whole of Britain,' he wrote, 'was changing into a poorer, more violent place.'[40]

There was, of course, another way of looking at all this. Punch-ups on a Saturday night would have come as no surprise to people a hundred years earlier. And in an international context the riots in Brixton and Toxteth were hardly exceptional. In the 1960s and 1970s hundreds of people had been killed and thousands injured in riots in the United States. Yet, in Britain's days of rage, not one person died. In some ways, then, the fact that people were so shocked was actually a testament to the remarkable orderliness of British life. But that, of course, was not how people saw it at the time. Indeed, as the summer wore on the headlines became ever more hysterical: 'Orgy of Fire and Fury', 'Britain in Turmoil', 'Riot Frenzy'. Perhaps the most powerful was the front page of the *Sun* on 6 July, which featured a striking image of policemen huddled behind riot shields in Tox-teth. 'To Think This Is England', lamented the headline. For more on the 'Fury in the Ghetto', the paper urged readers to 'see pages 2, 3, 4, 5, 6, 7'.[41]

Even before the first stones were thrown, fears of crime had already been running high. 'In the public mind, at least, violence in Britain, espe-cially among the young, has reached intolerable levels, and the statistical evidence shows that most forms of violent crime are increasing, in some cases dramatically,' began a long feature in *The Times* in the summer of 1980. In the last quarter of a century, the annual total of recorded offences had risen from 438,000 to 2½ million, while in just a decade the annual total of violent offences had more than doubled. There were more cases of wife-battering and child abuse, more reports of vandalism and criminal damage, even more assaults on policemen. What these figures did not show, said *The Times*, was the 'sheer horror and cruelty of some of the offences'. The National Society for the Prevention of Cruelty to Children warned that with rising unemployment and family breakdown, they were seeing far more shocking cases of neglect and child-beating. And after studying hundreds of instances of violent crime, the group Victims of Violence had found 'endless cases where helpless, often elderly victims of robberies, burglaries and random attacks have been subjected to such brutal treatment that they live constantly in fear'.

What on earth was going on? The director of education at the University of Exeter told *The Times* that the problem was a 'time bomb' of unemployed youngsters, who were 'likely to turn to vandalism or street gangs unless their predicament is tackled'. By contrast, a criminology professor at Edinburgh thought the causes were cultural rather than economic, blaming the 'decline in accepted common values and accepted attitudes to authority'. Either way, said the *Observer*, violence 'has seemed to be increasing':

> Most people over 35 can recall some moment – the casual beating up of a neighbour on the street in broad daylight, a suburban mother robbed and terrorised by her own son, the intermittently decipherable words of a punk lyric heard on the car radio – when it occurred to them that violence in our society might be not a departure from the norm, but the norm itself.[42]

Against this background, many people saw the riots in Brixton and Toxteth as proof that society was falling apart. For more conservative observers, the riots confirmed everything they had been saying for years about permissiveness, immorality and the decline of the family. Rioting was a 'law and order' issue, insisted Mrs Thatcher, who thought the chief cause was 'a weakening of authority in many respects of life over many, many years'. Other Conservative MPs invoked a favourite scapegoat, the state of Britain's schools. Ian Lloyd blamed the 'seditious sociological claptrap that is passed on in our schools as education', while the marvellously whiskered Rhodes Boyson, himself a former headmaster, considered that the riots were the inevitable result of 'destroy[ing] the authority of the headmaster and his staff'.

Merseyside's Chief Constable, Kenneth Oxford, blamed modern parents, who had lost sight of 'basic civilized discipline' and ought to have made sure that 'these kids are home and in their beds at midnight and not heaving bricks at policemen or in shop windows and going on an uncivi-lized rampage'. Mary Whitehouse, not unsurprisingly, blamed the BBC, warning that its news coverage 'creates excitement, teaches techniques and encourages imitation'. The columnist Ronald Butt blamed the race rela-tions industry, from more established groups that merely harped on the 'disadvantage of the immigrants', to 'much less reputable local bodies which fuel discontent instead of calming it'. And to complete the set, the Tory backbencher Sir Ronald Bell told readers of the *Sunday Express* that the blame lay with the politicians, many of them 'self-styled progressives' who had allowed so many immigrants to come in the first place. 'Their duty', he said, 'was to safeguard the nation, but over 20 years the nation has been betrayed.'[43]

On the left, the obvious culprit was Mrs Thatcher herself. Arguing that the rioters had been motivated by anger at unemployment, Michael Foot insisted that Liverpool was a 'monument to Thatcherism'. Edward Heath, too, thought the key issue was jobs. 'If you have a half a million people hanging around on the streets all day, you will have a massive increase in juvenile crime,' he explained. 'Of course you will get racial tension when you have young blacks with less chance of getting jobs.' And Labour's Shadow Home Secretary, Roy Hattersley, was in no doubt. Leading the attack in the Commons, he insisted that the riots had not been caused by racial prejudice or police harassment, but by 'social and economic circum-stances'. 'I repeat that I do not believe that the principal cause of last week's riots was the conduct of the police,' he told MPs on 16 July. 'It was the conditions of deprivation and despair in the decaying areas of our old cities – areas in which the Brixton and Toxteth riots took place, and areas from which the skinhead invaders of Southall came.'[44]

On the face of it, the link with unemployment seemed undeniable. Areas like Brixton, Toxteth and Moss Side all suffered from punishing youth unemployment rates. Bristol City Council's chief executive told *The Times* that the root cause of the St Paul's disturbances was 'resentment over high unemployment', and even suggested that the district's problems could be fixed with just 200 extra jobs. And when Willie Whitelaw talked to councillors in Liverpool after the Toxteth riots, they were, he reported, 'unanimous in agreeing that the underlying cause of the problems in Liverpool 8 was the extremely high level of unemployment in that district, particularly among black people'.[45]

Yet there was an obvious flaw in the argument that the riots were caused by high unemployment. If the real problem was the lack of jobs, then why were there no riots in Consett and Corby, which had been utterly devastated by steel closures? Why were there no riots in struggling areas such as South

Wales or the north-east of England, where unemployment was cripplingly high? On top of that, there was no historical evidence that unemployment inevitably led to urban rioting. Indeed, although some people were outraged when Norman Tebbit told the Tory faithful that his unemployed father 'didn't riot' but 'got on his bike and looked for work', he had a point. For if there really were a straightforward link between unemployment and riot-ing, why had there been no riots during the Depression, when times had been so much harder? As Frank Johnson mischievously asked readers of *The Times*: 'Who can forget the burning down of Jarrow in 1930?'[46]

Among the public, however, most people bought the argument that unemployment, rather than police harassment or institutionalized racism, was the principal cause. Even the teenagers at a south London school near to Brixton generally agreed with Roy Hattersley's diagnosis. The fundamen-tal cause of the riots, wrote 13-year-old Primrose, who was black, was that 'people don't have enough money and are out of a job. They don't even give the people a chance.' As it happened, she thought *Space Invaders* might represent a useful solution. The council, she explained, had tried to keep people off the streets 'by building a place which has Space Invaders and one-arm bandits, etc., but what's the use of building it if they haven't the money to play the game. They should try building some which you don't have to put money into them. That way they won't have so much trouble.'[47]

The opinion polls told a similar story. A survey for the *Evening Stand-ard* found that 40 per cent of Londoners blamed the riots on unemployment, with 22 per cent mentioning 'blacks' behaviour' and 18 per cent 'racial-ism', while only 13 per cent blamed the police. When Gallup's pollsters asked about the general increase in violent crime, most people blamed a general breakdown in 'respect for authority', followed by unemployment, softer laws and poor parenting. Asked whether they blamed white or black people for the riots, most blamed black people. Asked whether they sym-pathized with the police or the rioters, the overwhelming majority chose the police. And when Gallup invited them to name the most pressing social problems of the day, 83 per cent mentioned violent crime, 71 per cent teenage crime, 63 per cent drug-taking and 57 per cent 'coloured immi-grants'. Racism and police harassment barely featured at all; but 'coloured immigrants' did. It is worth emphasizing that most people were more likely to accept black neighbours, colleagues and friends than ever before. Even so, when millions of white Britons thought about black and Asian people in the abstract, they did not think of them as friends. They thought of them as a problem.[48]

The irony of all these efforts to discover what lay behind the riots was that there was clearly no single cause. In many cases, the most important factor was clearly the bad blood between the police and black residents. But no two situations were exactly the same. In Southall, for example, the key issue was the police's failure to protect the Asian community from racist attacks. As for the copycat riots in the days after Toxteth, the only common factor, as the *Observer* pointed out, was simply the presence of a lot of 'bored teenagers' who had seen the news footage on television and fancied 'an evening's smashing and burning'. Were they deprived and downtrodden, angry and alienated? Probably not. It was obvious to most witnesses that the rioters in West Yorkshire, the West Midlands and elsewhere were 'thoroughly enjoying themselves'. To put it crudely, rioting was fun.[49]

The idea of rioting being fun horrified many observers, from those on the right who shuddered at the prospect of lawless anarchy to those on the left who wrung their hands at the plight of the inner cities. And yet for many participants the riots were neither a shriek of rage nor a cry for help. The *Observer*'s northern correspondent Michael Nally, who had seen the fighting in Moss Side at first hand, thought only a few of the rioters were genuinely motivated by anger about jobs or the police. 'Many, if not most,' he wrote, 'were out either for kicks, emboldened by the excitement, drink and drugs, or to commit crimes.' This tallied with what other youngsters told the *Sunday Times*'s Ian Jack as he travelled across the country that summer. When Jack asked what they had made of the riots, most said simply that they were 'daft' or a 'laugh'. Rioting, said an apprentice miner from Yorkshire, was 'just like gang-fighting really. You've got one set of lads chucking bricks at another set of lads who're wearing a daft uniform and they're chucking bricks back at you.'

On the fringes of the fighting in Moss Side, Michael Nally encountered two white men wearing anti-Thatcher badges. They told him that the riots were 'all about' jobs and police harassment. But a girl nearby told a different story. The men with badges were 'Commies', only there to sell their newspapers. 'No one's taking much notice of them,' she added contemptuously. Also on the fringes was a 17-year-old black youth, 'high on the excitement and eager to join the fighting'. He told Nally that he had greatly enjoyed laying siege to the police station the night before: 'We had the bastards in there shitting themselves.' But he was not unemployed. He worked in a shop and generally minded his own business. At this point a friend of his, who was white, appeared and threatened Nally with a 'short wooden shaft'. 'You bugger off, you, and write what the hell you like,' he said angrily. 'Say it's all political or something. That'll explain it. What the fuck would you do if you lived here?'[50]

*

Lord Scarman published his report on the Brixton riots on 25 November. He called it a 'major challenge to the nation', and it made the front page of every newspaper except the *Sun*. The fundamental cause of the riots, Scarman concluded, was the simmering tension between the Metropolitan Police and the area's black residents. The police must recruit more black and Asian officers, make racial prejudice a sackable offence and emphasize 'community policing' instead of the self-conscious toughness seen in places like Brixton. Beyond that, with 'racial disadvantage' becoming an 'endemic, ineradicable disease threatening the very survival of our society', the government should seriously consider positive discrimination in education and employment. Unless black youngsters were given a stake in society they would drift towards the lawless margins. 'So it is the nation's choice,' said the next day's *Mirror*. 'Either act on Scarman or put it on the shelf with countless others. But if we decide on the shelf it will not be dust that this report gathers. It will be blood.'[51]

Although the government promised to implement Scarman's recommendations, change was slow. As the handling of the murder of Stephen Lawrence showed twelve years later, the culture of the Metropolitan Police remained defiantly unreconstructed, while the judge's call for positive discrimination never bore fruit. And while the hard left condemned the report as a whitewash, the most striking rejoinder came from the conservative Salisbury Group, which commissioned a rival report on what it called the 'real' victims of the riots, the 'elderly white people of Lambeth'. Its author, the young Charles Moore, duly trudged around the borough talking to people who felt embattled by social and cultural change. As might have been predicted, they tended not to be fans of their black neighbours. 'We did make a terrible mistake letting them in,' some said:

> To think our men died to let that lot in . . . They mugged an old lady here with a cataract who was helping a blind friend of hers back from church . . . Foreigners should live like us if they come here . . . They should go round and look for work, not riot . . . It's our country and our Queen. Why should we be afraid to go out?[52]

In Brixton, little changed. The council launched a campaign to revive local businesses, spent £100,000 to redecorate the town centre and invested thousands more in race-relations efforts and community projects. But when *The Times*'s Nicholas Timmins visited in the summer of 1982, he reported that Railton Road looked worse than ever, 'seedy, run down and crime ridden'. Teenage unemployment, already horrific, had risen by a further 60 per cent, half of Brixton's black residents were out of work and the waiting list for council housing still contained 17,000 names. In the press Brixton remained a byword for disorder, a place of 'illegal drinking and gambling dens, where soft drugs are sold openly'. The police still proclaimed their determination to root out the drugs pushers on Railton Road; local people still seethed at what they saw as intrusive stop-and-search measures on the Front Line. And when, in September 1984, Lord Scarman returned to Brixton for a Channel 4 documentary, he found that the crime figures were still atrocious, unemployment was worse than ever and the cannabis dealers had moved on to cocaine and heroin. Even the local police commander, Alexander Marnoch, agreed that the prospects for Brixton's youngsters were 'abysmal'. The best advice he could give a young school-leaver applying for a job was to 'put down his address as somewhere other than Brixton'.[53]

Yet this was not the complete picture. For all the talk of intolerance and alienation, attitudes were, slowly but steadily, changing for the better. Decades later, documentaries about the summer of 1981 invariably remarked on the fact that, when the riots were at their worst, the number one record in the country was the Specials' 'Ghost Town', set in a forbidding post-industrial landscape of abandoned shops, deserted clubs and menacing high-rises. Yet the success of a multi-racial ska band like the Specials, inspired by Jamaican music, formed in Coventry and committed to fighting prejudice, itself told a more heartening story. The very name '2-Tone', used for both the ska genre and the Specials' record company, captured the group's commitment to racial integration. So did the company's black-and-white chequerboard motif, which appeared on everything from ties and T-shirts to hats and badges, and became one of the abiding emblems of early-1980s pop culture. 'The Specials *et al* are by definition multi-racial, anti-racist,' wrote Garry Bushell in *Sounds* in October 1979, 'and the message is conveyed by their irresistible coaxing of feet to dance steps and lips to song.' Bands like the Specials, agreed the *NME* a year later, 'have done more to expose and eradicate petty racial squabbling in the UK than any number of self-righteous, overtly political organizations'.[54]

In fact, the Specials' success in the early 1980s – two Top Ten albums, two number one singles and five more Top Ten singles – suggests that the gulf between black and white youngsters was not as wide as the pessimists often claimed. A survey by two London School of Economics researchers in the winter of 1979–80 found that most black teenagers' ambitions were exactly the same as those of their white counterparts: a good job, a decent income, a happy marriage, a thriving family. Though they had harsh words for the police, they were generally positive about schools, colleges and even the media, and revealed 'no fundamental sense of alienation from British society'. They were not a revolutionary mob in the making, any more than their white counterparts were all potential recruits for the National Front.[55]

And while it is easy to find examples of prejudice in the early 1980s, it is equally easy to find examples of tolerance. Reflecting on life in Leamington Spa in 1981, the essayist Lincoln Allison noted that his neighbours now included 'Sikhs, Poles, Italians and Spaniards'. About one in five people, he reckoned, was a first- or second-generation immigrant. Yes, youths sometimes threw stones through the windows of Indian shops, or daubed 'Wogs Out' on the walls. But among the young, relations often struck him as 'tolerant and even friendly . . . Casual games of football and cricket or the walk to school in the morning know no colour bars.' No doubt some readers would have accused him of complacency. Yet when the *Mirror* interviewed a selection of white teenagers two years later, many of their answers were a far cry from the usual skinhead resentments. 'Black people aren't any different from us,' said 15-year-old Leigh Williams, from Chelsea. 'I've got some good mates who are coloured.' And 13-year-old Tanni Grey, a 'wheelchair schoolgirl' from Cardiff, spoke for many in rejecting the very idea of difference between black and white. 'Just think of all the problems that racial differences have brought,' the future Paralympics champion and baroness said scornfully. 'Just because of a tenth of a milligramme of melanin which makes people black.'[56]

In the long run, the future lay not just with Tanni and her peers, but with people like Harry and Nora Rose, a working-class couple from a council estate in Quinton, Birmingham. Both had left school at 14. Harry worked as a tea-boy, in the music halls and then as a British Leyland maintenance man, while Nora worked as a cleaner before retiring with emphysema. They had five daughters, one of whom, Debbie, became a teenage mother in 1978. The father of her two boys was her first boyfriend, Mervyn Lescott, whose parents had moved to Birmingham from St Kitts after the Second World War. At first Harry and Nora were taken aback. 'She was nineteen, and like she's always said, she didn't want to marry him,' Nora told the novelist Beryl Bainbridge.

But the colour of Mervyn's skin was never an issue. 'There was nothing to be bloody embarrassed about, was there?' Harry said defiantly.

It was irrespective of whether it had been Japanese, Chinese, Outer Mongolian or whatever . . . she was pregnant by somebody, and I look at it this way, it takes two to make a bargain. And I mean with a person like your own daughter in that predicament, what are you going to do? You're not just going to open the door and kick her out, just because she's carrying a black child. And if you look at them two kids now, how could you turn your backs on anything like that? The only difference between them two grandchildren and the others is the colour of their skin. They've got the same thoughts as me, they call me Grandad like the rest of them, they've got the run of the house like the rest of them, they get pocket money off me and all them perks, and I expect when they're grown they'll look back and they'll respect me for it, you know, irrespective of whether they're black or white.

Later, while little Aaron and Joleon were playing on the swing, Bainbridge wondered aloud whether their colour would count against them when they grew up. At this, Harry's mind turned to recent history:

They let them immigrants come in, which you can't blame; they were asked to come in, they were brought in, they were transported in. They've got families of their own now and they've intermarried, and them two thousand or so who were here in the middle fifties have expanded to thousands and thousands. And as long as there's stars in the sky those people will still be here. No good Maggie Thatcher or these other people offering them money to go home – they were born here, they were bred here, they're black and they're British.

Two decades later, Harry's grandson Joleon played football for England.[57]

## 22

# Showdown of the Century

*We want to get out of the European Common Market. We want
unilateral nuclear disarmament. We want to abolish the House
of Lords. And above all, we want to abolish capitalism ... The
person who best epitomizes that is Tony Benn.*

Arthur Scargill, interviewed by ITN, 27 September 1981

*The news that Harry Perkins was to become Prime Minister went
down very badly in the Athenaeum.*

Chris Mullin, *A Very British Coup* (1982)

It is the late 1980s, and the polls have closed in the general election. For
days the experts have been predicting a comfortable victory for the incum-
bent Conservative–SDP Government of National Unity. But as the first
results come in, it is obvious that something has gone terribly wrong.
South of the Wash, the Social Democrats are being wiped out, while
Labour are piling up huge majorities. On television, the screen shows the
Labour leader, Harry Perkins, a 'stocky, robust man, with a twinkle in
his eye', exultant in victory. Then a commentator lists the policies that
have won him the election: 'Withdrawal from the Common Market.
Import controls. Public control of finance, including the pension and
insurance funds. Abolition of the House of Lords, the honours list and
the public schools.' On top of that, Perkins has also promised to scrap
Britain's nuclear deterrent, dismantle all American air bases and give serious 'consideration' to leaving NATO.

In the Athenaeum Club in London, there are gasps of horror. 'Man's a
Communist,' says a retired banker. 'Might as well all emigrate,' agrees a
newspaper magnate. Then, on television, Perkins starts speaking:

Comrades, it is now clear that by tomorrow morning we shall form the
government of this country.

We should not be under any illusion about the task ahead of us. We inherit an industrial desert. We inherit a country which for ten years has been systematically pillaged and looted by every species of pirate, spiv and con man known to civilisation.

All we have won tonight is political power. By itself that is not enough . . . To win real power we have first to break the stranglehold exerted by the ruling class on all the important institutions of our country.

Our ruling class have never been up for re-election before, but I hereby serve notice on behalf of the people of Great Britain that their time has come.

'Scandalous,' murmurs the banker. 'South of France for me, old boy.' From Trafalgar Square comes the sound of celebratory firecrackers. But as Harry Perkins is about to discover, the ruling class are not going to give up without a fight.[1]

Chris Mullin first thought of Harry Perkins in the autumn of 1980, when he was coming home from Labour's tumultuous Blackpool conference. A left-wing journalist in his early thirties, the balding, bespectacled Mullin was a close ally of Tony Benn, and effectively ghostwrote his books *Arguments for Socialism* (1979) and *Arguments for Democracy* (1981). Mullin also produced a pamphlet entitled *How to Select or Reselect Your MP* (1981), though many MPs thought *How to Deselect Your MP* would have been more accurate. Now, on the train, Mullin and his friends Tony Banks and Peter Hain wondered what would happen if Benn became Prime Minister, as they dearly hoped. The result was his novel *A Very British Coup*, published in the autumn of 1982.[2]

*A Very British Coup* is nothing if not a Bennite fantasy. As Mullin told *The Times*, the premise was that the 'ruling class' was a much greater threat to parliamentary democracy than 'any obscure Trotskyist group'. If the people ever elected a left-wing Labour leader, he explained, 'senior members of the armed forces, the civil service, the intelligence services, leading businessmen, journalists and newspaper proprietors', backed by the Americans, would intervene to push him out. This is what happens to Harry Perkins. A former steelworker, he looks nothing like the patrician Benn. But when Mullin showed his mentor the first draft, Benn pointed out that Perkins 'drinks tea from a mug with a tea bag', just as he did. Mullin duly took out the mug and the tea bag. In his politics, however, Perkins remains true to his model. Withdrawal from the Common Market, import controls, unilateral disarmament, abolition of the House of Lords: all this was pure Benn.[3]

At the time, *A Very British Coup* made little impact. *The Times* enjoyed its 'speed and great credibility', but the *Guardian* afforded it just four lines, dismissing it as a 'cartoon'. Only at the end of the decade, when Channel 4 and Alan Plater turned it into a successful mini-series, did it really strike a chord. By that time, Mullin had become an MP himself, while the prospect of Benn becoming Labour leader had completely evaporated. Perhaps it had never been very likely anyway. But what had definitively destroyed Benn's chances was his role in one of the most melodramatic political campaigns in modern British history: his bid for the Labour deputy leadership.[4]

For Benn, the elevation of Michael Foot to the Labour leadership had been a major setback. Even before the first ballot, some of Benn's allies had warned that if Foot won the leadership, 'he would hang on to it, and I would not do very well in the electoral college'. Benn was inclined to agree. After Foot's victory, Benn told the new leader that he would like to serve in his Shadow Cabinet, ideally as Shadow Home Secretary. Unfortunately, his fellow Labour MPs had other ideas. In the annual elections he did not make the cut, pipped to the last place by Neil Kinnock.[5]

Although, at this stage, relations between Foot and Benn seemed reasonably cordial, both knew this was just a temporary truce. To Benn, his new leader was a trimmer, an appeaser, a conservative in socialist's clothing, who would never take a radical path if he could help it. And, to Foot, Benn was not just unreliable but deeply untrustworthy: a hypocrite, an opportunist, 'unctuous' and 'calculated'. Even their wives did not get on. The press often presented them as ideological twins or suggested that Foot was merely Benn's puppet, which was ridiculous. For, as Roy Hattersley remembered, his leader 'never missed an opportunity, in public or private, to demonstrate his distaste for Tony's behaviour'.[6]

Benn had no intention of settling down as just another Labour backbencher. In early January 1981 he went down to Bristol to present a clock to a veteran Labour ward secretary, Bill Isaac, who was 80. 'Thanks for the clock,' Mr Isaac said. 'My house is full of them. This one will do for the lavatory.' The old man then proceeded to lecture Benn about how much better Labour councillors had been in the old days, gesturing derisively at one of Benn's supporters from the Militant group. Then he leaned forward: 'My advice to you, Tony, is to pipe down. People don't know what you're saying. They say you are a communist and a Marxist and they don't know what you're up to. What are you up to anyway?'

It was a good question, and Benn, infuriated by Mr Isaac's boldness, did not answer it. The fact was that since Christmas he had been planning to challenge Denis Healey for the deputy leadership. On Sunday 25

January, while the Gang of Four were drafting the Limehouse Declaration, he invited his closest allies to Holland Park. The mood, he recorded, was 'victorious', with plenty of 'laughing and joking' before they got down to business. With the left having carried the day at Wembley and the Social Democrats on their way out, they agreed to go for broke, cementing their power at the top of the party.

'The nomination for the deputy leadership is the key,' said the young London councillor Tony Banks. 'We must link the issues, go for the deputy leadership and Tony [Benn] should make a statement now,' said Mullin. 'The framework for our campaign is the deputy leadership, and we need a person and a programme. We should link it all to Tony,' said the Campaign for Labour Party Democracy's Victor Schonfield. This was exactly what Benn wanted to hear. As he confided to his diary, he saw the deputy leadership as a crucial stepping stone, giving him 'the right of succession to Michael Foot and hence the claim to be the next Labour Prime Minister after him'. And when his allies reconvened a week later, the only question was the timing. He should wait, they decided, until the Social Democrats had gone. Then it would be time to strike.[7]

At Westminster, it was not long before rumours of Benn's challenge reached the ears of Michael Foot. On 24 March, appalled at the prospect of yet another bruising battle, Foot called Benn in for a chat. A challenge, he said, would 'lacerate the Party'. It 'would be deeply divisive, would ruin the annual Conference and would make it much harder for us to be elected in the next Election'. But Benn was not deterred. 'I don't regard elections as being divisive,' he said piously. 'I regard them as being quite unifying.' In any case, he added, 'I haven't finally made up my mind, but I think there is some support for a contest, and I will certainly take account of what you say.' Foot did not believe him. 'He was white and angry,' Benn recorded, 'as he always is.'[8]

Foot was right to be suspicious, since Benn's diaries show that his mind had been made up for months. One problem, though, was that his reputation inside the parliamentary party had never been lower. 'You are destroying the Labour Party,' the maverick Leo Abse yelled outside the Commons chamber, so loudly that 'everybody crowded round [and] the clerks in the Lobby heard every word of it'. Even Benn's allies in the soft-left Tribune Group were horrified by the rumours. 'What's this I hear about you standing for the deputy leadership?' his former Cabinet colleague Stan Orme asked him on 30 March. 'It would be a disaster.'

Benn promised that before deciding anything he would talk to Orme about it. But two days later, he told Foot he was definitely going to stand. 'I think that is most inadvisable,' Foot said grimly. At the very least, could

Benn postpone the announcement for a week? It was only a few days since the launch of the SDP, and the publicity would be dreadful. Benn said no. That evening, when another Labour MP, his old friend Joe Ashton, begged him not to do it, he remained implacable. 'I am not doing it for myself anyway,' Benn said. 'I am not worrying about what is going to happen to me but I think somebody has got to advocate Party policy in Parliament.'

By now the Commons, packed for a three-line whip, was buzzing with excitement. It was gone midnight, but downstairs the Tribune Group were holding an emergency meeting, hoping to organize an open letter that would persuade Benn to think again. When Benn got word of it, he moved fast. Taking refuge in the Commons library, he sealed letters to his fellow MPs confirming his intention to stand, and sent a short statement to the press gallery to make it public. It was 3.30 in the morning, hardly the obvious time to launch a bid for the deputy leadership of the party. But Benn was hardly a conventional candidate. Half an hour later, the Tribune Group's Robin Cook arrived at the Press Association's office with a copy of their open letter. He was too late. Benn's statement had gone out on the wires just minutes earlier.[9]

Even by Benn's own standards, his decision to announce his challenge at a time when the British people were fast asleep seemed almost dementedly unorthodox. To the next day's papers, it was utter madness. 'Don't Do It, Tony!' begged the *Mirror*'s front page, while the *Express* thought Benn 'a fanatic', who was 'destined only to destroy' his party. In the next few days, he was bombarded with messages from MPs and trade union leaders urging him to think again. Neil Kinnock tried to organize a round-robin letter among the staff at party headquarters, while at the next Tribune meeting the infuriated Orme told Benn that his decision would 'only divide the left'. The TGWU's deputy general secretary, Alex Kitson, who was the Labour Party chairman for 1981, sent Benn an open letter urging him to withdraw. ASTMS's mercurial Clive Jenkins even invited him to lunch and presented him with a porcelain loving cup. On one side an inscription read: 'Elections can be poisoned chalices, Tony'; on the other, it said simply: 'Don't do it, Tony'.[10]

But it was no good. The reaction, Benn wrote, had been 'completely hysterical'. His only goal was to 'force people to make choices. That's what's called polarisation, divisiveness and all the rest, but it's true. You can't go on for ever and ever pretending you're a socialist party when you're not, pretending you'll do something when you won't, confining yourself to attacks on the Tories when that's not enough.' In itself, this was not unreasonable. It was true that Labour often said one thing and did another. It was also true that many of Benn's fellow MPs preferred bashing the Tories to thinking seriously about what socialism meant in an age of globalization and technological change. But there was a world of difference between launching a debate about the future of socialism and launching a divisive bid for the deputy leadership. Alas, the more Benn's fellow MPs protested, the more they revealed their bad faith and ideological treachery. 'You know what this is really about, don't you?' one of his supporters whispered during the Tribune meeting. 'It is really about who is to be the leader of the left, and they don't want to concede it to you.'[11]

From the outset, Benn insisted that the campaign was a clash of policies, not personalities. This was not entirely true, since his policies were so strongly identified with his personality. What is true, though, is that he rarely attacked Healey personally. Instead, he talked unceasingly about his plan for national revival: the restoration of full employment through import controls and a siege economy; a massive spending spree on health and welfare; the restoration of trade union privileges; the abolition of the House of Lords; withdrawal from the Common Market; unilateral nuclear disarmament; and the removal of all American bases. In essence, this was the classic hard-left wish list, although it is telling that Benn never talked about the implications for borrowing, taxes and inflation. Nor did he admit that there might be difficulties or downsides. In fairness, few politicians ever do, but other Labour MPs were infuriated by Benn's penchant for playing to the gallery. 'He's telling everyone that if you just sack the manager you can win the League and the FA Cup straight away,' one left-wing MP told the *Guardian*. 'If we say, "look, international capitalism is going to be bloody hard to beat," the crowd says "rubbish, useless, gerrof."'[12]

What was really extraordinary about Benn's campaign was that it was fought in the country. Never before had a candidate for the Labour leadership – let alone the deputy leadership – taken his cause directly to the people. And while Healey's campaign managers relied on their contacts in the trade unions, the basis of Benn's campaign was the hard-left Rank and File Mobilising Committee. Above all, the Bennites relied on the RFMC's vast card index of activists in almost every part of the country. 'News and information sent in by these people is monitored in precise detail,' wrote the *Guardian*'s Simon Hoggart. 'When pressure has to be exerted, it always comes from a supporter in the relevant area or union.' In this respect, it was Benn's campaign that was the future, while Healey's seemed almost antediluvian.

None of this, however, would have been much use without Benn himself. No politician since Joseph Chamberlain had thrown himself so vigorously into a nationwide tour, sometimes addressing three or four meetings in a single evening. As the awestruck Hoggart recorded:

> On a fairly typical weekend . . . he took a train to Liverpool to speak at a march. Then he drove to his constituency in Bristol, then back to London, back to Bristol, London, Bristol a third time for the local election campaign, to London once more, up to Glasgow for a rally, followed by another meeting in West Lothian, and then to Blackheath on the Monday for a speech about the Peasants' Revolt.

At every stop he spoke passionately but calmly, with a ready smile, flashes of wit and a nice line in irony, his voice reassuring as he laid out the road to salvation. Even sceptics said what a nice man he was. In this respect, he seemed more like an American evangelist than a British politician. And like any good televangelist, he knew exactly what his audience wanted to hear, playing with consummate skill on their dreams of full employment, total equality and world peace. 'Lots of politicians will tell you there are no easy answers,' Hoggart wrote. 'Tony Benn tells you there are plenty.'[13]

In the meantime, Denis Healey contemplated the prospect of yet another campaign. In public, he remained as boisterous as ever, but one of his aides recalled that he 'suffered a lot of black dog, anger and frustration'. As luck would have it, he had just been offered the post of NATO Secretary General. By comparison, the deputy leadership was a non-job, with little status and no power. Few people would have blamed Healey for escaping the snake-pit. But, as he saw it, he had no choice. As deputy, Benn would be perfectly placed to take over when Foot retired. Healey knew the campaign would be awful. But he was determined, he said, 'to do my duty'. To a man who had experienced the landings at Anzio, Tony Benn's fan club held few terrors.[14]

Having pulled his punches during the last contest, Healey kicked off the campaign against Benn in his more familiar style. The Bennites, he announced, were 'a minority of authoritarian extremists', who did not care how many people were repelled by their 'sour and intolerant sectarianism'. A few weeks later, addressing the electricians' union, he went further, accusing the Bennites of telling 'barefaced lies', consorting with 'Communists and Trotskyists', pandering to the IRA and wanting to turn Labour MPs into 'grovelling zombies'. Other MPs, too, lined up to hurl abuse at Benn. Roy Hattersley claimed that he was driven by 'personal ambition and ideological fanaticism', while Walter Johnson urged transport workers to reject the 'bigotry, ill feeling and viciousness' of the Benn camp. Even Benn's old friend Peter Shore told the USDAW conference that the challenger was a 'contemporary Robespierre', whose hunt for traitors recalled the Nazis in Weimar Germany. Once, as Harold Wilson's modernizing protégés, Benn and Shore had been great pals. Not any more.[15]

Benn would not have been human if he did not feel the pressure. The very next day he made an ominous entry in his diary: 'I wasn't feeling very well today. I have had this tingling in my legs and now my hands, and my face has been very hot and my skin has been rough.' Three days later, after exulting at Labour's victory in the Greater London Council elections, he still had a 'tingling' in his arms and legs. But he was on the merry-go-round now, and could not stop. Wednesday 13 May brought another blazing row with Foot, this time about Northern Ireland, where Benn wanted to support the hunger strikers in the Maze prison. Afterwards, he again recorded feeling ill, and the next morning he visited his doctor, complaining that walking was like wearing 'wellington boots full of water with a sponge in the feet'.

But within hours he was on the train to Wolverhampton, to meet hundreds of demonstrators on the People's March for Jobs. Here, more than ever, Benn's adventure seemed more like a religious crusade than a political campaign. Tailed by two television crews, he came to Wolverhampton as a preacher, rekindling the spirits of the faithful. Many of his listeners were the stereotypical activists in beards, T-shirts and leather jackets, but there were also young black women and craggy white pensioners, unemployed working-class men in their shirt-sleeves and local trade unionists in their best suits, united by their enthusiasm for the socialist gospel. And even by his own standards Benn was in extraordinarily evangelical form, his voice trembling with passion, his eyes blazing with enthusiasm. 'What we are seeing is the rebirth of hope,' he told a rally on the steps of St Peter's Church. 'It is a march for human dignity, and against those forces which still try to persuade us that men and women should be crucified on a cross of gold in the name of monetarism and profit and loss.' Afterwards, as Benn clapped along while the Spinners, a radical folk group, sang 'We Shall Overcome', his eyes glistened with tears.[16]

Reading Benn's diaries, it is clear that the battle for the deputy leadership was the campaign of his dreams, a lonely struggle against the forces of evil. Almost every day saw him in a different part of the country; in one week in May he travelled more than 1,000 miles. Every time he delivered the same catechism: the Alternative Economic Strategy, trade union rights, withdrawal from the EEC, unilateral nuclear disarmament. Yet all this was taking a punishing toll. 'I am feeling really weak at the moment, I can't run or jump, and I feel as if I am walking in heavy wellingtons; my throat is getting constricted, and my hands are tingling,' he wrote on

19 May. But he never faltered. Indeed, by early June *The Times*'s labour editor Paul Routledge thought Benn was inching ahead. Already his efforts had secured the support of the train drivers, the bakers and the furniture workers, as well as the white-collar ASTMS union and the printers' union SOGAT. He had begun as the outsider. But now, wrote Routledge, he had a 'very good chance of emerging as the winner'.[17]

To Michael Foot, Benn's campaign was both a humiliating personal insult and a devastating blow to his hopes of unity. In private, the Labour leader told friends that Benn was a liar and a coward. All through May his fury grew, and at last, on 3 June, he snapped. After another rancorous Shadow Cabinet meeting, Foot suddenly produced a long statement that he was releasing to the press. It began with a challenge of his own: 'In view of what he has said and done over recent weeks . . . I have told Tony Benn that, in my judgement, his only course now is to stand against me.' For the next twenty minutes, Foot listed what he saw as Benn's betrayals: his contempt for collective responsibility; his breaches of the line on economic policy, Europe and Northern Ireland; his 'sectarian intolerance'; his 'ruthless pursuit of internal feuds'. His colleagues were delighted, but to Benn it came as a terrible shock. At the end, he wrote grimly, 'there was a lot of banging on the table by Shadow Cabinet people . . . the hatred there was unbelievable.' Afterwards, feeling thoroughly wretched, he staggered back to his office to listen to the first reports of Foot's ultimatum. He had no intention of accepting it.[18]

That night, Benn found it hard to sleep, his legs more painful than ever. When, after a wretched night, he surfaced to get breakfast for his wife, he found two television crews and a horde of photographers outside his front door. His son Hilary went to fetch the papers, but the headlines were awful. 'Come Out and Fight with Me!' roared the *Express*, calling it 'the political showdown of the century'. The *Mirror* preferred 'Foot Tells Benn: FIGHT ME!' and thought it merely 'one of the most dramatic moments in the 81-year history of the constantly feuding Labour Party'. All the papers thought Foot had shown tremendous courage; all agreed that Benn had been 'humiliated'. Somehow Benn found the energy to make a statement to the cameras, explaining that he had no intention of fighting Foot and repeating that all that mattered was 'how to get out of the Common Market, how to get rid of American nuclear missiles, how to get back to full employment and how to abolish the House of Lords'.[19]

Then Hilary drove him to the Charing Cross Hospital, where tests confirmed Benn's fears. He had a rare viral infection, Guillain-Barré syndrome, requiring immediate hospitalization. Nurses wheeled him to the tenth floor, where a private room was quickly found. As Benn admitted, he was desperate for a rest: 'I am not saying that it caused the viral infection, but I have been grossly overdoing it for ages.' On his little television, the news bulletins were still reporting Foot's challenge. But messages of support soon poured in. Two punks delivered a Mars bar 'from the Tony Benn fan club', while the hospital's shop stewards invited him to address them the following week. 'The nurses are extremely nice,' recorded Benn the next day, 'and all the cleaners are members of NUPE ... It's really nice. The good old health service.'

It was lucky he enjoyed it, because he ended up staying for almost two weeks. He was not discharged until 17 June, though he was still under strict orders to rest. He brought home five sacks of unanswered letters. When he opened the door, the CLPD's Jon Lansman was already there, poring over plans for the campaign.[20]

For Michael Foot, Benn's hospitalization was the first bit of good news for months. In the press the Labour leader's image had deteriorated from very bad to downright abysmal. Whenever Foot's name appeared, recalled Austin Mitchell, it was invariably in the context of utter 'incompetence and irrelevance'. His poll ratings were absolutely abject, with just two out of ten people saying that he was doing a decent job. By these standards, even Mrs Thatcher looked popular. In the unions many senior figures had given up on him. At a dinner in Westminster the AUEW's moderate general secretary, Sir John Boyd, told Foot to his face that he would never win an election unless he ditched unilateral disarmament. Even the *Guardian*, which never failed to praise his decency and erudition, thought he was completely out of his depth, describing his blustering performance in one economic debate as simply 'awful'.[21]

By now even some card-carrying Conservatives felt sorry for him. Watching Foot addressing the steelworkers' union that summer, Frank Johnson thought the Labour leader looked like 'any other old age pensioner from the traditional public service class enjoying Bournemouth this week: white-haired, courtly, still with his wits about him though occasionally a little forgetful, and perhaps rather out of place'. After a ritual denunciation of the government, Foot ambled around Bournemouth with his walking stick, chatting amiably with his 'fellow senior citizens' ('Where are you off to? ... splendid ... hope it keeps fine ... jolly good ... carry on'), before pottering home. 'What thoughts', Johnson wondered, 'are going through that noble old head as all this is going on? What does he make of this modern world of ours?' Even *Private Eye*'s Denis Thatcher feels a pang of sympathy. 'I must say, my heart goes out to poor old Foot,' he tells his friend Bill. 'There he could have been still, wandering about on Hampstead Heath, taking the dog for a walk, browsing through his second-hand bookshops, not a care in the world: instead he must be up at the crack of dawn, hardly time for a shit and a shave, and straight into battle with Benn or the Boss. What a life!'[22]

Almost every week brought more terrible headlines. On 16 July Labour's vote fell by 13 per cent in the Warrington by-election, while the SDP seemed to be surging from strength to strength. Meanwhile, wherever Healey went he was heckled by Communists, Trotskyists, fans of the Provisional IRA and even a group called the Posadists, who believed that the revolution would be brought to earth by aliens in flying saucers. He gave as good as he got, telling the *Guardian* that the Bennites were 'bully boys' preaching the 'doctrines of sectarian hate'. But to most people all this looked dreadful. Instead of offering an alternative to Thatcherism, complained *The Times*'s David Watt, Foot's party had descended into a 'moral orgy', the tone set by 'all sorts of ayatollahs peddling absolutes and denouncing betrayals of socialist morality'. It was a disgrace, agreed the *Mirror*'s Terence Lancaster, that 'the defects of Mrs Thatcher's government' had been relegated to a 'sideshow' compared with the 'blood-letting' on the left. And Lancaster knew who was to blame: Tony Benn, who was busy 'ending the Labour Party as we have known it'.[23]

Yet Benn never doubted that he was doing the right thing. On 3 September, looking 'fit and suntanned', he made his first public appearance since leaving hospital, addressing a meeting of NUPE's London branches. Far from moderating his rhetoric, the enforced break had only intensified it. The SDP, Benn said, had been set up by the Establishment 'with the full support of the mass media to syphon off anti-Government feeling'. Talk of law and order after the summer's riots was merely a ruse to allow the 'imperialist' government to establish a 'police state'. And while his opponents claimed that Benn was handing the next election to the Tories, he knew the reverse was true. 'The Prime Minister, the Cabinet, their allies in business and the City are beginning to panic,' he insisted, 'for they now realise that the Labour Party could win a landslide victory at the next general election.' Soon, he told a crowd in Bridgend, 'we will rebuild our industries and services and we will leave the Common Market and get rid of American nuclear bases'. Even Britain's role in the Cold War might soon be over. 'I will never forget until the day I die', Benn said, 'that the liberties that we enjoyed were bought with Russian blood.'[24]

Among Benn's supporters, the excitement of his campaign was approaching a peak of millenarian ecstasy. In a manifesto published on 1 September, a group of close allies, including his former special advisers Francis Cripps and Frances Morrell and the sociologist Peter Townsend, gave a detailed preview of a Benn government. Britain, they explained, had become a 'subject nation, unaware of its own subjection' to the forces of global capital. So the first step, 'the moment any future Labour government comes into office', would be to 'impose emergency controls on the City and banking system to block movements of funds out of sterling and fix the exchange rate'. Only then would they move on to the abolition of private schools and private healthcare, the 'social ownership of concentrations of wealth' and a statutory maximum wage set at £28,000 a year, the equivalent of about £143,000 today.[25]

All this would, of course, have been far too much for many people in the Bennites' party. But the doubters would soon be on their way out. 'The sooner a lot of them get out the better: the better for the rest of us who are remaining in the Labour Party who are really committed to Labour Party policies,' explained the young Valerie Wise, the Greater London Council's answer to *La Pasionaria*. She was talking not just about the likes of Healey and Hattersley, but about soft-left types like Neil Kinnock and Stan Orme. Either they backed Tony Benn or they must 'go and join their friends in the SDP'. 'I think the sooner they go the better', Wise said bluntly, 'because the trouble with these people is that they are very much identified with the last Labour Government and previous Labour Governments who betrayed the working people of this country.'[26]

Even on the Labour left, many MPs thought Benn had gone too far. Most damagingly for his cause, soft-left MPs like Kinnock were 'incandescent' at what they saw as his ideological narcissism and contempt for collective responsibility. In response, Kinnock and his friends in the Tribune Group had decided to rally behind a third candidate, the perennially optimistic John Silkin, even though he stood little chance of winning. In the meantime, Kinnock blazed away at Benn's allies: 'insignificant ravers' peddling 'a fantasy that insults adult intelligence, invites derision and guarantees disappointment'. His favourite target was the Yorkshire miners' leader Arthur Scargill, one of the few men who could match his way with words. When Scargill told the Scottish Miners' Gala that the Tribune MPs were 'sabotaging' the cause of socialism, Kinnock accused him of trying to bully people into voting his way. It was, he said a few weeks later, 'the strutting demagoguery of that statement in Scotland which finally convinced me not to vote for Tony Benn'.[27]

On Fleet Street, Benn the bogeyman had now assumed horrific proportions. Six years earlier, during his ill-fated stint at the Department of Industry, the press had portrayed him as a Marxist fanatic who wanted to nationalize everything in sight. Now, with the prospect of Benn as Prime Minister looming ever larger, they called him an ayatollah, a mullah, a lunatic, even a Nazi. 'Mr Benn – Is He Mad or a Killer?' wondered a *Sun* headline on 22 May. 'A cross on the ballot for a party which has Benn waiting in the wings for its top job', the paper said, 'is a cross for the bleak and cold regimes of Eastern Europe and for a government on their model.'

For the *Daily Express*'s Denis Lehane, Benn's manifesto was 'the philosophy of class hatred and envy', which 'would inevitably lead to civil conflict and strife'. Reviewing Benn's book *Arguments for Democracy*, Lehane claimed that 'not since Adolf Hitler published *Mein Kampf* has a revolutionary leader in the West set out so clearly his intentions of destroying the society he seeks to lead'. And in the *Express*'s Sunday stablemate, Michael Cummings drew Benn as a Nazi, sporting a CND badge and a hammer and sickle on his armbands, and wearing medals with the legend 'Ein Volk, Ein Reich, Ein Führer'. Perhaps it was no wonder that, when the *Guardian*'s Jill Tweedie interviewed Benn that September, she was half-expecting to meet a madman, 'lips split in demented smile, eyes spinning like Catherine wheels'. Entirely predictably, though, she came away converted. 'No one has been so misrepresented', she reported, 'since Robert Mugabe.'[28]

Whatever else people said of Benn, nobody could doubt his resilience. The pressure was unrelenting, the criticism merciless, but he kept going: a trade union meeting here, a left-wing rally there, never wavering, never losing his temper, always alight with ideological enthusiasm. The more the press abused him, the more it reinforced his self-image as the tribune of the plebs, standing up to the forces of international capitalism. It was all the more ironic, then, that ordinary people overwhelmingly supported his opponent. In June, a *Sunday Times* poll found that three out of five Labour voters supported Healey, while only one preferred Benn. In the industrial working-class heartlands of the North, Scotland and Wales, Healey was streets ahead. By contrast, Benn's strength was concentrated in university towns, inner cities and the suburbs of southern England, wherever two or three people with sociology degrees were gathered in his name.

Despite the sound and fury of the campaign, this picture never changed. In late September, another poll of Labour voters put Healey on 61 per cent, Benn on 20 per cent and Silkin on 12 per cent. A survey of trade unionists, meanwhile, put Healey on 56 per cent and Benn on 22 per cent. Only among hard-core activists was Benn ahead. According to one Gallup poll, he would probably win by as much as seven to two in the constituencies, with Silkin trailing in a very poor third. Not for the last time, a vast gulf yawned between the men and women at Westminster and the activists on the barricades.[29]

As a result, everything depended on the unions, with their hard-won 40 per cent of the electoral college. And even though rank and file trade unionists preferred Healey, that meant nothing. Confusingly, each union had its own way of deciding how to deliver its block vote, which made predictions impossible. The public health union NUPE, for example, was nominally on the left, but a ballot of its members favoured Healey, which meant he was likely to pick up all 600,000 votes. The engineers and the railwaymen also pledged their block votes to Healey. So did the General and Municipal Workers, whose 'internal consultation' found that nine out of ten regions preferred Healey, giving him another 650,000 votes. But the miners, who held pithead ballots, voted by 189 branches to seventy-nine to throw their 244,000 votes to Benn, thanks not least to a vigorous lobbying campaign by his friend Arthur Scargill.[30]

The battle for the unions culminated at the TUC conference in Blackpool, where on 10 September the three candidates held their only set-piece debate. In keeping with the mood of the campaign, it was an unmitigated shambles. Technical problems with the loudspeakers, which had been provided by the magazine *New Socialist*, caused a ten-minute delay, during which the 1,000-strong crowd booed, jeered and clapped their hands. When the debate got underway, the loudspeakers still buzzing loudly, it went exactly as expected. 'Mr Benn manifestly loathed Mr Healey,' wrote Frank Johnson. 'Mr Healey clearly regarded Mr Benn as light in the head. The only thing the two could agree about was Mr Silkin, who held an equally low opinion of both of them.' But in Johnson's view, 'Mr Benn carried all before him . . . He rang all the ideological bells, pressed all the buttons, pulled all the chains.' By contrast, Healey was jeered throughout. When, in closing, the former Chancellor said: 'This Labour movement of ours is a brotherhood or it is nothing,' people shrieked: 'IMF!' Afterwards, Benn recorded that it had been 'a good meeting'.[31]

Healey's treatment in Blackpool was par for the course. When the candidates appeared on *Panorama*, the audience heckling was so vociferous that the programme had to be carefully re-edited for broadcast. But the nadir came in Birmingham on Saturday 19 September, at an event that ranked among the least edifying moments in Labour's history. The occasion was an open-air rally in Aston Park, designed to show the party's 'unity over unemployment'. The organizers had hoped for 50,000 people, but only 8,000 turned up. The first signs of trouble, reported the *Guardian*, came during Michael Foot's address, which was interrupted by a dozen young men 'shouting slogans about Northern Ireland mixed with obscenities'. Then came Benn, who launched into a blistering attack on the media. The crowd loved it, chanting his name. And then it was Healey's turn.

Even before Healey stepped on to the platform, people were chanting: 'Out! Out!' He managed a few sentences before he was drowned out by the jeers of 'Tory, Tory, Tory!' To screaming from the crowd, he stepped back and Michael Foot took the microphone. 'We belong to a democratic party!' he yelled at the demonstrators. 'Those of you who have been shouting Denis Healey down have been playing the Tory game . . . You are a disgrace to the Labour movement!' The noise slackened, Healey came forward – and the jeers redoubled. But Healey was in no mood to retreat. 'When people watch these disgraceful scenes,' he bellowed, his face scarlet with rage, 'they will cast their votes for freedom and free speech in even greater numbers. I am grateful for those who are yelling now for proving the truth of what I have been saying for the last six months. Thank you very much. I shall see you at Brighton!'[32]

To Healey's supporters, Birmingham was a gift. 'It was manna from heaven,' recalled the indefatigable John Golding, who hoped 'Benn would get the blame'. Unfortunately, Healey shot himself in the foot the next day, telling *Weekend World* that the barracking had been 'led and orchestrated' by the CLPD's young organizer Jon Lansman. In fact, Lansman had not even been in Birmingham, and Healey had to issue an embarrassing apology. Even so, the furore probably worked in his favour, keeping Birmingham in the headlines and reminding voters of what the papers called Benn's 'wreckers'. And since Benn refused point-blank to condemn the hecklers, his critics went for him with extraordinary savagery.

'The bully boys of the Left who support Benn', Golding told the press, 'were acting like the Hitler Youth.' The attack had been 'deliberately organized and encouraged', agreed *The Times*, which thought Benn and his supporters were mounting an 'attack upon the principle of free speech'. And in the *Mirror*, Roy Hattersley was given a double-page spread to explain why Birmingham had been a 'catastrophe' for the Labour Party:

> Thanks to television, the screaming mob that shouted Denis Healey down spewed its contempt for free speech into half the homes of Britain.
>
> The orgy of intolerance must have cost Labour a million votes. Watching the late night news, I imagined Margaret Thatcher smiling with delight and Roy Jenkins rubbing his hands with glee . . .
>
> The mobsters who dishonoured us last Saturday pushed and shoved their way to the front of the march in the name of Tony Benn.
>
> I cannot believe that he wants or welcomes their support. It is essential that the man they hero worship renounces both their beliefs and their behaviour . . . [which] would not have been out of place at a Nuremberg rally . . .
>
> Some of the scenes can only be described as the cult of the personality. Joe Stalin must have turned in his grave with envy.

Benn did not mention Hattersley's attack in his diary. But even for some-body used to criticism, it must have been a shock to find himself likened to both Hitler and Stalin – and by one of his front-bench comrades, to boot.[33]

Although Birmingham did immense damage to Benn's public image, all that mattered was the arithmetic of the electoral college. By late September, it was clear that everything depended on the Transport and General Workers' Union, with its colossal 1¼ million votes. Since the TGWU backed Common Market withdrawal and unilateral disarmament, it might have been expected to vote for Benn, which would leave the election too close to call. In fact, a ballot found that 767 TGWU branches backed Healey and only 363 backed Benn, with a further 340 supporting Silkin. In all, seven of the TGWU's ten regions preferred Healey, while only London, Scotland and the north-west went for Benn. 'Many of our members simply don't like the way Mr Benn has campaigned,' an official explained. 'He has turned the Labour Party upside down in order to get himself elected deputy leader . . . They don't think he should have stood.'

Unfortunately for Healey, the vote was merely consultative. The union's left-wing executive had no love for the former Chancellor and felt under no compulsion to follow the members' wishes. To complicate matters further, the TGWU's delegates to the Labour conference were not obliged to follow the executive's advice but were free to decide for themselves. As a result, by mid-September speculation about the TGWU's intentions was approaching fever pitch. Most observers expected them to back Silkin on the first ballot, which was a bit of a cop-out. The word was that they would abstain on the second ballot, allowing Healey to claim the prize. But then, on the evening of 21 September, Benn had the phone call he wanted. The TGWU executive, he wrote, 'had decided to support me in the second ballot. All hell broke loose.' Within minutes, the press were camped outside his front door. 'The Healey campaign has backfired in his face,' Benn wrote with barely contained excitement. 'So it is possible now that I might actually win. The BBC news at 9 was a funeral oration.'[34]

Thanks to the TGWU's announcement, the final days were the most febrile of all. In a last, desperate intervention, Michael Foot took two pages in the *Mirror* to condemn the 'planned hooliganism' of the hecklers in Birmingham, about which Benn had been far 'too feeble and temporising'. The contest, he said, had proved a 'bitter divisive distraction', and Benn 'must bear the primary responsibility for the deep wounds inflicted on our movement'. Labour's Chief Whip, Michael Cox, weighed in too, joining more than a dozen Bristol MPs and councillors to warn that it would be 'little short of a disaster' if his parliamentary neighbour won.

*The Times* declared that Benn's victory would mean the triumph of 'violent rhetoric, street marches and the clenched fist salute'; the *Observer* warned that if Benn won, it was 'inconceivable that the party could ever recover the confidence of voters'. But amid all the hysteria there was a thin ray of sunshine for Healey. Despite increasingly strident threats from Benn's Rank and File Mobilising Committee, dozens of soft-left Tribune MPs were considering abstaining on the second ballot. If they did, they might just deny Benn victory. But would they stick to their guns?[35]

Benn's train pulled into Brighton just before midday on Saturday 26th. Physically exhausted, he was running on pure adrenaline. The rival camps were already out in force for the party conference, the Healey supporters wearing stickers proclaiming their support for 'Michael Foot and Denis Healey', while Benn's supporters handed out sheriff-style badges reading 'Tony Benn for Deputy'. 'What an incredible time!' Benn wrote. 'It is pouring with rain but I am really looking forward to it.' In their rooms at the Grand Hotel, his son Joshua was hunched over his computer, which forecast that with the support of the TGWU, 'a few more MPs and a few more constituencies', the prize was theirs. If, by some miracle, NUPE threw its block vote to Benn, he might even prevail on the first ballot. Among his supporters on the streets, the mood was electric. 'The word is going round now', Benn recorded that evening, 'that we are going to win.'

On Sunday morning, Benn awoke to a hubbub of activity. There were photographers everywhere, and the streets were lined with hundreds of demonstrators, most of them waving placards carrying his name. He was so busy with last-minute meetings that he did not have time to glance at the papers. That was probably just as well, since they were not exactly overflowing with generosity. Benn and his 'fist-clenching comrades', wrote John Junor in the *Sunday Express*, were 'rats attacking our society from within. And in the end they will destroy us if we do not destroy them.' Junor recalled the words of Ken Livingstone, 'the IRA-loving, poof-loving Marxist leader of the GLC', who had predicted that soon a 'Right wing Government would send militants to the gas chamber'. 'I wouldn't go as far as that,' Junor said mildly. 'But might we not all be a lot safer if at least half of them were in clink?'[36]

Late that afternoon, Benn went across to the colossal concrete conference hall. As on previous occasions, the MPs were corralled like defendants at a show trial, with members of the National Executive above on the platform. The air was thick with tension; 'the press were hysterical, people were cheering and shouting'. But there was bad news for Benn: the NUPE delegation had decided to honour their members' vote after all. He collected his voting papers, and suddenly a rumour swept around the hall. The thirty-nine-man TGWU delegation had been meeting that afternoon at the Old Ship Hotel: apparently they had decided to abstain on the second ballot, instead of voting for Benn. 'Well,' Benn wrote, 'that was a body blow!'

But the rumour was not true. The TGWU delegation was split right down the middle and had left the Old Ship without a decision. Having walked across to the hall, they started taking another vote outside, but then the first ballot started and they had to take their seats in a hurry. All was chaos; all was excitement. From the rostrum, somebody was droning on about a conference smoking ban. Then, at last, it was time for the first ballot.

The result was almost exactly as Joshua's computer had predicted. With 125 MPs and the majority of the trade unions, Healey had taken 45.4 per cent, not enough for an outright victory. Benn, whose strength lay entirely in the constituency parties, had 36.6 per cent. Silkin was a decent third with 18 per cent, which he owed to the TGWU and the soft left. So Silkin dropped out, and everything depended on where his votes would go. If the TGWU abstained, Healey was safe. On the platform, one of Healey's union allies warned him that the TGWU would never miss the chance to promote Benn. No more than a few yards away, the delegation were passing a sheet of paper from hand to hand. Back on the platform, somebody handed Benn a message, telling him he was going to win. Then another victory message came; then another. On the rostrum, somebody was talking about South Africa. It was 8.30, the counting was almost over and the future of the Labour Party hung in the balance. On the platform, Benn and Healey took their seats. The latter's chief lieutenant, Giles Radice, was in utter despair. Not far away, Neil Kinnock, who abstained in the second ballot, felt sick that he had not voted for Healey. The chief teller stepped to the microphone, and there was absolute silence.

'The final decision,' the teller said in his flat Yorkshire tones, 'and I'll say this now, the votes have been counted three times. Tony Benn' – and on television, the picture showed a close-up of Benn, deathly pale, intent on something he was scribbling – 'Forty-nine point five seven four.' There were scattered cheers in the hall. 'Denis Healey' – and there he was, florid as ever, also scribbling away – 'Fifty point four two six!' At that, a great roar crashed around the hall. On television, Healey gave the slightest hint of a smile, took off his glasses and glanced across at his supporters. The camera cut to Benn, still scribbling, his face caught between a smirk and a grimace. A few seconds later, Healey was surrounded by grinning supporters. He had done it.[37]

Afterwards, reporters pored over the details: the TGWU's decision to back Benn, the abstention of thirty-five MPs who had voted for Silkin and, above all, the sheer closeness of the outcome, which would have been different if just four MPs had changed sides. But in the press room, Edna Healey murmured to herself: 'Denis has won. Nothing else matters.' She and her husband decamped to the Old Ship, where the press found them drinking champagne. Benn, meanwhile, took his wife to a fish and chip shop, where Chris Mullin persuaded the photographers to give them some peace. In his diary Benn called it 'a staggering result with all the media against us, the most violent attacks by the Shadow Cabinet, the full inter-vention of Michael, the abstention of a group of Tribune Group MPs'. He said much the same to his supporters after getting back from the chip shop. 'I think everyone here knows', he declared, 'that what happened here today was an enormous victory for us. It was a victory because, from the beginning, right through to the end, and we are nowhere near the end, we have won the argument.' That was Benn to a tee. He was not defeated; he had just won a different kind of victory.[38]

Was Benn's result genuinely a moral victory, though? His support among the activists was certainly spectacular: in the second ballot he won more than 24 per cent out of a maximum of 30 per cent, almost enough to outweigh his weaknesses elsewhere. But in the first ballot he had come a very poor third among the MPs and an even poorer third in the unions, who awarded him less than 6½ per cent of their 40 per cent share. The only reason he had come so close was that the TGWU had ignored its members. Had the TGWU honoured its consultation, Healey would have prevailed by a comfortable margin. But the real irony, as Golding pointed out, is that if Benn had supported the Tribune Group's formula at the Wembley conference, which proposed to divide the electoral college equally, he would have won. By giving the unions more weight than the constituency parties, he had inadvertently handed victory to Healey – who was by far the most popular candidate in the country anyway.[39]

For the left, there were two ominous lessons. First, the results showed that the trade unions were nothing like the militant caricatures pilloried in the *Mail* and the *Express*. In fact, the unions were the single biggest force pulling Labour back to the centre ground. Second, the results showed that among Labour's MPs a gulf had opened up between the hard and soft left. If just four of the sixteen Tribune Group abstainers had voted for Benn, he would have won. Some observers had seen this coming for a while. Six days earlier, the radical journalist Christopher Hitchens had predicted that the Tribune Group might deny Benn victory. If, in the final days, Benn had moderated his tone, distanced himself from his more strident acolytes and worked harder to win the Tribune Group over, he might have prevailed. But that was not his style.[40]

The recriminations began immediately. Talking to the BBC, the hard-left MP Reg Race blamed the union leadership, which should have *told* its members how to vote instead of allowing them to be brainwashed by the media. But other Benn supporters blamed the Tribune abstainers. Some talked of compiling a hit list for deselection, with Kinnock a favourite target. Confronting the Welshman on television, Arthur Scargill insisted that the soft left had 'betrayed not merely their supporters but the fight that's taken place over many years'. 'If anybody lost him that deputy leadership election yesterday,' Kinnock shot back, 'it was you by the attitudes you espouse and the people like you who espouse them. We're not having them in the Labour Party, mate.' But one young activist from Islington, addressing a fringe meeting alongside Tony Benn and Ken Livingstone, insisted that it was time to punish the MPs, who should 'expect some discomfort from the rank and file in their own constituencies'. His name was Jeremy Corbyn.[41]

For Kinnock, the promised discomfort was not long in coming. When he spoke at Wednesday evening's Tribune rally, hecklers interrupted him with shouts of 'Judas!' Chief among his accusers was his fellow MP Margaret Beckett, who had earlier been spotted screaming 'Traitors!' at Healey supporters. Now she gave what the *Observer* called a 'speech dripping with venom', clearly aimed at Kinnock, though she could not bring herself to utter his name. Two days later, a young Benn supporter followed Kinnock into the toilets at the Grand Hotel and 'lashed out at him with his foot', catching him on the elbow. Unfortunately, the would-be assailant had misjudged his man. As the future Labour leader put it, 'I beat the shit out of him . . . there was blood and vomit all over the place.'[42]

Kinnock's little altercation captured the tone of what everybody agreed had been a spectacularly unpleasant occasion. Back in March, Benn had assured Foot that the contest would be 'quite unifying'. He was right: the contest had unified most of the country in revulsion. A poll for the *Observer* found that 51 per cent of the electorate said the campaign had made them think worse of Labour, while only 6 per cent said it had improved their opinion. And the contest's most abiding legacy, for which many of Benn's colleagues never forgave him, was the devastation wreaked on Labour's general election prospects. In the summer of 1980, they had been about 5 per cent ahead of the Tories. Even after Foot's coronation, Labour's lead had been in double figures, and as late as the summer of 1981 they were still ahead in some polls. But then, as Benn took over the headlines, Labour's reputation went into free-fall. In December 1980 it had been on 47½ per cent. A year later, it was down to just 23½ per cent, the most dramatic decline for an opposition party in history. Benn blamed Foot, Healey, the Social Democrats, the soft left, the unions and the press. Everybody else blamed Benn.[43]

For Benn's supporters, his defeat was one of the great missed opportunities of modern political history. Had he become deputy leader and then, presumably, leader, perhaps Labour would have done better in 1983. Perhaps a hard-left Labour Party was what the British people wanted. Perhaps he might even have won, taking Britain out of Europe, restoring full employment and reversing the tide of economic change.

Given the effect of Benn's campaign on public opinion and his uniquely divisive national reputation, however, a less rosy outcome seems more likely. In reality, Labour would probably have sunk much further and faster. Almost certainly Benn would soon have moved to take the leadership from Foot, triggering an even bloodier bout of factional infighting. Had Benn won again, there would undoubtedly have been more losses to the SDP, with MPs, councillors, party members and probably some trade unions defecting en masse. In Hattersley's words, 'thousands of moderates would have deserted Labour', leaving the party as a ragbag of 'Trotskyites, one subject campaigners, Marxists who had never read Marx, Maoists, pathological dissidents, utopians and, most dangerous of all, sentimentalists'. And had Benn been leader during the 1983 election, then Labour would almost certainly have come third in the popular vote behind the Alliance, which finished only 680,000 votes behind as it was.[44]

In reality, Benn's campaign brought a decisive shift in momentum inside the Labour Party. Intoxicated by their own enthusiasm, his allies had fatally overplayed their hand. As Shirley Williams put it, this was 'the moment the soft left woke up'. It was no accident that, just two days after Benn's defeat, the hard left suffered a stunning setback in the National Executive elections, with five Bennites, including the outraged Margaret Beckett, being ousted by five moderates. Even Benn thought it was a 'disaster'. But it was a disaster for the SDP, too. To succeed, they needed a Labour Party descending into sectarian extremism, not a Labour Party dragging itself back towards the centre. At the end of the year, Foot even set up an inquiry into Militant, though that unhappy saga would drag on for years. Characteristically, Benn thought he was making a 'tragic mistake'.[45]

Benn had not, of course, gone away. On 10 November he ignited a new storm by telling the Commons that a future Labour government would nationalize North Sea oil without compensation. The next day, white with

To the Conservative press, Michael Foot's inability to control Tony Benn was a sign of his fundamental weakness as a leader. This is Clive Collins in the *Sun*, 14 November 1981.

rage, Foot opened the Shadow Cabinet meeting by reading a long statement denouncing Benn for his total lack of 'common sense and comradeship'. It was 'horrible, the atmosphere icy, and Michael was angry,' Benn wrote afterwards. 'I am used to it now. The things they said were extreme, but of course they are frantic. After that, it is quite clear that it is the end of me.' But there was more to come. When Foot asked for loyalty at a meeting of Labour MPs the next day, Benn refused to apologize and wondered if the Shadow Cabinet had the right to ignore party policy. At that, he recorded, there was a lot of 'shouting . . . jeering and baying'. He was kicked, recalled a satisfied John Golding, 'from pillar to post'.[46]

A week later, Benn's colleagues voted him out of the Shadow Cabinet. In public, he blamed Foot and the press. In private, he claimed to be 'glad'. Yet given that in late September he had been on the brink of the deputy leadership, it must have felt like a terrible comedown. A few weeks later, he made one last, disastrous attempt to recapture the initiative. Emerging from a meeting of the party's National Executive, Benn suddenly announced to the waiting journalists that he was now 'Deputy Leader of the Labour Party, because of course Denis Healey's entire majority has now defected to the SDP'. His admirers were mortified; his enemies could barely contain their amusement. Healey wondered whether 'Benn might next assume some other role such as Pope or even Queen'. Even his wife thought it was time for a rest. 'Caroline has persuaded me', Benn wrote that December, 'that I am so damaged by my single-handed combat against Denis Healey and Michael Foot that I'm a bit of an embarrassment to the left. So I shall pull out a bit and see how things develop.'[47]

Michael Foot's personal ordeal was not over. It had, he recalled, been a year of 'futility and shame'. Even *The Times* wondered if there was a 'sadder figure in British politics today than Michael Foot', once such a firebrand, now 'beleaguered and apparently impotent'. But the worst was yet to come. On 8 November, Foot was due to attend his first Remembrance Sunday service as Leader of the Opposition. Knowing his fondness for scruffy old pullovers, his wife had issued him with a new coat, chosen specifically to smarten up his image. But when he reached the Cenotaph, things did not quite go to plan.[48]

Afterwards, in a rare diary entry, Mrs Thatcher recorded that it had been a 'wonderful service', although 'it was Michael Foot's first attendance and he was a little uncertain what to do'. She was being unusually generous. The television footage shows that at one point she virtually had to manoeuvre Foot into place. And while the other politicians gazed firmly ahead, as if contemplating the sacrifice of the fallen, Foot seemed oddly distracted, peering up at the sky, twitching his head oddly from side to side, and appearing generally miserable and ill at ease. Even when it was his turn to lay his wreath, he seemed to shamble forward against his will, like an overgrown schoolboy under the eyes of a formidable headmistress.

In the next few days, Foot drew unrelenting flak for having worn, of all things, a donkey jacket, as modelled by various burly men warming their hands around picket-line braziers. In fact, his infamous coat was really a dark green, slightly shapeless woollen overcoat, such as a man of advancing years might wear on an outing to Aldermaston. Later, Foot insisted that the Queen Mother had gone out of her way to commend it: 'Oh, hello, Michael. That's a smart sensible coat for a day like this.' Yet taken in conjunction with his tartan tie, scruffy rubber-soled shoes and general air of preoccupied bewilderment, it did look as if Foot had dressed for a car-boot sale. In the *Guardian*'s words, he looked 'as if he had just completed his Sunday constitutional on Hampstead Heath'.[49]

That was about as kind as it got. 'An old man with a green donkey-jacket, flapping trousers and casual shoes stood looking vaguely about him, like a bored tourist at a bus-stop,' wrote Charles Moore in the *Telegraph*, 'and when his turn came, he laid his wreath of poppies with all the reverent dignity of a tramp bending down to inspect a cigarette end. This was the Leader of Her Majesty's Opposition paying his party's tribute to the nation's dead.' This was perhaps a bit strong, though no stronger than what some of Foot's colleagues thought. The right-wing Labour MP Walter Johnson, a former serviceman, claimed that Foot looked like an 'out of work navvy . . . as if he was taking part in a demo rather than a solemn act of respect'. 'He seemed to have no inkling', fumed John Golding, 'of how important the idea was to working-class people that when you went to church you must wear your best suit and overcoat.'[50]

Even after a year of extraordinary drama, the donkey jacket cut through. In the next few days, poor Foot was deluged with letters, some offering vouchers and even money to buy himself a new coat, others more damning ('You looked, and behaved, like an oaf and a tramp . . . Why don't you depart for Russia and join your comrades there?'). One Savile Row tailor, no doubt fancying some publicity, wrote to offer his services as an image-maker. But perhaps the most imaginative response came from the *Daily Mail*, which printed a double-page spread giving readers the chance to 'dress your own Michael Foot doll'. Readers were presented with various outfits to cut out, including a pair of underpants with a 'CND motif', some bovver boots for 'fraternal meetings with the extreme left' and, bizarrely, a top hat and tails, to make him look 'like the real leader of an actual party. Probably the way Mrs Foot secretly dreams of seeing him.'[51]

A few weeks later, Foot went to Hull. Opening a new technology centre, this erudite, civilized and beleaguered man confounded his handlers by crossing the road to congratulate a group of demonstrators, who were protesting about local education cuts. Then he went to the Central Methodist Hall, where he was due to talk about building a 'tolerant, decent and compassionate Labour Party'. Unfortunately, the *Guardian* reported, Foot had only just started walking across the stage when he 'suddenly disappeared. His head and shoulders reappeared between the feet of the platform party, then he climbed out of the organ well and assured would-be helpers that he was all right.'

It had been that sort of a year. 'What fools we were', the left-wing Eric Heffer said, 'not to vote for Denis.'[52]

# 23

# The March of Death

*I cannot see Thatcher yielding on this. I don't see the Government backing down . . . There are ripple effects everywhere and if I were allowed to die there would be a tremendous upsurge of Welsh nationalism.*

Gwynfor Evans, quoted in the *Guardian*,
1 September 1980

*I am standing on the threshold of another trembling world. May God have mercy on my soul.*

Bobby Sands's diary, 1 March 1981

In the early hours of Thursday 13 December 1979, a fire broke out in an empty farmhouse in Llanrhian, between St David's and Fishguard, just inland from the Pembrokeshire coast. When the fire engines arrived, it was already too late. The house, which belonged to an English couple who had been renovating it for the past eight years, was completely gutted. A few hours later, as the firemen were wearily returning to the station, another call came in. A second house in Llanrhian had just gone up in flames.

Even as fire engines rushed to the scene, there were reports of two similar blazes some 150 miles to the north. In the remote village of Mynydd Nefyn, on the mountainous Lleyn peninsula looking out towards Anglesey and the Irish Sea, another fire had broken out on yet another converted farm a few hours earlier. And no sooner had the local fire brigade arrived there than a fourth call had come through. This time the target was a holiday house in Llanbedrog, on the same peninsula, where somebody had smashed a window and thrown a primitive incendiary bomb inside. Once again the building was completely destroyed. By dawn, all four were smoking ruins.[1]

So began a campaign that was never truly explained. In the next thirteen years there were almost 200 arson attacks on English-owned properties, estate agents and Conservative Party offices, the vast majority of them in North Wales. Fortunately, nobody was killed. At first the police seemed completely at a loss. But in January 1980, after twelve attacks, a letter arrived at the BBC newsroom at Bangor. It bore the eagle crest of the Free Wales Army, a minuscule paramilitary group that had come and gone in the mid-1960s, and appeared to be written by their successors, the self-styled Cymric Army. According to the letter, they had the support of the Irish Republican Army and the Basque separatist group ETA. 'What the IRA has achieved,' the letter said ominously, 'so shall we.'

To the police, the recent attacks had been so clumsy that it was hard to take the Cymric Army seriously. After an attack on a cottage in Bala, said the *Guardian*, the sight of 'paraffin poured through a letter box and an unlit candle left on a doorstep' suggested an incompetent hoax rather than a terrorist operation. The police thought the first fires had been lit by locals infuriated by the growing number of English-owned holiday homes – at least 25,000 at the last count – at a time when unemployment was surging, interest rates were punitively high and council rents were going up. The later fires, they thought, were probably due to a 'knock-on effect, the work of imitators unconnected with any organisation'.[2]

Yet the attacks kept coming. Late on the evening of 1 February, Angela Southwood, a sculptress who lived just over the border with Shropshire, returned to her cottage to find that somebody had broken in. She called the police, but nothing had been taken. Then, just as she was going to bed, there was an explosion. The burglars had wrapped an incendiary device in her curtains and stuffed them under the stairs. She survived unhurt. Even so, the fact that the arsonists had sprinkled spirits throughout the house, in an effort to intensify the blaze, was terrifying enough.

By now the police knew they were not just dealing with copycat gangs. But there were no leads. They set up a confidential hotline so that local people could give information without fear of reprisals. Still nothing. At the end of March, they launched a string of pre-dawn raids, arresting more than twenty-five people, including several schoolteachers, a lecturer, a publisher, a former trade union official, a farmer and four former Plaid Cymru parliamentary candidates. But the suspects were released without charge. The next day, *Not the Nine O'Clock News* ended with a clip of flames flickering over a pile of blackened wood, parodying the Coal Board's recent adverts for coal fires. 'Come home to a real fire,' says Rowan Atkinson's reassuring voiceover. 'Buy a cottage in Wales.'[3]

Although the culprits were never caught, attention eventually focused on a single group, who called themselves Meibion Glyndŵr ('Sons of

Glendower'). The police claimed they were a handful of fanatics. But this was not quite true. Some polls suggested that in Welsh-speaking areas they enjoyed considerable sympathy, while nationalist students wore T-shirts that proclaimed 'Taniwch dros Gymru!' ('Light for Wales!') or 'Ta ta tŷ ha' ha ha' ('Bye bye, summer house, ha ha'). When visitors asked about them, plenty of people said they sympathized with the arsonists. In the summer of 1982, Paul Theroux could not find 'anyone in Wales who objected to the burning of English-owned cottages'. 'They burn these cottages, the Plaid Cymru,' said a landlady in St Dogmael's, Pembroke-shire. 'Some of the chaps are very tough, you know. That's what I don't understand – there are still so many English cottages! The chaps do try, but they haven't been successful.'

The arson campaign did not come out of nowhere. Household incomes in parts of North Wales were barely two-thirds of the national average, while in Gwynedd, where there were an estimated 7,500 holiday homes, some 4,300 people were on the council-house waiting list. But the decisive factor was not economic; it was something more primal. When national-ists talked of 'English occupation', they were talking not just about people buying holiday homes; they were talking about the remorseless spread of English expressions, habits and customs, the decline of the Welsh lan-guage, the steady drift of cultural and economic power to London. To nationalists, the holiday homes were symbols of something deeper. In the Welsh magazine *Arcade*, one reader claimed that anybody 'with a modi-cum of sense coupled with patriotism' could see 'that we are witnessing genocide by substitution'. 'Large areas of west and north Wales', agreed the Plaid Cymru MP Dafydd Wigley, 'are in danger of being no more Celtic in character than is the Lake District or Cornwall today. What military conquest has failed to do over two millennia is now being accom-plished by the cheque-book invasion in two decades.'[4]

In hindsight, the striking thing about Wales and Scotland in the early 1980s is the nationalists' total failure to profit from the economic down-turn. In industrial working-class areas, the recession had fallen like a hammer-blow. British Steel employment in South Wales plunged from 66,000 in 1973 to less than 20,000 ten years later. In Scotland the collapse of textiles, coal, steel and shipbuilding similarly felt like the death sentence for an entire working-class ecosystem. In Kilmarnock and Paisley, as in Port Talbot and Newport, the headlines were dominated by factory clo-sures, job losses, poverty and deprivation. And in both countries Mrs Thatcher's middle-class Englishness, as well as her rhetorical stridency and the standing affront of her gender, made her an irresistible hate figure. 'Scotland's ruled by the bloody English,' a purple-faced man shouted at

Paul Theroux in a pub in Dunbar, East Lothian. 'They dropped Exchange Control so they could spend our money abroad – they don't spend it in Scotland, though they stole it from us in the first place by stealing our oil resairves [*sic*] . . . I'm a freedom fighter – don't let these tweeds fool you. You can ask my wife if you don't believe I'm a freedom fighter.'[5]

In reality, self-styled freedom fighters were surprisingly few on the ground. After having made great strides in the early 1970s, both the Scottish National Party and Plaid Cymru had gone backwards. The failed devolution referendums of 1979 had punched a gaping hole in their morale. In the general election a few weeks later, Plaid Cymru won just 8 per cent of the Welsh vote and two seats, down from 11 per cent and three seats in October 1974. Even more strikingly, the Scottish Nationalists collapsed to 17 per cent and two seats, down from 30 per cent and eleven seats. Demoralized and bitterly divided, Plaid Cymru lost one in four members almost overnight. And as both parties sank into introversion and faction-fighting, they conspicuously failed to exploit the Conservatives' unpopularity and Labour's divisions, not least because they could not decide whether they were vehicles for middle-class nationalism or parties of the radical left. In 1983, thanks partly to the emergence of the Alliance, they went even further backwards in vote share, though both clung on to their two seats. As a parliamentary force, nationalism seemed close to extinction.[6]

In a broader sense, however, nationalism remained very much alive. A survey in Wales in 1979 found that, if forced to choose, 57 per cent described themselves as Welsh and only 34 per cent British. And given what had happened in Northern Ireland, few people treated national sentiment as lightly as they had done a decade earlier. Even the Conservatives, the party of the Union, were careful not to dismiss it out of hand. In the general election of 1979, they explicitly promised that to reverse the precipitous decline in the Welsh language they would establish a separate Welsh television service, to run for twenty-five hours a week on the new fourth channel. In September 1979, however, they changed their minds, partly because it would be very expensive, partly because Wales's independent channel HTV lobbied fiercely against it, but also because many Welsh-speakers feared the new channel would become a 'ghetto'. Instead, Willie Whitelaw announced that, every week, they would split twenty-two hours of Welsh programmes between BBC2 and the fourth channel. That, he thought, would be a reasonable compromise.[7]

Unfortunately, many nationalists saw Whitelaw's plan as a monstrous betrayal. On 5 May 1980 Plaid Cymru's veteran president, Gwynfor Evans, told the press that the government had five months to reverse its plans. If not, on 6 October he would begin a hunger strike, and he planned to continue until he died. At first some people thought he was joking. One Tory MP offered to sponsor him. Evans himself remarked that the only thing that really worried him was the agony of smelling his wife's gammon. But it soon became clear that he was in deadly earnest. Depressed by the stagnation of the nationalist cause, he had decided that in 1980 his people would 'raise themselves to the level of history'. 'The Government has shown such contempt for us in Wales', he said, 'that there is no other way.' His old friend Sir Goronwy Daniel, the former head of the Welsh Office and vice-chancellor of the University of Wales, warned Whitelaw that Evans was not joking. 'Anybody who knows anything about Wales', he said, 'will tell you he means it.'[8]

In London, it seemed inconceivable that Evans would starve himself to death in order to get twenty-five hours of Welsh-language television on one channel rather than twenty-two hours on two channels. But Evans was not a frivolous person. Having led Plaid Cymru for the last thirty-five years, he had become the party's first MP at the Carmarthen by-election in 1966 and held the seat again in the late 1970s. Tall, white-haired, a committed Christian and fervent pacifist, he made a very plausible martyr. And now, single-handedly, he turned an obscure disagreement about a television channel into a matter of life and death. When the Welsh Secretary, Nicholas Edwards, arrived at the Eisteddfod in August, he was attacked by members of the Welsh Language Society, who besieged him in his car, beating on the windows with their fists, and laid waste to the nearby HTV Wales stand. All the time, dozens of robed druids looked on approvingly.

Until now, the dispute had seemed like the plot of a 1950s comedy. But, as the *Guardian* remarked, it could no longer be shrugged off as a joke. Given the growing mood of 'anger and resentment', as well as the arson campaign against English-owned homes, there was a 'widespread feeling that breaking point cannot be far off'. The Commons Select Committee on Welsh Affairs warned that 'public disorder could break out' unless the government acted, with Evans's hunger strike acting as the 'detonator for an all-Wales explosion'. Even the fiercely anti-nationalist Labour MP Leo Abse feared Evans's hunger strike could turn into a national crisis. There was a serious risk, agreed the *Observer*, of 'old racial hatreds' escalating into bloodshed, just as in Northern Ireland.

> Wales has gone a small but significant way down the road to terrorism in the past year. Attacks on TV transmitters and English-owned cottages, incendiary devices left here and there, the smell of violence at this month's National Eisteddfod; the threat of a 'fast to death' by Gwynfor Evans, Welsh nationalism's peaceful patriarch and mentor – all these are warning signs.[9]

Evans himself believed Mrs Thatcher would never countenance a U-turn. On 1 September, his sixty-eighth birthday, he told the *Guardian* that he genuinely expected to die. In Cardiff a few days later, thousands marched in his support – and his hunger strike was still a month off. At the Welsh Office one junior minister wrote in his diary that Evans was determined to become a martyr, was bound to become a national hero and might well 'inspire a less able breed to violence'. Even Nicholas Edwards was now persuaded that unless they backed down there would be 'intolerable consequences'. On 15 September he and Whitelaw told Mrs Thatcher that Evans was genuinely going to kill himself. That would be 'disastrous', she said. 'The last thing the Government needed was to inflame nationalism again.' They had made a mistake, and must change course.[10]

Two days later, the government announced that Wales would get its own channel, the future S4C, after all. The hunger strike was off. At a rally near Evans's Pembrokeshire home, almost a thousand people gathered to cheer their hero. Deep down, though, Plaid Cymru's president was a little disappointed. He had never expected Mrs Thatcher to give in so quickly, robbing his party of a unique propaganda coup. But as Nicholas Edwards told the press, the danger of provoking nationalist violence had proved decisive. The hunger strike had worked. Across the Irish Sea, another group of radical nationalists drew the inevitable lesson. Five weeks later, they began a hunger strike of their own.[11]

Not long after Mrs Thatcher had come to office, her first Northern Ireland Secretary, Humphrey Atkins, sent his colleagues a paper on the situation in the United Kingdom's smallest country. Even though Northern Ireland's interminable saga of killings and bombings was more than a decade old, it made for sobering reading. Of the province's 1½ million people, Atkins wrote, about two-thirds were Protestants, most of whom were fiercely loyal to the union with Great Britain. The remainder were Catholics, many of whom dreamed of unification with the Republic of Ireland. These were distinct and often antagonistic communities, divided by 'housing, education, ways of life, culture and attitudes to history . . . People know to which community they belong and they live, and vote, accordingly.'

After the outbreak of fierce inter-communal violence at the end of the 1960s, the British Army had been sent in to restore law and order. But their intervention had seen the conflict escalate into a low-level guerrilla war, peaking with the deaths of 480 people in 1972. Two years later, a general strike by militant Protestant workers had brought down the power-sharing Northern Ireland Executive, and since then the province had been governed directly from Westminster. Yet the security situation, Atkins reported, had greatly improved in recent years. Bombings, attacks on civilians and army casualties had fallen sharply, with civilian deaths down from 207 in 1976 to just thirty-seven in 1979. And contrary to the stereotype that children in Northern Ireland came into the world wearing a balaclava, most of the country was 'almost permanently free' from terrorism.

Quite apart from the violence of the Provisional IRA and the various loyalist vigilante groups, Northern Ireland was not a happy place. Nowhere in the United Kingdom had been harder hit by the decline of heavy industry; nowhere was poverty more endemic, insecurity greater or alienation more entrenched. Even before the recession, more than one in ten people were out of work; in some areas, such as Catholic west Belfast, the jobless rate among adult men was closer to 50 per cent. Housing conditions were far worse than in Britain, infant mortality was higher and average weekly household income was only £79, compared with £93 in Britain. In some parts of Belfast and Londonderry, living standards were so low that they reminded observers of southern Italy. This was the environment in which paramilitary groups found willing recruits.

The prospects for recovery, meanwhile, were bleak. Historically, Northern Ireland's economy had rested on agriculture, shipbuilding and textiles, all of which were in deep decline. Successive governments had poured in torrents of money, but with four out of ten people employed by the state, the province was already more reliant on public sector jobs than anywhere else in Western Europe. By the turn of the decade, Northern Ireland took more than £1 billion a year from Westminster, which amounted to at least a quarter of the province's GDP. Every single job at the giant shipbuilder Harland and Wolff, long a pillar of Protestant working-class identity, was subsidized by British taxpayers to the tune of £7,500 a year, the equivalent of at least £40,000 a year today. Atkins did not see any solution. Neither did anybody else. In ten years, more than 140,000 people had left Northern Ireland to build new lives overseas, the highest emigration rate in the Western world.[12]

To most outside observers, the stark facts of Northern Ireland's economic plight paled beside the horrors of terrorist violence and sectarian hatred. Paul Theroux, who visited the province during his journey around the coastline of Great Britain, was entirely typical. Almost despite himself, Theroux could see that for most people life went on as normal. In supposedly strife-torn Londonderry, for example, he went to a festival where thousands enjoyed bicycle races, a talent show and cookery demonstrations. But like most visitors, he was drawn to the signs of abnormality: the graffiti in Protestant areas that said, of the republican hunger strikers, 'Let Them Die'; the people in Derry who said that the British were 'brutes' and 'murderers'. And he found Belfast 'demented and sick', with soldiers, fences and metal detectors everywhere; a city of 'bellicose religion, and dirt, and poverty, and narrow-mindedness, and sneaky defiance, trickery and murder, and little brick terraces, and drink shops, and empty stores, and barricades, and boarded windows, and starved dogs, and dirty-faced children'. It was, he concluded, 'the blackest city in Britain, and the most damaged'.[13]

Theroux probably saw what he had always wanted to see. But he was far from alone. At the end of December 1979, reflecting on the last ten years in Northern Ireland's history, *The Times*'s correspondent, Christopher Thomas, struck a similarly bleak note. Even now, after the death toll had fallen, four people were killed by bombs and bullets every week. 'The deprivation in parts of Belfast is frightening,' he wrote. 'Anybody who feels like risking a drive through Turf Lodge, Whiterock, Ballymurphy or the Lower Falls district cannot avoid being moved. There, fear is the master.' The city had long since been carved up into Catholic and Protestant areas; to wander into the wrong street, depending on your surname, could literally mean death. 'But wherever you are', Thomas went on, 'the scene is the same: relentless rows of centuries-old terraces, some of them bombed and bricked up; Army vehicles everywhere; barbed wire and great walls of corrugated iron protecting vital installations; roads strewn with bricks and stones that have been hurled a thousand times at military vehicles. Hope, tragically, is in short supply.'[14]

To millions of ordinary Britons, all this confirmed Northern Ireland's image as an alien and violent place: a 'bloodstained land', said the *Express*, 'which seems to be cursed by the God they worship so assiduously'. *Private Eye*'s Denis Thatcher jokes that the only solution is to 'get the hell out of Ireland and leave the little monkeys to pelt each other with droppings in perpetuity'. The real Denis Thatcher thought much the same. 'If the Irish want to kill each other', he once remarked, 'that does seem to me to be their business.' His wife, meanwhile, never pretended to take much interest in Northern Ireland. As a self-conscious patriot, Mrs Thatcher never wavered in her support for the army and the Royal Ulster Constabulary. But she found the Irish in general annoying, intractable and bewilderingly un-English. In theory she was a committed Unionist, but she made no secret of her exasperation with the actual Unionists and often asked her ministers why she could not just hand Catholic areas over to the Republic of Ireland. Later, her critics painted her as the reincarnation of Oliver Cromwell, thirsting for Irish blood. In fact, as her biographer observes, it would be better to describe her as someone who just wished the entire problem would go away.[15]

Mrs Thatcher's hatred of terrorism, however, carried an electric charge.

Her antipathy to the bombers was not just political; it was intensely personal. On 30 March 1979, only a day into the general election campaign, her Shadow Northern Ireland Secretary, Airey Neave, had been killed by an Irish National Liberation Army car bomb at the Houses of Parliament. A decorated war hero who had escaped from Colditz, Neave had managed her campaign for the party leadership. Even years later, her voice throbbed with emotion whenever she said his name. 'Some devils got him,' she said to the press afterwards, fighting back tears. 'They must never, never, never be allowed to triumph. They must never prevail.'[16]

She was under no illusions, though, that victory would be straightforward. Indeed, less than four months into her premiership, the Provisional IRA pulled off an even more spectacular coup. On the morning of 27 August, the 79-year-old Lord Mountbatten of Burma, the Queen's cousin, formerly Supreme Allied Commander in South-East Asia, Viceroy of India, First Sea Lord and Chief of the Defence Staff, was on holiday at Classiebawn Castle, County Sligo, just over the border in the Republic of Ireland. A few moments after his wooden boat had pulled out from the harbour for a day's fishing, the IRA detonated a radio-controlled bomb hidden aboard the previous evening. Mountbatten was killed instantly; so were his 14-year-old grandson Nicholas and a 15-year-old deckhand, Paul Maxwell. Another passenger, the 83-year-old Lady Brabourne, died the next day.

There was more. Just hours after Mountbatten's death, the IRA struck again, detonating a gigantic fertilizer bomb as a British Army convoy was passing Narrow Water Castle near Warrenpoint, County Down. Six men of the Parachute Regiment were killed, but as reinforcements rushed to the scene they were walking into a trap. Half an hour later, another bomb killed twelve more soldiers who had set up a base in a gatehouse across the road, just as the IRA had anticipated. The future General Sir Mike Jackson, then a company commander, recalled seeing the grass verge littered with 'red flesh . . . torsos, limbs, heads, hands and ears'. Jackson was asked to identify one friend from the remains of his face, which had been ripped off his skull by the blast and was found by divers in the Newry River. The body of the commanding officer, Lieutenant-Colonel David Blair, had been completely destroyed. All that was left was one epaulette.[17]

Coming on the same day, the murder of the Queen's beloved cousin and the horrific ambush at Warrenpoint were a terrible shock to British pride. The symbolism of Mountbatten's death, in particular, could hardly have been more powerful: the former master of British India, blown to pieces in an Irish fishing boat. In a statement suffused with ghoulish glee, the IRA claimed to have taken revenge for the British 'oppression of our people and torture of our comrades', and boasted that they would 'tear out their sentimental, imperialist heart'. The next day's newspapers were apoplectic. The IRA, said the *Mirror*, were the 'enemies of man . . . the enemies of civilisation'. 'THESE EVIL BASTARDS', said the front page of the *Express*, mourning 'Britain's blackest day in Ireland for a decade'. Mountbatten, the paper said, had 'personified the greatest qualities of the British – courage and nobility. He was, above all, a very gallant gentleman . . . By killing him, the Irish terrorists have struck at the very heart of Britain.' But the *Express*, like other papers, remained defiant. 'They grossly underestimate the British people if they think they will ever attain their wicked purposes by these foul means . . . Irish unity will never be brought about by bombs and bullets.'[18]

Mrs Thatcher was deeply shaken by what happened on 27 August. Two days later, she flew to Northern Ireland. After a brief walkabout in Belfast, where Protestant passers-by told her she should bring back hanging, she took an army helicopter to Crossmaglen, South Armagh, in the heart of so-called 'Bandit Country'. There, in a gesture calculated to show the troops she was on their side, she pointedly put on a flak jacket of the Ulster Defence Regiment. A few minutes later, her host, Brigadier David Thorne, placed the Warrenpoint colonel's epaulette on the table beside her. 'This, Prime Minister, is all that is left of Colonel Blair,' he said. At the end, he said quietly: 'I would now like briefly to come back to the human factor. David Blair has a son. I have a son' – and then broke off, unable to continue.

It was the kind of dramatic gesture Mrs Thatcher always appreciated. And even at this stage, only a couple of months into her premiership, she was completely at home with the soldiers, 'her boys', as she called them. Years later, one officer remembered her charging in like a 'blue tornado', greeting the men with real enthusiasm, offering them 'very strong words of encouragement' and telling them 'how determined she was to defeat terrorism as best she possibly could'. They had heard it all before, of course, but rarely had anyone said it with such conviction. Afterwards, the British commander in Northern Ireland told her that her visit had been a 'tremendous boost to all my soldiers . . . As a result of your personal interest, we are all full of hope for the future.'[19]

Despite the horror of Warrenpoint, the security situation was actually better than it had been for years. Since 1976 the Callaghan government had been pursuing a successful 'criminalization' strategy, treating the conflict as a containable campaign against criminal gangs. With the Royal Ulster Constabulary (RUC) taking the lead and the British Army moving back from the firing line, fewer soldiers were dying. By the time Mrs Thatcher took over, people no longer talked of Northern Ireland as Britain's Vietnam. Meanwhile, Callaghan's pugnacious Northern Ireland

Secretary, the former miner Roy Mason, had been giving the IRA a ferocious beating. In effect, Mason allowed the RUC to be as aggressive as
they liked, as long as they got results. Catholics complained that he was
turning a blind eye to torture, and an Amnesty report claimed that prison
officers were licensed to abuse their republican inmates. But Mason's
methods seemed to work. Arrests were up; bombings and casualties were
down. With the authorities taking such a hard line, loyalist recruitment
virtually dried up. And Mason made no apology for 'being as tough as I
could be'. 'Words cannot express the disgust I felt', he wrote, listing the
IRA's atrocities, 'when the people responsible for such evils bleated about
the alleged erosion of their human rights.'[20]

To the IRA, who saw themselves as freedom fighters, the Callaghan
government's decision to treat them like common criminals seemed an
intolerable affront. In particular, they were outraged that in 1976 the
authorities had scrapped 'political status' for convicted terrorists. Until
then, republicans and loyalists had been treated as prisoners of war, incar-
cerated in old Nissen huts at the disused Long Kesh air base, where they
were free to wear their own clothes and answered to their commanding
officers. But under the new regime they were treated as common-or-garden
thugs and killers. The barbed wire compounds were replaced by purpose-
built 'H-blocks',* while Long Kesh was renamed HM Prison Maze. Above
all, IRA prisoners were expected to wear prison uniforms and undertake
prison work, just like everybody else.[21]

In September 1976 the first IRA prisoner convicted under the new
guidelines, a teenage carjacker called Kieran Nugent, refused to wear a
prison uniform and spent three years naked under a blanket instead. Other
IRA prisoners followed his example, launching what became known as
the 'blanket protest'. In March 1978 this escalated into a 'dirty protest'
when prisoners refused to leave their cells to wash and use the toilets,
claiming that they were being beaten by the warders. Eventually they
ended up using chamber pots and smearing their own excrement on the
walls, which inevitably ensured horrified coverage in the media. The
Catholic Archbishop of Armagh, Tomás Ó Fiaich, an ardent republican,
told the press that with their 'stench and filth' the H-blocks reminded him
of the 'sewer pipes in the slums of Calcutta'. Even Mason admitted that
'the image of prisoners naked in their cells with nothing for company but
their own filth' was hugely embarrassing. But to give in would 'appal the
law-abiding majority in Northern Ireland' and hand 'the IRA its biggest

---

* They were called 'H-blocks' for the banal reason that the cells were arranged in four wings,
linked by a central administrative section.

victory in years'. 'Whatever happened,' Mason wrote, 'I was determined not to budge. The prisoners were criminals and as far as I was concerned would always be treated as criminals.'[22]

Having inherited Mason's policy in 1979, Mrs Thatcher was determined to stick to it. As Humphrey Atkins assured his colleagues, there would be 'no return to special category status for terrorist prisoners'. But the prisoners' frustration was growing. In January 1980 they published what they called 'the Five Demands': the right not to wear prison uniform, the right not to do prison work, the right to associate freely with other prisoners, the right to a weekly visit and letter, and the restoration of remission lost through the protest. The demands had been designed to look as reasonable as possible, with nothing overtly sectarian. But Atkins, like Mason, refused to budge. So, in October, seven prisoners announced that they were beginning a hunger strike to win back their political status. The government dismissed them as tools of the IRA. In reality, the IRA leadership had strongly opposed a hunger strike, believing it would end in disastrous failure. But the shared experience of prison had given the men in the Maze a close-knit identity of their own. 'By that stage,' one told the BBC's Peter Taylor, 'the comradeship had built up so much that this had become totally our world . . . So the IRA had to go along with it.'[23]

Hunger strikes had a sacred place in Irish history. The figure of the Irish martyr suffering in a British prison had long played a central part in republican iconography. The revolutionary Thomas Ashe had died on hunger strike in British captivity in 1917; so had the Lord Mayor of Cork, Terence MacSwiney, in 1920. From the start, however, Mrs Thatcher and her ministers were adamant that they would never abandon the principle that terrorists were criminals, not prisoners of war. At a Cabinet meeting on 23 October, just before the strike was due to start, they agreed that the prisoners could wear approved 'civilian-type clothing'. But even though Atkins warned that there would be deaths by Christmas, they also agreed that under 'no circumstances' would IRA prisoners regain their political status. In this, as so often, the tone was set by the Prime Minister. 'I want this to be utterly clear,' Mrs Thatcher told the Commons. 'The Government will never concede political status to the hunger strikers.'[24]

At first it seemed that her intransigence had won the day. Although the seven hunger strikers maintained their fast for an agonizing fifty-three days, none of them died. Instead, they settled for a deal, concocted in great secrecy using existing channels between MI5 and the Provisional IRA, under which all prisoners in Northern Ireland would wear the approved 'civilian-type clothing' during the day and their own clothes during family visits. If nothing else, the deal, approved by Mrs Thatcher, gives the lie to her claim that she never negotiated with terrorists. She did; though always through secret intermediaries, never directly.

On 18 December the prisoners called off the strike. At the Northern Ireland Office, Atkins's officials congratulated themselves that victory had been down to the government's 'firmness of purpose', as well as to the fact that 'the seven hunger strikers just did not have the will to die'. But victory proved short-lived, because within weeks the settlement was breaking down. The problem was that the deal was not quite what the hunger strikers had been led to believe. They had been told that the British had caved in. Yet the government had not accepted any of their Five Demands, and especially not their claim to political status. Even the deal about clothes was not quite what they had originally imagined, since they wanted their *own* clothes, not clothes approved by their British oppressors.[25]

Eventually, after weeks of argument, the Maze authorities agreed that the prisoners' families could bring in their own clothes. But the authorities were not prepared to hand them over until the IRA men agreed to end their dirty protests, move into clean cells and make themselves available for work, like ordinary criminals. And by the end of January 1981 the prisoners' patience had run out. 'The Brits', one said, were 'intent on humiliating us once again'. On 7 February the Sinn Fein newspaper published a statement from the protesters' leader in the Maze, Bobby Sands, announcing a new hunger strike to begin on the first day of March. They had 'had enough', the statement said, 'of British deceit and of broken promises'. This time, though, the strike would be staggered, with men joining it every few weeks. The first would be Sands himself. And this time, he told his friend Gerry Adams, he was 'prepared to die'.[26]

At first the news that the men in the Maze had resumed their hunger strike provoked surprisingly little comment. As the BBC's Peter Taylor subsequently wrote, most reporters assumed this latest campaign would end in another deal. But 'all of us', he went on, 'underestimated Mrs Thatcher'. She knew that, this time, Bobby Sands and his comrades were intent on martyrdom. But on a brief visit to Northern Ireland, just four days into his fast, she made her position absolutely clear. 'We will not compromise on this,' she told an audience in Belfast. 'There will be no political status.' And when an interviewer pressed her the next day, she was even more obdurate. 'I am deeply sorry there is another hunger strike,' she said. 'It is to try to achieve political status for criminals. It will never achieve that status . . . Murder is criminal. Violence is criminal. It will stay that way. That hunger strike will achieve nothing.'[27]

In Bobby Sands, however, Mrs Thatcher found an antagonist whose determination more than matched her own. Born into a working-class Catholic family in 1954, Sands had grown up in the violent Rathcoole estate, where his family were harassed by loyalist gangs. After joining the Provisional IRA as a teenager, he was imprisoned in 1973 for armed robbery. In prison he fell under the influence of Gerry Adams and learned Irish; on his release in 1976, he resumed his role in the IRA. That October he joined five other Provos in blowing up a furniture showroom, but was caught and was sent back to prison. By this time, special category status had been abolished, and Sands threw himself into the blanket and dirty protests. He was a keen autodidact, who used his time in prison to read Irish history and write articles for republican newspapers. He also became a great poetry enthusiast, specializing in maudlin verses written on toilet paper and hidden up his rectum. His supporters saw him as a romantic hero, an idealistic outlaw with a heart of gold. But as the historian Richard English remarks, the image of the 'prisoner-scholar' may be a bit oversold. In 1979 Sands sent a fan letter to the Irish writer Ethna Carbery, urging her to write a poem in support of their campaign. Unfortunately, she had been dead since 1902.[28]

Although Sands was a man of immense resolve, his greatest asset was his apparent ordinariness. The only widely circulated photograph of him, taken a few years earlier, showed a grinning young man with long brown hair, who looked 'more like a drummer in a rock band than a ruthless terrorist'. From the IRA's perspective, this image, allied to the fact that Sands had never personally killed anyone, made him the ideal front man. And just four days into his hunger strike, fate handed him an extraordinary opportunity. On 5 March the independent republican MP Frank Maguire, who represented Fermanagh and South Tyrone, died of a heart attack. Although the Provisionals had always set their face against participation in British electoral politics, this was too good a coincidence to ignore. With other Catholic candidates encouraged to pull out, the field was clear for Sands to stand under the 'Anti-H-Block' banner, even though he had no connection with the constituency, was still on hunger strike in the Maze and had no intention of taking his seat, even if he had been able to do so.

Everybody knew the result would be tight, since the voters of Fermanagh and South Tyrone were split almost fifty-fifty between Catholics and Protestants. Even so, the result on 9 April could hardly have been a more resounding signal of Catholic support for the hunger strikers. With 30,493 votes, Sands had won a majority of 1,147 over the former Ulster Unionist leader, Harry West, and was duly elected as a Member of Parliament. Most Protestants were horrified; even the leader of the liberal Alliance Party, Oliver Napier, called it a 'black day for Northern Ireland', marking the triumph of 'the real evil of naked sectarianism'. In Whitehall, there was talk of expelling Sands from the Commons as a convicted terrorist, but the government wisely judged that this would be far too inflammatory. Even so, the fact that he was now an MP turned the hunger strike into an enormous international story. Almost overnight, said the *Guardian*, the voters of Fermanagh and South Tyrone had turned Sands's lonely struggle into a massive 'political triumph for the IRA'.[29]

By this point, Sands was forty days into his hunger strike. His weight was falling fast, down by two stone since March, and he was complaining of severe fatigue, dizziness and headaches. In the next few weeks, as the world's media descended on Belfast and he sank towards oblivion, the pressure mounted. On 13 April, John Hume, leader of the moderate Social and Democratic Labour Party (SDLP), told Mrs Thatcher that the 'situation in Northern Ireland was the worst he had ever known'. With support for Sands rising every day and the IRA clearly 'winning the propaganda battle', she must make concessions before it was too late. No, she said: 'Any wavering on the issue of political status would be to give a licence to kill.' Hume, clearly in despair, told her that 'if this was all [she] had to say, the problems for Northern Ireland would be serious indeed'. But she remained adamant. Hume was 'asking for total surrender. To give political status would be to act as a recruiting sergeant for the PIRA.' A week later, talking to the cameras after a trip to the Middle East, she repeated that she would not bend. 'Crime is crime is crime: it is not political, it is crime, and there can be no question of granting political status,' she said firmly. 'I understand Mr Sands is still on hunger strike, and I regret that he has not decided to come off it. There can be no possible concessions on political status.'[30]

Early on the morning of Sunday 3 May, Sands lapsed into a coma, from which he never recovered. He died just after one in the morning the following Tuesday, after sixty-six days without food. For the IRA, his death was the greatest propaganda coup in their modern history, a horrifying symbol of their determination to resist the British state. Around the world it was front-page news. In Oslo protesters threw balloons filled with ketchup at the Queen; in Zurich a British car showroom was firebombed; in Toulouse someone threw a petrol bomb at a Dunlop tyre warehouse; even in Florence firebombs were thrown at British-owned businesses. In Britain there were small protests in Birmingham, Manchester, Leeds and Edinburgh, while a crowd picketed outside Downing Street. And in Belfast rioting broke out almost immediately, with petrol bombs thrown at police stations, factories and even a Methodist church. Throughout the day, reported the Northern Ireland Office, came news of 'petrol and acid bombs, barricades, hijackings, malicious fires and even bolts from a crossbow'. In the most shocking incident, a Protestant milkman, Eric Guiney, and his 14-year-old son Desmond were seriously hurt when their float overturned after being attacked by a mob. Both died a few days later of their injuries. But the world had eyes only for Sands.[31]

Few British papers mourned Sands's passing. In a full-page editorial on the 'propaganda of death', the *Express* argued that the historical figure he most resembled was the Nazi stormtrooper Horst Wessel, whose murder by Communists in 1930 had made him a far-right martyr. 'Robert Sands', the paper said, 'was a fanatic who would have been unnoticed in life but imagined – God help us! – that he would serve Ireland in death. His sad credulity provides his political masters with the propaganda bonanza they have long planned. How Dr Goebbels would have approved.' An accompanying cartoon showed a memorial to the IRA's 2,094 victims, marked with the words 'They Had No Choice'. The *Mirror*, too, felt little pity. At Sands's funeral, which drew tens of thousands of republican supporters, the paper's chief reporter was struck by the presence of so many IRA men in combat jackets and masks, 'urging the mood of the people to its lowest and angriest levels'. And in the Commons, Mrs Thatcher never wavered. 'Mr Sands was a convicted criminal,' she said curtly. 'He chose to take his own life. It was a choice that his organisation did not allow to many of its victims.'[32]

**Who died that others might die**

The newspapers shed few tears for Bobby Sands. This is Mac in the *Daily Mail*, 6 May 1981.

Among Northern Ireland's Catholics, Mrs Thatcher's inflexibility seemed positively monstrous. To tens, perhaps hundreds of thousands of people, the hunger strikers were not the killers and bombers portrayed in the British press. They were, as one IRA activist put it, 'ordinary men . . . from the republican community': young men, generally in their twenties and thirties, with friends, neighbours, wives and mothers, who looked no different from their counterparts anywhere else. Not even Mrs Thatcher questioned their courage: a coward does not go on hunger strike. And here, as so often, the fact that she was a woman came into play. She was not just a politician; she was a *mother*. How could she allow another mother's son to starve himself to death? 'I didn't believe she'd let them die,' one Catholic teenager wrote later. 'Day after day she heard reports; she could have prevented it, but she didn't.'[33]

After Sands's death, many of Mrs Thatcher's critics assumed she would now see the error of her ways. But they did not understand her at all. The hunger strikes went on, and nothing changed. And so, just as Sands and his comrades had planned, they became a march of death. The second hunger striker, Francis Hughes, died on 12 May. Raymond McCreesh and Patsy O'Hara died on 21 May, but still Mrs Thatcher remained unyielding. 'Faced with the failure of their discredited cause,' she said in Belfast a week later, 'the men of violence have chosen in recent months to play what may well be their last card. They have turned their violence against themselves through the prison hunger strike to death. They seek to work on the most basic of human emotions – pity – as a means of creating tension and stoking the fires of bitterness and hatred.' But they would never succeed. 'What they want is special treatment, treatment different from that received by other prisoners. They want their violence justified. It isn't, and it will not be.'[34]

To her critics, Mrs Thatcher's stern implacability, her refusal to offer pity or sympathy, seemed deliberately incendiary. The Northern Ireland Office's David Blatherwick reported that her words had 'gone down in the Catholic community like a lead balloon', while Humphrey Atkins warned that with an 'indefinite run of deaths' now likely, 'the danger of losing the support of the Catholic community is now very real'. Yet when the cameras were off, she *was* prepared to compromise. We know now that, in early July, the Prime Minister authorized secret contacts with the IRA leadership about a deal, under which the government would make concessions on clothing, remission and prison work, but without conceding political status.

For reasons that remain bitterly contested, however, the deal collapsed, possibly because the IRA thought they were being led down the garden path, or perhaps because the leadership did not want to lose such a valuable propaganda weapon. Later, one former IRA prisoner, Richard O'Rawe, claimed that the men in the Maze had been eager to accept Mrs Thatcher's deal. According to O'Rawe, they considered it a 'fantastic offer', but were overruled by their commanders outside the prison, notably Gerry Adams. This certainly sounds plausible. The hunger strikes had generated enormous worldwide publicity for the IRA, and a cold-blooded tactician might well have calculated that it was better to keep them going, whatever the cost. But other IRA veterans dispute this, and there is no hard evidence either way. The truth will probably never be known.[35]

In any case, the march of death went on. On 8 July, Joe McDonnell became the fifth republican prisoner to die, and he was followed by Martin Hurson on 13 July, Kevin Lynch on 1 August and Kieran Doherty the following day. For Northern Ireland's Catholics, each new casualty was proof of Mrs Thatcher's inhuman cruelty. Yet, far from the momentum steadily mounting, the deaths were becoming normal. Like the bombings that had dominated the headlines for a decade, they were being absorbed into the general narrative of Northern Ireland. People died; these things happened. And although each death was followed by riots and protests, none attracted the same publicity as Sands's demise back in May. Even attendance at their funerals had fallen dramatically. By late summer, even many Catholics were beginning to wonder if the strikers were throwing their lives away. Given that Mrs Thatcher had not wavered after six or seven deaths, not even the most optimistic republican believed she would crack after eleven or twelve. If she were going to yield, she would have done so already. Even if every single man in the Maze starved himself to death, she would never restore their political status.

By now the prisoners' families, supported by the Catholic Church, were beginning to speak up. If Mrs Thatcher was never going to give in, what was the point of their sons killing themselves? On 31 July, Paddy Quinn's mother requested medical intervention to save his life. Three weeks later, Pat McGeown's family followed suit. Then Matt Devlin's family; then Laurence McKeown's; and now a trickle was becoming a stream. The strike was crumbling. On 26 September, Liam McCloskey became the fifth man to be taken off hunger strike at his family's request. At last, on 3 October, after seven months and ten deaths, the IRA bowed to reality and called off the strike. They had been 'robbed of the hunger strike as an effective protest weapon', they said bitterly, 'because of the successful campaign waged against our distressed relatives by the Catholic hierarchy, aided and abetted by the Irish establishment'.

But this was a smokescreen. The fact was that they had expected Mrs

Thatcher to crack, and had no answer when she refused to do so. Three days later, the government announced that all prisoners in Northern Ireland could wear their own clothes, would enjoy free association and would get some remission for time lost protesting. In essence, this was much the same package that the IRA leadership had rejected back in July. The same thing was missing: the prisoners' political status.[36]

For Mrs Thatcher, the hunger strike was a defining moment. Ever since becoming Conservative leader, she had boasted of her steadfastness under fire, her refusal to change course and her contempt for those who did so. Now, faced with young men starving themselves to death in a Northern Irish prison, she had lived up to her rhetoric. No matter what the pressure, she would not bend. To the IRA, she was the Oliver Cromwell of the modern age, a woman harder and crueller than any man. To her admirers, she stood alone as the supreme defender of Britain's interests, the Iron Lady who would never turn. Mrs Thatcher had won a 'resounding victory', declared the *Sunday Express*, noting that it was also a 'victory for common sense and firm moral purpose, over the confused, tortured mentality of appeasement'. There was a lesson here, the paper said, for her Conservative critics. 'Mrs Thatcher feels just as passionately about the rightness of her policies against inflation as she did about the hunger strikes. Can anyone be sure now that her determination to stay the course will not serve her and us just as well again?'[37]

Yet if the end of the hunger strikes was a personal victory for the Prime Minister, it came at a heavy cost. For the very fact of the hunger strikes – and, in particular, the death of Bobby Sands – meant that, in the eyes of the world, the IRA prisoners *had* won the title of political prisoners, if only unofficially. In the United States the strikes played into the hands of the Irish lobby, confirming the image of the British as bullying oppressors. And in Northern Ireland the identification of the hunger strikers as Christ-like martyrs, sacrificing themselves for their belief in Irish unity, struck a powerful chord even among Catholics who hated violence. Crucially, the IRA had contrived a situation in which they were seen exclusively as the *victims* of suffering, rather than as the perpetrators. The emaciated figure of the dying hunger striker was a far more sympathetic figure than the cold-blooded bomber.

All the time, almost overlooked amid the fascination with Sands and his comrades, the IRA's own march of death had gone on. On 7 April a gunman killed a Londonderry woman, Joanne Mathers, who had taken a part-time job as a census collector. The IRA had ordered Catholic families to boycott the census, which they saw as a front for British intelligence.

Later, a Special Branch agent who had infiltrated the local IRA claimed that the future Sinn Fein leader Martin McGuinness had ordered her death personally. She left a husband and 1-year-old son. Even by the standards of the IRA it seemed horrifyingly cruel. Yet it was a reflection of the mood that, although Mrs Mathers's killing came two days before the Fermanagh and South Tyrone by-election, it made no difference to the outcome. It was Bobby Sands, a member of the organization that murdered Joanne Mathers, whose death was commemorated in films, poems, biographies and murals. Hers was not. He was a martyr. She was just another victim.[38]

In later years, some commentators suggested that Mrs Thatcher should have made more effort to find a deal and blunt the hunger strikers' appeal to the Catholic community. Perhaps this might have worked, though Protestants would inevitably have seen it as a sign of surrender, and it might have encouraged the hunger strikers to push for more. In any case, the fact is that she *did* offer the IRA a deal, albeit one that fell short of their demands; but they turned it down. Still, there is no doubt that the events of 1981 played a central role in reviving the republican cause. Even in mid-August a confidential report by the Northern Ireland Office warned that public morale had reached an 'all-time low', with a surge of 'alienation, bitterness and frustration' in Catholic areas:

> Out of a community of some half-million [Catholics], nearly all know families with members in the Maze. Many protestors are from decent homes, and their neighbours find it hard to accept that they are the criminals described by 'the Brits'. The Provos and their friends have played cleverly on Irish history and tradition to show that the strike is the latest phase of a noble cause and that at bottom the British are responsible . . .
>
> The gap between the communities has widened. Catholics are retreating in upon themselves. Many Protestants were dismayed at Sands's election, and are angry at Catholic sympathy for the hunger strikers . . . The prospect of agreement on the political future of Northern Ireland seems further off than ever . . .
>
> A new generation of children has been infected with rampant Anglophobia. New heroes and myths have been created and new wounds opened which will take years to heal.

There was another consequence, too. Sands's election suggested that, in an embittered political landscape, a radical republican party might poll better than anybody thought. Sinn Fein drew the inevitable lesson. On their return to electoral politics in 1982 they won more than 10 per cent of the vote in the elections for the Northern Ireland Assembly, and a year later they won more than 13 per cent in the Westminster general election. Their new political direction was clear. As one activist put it, their new strategy was to 'take power in Ireland' with 'a ballot paper in this hand and an Armalite in the other'.[39]

In the meantime, the violence continued. Some 114 people were killed in 1981, a further 111 in 1982 and eighty-four the following year. Most of the deaths came in Belfast, but not all of them. In the autumn of 1981, the IRA set off bombs at Chelsea Barracks, the Royal Artillery Barracks in Woolwich and in the basement of a Wimpy burger restaurant on Oxford Street. At the Wimpy restaurant, a bomb disposal officer, Kenneth Howorth, was killed instantly while trying to defuse the device. He had two children. On and on the murders went. The following July, bomb attacks in Hyde Park and Regent's Park killed eleven soldiers and wounded about fifty, and in December 1983 a car bomb outside Harrods killed six people and wounded almost a hundred. Individually, each story seemed utterly heartbreaking. Cumulatively, they had lost the power to shock. The conflict had become normal, even banal; the news of some atrocity in Belfast or Londonderry, or even a bomb scare in a London department store, was a sad but inevitable part of the soundtrack of everyday life. To put it bluntly, people had long since come to take them for granted.

So they did not work. Even though the IRA had been bombing Britain for almost a decade, they had completely failed to change the political momentum. In reality, the vast majority of British people knew absolutely nothing about Northern Ireland, cared even less and could not be bombed into caring. Far from feeling an atavistic attachment to the province, most would have been perfectly happy to wave it goodbye. In December 1980 a poll found that 50 per cent of Britons would like to see Northern Ireland leave the United Kingdom, while only 29 per cent wanted to keep it. Indeed, surveys since the early 1970s had consistently shown that about half the electorate would like to see the British Army pull out, not because they thought Britain was in the wrong, but because they were heartily sick of the whole business. During the hunger strike, for instance, one poll found that six out of ten would like to see the troops brought home, while only three out of ten thought they should stay. Even Conservative voters, by a small margin, wanted the army to come home. Extraordinarily, this meant British Conservatives were more likely to want the troops out than Northern Ireland's Catholics, most of whom feared it would mean civil war. The reality of Northern Ireland, in other words, was much messier than the rhetoric.[40]

But although many people would have agreed with the joke that the two most boring words in the English language were 'Northern Ireland', some cared very much indeed. A good example was a young Londoner who had no family connections with Ireland but had read about its history in the 1970s and had come to believe that the conflict was a brutal imperialist war between the British Establishment and the Irish working class. Sinn Fein, he thought, were not apologists for terrorism; they were the anti-colonial resistance. The IRA were not murderers; they were freedom fighters. For, as he explained to his biographer, Britain's 'appalling record' was 'worse than all the Boers have done to the blacks in South Africa', comparable 'with the way some of the Middle Eastern races have been liquidated by the Turkish Empire or the Russians', and 'as bad in those 800 years as what Hitler did to the Jews in six'. To many people, such remarks were not so much offensive as utterly intolerable. But it was not the last time that Ken Livingstone would find himself in hot water after making remarks about Hitler and the Jews.[41]

# 24

# The Commissar of County Hall

*The harsh realities of life confront Kenneth Livingstone soon after he crawls from under his pink-patterned duvet in the simple bed-sitting room, which shakes every time a train passes on the Bakerloo line below.*

Daily Telegraph, 15 June 1981

*London has endured fire, plague and the blitz. It should not have to endure Mr Livingstone at the head of its affairs for one more day.*

Daily Express, 13 October 1981

Saturday 10 October 1981: a breezy autumn day in west London, and Nora Field had almost finished her shopping. At the age of 59, Mrs Field, a widowed grandmother, worked as a civil service typist and lived alone in a council flat on Vauxhall Bridge Road. She had just popped out to get some groceries for her bedridden mother, who was in her nineties and lived nearby. At the pedestrian crossing on Ebury Bridge Road, Mrs Field stopped to talk to another local woman, Hazel Cole, who was six months pregnant. Nearby, John Breslin, an 18-year-old photographic technician, was sitting on a wall, a few yards from a parked white laundry van.

The clock ticked towards half-past twelve. In the distance, a bus carrying dozens of Irish Guardsmen back to Chelsea Barracks from the Tower of London turned into the street. Further down the road, with a clear view of the pedestrian crossing, a man from Belfast waited, his finger poised on a detonator. The bus came closer. The bomber pressed the button. From his command device, the signal ran down a wire hidden in scaffolding along the street to a colossal gelignite nail bomb hidden in the laundry van. A split second later, the van exploded.

Nora Field was killed instantly, her heart pierced by a six-inch nail bent into a U-shape to fit into the bomb. The top of John Breslin's head was ripped off by the blast, though he did not die until four days later. Hazel Cole survived; she had been shielded by Mrs Field, who had taken the full impact of the blast. The street was littered with nails, bolts, glass and bodies; at least a dozen other passers-by had been injured, among them a 5-year-old boy and his 2-year-old sister. On the bus, horribly damaged by shrapnel, nobody had been killed, though several soldiers were badly injured. In a pub nearby, drinkers had been hurled to the floor, covered with glass from the blown-in windows. 'It was horrible,' a local travel agent told the press. 'There was a middle-aged woman lying on the ground screaming with a nail through her leg. There were people falling all over the place.'

Later, a spokesman for Westminster Hospital said the injuries were the worst they had ever seen. Some of the victims had arrived with their skulls split open; others had nails embedded in their wounds. It was a miracle that only two people had been killed; but that, of course, was no consolation. Nora Field, said her devastated brother Patrick, had been a 'dear, sweet innocent woman. She had never done anyone any hurt and never had any strong political views. This is so unfair. So unjust.' As for John Breslin, the horrible irony was that he came from an Irish family. 'It's their own people they are killing,' said his father Kevin, who had moved to England from County Roscommon. 'They are Irish. I am Irish and they killed my son.'[1]

The next day, the Provisional IRA claimed responsibility for the attack at Chelsea Barracks. They had struck a blow, they said, for the 'oppressed Irish people . . . We await the hypocrisy which will undoubtedly follow from British political leaders whose attitude to Irish victims of their violence in our country only strengthens our conviction in our cause and methods.' But the newspapers did not see it that way. 'Mrs Field didn't die in a just war,' said an editorial in the *Mirror*. 'She was the victim of a black wickedness.' And speaking to the press after taking flowers and chocolates to the wounded children in hospital, the Prime Minister visibly fought back tears. It seemed barely conceivable, Mrs Thatcher said, her voice thick with emotion, 'that any human being would have wrapped nails round these bombs to inflict maximum damage . . . The people who did this were murderers, murderers . . . These people are just criminals without regard for human life and limb. I shall never, never give them political status, never.'[2]

Everybody agreed that it had been a uniquely cruel and criminal attack; or rather, almost everybody. Two days after the Chelsea Barracks bomb, the new leader of the Greater London Council was in Cambridge. Although a Labour politician, he had agreed to give a talk to the university's Tory

Reform Group. And when a student asked about his views on the IRA, he did not hold back:

> They are not criminals or lunatics running about. That is to misunderstand them . . .
>
> Nobody supports what happened last Saturday in London. But what about stopping it happening? As long as we are in Ireland, people will be letting off bombs in London. I can see that we are a colonial power holding down a colony. For the rest of time violence will recur again and again as long as we are in Ireland. People in Northern Ireland see themselves as subject peoples. If they were just criminals and psychopaths they could be crushed. But they have a motive force which they think is good.

'This Damn Fool Says the Bombers Aren't Criminals', said the front page of the *Sun* the next day. 'This morning the *Sun* presents the most odious man in Britain. Take a bow, Mr Ken Livingstone, Socialist leader of the Greater London Council.'

Livingstone had been in his job for less than six months. A year earlier, few people had heard of him. Now, to the newspapers, he was the 'most odious man in Britain', the chief defender of the 'criminal murderous activities of the IRA', an 'alien in his own country'. The paradox was that, as most commentators agreed, he was also a remarkably cunning political operator, with an unmatched thirst for publicity. Not only did he turn the Greater London Council into the single best-known vehicle of opposition to the Thatcher government, he championed a whole series of issues, from anti-racism to gay rights, that were initially dismissed as outlandish but eventually flowed into the mainstream. Unlike most Labour politicians who emerged during the 1980s, he was that rare beast, a genuine national celebrity. The problem, though, was that he could not stop talking.[3]

The first thing people noticed about Ken Livingstone was how ordinary he was. With his nasal voice, his enthusiasm for science fiction, his fondness for snakes and salamanders, even his little moustache, he looked like exactly what he was: an affable, cheeky, nerdy man from the capital's suburban fringe. He was born in Lambeth in 1945. His mother was a former music hall dancer, while his father was a merchant seaman, then a trawler-man, then a window cleaner. The Livingstones were working-class Conservatives who saved to buy a house in suburban West Norwood. As their son recalled, they gave him a 'clear sense of right and wrong', but rarely talked about politics or religion. 'Our neighbours all seemed to be called Henry, George, Albert, Agnes, Gladys or Bessie,' he wrote, 'and respectable working-class values were reinforced in our house by the *Daily Express*.'[4]

Young Ken did not seem an obvious candidate for political stardom. Small and shy, he failed his 11-plus and left Tulse Hill Comprehensive with just four O-levels. His real passion was for reptiles and amphibians. By his teenage years, his bedroom was lined on three sides by tanks, which housed 'bullfrogs, newts, salamanders, snakes, lizards' and even a small alligator. But after a few years working as a laboratory technician, he discovered an even more eccentric interest: politics. On a hitchhiking trip to West Africa in 1966, he met various left-leaning young volunteers, who talked to him about Biafra and Vietnam. By the time he returned, he was fully committed. In particular, he was passionate about fighting racism, much in the news thanks to the riots in the United States and the impact of Enoch Powell. And in February 1969 he joined the Norwood Labour Party: a 'rare example', he remarked, 'of a rat joining a sinking ship'.[5]

Like many London branches in the late 1960s, Norwood's Labour Party was in a desperately moribund condition, with many younger members having left in protest at Harold Wilson's refusal to condemn the Americans' war in Vietnam. At Livingstone's first meeting there were only twelve people, and he was one of only three who were not pensioners. At his second meeting he was made chairman and secretary of the Young Socialists. At his third he became the Norwood membership secretary and was invited to join the local executive committee. But this was hardly an exceptional story. Labour had been obliterated in the local elections of 1968, clearing out hundreds of older working-class councillors and opening the way for a radical new generation. At the grass-roots level, the party was tipping towards what academics called the 'new urban left'. More middle-class, better educated and burning with righteous anger, these were Tony Benn's future supporters, as well as the models for the BBC's 'Wolfie' Smith, the Che Guevara of Tooting.[6]

All this reflected a bigger picture. The London that had voted for Herbert Morrison in the 1930s was no more. In ten years after 1964 the capital had lost almost half its manufacturing jobs; in the next ten years the total was halved again. As older working-class families moved out to the suburbs, young middle-class men and women, often working in the public sector or service industries, were moving in. It was in London that the women's liberation movement had first seriously established itself in the early 1970s; it was in London that feminists had first set up childcare centres, discussion groups and support networks; it was in London that the gay rights campaign had become most vocal and visible. What was more, immigration had changed the very look of the city: by 1981, one in five people in the inner boroughs was black or Asian. After years of relative quiescence, black and Asian Londoners were pressing for change. Against this background, a committed young man, brimming with energy, outspokenly committed to feminism, anti-racism and gay rights, was bound to do well.[7]

Livingstone rose quickly. By 1971 he had become a Lambeth councillor. Two years later, he was elected as Norwood's representative on the Greater London Council, and by 1974 he had become vice chairman of the GLC's housing committee. By now he was already associated with hard-left sects like the International Marxist Group, the Chartists and the Campaign for Labour Party Democracy, and especially with Trotskyists such as Lambeth's future leader Ted Knight. Later, Livingstone claimed that he had never read a word by Karl Marx, although he once told *The Times* that he had read the *Communist Manifesto*. He was happy to borrow ideas from his Trotskyist allies, which led some papers to mock him as a self-taught 'paperback Marxist'. But despite the 'Red Ken' image, he remained his own man: a free-floating attention-seeker, a troublemaker, a nuisance. '"Red Ken" was always a bit of a joke,' Neil Kinnock told Livingstone's biographer Andrew Hosken. 'I don't think he's even a Red . . . He's a "Kennist".'[8]

Like his Trotskyist friends, Livingstone took it for granted that capitalism was doomed, and had nothing but contempt for traitors such as Harold Wilson and Jim Callaghan ('an awful right-wing lot . . . a disgrace'). At this stage, though, he aimed most of his fire at enemies closer to home. In 1975 he launched a pressure group called Labour Against the Cuts, campaigning against housing cuts and fare increases by the GLC's Labour administration. And at the end of 1979 he and his friends launched a newsletter, *London Labour Briefing*, designed to circulate information among hard-left activists. True to form, it was preoccupied with heretics within Labour's ranks, identifying councillors who had voted against the left's prescriptions and revealed themselves as traitors. Later, one of Livingstone's own advisers described the *Briefing* team as a 'vitriolic, sectarian grouping that drove Labour in London to the brink of extinction, the distillation of all that turned the public off about Labour in the eighties'. In principle it was run by an editorial collective. But 'its guiding spirit', reported *The Times* in 1981, 'is Mr Jeremy Corbyn, aged 31, *Briefing*'s founder, an official of the National Union of Public Employees'.[9]

Even at this stage, Livingstone had a reputation for irresponsible grandstanding. After Livingstone had served briefly as Camden's housing committee chairman, the borough's veteran Labour leader, Roy Shaw, accused him of 'using the position as a platform to get publicity for himself' and of playing to 'the left-wing gallery, the trades union gallery,

THE COMMISSAR OF COUNTY HALL

whatever gallery would help him at any particular moment'. Livingstone's favourite tactic, Shaw said, was 'to put forward an outrageous proposition, knowing full well that it would not be accepted – not really believing it himself. It would be defeated in the [Labour] group. He could then turn round and say: it's all the fault of those right-wing bastards; if it had been left to me I would have done so and so.' But this was clever politics, bolstering Livingstone's image as the champion of the left. And even his opponents admitted that his impudence made him hard to dislike. 'To go out for a drink with Ken was a pleasure really,' said Shaw's deputy, who once had to fight off a Livingstone challenge for his own job. 'He was always full of stories and jokes.'[10]

For all his bonhomie, Livingstone was a supremely ruthless operator. He once joked that he identified with his collection of poisonous salamanders, and nothing captured his cold-blooded cunning better than the way he seized the leadership of the GLC. In 1977 the Conservatives had won control of the council under the flamboyant Horace Cutler, but by the turn of the decade Labour were overwhelming favourites to regain power. In April 1980 the Labour group had chosen a new leader: Andrew McIntosh, an Oxford-educated academic who lived in Highgate and ran a market research firm. A mild, donnish figure, McIntosh had only beaten Livingstone by a single vote, and was so unworldly that his close colleagues soon regretted their choice. Meanwhile, Livingstone made no secret of his plan to challenge McIntosh straight after the GLC elections. 'Look, Andrew,' he told his rival early in 1981, 'I am going to beat you, however many seats we win; if there is a Labour administration, it will elect me leader.'[11]

None of this was lost on Labour's opponents. The Conservatives' GLC manifesto claimed that the 'old Labour Party' had been taken over by 'Marxists and extremists', while Horace Cutler warned that McIntosh would be ditched after the election and urged voters to 'Keep London out of the Red'. A week before polling day Cutler issued an appeal in the *Daily Express*, 'Why We Must Stop These Red Wreckers', warning that Livingstone was poised to 'establish a Marxist power-base in London from which support can be given to the wider movement to take over the Labour Party'. And the *Express* was in no doubt that if Labour won, McIntosh would be dumped for the 'Bennite' Livingstone. 'Vote to keep the Marxists out of your town halls,' it begged its readers. 'Vote to keep your rates from soaring out of control. Vote to keep Britain out of the Red.'[12]

On 7 May 1981 voters across England and Wales went to the polls. Given the government's atrocious public standing, everybody knew Labour would do well. When the results were counted, they had gained almost a thousand council seats nationwide, winning control of Greater Manchester, Merseyside, the West Midlands and West Yorkshire, as well as counties such as Derbyshire, Lancashire, Nottinghamshire and Staffordshire. Most attention, however, was focused on London. But to general surprise, there was no landslide; indeed, the Tories held on to many more seats than the polls had predicted. Perhaps Cutler's warnings had made a difference. Still, the final tally gave Labour fifty out of ninety-two seats, enough for a working majority. At County Hall, where McIntosh held his victory party, Michael Foot raised his glass to offer a toast. 'It's going to be fine,' Foot said reassuringly, 'because you, Andrew, are in charge, and you know the machine.'

Given Foot's recent record, McIntosh should probably have taken that as the cue to clear his office. Yet when he returned to County Hall the following morning, he had no inkling of what was coming. When journalists asked about rumours that Livingstone was planning a challenge, McIntosh said blithely that he was 'going to win', because the local elections showed that Londoners 'wanted a Labour administration of responsible and realistic people'. But then everything began to fall apart. McIntosh expected a quick vote at nine that morning, after which he would get down to business. But Livingstone persuaded the party executive to postpone it until later that afternoon. At 3 p.m. he held a left-wing caucus, where he and his friends agreed a slate for the various committee posts. Then, two hours later, came the showdown.

With McIntosh completely unprepared, the meeting took only a few minutes. First the councillors voted for the leader, and Livingstone won by ten votes. Then they turned to the committee chairmanships. Since McIntosh, now in a state of shock, had not even prepared a list, Livingstone's nominees swept the board. It was less a victory than a massacre: of the twenty-nine people who voted for Livingstone, twenty-four were rewarded with senior positions. But for the Labour right, it came as a total, crushing surprise. McIntosh left the room in tears. Later, when a GLC planner saw him with his wife in the car park, he was still crying. 'People always laugh when I tell them this,' said Livingstone, 'but I really felt sorry for Andrew.' Still, that was the game. He played to win.[13]

The sheer ruthlessness of Livingstone's coup made him a household name overnight. The *Sun* told its readers that victory for 'Red Ken' meant 'full-steam-ahead red-blooded Socialism for London'; the *Mail* called him a 'left-wing extremist'; the *Express* claimed he had had 'no proper job' for six years. But on the left all was jubilation. To his supporters, Livingstone was Tony Benn's vicegerent in London, laying the foundations for the revolution. And, for the first time, the new left had some real power.

That weekend they celebrated at a party in the Barbican flat of the hard-left ex-MP Audrey Wise, whose daughter Valerie was one of Livingstone's closest allies. There, Livingstone recalled, they heard the news that François Mitterrand had won the French presidential election on an unashamedly high-spending, high-taxing socialist platform. History was moving in their direction. 'As we talked excitedly about our plans for London', Livingstone wrote, 'I truly believed that the elections of Thatcher and Reagan would be just a temporary setback in the long march to build a better world.'[14]

The obvious thing to say about Ken Livingstone's arrival as leader of the GLC is that in some ways it was entirely predictable. These might have been troubled times for the Labour Party at Westminster, but they were days of intense excitement among grass-roots activists. Sales of left-wing books and socialist papers were booming, and across the country thousands of idealistic young men and women were devoting their evenings to local community associations, women's groups and peace committees. And once Margaret Thatcher took office, it was inevitable that at least some councils would swing to the left. Even before most people had heard of Ken Livingstone, the hard-left playwright Jim Allen was already working on a story about a group of Labour councillors in Gateshead, who refuse to impose the government's welfare cuts and rate rises, provoking a savage police crackdown. It eventually went out on BBC1 as a *Play for Today*, 'United Kingdom', in December 1981. By this point, the looming conflict between national and local government was becoming a familiar theme. 'Who would say', mused *The Times*'s critic, 'that it could not happen here?'[15]

For all Livingstone's notoriety, he was not the only young left-wing council leader. In May 1980 the West Midlands industrial town of Walsall had elected a hard-left Labour administration under Brian Powell, a former print worker. Powell's brand of socialism was very different from Livingstone's: he described himself as 'puritanical', and had little time for feminism, minority interests or middle-class graduates. His chief innovation was a drive to bring local government into the streets, with the council sending 160 officials out to thirty-four 'neighbourhood offices' – many of them Portakabins – equipped with new computer terminals containing details of every house owned by the council. According to Powell, this would banish the 'faceless bureaucracy' of the past and show working people that the council was working in their interests.[16]

Although Walsall's experiment anticipated later initiatives by other councils, it soon ran into trouble. Council officials were deluged with complaints, the repair and rent arrears bills shot up, and the other parties promised to shut the experiment down. And like Livingstone, Powell was his own worst enemy, provoking outrage by sacking four dinner ladies who had refused to join a union under the council-approved closed shop. In one of his more eye-catching proclamations, he announced that the council would only employ 'working class applicants' who supported 'radical change', because only people 'aware of the basic ideals on which socialism is based . . . can grasp the structural changes that are necessary here'.[17]

The local press were horrified, accusing him of trying to build a 'little Kremlin in the heart of England'. Powell was unrepentant. 'What we're trying to do is reverse the capitalist system,' he insisted, 'and it's been there for a sodding thousand years.' Unfortunately, the people of Walsall did not want to reverse the capitalist system. They just wanted the council to fix the potholes, paint their fences and send somebody round to mend the boiler. In May 1982, after just two years, Powell lost control of the council to a Conservative–Liberal coalition. The dismantling of capitalism would have to wait.[18]

The most obvious parallel with the GLC, though, came further north. Sheffield, wrote the *Guardian*'s Peter Jenkins in 1981, was the 'most pro-letarian of cities', a self-consciously working-class place with a smaller middle class than Birmingham, Manchester or Leeds. As a result, outsiders often found it remarkably traditional, even backward-looking. The Steel City's people were literally older than their counterparts elsewhere; no other major city in Britain had a lower birth rate or a higher proportion of pensioners. And if many of them preferred to look back rather than look around, it was hardly surprising. South Yorkshire's traditional steel and textile industries had been under pressure for years, and the recession took a devastating toll. In five years after 1979, the number of steel jobs fell by half, while unemployment surged towards 20 per cent. It was no wonder that the head of the council's employment department talked of feeling 'under attack, under siege'.[19]

Sheffield had always been a Labour stronghold. The local party was one of the city's most important institutions, inextricably entwined with its steel mills, Methodist churches, football clubs and trade unions. Labour had run the city council since 1933, with only a brief Conservative inter-lude in the late 1960s. As in London, however, the mood of the local Labour Party had changed. Previously dominated by older, more conserva-tive trade union stalwarts, it had moved sharply to the left, thanks to the emergence of a younger group spearheaded by the ambitious David Blun-kett. There, was, however, a difference between the new left in Sheffield and their London counterparts. While many of Livingstone's supporters were middle-class graduates, the key figures in Sheffield's Labour group invariably came from manual working-class backgrounds and were acutely conscious of their origins. And unlike some activists elsewhere, they were not ashamed of belonging to a long local tradition. As the party whip told the *Guardian*, Sheffield's Labour history gave them a 'continuity and experience' which few other councils could match.[20]

As in London, Sheffield's new left benefited from the leadership of an engaging front man. But Blunkett was very different from his southern counterpart. Born into a working-class Sheffield family in 1947, he had known tragedy from an early age. When he was 12, his father, a Gas Board foreman, fell into a vat of boiling water, leaving David's mother to bring him up on a widow's pension. Blind from birth because of a rare genetic disorder, he was sent to a specialist state boarding school near Shrewsbury, where the only career options were piano-tuning, lathe-turning and secretarial skills. Blunkett chose the third. He studied in his spare time to pass his O-levels, returned to Sheffield, took more evening classes to get three A-levels and finally won a place to study politics at the local university. These were the late 1960s, when Livingstone was discovering the joys of progressive politics. But Blunkett had little time for the fashionable causes of the day. His blindness and his background made him a man apart; as he later told *The Times*, he felt a 'distaste for the trivial concerns of his fellow students'.

Blunkett was always passionate, though, about the Labour Party. In 1970, aged just 22, he became the youngest councillor in Sheffield's history; ten years later, he became the youngest council leader in Britain. Even then it was obvious that he would play a major role in the Labour Party for years to come. 'He may be young', one colleague said, 'but David has thought longer and harder than many politicians 20 years older than himself.' Interviewers unanimously commented on his resilience, memory and work ethic, which had seen him defy misfortunes that would have destroyed a lesser man. His fellow councillors, reported *The Times*, were often 'infuriated by the hundreds of memos he dictates each week'. Yet even his critics were invariably 'charmed by his disarmingly sensible persuasion', and left his office having forgotten the 'complaint they had intended to make'.

In theory Blunkett was on the left. Like Livingstone, he supported the Bennite campaign for greater party democracy, wanted Britain to leave the Common Market and advocated workers' control in industry. Councils like Sheffield, he said, were 'beacons' of socialism, advertising an 'alternative vision of the world'. He hated having to sell council houses to

their tenants, and invested some of the council's money in local co-
operatives, insisting that they make 'socially useful products'. Like
Livingstone, he tried to run his own foreign policy, subsidizing anti-nuclear
plays, protests and vigils. He named one street Donetsk Way to honour
Sheffield's Soviet twin city, and even signed a 'peace treaty' with Donetsk.
And there were a couple of other gestures that would have seemed familiar
to observers of the GLC. The oak-panelled Lord Mayor's Parlour, for
example, was converted into a crèche. But children hoping to come away
with a packet of Rolos were in for a disappointment: Blunkett ripped out
the Rowntree's machines from the Town Hall, as punishment for the firm's
South African connections.[21]

The most emblematic of all Blunkett's policies, though, was his commitment to cheap bus fares. Since 1975 South Yorkshire's bus fares had
been frozen, despite inflation having twice gone above 20 per cent.* So
in 1981 a four-mile journey from Sheffield still cost only 9p. By contrast,
the same journey in Newcastle cost 25p, in Birmingham 30p and in Manchester or Glasgow 40p. This was obviously excellent news for the poor,
who depended on public transport, as well as pensioners, who travelled
for free. Indeed, South Yorkshire's buses carried more passengers, proportionately, than any other system in Britain, including London. But cheap
fares did not, in fact, come cheap. In 1974 the council subsidy had come
to £3.4 million; by 1981 it had reached a whopping £53 million, with local
ratepayers footing the bill. In Sheffield, domestic rates rose from 136p in
the pound in 1980 to 233p by 1982, while the commercial rate soared
from 154p in the pound to almost 252p.

Local businessmen naturally complained, while the Conservatives
claimed that the annual rate increases, sometimes as high as 45 per cent,
were deterring new firms from moving to the area. When Peter Jenkins
visited the local mills, people told him that Sheffield's high business rate
added £7 to the price of a ton of steel. But Blunkett insisted that this was
a genuinely 'alternative socialist strategy', giving ordinary people what
they wanted and getting businesses and the middle classes to pay for it.
The government accused him of overspending. But to stay within their
spending limits, Blunkett said, would mean cutting £20 million worth of
services. If the government cut Sheffield's grant, he would put the rates up
even higher. And if they tried to cap local rates, he would fight them all

---

* The buses were run by South Yorkshire County Council, rather than Sheffield City Council. But there was obviously an extremely close relationship between the two. The city council
strongly supported the subsidized fare scheme, and it was Sheffield's rates that paid for most
of it.

the way.* 'Our claim', he said defiantly, 'is that we have a right to act to protect the local community . . . Local government must be upheld.'[22]

Blunkett's defiance confirmed his image as one of the chief standard-bearers of the new left. Yet his politics were more complicated than they appeared. His view of socialism, one profile said, was 'more deeply rooted in Methodism than in Marx, in municipal realism rather than in vanguard militancy'. Unlike almost every other Labour councillor in Britain, he made no secret of his admiration for Margaret Thatcher, even though he abhorred her policies. Indeed, when he poured scorn on the notion that 'people should be told and given what is good for them', he might have been singing from her hymnbook. A former Methodist lay preacher, he had little interest in what he saw as chattering-class fads, describing femin-ism as a 'diversion' that would 'sap the energy of the class struggle'. Ken Livingstone claimed that, when Blunkett first heard about the GLC's plans for a women's committee, he was so shocked 'he almost fell backwards off his chair'. And in what modern academics clearly regard as an abomin-able stain on Sheffield's reputation, the city council's official publications did not acknowledge the existence of lesbianism until 1987.[23]

Blunkett and his allies were not, of course, without their critics. At the turn of the decade, the leader of the small Conservative group on the county council, the immensely right-wing Irvine Patnick, suggested that it should be renamed the 'Socialist Republic of South Yorkshire', and the label stuck. By 1981 two Labour councillors had started selling 'Socialist Republic' badges, with the proceeds going to local party funds. To be a 'Socialist Republic', said one Sheffield MP, was a 'term of praise', although 'we wouldn't like it to be interpreted to suggest South Yorkshire is a microcosm of some state in Eastern Europe'. Given the treatment dished out to Livingstone and the GLC, they were right to be wary. Yet the national press only rarely mentioned the Socialist Republic. And although the newspapers shook their heads at Sheffield's rate rises, Blunkett and his colleagues never attracted the abuse directed at their southern counter-parts. Even the *Express*, which called him a 'hard line Left-winger', admitted that Blunkett was 'a remarkable young man'. It would never have said that about Ken Livingstone.[24]

County Hall stands on the south bank of the River Thames, almost directly facing the Houses of Parliament. A six-storey monument to the

---

* Although Blunkett became an unofficial leader of the rebellion against rate-capping in 1984–5, he did back down eventually – an early sign that he was much more pragmatic than his reputation suggested.

grandeur of Edwardian Britain's imperial capital, this was the home of
the Greater London Council. Everything about it suggested size, importance, the intoxicating swagger of power: the 1,200 rooms, the 3,000
windows, the twelve miles of corridors, one of them stretching for a quarter of a mile. Here was a fitting headquarters for the largest local authority
in Europe, employing 35,000 staff to serve almost 8 million people. To
walk into the council chamber, with its 'imported oak, Portland stone and
Italian marble', wrote Livingstone, was to feel the weight of history. As
in most other councils, meetings started with a prayer by the chairman's
personal chaplain. The first thing Livingstone did was to abolish it, but
the outgoing Conservative chairman insisted on one last prayer. 'I have
been told to be brief,' the chaplain said, 'so I shall simply beseech Almighty
God to watch over those who have chosen to walk a crooked path.'[25]

For all its grandeur, though, the façade along the South Bank was not
so much the face of power as the mask of weakness. The GLC had been
set up in 1963 to give the capital an overarching metropolitan authority.
But its day-to-day responsibilities were less extensive than many people
realized. Most services, from libraries and cemeteries to street cleaning and
food safety, were provided by London's thirty-two borough councils. That
left the GLC handling main roads, traffic management, flood prevention,
the fire brigade and land drainage, hardly the most glamorous responsibilities in the political world. In effect, it was squeezed between the borough
councils, which jealously guarded their daily responsibilities, and Westminster, which insisted on taking major strategic decisions itself. Even in
the mid-1970s, some observers wondered whether there was any point to
the GLC at all. The government, said The Times, could easily save millions
by getting rid of it, 'at no cost to public convenience or competent administration' – and this six years before Livingstone took office.[26]

Livingstone's mandate was weaker than it looked. Despite Mrs Thatcher's travails, Labour had won less than 42 per cent of the vote, just 2 per
cent ahead of the Conservatives. By contrast, when the Conservatives
had won in 1977, the gap had been almost 20 per cent. Talk of 'Red
Wreckers' and higher rates had clearly alienated suburban voters, and
most analysts agreed that, if the SDP had been organized enough to mount
candidates of its own, Labour would not have had a hope. 'If London
again proves to represent the nation,' wrote the elections expert Ivor
Crewe, 'Labour is in serious trouble.' Yet Livingstone's supporters had no
intention of letting electoral reality stand in the way of building socialism.
'After the most vicious GLC election campaign of all time, Labour has
won a working majority on a radical socialist platform,' boasted London
Labour Briefing. The headline read simply: 'LONDON'S OURS!'[27]

At first Livingstone's radicalism was limited to a series of eye-catching gestures. He returned his limousine to the car pool, announced he would only use public transport and asked his staff not to call him 'Leader'. The word 'lead', he explained, 'isn't a term which we go along with on the left of the Labour Party'. On the top of County Hall, which some journalists nicknamed the 'People's Palace', he hung a banner, showing how many Londoners were currently unemployed. His only regret, he said, was that they could not afford the electronic version, which would have updated the figures every hour. He threw open County Hall to the People's March for Jobs, putting the demonstrators up at a cost of some £14,000. And in the most striking sign of change, he promoted a new generation to run the GLC's committees. The youngest, Paul Boateng, was only 29. Born to Ghanaian and Scottish parents, Boateng had spent much of his childhood in Accra and had worked as legal adviser to the Scrap Sus Campaign. Now he was in charge of the police committee.[28]

On Fleet Street, Livingstone's gestures confirmed his reputation as a bogeyman of Tony Benn proportions. Later, he complained that the press had set out to smear him, but there is no doubt that his hunger for publicity made matters worse. On just his second day in the job, he agreed to an interview with the *Evening Standard*'s Max Hastings. In an oddly tragicomic little scene, Hastings arrived at Livingstone's flat in Maida Vale to find the leader ironing his shirts. The resulting picture was not complimentary. Livingstone came over as a lonely, ascetic and almost fanatical man, who lived alone with 'a portable snooker table, a tank of salamanders, a wardrobe, a bed, a suitcase, a couple of chairs and a portable TV'. One of his GLC colleagues described him as 'utterly ambitious, mean, ruthless, a brilliant organiser of caucuses'. Another recalled that, after Livingstone had separated from his wife, he had told him: 'I don't need anybody. I can cope.' The new leader was 'not interested in ordinary human relations – simply in getting to the top of the greasy pole'. And these were his own comrades talking.[29]

The *Evening Standard*'s interview set the tone. For press and public alike, Livingstone's image was fixed: a strange, slightly sad man, alone with his snooker table, his salamanders and his socialism. 'Bedsitter Vision of the Socialists' Mr London,' read the headline on the *Telegraph*'s profile, which explained that at his '£20 a week room in Maida Vale he is just one of the tenants who have to share the lavatory. To the neighbours he is the bizarre character who spends his free time searching the local terrain for slugs and woodlice to feed his pet lizards.' Once again the article juxtaposed the depressing banality of Livingstone's bedsit, the snooker table again very prominent, with what it saw as the fanaticism of his 'Socialist dream for London'. It drew down the curtain 'close to midnight, when Livingstone comes up the steps at Maida Vale station and stops to buy a packet of chips on the way to his room and his seven cold-blooded friends'. It was talking about his salamanders, not his colleagues.[30]

Although none of this was exactly flattering, it was hardly disastrous. There are worse things than playing snooker or owning salamanders. *Private Eye* mocked him as 'Ken Leninspart', his life consisting of feeding newts and allocating funds to 'special bus shelters for disabled gays', but this was not so much brutal satire as a mild exaggeration of his daily routine. The *Sun*, meanwhile, got hold of some rumours that Livingstone had a taste for schoolgirls and had attended an orgy where, apparently, 'he was buggered by six men in succession'. Unfortunately, none of them turned out to be true. When the paper's editor Kelvin MacKenzie told his news team to dig up some dirt, they reported that Livingstone 'kept newts and lived extremely modestly'. 'Fucking newts!' MacKenzie exploded. 'All you can find is newts!'[31]

At this point, Livingstone was still a vaguely comic figure. But then, in early July, came the riots in Toxteth, Southall and Moss Side, and with them the first sign of his instinct for controversy. Addressing the Anti-Nazi League in Lambeth on 10 July, Livingstone told a boisterous crowd that the real culprits were Mrs Thatcher and her press allies, who had been 'pumping out a daily diet of filth and making racism respectable'. The next day, he added the Metropolitan Police commissioner to the list, telling LBC radio that Sir David McNee had 'views which I frankly consider to be racist'. This, he said, had 'set the scene for a worsening of police–black relations'.

On the hard left, these views were not remotely controversial. After the Brixton riots, Livingstone's friend Ted Knight, the leader of Lambeth Council, had declared that the police were an 'army of occupation' and urged them to 'withdraw' immediately to avoid future disturbances. A future Labour government, Knight said, must replace the Metropolitan Police with a new force, 'responsible and answerable to the working-class people'. *London Labour Briefing* went even further. 'The street fighting was excellent, but could have been (and hopefully will be in future) better organised,' an editorial remarked of the Brixton riots. 'Some of us feel there are occasions when, in defence of genuine legality and democracy, insurrectionary methods become necessary . . . The task, surely, is to break the Metropolitan Police as presently constituted.'[32]

Among the public at large, however, views like these were positively inflammatory. When Mrs Thatcher told the Commons that *London Labour Briefing*'s editorial would be 'repugnant to most people in Britain', she was stating the obvious. And when Livingstone blamed the riots on unemployment, bad housing and police racism, demanding that responsibility for the Metropolitan Police be handed over to the GLC, the tabloids joyfully whipped themselves into a lather of rage. The *Evening Standard* claimed Livingstone wanted to 'handcuff' the police; the *Sun* said he wanted to 'destroy' them; the *News of the World* accused him of acting as 'a cheer leader to trouble'. Here, said the *Mail*, was the 'Commissar of County Hall', the 'face of a dogmatic zealot' hidden behind the 'mask of reason'.[33]

But what really did for the Commissar's reputation was Northern Ireland. There is no reason to doubt that his position was absolutely sincere. Nobody interested only in playing to the gallery would have adopted such a toxically unpopular cause. But like his allies in hard-left London politics, such as the young Jeremy Corbyn and John McDonnell, Livingstone believed Northern Ireland was a simple question of right and wrong. The conflict, he thought, was fuelled by racism and colonial exploitation. The IRA were freedom fighters, the Unionists were the running dogs of imperialism and the best thing for everybody would be a united Ireland. And although Livingstone knew these views would horrify millions of voters, he was not going to suppress them for political self-protection. 'There wouldn't be one per cent of doubt in my mind about sacrificing the whole of British local government', he explained, 'if it meant we got out of Ireland.'[34]

To most people, however, anything that smacked of sympathy for the IRA was beyond the pale. So when, on 21 July, Livingstone welcomed Alice McElwee to County Hall, he should have known what was coming. Mrs McElwee's son Thomas was on the forty-fourth day of his hunger strike. He was serving a twenty-year stretch in the Maze, having planted an incendiary bomb in a clothes shop in Ballymena, County Antrim, in October 1976. When the bomb went off, the proprietor, 26-year-old Yvonne Dunlop, shouted a warning to her 8-year-old son, who managed to escape from a window. But Yvonne was burned to death, leaving three young children. So when, two days before what would have been her birthday, her family saw Livingstone shaking hands with her killer's mother, they were understandably outraged.

What was even worse was what he said. 'The H-block protest', Livingstone told the *Evening Standard*, 'is part of the struggle to bring about a free, united Ireland.' The hunger strikers, he added, were not criminals but 'fighters for the freedom of their country . . . I have been consistently in favour of withdrawal from Ireland and to get away from the idea that it is some sort of campaign against terrorism. It is in fact the last colonial war.' At a press conference he went further. Successive governments, he said, had pursued in Northern Ireland a 'campaign of repression the like of which has not existed anywhere else in the world'. Then, donning his Trotskyist spectacles, he looked forward. 'The eventual freedom and unity of Ireland for the whole working class', he insisted, would be a 'major blow against international capitalism and the rulers of our state'.[35]

For Livingstone's public image, the McElwee meeting was a catastrophe. The tabloids were merciless: the *Sun* declared that Livingstone had 'proved himself a menace to stability in public life'. Mrs Thatcher even told the Commons that his denunciation of British policy was 'the most disgraceful statement that I have ever read'. To make matters worse, the furore coincided with a leaked report that Livingstone had warned Labour politicians that the GLC would have to raise rates by a whopping 120 per cent to pay for his manifesto promises. He had been exposed, said the *Mail*, as a 'doctrinaire clown', whose administration was a 'grotesque portent of things to come; of what could happen to all of us if we let the New Left misrule Britain tomorrow as they are misruling London today'.[36]

This was merely the beginning. The day before the Royal Wedding, Livingstone welcomed eight members of the H-Blocks Armagh Committee, who staged a two-day fast on the steps of County Hall. Then, after a fortnight's holiday, he returned to the fray with a speech to the Harrow Gay Unity Group, assuring them that 'everyone is bisexual' and that 'almost everyone has the sexual potential for anything'. The papers could barely believe their luck. The *Sun* ran the memorable headline: 'Red Ken Speaks up for the Gays – I'll Get Them Jobs and Homes, He Says.' The *Mail*, meanwhile, consulted 'three leading psychologists' to discover why 'this weird creature' would say such outlandish things. One suggested that Livingstone, as an 'only son' of working parents, had 'suffered a lack of attention' and felt driven to act like a 'naughty boy'. 'The desperate need for attention is the hallmark of the hysteric,' explained Dr Dougal Mackay. 'Mr Livingstone is in the same category as a punk rocker who wears outlandish clothes.'*[37]

By this stage, almost any other politician, except perhaps Tony Benn, would have realized it was time to keep his head down. Even Livingstone's GLC colleagues begged him to stop talking. But he just could not stop himself. On 21 August the Unionist mayor of Ballymena arrived in London with Yvonne Dunlop's three sons. So began a media circus of almost mind-boggling ghastliness. Hearing that Livingstone planned to greet the

---

* Dr Mackay complained vociferously that the paper had put words in his mouth. He said he had been talking about a hypothetical character type, not a specific individual, and had never even heard of Livingstone until he read the article.

boys at Victoria station, the GLC's Tory whips intercepted them at Gat-wick Airport and took them for a boat trip down the Thames. Eventually the boys arrived at County Hall, where, bizarrely, Livingstone posed for pictures with his arms around them, like an affectionate uncle. The oldest boy, 13-year-old Denis, told Livingstone that the hunger strikers had a choice whether to live or die, a choice the IRA had denied his mother. But Livingstone was having none of it. When reporters invited him to say something about the IRA, he insisted that he was 'not going to condemn violence by only one section of the community'. Afterwards, the Tories scooped the boys back up and took them to Hamley's, before organizing a farewell whip-round. They went home with £5 each.[38]

Two days later, utterly unabashed, Livingstone was back in the news, this time after appearing on an LBC radio phone-in. Not content with predicting a military coup and demanding state control of the press, he insisted that Northern Ireland 'does not exist' and said it was 'nonsense' to call the IRA 'criminals and murderers'. A few days later, he surfaced on the British Forces' Broadcasting Service, with a message for 'everybody who's got arms and is carrying arms in Northern Ireland, whether they are in the British Army or the IRA . . . Put those arms down and go back to your home. I think there would be no greater move for peace than if the British Forces just packed up and went home.' Even the *Observer*, which broke the story, thought he was sailing perilously close to the wind, while some papers called for his prosecution under the Incitement to Dis-affection Act of 1934. 'Nothing seems beyond our Ken – except common sense, that is,' said the *Express*. 'Marriage, bisexuality, homosexuality . . . and of course his all-time favourite, Northern Ireland. There is hardly a subject on which he has not put both feet in his mouth.'[39]

It was against this background that, just six weeks later, Livingstone made his inflammatory remarks on the bombing at Chelsea Barracks. A more tactful, cautious politician would surely have judged that, under such horri-fying circumstances, it would be better to play down his private views. But that was not in Livingstone's nature. He had got this far without being tact-ful, and he was not going to change now. He also felt, not entirely wrongly, that his remarks had been deliberately exaggerated. 'I abhor all violence,' he explained in a letter to *The Times*. 'Murder on London's streets is shocking and it is unacceptable . . . The point I was trying to make was that to crush the IRA as if they were simply criminals or lunatics will not work. It is the policy that has been tried for generations and still the killing persists.' A 'political solution', he insisted was 'the only way to bring about lasting peace'.[40]

Many people would probably have agreed with some of this. But when it emerged that Livingstone's GLC colleague John McDonnell had called for talks with the IRA about 'peace in London', even many Labour councillors thought they had lost their moral compass. While most people were now 'hardened to the fact that the man who runs London can be by turns sinister, unpleasant or merely foolish', said the *Evening Standard*, this latest blunder was 'worse than folly. It is criminal.' The *Mail*, meanwhile, considered it 'the behaviour of a man who through Marxist dogma has become an alien in his own country, blind to the IRA's bloodiest crimes even when committed on his own doorstep. He is certainly not fit to rule Britain's capital city.' In the same paper, a cartoon showed a group of villainous-looking men in balaclavas, huddled in a cellar and writing a letter: 'Dear Mr Livingstone. With the price of nails being what it is, we wondered whether the GLC . . .'[41]

But the most blistering comment came in the *Sun*, its front page famously branding Livingstone the 'most odious man in Britain'. That was just the beginning:

For most papers, Ken Livingstone's remarks after the Chelsea Barracks bombing crossed a line. In the *Sun* (14 October 1981), Clive Collins was especially scathing.

In just a few months since he appeared on the national scene, he has quickly become a joke. But no one can laugh at him any longer. The joke has turned sour, sick and obscene. For Mr Livingstone steps forward as the defender and the apologist of the criminal, murderous activities of the IRA . . .

Among the Socialist members of the GLC there must be many who are as outraged and disgusted by Mr Ken Livingstone as the rest of us. While he continues as their leader he is making the name 'Socialist' stink in people's nostrils. They should kick him out. *And right this minute.*

Even for somebody with Livingstone's thirst for attention, the *Sun*'s attack hit home. Hate mail poured in, a common theme being that he should 'go back to Russia'. 'What a slimy hypocrite you are,' wrote one retired major from the South Coast. The police advised Livingstone to be vigilant, but the day after the *Sun*'s broadside he was on his way to a talk in the City of London when a man sprayed red paint in his face. A few days later, he was attacked in a pub in Hampstead by skinheads calling him a 'Commie bastard'.[42]

The Chelsea Barracks furore set the seal on a disastrous first six months for Livingstone and the GLC. One poll late that summer found that only 35 per cent of Londoners supported him, with 52 per cent opposed; another found that just one out of five voters thought he was doing a good job. But his stance on the IRA was only part of the story. After coming to power with such high hopes, he had achieved virtually nothing. Among a string of abortive pledges or abandoned promises, he and his Labour comrades had not yet managed to set up a Greater London Enterprise Board, had failed to stop the transfer of GLC council houses to the London boroughs and had failed to block the sale of houses to private individuals. They had even failed to cut the price of school meals.[43]

By far the biggest setback, though, was the debacle of Livingstone's attempt to copy David Blunkett's public transport policy. By 1981 South Yorkshire's experiment had won praise from left-wing activists across the country, and during the local elections every big-city Labour group had promised either to freeze or to cut fares. In the capital, some activists argued for the total elimination of Tube and bus fares, allowing poor Londoners to travel for free with ratepayers picking up the bill. But under pressure from the unions, who were worried about bus conductors' jobs, Livingstone decided that fares should be cut by a quarter and then frozen indefinitely. By the time he had settled into the leader's office, the inner London boroughs had persuaded him to raise the cut to 32 per cent, which was unveiled to the public under the slogan 'Fares Fair'. The problem, however, was that this would cost some £117 million, far more than originally planned. So under the government's new grant system, which heavily penalized councils for overspending, ratepayers faced a £228 million bill.[44]

Contrary to what is often thought, Fares Fair was exceedingly unpopular. In August 1981, one poll found that fully 77 per cent of Londoners were against it. But Livingstone pressed on, and on Sunday 4 October 1981 it came into effect. Overnight the cost of short bus journeys fell from 12p to 10p, while maximum bus fares fell from 70p to 40p. Underground fares, meanwhile, were cut across the board, with journeys costing 20p across one zone and 30p across two. The *Daily Express* claimed that the new fares had turned 'rush hour into crush hour', with staff besieged by queues for the new cheaper season tickets. But that was an exaggeration: after the first week, other papers reported that there had been little discernible change.[45]

That was not, however, much consolation to the outer London borough councils. Even though their residents were much less likely to use public transport, they had to pay the lion's share of the higher rates. To Labour activists, this was a textbook example of the redistribution of wealth. But to the Conservatives who ran, say, Bromley Council, it was an outrage. At one public meeting, the Bromley Council leader remembered, there was a mood of 'mass hysteria' at the thought of paying higher rates for cheaper fares. But then he and his colleagues spotted a loophole. In the small print of the Transport (London) Act of 1969 was the stipulation that the GLC must try to make the Tube break even. To Livingstone's disbelief, therefore, Bromley took the GLC to court.

The case wound its way through the lower courts, and on 10 November the Appeal Court found in Bromley's favour, with Lord Justice Oliver concluding that, under the law, the GLC was obliged to run London Transport on disciplined business lines. Livingstone promptly appealed to the House of Lords. But on 17 December the five Law Lords agreed that Fares Fair was illegal. For Lord Scarman, the GLC had 'abandoned business principles' and committed a 'breach of duty owed to the ratepayers'. For Lord Diplock, meanwhile, their decision to overspend and incur a massive government penalty was a breach of the 'fiduciary duty' they owed the people of London. Fares Fair was dead. On 12 January 1982 the GLC reluctantly voted to obey the law. Livingstone himself, entirely typically, voted against. 'I think Ken was opportunistic,' remarked his deputy, Illtyd Harrington, 'because he knew that the law would have to be obeyed, but he knew other people would see to it that it was done.' Afterwards, Harrington sarcastically asked what they should do now. 'We fucking carry on,' Livingstone said, and slammed his office door.[46]

There was a farcical coda to the Fares Fair imbroglio. Outraged by the Law Lords' judgement, Livingstone's closest allies launched a 'Can't Pay, Won't Pay' campaign, urging Londoners to hand over protest notes instead of the new, higher fares. But when the campaign kicked off at the end of March 1982, it was a complete flop. When the head of the GLC transport committee, Dave Wetzel, refused to pay the full fare for his bus journey to County Hall, the other passengers and the conductor joined forces in throwing him off the bus. Undeterred, Wetzel claimed that this had been a triumph for democracy, since 'when I got off all the passengers were talking to each other instead of just reading papers'. As victories go, this was surely very well disguised. Across the network, the vast majority of commuters totally ignored the boycott, with most stations reporting barely a dozen protesters. Of 10,000 people who boarded the Tube at Charing Cross, said the next day's *Guardian*, just four refused to pay.[47]

Had Livingstone been just another politician, the Fares Fair fiasco might have finished him off. Opinion polls consistently found that most Londoners disapproved of his record in office, regretted voting for him and would not vote for him again. At Westminster, few Labour MPs had a good word to say about him. Even he privately feared he had 'blown it'. Yet it speaks volumes about his resilience and self-belief that he treated the disaster of his first year as a chance to mount a spectacular comeback. In some ways he was a modern version of the irrepressible Denry Machin in Arnold Bennett's novel *The Card* (1911), who rises to become mayor of his local town through a mixture of tricks, gambles and stunts. Another councillor says of Denry that he is 'identified with the great cause of cheering us all up'. And whatever they thought of his politics, Livingstone often cheered people up. 'He is a card,' said a *Times* profile nearly two years into his tenure, comparing him to an 'infuriatingly bright schoolboy for whom nothing in the world has yet gone wrong'. Only Livingstone could have emerged from a tense first meeting with the Transport Secretary, Norman Fowler, to tell the press: 'He asked to see me again. I think he must want me for my body.'[48]

Above all, Livingstone was a superb television performer: relaxed, down-to-earth and self-deprecating, with a rare ability to talk to people in language they understood. The more people saw of him, the more they forgave him, and at the end of 1982 he finished second in the BBC's annual Man of the Year poll, beaten only by the Pope. By the following summer *The Times* thought him 'the best-known socialist politician in the country', although Tony Benn might have had something to say about that. Even people who loathed his politics found him hard to dislike. The Tory

MP Julian Critchley thought him the 'smiling, jolly face of fairly extreme socialism'; the ultra-reactionary Kenneth Williams, who met him at County Hall in May 1982, found him 'charming' and 'v. attractive'. And after a long chat on a train a month later, the journalist Hugo Young recorded that Livingstone was 'humorous, decent, open, extraordinarily detached, very committed . . . A good political analyst. Very adept and knowledgeable with electoral figures . . . I think he will be leader of the Labour Party before the end of the century.'[49]

With his unerring instinct for controversy, however, Livingstone was already beginning to make a mockery of Young's prediction. After the collapse of Fares Fair he needed a new direction, and he found it in his long-standing commitment to feminism, anti-racism and gay rights. 'I came into politics because I wish to change society. And that means changing the hearts and minds of people. You start from an unpopular position and you plug away consistently,' he told one biographer.

> I've no doubt at all that by the end of this century, if we continue to fight for it, we will be living in a Britain where there will be complete tolerance towards sexual preference . . . If the leadership of the party, as one of their standard positions, argue for women's rights, gay rights and a proper equal opportunities policy for blacks, we'll eventually change attitudes nationally.[50]

Livingstone was as good as his word. In June 1981 he set up the GLC's first ethnic minorities committee, with a budget of almost £3 million. He pledged to boycott goods from South Africa and instructed the GLC Staff Association to monitor how many women and black people were employed in each department. He even introduced a code of conduct to outlaw racial and sexual harassment. But his most eye-catching innovation came in February 1982, at the moment when his public standing seemed to have reached its lowest ebb. At a meeting on 17 February, he approved what the *Guardian* called a 'new wheeze', a 'Women's Committee which will monitor all council activities to check that they are looking at things from a woman's as well as a man's point of view'.[51]

To run it, Livingstone appointed the ultra-Bennite Valerie Wise, the youngest of his close associates. Even Livingstone admitted that 'with her Lancashire accent and huge glasses', Wise came across as 'too serious by half', though she later proved to have a remarkable appetite for photo opportunities. The tone was set on 11 May, when Wise kicked off the first meeting by asking to be called 'chair' rather than 'chairman', which even the *Guardian* thought outlandish. Because there were few women GLC councillors, she had to co-opt eight extra members, and at first somebody suggested that all eight should be black. That fell by the wayside ('token-ism', said Wise), but then somebody else suggested that all eight must be Labour members. That caused even greater argument, and was also dis-missed. Within weeks, however, they had set up seven working groups, covering the core issues of health, industry, planning, childcare, violence against women, black women and lesbians. At just £332,000, the budget was tiny by GLC standards. But the potential for publicity – which meant outrage – was enormous.[52]

What really exercised the press about Wise's committee was its enthu-siasm for doling out public money. Under the Local Government Acts, authorities were allowed to support community groups as they saw fit, and at Livingstone's prompting more than a dozen GLC committees seized the opportunity. Contrary to myth, the sums involved were pretty small: even at their peak in 1985, when the GLC handed out almost £80 million, this was no more than 2 per cent of the authority's total budget. And despite later controversies about the handouts to, say, Babies Against the Bomb, the Black Female Prisoners Scheme or the Lesbian Feminist Writers Conference Planning Group, most grants went to mainstream groups such as the British Judo Association, Save the Children or the Town and Coun-try Planning Association.

Yet even at a very early stage the tabloids' knives were out. In February 1982, under the decidedly non-right-on headline 'Red Ken Hands out Cash with Gay Abandon', the News of the World complained that the GLC had given £8,000 to Women Against Rape and £750 to Lesbian Line. The Mail warned that taxpayers' money was going to 'militant lesbians, babies for peace, Irish and black extremists, prostitutes' collectives, left-wing theatre groups and revolutionary "creators" of all kinds'. The Sun, mean-while, told its readers that the GLC had become a 'hand-out machine for the feckless and freaky'.[53]

Had Livingstone been merely an opportunist, he would never have pursued a strategy guaranteed to attract so much abuse. But his radical commitments were not merely for show. 'It is impossible to spend any time with Livingstone', wrote his biographer John Carvel, 'without being con-vinced that he does indeed boil with outrage at the record of British colonialism in Ireland, at the racism he sees around him in London, at the intolerance shown to gays and lesbians.' The problem, though, was not just that these causes were deeply unpopular with millions of voters. It was the way Livingstone pursued them, dramatic, divisive and confron-tational to the point of recklessness. Today his efforts on behalf of black and gay Londoners look ahead of their time. Yet even some of his admirers thought he preferred self-indulgent posturing to patient coalition-building.

598

WHO DARES WINS

Not only did he pander to his most strident supporters, he deliberately baited his critics by handing out public money to fringe groups. In essence he was a superannuated teenage rebel, forever kicking against the Establishment. The title of his autobiography, *You Can't Say That*, says it all.[54]

Nothing captured this better than his attitude to Northern Ireland. Almost any other Labour politician would have learned to downplay his personal convictions. But Livingstone just could not hold back. Even as the IRA bombed Oxford Street, Knightsbridge, Hyde Park and Regent's Park, he continued to parade his support for the republican cause. In December 1982 he became embroiled in a fresh storm after the GLC organized a letter inviting Sinn Fein's Gerry Adams and Danny Morrison to London for 'fraternal' talks about how they could secure 'British withdrawal and a united Ireland'. On the night the letter was made public, terrorists detonated a bomb at a packed disco in Ballykelly, County Londonderry, killing eleven off-duty soldiers and six civilians, three of them teenagers, as well as badly injuring thirty others. Immediately Livingstone came under pressure to cancel the invitation. One Conservative MP was so outraged that he got hold of debris from the explosion – a girl's white dancing shoe, a smashed disco light and the sleeve of the record playing when the bomb went off – and personally delivered them to Livingstone's office.[55]

Eventually the government let Livingstone off the hook by banning Adams and Morrison from entering mainland Britain under the Prevention of Terrorism Act. All the same, the publicity was terrible. Denis Healey described Livingstone's behaviour as 'grotesque'; the *Mirror*'s front page deplored 'An Insult to the Memory of IRA Victims'; the *Sun* called him simply 'the most hated man in Britain'. Even his admirers thought he had been criminally insensitive, while most commentators thought he had shown a total lack of moral perspective. Yet he remained unrepentant, writing an article for *The Times* denouncing the 'hysteria whipped up by the press'. And he did get his meeting eventually. In February 1983 he flew to Belfast as the guest of Sinn Fein. Five months later, he managed to return the favour, inviting Gerry Adams, who had since been elected as MP for Belfast West, to London. The visit's co-sponsor was his old friend Jeremy Corbyn.[56]

So the controversies went on. In February 1983 Livingstone reluctantly withdrew a proposed £53,000 grant to the Troops Out movement after an incandescent Michael Foot personally ordered him to scrap it. And a few months later, he returned to one of his favourite analogies, telling an Irish radio station that 'what Britain has done for the Irish nation, is, although it is spread over 800 years, worse than what Hitler did to the

Jews'. The only difference, he said, was that Hitler's activities had been 'compacted into a short period of time', which made them look worse.

The reaction at home was unbridled outrage. Until now, said the *Express*, Livingstone had been treated with the 'humorous contempt normally reserved for amiable eccentrics'. But these 'despicable' remarks put him 'beyond the pale'. Among senior Labour politicians, Roy Hattersley told the press that he found the Nazi analogy 'both absurd and offensive', while Peter Shore said the GLC leader had brought 'shame on the whole Labour Party'. But Livingstone never dreamed of apologizing. He had meant every word.[57]

# 25

# Attack of the Sloanes

*They tell us the British economy is declining. Well, if it is, the*
*British certainly know how to go down in style.*
    Japanese bank official, quoted in *The Times*, 30 July 1981

*It is hard to believe that only five years ago it was smart to look*
*poor. Frayed jeans, peasant patchworks and Third World hand*
*weaves have now been overwhelmed by a tidal wave of rich velvet,*
*ritzy brocade and grand glitter.*
    *It is now fashionable to look very, very rich.*
        Suzy Menkes, *The Times*, 10 November 1981

A few days after Ken Livingstone had taken control of the Greater London
Council he was invited to a wedding. On 29 July Prince Charles was due
to marry Lady Diana Spencer at St Paul's Cathedral, and the great and
the good would be out in all their finery. Livingstone did not hesitate: he
turned it down. He had 'better and more important things to do', said one
of his allies, than to attend the wedding of the heir apparent. But on Radio
Four, Livingstone tried to strike an emollient note. A fervent republican,
he claimed to respect the affection most people had for the Queen, but
had no desire to dress up in a 'funny suit'. 'No one elected us to go to
weddings,' he said. 'We were elected to run the buses.'

If he had stopped there, he might have got away with it. But Livingstone
being Livingstone, he could not leave it at that. 'I would like to see the
abolition of the monarchy,' he went on. 'Some of the characters who are
hangers-on and living off public expense are really quite revolting.' Who
could he possibly have in mind? 'What earthly use the country gets out
of Princess Anne, I really do not know. She comes over as a horribly arrogant person. And some of the other characters around there . . . no way
can you justify those being paid out of the public purse.' So he would be
spending the day at work, 'looking after the unemployed, the homeless,

the disadvantaged and the traffic' – this last a marvellously bathetic touch. 'A more churlish piece of manners', said the *Express*, 'you would be hard-pressed to find.'[1]

Ever since February, when Buckingham Palace had announced the engagement, public anticipation had been mounting. For years Prince Charles's marital future had been the subject of intense speculation, with gossip columnists linking him to a succession of European aristocrats and upper-class debutantes. But from the perspective of the press, Lady Diana was perfect. At only 19, pretty, shy and fresh-faced, she looked like a princess from a children's story. The daughter of the Queen's former equerry, Earl Spencer, she had grown up in aristocratic comfort but was not entirely cocooned from life's realities. Her parents had divorced when she was 7; she had twice failed her O-levels, worked as a teaching assistant in a Pimlico nursery school and shared a flat with three friends in Earl's Court. And for the first few months the newspapers presented her as a timid, blushing country girl, an 'English rose' to whom ordinary people could relate. 'She's a Shy, Nervous Girl with Very Pretty Eyes', the *Mirror* said, describing her as a 'thoroughly nice, civilised, non-snooty young girl', such as 'one often meets at smartish London parties'.[2]

As on every major royal occasion since Princess Anne's wedding in 1973, the newspapers were full of gloomy predictions that Diana's big day was going to be a flop. When reporters visited King's Lynn, near Sandringham, a few days before the wedding, they found that souvenir shops had slashed prices on their mugs, medallions and biscuit tins to get rid of their stock. As always, though, public interest surged in the last few days. The tipping point came on the Sunday before the wedding, when the Oxford Street Association threw 'the world's longest street party', attracting an estimated 200,000 people, with thousands of schoolchildren treated to ten tons of free food on trestle tables along the mile from Marble Arch to Tottenham Court Road. The 'sight of black children dancing in rings with policemen, policewomen and police cadets', said the *Guardian*, was a reminder that the recent riots did not reflect the entire picture of life in the capital.

By Monday 27th, London was so crowded that the pavements in some areas were impassable. Keen monarchists, armed with flasks and sleeping bags, were already staking their claim to prime spots along the route to St Paul's. On Ludgate Hill, hundreds had turned their spots into 'personal sanctuaries guarded by elbows, Union Jacks and *bonhomie*'. One 'large lady squeezed into a frail aluminium chair' said this was the first time she had slept in the street since the wedding of the Queen and Prince Philip, more than three decades earlier. 'People were very friendly and they felt that it all mattered,' she said. 'I am glad it still seems to be the same now.'

The *Mirror* interviewed a mother and daughter from Guernsey, who had arrived three days early specifically to get a good spot. 'I was never very interested before but since Lady Diana has come on the scene the Royal Family have sort of come alive for me,' said 18-year-old Rosemary Harrison. 'Lady Diana seems so natural and young, you can identify with her in a way. You feel you could go up and say something quite normal to her.' But her mother, 54-year-old Avril, had always been a fan of the Royal Family. 'And I think everyone likes a wedding,' she said. 'There's so much misery going on with all the riots and unemployment. This is just what we needed to cheer us up.'[3]

By Tuesday, it was obvious that the big day was not going to be a flop after all. The Poet Laureate, Sir John Betjeman, published a remarkable wedding ode:

> I'm glad that you are marrying at home
> Below Sir Christopher's embracing dome . . .
> Blackbirds in City churchyards hail the dawn,
> Charles and Diana, on your wedding morn.

A friend explained that Betjeman was 'not very well'. But his poem was positively tasteful compared with the interview the happy couple gave to the BBC and ITN on Tuesday evening. Watching Charles and Diana sitting there, so stiff and awkward, a sceptic could have been forgiven for assuming that they had only just met. Diana said she was 'looking forward to being a good wife' and praised her fiancé as a 'tower of strength'. Charles, though, seemed much more interested in the music: 'I have always longed to have a musical wedding . . . I shall, I think, spend half of the time in tears.'

But few people were in the mood for scepticism. That night, in front of an estimated half a million people in Hyde Park, Charles lit a colossal celebratory beacon, the first in a chain of 101 bonfires reaching all the way to Balmoral. That was the cue for what one paper called the 'most elaborate firework display of the century', costing some £65,000 and funded by television companies from Australia to Brazil. To gasps from the crowd, it culminated with a giant Catherine-wheel sun, blazing with the monograms of Charles and Diana and the message VIVAT. The show had apparently been modelled on the spectacle in 1749 that marked the end of the War of Austrian Succession. On that occasion, one spectator died after falling out of a tree, while another fell into a pond and drowned. This time there were loud complaints about 'inadequate exits and a lack of signposts', while dozens of people injured themselves trying to climb over the fences. Still, nobody died, so that was something.[4]

The wedding day dawned warm and bright. 'Happy Britain Greets Our New Princess', gushed the *Express*'s wraparound cover. 'DIANA, THIS IS YOUR DAY', read the front-page headline. *The Times*, too, was, in its own way, thoroughly overexcited. 'The marriage of princes has always been the stuff of fairy tales and politics,' said an editorial, hoping that the day's festivities, 'symbolic of the nation's unity', would lift 'the spirits of a people depressed by persistent economic malfunctioning' and by the 'shocking and mysterious outbreaks of street violence this summer'. Yet the paper found space for a contrary view from the travel writer Jan Morris. 'I would like to put on record in *The Times* of July 29, 1981,' she wrote, 'one citizen's sense of revulsion and foreboding at the ostentation, the extravagance and the sycophancy surrounding today's wedding of the heir to the British throne.'[5]

Morris was not, of course, alone in her distaste for the pageantry of the day. Tony Benn watched the proceedings on television, steadfastly ignoring the reporters banging on his door. 'The image presented to the rest of the world', he recorded, 'was of a Britain about as socially advanced as France before the French revolution! . . . It was feudal propaganda, turning citizens into subjects.' As promised, Ken Livingstone spent the day working at a deserted County Hall, where he advised the press that there was 'always the possibility of the right-wing military element using royalty to justify a coup'. Meanwhile, a group of more than a hundred left-wing activists, among them such dangerous Bolsheviks as the young Peter Mandelson and Harriet Harman, took a cross-Channel ferry to Boulogne, where the local mayor fed them on cheap wine and steak frites. To the amusement of the accompanying journalist Frank Johnson, many of them spent the crossing attacking one another as sell-outs, a particular target being the organizer, the Labour MEP Richard Balfe, apparently 'an opportunist, a careerist and a creep'. As so often, Johnson thought, 'one of the most refreshing things about Labour activists who believe in the brotherhood of the human race is that they seldom speak well of any particular member of it'.

But most of the day's anti-royalist activities proved lamentably unsuccessful. The dampest squib of all came in Clay Cross, Derbyshire, which had been regarded as a socialist hotbed since the early 1970s, when local councillors had defied the law and refused to increase council-house rents. The council leader, Labour's Cliff Fox, had promised to organize a Republic Day, explaining that the House of Windsor was a 'bloody parasite on the backs of the working class'. Amid an intense backlash, one man suggested that Councillor Fox should be 'hauled to the top of his Red Flag pole to show that only a minority of local people were mad'. And when a reporter from the *Guardian* pitched up, he found plenty of patriotic bunting, no evidence of republican sentiment and Councillor Fox missing, presumed on holiday in Blackpool. At the Red Lion, the *Guardian*'s envoy asked what the people of Clay Cross really thought of the Royal Wedding. The landlord pointed at the hundreds of Union Jacks hanging from the ceiling and the scores of customers in red, white and blue outfits. 'Just look around you,' he said.[6]

The epicentre of the national celebrations was, of course, the capital. With fears of the IRA running high, armed police had been guarding St Paul's for days, while the procession route was lined with policemen every four steps and soldiers every six steps. But by mid-morning, when the Queen, Prince Philip and Prince Charles left Buckingham Palace for the City, the patriotic excitement had banished any anxieties. The crowds were colossal: at least a million strong, some observers said, though nobody knew for sure. As early as eight in the morning, they had been so thick from Trafalgar Square to the Mall that 'it was impossible to move', yet the mood was 'a riot of colour, good humour and fun'. 'Every square inch of pavement, balcony, step, wall, tree and even telephone kiosk roof was occupied,' reported the *Guardian*. Yet most people loved it. 'I'm hoarse with singing, dancing, laughing and eating,' a Yorkshirewoman from Thirsk told *The Times*. 'If I had known it would be as good as this,' agreed her sister, 'I would sit on a pavement every time I went on holiday.'[7]

Excitement at the wedding was not confined to central London. Although there were fewer street parties than at the Silver Jubilee in 1977, the likely explanation is that, four years on, people were less inclined to see it as a once-in-a generation collective event, and preferred to watch it on television. Yet almost every village organized some sort of celebration. In Tynemouth, the council staged a 'harbour spectacular, complete with commandos storming the cliffs'. In Harrogate, the Great Yorkshire Showground hosted a medieval joust, motorbike stunts and a firework display. At Caernarvon Castle, hundreds gathered to watch the 'largest portable colour television screen in the world'. In Romsey, Hampshire, where the couple spent their first night of married life, some 30,000 people turned out to cheer their black Rolls-Royce, among them a landlord who had decorated his pub with colossal eight-foot portraits of Charles and Diana, and a butcher who 'modelled wedding rosettes from breast of lamb, garnished with the initials C and D in liver'.* And in battle-scarred Brixton,

---

* Why Romsey? It was the location of the late Louis Mountbatten's country house Broadlands. Charles's parents had spent their honeymoon there, and he was keen to do the same.

a Rastafarian record-shop owner organized a street party on Railton Road, with hundreds of people dancing to reggae music. People in Brixton were fond of Prince Charles, he said, because he had visited Lewisham earlier that year to open a social club. 'People like him being married to Lady Diana. That is why we are holding a peace dance so that we can get the community back together and generate some spirit.'[8]

The television audience was simply phenomenal. More than 28 million people watched the coverage in Britain, as well as an estimated 750 million worldwide. Almost all of Mass Observation's correspondents were among them. In Lambeth, Margaret Bradshaw put on a 'red, white and blue jumper' and settled down to watch with her husband and elderly mother, while friends and neighbours popped in and out all day. 'Fantastic,' she wrote. 'Proud to be British . . . Something cheerful in the gloom of redundancy, youth unemployment and riots.' In Chelmsford, Jean Carr and her family spent the day in front of the television. 'It was a lovely and joyful day,' she wrote, 'one that will be always remembered . . . Lots of people were glad of the wedding and it took their minds for a little while of the ressesion [sic].'[9]

In Darlington, Susan Gray dressed her 4-year-old daughter in a red, white and blue pinafore before heading over to her own father's to watch the show. Not only had Susan prepared a wedding scrapbook for her daughter, she had also bought her a special wedding mug, to be brought out as a surprise with her 'wedding day elevenses'. The whole family enjoyed the day, even Susan's adult brother, who originally claimed he would rather spend the time with his model aircraft. Her father, husband and brother were 'really taken' with Diana's dress, and agreed that she was 'bringing prettiness back into clothes'. For her part, Susan noted that although Darlington was a Labour stronghold there was no talk locally of 'flying the red flag or having anti-wedding events'. Her husband reported that even the 'most staunchly Socialist of his immediate colleagues had watched the whole thing on television and said that "it was all worth it"'.[10]

Down in Devon, Mary Richards watched the wedding with her husband and daughters. Since it was a special occasion, she had splashed out on a bottle of wine, something usually reserved for Christmas. 'We girls are all very fond of Charles,' she wrote:

> We are happy to see him married to such a lovely girl. Wished we could have been in London . . . We all helped ourselves to food watching the telly all the time, we didn't miss anything. (The music made our hair stand on end.) We opened the wine and toasted the royal couple . . . Wished we could have been there cheering with the crowds.

That evening, they walked the one and a half miles into Newton Abbot ('buses are too pricy') to see the council's official pageant. The programme for this event was close to parody: while a concert by the Royal Marines was fair enough, some of the other events – a 'display of movement to music' by the Kingsteignton Ladies Keep Fit Group, a 'Motor Cycle Gymkhana' or an 'Exhibition of Fire Eating by Mr W. E. J. Lane (weather permitting)' – seemed like something from *Private Eye*. But Mary adored 'every minute of it. Thousands of people in town all friendly, like Christmas . . . It was a wonderful day. A day to remember.'

Afterwards, Mary felt moved to record some thoughts about the day and what it meant. She began with her friends and family:

> *Trade union leader we met.* It was very nice but! One of Diana's presents cost twice as much as the house your Debbie is buying on a mortgage.
>
> *Daughter aged 20.* I would rather see them spend our money like this than on bombs and missiles . . .
>
> *Daughter aged 19.* I think I am a royalist? Yes, I know I am. The Americans must be green with envy, they will have their majorettes out tomorrow.
>
> *My husband* watched TV all day, more than I had time to, and his comment was 'What a load of rubbish!' He started watching the wedding an hour before we could. We did not believe what he said he had obviously enjoyed every minute of it.
>
> *8 year old daughter.* I shall marry a prince when I grow up. I am going to be posh!
>
> *My comment.* A great day – Wonderful! Going to watch it all over again Sunday evening.

The wedding, Mary explained, was 'a good excuse for some fun and games' and 'an escape from the depressing times we are going through'. She did not begrudge the cost of the House of Windsor; if Britain became a republic, 'it would be spent on bombs'. As for the principle of the monarchy, she was all for it:

> Royalty is like an extended family to many people. People know and can relate to members of the Royal Family, they have problems just like us and celebrations that we can join in.
>
> Working people I know did not find it a bore. We escaped for a day and joined the Royal Family in their happiness. We worried with the Queen hoping no one would be killed or injured by some mad fool.
>
> Everything went well we enjoyed the few mistakes our Royalty made, it was just like our very own big family day.

We don't want a President or a Dictator or anything like that. We love
our Royal Family and [are] looking forward to the next big happy event in
their lives.

Over the page, there was a poignant little addition. 'Royalty on the whole
set high standards of morals and are an example of old fashioned family
life,' she wrote. 'Nearly everyone I know think the Royals are great and
often talk about them like they talk about their own families.' Poor Mary
was in for some disappointments in the years ahead.[11]

Of course not everybody was carried away. The ever-jolly Kenneth
Williams thought the dress 'badly designed', the music 'rotten' and the
'speakers of prayers & addresses all very bad indeed'. Yet that other great
diarist of the age, Adrian Mole, had a thoroughly good time. 'How proud
I am to be English!' he wrote. 'Foreigners must be as sick as pigs! We truly
lead the world when it comes to pageantry! I must admit to having tears
in my eyes when I saw all the cockneys who had stood since dawn, cheering heartily all the rich, well-dressed, famous people going by in carriages
and Rolls-Royces.' Disappointingly, Adrian missed the exchange of rings
because his grandmother had started crying and he had gone to fetch some
toilet roll. But they had a wonderful street party afterwards, complete
with 'jam tarts, sausage rolls and sausages on sticks', while a Des O'Connor
album played on the stereo. At the end, 'Mr Singh made a speech about
how great it was to be British. Everyone cheered and sang "Land of Hope
and Glory". But only Mr Singh knew all the words.'[12]

What did it all mean? Among most people's memories of the day were
the glamour of Diana's dress, the fact that both Charles and Diana stumbled while reciting their vows, and of course the kiss on the palace balcony.
Many also remembered the words of the Archbishop of Canterbury, Dr
Robert Runcie, who called the wedding 'the stuff of which fairy tales were
made'. In fact, he was pointing out that while fairy tales typically end with
a wedding, a real wedding is the beginning of an adventure, not an end.
Unfortunately, most people heard only the words 'fairy tale', which were
to be cruelly replayed for years to come.

Yet amid the pageantry, few commentators forgot the terrible headlines
of the last few months. 'In a grey world, for a troubled nation smarting
from a crown of social and political thorns,' said the front page of *The
Times*, 'it was a day of unbridled romance, colour and celebration, shared
with half the globe.' The royal historian Robert Lacey was less cheerful.
'We are travelling a hard road this summer,' he wrote in the *Express*. 'The
ruined streets of Toxteth, Southall and Northern Ireland make a bleak
backdrop to the carriages, fine clothes and flowers.' But 'if the shattered

shop windows of Toxteth remind us of humanity's greed, selfishness and imperfection, this marriage of two young people reminds us of the best, the freshest, the most idealistic of human impulses.'[13]

Even the ultra-conservative George Gale did not forget the woes of recent months. Wednesday, he said, had belonged to the 'ordinary people', not the rioters, strikers and law-breakers:

> They were saying, as they sang and cheered and laughed and waved their flags, that they did not hate their police, that they admired their soldiers, that marching military bands could constrict their throats and wet their eyes, that they loved their country.
>
> They were saying that they were the majority and that they did not riot in the streets or vandalise housing estates or loot shops or mug old women or fight on football terraces or maraud the country in packs of motorcycles.
>
> They brought along their children; no one would be hurt; there would be no need to board up shop fronts; there would be no call for riot shields, CS gas canisters, flaying truncheons.

Even Gale admitted that 'a royal wedding does not improve decaying city centres. It does not wipe out racial hostilities. It does not make the deprived and disaffected suddenly love the forces of law and order.' But it proved, he thought, that 'there is more to Britain than riots in Brixton and Toxteth, that in city centres there can be dancing as well as rioting, that the police are friends and not enemies, that the country can relax and enjoy itself, that patriotism and tolerance are still alive – and both doing well.'

All this was predictable enough. But what was a bit less predictable, and made for a contrast with the Silver Jubilee in 1977, was the defiant, supercharged patriotism of some of the editorials. It was as if every bleak headline about unemployment and violence had made it all the more urgent to broadcast Britain's virtues from the rooftops, as if every step down the ladder had made it all the more important to boast about how high Britain stood. 'London may no longer be the most important of cities,' said the *Express*, 'but it is still the capital of pageantry and yesterday it was the focus of all attention.' The *Mirror* offered a similar blend of self-pity and self-importance. 'Our politicians are wrong almost as often as our weathermen,' it admitted. 'We build cars with more faults than a McEnroe line judge. Motorways with more cracks than a stand-up comic. Our cricketers need wider bats. Our soccer players wider goalmouths to aim at. Our golfers are bunkered.' But 'at one thing we CAN still beat the rest. We know how to throw a wedding. The pageantry, splendour, timing and organisation of Wednesday's great show was the envy of the world.'

Unfortunately, the paper went on, the forecast for the next few years was 'gloom and doom . . . on all fronts'. So all true patriots should hope for another Royal Wedding. 'Come on, Prince Andrew! Your country needs you!' It had clearly not occurred to the *Mirror* that fate might provide an even more effective way of stoking patriotic sentiment than a wedding. But in July 1981 nobody was expecting a war.[14]

The excitement of the Royal Wedding took a long time to fade. Afterwards, hundreds of thousands of letters poured into Buckingham Palace, while stores were deluged with orders for copies of Diana's dress. A month later, the BBC's official *Album of the Royal Wedding* sold more than 130,000 copies to top the charts for two weeks, while the video recording raced straight to the top of the video charts. And when, on 5 November, the palace confirmed that Diana was expecting a baby, the newspapers were beside themselves. 'The Happiest News of the Year', said the *Mirror*. 'What Wonderful News!' said the *Express*. 'Naturally,' said the prospective father, 'my wife is overjoyed.'[15]

There had, of course, always been enormous interest in the Royal Family. Even so, the enthusiasm for Charles and Diana went far beyond the fascination with Princess Margaret or Princess Anne. One explanation is that the appetite for patriotic escapism was simply much greater in the summer of 1981, partly because of the shock of the recession and the riots, but also because, after years of being lectured about how low their morale had sunk, the British people were desperate to feel good about themselves. But there was obviously another element, captured in that *Daily Express* headline: 'DIANA, THIS IS YOUR DAY.' The X-factor was Diana herself.[16]

Looking back, it is easy to spot the signs of trouble ahead. At the age of 32, Charles had had numerous aristocratic girlfriends, among them the future Camilla Parker-Bowles. In essence, he only married Diana, who was almost thirteen years his junior, because the pressure was mounting and she seemed reasonably suitable. Few people close to the couple were under any illusions, except perhaps the girlish Diana. Even in their famously excruciating interview to publicize their engagement, they sat at opposite ends of a sofa and seemed at best politely affectionate. When the interviewer asked if they were in love, Diana murmured softly, 'Of course.' But Charles, in a moment of overwhelming awfulness, gave a thin smile, as if the idea were faintly ridiculous, and said: 'Whatever "in love" means.' Diana laughed – at the time.[17]

In other circumstances, this might not have been an insuperable problem. But no royal couple in modern times had been under such pressure from the media. At the turn of the 1980s, Fleet Street was in the throes of change, with the *Sun*, the *Mirror* and the new *Daily Star* locked in fierce competition to woo working-class readers. Tellingly, it was the ultra-patriotic, anti-deferential *Sun*, on 8 September 1980, that first revealed Diana's relationship with the Prince, using a photograph of the two at a polo match. Within days reporters had descended on her London kinder-garten, cynically photographing her with the sun directly behind her, so that her legs would be visible through her thin skirt. The next day, the *Mirror* ran a front-page comment on 'Lady Diana's slip', advising her to wear a petticoat if she wanted to avoid such embarrassment again.[18]

Right from the beginning, therefore, the 19-year-old Diana was the equivalent of a hunted animal. Journalists lurked outside her west London flat at all hours, sometimes literally chasing her flatmates down the street. One intrepid reporter tried to break into the kindergarten through a lav-atory window, while the *Sunday Mirror* persuaded the Spencers' former butler to sell a story about her fondness for teenage pranks. When the same paper claimed that Diana had enjoyed a nocturnal assignation with Prince Charles on the Royal Train, Buckingham Palace threatened to sue. Her mother wrote to *The Times* demanding to know whether editors thought it 'necessary or fair to harass my daughter daily, from dawn until well after dusk', while some forty-five MPs signed an early day motion deploring the press's misbehaviour.[19]

It was no wonder, then, that Diana struggled to cope. When the engage-ment was announced in February, she was moved into Clarence House, supposedly to protect her from the press. But this only fuelled her sense of being a prisoner. And by July her mood had visibly changed. At a polo match in Hampshire, the Saturday before the big day, she fled in tears from crowds of reporters. The next day, watching Charles play polo again at Windsor, she looked pale and miserable. She was 'very tired and very nervous', a palace aide explained. But the papers agreed that she had lost a worrying amount of weight: so much, in fact, that her dress designers had to make almost daily alterations. 'Darling Di, You're Lovely', declared the front page of the *Sun*, the day before her wedding, 'But Promise Us You Won't Lose One More Pound.' Later, after her marriage collapsed, the newspapers blamed Prince Charles, and there were certainly millions of easier families to marry into than the Windsors. But how many brides could have tolerated such headlines without throwing themselves off a cliff?[20]

The paradox is that the same papers that hounded Diana about her weight also elevated her into a symbol of Britishness itself. By nightfall on 29 July her image was already evolving from the blushing English rose to the coolly poised embodiment of elegance and glamour. She was a star. But she was a particular kind of star, the epitome of a type. 'The Princess of Wales', declared one bestselling book, 'is the 1980s Supersloane. When Diana Spencer began to appear in newspapers in the summer of 1980, the Sloane Ranger style started its gallop down the high streets, What the papers called the "Lady Di look" . . . was actually pure SR – a walking lesson in Mark II Sloane style at its best.'[21]

So said *The Official Sloane Ranger Handbook* (1982), one of the strangest and most revealing publishing phenomena of the age. Although it is always associated with Princess Diana, the Sloane Ranger nickname had been invented in 1975 by *Harpers & Queen*'s features editor Ann Barr and the marketing consultant Peter York. They used it to describe the kind of upper-class, slightly dim-witted girls who had grown up in farms and manor houses, had been to boarding schools and now shared flats around Chelsea's Sloane Square. It soon caught on, and by the turn of the decade the label regularly appeared in the appointments pages of *The Times*. 'A really "cushy number" . . . would suit young, married Sloane Ranger,' explained one advertisement for a secretary to a property firm, though it paid less than the next advert, which called for a 'Dishy Secretary with Brain'. 'SLOANE RANGER: Much photographed ad agency reception requires a thinking receptionist/telephonist who will add to, rather than detract from, the picture,' read another advert. 'SLOANE RANGER,' began a third advert. 'Young Secretary needed by a highly prestigious firm of Estate Agents. Beautiful offices: good secretarial skills and a public school education essential.'[22]

For Barr and York, the advent of Princess Diana was the equivalent of a genie throwing open the doors of a bank vault and inviting them to help themselves. York, in particular, was *everywhere* in the early 1980s, as he would have put it. He was always popping up to offer a few heavily italicized insights into everything from Bryan Ferry's taste in antique furniture to the alleged craze for 'knickerbockers for men' – which like many of York's discoveries, never quite made it to Stoke-on-Trent. But nobody would have listened to him if he had not had acute things to say. And even decades on, much of the *Official Sloane Ranger Handbook* still rings true. The name 'Diana' might have fallen from grace, but there are still plenty of Charlottes, Georginas, Henrys and Archies. The heirs of the Sloane Rangers still share their fondness for 'BMWs, powerboats and new garden machinery'. And Barr and York even spotted the trend for upper-class actors, noting that 'public-school boys are working like navvies to people all the television dramas of high life'. Crucially, they recognized that what really made the Sloanes tick was not their obsession with horses or even their enthusiasm for Range Rovers, but their ruthless commitment to their own privilege. On the back cover, a little first-place rosette perfectly captures the Sloane ethos. The words around the edge read: 'Who Sloanes Wins'.[23]

To some extent the Sloane Rangers had always been there. But York was right to spot a shift in the cultural temperature, which he called 'Reactionary Chic'. In effect, the Sloanes had become louder, more confident and more visible, while their style and values had begun to filter into the mainstream. 'Over the last six or seven years', he wrote in 1984, 'there's been this box opened, and unbelievably, out have come the most incredible sentiments – now hold on – the most insensitive language, the most extraordinary symbols of . . . what? Forward into the past, backward into the future.'

For York, Reactionary Chic was an inevitable backlash against the self-consciously right-on 'social-worker-speak' of the late 1960s and early 1970s. It was a new 'aggression and divisiveness: an instinct, one way or another, against the melting-pot, against the style of pluralism which by then was the everyday reality of Britain'. Partly it was born of frustration with the downbeat, defeatist political culture of the Heath, Wilson and Callaghan years. But there was also an element of overt anti-egalitarianism, as well as an impatience with the moralizing, apologetic cultural tone after Suez and Vietnam.

When, only a few months after becoming Conservative leader, Mrs Thatcher had issued a full-blooded attack on egalitarianism, emphasizing 'the right to be unequal' and promising to let 'our children grow tall and some taller than others if they have the ability', many commentators had been shocked. But even in 1975, York thought, the cultural mood had been turning in her favour. 'It was the end of guilt,' he wrote. 'Money style, *le style Ritz*, looked attractive when there seemed to be less around. From the mid-seventies a Grand Hotel or country house was the backdrop for every other fashion shot.' And by the turn of the 1980s Reactionary Chic, 'an imaginary upper-class style', had reached its 'fullest flowering . . . Never had there been so much swirling of taffeta, so much planning of balls, such a cottage industry in gossip columns, such eagerness to get into what the columns still called . . . stately homes.' Hence the Orchestral Manoeuvres in the Dark video at Blenheim and Stowe; hence Duran Duran on their yacht; hence all those interviews with Gary Kemp, not feeling 'guilty because I've made enough money to own my own home'.[24]

Tempting as it might be to dismiss all this as marketing waffle, there was undoubtedly something to it. In February 1981 the *Sunday Times Colour Magazine* sent Ian Jack to Oxford for an article about 'the return of the bright young things'. This was not Jack's natural territory. He had grown up in working-class Fife, while the *Sunday Times* had a reputation for encouraging grammar-school-educated meritocrats. But the vaguely egalitarian values he took for granted left him 'completely unprepared for the animal spirits of the students I met at Oxford', young people who 'talked in a way I'd never heard them talk before'.

To Jack's astonishment, the young men and women he met in Oxford betrayed no hint of guilt about their privileged backgrounds. He began with a modern languages student, Paul Golding, the son of a businessman in the Canary Islands, who wore glittering make-up and dreamed of becoming an interior designer. Golding explained that he was 'much more sophisticated than the average English child'. He and his friends were not ashamed of having 'a fun time . . . I suppose if I looked on it from the outside I'd loathe it, but the fact is that most of these people are very talented, very nice and very beautiful.' Golding was talking about people like Nigel Lawson's daughter Nigella, Christopher Soames's son Rupert and the critic Milton Shulman's daughter Nicola. 'They form clubs and elect themselves to office,' wrote Jack. 'They are photographed for *Tatler* magazine. Friendships formed at Eton or Winchester (Harrow at a pinch) are their basis; female qualification for membership is usually wealth, wit and beauty. The women enjoy dressing-up. The men enjoy getting drunk: "hog-whimpering drunk" in the words of Rupert Soames.'

Some of this, of course, was just posturing. Some of it was typical youthful high jinks, only with 'Muscadet, Côtes du Rhône, Burgundy, Sauternes, port and "limitless" champagne' in place of the beer ordinary students might have drunk. But *Tatler*'s young editor Tina Brown, who had graduated from Oxford a few years earlier and had devoted gallons of newsprint to the emergence of Diana, thought it reflected a deeper trend. 'What has changed in Oxford', she explained, 'is that it's fashionable again to be rich and smart . . . In the Sixties and Seventies the rich and smart went on existing but were rather more on the defensive.' Rupert Soames, the most affable of Jack's interviewees, said much the same. 'You see, students went through the Sixties thinking the world was organised in a bad way and that they could do something about it,' he said. 'Absolutely wrongly, as it turned out. Now people take themselves less seriously, which is very, very attractive.' For his part, Soames's ambition was 'to be rich and to love and marry a beautiful woman.' How rich? 'Very, very rich. As rich as one can possibly be.'*

---

* Soames was as good as his word. Thirty years later, as chief executive of the power generation firm Aggreko, he earned almost £8 million in a single year.

Perhaps the most striking interviewee was a third-year history student called Caroline Kellett, who had already appeared in *Tatler* and later worked as the *Evening Standard*'s fashion editor. The new Oxford elite, she said, was not about 'money particularly, it's much more a hierarchy based on style'. Jack asked her to elaborate. 'It's panache, élan, flamboyance and a certain amount of intelligence,' she said exasperatedly. 'For God's sake, it's a cultural and aesthetic standard as well as a question of self-projection. You can come from any class and have it.' She belonged to an exclusive drinking club, the George. By an amazing coincidence, its members had all been to private schools. It seems unlikely that many of them spent much time cheering on the People's March for Jobs. And although Kellett denied that they were in any way political, her next remarks told a different story. 'Our generation believes that the future lies in self-belief,' she said. 'Everyone here, even the Northern chemists, are out for themselves. If you're at all bright you know that you fuck other people before they fuck you.'

In the published piece, Jack changed 'fuck' to 'screw', and explained that 'Northern chemists' was shorthand for 'drudges in the sciences, up from comprehensives'. Oddly, he resisted the temptation to point out that the most famous 'Northern chemist' in Oxford's history was the current Prime Minster. And although it is tempting to see Kellett and her friends as Mrs Thatcher's children, the truth is more complicated. The date was February 1981; they had arrived at Oxford well before she entered Downing Street. If Michael Foot had been Prime Minister, their views would not have changed. And although Mrs Thatcher's critics maintained that Kellett's mantra was the kind of thing she secretly believed, the Methodist alderman's daughter would surely have recoiled from anything so obviously self-interested. Rereading the conversations decades later, Jack thought they showed 'how much the entitled prized their entitlement and how they intended to increase it'. But this was not quite the same as Thatcherite aspiration. The arrogant complacency of the entitled elite was one of the things Mrs Thatcher had set out to destroy – in her own mind, at least.[25]

In this respect, she clearly failed. Quite apart from the fact that policies such as tax cuts and mortgage interest relief played into the hands of people who were already rich, the cultural tide was always running in the upper classes' favour. The biggest influence, obviously, was Diana, 'the 1980s Supersloane'. But the vogue for New Romantic fashion undoubtedly had something to do with it, too. By the spring of 1981, dressing up, always easier when you have a lot of money, was the order of the day. As early as March, *The Times* reported that London's fashion houses were knee-deep in breeches, taffeta and lace, having been 'given an almighty push by Lady Diana Spencer's taste'. A few weeks later, it claimed that London was now 'the evening capital of the world, with the ball gown sweeping all before it'. Even Vivienne Westwood, the woman who had dressed the Sex Pistols, yielded to the new trend; indeed, she had been one of the first to embrace it. Fashion, she told *The Face* at the beginning of 1981, was heading upmarket. 'The children shall inherit the earth,' she explained: 'they should be allowed to cover themselves in gold dust if they wish. To look rich is *great*.'[26]

The magazine that really captured the mood, though, was *Tatler*. Formerly a moribund high-society monthly, it had recently been relaunched by the ferociously ambitious Tina Brown, who described it as an 'upper-class comic'. And just as the *Beano* had Dennis the Menace, the *Eagle* had Dan Dare and *2000 AD* had Judge Dredd, so *Tatler* had Lady Diana. 'The season's surprise fashion success is the Lady Di look,' the magazine announced in May 1981. 'Girls all over the country are frenziedly cloning themselves: Lady Di hairstyles, Lady Di hacking jackets, Lady Di knickerbockers, and the quintessential Lady Di blouses with the pie-crust frilled necks.' Of course *Tatler* hardly spoke for the man and woman on the Clapham omnibus, but the Lady Di look was already trickling down to the high street. 'Fashion is putting a little romance back in our lives,' declared the *Express* a few weeks later. 'After seasons of functional blue jeans, downbeat dungarees and low-key khaki, the mood is for frills, flamboyance and frivolity. Lady Diana Spencer has blazed the trail with her choice of romantic ruffles and frothy frills. And now the new, softer, prettier look has arrived, I believe it's here for quite a while.'[27]

On the train to see Oxford's 'bright young things', Ian Jack had started reading a paperback copy of Evelyn Waugh's *Brideshead Revisited* (1945). Both a lament for the dying world of the country house and an exploration of the workings of divine grace, it had become an 'etiquette manual for a certain kind of upper-class male'. It appealed to the sort of Oxford student impressed by Waugh's Sebastian Flyte, who introduces himself to the narrator by vomiting through a college window. It also appealed to executives at Granada, who had spent the last four years working on a television version, starring Jeremy Irons, Anthony Andrews, Diana Quick, Laurence Olivier, John Gielgud and Claire Bloom.[28]

As Granada saw it, *Brideshead Revisited* had all the ingredients to match *The Forsyte Saga* (1967), which had tapped a growing nostalgia for a vanished age of tradition and hierarchy. But *Brideshead* had an exceptionally troubled birth. After location filming on the island of Gozo, a strike shut down production for four months. The director had to leave for another job and was replaced by the novice Charles Sturridge, who was still in his late twenties. Sturridge and his producer, Derek Granger, promptly decided to expand the series from five hours to eleven hours, an extraordinary decision that would be impossible today. That meant they were filming and writing at the same time, spending their evenings scribbling dialogue for the next day.

By Christmas 1979 the script was finished, and the next few months were plain sailing. But then another disaster struck. Because of the previous hiatus, Granada had renegotiated all the actors' contracts, and Jeremy Irons had been promised time off if he was cast in *The French Lieutenant's Woman*. Since Irons, who played the hero Charles Ryder, was in almost every scene, production had to be shut down until the autumn of 1980. So the last scenes were not filmed until early 1981, more than a year and a half after the cameras had first rolled, while estimates of the total cost ranged from almost £5 million (according to Granada) to more than £11 million (according to the newspapers). As *The Times* put it, 'the operation of divine grace has proved breathtakingly expensive ... Nothing could sound more like a recipe for disaster.'[29]

In fact, it was a recipe for triumph. Before broadcast, the novelist Anthony Burgess wrote a preview for the house magazine of Exxon, the oil giant which had invested some $300,000 in the production. Burgess proclaimed it not merely 'the best piece of fictional television ever made', but 'even better than the book'. And many viewers seemed to agree. When the first episode went out on 12 October, some 10 million people tuned in, an astonishing figure given that Waugh's novel is hardly an obvious crowd-pleaser. 'We've had letters about the fashions, the morals, the cookery, the furniture, the interior decorations, the gardens, even the place settings at dinner,' said Granger. 'We really have touched a nerve.'[30]

The *Guardian* claimed that the series had 'divided the nation'. In reality, critical voices were vanishingly rare. *The Times* thought it 'gorgeous' and 'irresistibly seductive'; the *Guardian*'s own Nancy Banks-Smith thought it 'splendid' and a 'great cut-and-come-again fruit cake of longing'. By mid-December, when the series ended, it had become one of the cultural landmarks of the age: 'the drug of the middle classes', according to the *Express*. With dinner bookings down on Tuesday nights, the nation's restaurateurs were praying for the series to end. But everybody else was cashing in. The paperback version of Waugh's novel sold 200,000 copies and topped the bestseller list for six weeks, while the soundtrack album sold 75,000 copies. At an exhibition to promote the series at the National Theatre, the giant posters of Jeremy Irons and Anthony Andrews kept being 'stolen by teenage girls'. Admissions at Castle Howard in North Yorkshire, which doubled as Brideshead, had soared beyond the owners' wildest dreams. Even sales of teddy bears had reportedly boomed, with viewers wanting their own version of poor, doomed Sebastian's bear, Aloysius.[31]

Why was *Brideshead* such a hit? It looked sumptuous, the performances were exceptional and it obviously fulfilled a need for escapism, conjuring up the reassurance of a lost world of wealth and privilege. Later, it became common to say that *Brideshead* had ignited a national love affair with the country house. But it would be more accurate to say that it reflected trends that had been building for years. As bestsellers like Edith Holden's *Country Diary of an Edwardian Lady* (1977) and Mark Girouard's *Life in the English Country House* (1978) had proved, there was already an enormous appetite for country-house nostalgia. In 1980 Britain's historic houses had welcomed a staggering 29 million visitors, while National Trust membership had surged from 158,000 in 1965 to more than 539,000 in 1971, reaching 1 million in May 1981.

Middle-class homeowners did not need *Brideshead Revisited* to give them a taste for chintz fabrics, William Morris-inspired wallpaper and the 'country farmhouse' look, all of which had been popular since the mid-1970s. Even in 1977, four years before *Brideshead* reached the screens, Laura Ashley had shifted £8 million worth of stock, the firm's founder explaining that 'people in the cities' wanted a 'pastoral romantic' aesthetic. The *Brideshead* look was rather grander, of course. But it was part of a trend for what the historian Raphael Samuel called 'retrochic', embodied by everything from Victorian-style conservatories and farmhouse kitchens to 'authentic' brickwork, cobbled streets, 're-traditionalized' pubs and even neo-Victorian street lamps. Already the critics that Samuel mocked as 'heritage-baiters' were sharpening their knives. In 1983 another historian, David Cannadine, launched an early attack on the 'worship of wistfulness', complaining that 'depression is the begetter of nostalgia, disenchantment the handmaid of escapism'. Full-scale battle about the meaning of the heritage boom, though, would have to wait until later in the decade.[32]

But *Brideshead* undoubtedly had an effect, not least on the way people looked. By Christmas 1981, *Harpers & Queen* had already advised its readers to 'make a bid for decadence' by adopting the 'Brideshead look', while *Menswear* magazine thought trend-setting men should go for 'an indulgent, extravagant look – wider ties, cravats and bow ties . . . stripes, polka dots, Panama felt hats, braces and armbands for shirts'. By the following February the *Guardian* was advising its readers that an aspiring man-about-town should invest in such garments as a 'traditional cricket sweater trimmed in ... soft pastel colours', a 'classic oxford [shoe] in grained leather' and even 'a cricket shoe', which sounds remarkably similar to the Edwardian cricketing outfit Peter Davison had unveiled in *Doctor Who* a few weeks earlier.*[33]

Not everybody welcomed the *Brideshead* ethos. As the television critic James Murray pointed out, Sebastian Flyte, a weak, tortured and deeply unhappy man who dies alone in a North African monastery, was hardly an obvious role model. And even on the fashion pages some writers felt uncomfortable about glorying in glamour at a time when so many people were out of work. 'The poor may be always with us, but so are the rich, and the tinsel glitter of the rest of us seems to have inspired them to come out of the closet,' wrote *The Times*'s fashion editor, Suzy Menkes. Everywhere she saw 'glamorous ball gowns and mummy's jewellery', reflecting the trend for looking 'very, very rich'. It was tempting, she thought, to be struck by 'parallels with the 1920s, a rerun of Brideshead on the dole money of the unemployed. I feel genuinely uneasy when I sit in a Bond Street boutique and watch women buying £2,000 worth of clothes.' But since the vogue for 'ruffled blouses, cavalier frills, dashing knickerbockers and swinging skirts' was not going away, the only thing to do was to embrace it. 'Throw out the worthy wooden bangles. No-one wants to look poor any more.'[34]

Did the pendulum swing back again? Did the public tire of taffeta and lace? Was there a groundswell of revulsion at the excesses of the Sloane Rangers, the entitlement of the Oxbridge elite and the rise of the cricket jumper as a fashion accessory?

The answer, at least in the short term, was no. Fashion took new turns, but looking 'very, very rich' never lost its lustre. In the summer of 1982, the *Guardian* suggested that feminists should embrace the trend for 'glitter, glamour and outrage'. In the autumn of 1983, *The Times* announced that the new image for men was the 'honourable schoolboy, upper class chic spiced with cheek'. And that same autumn, *Harpers & Queen*'s Ann Barr discovered a new group to rival the Sloane Rangers. These were the 'Nooves', middle-class people who had made their money as accountants, in 'videos and home computers' or by renovating old buildings. They bought houses with paddocks for their new ponies; they went to the Brompton Road and South Molton Street, and came home with the right

* In fact, the show's production team had decided on Davison's outfit in the spring of 1981. Perhaps they had taken the TARDIS for a spin to find out what was coming. Tellingly, the other options for his new costume included a morning suit with a top hat and a polo outfit with matching jodhpurs.

sort of carrier bags, which they used for their sandwiches. Some commentators might have worried that they were too greedy, too ambitious, too indifferent to their fellow Britons. But Barr had spotted another, darker failing. 'If they take over,' she said grimly, 'the difficulty with them is that they haven't a feeling for country sports.'[35]

At around the same time that Ann Barr was contemplating the rise of the Nooves, the *Sunday Times* asked Ian Jack to write about how young people found love in the capital. His research took him to a dinner party in west London, thrown by four girls – 'Fiona and Nicki, Claire and Annabel' – who had been to the same boarding school and now worked as secretaries at auction houses, or for advertising firms, or in the City. To all intents and purposes, they were four little Lady Dianas. Young men arrived, 'Jamie and Hugh, Simon and Mark', wearing 'corduroys and roll-neck sweaters'. The men were all very much of a type: they put on comic voices, talked in quotation marks, spoke of getting 'wazzocked' after work and discussed how much easier it was to have an overdraft when you banked in the country.

At one point Jack asked one of the girls if 'she ever encountered members of the working class'. 'Not really,' she said, 'but I did sociology to A-level so I've got a fair idea about how they live.' She was not joking.[36]

# 26

# The British Are Coming!

*England won against odds that were at one stage quoted at 500 to one. Perhaps, reflecting on that apparent impossibility, Mrs Thatcher may sleep a little easier.*

*Daily Telegraph*, 21 July 1981

*If you want to change nappies, change nappies. It's a free world. That's why my father fought in the Second World War.*

Ian Botham on BBC2's *Open to Question*,
20 October 1986

The year was 1977, and in his rented house in Malibu, the film producer David Puttnam was feeling sorry for himself. Having moved across the Atlantic for tax reasons, he had never really settled in Hollywood and had come down with a nasty bout of flu. To cheer himself up, he reached to the bookshelf and pulled down one of the owner's books, a history of the Olympic Games.

When Puttnam reached the 1924 Games in Paris, and in particular the story of the Scottish athlete Eric Liddell, he realized he was looking at a brilliant premise for a film. When he returned to London, he commissioned a script from the television dramatist Colin Welland. Getting the money, however, was a problem. Everybody agreed that Welland's script was excellent, but Britain's film industry was in ruins, with annual production down to a pitiful sixty-one films in 1979, thirty-one films in 1980 and just twenty-four in 1981.* To put it bluntly, nobody wanted to make British films. But at last Puttnam managed to scrape a £4 million budget together. Half came from Twentieth Century Fox; the other half, bizarrely, came from the Egyptian playboy Dodi Fayed, who fancied himself as a film producer. Later, Fayed had to be banned from the set after Puttnam

---

* For comparison, the all-time peak came in 1936, when Britain produced 192 films.

accused him of offering cocaine to the actors. He was, Puttnam said, 'one of the laziest human beings I've ever come across'.[1]

In April 1980 the cameras rolled on Puttnam's Olympic project. After various rewrites, Welland had decided to concentrate on two British runners, Eric Liddell, an evangelical Presbyterian missionary, and Harold Abrahams, the ultra-competitive son of a Jewish immigrant. His aim was to show them not as flag-waving national icons, but as men 'fired by their own purpose, inspired by their own dreams and seeking only to test themselves, on their *own* behalf, against the fastest, the strongest, the highest on earth'. But when *Chariots of Fire* reached the screens a year later, it was its nostalgic patriotism that impressed the critics. *The Times*'s David Robinson thought it was 'proudly and uncompromisingly British', while the *Financial Times*'s Nigel Andrews hailed the 'mythic nostalgia' of its 'patriotism and idealism'. The *Evening Standard*'s Alexander Walker even thought it 'the kind of film that I'd almost given up hope of ever seeing in Britain again', reawakening 'sentiments that had so long lain publicly unexpressed one had begun to wonder if they ever existed: love of country, fear of God, loyalty to the team, unselfish excellence in the pursuit of honour, becoming modesty in the moment of victory'.

On the face of it, *Chariots of Fire* does seem an immensely nostalgic film. The opening scene, a memorial service for Harold Abrahams in 1978, sets the tone. 'Now there are just two of us,' says an aged Nigel Havers, 'young Aubrey Montague and myself, who can close our eyes and remember those few young men, with hope in our hearts and wings on our heels.' As his words die away, the troubles of the present fade into nothingness, and we are back in the 1920s. The Trinity Great Court Run, the Cambridge Gilbert and Sullivan Society, even the 'heather on the hills' of Liddell's beloved Scotland, seem perfectly calculated to stir a misty-eyed longing for a lost golden age. The bicycles clatter through Cambridge; the national anthem rings out over the conquered stadium; the crowds cheer their returning heroes. In many ways the atmosphere recalls George Orwell's words about the world of boys' weekly papers in the 1940s: 'The King is on his throne and the pound is worth a pound . . . Everything is safe, solid and unquestionable. Everything will be the same for ever and ever.'[2]

In fact, the men behind *Chariots of Fire* never thought of it as a conservative film. Puttnam was a keen Labour supporter. So was the director, Hugh Hudson, who had been educated at Eton but 'hated all the prejudice' of his class. As for Colin Welland, he had worked with Ken Loach and written several instalments of the BBC's immensely earnest *Play for*

*Today*, and was very firmly a man of the left. As the historian James Chapman has shown, Welland's original treatment envisaged the film as a struggle between the 'privileged few' and the 'postwar generation', who were 'determined to win through in their own right for what they, and they alone, believe is worthy'. The filmmakers even saw a parallel between Liddell, defying the authorities' demands that he run on the Sabbath, and the athletes who were defying Mrs Thatcher's call to boycott the Moscow Olympics. The film, wrote Welland, would tell the story of two men who, 'riding their "Chariots of Fire" . . . fight against and eventually sweep aside those newly emerging Goliaths, nationalism and political expedience, those same monsters which today have resurfaced in the probable demise of the whole magnificent ideal'.[3]

It is all the more ironic, then, that *Chariots of Fire* is often seen as a Thatcherite film. With her deeply romantic sense of history and intense belief in Britain's unique destiny, Mrs Thatcher would have relished the loving shots of chapels and courts, not to mention all the Gilbert-and-Sullivan-singing and Union Jack-waving. And it is easy to imagine her pride at seeing Abrahams and Liddell secure their medals, not just because they were British, but because both made satisfying Thatcherite heroes. As a strict Presbyterian who spent most of his later life as a missionary in China, Liddell was driven by similar convictions to the austere Methodism that had shaped the young Margaret Roberts. As for Abrahams, Mrs Thatcher always had a soft spot for Jews. As Hugo Young puts it, she particularly prized their 'belief in self-help', their enthusiasm for 'ambition and self-advancement' and their 'moral code for upward mobility', qualities that the film's Harold Abrahams has in abundance. For as Hudson told the critic Alexander Walker, *Chariots of Fire* 'wasn't about winning, but striving'.[4]

The most illuminating scene of *Chariots of Fire*, which most firmly places it at the turn of the 1980s, comes halfway through. The patrician Masters of Trinity and Caius, played by John Gielgud and Lindsay Anderson, have summoned the brooding Abrahams, played by Ben Cross, to dinner. All three are in black tie, savouring their port in a wood-panelled college room. The Master of Trinity launches into a paean to sport's role in the 'education of an Englishman', explaining that it fosters an 'unassailable spirit of loyalty, comradeship and mutual responsibility'. Then he changes tack. In his 'enthusiasm for success', Abrahams has 'lost sight of some of these ideals'. In particular, the Master has heard rumours that he is employing a coach: not merely an Italian but, worse, a professional. 'The way of the amateur is the only one to provide satisfactory results . . . You've adopted a professional attitude. For the past year, you've concentrated wholly on developing your own technique in the headlong pursuit, may I suggest, of individual glory.'

At that, Abrahams bridles, but the Master of Caius chips in: 'Your aim is to win at all costs, is it not?' 'At all costs, no,' says Harold. 'But I do aim to win within the rules. Perhaps you would rather I play the gentleman and lost?' 'To playing the tradesman, yes,' snaps the Master of Caius. 'My dear boy,' says the Master of Trinity with smooth condescension, 'your approach has been, if I may say so, a little too plebeian. You are the elite, and are therefore expected to behave as such.' That is too much for Abrahams. 'You know, gentlemen, you yearn for victory just as I do,' he says coldly, pushing back his chair to leave, 'but achieved with the apparent effortlessness of gods. Yours are the archaic values of the prep-school playground. You deceive no one but yourselves. I believe in the pursuit of excellence. And I'll carry the future with me.'

As the door closes behind him, the Master of Trinity murmurs complacently: 'There goes your Semite, Hugh.' But it is not Abrahams's Jewishness that they object to. It is his professionalism, his individualism, his modernity. They might have been Lord Carrington and Sir Ian Gilmour, shaking their heads at the folly of another impatient outsider.[5]

Of all *Chariots of Fire*'s virtues, the most important was its timing. Conceived in the late 1970s, it reached the screens at precisely the moment when audiences were tired of feeling depressed and thirsting for patriotic reassurance. Released in the spring of 1981, it proved that rare thing, a genuine word-of-mouth hit, with takings growing as the weeks went by. What was really striking, though, was how well it was doing in the United States, where most reviewers loved it. At the time, Alexander Walker thought it had tapped into two fashionable American enthusiasms: jogging and God. But a more obvious explanation is that it fulfilled middle-class Americans' expectations of a British picture, all country houses, Cambridge colleges and cut-glass accents. It was 'something more even than a thinking man's *Rocky*', said *Time* magazine, calling it 'a wonderful historical restoration' of a 'more gracious and perhaps more innocent time'.[6]

Even so, Puttnam, Hudson and Welland could scarcely have anticipated the bounties that flowed their way on 29 March 1982, when they arrived at the Los Angeles Music Center for the Academy Awards. The runaway favourite was Warren Beatty's Russian Revolution drama *Reds*. The big winner, though, was *Chariots of Fire*, which picked up awards for its screenplay, costume design and music, as well as the coveted title of Best Picture. It was thirteen years since the last entirely British-made winner,

*Oliver!*, so Welland could be forgiven for getting carried away. 'The British are coming!' he exclaimed.* And when he flew home it was to front-page headlines that easily dwarfed the column inches devoted to Britain's previous Oscar winners. After all the dire economic news – and the coldest winter since the 1940s – it was a relief to have something to cheer.[7]

In the wake of the Oscars, the distributors gave *Chariots of Fire* another whirl in the cinemas. But by now events in the South Atlantic had taken a hand. Four days after Welland's call to arms, Argentina invaded the Falkland Islands. Suddenly there was a new charge to the moment when the Master of Caius pays tribute to the fallen of the First World War, 'the flower of a generation', who 'died for England and all that England stands for'. And as the Task Force fought its way towards Port Stanley, dozens of people wrote to Puttnam to thank him for such an 'inspiring' film. 'I left the theatre feeling completely uplifted,' wrote one old acquaintance, 'proud of having been to Cambridge, of being British and of knowing you.'

Even the Prime Minister found it a source of encouragement. Over the weekend of 24 and 25 April, with British troops preparing to retake South Georgia, Mrs Thatcher arranged a special screening at Chequers. Had the landings unfolded differently, the film might have seemed a blackly ironic rebuke to its audience's surging patriotism. But things could hardly have worked out better for David Puttnam's accountants. By the end of 1982 *Chariots of Fire* had sold more tickets than any other film that year, with the sole exception of Dudley Moore's comedy *Arthur*. Perhaps people just liked watching John Gielgud.[8]

There was another obvious reason why *Chariots of Fire* appealed to so many cinemagoers in the early 1980s. Although the Corinthian ethos was in deep decline, athletics was enjoying a tremendous boom. Colour television had brought new blood, new attention and new money; and, after years in the doldrums, Britain's athletes were finally recapturing the vanished lustre of Liddell and Abrahams. By any reasonable standard, their recent record had been abject. At Munich in 1972 Britain's athletes had won just four Olympic gold medals, while at Montreal in 1976 they won just a single bronze. At this point, a story about all-conquering British runners would have seemed cruelly implausible.[9]

Four years later, however, the story was very different. 'SMASHING FOR BRITAIN', screamed the front page of the *Express* on 2 July 1980:

* He was consciously echoing the legendary words of the American independence fighter Paul Revere, though Revere never actually said them.

## Gloom-Beaters Ovett and Coe Stun the World

Super athletes Sebastian Coe and Steve Ovett put the life and fire back into gloomy Britain last night.

The Olympic rivals smashed a world record apiece in the space of an hour.

Between them, the pair now hold FIVE world records – all in the name of Britain, which is a great tonic for a country suffering the economic blues.

Coe and Ovett put on their world-beating show in faraway Oslo. But their sensational win double was just the thing to lift the temperature at home on one of the coldest, wettest July days ever . . .

In a month's time they will run each other into the ground in Moscow. But last night they were both winners. And so was Britain.

Here was a rivalry worthy of Puttnam's heroes. The *Financial Times*'s athletics writer Pat Butcher, who later wrote a book on the Coe–Ovett relationship, called them 'the Toff and the Tough': 'Coe, slight, elegant, intense, fear of failure investing his every move. Ovett, the barrel-chested bruiser, strolling around the track like the very incarnation of Kipling's dictum to accept victory and defeat with equal panache. Hollywood could not have conceived it better.' Puttnam might have had something to say about that.[10]

As in *Chariots of Fire*, what made the struggle between Steve Ovett and Sebastian Coe so compelling was that it was not just a question of sport. It was one of style, culture and social class. They were born less than a year apart: Ovett in Brighton in October 1955, Coe in London in September 1956. In the press they were portrayed as polar opposites: Ovett the self-made striver, Coe the embodiment of effortless privilege. Yet both images were very misleading. Despite his gritty reputation, Ovett was a preternaturally gifted prodigy, so good that when he was just 14, an experienced coach told his parents that he was likely to run at the Olympics. Coe was much slower to develop. As late as 1979, when he graduated from Loughborough University, he was still planning a career in the City. But then, that summer, he broke not one but three world records. It was obvious the financial world would have to cope without him.

There is no denying, though, that there was a class dimension to the Ovett–Coe rivalry. Ovett's background had been far from comfortable. His father was a roof tiler, his mother was just 16 when he was born, and he was effectively brought up by his grandparents. From the moment he broke through, he had a reputation for being a man of steely will and stubborn opinions, the 'bad guy' of British athletics. It is perhaps a stretch to compare him with Smith, the extravagantly talented rebel in Alan

Sillitoe's story 'The Loneliness of the Long-Distance Runner' (1959), since
Ovett did actually finish, and indeed win, his races. Yet in his crabby,
outspoken independence, Ovett recalled the lean and hungry heroes of
the late 1950s. If he had been born fifteen years earlier, Fleet Street might
have hailed him as a people's champion. But at the turn of the 1980s,
working-class heroes were out of fashion. Instead, wrote *The Times*'s
Simon Barnes, he was the 'pressmen's monster', a 'truly dangerous young
man . . . the horrid bully who might beat lovely Sebastian'.[11]

What of the lovely Sebastian? The press made him sound like *Brideshead Revisited*'s Sebastian Flyte, but in reality Coe's father was a
production engineer in a Sheffield steel firm, while his mother was a half-
Indian former actress. If his background was middle-class, it was hardly
patrician. He spent his teens in South Yorkshire, not exactly the height of
metropolitan glamour, and went to his local secondary modern. His father
Peter, an exceptionally intense man with sensationally right-wing opinions, made sure Sebastian was well mannered and well spoken, which
meant people thought he was better off than he was. But his athletic success was only partly a question of natural talent. It was also the result of
his father's gruelling training programme, which had him pounding up
the hills of Sheffield in driving snow. 'He ran Seb's life like a project,' a
friend said. According to Butcher, Peter Coe even took an evening class
in statistics, 'so that he could better map out the future'.

In this respect, Coe reflected the temper of the times. As *The Times* put
it, he was not merely the 'nice, friendly, modern successor to the Brylcreem
boys'; he was an innovator, who trained relentlessly and used the latest
scientific techniques to better himself. His young rival Steve Cram, who
thought the public had got Coe and Ovett completely wrong, found him
'cool and calculating'. No doubt *Chariots of Fire*'s Cambridge dons would
have thought his methods distressingly professional, not to say plebeian.
And if they were suspicious of Harold Abrahams's Italian coach, what
would they have made of Peter Coe's stage whisper at his son's press conference in Moscow, after Sebastian had lost the 800 metres final to Ovett?
'You ran like a cunt,' Peter said. Even the reporters were shocked by that.[12]

Coe had the last word, though. Six days later, with millions riveted to
their televisions, he stormed to gold in Ovett's favoured 1,500 metres. Yet
even though the two men are remembered as deadly rivals, they only faced
each other six times. By and large, they insisted on being kept apart, either
by choosing different meetings or running in different events. As a result,
this was a duel fought out at second hand, with personal bests and world
records as the weapons. In just forty-one days in 1979, for example, Coe
demolished the records in the 800 metres, the mile and the 1,500 metres,

a feat previously thought impossible. A year later, the two men broke world records on the same night in Oslo. And a few weeks after that, just before they went to Moscow, Ovett equalled Coe's record in the 1,500 metres.

The climax came in nine astonishing days in August 1981. On the 19th, Coe set a new world 1,500 metres record in Zurich. Seven days later, in Koblenz, Ovett beat it. In Sheffield, where reporters besieged the Coe family home, his mother snapped that he had 'gone to bed. He is not concerned about what Steve Ovett does.' Just two days later, however, Coe went to Brussels and took the record back. The next day's papers gave him front-page treatment. 'COE THE HERO!' roared the *Mirror*, and no wonder. Never had British athletes scaled such peaks. Certainly none had ever commanded such publicity or become such ambassadors for patriotic renewal. 'Throughout this red-hot summer of athletics,' exulted the *Express's* David Miller, 'they have blazed their separate yet interlocked record-breaking trails across Europe, while a global sporting audience has watched enthralled – these two so different, so exceptional Englishmen.' And after so many years of feeble performances, it was the two men's *Englishness* that seemed the most surprising thing of all. For years, said *The Times*, people had been expecting a 'Super Runner' to obliterate the records of the past. But everybody had assumed that he would 'come from the other side of the Andes or out of Africa's darkest and densest jungle. Not from Sheffield.'[13]

The remarkable thing was that, at a time when Coe and Ovett were two of the best-known young men in the country, both were still technic-ally amateurs. Under the antediluvian rules of the International Amateur Athletic Federation (IAAF), athletes were banned from accepting prizes and endorsements. Even at the height of his career, Coe was still living in digs with a university friend. Legend has it that when they were preparing for the 800 metres in Moscow, Ovett muttered to his rival: 'It's odd to think that we could fill a stadium on our own and yet here we are running for nothing.'

A few days after Coe's miraculous performance in Brussels, the IAAF agreed that athletes could accept advertising and endorsement deals, which meant they could aspire to the financial status of their fellow sports-men. Yet the new financial opportunities of the 1980s brought anxieties of their own. Ovett had already weathered fierce criticism in Moscow, where his exclusive deal with the *Sunday People* infuriated its Fleet Street rivals. And although Coe's golden-boy image gave him a degree of protec-tion, he was not immune from the pressures that came with professionalism. In August 1982 the *Observer* accused him of snubbing his home crowds for the well-heeled European promoters, who waved fat rewards for world-record attempts in Oslo and Zurich. 'What it boils down to', said the paper sternly, 'is that athletics is going through a period of rapid change. Coe and Ovett are now, to all intents and purposes, professional athletes. As professionals, they owe much to those who support the sport in this country.'[14]

Like *Chariots of Fire*'s Liddell and Abrahams, then, Coe and Ovett faced two ways. As pale, serious, impeccably patriotic young men, raising the Union Jack over the stadiums of the world, they looked like throwbacks to a lost age of sporting empire. 'Their personality, their style, their will to win are typical,' enthused the *Express*, 'and show that in sport, at least, Britain can still take on the world, and win.' Yet they were also representatives of change, not just as professionals in a hitherto amateur sport, but as individualistic heroes in a society where collective loyalties had frayed. Their triumphs were built on 'character', boasted the *Express*, not 'massive State or private financial backing'. The obvious implication was that if they could beat the world without Whitehall's assistance, then so could Britain's businessmen.

They were not alone, though. One of the pleasures of following British sport in the early 1980s was that it was full of self-made men and women who were no longer content to play the gallant loser, from Tessa Sanderson and Fatima Whitbread to Jayne Torvill and Christopher Dean. Among them was a young man from Notting Hill who has a good claim to be the most ferociously competitive athlete Britain has ever produced. 'Winning', Daley Thompson once said, 'is the only prize anybody cares about in this world.' That would not have gone down well with the Master of Trinity.[15]

Like Harold Abrahams, Daley Thompson defied the stereotype of the blue-blooded Anglo-Saxon athlete. His father had moved to London from Nigeria; his mother came from Dundee. He was born in Notting Hill in October 1958, just weeks after the riots that brought the scruffy west London neighbourhood to national attention, and grew up alongside children from a bewildering variety of ethnic backgrounds. But he had little sense of belonging to a minority, and always described himself as a British athlete, not a black athlete. 'People don't regard themselves as black or white in Notting Hill,' his brother Frank told his biographer. 'You're just from the area.' As for Thompson's mother, she thought that while Notting Hill was a 'dump', it was a 'happy dump'. 'We're not actually a black family,' she added. 'We're a mixed family. I think, being mixed, we're accepted more than if we were completely black.'[16]

Young Daley was not an easy child. A 'terror from the minute he was born', in his mother's words, he was a hyperactive little boy, always getting into fights. His parents worked long hours, and in 1965 his mother sent him to a state-approved boarding school in Sussex. Farney Close specialized in coping with 'troubled' children, with fees paid by their local authority. So at the age of just 7, writes his biographer Skip Rozin, Daley Thompson 'found himself there, alone, younger than most of the other students, the only black child, and without any sense of who he was or where he was going'.* He settled well: his teachers remembered a 'normal, active, naughty child, always very popular, always very able'. But after five years there came an almighty shock. When Thompson was 12, his mother rang with the dreadful news that his father had been shot dead in Streatham. And all this left its mark. As an interviewer wrote decades later, Thompson was defined by two apparently contradictory things: 'a desperate need to be noticed, and an even more powerful desire to be left alone'.[17]

It was at Farney Close that Thompson discovered sport. Competition provided a channel for his restless energy; victory gave him a sense of meaning. By the time he left, at the age of 16, his path was set. Initially he dreamed of becoming a footballer, but a coach at the Essex Beagles athletics club suggested he try the decathlon. His mother was horrified: she wanted him to stay at college and get a part-time job. When he said no, she threw him out. At first Thompson moved in with his coach, but eventually his mother's best friend, whom he knew as 'Auntie Doreen', agreed to take him in. And all the time, relentlessly, unceasingly, he trained. Other young athletes fell by the wayside, but he never gave up, even when the skies were black and the wind whipped around his ankles. 'I refuse even to contemplate defeat,' he said a few years later. 'I was talking to Steve Ovett one day about what drove us on and I told him that really I was the kind of guy who felt he should have been born Sir Somebody and now I was out to show that I deserved recognition through sheer ability.' Ovett nodded: 'Yes, that's your working-class syndrome showing through.'

Thompson's breakthrough came in 1978, when he turned 20, won silver at the European Championships in Prague and won gold at the Commonwealth Games in Edmonton. Almost unbelievably, it was only three years since he had taken up the decathlon, and he was still living on a pittance from the athletics authorities. Afterwards, he had scholarship offers from dozens of American universities, but he preferred life with Auntie Doreen.

* In a later interview, Thompson remembered that there *was* one other black child at the school, but the basic point stands.

That was good news for Britain's sportswriters, who found themselves with an extraordinarily engaging new subject. Thompson was a born showman. When he won Commonwealth gold, he celebrated by persuading his beaten rivals to join him in a lap of honour. Then he went out on the town, accompanied by the ubiquitous Doreen, and enjoyed a lavish meal with bottle after bottle of champagne. The bill came to several hundred Canadian dollars, a colossal amount of money in 1978, but the manager refused to accept his money. Thompson was thrilled. 'This was my first taste,' he said, 'of what stardom is all about.'[18]

For a young man who had lost his father and spent much of his childhood at boarding school, and whose skin colour marked him out as an outsider, all this was naturally intoxicating. If nothing else, Thompson's newfound fame was a perfect example of the way television could transform a nobody into a somebody almost overnight. Liddell and Abrahams might have been well known, but very few people had ever seen them compete. But Thompson was a celebrity. Newspapers promoted his 'exercise plan'; the BBC invited him to present a weekly sports show; eventually there was even a bestselling computer game, *Daley Thompson's Decathlon*, for the ZX Spectrum and Commodore 64. At first Thompson loved it. 'This kind of adulation and fame was what I had been working for all my life,' he told Rozin. 'The recognition, the autograph hunters – it's great.' But the novelty soon wore off, and by 1984 he was complaining that he could not visit his local McDonald's without being pestered. 'There is a feeling that anyone who performs in public becomes public property,' he lamented. 'I do not believe that.' Evidently adulation and fame were not such fun after all.[19]

Why did millions of people, who had never shown the slightest interest in the decathlon, embrace Thompson with such enthusiasm? The answer is not just that he won, but that he did so with such irreverent ebullience. In the early years, the flow of jokes made for a stark contrast with the grim seriousness of Ovett and Coe. At the Olympic village in Moscow, reporters found him 'at his ease and toasting the crumpet with his smile'. And even in the heat of competition, he rarely lost his sense of fun. When he walked out in Moscow for the decathlon's concluding 1,500 metres, he was so far ahead of his rivals he was already guaranteed gold. So he treated the race as four laps of honour, slowing down at the end to wave to friends in the crowd. To many viewers, this was barely believable. British athletes did not coast insouciantly to victory; they battled grimly against overwhelming odds. If by some miracle they won, they had the decency to look embarrassed about it. Yet here was an Englishman who not only treated success as his birthright but positively gloried in his superiority.

Among the press corps, some lamented Thompson's 'brashness' and 'arrogance'. But the public loved it. A cheeky patriotic champion: what could be better? Thompson was that rare beast, said *The Times*, a supreme athlete with a 'disarming twinkle in his eye . . . People are taken not only with his winning but with the way he wins. They are excited by his display of emotion, the fist pumped into the air in victory, the despair at a poor performance.' But there were virtually no poor performances. In the first half of the decade, Thompson did not lose a single decathlon. When he literally strolled to victory in the 1982 Commonwealth Games, so far ahead that he again jogged around the track during the final event, one rival remarked that it was 'a pity' they had been born in his era. And by now he had already joined the pantheon of national sporting heroes. For Rozin, 'he seemed to embody a fighting spirit that reminded his countrymen of a time when the influence of England was unparalleled around the world'.[20]

The twentieth century had, of course, thrown up a host of sporting idols. But there was something different about Daley Thompson. Technically, he was mixed-race, but to the public he was black. The first time his name appeared in a newspaper, he was described as a 'dusky youngster'. He came of age at a time when racial tensions were rarely far from the headlines, and was all too aware of the impact of prejudice. His old friend David Baptiste remembered that black faces were very rare on the athletics circuit in the 1970s. 'It did get nasty a few times,' he recalled. 'Some meetings you could tell you weren't at home, in the north, and on the coast. In the north it was plain nobody wanted to speak to you, but in some places it was a real hassle.'[21]

Against this background, a different athlete might have seized the opportunity to become a champion of black rights. Impressed by Thompson's self-confidence, Frank Keating tipped him 'to be a local leader of the emerging community of young black sportsmen in Britain', such as the footballers Viv Anderson and John Barnes, the boxer Frank Bruno and the javelin thrower Tessa Sanderson. But that was not Thompson's way. He consistently rejected invitations to speak up for black, Asian or mixed-race Britons, and when journalists asked him to comment on South Africa, he told them it was 'a shame on you that you try and intrude politics into something as beautiful as the Olympic concept'. Invitations from civil rights groups invariably ended up in the bin: as Thompson told his biographer, 'They only want me because I'm famous, and you can't get famous by attending all that rubbish.' And when a researcher preparing a book on black sportsmen approached him for an interview, his reply was emphatic: 'What do you want to talk to me for? I'm not black. I'm just Daley Thompson.'[22]

'I'm just Daley Thompson.' Even in the 1980s few people more una-shamedly proclaimed the value of self-interest. He owed the public nothing, he said: no 'favours, autographs, valuable time, public comment', other than to be the best he could be. The controversy over the Moscow Olympics passed him by. He 'didn't really care' about the politics of it; he 'didn't give a damn who was going'. Even some of the world's biggest brand names, waving cheques for tens of thousands of pounds, found it hard to penetrate his self-imposed isolation. 'I'd like to earn a million,' he told the press after Moscow, 'but I'm a sportsman first and foremost.' And although he signed deals to promote Brut, Adidas, Lucozade and Hertz, competition mattered more to him than money. His agents, he complained, were always pestering him about 'business arrangements'. But 'my commitment is to sport, not money . . . I spend all my days just training and travelling for sport. Everything else is secondary.'[23]

Perhaps even more than his racial background, his cheeky insouciance or his political indifference, it was this single-mindedness, this competitiveness, this obsession with *winning*, that made Daley Thompson one of the most richly symbolic figures of the age. 'Winner. That was all he ever wanted to be,' wrote Rozin. 'Winner in football. Winner in running. And finally, winner of the decathlon.' What defined him, agreed the sports-writer Norman Fox, was his 'driving ambition', his 'almost unbearable' dedication. 'Every morning,' explained one profile, 'Thompson pores over his books and journals on exercise and technique, grabs a breakfast of cereal and milk and is at the track by 10.30 am. He breaks for lunch at about 1.30 pm, returns by 3 pm and works until dark.' Training, he said, was 'everything . . . like being a monk. Not because you abstain or anything, but just because there is nothing else . . . It's all directed towards one thing.'[24]

Yet, if Thompson's dedication brought him glory, it also made him a strikingly solitary figure. When the crowds had departed, there was something oddly melancholy, almost Ken Livingstone-esque, about his routine: the bedroom lined with several years' editions of *Athletics Weekly*, the colossal cupboards stuffed with training gear, the 400 different pairs of athletics shoes. 'Usually I am alone,' Thompson said. 'I leave in the morning alone and come home alone. I eat most of my meals alone. I spend between two and three hours a day driving and that is alone.' But he never wavered. 'Competition is my life,' he told the press before the Los Angeles Olympics in 1984: 'winning is my goal.' He was, of course, as good as his word.[25]

Although Daley Thompson has a good claim to be the greatest athlete Britain has ever produced, not even he could match the popularity of the best-known sportsman of the 1980s. A state-educated working-class Tory, Ian Botham burst into the cricketing world with a swagger and glamour that had been absent for decades. With his sandy moustache and gigantic frame, he was immediately familiar even to people who could not care less about the difference between short leg and silly mid-off. Self-confident, aggressive and never far from the limelight, Botham organized high-profile walks for charity, was embroiled in a string of scandals and gladly embraced the new commercial culture of the game. To his biographer, the cricket writer Simon Wilde, he was the quintessential 'man of the people', the incarnation of Thatcherite ambition. To one of his teammates, he was simply 'a bricklayer who happened to be good at something else'.

Like Steve Ovett, Botham saw himself as an ordinary man misunderstood and mistreated by a patrician Establishment. His father had spent twenty years with the Fleet Air Arm before taking a job at the Westland helicopter firm; his mother had worked as a volunteer nurse during the war before starting a family. Born in 1955, young Ian grew up in a semi-detached house in Yeovil and went to the local comprehensive school. His parents were intensely patriotic, a legacy of their wartime service, as was their son. 'He sings the national anthem with his hand on his heart,' explained one of Botham's friends. 'He's incredibly, unbelievably, patriotic. He celebrates St George's Day and he's a huge monarchist. If there was a war tomorrow, he'd sign up to defend his country.'[26]

A fine cricketer as a boy, Botham left school at 16 to work as a junior member of the ground staff at Lord's, though his dream was to play for his local county, Somerset. Even at this stage, he was a young man of very traditional views. At a time when many youngsters were delaying getting married until their late twenties, he proposed to his girlfriend, Kathy, when he was just 18. They were married two years later and settled down in her native Lincolnshire, where he could pursue his dream of a rural life 'defined by family and friends, domesticated animals and rolling acres'. Even as a parent, he prided himself on being 'a bit old fashioned'. He voted for Mrs Thatcher's party in 1979 and never wavered in his loyalty. 'I do believe in free enterprise,' he told a group of Scottish sixth-formers a few years later. 'And I do believe that if a guy gets off his backside and wants to go out and try to make something of his life, he should have that opportunity. Unfortunately, under the Labour Party . . . I feel it would be too easy for people to sit down and do nothing and get paid for it.'[27]

Like many working-class Conservatives, Botham was at once fiercely proud of his background and very sensitive to criticism from his more privileged peers. His biographer points out that, despite his apparent self-confidence, he had a 'deep-seated anxiety for acceptance'. Unfortunately,

English cricket was still run by an upper-crust elite, with whom Botham never felt entirely comfortable. His predecessor as England captain, Mike Brearley, had been educated at the City of London School and Cambridge, while even at Somerset there were plenty of public schoolboys, such as Peter Roebuck (Millfield and Cambridge) and Vic Marks (Blundell's and Oxford). When Marks described Botham as a 'hooligan in the nicest sense of the word', he meant it affectionately. Yet this surely explains why Botham was drawn to outsiders like Somerset's young West Indian batsman Viv Richards, who became one of his closest friends in the game. At one point Botham even copied Richards's habit of wearing Rastafarian wristbands, a sign of his self-image as an underdog.[28]

When Botham took his first steps in the early 1970s, some coaches saw him merely as a slogger. But his sheer competitiveness set him apart. Viv Richards thought Botham 'made himself into a great player' through pure determination, ignoring the 'mumbo-jumbo' of the coaches and playing with untutored freedom. Later, Botham told *The Times* that, unlike many cricketers, he never tried to analyse his technique. 'You've got to enjoy it, let it go, let it speak for itself,' he said. 'It's basically a very simple game: three sticks stuck in the ground, a ball to knock them down, a big stick to protect them by hitting the ball.'[29]

By 1977 Botham's youthful heroics had caught the attention of the England selectors, and he soon became a fixture of the national side. To the public, he seemed an effervescent all-rounder unburdened by the fear of failure: in twenty Tests between the summer of 1978 and the spring of 1980, he scored 1,099 runs and took 112 wickets. In one unstoppable performance in Bombay in February 1980, he scored 114 runs in a single innings and took thirteen wickets, a combination unprecedented in Test history. To the press, he seemed a force of nature, a 'colossus', a rampaging lion in all his glory. 'BIONIC BOTHAM!' roared the *Daily Mirror*, reporting that he had 'scythed through India's ranks' to send the 'little men from the East' packing. By now he was more than just another cricketer. He was a phenomenon, so well known that the *Mirror*'s women's page ran a long profile of him and his wife Kathy. Apparently without irony, the headline described him as 'The Perfect Husband'.[30]

Botham was not perfect. Right from the start, profiles noted that he could be brash and aggressive, and was never shy of using his fists. But after a decade of sporting sterility, the papers were delighted to see somebody with a bit of spirit. Botham was 'wholly a fighter', said the *Express* in 1978, reporting that on a club tour of Australia the young Somerset all-rounder had 'physically cleared' a bar of local supporters. As the *Observer*'s Hugh McIlvanney remarked, Botham had 'a vitality which often appears to compare with that of ordinary men as Niagara does with a bathroom tap', even if it ended in punch-ups worthy of a Western saloon. When he first toured Pakistan, he got into a fight with the cricket correspondent of the *Sun* after drinks at the British High Commission in Islamabad. On subsequent tours, records his biographer, he invariably 'shoved people into swimming pools ... singed their hair with cigarette lighters, and, with breathtaking predictability, turned up to Christmas fancy-dress parties as a gorilla'.[31]

Botham's gorilla costume was aptly chosen. At a time when the newspapers were full of men in make-up and women in trousers, he was an old-fashioned, red-blooded alpha male. He liked hunting, shooting, fishing and drinking. He expected Kathy to stay at home and look after their children, and freely admitted that he was not a hands-on father. Interviewed about his parenting skills, he said cheerfully: 'I had a few backhanders in my time. It didn't do me any harm. Children must obey their parents. That is what is lacking in a lot of the youth today.' Profiles invariably came back to Botham's unreconstructed masculinity, all the more bracing when the same papers were running stories about the GLC women's committee or Duran Duran's taste in mascara. McIlvanney, for example, marvelled at his 'vast thighs', 'thick, impressive torso' and powerful forearms, 'huge, flexible slabs of bone and muscle'. Even his Somerset teammate Peter Roebuck, who thought him 'a very nice and generous man', added that he was 'like an animal hunting' – and, of course, 'a man's man'.[32]

To the tabloids, all this made Botham irresistible. He was a great character, a man of immense physical courage and commitment, who wore his heart on his sleeve, fought until the sweat streamed from his brow and would gladly have shed his blood for his country. It was no wonder that he became a columnist for the *Sun*, where he joined other populist rebels such as the footballers George Best and Jimmy Greaves, the showjumper Harvey Smith and the wrestler Mick McManus. Even his nickname, 'Beefy', might have been chosen specifically to cement his reputation as a national hero who could have stood beside Wolfe at Quebec or Nelson at Trafalgar. Some of his teammates referred to him simply as 'Beef'. And it was only too tempting to imagine him roaring out the chorus of Henry Fielding's 'The Roast Beef of Old England' (1731) after smashing the foreign foe for six:

> Oh! The Roast Beef of old England,
> And old English Roast Beef![33]

\*

In the summer of 1980, Botham's career reached its apogee, as the selectors appointed him England's youngest captain for almost a century.

Almost immediately there were mutters that he was too exuberant, too cocky, a great individualist rather than a leader of men. Above all, his critics warned that he was too immature, a rebel never far from flying off the handle. Yet Botham never doubted that he was the right man to lead his country. 'All through my career people have been saying that I'm too young . . . too young to do this, too young to do that,' he said defiantly. 'Let's wait and see just what happens.'[34]

What happened was worse than anybody could have imagined. England played six Tests against the West Indies and Australia in 1980, and failed to win one. 'Perhaps it was a mistake to push him into the deep end,' said an editorial in *The Times*. Then, in the spring of 1981, Botham took his team to the Caribbean for five more Tests against the West Indies. It was an utter disaster. One match was cancelled after the Guyanese government objected to England's Robin Jackman, who had played in South Africa. The other four went ahead, but again England failed to win a match, losing two and drawing two. By now Botham's teammates were losing confidence in their leader. Some complained that he was still trying to be 'one of the lads'; others muttered that he was training less and had put on weight. At the airport on the way home, seething with frustration, he lashed out at the BBC's Henry Blofeld. The other cricket writers agreed to draw a veil over it, but the *Sunday People* got hold of the story and ran it on the front page.[35]

Off the field, the captaincy did Botham no good at all. In December 1980 he was banned from driving after the police had intercepted him doing 120 m.p.h. on the way to a team meeting before his first Test as captain. His solicitor explained that he had been a 'little bit excited'. Two weeks later, Botham was on a night out in Scunthorpe when he got into a scuffle with a teenage seaman who was annoyed that Botham did not want his autograph.* To cut a long story short, the seaman went to the police and Botham was charged with assault, though the trial collapsed when the jury failed to reach a verdict. Given that the England captain was expected to be a pillar of Corinthian sportsmanship, the publicity was dreadful. Even one of Botham's greatest champions, *The Times*'s veteran correspondent John Woodcock, lamented that he had 'confirmed the worst fears of those who felt that at the tender age of 24 it was too much for him'.[36]

The summer of 1981, therefore, found Botham under horrendous pressure. His form had collapsed under the weight of responsibility, his batting average down from more than 40 runs to barely 14. To journalists he

---

* This is not a misprint. The seaman wanted Botham to take his autograph, not the other way around.

seemed deeply unhappy. 'Having been glad when he got the job,' wrote Woodcock, 'I would be sorry now to see him keep it.' But there was no let-up. On 18 June, England were due to begin the defence of the Ashes against their deadliest rivals, Australia. Amid intense speculation, the selectors announced that Botham would captain the side in the first Test at Trent Bridge, but not necessarily in the rest of the series. 'One Test is better than none at all,' he told the press. 'If we win the match there will be no pressure. But anyway, pressure never bothers me.' This was patently not true. Morale in the England camp was at rock bottom, and the players no longer bothered with drills or meetings, which Botham regarded as pointless. The selectors, wrote the *Express*'s Alan Thompson, 'have piled the pressure on Botham to such a degree that if he does not win the Trent Bridge Test single handed either with bat or ball or by captaincy he could be out on his ear'.[37]

Botham did not come close to winning the Trent Bridge Test, single-handed or otherwise. In miserably damp weather, he scored just 1 and 33, took just three wickets, dropped three catches and watched in listless confusion as the Australians ground out a narrow victory. Afterwards, Kathy urged him to step down, but the selectors decided to give him a last chance in the second Test at Lord's. Botham proclaimed himself 'delighted' and insisted that he still had the backing of 'the man in the street'. But Fleet Street saw matters differently. On 2 July, the opening day of the Lord's Test, the *Evening Standard*'s headline read: 'Botham Must Go'.[38]

The fates were not with him. At Lord's, where the match petered out into a drab draw, Botham scored 0 and 0. When he walked back to the pavilion after his second duck, the Marylebone Cricket Club's patrician members did not even look him in the eye. 'It was the feeling of being deserted which affected me so deeply,' he remembered. 'I've never felt as lonely as I did that day.' Nobody doubted that Botham was finished. He had led England twelve times without a victory, the worst record of any captain in Test history. When the match was over, the chairman of the selectors, Alec Bedser, took him aside. They agreed that Botham would tell the press he had resigned, but as the next day's papers gleefully reported, Bedser was going to give him the boot anyway. Kathy complained that her husband had been 'crucified' by the press. But the *Express* was not in a forgiving mood: 'It was inevitable that Ian Botham went. He should not have been made captain in the first place.'[39]

Botham's humiliation seemed a symptom of a wider malaise. The late 1970s had been atrocious years for Britain's established team sports. In football, England's manager Don Revie had controversially defected to the United Arab Emirates. In cricket, England's captain Tony Greig had been sacked after secretly recruiting players for Kerry Packer's breakaway

World Series Cricket. By these standards, for Botham to lose his position because of mere ineptitude was barely a story at all.

And in a broader context, his fall from grace was only too predictable. Britain was a country in which people were *always* falling from grace: a country, said the tabloids, in which nothing worked properly, the governing class had lost their backbone, the workers were always on strike and anyone with any ambition had long since jumped ship. On top of all that, Botham's fall came at the very moment when his political heroine's popularity was at an all-time low and her dream of national revival seemed to have turned into a living nightmare. In an excruciating accident of timing, the second Test coincided with the riots in Toxteth and Southall, which meant the news of Botham's resignation was literally juxtaposed with images of the inner cities burning. On one front page, the headlines read 'NEW RIOTS HIT LONDON' and 'I QUIT! SKIPPER BOTHAM BEATS THE AXE'. Another had 'SPOILS OF A LOOTER' and 'BOTHAM'S AGONY'. In essence they were aspects of the same story: the sad, embittered decline of a country that had once led the world, and had now become its whipping boy.[40]

And then: resurrection.

Even decades later, the story of the third Test at Headingley, which began nine days after Botham's humiliation, seems scarcely believable. As captain, the selectors brought back his predecessor, the cerebral Mike Brearley, while Botham returned to being one of the boys. Yet for the first three days, it was the same old story. In the damp gloom of a Yorkshire summer, Australia kicked off with a solid 401. England responded with a derisory 174, which meant they had to bat again immediately. Only once in history had any Test side recovered from such an abject start, and it seemed highly unlikely to happen again. By teatime on day three, a Saturday, Ladbrokes were quoting 500–1 for an England victory. To cap it all, when the umpires abandoned play early because of bad light, the spectators threw cushions on to the pitch in protest, and some even barged into the pavilion to harangue the officials. The *Observer* thought it had been a 'bitter letdown'; the *Sun*'s headline read simply: 'PATHETIC!' In other words, it had been a typical English day out.[41]

That night, Botham, who had scored a respectable 50 in the first innings, invited both teams to a barbecue at his Lincolnshire cottage. Sunday was a rest day, so England's players stayed up into the small hours, drowning their sorrows. On Monday battle resumed at Headingley, though not until after Botham and some of his teammates had checked out of their Leeds hotel, since they knew defeat was certain. By mid-afternoon, England were on 135 for 7, still some 92 runs behind Australia's first-innings total. With Botham the only vaguely decent England batsman still standing, the match was drifting towards the inevitable conclusion.

At this point, Botham was joined at the crease by Graham Dilley, a young fast bowler who had played poorly and was sure he was going to be dropped. With nothing to lose, Dilley came out swinging. In seventy-five balls he scored a stunning 56, including nine fours, and his enthusiasm proved contagious. As his captain amusedly recalled, there was nothing Botham liked more than some old-fashioned 'village-green slogging'. So he began to bash the ball as only he could, hitting twenty-seven fours and a six. He rode his luck, of course; but suddenly he was his old self again, relaxed, almost insouciant, free from the cares of the last few months. At last, Dilley fell; then Chris Old put on another 29 and Bob Willis another 2, while all the time Botham walloped away like a teenager in the nets. By the time England were all out, early the following morning, he had scored 149 not out. In the pavilion, the photographer Adrian Murrell captured him, still padded up, his hair tousled with sweat, apparently deep in thought and about to light a cigar. For the first time in two years, he looked like a man at peace.[42]

Even after Botham's heroics, victory seemed unlikely. The Australians needed only 130 to win. When play began on the fifth day, there were barely 2,000 people in a ground holding some 16,000, and the Australian batsmen seemed perfectly capable of handling the pressure. Not long before lunch, they were on 56 for 1, and heading for victory. Then Brearley told his gangling, shaggy-haired bowler Bob Willis to bowl downhill, as fast as possible. Three wickets followed before lunch, and with the score 58 for 4, there was a palpable shift in the momentum. By two o'clock, the mood was running in England's favour. The Australians, once so certain of success, were wobbling; the stands were filling up; the English players had an unaccustomed spring in their step. And with Willis raining down missile after missile, and the Australians in a state of panic, the impossible began to look distinctly probable. Suddenly it was 68 for 6, then 74 for 7, then 75 for 8. Later, there were stories of people gathering outside high-street electronics shops, hypnotized by the prospect of the unlikeliest victory in England's history.

At last, shortly before half-past two, Willis fired another deadly ball down the wicket and Ray Bright's middle stump exploded out of the ground. It was all over: Australia were all out for 111, and England – joyously, impossibly, gloriously – had won by 18 runs. On television, the pictures showed hundreds of delighted youngsters pouring on to the field, while England's players ran for the safety of the pavilion. Beneath the changing rooms, a small crowd chanted 'England!' and sang 'Jerusalem'.

At last, to roars from the crowd, the players reappeared, wreathed in smiles. The man of the match award, inevitably, went to Botham. The crowd, equally inevitably, sang: 'There's only one Ian Botham.'[43]

Although Headingley is remembered as a moment of glorious national triumph, what it really reflected was how low Britain's morale had sunk. A more self-confident country would hardly have celebrated an unlikely victory in a single Test match as if it were the Battle of Waterloo. Yet after all the dreadful headlines about padlocked factories and smouldering streets, people were desperate for good news. Bloodied but unbowed, Britain had dragged itself off the canvas, and of course the next day's papers loved it. 'We need heroes,' said *The Times*, 'and we need the sudden joyous satisfaction of enjoying a prize that we had thought far beyond our grasp. It is because they provided all of these that Ian Botham and Bob Willis have brought a little sunshine far beyond the city of Leeds.' But the tabloids had eyes only for Botham, a 'colossal cricketer for whom nothing seems impossible'. Even the typically caustic Jean Rook was beside herself. 'Normally cricket bores me to the stumps,' she told her readers. 'But Ian Botham yanked me out of my armchair like belted wickets . . . This was the banging, smashing, splintering stuff I've waited for what seems a lifetime of TV cricket matches . . . and never hoped to see.'[44]

Headingley was, of course, just one match, and there were still three Tests to go. But when the players reassembled at Edgbaston on 30 July, it was clear that something had changed. The day before, tens of millions had been glued to the Royal Wedding, and as the crowds arrived in suburban Birmingham they were still brimming with patriotic enthusiasm. Once again England started poorly, and by lunchtime on the fourth day, Sunday, Australia needed just 37 runs to win. Then Brearley handed the ball to Botham.

What followed was the stuff of a *Boy's Own* story. With his third ball Botham bowled the Australian wicket-keeper Rodney Marsh, and as the crowd roared, he never looked back. In twenty-eight balls he conceded just one run and took five Australian wickets, an exhibition of concentrated ferocity almost unprecedented in cricketing history. 'He just charged in and made it happen,' thought Peter Roebuck, 'shaping the outcome of the match by the sheer force of his personality.' Even to his captain, Botham seemed a man possessed, driven as much by his demonic will to win as by the fervent passion of 10,000 spectators. 'Each time he took a wicket,' Brearley recalled, 'his arms reached up, his chest filled, waist drawn in.' 'He plucked that game from nowhere,' agreed his teammate Graham Gooch. 'He won it with sheer magnetism.'[45]

With another improbable victory sealed, the action moved to Old

Trafford, and by now the script was almost predictable. England again started poorly, and Botham was caught facing his very first ball. Australia promptly fell apart, Botham and Willis ripping through them once again, and then England's batsmen came out for their second innings. At first they made little headway. But then came Botham, and his blood was up. After a careful start, he surged into form, smashing 118 runs off just 102 balls, including thirteen fours and six massive sixes, to help England into an impregnable lead. It had become a familiar story: glory from the jaws of ignominy, the crowd a 'mass of dancing people and waving flags'. 'Botham's innings was, of its kind, perhaps the greatest ever played,' wrote *The Times*'s John Woodcock two days later. 'I refuse to believe that a cricket ball has ever been hit with greater power or rarer splendour.'[46]

England's victory at Old Trafford, which ensured they retained the Ashes, cemented Botham's place in the national imagination. A callow failure only weeks earlier, he was now the Nelson of the cricket field, before whose dauntless courage mere foreigners quailed in terror. One back page hailed 'BLOCKBUSTER BOTHAM'; another called him 'Roy of the Rovers . . . our fairytale champ', who could produce 'miracles almost to order'. In fact, Brearley, Willis and the rest had more than played their part, while Botham's early performances hardly suggested a man who could do no wrong. Yet, in the euphoria of victory, all doubts were swept aside. 'The Ashes Belong To Ian', declared one headline. 'Never in the field of cricket conflict between England and Australia', began a story in the *Express*, 'can one team have owed so much to one man.' 'He was the difference,' agreed the *Mirror*, 'a throwback to cricket's golden age of Grace, Hobbs and Empire.'[47]

No English cricketer since the war had inspired such enthusiasm. In the *Observer*, Hugh McIlvanney suggested that Botham had the unique ability to captivate people who believed that 'cricket is only slightly less boring than watching celery grow or car bumpers rust'. In a crowded Glasgow pub, McIlvanney watched as all eyes turned to the television when Botham appeared. 'For a man in cricketing whites to hypnotise such an audience into awed admiration', he wrote, 'is a small miracle.' Yet McIlvanney was not surprised: 'No one anywhere in contemporary sport more spectacularly channels immense animal vigour and a fierce hunger for winning into an overwhelming effectiveness on the field.'[48]

There were downsides to Botham's heroic status. Some observers thought that after 1981 his boyish self-confidence coarsened into outright hubris. As long as he believed in his own ability, 'things would inevitably come right in the end', no matter how badly he had prepared. He remained a supremely gifted player, but as he became distracted by his celebrity off the field, and less inclined to spend time practising, so his form declined.

As the sportswriter Simon Barnes puts it: 'The England team became based around an Inner Ring, with Botham at its heart: Botham, self-justified by his prodigious feats during that unforgettable summer. To be accepted, you had to hate the press, hate practice, enjoy a few beers and what have you, and generally be one hell of a good ol' boy.' As a result, Barnes considered the summer of 1981 'one of the greatest disasters' that had ever befallen English cricket.[49]

But nobody could have known that at the time. Instead, Botham stood unchallenged as the incarnation of the bulldog spirit, the amateur who hit first and thought later, the hero who waited until things were really desperate before smashing boundary after boundary. The irony was that, at a time when Sebastian Coe and Daley Thompson were conquering the world through meticulous hard work, he was the exact opposite, a throw-back to a vanished age. It is hard to imagine him pounding along the beach at St Andrews with Liddell and Abrahams. It is harder still to picture him getting up to run through Sheffield in the snow, or poring over training manuals as the night drew in.

But perhaps this explains why Botham loomed largest in the national imagination. When he retired in 1993, the journalist Jonathan Margolis wrote that with his raw energy, driving ambition and 'anti-Establishment, outspoken' style, he had been the embodiment of Mrs Thatcher's Britain, a 'new type of Boy's Own Paper hero – really a Yob's Own Paper icon'. But he was also a reassuringly nostalgic figure, a rumbustious bruiser who would have been at home in the eighteenth century. 'In much of what he did, on and off the field, he was excessive,' admitted the cricket writer Derek Hodgson:

> but Regency England would have recognised him instantly as the man who could ride to hounds from dawn, fight 25 rounds bare-knuckle of an after-noon, dine on a mountain of boiled mutton, roast beef, plum duff and cheddar cheese, washed down by ale and claret, and top it off with a bottle of brandy: a man who proclaimed one Englishman worth 10 scurvy foreign-ers. For Ian Botham read John Bull.[50]

Even at the time, some people found the Botham phenomenon a bit ridicu-lous. In a mocking article in August 1981, Miles Kington could not resist conflating his heroics at Edgbaston with the scenes at St Paul's a few days earlier:

> 'It's like a fairy tale,' said the American lady. 'Only the British can do it this way,' said the *Tokyo Evening News*. 'Es mucho hombre,' they were saying throughout Latin America. Yes, over 750 million people are thought to have

been glued to their sets as Ian Botham single-handed rescued England yet again from disaster. What a man! What a giant! . . .

This is the kind of simple but moving ritual that the British still do best. Who can ever forget those images? Botham, leaping high in the air in triumph. Botham, standing silently and reverently in the slips beside Mike Brearley, his father. Botham, a stump held aloft in the final act . . .

It seemed as if the whole population of Birmingham was there to greet their idol. Some had slept out the night before rolled in Union Jacks, some had queued all morning at the local off-licence, but all came together in one vast crowd as they simply but movingly flowed across the field and trampled the pitch underfoot.

With 'men like Botham around', claimed Kington, 'it shows that Britain cannot yet be counted out'. It was 'up to Ian now' to 'get the economy on a sound footing. But given what he has done already, there's no reason why he should not do this as well.'[51]

It was absurd, of course. Yet, in the summer of 1981, many people wanted to believe it. Perhaps not since the Second World War had there been such a demand for patriotic heroes. 'Back Flows the Powerful Tide of British Pride', roared the *Express*'s George Gale nine days later, claiming that the victories at Headingley and Edgbaston ('Botham forgot he was British and played to win') reflected a deeper revival of national self-confidence. Even at this stage, Gale thought the decades of decline were over. 'Our industrial relations show a very marked improvement. Strikes are fewer. The work force is leaner. The unions are less arrogant. Even the dark cloud of unemployment has its silver lining . . . Good news keeps breaking in. We cannot quite credit it, but there it is.'

Even the SAS were in the news again. Among the guests at the Royal Wedding had been the President of the Gambia, Sir Dawda Jawara, who returned home to find that Marxist rebels were holding his wife and children hostage in the capital's main hospital. Mrs Thatcher duly despatched a three-man SAS team, who disguised themselves as doctors, infiltrated the hospital and rescued the President's family. To the press, it was yet more proof that when the chips were down, you could always count on Britain. 'Who needs James Bond and "M" when you've got the SAS?' enthused the *Express*. 'Once again Britain's crack regiment carries out a remarkable rescue operation.' As usual, the paper noted that the regiment was famous for its 'total secrecy . . . Never knowing who is a member adds glamour to the incredible escapes it organises.' But it could not resist suggesting one name, a man who had already proved himself capable of miracles. 'Could it be that Ian Botham . . . ?'[52]

# PART FOUR

# The British Are Back!

# 27

# She Came, She Saw, She Clobbered

*You know, Geoffrey, the trouble with this government is that it isn't fun any more. I don't know why we do it.*
> Christopher Soames, *c.* July 1981,
> quoted in Geoffrey Howe, *Conflict of Loyalty* (1994)

YOUNG WOMAN: *The things she's done to people, she must be callous not to see how it's hurting everyday people, in the family, in the home.*
DAVID DIMBLEBY: *What do you think of yourself, for having voted for her?*
YOUNG WOMAN: *Pretty dreadful – it's the worst thing I done, really. I'm never doing that again.*
> Young working-class woman interviewed on
> BBC1's *Panorama*, 12 October 1981

An evening in the summer of 1981, and at 10 Downing Street the phone is ringing. 'I'll get it, Denis,' says a familiar voice, and, pulling off her rubber gloves, Margaret Thatcher opens a kitchen cupboard to reveal an official-looking red phone. 'Mr Bond on the line, Prime Minister,' says a patrician voice. 'Ah, Mr Bond!' says Mrs Thatcher. 'I wanted to call you personally to say how pleased we all are that your mission was a success. Thank you.'

'Thank you!' a voice squawks back – unfortunately, not the voice of Britain's finest, who is actually enjoying a naked swim with Carole Bouquet, but that of his girlfriend's parrot. But as Mrs Thatcher's officials know, she is not easily deterred when in full flow. 'Don't thank me, Mr Bond,' she says earnestly. 'Your courage and resourcefulness are a credit to the nation. Denis and I' – and at this point she notices an addled-looking Denis, wine glass and cigarette in hand, reaching into the salad bowl, and gives him a smart slap on the wrist – 'look forward to meeting you.

Meanwhile, if there is anything I can do for you –' 'Give us a kiss!' inter-
rupts the parrot. 'Give us a kiss!' A look of surprised, almost coquettish
pleasure crosses the Prime Minister's face. 'Well, *really*, Mr Bond,' she
says delightedly, 'ah, ha, ha!' 'I think we're having a little trouble with the
line, madam,' the official voice says desperately, and at the headquarters
of the British Secret Service, the Minister of Defence pulls the plug.[1]

Probably not even Mrs Thatcher's greatest fan would claim that her
appearance in *For Your Eyes Only*, courtesy of the impersonator Janet
Brown, ranks among the high points in British cinematic history. Still, it
spoke volumes about her impact on the international imagination. Never
before had a Prime Minister appeared in a Bond film: sadly, it had never
occurred to the producers to have Edward Heath popping up on the train
at the end of *Live and Let Die* (1973). What is really remarkable, though,
is that although *For Your Eyes Only* was released in June 1981, the scene
had been shot at the end of 1980, when Mrs Thatcher had been in power
for barely eighteen months. At the time, she was still a newcomer on the
world stage. But she was a novelty, a sensation, the 'nation's most prodigious housewife-superstar', as the *Guardian* put it. And as the producers
knew, the first woman elected to lead a major Western power would be
instantly recognizable, not just to her fellow Britons, but to audiences all
over the world.[2]

The irony is that at precisely the point when Mrs Thatcher became the
unlikeliest Bond girl in history, her domestic popularity had sunk into the
abyss. For much of 1981 her Gallup approval rating was about 30 per cent,
and in August it fell to just 28 per cent, a nadir matched only by Harold
Wilson in 1968. There was some good news: nine out of ten people thought
she was a strong personality and spoke her mind, while eight out of ten
said she was trying her best and was a good speaker. Yet seven out of ten
thought she was divisive, self-centred and 'not in touch with ordinary
people', and a similar proportion considered her ideas 'destructive'. As for
her party, the Tories' private polls put their support at about 25 per cent,
the lowest figure in the party's modern history. When Gallup asked which
party people *expected* to win the next election, just 13 per cent of respondents in July 1981 named the Conservatives.[3]

No wonder, then, that although Mrs Thatcher never betrayed a hint of
strain in public, her closest aides thought she seemed harried. After a
Downing Street party that summer, Alan Clark recorded that she seemed
'a little bit triste and blotchy, which I recognise as being one of her stress
symptoms'. Her diary secretary, Caroline Stephens, was 'so worried about
the Prime Minister's physical and mental exhaustion, harsh public image
and alienation from her friends' that she asked Ronnie Millar to come for

lunch, with instructions to cheer her up. Perhaps she should have invited Roger Moore.[4]

With the Budget controversy behind her, Mrs Thatcher was hoping for a quieter life. But the next few months were even worse, the events piling up with melodramatic speed. On 9 April, Bobby Sands was elected MP for Fermanagh and South Tyrone. The following evening, the first reports of rioting came in from Brixton. In the early hours of 5 May, Sands died in the Maze; on the 8th, Ken Livingstone took control of the Greater London Council. On the 30th, England's football fans ran amok in the Battle of Basle; on the 31st, some 100,000 people joined the TUC's March for Jobs in Trafalgar Square. In the background, a grim soundtrack intoned the latest jobless figures, each month's total worse than the last. Ireland, inflation, unemployment; rioting, fighting, demonstrations: it felt like the Heath years all over again, the government lurching from crisis to crisis, the headlines ever more depressing, the atmosphere ever more conflicted.

But there was a difference. Even under pressure, Heath's crew had remained unswervingly loyal. But Mrs Thatcher captained what *The Times* called 'the most divided Conservative administration within memory'. And although the Wets had failed to influence Howe's Budget, there was a sense in the early summer of 1981 that they were, at last, beginning to stir. When, on 17 June, the Cabinet discussed Howe's latest public spending plans, Peter Carrington, Francis Pym and Peter Walker joined Jim Prior in opposing more cuts, while Willie Whitelaw even warned of 'future Brixtons' unless they turned the economy around. Bernard Ingham told the press that Mrs Thatcher had wiped the floor with them. 'She came, she saw, she clobbered,' claimed the *Mirror*. But her ministers did not see it that way. When Walker addressed businessmen in New York six days later, he went out of his way to dismiss the monetarists, warned that unemployment would breed a generation of criminals, praised the 'industrial strategy' of Japan and West Germany and could not bring himself to mention Mrs Thatcher's name. For perhaps the first time she seemed vulnerable. Perhaps, suggested *The Times*, she was not such a decisive leader after all. 'Invective against U-turns', the paper remarked, 'is not an adequate substitute for leadership and explanation.'[5]

The temperature rose, and things got worse. On the first Friday in July, riots broke out in Southall. Then came Toxteth, and then copycat riots across the country. What on earth was going wrong? What was happening to Britain? The answer, wrote *The Times*'s David Watt a few days later, was that all this reflected a deep-rooted collapse of political authority. It was hard, he told his readers, 'to respect a government that is divided and apparently unable to deliver economic success . . . What we need, and what we have not had for 20 years, is a settled spell of good government and moderate, persuasive political leadership.'[6]

His message was obvious. 'Most of the press, and indeed, most of the Cabinet, have been waiting for "rioting" to follow The Lady's economic policies,' grumbled Alan Clark. 'Now that they have got rioting – though for different reasons – they are delighted to be able to link the two and use it to proselytise their own arguments.' The situation, he thought, was 'desperately dangerous . . . I do not think it is exaggerating to say that if this continues the Government, or at any rate The Lady, could very easily fall . . . If the disturbances maintain their present pitch she could be forced into consultations with leaders of other parties, followed rapidly by a coalition.'[7]

Of course this never happened; still, the mood in Whitehall was simply awful. 'The consensus can be summarised in two words: deeply worried,' reported Bernard Ingham on 8 July, adding that the combination of the recession and the riots seemed likely to send the Conservatives away for the summer 'in a state of profound agitation, depression and gloom'. Ingham urged Mrs Thatcher to strike a more positive note, and indeed she was due to deliver a televised party political broadcast that very evening. Unfortunately, she had recorded her speech before seeing Ingham's note, and not in happy circumstances. Suffocating under the pressure, her aides had spent the last few days arguing viciously about whether she should mention Toxteth at all. John Hoskyns and Ronnie Millar urged her to go to Liverpool and record a special address to the nation. That would 'look like panic', she said. 'What could we say about it beyond a couple of paragraphs? How could we fill 4 minutes and 40 seconds?' At that, Hoskyns lost his temper. 'Why can't you just believe Ronnie's right?' he snapped at Ian Gow. 'Why can't you just drop these fucking stupid arguments?' There was a sudden, horrified silence. Later, when Hoskyns apologized to Mrs Thatcher, she said simply: 'I'm quite accustomed to it.'[8]

Hoskyns's mood that summer was close to despair. Ironically, he was at last becoming more optimistic about the economy, and towards the end of July he sent his boss a long note arguing that, despite her ministers' misgivings, 'in purely economic terms, we are doing better than many of them think. Despite the agonisingly slow bottoming out, the indications are that the recession is turning. The rise in unemployment *is* decelerating. Productivity *is* rising. Inflation *is* falling.' But he was tired of fighting to be heard, and tired, too, of Mrs Thatcher's abrasive style. To put it simply, he was no longer enjoying himself.

A few weeks later, Hoskyns persuaded Ronnie Millar and David

Wolfson to put their names to a 'blockbuster' memo, confronting the Prime Minister with her own failings. He sent it to her in August, just before she went away, and even by the standards of most holiday block-busters it made for excruciating reading. One section, for example, bore the headline 'You lack management competence'. Another, which began 'Your own leadership style is wrong', could scarcely have been more damning:

> You break every rule of good man-management. You bully your weaker colleagues. You criticise colleagues in front of each other and in front of their officials. They can't answer back without appearing disrespectful, in front of others, to a woman and to a Prime Minister. You abuse that situation. You give little praise or credit, and are too ready to blame others when things go wrong . . .
>
> *The result is an unhappy ship* . . . This demoralisation is hidden only from you. People are beginning to feel that everything is a waste of time, another Government is on its way to footnotes of history . . . But no one tells you what is happening, just as no-one told Ted.

If Mrs Thatcher had listened, the story of her administration might have been different. But as Charles Moore remarks, 'almost no human being', especially one under such merciless pressure, could have been expected to take all this on the chin. She did not mention the memo to Hoskyns until a few weeks later, when they were gathering for a meeting in her study. 'I got your letter,' she hissed. 'No one has ever written a letter like that to a prime minister before.' 'Margaret, we're trying to help you,' Hoskyns said. But their relationship was never the same again.[9]

In the meantime, the bad news kept coming. On 16 July the SDP made its electoral debut at the Warrington by-election, with Roy Jenkins surging from nowhere – or at least from Brussels – to within a whisker of victory. The Conservative vote, meanwhile, collapsed to 2,102, down from 9,032 only two years earlier. For dozens of MPs in marginal seats the threat of the Social Democrats, now almost 20 per cent ahead of the Tories in the polls, seemed horribly real. Even the newspapers' back pages offered scant consolation. Two days after Warrington, England's cricketers were bowled out in the third Ashes Test and forced to follow on. And even the miracle of Headingley gave ammunition to Mrs Thatcher's backbench critics. 'Has my right hon. Friend noticed that England has just won the Test Match?' wondered the ultra-Wet Charles Morrison. 'Does not their achievement demonstrate again how often it is possible to snatch victory out of the jaws of defeat by a combination of applied ability and changed tactics?'[10]

On 23 July, three days after Botham's heroics, Mrs Thatcher's teammates assembled to consider Howe's future spending plans. To put it simply, the Chancellor was keen to cut taxes in his next Budget, especially as there might well be an election the following year. Since market confidence was so fragile, however, he was convinced that spending would have to come down by as much as £5 billion to justify it. Both he and Mrs Thatcher knew this would test their colleagues' patience. Less than three weeks after Toxteth and just seven days since Warrington, most were desperate to offer the nation some much-needed respite, not another course of shock therapy. Indeed, when the Treasury added up all the requests for extra money, they came to a whopping £6½ billion. But Mrs Thatcher's mind was made up. 'Before I went down to the Cabinet Room that morning,' she remembered, 'I had said to Denis that we had not come this far to go back now. I would not stay as Prime Minister unless we saw the strategy through.'[11]

What followed, however, was even worse than she had anticipated. After the Chancellor had opened the batting, Michael Heseltine took the ball and rained down bouncer after bouncer. Howe's measures would do nothing for the inner cities, nothing to bring more jobs and nothing to calm the growing tension. 'Colleagues simply don't understand how bad it is . . . We have a society which is close to much more violence.' This was a key moment. Although on the interventionist left of the party, Heseltine was not usually regarded as a Wet. But once somebody with his energy and charisma had dared to speak up, more timid souls followed suit. 'All at once the whole strategy was at issue,' Mrs Thatcher recalled. 'It was as if tempers suddenly broke.' The situation was 'desperate', agreed Peter Walker, who liked Heseltine's idea of a pay freeze and suggested reviving the planning programmes of Edward Heath's day. Howe's proposed cuts would mean 'the decline and fall of the Tory Party', said Ian Gilmour. 'However beautiful the strategy, you should occasionally look at the results.' Unless they changed course, agreed Jim Prior, the situation might 'overwhelm us, and destroy what we stand for as a party and as a country'.

For Mrs Thatcher and her Chancellor, this was a dreadful moment. But then it got worse. To their horror, two of their usual allies, John Nott and John Biffen, joined the chorus of condemnation. The government had cut spending to the bone already, Biffen said. 'Enough was enough.' Then the big guns joined the assault. Lord Soames agreed with Heseltine. Lord Carrington said the party's support was collapsing in the country. Even Willie Whitelaw, usually the soul of loyalty, announced: 'There comes a time in politics when you have pushed the tolerance of a society too far. We aren't there, but we aren't far from it . . . We just aren't going to make these cuts.' And to cap it all, the 73-year-old Lord Chancellor, Quintin

Hailsham, added his voice to the chorus. The situation reminded him of American politics half a century earlier, when Herbert Hoover had been struggling to cope with the Great Depression. 'Hoover succeeded in destroying the Republican Party,' Hailsham said ominously. 'We are in danger of destroying our own.'[12]

Later, piecing together what happened from various off-the-record accounts, Hugo Young wrote that Mrs Thatcher had been 'shattered' by the criticism. Faced with a full-scale Cabinet revolt, she became, by her own account, 'extremely angry'. 'We have been here before,' she said bitterly, harking back to the great U-turn under Ted Heath in 1972. 'The most frightening thing I've heard is that we should abandon [the] policy of keeping inflation down.' All the same, she agreed that Howe should go back to the Treasury and compile arguments for and against the cuts, and on that note the meeting broke up.

'The whole tenor of the meeting had been a great shock to us,' the Chancellor recalled. 'Margaret and I discussed it more than once in the days that followed.' As a furious Mrs Thatcher saw it, she had been betrayed by men she had trusted. 'I had thought that we could rely on these people when the crunch came,' she wrote. But now she knew better. 'I was determined that the strategy should continue,' she recalled. 'But when I closed the meeting I knew that there were too many in Cabinet who did not share that view. Moreover, after what had been said it would be difficult for this group of ministers to act as a team again.' She would not change her mind. She would change her ministers.[13]

The ordeal did not end there. Later that afternoon, Mrs Thatcher addressed the backbench 1922 Committee, where she rattled off a detailed defence of her record, complete with statistics. She ended on a typically patriotic note, once again quoting Drake's prayer at Cadiz: 'Oh Lord God, when Thou givest to Thy Servant to endeavour in great matter, grant us to know that it is not the beginning but the continuing of the same until it be thoroughly finished, which yieldeth the true Glory.' It was good rousing stuff, and her listeners dutifully thumped the tables, but it changed nothing. Even Alan Clark, usually so loyal, thought the mood was 'gloomy, sepulchral almost', and her speech 'lacklustre'.

And when, a week later, Ian Gow scribbled some notes on the latest meeting of the 1922 executive, there was no mistaking the anxiety. Again and again the same three letters recurred, like a bell tolling a message of disaster. 'IS TIME RUNNING OUT . . . SDP now occupying centre of stage. Govt is perceived NOT TO CARE . . . Take SDP seriously . . . MUST CARE . . . MIDDLE GROUND . . . SDP . . . SDP . . .'[14]

*

Outside Westminster the summer holidays were in full swing. At St Paul's, Prince Charles married Lady Diana Spencer. The next day, at Edgbaston, England opened the batting in the fourth Test against Australia. Yet to outside observers the celebrations had an almost neurotic quality, as if the crowds waving their Union Jacks were trying a little too hard to banish Brixton and Toxteth. From his concrete fastness in Grosvenor Square, President Reagan's ambassador, John Louis, filed a bleak report on the 'troubling political, social, and economic drift' in Britain. Mrs Thatcher had clearly 'lost her grip on the political rudder', while the Labour Party 'could prove harmful to our security interests'. Whatever happened next, Britain was facing a future of 'political turbulence' that could seriously damage 'the country's reliability as a U.S. ally'.[15]

The ambassador's opposite number, Nicholas Henderson, was also in London that summer. Two years after filing his infamous despatch, Henderson was struck by how little had changed. The news, he wrote in his diary, was 'unredeemably bad: economic decline, rising unemployment, hunger-strike deaths and violence in Ulster, riots in many towns in England. I find that the hopes I entertained exactly two years ago that we might be going to turn over a new leaf under Maggie have been dashed.' Indeed, things were even worse now than during the Winter of Discontent, 'because we appear to have tried something new and it has failed'. Yet Henderson remembered people saying, when Mrs Thatcher was elected, 'that it would need time, that there would be great difficulties and that the most important and the most difficult moment would be when everyone started to say that the sacrifices being asked for were too high and that the policy therefore had to be changed'. So this, the ambassador thought, was not 'the moment to lose faith in her'. And part of him still felt, deep down, that it might 'come right in the end'.[16]

Mrs Thatcher never doubted it. She spent much of August walking on the north Cornish coast and relaxing in one of her favourite boltholes, a rented flat at Scotney Castle, Kent. But she never stopped thinking about politics. Even before that disastrous meeting on 23 July, her backbenchers were talking of the 'urgent need' for a Cabinet purge. Ian Gow confided to Alan Clark that 'there would be a major reshuffle in the autumn and that The Lady would be bringing in many of her friends'. And as rumours of the Cabinet bust-up swept through Fleet Street, *The Times*'s deputy editor Charles Douglas-Home sent her a forthright personal letter. After talking to Whitelaw, Prior, Pym and Nott, he wrote, 'I was left with an overwhelming feeling that you cannot let them go on like this: the whole thrust of the government is crippled – even subverted – by your ministers parading their consciences, frustrations, hysteria, snobberies, masculinity or ambitions before an audience.' But Mrs Thatcher needed little persuasion. She was convinced, she wrote later, that 'a major reshuffle was needed if our economic policy were to continue, and perhaps if I were to remain Prime Minister'. The 'dumb bunnies', as she called them, would have to go.[17]

She made her move on 14 September. If she needed to focus her mind, a long story in that morning's *Times* reported that the Tories were still stuck on just 25 per cent in the opinion polls, with Labour on 31 per cent and the Alliance on 41 per cent. The bloodletting began at half-past nine, and her first victim was her most biting critic, Sir Ian Gilmour. Their interview took place in her study; to Gilmour's discomfiture, she insisted on standing while he sat awkwardly in front of her. Perhaps she thought this would make him feel like a small boy being admonished by his headmistress, though, as she remembered it, he became very 'huffy' when she broke the bad news. In fact, Gilmour had long reconciled himself to the boot and had already prepared a statement demanding changes in economic policy. 'It does no harm to throw the occasional man overboard,' he observed, 'but it does not do much good if you are steering full speed ahead for the rocks.' It was a good line. But it would have been more effective if he had said it after storming bravely out, rather than after waiting ineffectually to be sacked.[18]

Then came Jim Prior. For weeks there had been rumours that the Industry Secretary was facing relegation to Northern Ireland, where he would be cut off from the daily realities of economic decision-making. Prior's friends had urged him to stand firm, and so, in a hapless attempt to show his resolve, he had gone around telling everybody that under no circumstances would he go to Belfast. 'I Will Resign, Prior Warns', declared the *Observer* the day before the reshuffle. But as Prior admitted, this was a colossal own goal. When he went to see Mrs Thatcher, she told him he was moving to . . . Northern Ireland. This was his moment, his very last chance to walk out of the government on principle. Yet again he missed it. After a great deal of huffing and puffing, he went to see Willie Whitelaw and told him he wanted to quit. But Whitelaw gave him 'the old guff, as you would expect: how important it was that I should do it, how she really wanted me to do it, what a blow it would be to the party if I didn't'. Prior pointed out that he had said publicly that he had no desire to go to Belfast. 'Oh, they don't mind that sort of controversy over there,' Whitelaw said blithely. 'In fact, they rather like that sort of thing.' So Prior took the post.[19]

Of the reshuffle's other major losers, the nondescript Education Secretary, Mark Carlisle, took his sacking relatively calmly, but the Lord President of the Council, Christopher Soames, had no intention of going quietly. As Churchill's son-in-law, as well as a former ambassador to France, European Commissioner and Governor of Rhodesia, the Old Etonian Soames was the incarnation of Establishment entitlement. When Mrs Thatcher told him that he was out, he let rip, roaring at her for twenty minutes with such vehemence that the tourists could hear him in Horse Guards Parade. Evidently she gave as good as she got, since Soames later complained that he had never been spoken to so rudely by a woman. In a moment of exquisite non-self-awareness, he added that he would have treated one of his gamekeepers with more courtesy. Evidently it did not occur to him that a grocer's daughter was more likely to empathize with the gamekeeper than with the gamekeeper's employer. 'I got the distinct impression', she wrote later, 'that he felt the natural order of things was being violated and that he was, in effect, being dismissed by his house-maid.' She must have loved every minute of it.[20]

There was one other loser from the reshuffle. After his nightmarish stint at the Department of Industry, Sir Keith Joseph was probably relieved to be moved to the quieter waters of Education. The days when Joseph had been seen as the power behind Mrs Thatcher's throne were long gone; by now, he had effectively yielded the mantle of Thatcherism's chief thinker to Nigel Lawson, who became Energy Secretary. Clever, louche and immensely self-assured, Lawson had been at Sir Geoffrey Howe's side since 1979, waiting impatiently for a Cabinet post of his own. And now Mrs Thatcher gave him a simple and very telling instruction: 'Nigel, we mustn't have a coal strike.'[21]

The most eye-catching newcomers were two men who personified the self-reliance and aspiration that Mrs Thatcher prized so highly. One was Norman Tebbit, who took Prior's old job at Employment. Born to working-class parents in Enfield, north London, Tebbit had gone to his local grammar school before becoming a pilot and entering the Commons in 1970 as MP for Epping in Essex and then Chingford in north-east London. The *Observer* called him the 'conscience of the Tory suburbs', a 'plain man who speaks his mind, with views that go down well at the golf club . . . in language that would please Alf Garnett'. In the public mind, he was the scourge of the permissive society, the hammer of the BBC, the sworn enemy of judges, social workers and all things European. The satirical puppet show *Spitting Image* portrayed him as a bovver boy in a leather jacket. To some extent Tebbit brought this on himself. As one of Mrs Thatcher's attack dogs in the late 1970s, he had accused Michael Foot of 'pure undiluted Fascism' because of his support for the closed shop. Foot hit back by calling him a 'semi-house-trained polecat', and the label stuck. Later, after he had been ennobled, Tebbit chose a polecat for his coat of arms. As the ultra-Wet Julian Critchley remarked, 'his was the wisdom of the saloon bar transported into the corridors of power'.

But the so-called 'Chingford Skinhead' was a more interesting figure than the caricatures suggested. Crucially, he was one of the few Thatcherite ministers who had been a trade unionist, having served as an official in the pilots' union in the 1950s. That, Critchley thought, gave him an understanding of 'people who were once automatically trade union members': the kind of people who had bought their own homes, or wanted to, who felt squeezed by inflation and incomes policies, and who were wary of moral and cultural change. As an aspirational suburban Conservative, Tebbit 'looked at the working-class shoppers wheeling their laden trollies to the boots of their cars in the supermarket car parks and knew that here were Tory voters'. In this respect, he was a thoroughly modern politician, an instinctive populist with a keen sense of ordinary voters' hopes and fears. By the mid-1980s, that made him Mrs Thatcher's likeliest successor. The irony, wrote Critchley, is that 'if Tebbit had entered politics a decade earlier, the Conservative Party would have been embarrassed by him'.[22]

If Tebbit seemed a Dickensian embodiment of social aspiration, then what would the novelist have made of his friend Cecil Parkinson? Nothing in the new party chairman's matinee-idol looks, his Brylcreemed hair or his suavely reassuring tones hinted at the truth of his background. Yet Parkinson, too, was a working-class grammar-school boy, the son of a Lancashire railwayman and an Irish Catholic immigrant. At school he belonged to the Labour Party and refused to join the cadet corps. But at Cambridge, where he studied English under the formidable critic F. R. Leavis before switching to law, he began to shed his Lancashire accent. Then, after moving into the City, he reinvented himself as a Home Counties Tory, forming a close alliance with the similarly ambitious Tebbit. To the delight of subsequent profile-writers, the two men climbed the local politics ladder together; supposedly Parkinson would get his friend to sit at the back and heckle him to enliven their public meetings.

The irony is that, in their public personas, the two men could hardly have been more different. Tebbit was rough, Parkinson smooth. Tebbit sought confrontation, Parkinson relied on charm. Tebbit retained his accent, Parkinson lost his. But like his friend, Parkinson was an irresistibly symbolic figure, a self-made man with a ten-bedroom Queen Anne rectory and an apartment in the Bahamas. In many ways he was like the hero of a novel by Arnold Bennett: he even wore monogrammed Turnbull & Asser shirts, because a friend had told him it was 'the most *nouveau riche* thing you could possibly do'. All this made the old guard sniffy, but Mrs Thatcher adored him. Like Ronald Reagan, Parkinson spoke to her as a man to a woman, courteous and respectful with just a hint of flirtation. Satirists mocked him as an oleaginous womanizer, but Hugo Young thought Parkinson was one of the few ministers whom she genuinely respected. He had, Young wrote, 'excellent instincts for assessing any situation, and going straight to the heart of the Conservative interest in it'. And, in the heat of battle, he had the crucial knack of calming Mrs Thatcher down, making 'a fussing, worried, preoccupied woman feel rather luxuriously at ease'.[23]

The promotion of Lawson, Tebbit and Parkinson was a key moment in the Thatcherite project. As the sons of, respectively, a Jewish commodities trader, an Enfield jeweller and a Lancastrian railway worker, none of them fitted the traditional Tory mould. Yet in the political imagination, Tebbit and Parkinson, in particular, became figures of vast symbolic importance, perfectly capturing the ambition and energy that supposedly defined the age. Even their names told a story of social change. They had grown up, wrote Critchley, 'in an England rich with Normans and Cecils, where young men Brylcreemed their hair and the excitement of the week was going to the pictures on Saturday night'. That gave them a connection to ambitious young voters that patricians like Soames and Gilmour could never understand. For 'out there in the suburbs', wrote Critchley, 'the party was being run by the Normans and the Cecils who knew that the Lord helps him who helps himself'. Still, not everybody approved of the new meritocracy. 'You don't know what it's like,' Willie Whitelaw told his friends. 'I'm sitting around the Cabinet table with the most ghastly people.'[24]

Reshuffles are always risky, but Mrs Thatcher's purge was a political triumph. Even the *Mirror*, under the tremendous headline 'All Mopped Up', thought that she had 'squelched' the Wets, while the *Mail* thought it 'the most magisterial demonstration of a prime minister's authority since the Night of the Long Knives'.* Yet it came when, thanks to her government's abysmal public standing, she ought to have been most vulnerable. That speaks volumes about the weakness of the Wets, as well as her resilience and opportunism. Inside the Cabinet the momentum had very clearly shifted in her favour. For with Gilmour and Soames in the cold, Prior in exile and Whitelaw isolated, there was no hope now of persuading her to accept a one-way ticket back to Grantham. From now on, recalled Geoffrey Howe, 'her instinct, her thinking, her authority, was almost always present, making itself felt pervasively, tenaciously and effectively. It came gradually to feel, as the months went by, as though the Prime Minister

---

* Presumably the *Mail* meant Harold Macmillan's purge of seven Cabinet ministers in 1962, not the goings-on in Germany in 1934.

was present, unseen and unspeaking, at almost every meeting.' She was the boss. And if she went down, she would go down fighting.[25]

Summer gave way to autumn, and every week brought little signs of cultural and economic change. The first women arrived at the Greenham Common peace camp, drivers caught their first glimpse of Ford's new Sierra and the first episodes of *Postman Pat* and *Only Fools and Horses* went out on BBC1. Soft Cell reached number one with 'Tainted Love', Granada unveiled *Brideshead Revisited* and Bryan Robson broke football's transfer record, moving from West Bromwich Albion to Manchester United for what seemed a staggering £1½ million. And yet all the time, week after week, month after month, thousands of people were still losing their jobs. In July the official unemployment total was 2.85 million. In August it was 2.94 million. In September it was 2.99 million. And although, strictly speaking, the recession was over, it did not feel like it. When asked, almost half the country expected things to get worse in 1982.[26]

That autumn *The Times* ran a series investigating the state of British industry in the aftermath of the recession. The picture could hardly have been gloomier. The machine-tools industry was in a state of virtual collapse, with production down by half in just ten years. In the appliances market, about half of all new washing machines and fridge freezers were now made abroad. Hoover, having already announced plans to close its Perivale factory, was preparing to shed a quarter of its workers. Thorn had already laid off one in five; Electrolux had cut its staff by half. And then there was one of the saddest stories of all, the textile industry, once synonymous with the Industrial Revolution. Only a quarter of a century earlier, it had employed some 200,000 people; now it employed 45,000, a total falling all the time. 'About 700 workers a month are joining the dole queues', said *The Times*, 'as the mill doors slam shut for ever.' Managers did not blame Mrs Thatcher alone: the textile industry had been in deep decline for years, squeezed by excess world capacity and cheap imports. But its products, they insisted, were better than ever. Unfortunately, high interest rates, high labour costs and the cripplingly high exchange rate meant nobody was buying them.[27]

On 14 September, alarmed that sterling was falling too quickly, Howe put interest rates back up by two points to 14 per cent. Two weeks later, he raised them to 16 per cent. That same day, 1 October, the Tories' latest private poll found that fully two-thirds of voters said they disapproved of the government's record, some seven out of ten were dissatisfied with Mrs Thatcher, and just 16 per cent said they would vote Conservative at the next election. Even by Mrs Thatcher's own standards, these figures were practically off the scale. And now, for the first time, there was a sense that the bonds of partisan loyalty had disintegrated. In *The Times*, the disgruntled Gilmour published a call to arms, warning that Mrs Thatcher's 'erroneous convictions' had 'left the centre ground of politics wide open to the SDP'. And at a dinner in the Commons, the backbench dissident Hugh Dykes told a Conservative meeting that they were heading either for 'the sharpest, most involuntary U-turn in history' or for crushing electoral humiliation.[28]

Early October found Mrs Thatcher in Australia, where the Commonwealth leaders had assembled for their biennial row about South Africa. And it was now, with impeccable timing, that her most dedicated enemy sailed back over the horizon. Having been laid low for several months with a thyroid problem, Edward Heath resurfaced on 6 October to address the Federation of Conservative Students in Manchester. Ordinary people, Heath said bitterly, had been pushed to breaking point by the 'unacceptable' price for Mrs Thatcher's monetarism. How was it that 'more than three million unemployed are necessary to get inflation down to a level higher than it was two and a half years ago'? There *was* an alternative: a 'dramatic change in policies' which would involve Britain joining the European Monetary System, restoring exchange controls, cutting interest rates, spending more on capital investment and funding a 'massive retraining programme' to get youngsters off the streets. Of course this would mean more borrowing and higher inflation. But 'how dare those who run the biggest budget deficit in history reproach others with the heinous crime of "printing money"'?[29]

Although Mrs Thatcher was on the other side of the world, word of Heath's attack reached her soon enough. Hoping to forestall her likely reaction, Sir Geoffrey Howe sent her a message urging her to 'avoid making too much of all this'. He had discussed it with Whitelaw and Parkinson, he said, and they all thought it was best 'not to raise the temperature'.[30]

He was wasting his time, of course. Giving a speech at Monash University, Mrs Thatcher added a new section pouring scorn on one of Heath's most hallowed principles:

> I count myself among those politicians who operate from conviction. For me, pragmatism is not enough.
>
> Nor is that fashionable word 'consensus' . . . To me consensus seems to be the process of abandoning all beliefs, principles, values and policies in search of something in which no one believes, but to which no one objects; the process of avoiding the very issues that have to be solved, merely because you cannot get agreement on the way ahead.
>
> What great cause would have been fought and won under the banner 'I stand for consensus'?

To the left of the Conservative Party, this was a declaration of war. Two days later, Heath's old ally Geoffrey Rippon told Tory students that the only 'alternative to consensus is confrontation. That way lies disaster for us all.' It was time, Rippon declared, for 'the younger generation' to 'stand up and fight' against the 'simplistic, deeply irrational, inherently divisive and ultimately destructive' dogmas peddled by Mrs Thatcher – a woman who, by a complete coincidence, had sacked him from the Shadow Cabinet the day after she became leader.[31]

Mrs Thatcher flew back from Australia to a party in ferment. She was, said the *Guardian*, facing the 'nearest thing to a co-ordinated Conservative revolt' since the start of her premiership, reflecting a growing panic that dozens of MPs could be swept away in a rush to the Alliance. In the *Mirror*, a *Jaws*-themed cartoon showed Heath as a shark poised to devour a bikini-clad Mrs Thatcher. In the *Observer*, the former Conservative peer John Grigg wrote that unless she ditched the 'masquerade of doctrinal purity . . . she will be condemning her party to one of the most comprehensive defeats in its history'.

To make matters worse, on 12 October the BBC screened a special edition of *Panorama* to mark the midpoint of her five-year term. The programme focused entirely on young skilled workers who had voted Conservative in 1979, many of whom were women. They had voted for Mrs Thatcher because they liked the idea of a woman, wanted a change, hated the unions and were sick of strikes. But now their voices were a chorus of disappointment: 'She didn't fulfil any of those promises she made. She fell down on nearly all of them . . . She won't take advice from her advisers . . . Callous . . . I don't think she cares . . . She doesn't care about the consequences . . . Diabolical . . . Unbendable . . . Dreadful . . . Lousy.' Not one was planning to vote for her again.[32]

She did, of course, still have her supporters in the Tory tabloids. The *Sun* ran the rule over her potential replacements and found them all wanting:

> Willie Whitelaw, noted for agreeing with the last person he talked to. Peter Walker, who thinks and speaks like Ted Heath. Jim Prior, who even looks like him – if people spurn the organ grinder, they certainly do NOT want the monkey! Francis Pym, the original faceless man, who has all the inspirational qualities of a glass of warm water.

But, as *The Times* noted, the fact remained that she was now 'the most unpopular Prime Minister since polls began'. Only a 'super-optimist', said the young Tory MP Chris Patten, could expect victory at the next election. 'The prospects for a full Conservative recovery', agreed the elections expert Ivor Crewe, 'now look very slim.' And it was against this background, with excruciating timing, that the action moved to Blackpool, where the Tory faithful were gathering for their annual conference.[33]

Mrs Thatcher flew into Blackpool on the afternoon of Monday 12 October, a few hours before the BBC's damning *Panorama* went out. Perhaps judging that she could do with a bit of the tickling stick, her staff had arranged for her to spend the evening watching Ken Dodd's *Laughter Spectacular* at the Opera House. But although he did his best to cheer her up, the mood among the party faithful was awful. As at Brighton a year earlier, the Winter Gardens felt like an armed camp, with lines of policemen protecting the sleekly prosperous delegates from the crowds outside. Writing in her journal, John Hoskyns's wife Miranda captured the atmosphere:

> Hundreds of police were there lining the route, and trying to keep the Right to Work marchers at bay; but as they spotted us they began to throw things, as well as abuse, and I found myself looking into the faces of young fellows who spat, stuck out their tongues and thumbed their noses at me . . .
>
> Even stranger was one older man who'd got inside the cordon and was standing quietly outside the doors as we went in. Very quietly, under his breath, he said, 'You should be ashamed of yourselves, coming to this conference, wearing a Tory badge, at a time like this.'

The media, however, were more interested in the enemies within. The conference theme, said the *Express*, was 'Thatcher at Bay . . . Her popularity is at its lowest ebb. Many in her party doubt the wisdom, many others lack the courage, of her convictions.' For this the paper blamed Ted Heath, a Tory in 'name and ambition' alone, and his 'wet, gutless and disloyal' supporters. 'This week', it said firmly, 'the Iron Lady must steel herself to crack the whip.'[34]

Funnily enough, flogging did dominate the first day, with speaker after speaker urging the government to bring back the birch to deter future riots. But the next day's headlines belonged to, of all people, Norman St John-Stevas, who had not forgiven Mrs Thatcher for booting him out at the turn of the year. Now, belying his foppish reputation, St John-Stevas struck back with interest. The Tory Party, he said, should be a broad church, 'not a sect and . . . not a community of saints following a Messianic vision'. If they had any sense, the Thatcherites would abandon their 'callous chatter about a leaner, fitter British industry'. Instead, unthinkingly 'sticking to the carcasses of dead policies', cocooned in the 'ignorant pride of a false consistency', they were facing 'an electoral catastrophe'.[35]

This was strong stuff by any standards. The fact that it came from St John-Stevas, usually such a prize drip, made it all the more biting. But he was merely the warm-up man for Edward Heath, who addressed a fringe event the next day. Monetarism, Heath said, had now had a fair test, and everybody could see the results: 'massive unemployment of over 3 million and still rising, and a massive number of liquidations and bankruptcies'. This kind of unemployment was 'morally unjustified. No society can tolerate that position and as a party we have to be absolutely clear about this . . . That is not what we want in the Conservative Party and not what many of us have devoted our political lives to working for.' Indeed, if they were not careful they would soon be presiding over a second Great Depression, with high unemployment resurrecting the corpses of the dictators. 'That is not the path any of us want to tread again.'[36]

Mrs Thatcher's allies did not take this lying down, and her young guns immediately returned fire. What the Wets were offering, Nigel Lawson said scornfully, was higher borrowing and higher inflation, with no mention of the costs. It was 'little more than cold feet dressed up as high principle . . . bribery dressed up as statesmanship'. They should 'drop their high moral tone, because there really is nothing that is moral or compassionate in prescribing policies which would engulf this country in a holocaust of inflation'. But the speaker who really seized people's attention was Norman Tebbit, who reminded the conference that the government was already spending some £1½ billion on special employment measures to keep people out of the dole queues. It was outrageous, Tebbit said, for their critics to claim that high unemployment had caused the riots in Brixton and Toxteth. 'I grew up in the Thirties, with an unemployed father. He didn't riot. He got on his bike and looked for work, and he kept looking till he found it.'

Contrary to what is often thought, Tebbit did not tell the modern-day unemployed to get on their bikes. He was using his father's story to defend the government against the accusation that unemployment inevitably meant rioting. But his phrase hit home. To the government's supporters it became a symbol of Mrs Thatcher's commitment to individual self-reliance. To its critics it captured her callous disregard for the poor and unlucky. For Tebbit himself, his father's bicycle became a central element of his abrasive image. Only a few weeks earlier, the *Observer* had called him a 'hard-faced man who did well out of the class war'. Now the *Guardian* declared that he had the 'air of a prison office manqué'. That was a bit unfair, but in a single sentence he had cemented his position as the man the chattering classes loved to hate.[37]

By the time the conference broke up, most neutral observers thought it had been the most fractious Tory meeting since the chaos following Harold Macmillan's resignation eighteen years earlier. 'By the end of the week', wrote the *Guardian*'s Peter Jenkins, 'the government was in open disarray, the Imperial Hotel had become a mill of rumour and malice and it was scarcely possible to wander through its corridors without encountering fringe meetings of the Cabinet at which the bitterness and deepness of the divisions became more and more open.' Even ordinary activists struck him as almost Bennite in their fervour and animosity; never had Jenkins heard people speaking with such venom of the 'unions, blacks and foreigners' they blamed for the nation's woes.

Instead of lifting the mood, Mrs Thatcher's speech on Friday was as dull as ditchwater, a predictable parade of what Hosykns called 'clichés' and 'wallpaper'. *The Times* thought it 'empty of new ideas'; the *Guardian* judged it 'second class stuff, more Morecambe than Blackpool'. 'Nothing is beyond this nation,' she ended grandly. 'Decline is not inevitable . . . There are those who say our nation no longer has the stomach for the fight. I think I know our people and I know they do.' But her listeners had now heard this sort of thing so often they could probably have recited it in their sleep.[38]

As the Conservatives headed home from Blackpool, there was, perhaps, one consolation. For all the bitterness, their conference had been a model of harmony compared with the chaos at Brighton, where Labour's annual festival of socialist brotherhood had been dominated by the titanic battle between Denis Healey and Tony Benn. But by this stage few Tories were particularly bothered about Labour. What worried them was the Alliance, which had made inroads into every social group and still commanded almost 40 per cent of the vote in the opinion polls. In the next six weeks, the Conservatives would face two stiff challenges in the Croydon and Crosby by-elections. If one fell to the Alliance, that would be bad. If both fell, it would be time to panic.[39]

The first test came in Croydon North West. This was safe Conservative territory: in 1979 their candidate, Robert Taylor, had won by almost 3,800 votes. After Taylor's death in June 1981 triggered a by-election, the Tory managers postponed it until 22 October, hoping that a successful conference would give them enough bounce to retain the seat. In this they were completely mistaken. Although the Alliance's campaign began with a row about who was actually going to contest the seat – the SDP fancied it for Shirley Williams, but the Liberals demanded that their local candidate, Bill Pitt, be given a free run – its momentum proved irresistible. By polling day, about a thousand Alliance volunteers had flooded into Croydon, and reporters found plenty of people happy to discuss their decision to switch. 'I think Mrs Thatcher's policy is too extreme and the Labour Party is in too much of a mess,' said one housewife, who had voted Tory in 1979. 'It's worthwhile giving the Alliance a try. When you are right at the bottom you have nothing to lose,' said a commercial artist who usually voted Labour. 'I don't like the way the Labour Party is going', agreed a local roofer, 'and I don't like Benn.'[40]

It was a sign of the Alliance's impact that when the result in Croydon was declared, few people were surprised to hear Pitt had won. Even so, the fact that he had increased his vote fourfold in barely two years, turning a 3,769 Conservative majority into a 3,254 Liberal one, was a stunning blow to the two major parties. The Tories remained relatively sanguine: governments often lose by-elections, and at least they had finished second. The other big losers, though, were Labour, who found themselves on the wrong end of a 14 per cent swing to the Liberals. In other circumstances, Croydon might have been a Labour gain, but this was precisely the sort of affluent, suburban seat in which their supporters were stampeding for the exits. Echoing many local activists, Michael Foot blamed Ken Livingstone's 'pronouncements on the IRA'. But the real blame, said Foot's employment spokesman, Eric Varley, a Chesterfield miner's son, lay with those who had 'cynically denounced the Labour governments in which they served'. Everybody knew whom he meant.[41]

Barely had the dust settled in Croydon than the circus moved on, pitching its tent in Crosby, Merseyside. Once again the death of a veteran backbencher had triggered a competition in a safe Conservative seat. With its suburban mock-Tudor mansions, prep schools and golf courses, its affluent commuters, pensioners and small businessmen, Crosby had been Tory territory since the end of the First World War. From the Alliance's point of view, though, it was perfect. Precisely because it was a safe Tory seat, even coming second would be seen as a victory. On top of all that, Crosby had one of the largest proportions of Catholic voters in the country. And, as luck would have it, Shirley Williams happened to be one of the most prominent Catholic politicians in the land. At first she hesitated: Crosby was a long way from London. But having declined to fight in Warrington, she could not sit on the sidelines again. She had to overturn a Tory–Liberal gap of more than 25,000 votes in 1979. But if there was 'one member of the SDP or the Liberal Party who could pull off the impossible', said the *Guardian*, it was Shirley Williams.[42]

Even at the time, Crosby seemed destined for a place in political legend. Williams seemed to be everywhere, campaigning for fourteen hours a day, banging on doors, greeting voters outside supermarkets, handing out leaflets in the street, always late, always cheerful, always smiling. Her activists called her the 'tiny tornado', and wherever she went loudspeakers pumped out the theme from *Chariots of Fire*. Her modus operandi, as the sceptical Frank Johnson observed, was to base her campaign on personality rather than policy:

> Mrs Williams bustles up to a group of willing voters outside some shops as if she is also a woman who can't stop now because she's got some shopping to do ... Breathlessly, she finds time to tell them that there are no easy solutions, that these are terribly difficult problems, but that one thing is certain: neither Mrs Thatcher nor Mr Benn have the answers.

This was smart politics: most people voted for the SDP because of what it was against, not what it was for. After so much economic misery and political factionalism, explained the *Express*'s George Gale, 'the public has been yearning for a ready excuse, and somebody to blame'. And in Shirley Williams they had found somebody who could give them both.[43]

Polling day was 26 November. A week beforehand, Mrs Thatcher's factotum Ian Gow visited Crosby and was appalled by what he found. The mood was so bad, he told Alan Clark, that 'our candidate was now completely shell-shocked, would not meet the press, could not bring himself to talk to strangers, etc.' And when the ballots were counted, Shirley Williams had achieved the impossible. With 28,118 votes, just over 49 per cent of the total, she had beaten the Conservative candidate by more than 5,000 votes, a result inconceivable only months earlier. The Labour candidate was completely blown away, winning barely 9 per cent of the vote and losing his deposit. It was, by any standards, a stunning result. And after all their sneers about her scruffiness and scattiness, Fleet Street's finest seemed overjoyed that her decency had won the day. Watching the mud-splattered, exhausted but exhilarated Williams tuck into breakfast the next morning, the *Mirror*'s John Edwards thought she had 'a lot of class, the class of dynamic ordinariness'. 'Against such a goddess', agreed the *Express*'s John Warden, 'mortal men had no chance.'[44]

Political history is littered with supposedly seismic and unprecedented by-elections, but Crosby really was something else. Not only was this the first time somebody in the SDP colours had been elected to Parliament, it had seen the biggest turnover of votes in electoral history. As amateur psephologists pointed out, a similar result at the next General Election would give the Alliance 533 seats, Labour seventy-eight and the Conservatives just four. And although nobody thought this was a serious possibility, the last three mainland by-elections had produced Alliance totals of

42 per cent, 40 per cent and 49 per cent. Some bookmakers made the SDP evens favourites to win the next general election, with both the Tories and Labour nine to four against. 'The mould of British politics has been totally broken', Williams declared in the first flush of victory, 'and it will never be the same again . . . This is not for us a party but a crusade, an attempt to find a democratic alternative to what we believe to be the growing extremism of politics in Britain . . . We are making a new beginning for Britain, a new vision for Britain in the world.'[45]

Some listeners might have thought this a bit over the top, but the next day's papers were in no doubt. 'Nothing in recent history', said *The Times*, could match 'the astonishing performance of Mrs Shirley Williams at Crosby'. 'SHIRLEY THE FIRST', gasped the front page of the *Mirror*, which thought the Alliance must now be 'favourite to be the largest party in the next Parliament'. As the paper's veteran political editor, Walter Lancaster, explained, Britain was now facing 'the biggest smash-up of its political system since 1931 when the Labour Party broke in two and its leaders helped form a National Government. Nobody knows what will happen at the general election.' And even the usually waspish George Gale agreed that the Alliance was poised to become, at the very least, the main opposition party. In the future, he told readers of the *Express*, 'the Labour Party will continue to wither away until only a rump is left. Healey and Hattersley must now wish they had joined the SDP. More Labour MPs soon will . . . We are gaining a new Opposition, a new alternative Government. We are losing Michael Foot, along with his heap of old rubbish.'[46]

The heap of old rubbish did not take its humiliation gracefully. 'They have not got any policies,' complained Michael Foot, though he promptly contradicted himself by describing the SDP as a 'kind of Margaret Thatcher Mark II'. By contrast, the Tories were so shell-shocked they could barely muster a satisfyingly bitchy reaction, at least in public. In private, however, it was a different story. 'How fickle and spastic the electorate are,' spat Alan Clark. 'How gullible, to be duped by someone as scatty and shallow as Shirley Williams.' Even *Private Eye*'s Denis Thatcher was beside himself with rage. 'I can't understand what they see in the Williams woman, not to mention that smarmy little GP or the fat cat from Brussels with the speech impediment,' he writes furiously to his friend Bill. 'If ever there was a set of hopeless hand-job merchants those are they.' To make matters worse, when Denis slips away from Number 10 for a stiff drink, he still cannot escape the shadow of the new party. 'I was not in the best of moods as I piloted the Rolls back to the sanctuary of Downing Street,' he adds, 'only to find some joker had plastered the roof with damnfool stickers for the SDP.'[47]

*

Mrs Thatcher had watched the Crosby result in the Number 10 flat with
Ian Gow, the latter seething at the spectacle of the 'ghastly Shirley
Williams'. But there was an even ghastlier spectacle to come: the sight of
the Conservative Party's former helmsman touring the television studios
the next day, delightedly telling everybody how sorry he was. The Alliance's victory, explained Edward Heath, 'shows that we have alienated a
very large number of people . . . You can't kid the electorate . . . If you go
on with Crosby after Crosby after Crosby until a general election you will
get another sort of Government.' So what was Heath going to do now?
Challenge Mrs Thatcher for the Tory leadership? Or would he and the
Wets consider a coalition with the Alliance? 'I'm prepared to help my
country wherever I think I can be of service,' he said. And if there were a
hung parliament in 1983 or 1984, 'there might be one or two invitations
which might be acceptable'.[48]

"Gracious lady! May I offer you the benefit of my unrivalled military know-how?"

The *Express*'s Michael Cummings took a predictably dim view of the prospect
of a rapprochement between Edward Heath and the SDP–Liberal Alliance.
Incidentally, this cartoon also shows how quickly poor Bill Rodgers disappeared
from the public consciousness: here he has been supplanted by the Liberal leader
David Steel (*Sunday Express*, 29 November 1981).

In retrospect, this was the moment for Heath to make a decisive break and raise his ensign alongside that of his former Balliol contemporary Roy Jenkins. But he never did. Jenkins found this baffling, later accusing his old friend of putting 'the telescope to his blind eye'. But, as Heath's biographer explains, he saw himself as 'fighting Mrs Thatcher for the soul of the Tory party', and was determined not to leave her in unchallenged command. After Crosby, he was more convinced than ever that his old shipmates would come to their senses and kick out Grantham's answer to Fletcher Christian. That would allow him to return to the bridge as a much-loved elder statesman, vindicated after years in exile, brokering a moderate coalition with his friends in the Alliance. In interviews he remembered how the Tories had installed Churchill as Prime Minister in 1940 because their coalition partners would not work with Neville Chamberlain. In Heath's own mind, Churchill was almost as considerable a figure as he was. 'So it has happened in the past,' he said happily, 'and it could happen again.'[49]

Heath's optimism was not entirely delusional, since by now parliamentary discipline seemed perilously close to breaking down. On 25 November two dozen Tory backbenchers signed a letter to the Chief Whip, Michael Jopling. If the government attempted another dose of spending cuts or tax rises, they said, they would vote against it. 'We have got far more dissidents than I expected,' Jopling warned Mrs Thatcher nine days later, 'and some of them are very unhappy indeed.' In total, he thought there were forty-five potential rebels – a 'very serious situation', given that the government had a majority of just forty-four. Yet the rebellion never materialized. If it had, political history would have taken a very different course. But a genuinely effective coup would have required considerable ruthlessness and opportunism, which were not qualities people associated with the likes of Gilmour or St John-Stevas. They were, however, qualities people associated with Margaret Thatcher. That was why she was in Number 10, and Gilmour and St John-Stevas weren't.[50]

Even so, there was only so much punishment Mrs Thatcher could take before her position disintegrated. By early December Gallup had the Alliance on 50½ per cent, Labour on 23½ per cent and the Tories on 23 per cent, while the government's approval rating had collapsed to just 18 per cent. Mrs Thatcher's own reputation, meanwhile, had descended to frankly diabolical depths. By Christmas, only one in four people said they were satisfied with her performance, the worst figure for any Prime Minister in history. At Conservative Central Office the mood was apocalyptic; according to the party's research department, the 'electoral and poll evidence' suggested that the Alliance was poised to 'sweep the

Conservative party into a small minority position, worse than anything we have experienced for over one hundred years'.[51]

In public, Mrs Thatcher never wavered. But she would not have been human if she had not had doubts. 'Willie, Geoffrey, Cecil and Norman I can count on,' she remarked to the *Sunday Express*'s editor, John Junor, but the others were 'in an utter funk about the election'. 'She doesn't know who to trust,' Denis said. 'Her authority is being eroded . . . She feels like jacking it in.'

But she kept going. Something, surely, would turn up.[52]

# 28

## The Shadow of the Past

*We are increasingly two nations, riven between employed and unemployed, north and south.*

Guardian, 28 August 1980

*The northern cities may offer little other than soot, football, and urban decline, but the surrounding countryside will make your northern expedition worthwhile.*

Let's Go, 1982: The Budget Guide to
Britain and Ireland (1982)

In the autumn of 1981, the children's authors Janet and Allan Ahlberg published one of the great masterpieces of the age. Set in a terraced working-class house during the Second World War, *Peepo!* is the story of a baby, glimpsed through his eyes. The first thing he sees is his parents' bedroom, his father asleep in the 'big brass bed' beside his mother, a 'hairnet on her head'. A kitchen scene shows his mother making porridge, his father carrying in coal from the yard, his grandmother hanging out the washing. A bonfire burns across the road; an air-raid warden does his rounds; his sisters hunt for a tin 'to take up to the park / And catch fishes in'. Later, his mother dozes with the *Picture Post*, while his father, in green battledress, pours the tea. The baby has a bath in a tin tub; his nightgown warms on the door of the oven; his sisters play under a clothes horse hung with washing. In the final pages, his parents carry him to his cot, his father clearly about to leave for the front. Our last glimpse is of the baby tucked up, 'fast asleep and dreaming / What did he see?'[1]

Quite apart from its virtues as a book for small children, *Peepo!* is a beautifully observed portrait of family life at the middle of the century. In many ways it is a toddler's version of George Orwell's cosy portrait of working-class life in *The Road to Wigan Pier*. Musing on the differences between working-class and middle-class, Orwell had claimed that in a working-class household, 'you breathe a warm, decent, deeply human atmosphere which it is not so easy to find elsewhere'. He imagined the living room of a terraced house:

> on winter evenings after tea, when the fire glows in the open range and dances mirrored in the steel fender, when Father, in shirt-sleeves, sits in the rocking chair at one side of the fire reading the racing finals, and Mother sits on the other with her sewing, and the children are happy with a pennorth of mint humbugs, and the dog lolls roasting himself on the rag mat.

As the historian Robert Colls remarks, there was plenty of 'sentimentality and contrivance' in all this. Yet as sentimental dreams go, Orwell's picture proved immensely influential: an idealized vision of an unchanging world, bound together by collective solidarity and domestic commitment, hard work and family values.[2]

At the very moment when Orwell's landscape was crumbling into dust, Allan Ahlberg had written *Peepo!* as a tribute to his own working-class childhood. Born to an unmarried mother in Croydon in 1938, Ahlberg had been adopted by a family from Oldbury, in the Black Country. His father was a manual labourer; his mother was an office cleaner. He had grown up in a world of brick back-to-backs, tin baths and coal fires, a pub on every corner and a football in every street. But he did not romanticize it, recalling a 'fair few clips round the ear, no books and not much conversation'. His driving ambition was to get out: he scraped into the local grammar school and eventually became a teacher. Only in his late thirties, prompted by Janet, an illustrator, did he begin writing children's stories. Many of their books – *Burglar Bill* (1977), *Cops and Robbers* (1978), *Each Peach Pear Plum* (1978), *Funny Bones* (1980), *The Jolly Postman* (1986) – became children's classics, thanks not least to Janet's wonderfully funny pictures, and by Allan's own account they 'made an absolute fortune'. Yet he never left the Black Country behind. 'When I was young my ambition was to leave and I did when I was 18, but now I go back, and I love it,' he said later. It might be a 'poor, blighted, devastated landscape', but it was 'the only patch of the world that I love'.[3]

For more than a century, the world Ahlberg described, the great foundry of the West Midlands, had been synonymous with Britain's industrial might. This was the landscape that had shocked the future Queen Victoria, horrified Charles Dickens and inspired J. R. R. Tolkien, whose nightmarish visions of industrial modernity, 'wheels and outlandish contraptions . . . a-hammering and a-letting out a smoke and a stench', might have come directly from the streets of West Bromwich. It was also the landscape that had given heavy metal to the world. Judas Priest's lead

THE SHADOW OF THE PAST


singer Rob Halford, whose father worked for a Walsall metalworking firm, recalled that at school:

> We'd be doing English, and we'd be next to a metal foundry, and the steam hammers would be banging up and down, and the whole desk would be shaking . . . Walking home, the air was full of all these bits of metal grit, and you could taste it, and you could breathe it in . . . You literally breathed in metal.

His bandmate Glen Tipton, who worked as an apprentice at British Steel, agreed. 'We really did grow up in a labyrinth of heavy metal. Huge foundries, big steam hammers,' he remembered. 'You could always hear the steam hammers. There was always a steel mill within audible distance.' The title of the band's most successful album, *British Steel*, released in April 1980, said it all. 'Pounding the world like a battering ram / Forging the furnace for the final grand slam,' runs 'Rapid Fire'. 'Hammering anvils straining muscle and might / Shattering blows crashing browbeating fright . . .'[4]

Yet at precisely the moment *British Steel* reached the record shops, that world was falling apart. For decades, the industrial towns of the West Midlands had prided themselves on their prosperity, work ethic and collective spirit. In 1975 the unemployment rate in the Black Country had been just 1.1 per cent. But then everything changed. By 1980 it had reached double figures. In some towns, one in four people was out of work. In the borough of Sandwell, which included West Bromwich, Smethwick, Oldbury and Tipton, 'metal-based manufacturing' accounted for almost half of all jobs. But most were either in gigantic firms such as Lucas and GKN or in tiny, family-run companies making one or two components for the big beasts. So when the recession came, its scale and speed were devastating. The first half of 1980 brought thousands of redundancies every month: some 30,000 people, who had once made things like steel bolts, pumps, pressure vessels, brass stampings and electrical components, were thrown on to the dole queue almost overnight. Six months earlier, the local *Evening Mail* had called 1979 'the year they tore the heart out of Sandwell'. Never did it imagine that 1980 would be even worse.

For many of the area's Labour MPs, the fault lay with the government. But many local businessmen recognized that there were deeper forces at work, too. For years, said *The Times*, they had warned of growing levels of cheap imports: taps from Italy, carpets from the United States, 'even Christmas cards from the Soviet Union, which are regarded as a threat to jobs at Kenrick and Jefferson of West Bromwich'. Many Midlands towns suffered from a perilously narrow industrial base: Bilston depended on the local steelworks, Kidderminster on carpets, Stoke on pottery. In Coventry, tens of thousands of jobs depended on companies such as Rolls-Royce and British Leyland – precisely those companies hardest hit by the high pound, feeble productivity and foreign competition. 'That makes us very vulnerable,' admitted the head of the town's Chamber of Commerce. But it was too late to do anything about it now.[5]

Not even the most pessimistic observers envisaged how bad things would get. Even two years after the end of the recession, unemployment across the West Midlands was stuck at about 17 per cent. Once, said the *Sunday Times*, 'Coventry was the most prosperous city in Britain; Wolverhampton, West Bromwich and Wednesbury the grimy foundations on which the full employment economy rested'. But now the area had become 'Britain's most devastated industrial wasteland', while 'the names of firms which have slashed jobs or shut plants reads like a roll-call of the biggest names in British industry: British Leyland, BSA, Swan, Alfred Herbert, GKN, Lucas, Typhoo, Bird's, Dunlop.' In just four years, the jobless figures in Wolverhampton had swelled from 8,000 to 26,000. In Coventry, unemployment had leapt from 15,000 to 40,000; in Walsall it had gone from 9,000 to 31,000; in Sandwell and Dudley, from 11,500 to 53,000. For every new job that opened up, almost fifty people were out of work.[6]

In Tipton, once the home of James Watt's ground-breaking steam pumping engine, a visiting reporter found the factories boarded up, the scrapyard for sale, the canals eerily silent. There was only one place where there were 'people visibly at work'. Fifteen minutes' walk from the station, the reporter found the terraced streets crowded, the old-fashioned pub serving faggots and peas, a chain-maker hammering red-hot metal, the ironworks bustling with activity. It was as though he had been transported back in time. He had. This was the Black Country Living Museum, the architectural equivalent of the Ahlbergs' *Peepo!* Its open-air recreation of the Victorian era had opened in 1978 on twenty-six acres of derelict land, complete with disused mine shafts and sewage works, with the aim of rebuilding 'stone by stone and brick by brick, the Black Country when it was at its most industrious and its heart was sound'. At the time, nobody could have envisaged how poignant those words would seem.

Today, when post-industrial dilapidation has become a familiar feature of our national life, it is hard to recapture the shock as people's neighbourhoods crumbled around them. Even children of the age of affluence had never imagined that this world would be swept away so quickly. No doubt this helps to explain the success of the Black Country Living Museum. By 1982 it was already attracting some 120,000 visitors a year, rising to 250,000 three years later. For many people, its forges and kilns, its

Victorian pub and old-fashioned sweet shop, seemed moving reminders of the world they had lost. Many years later, the columnist Caitlin Moran, who grew up in Wolverhampton in the 1980s, recalled her father's words whenever they drove into town in the mornings. 'When I was a kid, at this time of the day, all you'd hear was the tramp, tramp, tramp of people's feet as they walked to the factories,' he would say. 'Every bus would be full, the streets would be seething. This town had something to do and money in its pocket. People used to come here for work and get it the same day. Look at it now . . . A ghost town. Where have they gone? Where have they all gone?'[7]

What happened to the Black Country was not unique. It was much the same story half an hour north, in the heart of the Potteries. Reflecting on a long walk through the Six Towns in the autumn of 1980, the essayist Lincoln Allison thought few places in England better lived up to the 'mistily nostalgic vision of industrial society, a world of clogs clattering on the cobbles, coals burning in the grate, street parties on Jubilee day, and hot buttered crumpets and a mug of tea without pausing to take your muffler off when you come back from the match on a Saturday'.

But in the Potteries, as elsewhere, change was irresistible. Unemployment might be lower here than in the Black Country, but one in ten people was still out of work. 'Folks round here could either be miners or potters. Nothing else for it,' wrote Beryl Bainbridge when she visited Stoke three years later. Not any more, though. When she visited the Chatterley Whitfield colliery, once the largest mine in the North Staffordshire coalfield, she found weeds growing from the power house, the window frames rotting in the repair shop, grass growing on the slag heap. After more than a hundred years, it had closed in 1977. Now it was Britain's first underground mining museum.[8]

Even in London, once a great industrial city, visitors found the same melancholy picture. Trudging across the Isle of Dogs in the summer of 1979, Allison found an 'eerie silence', broken only by the occasional sad hoot from the Thames. Thanks to the rise of containerization and the establishment of huge new terminals downriver, the docks were virtually dead, the workforce falling from 35,000 men to just 2,000 in barely two decades. 'There wasn't a human being in sight,' wrote Jonathan Raban, who wandered through the 'miles of corrugated iron and slag-piles' three years later. 'It looked as if the great work of destruction had been set in train years ago, then suddenly abandoned on a whim.' By this stage, Michael Heseltine had established the London Docklands Development Corporation (LDDC), and, across the Thames, Raban spotted the first signs of redevelopment: warehouses converted into flats, forests of estate agents' signs, the promise of a fashionable new existence amid the ruins of industry. But not everybody welcomed the new order. On a 'lone atoll of redevelopment', Raban spotted some graffiti: 'SOD OFF LDDC. THESE ARE OUR BACK GARDENS NOT YOURS. WE WANT HOUSES FOR LOCAL PEOPLE, NOT PALACES FOR PLAYBOYS.'[9]

'These are our back gardens not yours.' Here spoke millions of people, bewildered and alienated by social and economic change. Gazing down from the hills above Bolton, Jeremy Seabrook thought the skyline looked the same as ever, 'the towers of churches, the rectangular mass of mills, the black cylinders of chimneys'. Only when he walked down into the town did he realize that everything had been transformed, 'mills into garages and warehouses, churches into stores or car showrooms'. Even the refurbishment of thousands of mouldering pubs, made lighter and more welcoming for a new generation, seemed a rebuff to the working-class men who had been regulars for decades. In 1982 the Three Tuns in Eastwood, Nottinghamshire, immortalized as the Moon and Stars in D. H. Lawrence's *Sons and Lovers* (1913), underwent a £25,000 renovation to cater for younger drinkers, complete with fruit machines and *Space Invaders* games. But the regulars did not like it at all. 'It's wicked,' said one old miner, sitting beneath a loudspeaker pumping out the Stranglers, Meat Loaf and Adam and the Ants. He did not mean it as a compliment. 'They have done it up for the young 'uns. I've been coming here for 53 years, and this bar has not been changed above 20 years since.'[10]

Hundreds of miles away, on the shores of the Firth of Forth, another elderly man was gazing sadly at a changed world. Harry Jack had been born into a working-class family in a Scottish lowland mill town in 1902, the year the Boer War ended. His life had been defined by work: work in textile mills, down a coal mine, on a cargo steamer, in a lead factory, in a hosepipe factory. 'He ended his working life only a few miles from where he had begun it, and in much the same way,' Ian Jack wrote after his father died in 1981: 'in overalls and over a lathe and waiting for the dispensation of the evening hooters, when he would stick his leg over his bike and cycle home.' Harry had inhabited a world steeped in tradition, in which the past was always present. He 'embodied it and spoke of it continually . . . it came home from work every evening in its flat cap and dirty hands and drew its weekly wages from industries which even then were sleepwalking their way towards extinction.'

Yet now Harry's world was gone. The cargo steamer had been scrapped; the coal mine was a field; the mills had become car parks. His old school had become a supermarket; his old house had made way for a traffic island. In the village of North Queensferry in Fife, where he spent the final decades of his life, everything seemed different. The neighbours died; new people moved in, 'wives who wore jeans and loaded small cars at the nearest supermarket, husbands who drove what twenty years before would have seemed an impossible distance to work'. The newcomers gutted the old cottages, knocked down walls or painted them white, 'hung garlic from their kitchen shelves'. They called their dinner 'lunch', their tea 'supper'. They set up a heritage trail and revived the village's annual gala day, yet at the same time the shops closed and the grocery vans stopped calling. Even the newspapers no longer made sense: one day, Harry threw down the local weekly in disgust, with the words: 'There's nothing in here but sponsored walks and supermarket bargains.' It was as if the past had been destroyed, every remnant changed or obliterated. By the time Harry Jack died, it might never have existed.[11]

In some ways, therefore, the story of Britain in the early 1980s was one of shattering loss. In Margaret Drabble's state-of-the-nation novel *The Middle Ground* (1980), the forty-something magazine columnist Kate Armstrong visits her old home in working-class east London, only to find everything 'changed forever', the narrow streets of artisans' houses replaced by 'a wilderness of flyovers and underpasses and unfinished supports . . . raw, ugly, gigantic in scale'. And two years later, in the final episode of *Boys from the Blackstuff*, Alan Bleasdale gives the ailing George, the last link with Liverpool's industrial past, a moving eulogy to the vanished age of working-class optimism:

> Ah Chrissie, it just seems like soddin' yesterday, the midday gun. The women sandstoning the steps and the flags. The kids playing alley-oh, the little shops on the corner where you got the three pennyworth of fine Irish, the old snuff, and the twist of tobacco, and your old gran had a flat top cart there, used to sell salt fish and a big barrel of ribs, straight off the pig's back, from the Irish boats and on the third Saturday an organ grinder and his monkey . . . And there we'd be pilin' into Effin' Nellie's or Peg-leg Pete's for a couple of pints of good beer, maybe the first of the week and the crack . . . the crack . . . we'd talk of many things . . . Of politics and power and come the day when we'd have inside toilets and proper bathrooms . . . of Attlee and Bevan, Hogan and Logan, the Braddocks and Dixie Dean . . . and Lawton and Liddell and Matthews and Finney . . .

For George, the end of everything he knew and loved comes as a devastating blow. 'I can't believe there is no hope, I can't,' he says desperately. But a moment later, he is dead.[12]

Twenty years earlier, the Beatles' home town had been feted across the world as the city of the Cavern Club and the Mersey Sound. But those days were long gone. With Liverpool now a byword for urban decay, mass unemployment, family breakdown and juvenile crime, it had become an essential destination for writers seeking apocalyptic colour about the state of the nation. Almost without exception, they agreed that it was uniquely forlorn, a doomed city stranded on the edge of England. Very rarely did they visit its middle-class suburbs; instead, they made straight for the very shabbiest, most poverty-stricken areas. Walking towards Everton from the Pier Head, Lincoln Allison found himself in 'deserted streets surrounded by factories and warehouses and occasional heaps of rubble . . . The silence is eerie, frightening. You hardly get silence like this anywhere on earth.' But there was worse to come:

> Going up Stanley Road towards Bootle, the townscape degenerates into the most sordid I have ever seen. Urban life cannot get any more raw than this. Nowhere else have I seen men pissing in the street in such a public way. There's a lot of vomit on the streets, most of it apparently special fried rice, though I don't examine it too closely. All the shops are boarded up. This isn't because they are closed; it is because Rule One of life round here is that glass gets broken. Rule Two is that any other surface gets written on, politically for the most part, with the UDA, UVF, SAS, SWP and IRA well represented.

Never before, in England, had Allison seen such a 'concentration of rock-bottom urban circumstances'. Only in the United States had he witnessed urban dereliction to match it – and in Scotland.[13]

Liverpool's problems were not, of course, unique: the people of Glasgow, Detroit, Naples and Marseilles would have found them very familiar. Were they exclusively Margaret Thatcher's fault? Obviously not. But she made an irresistible scapegoat, partly because she was so clearly implicated in the recession, but also because she so obviously lacked the slightest sentimental attachment to the traditions of working-class Britain. And since images of working-class Britain tended to be so masculine – the flat cap, the factory, the pub, the football crowd – it surely mattered that she was a bossy middle-class *woman*, the perfect personification of the social and economic changes undermining the foundations on which an entire world had rested.

Even so, it is sheer fantasy to imagine that, if she had never come to power, the world of *Peepo!* would have survived unscathed. In many ways it was dead already. Across the country, hundreds of thousands of Victorian terraced houses had already been demolished and their residents decanted into tower blocks. Football crowds were already in free-fall;

chapels were already deserted; pubs were already closing; the great manufacturing industries were already shedding workers; and, most profoundly, the social and cultural assumptions of Allan Ahlberg's childhood had already begun to crumble. Ahlberg's own story, that of a bright boy trying to escape from the world he celebrated, was part of this transformation. Indeed, there is a case that what really destroyed the landscape of *Peepo!* was not so much economic decline as economic affluence. Men did not stop going to the pub because they had run out of money; they stopped because they were watching television. Even the fate of Harry Jack's old school, demolished to make way for a supermarket, tells a story of affluence as much as one of loss.

By the time Mrs Thatcher came to power, Jeremy Seabrook had been writing about the erosion of working-class culture for more than a decade. As far back as 1971 he had visited Blackburn to find a world of 'derelict streets and decayed mills', where older residents, confused and alienated by the changes brought by economic growth and social mobility, directed their frustrations at their Pakistani neighbours. A few years later, he was shocked by the 'abbreviated terraces and derelict sites' of Wigan, while he found parts of Bradford virtually abandoned, 'as though the people had deserted the worn-out housing and exhausted landscape and gone elsewhere'. And as he watched people parking outside their new suburban houses, queuing for takeaways and swarming through the new shopping arcades, he seethed with anger that they had been encouraged, as he saw it, to abandon the 'working-class past' as 'something ugly and shaming'.[14]

Seabrook did not blame 'the desolation of ruined communities' on unemployment and poverty. He blamed them on affluence and individualism, trends that had brought Mrs Thatcher to power rather than ones she had called into being. It was affluence, he thought, which had inculcated a fatal 'dependence on commodities' in place of the 'capacity for caring, the wisdom won through pain and struggle in adversity; the stoicism and pride' that had supposedly characterized working-class life before the advent of the washing machine. Indeed, for Seabrook, even the grinding poverty of Orwell's Wigan had been better than the relative comforts of working-class life in the 1980s, because it was more authentic, more *real*. 'Even the food was different – the stew with its neck of lamb and three penn'orth of pot-herbs was not the same as the Colonel Sanders chicken in its red cardboard box and the saffron gravy in the tinfoil from the takeaway,' he wrote. 'The open fire was a living comfort, the old boots warming in the hearth and the lore and pictures in the flames had a consoling influence which the underfloor heating which cannot be regulated does not.'[15]

The open fire, the old-fashioned cooking, the boots in the hearth: all this was pure Orwell. And like Orwell – an Old Etonian who had been taught as a boy that working-class people smelled – Seabrook, a North-ampton grammar-school boy who had gone to Cambridge, wrote about working-class Britain with a strong sense of his own guilt. In January 1982 he published a bitterly self-flagellating article in the *Guardian*, lambasting his generation, who had risen by their own efforts into 'teaching, social work, the media, administration', for betraying their working-class roots. By abandoning their elders in the debris of the industrial landscape, he wrote, they had contributed to 'the spoliation of the working class [and the] loss of continuity'.

In a particularly telling passage, he pictured his meritocratic peers returning to see 'those old people, our parents' and listening to their endless 'monologues of loss':

> In desperation, you pick up a copy of the local newspaper – the Sunderland Echo, the Wolverhampton [Express and] Star – and on the front page there is a story of the closing down of one of those factories you were never supposed to go into. And then there is a report of violence or a mugging, which only gives rise to another cascade of oblique reproach, and they will tell you that it isn't safe to go out even in the daytime now, let alone at night, and that once upon a time you could leave your doors open day and night without fear of anyone stealing from you.

The obvious rejoinder, he knew, was that most people were richer than ever. And yet, he wrote, 'there has been a sustained and one-sided insistence on this single aspect of their lives, while a great silence has lain over all those felt losses'. When elderly people turned on the television, they heard people saying how lucky they were to live at a time of such comforts. Yet things they cared about just as much – the integrity of their families, the survival of their communities, respect for their traditions, a sense of purpose and belonging – had been brushed aside as trivial. 'We thought we were keeping faith,' Seabrook wrote, 'and all the time we were taking something away.'[16]

But there was, of course, another Britain: not broken, brooding, abandoned or alienated, but conservative, aspirational, prosperous and contented. This was the Britain of *Terry and June*, *Bergerac* and the *Antiques Roadshow*: microwave oven Britain, home computer Britain, Marks & Spencer's Britain. It was the Britain of sleepy suburbs and market towns: Watford, where unemployment never rose above 5 per cent; Taunton, with its booming light industrial estates, huge new ITT factory and gargantuan new Asda; Daventry, with its prosperous housing estates and busy distribution centres, where in the summer of 1981 the local Job Centre had so many vacancies that adverts carried the heading 'Urgently Needed'.

Nobody ever wrote a song about Redditch, which saw its population surge by 63 per cent in just ten years. No pop group immortalized Tamworth, where the population grew by almost two-thirds, or Basingstoke, a 'conglomeration of offices, factories and housing estates, characterised by a monotony and lack of inspiration that is probably unsurpassed anywhere in Britain', according to the journalist John Young. Yet although Young hated the Hampshire town's roundabouts and office blocks, Basingstoke had superb transport links, miles of new roads and a shiny new shopping centre. Even more strikingly, it had no unemployment to speak of, even though its population had trebled in less than thirty years. Nobody ever romanticized Basingstoke. But Basingstoke was a success story. Basingstoke was the future.[17]

Was there a formula for success? The most important thing was geography. 'I don't think we are doing anything right,' said Berkshire's county planning officer. 'It's just because of where we are.' The towns along the M4 corridor – Newbury, Reading, Bracknell, Wokingham – did not receive a penny in regional aid. They did not need to. They were close to London, close to Heathrow and close to the government research centres into weapons, aircraft, nuclear fusion, atomic energy, transport and meteorology. Many former government scientists had set up their own laboratories, attracting firms such as Ferranti, Racal and Hewlett-Packard to move in too, as well as bright, ambitious young men and women from the declining North and Midlands. 'It's an incestuous kind of thing,' explained Newbury's chief planning officer. 'They head-hunt each other, work and socialise together . . . Tonight's good idea means two more jobs on the lab bench tomorrow.'

Here, declared the *Guardian*, Mrs Thatcher's dream of a hi-tech Britain had become a reality: 'In the wake of the computer industry come the service industries, the precision engineering shops, the banks and insurance services.' No planner had earmarked Newbury as a pharmaceuticals centre, yet in the middle of 1982 the German giant Bayer was building a massive new complex that would be its British base for the next three decades. Across the county, in fact, business was booming. Half of all Berkshire's firms told a council survey that they were planning to take on more staff; barely one in ten expected to lay anybody off.[18]

It is telling, though, that few observers had kind words for places like Newbury and Reading. Imaginatively, most commentators were still

Victorians at heart. Work was something done by men in a factory, not women in an office. Streets should be lined with brick back-to-backs, not suburban bungalows. Town centres should be full of stone churches and Victorian town halls, not glass office blocks and concrete roundabouts. As a result, success stories were often treated like alien intruders in a landscape of decline. When Beryl Bainbridge went to Milton Keynes, she could barely contain her horror. 'If I had to describe the area in one sentence,' she wrote, 'I would say it was a series of motorways circled by endless roundabouts, with the houses hidden behind clumps of earth.'[19]

Yet Milton Keynes was the greatest urban achievement of the age. Since 1967, when the government had unveiled its plans for a New Town of some 250,000 people in the north Buckinghamshire countryside, its growth had been little short of sensational. Outsiders mocked the grid layout and concrete cows. But few could have looked at its growth figures, the best in the land, without feeling intensely jealous. In two decades, the area's population had more than doubled, while the number of jobs had risen from just 18,000 to more than 50,000. Two-thirds of the new jobs were in services; three-quarters of the local workforce were professional, managerial or skilled workers; more than half were aged under 40. In March 1981, when much of industrial Britain was shivering in the recession, the *Guardian* profiled two small firms that had just moved to the area. The first, a two-man band making vacuum systems for research laboratories, was doing so well it had just taken on fourteen precision engineers to cope with the demand. The other firm made moulded kitchen and bathroom fixtures, the perfect product for a home-centred age. There was no better location in the country, the boss said, 'for serving the country's best markets. It's simply a sensible place to be.'[20]

But there was more to Milton Keynes than work. Contrary to what its critics claimed, it was not some suburban wasteland, devoid of culture or community, 'all concrete and no soul'. The town's £300,000 advertising campaign called it 'Ambridge with all mod cons', and new residents waxed lyrical about the wonderful leisure facilities, the friendly neighbours, the sense of camaraderie and common endeavour. For elderly people moving to the area, the council had organized a 'good neighbour' programme, with staff to help the newcomers settle in, organize their shopping trips and even take them to doctors' appointments. For the youngest residents, there was a special pack containing a letter from the mayor, a badge, a certificate, a local quiz and a poster map of the area with stickers so they could mark off the different 'attractions'. No doubt critics would have scoffed at that last word; yet as one local man told *The Times*, 'I don't know of another place this size with all our facilities.'

He was not wrong. In March 1981, when the town was just 14 years old, the *Guardian* counted 104 football clubs, fifty-five pubs and bars, two rival English Civil War re-enactment groups, countless flower-arranging societies, toddlers' groups and youth clubs, and even a *Scrabble* group. The Milton Keynes Bowl could seat at least 50,000 people; there were two large leisure centres; there were riding, canoeing, hang-gliding and kung fu clubs. Every weekend on the landscaped lakes, people went angling, sailing, windsurfing and water-skiing. And despite what outsiders claimed, Milton Keynes did have a history. Local archaeology enthusiasts had already uncovered two Roman villas, several farmsteads, two Iron Age enclosures and a demolished seventeenth-century manor house. 'We watch the town grow', said one retired woman, who loved her weekly pensioners' club meetings, 'and wonder why we lived in London for so long.'[21]

Perhaps the most surprising success story, though, was just over an hour away on the other side of the M1. Here, in one of the most unglamorous corners of England it was possible to imagine, a reporter from *The Times* came across another outlandish vision of the future:

> You get the first impression that there is an unBritish air to the place as you approach it over the flat, black, fertile agricultural land: a mass of bright new factories, office blocks and housing is tucked amid a host of new trees and a modern road network. A new golf course has had hillocks piled up by bulldozers to relieve the flatness and a six-mile stretch of the River Nene has been declared a park, complete with an artificial steam railway. The image is Dutch, or Canadian.

This was Peterborough, a sleepy East Anglian cathedral city that had been designated as a New Town in 1967. In just over a decade it had seen its population surge from 81,000 to 120,000 and had built 17,000 new houses, more than 5 million square feet of new factory space and more than 1 million square feet of new office space. It even had a £250,000 advertising campaign, trumpeting what the city planners called the 'Peterborough Effect'.[22]

Even at the time, the thought of a 'Peterborough Effect' seemed faintly comical, because places like Peterborough were supposed to be so preternaturally boring. But in some ways Peterborough was one of the most interesting places in Britain. It was an advertisement for the judicious use of public money: since the end of the 1960s, successive governments had invested an estimated £255 million in Peterborough, including £12,500 in housing and infrastructure for every new job created. In an era when many people were obsessed by the apparent decline of traditional communities, it was also an advertisement for social and geographical mobility. Peterborough was a city of migrants: by 1983, three out of four residents had been born elsewhere. Half came from London, the rest from the Midlands and the North. But there were also sizeable communities of people from overseas: some 2,000 Ugandan Asians, for example, as well as 5,000 Italians, hundreds of Eastern Europeans and even some 125 Vietnamese boat people. But there were virtually no racial tensions. At the local Asian centre, Hindus, Muslims and Sikhs worshipped together perfectly happily, with scarcely a hint of inter-communal tension or hostility from their white neighbours. As the local bishop's community relations chaplain confidently declared: 'Race relations are not a problem in Peterborough.'[23]

When visitors came to places like Peterborough and Milton Keynes, they often described them as 'American'. They never meant it kindly. But to many of the newcomers, Peterborough's supposed 'Americanness' – the sense of space, the clean air, the absence of industrial conflict, the transport links, dual carriageways and suburban houses – was its greatest asset. The drinks firm SodaStream had moved to Peterborough in 1975 and saw production grow from 60,000 units to 415,000 units in just four years. For the firm's managing director, this was the Peterborough Effect in action:

> There's an American style get-up-and-go atmosphere here, an inbuilt sense of optimism helped by the fact that we all know we are paying our own way . . . The houses are good, the roads are good, and great effort has gone on providing the amenities while the expansion programme has been under way and not afterwards, like so many other places. When people live in pleasant houses and have a lot of attractions around them they have a basic goodwill towards life in general and all the new firms here will tell you how high productivity is.

In fact, a *Guardian* survey found that firms which had moved from London thought their productivity was 30 per cent higher in Peterborough, even though most had kept the same staff. The city was not immune from the recession: by 1983, the unemployment rate had reached double figures. But the authorities remained calmly optimistic. Given that they had already attracted some 200 new firms in just over a decade, they had good reason.[24]

Above all, Peterborough promised young families that, if they moved to East Anglia, their everyday lives would be tangibly better than if they stayed in London or Birmingham. The park, golf course and boating lake were designed to attract white-collar workers with children, as was the £24 million Queensgate shopping centre, with its large new John Lewis, 'better than anything short of North London's Brent Cross'. In the leafy Bretton area, the council raised money for a social and recreation centre, the Cresset, boasting a concert hall, sports facilities, meeting rooms, play areas, restaurants and shops. Most importantly, people wanted somewhere to live, and the council duly provided. New houses, although traditional in style, were arranged in suburban townships, linked by what the *Guardian* called 'parkways – fast American-style dual carriageway roads'. At the turn of the 1980s, there was so much housing that virtually everyone moving to Peterborough was guaranteed a home of their own, a potent lure for young couples stuck in rented London flats.

And with the right to own your own home becoming one of the great political totems of the day, Peterborough was ahead of the pack. The city's long-serving council leader, Charlie Swift, had pioneered an East Anglian version of the Right to Buy as far back as the 1960s. Interestingly, though, he was not persuaded by Mrs Thatcher's version. It was not Westminster's place, he thought, to tell local authorities what to do with their housing stock. Even more interestingly, he was a member of the Labour Party. But most of his new neighbours saw their political future rather differently. For decades, Peterborough had been a knife-edge marginal, but in 1979 the Conservatives took the seat with a majority of 5,000. In 1983, even after the recession had dented Peterborough's momentum, they doubled their majority to more than 10,000. Like Milton Keynes, this was Margaret Thatcher country now.[25]

On the face of it, the contrast between places like Liverpool and places like Peterborough was the perfect illustration of the vast chasm between North and South. The facts told the story. Of the fifteen most prosperous towns in Britain in the mid-1980s, reported the *Sunday Times*'s economics editor, David Smith, all fifteen were in the South, the top five being Milton Keynes, Newbury, Didcot, Welwyn and Aldershot. Of the fifteen least prosperous, however, all fifteen were in Scotland, Wales or northern England, the bottom five being Cardigan, Pembroke, Barnsley, Mexborough and Holyhead. Death rates in the North, and particularly in Scotland, were higher than in the South. High blood pressure was more common in northern industrial towns than anywhere else, so heart disease and strokes were more common, too. Northerners were more likely to be smokers, and the Scots the most likely of all.

People in Scotland, northern England and Wales spent a higher proportion of their income on alcohol than their southern counterparts. Rates of burglary, theft and criminal damage were much higher in the North and in Scotland than in southern England. Even morally there was a clear divide. Northerners tended to be more disapproving of drugs and adultery, although they claimed to have more sex; conversely, illegitimacy was much more common in the North. Nationally, about one in five babies was born out of wedlock. In the south-west, this fell to 17 per cent; in the north-west, it rose to 27 per cent. Little wonder that Beryl Bainbridge, who had moved from Liverpool to London, began her *English Journey* believing that 'North and South had long since merged', only to discover that 'they were separate countries'.[26]

This was nothing new, of course. As David Smith noted, the story of the North in the twentieth century had been one of apparently inexorable relative decline. Its public image seemed trapped in the era before the Second World War: hence the success of *Coronation Street*, an idealized, nostalgic community where everybody knows their neighbours. Indeed, the North–South divide was as much a frontier of the imagination as it was a border built of facts and figures. Of the suburban middle-class sitcoms that drew enormous audiences in the early 1980s, *Terry and June* was set near Croydon, *Butterflies* in Cheltenham and *Ever Decreasing Circles* in Surrey. By contrast, the most self-consciously northern of all sitcoms, *Last of the Summer Wine*, was about three old men in flat caps and tweed who might have been preserved in aspic from Orwell's day. The decade's most searing depiction of unemployment and poverty, *Boys from the Blackstuff*, was set in Liverpool. But its most unashamed celebration of wealth and aspiration, *Howards' Way*, was filmed on the Hampshire coast, almost as far south as it is possible to go in mainland Britain.[27]

There was, of course, an awful lot of myth-making in all this. For although the image of Britain as two nations has become a staple of historical writing about the 1980s, it represents only a simplistic version of what was a complicated picture. For one thing, it was never clear where places like the Midlands fitted in, let alone the more prosperous areas of Scotland. And even at the time, astute observers recognized that the idea of a North–South divide could be very misleading. 'England is divided' wrote the *Guardian*'s Peter Jenkins after a long journey across Yorkshire in the winter of 1981, 'but not quite as people imagine. The class war isn't a north–south affair. Great parts of the country remain prosperous in spite of the high unemployment and the worst effects of the recession are concentrated in the areas of deep-seated industrial decline.' For all the talk of provincial alienation, Jenkins thought people in the capital routinely exaggerated the 'political and social impact' of the downturn. He did not deny that the unemployed and the poor were suffering, which was 'tragic for them'. But they were always in a minority. Above all, he thought, 'there is no single pattern to affairs but only variety'.[28]

While the black-and-white figures of the North–South divide undoubtedly reflected underlying trends, they also obscured the nuances of people's daily lives. Even in the depths of winter, there were always green shoots: an expanded IBM factory in Greenock, the new Sanyo factory in Lowestoft, the massive new Nissan works in Sunderland. Even in the sunshine of the boom towns, there were still individual tragedies: a long-serving employee laid off, a family firm that went under, a marriage that collapsed under financial strain. It has become a commonplace that in the 1980s Britain was carved up into winners and losers. But most people did not define themselves as either, any more than they saw themselves as combatants in a class war. On any given street, one family might be struggling to come to terms with redundancy, another struggling to work their new video recorder. One brother might be heading out on a Right to Work march, another might be finishing the paperwork for the Right to Buy. Aspiration and anxiety often lived under the same roof: the same people who lamented the death of community and the decline of traditional morality might be looking forward to a night in with a rented film or a summer break in Yugoslavia.

The place that really summed this up, ironically, was Wigan. People always said that Wigan was a terrible place. Its very name had been a shorthand for industrial grit since Orwell's visit in 1936. Fifty years on, it seemed that, under some little-known UN convention, anybody writing about England, poverty, unemployment or working-class life was obliged to go to Wigan, a battered copy of Orwell's book in their suitcase, and shake their head sorrowfully at the disused mills and terraced houses. And if the town turned out to be less grim than advertised, that just proved that things were grimmer than ever.

When Paul Theroux visited in 1982 he thought the 'dark red terraced houses' and pubs with 'bright mirrors and brasswork' had not changed for a hundred years. But Wigan struck him as 'lifeless'; instead of the 'grubby vitality' of Orwell's day, there was only an 'overwhelming emptiness . . . a deadly calm – which was also like panic'. In place of the 'smoke and the slag-heaps and the racket of machines', he was appalled by the 'clear air and the grass . . . and the great silence'. Ian Jack, who visited in the same year, was similarly struck by the silence. As he noted, the cotton mills had closed, the coalfield was exhausted and unemployment was almost 20 per cent. One day, Jack drove out to Pemberton Colliery, where Orwell had gone down the pit. But the colliery had vanished. There was nothing there: 'no sign that here generations of men had toiled underground for miserable wages . . . No winding gear, no spoil heaps, no shaft, nothing but green.'[29]

But Jack was too shrewd to leave it at that. He was not struck by how awful Wigan was. In fact, he found it perfectly pleasant. Coming from London, he thought Wigan was a 'very *clean* town: no graffiti, not much litter, little smoke'. The mills and mines might be gone, but eight out of ten people still had jobs, so it was simply not true that there was no work. Since 1959 Wigan had been home to the largest food manufacturing plant in Europe, churning out Heinz baked beans for the masses, a staggering 960 million tins of processed food a year. Evidently all those beans had a calming effect: despite the closures and the dole queues, Jack detected no burning anger, no simmering alienation, no sense that a bold cry of 'Justice and Liberty!' would bring the townsfolk rushing into the streets. 'Wigan', he wrote, 'seems about as close to revolt as Weybridge.' The market was busy; the bakery windows were piled high with scones and doughnuts; the shops seemed happy and prosperous. 'Bewildering, isn't it?' said Sydney Smith, the owner of the town's largest newsagent. 'All these folk on the dole and yet trade still prospers.'

Like Orwell, Jack had sought out the cheapest lodgings he could find. Yet 'of the squalor that shocks', he wrote, 'I could find no trace'. Even his landlady's toilet roll was 'encased in knitted wool with a plastic fairy on top', an unmistakeable sign that 'middle-class gentility' had seeped into the hearts of the English working class. Did the people of Wigan feel a sense of kinship with their proletarian brethren in neighbouring towns? Hardly: 'nearly everybody spoke of Liverpool and its inhabitants with dread'. 'They should build a wall round the place,' one man told him, 'just like the one they have in Berlin.' There was no 'real solidarity', lamented the secretary of the local Labour Party. These days, people preferred to retreat behind their castle walls with their 'computers, video machines and roof repairs'. And perhaps most revealing of all, in this staunchly Labour working-class town, were Sydney Smith's sales figures. Every month he sold seven copies of *Tribune*, twelve copies of *Labour Weekly* and thirteen copies of the *New Statesman*. But he also sold twenty-two copies of *The Economist*, twenty-two *Investor's Chronicles* and – amazingly – thirty-six copies of *The Lady*. All these, however, were dwarfed by the 2,500 copies he sold every month of various computer magazines. And this not in Weybridge, but in Wigan.[30]

Wigan was not an anomaly. Wherever Jack went, he found the same picture. In almost every corner of the country, hope and anxiety, nostalgia and ambition, were so tightly woven together it was hard to pick them apart. During the steel strike of 1980, he went to Port Talbot, the archetypal South Wales steel town, a place where every 'mention of Mrs Thatcher or Sir Keith Joseph' was suffused with 'total hatred'. On a grey council estate, the front gardens invariably paved over to accommodate stately British Leyland saloons, Jack visited Owen Reynolds, who worked in the shunting yard of the local steelworks.

Owen, who was out on strike, was not a rich man. Now 51, he had worked since he was 14, had no savings and did not own his home. Usually he made £108 a week before tax, the equivalent of perhaps £650 a week today. Inside his house were 'a telephone, a colour television, quantities of bright, curved and spongy furniture, a gilt mirror which celebrates Wales's grand slam in the rugby internationals – and a bar stocked with bourbon, brandy, Cointreau'. The television was rented, and he still had to pay off the car. But he had far higher ambitions than his elderly father, who had worked in punishing heat in the rolling mill. 'You see in the old days you felt differently,' Owen explained. 'There are no poor people if you're all poor people. It's only when you see the rich that you realise "God, I'm poor" and in those days in Port Talbot you never met them.'

Owen and his brother Patrick had grown up in a slum in the 1930s, with candles and oil lamps, an outside toilet and a cold tap in the yard. When Jack invited them to list the 'essentials for a decent life', they began modestly: a fair wage, a roof over your head, enough food. 'But then the list grew. A car? Yes. A telephone? Yes. A fridge? Certainly.' They were not greedy or materialistic men, and neither were they rampant individualists. Indeed, Owen called himself a 'middle-of-the-road socialist'. They were simply men of their time, whose horizons had been expanded by social, cultural and technological change. They may not have been Thatcherites, but their ambitions nevertheless reflected the social trends that had brought her to power.

So did the words of Owen's son Alan, aged 24, who had just got back from picket duty. Alan had been at Sheerness in Kent, where he had seen policemen kicking strikers on the ground, and it had really shocked him. Since he had only recently started at the steelworks, he knew he was bound to lose his job in the next round of redundancies. Now he told Jack about his great ambition: to buy his own house. 'It's an investment, something you can pass on to your children,' Alan said. 'I'm not being snobbish about council houses, but I just want something better than the place I was brought up in. It's only natural, isn't it?'[31]

Here was the paradox of life in Mrs Thatcher's Britain. Literary travellers invariably looked back to the 1930s, invoking the dole queues and the hunger marchers. It was an apt comparison, but not necessarily for the reasons they imagined. For the 1930s had not just been the decade of the Depression; it had also been a decade of cinemas, dance halls, whodunnits and Butlin's. It was a decade of immense hardship but *also* one of unprecedented prosperity. Even Orwell, who did so much to fix the popular memory of the decade, had been acutely conscious that the innovations of the age, such as 'invisible heaters' and 'rubber, glass and steel' furniture, would soon transform his idealized working-class family beyond recognition. It is true, of course, that all moments are poised between past and future; there are always reminders of the world of yesterday and glimpses of the world of tomorrow. But there are some moments when the contrast is especially sharp. The mid-1930s was one, the early 1980s another.

Nobody saw this more clearly than Ian Jack, the most astute of the writers who travelled the country during the darkest days of the recession. The winter of 1982 found him in the Hebrides, lost in the snow on the island of Eriskay. He was searching for a croft where, he had been promised, the crofter would tell him all about 'the old days'. At last, he found it; and there, huddled in the warm, he listened to the man's memories. Yet all the time he was acutely conscious of the blaring television in the corner, the man's wife having refused to turn it off. So, as Jack later wrote, 'memories of the ceilidhs and the Sunday visiting and the cloth you had to tie over the bucket when you brought water from the well otherwise the water would simply blow away' were 'punctuated by *Falcon Crest* and then *Tenko* and then some other stuff about people getting married in Los Angeles and not enjoying it very much'. *Falcon Crest* in the Outer Hebrides: if there is one story that captures what was happening to Britain, perhaps that is it.[32]

# 29

# The Land of Make Believe

*I don't want love. I want consumer goods.*
Linda Craven (Susan Littler),<br>in Alan Bennett, Enjoy (1980)

*The best thing that can be said about 1981 is: Thank heavens it is 1982 tomorrow.*

*This has been a year dominated by the crack of the assassin's bullet, the cracks in the Labour Party and the crackpot ideas of Mrs Thatcher's team.*
Daily Mirror, 31 December 1981

Christmas came, and it was a season to forget. The fact that almost 3 million people were out of work was bad enough, but to cap it all, the weather was atrocious. In mid-December, blizzards left hundreds of thousands of homes in Wales and the West Country without electricity. And then, after days of freezing fog and driving rain, the snow came down. From the highlands of Scotland to the suburbs of London, roads were closed, train services cancelled and thousands of motorists stranded. In Derbyshire, entire towns were completely cut off; in Sussex, drivers abandoned their cars in deep snowdrifts; in Wales, sheep farmers struggled to save thousands of ewes trapped by the terrible weather. In major cities, cars crawled nervously through the murk; on the high streets, shoppers picked their way past great puddles of slush.

Flights, football matches and horse races were called off, patients airlifted from snowbound hospitals, fishermen swept out to sea by towering waves and howling gales. In the Shropshire hamlet of Preston Brockhurst, an amateur meteorologist found the thermometer reading minus 29.8 degrees centigrade, the lowest reading in Britain's history. In London, Big Ben's clock ground to a halt, unable to move because of the ice. In the New Forest, a man's frozen body was found in a bus shelter, where he had apparently tried to spend the night. In Whitby, North Yorkshire, an old man was found dead in a snowdrift, having tried to walk home after a Saturday evening out. And on a visit to an agriculture college in Baschurch, Shropshire, Mrs Thatcher held an impromptu snowball fight with the accompanying reporters, exhibiting a remarkably good eye by hitting one of them directly in the mouth.[1]

'Oh! It is unrelieved gloom!' recorded Kenneth Williams, consoling himself with sherry and crisps, and gleefully contemplating 'the dire state of the country in the grip of the freeze, with cattle dying and travellers stranded'. But while most of the papers wallowed in the 'Big Freeze', the *Mirror*'s Keith Waterhouse refused to get carried away. Why worry about the weather? 'Nothing works here whether it is snowing or not. I took a tube journey through the Arctic wastes of London on Friday. The ticket machines didn't work. The automatic barriers didn't work. The escalators didn't work. The train indicators didn't work. The busker's violin didn't work.' Even when there was no snow, he grumbled, the capital was 'getting to look like East Berlin just after the war'.[2]

Little wonder, then, that many people were desperate to get away, with tour operators reporting record sales to 'destinations ranging from Hawaii to ski-ing resorts'. Even twenty years earlier, the idea of flying to Hawaii would have struck most people as the stuff of fantasy. But despite the shock of the downturn, expectations had changed. Britannia Airways, owned by the holiday firm Thomson, estimated that about 100,000 people had booked flights to Malta, Morocco and the Canary Islands, while Laker Airways said their Christmas and New Year flights had been booked solid since early November. As a spokesman for Cosmos explained, 'people seem to have decided that they are going to have a good Christmas in the sun and forget about the depressing weather, political situation and so on'.[3]

For those staying at home, the obvious temptation was to curl up in front of the television. But as if determined to crush any remaining embers of good cheer, the BBC kicked off Christmas week with the last episode of its science-fiction series *Blake's 7*. After four years and an awful lot of alien quarries, it ended with the entire cast of heroic freedom fighters being massacred by their totalitarian foes. Given what was happening in Poland, where the Communist regime had just attempted to crush the Solidarity movement by declaring martial law, perhaps the production team should have been congratulated on their prescience. But the *Radio Times* was deluged with what the editor called an 'unusually large number' of angry letters.

'The BBC must know that the programme is a favourite with many children and that in the Christmas holidays more of them than usual would watch. Yet they chose this episode to kill off all their heroes, one by one,' fumed Mrs Peat from Rickmansworth, Hertfordshire. 'With only three days to go before Christmas, I had all my illusions about their fantasy world cruelly shattered,' agreed Mrs Street from Brixham, Devon. 'Was the writer really at such a loss that he had to have them all shot?' But it was Geoffrey Bowman from Bangor, County Down, who posed the questions that Mrs Thatcher's opponents had been asking ever since she first walked into Downing Street: 'Is nothing sacred? Must evil and tyranny inevitably triumph over good and freedom? Why did it all have to end this way?'[4]

In the *Daily Mirror*, the journalist Tony Pratt was asking himself something very similar. What on earth, he wondered, had happened to the time-honoured family Christmas? 'My son absorbs himself in the latest electronic game and my daughter pours her new Bruce Springsteen tape into her earphones.' But Pratt was determined to stick to ancient tradition: the last edition of Larry Grayson's *Generation Game* to begin with, followed by *Paul Daniels's Magical Christmas*, *The Two Ronnies* and *Game for a Laugh*. The *Guardian*'s critic, too, recognized that Paul Daniels was essential viewing, but thought his readers might also enjoy highbrow fare such as the special editions of *Last of the Summer Wine* and *It'll Be Alright on the Night*. But some, no doubt, preferred to spend their Christmas with the *Guardian*'s spoof board game, *Theseus and the Monetaur*. Typical squares included 'Nigel Lawson becomes Governor of the Bank of Crete. Miss 2 turns', 'Tony Benn complains of persistent Medea distortion: Miss a turn' and 'Professor Walters resigns to join the Argonauts. Take an extra turn.' As the instructions sternly pointed out: 'THERE WILL BE NO U-TURNS.'[5]

For London's shopkeepers, the fog and snow could not have come at a worse time. 'Only a last-minute shopping rush', warned the *Express*, could save the festive season from being 'the most frugal since wartime rationing'. Some retailers blamed the weather; others thought the recession had created a nation of 'Scrooge shoppers'. But Debenhams' managing director thought fears of terrorism had much to do with it. After four IRA attacks on the capital since October, people were staying away from the West End. Even food sales were down: a sign, suggested one supermarket spokesman, that 'the days of Christmas spending sprees are a thing of the past'. Indeed, when the *Express* approached a major West End store for comment, its spokesman was too disheartened to discuss the subject at all. 'It merely leads', he said grimly, 'to gloom and despondency.'

And then, with just days to go till Christmas, came the rush, and all

the gloom was forgotten. Over the last weekend before the holiday the
snowstorms eased, and suddenly the streets were packed with shoppers.
On Saturday 19 December, so many people descended on Oxford Street
that the major West End stores took more money than on the same day
in 1980, despite the recession. In the north of England, the Morrisons
supermarket chain defied the law to open on Sunday, explaining that after
being so 'badly hit by the heavy snowfalls', they had no choice but to make
up for it. The manager of Woolworths in Slough followed suit. At first,
he said, he planned 'just to open the sweet counter but in the end I opened
up the lot and did a roaring trade'.

Not even the deepest recession since the war could dent the British
people's love of shopping. For the first time, reported the *Mirror*, Britain
was set to spend more than £1.2 billion on alcohol over the holiday. There
were 'now 25 million wine-drinkers in Britain', and the paper advised
them to invest in a new-fangled 'three, four or five litre box', with wine
'ready to drink at the turn of a tap'. Indeed, the *Mirror*'s Christmas party
suggestions would surely have astonished its working-class readers a few
decades earlier. The look this Christmas, it said, was 'frothy, romantic',
with 'pearls', 'frills' and 'flounces'. 'Brash neck ornaments which mix with
matching earrings are THE jewellery to wear,' its fashion columnist
advised. 'Adorn yourself with "rich" looking jewellery, anything that glit-
ters or jingles.' Among the nation's teenagers, meanwhile, the New
Romantic look was approaching its peak. When, a week before Christmas,
Duran Duran played the Hammersmith Odeon, the *Guardian*'s critic
could barely move for youngsters in their 'frilled shirts, floppy hair,
scarves, headbands', casting 'sidelong glances into mirrors, checking their
eyeliner'.[6]

With one in ten people out of work and so many families counting every
penny, all this talk of frills and glitter could easily sound insensitive. Yet
even as people told pollsters how much their hearts bled for those on the
dole, they continued to splash out. Food sales were higher than ever, with
families gorging on a record 13 million turkeys and 5 million chickens.
And as the hours ticked down until Father Christmas's arrival, many
stores could scarcely believe how well they were doing. Demand for consumer electronics, for example, was unprecedented. Rumbelows reported
that sales of video recorders and Teletext-enabled televisions had trebled
since 1980, while, in a sign of the times, sales of the new Sinclair ZX81
and Commodore VIC-20 computers were running at a record 5,000 a
week.[7]

Even more striking, though, was how much people were spending on
toys. Many parents, Susan Gray told Mass Observation, 'go mad when

buying for their children'. Her daughter, with a Christmas haul worth £15, the equivalent of at least £80 today, was 'well behind in the loot stakes'. By contrast, her 8-year-old nephew had been given presents worth '£60, if not £100' from his parents alone. And he was not alone in collecting so much booty. For every child under the age of 10, parents in the early 1980s typically spent at least £35 on Christmas presents. As is traditional, older observers were convinced that the greedy little monsters were being spoiled to the point of decadence by their weak-willed parents. One woman recalled that, as a child, she had had 'a doll made from an old gippo's clothes peg and I loved her'. By contrast, she said, her granddaughter did not 'know how many dolls she's got, ugly bloody things they are as well, all painted and dressed up like whores'.

Meanwhile, another Mass Observation correspondent, Sheila Parkin, had been helping her sister-in-law cope with the Christmas rush in Zodiac Toys, Ilford. In the final weeks, Sheila wrote disapprovingly, their takings had been '£2,000 over target', with many customers using their credit cards to buy the latest electronic games. 'It seems children cannot go without anything they want these days,' she lamented. 'Bit different from the war years when we were content with anything. Personally, both my children and grand-children are given only what I can afford *after* I have paid all my bills.'[8]

When the Oxford Street stores threw open their doors for the New Year sales, the crowds were as big and boisterous as ever. As early as Christmas Day, hundreds had been queuing in the cold, wrapped in scarves and anoraks. One couple were hoping to get a fitted kitchen for their new house, knocked down from more than £2,000 to just £199. Even the retailers seemed amazed at the demand. According to a spokesman for Army & Navy, people were determined to spend 'their money on things for the home – furniture, TV and videos'. But the woman at the front of the Debenhams' queue, Mrs Imelda Saich, had her eye on a coat. 'There's a mink reduced from £3,000 to £300,' she said firmly. 'I'm having that.' Something went terribly wrong, though. Within moments of the doors opening, Mrs Saich had become embroiled in a full-on fight with a secretary over the coat, and eventually the two had to be dragged apart by security guards. Tragically, Mrs Saich had to settle for a lesser coat, once £395, now just £39.50.[9]

As Mass Observation's correspondents confirmed, the Christmas and New Year spree was not just a London phenomenon. In Basildon, Peter Hibbitt wrote that he was looking forward to 'a good blow out and [a] few luxury foods and drinks', while his neighbours seemed to be 'spending as though there was no tomorrow'. In recession-hit Darlington, Susan

Gray spent £137.35½ on presents for her relatives, from old favourites such as chocolates, cigars, alarm clocks and jigsaws to relatively new-fangled treats such as a '3D viewer' and the inevitable '*Star Wars* model'. She and her husband were 'stunned' when they totted it all up, and this did not include food, wine or their New Year's Eve buffet party for a dozen friends. In the local off-licence, her husband was astonished to see a man handing over £50 for wines and spirits, and when they went to MFI for the New Year sales, they were again 'amazed' to see so many people pushing trolleys 'piled high with boxes of self-assembly furniture'. Wherever she went, battling through the crowds, Susan heard the same refrain: 'You wouldn't think there was a recession on, would you?'[10]

How on earth did people pay for all this? 'We're wondering where all the money is coming from,' a Selfridge's spokesman remarked during the New Year sales. But he must have known perfectly well. For the nine out of ten people who were still in work, the recession had brought only a slight fall in their real incomes. Many were better off than they had ever been. And even those who had taken a hit made up for it by borrowing, a habit they had acquired during the 1960s and 1970s. People had become used to the good life, to a world of rising living standards and rising expectations, to a lifestyle funded by Access and Barclaycard. In 1981, said *The Times*, 'people in Britain borrowed more than they have ever done before'. In just twelve months, personal lending had risen by a fifth, reaching its highest level since the credit boom of 1973. For the government, this was a mixed blessing. In *The Times*'s words, the explosion of borrowing had driven a 'coach and horses' through the Treasury's money supply targets. Yet at the same time, it had 'enabled people to maintain their spending . . . preventing the recession from being even deeper'. In that respect, perhaps Mrs Thatcher was lucky that people did not listen to her.[11]

One of the great ironies of Mrs Thatcher's legacy is that she is so often blamed for turning Britain into a nation dependent on credit. With the government lifting many of the old restrictions, this was an age of credit cards, loans and mortgages, and during her time in office personal borrowing rose sevenfold. Yet with the notable exception of her enthusiasm for home ownership, it is almost impossible to find examples of her encouraging people to borrow. Quite the reverse: more than almost any other politician of the age, she loved to talk about saving, prudence and thrift. One reason she hated inflation, after all, was that it encouraged the profligate and undermined the frugal. Inflation, she told one audience in 1980, 'cuts the value of every pound the thrifty have saved. It means spending money you can't afford, haven't earned and haven't got.' She herself hated the thought of debt and never owned a credit card. In private, remarked the Tory monetarist Jock Bruce-Gardyne, 'the PM gets very emotional about the plastic cards and she thinks it's all very damaging and dangerous'.[12]

She was not alone. In the spring of 1982, Sheila Parkin recorded that she owned neither a credit card nor a chequebook, and did not want them. She worked in a camping shop and had been astonished by the Christmas trade: up 40 per cent, she thought, on 1980. She was troubled, though, by the 'live now, pay later' attitude of her customers, many of whom paid with cheques or credit cards. Some 'admitted to owing money on mortgage-gas-electricity, yet [were] still getting into more debt for Christmas'. But like Mrs Thatcher, Sheila was out of touch with the mood of the moment. People in their twenties and thirties had grown up in an affluent society, where hire purchase offers or credit cards were easily obtained. To them, debt was simply a fact of life, to be rolled over from month to month until it could eventually be paid off. It was no longer a source of shame.

As for Jenny Palmer, the mature student from Lancaster, she confessed to being 'haunted' by her father's words: 'If you have to use the "never never" then it means you can't afford it. You must save up until you can afford it.' She did not think credit cards were a 'good thing', having heard too many 'middle class students at university boasting about how mummy or daddy let them put their purchases on their credit card'. And yet, by the summer of 1984, she and her husband had a Barclaycard, a Visa card, a Debenhams' charge card and an Austin Reed card. They had no choice, she explained, but to rely on credit in order 'to maintain something like what I would consider a reasonable lifestyle – which I feel that now in our 40s we are entitled to'. That telling word 'entitled', which owed as much to the 1960s as the 1980s, was something her father would never have understood. But she was simply a woman of her time.[13]

There was nothing unusual about the roaring sales at the end of 1981. Every Christmas in the 1980s broke records of one kind or another. Every year brought awestruck articles about the surging popularity of imported liqueurs and luxury chocolates, colour televisions and video recorders, microwave ovens and home computers. Given that the same pages often carried doom-laden essays about the shadow of George Orwell and the parallels with the 1930s, this might have seemed incongruous. But even Orwell had remarked on the 'cheap luxuries' that so many working-class families enjoyed during the Depression: the 'fish-and-chips, art-silk stockings, tinned salmon, cut-price chocolate (five two-ounce bars for sixpence), the movies, the radio, strong tea, and the Football Pools' that had, he thought, 'averted revolution'. But in the early 1980s these things were not cheap luxuries. They were cheap staples.[14]

The truth is that, despite the hardship of the towns blighted by unemployment, Mrs Thatcher's Britain remained one of the most prosperous countries in the world, an affluent consumer society in which even modest working-class households generally owned washing machines, fridges and cars. Of course this did not mean everybody had been liberated from poverty, anxiety or debt. But, as *The Times*'s Louis Heren pointed out, it did mean that by the time she took office even 'the average working-class family enjoyed what Orwell would have defined as a middle-class life'. Even in the darkest hours of the downturn, sales of central-heating installations, tumble dryers, fridge freezers, toasters and microwaves continued to break records. Between 1978 and 1982, sales of coffee makers went up by 238 per cent. In the next twelve months, sales of colour televisions went up by 31 per cent, deep fat fryers by 30 per cent and microwave ovens by 70 per cent. Of course there was more to life than buying and owning things. Yet as Ian Jack wrote a few years later, these everyday appliances reflected the underlying reality that 'most people in Britain are better off than they have ever been'.[15]

In the summer of 1981 the *Guardian*'s young foreign correspondent Alex Brummer returned to Britain after two years in Washington, DC. Travelling around the country, he was shocked by the decline of Britain's cash-strapped public infrastructure: the 'increasingly shabby transport system, cracking pavements, potholed roads, mounds of rubbish [and] crowded hospitals'. Yet, when he went shopping, Brummer found a far more reassuring picture. 'It may be the worst recession since the 1930s,' he wrote, 'but Marks and Spencer, Boots, British Home Stores and Mothercare get bigger and better and look as crowded as ever.' Waiting to pay at the Marks & Spencer till, he found it hard to credit that this was the same 'riot-torn Britain' he had seen on American news bulletins. 'The shopping centres appeared busy, the mood buoyant . . . Notes changed hands as if everyone, despite the 10 per cent plus unemployed, had enough to spend.' The *Guardian* gave his piece the headline 'Garbage and greed'. But the people queuing for cosmetics in Boots or baby equipment in Mothercare were hardly greedy. They were simply doing what people had done for centuries: buying things to make their lives better.[16]

Criticism of consumerism is as old as consumerism itself. On the left and among middle-class progressives there had always been plenty of people who shared the critic Richard Hoggart's distaste for the 'shiny barbarism' of modern mass culture, or who nodded approvingly at Aneurin Bevan's view that the 'so-called affluent society' was a 'society in which priorities have gone all wrong'. Jeremy Seabrook was a classic example. His long *Guardian* essays on the plight of the poor often referred to shops and shopping, but only ever in the most damning terms. It was the tyranny of consumerism, Seabrook told his readers, that lay behind the riots of the summer of 1981. Brainwashed by 'the invasive quality of the market place ... the praise of commodities and hymns to materialism ... the shrill insistence on buying all the things that have become indispensable', people had simply lashed out in fury at the downturn.[17]

For writers like Seabrook, the supreme symbol of this meretricious Britain, the high altar of the marketplace, was the American-style shopping mall. From north London's Brent Cross to Dudley's Merry Hill, the new shopping centres built between the mid-1970s and mid-1980s embodied everything left-leaning writers loathed about Mrs Thatcher's Britain, which probably explains why they could never resist visiting them. Beryl Bainbridge, for example, made a pilgrimage to the enormous £24 million shopping centre in Milton Keynes, which had been opened in September 1979 by the Prime Minister herself. To Bainbridge, this 'glittering hall of glass' was 'a church, a cathedral dedicated to the worship of the credit card, a place where people could come and pay their respects to the consumer society'. To her surprise, she rather admired its 'cleanliness and brightness'. When she got outside, though, her enthusiasm ebbed and she began 'to despise the place all over again'.[18]

Yet Milton Keynes's shopping centre had plenty of admirers. The architecture critic Deyan Sudjic was impressed by the 'restrained opulence' that made it 'a worthy successor to Mies van der Rohe's austere elegance', while the environmental writer Tony Aldous thought it offered 'the pleasantest and most convenient covered shopping in Britain'. Above all, as Aldous pointed out, it was enormously popular. On Saturdays, its familiar names – John Lewis, Marks & Spencer, Boots, Woolworths – were packed with 100,000 people, some from nearby Bedford and Northampton, but some brought by coach from as far afield as South Wales. The Milton Keynes Development Corporation used the shopping centre in their full-page magazine adverts, which pictured a genuine couple, Mr and Mrs Davies, who had come for the day from the nearby village of Silsoe, Bedfordshire. 'For us,' the caption read, 'Milton Keynes city centre is like a glimpse of the future.' But as Mrs Davies explained, she had been slightly misquoted. 'We didn't actually say *those* words,' she told the *Sunday Times*. 'We said we liked the shopping centre.'[19]

What Milton Keynes's architects had grasped, and what writers like Seabrook never recognized, is that people like Mr and Mrs Davies did not go shopping to stuff their homes with commodities and dull the pain of their economic alienation. Often they just wanted a warm day out. So when, at the turn of the decade, Chapman Taylor Partners were asked to develop the new £23 million Ridings Centre in Wakefield – which, revealingly, occupied the site of a former pub, a dance hall, a Salvation Army hall and a public toilet – they designed it as somewhere families would go for fun. The model was unapologetically North American, and the council's planning officer even went on a fact-finding mission to New York, Boston, Atlanta and Toronto, which must have been a real comedown after Wakefield. The results, though, were widely praised. Even the *Guardian*, not always notable for its close attention to the West Yorkshire shopping scene, thought the Ridings would 'set the pattern for shopping centres in the future'.

The Ridings boasted three levels, with daylight flooding in from a glazed roof, while a glass lift, inspired by the elevator in the Hyatt Regency in Atlanta, carried shoppers up through a central atrium. Around the food court – 'an Edwardian style garden, complete with a band-stand, trees, a waterfall, sun umbrellas, and tables and chairs for over 300 people' – there was a professionally run playgroup, a nappy-changing room and ten different food outlets, including an Indian restaurant, a pizzeria, a patisserie and a seafood bar. Meanwhile, glass and mirrors accentuated what the *Guardian* called the 'sense of lightness and activity'. Wasn't it just a shopping centre? Not to the people of Wakefield. When, on 16 October 1983, the Ridings opened for the first time, some 4,000 people walked through the doors – even though they could not buy anything, because it was a Sunday. The next day, when the shops did open, local schools declared a half-day so that Wakefield's consumers of the future could look around for themselves. Jeremy Seabrook would have had something to say about that.[20]

The rising popularity of shopping centres, especially malls such as Dudley's Merry Hill or Gateshead's Metro Centre, established on former industrial sites that had been designated as Enterprise Zones, posed a formidable challenge to Britain's retailers. Ever since Alan Sainsbury had pioneered 'Q-less' shopping in 1950, the pace of change had been set by Britain's supermarkets. Thirty years later, these temples to the affluent society had become part of the fabric of everyday life, a weekly destination for rich and poor alike. Like other post-war institutions, though, supermarkets were changing. Originally they had cultivated an image of industrialized, mass-produced homogeneity. But by the beginning of the 1980s, very few people still saw frozen fish fingers as the height of modernity. As one report noted in March 1981, aspirational shoppers no longer wanted mass-produced sliced white loaves and square slices of ham in plastic packages. They wanted 'real' bread produced in an 'in-store bakery' and 'real' meat 'prepared by staff in striped aprons, visibly sawing and chopping in the background'.[21]

In effect, this meant that supermarkets were not merely usurping high-street greengrocers, they were passing themselves off as butchers and bakers, too. Once again Sainsbury's – 'the country's biggest wine merchant, biggest butcher, biggest greengrocer', according to the *Guardian* – was in the vanguard. The supermarket chain had weathered the recession better than any of its rivals, largely because its stores were concentrated in the south of England. There was only one Sainsbury's in Wales, and none at all north of Leeds. The chain's bosses, however, like those of its competitors, were conscious that customers' habits were changing. Crucially, people no longer walked to the shops; they drove. Customers' single biggest grievance, executives admitted, was the lack of car parking, so they planned to open new branches only where parking was readily available.

What people bought, too, was changing. With customers demanding more obviously 'worthy' food, Sainsbury's was now pushing 'muesli and yoghourt, wholemeal bread and skimmed milk'. With more people living alone and old-fashioned family meals in decline, meanwhile, it was stocking more 'sandwich fillings, sliced brown bread, small pork pies' and 'individual servings of chocolate mousse or ice cream'. Above all, it was seriously worried by the rise of Marks & Spencer, which, thanks partly to its chicken Kiev, was positioning itself as the fashionable destination for middle-class shoppers who wanted both convenience and quality.

So when, in February 1982, the biggest new Sainsbury's for years opened in Nine Elms, south London, its management trumpeted its '50 varieties of fresh fish', '60 different types of bread' and even its 'fresh orange juice . . . squeezed and bottled under customers' eyes'. It clearly worked. By late 1983 Sainsbury's customer base had grown by almost half again in just five years, while sales had doubled and profits were up by a staggering 220 per cent – and this despite the recession. The chain was now so popular, remarked *The Times*, that it need 'never invest in another newspaper advertisement or TV commercial. Britain's leading food retailer has such a high reputation for quality and value that its most vocal salesmen are its customers.'[22]

For every supermarket or shopping centre that succeeded, however, there were dozens of independent, family-run shops that suffered. Thanks to the ruthless expansion of the supermarket chains, almost half of Britain's grocer's shops had closed in the 1970s, and few of the survivors made it to the end of the next decade. Chain stores were the future: as Margaret Bradshaw reported to Mass Observation in the spring of 1981, two of her local shops, a DIY store and a decorating shop, had just closed down. The culprit was 'the large new Sainsbury Home Care shop at Croydon [actually the first Homebase in the country]. They seem to undercut considerably and many young folk who are doing home improvements all the time are going there.'

Even the grandest names were vulnerable to the tides of history. In London, the Bayswater department store Whiteley's, which had first opened in 1911, closed its doors in September 1981. The Swan & Edgar store, founded in the early 1800s, once famous for its aristocratic customers and grand Piccadilly Circus façade, disappeared behind 'To Let' signs a few months later. And when the *Guardian* sent a reporter to Oxford Street's art deco Bourne & Hollingsworth store in April 1982, she painted a thoroughly depressing picture. Venturing upstairs on the 'rickety, ancient wooden escalator', she found the upper floors empty of customers, despite the notices promising 'fantastic', 'amazing' and 'unrepeatable' bargains. 'There just isn't the supply and demand any more for a store of this size,' the manager said sadly. Within a few years, it was as if the store had never existed.[23]

The first weeks of 1982 brought more snow, more travel chaos and more miserable headlines. With temperatures dipping well below freezing, major roads were closed, trains and flights cancelled and thousands of people trapped far from home. In South Wales, some 500 men were even snowed in at the Port Talbot steelworks. 'Going to school with the children proved almost impossible,' wrote Carol Daniel in Romford. 'Many babies in pushchairs were crying with the cold.' In Lambeth, Margaret Bradshaw lamented that the roads were so icy that one friend had slipped and broken his wrist, another had broken her arm, a third had badly bruised her leg, a fourth had landed 'on her face and grazed it badly' and, to cap it all, a fifth had fallen, suffered a heart attack and died. 'Suddenly, the weather isn't funny any more,' said the *Mirror*. 'It is no longer a case of grit and bear it . . . Locally and nationally, the expensive consequences of the blizzards will be with us for a long time. Unemployment will get even worse. Industry will pay a high price.' Perhaps it was no wonder that the first new number one of the year, topping the chart on 16 January, was Bucks Fizz's whimsical 'The Land of Make Believe'. With the roads blocked by snow, the prospects so bleak and the credit card bills looming, make-believe had rarely seemed so appealing.[24]

For Mrs Thatcher, it was a grim start to the year. As she well knew, the weather matters in politics. Perhaps remembering how Jim Callaghan had misjudged the public mood during the Winter of Discontent, Bernard Ingham urged her to 'dispel the gloom and accentuate the positive', because 'the British public will want to hear a calm, cool, collected Prime

Minister who is manifestly in control'. She did her best, trying hard to sound upbeat in her interviews to welcome the New Year. There was, she insisted, 'much more hope ahead this coming year than there has been at the depth of [the] world recession . . . I think we are through the worst.'[25]

In broad economic terms she was right. The recession was over, the economy was growing, productivity was improving and profits were rising. But the bad news kept coming. On 26 January, official figures showed that unemployment had reached the dreaded milestone of 3 million. In the Commons, Labour's Eric Varley bitterly recalled Mrs Thatcher's prayer on her first day at Number 10, wondering 'what St Francis would have said about 3 million unemployed'. The furious Dennis Skinner, meanwhile, told the 'Westminster Ripper' that 'she and the Government have created more havoc in the British economy than the German High Command in the whole of the last war'.

'WASTE OF THE MILLIONS', read the headline in the next day's *Mirror*, appalled not just by the figures, but by the fact that people seemed to be getting used to them:

> Three million unemployed. Shocking? Yes, but it is failing to shock. Intolerable? Yes, but it is being tolerated. Unacceptable? Yes, but it is being accepted.
>
> The senses are dulled by years of economic failure . . .
>
> Mrs Thatcher says the Government deplores the tragedy of unemployment, as if it were nothing to do with her. Yet it has much more than doubled since she was elected . . .
>
> We are wasting the talents of three million people. We are wasting money spent on keeping them out of work. We are wasting the future. We are wasting the nation.

Yet still unemployment kept rising. By July it had reached almost 3.2 million, some 304,000 of them school-leavers. That summer, later remembered as the summer of victory, half of all youngsters leaving school walked straight on to the dole queue.[26]

By now even many of Mrs Thatcher's supporters conceded that her economic offensive had come at a punishing cost. Writing in the *Journal of Economic Affairs*, the monetarist David Laidler admitted that the experiment in controlling the money supply had been 'clumsy to the point of incompetence', and claimed they should have adopted Monetary Base Control instead. The great guru of monetarist theory, Milton Friedman, seemed to agree with him. Britain's economic performance under Mrs Thatcher, Friedman told the BBC in February 1982, had been 'terrible'.

With unemployment at 3 million, Trog could not resist looking back to the
'Labour Isn't Working' poster (*Observer*, 31 January 1982). Here the glowering
Norman Tebbit, complete with bike, makes a few tweaks to the message.


Her only success, he thought, was in cutting inflation. Not only had she
failed to bring taxes down, she had failed to cut government spending and
failed to roll back state interference in the economy. So even now Britain's
economy was 'desperately sick . . . I don't see how you can use any other
term.'

Unlike some of Mrs Thatcher's critics, though, Friedman maintained
that things could yet improve. The shock to British business, he conceded,
had been 'too costly', but the economy would see the benefits eventually.
And he still believed Mrs Thatcher and her team were the only people
who could turn Britain around. Indeed, he 'would not be surprised if, in
the next two or three years, Britain experienced a rather significant
revival'.[27]

Whether Mrs Thatcher would still be in Downing Street to see it, however, remained very uncertain. 'The Conservative Party faces grimmer
prospects than at any time since the end of the second world war,' began
a memorandum from her Minister of Agriculture, Peter Walker, in mid-
February. 'We are presiding over 3 million unemployed and, now, falling
living standards for those still at work. We are confronted with the emergence of the SDP/Liberal alliance, the most ominous third-party threat
in modern times. The potential for an electoral disaster for the Conservatives is clear.' Walker's suggestions included pumping money into the
economy and bringing back incomes policies, neither of which was
remotely likely. But he was not alone in his pessimism about the next

What NEXT?

17. Country casuals. *Above left*, a honeymooning couple model the new nostalgic chic, 1981. *Above right*, the Next catalogue follows their lead. But Spandau Ballet's look, *below*, is less *Brideshead Revisited* and more *Blake's 7*.

# H₂ Eau.

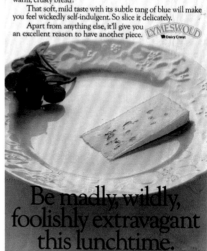

Dare we suggest you treat yourself to a little Lymeswold? With perhaps just a sprig of watercress, an apple or some warm, crusty bread?

That soft, mild taste with its subtle tang of blue will make you feel wickedly self-indulgent. So slice it delicately.

Apart from anything else, it'll give you an excellent reason to have another piece.

LYMESWOLD
Dairy Crest

Be madly, wildly, foolishly extravagant this lunchtime.

18. While industrial Britain buckled, suburban Britain was booming. For shoppers in the early 1980s, life offered few pleasures to rival a bottle of Perrier, a piece of Lymeswold, the Habitat catalogue and the Sony Walkman.

THE BOOK-KEEPER.

THE COOK.

THE CHILD-MINDER.

# Meet the ultimate home-help.

THE GARDENER.

THE SECRETARY.

THE TEACHER.

Above are just some of the ways you could use a BBC Micro computer.

And we say 'you' advisedly. For, contrary to popular misconceptions, you don't have to be a technical wizard to use a micro—especially a BBC Micro. Nor do you need any complex equipment.

All you need is an ordinary TV set and a cassette player.

Then with a few basic instructions you can run programs like those above.

There is a huge range of these programs available for the BBC Micro covering games, education and business applications as well as those closer to home.

But, of course, the more you get used to the computer and its language, the more you can get out of it.

To help you do just that, you will receive a step by step User Guide which explains the full capabilities of your micro and shows you how to construct useful programs of your own.

You will also receive a free "Welcome" cassette which contains different programs for you to experiment with, ranging from Music and graphics, to games like Kingdom and Bat 'n Ball.

The BBC Micro is at the heart of the BBC's massive Computer Literacy Project; it is also the most popular and successful machine being ordered by British schools, under the current DOI scheme.

So it is the ideal micro to introduce you – and the family – to home computing. (Although if you have children at school you may find them ahead of you already.)

The BBC Micro costs less than the average video – only £399. It is available from WH Smith Computer Shops, Boots, John Lewis and local Acorn stockists.

However, if you would like to order one with your credit card, or if you want the address of your nearest supplier just phone 01-200 0200.

## The BBC Microcomputer System.

Designed, produced and distributed by Acorn Computers Limited.

33

19. The future, 1982.

20. When Argentina seized the Falklands, Britain's decline into impotence and chaos seemed to have been confirmed. *Above*, the Royal Marine garrison surrenders to the invaders, 2 April 1982. *Below*, children watch as Argentine troops move into Stanley.

21. The departure of the Task Force was a moment of intense patriotic excitement. *Above*, soldiers on the *QE2* display their colours; *below*, a mother, son and Action Man wave their farewells.

22. The war cemented Mrs Thatcher's place in the international imagination. For the Argentine press, *top*, she was a 'pirate, witch and assassin'. Raymond Briggs drew her as 'the Old Iron Woman', *above left*. But *Battle* never doubted that she and her troops were on the side of the angels, *above right*.

23. The British commanders always knew they would suffer losses. *Top*, the *Sir Galahad* burns in Bluff Cove, 8 June 1982. But all the time their troops were tightening their grip, immortalized in this famous image of the Royal Marines yomping towards Stanley, *above*.

24. The nation's heroes return: Portsmouth, 17 September 1982.

election. In political and academic circles, the general consensus was that it would probably produce a hung parliament, leaving the Alliance as coalition kingmakers. That same month, the director of the Centre for Policy Studies, Alfred Sherman, warned the Prime Minister that he and his colleagues could only envisage a Tory majority if there were 'several major changes in the situation'. The 'most likely outcome', he thought, was 'a parliament where the Alliance holds the balance, one way or the other', so she should start thinking about coalition talks.[28]

One bit of good news for Mrs Thatcher was that talk of mass Tory defections to the SDP had at last died down, while Heath and Gilmour had temporarily retreated into the shadows. But if things went badly in 1982, they were bound to be back. And while the atmosphere in Number 10 lightened a little with the departure of the perennially disgruntled John Hosykns, who left with a knighthood to run the Institute of Directors, his replacement was astonished to find things so gloomy. The son of a baronet, educated at Eton and Oxford, the former *Spectator* journalist Ferdinand Mount came from an impeccable Tory background. Although he found Mrs Thatcher's radicalism invigorating, his languid scepticism felt very different from Hoskyns's apocalyptic urgency.

But when Mount toured Whitehall to talk to Mrs Thatcher's ministers, he was shocked by the sense of 'pessimism and sloth'. 'Only Kenneth Baker and Michael Heseltine', he remembered, 'showed any appreciable bounce.' But even Baker's bounce only went so high. A few months earlier, the technology minister had organized a sweepstake on the result of the next general election, the other contestants including young bloods such as Chris Patten and William Waldegrave. Mount predicted that the Conservatives would win 290 seats, Labour 270 and the Alliance eighty, which would mean a hung parliament. Later, he was amazed to learn that, of all the forecasts, his had been the most optimistic.[29]

Almost unnoticed amid the headlines about the big freeze, however, there had been a subtle change in the political temperature. In the Conservatives' private polls, their support had reached an all-time low of 23 per cent in early December. But then they began to recover. In early January they were back up to 25½ per cent, and by late January they had regained the dizzy heights of 30 per cent. Of course this was still pretty dire; even so, the momentum had definitely shifted. Mrs Thatcher's personal approval rating had risen, too, up from 18 per cent in December to 33 per cent by late January. Most striking of all, though, was the decline of the SDP, who – without doing anything wrong – were losing supporters by the week. In early December, they had been on 38 per cent, with the Liberals on 13½ per cent. But while the Liberals' backing held up, the SDP fell to 25 per cent by early January and were down to just 21½ per cent by mid-February. Even Mrs Thatcher's private pollsters found this puzzling, but the explanation is obvious. Despite all the hyperbole, the Gang of Four's support had always been soft. Now that their novelty value had worn off, voters were drifting back to their old haunts. And this, perhaps more than anything that happened in the South Atlantic, was the key to Mrs Thatcher's electoral recovery.[30]

'Take a sniff at the air this morning,' began a leader in the *Sunday Express* on 6 March:

> No matter what the weather is like there will be a different tang about it.
>
> From the gloom of winter there is emerging a whole new cycle of life.
>
> Suddenly there are crocuses springing up. The forsythia is in bloom. The grass is beginning to grow again. The birds are in full song. Everywhere the signs of a fresh beginning are to be seen.
>
> Is there anything quite so marvellous as a British spring?

The joys of spring would have come as little consolation to the thousands who had lost their jobs in the freezing winter months. And yet, as Sir Geoffrey Howe put the final touches to his fourth Budget, he had reason to feel optimistic. A few days earlier, the *Financial Times*'s regular survey of business opinion had found that confidence was higher than at any time for two years, with almost half of all firms feeling more cheerful than in the autumn of 1981. The stock market was growing, house prices were on the rise, interest rates were falling and, best of all, public borrowing was running below the Treasury forecasts. And when the *Sunday Express* invited its readers to imagine the Chancellor enjoying a pre-Budget stroll through the Surrey countryside ('Observe his easy stride, his relaxed manner, his calm expression'), the contrast with the feverish wrangling a year earlier could hardly have been more striking.[31]

Howe unveiled his Budget on Tuesday 9 March. By the standards of his previous efforts it was a comparative non-event, which came as a relief to many of his colleagues. The Chancellor's tone was upbeat: at last the economy was 'moving in the right direction', with borrowing budgeted to fall to £9½ billion in 1981–2. That meant he could relax the purse strings a little, raising income tax thresholds above inflation and cutting employers' National Insurance contributions, both of which were very well received. It was certainly enough to please the Tory benches, satisfy the financial markets and impress the next day's papers. Even the *Mirror*, usually so scathing, called it 'half a step forward'. The public seemed fairly happy, too. A poll for the *Daily Star* found that people were generally pleased with the Budget, with six out of ten saying it was better for them personally than expected and only two out of ten worse. Perhaps people had become so used to punishment that they treated even the slightest respite as a rare treat. Even so, it was striking that 48 per cent thought it would be good for the country, compared with 38 per cent who disagreed.[32]

A year earlier, Howe's third Budget had plunged the government into a slough of introspection and infighting. Now, as Francis Pym warned his colleagues, the Budget had been 'so well received that there could be danger in over-selling it'. But some of Mrs Thatcher's Fleet Street supporters seemed almost giddy with relief. Not only had her approval ratings regained the sunlit uplands of the early 30s, but the combined Alliance standing was now down to just 26 per cent, with the Tories on 37 per cent, four points clear of Labour. As the pain of the recession began, very slowly, to ease, voters were returning to Mrs Thatcher's banners. 'It is becoming daily more evident that she is going to win the economic battle,' exulted the *Sunday Express*. 'The party is uniting around her . . . Let no one doubt for one second that but for the courage and strength of purpose of this one remarkable woman the fight to restore economic sanity to Britain would have been, as it was so many times before, given up long ago.'[33]

There was, of course, a long road ahead. Millions were still out of work. Morale at Conservative high command remained desperately low. A week after the Budget, Mrs Thatcher became embroiled in a bitter row about the rising crime figures, with police spokesmen demanding that she bring back hanging. In the Glasgow Hillhead by-election, Roy Jenkins was campaigning hard, hoping to take the seat from the Tories and give the SDP a much-needed shot in the arm. 'The Alliance', said the *Guardian* optimistically, 'still has a reasonable hope of enough seats in the next Parliament to ensure that no one else gets an overall majority.' Victory for the SDP's Great Panjandrum, agreed the *Observer*, 'would not only advance its fortunes and revive morale but would more importantly secure in Parliament the one man who is capable of forging the Alliance into a united force at the next General Election'. There still seemed everything to play for; the future was still uncertain.[34]

And then, on 18 March, a group of Argentine scrap-metal dealers landed on the island of South Georgia.

# 30

# Tomorrow's World

*Do you actually need a computer? Is the computer a panacea, a plaything, a workhorse, a job destroyer, a profit maker, a job creator, or the overblown puff of a marketing manager's imagination?*

*Guardian*, 10 September 1981

*The image of four-year-olds keying in to computers for fun might seem to bear out George Orwell's wildest nightmares, but it is beginning to happen all over Britain.*

*The Times*, 29 November 1982

In the spring of 1982, a slight, red-bearded man, his eyes gleaming with a salesman's fervour, unveiled a little black box that, for millions of children, contained a world of almost unfathomable possibility. Designed in Cambridge, built in Dundee, Clive Sinclair's ZX Spectrum seemed a genuinely British success story. No home computer had ever made such a popular impact. 'Up and running in minutes, hours and hours of fun, invaluable in the years ahead,' promised the adverts – and thousands of people believed them.

Within just a year of its launch, the Spectrum had become a fixture of thousands of youngsters' bedrooms. By the end of the 1980s it had become easily the bestselling British computer in history, shifting an estimated 2½ million units in the United Kingdom, as well as a similar number abroad. At just £175 for the 48K version, it was astonishingly cheap: on the high street you might pay £250 for a hi-fi system, £350 for a large colour television or £500 for a video recorder. There was more to its appeal, though, than the price. Cheap computers were ten-a-penny in the 1980s. Yet the Spectrum stood out: a minimalist vision in sleek black plastic, the only flash of colour a neat rainbow stripe. Even the unconventional rubber keyboard suggested a thrilling space-age future, at least until you tried to use it. Other computers were more serious. But the Spectrum had been built to entertain. 'When you took the Spectrum out of the packaging,' remarks the writer Francis Spufford, 'you knew it was supposed to be fun, not good for you.'[1]

For anybody who grew up in the early 1980s, few products more immediately recall the spirit of the age than the Spectrum. Yet as children of the decade will know, it was not without its problems. The introduction to Dan Whitehead's book *Speccy Nation*, billed as a 'tribute' to a machine that 'changed the world', begins with a single word: 'Crap.' For the Spectrum owner, writes Whitehead, the gulf between promise and performance was cruelly wide. In theory the Spectrum could produce six colours, but on screen they would 'clash and flicker and generally fall to pieces'. It could make music, but 'in a squeaking squawking cacophony that only the truly besotted could appreciate'. Perhaps above all, the rubber keyboard, with its 'baffling surplus of specialist shift keys', might have been designed to drive owners into paroxysms of fury. Bewilderingly, each key had five functions: the letter K, for example, also denoted a 'plus sign, a "list" command, something called "screen" and LEN, whoever he was'.

Sinclair's machine never came close to matching the reliability of its chief British rival, Acorn's BBC Micro. Return rates often reached 30 per cent, and rumour had it that when people sent their Spectrums back, staff at the Dundee factory simply posted them straight out to other customers. Yet the fact that the Spectrum was plagued with problems only made its sales all the more impressive. In marketing terms, it was one of the great successes of the age.* By the summer of 1983, two out of every three computers bought in Britain carried the 43-year-old Sinclair's name.[2]

On the face of it, Sinclair made a very unlikely national hero. 'With his gentle, sometimes hesitant voice, tiny spectacles, narrow frame and disappearing ginger hair,' said one profile, 'he looks more backroom than boardroom.' His upbringing had been impeccably middle-class, and young Clive had been educated privately in the Home Counties. After leaving school, he became a technical journalist before setting up a small business, Sinclair Radionics, selling mail-order radio kits. In 1972, having moved into a converted flour mill in St Ives, Cambridgeshire, he had a huge popular hit with an £80 pocket calculator. Four years later, however, he launched a £25 digital watch, which proved such a disaster that he was forced to accept a £650,000 bailout from the National Enterprise Board.

---

* Not everybody liked it, though. Many BBC Micro owners tended to dismiss the Spectrum: the 11-year-old George Osborne, who spent his weekends painstakingly typing in the free programs in the magazine *Micro User*, reportedly regarded Spectrum owners as 'irredeemable dilettantes'.

This he sank into a new venture, a £100 pocket television, which was another catastrophe. By 1978 Sinclair Radionics was losing almost £2 million a year. Chafing under the supervision of the National Enterprise Board, Sinclair sold his house and his Rolls-Royce and walked away to focus on another of his little companies, Science of Cambridge, which he renamed Sinclair Research. This time he planned to make cheap home computers, beginning with a machine called the ZX80. A year later came the ZX81, then the Spectrum. By then, Sinclair was one of the most celebrated entrepreneurs in Britain.[3]

As Spectrum waiting lists lengthened, it seemed Clive Sinclair could do no wrong. Other well-known businessmen saw him as a role model. Sinclair was 'brilliant and daring' and 'somebody I admire enormously', wrote the founder of the Next clothing chain, George Davies, who thought he embodied the 'new spirit of entrepreneurialism in this country'. Yet in many respects Sinclair was far from being the ideal Thatcherite entrepreneur. His record, remarked the *Observer*, was 'littered with a multitude of close shaves, and several outright disasters', while many of his products had a reputation for cheapness, unreliability and downright shoddiness.

In the popular imagination, entrepreneurs were supposed to be outgoing, charming people, yet Sinclair cut a diffident figure, the stereotypical balding boffin. Employees testified that behind the mild-mannered image he could be an impatient and domineering boss. And far from incarnating the dignity of work, Sinclair boasted of being 'rather lazy'. Interviewed by *Practical Computing* in 1982, he said he was looking forward to the bank holiday weekend: 'Any excuse not to work!' To the *Guardian*, he confided that he himself did not use a calculator, let alone a computer. 'Sinclair refuses', the paper said admiringly, 'to fit the standard category of 1980s technocrat in any shape or form.'[4]

Yet, in the public imagination, Sinclair had revived a national tradition of scientific innovation. To the press, he was the embodiment of forward-thinking ambition, a one-man guide to Britain's technological future. In the broadsheets, interviewers lapped up Sinclair's presidency of Mensa, his love of Porsches, his decision to enrol as a mature economics student at Cambridge, even his then very unusual habit of rising early every morning to run seven miles before breakfast. In the tabloids, reporters solemnly echoed his predictions that soon 'computer doctors' would diagnose you in your own home, and that people would soon carry 'pocket telephones with unlimited range'.

Indeed, by the middle of 1983 Sinclair's pronouncements had become grander than ever. The next fifteen years, he said, would be 'among the most momentous in our economic history – a major turning point'. Soon the trade unions would wither away, manufacturing would virtually disappear and Britain would have to devote itself to the 'products of the mind'. Most economists refused to understand this, he said dismissively, 'because they expect the future to be like the past'. But he knew better. That he, Clive Sinclair, would play a major part in that future was beyond any possible doubt.[5]

The computer age had been a long time coming. As far back as 1955, the *Daily Mirror* had run a front-page series under the banner headline 'The Robot Revolution', announcing that 'another industrial revolution' was at hand, spearheaded by 'machines that can almost think'. Yet for the next twenty years most people never knowingly laid eyes on a computer. It was not until the development of the microprocessor – a computer 'brain' packed into a tiny integrated circuit – that people began to take seriously the prospect of computers in homes, shops and offices. 'The day is rapidly approaching', the *Observer* declared in 1978, 'when everyone can have their own household computer.' Indeed, the paper's science correspondent Nigel Hawkes had already caught a glimpse of the future. In California, he reported, there was now a craze for pre-assembled 'home computers', which could 'fit into the boot of an average car'. Interestingly, he was most impressed by a 'very attractive little computer' made by a firm called Apple, 'started by two young Californians, Steve Jobs and Steve Wozniak, in a garage'.

There was, however, an obvious caveat: 'What can home computers do?' Most American owners were hobbyists who used them 'to play sophisticated versions of the electronic TV games'. There was talk of education, household banking, diaries and address books; but people could do all that already 'without the help of computers'. As salesmen privately conceded, 'the home computer is a tool looking for something to do'. Even so, Hawkes thought it possible that one day, perhaps very soon, 'we will all want to rush out and buy our own computer. It sounds unlikely, but so did the horseless carriage.'[6]

For many observers at the end of the 1970s, however, computers seemed less like an intriguing distraction and more like a threat to people's livelihoods. On 31 March 1978 the BBC science series *Horizon* screened a documentary entitled 'Now the Chips Are Down', presenting an outstandingly bleak picture of a world transformed by computers. For too long, said the narrator, Britain had been blind to the advance of technology, its politicians deluding themselves about the terrifying implications for millions of jobs. There would, of course, be upsides: home banking, fancy watches, driverless tractors, robot-run factories. But what would happen to the 'men in today's jobs'? What would become of generations of school-children, cast on to the scrapheap as the computers moved in? 'Could this technology', asked the narrator, 'be the end of an age, the end of a line of evolution, and not a beginning?'[7]

A year later, in his ITV series *The Mighty Micro*, the psychologist Christopher Evans tried to present a more optimistic picture. Yet amid the robot doctors, computerized fridges and computer-controlled nuclear plants, there was still more than a hint of dystopia. The dashing Evans, who died of cancer just before the series went out, was a striking character in his own right. A close friend of J. G. Ballard, he had been the adviser to the tremendous children's science-fiction series *The Tomorrow People* (1973–9) and reportedly wore an Iron Cross under his open-necked shirt, which he was told to remove during filming.* Some of his predictions, like e-readers, tablets and word processors, were remarkably accurate. But what really struck him, in good Ballardian style, was the new technology's hypnotic power over the human mind:

> The one note of warning is sounded by the compelling nature of the computer itself. Increasingly, it will draw you into an obsessive embrace, where the world comes to you in your home. The current limitless fascination with microprocessor-based toys is but a tiny indicator of the trend towards an introverted society.
>
> With the computer as an increasingly interesting and useful companion, could the factories and office blocks empty, commuter lines fall silent, as we retreat into our own private universe?

People could not say they had not been warned.[8]

Although many viewers probably thought this was the stuff of science fiction, the microchip revolution was already gathering recruits. Britain's first amateur computer club was founded as far back as 1972, while the magazine *Personal Computer World* had made its corner-shop debut in 1978. For the computer historian Tom Lean, magazines like these were crucially important in building a network of hobbyists, many of whom went on to become developers themselves. There were even several hundred dedicated computer shops. The first, according to the *Observer*, was the Byte Shop in Ilford. Barely three months after opening in the summer of 1978, it had sold hundreds of computers costing up to 'several thousand pounds'. The most popular was the Commodore PET, which cost a whopping £695, the equivalent of at least £5,000 today. The manager, who claimed to sell about ten a week, reported that the buyers included

---

* The Iron Cross, that is, not the shirt. He was a 'character', not a Nazi.

'labourers, business people, a doctor, a dentist, an accountant and a couple of housewives'.

By common consent, though, computer enthusiasts were very particular kinds of people. As the *Guardian* remarked a year later, customers might range 'from the schoolboy, through the student and the businessman, to the retired engineer', but this was still a 'mainly male and young world'. Yet by the end of 1979 almost everybody agreed that home computers were poised to become very big indeed. Already there were an estimated 40,000 pre-assembled computers nationwide. Most were American, though a Japanese invasion was expected shortly. There were no significant British options, or at least none costing less than £10,000. Disturbingly, however, there were rumours that the French were building microcomputers of their own, backed by generous government funding. Unless the nation's computer lovers came up with something special, warned the *Guardian*, a generation of British children might be condemned to life with a Gallic keyboard.[9]

But a national saviour was at hand. Clive Sinclair had been thinking about a home computer since his days at Sinclair Radionics, but the real spur was an article he read in the *Financial Times* in May 1979, predicting that within the next five years somebody would make a user-friendly computer for less than £100, with a traditional keyboard and full-screen display. Sinclair saw that as a challenge. If the *Financial Times* thought it would take five years, he could do it in six months. He was right. Built by his chief engineer, Jim Westwood, the ZX80 was a slim white box which used a cassette recorder to load software and sent the picture to a television screen. The 'Britishness' of the machine, though, was a little ambiguous. Not only was the processor Japanese, but most of the memory chips had been imported from Texas Instruments. There was no sound, no colour and very little memory. On the other hand, it cost just £99.95 by mail order, a quarter of the cost of its nearest rival.

Even in January 1980, many critics had their doubts about Sinclair's cost-cutting compromises, from the ZX80's cheap membrane keyboard to its disturbing tendency to overheat. Sinclair told the press that it would probably be used for 'teaching children about computers'. But some observers doubted it would ever find a market. The economics commentator Hamish McRae, for example, was unconvinced that there were enough 'laymen who want to be embroiled in the intricacies of BASIC, the unbelievably complicated language that these things speak'. The ZX80 could only succeed, he thought, as a 'sort of up-market executive toy'.[10]

In reality, the ZX80 succeeded beyond Sinclair's wildest dreams. In a sign of things to come, the key thing was not so much the machine as the marketing campaign. Instead of being aimed at enthusiasts, it was targeted at people who knew nothing about computers. As the advertisements put it, 'the ZX80 cuts away computer jargon and mystique . . . and the grounding it gives your children will equip them for the rest of their lives'. This last point was crucial. The ZX80, Sinclair told the *Cambridge Evening News*, was the world's first 'computer for all the family', so simple 'any child of 10 with normal arithmetical ability could use it'. His own children, he said proudly, had helped him to test it. In this context, the fact that you had to connect it to a cassette recorder and a television was a real asset: as Tom Lean remarks, these were ordinary 'household items', and the effect was to turn the ZX80 into part of the living-room furniture. 'Inside a day', the adverts claimed, 'you'll be talking to it like an old friend.'

This was very dubious, of course; but as a sales pitch it was perfectly calibrated. With the expensive American imports aimed squarely at hobbyists, the ZX80 was the first affordable computer for the family market. Demand was unprecedented; even a year later, Sinclair was still producing machines at a rate of 10,000 a month, and by mid-1983 he had sold an estimated 100,000. Tellingly, more than half of them were for export. For the first time, a British computer manufacturer had not just broken into the domestic mass market, he was carrying the fight on to foreign soil – and winning.[11]

Even as Sinclair contemplated new conquests, Britain's politicians were adjusting to the new world. By the spring of 1978, Jim Callaghan had asked three government working parties to report on the 'social and economic upheaval that the microcomputer revolution is bringing'. Many experts believed Britain had been criminally negligent for at least a decade, and the director of the National Computing Centre warned a parliamentary committee that the nation was far behind its major rivals. Although the 66-year-old Callaghan was hardly an obvious convert to the creed of computing, he arranged a screening of 'Now the Chips Are Down' for his ministers, and launched a £55 million drive to inform businesses about computers' potential. In his final election press conference a year later, Callaghan even tried to present himself as the candidate for the computer age, talking earnestly about 'this trendy term we now have, the microprocessor revolution, and the silicon chip, which everybody talks about and hardly anybody has ever seen'. Yet still Britain seemed to be lagging behind. 'The UK is not in command of the situation,' warned the chief scientist at the Department of Industry, 'and those who lead the technology – the US and Japan – will use the processes of the free market to the full.'[12]

Given Mrs Thatcher's antipathy to state subsidies, she might have been tempted to let Britain's own free market do all the lifting. Yet right from the start, some of her ministers badgered her about the importance of embracing the new technology. A month after she had moved into Number 10, Sir Keith Joseph sent her a memo entitled 'Micro-Electronics'. There was, he wrote:

> almost universal acceptance that micro-electronics technology is of crucial importance to our future industrial and economic performance and our competitive position in world markets. In its way it is likely to be of the same sort of importance as was the steam engine with the difference that (a) it will be even more pervasive and (b) we are not in the forefront of its development. Because we are not in the lead, like Avis we have to try harder.*

As a result, Joseph wanted to honour Labour's plans for a major computer drive, pumping at least £125 million into the electronics industry over the next five years. 'As you know', he added, 'I am in principle strongly opposed to support of this kind'. But since other Western governments were investing in their own industries, 'we have little option . . . if we are to have the capability in this country to supply the needs of user industries and to achieve a reasonable share of the rapidly expanding world market'.[13]

Judging by the vehemence with which Mrs Thatcher scribbled the word 'No!' in the margin, all this came as an even bigger shock than Joseph's support for British Leyland. To John Hoskyns she 'dismissed [the] whole thing as socialism, a waste of money'. But Hoskyns thought it was a good idea. So did the Chief Secretary to the Treasury, John Biffen, who told her that if Britain did not change its ways then 'our relative competitiveness will suffer seriously'. Given the backwardness of Britain's computer industry, Biffen said, 'leaving it entirely to private sector initiatives' was not an option, so they must support their domestic manufacturers. That evidently did the trick, although not before an overwrought meeting between Thatcher and Joseph, in which the Prime Minister came 'close to tears of frustration'. 'Now, I've upset you, Keith!' Mrs Thatcher said at the end, her voice shaking with emotion. 'No, no, Prime Minister. I'm not sensitive about this. I'll come back again later,' Joseph said. 'No, Keith, I *have* upset you!' she burst out. 'If I've upset you, you're not to go away!' Who could have guessed that financial support for the electronics industry was such an emotive subject?[14]

---

* A reference to the car rental firm's then-famous advertising campaign, in which Avis claimed that, because they were second to their arch-rivals, Hertz, 'we try harder'.

Despite her misgivings, Mrs Thatcher's conversion to the microcomputer revolution was remarkably convincing. 'We have been slower in embracing new technology than other countries,' she told the *Sunday Times* in 1981, because people had been afraid that 'the jobs would go'. But now Britain would copy those 'countries that have gone hardest and fastest for technological change, notably the Japanese'. By now she appeared to be a fully paid-up computer enthusiast, with 1982 designated as the official Information Technology Year, with plans for conferences, exhibitions and even commemorative stamps. Indeed, far from being embarrassed by her financial support for the micro-electronics industry, she now positively gloried in it. Her industrial interventionism was different from Labour's, she told the CBI, because it was 'stimulating industries which do have a future, rather than shoring up lost causes – helping to create tomorrow's world, rather than to preserve yesterday's'.[15]

Her most eye-catching innovation came during the reshuffle of January 1981, when she appointed 'the world's one and only Minister for Information Technology', as he liked to introduce himself. This was the 46-year-old Kenneth Baker, previously one of Edward Heath's most devoted lieutenants. Later, *Spitting Image* depicted him as a slug, a tribute not just to the tremendous oiliness of his slicked-back hair but also to his undeniably oleaginous public persona. Behind the caricature, though, Baker was a bookish, good-humoured and irrepressibly energetic man. It was true, admitted the *Guardian*, that he was a former secretary of the Oxford Union and a member of the Carlton and Athenaeum clubs. But he was not quite your typical Tory. 'He wears jazzy ties and lightweight suits; he talks with unhealthy zeal about the need for rapid change in education and industry; and worst of all, he knows what's he's talking about.'

This was true. Before entering Parliament, Baker had been a business consultant specializing in computers, so he *did* know what he was talking about. Indeed, nobody could have thrown himself more eagerly into his new job than 'Mr Whizz' or 'Mr Chips', as the press called him, and the sight of the pinstriped minister grinning at a monitor became a familiar fixture in the newspapers. It was 'absolute balls', he insisted, to say that computers would throw millions out of work. 'The information technology industries', he told the *New Scientist*, 'are going to be the wealth creators in Britain – and therefore the job creators.' Was he worried that computers in schools were going to distract children from more serious subjects? Not at all. 'Just give the hardware to the kids and let them play around with it,' he said cheerfully, adding that using computers would soon be 'as important as reading or writing'.

What about arcade games like *Space Invaders*? Baker was all for them.

Children soon learned to recognize the patterns, he explained, and it helped them to get used to the technology. His own 11-year-old son, 'not exceptional, not a genius', had grown up with computers and was much better with them than Baker senior. The *Guardian* asked if Baker was worried that, one day, computers would 'outthink us'. Absolute balls again. All the really important decisions in life, he said, were about judgement, 'like falling in love', and 'the computer can't give judgements based on experience'. 'Never?' asked the interviewer. 'As long as man is on this planet . . .' Baker said thoughtfully. Like any good politician, he had left himself a loophole.[16]

Baker's real enthusiasm was for putting computers into schools. This had been mooted during the dog days of the Callaghan government, though it had done nothing about it. In April 1981, however, Mrs Thatcher unveiled Micros in Schools, the biggest secondary-school computer drive in the Western world. 'My generation has perhaps been too cautious about accepting new technology in micros,' she admitted, but now the computer would become 'each pupil's own personal teacher – a teacher with infinite patience which can work at his own pace'. And there was money to back up the rhetoric. Not only did the Department of Education stump up £9 million to train teachers in computing, but the Department of Industry agreed to find half the cost of every school computer, as long as the school paid the other half itself.

Schools could choose from two British models: the RM 380Z, made by the Oxford firm Research Machines, or the new BBC Micro, made by Cambridge-based Acorn. In the end, the vast majority went for the BBC Micro, which was cheaper, more modern and had the imprimatur of the national broadcaster. On the surface there seemed a hint of amateurism about the schools campaign, since it was run from a semi-detached house in Newcastle by a local education lecturer, Richard Fothergill, and three assistants. But they knew what they were doing. In just twelve months they organized courses for some 11,000 teachers, while almost every secondary school in the land had its own computer by the end of 1982. This was nowhere near enough, complained the *New Scientist*, which thought a typical sixth form needed at least twenty computers. Yet coming at a time when so many budgets were being slashed, the government's programme spoke volumes about Mrs Thatcher's newfound commitment to the microcomputer age.[17]

The BBC Micro had its own semi-legendary origin story. Even as the government was finalizing plans for the Micros in Schools programme, a second computer education drive was already underway. This was the work of the BBC's Continuing Education Department, which had been given some money by the Manpower Services Commission to raise public awareness of computers. In November 1979 the BBC decided to launch a Computer Literacy Project, modelled on an adult literacy drive starring the actor Bob Hoskins, which had been immensely successful a few years earlier. Specially commissioned research found that most people were keen to learn more about computers but had no idea where to start. So the BBC project would be aimed at the widest possible audience, 'women as well as men ... working-class viewers as well as middle class ... older age groups as well as younger'. And by the end of 1980 they had devised plans for a major ten-part series, a book and a thirty-hour teach-yourself-computing course, as well as nationwide networks bringing together teachers, lecturers, computer enthusiasts and interested viewers.[18]

There was one more element, the most important of all. Instead of using an existing home computer, the BBC decided to commission their own machine, with high-class sound and graphics and its own version of the computer language BASIC. This, they told the press, would be a machine that could do everything from 'domestic income tax accounts and car maintenance to stock control, Space Invaders and do it yourself horoscopes', a machine for 'the businessman ... amateur astronomer, musician and photographer'. Since it would carry the BBC's name, it would obviously have a gigantic advantage in the marketplace. Not surprisingly, executives were determined to award the contract to a British firm, but they were also acutely conscious that they might be criticized for favouring one private company over its rivals.

The answer was to pick a firm that was already publicly funded. The first choice was Newbury Laboratories, which was backed by the National Enterprise Board and was working on a machine called the Newbrain. But by December 1980 it was clear the Newbrain was not going to be ready in time. With the clock running, an alternative manufacturer would have barely a year before it had to go into mass production. So the BBC hurriedly drew up a list of specifications – colour graphics, interfaces for a cassette recorder and a disk drive, decent sound, lots of peripheral ports – and sent them to half a dozen firms, who were asked to present their pitches in the New Year.[19]

The obvious candidate was Clive Sinclair. No other manufacturer had his name recognition or nationwide reach; indeed, he had just struck a deal with W. H. Smith to sell his forthcoming ZX81. But when the BBC visited Cambridge at the turn of 1981, he treated their specifications with open disdain. His designers were already working on the Spectrum, and Sinclair insisted that the BBC should take that instead, rubber keyboard and all. Would he consider making a new machine? No: it was the Spectrum or nothing. Would he give it more memory? No: that would be too expensive. Would he produce a custom-made version of BASIC? No: that would undermine the rest of the Sinclair family. Would he allow them access to his network of retailers? No: his contacts were for Sinclair-branded machines only. Sinclair thought he was negotiating from strength. Nobody could match his experience; he was confident that the BBC had nowhere else to go. But they did. They had been there earlier that day.[20]

At the turn of the 1980s, Cambridge was already established as the epicentre of the emerging British computer industry. Every year the local university was producing dozens of clever young graduates with interests in science, engineering and computing, while the opening of a new Science Park in 1975 had cemented the city's reputation as the place for technological entrepreneurs to set up shop. Among hundreds of new hi-tech firms was one called Acorn Computers. Then almost completely unknown, it had been founded by two men in their early thirties: Chris Curry, who had worked for Sinclair until the late 1970s, and his Austrian-born friend Hermann Hauser, a Cambridge physics graduate.

Curry, who became Acorn's public face, had dabbled in politics, standing for Parliament in Cambridge in October 1974 on behalf of the United Democratic Party, a fringe assortment of hard-right Eurosceptics who were disillusioned with Edward Heath.* The Cambridge electorate's loss, however, was the computer industry's gain. Eager to emulate the start-ups he had seen in California, Curry parted company with Sinclair at the end of 1978, and the result was Acorn. Its first significant product, the Atom, sold about 35,000 units in four years: not spectacular, but not bad either. This inevitably meant direct competition with Sinclair, yet at first theirs was a relatively friendly rivalry. Nobody had heard of Curry, or indeed of Acorn, whereas Sinclair was becoming a household name. What could he have to fear from his former protégé?[21]

For Acorn, the prospect of a deal with the BBC was a spectacular opportunity. In stark contrast to his old boss, Curry strained every sinew to match the corporation's specifications, even though most of his team thought it was completely impossible. They had already been working on a follow-up to the Atom, called the Proton. But the tight deadline gave them only three days to put together a prototype before the BBC arrived to inspect it. They worked flat-out, yet computing legend has it that the evening before the BBC were due to arrive, the machine was still not

---

* He came last, winning just 885 votes. In fairness, this was a lot more than any of the party's other twelve candidates managed.

working. Then, almost in desperation, Hauser cut the earth wire, and the prototype sprang into life. Whether this was true or not, the BBC liked the machine. Even more importantly, they liked Acorn's enthusiasm, eagerness and can-do spirit. In the afternoon, the BBC delegation visited Sinclair; in the evening, they went to the pub with the team from Acorn. On 13 February 1981 the BBC rang Acorn and told them the contract was theirs. The Proton was no more; the BBC Micro was born.[22]

Sinclair was outraged. How could this have happened? 'I was, and still am, disgusted at the way the BBC handled things,' he said later. 'Acorn quite reasonably got the business and good luck to them. I am not complaining about that, I am complaining about the BBC's behaviour.' Precisely what the BBC had done wrong was never clear: the most likely answer is simply that they had given the contract to somebody else. The computer-game historians Magnus Anderson and Rebecca Levene suggest that if they *had* given it to Sinclair, then 'Britain would have emerged from the eighties with a single, strong computer brand with real survival power'. But the BBC had good reasons for overlooking him, and the result was a manifestly more powerful and versatile product. Indeed, given how quickly Acorn turned the BBC Micro around, it is remarkable how good it was. On the outside it was a big beige typewriter with a proper keyboard and a reassuringly sturdy feel. But inside it came with an unparalleled advantage: the 'unusually intuitive and friendly' BBC BASIC, accessible to children and casual users. Even I got the hang of it, and that is saying something. 'If there is a single tool that opened up computing in Britain in the eighties, and that laid the foundations for its vibrant games scene,' write Anderson and Levene, 'it is BBC BASIC.'[23]

For the rest of 1981, Acorn's engineers worked frantically to get the new machine ready for its television debut. The potential rewards were enormous, yet even before the BBC Micro reached the shops, there were rumours of trouble. Acorn were a very small outfit, with thirty-six employees and a turnover of just £1.3 million. They had very little capital and, like Sinclair, used subcontractors to build their computers. But they were facing two gigantic challenges, because the BBC Micro had *also* been chosen as one of the approved secondary-school computers. The schools contract required them to produce 535 working machines by September and 3,000 a month thereafter, while the BBC series was bound to bring thousands of orders on top of that. And as early as June 1981, some critics were predicting disaster. The *Guardian*'s economics editor, Victor Keegan, rang the company to get a reaction. But 'it took the best part of a week to get through to them', he reported, 'as the phone was always either engaged or not answering. I wondered whether I would have persevered if I had been a customer.'

The critics were right. Not only had Acorn underestimated the level of demand, they had disastrously overestimated their ability to cope with it. At first they expected to make about 12,000 machines for the private market, yet by Christmas 1981, before a single episode of the BBC series had been transmitted, their order book was full. Months before, Curry had talked grandly of having multiple factories making the new computer – three in Britain, one in Hong Kong, one in the United States and one in Australia – but this was hot air. In fact, there were only two, in Staffordshire and South Wales. Even at this early stage, Acorn were grasping for excuses, telling reporters that it was all the BBC's fault for misreading the demand. As a result, the BBC had to postpone the series for a month, because none of their viewers had been able to get hold of the new machines.* 'Once again', the *Guardian* said gloomily, 'a small British company, challenging the Americans and the Japanese for the rich market of home computers, has – like Sinclair – underestimated the initial demand.' It would become a sadly familiar story.[24]

On 11 January 1982 the former *That's Life!* presenter Chris Serle, smartly dressed in a sports jacket and tie, stepped in front of the camera to welcome BBC2 viewers to the first episode of *The Computer Programme*. 'You may have noticed,' he said affably, '1982 is Information Technology Year. There's a Minister for Information Technology, and the government's even spending a great deal of money on publicising it.' So what was information technology? Well, Serle said, 'all it really means is the world of computers. But why have they suddenly become so important? And what should we, as non-computer experts, know about them?'

Making the series had been an immense technical challenge, not least because the computers themselves arrived so late. All the same, *The Computer Programme* was a resounding success. The accent was firmly on the everyday, showing how computers could do everything from booking a holiday to running a sweet shop, while Serle was perfectly cast as the curious everyman. According to a BBC report, some 7 million people watched at least part of it, and the audience defied the stereotypes. Almost half of all viewers were women, while one in four was aged over 45. By the summer, the accompanying *Computer Book* had sold more than 60,000 copies, while viewers sent in an estimated 2,000 letters a week. Given that only a few years before most people had barely heard of computers, these figures were extremely impressive. As the BBC report put it,

* Broadcasts for schools began as expected on the morning of 11 January 1982, but weekend broadcasts were postponed until 14 February and evening repeats until 22 March.

the days of 'computer anxiety' were over; the age of 'computer enthusiasm' was at hand.[25]

There was, however, a problem. Everybody agreed that the BBC Micro was an excellent machine, but very few people could get their hands on it. By April 1982 Acorn had produced only 10,000 machines, far short of their original estimate, while the waiting list stretched to a staggering 20,000 names, some of whom had been on it for months. As BBC executives reported, the Cambridge company had been completely unprepared for the mass market, which meant a twentyfold increase in its turnover. But Acorn had also misjudged people's willingness to spend a lot of money. Curry had assumed that, given the grim economic situation, most people would want the cheaper Model A, which cost £235. But in fact most wanted the more powerful Model B, which cost an extra £100.

Acorn's co-founder Herman Hauser pointed out that the current production rate, 1,500 machines a week, still put Acorn in the top three computer firms in the world. Yet not until October, when sales finally passed 50,000, did Acorn manage to clear their backlog. For almost a year, therefore, they were completely unable to tap the world export market. There was nothing wrong with their product: pound for pound, it was probably the best home computer in the world. But they would never have such an opportunity again.[26]

In one area, though, Acorn could congratulate themselves on an unqualified success. In schools, the government's computer drive had prospered beyond anybody's wildest dreams. By the autumn of 1982, almost all of Britain's 5,000 secondary schools had at least one computer, and now the scheme was extended to the nation's 26,000 primary schools, with the Department of Industry again paying half of the cost. As before, schools were limited to British-made machines: the BBC Micro and the upgraded RM 480Z, with Sinclair's ZX Spectrum later added to the list. For about three out of four schools, the obvious choice was the BBC Micro, not least because of the association with the Computer Literacy Project. 'For most of a generation of children,' writes Tom Lean, 'the BBC was effectively *the* school computer.' The typical school had nine computers to be shared between hundreds of pupils, with many machines spending their days 'trundling between classrooms on trolleys' while crowds of children gathered for a demonstration. Yet this was better than nothing. No other country in Europe came close to matching Britain's investment in school computers.[27]

Even at this point, many observers were struck by the new machines' potential. In Cleveland, one primary school teacher used the Prestel online service to fix her pupils up with electronic pen pals at a school in

Buckinghamshire, breaking down the 'mutual misconceptions' between North and South. In west London, another primary school teacher was an early convert to the power of word processing, arguing that it enabled children to 'become the controllers of their words; they own their own text, and are proud of its appearance'. And in Crowthorne, Berkshire, *The Times* found teenagers queuing up to board the council's 'Computerbus', which shuttled fourteen machines between local schools. One 'remedial group', aged 12 and 13, played a version of Hangman. An English class played a spelling game that invited them to shoot through a brick wall; another remedial group played a maths game called *Car Wash* which required them to manage a car-wash company; a first-year maths group played a times-tables game that the headmaster had written himself. (No commercially available game, he explained, was as good as his.) Did they like computers? 'Yes,' one boy said earnestly, 'it's better than doing work.'[28]

For the chief evangelist of the gospel of work, the popularity of computers was a welcome sign that the younger generation were prepared to embrace the spirit of radical change. Presenting a hundred Sinclair computers to the Portuguese government, Mrs Thatcher could not resist boasting about 'British achievements in this field'. 'These marvellous machines', she told her hosts, 'now seem second nature to our children. Our aim is that every schoolchild in Britain should have access to a computer. Per head of population, Britain has the highest use of home computers in Europe. They are not only useful, they are fun to use!'

This last remark suggests that she had never wasted an afternoon trying to type in a program from a computer magazine. Indeed, barely a month went by in 1982 or 1983 without her popping up to proclaim the virtues of British computers and the wisdom of her government in promoting them. On a trip to Japan in September 1982, for example, she made a point of presenting her Japanese counterpart with one of Sinclair's new Spectrums. 'This', she said slowly and firmly, like a British tourist addressing an uncomprehending waiter, 'is a small home computer.' The Japanese Prime Minister, of all people, probably knew what a computer was.[29]

At home, Mrs Thatcher seized on the computer revolution as proof that, despite the gloom, a brighter, more entrepreneurial future lay ahead. 'There's no point in looking back,' she remarked on one occasion:

> We must be way up front in the new industries, the new products, the new services. For new technologies bring new opportunities as well. That's where the new jobs will come from. That's where they've always come from.
>
> Think of the successful new businesses which did not exist ten years ago and were not dreamt of twenty years ago. Think of Clive Sinclair and his

microcomputers – virtually every secondary school in the country now
has a microcomputer as a result of this Conservative Government's
programme.

And that created a lot of business too. For the parents feel they have to
buy computers to keep up!

Mentioning Sinclair was no accident. As a lone entrepreneur, cutting costs,
defying convention and being rude about the trade unions, he was the
Prime Minister's sort of person. Interviewed by the *Observer*'s Kenneth
Harris, she embarked on a lengthy tribute to the 'successful, enterprising,
thrusting, driving, vigorous, dynamic' American economy, supposedly
such a contrast with sluggish, sclerotic Britain. Fortunately, she added,
things were changing. Harris asked for an example. 'The obvious and
quick one is the Sinclair home computers,' she said happily, remembering
her trip to Japan months earlier. 'I knew I was going right into the heart
of electronics. I thought, what can I give Mr Suzuki, the Prime Minister?
And I took with me a Sinclair home computer and I gave it to Mr Suzuki
in front of all the television companies – look, there we are, first with it.'

Mrs Thatcher's conviction that British computers led the world never
wavered. 'This country is in as good a position as any of its competitors
to benefit from the new possibilities information technology has to offer,'
she told a conference to round off the Information Technology Year in
1982. 'We are a major producer, with skills and ingenuity second to none,
and sought after throughout the world. We are world leaders in the writing
of software . . . We are the first country in the world to put a computer
into every secondary school . . . The information technology revolution is
our revolution: let us make the most of it!'[30]

There was, of course, a fair bit of spin in all this. Turning self-made
entrepreneurs like Sinclair into national heroes was a way of reinforcing
some of Mrs Thatcher's favourite themes: hard work, ambition, seizing
the day and standing on your own two feet. As the academic Maureen
McNeil points out, men such as Sinclair were 'prototypes in the popular
capitalism the Conservative government pioneered', their stories 'mythical
tales of private investment, risk taking, concern for the national interest
and reward'. This was certainly how Sinclair saw himself, but it was not
the whole story. In many ways the computer boom was a textbook example of effective government intervention. Even Sinclair, after all, had once
benefited from a bailout by the National Enterprise Board. And many
other firms were dependent on government help. The computer-monitor
firm Microvitec, for example, was founded in Bradford in 1979 with backing from the Department of Industry. After two years it was already

making a healthy profit, and by 1984, with Microvitec monitors installed in almost every single school in the country, sales had reached almost £10 million a year.[31]

Underpinning all this was the fact that demand for computers did not miraculously appear in response to Sinclair's adverts. Had the government not put computers into schools, and had the BBC not launched its Computer Literacy Project, public enthusiasm would probably have been much weaker. And despite her image as the sworn enemy of government intervention, Mrs Thatcher was very keen to take the credit. Private enterprise had played its part, she told the information technology conference in 1982. But 'if such enterprise is to flourish, the Government itself also has a job to do'. This, she said proudly, was 'why our support for Information Technology in schools and higher education is so vital', and why the government was spending millions to support 'the Research and Development that must be carried out if industry is to bring successful products to the market'. And her minister for computers freely admitted that in this respect there was more continuity between the Callaghan and Thatcher governments than people recognized. There was nothing wrong, Kenneth Baker said, in handing out 'catalyst money' to create 'the climate of change'.[32]

On the face of it, the story of the British microcomputer industry was a tremendous vindication of the government's strategy. Francis Spufford suggests that it achieved 'levels of success in the global market not seen since the 1870s', and indeed some firms enjoyed spectacular export sales. The Dragon 32, built in Port Talbot with backing from the Welsh Development Agency, won the contract for Spain's school computer project, while the Oric-1, designed in St Ives and built in Berkshire, was briefly France's bestselling computer. Indeed, even the *Guardian*'s Victor Keegan thought Mrs Thatcher was perfectly justified in praising the achievements of the British computer industry. 'If you were looking for evidence of industrial resurgence in the UK', he wrote, 'you would be hard pushed to find a better example.' And he agreed that Clive Sinclair deserved credit, too, not merely because of the huge influence of machines like the ZX80, but because his formula – 'designing a machine from the world's most advanced components . . . and then contracting out the business of manufacturing' – meant he and his rivals could avoid 'the worst excesses of the British disease'.[33]

Yet even at this early stage, sceptics wondered whether the emperor's new clothes were quite as advertised. *The Times*, for example, was struck by the adverts for Sinclair's ZX80, which claimed it could 'do quite literally anything from playing chess to running a power station'. But this was quite literally untrue: in no meaningful way could such a primitive machine run a power station. It did not even have a decent keyboard. The only way for most users to save their work was through a painfully slow connection to a cassette recorder, while loading even the most basic program might take at least ten minutes – that is, if it loaded at all. Nobody who owned a home computer in the early 1980s will easily forget the agonizing frustration that accompanied loading and saving. Impatience, wrote the journalist David Hewson, was 'an integral part of being a home computer owner'. He could 'testify from personal experience that one hour of rerunning the same tape without success does not make one feel an advance guard of the new electronic generation, particularly if the programme concerned is Motorway Mania and an impatient child is tapping her foot by your seat'.[34]

There were other caveats. As Victor Keegan pointed out, the 'Britishness' of the industry was more ambiguous than the government liked to admit. A survey by the *Observer* in March 1983 suggested that a third of Britain's 1.35 million home computers had been built abroad. Even machines nominally made in Britain had often been pre-assembled in the Far East. Indeed, the government's approach to all this was a bit of a mess. If companies wanted to build their machines in Britain, as Sinclair did in Dundee, they had to pay 17 per cent duty to import American or Japanese microchips. But if the machines were fully or partly assembled abroad, they only needed to pay 6 per cent to bring them into the country. It made sense, in other words, to make them abroad. But this led to a further inconsistency. As far as the government was concerned, Acorn's machines, which were often built entirely abroad, were completely British, and could be used in schools. Yet Commodore's machines, which were made in a Corby factory built with assistance from the Department of Industry, were not British, and could not. There was a kind of logic here, because Commodore's machines were designed in Pennsylvania. Yet given what had happened to Corby since the turn of the decade, the government could have been forgiven for stretching its definition.[35]

The bigger problem, though, was that the foundations of the computer boom were weaker than they looked. It was true that Britain was now the only country in the world, apart from the United States and Japan, with a serious home computer industry. No other country, in fact, enjoyed such success selling low-specification microcomputers to middle-class families. But it was an industry made up of some fifty tiny, squabbling manufacturers, most of them run by people in their twenties and thirties with little business experience. The fact that almost all of them struggled to meet public demand told its own story. As the *Guardian*'s technology correspondent Peter Large predicted in 1983, the computer market was bound to become more globalized in the years ahead. Yet most of the British firms were far too small and under-capitalized to handle worldwide competition. It was, he thought, only a matter of time before the American and Japanese corporations moved into the home computer market, offering more sophisticated machines for similarly low prices. Then the British firms would be blown away.

And despite their boastful advertising, the British firms knew it. Almost unnoticed by the press, which preferred to run long articles about Clive Sinclair's business acumen or Chris Curry's technical flair, the British Microcomputer Manufacturers' Group asked the government in December 1982 to consider banning American and Japanese computers for a year, in order to save Britain's computer industry 'from virtual elimination by unfair competition'. The government refused: Mrs Thatcher was not in the business of banning imports. But it was a sign of things to come.[36]

Clive Sinclair never forgave the BBC for picking Acorn to make their new computer. Still, he consoled himself with the sensational success of the ZX81, which had broken almost every conceivable sales record since its launch in March 1981. It was remarkably cheap: at just £49.95 for a kit and £69.95 for a fully assembled machine, it was less than a fifth of the price of his calculator almost a decade earlier, when inflation was taken into account. It was also good-looking: a small black box with a mere kilobyte of memory, it had been designed to look 'high-tec and desirable' when visitors saw it 'in the bedroom or the lounge'. But its real asset was the swagger of Sinclair's marketing campaign, which sold it as a lifestyle choice, even a status symbol. Mocked-up screenshots, which bore remarkably little relation to reality, showed the ZX81 running home banking programs, recipe databases, diaries and address books. As one advert put it, owning a ZX81 would give you 'a firmer grip on the way the world works, an opportunity to join what is certain to be a British way of life'.

The campaign clearly struck a chord. As early as June 1981, Sinclair was selling about 10,000 machines a month, many of them at home, but the vast majority to France, Germany, Japan, Australia and, above all, the United States. By Christmas, total sales had reached 250,000, and by the spring of 1982 they stood at almost half a million, giving Sinclair the largest unit sales in the world. And then, that April, he launched the most popular British computer of all, the Spectrum.[37]

The advent of the Spectrum could hardly have been better timed. Thanks to the BBC's Computer Literacy Project, public interest in computers had never been higher. Indeed, judging by the volume of stories in the newspapers, the second half of 1982 was the moment when home computers definitively broke out of the hobbyists' club into the mainstream. It is worth remembering, though, that while computers were cheaper than ever before, they still cost quite a lot of money. Using average earnings as a yardstick, a Spectrum cost the equivalent of about £800 today, while a BBC Micro cost about twice that. So why did people bother? If you bought a microwave, you could heat up some beef stroganoff. If you bought a video recorder, you could watch *Minder* again and again. But why fork out for a home computer? 'Do you actually need a computer?' wondered the *Guardian*, and even the designers struggled to find a convincing answer. After all, what could you actually *do* with it? Copy out your address book? Print out a knitting pattern? What could the Spectrum or the BBC Micro possibly offer that justified spending such a lot of money?[38]

To readers of a certain age, like me, there was an obvious answer: games. But in the summer of 1982, computer advertisements barely mentioned games at all. Very few parents, no matter how well off, were likely to spend hundreds of pounds so that their offspring could waste their weekends playing *Manic Miner*. Instead, adverts played relentlessly on middle-class parents' fears of their children being left behind in an age of dizzying economic and technological change. As Tom Lean points out, the fact that most parents saw computers as 'a mystery from the future', to quote the adverts for the Dragon 32, made them susceptible to emotional blackmail. 'We live in an age of computers,' proclaimed the advert for the Commodore VIC-20. 'Coming to terms with them is part of coming to terms with the twentieth century.'

What decent parent would want to stop their children learning what BBC Micro adverts called 'the language of the future'? One Acorn advert even purported to show a gang of previously unemployed teenagers, who 'didn't have to burden the state much longer' after they had signed up for computer education. Of course this was largely fantasy, but with record youth unemployment in the headlines, and both the government and the national broadcaster banging on about Britain's silicon future, who wanted to take the risk? As Lean remarks, 'it became an article of faith that the cleverest children had a computer in the house, and would have a vital lead over those who didn't . . . The cost of a computer might have been falling, but so was the price of not having one.'[39]

The moment when computers really found their place on the high street came at Christmas 1982. As *The Times* observed, the computer was now 'established as a family purchase with a market which peaks at Christmas', with somewhere between 600,000 and 1 million machines already installed in homes across the country. No longer a machine for the dedicated hobbyist, it was bought by 'mums and dads', convinced that a home computer would turn their listless little darling into an all-conquering prodigy. And when the Christmas rush began, sales exceeded all predictions. Sinclair sold some 198,000 machines, followed by Commodore (32,600), Acorn (32,000) and Dragon (30,000). In fact, the demand was so high that W. H. Smith and Dixons sold out of the most popular brands, while smaller firms such as Dragon, Oric and Grundy found orders doubling every couple of months. Many shoppers, it seemed, did not care which computer they bought. All that mattered was to come home with *something*.

Even after the festive glow had faded, the rush continued. In the early months of 1983, industry experts estimated that people were still buying about 62,000 machines a month. By February, Sinclair had sold about a million ZX81s and Spectrums combined, while Commodore claimed to have shifted a million VIC-20s and Acorn had sold just under 100,000 BBC Micros. All three were struggling to cope with such rapid expansion. In just twelve months, Acorn's output had increased by a staggering 243 per cent, while Sinclair's rate of growth was even higher at 255 per cent. Indeed, almost every week brought an awestruck feature in the broadsheet business pages, the writer swooning in disbelief at the nation's enthusiasm for home computers.

'The rush, predominantly among the middle classes, determined to ensure that they and their children quickly learn this central skill of the future, is unmatched anywhere else in the world,' the *Guardian* reported proudly. This was no exaggeration. Britain now had the world's highest rate of home computer ownership, well ahead of both the United States and Japan, with one machine in every six homes by the spring of 1983. Here was a new Britain indeed. 'There's no doubt about it,' one newsagent admitted to the *Observer*, contemplating the shelves stuffed with computer magazines. 'Computers are now more popular than porn.'[40]

The boom seemed unstoppable. 'We are not placing any limits on the size we can grow to,' declared Acorn's Chris Curry, setting out his plans to dominate the education market, secure 'half the home computer market' and capture the market for business machines, winning over 'all the people who are buying Apples'.* As for Sinclair, he seemed the master of all he surveyed. With turnover now £50 million, his personal worth was estimated at a staggering £130 million. 'Today', declared the *Observer*, 'a Sinclair computer drops off the end of the production line every four seconds.' The *Guardian* crowned him the Young Businessman of the Year;

---

* The Californian firm had introduced the Apple II as early as 1977, but at a cost of £1,200 it generally appealed only to businesses.

the government awarded him a knighthood. 'Where will it end?' wondered the *Guardian*. Perhaps the answer lay in 'the gleam in Mr Sinclair's eye', his plan for a 'cheap electric car' that could revolutionize transport forever. 'If it was anyone but Clive Sinclair,' said a spokesman for a rival firm, 'we should be laughing. But what that man does we have to take seriously.'[41]

In the spring of 1984, Sinclair reached his apotheosis. Invited to Washington to address an American congressional symposium, he told them that in decades 'we will be able to assemble a machine as complex as the human brain'. Soon 'machines of silicon will arise first to rival and then surpass their human progenitors'. Computers would become teachers, even doctors. There would be 'totally automatic personal vehicles', travelling at more than 200 miles an hour; there would be 'truly personal telephones . . . wireless devices [that] would allow us to telephone and be telephoned wherever we choose'. Mankind, Sinclair said grandly, was on the brink of an age of 'art, music and science . . . as golden as that of Greece'. And afterwards? It was time to talk seriously about building a 'vast, man-created world in space, home to thousands or millions of people'. And then 'we may begin in earnest the search for worlds beyond our solar system and the colonisation of the galaxy'.[42]

First, though, came his electric car. But that, as it turned out, was a rather less inspiring story.

# 31

# Strangers in the Night

*The news was all rubbish apart from a scurry in the Falkland Islands where some impertinent Argentinians are pinching scrap metal or something.*

Kenneth Williams's diary, 29 March 1982

'*We've lost the Falklands,' I told Jane. 'It's all over. We're a Third World Country, no good for anything.'*

*She is used to my suddenly taking the* apocalyptic *view. Didn't say much.*

Alan Clark's diary, 2 April 1982

Saturday 27 March 1982: a sunny afternoon in Oxford, and Simon Winchester had just lit a bonfire in his back garden when the phone rang. It was the *Sunday Times*. 'We think you should stand by to go to the Falkland Islands,' said the voice at the end of the line. Winchester's first reaction was not enthusiastic. All that way for a story about some scrap-metal dealers! Still, by the following afternoon he was on a flight to Madrid. And by the time he touched down in Spain he was halfway through the file of clippings about the people who lived on these remote islands in the South Atlantic, the 'sturdy breed of sheep farmers and mullet fishermen who kept the Union Jack flying all those thousands of miles from home'.

On Monday morning, Winchester arrived in Buenos Aires. That evening, he had a quick chat with the British ambassador, Anthony Williams, who admitted that the imbroglio on South Georgia – a bizarre row about a group of scrap-metal dealers who had landed illegally and were refusing to leave – was 'damned exasperating, no doubt about it'. The following day Winchester and a couple of other reporters set off to the Falkland Islands' tiny capital, Stanley. It was very cloudy, he remembered, and he saw nothing until the last few moments of the flight – 'and then, suddenly, beneath the wheels, came the landscape we had been expecting. Rain-sodden, windswept, bleak – all green and black and grey, scrubby grassland dotted with sheep, curling clouds of gulls wheeling over the low cliffs.' When he disembarked it was raining, and there was a faded portrait of the Queen over the immigration desk in the aerodrome. A Land Rover took him to the island's only hotel, the Upland Goose on Ross Road. There he 'sat down to tea and cakes, and looked out at the rain'. 'Everything was so Scottish!' he thought. And then two Royal Marines from the island's garrison went past, and he remembered that he was not in Scotland after all.[*1]

The Falkland Islands have not always enjoyed a very good press. Samuel Johnson, who never visited them, wrote scornfully of their 'bleak and gloomy solitude'. Charles Darwin, who did, was struck by their 'desolate and wretched aspect', their 'peaty soil and wiry grass, of one monotonous brown colour'. Another great British thinker, Denis Thatcher, remarked simply that they were 'miles and miles of bugger all'.[†] 'When you first set foot in the Falklands', the BBC's Latin America correspondent told Radio Four listeners in March 1982, 'you feel a sense of isolation, like you're at the end of the earth, which is where you nearly are . . . There's no television, and no roads to speak of outside the capital . . . But there is a lot of drunkenness, a high divorce rate and a shortage of women.' No doubt Dr Johnson, too, would have thought the islands very Scottish.[2]

The history of the islands is immensely complicated. First visited by the English but first settled by the French, they changed hands several times in the eighteenth century, ending up with Spain. During the Napoleonic Wars the Spanish abandoned them, but left a plaque insisting that they still belonged to the Spanish crown. When Argentina declared independence in 1816, it claimed sovereignty over the Malvinas, as they were known in Spanish, and eventually established a small colony. However, the British had not abandoned their own previous claim and in 1833 moved in and re-established control. For the next 150 years the Falklands were British, though the legal situation remained very ambiguous. For the Argentines, the case was simple: the Malvinas were part of their inheritance and had been stolen by 'pirates'. But the British insisted that the islands had been up for grabs after the disintegration of the Spanish Empire. What was more, Britain had now owned them for longer than most modern

---

* As assignments go, Winchester's trip to the South Atlantic was remarkably eventful. Having been thrown off the Falklands after the invasion, he was arrested in Tierra del Fuego for spying and held in an Argentine prison for the next seventy-seven days, before being released at the end of the war.

† The real Denis, not the *Private Eye* one, though they were so similar it hardly matters.

nation-states had existed. And the islanders had lived there for generations, longer than most Argentine families had been in South America,
and overwhelmingly wanted to remain British.[3]

The real question is why anybody cared. The Falklands had no Argentine cultural connections and few natural resources, and were hundreds
of miles from the South American mainland. But the issue had become
inextricably entwined with Argentina's sense of national self-worth, especially after the Second World War, when Juan Perón stoked nationalist
feeling to fever pitch. Like most authoritarian populists, Perón thrived on
enemies, none more diabolical than the British, whose economic bucca-
neers had supposedly been robbing the Argentine people for decades. For
Perón, as for his successors, regaining the Malvinas from the Anglo-Saxon
pirates carried immense symbolic resonance. The islands became a totem
of national independence; they had been stolen, and without them Argentina would never be whole. 'Englishmen,' read the banners in Buenos Aires
during Perón's years in power, 'give us back the Malvinas!'[4]

The irony of all this is that, deep down, most British politicians would
have been delighted to return them. Although the Falklands had taken
their place in British naval legend as the site of victory over the Germans
in 1914, they had little strategic or economic value. From a peak of 2,392
in 1931 the population had slowly declined, dipping to 1,813 fifty years
later. By the late 1960s the islands' days seemed numbered. The problem,
though, was that while the Foreign Office was very happy to transfer
sovereignty to Buenos Aires, the islanders were dead against it. They might
rely on Argentina for their flights, their post, their medical services and
even their petrol, but they were damned if they would become Argentines.
Quite apart from their anxieties about Argentina's economic and political
instability, they saw themselves as British, so attached to their mother
country that they had donated £50,000 from their own funds to buy
Spitfires during the Second World War.

As another visiting reporter, the ubiquitous Ian Jack, told his readers
in 1978, this was not some weird self-delusion. The Falkland Islanders,
or 'Kelpers', looked British, sounded British and even ate British. They
drove Land Rovers and drank Tennent's. At the quayside, fish fingers
arrived every three months on a boat from Tilbury. At the Upland Goose,
Mrs King served onion soup, mutton stew and crème caramel made in a
British factory. At the Philomel Store, Mr Peck sold cans of beer, tubes of
Smarties and stickers reading 'Keep the Falkland Islands British'. The
islanders had their grievances, of course: the stagnant economy, the falling
population, the depressing tendency of local girls to marry Royal Marines
and move to England. But most insisted that they would never surrender

their birthright. 'I'd go,' one said flatly when Jack asked about the prospect of Argentine sovereignty. 'I'd quite definitely – what, stay here under some lousy Latin American dictator? Not likely.'[5]

By this point, though, the Argentines were running out of patience. The mid-1970s had been horrendously violent and turbulent years for Argentina, and the ruling military junta craved a grand gesture of patriotic self-assertion. In December 1976 their air force landed a little party on the uninhabited British dependency of Southern Thule, some 1,200 miles south of Stanley, and refused to budge. The Labour government lodged a formal protest, but otherwise did nothing. A year later, Jim Callaghan was so concerned about Argentina's aggressive rhetoric that he sent a submarine and two frigates to patrol the South Atlantic. Years afterwards, Callaghan claimed that if only Mrs Thatcher had done the same she could have deterred Argentina from invading the Falklands. In reality, the junta never knew about his little flotilla because the British government kept it secret. And at least one of Callaghan's ministers feared that if the worst happened Britain would never have the guts to fight back. This 'ghastly fascist military dictatorship', wrote Tony Benn, was 'determined to get hold of the islands'. And when it did, the 'total spinelessness of the Foreign Office and the general decay of Britain will have combined to put us in a position where we will be unable to do anything to defend the 1950 people who live there'. Needless to say, he took a rather different view five years later.[6]

For Mrs Thatcher, the Falklands were never a priority. Compared with her enormous domestic difficulties, they were barely even a sideshow. But they would not go away. As early as October 1979, Lord Carrington warned his colleagues that unless they found a solution there was a 'serious threat of Argentine invasion which would require the long-term commitment of substantial British forces'. If the Argentines did invade, recovering the islands would be 'extremely difficult', because they were so far away that it would be impossible to resupply any expedition. But Mrs Thatcher did not seem wholly convinced. Underlining a passage about the islands' importance to Argentine national honour, she wrote crossly: 'Acc. to the Foreign Office our national honour doesn't seem to matter!' And beside Carrington's warnings of an invasion, she scribbled: 'These conclusions are debatable . . . *What evidence?*'[7]

In June 1980 Carrington returned to the subject. They really ought to settle the issue, he said, not least because the 'uncertainty' was damaging the islands' economy. The obvious solution was to hand over sovereignty to Argentina in return for a 'leaseback' deal, whereby Britain would continue to administer the Falklands for an agreed period. That way, the

Argentines could claim they had regained ownership of the islands, while the islanders would be reassured by living under British rule for the foreseeable future. And at first his scheme looked very promising. In November he reported that preliminary discussions with Argentina had gone well, with talk of a lease lasting ninety-nine years. Mrs Thatcher was still very wary. 'We can't afford to defend them,' she told her ministers, but 'surrender of sovereignty' would be 'very difficult' to sell. 'We should do nothing,' she added, 'without [the] consent of the islanders.' Fortunately, the Foreign Office had a plan. It proposed to send Carrington's junior minister, Nicholas Ridley, to win them over.[8]

Ridley's visit to the Falklands, which took place at the end of November, was an unmitigated disaster. The son of a viscount and the grandson of the architect Sir Edwin Lutyens, Ridley was an enthusiast for fishing, painting and smoking, with an arrogant manner and an aristocratic relish for saying what people did not want to hear. When he was invited to address a public meeting at Stanley Town Hall, things did not go well at all. 'I don't think we should give them sovereignty. We're giving up our birthright,' one man said. 'Well then,' said Ridley, 'you take the consequences, not me.' The man, evidently astonished, said: 'That's a pretty bald statement.' But Ridley was unrepentant. 'If you can't get the communications, if you can't get the medical services and the educational services, if you can't get the oil,' he said, 'then it's you who suffer, not us.' 'We know that,' the man said angrily, 'we realise that, we're not nits.'

At one point somebody asked: 'If the Argentines invaded, what is Britain going to do?' 'Kick them out!' Ridley said, at which there was a burst of mocking laughter. 'Of course we will!' he exclaimed, raising his voice above the din:

> Goodness me – that's not the problem. The problem is, do you want the Argentinians invading you and us kicking them out in a state of perpetual war? That's what you've got to think about. I mean, it's all very well sitting here saying someone else must come and kick the Argentinians out. Of course we will, but is that good for sheep-farming, for fishing, for looking for oil, for all your futures, for your children, and your grand-children and your great-grand-children? Is that the way you want to live? – That's what you've got to think about.

Ridley was never going to win any prizes for tact, but everything he said was true. The problem was twofold: the islanders did not want to hear it, and he was entirely the wrong person to persuade them. When he left to fly home, they saw him off with a loudspeaker playing 'Land of Hope and Glory', 'This Land Is Our Land' and 'We Shall Not Be Moved'.[9]

What really killed off the leaseback idea, though, was the reaction in the Commons. By the time Ridley reported back on 2 December, the small pro-Falklands lobby had got to work, and the result was a terrible thrashing. For true-blue Conservatives, the issue was an opportunity to flaunt their patriotism; for Labour, it was simply a chance to have a go at the government. One by one, MPs leapt up to denounce this shameful sell-out. The islanders' wishes must be 'paramount', said Labour's Peter Shore. The plan was an 'insult' to people 'wholly British in blood and sentiment', thundered the Conservative backbencher Sir Bernard Braine. 'Whatever the Government', declared Labour's Tom McNally, 'there will never be a majority in this House to give this historically separate people and these separate islands to the Argentine.' Eighteen MPs spoke; none had anything but contempt for the Foreign Office's plan. So that was that. And with leaseback dead, the government reverted to what the Falklands War's official historian, Sir Lawrence Freedman, calls 'Micawberism': waiting for something to turn up.[10]

When Mrs Thatcher remarked that Britain could no longer afford to defend the Falklands, she had not been joking. For a quarter of a century, governments of both parties had been whittling away at the defence budget, endeavouring to reconcile the demands of the Cold War with the reality of Britain's overstretched finances. In the autumn of 1980, Sir Geoffrey Howe had tried to cut defence spending even further, but her first Defence Secretary, Francis Pym, had fought a dogged rearguard action to protect his budget. So in January 1981 Mrs Thatcher brought in a new Defence Secretary, the saturnine, prickly and impeccably dry John Nott.

A man who always looked as though he had missed his calling as a Bond villain's accountant, Nott duly sharpened his axe. Given Britain's commitments in West Germany, the obvious target, he told Mrs Thatcher, was the Royal Navy. By the summer, he had decided on 'radical adjustment', scrapping much of Britain's surface fleet, closing the dockyards in Chatham and Gibraltar, shutting down much of the Portsmouth dockyard and slashing naval manpower by at least a third. Not only was Nott eager to get rid of two of Britain's three aircraft carriers, HMS *Hermes* and HMS *Invincible*, he was also keen to sell the assault ships *Fearless* and *Intrepid*, as well as at least twenty destroyers and frigates. The navy, not surprisingly, were aghast. The First Sea Lord, Sir Henry Leach, visited Mrs Thatcher in Number 10 and told her she was making a 'serious miscalculation'. Such cuts, he said, would 'unbalance our entire defence capability, and once the ships were gone, we should probably not be able to recover this century'. But he was wasting his breath. Nott thought Leach was a romantic fantasist. What Leach thought of Nott was barely printable.[11]

For the Falkland Islanders, much of this was academic. But one ship did matter to them. This was HMS *Endurance*, the ageing ice patrol vessel that had been keeping watch over the South Atlantic since 1968. In itself *Endurance* was pretty useless, and the Ministry of Defence had been talking about getting rid of it for years. The Foreign Office thought it was an important symbol of Britain's determination to defend the Falklands, while the islanders themselves found it reassuring. But it was an obvious target for Nott's axe, not least because it was overdue for an extremely expensive refit. From the Foreign Office, Lord Carrington warned that scrapping *Endurance* 'would be interpreted by both the Islanders and the Argentines as a reduction in our commitment to the Islands and in our willingness to defend them'. But nobody at the Navy really wanted to fight for the ship, especially if scrapping *Endurance* helped to save another frigate. As Mrs Thatcher herself put it, *Endurance* was a 'military irrelevance', which 'would neither deter nor repel any planned invasion'. So it had to go.[12]

As it turned out, the decision to scrap *Endurance* was one of the most expensive Mrs Thatcher ever took. Later, even the Franks Committee's report on the origins of the war, which was widely seen as a bit of a whitewash, agreed with the Foreign Office view that the ship had been an emblem of Britain's 'commitment to the defence of the Falkland Islands', and that getting rid of it was a bad mistake. The obvious counter-argument is that if the government had retained *Endurance*, it would have had to get rid of something else. Yet, as the archives show, Carrington repeatedly warned his colleagues that this particular cut would be seen as an invitation to Argentina. Indeed, although Carrington later took the blame for the invasion, he was the only senior minister who recognized that storm clouds were gathering. In September 1981 he told his colleagues, yet again, that the Argentine regime was under 'strong domestic pressure to show results' and was betraying 'renewed impatience' with the failure to agree a deal. They should not 'discount the risk', he wrote, that 'we might become involved in a military confrontation with Argentina'. And if they did, 'defending the Islands would be both difficult and costly'.[13]

All this gives the lie to the Franks Report's claim that the Argentine invasion of the Falklands could not reasonably have been foreseen. It *was* foreseen. That said, it is hard to know what Mrs Thatcher's government should have done differently. The islanders themselves had rejected the leaseback idea; if the government had handed them over to Buenos Aires

against their will, it would have been pilloried by the press, the Labour
Party and its own backbenchers. Some historians, such as Mrs Thatcher's
biographers Hugo Young and John Campbell, argue that the government
should have deterred the Argentine invasion by sending more ships to the
South Atlantic. Of course it is easy to say that now. But if Mrs Thatcher
*had* sent more ships, she would have scuppered any chance of settling the
issue through negotiations. What was more, in the autumn of 1981 a
report for the defence chiefs concluded that to 'deter a full-scale invasion',
Britain would have to send a 'large balanced force' including at least four
destroyers and an *Invincible*-class aircraft carrier, as well as numerous
supply ships and a brigade to reinforce Stanley's garrison of Royal Marines.
Not only would this be extremely expensive, it 'could well precipitate the
very action it was intended to deter'. And if Mrs Thatcher had sent the
ships and Argentina had reacted, history's verdict would not be kind.[14]

None of this, of course, means the government was blameless. Back in
1976, in the first line of the speech that earned her the Iron Lady nickname,
Mrs Thatcher had proclaimed that 'the first duty of any Government is
to safeguard its people against external aggression'. In the Falklands she
conspicuously failed to deliver on that promise. Scrapping *Endurance*, in
particular, now looks like a terrible mistake. It is true, of course, that she
was dependent on advice from the Ministry of Defence, much of which
proved unforgivably complacent. But as she well knew, the buck always
stops at the top. If the invasion had happened under Labour, she would
not have cut Jim Callaghan or Michael Foot an inch of slack. It happened
on her watch, so she gets the blame.[15]

In a wider sense, though, this is beside the point. Much of the historical
discussion about the Falklands, like much of the discussion of the 1980s
in general, is absurdly parochial. Contrary to what some of her critics
claimed, Mrs Thatcher did not want a war in the Falklands. Her government, like its predecessors, believed the islands' future lay in a closer
relationship with Argentina. She certainly made mistakes, but getting
rid of a burglar alarm is not the same thing as burgling a house. The first
shots in the conflict were not fired by British soldiers; they were fired
by Argentines. Whatever her critics said, the war was not made in London.
It was made in Buenos Aires.

To most people in Britain at the turn of the 1980s, Argentina was so
remote it might as well have been on the moon. In the popular imagination
it seemed an intoxicating, passionate place, the land of tango and steak,
pampas and gauchos, the vast wilderness of Patagonia and the crumbling
grandeur of Buenos Aires. But to readers of *The Times* or the *Guardian*,

it was the unsettling instability of Argentine life that loomed largest: the bombs, the death squads and the triple-digit hyperinflation. When a military coup deposed the floundering Isabel Perón in 1976, *The Times* hoped Argentina's new masters might banish its 'nightmare of bloodshed, corruption, administrative paralysis and economic disaster'. They did indeed restore order, though at a horrifyingly high price. During the so-called Dirty War, tens of thousands of Marxists, trade unionists, clergymen, students and journalists were variously kidnapped, imprisoned, raped, tortured, shot or simply dropped into the Atlantic. None of this was a secret. Another *Times* editorial, in July 1981, noted that the junta's campaign had come at an 'enormous cost in human suffering'. After the 'brutal repression which has been carried out in the name of combating terrorism', the paper said sadly, 'Argentina needs a return to normality'.[16]

Normality, however, was some way off. At the beginning of 1982, the Argentine economy was still in a terrible mess, with production and earnings in free-fall and inflation at lunatic levels. The workers were restive; the mood was febrile. It was against this background that the head of the army, General Leopoldo Galtieri, took over as the junta's third president. Tall, rugged and hard-drinking, Galtieri was the son of Italian immigrants and had spent his entire adult life in the military. He was a man of action, not ideas; a gambler, not a strategist. For strategy, he relied on his chief ally, Admiral Jorge Anaya, who ran Argentina's navy. The two men had been friends since their days at the National Military College, and it was Anaya who urged Galtieri to settle the Falklands issue once and for all. With the islands back in Argentine hands, Anaya argued, their domestic popularity would be assured.[17]

At the time, Anaya's plan seemed rational enough. If the junta could regain the islands by January 1983, which would mark the 150th anniversary of the British takeover, the Buenos Aires crowds would cheer them to the skies. But given the fate of Ridley's initiative, any chance of a negotiated settlement seemed extremely remote. So on 15 December 1981, Anaya told his chief of naval operations to draft a secret contingency plan to seize the islands, and by late January they had a very rough outline. Ideally they would strike in the second half of 1982, after the British had withdrawn the *Endurance*. Taking the islands would be fairly straightforward: once their troops had landed outside Stanley, it would be easy to overpower the tiny garrison of Royal Marines.

As for the British, Anaya never expected them to hit back. Everybody knew they had lost their fighting spirit, while Mrs Thatcher's plan to scrap the *Endurance* showed she no longer took the defence of the islands seriously. And if she did make a fuss, so what? She would never dare to move without American support, yet Argentina was one of Washington's most reliable partners. General Galtieri had even been trained at West Point. Nobody seriously doubted that if it came to the crunch President Reagan would side with his friends from Buenos Aires.[18]

Although the plan was supposed to be secret, rumours soon spread. Perhaps the junta hoped that, if they rattled their sabres loudly enough, the British would roll over. On 24 January the newspaper *La Prensa* ran a story, later picked up by the *Guardian*, claiming that the Galtieri regime was running out of patience with the talks and was seriously considering military action. On 2 March, Britain's defence attaché in Buenos Aires warned that a full military attack was not beyond the realms of possibility. And on the next day the Foreign Office forwarded to Number 10 a cable from Britain's ambassador in Buenos Aires reporting on the intransigent rhetoric coming from the Argentine Foreign Ministry. On the top, Mrs Thatcher scrawled: 'We must make contingency plans.' But none of her officials did anything about it. In Whitehall, nobody believed – or wanted to believe – that the Argentines were serious.[19]

By this point, Anaya's men had drawn up a preliminary landing plan. On 2 March, the day before Mrs Thatcher made her anxious little note, Galtieri told one of his brigadier-generals, Mario Benjamin Menéndez, that they would soon reclaim the Malvinas and that he would be the islands' first military governor. But at this stage they had no plans to invade before September. Some of Anaya's officers believed it was 'only a contingency plan', and Rear Admiral Carlos Büsser, who led the invasion, told the historian Martin Middlebrook that he expected to be working on it until the final months of 1982. The 'main emphasis', Büsser claimed, was 'always on recovering the islands by negotiations'. Since negotiations had stalled, this seems a bit disingenuous. Probably the junta were always going to invade; the only question was when. This was where the South Georgia scrap-metal dealers came in.[20]

The occupation of South Georgia was a very odd business, and even now it is hard to untangle the details. The island itself, some 800 nautical miles to the east of Stanley, is even more remote than the Falklands. First claimed for Britain by Captain Cook in 1775, it was now effectively deserted, save for the British Antarctic Survey's tiny research station at King Edward Point. But the island's former whaling stations, where the explorer Ernest Shackleton had famously sought help in 1916, were littered with the rusting relics of whaling ships and oil processing plants. And in 1978 an Argentine wheeler-dealer, Constantino Davidoff, approached the nominal owners, a company based in Edinburgh, to ask if he could carry off the old equipment for scrap.

To cut a long story short, the company agreed, the Foreign Office gave its permission and Davidoff got his contract. However, when he first visited South Georgia in December 1981 to see exactly what was there, his men behaved badly, not getting the right clearance, scrawling '*Los Malvinas son Argentinas*' on a wall and generally making a nuisance of themselves. The damage was spotted by the British Antarctic Survey, and a shamefaced Davidoff duly went to the British Embassy in Buenos Aires to apologize. The Embassy agreed to give him another chance, and on 18 March 1982 the *Bahia Buen Suceso* sailed into the former whaling station of Leith, South Georgia, nominally to collect the equipment. But now the story took a very strange turn. When a British Antarctic Survey team came across Davidoff's men in Leith the next day, they discovered that not only were some dressed in paramilitary uniforms, but they had again vandalized the British Antarctic Survey station, were flying the Argentine flag and were even barbecuing a local reindeer, which was a protected species. Even by the standards of South American scrap-metal dealers, this seemed pretty poor form.

But Davidoff's men were not just scrap-metal dealers, or at least not all of them. In effect, his expedition had been co-opted by the Argentine Navy, who had offered him the use of their ships, free of charge, to bring the scrap back to the mainland. Their motives, however, were not entirely charitable. Argentina had laid claim to South Georgia since 1927, and Davidoff's scheme gave them a chance to establish a presence on the island, as they had already done on Southern Thule. Under their plan, known as Operation Alpha, a group of naval personnel had joined Davidoff's workers and were planning to stay behind after the scrap merchants left. Once they had a foothold on the island, they would be joined by a second party of Argentine Marine commandos, who would establish a permanent military base. By the time the British noticed, they hoped, South Georgia would be in Argentine hands.[21]

On the face of it, Operation Alpha was a perfectly workable plan. It was basically a Southern Thule-style military escapade, and there was no reason to expect drastic consequences. The problem, however, was that it muddied the waters for the plan to invade the Falklands, which was an entirely separate undertaking. Indeed, some of Admiral Anaya's senior commanders thought they had persuaded him to postpone Operation Alpha and were horrified to hear it had gone ahead. There was obviously no chance now of an early breakthrough in the negotiations, because the British were furious. Worse, with Britain's attention now focused on the South Atlantic, Anaya's commanders were in danger of losing any element of surprise. The irony is that if Anaya had shut down the stunt in South

Georgia he could have launched the conquest of the Falklands a few weeks later, when the weather would have made a successful British expedition almost impossible. But as it was, the British reaction forced him to bring the invasion plans forward. And although she could hardly have known it, this was Mrs Thatcher's great stroke of luck.[22]

Over the next few days, the crisis in South Georgia spiralled out of control. The Governor of the Falkland Islands, Rex Hunt, ordered the intruders to haul down the Argentine flag and retreat to their ship, and asked the government to send *Endurance* from Stanley with a detachment of Royal Marines. Eventually the Foreign Office agreed, while in the meantime the Argentines seemed to pack up and leave. But by 22 March it was obvious that some of them, at least, were still on the island. The Argentines were clearly up to something, and Hunt urged the Foreign Office to deter future incursions with a show of strength. In Whitehall, however, the feeling was that Britain should do nothing to inflame the situation. The ambassador in Buenos Aires, Anthony Williams, thought talk of military action ridiculous and assured his superiors that the junta were 'much too intelligent to do anything so silly'. So when the Foreign Office minister Richard Luce reported on the affair to the House of Commons, he deliberately played it down. There had been a bit of a contretemps, he said, and 'a small number of men and some equipment remain. We are therefore making arrangements to ensure their early departure.'[23]

Had Britain been a dictatorship, like Argentina, the Foreign Office might have got away with taking such a soft line. But the Commons was fractious. Even before Luce's speech, the ever-dramatic Alan Clark had recorded his unease at the situation in South Georgia. 'If we don't throw them out, preferably shedding blood at the same time,' he wrote, 'they will try their luck in the Falklands.' When Clark discussed his fears with other backbenchers in the smoking room, they agreed that 'it's all down to that fucking idiot Nott, and his spastic "Command Paper", which is effectively running down the Royal Navy so as to keep the soldiers in Rhine Army happy'. 'Surely Margaret must sympathise?' said Clark. 'Don't bet on that, Alan,' said the similarly ferocious Nicholas Budgen. 'She is governed only by what the Americans want. At heart she is just a vulgar, middle-class Reaganite.'[24]

The result of all this armchair sabre-rattling was that when Luce made his statement on 23 March he was besieged by speakers demanding a tougher response. The government must realize, thundered Jim Callaghan, that the plan to withdraw *Endurance* was a 'gross dereliction of duty'. *Endurance* was in the area, Luce said feebly, and 'in a position to help if necessary'. But that was not good enough. The events in South Georgia were 'tantamount to the invasion of an independent country', insisted the Conservative backbencher Nicholas Winterton. Britain must send 'tangible support to the Falkland Islanders', agreed Sir Bernard Braine, while a third Tory, John Stokes, demanded that they send 'sufficient armed forces – naval, military or air – to defend the Falkland Islands'. 'We've got the whole thing opened now,' Clark recorded happily. 'Clearly the Labour Party are also indignant, and if she doesn't get the Argentines out by next week there will be a major disturbance.'[25]

Unknown to Clark, one of the spectators in the public gallery was an official from the Argentine Embassy. And now came one of the crucial moments in the whole story. A few hours later, Galtieri, Anaya and their senior colleagues met in Buenos Aires. The confrontation was clearly getting out of hand: British suspicions had been roused, the *Endurance* was heading for South Georgia's main harbour, Grytviken, and Mrs Thatcher's backbenchers were urging her to send reinforcements to the South Atlantic. As the junta saw it, they were about to be humiliated. Worse, if they did not act now, they might lose any chance of regaining the islands in the foreseeable future. They could not back down. This was their moment; they must seize it.

That evening, Anaya ordered another ship, the *Bahia Paradiso*, to sail directly for South Georgia with a group of armed marines, as per the plan in Operation Alpha. In the first of several public relations calamities, the commander was Lieutenant Alfredo Astiz, nicknamed the 'Blond Angel of Death' for his gruesome record during the Dirty War. Wanted by the French for torturing and killing two Catholic nuns, Astiz was the worst possible advertisement for the Argentine military and a gift to the British tabloids. Meanwhile, Anaya ordered his planners to bring forward their timetable. For the next two days they worked without a wink of sleep, and on 25 March they reported that they could sail in three days' time. The next day, the junta held one last meeting. If there were any lingering doubts, the fact that the Argentine unions had just called a general strike decided the issue. They could not afford to be humiliated. The British would be furious, said Galtieri's foreign minister, but if the invasion went according to plan, they would be powerless to react: 'Let's do it quickly.'[26]

At dawn on Sunday 28 March the first Argentine troops boarded their ships at the naval base in Puerto Belgrano, south of Buenos Aires. It was, remembered Rear Admiral Büsser, a lovely sunny day, a 'nice autumn day without wind'. The soldiers had been told they were going on exercise in Patagonia. But with so much ammunition and so much secrecy, many suspected the truth. Some had packed large quantities of Argentine flags to hand out to the islanders, who would naturally be thrilled to be liberated from their piratical overlords. 'Those of us who knew where we going', Büsser recalled, 'were very proud. We felt very lucky that we had been chosen and extraordinarily fortunate to have the opportunity to regain the Malvinas.' At midday all was ready. The ships sailed. That evening, on the military landing ship *Cabo San Antonio*, Büsser's troops celebrated Mass and prayed for victory.[27]

In London there was still no sense of urgency. Four days earlier, on 24 March, Lord Carrington had warned Mrs Thatcher that they might 'face the prospect of an early confrontation with Argentina', but the worst he imagined was that Buenos Aires might cut off services to the Falkland Islands. On 25 March the matter came up at Cabinet. Carrington said South Georgia was escalating into 'something which may be very difficult', but using force might provoke a rash Argentine reaction. If they threatened the Falklands, he added, 'Britain would face an almost impossible task in seeking to defend the Islands at such long range'. The next day, the Ministry of Defence presented Mrs Thatcher with a hastily drafted contingency plan, envisaging sending a small fleet to deter an Argentine invasion. But it would take weeks to arrive; if the Argentines attacked in the meantime, 'there would be no certainty that such a force would be able to retake the dependency'. 'You can imagine', Mrs Thatcher said later, 'that turned a knife in my heart.'[28]

On Monday, Mrs Thatcher and Lord Carrington flew to Brussels for a European summit. On the plane, they decided to send a submarine to South Georgia, but still they did not believe an invasion was imminent. On the same day, *The Times* published its first editorial about the crisis in the South Atlantic. The 'presence of the Argentine scrap-merchants', it said, was clearly meant as a 'direct challenge to British sovereignty'. But the bigger issue was obviously the Falklands. 'The Falklands Islanders', the paper said, 'have to face the unpleasant fact that Britain is no longer a world power and that the rest of the world is unlikely to come to their rescue. If they are to stay where they are in the next century it can only be on the basis of an arrangement with their South American neighbours.'[29]

The next day, a storm broke over the South Atlantic. On the overcrowded *Cabo San Antonio*, pitching wildly in the roiling waters, the Argentine troops were violently seasick, and their commanders agreed to delay the landing for a day or so. In Westminster, Mrs Thatcher was not back from Brussels, so Willie Whitelaw deputized at Prime Minister's Questions. Most of the questions touched on familiar themes: youth unemployment, the Scarman Report, the 'extraordinary behaviour' of Ken Livingstone. But one MP asked about the *Endurance*, and another about arms sales to Argentina. Whitelaw fielded their questions with character-istic stolidity, but now the first rumours of Argentine ship movements were beginning to seep through the fog of complacency. That afternoon, Rich-ard Luce assured the Commons that Britain was still seeking a diplomatic solution to the South Georgia dispute, and would 'support and defend the islanders to the best of our ability'. But he 'knew deep down', he said later, 'how dangerously empty those words had become'.[30]

The following day was Wednesday 31 March. Late that afternoon, John Nott told Mrs Thatcher that he needed to see her urgently about the Falklands. She knew immediately that something was wrong. By about six, her Commons room was crowded with people, including Nott, Luce, the latter's Foreign Office colleague Humphrey Atkins and a gaggle of senior civil servants. The news, Nott said quietly, was terrible. British intelligence had intercepted an Argentine signal that left no room for doubt: an enemy fleet was approaching the Falklands and would invade on Friday. There was nothing they could do to stop them, and the Ministry of Defence's view was that 'the Falklands could not be retaken once they were seized'. It was, Mrs Thatcher said later, the worst moment of her life: 'I could not believe it: these were our people, our islands.' She looked around the room, but the expressions were hopeless. 'If they are invaded, we have got to get them back,' she said desperately. 'We can't,' Nott said. 'You'll have to,' she said.[31]

It was at this point, in a twist worthy of a Hollywood blockbuster, that the door opened and the First Sea Lord, Sir Henry Leach, strode in, dressed in his admiral's uniform. After inspecting ships in Portsmouth, Leach had just got back to hear the news about the Falklands. Having failed to find Nott at the Ministry of Defence, he made for the House of Commons, where the ushers in the central lobby initially refused to let him through. But Leach's blood was up. All his life he had been waiting for a moment like this. His father had been a naval officer, killed on HMS *Prince of Wales* during the Japanese invasion of Malaya. Leach, who worshipped his father, had joined the navy at the age of 13 and yearned to show what his fleet could do. Now, after gauging the temperature of the room, and with half an eye on the despised Nott, he seized his chance.

The obvious answer, Leach told Mrs Thatcher, was to assemble a naval task force at once. There was a shocked silence, and then she asked what that meant. Without wasting a breath, Leach listed what he would need: carriers, destroyers, assault ships and submarines, as well as a large force of Royal Marines supported by the army. 'How long will it take to assemble?' she asked. 'Three days,' Leach said. 'How long to get there?' 'Three weeks.' 'Surely you mean three days,' Mrs Thatcher said. 'No, I don't.' Then came the crucial question: 'Can we do it?' Leach's answer, of which there are numerous slightly different versions, has gone down in naval and political legend. 'Yes, we can, Prime Minister,' he said, 'and though it is not my business to say so: yes, we must . . . If we do not, or if we pussyfoot in our actions and do not achieve complete success, in another few months we shall be living in a totally different country whose word will count for little.'

At that, Leach remembered, there was another long silence. Nott looked stunned. Mrs Thatcher, however, gave a very slight smile. He had told her precisely what she wanted to hear. Britain could fight; Britain could win. After that, her decision was never really in doubt. By the time the meeting broke up, Leach had the go-ahead to mobilize his task force, while she had recovered some of her composure. 'Before this,' she wrote:

> I had been outraged and determined. Now my outrage and determination were matched by a sense of relief and confidence. Henry Leach had shown me that if it came to a fight the courage and professionalism of Britain's armed forces would win through. It was my job as Prime Minister to see that they got the political support they needed.

All her life she had seen herself as a fighter. Now she would have a chance to prove it.[32]

In the South Atlantic, Thursday 1 April dawned clear and bright. The wind had dropped. Out at sea, the Argentine commanders made their final preparations. In Stanley, the townspeople were going about their daily business, blissfully ignorant of what was coming. The evening before, Governor Hunt had hosted a dinner party to mark the retirement of the islands' senior magistrate. After dinner, with unconscious irony, he had shown his guests a video of a recent ITV film about the Falklands' history. The title was *More British Than the British*. Not surprisingly, they loved it.[33]

At the age of 55, Rex Hunt was a bluff, jolly, stocky fellow, as if playing a British colonial governor in a Peter Sellers comedy. A career diplomat, he had knocked around the tropics for years before accepting the governorship of the Falklands in 1980. As postings go, it scarcely qualified even as a backwater. But he fancied the idea of a change, not least because he would get to do some flying, which he had loved since his days in the RAF as a young man. His superiors expected him to sell the idea of a closer relationship with Argentina. But as soon as Hunt and his wife Mavis arrived, they threw themselves wholeheartedly into Falklands life. Pottering around the islands in his official car, a red London cab, Hunt shook countless hands, judged innumerable sheepdog trials, accepted endless cups of tea and generally made himself at home. By the time Ridley visited in 1981, Hunt was so committed to the islanders' cause that he had become one of their greatest champions. In the Foreign Office, people said he had gone native.[34]

Now, as the Argentine fleet steamed towards him, Hunt went about his usual routine. He spent the morning doing paperwork in his sprawling Victorian residence, Government House, before lunch with his family. There was good news: his son Tony, on holiday from boarding school, seemed 'at long last to be getting down to serious study for his A-levels'. Then Hunt did a spot more paperwork. At 3.30, there came a knock at the door. His radio operator was holding a telegram. 'We have apparently reliable evidence', Hunt read in horror, 'that an Argentine task force will gather off Cape Pembroke early tomorrow morning, 2 April. You will wish to make your dispositions accordingly.' The signals man said ruefully: 'They might have added goodbye and the best of British.'[35]

Hunt stayed calm. He ordered his staff to burn all classified papers, and immediately called the two senior officers in the island's Royal Marine garrison. 'It looks as if the buggers really mean it this time,' he said. He asked the education superintendent to cancel school the next day, warned the chief medical officer to prepare for 'heavy duty tomorrow', and told Mavis and Tony to stay with friends, because the Marines would be setting up camp in Government House. Then, at 8.15 that evening, he telephoned the local radio station to break the bad news to the islanders. The Argentines were coming, but people should 'keep calm and keep off the streets ... Please, do not take the law into your own hands. Let us show our visitors that we are responsible, law-abiding and resolute citizens.' Then he handed back to the regular presenter. 'Well, as it says in those large, frenzied letters on the cover of *The Hitchhiker's Guide to the Galaxy*, "Don't panic!"' the presenter said. With impeccable timing, he reached for his next record: 'Strangers in the Night.'[36]

Showing remarkable sangfroid, as if determined to emulate Sir Sidney and Lady Ruff-Diamond in *Carry On Up the Khyber*, the Hunts had dinner before saying their goodbyes. When his wife and son were safely gone, the Governor went to get his shotgun, only to find that his faithful driver had beaten him to it. 'I've left the flag up tonight, sir,' the driver said, 'and I'll shoot any Argie bastard who tries to take it down.' By his own account, Hunt was so choked with pride at this that he turned away to hide his tears, and his driver offered to fetch him a stiff drink. But Hunt preferred to keep a clear head if there was going to be shooting. A few hours later, he called the radio station again and warned that the Argentines were probably only hours away. 'Now please don't be inquisitive and go and see for yourselves,' he said. 'You'll just get in the way.' And then, almost unbelievably, he went to bed.[37]

By the time Hunt awoke, after a couple of hours' sleep, his house had been turned into a makeshift Marine defence post, crammed with automatic weapons and ammunition boxes. Installing himself by the peat fire in the drawing room, clutching a pistol handed him by the Marines, the Governor told himself that he would use it on the 'first Argie that came through the door'. At 3.30 in the morning, another message came in from the Foreign Office. General Galtieri, it said, had personally rejected President Reagan's entreaties to call off the landings. So Hunt broadcast again to the islanders, declaring a state of emergency and again imploring them to stay indoors. Then he settled back down by the fire. He had had a 'hugely enjoyable, interesting and satisfying life', he thought. He had been too young to fight in the Second World War, and had always felt a bit 'restless and unfulfilled' as a result. But now 'it was a relief to find that I could face the prospect of death with equanimity'.[38]

News of the first sightings of Argentine landing craft reached Government House shortly after five. Then, just under an hour later, there came a series of tremendous bangs and the sound of automatic gunfire. Hunt dived under the desk for cover. 'The noise for a while was deafening,' he recalled. 'Outbursts of automatic and rifle fire interspersed the bangs . . . Our Royal Marines were obviously firing back at the enemy.' Eventually he lifted his head and peered out:

> It was still dark but there was the faintest glimmer of dawn. More bangs close by sent me under the desk again and then, in a lull in the firing, a weird, unearthly voice, distorted by a loudhailer, called out in a thick Spanish accent: 'Meestair Hurnt – You are a reasonable man. Come out and surrendair.' To which a Royal Marine responded, with commendable initiative and choice lower-deck language, 'F . . . off you bloody spic!' followed by a burst of automatic fire. The shooting then intensified on both sides . . .

The Marines were, however, horribly outnumbered. There were only sixty-nine of them on the entire island, facing almost ten times as many Argentines. They could not win, and they knew it. Even after they had repulsed the first attack on Government House, firing relentlessly from doorways and windows, their commanding officer was under no illusions. As he told the Governor, the enemy had artillery that could 'knock the shit out of us and we can't do a thing about it'.[39]

By now it was light, and the local radio was already fielding calls from islanders who had spotted Argentine armoured cars from their bedrooms. At Government House the battle went on, the Marines having taken three Argentines captive and fatally wounded a fourth. But deep down, Hunt knew the islands were lost. He rang the local representative of the Argentine state airline and persuaded him to act as a go-between. And eventually, after various toings and froings, the door of his office opened, and in strolled the tall figure of Rear Admiral Büsser, holding out his hand in greeting.

Later, Hunt admitted that his first reaction was an overpowering 'desire to pull my pistol out of the drawer and empty the magazine into his chest'. Büsser dropped his hand in disappointment, and Hunt immediately felt ashamed of himself. Yet Büsser, a veteran of the Dirty War, was magnanimous in victory. He was a 'soldier merely obeying instructions', he said, and while he complimented the Royal Marines on their 'bravery and professionalism', they should lay down their weapons to avoid bloodshed. Hunt knew he was right. 'With a heavy heart', he turned to the Marine commander and gave the order.[40]

A few moments later, as Hunt was preparing to broadcast to the islanders for the last time, came the most celebrated moment of the invasion. Understandably enough, one of the Argentines' priorities had been to seize the radio station. What they did not expect, though, was that the presenter, Patrick Watts, would keep broadcasting after they came in, so the whole island could hear what was happening:

> WATTS: Well, the radio station has now been taken over. I still hope we can get His Excellency the Governor's message to you. Sir, what do you want – do you want to speak to the people?
>
> ARGENTINE SOLDIER: Tell the people to wait – tell them now, they are wishing us to wait some minutes; in some minutes the Chief is going to communicate to them what we want for the population –
>
> WATTS: Just a minute – [*Shouting in Spanish*] – Well, just a minute. If you take the gun out of my back, I'm going to transmit this news, if you take the gun away. But I'm not speaking with a gun in my back – [*More shouting in Spanish*] – Well, there's an argument going on now between the three Argentines. They've disappeared; they've left me alone in this room. They're having an argument between themselves.

At this point, with glorious timing, the phone rang. It was Rex Hunt. 'Sir, I've just been taken over by the Argentines,' Watts said. Then, holding the phone to the microphone, he asked Hunt to go ahead.

In a tone of long-suffering exasperation, as if bringing bad news about the sheepdog trials, Hunt delivered his final message:

> Hello, Kelpers and Islanders. I hope that you can hear me on the phone. The machine here doesn't work. I'm sorry it happened like this ... The Admiral came along to me and I told him that he had landed unlawfully

on British sovereign territory and I ordered him to leave forthwith. He refused, claiming that he was taking back territory that belonged to Argentina . . . I said that it was reprehensible that Argentina should have seized the Islands by force . . .

I'm sorry it's happened this way. It's probably the last message I'll be able to give you, but I wish you all the best of luck. And rest assured that the British will be back.

A moment later, the phone went dead. Not long afterwards, a local historian, John Smith, made an entry in his journal: '*1017 Hours*. The Argentine national anthem has been played over the radio. It now seems final. The Argentines have got us.'[41]

At 10.30 a.m., two helicopters landed on Stanley's football field, not far from Government House. 'Out poured a horde of red-hatted, gold-braided gentlemen,' Hunt drily recalled, 'who proceeded to hug, kiss and embrace each other in typical Latin fashion.' 'Just look at the silly buggers,' his driver said. 'You'd think they'd won the World Cup.' After a short interval, Hunt agreed to go to the Town Hall to meet the newly arrived General Osvaldo García, commander of the Argentine land forces. There Hunt was presented to a 'sallow little man' with a 'fixed, sickly smile on his face', his hand outstretched. Again he did not shake it.

'It is very ungentlemanly of you to refuse to shake my hand,' García said through an interpreter. 'It is very uncivilised of you to invade my country,' Hunt replied. 'You have landed unlawfully on British territory and I order you to remove yourself and your troops forthwith' – a bold thing to say, given that he was surrounded by men with automatic weapons. At that, García shouted: 'We have taken back what is rightfully ours and we shall stay FOREVER!' Then he told Hunt he would be flown out at four. Impossible, Hunt said. 'You didn't tell us you were coming. So we haven't packed.'[42]

For all his defiance, the Governor and his family were indeed flown out of Stanley later that afternoon. So were the Royal Marines, who, in a moment of bitter humiliation, had been photographed face-down on the ground beneath their armed captors. In a final touch of bravado, Hunt insisted on wearing his full ceremonial uniform, complete with sword, gold braid and gigantic ostrich-feathered hat, and drove to the airport in his red cab, the Union Jack fluttering proudly on the bonnet. It was, he remembered, a sunny afternoon, and the streets were lined with islanders who had come to wave goodbye, many of them in floods of tears. At the airport, his wife Mavis, incongruously clutching a Dick Francis novel, burst into tears, too. 'I feel as if we are deserting these people,' she said.

STRANGERS IN THE NIGHT 751

'We should be staying with them. What is going to become of them all?' Then they boarded the plane. The last thing Hunt saw, as the Falklands fell away beneath them, was the 'blue and white flag of Argentina, usurping the Union Jack on the airport flagpole'.[43]

In London, five hours ahead of Stanley, it was evening. For Mrs Thatcher and her ministers, Thursday had been a day of agonizing inevitability. Early that morning, she had broken the news to the Cabinet at Number 10. Nott reported that the defence chiefs were already assembling a 'large amphibious task force', which could sail within days. The Leader of the House, Francis Pym, asked why she had not already issued the order to sail. 'I don't wish to close options,' Mrs Thatcher explained. Sir Geoffrey Howe thought even this was too belligerent, since it would give the public 'the impression that we are in a position to reverse or reconquer. We ought to convey the opposite impression.' But Nigel Lawson, more presciently, thought people would demand action: 'Public opinion won't regard this as a faraway island.'[44]

Even as Hunt and his Marines were besieged in Government House, the government remained in total confusion. At 11 a.m. on Friday, the Foreign Office minister Humphrey Atkins made a short statement in the Commons, admitting that there was a 'real expectation' of an Argentine attack, but claiming that they had just been in touch with Hunt and that no Argentine troops had yet landed. This was obviously untrue: not only had the government lost control, it had completely lost its bearings. At about lunchtime, the British Antarctic Survey told the Foreign Office that they had intercepted radio reports indicating that Argentine ships had reached Stanley and that armoured troop carriers had been seen on land. Yet even now, as rumours spread of cheering crowds in Buenos Aires, there came no word from the government. Indeed, at 2.30 a visibly unhappy Pym told the Commons that there was still no news from the South Atlantic. If news came, he added, the Commons would be recalled the next day, even though it was a Saturday.[45]

By this point, Hunt was already preparing to surrender, yet still the government hesitated. 'From the BBC in London', John Smith noted sardonically, 'we hear they think the Falkland Islands *may* have been invaded. Words fail us – this is the age of the train, rockets to the moon, computers and microchips and they only *think* that the Falklands may have been invaded. God help us all.' At last, at six that evening in London, the BBC announced that the islands had fallen. A few moments later, their faces ashen, Carrington and Nott appeared in front of the cameras at the Foreign Office and admitted that the Falklands had been lost. When one reporter asked if they had offered their resignations, Nott paused, and then said it was 'ridiculous and quite untrue'. But Carrington merely shook his head, and said nothing.[46]

Two hours later, the Cabinet reassembled in Number 10, joined by Sir Henry Leach. The Foreign Office had now sent across a preliminary assessment, which suggested that Britain would not win international backing for using force. Even the United States, it predicted, would remain neutral, and as for the British public, it would be 'hard to persuade people that the game was worth the candle'. Mrs Thatcher could scarcely believe her eyes. Here, in black and white, was proof that the Foreign Office would always appease foreign dictators, just as she had feared. 'When you are at war', she recalled, 'you cannot allow the difficulties to dominate your thinking: you have to set out with an iron will to overcome them. And anyway what was the alternative? That a common or garden dictator should rule over the Queen's subjects and prevail by fraud and violence? Not while I was Prime Minister.'[47]

In the Cabinet Room, the consensus was that the Task Force must sail as soon as possible. Leach said that while victory was never guaranteed, with the 'anti-air capability we could provide, I would feel confident of success'. Almost everybody thought they should go for it: as Carrington remarked, nobody would believe a word they said unless the fleet was sailing. 'We should lose a vote of confidence if we don't sail,' agreed Michael Heseltine, although 'we don't know where we are going'. Only one minister, the independent-minded John Biffen, was against sending the Task Force. Leach thought he was a 'little runt of a man'.[48]

Saturday was a gloriously bright spring day. From breakfast, MPs were pouring into Westminster for the emergency debate, the first time they had met on a Saturday since Suez. The queue for the public gallery was the longest many journalists had ever seen, and even by parliamentary standards the atmosphere was electric, the anger almost tangible. The morning headlines left no room for doubt about the mood. Argentina's action, declared *The Times*, 'threatens the right to self-determination of all island peoples throughout the world . . . We no longer "rule the waves". But . . . we can inflict severe damage on the Argentine navy if we have to reply to force with force. It should be clear that we are prepared to do that if the invaders are not withdrawn.' The *Express* carried the same message in a single front-page image: a large photo, taken in happier times, of all 1,813 Falkland Islanders gathered outside Government House, laughing and waving Union Jacks. 'Our Loyal Subjects,' read the headline: 'We MUST Defend Them.'

But every paper also agreed that this was a dreadful, almost unprecedented disgrace, for which Mrs Thatcher's government had been unforgivably culpable. The *Guardian* thought Friday had been a 'day of spectacular military and diplomatic humiliation', while the *Sun* urged Mrs Thatcher to 'Sack the Guilty Men'. Even the *Express*, always so loyal, was in no doubt. 'Mrs Thatcher's government', it said, 'was reeling last night amid the wreckage of Britain's biggest disaster since Suez.' Now she was 'on the spot, her whole defence policy under fire and two of her most senior Ministers facing the sack'. This, it predicted, would be 'the most humiliating day of her life'.[49]

By mid-morning the Commons was packed: as Tory MPs gathered, many were muttering that Nott and Carrington would have to go, and perhaps even Mrs Thatcher herself. In a gloomily bathetic note, Humphrey Atkins kicked off with a short statement apologizing for misleading the House the day before, which strengthened what Alan Clark called 'the general impression of almost total Government incompetence'. Then came Mrs Thatcher. 'Mr Speaker,' she began quietly, 'the House meets this Saturday to respond to a situation of great gravity. We are here because, for the first time for many years, British sovereign territory has been invaded by a foreign power.'

At first, wrote Clark, she spoke 'very slowly and didactically'. Then, while describing the invasion, she said: 'We sent a telegram' – and the Labour benches 'started laughing and sneering'. That threw her: 'she changed gear and gabbled'. David Owen, too, thought she was 'clearly shaken', with 'none of the self-confident hectoring that we were used to'. Yet what she actually said left little room for compromise. The Argentine occupation could not be tolerated. The Task Force would sail. 'The people of the Falkland Islands, like the people of the United Kingdom, are an island race. Their way of life is British; their allegiance is to the Crown. They are few in number, but they have the right to live in peace, to choose their own way of life and to determine their own allegiance.'[50]

Then Michael Foot rose to speak, and the Tories braced themselves. But although the Labour leader had nothing but scorn for the government's handling of the crisis, what most struck his listeners was his passionate commitment to the islanders' cause. The Argentine junta, he said, was a regime in which 'thousands of innocent people . . . have been tortured and debased. We cannot forget that fact when our friends and fellow citizens in the Falkland Islands are suffering as they are at this moment.' The islanders had been faced with an 'act of naked, unqualified aggression, carried out in the most shameful and disreputable circumstances'. They had the 'absolute right to look to us at this moment of their desperate plight, just as they have looked to us over the past 150 years'. It was Britain's duty to ensure that such 'foul and brutal aggression' did not succeed.

Foot sat down to roars of approval. 'He got a tremendous cheer from the Tories,' noted a shocked Tony Benn. Alan Clark thought he was 'excellent', while the next speaker, the Conservative Edward du Cann, declared that 'the Leader of the Opposition spoke for us all'. By contrast, many of Foot's friends were shocked that he had taken such an uncompromisingly patriotic line. But, as he saw it, the issue was simple. The islanders were British, and had never harmed anybody. The Argentines were fascists, with a hideous record of torture and repression. As a young man Foot had made his name as a critic of appeasement; he was damned if he was going to become an appeaser now. Later, when the Eton-educated Labour maverick Tam Dalyell accused him of indulging his inner jingoist, Foot had a simple answer: 'I know a fascist when I see one.'[51]

Foot's speech set the tone for the next ten weeks. This was not just a spat in the South Atlantic. It was the Second World War all over again, a titanic moral clash between the defenders of liberty and the forces of fascism, between a beleaguered island people and a blood-soaked military dictatorship. And now, one by one, speakers rose to pledge support for the fleet. 'Let us hear no more about logistics – how difficult it is to travel long distances,' insisted du Cann. 'I do not remember the Duke of Wellington whining about Torres Vedras. We have nothing to lose now except our honour.' Only victory, agreed Julian Amery, could 'wipe the stain from Britain's honour'. As for the Argentine leadership – a 'Fascist, cruel and corrupt regime', a 'jumped-up junta of barbarous men', led by a 'man who wears upon his chest the medals that he won in repressing his own people' – most speakers had nothing but contempt. 'The very thought that our people, 1,800 people of British blood and bone, could be left in the hands of such criminals', thundered Sir Bernard Braine, 'is enough to make any normal Englishman's blood – and the blood of Scotsmen and Welshmen – boil.'

Yet while the Commons worked itself into a frenzy of patriotic outrage, at least some people were horrified. For Tony Benn, who could not even bring himself to speak, the atmosphere was 'awful', the Commons 'in the grip of jingoism'. 'I came away full of gloom', he wrote afterwards, 'because it is obvious that a huge fleet of forty or so warships will set sail for the Falklands . . . and then there will be a major battle.' The *Guardian*'s Peter Jenkins, too, could 'scarcely believe my ears . . . Listening to the debate in the country, from a portable radio on the kitchen table, it seemed to me that the place had taken leave of its senses.' He expected this sort of thing from the Tories, 'but it was the bipartisanship of the patriotic passion which dinned the ears that morning'. And the writer Jonathan Raban was so shocked he had to turn off his set. 'It wasn't a debate,' he thought, 'it was a verbal bloodletting . . . Listening to it, I felt that I'd been eavesdropping on the nastier workings of the national sub-conscious; I'd heard Britain talking in a dream, and what it was saying scared me stiff.'[52]

Under the circumstances, Mrs Thatcher got off lightly. She was lucky that the House preferred to vent its fury at the hapless Nott, whose closing speech, stuttering, peevish and unduly partisan, was such a disaster that he sat down with cries of 'Go!' ringing in his ears. For Mrs Thatcher, though, the most painful moment had come earlier, thanks to the man some saw as her John the Baptist. As Enoch Powell got to his feet, recalled Alan Clark, she bowed her head, her entire being '*knotted* with pain and apprehension'. The Prime Minister, Powell reminded them, had been nick-named the Iron Lady, and 'there was no reason to suppose that the right hon. Lady did not welcome and, indeed, take pride in that description'. But this, he said, was the test. 'In the next week or two, this House, the nation and the right hon. Lady herself will learn of what metal she is made.'[53]

That weekend the Task Force mobilized for war. On Friday morning, even before the Cabinet had given the go-ahead, Leach had sent a signal to Rear Admiral Sandy Woodward, on exercise in the mid-Atlantic, ordering him to prepare to head south. By Saturday a small team were heading for Gibraltar, preparing to requisition the vast P&O cruise liner *Canberra* for use as a troopship, while columns of supply trucks were streaming towards the South Coast. At the Royal Marine barracks in Plymouth, senior offic-ers were poring over maps of the Falklands, while in scenes that reminded older people of the Second World War, posters had gone up in major railway stations, urging members of the Parachute Regiment's 3rd Bat-talion to report immediately. And at Portsmouth, where Harrier jump jets and Sea King helicopters were already being loaded aboard the carriers *Hermes* and *Invincible*, journalists found a 'heady whiff of war in the air'. For sailors and soldiers alike, this was the kind of adventure they had been dreaming of since boyhood. 'We are all keen to get to the Falklands,' one naval lieutenant told the *Express*. 'Just let us at 'em,' agreed a young Royal Marine. 'We're raring to go.'[54]

In the South Atlantic, General Galtieri's troops were strengthening their grip. By Saturday morning, transport planes were already landing vast quantities of equipment, including radar technology and heavy machine guns, while more armoured cars were thundering along the roads into Stanley. The islanders themselves were in total despair. Watching the Argentines 'rushing and roaring about all over the place, knocking down fences, breaking up the roads', John Smith thought it was 'like a living nightmare'. Worse was to follow. By mid-morning, the rebranded Radio

Nacional Islas Malvinas had announced that all schools, shops and pubs would be closed indefinitely. Any citizens who ignored these instructions could expect 'personal misfortunes'. Then came a blizzard of announcements. Stanley was now Puerto Argentino. British currency was no longer valid, the islands' official language was now Spanish and all transactions must use metric measurements. Flicking V-signs at Argentine soldiers carried a penalty of thirty days' imprisonment, while disrespect for the Argentine flag meant sixty days. And all cars had to drive on the right, much to the islanders' fury. 'Which would you prefer,' said an Argentine officer, 'that our eighteen-year-old conscripts, with their big lorries, should try to drive on the left, or that you, with your little vehicles, change to the right?'[55]

As it turned out, the occupiers were less bloodthirsty than their new subjects had feared. Some islanders were threatened, and some even forcibly detained. But none was tortured, raped or murdered, which by the standards of the Argentine military represented extraordinary self-restraint. Yet none of this came as much consolation to the islanders, many of whom openly wept as the armoured cars rumbled past their front doors. Nor did it cut much ice with the British press. Without exception, the papers agreed that the Argentines had revealed themselves to be strutting, sadistic bullies. And by Monday morning, all but the *Guardian* and the *Mirror* were in the mood for battle.[56]

That morning, *The Times* cleared the decks for a colossal 68-column-inch leader, written by its editor Charles Douglas-Home and entitled 'We Are All Falklanders Now.' The central issue, the paper said, was simple: 'The Falkland Islands are British territory, inhabited by British citizens. They have been invaded by enemy forces. These forces must be removed.' The obvious parallel was with Hitler's invasion of Poland. As in 1939, Britain had a duty to 'prevent the expansionist policies of a dictatorship affecting our interests'. But there was another issue. 'The Poles were Poles; the Falklanders are our people . . .When British territory is invaded, it is not just an invasion of our land, but of our whole spirit. We are all Falklanders now.'

So this was a test not just of Mrs Thatcher's government, but of every man and woman in Britain; a test of 'the national will to defend itself . . . in a dangerous and unpredictable world'. And in its conclusion, *The Times* became positively lyrical:

> We are an island race, and the focus of attack is one of our islands, inhabited by our islanders. At this point of decision the words of John Donne could not be more appropriate for every Briton, for every islander, for every man and woman anywhere in a world menaced by the forces of tyranny:

'No man is an island, entire of itself. Any man's death diminishes me, because I am involved in mankind; and therefore never send to know for whom the bell tolls; it tolls for thee.'
It tolls for us; it tolls for them.

Here, echoing Michael Foot's rhetoric in the Commons on Saturday, were all the themes of the next ten weeks: the island race, the crusade for democracy, the test of the nation's will, even the parallel with the Second World War. Later that summer, in a fervent polemic, the writer Anthony Barnett claimed that Britain had succumbed to 'Churchillism', its themes being 'the cruel seas, a British defeat, Anglo-Saxon democracy challenged by a dictator, and finally the quintessentially Churchillian posture – we were down but we were not out'. There was a lot of truth in this. On the same day that *Times* editorial appeared, the *Sun* mockingly depicted Lord Carrington, a mouse, alongside Winston Churchill, a lion. In the *Sun* newsroom, executives had already put up Churchill's portrait.[57]

For Carrington, the papers made agonizing reading. He had spent the

To the newspapers, the Falklands invasion set the seal on Britain's decline into impotence and insignificance. This is Stanley Franklin in the *Sun*, 5 April 1982.

weekend wrestling with his conscience, and Monday morning's editorials
were even worse than he had feared. *The Times* thought he should 'hon-
ourably resign'; the *Mail* urged Mrs Thatcher to 'sack him and his whole
rotten gang'; the *Express* claimed that he and Nott, 'Thatcher's guilty
men', had 'misled themselves, the Cabinet, Parliament and the country'.
The Foreign Office itself came in for scathing treatment. 'Rotten to the
core, rotten with appeasement', said the *Mail*, while the *Sun* urged Mrs
Thatcher to clean out the 'appeasers' and surround herself with 'men of
iron'. Carrington had drafted a resignation letter the night before. When
he got to his Whitehall office, he sent it. Mrs Thatcher knew there was no
point in arguing. At midday, the government announced that Carrington,
Luce and Atkins had resigned.[58]

While Fleet Street rejoiced, Mrs Thatcher mourned the loss of a man
whose loyalty and gallantry she had much valued. ('Your old Cabinet
colleagues continue to miss you very much,' she told Carrington a few
weeks later, 'and me most of all.') His replacement as Foreign Secretary,
however, was rather less to her taste. Cautious, serious, always looking
for compromise, the Eton-educated Francis Pym embodied what she saw
as the very worst qualities of the old guard. What was more, he was widely
regarded as the most likely successor if the Tories got rid of her, which
meant she was promoting her most dangerous rival. But not only did Pym
know how to handle the Commons, he had served as her first Defence
Secretary and was a decorated veteran of the campaigns in North Africa
and Italy. 'Margaret, you mustn't do that,' Carrington said when she told
him. 'You hate him. It'll all end in tears.' 'I know,' she said, 'but he's the
only one with the experience.'[59]

There was, of course, one more guilty man. When, before lunch on
Monday, John Nott heard that Carrington was going to resign, he was
furious that nobody had warned him. If the Foreign Secretary was going,
he told Mrs Thatcher, he would go too. Otherwise he would look like a
dishonourable creep, clinging to office after Carrington had graciously
fallen on his sword. But Mrs Thatcher turned him down flat. Nott could
not possibly go 'when the Task Force was on the ocean'. In fact, she probably kept him on because, if he went, the pressure on her would become
even more intense; what was more, she needed a loyalist at the Ministry of
Defence. 'Thank goodness I didn't accept it,' she wrote a year later, in a
private memoir of the war. 'John was splendid throughout the campaign.'

Even so, Nott insisted that Number 10 tell the press his resignation had
been refused, and even asked them to publish his resignation letter. But
he never forgave Mrs Thatcher for making him look dishonourable, and
with good reason. Despite the publication of his letter, many people were

convinced, quite unfairly, that he had clung on like a limpet. The Wets, wrote Alan Clark, were furious at Carrington's resignation and were 'taking it out on poor old Notters, saying he should be sacked, that it was intolerable that he should have survived, etc.' Even some of the public agreed. The difference between Carrington and Nott, Peter Hibbitt told Mass Observation, was 'the difference between an honourable man and a power-seeking careerist'.[60]

That afternoon, as the first ships in the Task Force sailed for war, Mrs Thatcher went to Westminster Abbey for the memorial service for the former Tory grandee R. A. Butler, who had died a month earlier. With blackly ironic timing, Carrington had promised to read the first lesson: the order of service still billed him as Foreign Secretary. 'To his credit, he read the text with great aplomb,' admitted Alan Clark. But the ironies were unavoidable. As a central figure in the Conservative governments of the 1950s, Butler had been the incarnation of the liberal, patrician values that Mrs Thatcher blamed for Britain's decline. But he had also belonged to a vanished age, the heyday of economic optimism and full employment, as well as the twilight of Empire, when the map had still been splashed with pink. In his address, the Reverend Harry Williams reminded the congregation of Butler's unhappiness during the Suez crisis, when he had never made the mistake of 'letting his heart rule his head'. Butler, he said, had never forgotten that the 'hot-headed ringing of bells' was 'often followed by the wringing of hands'. Few of his listeners missed the implication.[61]

A few hours later, Mrs Thatcher went on television, where she presented an image of implacable self-possession. 'We have to recover those islands, we have to recover them for the people on them are British,' she told ITN. What about the risks? 'When you stop a dictator there are always risks,' she said, 'but there are great risks in not stopping a dictator. My generation learned that a long time ago.' What about if she failed? Would she resign?

> I am not talking about failure, I am talking about my supreme confidence in the British fleet . . . superlative ships, excellent equipment, the most highly trained professional group of men, the most honourable and brave members of Her Majesty's service.
>    Failure? Do you remember what Queen Victoria once said? 'Failure – the possibilities do not exist.'

Yet everybody knew that the stakes were higher than ever. In a matter of weeks, either she would be a national hero, or she would be finished.

Watching her in the Commons the next day, Frank Johnson wrote that 'she had about her an almost visible aura of being alone . . . between triumph and tragedy'. And two days later, her factotum Ian Gow scribbled her a private letter. He had been talking to Sir Geoffrey Howe, and they both felt she was confronting 'the worst and most daunting situation faced by any Prime Minister since Suez, 26 years ago'. But, Gow went on:

> We also said that there is no one in the Kingdom better qualified than you to lead Party and Nation.
>
> I think I understand a little of the loneliness of your task and of the enormity of the responsibility which you carry.
>
> The purpose of this note is just to remind you that there are many of us who, whatever the future holds in store, will be forever thankful for having had the privilege of trying to help the finest chief, the most resolute and far sighted leader and the kindest and most considerate friend that any man could hope to serve.

He was, of course, trying to reassure her. But it was obvious that even he feared the end was coming.[62]

# 32
## We'll Show 'Em We're British

*We have faith in Margaret Thatcher. She has the nation behind her.*
                                                         *Sun,* 6 April 1982

*One 17 year old girl who had passed O level Geography had never even heard of the Falkland Islands and now it seems we are heading for war over something ordinary people hardly knew existed.*

            Mary Richards to Mass Observation, 20 April 1982

On the morning of Monday 5 April the aircraft carrier *Invincible* slipped its moorings and eased into Portsmouth Harbour, bound for the South Atlantic. It was barely ten o'clock, yet the shoreline was packed with tens of thousands of flag-waving onlookers, roaring and cheering for all they were worth, many of them in tears. From every building in sight flew the Union Jack, while well-wishers brandished dozens of homemade placards and banners: 'God Bless, Britannia Rules', 'Don't Cry for Us, Argentina.' In the harbour, a flotilla of little boats, crammed with spectators, bobbed with patriotic enthusiasm. And as the band played and the ship's horn sounded, red flares burst into the sky.

Half an hour later, a second carrier, *Hermes,* followed the *Invincible* into the Channel. Watching on a battered black-and-white television, the sceptical Jonathan Raban thought it seemed a spectacle from history: 'pipe bands, bunting, flags, kisses, tears, waved handkerchiefs', thousands of little Union Jacks fluttering as Nelson's heirs headed for the Falkland Islands. The cameras tracked across the faces left behind. 'Girls, their shoulders quaking, searched for their powder compacts; the grandfathers frowned at a memory; the infants shook their happy flags like rattles.' And suddenly, as the picture blurred, Raban realized that he was in tears. It was 'absurd', he thought, 'like crying over a bad movie in an empty cinema'. But he could not help it. 'The families on the shore, the receding ships, the bands and streamers had me blubbering with silly pride in Queen and Country.'[1]

The departure of the Task Force, carried on a tide of pomp and patriotism, was one of the great public spectacles of the age. For the last few days, all roads leading to Portsmouth's naval dockyards had been clogged with traffic. The pubs had stayed open on Sunday night, packed with sailors and Marines, but every few minutes lorries thundered towards the docks, carrying artillery, ammunition and explosives. The *Mirror* thought it a 'scene every Briton prayed we would never see again'. Yet the Task Force was terrific theatre: the cranes on the quaysides, the columns of trucks, the colours and crowds. And despite all the tears, it carried an extraordinarily patriotic charge. The *Daily Mail* interviewed a veteran of the First World War, Tommy Mallen, for whom it had been a day of catharsis. 'I thought England was done for, spineless, a doormat for the world,' he said. 'I'd pass the war memorials or see Nelson's *Victory* and wonder what it had all been for. But I was wrong, thank God. We are still a proud country, and we'll still protect our own.'[2]

Four days later, in Southampton, came the sequel. This time all eyes were on the hastily requisitioned *Canberra*, home to the vanguard of the land force charged with recapturing the Falklands: Brigadier Julian Thompson's 3 Commando Brigade, consisting of three Royal Marine battalions and two Parachute Regiment battalions, some 3,500 men in all. Once again cheering crowds packed the quayside; once again the bands played, the flags waved and the tears flowed. As the *Canberra* steamed away, sailors on nearby ships lined the decks, shouting three cheers. The *Evening Standard*'s Max Hastings, who had grabbed one of the few places on board for journalists, stood by the rail, listening as 'Rule Britannia' drifted up from the quay. 'Now I know this is serious,' a Marine officer muttered. 'You can't let the nation see us go off to war with bands playing and then bring us back without doing anything.'[3]

Yet to many of the young men settling into their berths on the *Canberra* that night, the expedition still seemed 'unreal, almost a joke'. One young paratrooper, Ken Lukowiak, had cheered when 2 Para's commanding officer, Colonel Herbert ('H') Jones, told them they were going to the Falklands. But as they pulled away, Lukowiak recalled, the fear was that 'nothing was ever going to come of it. We were going to get there, do a bit of sabre rattling, the Argies would piss off back to Argentina and we'd all sail home disappointed.' Even some of their families thought so. When 3 Para's Vincent Bramley told his parents he was heading for the Falklands, they 'seemed more concerned about the weather'. A few hours before the *Canberra* was due to leave, Bramley rang to ask if they were coming to see him off. 'Vince,' they said, 'you'll be home shortly' – and, in any case, they had visitors.

Yet as the lights of the South Coast receded into the dusk, the mood changed. 'I watched from the deck', Bramley recalled, 'and an almost eerie silence took over as we moved away from the dock. The only noise now was the rushing of water as the great liner cut a path through the Channel. Gone was the sound of cheering families and friends. Almost gone, too, was the sight of England.' Then, as the coastline disappeared, he heard men singing below. Leaning over the rail beside him, a Marine said: 'Looks like something from a film, don't it, mate?'[4]

Few expeditions had ever left British shores amid such passionate enthusiasm. According to the first polls, some eight out of ten people agreed that Mrs Thatcher's government had been caught badly off guard, but eight out of ten also thought Britain must get the islands back. On 5 April, the day the Task Force sailed, a poll for *News at Ten* found that 88 per cent thought Britain had an obligation to support the Falkland Islanders, 70 per cent would sink Argentine ships if necessary and 41 per cent wanted the government to use force right away. The next day, a poll for the *Daily Mail* found that 69 per cent thought it was 'very important' to regain the islands, while 53 per cent wanted to fight immediately. And two days later, a poll for *Weekend World* found that even if the islanders themselves were happy to accept Argentine rule, almost one in five people thought Britain should go ahead and fight anyway.

Far from abating as the days went by, public attitudes almost visibly hardened. A survey published in *The Economist* on 17 April found that 51 per cent of people claimed to 'care very much' about the fate of the islands, with 32 per cent caring 'a little'. Almost nine out of ten thought the government should ban Argentine imports, eight out of ten backed sending the Task Force and seven out of ten wanted to break off relations with Argentina. Perhaps most strikingly, almost a third wanted to bomb Argentine military bases. And two out of ten people thought Britain should invade Argentina itself – a prospect that was never remotely likely.[5]

To the expedition's critics, the public fervour seemed utterly bewildering. Outside the hard left, few people in 1982 thought of Britain as an especially warlike nation. With the end of National Service twenty years earlier, only a tiny minority had direct contact with the military. And with the exception of their involvement in Northern Ireland, the armed forces had been relegated to the fringes of the national imagination. When young men joined the army, they tended either to come from military families or to be escaping deprived, abusive or unhappy backgrounds. Many of those who sailed to the Falklands had been in trouble as teenagers; they had joined the army as a way of finding a purpose and seeking adventure, not because they seriously expected to fight on a foreign field. Indeed, to most children of the 1960s the prospect of Britain ever fighting another war on its own, especially so far from home, seemed utterly fantastical.[6]

Only a few days earlier, many people had never heard of the Falkland Islands. When Adrian Mole bursts in to tell his father about the invasion, the latter leaps 'out of bed because he thought the Falklands lay off the coast of Scotland'. He was not alone. Having heard other boys discussing the crisis at school, I was astonished when my parents told me that the Falklands were not, in fact, somewhere near the Shetland Islands, but were off the South American mainland. 'Like many people I know,' Mary Richards told Mass Observation, 'we thought they were off Scotland.' 'What's all this crap about the Spicks invading Scotland?' one young Para asked Vincent Bramley. And even Ken Lukowiak had 'never heard of them and so, for some reason, assumed that they must lie off the coast of Scotland'.[7]

It is all the more striking, then, how quickly the Falklands assumed a near-sacred place in the national imagination. Back in Britain after being kicked out by the Argentines, Rex Hunt was astounded to find 'ordinary people from all walks of life, young and old', writing him letters of support or coming up to him in the street. On one occasion, he was even accosted by a tramp under Charing Cross Bridge, who insisted on shaking his hand with the words, 'Well done, Guv!' And when, during the first weekend of the crisis, Jonathan Raban went for a drink at Plymouth's Royal Western Yacht Club, he found the regulars suffused with patriotic excitement. 'It's exactly as if Russia had come over and occupied the Isle of Wight without a by-your-leave,' one man said. 'Exactly the same. No difference at all. It's British soil.' 'Well, is it, quite?' Raban asked. 'Of course it is,' the man said. 'Sovereign territory. British soil. The Falklanders are as English as I am. To a man.'[8]

Later, Mrs Thatcher's critics claimed that this was the last colonial war, driven by her atavistic desire to rebuild the British Empire. On 10 April the cover of the American magazine *Newsweek* depicted HMS *Hermes* sailing south beside the blazing headline 'The Empire Strikes Back'. And when intellectuals condemned the war, the word 'imperialism' came up again and again. But this is not convincing at all. The Falklands campaign was very different from most colonial wars. It was not a war of conquest, nor a defence of white imperialists against a nationalist uprising, but the defence of a tiny island population against an unprovoked invasion. The sheep farmers of the Falklands were hardly a colonial elite; in any case, they had been there since 1833, when the islands had been largely unin-habited. And the Argentines were hardly downtrodden natives: indeed, as the heirs to the Spanish Empire, they had actually exterminated most of their own native population centuries earlier.

Even the argument that Mrs Thatcher wanted to restore the British Empire does not stand up. Both in public and in private she often talked about the Second World War, but she almost never talked about the Empire. She adored Kipling, but she loved him for his patriotism, not his imperialism. Like many Conservatives, she enjoyed making misty-eyed tributes to Britain's brethren in Canada, Australia and New Zealand, but there was rarely any sense of personal investment. Her family had no colonial connections, and she never evoked the glory of the Raj, the veldt of southern Africa or the jungles of Malaya. In that respect, she was absolutely typical. As surveys consistently found, people were *not* nostal-gic for Empire. Most knew very little about it and cared even less. They did not even care about the Commonwealth.[9]

So why did they care about the Falklands? The answer is obvious. The islanders, wrote Jonathan Raban, were 'visibly, audibly, our kith and kin'. As the *Sunday Telegraph*'s Peregrine Worsthorne wrote with brutal frankness, it would have been a different story if they had 'black or brown skins, spoke with strange accents or worshipped different gods'. But when a Falklands family, trapped in Britain during the inva-sion, appeared on television, Raban thought they sounded like people from the 1950s, their voices evoking 'gin and tonic, cavalry twill, the next monthly mortgage repayment, brussels sprouts, tea cosies, *Jour-ney's End* at the amateur dramatic society, the Magimix in the kitchen and the Queen's head on the stamp'. To the public, 'the Falklanders *were* us', in nostalgic miniature.

As Mrs Thatcher had told the Commons, the people of the Falklands were an 'island race'. They were little people: farmers and shopkeepers, parochial, unassuming and old-fashioned, like J. R. R. Tolkien's hobbits. And at a time when the very idea of Britain seemed besieged by economic decline and cultural upheaval, that made the islands the perfect cause. The Falklands, wrote Raban, reflected 'all our injured belittlement, our sense of being beleaguered, neglected and misunderstood . . . They meant Trad-ition, Honour, Loyalty, Community, Principle – they meant the whole web and texture of being British.'[10]

Not everybody, of course, was equally gung-ho. The *Guardian*'s Peter Jenkins, one of the great champions of bien-pensant opinion, thought the very idea of fighting for the Falklands 'preposterous and disproportionate'. To regard the islanders' rights as paramount was 'romantic and far-fetched'. Britain simply did not have the strength to build a 'world safe for South Atlantic sheep-shearers', so the only solution was to negotiate a face-saving deal. Above all, the enfeebled British military had no chance of winning. 'Perhaps', he wrote, 'the Prime Minister has a daring and unconventional plan, but it isn't going to be as simple as recapturing the Iranian Embassy. Unfortunately the Falkland Islands are not in Knightsbridge.'[11]

Among Mass Observation's correspondents, there were several sceptics. Carol Daniel thought the operation a waste of money: if the Falkland Islanders wanted to 'call themselves British', then 'they should live in Britain not an island off the coast of Argentina'. Lesley Hughes felt sickened that anybody should die for the islands, especially the 'young lads of the Navy, Army & RAF who are so loyal to their country'. 'How would I feel if it were one of my lads,' she wrote. 'What's it all about. It's a power struggle.' And Mary Richards could not forgive the government for letting it happen in the first place. 'If Mrs Thatcher had spent more time on things that matter and less time figuring how to get the last penny out of us,' she explained, 'it would never have happened, it's just bad politics.' Only younger people could welcome war, because they had no idea how terrible it was. 'I talked to two working men of my age group yesterday,' she wrote on 23 April: 'they had terrible memories of the last war and like me hope nothing too bad comes of this. It is rare that men talk about the last war but they said they can never forget.'[12]

But voices like these were heavily outnumbered. 'Yes it was mishandled from the start,' wrote Margaret Bradshaw. 'Yes we should act. Fight.' In Darlington, Susan Gray recorded that most people felt 'we had to fight', because the alternative would be 'appeasement'. And in Lancaster, Jenny Palmer, who was deeply opposed to the war, was very conscious of being in a tiny minority. 'We have to fight, don't we,' said her chiropodist, a widow in her late fifties, 'because the Russians will step in if we don't.' The next day, Jenny was on a shopping trip when she overheard a group of elderly men talking about the crisis. 'She's a grand lass,' one said of Mrs Thatcher, to general approval. 'We'll show 'em we're British, eh?'[13]

At his lorry depot in Basildon, Peter Hibbitt canvassed eight of his colleagues. 'Their collective opinion, which agrees with my own, is that there is nothing to negotiate about,' he reported. 'Perhaps our view is coloured by all being able to remember to some degree Neville's bit of paper at Croydon airport.'* Unlike Mary Richards, he thought older people were

---

* Actually, Neville Chamberlain returned from Munich to Heston Aerodrome, which is in Hounslow – not Croydon.

much more robust than their weedy, 'pacifistic' juniors. 'In my own little circle', he wrote, 'the old Dunkirk/Blitz spirit is re-emerging.' As for what Britain should do next, he had it all worked out:

> We should start by retaking South Georgia, which would give us a long range forward base. We should then blockade by air and sea the Falklands themselves, shooting down or sinking as necessary, and then follow this up with a large scale assault and attacks on Argentinian mainland military and naval installations . . .
>
> If we 'bottle out' of taking any direct actions, then we abdicate as a world power. We should then reduce our armed forces to a Home Guard and a few Home Defence fighter squadrons. Redundant servicemen could be retrained as morris dancers, potters and basket weavers, in fact any quaint pacifist pastime, perhaps we could then be a world power in tourism. Maggie has already seen us off as an industrial power.

Sometimes it was easy to forget that he was a great enthusiast for Tony Benn.[14]

For those who did not share the belligerent mood, the whole experience was deeply disturbing. The *Sunday Times*'s Hugo Young found it 'strange and improbable and not a little mad'; the veteran columnist James Cameron, who had covered the wars in Korea and Vietnam, told Radio Four listeners he had never seen a 'sillier, dottier, [more] insultingly fatuous episode', a 'bit of post-imperial exhibitionism that shows we have reached our dotage as a nation'. The crisis, thought Jonathan Raban, had brought out 'all the crabbiness, the xenophobia . . . the hunch-shouldered go-it-alone-ism' that he had left Britain to escape. Even the Conservative MP Matthew Parris, astounded by the 'warlike streak' in his constituents, felt as if 'stranded on a sandbank, and almost completely alone'. When he told an audience in Matlock, Derbyshire, that he hoped for a negotiated solution, some hissed him, one man ('*a member of the party*', he wrote in disbelief) shouted 'Boo!' and another literally walked out. 'I left Matlock really shaken,' Parris recalled. 'I had learned something about my countrymen which I will not now forget.'[15]

Although the Falklands is typically remembered as a 'Thatcherite' war, the reality is more complicated. Many card-carrying Thatcherites were very anxious about fighting and would have preferred to reach a deal. Parris was astonished when, as the guest of honour at a meeting of the East Midlands Conservatives, Norman Tebbit told them that the Argentine troops looked like 'callow youths'. If 'a bit of willingness to negotiate' could save their lives, Tebbit said, 'he would be pleased to see the politicians try'. The reaction was a 'baffled and complete silence'. As Parris wrote, he had 'never been able to dislike him since'.[16]

Behind the scenes, some of Mrs Thatcher's closest advisers thought the war appallingly risky. Her retiring policy chief, John Hoskyns, was worried that 'we are about to make almighty fools of ourselves', and thought the war could wreck everything they had worked for. Most famously, Alan Walters regarded the operation as absurdly jingoistic, and pestered his colleagues with elaborate plans for bribing the islanders to emigrate, either to Britain or to New Zealand. One memo, recalled Ferdinand Mount, suggested giving them £1 million each. Even after the war was over, Walters presented Sir Geoffrey Howe with a plan to let Argentina buy out the sovereignty of the islanders, as in a 'contested corporate takeover bid'. In Walters's view, it would take just £50,000 apiece to persuade the islanders to vote for Argentine sovereignty. 'It was certainly an ingeniously simple idea,' Howe thought. But by this stage it would have been political suicide.[17]

In the Commons, many Conservative MPs made no secret of their misgivings. On 6 April the Chief Whip reported that there were plenty of doubters. One backbencher told him that 'when the blood of our own troops is shed . . . the country will forsake us', while Chris Patten and Julian Critchley thought the 'military difficulties may be insurmountable'. 'We are making a big mistake,' said Sir Ian Gilmour. 'It will make Suez look like common sense.'[18]

The next day, Alan Clark recorded that 'people who should know better' were stalking the Commons corridors, telling anyone who would listen that the whole thing was going to be a disaster. 'It is monstrous that senior Tories should be behaving in this way,' he wrote, blaming their 'implacable hatred' of Mrs Thatcher. 'They are within an ace, they think of bringing her Government down. If by some miracle the expedition succeeds they know, and dread, that she will be established for ever as a national hero.' The irony was that Clark had his doubts, too, but he was determined to keep them to himself. 'If we are going to go,' he wrote, 'let us go out in a blaze – then we can all sit back and comfortably become a nation of pimps and ponces, a sort of Macao to the European continent.'[19]

The Labour Party was no less divided. Some senior figures agreed with Michael Foot that the Argentine junta were fascists and must be fought. Yet to many of Foot's friends, his red-blooded intervention had been deeply shocking. In *Tribune*, which considered the expedition 'complete and utter madness', a Sheffield academic sent Foot an open letter, calling it a 'war of petty prestige and the crudest chauvinism', and expressing amazement that he had joined 'this tide of revived imperialist fervour'.

Yet although Foot did tone down his rhetoric, he never wavered in his belief that Britain was in the right. 'Jingoism was not to be confused with the protection of our people,' he told Labour's National Executive. 'We must be prepared to use force as we did in Borneo,* otherwise Galtieri's fascists would have won.'[20]

On the hard left, this confirmed that Foot was just a Tory. Ken Livingstone's *Labour Herald* refused to use the word 'Falklands', and insisted that the 'only credible claim to sovereignty of the Malvinas is that of Argentina'. 'A tide of jingoism is sweeping the country,' Livingstone's friend Jeremy Corbyn told a Hornsey Council meeting. 'It is a nauseating waste of money and lives . . . The whole thing is a Tory plot to keep their money-making friends in business.' But by far the most outspoken public face of opposition to the war was, inevitably, Tony Benn. It was 'very foolish', he wrote, for Foot to have backed the expedition. The Falklands were 'a colony we grabbed years ago from somebody and we have no right to it', while 'some 1800 British settlers do not constitute a domestic population whose views can be taken seriously'.†

Benn thought Britain should cede the islands to the United Nations while talks took place, even though this would leave the Argentines in possession. And although the polls suggested that the public wanted action, he knew better. 'A majority of the British people are against the war with Argentina,' he recorded, 'but the media are preventing that view becoming apparent.' To some of his Labour colleagues, this simply proved he had lost his marbles. The soft-left Birmingham MP Jeff Rooker took great pleasure in quoting Benn's speech a few weeks earlier about the merits of Marxism, in which he had explicitly endorsed the right to 'take up arms . . . to defeat a foreign invasion, or repel those who have successfully occupied a part of our territory'. And his old ally Eric Heffer had no time for Benn's position at all. 'Was Tony in favour of fascist regimes taking over?' he demanded at a meeting in mid-May. 'The people were not with us – the majority wanted the Task Force to go . . . The Shadow Cabinet didn't like jingoism, but we would have been called the Munich Party if we'd done nothing.'[21]

The biggest losers from the war were the Alliance. On 25 March, Roy Jenkins had won a sensational victory in the Glasgow Hillhead by-election, reinforcing his claim to lead the SDP. His disciples rubbed their hands with anticipation at his return to the Commons, but the Falklands crisis was a

---

* In a conflict virtually hidden from the general public, some 17,000 British troops had served in Borneo during the mid-1960s, defending Malaysia against its neighbour Indonesia.

† That word 'settlers' is very revealing. Many of the islanders were not, in fact, settlers, since they had been born on the Falklands, as had their parents and grandparents.

disaster for him. While David Owen's patriotic enthusiasm went down very
well with the general public, the former President of the European Commission, a 'soft man in tough times', seemed utterly out of his depth. As
Frank Johnson wryly put it, Jenkins was a one-man Switzerland, 'prosperous, comfortable, civilized and almost entirely landlocked. His only previous
contact with the high seas has been in various good fish restaurants.'

In the Commons, Jenkins seemed at once pompous, nervous and painfully uncomfortable. On television he was almost comically stiff and
portentous, more at home in 1882 than 1982. In truth, he hated the war
and was baffled by the public mood. It was absurd, he said later, to treat
the Falklands campaign 'like a latter-day recapture of Khartoum by Kitch-
ener'. But in some ways, that is precisely what it was: a flag-waving
campaign to restore the nation's honour, fought in a far-off land of which
most people knew nothing. Indeed, since Britain could hardly claim to
have been fighting for self-determination at Khartoum, Jenkins's historical
analogy was singularly ill chosen. The truth is that, like many other self-
consciously liberal, cosmopolitan people, he was completely at odds with
the great majority, and he never managed to disguise it.[22]

There was, inevitably, a class dimension to the Falklands debate. The
*Guardian*'s Peter Jenkins wrote later that it had divided the nation between
the 'educated middle classes and the patriotic working classes', though
quite a lot of the former supported the war, too. He had 'few friends or
acquaintances who supported the war or knew people who did', but canvassers in local elections 'found few working class households who were
against it'. And there was also a pronounced cultural dimension. In many
ways the public reaction was a perfect example of the old schism between
what Michael Frayn called the *Guardian*-reading Herbivores, 'who look
out from the lush pastures which are their natural station in life with eyes
full of sorrow for less fortunate creatures, guiltily conscious of their
advantages', and the *Express*-reading Carnivores, who believed that 'if
God had not wished them to prey on all smaller and weaker creatures
without scruple he would not have made them as they are'. On the one
hand, the citizens of the world; on the other, the people.[23]

The most entertaining glimpse of the nation's divisions was a book
entitled *Authors Take Sides on the Falklands*, inspired by a volume published during the Spanish Civil War. Why authors should have had
anything worthwhile to say about the Falklands is an intriguing question.
In any case, the editors received 106 contributions, of which fifty-nine
opposed the government line, thirty-nine supported it and eight were
neutral. Of the contributions opposed to the war, many were frankly
extraordinary. Brian Aldiss 'would like to see the islands sink below the

waves'. John Arden believed the war had been deliberately engineered to 'replenish some of the international reputation lost by Britain' during the Belfast hunger strikes. Alan Brownjohn believed the war was an 'electronic rehearsal' for an imminent nuclear conflict. The poet David Gascoyne sent in a splendidly pompous essay, ending with the terrifying words 'I now append a short poem . . .' And another poet, Michael Horovitz, suggested that both armies be compelled to put on neutral uniforms before being randomly reshuffled. If that failed, a dedicated 'area of the planet' should be set aside for people who wished to carry on fighting. Alas, he lamented, 'this will get slagged as Utopian dreaming'.[24]

Among the saner objections, the prevailing theme was sheer horror at the resurgence of patriotic feeling. Peter Cadogan was shocked to have 'discovered the meaning and scale of British tribalism'. Margaret Drabble thought the war a 'frenzied outburst of dying power'. Kathleen Raine deplored the 'unlooked-for upsurge of the worst kind of imperialist jingoism', while Polly Toynbee claimed that 'after the first taste of blood', the government had discovered 'the joys of singing Rule Britannia to the accompaniment of rising opinion polls'. (Actually, much of the government's surge in the polls came *before* the first casualties, not afterwards.) And as so often, one of the most memorable contributions came from Salman Rushdie, riding high after winning the Booker Prize for *Midnight's Children* (1981). The war was 'xenophobic militarism', he said, 'the politics of the Victorian nursery; if somebody pinches you, you take their trousers down and thrash them'. 'The huge support given by the British people to this war doesn't need much discussion,' he added loftily. 'I wish only to say that it has made me feel ashamed.'[25]

The authors who supported the government were a similarly eccentric bunch. Kingsley Amis thought the very question 'How, in your view, should the dispute in the South Atlantic be resolved?' betrayed a left-wing bias. Roald Dahl believed that 'excessive socialism seems to have nurtured a flabby and idle breed of people who would rather compromise than fight'. Francis King, a pacifist in the Second World War, had now lost his faith and supported the Task Force, as did Spike Milligan, Alan Sillitoe and Muriel Spark. Mary Renault demanded to know whether France would be justified in seizing the Channel Islands ('Do you really think the issue controversial? You surprise me.') And Patrick Moore claimed that if the Argentines were allowed to 'get away with it', then 'Gibraltar would be the next to go – followed, possibly, by the Isle of Wight'.

But the most striking contribution of all came from Jilly Cooper, writing after the end of the war. 'All I can say is I think Mrs Thatcher was magnificent, our troops even better,' she wrote. 'I'm desperately sorry for the families of all those who died on both sides. But I have to confess some of those Argentinian officers are so frightfully good-looking one might almost enjoy being taken prisoner by them.'[26]

While Jilly Cooper fantasized about the pleasures of an Argentine prison, the most influential newspaper in Britain had no doubt that the Falklands was the great moral battle of the age. The deputy editor of the *Sun*, Roy Greenslade, had been on holiday in Malta during the invasion. When he went into the office on Monday morning, he found it on a war footing. The news editor was wearing a naval officer's cap and insisted on being called 'Commander', while a giant map of the South Atlantic had been pinned up beneath the newly installed portrait of Sir Winston Churchill. Greenslade told his colleague Wendy Henry that he thought the whole business ridiculous. She laughed. 'Be careful, pet,' she said, 'that's a very unpopular view to hold round here.'[27]

Four years after overtaking the *Mirror*, Rupert Murdoch's *Sun* was the most popular paper in the country, with an estimated 12 million readers, the vast majority of them working-class and many of them under 30. The key to its success was its brash, shameless, fun-loving populism. It had no time for stuffy patricians or sneering snobs, and had famously thrown its weight behind Mrs Thatcher, who offered 'FREEDOM to run your life as YOU want to run it'. But at the turn of the 1980s the *Sun* had come under pressure. Its formula was looking stale, sales had dipped and the *Mirror* was mounting a comeback. Worse, the *Express* group had launched an aggressively populist tabloid of their own, the *Daily Star*. Billed as a 'socialist *Sun*' for the northern working classes, the *Star* offered a similar formula of punning headlines and topless women. Its ethos, said its editor, was 'tits, bums, QPR and roll-your-own fags'. He forgot to mention bingo, which added hundreds of thousands of extra sales. For the first time, the *Sun* was worried.[28]

In the spring of 1981, Murdoch made two changes. First, the *Sun* introduced its own bingo competition; second, and more important, he brought in a new editor, the 34-year-old Kelvin MacKenzie. One colleague called MacKenzie 'driving, youthful, modern-minded, brash', while his deputy Roy Greenslade called him a 'workaholic, manic, abusive, obnoxious, socially gauche bully-cum-comedian with a singular talent for editing a populist tabloid'.* MacKenzie, who had left his direct-grant grammar

---

* Greenslade also noted, though, that MacKenzie was straightforward, good-humoured and 'rarely held grudges ... He was far kinder and more understanding in private than in public.'

school with a single O-level, had a clear vision of his ideal reader. 'He's the bloke you see in the pub,' he said, 'a right old fascist, wants to send the wogs back, buy his poxy council house, he's afraid of the unions, afraid of the Russians, hates the queers and the weirdos and drug dealers.' And although more high-minded souls shuddered, MacKenzie's formula worked. By April 1982, boosted by bingo, the *Sun*'s sales had risen by more than half a million copies in just twelve months.[29]

When the Falklands crisis broke, MacKenzie saw an unmissable opportunity to confirm his paper's hold over working-class Britain. On Tuesday 6th, declaring that the 'worms are already coming out of the woodwork', the *Sun* attacked the 'ailing *Daily Mirror*' for its cowardice in urging a negotiated settlement. On the 7th it laid into another 'political termite . . . No.1 left-winger Tony Benn', as well as the 'whining namby-pamby ultra-Left, who always run scared at the first sign of a crisis'. And on the 8th it ran a double-page spread ('LEST WE FORGET') showing the Marines surrendering during the Argentine invasion. 'It was a black moment in our history,' the *Sun* said sententiously. 'But now our troops are on their way . . . to wipe out the memory and free our loyal friends.'[30]

Every day brought more of the same. As the future bestseller writer Robert Harris explains in his book *Gotcha!*, this was 'the first time old-fashioned jingoism had been allied in wartime to a modern, mass-circulation British tabloid'. No joke was too tasteless, no stunt too contrived, no headline too sensational. Later, *Private Eye* produced a brilliant *Sun* front page, including the timeless offer 'KILL AN ARGIE – and Win a Metro'. But it was hard to tell the difference between the parody and the original. MacKenzie and his team airlifted fifty gigantic posters of Page Three girls to the RAF base at Ascension Island, in the middle of the South Atlantic, and had them dropped by helicopter on to the *Invincible*. They mounted a campaign to persuade housewives 'NOT to buy corned beef produced in the Argentine'. They promoted a video game that allowed players to torpedo Argentine ships. They ran a daily 'Argy-Bargie' joke column, and offered £5 and a tin of 'non-Argentinian' corned beef for every successful entry. They even featured Page Three girls, 'all shipshape and Bristol fashion', wearing knickers displaying the names of Task Force ships ('Britain's secret weapon').

All the time they searched for ever more outrageous puns, culminating in one of the most famous headlines in the paper's history, referring to the latest impasse in diplomatic negotiations: 'STICK IT UP YOUR JUNTA.' MacKenzie enjoyed the joke so much that, a few days later, he offered readers the chance to 'give those damn Argies a whole lot of bargie' by

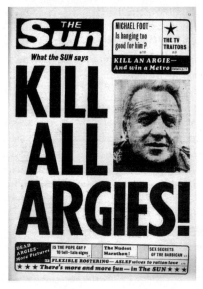

Appearing in the issue of 21 May 1982, *Private Eye*'s version of the *Sun* front page was one of the best things it ever did, not least because it was so hard to tell it apart from the originals. When MacKenzie saw the 'KILL AN ARGIE – and Win a Metro' competition, he remarked: 'Why didn't we think of that?'

buying a 'Sunsational' STICK IT UP YOUR JUNTA T-shirt. The next day, he ran a version of the headline again, though this time it proved much more controversial:

### STICK THIS UP YOUR JUNTA!

*A Sun Missile for Galtieri's Gauchos*

The first missile to hit Galtieri's gauchos will come with love from the Sun.

And just in case he doesn't get the message, the weapon will have painted on the side 'Up Yours, Galtieri', and will be signed by Tony Snow – our man aboard HMS Invincible.

The Sun – on behalf of all our millions of patriotic readers – has sponsored the missile by paying towards HMS Invincible's victory party once the war is over.

Even many of the men in the Task Force were appalled. 'There was a general feeling', said another reporter on the *Invincible*, 'that it was a sick thing to do.' Some complained to the Ministry of Defence's press office.

But since there was nothing they could do, the 'Paper That Supports Our Boys' roared on regardless.[31]

The irony of all this is that, far from boosting sales, the *Sun*'s rhetoric probably put some readers off. Across Fleet Street, newspaper sales barely rose during the war, but the *Sun*'s circulation actually dropped by 40,000 copies. Yet even though the *Sun*'s own reporters were mortified by some of its coverage, it was MacKenzie's paper that set the tone. The *Daily Star* eagerly followed its example, urging Mrs Thatcher to 'throw the invading Argentines into the sea', and devoting one front page to an attack on Tony Benn and nine other Labour traitors, 'no friends of their country, of freedom or of their own party'. At one point the *Star* warned Benn not to 'abuse' the privilege of free speech 'by continuing with your dangerous attacks on the Task Force', and commissioned a lawyer to examine his speeches. The lawyer duly reported that Benn 'might be considered as preaching something very like treason'.[32]

For people who were already minded to look down on the tabloids, all this merely confirmed their unforgivable vulgarity. Jonathan Raban considered the *Sun*'s headlines 'infantile' and 'grisly', while almost every day the *Guardian*'s diarist, Alan Rusbridger, had something to say about 'Rupert's boys at the Sun', who lacked even a 'soupçon of sensitivity'. In early May the *Guardian* ran a long essay by the veteran journalist Tom Baistow, attacking the tabloids' 'nastiness and bathos', their 'vicious, undemocratic tripe' and 'Yobspeak headlines'. (That word 'Yobspeak' is, of course, very revealing.) Some observers thought this absurdly precious. The *Sun*'s approach might have upset 'the intelligentsia in London', wrote a scornful David Owen, 'but in the provinces it was taken in good heart'. Plenty of people, though, thought MacKenzie had crossed a line. On his return from the South Atlantic, Admiral Woodward deplored the 'lunatic nationalist pride' of the tabloids, singling out the *Sun* in particular. No doubt he was just another a whining namby-pamby.[33]

In the newsroom of the *Sun*, victory was never in doubt. But at Northwood Headquarters, where Mrs Thatcher's military chiefs pored over their options, things seemed less clear-cut. Every element of the campaign was fraught with danger: the towering waves, the freezing cold, the howling winds – and that was just the weather. And precisely because of the weather, the margins were painfully tight. Even in late April the seas were likely to be stormy, and by late May winter, bringing rain and gales, would have arrived on the Falkland Islands. Even for elite units like the Marines and the Paras, the conditions would be awful. And given how long it took to get to the islands, Northwood's planners calculated that they had a ten-day window to move the troops off the ships and on to dry land, from 14 to 23 May. If anything went wrong, the operation would be in real trouble.[34]

That was not all. As the Task Force approached the Falklands, it would be acutely vulnerable to attack, especially by Argentina's warplanes, with their Exocet anti-ship missiles. Even if the fleet arrived without disaster, an amphibious assault on Stanley was far too dangerous because the Argentines had concentrated at least 9,000 troops around the town and had mined the nearby beaches. So British troops would have to land elsewhere and establish a bridgehead before moving over rough terrain towards the capital. The landing alone would be dauntingly risky, and early estimates suggested they might lose one in five men, about 900 in all. Even if they made it on to the islands, wet, cold and exhausted, they would be facing about 13,000 Argentines, who would have had weeks to bring in supplies and prepare their defensive positions. The naval commander-in-chief, Admiral Sir John Fieldhouse, told Mrs Thatcher that they might incur 3,000 casualties, but nobody knew for sure. In his own words, 'this is the most difficult thing we have attempted since the Second World War'. And not even Britain's closest allies were convinced they could do it. Given the 'logistical problems' facing the British, the CIA told President Reagan, they would 'be hard pressed to oust a force of the size anticipated'.[35]

At Westminster, many of Mrs Thatcher's ministers had strong doubts about the wisdom of such a complicated operation. Later, Willie Whitelaw admitted that he was 'haunted by Suez', when another Conservative government had gambled and lost. Like some of his colleagues, Whitelaw had seen war at first hand, and knew that things always went wrong. Indeed, among the seasoned Tory patricians, there was a strong feeling that a woman who knew nothing of war had rushed into a decision that could have terrible consequences. 'She wouldn't have done it if she'd been a man and if she'd been in the armed forces during the war,' reflected Philip Goodhart, a former junior defence minister who had served in the Paras. 'Then she'd have been aware how dreadfully wrong everything was likely to go.'[36]

In this instance, the fact that Mrs Thatcher was not a man proved an enormous asset. Since she could not be expected to know anything about war, she had no problem deferring to people who did. On 7 April she called the first meeting of her War Cabinet, which consisted of Whitelaw, Francis Pym, John Nott and Cecil Parkinson. The first three picked themselves. If nothing else, Whitelaw had won the Military Cross in Normandy, Pym had won it in Italy and Nott had been an officer in the Gurkhas in

Malaya. But Parkinson, the party chairman, was a more controversial choice. To Mrs Thatcher's critics, this revealed her obsession with presentation, as well as her determination to politicize the conflict. In reality, she needed Parkinson to give her a majority against Pym and Whitelaw, whom she suspected of being instinctive appeasers. As she told him when she offered him the job, there was 'no room for fainthearts'.

After the war, everybody agreed that Mrs Thatcher's handling of the War Cabinet had been a model of political management. They met every weekday at Number 10 and at Chequers at weekends, joined by their military chiefs and senior officials. For perhaps the only time in her premiership, wrote Hugo Young, Mrs Thatcher 'listened more than she spoke', always deferring to her commanders on the details, but remaining totally clear-sighted about the wider objectives. Whenever the military asked her for a decision, she swiftly obliged. But she always recognized that they knew far more about it than she did, and listened to the Chief of the Defence Staff, Admiral Terence Lewin, with immense respect. Many insiders thought she regarded the armed forces with a kind of nostalgic awe. Yet at the same time she saw her soldiers and sailors as paragons of her ideal forward-looking Britain, professional, classless, gallant and decisive, in stark contrast to the spineless fops at the Foreign Office. As Alan Walters laconically recorded at the end of April: 'PM loves the forces.'[37]

But while the Falklands brought the best out of Mrs Thatcher, the political effort was far from a one-woman show. Later, she recognized a particular debt to her ambassador to the United Nations, the urbane Sir Anthony Parsons. As early as the evening of Saturday 3 April, Parsons had called a meeting of the Security Council and introduced Resolution 502, which called for talks to resolve the crisis and, crucially, the withdrawal of all Argentine forces. Twenty-five minutes before the vote, though, Parsons was still not certain of getting the necessary two-thirds majority. So Mrs Thatcher rang King Hussein of Jordan, and begged him to back it. He agreed. 'You're very kind and a wonderful ally,' she said breathlessly. The resolution passed, with ten countries voting for it, the Soviet Union, China, Spain and Poland abstaining and only Panama voting against. From now on Mrs Thatcher could point to the support of the United Nations, including its Charter's endorsement of the right of self-defence. The crisis was only a day old, and already she had seized the moral high ground. After the vote, the Soviet ambassador murmured to Parsons: 'You should get the Garter.'

In Buenos Aires, Resolution 502 came as a terrible shock. Almost incredibly, the Argentine generals had given little thought to what would happen next, simply assuming that the British would roll over. They had no plans for fighting a long campaign, while their nationalist rhetoric had made it impossible for them to compromise without appearing fatally weak. After the explosion of joy that had followed the initial conquest, to pull back now would be an utter fiasco. Above all, they had completely failed to line up international support. A few Western countries, notably Ireland, Spain and Italy, sympathized with the Argentines for historical or cultural reasons. But most were shocked by the invasion and felt sorry for the Falkland Islanders, while Commonwealth countries like Canada, Australia and New Zealand were firmly pro-British. As for the Soviet Union, it had no dog in the fight: as far as it was concerned, it was a shame both sides could not lose.[38]

From Mrs Thatcher's perspective, three countries were particularly vital. One was Argentina's neighbour Chile, ruled by another authoritarian right-wing regime under General Augusto Pinochet. Despite their ideological affinity, the Chileans absolutely despised the Argentines. Only four years earlier they had come close to war, and it was an open secret that Argentina's military was itching to move against Chile. Almost immediately, therefore, Pinochet agreed that the RAF could use an air base in southern Chile, while his intelligence agencies promised to hand over details of Argentine naval movements and to help the British break the enemy's signals. Neither side was keen to advertise these arrangements: the Chileans were flouting the code of Latin American solidarity, while Pinochet's record of violent repression made him an uncomfortable ally. But Mrs Thatcher did not forget it. When Pinochet was detained on human rights charges in London in 1999, she made a point of visiting him to say thank you.[39]

The second key ally was France. On the evening of Saturday 3rd, while Mrs Thatcher was awaiting the vote at the United Nations, President Mitterrand rang to offer his support. 'I wouldn't wish you to think', he said, 'that France, as a very close friend and neighbour, was not absolutely with you in thought and freedom . . . If there's anything we can do to help, we should like to.' He was as good as his word. In the past, France had made a lot of money selling Super Étendard fighters and Exocet anti-ship missiles to Argentina. Now Mitterrand told his staff to hand over all the necessary specifications to the British, and blocked the sale of more missiles to Peru, which was likely to pass them on to Buenos Aires. He was 'the staunchest of our friends', recalled Mrs Thatcher, who 'never forgot the debt we owed him for his personal support'. It did not mean she gave him an easier ride at European summits, though.[40]

The most important country of all was Britain's closest military ally, the United States. With British forces operating in the Western hemisphere, access to American intelligence, satellite reports and communications technology would be vital, while the Task Force would need to refuel halfway across the Atlantic at Ascension Island, a British colony which the Americans were using as a military base. President Reagan's natural sympathies lay with Mrs Thatcher, while his Secretary of Defense, Caspar Weinberger, saw the Washington–London axis as the 'bedrock' of the Western alliance. Almost from the first, therefore, Weinberger ordered his officials to give the British whatever they wanted, including the latest Sidewinder air-to-air missiles. As Reagan privately remarked a few days later, they should 'give Maggie everything she needs to get on with it'.[41]

But not all of Reagan's officials shared his views. Most worryingly for Mrs Thatcher, his ambassador to the United Nations, Jeane Kirkpatrick, was a great fan of General Galtieri's regime, which she regarded as a bulwark against Communism. To avoid alienating their allies in Latin America, she told Reagan on 7 April, it was vital 'not to be seen to be favouring the British'. That went down very badly with some of her colleagues. But Reagan, despite his personal inclinations, appreciated the dilemma. 'The main thing we have to do', he told his staff, 'is to get these two brawlers out of the bar room.' To do it, he turned to his Secretary of State, the immensely self-confident Alexander Haig. Formerly NATO's Supreme Commander in Europe, Haig leapt at the chance to promote himself as a world statesman. It would take him two weeks, he told Reagan, to broker a deal. 'There will not', he promised, 'be a war in the South Atlantic.'[42]

On 8 April, Haig and his team arrived in London. At the airport, an embassy official warned him that Mrs Thatcher would never bend: 'If you think you can sway her you're dead wrong.' But Haig was not deterred, and late that afternoon he went in to see the Prime Minister, Pym and Nott. Mrs Thatcher kicked off with a gesture that came close to self-parody, ostentatiously showing her guests a pair of portraits that she thought 'very appropriate'. One was Nelson, the other Wellington. Then she got down to what Haig's aide Jim Rentschler called the 'nut-cutter nitty-gritty'.

Haig suggested that a possible deal might see the Argentine forces withdraw and an interim 'multilateral entity' take charge of the islands until the two sides sorted out the question of sovereignty. But Mrs Thatcher, the colour rushing to her face, did not like that at all:

> I am pledged before the House of Commons, the Defense Minister [sic] is pledged, the Foreign Secretary is pledged to restore British administration. I did not dispatch a fleet to install some nebulous arrangement which would

have no authority whatsoever. Interim authority! – to do what? I beg you,
I beg you to remember that in 1938 Neville Chamberlain sat at this same
table discussing an arrangement which sounds very much like the one you
are asking me to accept; and were I to do so, I would be censured in the
House of Commons – and properly so! We in Britain simply refuse to reward
aggression – that is the lesson we have learned from 1938.

'Tough lady,' Rentschler thought, while Haig sat chain-smoking and 'nervously tapping his leg'. But Mrs Thatcher knew exactly what she was doing.
As the meeting broke up, she said she hoped the Americans realized that
this kind of candour was only possible 'among the closest of friends'. 'With
everyone else', she said sweetly, 'we're merely nice.'[43]

The next day, Haig sent Reagan a telegram summarizing the position.
Mrs Thatcher, he wrote, 'has the bit in her teeth . . . She is clearly prepared
to use force, though she admits a preference for a diplomatic solution.'
Even to Haig, however, it was obvious that Francis Pym was desperate for
a deal. Indeed, he was astonished how far the Foreign Secretary went 'in
showing this in her presence'. ('He's not long for this world,' Haig muttered to one of his aides.) But Mrs Thatcher was 'convinced she will fall
if she concedes on any of three basic points': the immediate withdrawal
of Argentine forces, the restoration of British administration and respect
for the self-determination of the islanders. On this, Haig thought, there
was little room for manoeuvre. Still, he was now off to Buenos Aires,
where perhaps the Argentines would prove more conciliatory.[44]

In reality, Mrs Thatcher was more pragmatic than Haig realized.
Although she found him annoying, his efforts were very useful, keeping
the Americans on side and showing the public that she was willing to
consider a settlement. But she had no intention of making it easy for him.
And when Haig got back from Buenos Aires on 12 April, having encountered an extraordinarily frosty reception, she was in fighting form. When
he suggested that the British fleet might hold back, she exclaimed:
'Unthinkable, that is our only leverage, I cannot possibly give it up at this
point, one simply doesn't trust burglars who have tried once to steal your
property! No, Al, no, absolutely not, the fleet must steam on!' Pym, clearly
embarrassed by her hard line, was almost literally 'wringing his hands in
anguish'. But Nott was determined to stand firm. 'I wouldn't [hold back],
Prime Minister,' he said, 'I'm against it, we've really conceded too much
as it is.'[45]

Even so, on 14 April, after a great deal of toing and froing, Mrs Thatcher
presented Haig's plan to her Cabinet. Both sides would pull out their troops,
while the Falkland Islanders would run their own affairs until the end of the

year, under the aegis of a joint British, Argentine and American commission. By that time, Haig wanted the two countries to have reached a lasting arrangement. Some ministers thought they should go for it: both Pym and Howe thought they were unlikely to get a better deal. But Lord Hailsham and Nigel Lawson were more hawkish. 'Britain had been the victim of unprovoked aggression,' recorded the minutes. 'The wider principle was even more important than the fate of the Islanders. If aggression was shown to pay, it would be a disastrous precedent for the world as a whole.'

Remarkably, though, Mrs Thatcher was less intransigent. She might have presented an unbending face to the world, but she was nothing if not a realist. The Argentines, she told the hawks, would only be getting 'one-third of a commission'. Summing up, she told her ministers that 'a diplomatic solution on the lines outlined would be a considerable prize. The withdrawal of Argentine forces would have been secured without military action . . . Repugnant as it was that the aggressor should gain anything from his aggression, this seemed an acceptable price to pay.'[46]

Acceptable to her, perhaps, but not to General Galtieri. For when Haig flew back to Buenos Aires the next day, he found the junta totally inflexible. Not only did they want the British fleet to turn back immediately, they demanded an Argentine governor for the islands and an Argentine flag, as well as a guarantee that negotiations would end with Argentine sovereignty. To the exhausted Haig, this was patently unrealistic. What was more, the Argentines treated his team with ostentatious contempt, his aides complaining of orchestrated jeering by crowds, poor treatment by Galtieri's staff and 'excessive rudeness' from his guards. The whole thing was a 'charade', Haig muttered to his aides the next day, 'a fucking charade – these guys are diddling me'. 'Of course they are,' the American ambassador said, 'they aren't hearing us, we can't negotiate with them, our relationship means nothing.'

By now Jim Rentschler was pressing Haig to ditch the talks and support Britain, 'our most important and forthcoming ally'. 'The Argies', he added, were not 'nice people'. Haig made a last effort, meeting Galtieri the next day, the 17th, and imploring him to compromise. But Galtieri was trapped, both by his own nationalist bombast and by his people's frenzied excitement. He had no intention of withdrawing his troops unless the British agreed to recognize Argentine sovereignty. In that case, Haig said, 'you are leaving us no choice but to break off our effort and throw our full support behind the British'.

Grimly he laid out the scenario. 'Within a matter of days, the British fleet will be upon you. These forces are capable of inflicting severe damage on yours. I do not for one moment question Argentine courage. But it cannot prevent your systematic defeat by sophisticated British surface, sub-surface, and air power.' Such a war, he said, would be 'ruinous for Argentina – politically, economically, and militarily. The British will not bear the onus, for you were the first to use force, and they made a reasonable effort to reach a peaceful settlement. There is no escaping historical responsibility for what now seems inevitable.' He was right. But he was wasting his time.[47]

Meanwhile, the Task Force sailed south, armed with its gigantic *Sun* pin-ups and mountains of letters from enthusiastic well-wishers. As they approached the Equator, the weather was getting hotter. As the *Canberra* 'ploughed through the vast emptiness of the ocean in warm evening sunshine', Max Hastings sat among a crowd of tanned young soldiers, listening to the band playing 'Rule Britannia', 'Hearts of Oak' and, inevitably, Rod Stewart's 'Sailing'. He thought of 'millions of people at home in Britain and around the world consumed with wonder and doubt about where we were, and what we were doing'. Writing home, he told his wife and children how much he missed them. But 'what man in England', he asked, 'would not give anything to be sailing with us into the South Atlantic today?'[48]

For the young men on board, though, life was becoming increasingly tedious. Every morning Vincent Bramley and his comrades pounded around the deck of the *Canberra* in full kit, sometimes doing twenty-four circuits in all, the equivalent of about six miles. They listened to endless lectures about the islands, the Argentines, the conditions, their weapons; they gossiped and bickered; they watched violent films and wrote letters home; they cracked dirty jokes and stared out to sea. Most had spent years training for this moment. Far from being frightened or reluctant, they were desperate to get on with it. What they really feared was that the politicians would reach a deal and call them back. 'Fuck the bloody twats sat there arguing,' Bramley thought. 'Let's get it done and over with. We love Maggie for giving us the chance to kill some Spicks. Just let's hope we get back in time for the World Cup and summer leave.'[49]

In Downing Street, Mrs Thatcher watched and waited, one eye on Haig's attempts to find a solution, the other on the colossal armada heading south. On 16 April, *Hermes* reached Ascension Island, midway between Britain and the Falklands. Most of the rest of the fleet – in total, some 127 ships, carrying just under 10,000 men – began to arrive in the next few days. All the time the clock was ticking. Yet the landings were still weeks away, and Mrs Thatcher was painfully aware that she needed *some* kind of success to satisfy the public and show that she meant what she said.

Almost from the moment the Task Force sailed, Mrs Thatcher's defence chiefs had agreed that the first objective would be South Georgia, where a small group of Argentine Marines had landed to reinforce the so-called scrap-metal dealers. If nothing else, recapturing South Georgia would please the voters and provide Britain with a possible bargaining chip. As Nott remarked, the operation was 'pure politics'. So, at Ascension, a small force of some 150 Royal Marines and seventy SAS men was detached from the main fleet, before secretly heading south towards South Georgia. The plan, drawn up at Northwood, was for them to strike on 21 April. But this raised a problem: should they attack while Haig was still trying to find a deal? On the afternoon of the 19th, the War Cabinet met to discuss the dilemma. On the proviso that the assault team would keep Argentine casualties to a minimum, they decided to go for it.[50]

Two days later, amid towering waves, driving snow and howling winds, helicopters dropped the first SAS team on South Georgia's Fortuna Glacier. The conditions, even for elite soldiers, were horrific. Lugging all their kit, it took them five hours to advance little more than 500 yards. When they tried to put up their tents, the first was ripped away by the blizzard, while the poles of the others snapped almost instantly. A handful of men forced their way inside, taking turns to crawl out and shovel snow away from the entrance; the others huddled together in the freezing night. The next morning, with the weather deteriorating, they decided to call it a day. But as the first Wessex 5 helicopter took off after picking them up, the pilot lost control and crashed into the snow. Somehow they all managed to scramble out and get aboard a second helicopter. But no sooner had the second helicopter taken off than it, too, smashed on to the glacier.[51]

News of the crash reached London that afternoon. There was no word of any survivors. For Nott, it was 'the worst moment of the war'. When he told Mrs Thatcher, she wept. Her aide Clive Whitmore said quietly: 'There's going to be a lot more of this.' It was an extraordinarily highly charged moment. As her biographer Charles Moore points out, this was not merely the first British action of the war, it was the first time Mrs Thatcher had sent troops into a situation where they might lose their lives. Not a shot had been fired, yet already it seemed to have ended in disaster. It was, she recalled, 'a terrible start to the campaign ... My heart was heavy as I changed to go to a dinner at the Mansion House to support the Civic Trust, and to speak. I wondered how I could conceal my feelings, whether this was an omen and was there worse to come. Was the task we had set ourselves impossible.'

Then came the twist. 'Just as I reached the bottom of the staircase', she wrote, 'Clive came rushing out of the office.' A third Wessex helicopter had gone back to the glacier, found the men and got them out. They were alive. For Mrs Thatcher, it was one of the sweetest moments of the war. 'I went out walking on air,' she remembered. 'Nothing else in the world mattered – the men *were safe*.' As so often, she had proved a supremely lucky politician.[52]

But there was no let-up in the pressure of events. Two days later, on the morning of 24 April, Francis Pym flew in from Washington with momentous news. After more talks with Alexander Haig, he had agreed a deal. In effect, it was almost exactly the same deal that Haig had been pushing all along, requiring Argentine forces to pull out and the British fleet to withdraw some 2,000 nautical miles from the Falklands. Meanwhile, the islanders would run their own affairs subject to the approval of a joint British, Argentine and American authority, until Britain and Argentina had sorted out the sovereignty issue. Mrs Thatcher was aghast. Contrary to everything she had promised, the document omitted to say that the islanders' wishes were paramount, rewarded Argentina for its aggression and carried the obvious implication that the islands would end up in Argentine hands. Haig had 'got at him', she thought – as indeed he had.

According to Pym, Haig had made it clear that if Britain rejected the deal 'we might be on our own'. But Mrs Thatcher thought Haig was bluffing. The terms were a 'complete sell-out', which would 'rob the Falklanders of their freedom and Britain of her honour and respect . . . I repeated to Francis that we could *not* accept them.' Pym wanted to put the terms to the War Cabinet that evening. Mrs Thatcher was appalled, but she could not stop him. 'A former *Defence Secretary* and present Foreign Secretary of Britain recommending peace at that price,' she recalled in disbelief. 'Had it gone through the committee I could not have stayed.'

At about six that evening her colleagues gathered outside the Cabinet Room, with Pym audibly 'trying to get their support'. If they overruled her and backed him, her premiership could be over within hours. She called Willie Whitelaw into her study and told him how she felt. She knew her man. An officer to the last, Whitelaw nodded. A few moments later, the meeting began. Mrs Thatcher got stuck in straight away, going through Pym's draft 'clause by clause', tearing holes in the plan. Then John Nott suggested an elegant solution. They should simply acknowledge Haig's plan, without accepting, and encourage him to put it to Buenos Aires. It was, Nott argued, 'virtually impossible' that the Argentines would agree to pull their troops out. Galtieri would get the blame, and Reagan would be free to back the British. 'So the crisis passed,' wrote a relieved Mrs Thatcher, 'the crisis of Britain's honour.'[53]

But it was not quite as simple as that. Mrs Thatcher always remembered that meeting as one of the turning points of the campaign, in which she saved the islanders from being betrayed by her Foreign Secretary. Yet only ten days earlier, she had told the Cabinet that a deal along these lines would be 'an acceptable price to pay' for peace. So why the outrage? Charles Moore suggests two reasons. One is that, in the immediate aftermath of the South Georgia helicopter rescue, she had become completely absorbed by the drama of the campaign. Having almost lost her young men on the glacier, she identified more closely than ever with the Task Force, and had no patience for the fudging of the Foreign Office. The second reason is rather simpler. For the past two years, people had been saying that she was doomed and that Pym, the old-school paternalist, was the favourite to replace her. Now he was putting himself forward as the peacemaker, while she would get the blame for betraying the islanders. There was no way she could ever accept it. Even at the height of a national crisis, she was still a politician.[54]

The next day, Sunday 25th, found Mrs Thatcher at Chequers, working as usual. But in South Georgia, the British forces were again preparing to strike. They began with a helicopter attack on the Argentine submarine *Santa Fe*, which had just unloaded reinforcements at Grytviken. Now, fatally crippled, it was forced back into port. A few hours later, while British naval guns pounded the shoreline, an improvised company of some seventy-five Marines, SAS and Special Boat Squadron commandos landed by helicopter. General Galtieri had boasted that his men would defend South Georgia 'to the last drop of blood'. But the Argentine Marine commander knew it was pointless. Having radioed Rear Admiral Büsser for approval, he wasted little time in raising the white flag. South Georgia had been reclaimed, and the British commandos had not fired a shot. Later, as dusk fell, in what looked like a 'scene from some ancient ritual', some three dozen dishevelled men appeared over the horizon, chanting songs and carrying makeshift torches. After more than a month on the island, cold, miserable and hungry, Constantino Davidoff's scrap-metal workers were ready to go home.[55]

Mrs Thatcher heard the news of South Georgia's recapture late that afternoon, just before she left for Windsor for an evening audience with the Queen. 'It was wonderful', she recalled, 'to be able personally to give her the news that one of her islands had been restored to her.' Then, back at Downing Street, she prepared to tell the world. With remarkable generosity, she decided that Nott, whose reputation had taken such a battering, should be the man to do it. At 8.45 that evening the door of Number 10 swung open and the two of them, flanked by policemen and aides, walked towards the flashing cameras.

'Ladies and gentlemen,' Mrs Thatcher said, 'the Secretary of State for Defence has just come over to give me some very good news and I think you'd like to have it at once.' With that, Nott, who looked thoroughly miserable, unfolded a piece of paper:

> The message we've got is that British troops landed on South Georgia this afternoon, shortly after 4 pm London time. They have now successfully taken control of Grytviken; at about 6 pm London time, the white flag was hoisted in Grytviken beside the Argentine flag. Shortly afterwards, the Argentine forces there surrendered to British forces. The Argentine forces offered only limited resistance to the British troops . . .
>
> So far, no British casualties have been reported. At present we have no information on the Argentine casualty position.
>
> The commander of the operation has sent the following message: 'Be pleased to inform Her Majesty that the White Ensign flies alongside the Union Jack in South Georgia. God save the Queen.'

At that, Mrs Thatcher allowed herself a small smile. Then, as they both turned towards the door, one of the reporters called out: 'What happens next?', and her eyes flashed. 'Just rejoice at that news', she said imperiously, 'and congratulate our forces and the Marines.'

'Are we going to declare war on Argentina, Mrs Thatcher?' the reporter asked. She was almost through the door, but there was time for one last word: 'Rejoice.' As the door closed, one of the reporters muttered: 'Hallelujah.'[56]

# 33

# The Day of Reckoning

*Never again ask the British, 'Where did it all go?' We never lost*
*it. Or, if we did, in six weeks we've tooth and clawed it all back.*
*Not our Empire. Not yet, the Falklands. But we've re-raised and*
*unfurled our spirit, self-respect, comradeship and guts.*

Jean Rook, *Daily Express*, 19 May 1982

*I have never known a more bleak, windswept and wet place in*
*my life . . . To be quite honest once we have given them a*
*hammering and put them back in their place the Argentines can*
*have the place. It really is fit for nothing.*

Sergeant Ian McKay to his parents,
8 June 1982, quoted in Jon Cooksey,
*Falklands Hero: Ian McKay – The Last*
*VC of the Twentieth Century* (2012)

Mrs Thatcher told the press to rejoice; and they did. 'Britain Seizes South
Georgia . . . Now Britain Is Striking Back', roared the *Express* on Monday
26 April, urging its readers to rally behind 'all-action Maggie'. 'VICTORY',
read the single-word headline in the *Sun*, beside a large photo of Admiral
Woodward: 'We Didn't Lose a Man – Heroes Win at the World's End'.
Thousands of miles away, even Woodward, talking unguardedly aboard
his flagship *Hermes*, allowed himself to be caught up in the excitement.
'South Georgia was the appetiser,' he said. 'Now this is the heavy punch
coming up behind. My battle group is properly formed and ready to strike.
This is the run-up to the big match which, in my view, should be a
walkover.'[1]

There were, of course, sceptical voices, who pointed out that Britain
was still a long way from landing on the Falklands, and that a short skir-
mish with an outgunned Argentine garrison was not exactly the relief of

Mafeking.* But they were drowned out by the cheers of relief and delight. Indeed, if there was one moment when public opinion definitively shifted in Mrs Thatcher's favour, it was the reconquest of South Georgia. A Gallup poll before the landing had put the Conservatives on 31½ per cent, Labour on 33 per cent and the Alliance on 35 per cent. But once the island was taken, the trickle back to the Tory banners became a flood. By 30 April, five days after the landing, the Tories had surged to 43 per cent, while the Alliance share had fallen to just 25 per cent. Almost overnight, the political atmosphere had been transformed.[2]

Even to experienced observers the new mood seemed barely credible. 'Somehow, after nearly four weeks of it, the crisis still has a dream-like quality. Is it really happening?' wondered Frank Johnson in *The Times*. As he noted, what made even an operation like the retaking of South Georgia so startling was that it was completely at odds with the national narrative since the 1950s. What had happened to post-imperial decline? What had happened to the 'Sick Man of Europe'? 'Those of us who are essentially creatures of the world as it has been post-Suez', Johnson wrote, 'had been assured all our adult lives that Britain was no longer capable of doing this sort of thing. All the best people said so.'

And what was more, the public were all for it. For although polls found that people were still anxious about the prospect of British casualties, attitudes were hardening. In a poll for *The Economist*, three out of four people said they approved of Mrs Thatcher's handling of the crisis, yet approval for Labour's approach, which emphasized negotiations rather than conflict, had fallen to just one in four. More people than ever wanted to see British troops land on the Falklands; more people thought regaining the islands was worth the loss of British lives; and more people than ever, four out of ten, thought Britain should bomb the Argentine mainland.[3]

In the Commons, the atmosphere had changed completely. When MPs debated the war on 29 April, the anxious, friendless Mrs Thatcher of a month earlier now struck observers as 'confident and relaxed', pledging to 'intensify the pressure on Argentina' until its forces withdrew. And although Michael Foot had slightly retreated from his formerly aggressive position, the mood was clearly with her. Even Jim Callaghan told the House that she 'spoke with restraint and put her case in a way that I found unexceptionable'. 'He is just an old Tory warmonger,' fumed Tony Benn, who made a passionate speech claiming that this 'Victorian imperialism' was merely 'a diversion from the issues of unemployment and the destruction of the

---

* No British lives were lost. The only Argentine killed was Petty Officer Felix Artuso, a prisoner shot by a Royal Marine who thought he was trying to sabotage the *Santa Fe*.

Welfare State'. In a sign of the new mood, however, Benn could barely finish a sentence without being interrupted by Conservative hecklers. 'The right hon. Gentleman is quite mad,' shouted John Peyton. 'On a point of order, Mr Speaker,' said Tony Marlow. 'Is it in order for the right hon. Gentleman to act as apologist for the Argentine junta?'[4]

For Mrs Thatcher, the danger of a parliamentary revolt had completely evaporated. What did still worry her, though, was the continuing ambiguity of the American position. With Alexander Haig's peace deal still on the table, she and her ministers were still very nervous that General Galtieri would change his mind and accept it, which would put her in a tricky position. But she need not have worried. On 29 April, in the latest in a series of calamitous diplomatic miscalculations, the junta formally rejected Haig's peace plan. 'Argentines have been told & told & told,' recorded an official after Haig briefed Reagan's chief advisers.

In a letter to Mrs Thatcher that evening, Reagan promised that he would 'leave no doubt that Her Majesty's Government worked with us in good faith and was left with no choice but to proceed with military action based on the right of self-defence'. He was as good as his word. In the next two days, Haig told the world that while the British had been 'reasonable and easy to deal with', the Argentines had been completely intransigent. To Britain's tabloids, this was almost as great a victory as the taking of South Georgia. 'YANKS A MILLION', declared the next day's *Sun*. Inside, a cartoon showed Reagan being presented with a celebratory T-shirt, with the words 'You've earned this, Mr President!' The legend on the T-shirt read, inevitably, 'STICK IT UP YOUR JUNTA'.[5]

For Mrs Thatcher, these were extraordinary times. For the first time since the beginning of her premiership, she was no longer fighting the tide of public opinion, but being carried along by it. She was no longer a beleaguered domestic reformer; she was an international war leader, her image plastered on the front pages of the world's papers for day after day. The evening after she got Reagan's message, she went to Bedford, where she had promised to mark the fiftieth anniversary of the Mid-Bedfordshire Conservative Association. The turnout was enormous, the mood almost euphoric. Speaking off the cuff, confident that she was among friends, Mrs Thatcher unburdened her soul. Her critics talked about peace, she said, but there was 'one thing in the world more important . . . It is liberty and justice and duty.'

As a schoolgirl, she said, she had written an essay about Kipling, and she had loved his poems ever since. From memory, she quoted the final lines of his ultra-patriotic poem 'The Heritage' (1905), which celebrates the sacrifices made by Britons of old to defend their native land:

> Dear-bought and clear, a thousand year,
> Our fathers' title runs.
> Make we likewise their sacrifice,
> Defrauding not our sons.

That spirit, she said, still burned in British hearts. And 'we are still, still, the third largest naval power in the world. Those things haven't changed.' There were cheers and applause at that. Britain, she went on, had always been a land of 'might, right and majesty ... We still have the right, and we're not half bad when it comes to might either.' The Falklands crisis had united 'people of all politics, of all backgrounds', who 'weren't going to have this. This country was a free country and we weren't going to have other people walking all over British citizens even though they were 8,000 miles away.' More thunderous applause. She ended by recalling Dean Acheson's endlessly quoted remark, not long after Suez, that Britain had lost an Empire and not yet found a role. 'I believe Britain has now found a role,' she said fervently. 'It is in upholding international law and teaching the nations of the world how to live.'[6]

As a glimpse into Mrs Thatcher's patriotic imagination, this was unsurpassed. By her own account, she was 'given a rousing reception – but *more* than that. It was a very emotional time – Britain was being tested and the odds of weather & distance were difficult to overcome.' For what she knew, but could not say, was that even as she was speaking, the RAF's Vulcan bombers were preparing to launch their first air attacks from Ascension Island against Argentine positions in the Falklands. The next morning, having breakfast with the veteran Tory MP Sir Stephen Hastings and his wife amid the grandeur of Milton Hall, she was called to the telephone. 'Everything all right, Prime Minister?' Lady Hastings asked when she returned. Mrs Thatcher said nothing, but inwardly she was euphoric.

Later, writing to thank her hosts, she explained that the call had been to tell her that 'the air-strip at Port Stanley *had* been bombed by the Vulcans successfully'.* In fact, the raid was largely symbolic, since the Vulcans never managed to knock out the airfield completely. As a feat of sheer courage and ingenuity, though, it was unsurpassed: with the Vulcans covering a staggering 6,000 nautical miles, they had been refuelled several times in mid-air, which in itself was an almost dementedly risky undertaking. And for Mrs Thatcher, living every moment as if she were on the front line, it was a moment to savour. 'During the last week,' she told Sir Stephen

---

* Actually only one Vulcan: the other had to turn back.

Hastings, 'there has been an activity and tenseness I never thought to experience – but this has happened throughout history and it falls to us to make *our* contribution to liberty under the law.' As thank-you letters go, it could hardly have been more Churchillian.[7]

When Mrs Thatcher left Milton Hall on Saturday morning she made immediately for Chequers, listening intently for news on the car radio. She arrived for lunch, had meetings with the Attorney General and the naval commander-in-chief, Admiral Sir John Fieldhouse, and worked late into the night. The next day, as members of the War Cabinet were arriving for their afternoon meeting, Admiral Fieldhouse and the Chief of the Defence Staff, Sir Terence Lewin, asked to speak to her urgently. They had received a request from Admiral Woodward in the South Atlantic, who was becoming increasingly agitated about the threat to his ships from a circling Argentine task force. A few days earlier, he had already contacted them about the Argentine aircraft carrier *Veinticinco de Mayo*, requesting permission to attack if necessary. Now Woodward had ordered the nuclear-powered submarine *Conqueror* to sink another Argentine vessel lurking to the south. The order was immediately countermanded, as Woodward knew it would be, but he wanted to force his superiors into making a quick decision. The ship in question, an ageing cruiser carrying more than a thousand men, was the *General Belgrano*.[8]

To understand the sinking of the *Belgrano*, context is everything. After the recovery of South Georgia the government had declared a 200-nautical-mile Total Exclusion Zone around the Falklands, in which any Argentine ships would be 'regarded as hostile and liable to be attacked by British forces'. Contrary to what is often thought, however, this did not mean that Argentine ships could *only* be attacked if they were caught inside the Total Exclusion Zone. Indeed, the Ministry of Defence always made it very clear that any Argentine ships, even outside the exclusion zone, might be seen as hostile and treated accordingly. What is true, though, is that Admiral Woodward's rules of engagement did not allow him actively to attack Argentine ships outside the exclusion zone, which is why he had asked permission to sink the *Veinticinco de Mayo*. That was also why he had been forced to ask about the *Belgrano*, which was deliberately loitering just outside it.[9]

There was never any doubt that the *Belgrano*, a cruiser supported by destroyers with Exocet anti-ship missiles, posed a severe danger to the Task Force. After all, it was hardly sailing around the South Atlantic on a pleasure cruise. It later transpired that the Argentine fleet commander, Rear Admiral Jorge Allara, had planned a kind of pincer movement, with the *Belgrano*'s formation acting as a decoy to the south while the *Veinticinco de Mayo*'s group moved in from the north. Indeed, in the early hours of that morning Britain had intercepted signals suggesting that the Argentines were preparing a massive surprise attack against Woodward's fleet. This was a moment of maximum danger. The Task Force only had two aircraft carriers: to lose even one, as was eminently possible in an Exocet attack, might mean losing the war. Woodward himself was in no doubt. Neither was Mrs Thatcher. Cloistered with her senior ministers and military chiefs, she made up her mind in just twenty minutes. 'You don't wait', she later remarked, 'for them to get at your ships.'[10]

The slight complication is that by the time Woodward got the go-ahead the *Belgrano* had changed course. The wind had changed, and the planned Argentine strike on the British fleet had been called off. In the small hours of Sunday morning the *Belgrano*'s captain, Hector Bonzo, had been ordered to head west towards the mainland to 'await further orders'. But this obviously did not mean the *Belgrano* had ceased to be a threat: the next day it might easily head back again. So when, later that afternoon, the *Conqueror* glimpsed its quarry, its captain, Chris Wreford-Brown, did not hesitate. For two hours he worked his way into position. Twice the *Belgrano* seemed to be in his sights; then he lost contact. But at almost 3.15, local time, Wreford-Brown moved into firing position and ordered his crew to action stations. At 3.57 the *Conqueror* opened fire. Moments later, two colossal explosions ripped through the *Belgrano*.[11]

Three hundred and twenty-three men lost their lives that afternoon. About a third of the dead were conscripts, some still in their teens. Probably 200 were killed immediately by the explosions and the fireball that blazed down the ship's companionways. The others drowned. More than 700 men survived, drifting in life rafts until they were rescued late the following day. In human terms it was a tragedy. In military terms it was a triumph. With the *Belgrano* gone, Admiral Anaya ordered his fleet to return to port. In one action, the *Conqueror* had completely neutralized the threat of the Argentine Navy.[12]

Later, the sinking of the *Belgrano* became the stuff of various deranged conspiracy theories. The most common holds that Mrs Thatcher ordered the attack in order to torpedo a peace plan being drafted by the Peruvian government. According to the Labour MP Tam Dalyell, Mrs Thatcher 'coldly and deliberately gave the orders to sink the *Belgrano*, in the knowledge that an honourable peace was on offer'. But this is nonsense. The request for authorization came from Admiral Woodward, who knew nothing about a Peruvian peace plan and was interested only in protecting his fleet. If Mrs Thatcher had turned him down and the *Belgrano* had gone on to sink his ships, her name would still be reviled today in every port and harbour in Britain. What is more, she and her ministers did not even see the Peruvian peace plan, which was basically a reincarnation of Haig's proposed deal, until *after* they had given the go-ahead. And as the next few days proved, far from undermining the case for peace, the sinking of the *Belgrano* put Mrs Thatcher under immense pressure to accept it – as indeed she did.[13]

The real test, surely, is what the Argentines themselves thought. And, by and large, most Argentine officers thought Britain was well within its rights to sink the *Belgrano*. One senior officer, speaking anonymously, told the journalist Jimmy Burns that it 'was sunk because I think it was a threat. And there's nothing more to it.' Similarly, Rear Admiral Allara told the historian Martin Middlebrook that his men knew perfectly well that the 'entire South Atlantic was an operational theatre for both sides. We, as professionals, said it was just too bad that we lost the *Belgrano*.' Even the ship's captain, Hector Bonzo, maintained to the end of his life that there had been nothing illegitimate about the British attack. And as late as 2005, the former head of the Argentine Navy, Enrique Molina Pico, complained to a Buenos Aires newspaper about an article that had called it a war crime. 'It was not a war crime,' he wrote, 'but a combat action . . . The *Belgrano* and the other ships were a threat and a danger to the British . . . It was not a violation of international law, it was an act of war.' No doubt Admiral Molina Pico, too, was part of Mrs Thatcher's conspiracy.[14]

Back home in Britain the sinking of the *Belgrano* left many people open-mouthed in shock. Watching television in the lounge of a grimy bed-and-breakfast in Deal, Kent, the travel writer Paul Theroux was struck by the embarrassed silence when the news broke. 'Those poor men,' one woman said softly. 'They won't stand a chance in that water.' From Romford, Carol Daniel told Mass Observation that the sinking was wrong, partly because of the terrible death toll but also because Britain would lose 'the world's support'. 'I feel like crying thinking of those young Argentine men killed on the ship,' wrote Mary Richards the next day. 'Not a lot of people want to talk about what is going on, it was not mentioned once in work this morning.'

Even the men in the Task Force had mixed feelings. Ken Lukowiak recalled that he and his fellow paratroopers cheered when the news was announced over the *Canberra* tannoy: 'It was party time. Open the bars. "That will teach the fuckers to mess with us, a thousand less of the bastards for us to worry about."' But another paratrooper, Vincent Bramley, remembered that the news 'wasn't greeted with total enthusiasm. In the bar that night most of us were solemn. We now knew that war was inevitable.'[15]

Kelvin MacKenzie's *Sun*, which produced perhaps the most infamous headline in British newspaper history, had no such qualms:

### GOTCHA

*Our lads sink gunboat and hole cruiser*

The Navy had the Argies on their knees last night after a devastating double punch.

WALLOP: They torpedoed the 14,000-ton Argentine cruiser General Belgrano and left it a useless wreck.

WALLOP: Task Force helicopters sank one Argentine patrol boat and severely damaged another.

At this stage, *Sun* executives insisted afterwards, there was no news of any casualties. Later, after a change of heart, MacKenzie hurriedly redesigned the page around the marginally less tasteless 'DID 1,200 ARGIES DROWN?' But by then it was too late, since thousands of copies of the first edition were heading for Scotland, Northern Ireland and northern England. Even *Sun* executives admitted it had been an awful mistake, with which their paper would be forever associated. And as Ken Lukowiak later recalled, the 'GOTCHA' headline was the only time he and his mates felt genuine animosity towards the newspapers. It would have been all right, they thought, for soldiers and sailors to say it. 'But a person 8,000 miles away from the war has no right to write such a thing because they are risking nothing.'[16]

Nemesis came swiftly. On the afternoon of 4 May, two days after the sinking of the *Belgrano*, the destroyer *Sheffield* spotted what seemed like an aircraft approaching very swiftly from the west. Barely two minutes later, the officer of the watch exclaimed: 'My God, it's a missile.' Five seconds after that, the Exocet smashed into the ship's side. Because the *Sheffield* was at a state of heightened readiness, the corridors were clear and casualties were relatively light: of the crew of 281 men, only twenty were killed and twenty-six injured. But with acrid black smoke pouring from the hull and fires burning uncontrollably, the captain had no choice but to abandon ship. It was the first time the Royal Navy had lost a ship to enemy action since the Second World War, and across the Task Force the news brought gasps of disbelieving horror. In the bar of the *Canberra*, Vincent Bramley wrote, there was an 'almost sickening silence. Everything stopped.' All that mattered now, he recalled, was revenge. 'We all thought the same. What's the fucking brass up to now? Why can't we go in now?'[17]

The news about the *Sheffield* did not reach London until later that evening. Some 12 million people were watching the BBC's nine o'clock news when

the picture cut to Whitehall, where the Ministry of Defence's press spokesman, Ian McDonald, began reading a short, funereal statement. The
*Sheffield* had been hit, he said, and its crew had abandoned ship. 'It is
feared that there have been a number of casualties, but we have no details
of them yet. Next of kin will be informed first as soon as details are
received.' And that was it. In television terms, it could hardly have been
starker or more dramatic, the effect heightened by McDonald's extraordinarily slow, gloomy delivery. Watching in another Kentish hotel, this
time with a group of middle-aged salesmen, Paul Theroux remembered
another sudden silence, as their anticipation turned to horror. 'That'll take
the wind out of our sails,' one said at last.[18]

Mrs Thatcher took the attack on the *Sheffield* very hard. After John
Nott had confirmed the news to the Commons, she went upstairs with
Willie Whitelaw to her room, and wept. On his way out, Whitelaw told
her bodyguard: 'Don't let anyone in. She wants to be alone.' Far from
glorying in slaughter, she was well aware of the costs of war. As she told
Britain's ambassador to the United Nations, Sir Anthony Parsons, it would
be 'the most awful waste of young life if we really have to go and take those
islands'. And despite her steely reputation, many of her closest colleagues
were struck by her emotional reaction to casualties. Ronnie Millar remembered her clenching her fists and struggling to keep back the tears, while
the Attorney General, Sir Michael Havers, saw her bow her head to hide
her emotions when bad news arrived during a War Cabinet meeting.[19]

Even in public, she made no secret of it. A few weeks after the war, in
an extraordinarily open interview with *Woman's Own*, she recalled her
feelings:

> You agonise within. Your job is to keep up morale, and the moment you go
> out of the door or see other people your job is to keep up the morale in spite
> of the tragedy. There's no-one else to look to except your own few who are
> intimately with you. There are not many people you can show your inner-
> most feelings to. You need your own family desperately. Yes, it's very lonely.

The interviewer asked if she sometimes reached the point of tears. 'Oh
yes,' she said, 'you can't help it. They just come. But you pull yourself
together very quickly. You have to.' She remembered being in the garden
at Chequers during the war, looking around and thinking how strange it
was that ordinary life went on:

> The flowers grow. The garden looks the same. Of course it does. The sun
> shines. You think, how can it shine? . . . but someone has had terrible news
> that day . . . Everything looks lovely, and yet somehow you feel you ought

not to enjoy it because there are terrible things happening, and in a way it heightens the poignancy. You think of what's happened to someone who will go out on that same morning and see those same beautiful things. And it won't still their sad hearts because they will never see spring the same way again.

Her predecessors might have had similar thoughts, but it is hard to imagine them sharing them with *Woman's Own*.[20]

Abroad, the tragedies of the *Belgrano* and the *Sheffield* stunned world opinion. To most outside observers, the conflict had always seemed a faintly comic affair. But now that hundreds of men were dead, nobody was laughing. In Washington, Paris and Bonn there were growing murmurs of disquiet. To the American diplomat Jim Rentschler, the two combatants looked like a 'couple of staggering streetfighters, spastically-swinging at each other while blinded into fury by the flow of their own blood'. And in the days that followed, the international pressure to settle became almost overwhelming. As Sir Anthony Parsons recalled, Britain looked like a 'horrid NATO country', brutally clobbering a 'poor Third World' country.[21]

The irony, therefore, is that far from torpedoing the Peruvian peace plan, the sinking of the *Belgrano* had put Britain in a position where it could not afford to reject it. By 4 May, even before news came through about the *Sheffield*, Mrs Thatcher's government was already conceding ground. For the first time, Francis Pym told the Americans that Britain would consider a ceasefire, though he still insisted on the islanders' right to self-determination. Within hours, however, President Reagan sent Mrs Thatcher a blunt message. Pym's proposal was not good enough. Instead, Reagan urged her to accept Peru's deal, which was essentially the latest version of Haig's old plan. Both sides would withdraw their forces, while for the next year the Falklands would be run by a 'contact group', consisting of the United States, West Germany, Brazil and Peru, until Britain and Argentina concluded a sovereignty agreement. Crucially, there was nothing about the self-determination of the islanders. Instead, the plan promised only to take into account their 'aspirations and interests', which was meaningless. Almost certainly it would end with Argentine sovereignty over the Falklands.[22]

The next morning, Mrs Thatcher called an emergency Cabinet to discuss the Peruvian plan. Some ministers thought the loss of the *Sheffield* meant Britain had no choice but to accept. Willie Whitelaw warned that if they turned it down they would 'lose' the Americans. Others were more hawkish. Norman Fowler believed Britain would be 'giving up a great deal, e.g. on self-determination', while Michael Heseltine said they would be 'abandoning the things we set out to achieve'. But the key voice belonged to Mrs Thatcher – who, perhaps surprisingly, said they had to take it. She recognized that it was a compromise, and that they were giving up the principle of self-determination. But she also knew she could not afford to alienate the Americans. If Britain rejected the plan, recorded the minutes, 'she would be severely criticised by international opinion, which was already moving against her'.* So they had to go for it.[23]

For Mrs Thatcher, this was an immensely difficult moment. In effect, she had persuaded her own colleagues to do the one thing she had always set her face against: compromise on the core principle of the islanders' self-determination. The explanation is no mystery: in the aftermath of the *Belgrano* and the *Sheffield*, the pressure from her allies left her no choice. But there is no doubt that she found it stressful, even traumatic. Immediately afterwards she scribbled an extraordinarily emotional plea to Reagan, imploring him to see that the Falkland Islanders, who had lived under 'liberty and a just law', were being betrayed. It seemed terrible, she wrote, that she was expected to abandon these 'fundamental democratic principles', something she would have thought 'impossible while you are at the White House'. Tellingly, though, she never sent it. Instead, she sent a much more anodyne version, suggesting only cosmetic tweaks to the deal. 'In a word, Maggie accepts,' scribbled one of Reagan's White House confidants.[24]

And then, with stunning predictability, the Argentines let her off the hook. Only hours later, General Galtieri told his Peruvian counterpart that the plan was no good. 'They believe that time is on their side, that Britain's diplomatic support will dwindle and that with the onset of winter in the South Atlantic and possibly the sinking of another ship, we will buckle,' recorded Sir Nicholas Henderson, Britain's ambassador in Washington. But of course there was another factor, too. For Mrs Thatcher, a deal might have caused difficulties with the *Sun*, but it would not necessarily have been terminal. For the junta, however, withdrawal from Stanley would have been impossible to sell to the Buenos Aires crowds. In effect, they were trapped by their own nationalist rhetoric. Mrs Thatcher could hardly have wished for more maladroit opponents.[25]

Far beyond the South Atlantic, the loss of the *Sheffield* had come as a terrible shock. The collective shudder, wrote Sir Henry Leach, was almost

---

* 'She' in this case means Britain, not Mrs Thatcher.

*" Nothing except a battle lost can be half so melancholy as a battle won."*
*(The Duke of Wellington)*

Nicholas Garland's cartoon for the *Daily Telegraph* (6 May 1982) is a masterpiece
of its kind, at once compassionate, learned and patriotic. He was one of the only
cartoonists to mourn the *Belgrano* and the *Sheffield* in the same image.

tangible. For many people, 'this was the first real comprehension that the
country was *at war*'. In the Commons, recalled Julian Critchley, it was a
'terrible night'. After South Georgia, many Tory MPs had been giddy with
patriotic excitement; now they realized that this great adventure 'might
end badly – not just for the Tory Party, but for the nation and for everyone
involved in the task force'. The next day's *Sun* replaced its political cartoon
with a blank space, explaining that it was 'now considered inappropriate',
while the *Mirror* redoubled its appeals for peace, insisting that 'the killing
has got to stop'. In the *New Statesman*, Peter Kellner proclaimed that the
war was 'turning into a worse fiasco than Suez'.[26]

In Newton Abbot, Mary Richards told Mass Observation that the loss
of the *Sheffield* had made her feel physically sick. It brought back memories
of the Second World War: the air raids, when she was so frightened she
could barely breathe; or her father's long absences working on the railways, when they were worried that the Luftwaffe had got him. And in
Darlington, Susan Gray recorded that she and her husband had heard the
news just after they had got back from their folk-dance display practice
and were having supper with her father. 'At the end of the bulletin', she
wrote, 'none of us knew what to say.' He father had been on a ship attacked

by Japanese warplanes during the Second World War. Now he sat in silence, aghast. But a few days later, her brother told her that among his workmates the reaction was unanimous: 'We go in now.'[27]

In some ways it is remarkable that the public reaction to the loss of the *Sheffield* was so muted. Almost certainly things would have been different if there had been television pictures. But from start to finish, the Ministry of Defence managed the media with ruthless efficiency. Initially, remembering the American ordeal in Vietnam, they had wanted to forbid any reporters from travelling at all, and had only reluctantly allowed a handful to leave with the Task Force. Those who did were so deeply embedded, digging their own trenches, cooking their own rations, helping to carry military equipment and generally mucking in, that they sometimes seemed more like fans with typewriters. Indeed, by far the best known of the Falklands correspondents, the *Evening Standard*'s Max Hastings, openly told his readers that he was there to 'report as sympathetically as possible what the British forces are doing'. Having watched 'British ships burn to the waterline while British sailors fought to escape with their lives', he had no intention of letting the side down. 'Like the humblest marine, like most of my colleagues,' he wrote, 'I am impelled through the day by a brutish determination to see the Argentines driven from the Falklands.'[28]

The real contrast with Vietnam was the absence of television. The American experience, when the networks had beamed raw, visceral footage into people's living rooms for night after night, had taught the Ministry of Defence a potent lesson. As a result, the Falklands was, in Robert Harris's words, the 'worst reported war since the Crimea'. Since it took three weeks for film to get back to London anyway, there were no television images at all for the first fifty-four days. That meant the BBC and ITN had to rely on stills, artists' impressions, stock footage and even toy models. The first television pictures of the stricken *Sheffield* were not broadcast until 26 May, three weeks after the attack. And as Harris points out, one thing, above all, was completely missing from the television version of the Falklands War. There were no dead bodies; indeed, there were not even any still photographs of bodies. Hundreds of people died, but there was no blood.

Instead, the defining television image of the war was the face of Ian McDonald, the Ministry of Defence's lugubrious press officer, who delivered his reports so slowly and expressionlessly that the press called him 'McDalek'. *Private Eye*'s editor, Richard Ingrams, thought McDonald sounded like an 'especially gloomy dean reading the second lesson at Evensong in a huge and draughty cathedral'. The *Mirror*'s Keith Waterhouse, more tartly, thought he was 'the only man in the world who speaks in Braille'. But clearly some people liked him, since he received several proposals of marriage. One woman became so obsessed that she used to wait for him outside the Ministry of Defence. In the end, McDonald had to complain to the building's security men.[29]

Yet public attitudes to the war were never straightforward. Paul Theroux thought that while British newspapers were astonishingly jingoistic, the British people were not. Whenever television bulletins brought fresh news, most people reacted with 'great bewilderment'. They did not hate the Argentines, but regarded them as 'pathetic, ramshackle and unlucky, with a conscript army of very young boys'. And some disagreed with the whole business. In a pub in Bognor, one Mrs Hykeham, with 'an old scarf yanked on her head and puffy, smoker's eyes', started a great row at the bar by declaring that it was 'stupid for Britain to be killing fourteen-year-old boys'. And in Newton Abbot, Mary Richards got into an argument in the newsagents with 'another working-class woman', who attacked her for being unpatriotic because she did not want to see fighting. This was typical, Mary lamented. Nobody in Newton Abbot wanted to discuss the war, because 'if a word against it is said you will be accused of being unpatriotic'.[30]

Even inside the Task Force there were at least some who considered the entire operation misguided. The best known was the 25-year-old naval lieutenant David Tinker, who served on HMS *Glamorgan* and was killed during the battle for Stanley. Afterwards, his father Hugh, an eminent historian, published his letters and poems, which were then reprinted in the *Sunday Times*. Lieutenant Tinker had never approved of the war, which he thought 'barbaric and unnecessary', and was appalled by the press coverage. 'The newspapers all seem to be screaming "War, War",' he wrote home from the *Glamorgan*:

> It must be the same on TV and radio. They give the impression that the whole of Britain is under attack ... From the way Maggie Thatcher has reacted one would imagine that the Russians were already in Bonn: not that we were fighting for a rocky island which Mr Nott had planned to keep completely undefended from mid-April.[31]

Yet Tinker was in a minority. Even after the loss of the *Sheffield*, polls consistently found that most people backed sending the Task Force, believed the islands should be returned to Britain and would support a land war if necessary. 'The Falklands look like bloody Bodmin Moor, but I suppose we have to do something,' one man told Theroux in a Cornish bed-and-breakfast. 'We have to do it,' said a man on the train at Bristol. 'Our land's been taken. The Argies have to be stopped. They can't get away with it.

That's how Hitler got started!' And in Blackpool, Theroux met Mr Gummer, fishing on the pier, who thought Britain ought to flatten Buenos Aires immediately. 'After all, the Argies had captured a British sheep station. Those bloody bean-eaters had to be taught a lesson.' Mr Gummer said he had been a socialist all his life, 'but he had a lot of respect for the prime minister. She had guts, and he agreed that it was a good idea to call the British troops "our boys".'[32]

'Our boys.' That was what Mrs Thatcher called them, while the *Sun* marketed itself as 'the newspaper that supports our boys'. But to some people, those words sounded mawkish, jingoistic and plain wrong. Early in the conflict, the BBC's Brian Hanrahan had made a passing reference to 'our forces', which worried his editors. The radio news editor put up a notice reminding people to say 'British forces' instead, in order to avoid giving the 'impression that we are taking verbal sides'. 'NOT OUR TROOPS', began another note circulated in the news department. 'We should try to avoid using "our" when we mean British. We are not Britain, we are the BBC.'[33]

Clearly this was a tricky issue. As BBC executives saw it, the audience expected them to report the truth as objectively as possible. On the other hand, many viewers *also* expected them to reflect the nation, especially when Britain was at war. The BBC could not be expected to take their cue from the *Sun*, but many people felt that the words 'British Broadcasting Corporation' ought to mean something. The most controversial example came on Sunday 2 May, the day the *Belgrano* was sunk, when *Newsnight*'s presenter Peter Snow was discussing rival claims about what was happening in the South Atlantic. 'We cannot demonstrate that the British have lied to us so far,' he said, 'but the Argentinians clearly have. Until the British are demonstrated either to be deceiving us or to be concealing losses from us, we can only tend to give a lot more credence to their version of events.'[34]

To some viewers this was disgraceful. The fact that Snow had endorsed the British version was beside the point; what incensed them was his language ('lied', 'deceiving'), as well as the implication that the BBC saw itself as the arbiter between two potentially disingenuous combatants. Snow's words were 'totally offensive and almost treasonable', declared one Tory MP. *Private Eye*'s Denis Thatcher tells his friend Bill that he had been warning of the 'closet Marxists at the BBC' for years: 'If ever there was a state owned industry ripe for privatisation,' he remarks, 'it is that nest of Pinkoes and Traitors at Shepherd's Bush.' And in a case of life imitating art, the real Denis thought much the same. Later, he told his daughter that he had been 'livid with rage' that the 'bloody BBC [could] question the integrity of the military', and had 'hated them since that day'.[35]

Then, two days later, came the loss of the *Sheffield*. And with feelings running higher than ever, the BBC found itself cast as the enemy within. Invited to condemn the national broadcaster on 6 May, Mrs Thatcher agreed that when presenters talked of 'the Argentines' and 'the British', it 'gives offence and causes great emotion among many people'. Among her backbenchers, Winston Churchill, Britain's leading professional grandson, accused the BBC of peddling 'live propaganda out of Buenos Aires', while Robert Adley called it 'General Galtieri's fifth column in Britain'. The next day, the 7th, the *Sun* charged into battle. 'There are traitors in our midst,' began a long editorial:

> Margaret Thatcher talked about them in the House of Commons yester-day . . . The Prime Minister did not speak of treason. The Sun does not hesitate to use the word . . .
>
> What is it but treason to talk on TV, as Peter Snow talked, questioning whether the Government's version of the sea battles was to be believed?
>
> We are caught up in a shooting war, not a game of croquet. There are no neutral referees above the sound of the guns. A British citizen is either on his country's side – or he is its enemy.

What most infuriated the *Sun*, though, was the *Mirror*, a paper with 'no faith in its country and no respect for her people'. 'What is it but treason', it asked, 'for this timorous, whining publication to plead day after day for appeasing the Argentine dictators because they do not believe the British people have the stomach for a fight, and are instead prepared to trade peace with honour?'[36]

The *Mirror* did not take that lying down. The next day, it hit back with an editorial of its own, written in a white-hot fury by Harold Wilson's former press secretary, Joe Haines. Entitled 'The Harlot of Fleet Street', it called the *Sun* a 'coarse and demented newspaper' and claimed that, in falling 'from the gutter to the sewer', the paper was 'to journalism what Dr Josef Goebbels was to truth'. One Labour MP, Haines noted, had called for it to be prosecuted for criminal libel, but he thought it had 'the perfect defence: Guilty but insane.' Instead, the best thing would be for every copy of the *Sun* to carry an official government announcement: 'Warning: reading this newspaper may damage your mind.'[37]

It was against this background that, two days later, the BBC's current affairs flagship *Panorama* broadcast a short film by the journalist Michael Cockerell. The film explored the views of people opposed to the war, focusing on the Conservative MPs David Crouch and Sir Anthony Meyer and the Labour MPs George Foulkes and Tam Dalyell. Foulkes said it had been 'crazy' to send the Task Force. Dalyell asked why Britain had sold arms to Argentina for so long. Meyer, who had been severely wounded in a tank battle in Normandy, almost broke down as he talked of the deaths of his friends in the Second World War. Then up popped a journalist, based in Buenos Aires, who explained why the Argentines believed the islands belonged to them. Finally, Cockerell told the audience that among the Chiefs of Staff there had been 'reservations from the start' about the wisdom of the campaign.[38]

Even before a headline had been printed, many people were outraged by the *Panorama* film. Mrs Thatcher, who saw it that evening before going across to the House of Commons, was furious, especially about the allegations of dissent among the defence chiefs. Hundreds of viewers rang immediately to complain, some waiting on the line for as long as an hour to register their fury. The next day, all the usual suspects swung into action. At the Commons, a group of Tory backbenchers put down a motion attacking the BBC's 'anti-British broadcasting'. The *Sun*, claiming to have been contacted by 'dozens of patriots' lambasting *Panorama*'s '"despicable" Argie bias', inveighed against the 'pacifists, appeasers and elitists' who were 'sabotaging Britain's war against the Argentines'. And the inevitable Mary Whitehouse claimed that the 'arrogant and disloyal' BBC had deliberately 'spread alarm and despondency', a 'treasonable offence in the last war'.[39]

At Prime Minister's Questions that afternoon, the Tory backbencher Sally Oppenheim invited Mrs Thatcher to condemn the 'odious, subversive, travesty in which Michael Cockerell and other BBC reporters dishonoured the right to freedom of speech in this country'. 'I share the deep concern that has been expressed on many sides,' agreed Mrs Thatcher, adding that she knew 'how strongly many people feel that the case for our country is not being put with sufficient vigour on certain – I do not say all – BBC programmes'. That ignited the fiercest Commons row of the war. First the Labour MP David Winnick demanded that the Tories stop their 'constant intimidation' of the BBC, to which Mrs Thatcher snapped that she expected the 'case for freedom to be put by those who are responsible for doing so'. Then the ultra-patriotic Sir Bernard Braine weighed in, insisting that the BBC's fondness for presenting 'enemy propaganda' was a 'sort of treachery'.

At that, some Tory MPs were so quick to jab their fingers at Tony Benn and Tam Dalyell that they practically fell out of their seats. Amid tumultuous booing, Dalyell leapt to his feet with a point of order. 'Some of us who have been in the 7th Armoured Division, who have been gunner operators on tanks and many of whose contemporaries in training were shot up with the King's Royal Irish Hussars in Korea,' he said angrily, 'take it ill to be accused

of treachery and dishonour.' More howling and roaring followed, and with
MPs leaping up, pointing fingers and waving their fists all over the House,
the Speaker brought the session to a hasty close. On the way out, a group of
Tory MPs cornered Sir Anthony Meyer, their faces suffused with rage. Later,
Meyer recalled getting a telegram. 'I remember you at Eton,' it said. 'You are
a disgrace to our school, your regiment and my country.'[40]

The furore over the *Panorama* film was one of the lowest points in the
BBC's history. In the Conservative papers, cartoonists competed to find
the most damning images. The *Sun* had a BBC newsreader reading 'ze
latest unbiased news' with a sombrero and Zapata moustache, while the
*Express* showed a baffled footballer being interviewed by a BBC reporter.
'Are you sure you want to interview me about the World Cup?' the footballer says. 'I'm on England's side.' But there was no competing with the
same paper's Michael Cummings, the unrivalled master of reactionary
invective. One cartoon imagined the BBC's 'Traitorama' panel during the
First World War, consisting of the Kaiser, Admiral Tirpitz and Generals
Hindenburg and Ludendorff, with the journalist Peter Taylor in the chair.
'If Britain admits German sovereignty over the "British" Isles,' says Ludendorff, 'we'll stop the war!'[41]

"Shocking! Someone's written a dirty word!"

Whatever you think of the sentiments, this typically ferocious Cummings
cartoon for the *Daily Express* (30 May 1982) is very skilfully done. 'Mr Bennos
Aires' is a ruthlessly clever touch.

The *Panorama* story had a bizarre coda. On 14 May the show's presenter, Robert Kee, wrote to *The Times* and said that he actually agreed with much of the criticism. A former bomber pilot and prisoner of war, now a reporter and historian, Kee was a man of famously prickly integrity. But he thought the film had been edited so that it seemed to endorse the 'minority view it was claiming to look at objectively'. His letter went down well with Mrs Thatcher, who thought it 'very courageous', but rather less well with his BBC bosses. Given the state of public opinion, they could not afford to sack him publicly. But when the *Panorama* staff said they would not work with him again, he agreed to resign.

The irony is that, despite all the sound and fury, the fracas had little impact on the BBC's public image. Indeed, polls found that seven out of ten thought the corporation had covered the Falklands perfectly responsibly. Even among Conservative voters, more than half thought the BBC had been unfairly criticized. And even Prince Charles, whose brother Andrew was serving with the Task Force as a helicopter pilot, went out of his way to show his support. The British media, Charles told an audience at the Open University on the day Kee's letter was published, were 'independent personalities', not 'servants of the state machine'. They 'might get it wrong from time to time', but 'my goodness, you certainly can't please everybody'. He would soon find that out for himself.[42]

While Mrs Thatcher's backbenchers raged against the enemy within, the Task Force sailed implacably towards the Falkland Islands. With every day, all-out war loomed ever larger. And for the Prime Minister herself, the mantle of a war leader was becoming increasingly comfortable. Still only 13 when the Second World War had broken out, she had always worshipped Sir Winston Churchill. Now she had been given the chance to play the great man herself, and she threw herself into the part with gusto.

On 14 May, while Prince Charles was talking at the Open University, Mrs Thatcher addressed the Scottish Conservatives. 'As so often in our island's story', she said, the British people had been called 'to stand for freedom and the rule of law . . . The task has fallen to us but our service is to all who cherish liberty.' For too long, Britain had been 'drifting on the ebbing tide of history, slipping inexorably backwards under pressures we somehow felt powerless to resist'. But now the nation had turned a corner. 'Perhaps we have surprised even ourselves. And I know we have surprised all those who didn't think we had it in us. But in these things Britain still leads the world. The love of liberty in the rule of law and in the character of our people.'

After the chairman had thanked her, she returned to the podium. There was one more thing, she said:

> What really thrilled me, having spent so much of my lifetime in Parliament, and talking about things like inflation, Social Security benefits, housing problems, environmental problems and so on, is that when it really came to the test, what's thrilled people wasn't those things, what thrilled people was once again being able to serve a great cause, the cause of liberty.

The British people, she said, did not fight 'because they want more wages . . . or anything like that.' They fought for a cause greater than themselves, because 'we are a free country'. Some commentators were horrified, not least by that word 'thrilled'. Her audience loved every syllable.[43]

Yet despite her resounding words, Mrs Thatcher had still not closed the door on a deal. On Sunday 16th, the War Cabinet agreed a final offer to Buenos Aires. As Sir Nicholas Henderson recalled, the Prime Minister presented herself as the sworn enemy of compromise, constantly attacking the others 'for being wet, ready to sell out, unsupportive of British interests, etc.' Yet she actually approved far more concessions than her Scottish listeners might have expected. Under the British plan, both sides would withdraw their forces and allow the United Nations to administer the Falklands, in consultation with the locals, while the two sides discussed sovereignty. Some of her more ferocious backbenchers would undoubtedly have seen this as a sell-out, and Sir Anthony Parsons took her aside to check that she understood how much she was giving away. Even the United Nations Secretary General, the Peruvian Javier Pérez du Cuéllar, thought Britain's proposal offered Argentina 'a fair chance of gaining sovereignty in the Falklands'. The deadline for acceptance was 5 p.m. on 19 May. Needless to say, Mrs Thatcher did not expect the Argentines to say yes.[44]

In the meantime, Northwood's planners had been finalizing the details of the British assault. Given the strong Argentine defences around Stanley, the Chiefs of Staff had selected a site some sixty miles away: the sheltered bay of San Carlos Water, on the far side of East Falkland, which offered some semblance of protection against long-range Argentine air and naval attack. The plan called for 3 Commando Brigade to land on or just after 20 May and establish a bridgehead. Ten days later, they would be joined by reinforcements in the shape of 5 Infantry Brigade; then, moving across rough terrain, they would head for Stanley. It was not a perfect plan by any means, but it was the best available. On 12 May, Admiral Fieldhouse issued his operational order to the Task Force, and two days later the Chiefs of Staff briefed the War Cabinet.

The moment of decision came on the morning of 18 May. One by one,

Mrs Thatcher invited her military chiefs to give their thoughts. The Chief of the Air Staff, Sir Michael Beetham, was worried about the lack of air superiority, but was 'confident that the landing forces would achieve success'. Sir Henry Leach, bullish as ever, said they should go for it. 'If Britain hung back now,' he said, 'the erosion of her national standing, both in general and as regards negotiations in the present crisis, would be profound and long-term.' Finally came the Chief of the General Staff, Sir Edwin Bramall. He too was worried about the lack of air superiority, but there was 'now no option but to mount a landing'. If it went well, he added, 'Britain's status in the world, the respect shown to her and the strength and credibility of her deterrent strategy would be that much more enhanced for years to come'. After all that, there was really no doubt what the War Cabinet would do. The troops, they agreed, should land and repossess the islands as quickly as possible. The date was set for the night of 20–21 May.[45]

On the night of the 18th, Mrs Thatcher worked until two o'clock and slept for barely four hours before rising to read the latest reports. In the South Atlantic, the Task Force was making its final preparations. From New York, Sir Anthony Parsons reported that the Argentines had rejected Britain's final offer. The day went by in a series of oddly random engagements: an appearance on the *Jimmy Young Show*, a drink with Lord Carrington, lunch with Robert Mugabe. At 5 p.m. the British deadline expired. The next morning, the 20th, Mrs Thatcher told her full Cabinet that the troops were preparing to land. 'All agreed,' she said at the end, according to the Cabinet Secretary's notes. 'This is the most difficult time we have ever faced. Our job to stick together, and keep up morale. Total confidence in Task Force and every good wish.'[46]

That afternoon, Mrs Thatcher reported to the Commons. Although she said nothing about the plan to land that night, she was in sombre mood, and there was no mistaking the tension in the air. 'Difficult days lie ahead,' she said, 'but Britain will face them in the conviction that our cause is just and in the knowledge that we have been doing everything reasonable to secure a negotiated settlement.' Britain, she added, 'has a responsibility towards the islanders to restore their democratic way of life. She has a duty to the whole world to show that aggression will not succeed and to uphold the cause of freedom.'

This was the sort of stuff the Commons liked. For his part, Michael Foot thought she should keep negotiating, but did not oppose the use of force and hoped any action would be as 'swift and successful as possible'. For the SDP, David Owen wished her 'every success. We have given her unstinting support and will continue to do so in the pursuit of honourable objectives.' The speaker who caught the attention of the next day's papers, though, was their old boss, Jim Callaghan, who paid a generous tribute to Mrs Thatcher for her handling of the crisis. 'With regard to military action,' he said – and then paused, looked at the floor and said quietly: 'I think all that we can do at this stage is to wish our men God-speed.'[47]

There was one very bad omen for Mrs Thatcher. Somehow, in those hectic, anxious days, a press release found its way into her red box from a 'consultant astrologer' called Peter J. Clark. He had studied the signs and thought invading the Falklands was not a good idea at all. The Prime Minister's chart, he wrote, indicated that she could not expect military victory and was facing 'aggressive hostility and disarray with her colleagues'. As for her commanders, Admiral Woodward's chart was 'inauspicious for an invasion' while Admiral Fieldhouse's chart was very 'discouraging from now until at least after August'. But General Galtieri's chart was pretty good, at least until September.

Any other Prime Minister would have thrown it aside unread. Mrs Thatcher read it, underlined the key words and corrected the grammar.[48]

For the troops waiting in the South Atlantic, all that mattered now was to get on with it. Ever since the loss of the *Sheffield*, the mood had become increasingly tense, the conversations quieter, the tone more thoughtful. They knew they were very close, yet still Vincent Bramley could not 'quite believe the war was going to happen'. On 17 May his platoon commander called his NCOs together. 'Gents,' he said, 'it's the green light.' When Bramley told his men, they were wide-eyed with excitement. 'This is going to be one hell of a fucking exercise,' he said drily. Morale seemed high, but the 'laughing and joking', he thought, was 'partly to cover the fear. Not that anyone thought that death was going to hit him. That was for the guy you were talking to.'[49]

On 18 May the fleet sailed into the Total Exclusion Zone. The next day, the paratroopers made their final preparations before their transfer from the *Canberra* to the assault ship *Intrepid*. Then they sat in their cabin, waiting. Nobody said anything. The call came, and they joined the long line, shuffling down the grey steel corridor, the lights dimmed red. The door opened, and one by one they jumped into the little landing craft, bobbing in the freezing waters. Then, shivering, half soaked and carrying at least sixty pounds of gear each, they climbed on board *Intrepid*, already crowded with men and kit. Once again they waited. Silently, through thick white fog, the fleet sailed on towards San Carlos. At last, at midnight on 20–21 May, local time, they were in position. In Bramley's cramped cabin, the intercom crackled into life. This was it.

When Bramley's section arrived in the *Intrepid*'s galley, it was already crowded with men, packed together like football fans at a turnstile. The tension, he remembered, was almost unbearable:

> I looked around me at the hundreds of cammed faces, all with big wide eyes. Each face told its own story. Each soldier has his own thoughts of the coming battle as the lads quietly sat about waiting. Always waiting – the story of all soldiers. Myself, I couldn't help but think that it was still a joke and that we wouldn't be going ashore. My stomach was in knots and the nausea was hard to control. The nervousness running through me was the worst of all. Waiting, waiting for that fucking green light . . .

The green light came, and they squeezed into the *Intrepid*'s landing craft. After so long below decks, the first thing that hit them was the shock of the sea air. They moved towards land, the motor throbbing, bursts of tracer fire lighting up the darkness overhead. 'Sweat ran down through my hair,' Bramley wrote. 'My mouth was dry with nerves. I was longing to land now, even if we had to fight.'

The engine slowed, the ramp lowered and the paratroopers stumbled out on to a stony beach, hobbling under the weight of their kit. The Argentines were nowhere to be seen, though they soon heard planes overhead. Their officers screamed at them to keep moving, a 'bloody hard uphill slog'. About three-quarters of an hour later, streaming with sweat, they reached their position, a little valley known as Windy Gap. It looked even grimmer, Bramley thought, than 'Dartmoor and the Brecon Beacons put together'. They set their guns and started digging trenches. Then, with impeccable timing, it started raining. 'It was like having a bucket tipped over us,' he wrote. 'We sat there, on a bloody hill thirteen thousand kilometres from home, in our wet-proofs in the rain, wind and sleet, with an air attack in progress and our trench filling with water. What a lovely war. But we were still laughing.'[50]

In the tiny village of San Carlos, home to some thirty farm workers and shepherds, Royal Marine commandos were moving from house to house. In the farmhouse, the settlement manager opened the door warily, then exclaimed: 'You're British! We've been expecting you these last two or three nights.' 'We were getting fed up of waiting for you!' put in his wife. 'Every morning we've been saying, "Perhaps it'll be today!"' It was, in its way, the most British reaction imaginable. A few doors down, a bleary-eyed housewife offered Max Hastings a cup of coffee. 'We knew somebody would turn up sooner or later,' she said, 'but we didn't expect it to be here.' Not far away, an elderly farm worker was offering soup in a Silver Jubilee mug to the *Sunday Times*'s John Shirley. 'You a reporter?' the man asked. 'Tell me, did Leeds United get relegated?'[51]

In London, Mrs Thatcher waited anxiously for news. As luck would
have it, she had a long-arranged commitment in her Finchley constituency,
opening a new warehouse for a company that specialized in – of all
things – international removals. Her constituency agent recalled that she
arrived dressed in black, with a 'look of great depression'. With more than
a thousand people there, including a Guards band, she was expected to
make a speech. 'What could I say', she wrote, 'but that 8,000 miles was
really only a heart-beat away. And it *was* for *all* our people; not only those
whose family were in the Task Force. One felt the whole audience with
us. It was a matter of pride, respect, conviction and *being free* that meant
we must restore the Falklands.' Somehow she forced herself to inspect
everything, 'rode on a fork-lift truck, had lunch in an enormous warehouse
and then fled to the office to see if there was any news. *Not yet.*'

Late that afternoon, the Ministry of Defence contacted Number 10.
All major infantry units had been landed safely, and the fleet were beginning to move artillery and heavy equipment ashore. In Mrs Thatcher's
constituency office, where she was resting before her next engagement,
the call came through. When she put the phone down, her agent remembered, 'she stayed motionless for a full thirty seconds. Then her whole
body came alive again with a huge jerk, as she said: "That's it. That's what
I've been waiting for all day. Let's go!"'[52]

By the time she arrived for her next appointment, a reception at a local
school, the news had broken on television. The emotion, she recalled, 'was
*overwhelming*. The Union Jack was flying in San Carlos Bay. We had
returned to the Falklands. My heart was full but desperately anxious
about casualties.' In fact, the first few hours of the landing had been a
stunning success, without the loss of a single man. Once daylight came,
however, it was a different matter. With Argentine warplanes screaming
low over San Carlos Water ('Bomb Alley'), two ships, *Argonaut* and
*Antrim*, had been hit, while *Ardent* had been crippled with the loss of
twenty-two lives. Even so, the general feeling in London was a mixture
of optimism and relief. That night, Nott issued a public statement, confirming that 'British forces have now established a firm bridgehead on the
Falkland Islands'. And when Mrs Thatcher returned to Downing Street,
a small crowd had gathered, cheering and singing. 'These are nervous
days,' she told the cameras, 'but we have marvellous fighting forces:
everyone is behind them. We are fighting a just cause, and we wish them
Godspeed.'[53]

For Admiral Woodward, mourning his losses but immensely proud of
his fleet, it had been 'one of the most successful landings in military history'. 'We had got our forces ashore,' he proudly recalled. 'Casualties to

the land forces: Zero.' And like Mrs Thatcher, Woodward thought back
to the glories of Britain's past. 'What difference', he wondered, 'between
*Ardent*, crippled and burning, still fighting and Sir Richard Grenville's
*Revenge* all those centuries ago. Or between this and that October day
off Cape Trafalgar as Nelson and Hardy walked the quarter deck of the
*Victory* shortly after noon.' This was why he and his comrades had joined
the Navy. Not 'to attend courses and to make yourself a comfortable
career', but 'for this day, the day of reckoning'.[54]

'THE BRITISH ARE BACK!' roared the *Daily Mail* the next morning,
beside a picture of Marines raising the flag at San Carlos. The *Sun*'s front
page, which carried the gigantic headline 'WAR', was a shriek of aggression: '*Huge Battles Are Raging for the Falklands* – Troops storm the
islands – 5 Navy ships damaged – 14 Argy planes downed – 21 of our
boys are dead.' By this stage, however, the mood in San Carlos Bay was
darkening. During the next three days, the Argentines kept up their air
bombardment, putting the ships' crews and Sea Harrier pilots under enormous strain. Then, on Tuesday 25 May, came the climax. It was Argentina's
National Day, and the junta's pilots were naturally keen to give the crowds
in Buenos Aires something to cheer.

At two that afternoon, four Argentine planes swooped towards San
Carlos Water. Moments later, three bombs tore into the side of HMS
*Coventry*, like the *Sheffield* a Type 42 destroyer. 'There was a vicious
shockwave, a blinding flash and searing heat,' wrote the ship's captain,
David Hart Dyke. 'I felt as though I had been caught in a doorway and a
heavy door had been slammed against me.' When he came to, the air was
full of smoke, his radar screen was in fragments and his headset and
microphone had 'disappeared – burnt off me without a trace'. All Hart
Dyke could see were 'people on fire, like candles burning'. Somehow he
hauled himself up a ladder to the bridge, where he fell to his knees to get
some air. With the power gone and the *Coventry* listing badly, his men
were already abandoning ship. To their captain, still in shock, it was like
'watching a film'. When he was sure they were all safe, he climbed down
a ladder and jumped into the freezing water, and a petty officer dragged
him into a lifeboat. It was the same man, Hart Dyke noticed, who had
given him a card with a prayer of St Joseph on the journey south, promising that it would bring him luck. 'There you are, sir,' the petty officer said,
smiling broadly: 'it works.'[55]

Nineteen men were killed on the *Coventry*, all but two of them instantly.
That evening, Mrs Thatcher was working in her Commons office when
Nott, perfectly cast as the bringer of gloom, materialised with the news.
With casualty figures uncertain, they decided not to release the name of

the ship, which, as Mrs Thatcher later admitted, meant that '*every* navy family was anxious'. But there was worse to come. When she got back to Number 10, the duty clerk told her that the 13,000-ton merchant ship *Atlantic Conveyor*, carrying nine precious helicopters and tents for the entire army, had been hit too, with the loss of twelve lives. Later, Denis Thatcher walked into the bedroom at Number 10 to find his wife in tears. 'That's what war's like, love,' he said consolingly. 'I've been in one. I know.' But for Mrs Thatcher this was the 'worst night of all'. 'How many more tragedies could there be?' she asked herself. 'How many losses could we suffer . . . We learned the deep sorrows of war, but we had to go on to complete the task.'[56]

To the British commanders the events of 25 May came as a grievous blow. If they had another 'bloody day' like it, Woodward thought, they might lose the battle. 'We can't go on like this,' Nott muttered to Sir Henry Leach, 'losing all these ships.' Yet the Argentines had taken losses too, with ten Skyhawk and nine Dagger jets having been shot down since the landings began. And above all, despite the black smoke billowing over San Carlos Water, they had failed to stop the Task Force from unloading its equipment. The Argentines had suffered a fair amount of bad luck, with many of their bombs failing to go off because they were not fused properly. But they were facing a better-trained and more skilful adversary, not least in the Sea Harrier pilots, flying at the limit of their endurance to protect the fleet. And in the next two days, the momentum tilted back in Britain's favour. By the evening of the 27th the last ship, *Sir Galahad*, had almost finished unloading. More than 3,000 troops were safely ashore. The Battle of San Carlos was over. In the early hours of the following morning, in the tiny hamlet of Goose Green, the first land battle began.[57]

For the young British soldiers on the islands, the first few days ashore were just as cold, wet and miserable as everybody had predicted. Their surroundings, wrote the Marine commander Nick Vaux, seemed like some 'biblical wilderness', a bleak desolation of waterlogged moorlands, 'steep, slippery slopes', rugged crags and 'jumbled boulders'. Never had his men's kit felt heavier, as they trudged for hour after hour across the broken terrain. Somehow they kept going, splashing through rivers, staggering up hills, ignoring the pain in their aching shoulders and bleeding blisters. Before long, many were suffering from trench foot, their socks sodden, their toes blue and aching. Looking around at his fellow paratroopers, Vincent Bramley thought they resembled a 'rag-and-bone army', their faces thin and drawn, their boots battered and leaking, their 'uniforms matted and soaked'. Yet even as the sleet turned to snow and his boots filled with water, Bramley kept going. What drove him was not 'Queen and Country', nor even 'home and family'. It was his dread of 'letting the side down', of disappointing the 'lads you fight and work for . . . That fear kept me walking.'[58]

With the troops ashore, the question was what to do next. Although most of the Argentine forces were concentrated around Stanley, a smaller contingent, about a thousand strong, had taken up position in the narrow isthmus connecting the two halves of East Falkland, around the tiny settlements of Darwin and Goose Green. This smaller Argentine force posed no serious threat to the British beachhead, thirteen miles away, and the acting land commander, Brigadier Julian Thompson, planned simply to mask and isolate it.* His instinct was to move slowly and deliberately, husbanding his forces and waiting for reinforcements, rather than throwing lives away in the reckless pursuit of a quick victory. As he well knew, the Task Force had only 'one shot', and he did not propose to waste it.

On the ground, almost all of Thompson's senior officers shared his caution. But at Northwood his reluctance to leave the beachhead fuelled a growing sense of impatience. Given the international pressure for a ceasefire, it was imperative for the British to gain the upper hand and move against Stanley as quickly as possible. And, as Thompson later remarked, 'after the hammering the navy had been taking, there was a need for a victory, a tangible sign that we could win'. On the morning of 26 May he received fresh orders from Northwood. 'More action was required all round', while Admiral Fieldhouse wanted to see the Union Jack 'flying in Darwin'. And if Thompson refused to move against Darwin and Goose Green, the chiefs would find a new commander who would.[59]

The battle for Goose Green, the most celebrated of all of the Falklands land battles, was chaotic from start to finish. Thompson envisaged the attack as a raid. But 2 Para's commanding officer, Colonel 'H' Jones, had been renowned since his Eton days as a man of unusual energy, charisma, arrogance and recklessness. Thirsting for battle ever since the crisis had started, Jones saw Goose Green as his chance of glory. By the time he briefed his company commanders, at dusk on 27 May, what Thompson had described as a raid had turned into an all-out attack. And by the small hours of the following morning, Jones's paratroopers, almost 700 strong,

---

* Thompson was in charge because his superior officer, Major-General Jeremy Moore, was still sailing south on the *QE2* with 5 Infantry Brigade. Moore did not take over command of land operations until 30 May, when the Battle of Goose Green was over.

were in position at the top of the isthmus.* Most felt a thrill of excitement; as one recalled, he was 'electrified' by the sound of his mates fixing their bayonets, 'because I'm a soldier, and the thought of the fight to come and the idea of my mates out there preparing to do battle gave me a warrior's rush'.

At about two in the morning, the fighting started. To Jones's immense frustration, the Argentines proved tougher adversaries than he had hoped, and his men made slow, spasmodic progress down the isthmus, often being pinned down by devastating enemy fire. By dawn they were still a long way from Goose Green, and their momentum seemed to have ground to a halt. At about 8.30, Jones decided it was time for a dramatic gesture. 'Come on A Company,' he shouted, 'get your skirts off.' Then, armed with his sub-machine gun, he charged up the hill towards the nearest Argentine trench. To his men, and to the newspapers afterwards, it seemed like something from military legend, the kind of thing they might have expected from Alexander the Great or Henry V. But Jones had clearly not realized that he was running directly into the line of fire of another Argentine position, up the hill and slightly behind him. He was hit only a few feet from the enemy trench. When his men caught up with him, he was already slipping into unconsciousness. He died soon afterwards.

In reality, there had been no need for Jones to sacrifice himself. Although the British advance had stalled, it had not been reversed, and as the day wore on his men fought their way, inch by inch, along the isthmus. By nightfall they had the upper hand, and the following morning, after a battle that had cost eighteen British and about fifty Argentine lives, the Argentine commander surrendered. The British flag fluttered over Darwin; Northwood had its victory. 'You have kindled a flame in land operations', cabled a triumphant Admiral Fieldhouse, 'which will lead to the raising of the Union Jack in Port Stanley.'[60]

To the tabloids, Goose Green was a triumph to set beside Agincourt, Waterloo and El Alamein. 'WE'RE WINNING!' exulted the *Mirror*. 'VICTORY', screamed the *Sun*. The hero of the hour, naturally, was Jones, who was posthumously awarded the Victoria Cross. 'MY HERO', read the *Sun*'s headline on Monday 31st, above a picture of his widow Sara and a suitably stirring quotation: 'If he had to die, then I believe he would have liked to have died the way he did.' For the press, Jones was the first authentic fallen British hero since the Second World War, a throwback to a vanished

---

* To 2 Para's fury, the BBC World Service effectively gave away their position, telling listeners that they had moved towards Darwin before they had actually done so. The soldiers naturally felt that the BBC had betrayed them to the Argentines, but it probably made no difference to the course of the fighting.

age of courage and gallantry, a symbol of the nation's rekindled thirst for victory. The next day, remembering the sense of 'complete and utter humiliation' at the start of the war, Alan Clark could barely believe the transformation. 'Now not only have we redeemed everything that was at stake then,' he wrote, but Britain had 'advanced immeasurably in self-esteem and in the status accorded to us by the whole world'.[61]

Not everybody gloried in the advance of the British forces. Abroad, many people were horrified by the bloodshed, and Pope John Paul II, who was due to visit Britain at the end of May, called publicly for a ceasefire. Even President Reagan had not quite abandoned his vision of acting as a peacemaker. Two days after the Argentine surrender at Goose Green, he rang Mrs Thatcher to suggest a new peace initiative. From his very first words, he clearly knew he was on a sticky wicket, and Mrs Thatcher wasted little time in cutting him off. 'I didn't lose some of my finest ships and my finest lives,' she said icily, 'to leave quietly under a cease fire without the Argentines withdrawing.' There was no question 'of us quietly moving out of the island . . . I can't lose the lives and blood of our soldiers to hand the islands over . . . Just supposing Alaska was invaded, it's a long way away from you [and] you've put all your people up there to retake it . . . and you've lost a lot of men and your ships. You wouldn't do it.' 'Margaret, I have to say that I don't quite think Alaska is a similar situation,' Reagan said mildly. 'More or less so,' she snapped. As the exchange went on, Reagan's contributions gradually dwindled to 'Margaret, I –' and 'Yes, well –', while hers got longer and longer. 'Well, Margaret, I know that I've intruded,' Reagan said at last. 'You haven't intruded at all,' she said, sweetly but firmly. 'You know how you'd feel if you went through the same conflict.'[62]

In Stanley, the Argentines sat and waited, the tension rising as their adversaries trudged grimly towards them. 'The hour of the final battle has arrived,' Brigadier-General Menéndez told his troops on 1 June:

> The adversary is getting ready to attack Puerto Argentino, with the rash and hateful intention of conquering the capital of the Malvinas . . . Not only must we beat them, we must do it in such a way that their defeat is so crushing that they will never again have the impertinence to invade our land. TO ARMS! TO BATTLE!

Yet behind the rhetoric, Menéndez had already warned General Galtieri that without a massive air attack or a new landing behind British lines, he was doomed to defeat. No help came. He and his men were alone. Morale was abysmal. Most of Menéndez's troops were young conscripts from the barrios of Buenos Aires, treated with casual brutality by their own officers. Cold, exhausted, poorly trained and desperate to get home, many had no idea why they were there. 'I'd reached a point', one recalled, 'when I felt I was just falling apart from so much waiting and I felt that the sooner the British came the better because that way there would be some kind of definition.' Indeed, some even doubted the justice of their own cause. 'What, if anything, of all this really belongs to us Argentines?' one conscript wondered. 'The "natives" of these islands have shown us with their silence that we are the intruders.'[63]

In the meantime, the killing went on. On the afternoon of 8 June, the Welsh Guards were waiting to disembark from their transports at Bluff Cove, seventeen miles south-west of Stanley, when four Argentine planes screamed out of the sky. There was just time for someone to shout, 'Get down!' before the bombs landed. Two ships, the *Sir Tristram* and the *Galahad*, were badly hit. On the *Galahad*, which had been carrying white phosphorus mortar bombs, a fireball ripped through the centre of the ship, the heat devouring men where they stood. One young Welsh Guardsman, Simon Weston, remembered that there was no bang, just a 'ball of flame which came out of the wall at us'. With his body ablaze and his throat choked with smoke, Weston scrambled up the ladder, screaming with 'shock and agony', and collapsed on deck. 'Nobody can tell you how blood smells, or what it feels like to be engulfed in the thick pall of burning flesh,' he said later. 'You can't describe the sound of thousands of men all screaming at once . . . It was the colours that stayed with me the longest. The deep, swirling reds and oranges and yellows of the fire.'[64]

Some forty-nine men were killed in the Bluff Cove air attacks, including four Chinese crewmen, while a further forty were severely burned – many of them, like Weston, beyond recognition. For the paratroopers pulling the charred, blackened survivors ashore, it was like something from a nightmare. 'In the boat,' wrote Ken Lukowiak more than a decade later, 'there were men whose expressions and cries I can still see and hear today.' In London, Mrs Thatcher sat in silence for two minutes, tears running down her face. 'General Moore was grief-stricken,' she wrote. 'We all felt – *how* many more.' But she reluctantly agreed to her commanders' request not to release the casualty figures, in order to trick the Argentines into thinking that the Task Force had lost dozens, perhaps hundreds more men than it had. As a result, Ministry of Defence switchboards were jammed by soldiers' families desperately seeking information. In the press, some estimates suggested that hundreds might have been killed.[65]

In reality, General Moore was poised to tighten his grip. After their gruelling yomp over the Falklands moorlands, his troops were at last in position outside Stanley. For two days the British fleet pounded the

Argentine forces on the high ground to the west of the capital. Then, on the morning of 11 June, Moore's commanders briefed their men for the coming battle. The plan was for 3 Para, 42 Commando and 45 Commando to move overnight against the Argentine positions on Mount Longdon, Mount Harriet and Two Sisters, and press on to the next ridges when they had secured their objectives. 'I know that none of us expects a walkover,' read Moore's final message to his troops. 'There will be hard fighting but the reputations of all units in this formation are that they fight hard and they win ... May God go with you.'[66]

Moore's men went into battle late on the evening of 11 June. As with all night fighting, it was an experience of utter chaos and horror. The close-quarters combat was often exceptionally savage, as paratroopers and Marines fought their way from trench to trench with bayonets and grenades. Later, Vincent Bramley, who was in the thick of the action, remembered his uncontrollable nerves, his shaking knees and churning stomach, the 'deadly silence' as he and his mates climbed into position, the 'anguished moaning and crying' of the wounded in the darkness, the shock and terror as the shells rained down. He remembered the sight of shaking, sobbing Argentine prisoners; a dying man moaning in Spanish for his mother; a wounded Argentine who burst into tears when Bramley lowered his rifle and tried to help him; a fellow Para who lay dead in a broken heap, clutching a teddy bear given him by his sister before they left England. 'What a fucking game this is,' one of his mates said, as he tucked the bear into their fallen comrade's smock.

By now Bramley knew there was 'no glory in killing'. 'I've done all the training possible for this,' an army medic muttered grimly, 'and it still hasn't been what I thought.' Like the SAS and the Marines, the Paras had always seen themselves as harder than other soldiers, let alone the general public. Yet nothing had prepared them for the sight of a man literally cradling his intestines in his lap, a man with one leg hanging by a thread. Nor had anything prepared them for the shock as their friends fell dead beside them. Like all young men, they had thought themselves invincible. 'Only yesterday we had been celebrating Tim's 19th birthday and mine the week before,' one paratrooper reflected, 'and I thought, "What the fuck am I doing here? Tim's dead, I'm 8,000 miles from home, I'm being shot at and my mate is lying dead next to me."'[67]

Afterwards, when veterans published their accounts of the war, many readers were shocked by their casual brutality. Ken Lukowiak remembered an incident when, faced with a horrifically injured prisoner whose brains were literally falling out of his head, a sergeant told the others to stand back and fired a machine-gun burst into the Argentine's body. Bramley told a similar story about another sergeant shooting an injured Argentine, on the grounds that he might be rigged to a booby trap. He claimed that a paratrooper had bayoneted a wounded prisoner with the words 'Shut up, shut up, you cunt!' and that other paratroopers had shot their captives and thrown them over a cliff. Both writers confirmed that paratroopers had taken souvenirs from their dead opponents. One of Bramley's comrades picked up a skull with the brain still inside ('This is the ultimate souvenir. My missus will love this'), while others were reported to have cut off their dead adversaries' ears. At Goose Green, Lukowiak saw men posing for 'happy snaps' beside the Argentines they had killed. One man heaved up a dead Argentine, put a cigarette in his mouth and pretended to light it, while a friend snapped away on his camera. 'They both laughed,' Lukowiak wrote. 'I also laughed.'[68]

When these stories came out in the early 1990s, some critics insisted that they must have been grossly exaggerated. Yet none of the paratroopers' recollections would have been remotely surprising to men who had served in Malaya, Korea or the two world wars. Indeed, the fact that readers were so shocked speaks volumes about their ignorance of the realities of war, from which most people were now completely insulated. 'If young men are sent 8,000 miles from their homes, to fight a war in a place that none of them had ever heard of, then such things should be expected,' wrote Lukowiak. 'Their bravado was just a cover for their fear.' And as the historian Helen Parr points out, the surprising thing is not how many reports of atrocities there were, but how few. The most obvious fact about the Falklands War is that, by the sadistic standards of most twentieth-century conflicts, it was unusually clean – perhaps because it was so short, and because civilians were barely involved at all.[69]

By midday on the 12th, all three objectives had been secured. The British had lost twenty-three men on Longdon, eight on Two Sisters and another seven on Mount Harriet, the Argentines having fought more valiantly than is often remembered. The battle had also seen the last British naval losses of the war. While bombarding Argentine positions on Mount Harriet, HMS *Glamorgan* had been hit by an Exocet with the loss of thirteen lives, among them the young David Tinker. In Number 10, Mrs Thatcher, distraught that Britain was losing its 'bravest and best', found the news 'unjust and heartbreaking'. But there was little doubt now that the end was near.[70]

After a day's rest while reinforcements from 5 Infantry Brigade moved into position, General Moore renewed the attack. This time the targets were the next two Argentine positions, on Mount Tumbledown and Wireless Ridge. Once again the conditions were dreadful; once again, though,

British casualties were relatively light. Using 'rifles, bayonets, shovels and whatever came to hand', the Scots Guards fought their way through a driving blizzard to the summit of Tumbledown for the loss of nine lives, while 2 Para lost only three men in capturing Wireless Ridge. By first light, the Argentine survivors, exhausted, bedraggled and panic-stricken, were streaming back into Stanley, 'like men resurrected from their graves'. Defeat was inevitable, and they knew it.[71]

It was the morning of Monday 14 June, a damp, grey day. On Wireless Ridge, Max Hastings passed the abandoned Argentine positions, littered with weapons, ammunition and clothing, and sat down to type his latest despatch for the *Evening Standard*. Of all the reporters embedded in the Task Force, none had identified more closely with Britain's fighting men, or been more committed to the cause of retaking the islands. Now Hastings paid a handsome tribute to the paratroopers celebrating their latest victory. 'Their morale is sky-high,' he wrote. 'Their certainty that they have won and that the enemy is collapsing is absolute. They are very cold, very dirty, but in their mood this morning, they could march to London.' A moment later, he heard shouting: 'They're running away! It's on the radio! The Argies are running everywhere! Victory!'

Hastings hitched a lift on a Scimitar tank to the lip of the ridge, and looked down on to a narrow concrete road leading towards Stanley, its 'little houses and churches' laid out like a children's train set. It looked, he thought, like a 'prize lying open for the taking'. And as the men around him discussed the next advance, an idea took shape. 'There was a chance, just a chance,' he thought, 'that we could be first into Stanley. It would be the greatest scoop of my professional life.' They moved on. At the little racecourse, on the outskirts of the town, the exhausted paratroopers halted and began to brew up. Hastings wandered down to the road. One paratrooper asked what he was doing, but he kept walking. The road bent around to the right, and suddenly he realized he was passing Government House. He raised his hands in the air, one clutching a white handkerchief, and kept going. By the cathedral he saw a group of Argentine soldiers. 'Good morning!' he said cheerfully. They said nothing. Eventually he ran into an Argentine colonel, who proved remarkably cordial. 'Will you surrender East and West Falkland?' Hastings asked, hardly believing his luck. 'I think so,' the colonel said, 'but it is best to wait until your general meets General Menéndez.' Hastings asked if it was all right for him to talk to the islanders. 'Of course,' the colonel said.

Hastings walked on. He passed lines of Argentine soldiers, 'cowed, drained of hostility'. Some officers peered suspiciously at him from their vehicles, but they said nothing. Then, at last, he saw what he was looking

for: the Upland Goose, where ten weeks earlier, in another age, Simon
Winchester had eaten cake and watched the rain. Now Hastings went
inside, and found some twenty people in the bar. 'I'm from the task force,'
he said, and they burst into applause. 'We never doubted for a moment
that the British would come,' the landlord said. 'We have just been waiting
for the moment. Would you like a drink?'[72]

# 34

# We Are Ourselves Again

*A change has come about in Britain . . . The people of this nation*
*have discovered that they have a self, which the older among them*
*supposed had been lost forever, and the young, who never knew*
*it, have nevertheless recognized for theirs.*
Enoch Powell, *The Times*, 14 May 1982

*Mrs Thatcher makes great play with her feelings for the SAS*
*whose motto is 'Who dares wins.'*
  *In the Falklands crisis she dared. And won.*
Terence Lancaster, *Daily Mirror*, 16 June 1982

It was nine o'clock in the evening when Margaret Thatcher got the call.
On a scrap of notepaper she scribbled the time and date, and then a few
sketchy but momentous words. 'From Northwood – Gen. Moore pressed
forward – Enemy retreated . . . White flags flying over Stanley.' Then she
went over to the Commons, where rumours were spreading fast. In the
lobbies, wrote Alan Clark, 'I found the whole House, policemen, badge
messengers, etc., everybody bubbling with excitement.' Clark squeezed
through into the chamber, which was already heaving with anticipation.
Just after ten, Mrs Thatcher made her way in, 'radiant, and there was
cheering, bellowing indeed'. At 10.14, she got to her feet:

> On a point of order, Mr Speaker. May I give the House the latest informa-
> tion about the battle of the Falklands? After successful attacks last night,
> General Moore decided to press forward. The Argentines retreated. Our
> forces reached the outskirts of Port Stanley. Large numbers of Argentine
> soldiers threw down their weapons. They are reported to be flying white
> flags over Port Stanley. Our troops have been ordered not to fire except
> in self-defence. Talks are now in progress between General Menéndez and
> our Deputy Commander, Brigadier Waters, about the surrender of the

Argentine forces on East and West Falkland. I shall report further to the
House tomorrow.

At first she seemed extraordinarily calm. Only right at the end did she
relax, and allow herself a broad smile of relief. And at the words 'East and
West Falkland' a great roar of triumph rolled across the House.

When she sat down, the cheers were deafening. Then Michael Foot, so
influential in setting the tone at the beginning of the war, rose to speak.
There would, he said:

> be widespread, genuine rejoicing – to use the word that the right hon. Lady
> once used – at the prospect of the end of the bloodshed. If the news is
> confirmed, as I trust it will be, there will be great congratulations from the
> House tomorrow to the British forces who have conducted themselves in
> such a manner and, if I may say so, to the right hon. Lady.

In the future, Foot said, there would be time to debate the 'origins of this
matter . . . but I can well understand the anxieties and pressures that must
have been upon the right hon. Lady during these weeks. I can understand
that at this moment those pressures and anxieties may have been relieved,
and I congratulate her on that.' It was a generous thing to say; when he
had finished, more cheers of approval echoed across the chamber.[1]

As Mrs Thatcher made her way out, Clark rushed to intercept her.
'Prime Minister, only you could have done this,' he exclaimed: 'you did it
alone, and your place in history is assured.' But she looked a 'little startled.
Had she heard properly? She was still a little bemused by the triumph.'
Perhaps the emotion was now beginning to sink in; for all her composure,
this must have been an intensely heady moment. In her Commons office,
packed with well-wishers, Willie Whitelaw proposed a toast. 'I don't think
anybody else but you could have done it,' he said. At that, one observer
remembered, 'she wept, out of sheer relief', before the ever-reliable Denis
put his arm around her. 'Well done,' he said. 'Have a drink.'[2]

When the Prime Minister got back to Number 10, it was just after
midnight. As on that memorable afternoon three years earlier, when she
had first walked into Number 10, the cameras were waiting. Once again
she was wearing blue; once again she was flanked by policemen. Then she
had been the earnest reformer; now she was the conquering heroine. 'Just
wonderful news,' she said, clearly still elated, 'and it's *Great* Britain. Marvellous forces, every single one of them. It's just been – it's just been
everyone together, and that's what matters. We knew what we had to do,
and we went about it.' Then she gestured to the crowd, who were singing
'Rule, Britannia': 'Listen to everyone. I must go down and talk to them.'

Afterwards, in her private memoir, she remembered the moment:

Downing Street was full of people, young people. It was their generation who had done it. Today's heroes. Britain still breeds them.

As I went to sleep very late that night I felt an enormous burden had been lifted from my shoulders and future worries would be small compared with those of life or death which had been with us constantly for eleven weeks. It was a miracle wrought by ordinary men and women with extra-ordinary qualities. Forever bold, forever brave, forever remembered.

But as she well knew, victory had come at a cost. Two days later, she wrote a letter to Ray Stuart, a Tewkesbury man whose son Matthew had been killed on HMS *Argonaut* on his eighteenth birthday. The first lines were typewritten: 'Thank you for writing to me about your son Matthew. Since you wrote, of course, we have had the news of the victory of our forces . . . Nothing that I say can diminish your loss; you can, however, take pride that Matthew died that others may live in freedom and justice.' But then, in her own hand, she added a postscript:

I have had telegrams and letters from all over the world showing great respect, admiration and thankfulness for Britain's stand in this matter. King Hussein said, 'The British Forces acquitted themselves brilliantly on the field with determination, courage and skill. The souls of martyrs never die. It is only by upholding lofty principles that human dignity and rights may be upheld and a brighter tomorrow may be born.'

He was speaking of young men like Matthew.[3]

*

By the time the Cabinet met on the morning of the 15th, Major-General Moore's message confirming Menéndez's surrender had reached London. His final lines were a model of patriotic understatement: 'The Falklands Islands are once more under the government desired by their inhabitants. God save the Queen.' In the Cabinet Room, Lord Hailsham congratulated Mrs Thatcher on her 'courage and leadership', which had added 'new lustre to our arms and the spirit of our people'. Then she went back across to the Commons, where the congratulations continued to flow. For the watching Frank Johnson, 'her triumph was total: the most complete a British Prime Minister has achieved in a generation' – and she knew it.

Amid the derision and disbelief of Britain's sophisticated classes, she had vowed to the world all those weeks ago that she would free those islands. And now she had. As she sat there, much of the House must have pondered in relief, exultation or dismay: the old girl had actually done it. Meanwhile, she leafed through her notes, perhaps trying to give the impression that she regarded this as just another working day, from time to time smiling sweetly about her. But she knew that life and politics being what they are, she will never again have a day such as this.

One tribute meant more than any other. Back on 3 April, Enoch Powell had warned that the Commons would soon learn of what metal she was made. Now he announced that he had obtained a copy of a report 'from the public analyst . . . It shows that the substance under test consisted of ferrous matter of the highest quality, that it is of exceptional tensile strength, is highly resistant to wear and tear and to stress, and may be used with advantage for all national purposes.' Some observers groaned. But Mrs Thatcher loved it. Later, Ian Gow persuaded Powell to sign the transcript of his speech, which he had framed and gave her as a Christmas present.[4]

In the next few days, as furious crowds streamed into the streets of Buenos Aires and a humiliated General Galtieri announced his resignation, messages poured in from friends abroad. The Prime Ministers of Australia and New Zealand were quick to offer their congratulations, while President Reagan wrote to commend 'a brilliant military feat and a defense of our shared principle that disputes are not to be resolved by aggression'. The 'minimum loss of life and the generous terms of withdrawal', he added, 'were also in the finest British tradition'. An especially gushing letter came from the Canadian premier Pierre Trudeau, not previously a great fan, who had high praise for Mrs Thatcher's 'strength and integrity' as well as the 'measured and brilliant' British forces. The Prime Minister of newly independent Belize thanked her on behalf of the 'little people of the world', while Singapore's Lee Kuan Yew thought the war proved 'there is still that divine spark in the British people'. The most memorable message, though, came from El Salvador's Revolutionary Democratic Front, then embroiled in one of the world's most savage civil wars.

Dear Mrs Thatcher,

You have succeeded where we failed. Since the despatch of the Task Force to the Falkland Islands, 266 Argentine military advisers have been withdrawn from Central America.
Thank you.

Yours in the democratic struggle,
FDR – Revolutionary Democratic Front El Salvador

For good measure, the message came with a bunch of flowers.[5]

On Fleet Street all was ecstasy. 'WHITE FLAGS OVER STANLEY!' exulted the *Mail*. 'WE'VE WON!' roared the *Sun*. The front page of the *Express* showed a close-up of an imperious Mrs Thatcher framed within a colossal V for victory. 'We have done what we set out to do,' wrote George Gale, hailing 'The Hour of Our Triumph':

> We have brought about the restoration of British rule to the Falklands. That, above all, is what counts. We have defeated the Argentine invaders and despoilers of our territory . . . We have rejected the foreign body from our midst. Our flags now fly again from one end of the Falklands to the other. No Argentine flag flies, except the flag of surrender.

Had Britain 'done nothing', he said, 'we would have suffered a shameful defeat'. Thankfully, Mrs Thatcher had rejected the 'pacifists, appeasers, wobblers and wets'. Yet this was not merely her victory. It was the people's victory:

> We have seen in these weeks of crisis and battle a remarkable resurgence of patriotism. It has welled up from the nation's depth. We have undergone a sea-change . . .
>
> For years patriotism was written off – in the years since Suez, in the swinging sixties, in the slumping seventies.
>
> Yet it must always have been there, for we have seen it flooding back.
>
> Our troops have fought to regain our land. They have battled to defend our people and to assert our interests. The country has become engaged. It has been locked into the struggle. The blood has quickened and thrilled.

The British people, Gale said, had 'almost lost track of our history, had almost given up the roots of our past. But now we have fought again for what is ours, and the blood is up, the heart is strong.' Britain was reborn. Nothing was beyond it now.[6]

While the Conservative papers gloried in 'V-F Day', Mrs Thatcher's critics shook their heads in horror. For those still true to the spirit of the 1960s, the new national mood was almost too much to bear. 'Not English I feel now,' recorded the appalled Alan Bennett. 'This is just where I happen to have been put down. No country. No party. No Church. No voice. And now they are singing "Britannia Rules the Waves" in Downing Street. It's the Last Night of the Proms erected into a policy.' 'I have felt totally alienated from popular opinion', Jenny Palmer told Mass Observation, 'and so conscious of holding a minority view that in company I constantly hoped that the topic would not come up, especially with elderly relatives.' The war, she wrote, 'hasn't solved anything and it isn't over'. As for the jubilation in the media, she considered it 'disgusting . . . I thanked God for the *Guardian* – there were other people who felt the same way as my husband and myself.'[7]

Indeed there were. One *Guardian* reader, furious that the Argentine surrender had driven the unemployment figures off the front pages, wondered whether 'the Falklands Islands or the British Isles has the more sheep'. The paper's veteran columnist James Cameron maintained that the war had been a 'military and political debacle', conceived in the 'folly and arrogance' of an 'obsessed' Prime Minister. And some critics went even further. Addressing trade unionists in Dundee, the Scottish miners' leader Mick McGahey insisted that Mrs Thatcher's hands were 'covered in the blood of young British and Argentine boys', and accused Michael Foot of pandering to the 'jingoism' of the hour. Tony Benn, too, had harsh words for Foot, whose congratulations he thought 'odious and excessive'. The press, Benn wrote, 'has gone berserk – Union Jacks, "VF" day and the Queen smiling and Thatcher looking stern, and pictures of our troops and God knows what. I find it utterly distressing, but there you are . . . A bloody awful day.'[8]

There was, of course, still work to be done. In the next few days the British troops herded 11,313 weary, crestfallen Argentine prisoners to the quays for the journey home. Meanwhile, Stanley was a hub of activity. There were more than a hundred minefields to be cleared, power and water supplies to be reconnected, bodies to be buried, buildings to be repaired. Although Mrs Thatcher's boys were desperate to get home, most did not embark for weeks. But Rex Hunt wasted little time in returning to his post. After a ceremonial welcome in driving rain, he went straight to Government House, where he found that the Argentines (or perhaps the British?) had made off with all his wine. Still, his books had been left untouched, except for a volume of the *Illustrated London News* from the First World War, which Menéndez had apparently been reading for inspiration. The Argentine commander had also left behind his scented pink lip-balm and a pair of pyjamas. 'As they were thicker and warmer than mine,' Hunt recorded, 'I had no compunction about wearing them.'[9]

Was victory inevitable? On paper, the combatants had always been ludicrously ill matched. For all its travails, Britain was a vastly richer and better-governed country than Argentina, with a far more professional and better-equipped military. In the last forty years the British had fought Nazi Germany and imperial Japan, as well as the North Koreans, the Chinese and a host of guerrillas from Malaya to Aden. But despite their gold braid, the most senior Argentine officers had barely fired a shot in anger. They were very good at launching coups, wearing sunglasses and murdering dissidents, but they had no record of fighting wars, let alone winning them. In some cases their only experience of combat had been to apply electrodes to the genitals of left-wing poets. Most of their young conscripts, meanwhile, had never been outside Argentina and had no idea what they were supposed to be doing. Even before the British landing, many of them were desperate to pack up and go home.[10]

But things could easily have been different. Many experts had thought the campaign hideously risky: in Admiral Woodward's words, 'we fought our way along a knife-edge'. For all their weaknesses, the Argentines had the advantages of numbers and geography. And even after the Task Force had arrived in the South Atlantic, fate might have dealt Britain a different hand. If more Argentine bombs had gone off, Woodward wrote, he could have lost another half a dozen ships, and 'if they had hit either of our aircraft carriers, the British would have been finished'. In that case, the war would have gone down as the crowning debacle in Britain's inexorable fall from grace. But the bombs did not go off. The carriers remained unscathed. The landings went to plan. There was more to it than luck, but as so often in Mrs Thatcher's career, fortune was with her. As the Tory dissenter Julian Critchley remarked: 'She who dares, wins.'[11]

Victory did not, of course, come without a price. According to the official history of the campaign, the immediate cost was about £1 billion, while the cost of defending the Falklands over the next six years came to almost £4 billion. In purely economic terms, it would have been cheaper to abandon the islands and pay the residents £1 million each in compensation. But what preoccupied most people was the bloodshed. Some 253 British servicemen had been killed, while a further 775 were wounded.* In relative terms, these numbers were minuscule. Far more British soldiers had died in Malaya or Cyprus than in the Falklands. But in a comfortable, peaceful, post-imperial age, when war felt utterly remote from the national experience, the death toll seemed profoundly shocking.

To put it bluntly, young men's lives were more precious in 1982 than they had been thirty or forty years earlier. For more pacific observers, to lose as many as 253 seemed monstrously disproportionate. It was no accident, then, that Mrs Thatcher allowed grieving families to bury their

---

* Some sources give the figure as 255, but Sir Lawrence Freedman's *Official History* suggests 253. Of these, eighty-five served in the Royal Navy, twenty-six were Marines, one belonged to the RAF, eighteen were civilians serving with the fleet and 123 were serving in the army. Argentine casualties were much higher: 649 killed, more than 1,600 wounded and 11,313 taken prisoner. Of the Argentine dead, almost exactly half had been on the *Belgrano*.

sons at home, rather than in battlefield graves, as in previous wars. Instead
of being an inevitable part of a collective endeavour, each death was now
seen as an individual family tragedy. For the tabloids, the prime example
was 22-year-old Lance-Corporal Simon Cockton of Frimley, Surrey, who
had literally kissed his teenage wife Lindsay goodbye at their wedding
reception before leaving for the Falklands. He was killed by friendly fire
when HMS *Cardiff* shot down a British helicopter over East Falkland.
'Like the others who fought and died for his country,' Lindsay told the
papers, 'the least we can do is to bring him home. I want him to be buried
in St Peter's Church where we were married.'[12]

Few men returned from the South Atlantic without mental scars. Ken
Lukowiak's memories were dominated by the 'young men who had their
flesh ripped and punctured by flying metal, young men who screamed and
died in agony, young men who prayed for mercy'. Vincent Bramley, whose
battalion had lost almost two dozen men, had similarly little time for the
tabloids' triumphalism. 'Gone were the days', he wrote, 'when I had
thought of war as a game.' For almost a year, the faces of his dying friends
flashed before him as he slept, their agonies haunting his dreams. He felt
restless, hemmed in, dissatisfied, bitter. 'It all seemed so unreal,' he
explained:

> The odd thing was, I felt anger. Anger at everyone for doing their own thing.
> It was as if something in my head was urging me to shout at them as they
> walked along the streets, 'Hey, you lot, licking your fucking ice creams,
> there's a fucking lot of injured guys over there. Friends have been killed,
> but all you're interested in is yourselves.'[13]

When the historian Helen Parr, whose uncle Dave had been killed on
Wireless Ridge, interviewed his former comrades, they talked of their
unease at being described as conquering heroes, their alienation from
friends and family, their feelings of emptiness, guilt, even shame. A study
five years after the war suggested that almost one in four veterans had
severe post-traumatic stress disorder, while a similar proportion showed
other traumatic symptoms. Many had trouble sleeping and found it impossible to settle into civilian life. Reluctant to admit weakness, unable to
open up about their grief and guilt, some turned to drink or drugs, to
chasing women or to fighting in pubs. Later, the South Atlantic Medal
Association, representing Falklands veterans, claimed that more men had
taken their own lives than had died in the conflict. A Ministry of Defence
survey in 2013, however, suggested that only ninety-five veterans had
killed themselves since 1982, a lower suicide rate than among the civilian
male population.[14]

Still, there is no doubt that the war took a punishing psychological toll. When *Panorama* flew a group of former Welsh Guards back to the islands to mark the thirty-fifth anniversary of the conflict, many were still haunted by their experiences. 'Not a single day that goes by when you don't think about it, think about the boys, friends that we lost,' said Mick Hermanis, who had been only 19 and survived the attack on the *Sir Galahad*. 'As I grew older it started eating away at me,' said Nigel O'Keeffe, who had been just 18 and struggled for years with alcoholism and depression. Another who turned to drink, Paul Bromwell, said his experiences had 'marked me for the rest of my life . . . It's a devil really, because you can't see the injury, everyone thinks you're all right but underneath you're screaming.'[15]

But it was another young Welsh Guardsman who became the public face of the Task Force. Born in Caerphilly and brought up on a council estate, Simon Weston had joined the army at the age of 16 after getting into trouble with the police. Horrifically wounded during the attack on the *Galahad*, he suffered 46 per cent burns, easily enough to have killed him. As his face and hands melted in the heat, he lost his eyelids, one of his ears, part of his nose and some of his fingers. In the first moments after the attack, he begged one of his mates to shoot him and end his misery. When a doctor saw him, he said bluntly: 'God, you're ugly.' When Weston saw his own face, he said: 'Oh, you've got a lot of work to do on that.' On his way home, on the hospital ship *Uganda*, he got septicaemia, nearly lost his eyesight and became deeply depressed. When he was wheeled into the transit hospital at RAF Lyneham, his waiting mother said to his grandmother: 'Oh Mam, look at that poor boy.' Weston cried out: 'Mam, it's me!' and at that, he remembered, 'her face turned to stone'.[16]

The doctors worked on Weston for years. He required more than seventy operations and multiple skin grafts, many of them on his face, which was now utterly unrecognizable. In public, he presented an image of unrelenting optimism. 'He's a great one for jokes,' wrote Polly Toynbee after visiting him in October. 'He has become a kind of walking mascot at the Queen Elizabeth Military Hospital in Woolwich. His cheeriness defies belief.' To the public he was a hero, jolly and resilient, the embodiment of British valour. The newspapers adored him. It was 'humbling' to contemplate Weston's 'dignity and resilience', said the *Express*. But it could 'not publish a picture of Simon, because it would shock and horrify readers'.

In reality, Weston was suffering from severe depression. 'I was filled with self-loathing – drinking too much, waking up at night because I was still on fire, hearing the screams of people dying around me,' he later told *The Times*. 'The darkness inside was so bad, I could lose a whole weekend and not remember a thing. I was an incredibly sad, lonely person for a hell of a long time.' At last, alone one day in his room, he decided to end it all. 'I tried to top myself with a crossbow – cocked it and everything – but my damaged hands weren't strong enough to pull the twine back on the bow and the damn thing nearly took my fingers off.'

But his life turned around eventually. He got married, had three children and travelled the world as a motivational speaker. He befriended the Argentine pilot who had attacked the *Galahad*: a 'very kind and compassionate man', Weston said. Decades later, he remained one of the most admired men in the country. He still carried the mental scars, yet he never doubted that the cause had been just. 'It was a must, this war,' he told Polly Toynbee. 'Lives were lost, and I'm sorry, but dictators must be stopped. No two ways about it. We can't let dictators rule the world.'[17]

To people who had always opposed the war, the suffering of men such as Simon Weston merely confirmed that they had been right. Some saw the war as ridiculous, pointless, an absurd aberration. The *Buenos Aires Herald* thought it a combination of 'an Italian opera with a very British Ealing comedy'; the biographer John Campbell calls it a 'Gilbert and Sullivan or Monty Python war'. The journalist Simon Winchester thought it a 'terrible, ghastly and irresponsible mistake' and a 'blot upon our hopes for international respect'. The Argentine Nobel laureate Jorge Luis Borges remarked that the combatants looked like 'two bald men fighting over a comb', and suggested that the islands should be 'given to Bolivia so that it has access to the sea'. And another great writer of the age, the children's author Raymond Briggs, published a savagely grotesque satire, *The Tin-Pot Foreign General and the Old Iron Woman* (1984), which briefly topped the bestseller lists. Mrs Thatcher, 'an old woman with lots of money and guns', does not come out well. 'When this Old Iron Woman heard that the Tin-Pot General had bagsied the sad little island,' writes Briggs, 'she flew into a rage. "IT'S MINE!" she screeched. "MINE! MINE! MINE! I bagsied it AGES ago. I bagsied it FIRST! DID! DID! DID!"'[18]

For all Borges's brilliance, his analogy completely missed the point. There were more than 1,800 people living on the Falkland Islands, some families having been there for generations. The vast majority were desperate to remain British; all of them were shocked and frightened by the Argentine invasion. This was their home: when critics blithely suggested that they should be bribed to move halfway across the world, they were naturally outraged. In his final pages, Briggs depicted the Falklands as a bomb-shattered, corpse-littered wasteland, while Winchester was sure the islanders would soon regret living in an 'armed camp'. In reality, the islanders never wavered in their gratitude to Mrs Thatcher, and never faltered in their allegiance to the British flag. A survey on the fourth anniversary of the invasion found that more than 95 per cent of Falkland Islanders wanted to remain British. Only three people said they would accept Argentine sovereignty instead.[19]

It is true, of course, that the Falklands were a long way from London, and that defending them was very expensive. But given how long the islanders had been living there, it seems very odd to argue that they should have been denied the right of self-determination, or simply handed over to General Galtieri. When, in the autumn of 1982, Alan Clark visited the islands for the first time, he passed Port Stanley's infants' school, where 'out tumbled a lot of jolly, fair-haired children in their anoraks, to be collected by their Mums'. It was, Clark thought, a 'completely English scene. We could not possibly have abandoned these people and packaged them up in some diplomatic deal. This has been a real war of liberation . . . a battle fought in obedience to a blood tie.' He was so moved that when he got back he scribbled a letter to the Chief Whip. 'Seeing all those little fair-haired children in their anoraks', he wrote, 'brought home more effectively than anything else could have done what exactly we were fighting for, and how impossible it would have been to have abandoned them to a foreign power.' Whatever Clark's ideological peculiarities, on this issue millions of people would have agreed with him.[20]

The great majority of the men who fought for the Falklands believed the campaign had been worth it. Vincent Bramley might have learned a shattering lesson in the horrors of war, but he was 'fully behind the decision to send the task force' and 'wouldn't hesitate to fight again for our country and its beliefs'. At the military hospital in Woolwich, many of the patients assured reporters that they still believed in the cause. 'British soil had to be guarded and that's what we were doing down there,' said Denzil Connick, who had lost his left leg. 'We had to go down there and do it, or this country would never have lived it down,' agreed Mark Richards, who had suffered dreadful burns on the *Galahad*. 'We'd have had people taking over Belize and Gibraltar next.' And among the general public, the vast majority believed Mrs Thatcher had done the right thing. Victory had banished their misgivings: a poll for the *Sunday Times* after the Argentine surrender found that fully 81 per cent thought she had been right to fight for the Falklands.[21]

By October, when the City of London organized a military parade to celebrate victory, even some of Mass Observation's more sceptical correspondents had come round. Having originally questioned the cost of the war, Carol Daniel watched the parade on television and felt 'touched when the crowd burst into "Rule Brittianer [*sic*]"'. Similarly, Lesley Hughes, who had initially been 'horrified when our Task Force set sail' and had been so 'deeply depressed' by reports of casualties that she went to the doctor, actively 'looked forward to seeing the Victory March'. It was a 'glory to watch', she wrote, 'and I felt very proud of our forces . . . I was moved to tears when I saw the old Chelsea Pensioner in full regalia openly weep. And I also sobbed my heart out when the crowd joined in with "Rule Brittania [*sic*]"'. 'All my workmates and the over thirties who I talk to on CB believe we should have gone,' wrote Peter Hibbitt, 'and they are glad we won.'[22]

The biggest winners, apart from the islanders themselves, were 'our boys'. The decades since the Second World War had not been kind to Britain's armed forces, who had seen their budgets eroded, their numbers cut and their reputation damaged by the conflict in Northern Ireland. Many younger people shuddered to think of Britain as a warrior nation; some felt embarrassed by its imperial history. But now all that was forgotten. 'In defeating aggression,' declared George Gale, 'our forces have sustained us and enhanced us and all we stand for.' It had been a 'genuinely uplifting experience', wrote Max Hastings, to join the nation's fighting men on the road to victory. 'After so many years in which we have heard and said so much about British failure in so many areas of our national life, in the past few weeks I have been exposed to almost unbroken generosity, spontaneous kindness, patience [and] comradeship towards a common aim.' His readers never doubted it. After 1982, polls showed enormous public support for the armed forces. Peter York even announced that 'army surplus' was now the height of fashion. A few years earlier, people would have thought him insane.[23]

The other obvious winner was the woman at the top. Given her eagerness to cut defence spending, few senior officers had previously seen Margaret Thatcher as a natural ally. Yet as the Chief of the Defence Staff, Admiral Terence Lewin, wrote afterwards, the service chiefs were unanimous in their 'enormous admiration' for her 'determination and leadership', as well as her 'support and decisiveness when we needed difficult decisions'. Lewin himself had 'absolutely no doubt' that because of her grit and efficiency, 'many lives were saved and the job was finished more quickly'.[24]

Further down the chain of command, Mrs Thatcher's star shone even more brightly. Here, as so often, the fact that she was a woman mattered enormously. 'She felt a maternal, almost a romantic identification with the men whom she was sending into battle,' explains Charles Moore, 'and they responded with a chivalrous devotion, a desire to protect her as a

woman and as an embodiment of national spirit'. After she hosted a celebratory dinner that autumn, her guests' letters brimmed with admiration.
'If I may say so, during our days in the South Atlantic, some of them pretty
dark, it was good to feel that we had your resolution and the backing of
Great Britain behind us,' wrote Colonel Mike Scott, who had commanded
the Scots Guards at Tumbledown. 'None of us, on the ground in the
Falklands, of whatever rank, ever had any doubts or worries about the
hand on the helm back at home,' agreed Brigadier Julian Thompson. 'I
think that you saw on Tuesday the depth of respect and, if I may say so,
affection which we have for you.' And when she rose to speak at a celebratory lunch for the victors at the Guildhall, even she was taken aback by
her reception. 'Suddenly, before she could say anything,' Thompson
recalled, 'there was a standing ovation from the floor, started by the boys.
The other politicians couldn't believe what was happening. When Mrs
Thatcher had quietened everyone down, she said, "It is I who should be
down there, thanking you."'[25]

As for the officials who worked beside her during the ten-week campaign, they unanimously agreed that she deserved the credit. It is often
said that the war transformed Mrs Thatcher's faults into virtues, her
stubborn rigidity becoming steadfast resolve. But it is also true that under
immense pressure she raised her game. Gone were the lectures and tirades.
Conscious of her military inexperience, she did her homework and listened
respectfully to advice. She moved carefully and deliberately, always conscious of the risks; but if the military needed a swift decision, she never
hesitated. Her Private Secretary for Foreign Affairs, John Coles, previously
a sceptic, was enormously impressed by her 'courage and clarity'. 'Without
her,' he wrote afterwards, 'I doubt that the Task Force would ever have
sailed, or even if it had that it would have fought.'[26]

In just ten weeks, Mrs Thatcher's public reputation had been transformed.
She had always been seen as a fighter, but now commentators and cartoonists
saw her as Boadicea defying the Romans or Elizabeth I rousing her troops
at Tilbury. Abroad, she was universally seen as the embodiment of strong
leadership, the personification of British courage and bloody-mindedness.
'Now, as a result of events in those bleak and remote islands, Mrs Thatcher
is the most powerful and secure leader in Europe,' said the *Wall Street Journal*. The West German weekly *Der Stern* depicted her as a second Churchill,
chewing on a cigar and flashing a V for victory. The *Frankfurter Allgemeine
Zeitung* drew her as Britannia, holding the Union Jack aloft.[27]

And at home, for virtually the only time in her premiership, she briefly
transcended party politics to become a genuinely unifying patriotic figure.
'If things had gone wrong it would have been known as Thatcher's War,'

said the *Mirror*, which had spent the last three years damning everything she stood for. 'But now things have gone right nobody should deny her the credit ... The scale of her triumph, in both military and political terms, is amazing.' 'People can now finally see the point of Mrs Thatcher and feel more comfortable with her,' agreed the *Spectator*'s Alexander Chancellor. 'Set beside the Falklands conflict, even her economic policies appear no longer harsh but courageous.' At Westminster she reigned supreme. Alan Clark thought she had more 'freedom of action' than any Prime Minister since Churchill. And in the *Guardian*, Peter Jenkins wrote that she was 'soaring high on the wings of victory'. If an election were held that summer, he admitted, 'she would be queen of all'.[28]

In later years, historians often talked of a 'Falklands factor'. On the left, the war is seen today as a radical turning point, rescuing a doomed Prime Minister from inevitable defeat. And on the face of it the evidence is very striking. At the end of 1981, Gallup had put the Conservatives on just 23 per cent, behind both Labour and the Alliance. Many commentators thought the next election would produce a hung parliament; very few believed Mrs Thatcher could win a majority. And even though the Alliance's fortunes had ebbed in the first months of 1982, Roy Jenkins's sensational victory in Glasgow Hillhead showed that it was far too early to write it off.

But then came the war; and by the time it was all over, the political landscape looked very different. With every week, voters had flooded back from the Alliance to the government. After the recapture of South Georgia, the Conservatives had surged to more than 43 per cent. By the time the Argentines surrendered, they had reached 49 per cent, which would have seemed frankly incredible only months earlier. Other polls told a similar story. At the beginning of 1982, barely one in four voters had approved of the government's record; by the end of May, half of them did so. And Mrs Thatcher's own standing was completely transformed. By early June her personal approval rating had climbed to 53 per cent. By contrast, Michael Foot's rating had sunk to just 14 per cent – the lowest figure for any party leader in history.[29]

Yet despite the conventional wisdom that the Falklands radically redrew the electoral picture, the reality is more complicated. As we have seen, the Tories had been climbing back into contention even before the war began. With every slow, painful step towards economic recovery, their fortunes were improving. Just before the Argentines had landed on South Georgia, they were already on 31½ per cent, their best figure since 1979. Indeed, back on 7 May, the third anniversary of Mrs Thatcher's election, *The Times*'s David Watt had argued that the Falklands crisis was distracting attention from the fact that her government was now in remarkably good shape, with a united Cabinet, falling inflation, rising house prices, a buoyant stock market and improving business confidence. The public, he wrote, was 'getting used to a right-wing government'. The arguments about economic policy had died down, and on matters such as law and order and industrial relations, her instincts clearly matched public opinion. 'People admire her', Watt wrote, 'even if they do not like her' – and this before her troops had fired a shot.[30]

The most detailed analysis of the Falklands factor, published in the *British Journal of Political Science*, suggests that it has been enormously exaggerated. Even without the war, the combination of falling taxes, lower interest rates and rising consumer spending meant that the Conservatives were *always* likely to surge in the polls during the spring and summer of 1982. If the war made a difference, it was simply to accelerate a recovery that was already underway, and to strengthen the image of unbending certainty that Mrs Thatcher had been projecting for years. But of course this makes for a less dramatic story than one in which a failing Prime Minister was rescued from disaster by war in the South Atlantic. And it suited her opponents to pretend she had been saved only by the war, because then they could write her off as an extremist aberration, delivered from oblivion by a twist of fate. The alternative explanation – that millions of people actually supported her policies and genuinely preferred her to the alternatives – was too dreadful to contemplate.[31]

Yet *something* had changed. Everybody said so. 'Britain has said something to itself,' declared *The Economist*, for which the war represented a 'sort of cultural revolution', making it fashionable once again to love and fight for your country. In Whitehall, John Coles thought the war had fostered a 'new sense of vigour and achievement, a feeling that Britain had not lost its former capacity for action in defence of freedom'. At the Centre for Policy Studies, the conservative historian Hugh Thomas told Mrs Thatcher that 'with this defeat of the Argentines you have turned the tables too on the defeatism, negativism & spirit of withdrawal in our own country'. And in *The Times*, Simon Jenkins wrote that the war had brought back 'national self-respect and a reinvigorated belief in Britain's skill and efficiency', banishing for good the hysterical pessimism about a divided, ungovernable nation.[32]

In Mrs Thatcher's mind there was no doubt that the war had changed everything. Later, talking to *Woman's Own*, she tried to put it into a wider context, harking back, as so often, to the experience of standing alone against the Nazis:

Not since World War II had we had to undertake such a big operation . . .
In those 37 years we had gone from being a great Imperial power to being
a Commonwealth . . . So we had to prove to ourselves again that we could
do it, and this time we did it in a way more alone than ever before.

You ask if the national pride that was so evident at the time of the Falklands campaign can be maintained. I think it will be. Because it's always
there in the hearts of our people. I've always known and felt it was there.

You see, what the Falklands proved was that we could still do it, and do
it superbly. There was a feeling of colossal pride, of relief that we could still
do the things for which we were renowned. And that feeling will stay with
us for a very long time.

A year later, she welcomed the Russian writer Alexander Solzhenitsyn to
Downing Street. He was on typically gloomy form. The West, he said,
was weak, and 'the young did not seem to be prepared to defend their
country'. At that, Mrs Thatcher jumped in. 'Our young people were ready
to do this,' she corrected him. 'They had gone eight thousand miles to
defend the Falklands. There was a new pride in Britain.'[33]

That word 'pride' was crucial. Among the general public, said the
*Guardian*, there was immense 'pride in the professionalism of our troops.

This is Mac in the *Daily Mail*, two days after the Argentine surrender
(16 June 1982).

Pride that Britain can still kick back hard at those who kick us. Pride in the buoyant headlines and feeling of adventure.' For the *Daily Mail*'s Robin Oakley, the war was one of those 'moments which can lift a nation's mood and alter its history', marking the 'restoration of Britain's pride and self-confidence'. Even Tony Benn recognized that there had been a profound shift in the way that people thought about their country. 'I feel somehow that we are at a real turning point in politics,' he wrote at the end of July. 'I can't quite describe it. The military victory in the Falklands, Thatcher's strength, the counter-attack of the right of the Labour Party on the left, the fact that unemployment has weakened the unions, make me feel more than ever before that I need to pause and think and work out a new strategy.' He had been living 'in a dream world believing it wasn't really happening . . . I feel we have just come to the end of an era.' Another controversial prophet of national decline put it more concisely. 'A change has come about in Britain,' wrote Enoch Powell. 'We are ourselves again.'[34]

The irony of all this was that, before the crisis began, most people did not even know where the Falkland Islands were. In a broad strategic sense the war was a sideshow, which made no discernible difference to the lives of the vast majority who applauded it. Yet in psychological and political terms its impact can hardly be overstated. For as John Campbell points out, people did not see it merely as a struggle for some obscure islands in the South Atlantic. They saw it as a question of principle, a matter of honour and a crucial test of national spirit.

Context was everything. A self-confident economic superpower would probably have been able to shrug off the loss of the Falklands. But a nation that believed itself to be in deep post-imperial decline could never have done so. If Britain had failed to fight or had been defeated, thought John Coles, 'the consequences . . . would have been profound. The moral shock, the humiliation, for a nation which has still not come to terms with imperial withdrawal, would have been unbearable. The national decline would have been irretrievable.' It was, David Owen told a journalist years later:

> one of those moments when the whole way that a country sees itself can be changed. If we'd scuttled out of the Falklands . . . [it] would have been a huge defeat. These are the fundamental questions for a country. You have to decide, 'Is this country still capable? Is this country played out?' This was Thatcher's call. And she called it correctly.[35]

No event since the Second World War had a more lasting impact on Britain's self-image. 'It's Great Britain,' Mrs Thatcher told the cameras on the night of victory. 'Today,' said the *Evening Standard* a few hours later, 'the

Great is back in Britain.' In the last few decades, that word 'Great' had rung hollow. When Eden was humiliated at Suez, when Macmillan saw his European bid vetoed by the French, when Wilson was forced to devalue the pound, when Heath was defeated by the miners, when Callaghan took his begging bowl to the IMF, Britain had looked far from great. And in most respects Mrs Thatcher's first three years had been more of the same: strikes, bankruptcies, inflation, recession; unemployment, riots, hooliganism, Northern Ireland; failure, disaster, division, decline. For many of those involved in the Falklands drama, this history was always at the back of their minds. Max Hastings, for example, was tired of reporting on 'one aspect or another of national failure', and was itching 'to record a national success'. Even Vincent Bramley thought that 'we British had been kicked too often', and felt proud to stand up at last 'for our country and its beliefs'.[36]

The Falklands War, then, was a genuine turning point, the first for forty years. It banished the ghosts of Suez, and marked the end of an era defined by post-imperial introspection. It even provided a new national myth to rank alongside D-Day, Dunkirk and the Battle of Britain. In this respect, everything about it was perfect. No scriptwriter could have provided more endearing victims, a cast of harmless sheep farmers who might have just walked out of *The Archers*; or more fiendish adversaries, a South American junta who specialised in torturing their own people. Indeed, the look and feel of the conflict might have been designed specifically for a generation who had grown up with *The Dam Busters* and *Dad's Army*. The great spectacle of the Task Force ploughing through the Atlantic was perfectly calculated to stir the hearts of a seafaring people who had grown up with stories of Drake and Nelson. And the pictures of the little green figures with their enormous packs, trudging stoically across the windswept moorlands, played perfectly to the self-image of an indomitable island race, never happier than when the weather was miserable and the odds were against them. Once again Britain had been written off. Once again Britain had stood alone. Once again Britain had prevailed.

'It was a war', wrote Julian Critchley, 'which seemed to belong to an age long before Thatcherism. It was a campaign that Kipling, or the *Boy's Own Paper*, might have invented for readers of gripping yarns . . . the kind of war which people had thought could never happen again.' It was a campaign that banished thoughts of riots, recession, crime and permissiveness. It rekindled the spirit of Nelson at Trafalgar, the Little Ships at Dunkirk, Churchill during the Blitz. It even drove unemployment off the front pages. And that, of course, was why it struck such a chord.[37]

*

A week after the Falklands War had ended, as the nation basked in the glow of victory, Princess Diana gave birth to a boy. To the newspapers the arrival of Prince William, coming so soon after the liberation of Port Stanley, seemed a moment of almost unimaginable ecstasy. It was as if, after years of driving rain, the clouds had parted, the sun was shining and the green fields were wreathed in splendour. Who now could doubt that Britain was Top Nation once again?

'THE CROWNING GLORY', exulted the *Express*, whose columnist Peter McKay was beside himself with enthusiasm:

> What times we live in! The excitement surrounding a royal birth. A famous victory in the Falklands. A nation which, according to all recent opinion polls, exults in a common aim.
>
> There cannot have been a June like it for 30 years. Indeed, since June 1953 – the Queen's Coronation, coinciding with the conquering of Everest! And the Express headline over both events which said: 'ALL THIS – AND EVEREST TOO!'
>
> There will always be something ridiculous about a nation in the throes of self congratulation. Sometimes it is a dangerous condition.
>
> But surely, our triumphs of these days in the summer of '82 seem right and proper, a consequence of our having been a good and true people.

McKay recognized that the glow would fade eventually, and that people would revert to 'fighting one another, ridiculing each other'. Such was the British way. But 'we may have to wait for a long time', he wrote, 'to see the likes of this summer and the excitement of these days. Days in which we seemed incapable of defeat.'[38]

For Mrs Thatcher, these were days of glory. On 3 July, in her first major party speech since the end of the war, she addressed the faithful at Cheltenham Racecourse. The train drivers' union ASLEF was threatening an all-out strike in protest at British Rail's decision to bring in more flexible rosters, and most of her advisers had warned her not to exploit victory too obviously. But now she threw off the fetters:

> Today we meet in the aftermath of the Falklands Battle. Our country has won a great victory and we are entitled to be proud . . .
>
> Now that it is all over, things cannot be the same again, for we have learned something about ourselves – a lesson which we desperately needed to learn.
>
> When we started out, there were the waverers and the fainthearts. The people who thought that Britain could no longer seize the initiative for herself. The people who thought we could no longer do the great things

which we once did. Those who believed that our decline was irreversible –
that we could never again be what we were.

There were those who would not admit it – even perhaps some here
today – people who would have strenuously denied the suggestion but – in
their heart of hearts – they too had their secret fears that it was true: that
Britain was no longer the nation that had built an Empire and ruled a
quarter of the world.

Well, they were wrong. The lesson of the Falklands is that Britain has
not changed and that this nation still has those sterling qualities which shine
through our history.

More than any other speech she ever gave, this was her apotheosis. What
had always driven her, underpinning her beliefs in free enterprise and the
small state, was her unyielding faith in British greatness, and her horror
at its decline. But now Britain was reborn in battle. This was the true spirit
of the South Atlantic:

We have ceased to be a nation in retreat.

We have instead a new-found confidence – born in the economic battles
at home and tested and found true 8,000 miles away.

That confidence comes from the re-discovery of ourselves, and grows
with the recovery of our self-respect.

And so today, we can rejoice at our success in the Falklands and take
pride in the achievement of the men and women of our Task Force . . .

We rejoice that Britain has re-kindled that spirit which has fired her
for generations past and which today has begun to burn as brightly as
before.

Britain found herself again in the South Atlantic and will not look back
from the victory she has won.

Her audience loved it.[39]

All her enemies now seemed to be running up white flags. Two weeks
later, the train drivers' strike collapsed, the TUC having threatened to sus-
pend them unless they went back to work. 'SURRENDER', gloated the front
page of the *Express*. For the paper's labour correspondent, a bearded young
man called Peter Hitchens, this was proof that the trade unions' power had
been broken. The Winter of Discontent was a fading memory, the steelworkers had fought and lost, even Derek Robinson was yesterday's man. In part,
Hitchens admitted, this reflected the fact that 'most of our old industrial
battlegrounds are now industrial graveyards'. But it also reflected the new,
more conservative spirit at the top of the unions. There was, Hitchens
thought, just one exception: 'Mr Arthur Scargill of the Mineworkers,

desperate to have a fight with someone, about something, as soon as he has finished his holiday in Communist Cuba. One thing stands between him and what he wants, and that is the democracy of the Mineworkers' Union.'[40]

By now the Task Force was steaming home. On Saturday 10 July, Alan Clark flew out to welcome the *Canberra*, which was due to dock in Southampton the next morning. When he spotted the great liner's escort from his Sea Otter plane, he 'felt very moved':

> I saw that little frigate and thought how she and her sister ships had sailed the whole length of the world to uphold the honour of the country and of the Royal Navy. What a truly wonderful epic event in our history was that Falkland Islands war. I have said this so many times in so many places, and on each occasion I can still feel almost tearful. There will never again be anything like that.[41]

At dawn on Sunday morning the *Canberra* sailed into Southampton harbour. Aboard were more than 2,000 Royal Marines, as well as hundreds of other servicemen and members of the ship's original crew, who had volunteered to stay on board during the Falklands campaign. Also aboard was the *Mirror*'s Paul Callan, who described the scene the next day:

> At first they were only tiny white plumes in the 6 am heat haze hovering at that point in the Solent where the sky ended and the sea began.
>
> Then, as the wearied Canberra pushed herself home through the frisky sea, the wispy little shapes became definite.
>
> They were sailing craft of every conceivable size – sleek yachts, lumbering catamarans, even dumpy dinghies – and all were tearing through the waters to welcome home a liner more used to the luxurious murmur of world cruises than the ugly clamour of war . . .
>
> Out of the dawn's horizon [came] a joyful Dunkirk of a welcome – a mass of boats which grew into thousands as they bobbed and wobbled excitedly like children around a favourite parent.

Even the Marines were visibly moved. Some were so overcome they turned away and 'just stared out to sea, lost in the ocean of their own thoughts'. As the *Canberra* edged close to the quay, they could see the red, white and blue of the flags and hear the 'hoarse greetings of mothers, fathers, wives, children and lovers'. The returning heroes had clearly been keeping up with the news: on deck, one group displayed a banner that read 'CALL OFF THE RAIL STRIKE – OR WE'LL CALL AN AIR STRIKE!' And as they fell into the arms of their families, they were pleased to see that Britain had not changed. 'Cor,' one Marine muttered as a 'well-shaped young girl popped up topless from behind a blue flag'. 'Now that's a fine pair of welcomes.'[42]

As luck would have it, the Marines had made it back in time for what was surely the cultural highlight of the age. Broadcast from the London Coliseum on 18 July, ITV's *National Salute to the Falklands Task Force from the British Theatre* was a remarkable occasion by any standards. Vera Lynn was there, of course. So were Laurence Olivier, John Mills, Richard Todd, Christopher Lee, Roger Moore and Anthony Andrews. *Who Dares Wins*'s Lewis Collins was there, alongside Martin Shaw and Gordon Jackson, his fellow *Professionals*. Robert Powell, Ronnie Corbett, Adam Ant, Les Dawson, Paul Daniels, Alvin Stardust, Kim Wilde, Leslie Crowther . . . the 'galaxy of stars', as the programme modestly put it, just went on and on. Even Prince Charles was there, having torn himself away from his nappy-changing duties. At the end, to the palpable delight of the audience, the cast assembled on stage to sing 'Land of Hope and Glory'. But not everybody liked it. 'Thank goodness I didn't get mixed up in *that*!' recorded an appalled Kenneth Williams. 'It was excruciating: the sort of patriotic jingoism and amateur theatricals which leave you squirming.'[43]

There was one last Falklands story before the summer was over, though it was more like an episode of *Yes Minister* than a night at the London Coliseum. This was the official service of thanksgiving at St Paul's Cathedral, which was preceded by weeks of comical acrimony. The problem was that although Mrs Thatcher was keen to celebrate victory and mourn the fallen, the church authorities, many of whom had been passionately opposed to the war, were determined to suppress any mention of the Falklands at all. Every aspect, from the choice of hymns to the wording of the order of service, provoked intense bickering. The President of the Methodist Conference, Dr Kenneth Greet, who had attacked the war in the *Guardian*, said there should be no hint of celebration and did not want any members of the armed forces to read lessons. The Catholic cardinal Basil Hume refused to countenance the word 'liberation'. Most alarmingly for the government, the Dean of St Paul's, Dr Alan Webster, a pacifist with strong left-wing sympathies, seriously proposed that the service should be dedicated to 'reconciliation' with Argentina, with half of it conducted in Spanish.

To Mrs Thatcher, all this seemed beyond parody. When she heard about the Dean's plan, one aide said, 'her eyes widened in absolute horror'. As John Nott remarked, Dr Webster had completely missed the point that this was meant to be a service for the 'families of the British dead', who were unlikely to be consoled by hearing the Lord's Prayer in the language of General Galtieri. At one point Nott urged her to call the whole thing off and have a military service on Horse Guards Parade instead. But in the end they found a compromise. The churchmen agreed that Falklands veterans could read lessons after all, while Mrs Thatcher agreed to drop any mention of celebration. Dr Webster even abandoned his plan to read the Lord's Prayer in Spanish, though he made one last plea that a Spanish translation be included in the order of service. 'Why?' scribbled Mrs Thatcher.[44]

In the event, the service on 26 July passed off without a word of Spanish. But since the clergymen had made no secret of their misgivings, the press were spoiling for a fight. Their chosen target was a man who, ironically, knew more than most about the reality of battle. During the Second World War, the Archbishop of Canterbury, Robert Runcie, had served as a tank commander in the Scots Guards. His men affectionately called him 'Killer', and after leading an attack to knock out three German guns under heavy fire, he had been awarded the Military Cross. In a further irony, he had privately supported the Falklands War and explicitly told the congregation that sometimes force was necessary. But the deaths of so many young men, he added, were nothing to celebrate. He was 'thankful' the war was over, for it was 'impossible to be a Christian and not to long for peace'. And in words that many people interpreted as a rebuke to the press, he noted that it was sometimes 'those spectators who remained at home who continue to be most violent in their attitudes, and untouched in their deepest selves'.

To Runcie's critics, all this was absolutely disgraceful. In a striking sign of the times, the *Sun* branded him the 'Arch-Wimp of Canterbury'. The immensely right-wing Tory backbencher Sir John Biggs-Davison declared that it was 'revolting for cringing clergy to misuse St Paul's to throw doubt upon the sacrifice of our fighting men'. Another of Mrs Thatcher's MPs, the similarly ferocious Julian Amery, claimed that the sermon was typical of the 'pacifist, liberal, wet establishment' who had been 'shocked by our going to war and even more shocked at our winning victory'.[45]

Mrs Thatcher was widely reported to have hated the sermon, even though she made a point of congratulating Runcie afterwards. But most of her ministers were more generous. 'I felt he spoke exactly for me,' said Willie Whitelaw, who had fought alongside Runcie in Normandy. 'His words at St Paul's were those of a soldier who understood war, and he expressed his admiration for those who fought and gave their lives.' And even Alan Clark, who had fortified himself with a sticky bun from a café 'staffed entirely by black people', thought the service 'could have been worse'. His attention was monopolized by the grieving families behind him, not least because so many of the widows were 'raging beauties'. 'With the exception of the very young children, who were excited and jolly,' he wrote, 'most of the relatives looked deeply unhappy.' Many of them spent the service in tears. Later, on his way out, Clark passed 'row after row of next of kin. Anxiously I scanned their faces, but the only emotion I could see was anguish, sheer anguish.'[46]

In Newton Abbot, Mary Richards watched the service on television. She was relieved that 'it was not turned into Party Politics . . . I was taught God is love and the Church is right to try and teach us to love each other and forgive each other . . . I would not like to think the C of E represent Mrs Thatcher's views as I have never felt Mrs Thatcher and her followers are compassionate.' At one point that summer her grown-up daughter remarked: 'I don't know how Maggie Thatcher gets away with it.' But Mary just felt tired of the whole business:

> We are now fed up with it. Every time we turn the TV on something else is coming home. It's like a party political programme.
>
> I am just glad it's all over. Every time we watch all that pomp and glory I think of the boys that never came back and the wounded young men and the sorrow it has caused many families.
>
> Our family has not been involved in any of these celebrations and I don't know anyone else who has.
>
> Just glad it's over.

For Margaret Thatcher, though, it was never over.[47]

# Acknowledgements

This is the fifth book in my series about Britain since the 1950s. To my shame, the entire series, which was meant to be just three books, was supposed to have been finished well over a decade ago. So my greatest debt is to my editor, Simon Winder, who, as always, was endlessly encouraging, patient, astute and full of hilarious observations. I am glad that he now recognizes the merits of *For Your Eyes Only*. I am grateful to everybody at Allen Lane for their hard work, especially Maria Bedford and Ellen Davies. As usual, Jim Stoddart produced a splendid cover, while Cecilia Mackay came up with a vast array of superb illustrations. The copy editor, Kit Shepherd, who knows everything about everything, once again saved me from more hideous blunders than I care to remember. And I am immensely lucky to be represented by James Pullen at the Wylie Agency, the best in the business.

I was fortunate to write this book as a visiting professor at King's College London, and I am enormously grateful to Professor Richard Vinen for setting this up. My debts to the superlatively rich archives of the Thatcher Foundation, and to their omniscient editor, Christopher Collins, will be obvious to anybody who glances at my endnotes. For the Mass Observation material, I am indebted to the work of the University of Sussex's 'Observing the 80s' project. For a chance to air the arguments in this book, I am grateful to the universities, schools and societies which have hosted me in the last few years. Among many others, I would like to thank Dr Molly O'Brien Castro at the University of Tours for inviting me to speak at her conference on Margaret Thatcher; Professor Keith Gildart at the University of Wolverhampton for asking me to discuss popular culture and social change; Professor Robert Colls at De Montfort University for asking me to talk about sport in the 1980s; and Dr Ben Jackson and the Oxford University History Society for inviting me to debate Thatcherism. In every case, I came away recharged with ideas and enthusiasm.

At an early stage in the research, Kester Aspden offered me some invaluable advice, while Alistair Quarterman was a mine of information about the BBC Computer Project. My debts to other historians will be clear from my endnotes, but I want to pay particular tribute to the work of Charles Moore on Margaret Thatcher; Ben Jackson and Robert Saunders on Thatcherism; Jim Tomlinson and David Smith on economics; Peter King on housing; Jerry White on London; Simon Reynolds on pop music; Kenneth O. Morgan on the Labour Party; Ivor Crewe and Anthony King on the SDP; Gordon Burn and Clive Everton on snooker; Joe Moran on television; Mike and Trevor Phillips on race; Thomas Hennessey and Peter Taylor on Northern Ireland; Pat Butcher on athletics; Simon Wilde on Ian Botham; and Tom Lean, Magnus Anderson and Rebecca Levene on computers. On the Falklands, I am particularly indebted to the work of Max Hastings and Simon Jenkins, Jimmy Burns, Martin Middlebrook, Sir Lawrence Freedman and Helen Parr. And of the existing books covering the entire period, I learned most from Alwyn W. Turner's *Rejoice! Rejoice!*, an immensely entertaining read.

While I was writing this book, BBC Two asked me to make a television series about the 1980s, which drew on a lot of this material. Sue Ayton and her superb team at Knight Ayton drove a suitably hard bargain. As always, I was merely the risibly un-telegenic front man for an immensely amiable, clever and industrious team. The incomparable Louis Caulfield and Adam Scourfield, ably supported by Alex Webb, Hassan Ali and Tracey Li, did most of the real work. Jacqui Farnham co-ordinated the playing of video games, Kate Misrahi organized the consumption of meatballs, Chris Granlund kept the show on the road and Fatima Salaria did her best to save me from myself. For their wisdom and comradeship, I am especially indebted to two great men: the series producer, Alex Leith, and the series originator, Steve Condie, who also invited me to be the consultant for his splendid series about the life of Margaret Thatcher. Between them Steve and Alex have spent years listening to me talking about the 1980s. The crimes they must have committed in their former lives to deserve such punishment are too terrible to contemplate.

As a jobbing writer, I am indebted to the editors who, to the horror of the reading public, have kept giving me work. At the *Daily Mail*, I count myself lucky to work with Leaf Kalfayan, Andrew Morrod, Andrew Yates and Liz Hunt. I will forever be grateful to Paul Dacre for giving me such a wonderful opportunity, and it is a pleasure to write for his successor, Geordie Greig. I am lucky, too, to have worked for so long with the team at *BBC History*, especially Rob Attar, Charlotte Hodgman and Ellie Cawthorne. And I am, as always, immensely grateful to the *Sunday Times*'s Andrew Holgate for his friendship and counsel.

My deepest thanks, though, are to my family. It would take another thousand pages to express what I owe to Catherine and Arthur. To them, and to my father, Rhys Sandbrook, this book is dedicated, with love.

# Notes

Documents marked TNA are from the National Archives (Public Record Office) in Kew. Those marked PRONI are from the Public Record Office of Northern Ireland and can be found at the University of Ulster's Conflict and Politics in Northern Ireland (CAIN) website at https://cain.ulster.ac.uk/proni/index.html. References to Hansard are from the websites https://api.parliament.uk/historic-hansard/sittings/1970s and https://api.parliament.uk/historic-hansard/sittings/1980s. Documents marked TFW are from the Margaret Thatcher Foundation website at https://www.margaretthatcher.org/. And those marked MO are from the Mass Observation archive and can be found at the University of Sussex's 'Observing the 80s' website at http://blogs.sussex.ac.uk/observingthe80s/home/mass-observation/. Place of publication is London, unless otherwise stated.

## Preface: We're Still a Super Power

1. C. H. O'D. Alexander to Clive Whitmore, 'Terrorist Incident at Iranian Embassy', 30 April 1980, TFW; *The Times*, 1 May 1980, 2 May 1980, 5 May 1980, 6 May 1980; *Guardian*, 24 July 2002. 2. 'Written Statement on Mountbatten and Warrenpoint Murders', 27 August 1979, TFW. 3. 'No. 10 Record of Conversation (MT-Whitelaw)', 2 May 1980, TFW. 4. 'No. 10 Record of Telephone Conversation (MT-Whitelaw)', 3 May 1980, TFW. 5. *Daily Express*, 5 May 1980; *Guardian*, 24 July 2002; Mark Garnett and Ian Aitken, *Splendid! Splendid! The Authorized Biography of Willie Whitelaw* (2002), pp. 254–5. For a more detailed narrative, see Gregory Fremont-Barnes, *Who Dares Wins: The SAS and the Iranian Embassy Siege, 1980* (Oxford, 2009). 6. Nixon to Thatcher, 6 May 1980, TFW; TNA PREM 19/1137, Ramphal to Thatcher, 6 May 1980; TNA PREM 19/1137, William G. Davis to Thatcher, 6 May 1980; *New York Times*, 7 May 1980. 7. *Daily Express*, 6 May 1980, 7 May 1980. 8. *The Times*, 10 May 1980; *Guardian*, 15 May 1980, 9 May 1980, 12 May 1980. 9. 'No. 10 Note to Press Office', 8 May 1980, TFW; *Guardian*, 24 July 2002; Margaret Thatcher, *The Downing Street Years* (1993), p. 90. 10. Richard Vinen, *Thatcher's Britain: The Politics and Social Upheaval of the Thatcher Era* (2009), p. 102; *The Times*, 13 December 1980. 11. General Sir Robert Ford to Thatcher, 17 November 1982, TFW; David Stirling to Thatcher, 10 February 1983, TFW. 12. *The Times*, 12 November 1980, 15 October 1982. 13. *Los Angeles Times*, 9 May 1982; see also Lloyd's obituaries in the *Scotsman*, 16 July 2016, and at http://www.bfi.org.uk/news-opinion/news-bfi/features/euan-lloyd-1923-2016. On Lewis Collins, see *Daily Mirror*, 29 November 2013; *Daily Mail*, 29 November 2013; and the tribute at the Parachute Regiment website https://www.parachuteregiment-hsf.org/Lewis_Collins.html. 14. *Guardian*, 1 September 1982, 27 August 1982. 15. *The Times*, 3 September 1982; *Guardian*, 26 August 1982 16. *The Times*, 18 December 1982; *Los Angeles Times*, 9 September 1983. 17. Richard Ingrams and John Wells, *Dear Bill: The Collected Letters of Denis Thatcher* (1980), p. 74. 18. *Daily Express*, 7 May 1980; *Sun*, 20 April 1982; *Daily Mail*, 22 May 1982; Barbara Castle, *The Castle Diaries, 1974–76* (1980), p. 221. 19. *Sunday Times*, 3 August 1980; *The Times*, 25 October 1982.

## Chapter 1. Whatever Happened to Britain?

1. All this comes, of course, from the *Fawlty Towers* episode 'Waldorf Salad', first shown on BBC1 on 5 March 1979.   2. *The Times*, 18 August 1980, 1 September 1980; *Observer*, 2 September 1984.   3. *Let's Go, 1982: Britain and Ireland* (New York, 1982), p. 52; *Fodor's 1982 Guide to Great Britain* (New York, 1982), pp. v–vi.   4. Ibid., pp. 52–3; *Let's Go, 1982*, pp. 31–2.   5. Paul Theroux, *The Kingdom by the Sea: A Journey around the Coast of Great Britain* (1983), p. 219.   6. *Fodor's 1982 Guide to Great Britain*, pp. v, 50, 102, 151; *Let's Go, 1982*, pp. 36, 68, 57, 92; Theroux, *Kingdom by the Sea*, p. 13. For a similar take from a British perspective, see *The Times*, 24 September 1980.   7. *Fodor's 1982 Guide to Great Britain*, pp. v, 50; *Let's Go, 1982*, pp. 36, 68; Jonathan Raban, *Coasting* (1986), pp. 212–13, 236. 8. *Wall Street Journal*, 29 April 1975.   9. *Guardian*, 26 January 1979.   10. *Daily Express*, 30 April 1979; 'Speech to Conservative Rally in Bolton', 1 May 1979, TFW.   11. Memorandum of Conversation, President Ford and Henry Kissinger, 8 January 1975, Box 8, National Security Adviser's Files, Gerald R. Ford Library, Ann Arbor, Michigan; *Guardian*, 30 September 1975; Samuel H. Beer, *Britain Against Itself: The Political Contradictions of Collectivism* (New York, 1982), p. xi. See also *Time*, 19 May 1975; Robert Moss, 'Anglocommunism?', *Commentary* (February 1977), pp. 27–33; *The Times*, 8 May 1975; Bernard D. Nossiter, *Britain: A Future That Works* (1978), pp. 12–13.   12. *New York Times*, 15 October 1976. 13. Ibid., 3 December 1977, 16 July 1978, 10 December 1978.   14. Martin J. Wiener, *English Culture and the Decline of the Industrial Spirit, 1850–1980* (1981: Cambridge, 2004), pp. xv, 3, 165–6.   15. *Spectator*, 3 December 2011; Theroux, *Kingdom by the Sea*, pp. 13, 15.   16. John Eatwell, *Whatever Happened to Britain? The Economics of Decline* (1982), p. 12; Sidney Pollard, *The Wasting of the British Economy: British Economic Policy, 1945 to the Present* (1982), pp. 2–3. For a very critical view of the 'declinist' interpretation of modern British history, see Jim Tomlinson, 'Inventing "Decline": The Falling Behind of the British Economy in the Postwar Years', *Economic History Review*, 49:4 (1996), pp. 731–57; Jim Tomlinson, 'Mrs Thatcher's Macroeconomic Adventurism, 1979–1981, and Its Political Consequences', *British Politics*, 2:1 (2007), pp. 14–16.   17. Alan Clark, *Diaries: Into Politics, 1972–1982* (2000), pp. 163, 177; Tony Benn, *The End of an Era: Diaries, 1980–90* (1992), pp. 93–4. 18. Louis Heren, *Alas, Alas for England: What Went Wrong with Britain* (1981), pp. 2, 4, 8, 42, 168, 80, 166.   19. *The Economist*, 2 June 1979; *Guardian*, 2 June 1979; David Owen, *Time to Declare* (1991), p. 277.   20. Sir Nicholas Henderson, 'Britain's Decline: Its Causes and Consequences', 31 March 1979, TFW; *The Economist*, 2 June 1979.   21. *Guardian*, 2 June 1979, 23 May 1979; Richard Vinen, *Thatcher's Britain: The Politics and Social Upheaval of the Thatcher Era* (2009), p. 190; *Daily Telegraph*, 16 March 2009; and see Nicholas Henderson, *Mandarin: The Diaries of Nicholas Henderson* (1994: 2000).   22. *Daily Mirror*, 2 June 1979; *Guardian*, 2 June 1979, 23 May 1979; *Daily Express*, 23 May 1979; *The Economist*, 16 June 1979, 30 June 1979.   23. Andrew Gamble, *Britain in Decline: Economic Policy, Political Strategy and the British State* (Basingstoke, 1994), pp. xv, 15, 17; Catherine R. Schenk, 'Britain and the Common Market', in Richard Coopey and Nicholas Woodward (eds.), *Britain in the 1970s: The Troubled Economy* (1996), p. 193; Richard Coopey and Nicholas Woodward, 'The British Economy in the 1970s: An Overview', in ibid., p. 3; *Guardian*, 26 September 1978, 27 September 1978.   24. See Jim Tomlinson, 'De-Industrialization Not Decline: A New Meta-Narrative for Post-War British History', *Twentieth Century British History*, 27:1 (2016), pp. 76–99.   25. *The Economist*, 16 June 1979, 30 June 1979; Lincoln Allison, *Condition of England: Essays and Impressions* (1981), pp. 37, 64.   26. Theroux, *Kingdom by the Sea*, pp. 34, 42.   27. Allison, *Condition of England*, pp. 52–3; Heren, *Alas, Alas for England*, p. 150.   28. *Guardian*, 6 December 1980, 10 January 1983; John Sutherland, *Reading the Decades: Fifty Years of the Nation's Bestselling Books* (2002), pp. 114–15, 122–4, 132, 138.   29. *The Times*, 16 March 1981, 17 February 1982, 7 March 1983; *Guardian*, 8 December 1982.   30. MO R470, Summer Directive – Work, 1983; MO A883, Summer Directive – Work, 1983.   31. HMSO, *Housing in Britain* (1975), pp. 7–8; Arthur M. Edwards, *The Design of Suburbia: A Critical Study in Environmental History* (1981), pp. 243–4;

Lawrence James, *The Middle Class: A History* (2006), pp. 522–3; Phil Wickham, *The Likely Lads* (Basingstoke, 2008), pp. 16, 34.   **32.** MO D156, Autumn Directive – Housework, 1983; MO W633, Autumn Directive – Housework, 1983; MO G226, Autumn Directive – Housework, 1983.   **33.** Margaret Drabble, *The Middle Ground* (1980), p. 199.   **34.** MO W633, Autumn Directive – Housework, 1983; MO G226, Autumn Directive – Housework, 1983; MO G218, Autumn Directive – Housework, 1983.   **35.** Jeremy Seabrook, *Unemployment* (1982: 1983), p. 168; MO W633, Autumn Directive – Housework, 1983; MO G226, Autumn Directive – Housework, 1983.   **36.** *The Times*, 10 December 1981; *Guardian*, 11 December 1980. On electricity, see Gavin Weightman, *Children of Light: How Electricity Changed Britain Forever* (2011).   **37.** MO R470, Winter Directive – Christmas, 1983; MO W633, Winter Directive – Christmas, 1983; MO S496, Winter Directive – Christmas, 1983.   **38.** *Guardian*, 14 September 1982, 1 September 1981, 2 April 1982; MO D156, Summer Directive 1982.   **39.** Brian Harrison, *Finding a Role? The United Kingdom, 1970–1990* (Oxford, 2010), p. 89; *The Times* 6 April 1983; *Guardian*, 18 March 1982.   **40.** Ian Jack, *Before the Oil Ran Out: Britain in the Brutal Years* (rev. edn: 1997), p. xvii; *Guardian*, 3 October 1983. See also Harrison, *Finding a Role?*, pp. 19, 68, 101.   **41.** Ibid., p. 403; *The Times*, 24 June 1981, 30 November 1982, 5 October 1984. On video sales, see also *Guardian*, 3 February 1984.   **42.** Raban, *Coasting*, p. 12; Harrison, *Finding a Role?*, p. 101; Robert J. Wybrow, *Britain Speaks Out, 1937–87: A Social History as Seen through the Gallup Data* (Basingstoke, 1989), p. 137.   **43.** *The Times*, 8 May 1980, 27 February 1981, 15 September 1981.   **44.** Ibid., 4 November 1981, 21 January 1982, 1 April 1982, 9 November 1983.   **45.** Ibid., 2 May 1981, 8 November 1983; *Guardian*, 12 October 1982.   **46.** MO S496, Spring Directive 1982; *Guardian*, 3 December 1984, 23 December 2012; *Daily Mail*, 21 December 2012.   **47.** *New Statesman*, 6 March 1998; *Guardian*, 10 March 1978, 23 September 1981; *Daily Telegraph*, 20 December 2012; *Guardian*, 3 December 1984.   **48.** *Daily Telegraph*, 20 December 2012; *The Times*, 3 June 1981, 7 March 1984; and see Joe Moran, *Reading the Everyday* (Abingdon, 2005), pp. 145–7.   **49.** For two nice articles about Barratt's style and its appeal, see Joe Moran in the *New Statesman*, 6 March 1998, and Harry Mount in the *Daily Mail*, 21 December 2012.   **50.** *Observer*, 11 August 1985; Charles Moore, *Margaret Thatcher: The Authorized Biography*, vol. 2: *Everything She Wants* (2015), pp. 669–70; *Woman's Own*, 12 October 1985; 'Interview for *Mail on Sunday*', 30 August 1985, TFW.

## Chapter 2. The Line of Duty

**1.** 'Thatcher Arrives at Downing Street', 4 May 1979, http://www.bbc.co.uk/archive/thatcher/6328.shtml; 'Remarks on Becoming Prime Minister', 4 May 1979, TFW.   **2.** Ronald Millar, *A View from the Wings: West End, West Coast, Westminster* (1993), pp. 263–7; and see the invaluable article by the Thatcher Foundation's Christopher Collins at https://www.margaretthatcher.org/archive/StFrancis.asp.   **3.** Charles Moore, *Margaret Thatcher: The Authorized Biography*, vol. 1: *Not for Turning* (2013), pp. 419–20.   **4.** Ibid., pp. 308–9, 387; *Sunday Telegraph*, 29 April 1979, quoted in Brian Harrison, 'Mrs Thatcher and the Intellectuals', *Twentieth Century British History*, 5:2 (1994), p.p. 226–7; *Daily Mirror*, 9 January 1981; Alwyn W. Turner, *Rejoice! Rejoice! Britain in the 1980s* (2010), p. 163; Henry Root, *The Henry Root Letters* (1980: 1981), p. 15.   **5.** 'TV Interview for BBC *Campaign '79*', 27 April 1979, TFW.   **6.** Robert Saunders, 'The Many Lives of Margaret Thatcher', *English Historical Review*, 132:556 (2017), p. 645; Moore, *Not for Turning*, pp. 308, 410. See also Dominic Janes, '"One of Us": The Queer Afterlife of Margaret Thatcher as a Gay Icon', *International Journal of Media and Cultural Politics*, 8:2–3 (2012), pp. 211–27.   **7.** Ferdinand Mount, *Cold Cream: My Early Life and Other Mistakes* (2008), pp. 269, 324; Alan Hollinghurst, *The Line of Beauty* (2004), p. 376; Charles Moore, *Margaret Thatcher: The Authorized Biography*, vol. 2: *Everything She Wants* (2015), pp. 648–9.   **8.** Ibid., p. 665; Mount, *Cold Cream*, p. 290; Moore, *Not for Turning*, p. 388; Matthew Parris, *Chance Witness: An Outsider's Life in Politics* (2002: 2013), p. 177; *Guardian*, 8 October 2010.   **9.** Parris, *Chance Witness*, p. 213; Louis Heren, *Alas, Alas for England: What Went Wrong* *with Britain* (1981), p. 114; L. J. Sinclair, 'Summit Information Desk ("Who Me?")', *c.* 1 May 1983, TFW; Moore, *Not for Turning*, pp. 176, 342–3; *Observer*, 12 October 1975; Moore, *Everything She Wants*, pp. 637, 652; 'Interview for *News of the World*', 24 April 1980, TFW; *The Times*, 1 May 1980; Thatcher to Sir James Hanson, 8 July 1981, TFW; Ion Trewin (ed.), *The Hugo Young Papers: Thirty Years of British Politics – Off the Record* (2008), p. 189.   10. Moore, *Everything She Wants*, p. 636; *Guardian*, 30 May 1988; Parris, *Chance Witness*, p. 212; Harrison, 'Mrs Thatcher and the Intellectuals', p. 224; Trewin (ed.), *Hugo Young Papers*, p. 49.   11. Harrison, 'Mrs Thatcher and the Intellectuals', p. 208; Moore, *Not for Turning*, p. 342; Trewin (ed.), *Hugo Young Papers*, p. 273. Harrison's essay is a pretty comprehensive rebuttal of the idea that Mrs Thatcher was a philistine; for another example, written by a Labour supporter, see D. J. Taylor, *The Prose Factory: Literary Life in England since 1918* (2016), pp. 415–16.   12. Trewin (ed.), *Hugo Young Papers*, p. 49. On Mrs Thatcher's lack of empathy, see John Campbell, *Margaret Thatcher*, vol. 2: *The Iron Lady* (2003), pp. 247–8.   13. Parris, *Chance Witness*, p. 210.   14. *Guardian*, 6 June 1983, 28 May 1988; *Observer*, 13 September 1987.   15. Moore, *Everything She Wants*, p. 668; TNA PREM 19/474, Sally Rozario to A. Kennard, 'Expenditure of Refurbishing at No. 10 Downing Street', 25 June 1979; Moore, *Not for Turning*, p. 431; Jonathan Aitken, *Margaret Thatcher: Power and Personality* (2013), p. 265; TNA PREM 19/474, Edwards to Thatcher, 28 January 1981; and see the subsequent correspondence about the Welsh flat in TNA PREM 19/474.   16. 'Interview for *Living* Magazine', 9 January 1984, TFW; Moore, *Not for Turning*, pp. 361, 529–30; Aitken, *Margaret Thatcher*, p. 238; Sir John Coles, 'Appreciation of Margaret Thatcher', *c.* 14 June 1984, TFW; Campbell, *Iron Lady*, pp. 480, 482.   17. John Hoskyns, *Just in Time: Inside the Thatcher Revolution* (2000), p. 24; Mount, *Cold Cream*, pp. 287, 289–90, 323.   18. Moore, *Not for Turning*, p. 423; Coles, 'Appreciation of Margaret Thatcher', *c.* 14 June 1984, TFW; Aitken, *Margaret Thatcher*, p. 278; Trewin (ed.), *Hugo Young Papers*, pp. 149, 165.   19. 'Interview for *News of the World*', 24 April 1980, TFW; Harrison, 'Mrs Thatcher and the Intellectuals', p. 208; Coles, 'Appreciation of Margaret Thatcher', *c.* 14 June 1984, TFW; Campbell, *Iron Lady*, pp. 20, 479; Moore, *Not for Turning*, p. 438; David Waddington, John MacGregor and Peter Morrison to Thatcher, 31 July 1980, TFW.   20. Sue Townsend, *The Growing Pains of Adrian Mole* (1984: 2002), p. 147.   21. Parris, *Chance Witness*, p. 201; Aitken, *Margaret Thatcher*, p. 278; *Sun*, 3 November 2012.   22. 'Interview for *News of the World*', 24 April 1980, TFW; *Los Angeles Times*, 23 April 1979; Aitken, *Margaret Thatcher*, pp. 184, 188.   23. Ibid., p. 239; *Sun*, 2 November 2012.   24. Hoskyns, *Just in Time*, p. 380; Moore, *Not for Turning*, pp. 432, 434; Coles, 'Appreciation of Margaret Thatcher', *c.* 14 June 1984, TFW; Hailsham to Thatcher, 11 July 1984, TFW; Mount, *Cold Cream*, p. 324.   25. Frank Johnson, *Out of Order* (1982), p. 170. It has to be said that this story comes from the journalist Frank Johnson, who heard it from the journalist Sir John Junor, so it might be a bit exaggerated. Still, it is so good, and rings so true, that it would be a shame to question it.   26. Aitken, *Margaret Thatcher*, pp. 239–40; Campbell, *Iron Lady*, pp. 15, 17, 19; Moore, *Everything She Wants*, pp. 5, 523, 618; Mount, *Cold Cream*, pp. 324, 326; Cecil Parkinson, *Right at the Centre: An Autobiography* (1992), p. 217; Nigel Lawson, *The View from No. 11: Memoirs of a Tory Radical* (1992: 1993), p. 128; John Biffen, *Semi-Detached* (2013), pp. 374, 390–91; *Spectator*, 18 January 2014; Jim Prior, *A Balance of Power* (1986), p. 136.   27. Moore, *Not for Turning*, p. 422; Campbell, *Iron Lady*, pp. 16–17; George Walden, *Lucky George: Memoirs of an Anti-Politician* (1999), p. 191; Parris, *Chance Witness*, p. 188; Aitken, *Margaret Thatcher*, pp. 264–5. See also, for example, Roy Jenkins, *A Life at the Centre* (1991), pp. 493, 496.   28. Parris, *Chance Witness*, pp. 193, 205; Thatcher to Kirk Peters, 10 February 1981, TFW; Thatcher to unidentified boy, 1 July 1981, TFW.   29. Thatcher to David Liddelow, 1 April 1980, TFW. For David's original letter, as well as later press commentary, see *Daily Express*, 11 April 2013; *Daily Telegraph*, 17 April 2013.   30. 'Speech to Conservative Central Council', 15 March 1975, TFW; and see Robert Saunders, '"Crisis? What Crisis?" Thatcherism and the Seventies', in Ben Jackson and Robert Saunders (eds.), *Making Thatcher's Britain* (Cambridge, 2012), p. 29; Saunders, 'The Many Lives of Margaret Thatcher', p. 651; Matthew Bailey and Philip Cowley, 'Thatcherism: Not Made in Birmingham', 16 March 2015, http://www.

conservativehome.com/platform/2015/03/matthew-bentley-and-philip-cowley-thatcherism-not-born-in-birmingham.html.   31. Stuart Hall, 'The Great Moving Right Show', *Marxism Today* (January 1979), pp. 14–20; David Marquand, 'The Paradoxes of Thatcherism', in Robert Skidelsky (ed.), *Thatcherism* (1988), p. 160; Austin Mitchell, *Four Years in the Death of the Labour Party* (1983), p. 15.   32. For a good survey of this colossal subject, mercifully free of political-science jargon, see Saunders, 'The Many Lives of Margaret Thatcher'.   33. Lawson, *View from No. 11*, p. 64; 'TV Interview for BBC1 *Panorama*', 8 June 1987, TFW.   34. Ian Gilmour, *Dancing with Dogma: Britain under Thatcherism* (1992), p. 11; Woodrow Wyatt, *The Journals of Woodrow Wyatt*, vol. 1 (1998), p. 585; E. H. H. Green, *Thatcher* (2006), p. 33; Graham Stewart, *Bang! A History of Britain in the 1980s* (2013), p. 61.   35. 'Speech to Conservative Party Conference', 14 October 1983, TFW; and see Green, *Thatcher*, pp. 21–54; E. H. H. Green, *Ideologies of Conservatism: Conservative Political Ideas in the Twentieth Century* (Oxford, 2002), pp. 214–39; Richard Vinen, *Thatcher's Britain: The Politics and Social Upheaval of the Thatcher Era* (2009) p. 288; Stewart, *Bang!*, pp. 61–2.   36. 'TV Interview for BBC1 *Panorama*', 8 June 1987, TFW; Nigel Lawson, 'The New Conservatism: Lecture to the Bow Group', 4 August 1980, TFW.   37. Green, *Ideologies of Conservatism*, pp. 218–22, 224, 235; Green, *Thatcher*, p. 27; Vinen, *Thatcher's Britain*, p. 289; Lawson, *View from No. 11*, p. 14.   38. Kevin Bonnett, Simon Bromley, Bob Jessop and Tom Ling, 'Authoritarian Populism, Two Nations, and Thatcherism', *New Left Review* 147 (1984), pp. 32–60; Vinen, *Thatcher's Britain*, pp. 4, 275–6; 'Speech to Greater London Young Conservatives: Iain Macleod Lecture, "Dimensions of Conservatism"', 4 July 1977, TFW; Saunders, '"Crisis? What Crisis?"', pp. 28–9.   39. Moore, *Not for Turning*, p. 302; Vinen, *Thatcher's Britain*, pp. 282, 57; *The Times*, 31 March 1983; 'TV Interview for BBC *Campaign '79'*, 27 April 1979, TFW; *New York Times*, 29 April 1979; Coles, 'Appreciation of Margaret Thatcher', c. 14 June 1984, TFW; Hugo Young, *This Blessed Plot: Britain and Europe from Churchill to Blair* (1998), p. 307.   40. John Ranelagh, *Thatcher's People: An Insider's Account of the Politics, the Power and the Personalities* (1991), p. 71.   41. David Cannadine, 'Apocalypse When? British Politicians and British "Decline" in the Twentieth Century', in Peter Clarke and Clive Trebilcock (eds.), *Understanding Decline: Perceptions and Realities of British Economic Performance* (Cambridge, 1997), p. 262; Margaret Thatcher, *The Downing Street Years* (1993), p. 15; 'Message to the People of Britain', 16 April 1979, TFW; 'Speech to Conservative Rally in Bolton', 1 May 1979, TFW; 'TV Interview for BBC *Campaign '79'*, 27 April 1979, TFW.   42. Aitken, *Margaret Thatcher*, p. 268; Lord Hailsham, *The Dilemma of Democracy: Diagnosis and Prescription* (1978) pp. 15, 22; Sir Keith Joseph, *Solving the Union Problem Is the Key to Britain's Recovery* (1979), p. 5; Trewin (ed.), *Hugo Young Papers*, pp. 120–21; Green, *Thatcher*, p. 55; Thatcher, *Downing Street Years*, p. 10. Saunders, '"Crisis? What Crisis?"', pp. 30–31, is very good on all this.   43. Moore, *Everything She Wants*, pp. 6–7; 'TV Interview for De Wolfe Productions', 30 December 1982, TFW.   44. Moore, *Everything She Wants*, pp. 8, 6; Moore, *Not for Turning*, pp. 302, 577, 300; Campbell, *Iron Lady*, p. 250; Parris, *Chance Witness*, p. 204; 'TV Interview for BBC1 *Panorama*', 8 June 1987, TFW.   45. Mount, *Cold Cream*, pp. 287–8; '1979 Election Address: "The Britain I Want to See"', 11 April 1979, TFW.   46. 'Notes for Conference Speech ("Thoughts on the Moral Case")', 3 October 1979, TFW.   47. 'Notes for Conference Speech ("Virtue of a Nation")', 16 October 1981, TFW; 'Notes for Conference Speech ("Draft 2")', 16 October 1981, TFW.   48. 'Speech in Finchley (adoption)', 11 April 1979, TFW; 'Speech at St Lawrence Jewry', 4 March 1981, TFW; *The Times*, 5 March 1981; and see Matthew Grimley, 'Thatcherism, Morality and Religion', in Jackson and Saunders (eds.), *Making Thatcher's Britain*, pp. 84, 89; *Daily Telegraph*, 18 September 1984, quoted in Hugo Young, *One of Us: A Biography of Margaret Thatcher* (rev. edn: 1990), p. 352.   49. Eliza Filby, *God and Mrs Thatcher: The Battle for Britain's Soul* (2015), pp. 9, 14–15, 21; Moore, *Not for Turning*, p. 349; Moore, *Everything She Wants*, p. 447; Parris, *Chance Witness*, pp. 186–7.   50. Saunders, 'The Many Lives of Margaret Thatcher', p. 653; *News of the World*, 20 September 1981, quoted in Stewart, *Bang!*, p. 62. For a clip of the *Nationwide* interview, which went out on 20 April 1979, see the first episode of *The 80s*, 'The Sound of the Crowd' (BBC Two, 4 August 2016).   51. Brian Harrison, *Finding a Role?*

*The United Kingdom, 1970–1990* (Oxford, 2010), pp. 140, 406; Moore, *Not for Turning*, p. 308; Jon Lawrence and Florence Sutcliffe-Braithwaite, 'Margaret Thatcher and the Decline of Class Politics', in Jackson and Saunders (eds.), *Making Thatcher's Britain*, pp. 134–5, 142.  **52.** Ibid., pp. 139–43; 'Speech to Conservative Trade Unionists Conference', 11 March 1978, TFW.  **53.** John Campbell, *Margaret Thatcher*, vol. 1: *The Grocer's Daughter* (2000), p. 3; Green, *Thatcher*, p. 18; Anthony Sampson, *The Changing Anatomy of Britain* (1982: 1983), p. 41; *New York Times*, 29 April 1979; Saunders, 'The Many Lives of Margaret Thatcher', pp. 641–2; 'Remarks on Becoming Prime Minister', 4 May 1979, TFW.  **54.** Anthony King and Robert J. Wybrow (eds.), *British Political Opinion, 1937–2000: The Gallup Polls* (2001), pp. 198–9, 208; *The Times*, 10 October 1978; David Butler and Dennis Kavanagh, *The British General Election of 1979* (1980), pp. 323, 394, 163, 342–3, 345, 350; *Time*, 23 April 1979. On the polls, see also *Guardian*, 4 May 1979, 5 May 1979; *Sunday Times*, 6 May 1979.  **55.** *Guardian*, 4 May 1979; Trewin (ed.), *Hugo Young Papers*, p. 133; Mount, *Cold Cream*, p. 347.  **56.** 'Remarks on Becoming Prime Minister', 4 May 1979, TFW; *Daily Express*, 3 February 1975; 'Speech to Conservative Party Conference', 13 October 1978, TFW; Saunders, '"Crisis? What Crisis?"', p. 32; Campbell, *Iron Lady*, p. 5; *Spectator*, 11 May 1985; Mount, *Cold Cream*, pp. 325–6, 328.  **57.** Parris, *Chance Witness*, pp. 290–91. The City economist Roger Bootle, otherwise a keen admirer, made similar observations after Mrs Thatcher died: see *Daily Telegraph*, 8 April 2013.  **58.** Thatcher, *Downing Street Years*, pp. 24–5, 29; Aitken, *Margaret Thatcher*, p. 261; Moore, *Not for Turning*, p. 421; Campbell, *Iron Lady*, p. 27.  **59.** Tim Lankester, 'Summary of the General Post', 10 September 1979, TFW; Thatcher to Sellers, 18 May 1979, TFW; Grimley, 'Thatcherism, Morality and Religion', p. 299, fn. 92; Thatcher to Hayek, 18 May 1979, TFW; Thatcher to Friedman, 11 May 1979, TFW. On the messages in general, see Christopher Collins's guide at https://www.margaretthatcher.org/archive/1979-cac-releases-1.asp.  **60.** Moore, *Not for Turning*, p. 324; Mount, *Cold Cream*, pp. 330–32; Thatcher to Millar, 5 May 1979, TFW; Millar to Thatcher, 10 May 1979, TFW.  **61.** Thatcher to Millar, 25 August 1978. TFW.

## Chapter 3. You'd Look Super in Slacks

**1.** *Guardian*, 3 September 1982.  **2.** *Daily Express*, 12 August 1980; see also *Guardian*, 14 January 1981, 3 December 1988.  **3.** *Daily Express*, 12 August 1980; *Guardian*, 26 April 1981, 16 January 1980; *The Times*, 10 March 1981; *Observer*, 23 January 1983.  **4.** *Guardian*, 8 June 1978, 9 June 1978.  **5.** *Daily Express*, 13 June 1978, 19 June 1978.  **6.** Ibid., 14 June 1978; *Guardian*, 26 April 1981.  **7.** *The Times*, 9 August 1983.  **8.** 'Interview for *News of the World*', 24 April 1980, TFW.  **9.** *The Times*, 5 May 1980; *Sun*, 16 March 1979.  **10.** Brian Harrison, *Finding a Role? The United Kingdom, 1970–1990* (Oxford, 2010), p. 269; *Guardian*, 10 January 1983; *Financial Times*, 23 July 1984; *The Times*, 2 April 1981.  **11.** 'Interview for *News of the World*', 24 April 1980, TFW; 'Mayo Clinic Diet', 1 January 1979, TFW; *Sun*, 16 March 1979.  **12.** *Observer*, 12 October 1975; Charles Moore, *Margaret Thatcher: The Authorized Biography*, vol. 2: *Everything She Wants* (2015), pp. 671–2; John Campbell, *Margaret Thatcher*, vol. 2: *The Iron Lady* (2003), pp. 25, 475–6; Charles Moore, *Margaret Thatcher: The Authorized Biography*, vol. 1: *Not for Turning* (2015), pp. 41–2, 435; 'Interview for *News of the World*', 24 April 1980, TFW.  **13.** *Daily Express*, 11 May 1981; *Sunday Express*, 15 February 1981; *Daily Mirror*, 13 October 1980.  **14.** *The Times*, 10 March 1981; *Guardian*, 11 July 1979.  **15.** Ibid., 11 July 1979, 11 August 1981, 26 July 1982, 18 October 1983.  **16.** *Observer*, 7 February 1982; *The Times*, 24 August 1982.  **17.** 'Mrs McClusky Remembers Her School', 6 February 2008, http://news.bbc.co.uk/1/hi/entertainment/7231367.stm; *Guardian*, 23 October 1981; *Daily Mirror*, 24 October 1981.  **18.** Alwyn W. Turner, *Rejoice! Rejoice! Britain in the 1980s* (2010), pp. 6–7.  **19.** Ian Kennedy Martin, 'Juliet Bravo', http://www.iankennedymartin.com/page6.htm; *Daily Express*, 5 September 1981; *Daily Mirror*, 28 August 1980.  **20.** Peter Clarke, *Hope and Glory: Britain, 1900–1990* (1996), p. 363; Graham Stewart, *Bang! A History of Britain in* *the 1980s* (2013), p. 340; Hera Cook, *The Long Sexual Revolution: English Women, Sex, and Contraception, 1800–1975* (2004: Oxford, 2005), p. 336; Christopher Johnson, *The Economy under Mrs Thatcher, 1979–1990* (1991), p. 248; *Guardian*, 15 June 1981. **21.** *Financial Times*, 20 May 1992; *Guardian*, 12 August 1980. **22.** Harrison, *Finding a Role?*, p. 230; *Observer*, 8 April 1984; *Guardian*, 15 April 1985; and see the interview with Shirley, dated 21 October 2016, at https://www.director.co.uk/dame-stephanie-shirley-first-generation-immigrants-wealth-creators/. **23.** Beatrix Campbell, *Wigan Pier Revisited: Poverty and Politics in the 80s* (1984), p. 58. **24.** *Mail on Sunday*, 9 October 1983; Cate Haste, *Rules of Desire: Sex in Britain, World War I to the Present* (rev. edn: 1994), p. 287; *Guardian*, 22 July 1982; *The Times*, 23 February 1983; Daisy Payling, '"Socialist Republic of South Yorkshire": Grassroots Activism and Left-Wing Solidarity in 1980s Sheffield', *Twentieth Century British History*, 25:4 (2014), p. 617. **25.** Mary Abbott, *Family Affairs: A History of the Family in Twentieth-Century England* (2003), p. 164; Haste, *Rules of Desire*, p. 289; Sheila Rowbotham, *A Century of Women: The History of Women in Britain and the United States* (1997: 1999), p. 470. **26.** Haste, *Rules of Desire*, pp. 236–7; Harrison, *Finding a Role?*, p. 230; Chris Wrigley, 'Women in the Labour Market and in the Unions', in John McIlroy, Nina Fishman and Alan Campbell (eds.), *The High Tide of British Trade Unionism: Trade Unions and Industrial Politics, 1964–79* (new edn: Monmouth, 2007), pp. 56–7, 59–60, 66; Campbell, *Wigan Pier Revisited*, pp. 138–42. **27.** Beatrix Campbell, *The Iron Ladies: Why Do Women Vote Tory?* (1987), pp. 161, 152. **28.** *Daily Mirror*, 27 October 1981; Sue Townsend, *The Secret Diary of Adrian Mole Aged 13¾* (1982: 2002), pp. 17, 249. **29.** *Daily Express*, 29 October 1981; Campbell, *Iron Ladies*, pp. 162–3. **30.** *The Economist*, 8 September 1979; Clarke, *Hope and Glory*, p. 365; Laura Beers, 'Thatcher and the Women's Vote', in Ben Jackson and Robert Saunders (eds.), *Making Thatcher's Britain* (Cambridge, 2012), pp. 113–31; MO D156, Autumn Directive – Housework, 1983. **31.** Abbott, *Family Affairs*, p. 154; MO W633, Summer Directive – Work, 1983; MO S496, Summer Directive – Work, 1983. **32.** Haste, *Rules of Desire*, p. 289; Harrison, *Finding a Role?*, pp. 228–9; Rowbotham, *Century of Women*, pp. 488–91; *The Times*, 8 December 1982. **33.** *Guardian*, 18 June 1980; *The Times*, 26 November 1980, 27 November 1980, 8 December 1982; Alan Bleasdale, *Boys from the Blackstuff* (1982: 1985), p. 177. **34.** Ina Zweiniger-Bargielowska, 'Housewifery', in Ina Zweiniger-Bargielowska (ed.), *Women in Twentieth-Century Britain* (Harlow, 2001), p. 153; *Daily Express*, 21 May 1979; *Daily Telegraph*, 1 June 2016; *Guardian*, 2 June 2016. **35.** Ibid., 18 July 2007; *Observer*, 20 April 1980. **36.** MO C1191, Summer Directive – Well-Being, 1984. **37.** 'Speech on Women in a Changing World (1st Dame Margery Corbett-Ashby Memorial Lecture)', 26 July 1982, TFW; and see Campbell, *Iron Ladies*, pp. 235–6; Moore, *Not for Turning*, pp. 118–24. **38.** 'Interview for *Living* magazine', 9 January 1984, TFW; *Daily Express*, 26 July 1982. **39.** Campbell, *Iron Ladies*, p. 253; Turner, *Rejoice! Rejoice!*, p. 164; Harrison, *Finding a Role?*, p. 232; *Guardian*, 11 September 1984, 11 August 1988. **40.** *Observer*, 28 September 1980 (see also Katharine Whitehorn's *Observer* columns on 14 September 1980 and 3 February 1985); Campbell, *Iron Lady*, p. 26; Moore, *Everything She Wants*, p. 667; Moore, *Not for Turning*, p. 353. **41.** Barbara Castle, *The Castle Diaries, 1974–76* (1980), p. 309; Abbott, *Family Affairs*, p. 146; Turner, *Rejoice! Rejoice!*, p. 162; *Daily Telegraph*, 9 April 2013. **42.** Michael Billington, *State of the Nation: British Theatre since 1945* (2007), pp. 307–8; Rowbotham, *Century of Women*, p. 476; Campbell, *Iron Ladies*, p. 241; *Daily Mail*, 11 April 2013; *Guardian*, 19 September 2014; and see Caryl Churchill, *Top Girls* (1982). **43.** Sir John Coles, 'Appreciation of Margaret Thatcher', *c.* 14 June 1984, TFW; Jim Prior, *A Balance of Power* (1986), p. 138. On Mrs Thatcher as a woman, see also Richard Vinen, *Thatcher's Britain: The Politics and Social Upheaval of the Thatcher Era* (2009) p. 3; Charles Moore, *Margaret Thatcher: The Authorized Biography*, vol. 2: *Everything She Wants* (2015), pp. xvii, 41–2, 59, 60–65, 134; Moore, *Not for Turning*, pp. 183–4, 222–3; Robert Saunders, 'The Many Lives of Margaret Thatcher', *English Historical Review*, 132:556 (2017), p. 645. **44.** Ibid., p. 647; *Guardian*, 21 March 1980. On Servalan, see http://blakes7.wikia.com/wiki/Servalan, as well as Jonathan Bignell and Andrew O'Day, *Terry Nation* (Manchester, 2004), p. 173. **45.** Moore, *Not for Turning*, pp. 307–8, 333; Campbell, *Iron Lady*, pp. 471, 473; *Spectator*, 11 May 1985; John Simpson, *Strange Places, Questionable People* (1998), p. 250. **46.** Matthew Parris, *Chance Witness: An Outsider's Life in Politics* (2002: 2013), p. 202; Alan Clark, *Diaries: Into Politics, 1972–1982* (2000), p. 238. **47.** Ibid., p. 147; Moore, *Not for Turning*, p. 436; Kingsley Amis, *Memoirs* (1991), p. 316; Nott to Thatcher, 23 January 1983, TFW; Prior, *Balance of Power*, p. 139. For Christopher Collins's thoughts, see his essay on her private papers for 1983 at https://www.margaretthatcher.org/archive/1983cac1.asp. **48.** Campbell, *Iron Lady*, p. 472; Marcus K. Harmes, 'A Creature Not Quite of This World: Adaptations of Margaret Thatcher on 1980s British Television', *Journal of Popular Television* 1:1 (2013), pp. 53, 63; *Guardian*, 19 June 2000; Moore, *Everything She Wants*, pp. 638–40; Clare Ramsaran, 'So Who's Next in the Firing Line?', in Joan Scanlon (ed.), *Surviving the Blues: Growing up in the Thatcher Decade* (1990), p. 175.

# Chapter 4. No Money, Margaret Thatcher!

**1.** *The Times*, 27 December 1979; *Guardian*, 28 November 1979; *Daily Mirror*, 7 January 1980. **2.** *Observer*, 30 December 1979. **3.** Henry Root, *The Henry Root Letters* (1980: 1981), pp. 116–17, 119. **4.** 'No. 10 Record of Telephone Conversation: MT-Clark', 23 May 1979, TFW. **5.** John Campbell, *Margaret Thatcher*, vol. 2: *The Iron Lady* (2003), p. 14; Charles Moore, *Margaret Thatcher: The Authorized Biography*, vol. 1: *Not for Turning* (2013), p. 427. **6.** Campbell, *Iron Lady*, pp. 9, 11, 13; Jim Prior, *A Balance of Power* (1986), pp. 112, 114, 118; Campbell, *Iron Lady*, pp. 11, 13; Moore, *Not for Turning*, p. 457; Geoffrey Howe, *Conflict of Loyalty* (1994), pp. 147, 169. **7.** Campbell, *Iron Lady*, p. 8; Moore, *Not for Turning*, pp. 300–301, 429; Louis Heren, *Alas, Alas for England: What Went Wrong with Britain* (1981), pp. 103, 154–5; and see Graham Stewart, *Bang! A History of Britain in the 1980s* (2013), pp. 63–4. **8.** Alan Clark, *Diaries: Into Politics, 1972–1982* (2000), pp. 138–9. **9.** John Ranelagh, *Thatcher's People: An Insider's Account of the Politics, the Power and the Personalities* (1991), pp. 39, 45, 52, 55. **10.** Ibid., p. 253; Campbell, *Iron Lady*, p. 31; Julian Critchley, *Some of Us: People Who Did Well under Thatcher* (1992), pp. 130–31; and see Robert Harris, *Good and Faithful Servant: The Unauthorized Biography of Bernard Ingham* (1990). **11.** Ranelagh, *Thatcher's People*, p. 241; John Hoskyns, *Just in Time: Inside the Thatcher Revolution* (2000), pp. 3, 12, 93–4; 'Speech to the Institute of Directors', 24 February 1987, TFW; Tim Lankester, 'The 1981 Budget: How Did It Come About?', in Duncan Needham and Anthony Hotson (eds.), *Expansionary Fiscal Contraction: The Thatcher Government's 1981 Budget in Perspective* (Cambridge, 2014), p. 14. **12.** Howe, *Conflict of Loyalty*, p. 121; Nigel Lawson, *The View from No. 11: Memoirs of a Tory Radical* (1992: 1993), p. 16. **13.** Hugo Young, *One of Us: A Biography of Margaret Thatcher* (rev. edn: 1990), pp. 141–2; Frank Johnson, *Out of Order* (1982), p. 171; Moore, *Not for Turning*, p. 352. **14.** Howe, *Conflict of Loyalty*, p. 122; J. B. Unwin to Tim Lankester, 'Overall Economic Outlook: Note by the Central Unit', 4 May 1979, TFW. **15.** Hunt to Thatcher, 'Public Expenditure 1979–80: Cash Limits and Civil Service Manpower', 16 May 1979, TFW; see also *Guardian*, 24 February 1979; David Smith, *The Rise and Fall of Monetarism* (1987: 1991), p. 89; Lawson, *View from No. 11*, p. 28; Edmund Dell, *The Chancellors: A History of the Chancellors of the Exchequer, 1945–90* (1996), p. 446; Moore, *Not for Turning*, p. 455. **16.** *The Times*, 29 December 1979; Hoskyns, *Just in Time*, pp. 11, 8. On the broad economic inheritance in 1979, see also John Wells, 'Miracles and Myths', *Marxism Today* (May 1989), pp. 22–5. **17.** *Guardian*, 8 March 1979, 2 August 1979; and see Howe, *Conflict of Loyalty*, pp. 114–15; Moore, *Not for Turning*, p. 408; Prior, *Balance of Power*, p. 120; Dell, *The Chancellors*, pp. 459–60; Smith, *Rise and Fall of Monetarism*, pp. 86–7; Young, *One of Us*, p. 151; Christopher Johnson, *The Economy under Mrs Thatcher, 1979–1990* (1991), p. 102. **18.** Stewart, *Bang!*, pp. 186–7, 189–90; Johnson, *Economy under Mrs Thatcher*, p. 131; Bernard Donoughue, *Downing Street Diary*, vol. 2: *With James Callaghan in No. 10* (2008), p. 167; and see Christopher Harvie, *Fool's Gold: The Story of North Sea Oil* (1994). **19.** Dell, *The Chancellors*, p. 458; Campbell, *Iron Lady*, p. 7; Stewart, *Bang!*, p. 185; Richardson to Howe, 4 May 1979, TFW. **20.** TNA T 337/432, 'The Government's

Economic Strategy', 1 August 1979.   **21.** 'Speech to Conservative Central Council', 15 March 1975, TFW; Hansard, 26 March 1980.   **22.** *The Times*, 29 September 1976; for a summary from a Thatcherite perspective, see Lawson, *View from No. 11*, p. 29.   **23.** Milton Friedman, 'The Quantity Theory of Money: A Restatement', in Milton Friedman (ed.), *Studies in the Quantity Theory of Money* (Chicago, IL, 1956), pp. 3–21; Milton Friedman, 'The Role of Monetary Policy', *American Economic Review*, 58:1 (1968), pp. 1–17; Franco Modigliani, 'The Monetarist Controversy, or, Should We Forsake Stabilization Policies?', *American Economic Review*, 67:2 (1977), pp. 1–19; Alan S. Blinder, 'The Rise and Fall of Keynesian Economics', *Economic Record*, 64:4 (1988), p. 278; Smith, *Rise and Fall of Monetarism*, pp. 11–30. To get a sense of how its British advocates defined it at the time, see the summary by the monetarist Tim Congdon in *The Times*, 1 March 1980.   **24.** *Guardian*, 28 October 1977; Ian Gilmour, *Dancing with Dogma: Britain under Thatcherism* (1992), pp. 18–19; Howe, *Conflict of Loyalty*, p. 162; Smith, *Rise and Fall of Monetarism*, p. 59; Bernard Donoughue, *The Heat of the Kitchen: An Autobiography* (2003), pp. 249–50; David Smith, *From Boom to Bust: Trial and Error in British Economic Policy* (rev. edn: 1993), pp. 39–40; Dell, *The Chancellors*, pp. 419–20, 426, 457; and see Duncan Needham, *UK Monetary Policy from Devaluation to Thatcher, 1967–82* (Basingstoke, 2014).   **25.** Denis Healey, *The Time of My Life* (1989), pp. 382–3, 434; Austin Mitchell, *Four Years in the Death of the Labour Party* (1983), p. 18; Dell, *The Chancellors*, p. 454; *The Times*, 18 January 1982.   **26.** Dell. *The Chancellors*, pp. 449, 451, 453–4; Lawson, *View from No. 11*, p. 1042; Richard Ingrams and John Wells, *The Other Half: Further Letters of Denis Thatcher* (1981), p. 19. The *Yes Minister* episode 'The Quality of Life' first went out on 30 March 1981 on BBC2.   **27.** TNA T 337/432, Lawson to Howe, 'Sir Keith Joseph's Meeting on Public Attitudes to Pay', 18 July 1979; TNA T 337/432, 'The Government's Economic Strategy', 1 August 1979; *Sunday Times*, 1 May 1981.   **28.** Lawson to Thatcher, 19 July 1978, TFW; E. H. H. Green, *Thatcher* (2006), p. 66; TNA T 337/432, 'The Government's Economic Strategy', 1 August 1979; Hoskyns to Thatcher, 'Government Strategy: Paper No. 2', 18 July 1979, TFW.   **29.** Hoskyns, *Just in Time*, p. 94; Campbell, *Iron Lady*, p. 18; Lawson, *View from No. 11*, p. 20; TNA T 337/432, Cropper to Howe, 'The Government's Economic Strategy', 2 August 1979.   **30.** Lawson, *View from No. 11*, p. 32.   **31.** Johnson, *Economy under Mrs Thatcher*, pp. 108, 110; Young, *One of Us*, p. 146; 'Speech to Putney Conservatives', 17 February 1978, TFW; 'Conservative General Election Manifesto', 11 April 1979, TFW; 'General Election Press Conference', 23 April 1979, TFW. On tax and spending under Labour, see, for example, Noel Thompson, 'Economic Ideas and the Development of Opinion,' in Richard Coopey and Nicholas Woodward (eds.), *Britain in the 1970s: The Troubled Economy* (1996), p. 77; Edward Pearce, *Denis Healey: A Life in Our Times* (2002), p. 510; Jim Tomlinson, 'Economic Policy', in Anthony Seldon and Kevin Hickson (eds.), *New Labour, Old Labour: The Wilson and Callaghan Governments, 1974–79* (2004), pp. 59, 64–5.   **32.** Hansard, 12 June 1979; Howe, *Conflict of Loyalty*, pp. 128–9; Johnson, *Economy under Mrs Thatcher*, p. 36; Dell, *The Chancellors*, pp. 460–61; Jim Tomlinson, 'Mrs Thatcher's Macroeconomic Adventurism, 1979–1981, and Its Political Consequences', *British Politics*, 2:1 (2007), pp. 7–8.   **33.** Hoskyns, *Just In Time*, p. 32; Lawson, *View from No. 11*, p. 35; 'General Election Press Conference', 23 April 1979, TFW; Howe, *Conflict of Interest*, p. 116; Dell, *The Chancellors*, pp. 458–9.   **34.** 'Note for the Record (MT–Treasury Ministers)', 16 May 1979, TFW; Campbell, *Iron Lady*, p. 53; Moore, *Not for Turning*, p. 464. On VAT and inflation, see also Gilmour, *Dancing with Dogma*, p. 22; Howe, *Conflict of Interest*, p. 131; Lawson, *View from No. 11*, p. 32; Dell, *The Chancellors*, pp. 460–61.   **35.** 'No. 10 Record of Conversation (MT–Howe)', 22 May 1979, TFW.   **36.** Howe to Thatcher, 23 May 1979, TFW; Tim Lankester to Tony Battishill, 'No. 10 Record of Conversation (MT–Howe-Biffen)', 24 May 1979, TFW; Howe, *Conflict of Loyalty*, pp. 130–31.   **37.** Howe to Thatcher, 10 May 1979, TFW; Howe to Thatcher, 6 June 1979, TFW. For interest rates, see the Bank of England's Statistical Interactive Database at https://www.bankofengland.co.uk/boeapps/iadb/Repo.asp.   **38.** Tim Lankester to Tony Battishill, 'MT Meeting with Chancellor and Governor', 6 June 1979, TFW; Howe to Thatcher, 'MLR', 11 June 1979, TFW; Lankester to Battishill, 11 June 1979, TFW; and see Moore, *Not for Turning*, pp. 461–2, which is very good on all this.   **39.** Howe,

*Conflict of Loyalty*, pp. 132, 134; Hansard, 12 June 1979.  **40.** *Daily Mirror*, 13 June 1979; *Daily Express*, 13 June 1979; *Guardian*, 13 June 1979; *Observer*, 17 June 1979; Keith Britto, 'Public Opinion after the First Seven Months of the New Government', 21 November 1979, TFW.  **41.** Prior, *Balance of Power*, pp. 119–20.  **42.** Young, *One of Us*, p. 155; Stephen Nickell, 'The Budget of 1981 Was over the Top', 13 March 2006, https://www.bankofeng land.co.uk/-/media/boe/files/speech/2006/the-budget-of-1981-was-over-the-top; Tomlinson, 'Mrs Thatcher's Macroeconomic Adventurism', p. 10; *Guardian*, 6 November 1979; Johnson, *Economy under Mrs Thatcher*, p. 36; Campbell, *Iron Lady*, p. 52.  **43.** Moore, *Not for Turning*, pp. 465, 467; *Daily Express*, 13 August 1979.  **44.** Lawson, *View from No. 11*, pp. 41, 47; Hoskyns, *Just in Time*, pp. 121–2.  **45.** Thatcher to Howe, 24 June 1979, TFW; Howe to Thatcher, 'Mortgage Rate', 25 June 1979, TFW; Tim Lankester to Tony Battishill, 'Record of Conversation', 4 July 1979, TFW.  **46.** Howe, *Conflict of Loyalty*, p. 153; Lawson, *View from No. 11*, p. 77  **47.** See Pepper to Thatcher, 'Assessing the Budget', 16 May 1979, TFW; 'No. 10 Record of Conversation (MT-Gordon Pepper)', 18 May 1979, TFW; Thatcher to Howe, 18 May 1979, TFW; David Laidler to Pepper, 5 November 1979, TFW; Green, *Thatcher*, pp. 78–9; Moore, *Not for Turning*, p. 524; Jim Tomlinson, 'Thatcher, Monetarism and the Politics of Inflation', in Ben Jackson and Robert Saunders (eds.), *Making Thatcher's Britain* (Cambridge, 2012), p. 74; Lawson, *View from No. 11*, pp. 77, 79–81; Bank of England, 'Pepper on the Monetary Base', 5 July 1979, TFW; Tim Lankester, 'No. 10 Record of Conversation: Note on the Monetary Policy Seminar', 18 July 1979, TFW'.  **48.** Lawson, *View from No. 11*, p. 77; Green, *Thatcher*, pp. 78–9; Tomlinson, 'Thatcher, Monetarism and the Politics of Inflation', p. 74; Sir Geoffrey Howe, 'Public Expenditure: The Economic Background', C (79) 27, 6 July 1979, TFW; and see Howe, *Conflict of Loyalty*, pp. 144–5, 153–4; Moore, *Not for Turning*, pp. 471–2.  **49.** Hunt to Thatcher, 'Public Expenditure to 1983–84', 11 July 1979, TFW; Moore, *Not for Turning*, pp. 472–5; CC (79) 9, 12 July 1979, TFW; 'No. 10 Record of Conversation (MT-Prior)', 16 July 1979, TFW; Sir Geoffrey Howe and John Biffen, 'Public Expenditure: Proposals for the Years after 1980–81', C (79) 35, 7 September 1979, TFW.  **50.** Lawson to Howe, 'Economic and Financial Situation Report', 28 August 1979, TFW.  **51.** 'Speech to Conservative Party Conference', 12 October 1979, TFW; Howe to Thatcher, 'Economic Prospects', 12 October 1979, TFW; *Guardian*, 31 October 1979; 'No. 10 Record of Conversation (MT-Howe)', 5 November 1979, TFW.  **52.** David Kynaston, *The City of London*, vol. 4: *A Club No More, 1945–2000* (2001), pp. 561–2.  **53.** Ibid., p. 583; Howe, *Conflict of Loyalty*, pp. 140–41; Lawson, *View from No. 11*, pp. 38–9; Moore, *Not for Turning*, p. 478.  **54.** Lawson, *View from No. 11*, p. 40; Tim Lankester to M. A. Hall, 'Note for Record (MT Lunch with Treasury Ministers & Governor)', 24 September 1979, TFW; Howe, *Conflict of Loyalty*, p. 142.  **55.** Ibid., p. 143; Hansard, 23 October 1979; Tony Benn, *Conflicts of Interest: Diaries, 1977–80* (1990), p. 549; *Observer*, 26 October 1979; *Guardian*, 24 October 1979.  **56.** Lawson, *View from No. 11*, p. 41; Johnson, *Economy under Mrs Thatcher*, p. 37; Kynaston, *A Club No More*, p. 600; Brian Harrison, *Finding a Role? The United Kingdom, 1970–1990* (Oxford, 2010), p. 9.  **57.** Margaret Thatcher, *The Downing Street Years* (1993), p. 44; 'Speech at Lord Mayor's Banquet', 12 November 1979, TFW. On Mitterrand and controls, see *New York Times*, 17 May 1981, 5 June 1983; Jeffrey Sachs and Charles Wyplosz, 'The Economic Consequences of President Mitterrand', *Economic Policy*, 1:2 (1986), pp. 271, 275.  **58.** For exchange controls and the money supply, see Johnson, *Economy under Mrs Thatcher*, p. 37; Dell, *The Chancellors*, pp. 463–4.  **59.** Howe to Thatcher, 'Monetary Prospect', 5 November 1979, TFW; 'Note for the Record (Howe-MT Meeting), 5 November 1979, TFW; Tim Lankester to Tony Battishill, 'No. 10 Record of Conversation (MT-Howe)', 7 November 1979, TFW.  **60.** 'Note of a Meeting Held at 10 Downing Street', 9 November 1979, TFW; Moore, *Not for Turning*, p. 480.  **61.** *Daily Express*, 16 November 1979; *Daily Mirror*, 16 November 1979; Clark, *Diaries: Into Politics*, p. 136; *The Times*, 22 November 1979, 23 November 1979.  **62.** Hoskyns, *Just in Time*, p. 142; *The Times*, 15 December 1979, 20 December 1979; Sir Geoffrey Howe, 'The Economic Outlook and Public Expenditure', C (79) 61, 10 December 1979, TFW.  **63.** Gilmour, *Dancing with Dogma*, p. 23; Young, *One of Us*, p. 167.  **64.** 'Press Office Bulletin: Prime Minister at Chequers – Christmas 1979', 21

December 1979, TFW; *Sun*, 2 November 2012. **65.** *The Times*, 29 December 1979; *Observer*, 30 December 1979; *Daily Mirror*, 31 December 1979. **66.** *Sunday Express*, 30 December 1979. **67.** *Guardian*, 31 December 1979; *Sunday Express*, 31 December 1979; and see Tony Hendra, Christopher Cerf and Peter Elbling, *The 80s: A Look Back at the Tumultuous Decade, 1980-1989* (1979). **68.** *Daily Express*, 2 January 1980. **69.** *Daily Mirror*, 31 December 1979.

## Chapter 5. The Word Is . . . Lymeswold!

**1.** Jonathan Aitken, *Margaret Thatcher: Power and Personality* (2013), p. 261; Charles Moore, *Margaret Thatcher: The Authorized Biography*, vol. 1: *Not for Turning* (2013), p. 421. **2.** *Daily Mirror*, 3 February 1975; John Campbell, *Margaret Thatcher*, vol. 1: *The Grocer's Daughter* (2000), pp. 296-7. **3.** 'Interview for *Manchester Evening News*', 1 May 1975, TFW; Aitken, *Margaret Thatcher*, p. 187; Moore, *Not for Turning*, p. 328; 'Interview for *Barnet Press*', 9 September 1978, TFW. **4.** Moore, *Not for Turning*, pp. 431-2; 'Interview for the *Sun*', 28 February 1983, TFW; 'Interview for *Living* magazine', 9 January 1984, TFW. **5.** Beatrix Campbell, *The Iron Ladies: Why Do Women Vote Tory?* (1987), p. 179. **6.** MO C108, Special Report, 'Royal Wedding', 1981; MO N403, Summer Directive 1981. **7.** MO G226, Summer Directive 1981; MO W633, Summer Directive 1981. **8.** MO R470, Summer Directive 1981. **9.** Christopher Driver, *The British at Table, 1940-1980* (1983), pp. 58-9; *Guardian*, 9 April 1979; MO W633, Winter Directive – Food, 1982. **10.** Driver, *British at Table*, pp. 59, 135; *Guardian*, 25 January 1978; MO N403, Autumn Directive 1981. **11.** *The Times*, 20 May 1980; *Observer*, 24 February 1980; MO W633, Winter Directive – Food, 1982; MO R470, Winter Directive – Food, 1982. **12.** *The Times*, 24 May 1983; Driver, *British at Table*, p. 106. The Barnstaple review is quoted in *The Times* and comes from Lesley Nelson, *Vegetarian Restaurants in England* (Harmondsworth, 1982). **13.** *The Times*, 24 May 1983; Driver, *British at Table*, pp. 104-5. **14.** *Guardian*, 2 September 1983, 18 May 1983; Beatrix Campbell, *Wigan Pier Revisited: Poverty and Politics in the 80s* (1984), pp. 69, 11, 13. **15.** MO G226, Summer Directive 1981; *The Times*, 15 March 1980, 25 May 1983. **16.** *Guardian*, 15 June 1981; *The Times*, 10 December 1981, 17 September 1981. **17.** *The Times*, 21 November 1981, quoting Beryl Downing, *Quick Cook: Recipes in Thirty Minutes and Under* (Harmondsworth, 1981). **18.** Joe Moran, *Queuing for Beginners: The Story of Daily Life from Breakfast to Bedtime* (2007), pp. 150-54; *Independent*, 22 July 2009; *Daily Telegraph*, 10 October 2010; *The Times*, 2 January 1982. **19.** Driver, *British at Table*, pp. 142-4; *Observer Magazine*, 10 January 1982; *Sunday Times*, 28 March 1982. **20.** Driver, *British at Table*, pp. 144-5; *Guardian*, 9 April 1979. **21.** Arthur Marwick, *British Society since 1945* (1982), p. 242; Ian Jack, *Before the Oil Ran Out: Britain in the Brutal Years* (rev. edn: 1997), p. xvii; *The Times*, 9 May 1980; MO S496, Winter Directive – Food, 1982. **22.** Moran, *Queuing for Beginners*, p. 155; *Guardian*, 19 October 1978. **23.** Ibid., 4 August 1984, 6 October 1984; *The Times*, 11 December 1984; Margaret Thatcher, *The Downing Street Years* (1993), p. 21; 'Remarks visiting ASDA HQ', 7 December 1988, TFW. **24.** *Guardian*, 11 February 1980. **25.** David Kynaston, *The City of London*, vol. 4: *A Club No More, 1945-2000* (2001), pp. 424, 558, 712; Moran, *Queuing for Beginners*, p. 74. The parable of the jam sandwiches is recounted in Harry Hopkins, *The New Look: A Social History of the Forties and Fifties in Britain* (1963), p. 153. **26.** *Daily Mail*, 8 November 2006, 5 June 2010; *Guardian*, 1 March 1985. **27.** *Observer*, 18 May 1980; Moran, *Queuing for Beginners*, pp. 79-80. **28.** Christopher Driver (ed.), *The Good Food Guide, 1980* (1980), pp. 15-17; *The Times*, 25 May 1983; *Fodor's 1982 Guide to Great Britain* (New York, 1982), pp. 90-91, 96; *Let's Go, 1982: The Budget Guide to Britain and Ireland* (New York, 1982), p. 47. **29.** Driver (ed.), *Good Food Guide, 1980*, pp. 51, 87, 107; *Fodor's 1982 Guide to Great Britain*, p. 136; *Let's Go, 1982*, p. 81. **30.** Driver (ed.), *Good Food Guide, 1980*, pp. 93, 250, 258, 269, 378, 358-9. **31.** *The Times*, 24 May 1983; MO C108, Special Report, 'Royal Wedding', 1981. **32.** Driver, *British at Table*, p. 113; *Guardian*, 23 January 1982; *Observer*, 13 February 1983. **33.** Mark Batey, *Brand Meaning:*

*Meaning, Myth and Mystique in Today's Brands* (2nd edn: 2016), p. 96; Driver, *British at Table*, p. 161; *Guardian*, 27 July 1982, 15 November 1982. **34.** *Let's Go, 1982*, p. 81; Driver, *British at Table*, p. 90; *The Times*, 17 October 1983, 23 May 1983. **35.** Driver, *British at Table*, pp. 90, 88, 73, 77; *The Times*, 23 May 1983; Lincoln Allison, *Condition of England: Essays and Impressions* (1981), p. 189. **36.** *The Times*, 14 December 1976, 15 May 1976, 17 October 1983. **37.** *Guardian*, 24 May 1980; *The Times*, 21 June 1983, 17 October 1983. **38.** *Guardian*, 17 April 2013, 28 September 1982; *The Times*, 20 May 1980. **39.** *The Times*, 19 October 1981. My account of Lymeswold's origins also draws on an episode of Radio 4's history series *In Living Memory* (23 January 2013). **40.** *Guardian*, 28 September 1982. I transcribed Walker's words from *In Living Memory*, as above. **41.** *Guardian*, 3 November 1982, 9 November 1982; *The Times*, 18 November 1982. **42.** Hansard, 17 February 1983; *The Times*, 22 November 1982; and see *Independent*, 11 April 1997. **43.** *Guardian*, 31 May 1985; *The Times*, 20 July 1983. **44.** *Glasgow Herald*, 8 June 1982, 5 January 1983; *The Times*, 19 February 1983.

# Chapter 6. You Are Mad and We Hate You

**1.** *Guardian*, 19 March 1979, 25 January 1979, 9 October 1979; Tony Benn, *Conflicts of Interest: Diaries, 1977–80* (1990), p. 533. **2.** *Observer*, 4 November 1979; *Guardian*, 9 October 1979, 2 November 1979, 24 April 1980. On Frank Scuffham, a fascinating man, see *Church Times*, 15 November 2013. **3.** Geoffrey Owen, *From Empire to Europe: The Decline and Revival of British Industry since the Second World War* (1999), pp. 114, 133, 137–9, 149; *The Times*, 5 October 1977, 1 March 1976, 19 December 1977. **4.** Owen, *From Empire to Europe*, pp. 138, 142; Margaret Thatcher, *The Downing Street Years* (1993), pp. 108–9; John Campbell, *Margaret Thatcher*, vol. 2: *The Iron Lady* (2003), p. 98; Jim Prior, *A Balance of Power* (1986), p. 128; 'General Election Press Conference', 2 May 1979, TFW. **5.** 'TV Interview for LWT's *Weekend World*', 6 January 1980, TFW; David Parker, *The Official History of Privatisation*, vol. 1: *The Formative Years, 1970–1987* (Abingdon, 2009), pp. 15, 17, 27–51; E. H. H. Green, *Thatcher* (2006), pp. 83–4, 89–90, 98; *Sun*, 21 July 1978; Nigel Lawson, *The View from No. 11: Memoirs of a Tory Radical* (1992: 1993), p. 199; Hoskyns to Thatcher, 'Loss-Making Nationalised Industries', 15 September 1980, TFW; Charles Moore, *Margaret Thatcher: The Authorized Biography*, vol. 2: *Everything She Wants* (2015), pp. 34–6, 188–9. **6.** Stephen Milligan, *The New Barons: Union Power in the 1970s* (1976), p. 7; and see Chris Wrigley, 'Trade Unions, Strikes and the Government', in Richard Coopey and Nicholas Woodward (eds.), *Britain in the 1970s: The Troubled Economy* (1996), pp. 274–5; Owen, *From Empire to Europe*, p. 437. **7.** On the unions, see Robert Taylor, *The Fifth Estate: Britain's Unions in the Seventies* (1978), pp. 337–8, 353; Robert Taylor, 'The Rise and Fall of the Social Contract', in Anthony Seldon and Kevin Hickson (eds.), *New Labour, Old Labour: The Wilson and Callaghan Governments, 1974–79* (2004), pp. 92–3, 99, 101; John McIlroy and Alan Campbell, 'The High Tide of Trade Unionism: Mapping Industrial Politics, 1964–79', in John McIlroy, Nina Fishman and Alan Campbell (eds.), *The High Tide of British Trade Unionism: Trade Unions and Industrial Politics, 1964–79* (new edn: Monmouth, 2007), pp. 100, 106; Owen, *From Empire to Europe*, pp. 433–9. **8.** *Guardian*, 20 October 1979, 23 October 1979, 20 June 1979. **9.** 'Final Report of the Nationalised Industries Policy Group', 30 June 1977, TFW; 'Authority of Government Group Report', 22 June 1977, TFW; *The Times*, 18 April 1978; John Hoskyns, *Just in Time: Inside the Thatcher Revolution* (2000), p. 127. **10.** John Hoskyns and Norman Strauss, 'Stepping Stones', 14 November 1977, TFW (see esp. pp. S-1, 5, 6–7, 13, 17, 30, A12–A13); Hoskyns, *Just in Time*, pp. 42–3, 45–7, 86; 'Minutes of Leader's Steering Committee, 51st Meeting', 30 January 1978, TFW; 'Speech to Conservative Party Conference', 14 October 1977, TFW; John Campbell, *Margaret Thatcher*, vol. 1: *The Grocer's Daughter* (2000). **11.** Louis Heren, *Alas, Alas for England: What Went Wrong with Britain* (1981), pp. 120–21; Hugo Young, *One of Us: A Biography of Margaret Thatcher* (rev. edn: 1990), p. 109; Prior, *Balance of Power*, pp. 8, 10; *Daily Telegraph*, 12 December 2016. The affair in question is chronicled in Simon Raven, *Sound the Retreat* (1971). **12.** Prior, *Balance of Power*, p. 113; Young, *One of Us*, pp. 161, 310; Thatcher, *Downing Street Years*, pp. 28, 104; Ferdinand Mount, *Cold Cream: My Early Life and Other Mistakes* (2008), p. 289. **13.** Lawson to Thatcher, 1 March 1976, TFW; Green, *Thatcher*, pp. 113, 123–6; 'Memorandum by the Secretary of State for Employment: The Way Forward on Pay', C (79) 6, 15 May 1979, TFW; Moore, *Not for Turning*, pp. 458–9, 511. **14.** Prior to Thatcher, 14 May 1979, TFW; Prior, *Balance of Power*, pp. 158–9; Green, *Thatcher*, pp. 117–18; and see Campbell, *Iron Lady*, pp. 89–90; Moore, *Not for Turning*, pp. 460–61. **15.** Prior, *Balance of Power*, pp. 164, 158; Young, *One of Us*, p. 194; Thatcher, *Downing Street Years*, p. 105; Campbell, *Iron Lady*, p. 91. For a detailed chronology of the build-up to the steel strike, see Hoskyns to Thatcher, 'Steel Strike – Lessons Learned', 9 May 1980, TFW. **16.** Owen, *From Empire to Europe*. p. 143; Thatcher, *Downing Street Years*, pp. 109–11; *Guardian*, 22 June 2015; Hoskyns, *Just in Time*, p. 182. **17.** Ibid., pp. 146–7, 149; Joseph to Thatcher, 'BSC Steel Strike', 21 December 1979, TFW. The conspiracy-theory view of the strike is best captured in Ken Loach's ITV film *A Question of Leadership* (1980). **18.** 'No. 10 Record of Conversation', 8 January 1980, TFW; *Sunday Express*, 13 January 1980; Hansard, 17 January 1980; see also Green, *Thatcher*, pp. 113–14. **19.** Prior, *Balance of Power*, p. 126; Sherman to Thatcher, 'The Blockade of Britain – Decisive for British Democracy', 14 January 1980, TFW; Young, *One of Us*, p. 193; Alan Clark, *Diaries: Into Politics, 1972–1982* (2000), p. 144. **20.** Prior, *Balance of Power*, p. 163; *Daily Express*, 7 February 1980, 14 February 1980. **21.** Thatcher, *Downing Street Years*, p. 105; 'No. 10 Record of Conversation: Thatcher-Methven', 5 February 1980, TFW; Hoskyns, *Just in Time*, p. 152; Hoskyns to Howe, 'Trade Union Reform', 29 January 1980, TFW. **22.** Howe to Thatcher, 'Immunities for Secondary Industrial Action', 4 February 1980, TFW; Geoffrey Howe, *Conflict of Loyalty* (1994), pp. 165–6; Hoskyns to Thatcher, 'Jim Prior's Proposals Are Inadequate', 13 February 1980, TFW; Hansard, 14 February 1980; Prior, *Balance of Power*, pp. 164–5. **23.** *The Times*, 12 February 1980; Andrew Denham and Mark Garnett, *Keith Joseph* (2001: Chesham, 2002), p. 349. **24.** *The Times*, 15 February 1980, 20 February 1980; *Daily Mirror*, 15 February 1980; *Daily Express*, 15 February 1980; see also *Sheffield Star*, 9 April 2015. **25.** *Sunday Express*, 17 February 1980. **26.** Thatcher, *Downing Street Years*, pp. 107, 112; Moore, *Not for Turning*, pp. 511–12; 'No. 10 Record of Conversations', 17 February 1980, TFW. **27.** 'Minutes of Ministerial Committee on Economic Strategy: E (80) 6, Secondary Picketing', 18 February 1980, TFW; Prior, *Balance of Power*, p. 165; Thatcher, *Downing Street Years*, p. 107. **28.** Owen, *From Empire to Europe*, p. 143; Thatcher, *Downing Street Years*, pp. 112–13; Moore, *Not for Turning*, p. 513; Anthony Hayward, *Which Side Are You On? Ken Loach and His Films* (2004), pp. 161–2. **29.** Owen, *From Empire to Europe*, p. 144; Thatcher, *Downing Street Years*, pp. 113–14; Moore, *Not for Turning*, p. 513; Green, *Thatcher*, p. 114; Young, *One of Us*, pp. 196–7; Howe, *Conflict of Loyalty*, p. 164. **30.** Owen, *From Empire to Europe*, pp. 145, 444; Nicholas Comfort, *The Slow Death of British Industry: A Sixty-Year Suicide, 1952–2012* (2013), p. 112; Anthony Sampson, *The Changing Anatomy of Britain* (1982: 1983), pp. 407–8; Prior, *Balance of Power*, pp. 129–30; Ian MacGregor with Rodney Tyler, *The Enemies Within: The Story of the Miners' Strike, 1984–5* (1986: 1987), pp. 94–5. **31.** Owen, *From Empire to Europe*, pp. 144–5, 149; *The Times*, 16 June 1988; *Guardian*, 8 October 1988. **32.** Hoskyns to Thatcher, 'Steel Strike – Lessons Learned', 9 May 1980, TFW. **33.** *The Times*, 27 March 1980; *Daily Express*, 16 April 1980, 17 April 1980; *Sunday Express*, 11 May 1980. **34.** *Guardian*, 15 May 1980; *Daily Express*, 13 May 1980; *Daily Mirror*, 15 May 1980. **35.** Andrew Taylor, 'The Conservative Party and the Trade Unions', in John McIlroy, Nina Fishman and Alan Campbell (eds.), *The High Tide of British Trade Unionism: Trade Unions and Industrial Politics* (new edn: Monmouth, 2007), pp. 174–5; *Time*, 12 February 1979; Bernard Donoughue, *Downing Street Diary*, vol. 2: *With James Callaghan in No. 10* (2008), p. 452; *Daily Mail*, 12 February 1979; Alwyn W. Turner, *Crisis? What Crisis? Britain in the 1970s* (2008), p. 267. **36.** Keith Britto, 'Public Opinion after the First Seven Months of the New Government', 21 November 1979, TFW; Keith Britto, 'Public Opinion Background Note 132', 26 September 1982, TFW; Denis Healey, *The Time of My Life* (1989), p. 462; MO S496, Special

860 NOTES TO PP. 156-65

Report 404, 'Trade Unions', 1983.   37. *Guardian*, 26 January 1979; Hoskyns to Thatcher,
'CBI', 29 June 1979, TFW; Howe to Thatcher, 'Relations with Trade Union Leaders', 27
May 1980.   38. Louis Heren, *Alas, Alas for England: What Went Wrong with Britain* (1981),
p. 80; Sampson, *Changing Anatomy of Britain*, p. 61; *Observer*, 24 February 1980; and see
*Daily Telegraph*, 22 May 2004.   39. Sampson, *Changing Anatomy of Britain*, pp. 77–8;
*The Times* 16 September 1980.   40. Sampson, *Changing Anatomy of Britain*, p. 68; *The
Times*, 9 December 1980, 11 November 1980.   41. Alan Bleasdale, *Boys from the Blackstuff*
(1982: 1985), p. 243; Beatrix Campbell, *Wigan Pier Revisited: Poverty and Politics in the
80s* (1984), pp. 155–6; Jeremy Seabrook, *Unemployment* (1982: 1983), pp. 178–9, 181.
**42.** *The Times*, 9 March 1982; Sampson, *Changing Anatomy of Britain*, p. 78; David Butler
and Dennis Kavanagh, *The British General Election of 1979* (1980), pp. 163, 343, 345, 350;
Taylor, 'The Rise and Fall of the Social Contract', p. 97; Taylor, 'The Conservative Party
and the Trade Unions', p. 175; *The Economist*, 2 June 1979; *Observer*, 12 September
1982.   **43.** Campbell, *Wigan Pier Revisited*, pp. 155, 174.   **44.** Thatcher, *Downing Street
Years*, pp. 104–5; Campbell, *Iron Lady*, p. 164; Green, *Thatcher*, pp. 118–19; Moore, *Not
for Turning*, pp. 649–50; Norman Tebbit, *Upwardly Mobile: An Autobiography* (1988), pp.
233–41; *Daily Express*, 13 July 1983; Peter Dorey, 'Weakening the Trade Unions, One Step
at a Time: The Thatcher Governments' Strategy for the Reform of Trade-Union Law, 1979–
1984', *Historical Studies in Industrial Relations*, 37 (2016), p. 186.   **45.** Ian Gilmour,
*Dancing with Dogma: Britain under Thatcherism* (1992), p. 100; Campbell, *Iron Lady*, pp.
93–4; Green, *Thatcher*, p. 199.   **46.** *The Times*, 30 April 1981; *Observer*, 4 April 1982;
Owen, *From Empire to Europe*, p. 443; Sampson, *Changing Anatomy of Britain*, p. 59;
Brian Harrison, *Finding a Role? The United Kingdom, 1970–1990* (Oxford, 2010), p. 161;
Campbell, *Iron Lady*, pp. 90, 165; *Guardian*, 8 September 1983; *Daily Mirror*, 1 September
1980.   **47.** *Guardian*, 6 May 1983; *The Times*, 11 November 1980; Sampson, *Changing
Anatomy of Britain*, p. 379.   **48.** Christopher Johnson, *The Economy under Mrs Thatcher,
1979–1990* (1991), p. 312; John Wells, 'Miracles and Myths', *Marxism Today* (May 1989),
pp. 22–5; Owen, *From Empire to Europe*, p. 444; Harrison, *Finding a Role?*, pp. 168,
332.   **49.** Nicholas Crafts, *Britain's Relative Economic Performance, 1870–1999* (2002),
p. 86; Johnson, *Economy under Mrs Thatcher*, p. 15; Simon Wren-Lewis, 'On the Economic
Achievements and Failures of Margaret Thatcher', 10 April 2013, https://mainlymacro.
blogspot.co.uk/2013/04/on-economic-achievements-and-failures.html; see also, for example,
Paul Krugman, 'Did Thatcher Turn Britain Around?', 8 April 2013, https://krugman.blogs.
nytimes.com/2013/04/08/did-thatcher-turn-britain-around/; John Van Reenen, 'The Economic Legacy of Mrs Thatcher Is a Mixed Bag', 10 April 2013, http://blogs.lse.ac.uk/
politicsandpolicy/the-economic-legacy-of-mrs-thatcher-2/.   50. *Guardian*, 12 August 1980, 29
May 1981; *Observer*, 26 July 1981; 'Corby People Recall Steel Works Closure 30 Years Ago',
1 June 2010, http://news.bbc.co.uk/local/northampton/hi/people_and_places/history/
newsid_8715000/8715706.stm; see also Heather Behan, 'The Rise, Fall and Rise Again of
Corby', 22 July 2011, http://www.open.edu/openlearn/the-rise-fall-and-rise-again-
corby.   51. *The Times*, 15 March 1980, 13 June 1980, 19 June 1980; Peter Stredder to Tim
Lankester, 'Consett Steelworks', 6 October 1980, TFW.   52. *The Times*, 19 June 1980, 10
July 1980, 13 September 1980, 15 September 1980, 27 November 1980, 2 November 1981;
David Smith, *North and South: Britain's Economic, Social and Political Divide* (1989),
p. 132; *Guardian*, 26 March 1983, 12 February 1987.

## Chapter 7. Who Needs Enemies?

1. *Daily Mirror*, 5 March 1981; *Guardian*, 29 December 1983. In general, see Simon
Morgan-Russell, *Jimmy Perry and David Croft* (Manchester, 2004), but be warned. 'Before
looking at the ways in which *Hi-de-Hi!* expresses this liminality,' runs a typical sentence,
'it is worth elucidating briefly Bakhtin's definitions of carnival and the grotesque body.'
What would Ted Bovis say?   2. Paul Theroux, *The Kingdom by the Sea: A Journey around
the Coast of Great Britain* (1983), pp. 142–6.   3. Gordon Burn, *Pocket Money: Bad-Boys,*

*Business-Heads and Boom-Time Snooker* (1986), pp. 84–5; Miriam Akhtar and Steve Humphries, *Some Liked It Hot: The British on Holiday at Home and Abroad* (2000), pp. 51–2; Theroux, *Kingdom by the Sea*, pp. 53, 34; *The Times*, 2 July 1983, 22 August 1981. **4.** Ibid., 11 December 1980, 10 December 1981, 24 August 1981; *Guardian*, 23 November 1982; Robert J. Wybrow, *Britain Speaks Out, 1937–87: A Social History as Seen through the Gallup Data* (Basingstoke, 1989), p. 132; MO C108, Summer Directive 1981. **5.** *Guardian*, 23 November 1982, 12 December 1981; *The Times*, 24 August 1981; *Daily Express*, 3 February 1979, 12 March 1983. **6.** *Guardian*, 13 April 1981. **7.** Wybrow, *Britain Speaks Out*, p. 131; the quotation comes from the second episode of *Auf Wiedersehen, Pet*, 'Who Won the War Anyway?', which went out on 18 November 1983. **8.** Wybrow, *Britain Speaks Out*, pp. 124, 132. **9.** *Financial Times*, 18 January 2017; Anthony King and Robert J. Wybrow (eds.), *British Political Opinion, 1937–2000: The Gallup Polls* (2001), p. 301. **10.** Ibid., p. 301; Wybrow, *Britain Speaks Out*, p. 122; Gordon Reece to Richard Ryder, 28 November 1979, TFW; Keith Britto, 'Public Opinion Background Note 132', 26 September 1982, TFW. **11.** Wybrow, *Britain Speaks Out*, p. 121; MO C108, EEC Special, 1982; MO S496, EEC Special, 1982; MO D156, EEC Special, 1982. **12.** Charles Moore, *Margaret Thatcher: The Authorized Biography*, vol. 1: *Not for Turning* (2013), pp. 166, 237, 306; John Campbell, *Margaret Thatcher*, vol. 2: *The Iron Lady* (2003), p. 64; Hugo Young, *This Blessed Plot: Britain and Europe from Churchill to Blair* (1998), pp. 309–10; Hansard, 6 December 1978; 'Speech at Dinner for West German Chancellor', 10 May 1979, TFW; 'Speech to Conservative Party Conference', 12 October 1979, TFW. **13.** *The Times*, 2 October 1980; 'Speech in Harrogate', 26 May 1983, TFW. **14.** John Stanley to Thatcher, 12 February 1979, TFW; Hugo Young, *One of Us: A Biography of Margaret Thatcher* (rev. edn: 1990), p. 385; Campbell, *Iron Lady*, pp. 64, 302; Moore, *Not for Turning*, pp. 306, 487–8; Young, *This Blessed Plot*, pp. 309, 307, 323; Percy Cradock, *In Pursuit of British Interests: Reflections on Foreign Policy under Margaret Thatcher and John Major* (1997), p. 125; Roy Jenkins, *European Diary, 1977–1981* (1989), pp. 450, 511; and see Margaret Thatcher, *The Downing Street Years* (1993), p. 82; Campbell, *Iron Lady*, pp. 65, 301. **15.** Alan Clark, *Diaries: In Power, 1983–1992* (1993: 2001), p. 219; Campbell, *Iron Lady*, pp. 54, 56; Young, *One of Us*, p. 172; Moore, *Not for Turning*, pp. 429, 452–3. **16.** Young, *One of Us*, p. 185; Campbell, *Iron Lady*, pp. 56, 259; Geoffrey Howe, *Conflict of Loyalty* (1994), pp. 303, 394; Moore, *Not for Turning*, pp. 487–8, 502; Ian Gilmour, *Dancing with Dogma: Britain under Thatcherism* (1992), pp. 280–85. **17.** Sir John Hunt to Thatcher, 'European Issues', 4 May 1979, TFW; Young, *This Blessed Plot*, pp. 312–13; Roy Jenkins, *A Life at the Centre* (1991), p. 492. **18.** Ibid., p. 493; Campbell, *Iron Lady*, pp. 59–60; 'Speech at Dinner for West German Chancellor', 10 May 1979, TFW. **19.** Gilmour, *Dancing with Dogma*, pp. 287–8; Young, *This Blessed Plot*, p. 313; Campbell, *Iron Lady*, p. 61; Jenkins, *European Diary*, pp. 528–30. **20.** Moore, *Not for Turning*, pp. 312, 443–4; Thatcher, *Downing Street Years*, pp. 34, 70; Jim Prior, *A Balance of Power* (1986), p. 144; Young, *One of Us*, p. 187. **21.** Campbell, *Iron Lady*, pp. 61–2; Young, *One of Us*, p. 188; Jenkins, *Life at the Centre*, p. 494; Thatcher, *Downing Street Years*, pp. 63–4. **22.** Campbell, *Iron Lady*, p. 62; Moore, *Not for Turning*, pp. 445–6; 'Winston Churchill Memorial Lecture', 18 October 1979, TFW; and see Thatcher, *Downing Street Years*, p. 79. **23.** Ibid., pp. 80–81; Campbell, *Iron Lady*, pp. 62–3, 81; Jenkins, *European Diary*, pp. 519, 528–30; Jenkins, *Life at the Centre*, pp. 498–9; Young, *One of Us*, p. 187; Gilmour, *Dancing with Dogma*, p. 288; Young, *This Blessed Plot*, p. 314. **24.** Jenkins, *Life at the Centre*, p. 499; 'Press Conference after Dublin European Council', 30 November 1979, TFW; Young, *This Blessed Plot*, p. 317; John Simpson, *Strange Places, Questionable People* (1998), p. 250. **25.** Jenkins, *Life at the Centre*, p. 500; Moore, *Not for Turning*, pp. 490–91; Young, *This Blessed Plot*, p. 314; *Daily Mirror*, 1 December 1979; Hansard, 3 December 1979. **26.** TNA PREM 19/223, 'Note of Meeting between the Prime Minister and the Foreign Secretary', 20 February 1979; TNA PREM 19/223, OD (E) 4, 14 February 1980; 'Gow Notes', 18 March 1980, TFW. **27.** Young, *One of Us*, p. 189; Young, *This Blessed Plot*, p. 318; Jenkins, *Life at the Centre*, p. 504; Moore, *Not for Turning*, p. 493; TNA PREM 19/226, Carrington to Thatcher, 1 May 1980; 'Treasury Note: EEC:

Withholding', 29 May 1980, TFW.   28. Gilmour, *Dancing with Dogma*, pp. 292–5; *The Times*, 31 May 1980; *Sunday Express*, 1 June 1980; Moore, *Not for Turning*, p. 494; Young, *One of Us*, pp. 189–90; TNA CAB 128/67, CC (80) 21, 2 June 1980.   29. Campbell, *Iron Lady*, pp. 67–8; Young, *This Blessed Plot*, p. 318; Young, *One of Us*, p. 384; Thatcher, *Downing Street Years*, p. 81.   30. Campbell, *Iron Lady*, pp. 68, 305–6; Young, *This Blessed Plot*, p. 325; Moore, *Not for Turning*, p. 494; Howe to Thatcher, 'EC Budget Refunds', 12 September 1980, TFW; Walker to Thatcher, 'The Common Fisheries Policy', 24 May 1979, TFW.   31. 'Message to the Conservative Group for Europe', 16 January 1983, TFW; and see Young, *This Blessed Plot*, pp. 324–6, 337–8.   32. 'Speech at Conservative Party Conference', 16 October 1981, TFW; '1951 General Election Address', 8 October 1951, TFW; 'Speech at "Youth for Europe" Rally', 2 June 1979, TFW; and see Young, *One of Us*, p. 169.   33. 'Speech at Kensington Town Hall', 19 January 1976, TFW; Moore, *Not for Turning*, pp. 310–11, 320, 333, 553, 558–9; 'Speech to the National Press Club', 19 September 1975, TFW.   34. Moore, *Not for Turning*, pp. 370, 499; Young, *One of Us*, p. 121; 'Speech to the Foreign Policy Association', 18 December 1979, TFW; and see Jimmy Carter, *Keeping Faith: Memoirs of a President* (New York, 1982), p. 113; Thatcher, *Downing Street Years*, pp. 68–9; 'Sir Nicholas Henderson Diary', 23 December 1979, TFW. For 'Margaret R. Thatcher', see Christopher Collins's essay at http://www.margaretthatcher.org/archive/1981_PREM19.asp.   35. See Raymond Garthoff, *Détente and Confrontation: American–Soviet Relations from Nixon to Reagan* (rev. edn: Washington, DC, 1994), pp. 1017–19, 1023–46; Aleksandr Antonovich Lyakhovskiy, 'Inside the Soviet Invasion of Afghanistan and the Seizure of Kabul, December 1979', Cold War International History Project Working Paper No. 51 (January 2007), pp. 8–34, https://www.wilsoncenter.org/publication/inside-the-soviet-invasion-afghanistan-and-the-seizure-kabul-december-1979.   36. Carter, *Keeping Faith*, pp. 471–2; 'President Carter Phone Call to MT', 28 December 1979, TFW; Moore, *Not for Turning*, p. 561; Thatcher, *Downing Street Years*, pp. 87–8.   37. Carter to Thatcher, 20 January 1980, TFW; Thatcher to Follows, 22 January 1980, TFW; and see Thatcher, *Downing Street Years*, p. 88; Kevin Jefferys, 'Britain and the Boycott of the 1980 Moscow Olympics', *Sport in History*, 32:2 (2012), pp. 283–4; Paul Corthorn, 'The Cold War and British Debates over the Boycott of the 1980 Moscow Olympics', *Cold War History*, 13:1 (2013), pp. 46–8.   38. Jefferys, 'Boycott of the 1980 Moscow Olympics', pp. 282, 285; Corthorn, 'Boycott of the 1980 Moscow Olympics', pp. 49, 51–2; *The Times*, 3 January 1980; Thatcher to Follows, 19 February 1980, TFW; Stephen J. Solarz, *Journeys to War and Peace: A Congressional Memoir* (Waltham, MA, 2011), p. 90.   39. Hansard, 17 March 1980; *The Times*, 12 March 1980, 8 January 1980; *Church Times*, 25 January 1980, 1 February 1980; and see Corthorn, 'Boycott of the 1980 Moscow Olympics', p. 50.   40. *The Times*, 22 January 1980.   41. Ibid., 17 January 1980, 14 February 1980, 17 March 1980; *Daily Mirror*, 24 January 1980, 3 January 1980, 21 March 1980.   42. *Sunday Express*, 14 March 1980; *Daily Express*, 3 January 1980; Jefferys, 'Boycott of the 1980 Moscow Olympics', p. 290; Corthorn, 'Boycott of the 1980 Moscow Olympics', pp. 61–2; *Daily Mail*, 14 March 1980; Campbell, *Iron Lady*, p. 59.   43. *The Times*, 29 January 1980; *Observer*, 16 March 1980; see also Wybrow, *Britain Speaks Out*, p. 122.   44. Jefferys, 'Boycott of the 1980 Moscow Olympics', pp. 286–8; Thatcher to Follows, 19 March 1980, TFW; Thatcher to Follows, 20 May 1980, TFW; *The Times*, 4 March 1980, 6 March 1980, 14 March 1980, 26 March 1980; *Daily Express*, 26 March 1980; and see Corthorn, 'Boycott of the 1980 Moscow Olympics', pp. 53–4.   45. Jefferys, 'Boycott of the 1980 Moscow Olympics', pp. 292, 294, 297; Pat Butcher, *The Perfect Distance: Ovett and Coe: The Record-Breaking Rivalry* (2004), pp. 156–7; Skip Rozin, *Daley Thompson: The Subject Is Winning* (1983: 1984), p. 141.   46. 'UKE Moscow to FCO: The Olympics', 16 July 1980, TFW.   47. *The Times*, 14 June 1980, 26 May 1980.   48. Rozin, *Daley Thompson*, p. 150; *Guardian*, 25 July 1980.   49. *Sunday Express*, 3 August 1980; Jefferys, 'Boycott of the 1980 Moscow Olympics', p. 294; *Daily Express*, 11 August 1980; *The Times*, 4 August 1980.   50. 'Radio Interview for IRN', 31 December 1980, TFW; *Guardian*, 31 December 1980; *Daily Mirror*, 31 December 1980; *Observer*, 4 January 1981; *Daily Express*, 6 January 1981.

## Chapter 8. Mrs Thatcher's Final Solution

1. 'TV Interview for LWT *Weekend World*', 6 January 1980, TFW.   2. *Daily Mirror*, 7 January 1980; *Guardian*, 7 January 1980, 11 January 1980.   3. *The Times*, 19 January 1980, 26 February 1980, 27 February 1980; John Hoskyns, *Just in Time: Inside the Thatcher Revolution* (2000), pp. 161–2; Adam Ridley to Douglas Wass, 'The Monetary Situation and Related Matters', 22 February 1980, TFW; Lankester to Thatcher, 'Prescription Charges', 31 January 1980, TFW. The Thatcher Foundation website attributes Ridley's paper to Howe, but the signature at the foot of p. 2 suggests that Ridley wrote it.   4. Hoskyns, *Just in Time*, pp. 161–2, 164; *The Times*, 9 January 1980, 26 March 1980, 29 March 1980; Hayek to Thatcher, 24 April 1980, TFW; Hayek to Thatcher, 28 August 1979, TFW; Thatcher to Hayek, 13 May 1980, TFW; Thatcher to Hayek, 17 February 1982, TFW.   5. *The Times*, 12 February 1980; Gow to Gilmour, 14 February 1980, TFW. Gow's note contains the text of Gilmour's Cambridge speech. See also Hugo Young, *One of Us: A Biography of Margaret Thatcher* (rev. edn: 1990), p. 200; Charles Moore, *Margaret Thatcher: The Authorized Biography*, vol. 1: *Not for Turning* (2013), p. 522.   6. Young, *One of Us*, p. 198   7. *The Times*, 26 February 1980, 31 January 1975; John Campbell, *Margaret Thatcher*, vol. 1: *The Grocer's Daughter* (2000), p. 291; Ferdinand Mount, *Cold Cream: My Early Life and Other Mistakes* (2008), p. 303; Matthew Parris, *Chance Witness: An Outsider's Life in Politics* (2002: 2013), pp. 190–91; Young, *One of Us*, p. 331.   8. Campbell, *Iron Lady*, p. 110; Ian Gilmour, *Dancing with Dogma: Britain under Thatcherism* (1992), pp. 42–3; Young, *One of Us*, p. 199; Mark Garnett and Ian Aitken, *Splendid! Splendid! The Authorized Biography of Willie Whitelaw* (2002), pp. 235–6; Ion Trewin (ed.), *The Hugo Young Papers: Thirty Years of British Politics – Off the Record* (2008), p. 237.   9. Lord Carrington, *Reflect on Things Past: The Memoirs of Lord Carrington* (1988), pp. 309–10; Young, *One of Us*, p. 204; Garnett and Aitken, *Splendid! Splendid!*, p. 269.   10. Geoffrey Howe, *Conflict of Loyalty* (1994), pp. 170, 207; Nigel Lawson, *The View from No. 11: Memoirs of a Tory Radical* (1992: 1993), p. 137; Young, *One of Us*, p. 204; and see Campbell, *Iron Lady*, pp. 111–12.   11. Gilmour, *Dancing with Dogma*, pp. 37, 40, 56.   12. *The Times*, 26 February 1980, 29 September 1976; and see Edmund Dell, *The Chancellors: A History of the Chancellors of the Exchequer, 1945–90* (1996), pp. 462, 468–9.   13. Campbell, *Iron Lady*, p. 111; Dell, *The Chancellors*, pp. 476–7. On the alternatives, see David Wood's series in *The Times*, 1–3 June 1981.   14. 'Party Political Broadcast', 12 March 1980, TFW.   15. Hansard, 26 March 1980, 27 March 1980; *Daily Express*, 27 March 1980; *Daily Mirror*, 27 March 1980; *The Times*, 28 March 1980.   16. Howe, *Conflict of Loyalty*, p. 175; Richard Ingrams and John Wells, *Dear Bill: The Collected Letters of Denis Thatcher* (1980), p. 74.   17. Hansard, 26 March 1980; Christopher Johnson, *The Economy Under Mrs Thatcher, 1979–1990* (1991), pp. 37–8; Lawson, *View from No. 11*, p. 68.   18. *The Times*, 14 September 1978. Lawson, *View from No. 11*, pp. 67–9; Dell, *The Chancellors*, pp. 465–6; Moore, *Not for Turning*, pp. 504–5.   19. Tim Lankester to John Wiggins, 'No. 10 Record of Conversation', 7 March 1980, TFW; Biffen to Howe, 'Medium Term Financial Strategy', 4 March 1980, TFW; Dell, *The Chancellors*, p. 466; Johnson, *Economy under Mrs Thatcher*, pp. 39–41; *Observer*, 6 July 1980; Jim Tomlinson, 'Mrs Thatcher's Macroeconomic Adventurism, 1979–1981, and Its Political Consequences', *British Politics*, 2:1 (2007), pp. 8–9; Lawson, *View from No. 11*, p. 468; Howe, *Conflict of Loyalty*, pp. 163–4; Moore, *Not for Turning*, p. 505.   20. Johnson, *Economy under Mrs Thatcher*, pp. 38, 274; David Smith, *The Rise and Fall of Monetarism* (1987:1991), pp. 93, 106; Gilmour, *Dancing with Dogma*, p. 27; Lawson, *View from No. 11*, p. 72. Oddly, Johnson and Smith give slightly different figures for the monetary outcomes, even though they are using many of the same government sources.   21. David Smith, *From Boom to Bust: Trial and Error in British Economic Policy* (rev. edn: 1993), pp. 24–5, 29, 29, 40–41, 256; see also Tomlinson, 'Mrs Thatcher's Macroeconomic Adventurism', p. 10; Johnson, *Economy under Mrs Thatcher*, p. 39; Moore, *Not for Turning*, p. 524.   22. Lawson, *View from No. 11*, p. 72; Johnson, *Economy under Mrs Thatcher*, pp. 278, 281, 69, 73–4.   23. Jim Tomlinson, 'Monetarism and the Politics of

Inflation', in Ben Jackson and Robert Saunders (eds.), *Making Thatcher's Britain* (Cambridge, 2012), pp. 75, 76–7; Margaret Thatcher, *The Downing Street Years* (1993), p. 97; Campbell, *Iron Lady*, p. 80; Moore, *Not for Turning*, p. 507; Young, *One of Us*, p. 201; 'Speech at Press Association Annual Lunch', 11 June 1980, TFW.   24. *The Times*, 5 May 1980. 25. *Sunday Express*, 4 May 1980; *Daily Mirror*, 1 May 1980.   26. *The Times*, 17 May 1980. 27. Ibid., 22 May 1980; Biffen to Howe, 16 June 1980, TFW; Moore, *Not for Turning*, p. 525.   28. Hoskyns, *Just in Time*, p. 190; *The Times*, 22 May 1980.   29. Ibid., 23 May 1980; *Daily Mirror*, 23 June 1980.   30. *The Times*, 25 June 1980; Hansard, 25 June 1980.   31. *The Times*, 18 June 1980, 28 June 1980, 9 July 1980.   32. Ibid., 30 June 1980, 23 July 1980.

## Chapter 9. Your Boys Took a Hell of a Beating

1. 'MT Engagement Diary', 5 June 1980, TFW; 'Record of Conversation with Argentinian Minister of the Economy', 5 June 1980, TFW.   2. Daniel Ruiz, 'Squad Rotation, Tear Gas and a Bucketload of Medals: How England Flopped at Euro 80', 14 June 2016, http://www.fourfourtwo.com/features/squad-rotation-tear-gas-and-bucketload-medals-how-england-flopped-euro-80.   3. 'Remarks Visiting Liverpool Football Club', 18 June 1976, TFW; Thatcher to Emlyn Hughes, 27 February 1978, TFW.   4. *Daily Express*, 6 June 1980; Ruiz, 'Squad Rotation'; *Guardian*, 9 April 2013.   5. *Daily Express*, 12 June 1980. On Greenwood, see the profile in Jimmy Greaves with Norman Giller, *Don't Shoot the Manager: The Revealing Story of England's Soccer Bosses* (rev. edn: 1994), pp. 98–116.   6. *Daily Mirror*, 11 June 1980; *Sunday Express*, 8 June 1980.   7. *The Times*, 13 June 1980; *Daily Mirror*, 13 June 1980; *Daily Express*, 13 June 1980; *Guardian*, 13 June 1980.   8. *Daily Express*, 13 June 1980, 14 June 1980; Ruiz, 'Squad Rotation'; *Daily Mirror*, 13 June 1980; *Guardian*, 14 June 1980. 9. 'Press Conference after Venice European Council', 13 June 1980, TFW; and see, for example, *Daily Express*, 14 June 1980; *Guardian*, 14 June 1980.   10. *Observer*, 15 June 1980; *Daily Mirror*, 17 June 1980; and see James Walvin, *Football and the Decline of Britain* (Basingstoke, 1986), e.g. pp. 51, 63, 121.   11. 'Commentator's "Maggie Thatcher" Outburst Makes UNESCO List', 8 February 2012, https://www.thelocal.no/20120208/football-commentators-maggie-thatcher-outburst-makes-unesco-list.   12. *Daily Mirror*, 1 June 1981; *Sunday Express*, 31 May 1981; *Guardian*, 1 June 1981.   13. *Daily Mirror*, 1 June 1981; *Daily Express*, 1 June 1981; *Guardian*, 28 November 1981; Nick Hornby, *Fever Pitch* (1992), pp. 201–2; *Observer*, 15 June 1980.   14. *Guardian*, 24 June 1982.   15. *Observer*, 20 June 1982.   16. Lincoln Allison, *Condition of England: Essays and Impressions* (1981), pp. 123, 125; and see Walvin, *Football and the Decline of Britain*, pp. 1–14.   17. Allison, *Condition of England*, p. 125; Walvin, *Football and the Decline of Britain*, pp. 6–7, 10–12. Stephen Dobson and John Goddard, *The Economics of Football* (2nd edn: Cambridge, 2011), pp. 151–2; *Guardian*, 11 April 1980, 27 August 1981.   18. For a powerful example of the tendency to romanticize the pre-Premier League era, see Adrian Tempany, *And the Sun Shines Now: How Hillsborough and the Premier League Changed Britain* (rev. edn: 2016). In one passage, Tempany, a Hillsborough survivor, criticizes unnamed 'historians' who insist on painting the 1970s as an age when Britain was 'paralysed by the unions, powered by candles and drowning in rubbish' while 'we were stuffing our mouths with Black Forest gateau'. I am naturally saddened that anybody would object to such a rich and sophisticated view of the 1970s.   19. *The Times*, 8 September 1980; *Guardian*, 8 September 1980; *Daily Express*, 9 September 1980.   20. *The Times*, 19 September 1980; Bonds is quoted in Roger Hillier, 'Castilla Ghost Match', http://theyflysohigh.co.uk/castilla-ghost-match/4577286094. 21. Hornby, *Fever Pitch*, pp. 97, 141; Walvin, *Football and the Decline of Britain*, p. 51. 22. *Guardian*, 19 December 1979.   23. *Daily Express*, 1 June 1981; *The Times*, 11 September 1980; *Guardian*, 28 November 1981; *Independent*, 29 December 1992.   24. Eric Dunning, Patrick Murphy and John Williams, *The Roots of Football Hooliganism: An Historical and Sociological Study* (1988), pp. 17, 155; Allison, *Condition of England*, p. 128.   25. *Guardian*, 22 December 1979; *Observer*, 7 February 1982.   26. Geoffrey Pearson, *Hooligan: A History of Respectable Fears* (1983), pp. 220–21; Arthur Hopcraft, *The Football Man: People and*

*Passions in Soccer* (1968: Harmondsworth, 1971), pp. 156–7; and see Walvin, *Football and the Decline of Britain*, pp. 9–10, 12; Richard Holt, *Sport and the British: A Modern History* (Oxford, 1989), pp. 334–5, 342–3; Dunning, Murphy and Williams, *Roots of Football Hooliganism*, p. 132. 27. Bill Buford, *Among the Thugs* (1991), pp. 13–14, 15. 28. Ibid., pp. 21, 29, 30–31; for earnings, see *Guardian*, 26 June 1984. 29. Buford, *Among the Thugs*, pp. 32, 118–20. 30. Ibid., pp. 88, 114, 116, 195, 219–20. 31. Ibid., pp. 263–4. 32. *The Times*, 16 February 1981; *Observer*, 12 July 1981; Matthew Worley, 'Oi! Oi! Oi!: Class, Locality, and British Punk', *Twentieth Century British History*, 24:4 (2013), pp. 606–36; and see *Guardian*, 18 March 2010. 33. Buford, *Among the Thugs*, pp. 38–9, 44, 47–8, 52, 54, 65, 68, 89. 34. Ibid., pp. 96–7, 136–7. 35. *The Times*, 16 February 1981; *Daily Mirror*, 8 September 1980; and see Walvin, *Football and the Decline of Britain*, pp. 70–80. 36. Ibid., p. 121; *Guardian*, 22 December 1979. 37. *The Times*, 10 December 1980; *Guardian*, 4 February 1982; *Observer*, 7 February 1982. Among countless other examples, see, for instance, *Guardian*, 11 December 1980; *The Times*, 26 September 1981. 38. *Guardian*, 6 December 1986. 39. Ibid., 3 May 1982, 30 July 1985. 40. Ibid., 3 July 1982, 17 July 1982, 24 July 1982; *Observer*, 25 July 1982. 41. *Guardian*, 31 July 1982; *The Times*, 3 December 1982; David Harrison and Steve Gordos, *The Doog: The Incredible Story of Derek Dougan, Football's Most Controversial Figure* (Studley, 2008), pp. 141–63; and see Ian King, 'The Bhatti Brothers: Wolverhampton Wanderers', 15 May 2013, http://twohundredpercent.net/?p=23076. 42. *Guardian*, 23 April 1984, 16 January 1985, 30 July 1985, 31 July 1985, 2 November 1985. 43. Ibid., 30 July 1986, 6 December 1986.

# Chapter 10. A Bit of Freedom

1. *Romford Recorder*, 30 July 2013; and see Jerry White, *London in the Twentieth Century: A City and Its People* (2001), pp. 43, 57; Simon Donoghue and Don Tait, *Harold Hill and Noak Hill: A History* (Havering, 2013). 2. 'Remarks on Council House Sales', 11 August 1980, TFW; and see *Daily Mail*, 10 April 2013; *Daily Telegraph*, 14 April 2015. There are clips from the footage of Mrs Thatcher's visit in the fourth episode of *The 70s*, 'The Winner Takes It All, 77–79' (BBC Two, 7 May 2012). 3. Tony Travers, 'GLC Leaders, 1965 to 1986', London School of Economics HEIF2 Seminars paper (31 July 2007); 'First GLC Tenant to Buy, 1967' (British Pathé report), https://www.youtube.com/watch?v=945MuotYauE; for later reports on Harold Hill, see *Observer*, 6 December 2009; *Daily Telegraph*, 14 April 2015. 4. *Daily Telegraph*, 14 April 2015. 5. Pat Thane, *Foundations of the Welfare State* (1982), p. 196; Ian Gilmour, *Dancing with Dogma: Britain under Thatcherism* (1992), p. 175; Colin Jones and Alan Murie, *The Right to Buy: Analysis and Evaluation of a Housing Policy* (Oxford, 2006), pp. 12–15, 23; and see David Torrance, *Noel Skelton and the Property-Owning Democracy* (2010). 6. Charles Moore, *Margaret Thatcher: The Authorized Biography*, vol. 1: *Not for Turning* (2013), pp. 260, 262; 'Article for *Daily Telegraph*: The Owner-Occupier's Party', 1 July 1974, TFW; *The Times*, 11 September 1974. 7. Jones and Murie, *Right to Buy*, pp. 8, 52; Bernard Donoughue, *The Heat of the Kitchen: An Autobiography* (2003), pp. 172–3; Joe Haines, *The Politics of Power* (1977), pp. 96–100; and see Peter King, *Housing Policy Transformed: The Right to Buy and the Desire to Own* (Bristol, 2010), pp. 74, 86–7. 8. Peter Walker, *Staying Power: An Autobiography* (1991), pp. 140–41; Gilmour, *Dancing with Dogma*, p. 175; Simon Jenkins, *Accountable to None: The Tory Nationalization of Britain* (1995), p. 175; John Campbell, *Margaret Thatcher*, vol. 2: *The Iron Lady* (2003), pp. 232–3; Hansard, 15 January 1980. See also King, *Housing Policy Transformed*, pp. 56, 58; Jones and Murie, *Right to Buy*, p. 33; Moore, *Not for Turning*, pp. 260, 340, 469–71. 9. *Guardian*, 12 August 1980; *Daily Express*, 6 October 1980; *The Times*, 4 October 1980, 24 October 1980; Hansard, 25 November 1980. 10. *The Times*, 24 November 1979, 4 October 1980; Jenkins, *Accountable to None*, pp. 176–7. 11. *Observer*, 28 September 1980; *The Times*, 5 December 1979, 4 October 1980, 10 October 1980, 8 April 1981; *Guardian*, 9 April 1981. 12. Jenkins, *Accountable to None*, p. 178;

Gilmour, *Dancing with Dogma*, pp. 175–6; *The Times*, 16 April 1980, 10 October 1980; Ray Forrest and Alan Murie, *Selling the Welfare State: The Privatisation of Public Housing* (1988), pp. 213–15. **13.** MO R470, Spring Directive 1982; *The Times*, 3 June 1983; *Guardian*, 23 May 1983. **14.** Ibid., 23 May 1983; *The Times*, 3 June 1983. **15.** MO W632, Spring Directive 1982; MO H260, Spring Directive 1982. **16.** MO S496, Spring Directive 1983. **17.** *The Times*, 9 April 1981, 20 June 1981, 11 February 1982; King, *Housing Policy Transformed*, p. 67; Christopher Johnson, *The Economy under Mrs Thatcher, 1979–1990* (1991), p. 151; 'Speech to Conservative Party Conference', 8 October 1982, TFW; 'Interview for *The Times*', 24 March 1986, TFW. **18.** *The Times*, 1 November 1982, 2 November 1982, 9 April 1981, 19 May 1984. **19.** Ibid., 2 November 1982, 12 December 1984. See also Richard Vinen, *Thatcher's Britain: The Politics and Social Upheaval of the Thatcher Era* (2009), p. 203; Andy Beckett, *Promised You a Miracle: UK80–82* (2015), pp. 222, 224–5. **20.** King, *Housing Policy Transformed*, pp. 7, 107, 109–10; Mary Abbott, *Family Affairs: A History of the Family in Twentieth-Century England* (2003), pp. 155–6. **21.** *The Times*, 30 October 1984. **22.** Ibid., 2 November 1982, 26 October 1984. **23.** 'Interview for *The Times*', 24 March 1986, TFW; Geoffrey Howe, *Conflict of Loyalty* (1994), pp. 280–81; Howe to Thatcher, 'Tax Reliefs for Housing', 7 August 1980, TFW; and see Jenkins, *Accountable to None*, pp. 176, 181–2; Campbell, *Iron Lady*, p. 233. **24.** T. S. Callen and J. W. Lomax, 'The Development of the Building Societies Sector in the 1980s', *Bank of England Quarterly Bulletin* (November 1990), pp. 503–4; Johnson, *Economy under Mrs Thatcher*, pp. 148–9; *The Times*, 31 December 1983; Graham Stewart, *Bang! A History of Britain in the 1980s* (2013), pp. 418, 422–3. **25.** King, *Housing Policy Transformed*, p. 8; 'A Century of Home Ownership and Renting in England and Wales', 19 April 2013, http://www.ons.gov.uk/ons/rel/census/2011-census-analysis/a-century-of-home-ownership-and-renting-in-england-and-wales/short-story-on-housing.html; *The Times*, 9 July 1983, 24 August 1983, 12 December 1984. **26.** Forrest and Murie, *Selling the Welfare State*, p. 103; Jenkins, *Accountable to None*, p. 176; Moore, *Not for Turning*, p. 471; *The Times*, 3 June 1983. For an example of the 'creating a new demand' interpretation, see Beckett, *Promised You a Miracle*, p. 226. On the Right to Buy and the Tory vote, see E. H. H. Green, *Thatcher* (2006), p. 130. **27.** King, *Housing Policy Transformed*, pp. 1, 6, 67; Alan Murie, 'Housing and the Environment', in Dennis Kavanagh and Anthony Seldon (eds.), *The Thatcher Effect: A Decade of Change* (Oxford, 1989), pp. 213–25; Jenkins, *Accountable to None*, p. 179; Vinen, *Thatcher's Britain*, p. 202. **28.** Sir Kenneth Berrill to Ken Stowe, 'The Prime Minister's Talk with Mr Heseltine', 22 July 1979, TFW; Moore, *Not for Turning*, pp. 469–70; Jenkins, *Accountable to None*, p. 179; Nigel Lawson, *The View from No. 11: Memoirs of a Tory Radical* (1992: 1993), pp. 566–7. **29.** *The Times*, 6 February 1982, 21 May 1983; Gilmour, *Dancing with Dogma*, p. 177; Redwood to Thatcher, 'Housing Expenditure', 6 November 1984, TFW; Jones and Murie, *Right to Buy*, p. 19; Jess McCabe, 'Thatcher's Secrets', 4 April 2014, https://www.insidehousing.co.uk/insight/insight/thatchers-secrets-39472; James Meek, 'Where Will We Live', *London Review of Books*, 36:1 (9 January 2014); Moore, *Not for Turning*, p. 471. For house prices, see, for example, the Office for National Statistics' page 'Housing and Home Ownership in the UK', 22 January 2015, http://visual.ons.gov.uk/uk-perspectives-housing-and-home-ownership-in-the-uk/. **30.** Rob Baggott, *Health and Health Care in Britain* (Basingstoke, 1994), pp. 224–5; *The Times*, 11 December 1990, 2 November 1984. See also the good section on this in Stewart, *Bang!*, pp. 420–21. **31.** Gilmour, *Dancing with Dogma*, pp. 177–8; *The Times*, 1 December 1981; *Church Times*, 29 October 1982. **32.** *The Times*, 28 March 1986; Beckett, *Promised You a Miracle*, pp. 221, 225; Campbell, *Iron Lady*, p. 235; Moore, *Not for Turning*, p. 471; Anne Power and Rebecca Tunstall, *Swimming Against the Tide: Polarisation or Progress on 20 Unpopular Council Estates, 1980–1995* (York, 1995), p. 32; Vinen, *Thatcher's Britain*, p. 203; and see *Guardian*, 23 May 1983. **33.** *The Times*, 14 November 1980, 19 October 1981; Jones and Murie, *Right to Buy*, p. 78. **34.** *The Times*, 2 February 1983, 12 December 1984; King, *Housing Policy Transformed*, pp. 75–9; Stewart, *Bang!*, p. 420; Jones and Murie, *Right to Buy*, p. 86. **35.** Jeremy Seabrook, *Unemployment* (1982: 1983), pp. 28, 148–9. **36.** White, *London in the Twentieth Century*, pp. 73, 163–4; 'History of Broadwater Farm', 7 November

2018, https://www.haringey.gov.uk/libraries-sport-and-leisure/culture-and-entertainment/visiting-haringey/archive-and-local-history/history-broadwater-farm; Paul Harrison, *Inside the Inner City: Life under the Cutting Edge* (Harmondsworth: 1983), pp. 229–30, 382; *The Times*, 8 October 1985.  37. Seabrook, *Unemployment*, pp. 57–8.  38. *The Times*, 15 June 1981.  39. Ibid., 10 November 1981, 11 November 1981; Hansard, 14 November 1974; and see Peter Shapely, 'Social Housing in Post-War Manchester: Change and Continuity', 27 April 2013, http://personalpages.manchester.ac.uk/staff/m.dodge/pwm/Shapely-talk-PWM-symposium.pdf.  40. Peter Shapely, *The Politics of Housing: Power, Consumers and Urban Culture* (2007: Manchester, 2014), pp. 181–8; *The Times*, 10 November 1981, 11 November 1981; and see Shapely, 'Social Housing in Post-War Manchester'.  41. Ruth Glass, *Clichés of Urban Doom and Other Essays* (Oxford: 1988), p. x; Tony Benn, *The End of an Era: Diaries, 1980–90* (1992), p. 124.  42. *Guardian*, 13 November 1981.

# Chapter 11. She's Lost Control

1. See Deborah Curtis, *Touching from a Distance: Ian Curtis and Joy Division* (1995); Mick Middles and Lindsay Reade, *Torn Apart: The Life of Ian Curtis* (2006).  2. James Nice, *Shadowplayers: The Rise and Fall of Factory Records* (2010), pp. 22–23, 68–9; Simon Reynolds, *Rip It Up and Start Again: Post-Punk, 1978–84* (2005), pp. 180–81, 183; *NME*, 19 July 1979.  3. Curtis, *Touching from a Distance*, p. 142; Nice, *Shadowplayers*, pp. 91–2, 122; Reynolds, *Rip It Up*, pp. 187–9.  4. Mick Middles, *Factory: The Story of the Record Label* (2009), pp. 55–6; Dave Haslam, *Manchester, England: The Story of the Pop Cult City* (1999), p. xxiv.  5. Reynolds, *Rip It Up*, p. 173; Haslam, *Manchester, England*, pp. 124–6; *Sounds*, 26 May 1979.  6. Reynolds, *Rip It Up*, p. 174; Haslam, *Manchester, England*, p. 110; *The Times*, 2 November 1984.  7. *The Times*, 17 February 1982; Haslam, *Manchester, England*, p. xvii; Nice, *Shadowplayers*, pp. 36, 157; Middles, *Factory*, pp. 228–33.  8. Geoffrey Moorhouse, *Britain in the Sixties: The Other England* (Harmondsworth, 1964), pp. 95, 97; *The Times*, 11 September 1980; Beryl Bainbridge, *English Journey, or, The Road to Milton Keynes* (1984), pp. 58, 60–61; and see Ken Spencer et al., *Crisis in the Industrial Heartland: A Study of the West Midlands* (Oxford, 1986).  9. *The Times*, 30 June 1981, 17 February 1982.  10. Ibid., 31 August 1981, 1 September 1981, 3 September 1981, 4 September 1981, 5 September 1981.  11. *Guardian*, 28 August 1980.  12. Ibid., 19 November 1980; David Smith, *From Boom to Bust: Trial and Error in British Economic Policy* (rev. edn: 1993), pp. 253–4, 257; Ian Gilmour, *Dancing with Dogma: Britain under Thatcherism* (1992), pp. 67, 69; David Smith, *North and South: Britain's Economic, Social and Political Divide* (1989), p. 132; and see John Wells, 'Miracles and Myths', *Marxism Today* (May 1989), pp. 22–5.  13. Nicholas Comfort, *The Slow Death of British Industry: A Sixty-Year Suicide, 1952–2012* (2013), pp. 113–14; Geoffrey Owen, *From Empire to Europe: The Decline and Revival of British Industry since the Second World War* (1999), pp. 199–200; Smith, *North and South*, pp. 126, 127, 133; David Smith, *Something Will Turn Up: Britain's Economy, Past, Present and Future* (2015), pp. 41–2.  14. Geoffrey Howe, *Conflict of Loyalty* (1994), p. 199; Smith, *From Boom to Bust*, p. 19.  15. *Guardian*, 11 November 1980; Edmund Dell, *The Chancellors: A History of the Chancellors of the Exchequer, 1945–90* (1996), p. 472; Nigel Lawson, *The View from No. 11: Memoirs of a Tory Radical* (1992: 1993), pp. 184–5; *The Times*, 14 December 1981  16. Gilmour, *Dancing with Dogma*, p. 56; Dell, *The Chancellors*, p. 528; Lawson, *View from No. 11*, pp. 186–7.  17. Hansard, 21 March 1978; and see the excellent discussion in Graham Stewart, *Bang! A History of Britain in the 1980s* (2013), pp. 193–5. For a contrasting argument, see, for example, Simon Wren-Lewis, 'On the Economic Achievements and Failures of Margaret Thatcher', 10 April 2013, https://mainlymacro.blogspot.co.uk/2013/04/on-economic-achievements-and-failures.html.  18. William Keegan, *Mrs Thatcher's Economic Experiment* (1984), p. 171; Jim Tomlinson, 'Mrs Thatcher's Macroeconomic Adventurism, 1979–1981, and Its Political Consequences', *British Politics*, 2:1 (2007), p. 6. See also the very useful guide by Christopher Collins, 'The 1981 Budget: Background and Documents', at https://www.margaretthatcher.org/archive/1981_budget.asp.

19. Richardson to Howe, 'Exchange Rate Policy', 4 May 1979, TFW.   20. Lawson, *View from No. 11*, p. 59.   21. Christopher Johnson, *The Economy under Mrs Thatcher, 1979–1990* (1991), p. 38; Tomlinson, 'Mrs Thatcher's Macroeconomic Adventurism', p. 11; Jürg Niehans, 'The Appreciation of Sterling: Causes, Effects, Policies', 7 January 1981, TFW; Hoskyns diary, 9 January 1981, TFW; Walters diary, 8 January 1981, TFW. See also David Smith, *The Rise and Fall of Monetarism* (1987: 1991), pp. 96–7.   22. Howe, *Conflict of Loyalty*, p. 192.   23. Tomlinson, 'Mrs Thatcher's Macroeconomic Adventurism', p. 4; 'Speech to Conservative Rally in Birmingham', 19 April 1979, TFW; 'Conservative General Election Manifesto', 11 April 1979, TFW.   24. Tim Congdon, *Reflections on Monetarism: Britain's Vain Search for a Successful Economic Strategy* (Aldershot, 1992), p. 96; Dell, *The Chancellors*, p. 468; Hugo Young, *One of Us: A Biography of Margaret Thatcher* (rev. edn: 1990), p. 316; Lawson, *View from No. 11*, p. 55; Tomlinson, 'Mrs Thatcher's Macroeconomic Adventurism', pp. 4–5, 7.   25. See Jim Tomlinson, 'De-Industrialization Not Decline: A New Meta-Narrative for Post-War British History', *Twentieth Century British History*, 27:1 (2016), pp. 76–99; Smith, *North and South*, p. 88; Smith, *Something Will Turn Up*, pp. 31, 50.   26. Howe, *Conflict of Loyalty*, pp. 285–6; Dell, *The Chancellors*, p. 479.   27. Lawson, *View from No. 11*, p. 57; Owen, *From Empire to Europe*, p. 456; Wells, 'Miracles and Myths', p. 25.   28. Smith, *Something Will Turn Up*, pp. 12–13, 38–9, 45–6; *Guardian*, 2 July 1981, 10 May 1983.   29. John Wiggins to Tim Lankester, 'Economic Prospects in the Medium Term', 20 June 1980, TFW; *Sunday Times*, 3 August 1980.   30. Moore, *Not for Turning*, pp. 529–30; Christopher Collins, 'The Origins of the Budget in 1980', in Duncan Needham and Anthony Hotson (eds.), *Expansionary Fiscal Contraction: The Thatcher Government's 1981 Budget in Perspective* (Cambridge, 2014), p. 104; Brunner to Thatcher, 10 September 1980, TFW.   31. Moore, *Not for Turning*, p. 530; John Hoskyns, *Just in Time: Inside the Thatcher Revolution* (2000), p. 225; Collins, 'The Origins of the Budget in 1980', pp. 103–4; Smith, *From Boom to Bust*, p. 41; Howe, *Conflict of Loyalty*, p. 184; Tim Lankester, 'The 1981 Budget: How Did It Come About?', in Needham and Hotson (eds.), *Expansionary Fiscal Contraction*, pp. 16–17.   32. Burns to Howe, 'Economic Strategy – Latest Developments', 3 September 1980, TFW; Moore, *Not for Turning*, p. 531; 'No. 10 Record of Conversation (MT-Treasury-Bank of England)', 3 September 1980, TFW; Michael Pattison to Clive Whitmore and Tim Lankester, 3 September 1980, TFW; Pattison to Lankester, 8 September 1980, TFW.   33. Nigel Lawson, *View from No. 11*, pp. 84–5; Howe, *Conflict of Loyalty*, pp. 186–7.   34. Duncan Needham, Michael J. Oliver and Andrew Riley (eds.), 'The 1981 Budget: Facts and Fallacies', transcript of witness seminar held at Lombard Street Research, 27 September 2011, https://www.chu.cam.ac.uk/media/uploads/files/1981_Budget.pdf, p. 12; R. C. W. Mayes, 'Bank of England Record of Conversation', 19 September 1980, TFW.   35. Howe, *Conflict of Loyalty*, pp. 188, 190; 'Treasury Note of Conversation (Economic Strategy)', 22 September 1980, TFW; Kit McMahon to Gordon Richardson, 'Treasury Thinking on Economic Policy', 25 September 1980, TFW; Lankester, 'The 1981 Budget: How Did It Come About?', p. 19; and see Tomlinson, 'Mrs Thatcher's Macroeconomic Adventurism', p. 12; Lawson, *View from No. 11*, p. 63.   36. Howe to Thatcher, 18 September 1980, TFW; Hoskyns to Thatcher, 'Economic Strategy', 19 September 1980, TFW; Howe to Thatcher, 'Public Expenditure', 10 October 1980, TFW.   37. *The Times*, 1 September 1980, 29 September 1980, 14 October 1980, 17 October 1980.   38. *Daily Mirror*, 30 August 1980, 17 October 1980; *The Times*, 18 October 1980, 20 October 1980.   39. Hoskyns, *Just in Time*, p. 232; Moore, *Not for Turning*, p. 532.   40. *The Times*, 11 October 1980; *Guardian*, 11 October 1980.   41. Ibid.; 'Speech to Conservative Party Conference', 10 October 1980, TFW.   42. Dell, *The Chancellors*, p. 473; *Daily Express*, 11 October 1980; *Daily Mirror*, 11 October 1980; Ferdinand Mount, *Cold Cream: My Early Life and Other Mistakes* (2008), p. 330; Ian Gow to Thatcher, 'Party Conference Speech', 13 October 1980, TFW. On the memory of Heath's supposed betrayal, see E. H. H. Green, *Ideologies of Conservatism: Conservative Political Ideas in the Twentieth Century* (Oxford, 2002), p. 234.   43. Ridley to Howe, 'Policy Options', 13 November 1980, TFW; Hoskyns to Thatcher, 'Policy Options', 11 November 1980, TFW; McMahon to Richardson, 'The Roll-Over and Policy Generally: Tomorrow's Meeting with the Chancellor', 21 October 1980, TFW; McMahon

to Richardson, 'Policy and the Exchange Rate', 27 October 1980, TFW.    **44.** 'No. 10 Record of Conversation (Monetary Policy Seminar)', 13 October 1980, TFW. Goodhart's cake story is from Needham, Oliver and Riley (eds.), 'The 1981 Budget', p. 9.    **45.** Wass to Howe, 'Policy Options', 7 November 1980, TFW; 'No. 10 Record of Conversation (MT-Howe-Wass)', 12 November 1980, TFW; Collins, 'The Origins of the Budget in 1980', p. 112; Sir Geoffrey Howe, 'The Economic Prospect and Implications for Policy', C (80) 59, 22 October 1980, TFW; John Biffen, 'Public Expenditure Programmes', C (80) 58, 22 October 1980, TFW; Moore, *Not for Turning*, pp. 534–5; Minutes of Full Cabinet, CC (80) 37, 30 October 1980, TFW; Howe, *Conflict of Loyalty*, p. 195; CC (80) 38, 4 November 1980, TFW.    **46.** Peter Cropper, 'Conservative Party Finance Committee', 4 November 1980, TFW; Alan Clark, *Diaries: Into Politics, 1972–1982* (2000), p. 172.    **47.** *The Times*, 10 November 1980, 13 November 1980, 16 December 1980.    **48.** Taylor to Hugh Thomas, 17 October 1980, TFW; Collins, 'The Origins of the Budget in 1980', pp. 110–12; *The Times*, 10 November 1980.    **49.** *Guardian*, 11 November 1980, 12 November 1980; *The Times*, 12 November 1980.    **50.** Ibid.; *Daily Telegraph*, 10 May 2013.    **51.** Richard Ingrams and John Wells, *The Other Half: Further Letters of Denis Thatcher* (1981), p. 34; 'TV Interview for Thames TV *Afternoon Plus*', 6 January 1981, TFW.    **52.** Collins, 'The Origins of the Budget in 1980', pp. 113–14; Lankester, 'The 1981 Budget: How Did It Come About?', p. 17; Cropper, 'Conservative Party Finance Committee', 25 November 1980, TFW; Clark, *Diaries: Into Politics*, p. 178.    **53.** *The Times*, 26 November 1980; *Daily Mirror*, 26 November 1980.    **54.** Hansard, 27 November 1980; *The Times*, 28 November 1980.    **55.** 'Radio Interview for IRN', 28 November 1980, TFW.    **56.** Moore, *Not for Turning*, p. 535; Collins, 'The Origins of the Budget in 1980', p. 115; *Guardian*, 19 November 1980; Cropper, 'Conservative Party Finance Committee', 10 December 1980, TFW; *The Times*, 12 December 1980. In a very rare slip, the Thatcher Foundation website dates the minutes of the finance committee's meeting to 25 November, but the documents show that the meeting was on the 9th and that Ian Gow sent Mrs Thatcher Peter Cropper's minutes the next day.    **57.** *The Times*, 24 December 1980.    **58.** Robert J. Wybrow, *Britain Speaks Out, 1937–87: A Social History as Seen through the Gallup Data* (Basingstoke, 1989), pp. 162–3; Moore, *Not for Turning*, p. 535.    **59.** Howe to Thatcher, 'Government Strategy', 31 December 1980, TFW.    **60.** *Observer*, 28 December 1980; Moore, *Not for Turning*, p. 536.

## Chapter 12. Nice Video, Shame about the Song

**1.** *Guardian*, 18 February 2014; and see Stuart Maconie, 'The People's Songs: Are "Friends" Electric?', http://www.bbc.co.uk/programmes/profiles/2c2C2plDfXBMjD5wVb7rzMT/are-friends-electric; Simon Reynolds, *Rip It Up and Start Again: Post-Punk, 1978–84* (2005), pp. 323–4.    **2.** Ibid., p. 324; *Guardian*, 18 February 2014.    **3.** *Smash Hits*, 31 May 1979.    **4.** On Numan's chart success, see *Sounds*, 6 October 1979; *Smash Hits*, 15 November 1979.    **5.** *Daily Mirror*, 8 October 1979.    **6.** *Sounds*, 6 October 1979; *Melody Maker*, 29 September 1979; *Guardian*, 29 September 1979; *NME*, 8 September 1979, 11 September 1982.    **7.** On Numan's significance, see Simon Reynolds's excellent *Rip It Up and Start Again*, pp. 323–4, to which this chapter is greatly indebted.    **8.** Dave Laing, *One Chord Wonders: Power and Meaning in Punk Rock* (Milton Keynes, 1985), pp. 106, 109, 120; *The Times*, 18 November 1980; Peter York, *Style Wars* (1980), pp. 43–5; Paul Theroux, *The Kingdom by the Sea: A Journey around the Coast of Great Britain* (1983), p. 221; Sue Townsend, *The Secret Diary of Adrian Mole Aged 13¾* (1982: 2002), p. 19.    **9.** *Observer*, 30 April 1981; for the charts, see the data at www.everyhit.com.    **10.** *NME*, 20 December 1980.    **11.** Simon Reynolds, 'Song from the Future: The Story of Donna Summer and Giorgio Moroder's "I Feel Love"', 29 June 2017, https://pitchfork.com/features/article/song-from-the-future-the-story-of-donna-summer-and-giorgio-moroders-i-feel-love/; and see the superb BBC Four documentary *Synth Britannia* (16 October 2009).    **12.** *Observer*, 3 August 1980; Dave Rimmer, *New Romantics: The Look* (2003), pp. 95; Reynolds, *Rip It Up*, p. 328.    **13.** Ibid., pp. 151, 159, 320–21.    **14.** *Evening Standard*, 24 January 1980; *Observer Music Monthly*, 4 October

2009; Rimmer, *New Romantics*, pp. 12, 37, 52; Gary Kemp, *I Know This Much: From Soho to Spandau* (2009), pp. 93–4; Steve Strange, *Blitzed! The Autobiography of Steve Strange* (2002), pp. 39–40. See also David Johnson's fabulously detailed website, www.shapers ofthe80s.com, to which I am hugely indebted.  **15.** *Observer Music Monthly*, 4 October 2009; Kemp, *I Know This Much*, pp. 89–90, 93.  **16.** Ibid., p. 93; *Observer Music Monthly*, 4 October 2009; Reynolds, *Rip It Up*, p. 326  **17.** Peter York, *Modern Times* (1984), pp. 23, 76; *Observer Music Monthly*, 4 October 2009; Rimmer, *New Romantics*, p. 64.  **18.** Ibid., p. 52; *Observer Music Monthly*, 4 October 2009; Paul Theroux, *Kingdom by the Sea*, p. 148.  **19.** Rimmer, *New Romantics*, p. 67; *Evening Standard*, 24 January 1980; *Guardian*, 9 December 1980; *Daily Mirror*, 3 March 1980. For the *Newsnight* feature, see https://www.youtube.com/watch?v=8O56cequU32Q.  **20.** Kemp, *I Know This Much*, pp. 16, 19, 53–4, 85–6; *Guardian*, 2 February 1981.  **21.** Kemp, *I Know This Much*, pp. 88, 100; *Sounds*, 13 September 1980; *NME*, 29 November 1980; Martin Kemp, *True: The Autobiography of Martin Kemp* (2000), p. 54; *Sounds*, 13 September 1980.  **22.** Ibid.; *NME*, 29 November 1980.  **23.** Kemp, *I Know This Much*, pp. 103, 110, 120; *Evening Standard*, 16 October 1980; *Daily Mirror*, 22 October 1980; *NME*, 29 November 1980; and see *Observer Music Monthly*, 4 October 2009.  **24.** *Daily Mirror*, 22 October 1980.  **25.** *NME*, 29 November 1980.  **26.** *Sounds*, 13 September 1980; York, *Modern Times*, p. 73; *Observer Music Monthly*, 4 October 2009; and see *Guardian*, 2 February 1981; Kemp, *I Know This Much*, p. 102.  **27.** Paul Gorman, *The Story of The Face: The Magazine That Changed Culture* (2017), pp. 16–17.  **28.** Ibid., pp. 19–21, 70, 82; *Evening Standard*, 1 May 1980. See also David Johnson, 'The Face and i-D', https://shapersofthe80s.com/the-face-i-d-media/; for the first issue, see *The Face*, May 1980.  **29.** Gorman, *Story of The Face*, pp. 40–41, 43, 50–51; *The Face*, October 1980, November 1980.  **30.** Gorman, *Story of The Face*, pp. 6, 45, 61, 69; *Observer Music Monthly*, 4 October 2009; Reynolds, *Rip It Up*, p. xxviii. On videos, see *Observer*, 4 March 1984; *The Times*, 6 June 1985.  **31.** On 'Ashes to Ashes', see Rimmer, *New Romantics*, pp. 14–18. Bowie told the 'clown suit' story to an American camera technician called Michael Dignum, who posted it online at https://www.facebook.com/michael.dignum.1/posts/10153309716274071.  **32.** Shelton Waldrep, *Future Nostalgia: Performing David Bowie* (New York, 2015), p. 30; Strange, *Blitzed!*, p. 53; Rimmer, *New Romantics*, pp. 21, 23, 98; Reynolds, *Rip It Up*, pp. 326–7.  **33.** *Sounds*, 13 September 1980; Kemp, *I Know This Much*, pp. 124–5; and see *Observer Music Monthly*, 4 October 2009.  **34.** Reynolds, *Rip It Up*, p. 327; *Melody Maker*, 12 September 1981.  **35.** *Observer*, 15 March 1981; Reynolds, *Rip It Up*, p. 403.  **36.** Ibid., pp. 334–5; *New York Times*, 7 March 1982.  **37.** *NME*, 1 May 1982; Boy George with Spencer Bright, *Take It Like a Man: The Autobiography of Boy George* (1995), pp. 33–6, 139; Rimmer, *New Romantics*, pp. 20, 28, 30; Kemp, *I Know This Much*, p. 76.  **38.** Rimmer, *New Romantics*, pp. 43, 45–6, 88; Reynolds, *Rip It Up*, pp. xxii, 327.  **39.** *NME*, 13 June 1981; Reynolds, *Rip It Up*, pp. xv, xix; Rimmer, *New Romantics*, pp. 89–93.  **40.** *NME*, 20 December 1980.  **41.** *Observer*, 25 January 1981; *The Times*, 31 March 1981, 7 April 1981.  **42.** *Daily Mirror*; 7 April 1981; *The Times*, 24 February 1981; and see George, *Take It Like a Man*, p. 175.  **43.** *Sun*, 2 October 1981, quoted in Alwyn W. Turner, *Rejoice! Rejoice! Britain in the 1980s* (2010), p. 60.  **44.** *The Times*, 31 December 1980; *NME*, 19 December 1981.  **45.** Reynolds, *Rip It Up*, pp. xv, 335.  **46.** *Melody Maker*, 2 August 1980, 23 October 1982.  **47.** *The Face*, March 1981.  **48.** *NME*, 25 July 1981; *Melody Maker*, 13 November 1982; *The Times*, 8 December 1983; *Guardian*, 18 December 1981.  **49.** *Melody Maker*, 13 November 1982; *NME*, 23 July 1983.  **50.** *Melody Maker*, 28 February 1981; *Sounds*, 13 September 1980; *Guardian*, 25 March 2009.  **51.** George, *Take It Like a Man*, p. 212; *The Face*, August 1981; Kemp, *I Know This Much*, p. 102; *Daily Mirror*, 16 May 1981; *The Face*, December 1981; Turner, *Rejoice! Rejoice!*, pp. 64–5.  **52.** *Guardian*, 2 February 1981; *Sounds*, 13 September 1980; *NME*, 29 November 1980; *The Face*, August 1981.  **53.** Philip Norman, *Shout! The True Story of the Beatles* (1981: 1993), p. 157; Mark Lewisohn, *The Beatles: All These Years*, vol. 1: *Tune In* (2013), pp. 568, 647, 649; Fred Vermorel and Judy Vermorel, *Adam and the Ants* (1981), quoted in Andy Beckett, *Promised You a Miracle: UK80–82* (2015), p. 191; *NME*, 1 May 1982, 12 July 1980; *Sounds*, 20 March 1982, 11 September 1982.  **54.** Kemp, *I Know*

*This Much*, pp. 176–7.    55. *NME*, 20 December 1980, 17 October 1981, 14 March 1981; *Record Mirror*, 8 August 1981; Reynolds, *Rip It Up*, p. 9; *Melody Maker*, 13 November 1982; *Sounds*, 11 September 1982; *Smash Hits*, 18 February 1982; *NME*, 14 March 1981.    56. *The Times*, 5 December 1983.    57. *Guardian*, 26 March 1983; Reynolds, *Rip It Up*, pp. 409–10. On pop videos in general, see the thoughtful discussion in Graham Stewart, *Bang! A History of Britain in the 1980s* (2013), pp. 284–6.    58. *Daily Express*, 22 May 1980.    59. *Daily Mirror*, 30 July 1981.    60. *Observer*, 1 August 1982; *Daily Express*, 1 October 1982; *Guardian*, 26 October 1982; *City Limits*, 16 October 1981.    61. *Guardian*, 2 April 1983.

## Chapter 13. High Noon at Leyland

1. Michael Edwardes, *Back from the Brink: An Apocalyptic Experience* (1983), pp. 173–4, 176–8; *Observer*, 14 September 1980.    2. Edwardes, *Back from the Brink*, pp. 177–8, 180, 182; *Guardian*, 8 October 1980; *Observer*, 14 September 1980; and see Graham Robson, *Metro: The Book of the Car* (Cambridge, 1982).    3. *Guardian*, 13 October 1980; *Observer*, 14 October 1980; *The Times*, 10 September 1980; Edwardes, *Back from the Brink*, p. 183.    4. Ibid., p. 184; *Daily Express*, 15 October 1980; *Guardian*, 15 October 1980; *The Times*, 8 October 1980, 9 October 1980; *Observer*, 14 September 1980; Richard Ingrams and John Wells, *The Other Half: Further Letters of Denis Thatcher* (1981), pp. 41–2.    5. *Guardian*, 9 October 1980; the advert is on YouTube.    6. See, for example, the huge advert in *The Times*, 14 October 1980.    7. *The Times*, 3 October 1980, 4 October 1980; *Guardian*, 17 October 1980, 28 October 1980, 22 November 1980, 27 December 1980; *Daily Mirror*, 22 November 1980; *Daily Express*, 22 November 1980.    8. *Guardian*, 8 November 1980, 8 December 1980.    9. Louis Heren, *Alas, Alas for England: What Went Wrong with Britain* (1981), p. 91.    10. Stephen Wilks, *Industrial Policy and the Motor Industry* (Manchester, 1984), pp. 69–70, 76, 83–4; Geoffrey Owen, *From Empire to Europe: The Decline and Revival of British Industry since the Second World War* (1999), pp. 230–31, 236, 238.    11. Ibid., pp. 233–4; TNA CAB 129/183, C (75) 53, 'British Leyland: The Ryder Report', 23 April 1975; TNA CAB 128/56, CC (75) 22, 22 April 1975; *The Times*, 25 April 1975; Wilks, *Industrial Policy*, pp. 100–104, 107; *Daily Mirror*, 11 September 1979.    12. Edwardes, *Back from the Brink*, pp. 39, 13–15, 78, 90; Nicholas Comfort, *The Slow Death of British Industry: A Sixty-Year Suicide, 1952–2012* (2013), p. 65; Wilks, *Industrial Policy*, p. 113; Ian MacGregor with Rodney Tyler, *The Enemies Within: The Story of the Miners' Strike, 1984–5* (1986: 1987), p. 62.    13. Owen, *From Empire to Europe*, p. 233; Wilks, *Industrial Policy*, p. 272; Edwardes, *Back from the Brink*, p. 91; Henry Root, *The Henry Root Letters* (1980: 1981), p. 35.    14. *Daily Express*, 11 October 1979, 16 July 1980, 4 February 1985; *The Times*, 17 September 1981; for an excellent overview, see Owen, *From Empire to Europe*.    15. *News of the World*, 30 December 1979.    16. *The Times*, 8 October 1976, 15 December 1976, 26 October 1977; Anthony Sampson, *The Changing Anatomy of Britain* (1982: 1983), p. 393; *Observer*, 14 September 1980; *Time*, 14 November 1977; Edwardes, *Back from the Brink*, pp. 40–41, 45.    17. *The Times*, 17 January 1978, 23 January 1978, 1 February 1978, 2 February 1978, 21 August 1978; Edwardes, *Back from the Brink*, pp. 72, 55, 75, 80–81, 87, 74; Wilks, *Industrial Policy*, pp. 207–8.    18. John Hoskyns, *Just in Time: Inside the Thatcher Revolution* (2000), p. 88; Edwardes, *Back from the Brink*, pp. 211, 231, 221–2, 205–6; and see Hugo Young, *One of Us: A Biography of Margaret Thatcher* (rev. edn: 1990), p. 362; Charles Moore, *Margaret Thatcher: The Authorized Biography*, vol. 1: *Not for Turning* (2013), p. 514.    19. Andrew Denham and Mark Garnett, *Keith Joseph* (2001: Chesham, 2002), pp. 14, 24, 48–50, 55, 134, 274, 276, 324, 334, 352–3; *Observer*, 9 December 1984; Ferdinand Mount, *Cold Cream: My Early Life and Other Mistakes* (2008), pp. 276–8. On Joseph and Arthur Daley, see Manuel Alvarado and John Stewart, *Made for Television: Euston Films Limited* (1985), p. 94.    20. Denham and Garnett, *Keith Joseph*, p. 304; Norman Tebbit, *Upwardly Mobile: An Autobiography* (1988), p. 173; Heren, *Alas, Alas for England*, p. 156; Mount, *Cold Cream*, pp. 270, 278, 275–6.    21. Hoskyns, *Just in Time*,

p. 54; Mount, *Cold Cream*, p. 278; Denham and Garnett, *Keith Joseph*, pp. 328, 339–41, 350–51. **22.** Edwardes, *Back from the Brink*, pp. 96–7, 224; Wilks, *Industrial Policy*, pp. 214–15. **23.** Joseph to Thatcher, 'British Leyland', 7 September 1979, TFW; Margaret Thatcher, *The Downing Street Years* (1993), pp. 115, 117; Moore, *Not for Turning*, p. 514; Jim Prior, *A Balance of Power* (1986), p. 127; Hoskyns to Thatcher, 'British Leyland', 7 December 1979. **24.** Edwardes, *Back from the Brink*, pp. 98–9, 105–6; *Daily Mirror*, 11 September 1979; *Daily Express*, 2 November 1979. The text of Edwardes's 'Recovery Plan', as presented to British Leyland's workers, is included in Department of Industry, 'BL Closures', 12 September 1979, TFW. The official BL press release on the ballot result is in TNA PREM 19/71. **25.** Edwardes, *Back from the Brink*, pp. 108–10; *The Times*, 20 November 1979, 1 May 1980; *Daily Mirror*, 20 November 1979; *Daily Express*, 20 November 1979, 21 November 1979. **26.** Edwardes, *Back from the Brink*, p. 117; *The Times*, 20 November 1979, 8 February 1979; *Daily Express*, 11 October 1979. **27.** *The Times*, 20 November 1979, 6 February 1980; *Guardian*, 12 February 1980; John Bloomfield, 'Interview with Derek Robinson', *Marxism Today* (March 1980); and see Comfort, *Slow Death of British Industry*, pp. 67–8. **28.** Bloomfield, 'Interview with Derek Robinson'; *The Times*, 28 November 1979; Edwardes, *Back from the Brink*, pp. 110–11, 126; and see the interview with Edwardes in Peter Taylor's documentary *True Spies* (BBC Two, 2002), transcribed at http://news.bbc. co.uk/nol/shared/spl/hi/programmes/true_spies/transcripts/truespies_prog2.txt. **29.** Christopher Andrew, *The Defence of the Realm: The Authorized History of MI5* (2009), pp. 671–2; and see the interviews in *True Spies*, http://news.bbc.co.uk/nol/shared/spl/hi/ programmes/true_spies/transcripts/truespies_prog2.txt. **30.** *The Times*, 22 November 1979, 23 November 1979; *Daily Express*, 22 November 1979; *Daily Mirror*, 22 November 1979, 23 November 1979. **31.** Edwardes, *Back from the Brink*, p. 111; *The Times*, 26 November 1979, 27 November 1979; *Daily Express*, 27 November 1979. **32.** Edwardes, *Back from the Brink*, pp. 114–15; *The Times*, 28 November 1979, 29 November 1979, 30 November 1979; *Daily Express*, 28 November 1979. **33.** Robert Armstrong to Thatcher, 'British Leyland: E (79) 74', 7 December 1979, TFW; TNA PREM 19/71, Hoskyns to Joseph, 15 November 1979; Hoskyns to Thatcher, 'British Leyland', 7 December 1979, TFW; Sir Keith Joseph, 'Future of BL Ltd', 17 December 1979, TFW; TNA CAB 128/66, CC (79) 26, 20 December 1979; Moore, *Not for Turning*, p. 515; Young, *One of Us*, p. 201. **34.** *Daily Express*, 10 December 1979, 7 February 1980, 8 February 1980; *Daily Mirror*, 8 February 1980; *The Times*, 8 February 1980. **35.** *Daily Express*, 7 February 1980, 8 February 1980; *The Times*, 11 February 1980; *Daily Mirror*, 8 February 1980. **36.** *Guardian*, 12 February 1980; Comfort, *Slow Death of British Industry*, p. 69; *The Times*, 9 February 1980, 11 February 1980; Edwardes, *Back from the Brink*, p. 123. **37.** *The Times*, 21 February 1980; *Daily Mirror*, 21 February 1980; *Daily Express*, 21 February 1980. **38.** Hansard, 21 February 1980; *The Times*, 21 February 1980; *Daily Express*, 21 February 1980; *Daily Mirror*, 21 February 1980. **39.** *Observer*, 24 February 1980; *The Times*, 9 May 1980, 16 November 1981, 19 November 1981. **40.** *The Times*, 12 January 1983, 2 June 1983; *Guardian*, 16 November 1983. **41.** *The Times*, 11 February 1980, 14 February 1980. **42.** Ibid., 28 November 1979; Edwardes, *Back from the Brink*, pp. 124–7; Wilks, *Industrial Policy*, pp. 207–8, 211. **43.** 'Radio Interview for *The World This Weekend*', 4 January 1981, TFW; Thatcher, *Downing Street Years*, pp. 118–19; Edwardes, *Back from the Brink*, pp. 92, 96, 226; *Observer*, 4 September 1980; Hoskyns, *Just in Time*, pp. 174, 258. **44.** 'No. 10 Record of Conversation (British Leyland)', 22 May 1980, TFW; Edwardes, *Back from the Brink*, pp. 227–31; see also Edwardes to Joseph, 15 May 1980, TFW. **45.** Moore, *Not for Turning*, pp. 516–17; Thatcher, *Downing Street Years*, p. 120; 'No. 10 Record of Conversation (British Leyland)', 13 January 1981, TFW. **46.** Joseph to Thatcher, 21 January 1981, TFW; Joseph to Thatcher, 22 January 1981, TFW; Denham and Garnett, *Keith Joseph*, pp. 341–2; Edwardes, *Back from the Brink*, pp. 237–8, 240, 243. See also Wilks, *Industrial Policy*, pp. 218–20. **47.** Christopher Johnson, *The Economy under Mrs Thatcher, 1979–1990* (1991), pp. 185–6, 96; Moore, *Not for Turning*, pp. 517–18; Friedman to Harris, 2 July 1981, TFW; Morrison Halcrow, *Keith Joseph: A Single Mind* (1989), p. 149; Young, *One of Us*, p. 318; 'TV Interview for LWT *Weekend World*', 1 February 1981, TFW; Denham and Garnett,

*Keith Joseph*, pp. 342–3; Moore, *Not for Turning*, p. 517; Tebbit, *Upwardly Mobile*, p. 176.   **48.** Denham and Garnett, *Keith Joseph*, pp. 363, 356, 353–4; *Sunday Times*, 31 May 1981.   **49.** Hansard, 29 October 1980. As so often with Hansard, though, it does not perfectly capture what Foot *actually* said, which was less formal and therefore funnier: it is worth tracking down the recording, which used to be online but has recently vanished. **50.** *Guardian*, 14 May 1982.   **51.** Ibid., 30 September 1982; Wilks, *Industrial Policy*, pp. 206, 212; Edwardes, *Back from the Brink*, p. 127; *Sunday Times*, 21 March 1982; *The Times*, 19 October 1982.   **52.** Wilks, *Industrial Policy*, pp. 206–7; Owen, *From Empire to Europe*, pp. 241, 243; *Guardian*, 15 March 1982, 30 September 1982, 19 March 1982, 20 March 1982.   **53.** Wilks, *Industrial Policy*, pp. 75, 229; Owen, *From Empire to Europe*, pp. 241–2; *Guardian*, 30 September 1982; see also the similar verdicts in *Guardian*, 16 September 1982; *The Times*, 19 October 1982.   **54.** Joseph to Thatcher, 6 August 1980, TFW; Joseph to Thatcher, 30 September 1980, TFW; 'UKE Tokyo to FCO', 19 September 1982, TFW; Thatcher, *Downing Street Years*, pp. 496–7; *The Times*, 13 January 1984, 30 March 1984; *Observer*, 29 January 1984; 'Speech Opening Nissan Car Factory', 8 September 1986, TFW.   **55.** *Guardian*, 13 March 1984, 23 April 1985; *The Times*, 13 May 1991; and see Wilks, *Industrial Policy*, pp. 307–8.

# Chapter 14. A Really Angry Brigade

**1.** Philip Norman, *John Lennon: The Life* (2008), pp. 805–6. For a recording and transcript of Lennon's last interview, see http://www.beatlesarchive.net/john-lennons-last-interview-december-8-1980.html.   **2.** Norman, *John Lennon*, p. 806.   **3.** *Daily Mirror*, 10 December 1980, 11 December 1980, 15 December 1980; *Sun*, 10 December 1980; *The Times*, 10 December 1980, 15 December 1980; *Guardian*, 15 December 1980; *Daily Express*, 10 December 1980.   **4.** *Daily Mirror*, 10 December 1980; *Daily Express*, 10 December 1980; *The Times*, 10 December 1980.   **5.** *Daily Express*, 15 December 1980.   **6.** Lincoln Allison, *Condition of England: Essays and Impressions* (1981), p. 153; *The Face*, April 1981. On the turn away from the 1960s, see Simon Reynolds, *Rip It Up and Start Again: Post-Punk, 1978–84* (2005), p. xiv.   **7.** *The Times*, 2 February 1980, 10 December 1980. On Bond, see James Chapman, *Licence to Thrill: A Cultural History of the James Bond Films* (1999), p. 202.   **8.** *Guardian*, 8 December 1980, 9 December 1980.   **9.** Allison, *Condition of England*, p. 40; Jeremy Seabrook, *Unemployment* (1982: 1983), p. 74.   **10.** *Guardian*, 12 May 1981, 30 March 2012; *Observer*, 14 June 1981; *The Times*, 17 September 1981.   **11.** Alan Bleasdale, *Boys from the Blackstuff* (1982: 1985), p. 47; *The Times*, 6 October 1981; Tony Benn, *The End of an Era: Diaries, 1980–90* (1992), p. 257.   **12.** *Guardian*, 19 April 1979, 21 July 1981, 29 September 1981, 12 April 1980, 16 April 1980.   **13.** *Daily Express*, 25 October 1982.   **14.** Andrew Denham and Mark Garnett, *Keith Joseph* (2001: Chesham, 2002), pp. 291–6; Jacqueline McCafferty, 'Us over Here – Them over There', in Joan Scanlon (ed.), *Surviving the Blues: Growing up in the Thatcher Decade* (1990), p. 60.   **15.** Brian Harrison, 'Mrs Thatcher and the Intellectuals', *Twentieth Century British History*, 5:2 (1994), p. 239; *The Times*, 30 March 1981, 24 September 1983; Nicholas Timmins, *The Five Giants: A Biography of the Welfare State* (1995), pp. 383–4; *Guardian*, 23 September 1983, 23 May 1983; *New Statesman*, 3 June 1983; *Independent*, 12 June 1987; *Sunday Telegraph*, 10 January 1988; and see Charles Moore, *Margaret Thatcher: The Authorized Biography*, vol. 2: *Everything She Wants* (2015), pp. 635–7, 655, 657.   **16.** *Let's Go, 1982: The Budget Guide to Britain and Ireland* (New York, 1982), p. 210.   **17.** *Observer*, 10 February 1980.   **18.** *The Times*, 11 May 1981.   **19.** Sue Townsend, *The Secret Diary of Adrian Mole Aged 13 ¾* (1982: 2002), pp. 43, 159.   **20.** Jerry White, *London in the Twentieth Century: A City and Its People* (2001), pp. 393–4; David Kogan and Maurice Kogan, *The Battle for the Labour Party* (1982), pp. 122–5; *Observer*, 10 February 1980.   **21.** Tony Benn, *Conflicts of Interest: Diaries, 1977–80* (1990), pp. 157, 453; and see *Politico*'s profile of Primarolo, dated 21 July 1999, at https://www.politico.eu/article/tax-collector/.   **22.** Austin Mitchell, *Four Years in the Death of the Labour Party* (1983), p. 89; Roy Hattersley, *Who Goes Home? Scenes from* *a Political Life* (1995), p. 214.   **23.** Kenneth O. Morgan, *Callaghan: A Life* (Oxford, 1997), p. 707; *Observer*, 22 April 1979, 6 May 1979; Eric Hobsbawm, 'The Forward March of Labour Halted?', *Marxism Today* (September 1978), pp. 279–86.   **24.** John Golding, *Hammer of the Left: The Battle for the Soul of the Labour Party* (2016), p. 48; Ivor Crewe and Anthony King, *SDP: The Birth, Life and Death of the Social Democratic Party* (Oxford, 1995), pp. 14, 33; David Marquand, *The Progressive Dilemma: From Lloyd George to Blair* (2nd edn: 1999), p. 212; *The Times*, 5 May 1981.   **25.** *The Times*, 19 February 1983; and see Kogan and Kogan, *Battle for the Labour Party*, pp. 37, 71; Michael Crick, *Militant* (1984), esp. pp. 45–62, 78–94, 211, 62, 315; Nick Thomas-Symonds, 'A Reinterpretation of Michael Foot's Handling of the Militant Tendency', *Contemporary British History*, 19:1 (2005), pp. 27–51; Martin Pugh, *Speak for Britain: A New History of the Labour Party* (2010), pp. 366, 368.   **26.** Mitchell, *Four Years in the Death of the Labour Party*, pp. 21–2, 24; Anthony Sampson, *The Changing Anatomy of Britain* (1982: 1983), p. 87; Ian Bradley, *Breaking the Mould? The Birth and Prospects of the Social Democratic Party* (Oxford, 1981), p. 115.   **27.** *Guardian*, 26 September 1981; Benn, *Conflicts of Interest*, pp. 157, 453.   **28.** Crewe and King, *SDP*, pp. 16, 18; Mitchell, *Four Years in the Death of the Labour Party*, p. 35; *The Times*, 28 November 1981; *Daily Telegraph*, 12 June 1979.   **29.** *Guardian*, 10 December 1981; Stuart Hall, 'The Great Moving Right Show', *Marxism Today* (January 1979), pp. 14–20.   **30.** *Guardian*, 10 December 1981.   **31.** Kogan and Kogan, *Battle for the Labour Party*, p. 57; Mitchell, *Four Years in the Death of the Labour Party*, p. 28; Crewe and King, *SDP*, p. 16; *The Times*, 24 September 1981; Golding, *Hammer of the Left*, p. 31.   **32.** Mitchell, *Four Years in the Death of the Labour Party*, p. 20; Kogan and Kogan, *Battle for the Labour Party*, pp. 56–7; Crewe and King, *SDP*, pp. 13–14, 20–21; *The Times*, 5 June 1980; Edmund Dell, *A Strange Eventful History: Democratic Socialism in Britain* (2000), p. 476. The Hattersley line is from the first episode of BBC2's documentary *The Wilderness Years*, 'Cast into the Wilderness' (3 December 1995).   **33.** Kogan and Kogan, *Battle for the Labour Party*, pp. 22–3, 49; Benn, *Conflicts of Interest*, pp. 482, 485–8, 508; Morgan, *Callaghan*, pp. 711, 708.   **34.** Kogan and Kogan, *Battle for the Labour Party*, pp. 24–5, 31; Mitchell, *Four Years in the Death of the Labour Party*, pp. 38, 46; Crewe and King, *SDP*, p. 17.   **35.** Dell, *Strange Eventful History*, p. 481; Mervyn Jones, *Michael Foot* (1994), p. 440   **36.** Mitchell, *Four Years in the Death of the Labour Party*, p. 46; Benn, *Conflicts of Interest*, pp. 541, 504, 581; Kenneth O. Morgan, *Michael Foot: A Life* (2007), p. 374; *The Times*, 12 July 1980; Crewe and King, *SDP*, p. 33; the *Sun* quotation is from Golding, *Hammer of the Left*, p. 384.   **37.** Crewe and King, *SDP*, pp. 30–31, 17–18, 21, 48; Kogan and Kogan, *Battle for the Labour Party*, pp. 32–3, 42–3, 55–6; Golding, *Hammer of the Left*, p. 21; Denis Healey, *The Time of My Life* (1989), p. 470.   **38.** Kogan and Kogan, *Battle for the Labour Party*, pp. 39, 45–6, 28, 42; Golding, *Hammer of the Left*, pp. 19–20.   **39.** *The Times*, 12 May 1975; *Daily Mirror*, 9 May 1975.   **40.** *The Times*, 4 November 1982; Kenneth O. Morgan, *Labour People: Leaders and Lieutenants, Hardie to Kinnock* (rev. edn: Oxford, 1992), pp. 301–2. On Benn's strengths, see, for example, Crewe and King, *SDP*, p. 16; Golding, *Hammer of the Left*, p. 3.   **41.** Shirley Williams, *Climbing the Bookshelves* (2009), p. 276; Healey, *Time of My Life*, p. 471; Bill Rodgers, *Fourth among Equals* (2000), p. 189; Barbara Castle, *The Castle Diaries, 1974–76* (1980), pp. 126, 128, 109. See also Crewe and King, *SDP*, p. 28.   **42.** Golding, *Hammer of the Left*, pp. 3, 5; Robert Harris, *The Making of Neil Kinnock* (1984), p. 154.   **43.** *The Times*, 15 May 1981. On Benn the populist, see Morgan, *Labour People*, pp. 304–6, 311.   **44.** Benn, *Conflicts of Interest*, pp. 477, 549; Morgan, *Michael Foot*, p. 409; Brian Harrison, *Finding a Role? The United Kingdom, 1970–1990* (Oxford, 2010), p. 494; *The Times*, 28 May 1981, 24 September 1981.   **45.** Benn, *Conflicts of Interest*, pp. 484, 528, 560, 556; see also Golding, *Hammer of the Left*, pp. 6–10, which is merciless about Benn's leadership ambitions.   **46.** Ibid., p. 389.   **47.** *Daily Mirror*, 6 November 1979; *Daily Express*, 10 June 1980; *The Times*, 20 November 1981. On Benn and the media, see, for example, Benn, *End of an Era*, p. 79.   **48.** Michael Foot, *Loyalists and Loners* (1986), p. 119; Benn, *Conflicts of Interest*, pp. 498, 501, 516; Benn, *End of an Era*, p. 16.   **49.** Morgan, *Callaghan*, pp. 702–3; Healey, *Time of My Life*, p. 466; Edward Pearce, *Denis Healey: A Life in Our Times* (2002), pp. 531–2; Rodgers, *Fourth* *among Equals,* p. 188.   50. Benn, *Conflicts of Interest,* pp. 501–2, 504; *Observer,* 13 May 1979; Golding, *Hammer of the Left,* pp. 83–4.   51. *Daily Mirror,* 1 October 1979; *Daily Express,* 1 October 1979; Golding, *Hammer of the Left,* p. 94; *The Times,* 1 October 1979; Crewe and King, *SDP,* p. 31; Pearce, *Denis Healey,* p. 529; *Guardian,* 2 October 1979; Morgan, *Callaghan,* p. 711.   52. *Daily Mirror,* 2 October 1979; *Daily Express,* 2 October 1979; *Guardian,* 2 October 1979; Benn, *Conflicts of Interest,* pp. 542, 545.   53. *Guardian,* 2 October 1979; Benn, *Conflicts of Interest,* p. 545; and see Golding, *Hammer of the Left,* pp. 101–5.   54. Benn, *Conflicts of Interest,* p. 546; *Guardian,* 2 October 1979; *Mirror,* 4 October 1979; *Sunday Express,* 7 October 1979; *Daily Express,* 2 October 1979.   55. Benn, *Conflicts of Interest,* pp. 489, 568; 'Eric Hobsbawm Interviews Tony Benn', *Marxism Today* (October 1980), p. 6.   56. David Owen, *Time to Declare* (1991), pp. 430, 418; Harris, *Making of Neil Kinnock,* p. 141; Rodgers, *Fourth among Equals,* pp. 190–91; Kogan and Kogan, *Battle for the Labour Party,* p. 101; Healey, *Time of My Life,* p. 475; Golding, *Hammer of the Left,* p. 63; Crewe and King, *SDP,* pp. 22–4; *The Times,* 17 January 1980, 27 March 1980.   57. *Sunday Express,* 4 February 1980; *The Times,* 11 February 1980; Benn, *Conflicts of Interest,* p. 599; Kogan and Kogan, *Battle for the Labour Party,* pp. 73, 80–82.   58. *The Times,* 14 July 1980, 31 May 1980; Golding, *Hammer of the Left,* p. 108. The text of *Peace, Jobs and Freedom* is included as an appendix in Benn, *Conflicts of Interest,* pp. 626–32.   59. Golding, *Hammer of the Left,* p. 109; Benn, *Conflicts of Interest,* p. 599; *The Times,* 2 June 1980; Pearce, *Denis Healey,* p. 532; Crewe and King, *SDP,* pp. 39–40. On Fields, see his obituary in the *Guardian,* 1 July 2008.   60. *Guardian,* 2 June 1980; Owen, *Time to Declare,* pp. 435–6; Crewe and King, *SDP,* p. 40.   61. Golding, *Hammer of the Left,* pp. 117–20; Benn, *End of an Era,* pp. 5–10; Morgan, *Callaghan,* pp. 715–16.   62. Benn, *End of an Era,* p. 10; Rodgers, *Fourth among Equals,* p. 195; Crewe and King, *SDP,* pp. 45–6; Owen, *Time to Declare,* pp. 440–41, 445.   63. *Daily Mirror,* 16 June 1980; *The Times,* 16 June 1980, 18 June 1980, 24 June 1980; *Guardian,* 18 June 1980.   64. *Daily Mirror,* 23 June 1980; *Daily Express,* 19 June 1980.

## Chapter 15. Another Day of Feud and Fury

1. The episode is 'The Devil You Know' (BBC2, 23 March 1981). There is a slightly different version in Jonathan Lynn and Antony Jay, *The Complete Yes Minister: The Diaries of a Cabinet Minister by the Right Hon. James Hacker, MP* (1984), pp. 282–3.   2. Roy Jenkins, *A Life at the Centre* (1991), p. 444.   3. Ivor Crewe and Anthony King, *SDP: The Birth, Death and Life of the Social Democratic Party* (Oxford, 1995), pp. 56, 53; Austin Mitchell, *Four Years in the Death of the Labour Party* (1983), p. 69; *The Times,* 23 March 1982; John Campbell, *Roy Jenkins: A Well-Rounded Life* (2014), pp. 9, 523, 525; Shirley Williams, *Climbing the Bookshelves* (2009), p. 269.   4. Campbell, *Roy Jenkins,* pp. 28, 162–3, 476, 518; Jenkins, *Life at the Centre,* pp. 448–9.   5. Ibid., pp. 364, 388, 410, 416, 424–6, 493, 513–14; Ronald McIntosh, *Challenge to Democracy: Politics, Trade Union Power and Economic Failure in the 1970s* (2006), pp. 87, 120, 130; Campbell, *Roy Jenkins,* pp. 503, 506.   6. Jenkins, *Life at the Centre,* pp. 514–19; Campbell, *Roy Jenkins,* pp. 511–15.   7. Jenkins, *Life at the Centre,* pp. 514–15; Campbell, *Roy Jenkins,* p. 515; Hugh Stephenson, *Claret and Chips: The Rise of the SDP* (1982), pp. 21–2; *The Times,* 26 November 1979.   8. Ibid., 27 November 1979; Jenkins, *Life at the Centre,* p. 520; Campbell, *Roy Jenkins,* pp. 516–17; Bill Rodgers, *Fourth among Equals* (2000), pp. 199–200; Crewe and King, *SDP,* pp. 36–7, 67.   9. Ibid., pp. 71, 39; David Owen, *Time to Declare* (1991), pp. 426, 428; Stephenson, *Claret and Chips,* p. 31.   10. Crewe and King, *SDP,* p. 67; Campbell, *Roy Jenkins,* p. 544.   11. Owen, *Time to Declare,* p. 438; Crewe and King, *SDP,* pp. 40–41; *Financial Times,* 6 June 1980.   12. Alwyn W. Turner, *Rejoice! Rejoice! Britain in the 1980s* (2010), pp. 31–2; David Marquand, *The Progressive Dilemma: From Lloyd George to Blair* (2nd edn: 1999), pp. 196–7.   13. Mitchell, *Four Years in the Death of the Labour Party,* p. 74; Rodgers, *Fourth among Equals,* p. 194; Crewe and King, *SDP,* p. 38; Owen, *Time to Declare,* p. 624; Denis Healey, *The Time of My Life* (1989), p. 480.   14. Rodgers, *Fourth*

*among Equals*, pp. 192–3; Owen, *Time to Declare*, pp. 39–40, 452; Marquand, *Progressive Dilemma*, pp. 203–4; Campbell, *Roy Jenkins*, p. 554; *Guardian*, 9 January 1984.  **15.** Owen, *Time to Declare*, pp. 419, 425, 438–9; Crewe and King, *SDP*, pp. 41, 44; Williams, *Climbing the Bookshelves*, pp. 271–3; *Sunday Times*, 8 June 1980.  **16.** Stephenson, *Claret and Chips*, p. 142; Rodgers, *Fourth among Equals*, p. 207; Crewe and King, *SDP*, p. 36; *The Times*, 15 July 1980.  **17.** Louis Heren, *Alas, Alas for England: What Went Wrong with Britain* (1981), p. 73; Crewe and King, *SDP*, pp. 41–2; Williams, *Climbing the Bookshelves*, pp. 148–50.  **18.** Ibid., pp. 254, 210, 266–7, 271; Crewe and King, *SDP*, pp. 42–3; Ion Trewin (ed.), *The Hugo Young Papers: Thirty Years of British Politics – Off the Record* (2008), pp. 147–8.  **19.** Rodgers, *Fourth among Equals*, pp. 155, 191, 196–7; Owen, *Time to Declare*, p. 438; *Guardian*, 1 August 1980.  **20.** Ibid.; Owen, *Time to Declare*, p. 447; Crewe and King, *SDP*, p. 47; Tony Benn, *The End of an Era: Diaries, 1980–90* (1992), p. 23.  **21.** *The Times*, 10 June 1980; Jenkins, *Life at the Centre*, pp. 525–6; Crewe and King, *SDP*, p. 68; *Spectator*, 14 June 1980; Mitchell, *Four Years in the Death of the Labour Party*, p. 72; Campbell, *Roy Jenkins*, pp. 549–50.  **22.** Jenkins, *Life at the Centre*, p. 526.  **23.** Anthony Sampson, *The Changing Anatomy of Britain* (1982: 1983), p. 60. On Blackpool (and Morecambe), see *The Times*, 9 July 1980, 2 July 1983, 5 October 1983.  **24.** Peter Jenkins, *Mrs Thatcher's Revolution: The Ending of the Socialist Era* (1987: Cambridge, MA, 1988), p. 117; Rodgers, *Fourth among Equals*, p. 202; Williams, *Climbing the Bookshelves*, p. 276; Crewe and King, *SDP*, p. 49.  **25.** David Kogan and Maurice Kogan, *The Battle for the Labour Party* (1982), p. 105; Williams, *Climbing the Bookshelves*, pp. 276–7.  **26.** *Guardian*, 30 September 1980; *The Times*, 30 September 1980; and see Benn, *End of an Era*, p. 30.  **27.** *The Times*, 30 September 1980; *Daily Mirror*, 30 September 1980; *Daily Express*, 30 September 1980; Benn, *End of an Era*, pp. 30–31.  **28.** *Guardian*, 30 September 1980; *Daily Mirror*, 30 September 1980; *The Times*, 30 September 1980; Crewe and King, *SDP*, p. 50.  **29.** For the extraordinary events of Wednesday 1 October, see *The Times*, 2 October 1980; *Guardian*, 2 October 1980; *Daily Mirror*, 2 October 1980; *Daily Express*, 2 October 1980; as well as Crewe and King, *SDP*, p. 50; Mervyn Jones, *Michael Foot* (1994), p. 440; Owen, *Time to Declare*, pp. 451–2; Benn, *End of an Era*, pp. 31–2; John Golding, *Hammer of the Left: The Battle for the Soul of the Labour Party* (2016), pp. 131–2, 141.  **30.** *The Times*, 2 October 1980; *Daily Mirror*, 2 October 1980; Kogan and Kogan, *Battle for the Labour Party*, pp. 85–6; Golding, *Hammer of the Left*, pp. 141–2; Benn, *End of an Era*, pp. 33–4.  **31.** *The Times*, 3 October 1980; *Guardian*, 3 October 1980; Owen, *Time to Declare*, p. 451; Golding, *Hammer of the Left*, pp. 145–6; Kogan and Kogan, *Battle for the Labour Party*, p. 86; *Daily Mirror*, 3 October 1980.  **32.** Golding, *Hammer of the Left*, p. 111; Benn, *End of an Era*, pp. 34–5.  **33.** 'Speech to Conservative Party Conference', 10 October 1980, TFW; *Daily Mirror*, 2 October 1980; *Daily Express*, 2 October 1980.  **34.** *Guardian*, 4 October 1980 (and see the letters on 7, 8 and 10 October); *The Times*, 4 October 1980.  **35.** Owen, *Time to Declare*, pp. 450, 452–3, 457, 461, 467; Crewe and King, *SDP*, pp. 50, 69, 79; *The Times*, 4 October 1980; Stephenson, *Claret and Chips*, p. 36; Rodgers, *Fourth among Equals*, pp. 203–4.  **36.** Golding, *Hammer of the Left*, pp. 146–7; *Guardian*, 16 October 1980; 'No.10 Letter to FCO ("Conversation with Chancellor Schmidt")', 31 October 1980, TFW.  **37.** Benn, *End of an Era*, pp. 43–4, 35–6, 38; Kogan and Kogan, *Battle for the Labour Party*, p. 90.  **38.** *The Times*, 17 October 1980; *Daily Mirror*, 16 October 1980, 17 October 1980.  **39.** Simon Hoggart and David Leigh, *Michael Foot: A Portrait* (1981), pp. 5–6.  **40.** Kenneth O. Morgan, *Michael Foot: A Life* (2007), pp. 9–10; Jones, *Michael Foot*, pp. 21, 432–3; Hoggart and Leigh, *Michael Foot*, pp. 11–12.  **41.** Ibid., pp. 4–7; Jones, *Michael Foot*, pp. 448, 450–52; *Observer*, 19 October 1980; *The Times*, 21 October 1980.  **42.** *Sun*, 3 November 1980; Mitchell, *Four Years in the Death of the Labour Party*, pp. 49–50; *The Times*, 31 October 1980; Edward Pearce, *Denis Healey: A Life in Our Times* (2002), p. 541; Golding, *Hammer of the Left*, p. xxvii; Roy Hattersley, *Who Goes Home? Scenes from a Political Life* (1995), p. 223; Williams, *Climbing the Bookshelves*, p. 224.  **43.** Golding, *Hammer of the Left*, p. 151; Pearce, *Denis Healey*, p. 545; Crewe and King, *SDP*, pp. 73–4.  **44.** Pearce, *Denis Healey*, pp. 545–6; Benn, *End of an Era*, p. 46; Hoggart and Leigh, *Michael Foot*, pp. 1–2.  **45.** Benn, *End of an Era*, p. 46; Healey, *Time of My Life*, p. 478.  **46.** *The Times*, 11

November 1980; *Guardian*, 11 November 1980; Benn, *End of an Era*, p. 46; Hoggart and Leigh, *Michael Foot*, p. 2.   **47**. *Daily Express*, 11 November 1980; *Sun*, 11 November 1980; *The Times*, 11 November 1980; *The Economist*, 15 November 1980.   **48**. Hattersley, *Who Goes Home?*, p. 225; Crewe and King, *SDP*, p, 75; Pearce, *Denis Healey*, p. 543.   **49**. On the prospects for a party led by Healey, see Jones, *Michael Foot*, p. 449; Golding, *Hammer of the Left*, p. 151; Martin Pugh, *Speak for Britain: A New History of the Labour Party* (2010), p. 364.   **50**. Morgan, *Michael Foot*, p. 381; *Observer*, 17 January 1982; Hattersley, *Who Goes Home?*, pp. 227–8. For the offending essay on Dorothy Parker, see *Guardian*, 24 April 1982.   **51**. Mitchell, *Four Years in the Death of the Labour Party*, p. 50; Anthony King and Robert J. Wybrow (eds.), *British Political Opinion, 1937–2000: The Gallup Polls* (2001), p. 123.   **52**. Jones, *Michael Foot*, pp. 456, 497; *The Times*, 1 December 1982.   **53**. Mitchell, *Four Years in the Death of the Labour Party*, pp. 52, 51, 96; Jones, *Michael Foot*, pp. 497–8; Pearce, *Denis Healey*, pp. 540–41.   **54**. Roy Jenkins, *European Diary, 1977–1981* (1989), p. 643; Campbell, *Roy Jenkins*, p. 552; Crewe and King, *SDP*, pp. 76, 81; *The Times*, 15 November 1980; Morgan, *Michael Foot*, p. 394; Williams, *Climbing the Bookshelves*, pp. 278–9.   **55**. Rodgers, *Fourth among Equals*, pp. 204–5; Crewe and King, *SDP*, pp. 83–4.   **56**. Williams, *Climbing the Bookshelves*, p. 281; Crewe and King, *SDP*, pp. 85–7; Campbell, *Roy Jenkins*, pp. 553–4; Jenkins, *Life at the Centre*, p. 531; Owen, *Time to Declare*, p. 464.   **57**. *Guardian*, 3 December 1980.   **58**. Crewe and King, *SDP*, pp. 89–90; Owen, *Time to Declare*, pp. 476–8; *The Times*, 24 January 1981.   **59**. Owen, *Time to Declare*, pp. 478–9; *The Times*, 26 January 1981; Robert Harris, *The Making of Neil Kinnock* (1984), pp. 146–7; Golding, *Hammer of the Left*, pp. 158–61.   **60**. Kogan and Kogan, *Battle for the Labour Party*, pp. 87, 90, 92–3, 95–7; Golding, *Hammer of the Left*, pp. 161–2; Harris, *Making of Neil Kinnock*, pp. 147–9; *The Times*, 26 January 1981.   **61**. Healey, *Time of My Life*, p. 479; Morgan, *Michael Foot*, p. 393; *Daily Mirror*, 26 January 1981; Mitchell, *Four Years in the Death of the Labour Party*, p. 44; *Guardian*, 26 January 1981.   **62**. Kogan and Kogan, *Battle for the Labour Party*, p. 97; Benn, *End of an Era*, pp. 69–70.   **63**. Edmund Dell, *A Strange Eventful History: Democratic Socialism in Britain* (2000), p. 485; Mitchell, *The Battle for the Labour Party*, p. 45; Morgan, *Michael Foot*, p. 395; Hattersley, *Who Goes Home?*, p. 229; *The Times*, 26 January 1981.

# Chapter 16. When the Wind Blows

**1**. The file is TNA CAB 130/1169, MISC 53 (81), 'Wintex-Cimex 81 Committee'; see also *Daily Mail*, 25 February 2012.   **2**. *Time*, 5 February 1979; Daniel Yergin, *The Prize: The Epic Quest for Oil, Money, and Power* (New York, 1991), pp. 684–7; Robert J. Wybrow, *Britain Speaks Out, 1937–87: A Social History as Seen through the Gallup Data* (Basingstoke, 1989), p. 122.   **3**. *Sunday Express*, 7 January 1979; Sir John Hackett, *The Third World War: A Future History* (1978); I. F. Clarke, *Voices Prophesying War: Future Wars, 1763–3749* (Oxford, 1992), pp. 198–201.   **4**. Charles Moore, *Margaret Thatcher: The Authorized Biography*, vol. 1: *Not for Turning* (2013), pp. 552–7, 572; James Callaghan, *Time and Chance* (1987), pp. 554–6; 'No. 10 Record of Conversation (MT-Nott-Carrington)', 10 February 1981, TFW; Hansard, 24 July 1980.   **5**. Michael J. Turner, *Britain's International Role, 1970–1991* (Basingstoke, 2010), pp. 84–5; Moore, *Not for Turning*, pp. 557–8; 'No. 10 Record of Conversation (MT-Schmidt)', 11 May 1979, TFW; Pym to Thatcher, 'NATO Long-Range Theatre Nuclear Forces', 5 July 1979. TFW; Pym to Thatcher, 'US Ground Launched Cruise Missiles in the UK', 20 September 1979, TFW; *Daily Express*, 13 December 1979.   **6**. Angela Carter, 'Anger in a Black Landscape', in Dorothy Thompson (ed.), *Over Our Dead Bodies: Women against the Bomb* (1983), p. 150; *The Times*, 18 June 1980, 23 June 1980; Moore, *Not for Turning*, p. 553; Tony Benn, *Conflicts of Interest: Diaries, 1977–80* (1990), p. 575. On US bases in Britain, see Duncan Campbell, *The Unsinkable Aircraft Carrier: American Military Power in Britain* (1984).   **7**. Hansard, 17 June 1980, 13 February 1983; *The Times*, 18 June 1980, 14 February 1983; and see Simon Duke, *United States Military Forces and Installations in Europe* (Oxford, 1989), pp. 300–301. On the

American offer of dual control, see Pym to Thatcher, 'Nuclear Issues', 2 November 1982, TFW. **8.** Nott to Thatcher, 'Nuclear Issues', 20 October 1982, TFW; Nott to Thatcher, 'Basing of Cruise Missiles and Arms Control', 15 December 1982, TFW; 'Minutes of MISC 7 (83) 1st Meeting (Basing of United States Cruise Missiles)', 27 January 1983, TFW; 'Minutes of MISC 7 (83) 2nd Meeting (Basing of United States Cruise Missiles)', 8 March 1983, TFW; Hansard, 12 May 1983, 30 June 1983; MO D156, Autumn Directive – USA, 1984. See also Charles Moore, *Margaret Thatcher: The Authorized Biography*, vol. 2: *Everything She Wants* (2015), pp. 24–5. **9.** Hansard, 17 June 1980; *The Times*, 18 June 1980, 19 June 1980, 20 June 1980, 25 July 1980. On the choice of bases, see Robert Armstrong and R. M. Hastie-Smith, 'Basing of United States GLCMs in the United Kingdom' (OD (80) 42), 8 May 1980, TFW. **10.** *The Times*, 9 March 1981. **11.** 'Introduction', in John Minnion and Philip Bolsover (eds.), *The CND Story: The First 25 Years of CND in the Words of the People Involved* (1983), p 36; *The Times*, 2 June 1981, 11 December 1982; *Observer*, 18 January 1981. **12.** E. P. Thompson, 'Resurgence in Europe and the Role of END', in Minnion and Bolsover (eds.), *CND Story*, pp. 80–81; 'Introduction', in ibid., p. 36; *The Times*, 30 January 1980, 19 January 1980. **13.** Duncan Campbell, *War Plan UK: The Truth about Civil Defence in Britain* (1982), pp. 150–51; *The Times*, 7 February 1980; *Guardian*, 19 February 1980; Hansard, 20 February 1980; *New Statesman*, 27 June 1980. **14.** E. P. Thompson, *Protest and Survive* (1980), p. 26; Philip Bolsover, 'A Victory – And a New Development', in Minnion and Bolsover (eds.), *CND Story*, p. 89; *Guardian*, 31 May 1980. **15.** *The Times*, 23 June 1980; Tony Benn, *The End of an Era: Diaries, 1980–90* (1992), p. 12. Benn says there were 25,000 there, but this seems to have been an exaggeration. **16.** Benn, *End of an Era*, p. 20; David Griffiths, 'CND and the Labour Party', in Minnion and Bolsover (eds.), *CND Story*, p. 133; *The Times*, 3 October 1980, 4 October 1980; Austin Mitchell, *Four Years in the Death of the Labour Party* (1983), p. 59; *Guardian*, 11 November 1980. **17.** 'Introduction', in Minnion and Bolsover (eds.), *CND Story*, p. 36; *The Times*, 27 October 1980; Benn, *End of an Era*, pp. 40, 37. **18.** Ibid., p. 44; *Guardian*, 6 June 1981; MO D156, Autumn Directive – USA, 1984; Caroline Blackwood, *On the Perimeter* (1984), p. 101. **19.** Martin Anderson, *Revolution* (San Diego, CA, 1988), pp. 64–72; *Time*, 19 November 1984; John Lewis Gaddis, *The Cold War* (2006), p. 226; Paul Lettow, *Ronald Reagan and His Quest to Abolish Nuclear Weapons* (2005: New York, 2006); Moore, *Everything She Wants*, p. 588; Geoffrey Smith, *Reagan and Thatcher* (1990), p. 58; *The Times*, 22 September 1980; *Daily Mirror*, 6 November 1980. **20.** Jonathan Hogg, *British Nuclear Culture: Official and Unofficial Narratives in the Long 20th Century* (2016), pp. 137–9; Clarke, *Voices Prophesying War*, pp. 204, 209–10; Russell Hoban, *Riddley Walker* (1980: 2012), p. 19. **21.** *Guardian*, 8 January 1983; and see Robert Swindells, *Brother in the Land* (1984); Raymond Briggs, *When the Wind Blows* (1982). **22.** Rob Jovanovic, *Kate Bush: The Biography* (2005: 2006), pp. 112–14; the *Nationwide* interview (29 April 1980) can be seen on YouTube. **23.** Simon Reynolds, *Rip It Up and Start Again: Post-Punk, 1978–84* (2005), pp. xxv, 327; Pascal Bussy, *Kraftwerk: Man, Machine and Music* (1993), pp. 75–6; Johnny Waller and Mike Humphreys, *Orchestral Manoeuvres in the Dark: Messages* (1987), pp. 79–80; *Guardian*, 7 January 2013. **24.** *Observer*, 18 January 1981. **25.** 'Introduction', in Minnion and Bolsover (eds.), *CND Story*, pp. 37–8; Geoffrey Howe, *Conflict of Loyalty* (1994), p. 194. **26.** *Guardian*, 8 June 1981; Crispin Aubrey and John Shearlaw, *Glastonbury: An Oral History of the Music, Mud and Magic* (2005), pp. 57–62; and see George McKay, *Glastonbury: A Very English Fair* (2000), ch. 6. **27.** *Guardian*, 26 October 1981; Benn, *End of an Era* p. 162. **28.** *The Times*, 16 November 1981, 6 April 1983; *Guardian*, 16 November 1981; *Daily Mirror*, 26 January 1983; Michael Heseltine, *Life in the Jungle: My Autobiography* (2000), p. 244. **29.** 'Introduction', in Minnion and Bolsover (eds.), *CND Story*, pp. 39–40; *The Times*, 26 November 1982; *Church Times*, 13 August 1982, 22 October 1982, 18 February 1983; *Daily Express*, 18 October 1982. **30.** *Guardian*, 7 June 1982, 29 November 1982; Shipley to Cecil Parkinson, 'Some Brief Observations on Yesterday's CND Demonstration', 7 June 1982, TFW. **31.** 'Introduction', in Minnion and Bolsover (eds.), *CND Story*, p. 36; *Guardian*, 26 February 1981, 16 June 1981, 24 February 1982, 13 March 1982. **32.** Ibid., 24 February 1982; and see Rhys Evans, *Gwynfor Evans: A Portrait of a Patriot* (Talybont, 2008),

p. 436.  33. *Guardian*, 7 June 1982, 4 August 1982, 11 September 1981, 24 February 1982, 15 July 1982, 7 October 1982, 22 October 1983, 27 October 1983; Dorothy Thompson, 'Defend Us against Our Defenders: Democracy and Security', in Thompson (ed.), *Over Our Dead Bodies*, p. 67.  34. On London, see *Guardian*, 14 May 1982, 22 October 1983, 27 October 1983; Ken Livingstone, *You Can't Say That: Memoirs* (2011), p. 215; Andrew Hosken, *Ken: The Ups and Downs of Ken Livingstone* (2008), pp. 152–5. On Sheffield, see *Guardian*, 18 December 1982, 7 April 1983.  35. *The Times*, 4 August 1982, 1 August 1983.  36. *Daily Express*, 7 January 1983; *Sunday Express*, 1 November 1981, 6 June 1982; *The Times*, 29 November 1982.  37. *Guardian*, 15 November 1983; Christopher Andrew, *The Defence of the Realm: The Authorized History of MI5* (2009), pp. 673–6; Ann Pettitt, *Walking to Greenham* (Dinas Powys, 2006), p. 172.  38. *Independent*, 19 September 1999; *The Times*, 9 March 1985; *Guardian*, 21 February 1985, 27 November 1999.  39. 'Speech to Young Conservative Conference', 12 February 1983, TFW; 'MT Notes on USSR', 8 September 1983, TFW; 'Conservative Political Centre Report: Modernising Britain's Defences', 1 September 1982, TFW.  40. *The Times*, 26 November 1982; *Guardian*, 23 September 1982; Keith Britto, 'Public Opinion Background Note 132', 26 September 1982, TFW; Keith Britto, 'First State of Battle Survey – General Election 1983', 14 May 1983, TFW.  41. *The Times*, 31 July 1984; Russell Davies (ed.), *The Kenneth Williams Diaries* (1993), p. 685.  42. *The Times*, 9 October 1981, 3 December 1983.  43. 'Introduction', in Minnion and Bolsover (eds.), *CND Story*, p. 35; *Daily Mirror*, 11 November 1980, 5 March 1981; Andy Beckett, *Promised You a Miracle: UK80–82* (2015), pp. 95–6; *Daily Mail*, 23 January 1981.  44. *The Times*, 10 October 1984.  45. Anthony King and Robert J. Wybrow (eds.), *British Political Opinion, 1937–2000: The Gallup Polls* (2001), pp. 267–8; *The Times*, 1 August 1983; Sue Townsend, *The Secret Diary of Adrian Mole Aged 13¾* (1982: 2002), pp. 226–7.

## Chapter 17. The Gang's on Its Way!

1. *Observer*, 18 January 1981; Shirley Williams, *Climbing the Bookshelves* (2009), p. 282; Bill Rodgers, *Fourth among Equals* (2000), pp. 208–9.  2. David Owen, *Time to Declare* (1991), pp. 481, 92, 127, 210; *The Times*, 11 March 1980.  3. Rodgers, *Fourth among Equals*, p. 209; Williams, *Climbing the Bookshelves*, p. 282.  4. *The Times*, 26 January 1981; Hugo Young, *One of Us: A Biography of Margaret Thatcher* (rev. edn: 1990), p. 294; Ivor Crewe and Anthony King, *SDP: The Birth, Life and Death of the Social Democratic Party* (Oxford, 1995), p. 93; John Campbell, *Roy Jenkins: A Well-Rounded Life* (2014), pp. 557–8.  5. Owen, *Time to Declare*, pp. 481–2; Austin Mitchell, *Four Years in the Death of the Labour Party* (1983), p. 76; Hugh Stephenson, *Claret and Chips: The Rise of the SDP* (1982), p. 40.  6. Charles Moore, *Margaret Thatcher: The Authorized Biography*, vol. 1: *Not for Turning* (2013), p. 549.  7. *Spectator*, 31 January 1981; Stephenson, *Claret and Chips*, p. 47; Campbell, *Roy Jenkins*, p. 559; *Daily Express*, 26 January 1981, 27 January 1981.  8. *The Times*, 19 February 1981, 18 February 1981, 16 February 1981.  9. Ibid., 27 January 1981, 28 January 1981; *Daily Express*, 27 January 1981.  10. *Daily Mirror*, 28 January 1981; Tony Benn, *The End of an Era: Diaries, 1980–90* (1992), pp. 75–6.  11. *Guardian*, 5 February 1981; Stephenson, *Claret and Chips*, p. 48; Crewe and King, *SDP*, p. 94.  12. Benn, *End of an Era*, p. 83; *Guardian*, 9 February 1981; Owen, *Time to Declare*, p. 488; Stephenson, *Claret and Chips*, pp. 50, 89; Crewe and King, *SDP*, p. 94.  13. *The Times*, 10 February 1981.  14. Crewe and King, *SDP*, pp. 94, 100; Owen, *Time to Declare*, p. 488; Roy Jenkins, *A Life at the Centre* (1991), p. 536; Williams, *Climbing the Bookshelves*, pp. 282–3.  15. Owen, *Time to Declare*, pp. 493, 473; Crewe and King, *SDP*, pp. 98–9, 91–2.  16. Mitchell, *Four Years in the Death of the Labour Party*, p. 81; *Guardian*, 26 January 2016; Sue Townsend, *The Secret Diary of Adrian Mole Aged 13¾* (1982: 2002), p. 229.  17. Roy Hattersley, *Who Goes Home? Scenes from a Political Life* (1995), p. 235; Crewe and King, *SDP*, pp. 77, 84.  18. Ibid., pp. 105, 107–8, 110, 113.  19. Owen, *Time to Declare*, pp. 490–91; Rodgers, *Fourth among Equals*, p. 214; Crewe and King, *SDP*, pp. 99, 103; Campbell, *Roy Jenkins*, p. 561.  20. Hansard, 16

March 1981; Owen, *Time to Declare*, p. 496; Crewe and King, *SDP*, pp. 114–16; Jenkins, *Life at the Centre*, pp. 553–4; Campbell, *Roy Jenkins*, pp. 168, 190–92, 635; and see *Observer*, 6 December 1981.    **21.** *The Face*, December 1982.    **22.** Owen, *Time to Declare*, p. 503; Stephenson, *Claret and Chips*, pp. 5–6; Campbell, *Roy Jenkins*, p. 563; *Guardian*, 25 March 1981; Crewe and King, *SDP*, p. 102; Rodgers, *Fourth among Equals*, p. 211; Stephenson, *Claret and Chips*, pp. 5–6.    **23.** Williams, *Climbing the Bookshelves*, p. 284; Stephenson, *Claret and Chips*, p. 5; Owen, *Time to Declare*, pp. 504–5; *The Times*, 27 March 1981.    **24.** Ibid., 23 March 1981; *Observer*, 22 March 1981.    **25.** Stephenson, *Claret and Chips*, p. 9; Crewe and King, *SDP*, pp. 241–2, 135, 247; and see, for example, Andy Beckett, *Promised You A Miracle: UK80–82* (2015), p. 128.    **26.** Rodgers, *Fourth among Equals*, p. 213; Crewe and King, *SDP*, pp. 238, 103, 131, 133, 522.    **27.** Ion Trewin (ed.), *The Hugo Young Papers: Thirty Years of British Politics – Off the Record* (2008), pp. 162–3; Crewe and King, *SDP*, p. 141; Rodgers, *Fourth among Equals*, p. 210; Owen, *Time to Declare*, p. 505; *Observer*, 29 May 1981.    **28.** Crewe and King, *SDP*, p. 135; Williams, *Climbing the Bookshelves*, p. 285; Owen, *Time to Declare*, p. 487; Rodgers, *Fourth among Equals*, p. 211.    **29.** Crewe and King, *SDP*, pp. 70, 124, 151; Owen, *Time to Declare*, p. 558.    **30.** Campbell, *Roy Jenkins*, p. 554; Rodgers, *Fourth among Equals*, p. 201.    **31.** Crewe and King, *SDP*, p. 65; Williams, *Climbing the Bookshelves*, pp. 298–9; Campbell, *Roy Jenkins*, pp. 544–5, 156.    **32.** Crewe and King, *SDP*, p. 102.    **33.** Rodgers, *Fourth among Equals*, p. 207; Stephenson, *Claret and Chips*, pp. 40, 44, 174; Owen, *Time to Declare*, pp. 556, 510–11; *Guardian*, 24 November 1981; Campbell, *Roy Jenkins*, p. 565.    **34.** Owen, *Time to Declare*, pp. 482, 519; Campbell, *Roy Jenkins*, p. 573; Stephenson, *Claret and Chips*, p. 41.    **35.** Rodgers, *Fourth among Equals*, pp. 212–13; Stephenson, *Claret and Chips*, p. 26; Mitchell, *Four Years in the Death of the Labour Party*, pp. 79–80.    **36.** Crewe and King, *SDP*, pp. 135, 169; Williams, *Climbing the Bookshelves*, pp. 286–7; Owen, *Time to Declare*, pp. 508, 516.    **37.** *The Times*, 24 April 1981; Crewe and King, *SDP*, pp. 462, 464, 287, 291, 298; Owen, *Time to Declare*, p. 505.    **38.** Benn, *End of an Era*, p. 113; John Golding, *Hammer of the Left: The Battle for the Soul of the Labour Party* (2016), p. 176; Mervyn Jones, *Michael Foot* (1994), p. 463; Owen, *Time to Declare*, p. 486; Martin Westlake, *Kinnock: The Biography* (2001), p. 173.    **39.** Mitchell, *Four Years in the Death of the Labour Party*, pp. 81–2; Crewe and King, *SDP*, p. 254; *Guardian*, 12 September 1981.    **40.** Crewe and King, *SDP*, pp. 254, 260, 256–8.    **41.** Ibid., p. 272; *Daily Express*, 6 October 1981; *Observer*, 14 September 1986; Peter York, *Modern Times* (1984), p. 12; *The Times*, 13 October 1982; Stephenson, *Claret and Chips*, p. 30; *Spectator*, 1 December 1979, 31 January 1981; Campbell, *Roy Jenkins*, p. 559; *Sun*, 7 October 1981; Alwyn W. Turner, *Rejoice! Rejoice! Britain in the 1980s* (2010), pp. 40–41.    **42.** Crewe and King, *SDP*, pp. 273–6, 292, 246–7, 281; Brian Harrison, 'Mrs Thatcher and the Intellectuals', *Twentieth Century British History*, 5:2 (1994), pp. 223, 225.    **43.** Owen, *Time to Declare*, p. 534; Rodgers, *Fourth among Equals*, p. 217; Stephenson, *Claret and Chips*, pp. 170–71, 172.    **44.** Crewe and King, *SDP*, pp. 136–7; Williams, *Climbing the Bookshelves*, pp. 288–9; Stephenson, *Claret and Chips*, p. 68; *Sun*, 4 June 1981; *The Times*, 4 June 1981; Owen, *Time to Declare*, pp. 520–21.    **45.** Stephenson, *Claret and Chips*, p. 61; Jenkins, *Life at the Centre*, pp. 539–40.    **46.** Ibid., p. 542; Rodgers, *Fourth among Equals*, p. 216; Stephenson, *Claret and Chips*, p. 61; *Daily Express*, 10 July 1981.    **47.** *The Times*, 30 June 1981; *Guardian*, 2 July 1981; Campbell, *Roy Jenkins*, p. 579.    **48.** David Marquand, *The Progressive Dilemma: From Lloyd George to Blair* (2nd edn: 1999), p. 186; *The Times*, 6 July 1981.    **49.** *Guardian*, 17 July 1981; Stephenson, *Claret and Chips*, p. 63; *Daily Mirror*, 17 July 1981; Crewe and King, *SDP*, p. 138; *Sun*, 17 July 1981.    **50.** *The Times*, 6 August 1981, 5 October 1981; *Guardian*, 5 October 1981; Crewe and King, *SDP* pp. 140–41; Owen, *Time to Declare*, pp. 533–4.    **51.** *The Times*, 16 September 1981, 17 September 1981; *Daily Express*, 16 September 1981; *Daily Mirror*, 16 September 1981; Jenkins, *Life at the Centre*, p. 546; Crewe and King, *SDP*, p. 140.    **52.** *Guardian*, 19 September 1981; *The Times*, 19 September 1981; Jenkins, *Life at the Centre*, p. 547; *Daily Express*, 19 September 1981.

## Chapter 18. Up Yours from the Chancellor

1. 'Radio Interview for BBC Radio 4 *The World This Weekend*', 4 January 1981, TFW.
2. Millar to Thatcher, 6 January 1981, TFW; 'TV Interview for Thames TV *Afternoon Plus*',
6 January 1981, TFW.   3. John Campbell, *Margaret Thatcher*, vol. 2: *The Iron Lady* (2003),
pp. 105–6; *Daily Telegraph*, 5 March 2012; and see Christopher Collins's discussion of the
changes at https://www.margaretthatcher.org/archive/1981cac2.asp.   4. Thorneycroft to
Thatcher, 'The Public Image of the Government and Party', 19 January 1981, TFW; Alan
Clark, *Diaries: Into Politics, 1972–1982* (2000), pp. 202–3.   5. Sir John Hunt to Thatcher,
'Strategy for the Coal Industry: E (79) 45', 26 September 1979, TFW; David Howell, 'Strategy
for the Coal Industry: E (79) 45', 26 September 1979; *The Times*, 11 February 1981; Ingham
to Thatcher, 'Miners', 13 February 1981, TFW; Charles Moore, *Margaret Thatcher: The
Authorized Biography*, vol. 1: *Not for Turning* (2013), p. 539; *The Times*, 19 February
1981.   6. *Daily Mirror*, 19 February 1981; *Daily Express*, 19 February 1981; Moore, *Not
for Turning*, p. 539; Tim Lankester to Julian West, 'Coal: No. 10 Record of Conversation',
20 February 1981, TFW; John Hoskyns, *Just in Time: Inside the Thatcher Revolution*
(2000), p. 275.   7. *Guardian*, 5 February 1981; *The Times*, 14 February 1981; Gow to
Thatcher, 27 February 1981, TFW; Clark, *Diaries: Into Politics*, p. 205.   8. Moore, *Not
for Turning*, p. 550; Hoskyns diary, 5 March 1981, TFW.   9. *Daily Mirror*, 5 January 1981;
Tim Lankester, 'The 1981 Budget: How Did It Come About?', in Duncan Needham and
Anthony Hotson (eds.), *Expansionary Fiscal Contraction: The Thatcher Government's 1981
Budget in Perspective* (Cambridge, 2014), pp. 14–15; David Smith, *Something Will Turn Up:
Britain's Economy, Past, Present and Future* (2015), p. 91; *Daily Telegraph*, 5 January
2009.   10. Walters diary, 6 January 1981, TFW; John Ranelagh, *Thatcher's People: An
Insider's Account of the Politics, the Power and the Personalities* (1991), p. 227.   11. Jürg
Niehans, 'The Appreciation of Sterling: Causes, Effects, Policies', 7 January 1981, TFW;
Walters diary, 7 January 1981, TFW; Hoskyns diary, 7 January 1981, 9 January 1981, TFW;
Hoskyns to Thatcher, 5 February 1981, TFW; Hoskyns, *Just in Time*, pp. 256–7, 267–9;
and see Smith, *Something Will Turn Up*, p. 93; Lankester, 'The 1981 Budget: How Did It
Come About?', p. 20; Christopher Collins, 'The Origins of the Budget in 1980', in Needham
and Hotson (eds.), *Expansionary Fiscal Contraction*, p. 117.   12. Nigel Lawson, *The View
from No. 11: Memoirs of a Tory Radical* (1992: 1993), p. 94; Geoffrey Howe, *Conflict of
Loyalty* (1994), pp. 202, 204; Hoskyns, *Just in Time*, pp. 283–4, 264; Lankester, 'The 1981
Budget: How Did It Come About?', pp. 11–13, 21, 35; Collins, 'The Origins of the Budget
in 1980', p. 118; Edmund Dell, *The Chancellors: A History of the Chancellors of the Exchequer, 1945–90* (1996), p. 475. In general on all this, see Christopher Collins's invaluable
guide to the archives, 'The 1981 Budget: Background and Documents', at https://www.
margaretthatcher.org/archive/1981_budget.asp. For an alternative view, more favourable to
Hoskyns, see Moore, *Not for Turning*, pp. 627–8, though note that Lankester and Collins
both have disagreements with it.   13. Lankester, 'The 1981 Budget: How Did It Come
About?', pp. 13–14; Hoskyns diary, 25 February 1981, TFW.   14. Ibid., 17 January 1981,
TFW; Lankester, 'The 1981 Budget: How Did It Come About?', p. 24; Howe to Thatcher,
'Public Expenditure White Paper', 23 January 1981, TFW.   15. Howe to Thatcher, 'The
Budget', 5 February 1981, TFW; 'Treasury Minute (Chancellor's Meeting with Governor):
Monetary Policy and the Budget', 6 February 1981, TFW. For Howe's colleagues' demands
for more money, see Heseltine to Howe, '1981 Budget', 5 February 1981, TFW; Joseph to
Howe, 'The 1981 Budget', 30 January 1981, TFW; Prior to Howe, 'The 1981 Budget', 9
February 1981, TFW.   16. 'Note for the Record', 10 February 1981, TFW; Lankester, 'The
1981 Budget: How Did It Come About?', pp. 26–7; Walters to Thatcher, 'The Budget, etc.',
10 February 1981, TFW; Hoskyns diary, 10 February 1981, TFW; Hoskyns, *Just in Time*,
pp. 269–70.   17. Hoskyns diary, 11 February 1981, 13 February 1981, TFW; Walters,
Hoskyns and Wolfson to Thatcher, 'Budget Strategy', 12 February 1981, TFW; Hoskyns,
*Just in Time*, pp. 270–73.   18. Lankester to Thatcher, 'Meeting on the Budget', 13 February
1981, TFW; Lankester, 'The 1981 Budget: How Did It Come About?', p. 27; Hoskyns, *Just

*in Time*, p. 273; Moore, *Not for Turning*, p. 625; Hoskyns diary, 13 February 1981, TFW.   **19.** 'Note for the Record', 17 February 1981, TFW; Lankester, 'The 1981 Budget: How Did It Come About?', p. 27; Hoskyns diary, 17 February 1981, 18 February 1981, TFW; Walters diary, 20 February 1981, TFW; Walters, Hosykns and Wolfson to Thatcher, 'Budget Strategy', 20 February 1981, TFW; Hoskyns, *Just in Time*, pp. 274–6.   **20.** Lankester, 'The 1981 Budget: How Did It Come About?', pp. 29–31, 35; Walters diary, 24 February 1981, TFW; 'No. 10 Minute: Meeting with Chancellor and Wass', 24 February 1981, TFW.   **21.** 'Treasury Minute: Chancellor's Meeting', 25 February 1981, TFW; Margaret Thatcher, *The Downing Street Years* (1993), p. 136; 'No. 10 Minute: Meeting with Chancellor', 25 February 1981, TFW; Lankester, 'The 1981 Budget: How Did It Come About?', p. 32.   **22.** Ibid., p. 33; Walters diary, 25 February 1981, TFW; Walters to Wass, 'Budget', 26 February 1981, TFW; Hoskyns diary, 3 March 1981, TFW; Hoskyns, *Just in Time*, pp. 279–80.   **23.** Nicholas Henderson, *Mandarin: The Diaries of Nicholas Henderson* (1994: 2000), pp. 384–5; Hugo Young, *One of Us: A Biography of Margaret Thatcher* (rev. edn: 1990), p. 250.   **24.** Margaret Thatcher, *The Path to Power* (1995), p. 371; Ronald Reagan, *An American Life: The Autobiography* (New York, 1990), p. 204; Young, *One of Us*, pp. 251, 254–5; Lou Cannon, *President Reagan: The Role of a Lifetime* (New York, 1991), p. 25; Lou Cannon, *Governor Reagan: His Rise to Power* (New York, 2003), p. 139; Craig Shirley, *Reagan's Revolution: The Untold Story of the Campaign That Started It All* (Nashville, TN, 2005), pp. 34–8.   **25.** Moore, *Not for Turning*, pp. 571, 542; 'Department of the Treasury Memcon: Howe-Regan Meeting', 28 September 1981, TFW; *The Economist*, 24 October 1987. See also Young, *One of Us*, p. 251; Campbell, *Iron Lady*, pp. 270–71.   **26.** Young, *One of Us*, pp. 252–3; Cannon, *President Reagan*, p. 120; Campbell, *Iron Lady*, p. 262; Virginia Fraser (ed.), *Best Seat in the House: The Wit and Parliamentary Chronicles of Frank Johnson* (2009), p. 105; Moore, *Not for Turning*, p. 547.   **27.** Thatcher, *Downing Street Years*, p. 157; Moore, *Not for Turning*, p. 547; Campbell, *Iron Lady*, pp. 261–3; Geoffrey Smith, *Reagan and Thatcher* (1990), pp. 26, 51–2; Richard Aldous, *Reagan and Thatcher: The Difficult Relationship* (2012), pp. 49–50; Douglas Brinkley (ed.), *The Reagan Diaries* (New York, 2007), p. 32.   **28.** Ibid., p. 250; 'Remarks Arriving at the White House', 26 February 1981, TFW; 'Record of Phone Conversation' (Reagan-Thatcher), 21 January 1981, TFW; Thatcher, *Downing Street Years*, p. 159; Moore, *Not for Turning*, pp. 541, 544–5; 'State Department Briefing for President Reagan', 17 February 1981, TFW; Martin Anderson, 'Reaganism and Thatcherism', 26 February 1981, TFW.   **29.** Brinkley (ed.), *Reagan Diaries*, p. 5. See also Moore, *Not for Turning*, p. 545.   **30.** 'Exchange of Toasts at British Embassy Dinner', 27 February 1981, TFW; Moore, *Not for Turning*, p. 546; Aldous, *Reagan and Thatcher*, pp. 42–3; Richard Ingrams and John Wells, *The Other Half: Further Letters of Denis Thatcher* (1981), p. 70; Brinkley (ed.), *Reagan Diaries*, p. 5; Henderson, *Mandarin*, p. 390.   **31.** Ibid., p. 388.   **32.** 'Speech Accepting Donovan Award', 28 February 1981, TFW; Henderson, *Mandarin*, p. 388.   **33.** Moore, *Not for Turning*, p. 547; Henderson, *Mandarin*, pp. 387, 390; Brinkley (ed.), *Reagan Diaries*, p. 5; Thatcher to Henderson, 5 March 1981, TFW; Young, *One of Us*, p. 252.   **34.** *The Times*, 14 February 1981, 9 March 1981; *Sunday Times*, 15 February 1981; *Guardian*, 9 March 1981.   **35.** Jim Prior, *A Balance of Power* (1986), pp. 131, 140; Ian Gilmour, *Dancing with Dogma: Britain under Thatcherism* (1992), p. 44.   **36.** Hoskyns diary, 10 March 1981, TFW; Hoskyns, *Just in Time*, p. 281; Moore, *Not for Turning*, p. 629; Prior, *Balance of Power*, p. 140.   **37.** Hansard, 10 March 1981; *The Times*, 11 March 1981.   **38.** Keith Britto, 'Public Opinion Background Note 57', 24 March 1981, TFW; Ingham to Thatcher, 'Press Summary', 11 March 1981, TFW; *Guardian*, 11 March 1981; *The Times*, 11 March 1981, 12 March 1981; *Daily Express*, 11 March 1981; *Daily Mirror*, 11 March 1981; and see Howe, *Conflict of Loyalty*, p. 210.   **39.** 'Speech at Guardian Young Businessman of the Year Award', 11 March 1981, TFW; *Guardian*, 11 March 1981; *The Times*, 12 March 1981.   **40.** Ibid.; *Sun*, 12 March 1981, 13 March 1981; Howe, *Conflict of Loyalty*, p. 208; Ingham to Thatcher, 'Chancellor of the Duchy's Lobby', 13 March 1981, TFW; Moore, *Not for Turning*, pp. 629–30.   **41.** *The Times*, 30 March 1981; Robert Neild, 'The "1981 Statement by 364 Economists" Revisited', *Royal Economic Society Newsletter*, no. 159 (October 2012), pp. 11–14. The statement and a list of signatories are also reprinted in the appendix to Philip Booth (ed.), *Were 364 Economists All Wrong?* (2006), pp. 121–32.    42. *Daily Express*, 30 March 1981; *Daily Mirror*, 30 March 1981; *The Times*, 4 April 1981, 1 April 1981.    43. *The Times*, 4 April 1981; *Spectator*, 11 April 1981; *Daily Express*, 31 March 1981. See also Ferdinand Mount, *Cold Cream: My Early Life and Other Mistakes* (2008), pp. 283–4.    44. *The Times*, 1 April 1981; *Daily Express*, 3 April 1981; *Daily Mirror*, 2 April 1981.    45. David Kynaston, *The City of London*, vol. 4: *A Club No More, 1945–2000* (2001), p. 587; Howe, *Conflict of Loyalty*, p. 209.    46. Lawson, *View from No. 11*, p. 98; for comparison, see Alan Walters, *Britain's Economic Renaissance: Margaret Thatcher's Reforms, 1979–1984* (New York, 1986), p. 86.    47. Howe, *Conflict of Loyalty*, pp. 226–7; Lawson, *View from No. 11*, p. 98; Lankester, 'The 1981 Budget: How Did It Come About?', p. 36; Dell, *The Chancellors*, pp. 480–81. See also Terry Burns's comments in 'IEA Seminar: The 1981 Budget', 16 March 2006, TFW.    48. See ibid., as well as the essays in Booth (ed.), *Were 364 Economists All Wrong?*. For a more critical verdict, see Jim Tomlinson, 'Mrs Thatcher's Macroeconomic Adventurism, 1979–1981, and Its Political Consequences', *British Politics*, 2:1 (2007), pp. 3–19.    49. Stephen Nickell, 'The Budget of 1981 Was over the Top', 13 March 2006, https://www.bankofengland.co.uk/-/media/boe/files/speech/2006/the-budget-of-1981-was-over-the-top. See also Nickell's remarks in 'IEA Seminar: The 1981 Budget', 16 March 2006, TFW.    50. 'IEA Seminar: The 1981 Budget', 16 March 2006, TFW; and see Derek Scott, 'The 1981 Budget: A Turning Point for UK Macroeconomic Thinking', in Booth (ed.), *Were 364 Economists All Wrong?*, pp. 112–21.    51. *The Times*, 31 March 1981; and see Dell, *The Chancellors*, pp. 468–9.    52. *The Times*, 1 June 1981.    53. Ibid., 3 June 1981, 27 March 1980; and see TNA CAB 129/193, CP (76) 116, 'The Case for and against Import Controls', 30 November 1976. On the Alternative Economic Strategy, see Cambridge Political Economy Group, *Britain's Economic Crisis* (Nottingham, 1975); Stuart Holland, *The Socialist Challenge* (1975); Andrew Gamble, *Britain in Decline: Economic Policy, Political Strategy and the British State* (Basingstoke, 1994), pp. 158, 171–185; Tony Benn, *Against the Tide: Diaries, 1973–76* (1989), pp. 324–5, as well as Benn's paper, 'The Alternative Economic Strategy in Outline' (1975), reprinted in ibid., pp. 725–7. On the evasiveness of the Labour right and centre, see *The Times*, 27 March 1980, 18 January 1982; *Guardian*, 25 June 1981; Brian Harrison, *Finding a Role? The United Kingdom, 1970–1990* (Oxford, 2010), pp. 496, 531–2.    54. *Guardian*, 5 March 1984, 9 July 1984, 4 May 1984; Rod Kedward, *La Vie en bleu: France and the French since 1900* (2005), pp. 484–6, 491–5.    55. *The Times*, 9 March 1982. On Ireland, see, for example, Patrick T. Geary, 'Ireland's Economy in the 1980s: Stagnation and Recovery', *Economic and Social Review*, 23:3 (1992), pp. 253–81.    56. Lawson, *View from No. 11*, pp. 62–3; Scott, 'The 1981 Budget', pp. 112–15; Dell, *The Chancellors*, pp. 479–80, 486–7.    57. Keith Britto, 'Public Opinion Background Note 57', 24 March 1981, TFW; TNA PREM 19/423, Ingham to Pym, 'Economic Presentation', 19 March 1981.    58. Campbell, *Iron Lady*, p. 112; 'Speech to Conservative Central Council', 28 March 1981, TFW.    59. Hoskyns diary, 13 March 1981, 15 March 1981, 20 March 1981, TFW; Clark, *Diaries: Into Politics*, p. 217.    60. Thatcher to Fowler, 21 May 1981, TFW.

# Chapter 19. One in Ten

1. *The Times*, 30 April 1981, 2 May 1981, 5 May 1981, 15 May 1981; *Daily Mirror*, 13 May 1981; *Stoke Sentinel*, 16 May 2009.    2. *The Times*, 30 April 1981, 15 May 1981; Tony Benn, *The End of an Era: Diaries, 1980–90* (1992), p. 131; *Daily Mirror*, 29 May 1981.    3. *Stoke Sentinel*, 16 May 2009; *Church Times*, 22 May 1981; *Daily Express*, 5 May 1981; *Daily Mail*, 1 May 1981; *Daily Mirror*, 29 May 1981, 26 May 1981.    4. Ibid., 13 May 1981; *The Times*, 19 May 1981, 27 May 1981.    5. Ibid., 30 May 1981, 1 June 1981; *Sunday Express*, 31 May 1981; *Daily Express*, 26 May 1981; *Daily Mirror*, 1 June 1981.    6. *The Times*, 2 June 1981; Benn, *End of an Era*, p. 133.    7. Beatrix Campbell, *Wigan Pier Revisited: Poverty and Politics in the 80s* (1984), pp. 163–5.    8. 'Speech to Conservative Party Conference', 10 October 1980, TFW; *Guardian*, 17 February 1981.    9. *The Times*, 26 February 1981, 26

February 1981, 27 January 1982, 9 March 1982.  10. David Smith, *North and South: Britain's Economic, Social and Political Divide* (1989), pp. 92, 94, 132–3; *The Times*, 5 May 1981.  11. *Guardian*, 24 January 1981.  12. *The Times*, 5 June 1980; *Sunday Times*, 15 May 1983; Jonathan Raban, *Coasting* (1986), pp. 255, 258.  13. *The Times*, 1 September 1980.  14. *Guardian*, 24 January 1981, 26 January 1982; *The Times*, 15 July 1982, 25 March 1981, 27 December 1980, 27 January 1982, 8 September 1980.  15. Hansard, 9 November 1981; *The Times*, 25 November 1981.  16. Ibid., 12 February 1981, 25 November 1981, 30 December 1980, 20 May 1981, 15 December 1981; Christopher Johnson, *The Economy under Mrs Thatcher, 1979–1990* (1991), pp. 94–5.  17. *Daily Express*, 21 March 1981, 21 December 1981, 8 December 1981; *Sunday Times*, 14 February 1982; *The Times*, 23 January 1984, 20 May 1981; Campbell, *Wigan Pier Revisited*, pp. 11–14, 17. For another example, see Ian Jack, *Before the Oil Ran Out: Britain in the Brutal Years* (rev. edn: 1997), pp. 135–7.  18. *Daily Express*, 28 August 1981; *Guardian*, 28 August 1981.  19. *The Times*, 22 July 1981, 23 July 1981.  20. Ibid., 9 October 1981, 31 July 1984.  21. Jeremy Seabrook, *Unemployment* (1982: 1983), p. 142; Campbell, *Wigan Pier Revisited*, pp. 175, 179–80.  22. Sue Townsend, *The Secret Diary of Adrian Mole Aged 13¾* (1982: 2002), p. 175; Campbell, *Wigan Pier Revisited*, pp. 184, 190, 169, 61, 173; *The Times*, 6 May 1983; Seabrook, *Unemployment*, p. 3.  23. Alan Bleasdale, *Boys from the Blackstuff* (1982: 1985), pp. 66, 169, 176–7.  24. Ibid., pp. 9, 10–12; Lez Cooke, *British Television Drama: A History* (2015), pp. 139–40.  25. Ibid., pp. 141, 143; Bleasdale, *Boys from the Blackstuff*, pp. 97, 131, 197.  26. Ibid., pp. 187, 191, 218, 226.  27. Ali Campbell and Robin Campbell, *Blood and Fire: The Autobiography of the UB40 Brothers* (2005), pp. 55, 77, 4; *Daily Telegraph*, 14 February 2013.  28. *Daily Mirror*, 27 January 1982; Campbell, *Wigan Pier Revisited*, pp. 186–7, 175.  29. *The Times*, 28 November 1980; *Observer*, 9 August 1981.  30. Bill Williamson, *The Temper of the Times: British Society since World War II* (Oxford, 1990), pp. 202–4; Ben Pimlott, 'The North-East: Back to the 1930s?', *Political Quarterly*, 52:1 (1981), pp. 51–63; *The Times*, 29 September 1976, 2 February 1977, 23 February 1977.  31. John Campbell, *Margaret Thatcher*, vol. 1: *The Grocer's Daughter* (2000), pp. 395, 413.  32. *The Times*, 22 July 1981.  33. Johnson, *Economy under Mrs Thatcher*, p. 235; *The Times*, 9 March 1982.  34. See, for example, Paul Krugman, 'Did Thatcher Turn Britain Around?', 8 April 2013, https://krugman.blogs.nytimes.com/2013/04/08/did-thatcher-turn-britain-around/. For comparative economic figures, see the invaluable data sets maintained by the Federal Reserve Bank of St Louis at https://fred.stlouisfed.org.  35. Geoffrey Howe, *Conflict of Loyalty* (1994), p. 687.  36. 'Party Political Broadcast', 22 April 1977, TFW; John Campbell, *Margaret Thatcher*, vol. 2: *The Iron Lady* (2003), p. 85. For another example, see 'Speech to Conservative Rally in Birmingham', 19 April 1979, TFW.  37. See Bernard Porter, '"Though Not an Historian Myself . . .": Margaret Thatcher and the Historians', *Twentieth Century British History*, 5:2 (1994), pp. 255–6.  38. *The Times*, 30 June 1980. I counted the Orwell references using the newspaper archive at www.proquest.com.  39. *The Times*, 5 May 1980, 16 February 1983; *Guardian*, 19 February 1981. Methods of estimating unemployment figures have changed over time: for one set of figures, see James Denman and Paul McDonald, 'Unemployment Statistics from 1881 to the Present Day', *Labour Market Trends* (January 1996), https://www.ons.gov.uk/ons/rel/lms/labour-market-trends--discontinued-/january-1996/unemployment-since-1881.pdf.  40. Raban, *Coasting*, pp. 274–5; MO W633, Summer Directive 1981.  41. *The Times*, 25 November 1971; 'Party Political Broadcast', 22 April 1977, TFW; Anthony King and Robert J. Wybrow (eds.), *British Political Opinion, 1937–2000: The Gallup Polls* (2001), pp. 266–8.  42. Richard Vinen, *Thatcher's Britain: The Politics and Social Upheaval of the Thatcher Era* (2009), pp. 131–3; Austin Mitchell, *Four Years in the Death of the Labour Party* (1983), pp. 140–41.  43. *The Times*, 25 October 1982; Seabrook, *Unemployment*, p. 17.  44. *Guardian*, 18 May 1983.  45. Hugo Young, *One of Us: A Biography of Margaret Thatcher* (rev. edn: 1990), pp. 502, 534; Robert J. Wybrow, *Britain Speaks Out, 1937–87: A Social History as Seen through the Gallup Data* (Basingstoke, 1989), p. 123; Campbell, *Wigan Pier Revisited*, p. 161; Beryl Bainbridge, *English Journey, or, The Road to Milton Keynes* (1984), pp. 36–7.  46. MO A883, Summer Directive – Work, 1983; MO H260, Summer Directive – Work, 1983; MO D156, Summer

Directive – Work, 1983. On Labour, see *The Times*, 30 March 1983. On Mrs Thatcher and full employment, see, for example, 'MT Notes for Conference Speech (Draft)', 16 October 1981, TFW; 'Interview for *Sunday Times*', 22 February 1983, TFW; 'TV Interview for BBC1 *Panorama*', 31 May 1983, TFW; 'Interview for *The Times*', 3 May 1983, TFW.   **47.** MO R470, Summer Directive – Work, 1983.

# Chapter 20. Potting the Reds

**1.** The BBC footage of the 1981 world snooker final is on YouTube; see also Steve Davis, *Interesting: My Autobiography* (2015), ch. 1.   **2.** *The Times*, 21 April 1981; *Daily Mirror*, 22 April 1981; *Daily Express*, 22 April 1981.   **3.** *Guardian*, 21 April 1981; *The Times*, 21 April 1981, 22 April 1981; *Daily Express*, 22 April 1981.   **4.** Joe Moran, *Armchair Nation: An Intimate History of Britain in Front of the TV* (2013), pp. 256–7; Clive Everton, *Black Farce and Cue Ball Wizards: The Inside Story of the Snooker World* (2007: Edinburgh, 2012), pp. 47, 50; Gordon Burn, *Pocket Money: Bad-Boys, Business-Heads and Boom-Time Snooker* (1986), pp. 73, 98.   **5.** Ibid., pp. 166–7; Moran, *Armchair Nation*, pp. 256–7; Martin Kelner, *Sit down and Cheer: A History of Sport on TV* (2012), p. 121; *Guardian*, 3 April 1981.   **6.** Ibid.; Everton, *Black Farce*, pp. 56, 62, 68; Moran, *Armchair Nation*, p. 257; Burn, *Pocket Money*, p. 140; *Guardian*, 29 April 1978.   **7.** Rob Cole, 'Wales v England: The Remarkable Inside Story of the Most Explosive 13 Minutes in Rugby History', 5 February 2015, http://www.walesonline.co.uk/sport/rugby/wales-v-england-remarkable-inside-8584476; *Daily Mirror*, 18 February 1980.   **8.** *The Times*, 1 May 1980, 1 September 1980, 17 September 1980, 4 December 1980; Martin Williamson, 'Men Behaving Badly in the Lord's Pavilion', 28 August 2010, http://www.espncricinfo.com/magazine/content/story/474524.html.   **9.** *Guardian*, 3 April 1981; Burn, *Pocket Money*, pp. 29, 166; *Listener*, 28 April 1983; *Daily Mail*, 2 May 2011; Moran, *Armchair Nation*, pp. 258–9.   **10.** *The Times*, 29 April 1983; Moran, *Armchair Nation*, p. 259.   **11.** *The Times*, 29 January 1982; Everton, *Black Farce*, pp. 48–9, 51; *Guardian*, 3 April 1981; Burn, *Pocket Money*, pp. 120–21.   **12.** *Daily Mirror*, 17 May 1982, 18 May 1982; *Guardian*, 25 July 2010; Burn, *Pocket Money*, pp. 121–3; and see Bill Borrows, *The Hurricane: The Turbulent Life and Times of Alex Higgins* (2002).   **13.** *The Times*, 4 December 1980; *Daily Express*, 22 April 1981.   **14.** Everton, *Black Farce*, pp. 86–7, 365; Burn, *Pocket Money*, pp. 65, 68–9. For a different and more detailed version of Davis's sex–snooker dilemma, see *Daily Express*, 24 September 1985.   **15.** Burn, *Pocket Money*, p. 64; *The Times*, 9 May 1984; *Daily Express*, 9 May 1984.   **16.** *Guardian*, 4 May 1985; Burn, *Pocket Money*, pp. 103, 111, 30, 4, 8, 36; *The Times*, 3 April 1981, 7 July 1982.   **17.** Ibid., 29 April 1983; and see Burn, *Pocket Money*, pp. 30, 109; Everton, *Black Farce*, pp. 109, 111.   **18.** Burn, *Pocket Money*, pp. 104, 110–11.   **19.** *The Times*, 27 November 1981; *Daily Telegraph*, 11 February 2001, 18 September 2011; *Independent*, 13 December 2009.   **20.** *The Times*, 29 April 1983.   **21.** Burn, *Pocket Money*, pp. 108, 14–15; *Daily Express*, 18 April 1984.   **22.** Burn, *Pocket Money*, p. 30; Everton, *Black Farce*, p. 111; *Guardian*, 12 June 1984; 'Remarks on Council House Sales', 11 August 1980, TFW; and see http://www.romford-snooker-club.co.uk/about-the-club.html.   **23.** *The Times*, 9 November 1982; Burn, *Pocket Money*, p. 65.   **24.** Ibid., p. 106; *The Times*, 6 June 1983; *Guardian*, 6 June 1983; 'Speech to British Radio and Electronic Equipment Manufacturers Association', 11 December 1985, TFW; and see Davis, *Interesting*, ch. 13.   **25.** 'TV Interview for Thames TV *CBTV* ', 19 December 1983, TFW; 'Interview for *Sunday Mirror*', 1 October 1985, TFW.   **26.** *The Times*, 29 January 1982, 7 July 1982; Burn, *Pocket Money*, p. 31.   **27.** *Daytona Beach Morning Journal*, 14 July 1980; *Guardian*, 1 June 1981; *Yorkshire Post*, 2 April 2007. (The Daytona Beach paper contains a syndicated story from the *New York Times*, digitised by Google, in case anyone is wondering why Florida's daily papers were so interested in the Wakefield working men's club scene.)   **28.** *Daily Express*, 23 April 1981.   **29.** Burn, *Pocket Money*, p. 109; *The Times*, 7 July 1982; *Guardian*, 15 May 1982; *The Journal* (Newcastle-upon-Tyne), 15 November 2005.   **30.** *Daily Express*, 23 April 1981.

## Chapter 21. To Think This Is England

1. Mike Phillips and Trevor Phillips, *Windrush: The Irresistible Rise of Multi-Racial Britain* (1998), pp. 340–42; *Guardian*, 3 March 1981; see also the flyers and pictures at http://transpont.blogspot.com/2017/04/13-dead-and-nothing-said-new-cross-fire.html and http://www.eastlondonlines.co.uk/2017/03/photographs-uncover-1981-new-cross-march-for-racial-equality/.   2. *The Times*, 3 March 1981, 4 March 1981; *Daily Express*, 3 March 1981; *Sun*, 3 March 1981; Hansard, 5 March 1981; Alan Clark, *Diaries: Into Politics, 1972–1982* (2000), p. 209; and see Martin Kettle and Lucy Hodges, *Uprising! The Police, the People and the Riots in Britain's Cities* (1982), p. 21.   3. *The Times*, 20 January 1981, 30 January 1981, 4 March 1981; Phillips and Phillips, *Windrush*, pp. 323, 339–40, 342, 344–5.   4. *Evening Standard*, 7 May 2004, 18 January 2011; *The Times*, 23 April 1981, 1 May 1981, 14 May 1981; *Guardian*, 14 May 1981, 4 April 1981, 14 April 1981. For the leaflets see http://transpont.blogspot.com/2017/04/13-dead-and-nothing-said-new-cross-fire.html.   5. *The Times*, 23 February 1983, 3 March 1982; Kettle and Hodges, *Uprising!*, pp. 135–6; Beryl Bainbridge, *English Journey, or, The Road to Milton Keynes* (1984), p. 65; Sathnam Sanghera, *The Boy with the Topknot: A Memoir of Love, Secrets and Lies in Wolverhampton* (2008), p. 5.   6. *Daily Express*, 19 April 1978.   7. Kettle and Hodges, *Uprising!*, pp. 136, 138–9; *The Times*, 11 September 1980.   8. Ibid., 18 July 1980; 3 March 1982, 11 September 1980; Kettle and Hodges, *Uprising!*, pp. 141–2.   9. *The Times*, 30 May 1980; *Guardian*, 23 August 2001.   10. Paul Theroux, *The Kingdom by the Sea: A Journey around the Coast of Great Britain* (1983), pp. 25, 115, 203, 318.   11. Russell Davies (ed.), *The Kenneth Williams Diaries* (1993), p. 583; *The Times*, 8 October 1981.   12. Ian Jack, *Before the Oil Ran Out: Britain in the Brutal Years* (rev. edn: 1997), p. 108, 114–15; Jeremy Seabrook, *Unemployment* (1982: 1983), pp. 91–2, 107.   13. Kettle and Hodges, *Uprising!*, pp. 69–71; *The Times*, 3 March 1982, 6 February 1981.   14. Ibid., 14 April 1981; Roger Graef, *Talking Blues: The Police in Their Own Words* (1989: 1990), p. 133, 137, 138, 140–41.   15. Brian Harrison, *Finding a Role? The United Kingdom, 1970–1990* (Oxford, 2010), p. 200; David J. Smith et al., *Police and People in London*, vol. 4: *The Police in Action* (1983), pp. 113, 116; Jerry White, *London in the Twentieth Century: A City and Its People* (2001), p. 302; Graef, *Talking Blues*, pp. 124–5, 130–31; *The Times*, 24 September 1981.   16. White, *London in the Twentieth Century*, pp. 296–7; Kettle and Hodges, *Uprising!*, pp. 87, 91–3; John Benyon, *A Tale of Failure: Race and Policing* (Coventry, 1986), p. 40; Phillips and Phillips, *Windrush*, p. 302.   17. *New Statesman*, 27 June 1980; *The Times*, 20 March 1980, 30 June 1980. On *Babylon*, see, for example, Alexander Walker, *National Heroes: British Cinema in the Seventies and Eighties* (1985), pp. 239, 242–4. On Linton Kwesi Johnson, see *Guardian*, 4 January 1979, 5 June 1979.   18. Kettle and Hodges, *Uprising!*, pp. 23–30; *The Times*, 4 April 1980, 5 April 1980; *Guardian*, 5 April 1980.   19. *Daily Mirror*, 3 April 1980; *Daily Express*, 3 April 1980; Hansard, 3 April 1980; *The Times*, 5 April 1980, 21 June 1980; Kettle and Hodges, *Uprising!*, p. 31; *Sun*, 5 April 1980; *Sunday Express*, 6 April 1980.   20. *Observer*, 19 April 1981.   21. *Guardian*, 13 April 1981; Kettle and Hodges, *Uprising!*, pp. 89, 101; *The Times*, 15 April 1981; Lord Scarman, *The Scarman Report: The Brixton Disorders, 10–12 April 1981* (1981), p. 27–8.   22. Kettle and Hodges, *Uprising!*, pp. 89, 101–2; White, *London in the Twentieth Century*, p. 282; Scarman, *Scarman Report*, p. 11.   23. *The Times*, 10 April 1980, 23 July 1980; Kettle and Hodges, *Uprising!*, pp. 89, 94, 103; *Guardian*, 13 April 1981.   24. Kettle and Hodges, *Uprising!*, pp. 104–5, 98; 'TV Interview for Granada *World in Action*', 27 January 1978, TFW.   25. *Guardian*, 13 April 1981; Kettle and Hodges, *Uprising!*, pp. 98–9, 106–7.   26. Phillips and Phillips, *Windrush*, p. 359; Kettle and Hodges, *Uprising!*, pp. 107–9; *Guardian*, 13 April 1981.   27. Ibid.; *The Times*, 13 April 1981; Graeff, *Talking Blues*, p. 49; *Observer*, 12 April 1981; *Daily Express*, 13 April 1981.   28. Kettle and Hodges, *Uprising!*, pp. 100, 114; Graef, *Talking Blues*, p. 51; White, *London in the Twentieth Century*, p. 299; *Observer*, 19 April 1981; *Guardian*, 13 April 1981, 14 April 1981.   29. *Guardian*, 13 April 1981; *Daily Express*, 13 April 1981; Graef, *Talking Blues*, pp. 49, 52.   30. *Observer*, 12 April 1981; *Guardian*, 13 April 1981; *Daily*

*Express*, 13 April 1981.   31. Mark Garnett and Ian Aitken, *Splendid! Splendid! The Authorized Biography of Willie Whitelaw* (2002), p. 258; Whitelaw to Thatcher, 'Review of Potential for Civil Disturbance in 1981', 27 April 1981, TFW; *Daily Express*, 13 April 1981; *Daily Mirror*, 13 April 1981.   32. *Guardian*, 24 January 1981; *The Times*, 6 July 1981; and see Jacqueline Nassy Brown, *Dropping Anchor, Setting Sail: Geographies of Race in Black Liverpool* (Princeton, NJ, 2005), pp. 102–9. For some contemporary descriptions of Toxteth, see Bainbridge, *English Journey*, pp. 91–2; Kettle and Hodges, *Uprising!*, p. 93; Theroux, *Kingdom by the Sea*, p. 203.   33. Kettle and Hodges, *Uprising!*, pp. 158–60; *The Times*, 6 July 1981, 7 July 1981; Graef, *Talking Blues*, p. 54; *Daily Express*, 7 July 1981.   34. Graef, *Talking Blues*, pp. 53, 55, 58.   35. *Observer*, 5 July 1981; *The Times*, 6 July 1981.   36. Kettle and Hodges, *Uprising!*, pp. 164–5, 167; *Observer*, 12 July 1981; *The Times*, 13 July 1981; TNA PREM 14/484, HAC (81) 8, 'Brief for a Debate on Recent Outbreaks of Civil Disorder in Great Britain', *c.* 27 July 1981.   37. *Daily Express*, 7 July 1981.   38. Hugo Young, *One of Us: A Biography of Margaret Thatcher* (rev. edn: 1990), p. 239; 'Party Political Broadcast', 8 July 1981, TFW; *The Times*, 11 July 1981; *Observer*, 12 July 1981; Charles Moore, *Margaret Thatcher: The Authorized Biography*, vol. 1: *Not for Turning* (2013), pp. 635–6; *Daily Express*, 14 July 1981. See also 'No. 10 Record of Conversation (MT-Liverpool Community Leaders)', 13 July 1981, TFW; 'No. 10 Record of Conversation (MT-Liverpool and Merseyside Councillors)', 13 July 1981, TFW.   39. *Daily Express*, 6 July 1981; *The Times*, 10 July 1981.   40. Ibid., 13 July 1981, 17 August 1981; Davies (ed.), *Kenneth Williams Diaries*, p. 582; Theroux, *Kingdom by the Sea*, p. 221.   41. *News of the World*, 12 April 1981; *Daily Mirror*, 14 April 1981, 6 July 1981, 11 July 1981; *Daily Express*, 7 July 1981, 11 July 1981; *Sun*, 6 July 1981.   42. *The Times*, 30 July 1980, 2 June 1981; *Observer*, 12 July 1981.   43. Kettle and Hodges, *Uprising!*, pp. 182–9; Hansard, 14 July 1981, 9 July 1981, 16 July 1981; *The Times*, 8 July 1981, 9 July 1981; *Sunday Express*, 6 April 1980.   44. *The Times*, 12 August 1981, 2 July 1981; Hansard, 16 July 1981; and see Kettle and Hodges, *Uprising!*, pp. 192–7.   45. *The Times*, 8 July 1980; TNA PREM 14/484, C. J. Walters, 'Note of a Visit: Liverpool: 7 July 1981', 9 July 1981.   46. Kettle and Hodges, *Uprising!*, p. 123; *The Times*, 15 October 1981, 16 October 1981, 3 October 1981.   47. Ibid., 22 July 1981.   48. Robert J. Wybrow, *Britain Speaks Out, 1937–87: Social History as Seen through the Gallup Data* (Basingstoke, 1989), p. 125; *New Standard*, 11 May 1981, cited in Kettle and Hodges, *Uprising!*, pp. 197–200; and see Jack, *Before the Oil Ran Out*, p. 105.   49. *Observer*, 12 July 1981.   50. Ibid.; Jack, *Before the Oil Ran Out*, p. 105.   51. Young, *One of Us*, p. 234; Scarman, *Scarman Report*, pp. 106, 209–10; *Guardian*, 26 November 1981; *Daily Express*, 26 November 1981; *Daily Mirror*, 26 November 1981.   52. Ibid.; Patrick Wright, *On Living in an Old Country: The National Past in Contemporary Britain* (1985: Oxford, 2009), pp. 227–9, 230, quoting Charles Moore, *The Old People of Lambeth* (1982). See also Paul Gilroy, 'The Status of Difference: Multiculturalism and the Postcolonial City', in Ghent Urban Studies Team, *Post Ex Sub Dis: Urban Fragmentations and Constructions* (Rotterdam, 2002), pp. 199–200.   53. *Guardian*, 10 April 1982, 11 June 1983; *The Times*, 2 August 1982; *Observer*, 12 June 1983, 9 September 1984.   54. Simon Reynolds, *Rip It Up and Start Again: Post-Punk, 1978–84* (2005), pp. 283–9, 297, 299; *Sounds*, 6 October 1979; *NME*, 27 September 1980.   55. Kettle and Hodges, *Uprising!*, p. 152; *Observer*, 12 July 1981.   56. Lincoln Allison, *Condition of England: Essays and Impressions* (1981), pp. 148, 189, 193; *Daily Mirror*, 29 April 1983.   57. Beryl Bainbridge, *Forever England: North and South* (1987), pp. 157, 159, 171–2.

# Chapter 22. Showdown of the Century

1. Chris Mullin, *A Very British Coup* (1982: 2006), pp. 7–11.   2. *Guardian*, 7 March 2006, 10 August 2015; Chris Mullin, *Hinterland: A Memoir* (2016), pp. 100–101; and see David Kogan and Maurice Kogan, *The Battle for the Labour Party* (1982), pp. 65–6.   3. *The Times*, 20 August 1982; *Guardian*, 30 August 1982; Tony Benn, *The End of an Era: Diaries, 1980–90* (1992), p. 158.   4. *The Times*, 20 August 1982; *Guardian*, 2 September 1982.   5. Benn, *End*

*of an Era*, pp. 44, 49–50, 53; *The Times*, 5 December 1980.    6. Michael Foot, *Loyalists and Loners* (1986), pp. 110, 117, 121–2; Kenneth O. Morgan, *Michael Foot: A Life* (2007), pp. 396–7; Roy Hattersley, *Who Goes Home? Scenes from a Political Life* (1995), p. 230.    7. Benn, *End of an Era*, pp. 62, 64, 66, 69–72, 132.    8. Ibid., pp. 110–12.    9. Ibid., pp. 83, 113–15; Mervyn Jones, *Michael Foot* (1994), p. 467.    10. *Daily Mirror*, 3 April 1981; *Daily Express*, 3 April 1981; Benn, *End of an Era*, pp. 115, 118–20; *The Times*, 4 April 1981, 5 April 1981.    11. Benn, *End of an Era*, pp. 116, 122.    12. *The Times*, 3 April 1981, 19 June 1981; *Guardian*, 13 September 1981.    13. Ibid., 27 September 1981, 13 September 1981.    14. Edward Pearce, *Denis Healey: A Life in Our Times* (2002), pp. 549, 551, 553; Denis Healey, *The Time of My Life* (1989), p. 481.    15. *Guardian*, 13 April 1981; *The Times*, 13 April 1981, 13 May 1981, 27 April 1981, 12 May 1981; *Daily Mirror*, 4 April 1981.    16. Benn, *End of an Era*, pp. 125–6, 130–31; *The Times*, 15 May 1981. See also the terrific coverage in Thames Television's *TV Eye* documentary 'Benn's Bandwagon' (28 May 1981), which is on You-Tube.    17. Benn, *End of an Era*, p. 132; *The Times*, 3 June 1981.    18. Benn, *End of an Era*, pp. 134–5; Jones, *Michael Foot*, p. 469; *Guardian*, 4 June 1981; *The Times*, 4 June 1981.    19. Benn, *End of an Era*, p. 136; *Daily Express*, 4 June 1981; *Daily Mirror*, 4 June 1981; *The Times*, 4 June 1981.    20. Benn, *End of an Era*, pp. 136–9.    21. Anthony King and Robert J. Wybrow (eds.), *British Political Opinion, 1937–2000: The Gallup Polls* (2001), p. 213; Austin Mitchell, *Four Years in the Death of the Labour Party* (1983), pp. 92–3; *The Times*, 28 April 1981; *Guardian*, 25 June 1981.    22. *The Times*, 19 June 1981; Richard Ingrams and John Wells, *The Other Half: Further Letters of Denis Thatcher* (1981), p. 76.    23. Healey, *Time of My Life*, pp. 482–3; *Guardian*, 27 August 1981; *The Times*, 6 November 1981; *Daily Mirror*, 15 May 1981. On Labour's inadequacy as a party of opposition, see also Ronald Butt in *The Times*, 31 July 1981.    24. *The Times*, 3 September 1981, 20 July 1981, 5 September 1981; Benn, *End of an Era*, p. 144; *Guardian*, 5 September 1981.    25. *The Times*, 1 September 1981.    26. Kogan and Kogan, *Battle for the Labour Party*, p. 144.    27. Robert Harris, *The Making of Neil Kinnock* (1984), pp. 161, 153, 156, 157; Morgan, *Michael Foot*, p. 399; *The Times*, 4 September 1981; Jones, *Michael Foot*, p. 471; Martin Westlake, *Kinnock: The Biography* (2001), pp. 175–6, 180; *Guardian*, 25 April 1981. For Kinnock as 'incandescent', see the interview with him in the second episode of BBC2's documentary *The Wilderness Years*, 'Comrades at War' (10 December 1995).    28. *Sun*, 22 May 1981; Peter Chippindale and Chris Horrie, *Stick It Up Your Punter! The Uncut Story of the Sun Newspaper* (rev. edn: 2013), p. 154; *Daily Express*, 10 September 1981; *Sunday Express*, 30 August 1981; *Guardian*, 24 September 1981.    29. *Sunday Times*, 21 June 1981; *The Times*, 22 June 1981, 23 June 1981; Healey, *Time of My Life*, p. 482; *Guardian*, 25 September 1981, 23 June 1981.    30. *The Times*, 19 September 1981, 8 July 1981, 7 September 1981, 25 September 1981; *Guardian*, 23 September 1981; and see Kogan and Kogan, *Battle for the Labour Party*, p. 114; Pearce, *Denis Healey*, pp. 559–60; Benn, *End of an Era*, pp. 148, 150.    31. *The Times*, 11 September 1981. Highlights of the debate, or perhaps lowlights, were later shown by Thames Television on *TV Eye* (10 September 1981): see https://www.youtube.com/watch?v=mBycdYVRUZk.    32. *The Times*, 15 September 1981; *Guardian*, 15 September 1981, 21 September 1981; Pearce, *Denis Healey*, p. 557; *Observer*, 20 September 1981; *Sunday Express*, 21 September 1981.    33. John Golding, *Hammer of the Left: The Battle for the Soul of the Labour Party* (2016), pp. 195–6; *The Times*, 21 September 1981; *Daily Express*, 21 September 1981; *Daily Mirror*, 22 September 1981.    34. *The Times*, 25 September 1981; *Daily Mirror*, 19 September 1981; Kogan and Kogan, *Battle for the Labour Party*, p. 114; Pearce, *Denis Healey*, pp. 560–61; Benn, *End of an Era*, p. 151.    35. *Daily Mirror*, 24 September 1981; *The Times*, 26 September 1981, 24 September 1981; *Guardian*, 26 September 1981, 28 September 1981; *Observer*, 27 September 1981; and see Golding, *Hammer of the Left*, p. 199.    36. Benn, *End of an Era*, p. 153; *Guardian*, 26 September 1981, 28 September 1981; *Sunday Express*, 27 September 1981.    37. Benn, *End of an Era*, pp. 153–4; Kogan and Kogan, *Battle for the Labour Party*, p. 114; *Guardian*, 28 October 1981; Pearce, *Denis Healey*, pp. 561–2. For Kinnock, see the interview clip in 'Comrades at War'.    38. Pearce, *Denis Healey*, p. 563; Golding, *Hammer of the Left*, pp. 198–9; Benn, *End of an Era*, pp. 154–5; *The Times*, 1 October 1981.    39. Ibid.; Healey, *Time of My Life*, p. 483; Pearce, *Denis Healey*, pp. 562–3; Golding, *Hammer of the Left*, pp. 154–5, 162.   40. Pearce, *Denis Healey*, pp. 563–4; Westlake, *Kinnock*, p. 182; *The Times*, 1 October 1981, 21 September 1981.   41. Kogan and Kogan, *Battle for the Labour Party*, p. 116; *The Times*, 1 October 1981; *Guardian*, 1 October 1981; Harris, *Making of Neil Kinnock*, p. 164; Hattersley, *Who Goes Home?*, p. 231. The Corbyn clip is from the archives of *Newsnight*: see https://www.youtube.com/watch?v=uZKNCXxHL_g. 42. Harris, *Making of Neil Kinnock*, p. 165.   43. *Observer*, 27 September 1981; Mitchell, *Four Years in the Death of the Labour Party*, pp. 90–91; King and Wybrow (eds.), *British Political Opinion*, p. 14.   44. Hattersley, *Who Goes Home?*, p. 232. See Richard Heller, 'Tony Benn Was the Leader Labour Was Lucky to Lose', 17 March 2014, http://www.politics.co.uk/ comment-analysis/2014/03/17/comment-tony-benn-was-the-leader-labour-was-lucky-to-lose. 45. Westlake, *Kinnock*, p. 166; Shirley Williams, *Climbing the Bookshelves* (2009), p. 297; *Guardian*, 30 September 1981; Kogan and Kogan, *Battle for the Labour Party*, p. 119; Benn, *End of an Era*, pp. 155, 176; Pearce, *Denis Healey*, p. 563; Jones, *Michael Foot*, pp. 493–5; Morgan, *Michael Foot*, pp. 419–20.   46. Benn, *End of an Era*, pp. 166–8, 169; Golding, *Hammer of the Left*, p. 247.   47. Benn, *End of an Era*, pp. 174, 177; *The Times*, 20 November 1981, 17 December 1981; Golding, *Hammer of the Left*, p. 248.   48. Foot, *Loyalists and Loners*, pp. 122–4; *The Times*, 1 October 1981; Morgan, *Michael Foot*, p. 390.   49. 'MT Diary Note', 8 November 1981, TFW; *Guardian*, 10 November 1981.   50. *Daily Telegraph*, 9 November 1981; *Daily Mirror*, 9 November 1981; Golding, *Hammer of the Left*, p. 297. 51. Morgan, *Michael Foot*, p. 390; *Daily Mail*, 10 November 1981. The 'oaf and a tramp' letter has been posted online by Steven Fielding at https://twitter.com/PolProfSteve/status/ 1032207697503027200.   52. *The Times*, 5 December 1981; *Guardian*, 5 December 1981; Edna Healey, *Part of the Pattern: Memoirs of a Wife at Westminster* (2006), p. 216.

## Chapter 23. The March of Death

1. *Guardian*, 14 December 1979.   2. Martin Johnes, *Wales since 1939* (Manchester, 2012), pp. 385–7; *Guardian*, 30 January 1980.   3. Ibid., 11 February 1980, 31 March 1980. 4. Johnes, *Wales since 1939*, p. 386; *Guardian*, 11 February 1980, 24 March 1980; Paul Theroux, *The Kingdom by the Sea: A Journey around the Coast of Great Britain* (1983), pp. 172, 164.   5. Johnes, *Wales since 1939*, pp. 255–6; David Torrance, 'We in Scotland': Thatcherism in a Cold Climate* (Edinburgh, 2009), pp. 85, 38; Theroux, *Kingdom by the Sea*, p. 312. See also Richard Finlay, 'Thatcherism, Unionism and Nationalism: A Comparative Study of Scotland and Wales', in Ben Jackson and Robert Saunders (eds.), *Making Thatcher's Britain* (Cambridge, 2012), pp. 172–4.   6. Johnes, *Wales since 1939*, p. 298; Rhys Evans, *Gwynfor Evans: A Portrait of a Patriot* (Talybont, 2008), pp. 391, 394; Torrance, 'We in Scotland', pp. 94–5.   7. Johnes, *Wales since 1939*, pp. 285, 312–13; Evans, *Gwynfor Evans*, pp. 397– 400.   8. *Guardian*, 7 May 1980; Evans, *Gwynfor Evans*, pp. 408–9, 414–15, 417; *Observer*, 10 August 1980.   9. *Guardian*, 6 August 1980, 11 August 1980; Evans, *Gwynfor Evans*, p. 420; *Observer*, 17 August 1980.   10. *Guardian*, 1 September 1980; Evans, *Gwynfor Evans*, pp. 423–4; Johnes, *Wales since 1939*, p. 311; 'No. 10 Record of Conversation (MT-Whitelaw-Edwards-Whitmore-Pattison)', 15 September 1980, TFW.   11. *Guardian*, 18 September 1980; Evans, *Gwynfor Evans*, p. 428; Johnes, *Wales since 1939*, p. 314.   12. Humphrey Atkins, 'Memo to OD Committee: OD (79) 12: Northern Ireland: The Overall Situation', 5 July 1979, TFW; Henry Patterson, *Ireland since 1939: The Persistence of Conflict* (2nd edn: Dublin, 2006), p. 253; Jim Prior, *A Balance of Power* (1986), pp. 203–4, 210; Theroux, *Kingdom by the Sea*, p. 255.   13. Ibid., pp. 239, 238, 241, 230–31, 257.   14. *The Times*, 29 December 1979.   15. *Daily Express*, 29 August 1979; Richard Ingrams and John Wells, *One for the Road* (1982), letter dated 24 April 1981; Charles Moore, *Margaret Thatcher: The Authorized Biography*, vol. 1: *Not for Turning* (2013), pp. 587–8; Marc Mulholland, 'The Irish Question in the Thatcher Years', in Jackson and Saunders (eds.), *Making Thatcher's Britain*, p. 190.   16. 'Remarks on the Murder of Airey Neave', 30 March 1979, TFW. 17. *Guardian*, 28 August 1979; Peter Taylor, *Provos: The IRA and Sinn Fein* (1997), pp. 227–8; Peter Taylor, *Brits: The War against the IRA* (2001), pp. 221–3; Mike Jackson, *Soldier: The*

*Autobiography of General Sir Mike Jackson* (2007: 2008), pp. 158–60.   **18.** Richard English, *Armed Struggle: The History of the IRA* (2003), p. 220; *Daily Mirror*, 28 August 1979; *Daily Express*, 28 August 1979.   **19.** Moore, *Not for Turning*. pp. 482–3; 'Remarks Visiting Belfast', 29 August 1979, TFW; *Guardian*, 25 April 2000; Taylor, *Brits*, p. 224; Lieutenant General Sir Timothy Creasey to Thatcher, 29 August 1979, TFW.   **20.** Taylor, *Provos*, pp. 202–3, 207, 210; David McKittrick and David McVea, *Making Sense of the Troubles* (2000: 2001), pp. 118–19, 122–3, 130–31; Patterson, *Ireland since 1939*, p. 250; Peter Taylor, *Loyalists* (1999), pp. 157–62; Roy Mason, *Paying the Price* (1999), p. 206.   **21.** McKittrick and McVea, *Making Sense of the Troubles*, pp. 137–8; English, *Armed Struggle*, pp. 188–91.   **22.** Taylor, *Provos*, pp. 203–4, 220–22; Taylor, *Brits*, pp. 227–9; English, *Armed Struggle*, pp. 190–91; Mason, *Paying the Price*, pp. 200–201; McKittrick and McVea, *Making Sense of the Troubles*, pp. 139–40; and see Thomas Hennessey, *Hunger Strike: Margaret Thatcher's Battle with the IRA, 1980–1981* (Sallins, Co. Kildare, 2014), pp. 15–35.   **23.** Humphrey Atkins, 'Memo to OD Committee: OD (79) 14: Northern Ireland: Law and Order', 5 July 1979, TFW; Taylor, *Provos*, pp. 229, 231; Taylor, *Brits*, pp. 230–31; English, *Armed Struggle*, p. 194; McKittrick and McVea, *Making Sense of the Troubles*, pp. 139, 141; Hennessey, *Hunger Strike*, pp. 68–76.   **24.** English, *Armed Struggle*, p. 192; Hennessey, *Hunger Strike*, p. 69; TNA CAB 128/66 CC (80) 36; PRONI NIO 12/189, 'Statement by the Secretary of State for Northern Ireland', 24 October 1980; Hansard, 20 November 1980.   **25.** Moore, *Not for Turning*, pp. 599–600; Hennessey, *Hunger Strike*, pp. 117–18; PRONI NIO 12/196A, 'The Republican Hunger Strikes: 27 October–19 December 1980', *c.* December 1980; Taylor, *Provos*, pp. 235–6; English, *Armed Struggle*, pp. 196, 198.   **26.** Hennessey, *Hunger Strike*, pp. 125–6, 136, 150–51, 160; Taylor, *Provos*, pp. 236–7; English, *Armed Struggle*, pp. 195–6.   **27.** Taylor, *Provos*, p. 239; Hennessey, *Hunger Strike*, p. 155; Moore, *Not for Turning*, p. 607; 'Speech in Belfast', 5 March 1981, TFW; 'TV Interview for ITN', 6 March 1981, TFW.   **28.** *Guardian*, 6 May 1981; Taylor, *Provos*, p. 238; English, *Armed Struggle*, pp. 196–7.   **29.** Ibid., p. 196; McKittrick and McVea, *Making Sense of the Troubles*, p. 143; Taylor, *Provos*, pp. 240–41; Patterson, *Ireland since 1939*, p. 256; PRONI CENT 1/10/25, Atkins to Francis Pym, 8 April 1981; PRONI CENT 1/10/25, 'Protests and Second Hunger Strike: Weekly Bulletin No. 7', *c.* April 1981; *Guardian*, 11 April 1981.   **30.** Hennessey, *Hunger Strike*, p. 168; PRONI CIO 12/197A, 'Record of a Discussion Between the Prime Minister and Mr John Hume', 13 April 1981; 'Press Conference Ending Visit to Saudi Arabia', 21 April 1981, TFW.   **31.** PRONI CENT 1/10/36A, 'Protests and Second Hunger Strike: Weekly Bulletin No. 10', 7 May 1981; *The Times*, 6 May 1981.   **32.** *Daily Express*, 6 March 1981; *Daily Mirror*, 8 May 1981; Hansard, 5 May 1981.   **33.** Taylor, *Provos*, p. 242; English, *Armed Struggle*, pp. 200–201; Jacqueline McCafferty, 'Us over Here – Them over There', in Joan Scanlon (ed.), *Surviving the Blues: Growing up in the Thatcher Decade* (1990), p. 58.   **34.** 'Speech at Stormont Castle Lunch', 28 May 1981, TFW.   **35.** PRONI NIO 12/197A, D. E. S. Blatherwick, 'Where Next?', 1 June 1981; Humphrey Atkins, 'Memo to OD Committee: OD (81) 33: Northern Ireland Prisons Situation', 12 June 1981, TFW; 'MT Meeting with Northern Ireland Secretary', 8 July 1981, TFW; Hennessey, *Hunger Strike*, pp. 6–7, 300–329; Moore, *Not for Turning*, pp. 610–12; *Belfast Telegraph*, 27 March 2008; and see Richard O'Rawe, *Afterlives: The Hunger Strike and the Secret Offer That Changed Irish History* (Dublin, 2010).   **36.** Taylor, *Provos*, pp. 247–52; English, *Armed Struggle*, p. 202; Moore, *Not for Turning*, p. 616; Hennessey, *Hunger Strike*, pp. 448–53; *Sunday Times*, 4 October 1981; *The Times*, 5 October 1981, 7 October 1981.   **37.** Moore, *Not for Turning*, pp. 616–17; English, *Armed Struggle*, p. 207; *Sunday Express*, 4 October 1981.   **38.** McKittrick and McVea, *Making Sense of the Troubles*, pp. 146–7; English, *Armed Struggle*, pp. 203, 210; Taylor, *Provos*, pp. 241–2; *Belfast Telegraph*, 10 February 2014, 31 January 2017.   **39.** Taylor, *Brits*, p. 240; English, *Armed Struggle*, pp. 204–5, 224–5; PRONI CENT 1/10/66, D. E. S. Blatherwick, 'Local Effects of the Hunger Strike', 17 August 1981; Patterson, *Ireland since 1939*, p. 256.   **40.** *Guardian*, 22 December 1980, 22 April 1981, 30 August 1979; *The Times*, 28 October 1981.   **41.** John Carvel, *Citizen Ken* (1984), pp. 162–3; Andrew Hosken, *Ken: The Ups and Downs of Ken Livingstone* (2008), p. 164.

## Chapter 24. The Commissar of County Hall

1. *The Times*, 12 October 1981; *Daily Mirror*, 12 October 1981; *Daily Express*, 12 October 1981; *Guardian*, 12 October 1981; David McKittrick et al., *Lost Lives: The Stories of the Men, Women and Children Who Died as a Result of the Northern Ireland Troubles* (Edinburgh, 1999), pp. 881–2.   2. *Guardian*, 12 October 1981; *Daily Express*, 12 October 1981; *Daily Mirror*, 12 October 1981; *The Times*, 12 October 1981.   3. Ibid., 13 October 1981; *Sun*, 13 October 1981; *Daily Mail*, 14 October 1981; *Sunday Express*, 27 September 1981; John Carvel, *Citizen Ken* (1984), pp. 95–6.   4. Ibid., pp. 27, 32; *The Times*, 1 May 1981; Ken Livingstone, *You Can't Say That: Memoirs* (2011), p. 13.   5. Carvel, *Citizen Ken*, pp. 37, 39; Livingstone, *You Can't Say That*, pp. 25, 28, 76.   6. Ibid., p. 77; Carvel, *Citizen Ken*, p. 40; Andrew Hosken, *Ken: The Ups and Downs of Ken Livingstone* (2008), pp. 14, 16; Jerry White, *London in the Twentieth Century: A City and Its People* (2001), pp. 392–4.   7. James Curran, 'Rise of the "Loony Left"', in James Curran, Ivor Gaber and Julian Petley (eds.), *Culture Wars: The Media and the British Left* (2nd edn: 2018), pp. 6–8.   8. Carvel, *Citizen Ken*, pp. 177–8; *The Times*, 1 May 1981; Hosken, *Ken*, pp. 26–7, 29.   9. David Kogan and Maurice Kogan, *The Battle for the Labour Party* (1982), pp. 121–2, 124; Ion Trewin (ed.), *The Hugo Young Papers: Thirty Years of British Politics – Off the Record* (2008), p. 184; Livingstone, *You Can't Say That*, p. 130; Carvel, *Citizen Ken*, pp. 35, 60, 70–72; Hosken, *Ken*, pp. 73–4; *The Times*, 9 December 1981.   10. Carvel, *Citizen Ken*, pp. 65–6, 70–71, 74–5; Hosken, *Ken*, p. 59.   11. *The Times*, 14 May 1981; Carvel, *Citizen Ken*, pp. 10, 79–80; Hosken, *Ken*, pp. 76–7, 83.   12. Carvel, *Citizen Ken*, p. 10; *The Times*, 6 April 1981; *Daily Express*, 30 April 1981, 6 May 1981.   13. *The Times*, 8 May 1981, 9 May 1981; Carvel, *Citizen Ken*, pp. 13, 17–19; Hosken, *Ken*, pp. 85, 86, 89–90.   14. Carvel, *Citizen Ken*, pp. 16, 18–20; *Sun*, 9 May 1981; *Daily Mail*, 9 May 1981; *Daily Express*, 9 May 1981; Livingstone, *You Can't Say That*, pp. 169–70. Livingstone says this happened on the Saturday. But that is impossible, because Mitterrand was elected on the Sunday.   15. Andy Willis, 'Jim Allen: Radical Drama beyond *Days of Hope*', *Journal of British Cinema and Television*, 5:2 (2008), pp. 312–15; *Guardian*, 9 December 1981; *The Times*, 9 December 1981. On the booming left, see, for example, Martin Walker's essay in the *Guardian*, 10 December 1980.   16. *New Statesman*, 19 March 1982; *New Internationalist*, 1 July 1982; and see Colin Fudge, 'Decentralisation: Socialism Goes Local?', in Martin Boddy and Colin Fudge (eds.), *Local Socialism? Labour Councils and New Left Alternatives* (1984), pp. 195–8.   17. *New Statesman*, 19 March 1982; *New Internationalist*, 1 July 1982; *Guardian*, 5 September 1980, 22 September 1980, 16 March 1982, 23 March 1982; *Daily Mail*, 17 September 1980.   18. *New Internationalist*, 1 July 1982; *Guardian*, 8 May 1982.   19. Ibid., 19 February 1981, 25 March 1981, 1 July 1982, 25 July 1984.   20. Ibid., 6 January 1981; Daisy Payling, '"Socialist Republic of South Yorkshire": Grassroots Activism and Left-Wing Solidarity in 1980s Sheffield', *Twentieth Century British History*, 25:4 (2014), pp. 609–10.   21. *The Times*, 5 April 1984; 'Interview with David Blunkett', in Boddy and Fudge (eds.), *Local Socialism*, pp. 245–6; *Guardian*, 18 December 1982, 7 April 1983, 10 January 1983; Payling, '"Socialist Republic of South Yorkshire"', pp. 603, 614; see also the interview with Blunkett in the *Guardian*, 18 July 1998.   22. *Guardian*, 24 April 1981, 10 January 1983, 6 January 1981.   23. *The Times*, 5 April 1984; *Guardian*, 9 April 1981, 25 July 1984; 'Interview with David Blunkett', in Boddy and Fudge (eds.), *Local Socialism*, pp. 254–5; Livingstone, *You Can't Say That*, p. 212; Payling, '"Socialist Republic of South Yorkshire"', pp. 605, 612; Daisy Payling, 'City Limits: Sexual Politics and the New Urban Left in 1980s Sheffield', *Contemporary British History*, 31:2 (2017), pp. 267–8.   24. *Guardian*, 10 January 1983, 6 January 1981; *Daily Express*, 5 October 1983, 10 April 1981.   25. Carvel, *Citizen Ken*, p. 51; Hosken, *Ken*, pp. 38–9; Livingstone, *You Can't Say That*, pp. 103–4.   26. Carvel, *Citizen Ken*, pp. 48, 50–51; White, *London in the Twentieth Century*, pp. 387–90; *The Times*, 21 June 1975.   27. Ibid., 8 May 1981, 9 May 1981; Alwyn W. Turner, *Rejoice! Rejoice! Britain in the 1980s* (2010), pp. 78–9; Carvel, *Citizen Ken*, p. 24; *London Labour Briefing*, June 1981.   28. *The Times*, 14 May 1981, 18 May 1981, 30 May 1981, 1 June 1981; *Guardian*, 30 July 1981; Hosken, *Ken*, p. 114; *Daily Express*, 26

May 1981; *Sunday Express*, 31 May 1981.  **29.** Livingstone, *You Can't Say That*, pp. 178, 1890; Hosken, *Ken*, pp. 96–7.  **30.** *Daily Mail*, 30 May 1981; *Daily Telegraph*, 15 June 1981; Carvel, *Citizen Ken*, pp. 87–8; Hosken, *Ken*, pp. 97–8.  **31.** *Private Eye*, 5 June 1981; Hosken, *Ken*, pp. 98, 110; Ken Livingstone, *If Voting Changed Anything, They'd Abolish It* (1987), p. 163; Peter Chippindale and Chris Horrie, *Stick It Up Your Punter: The Uncut Story of the Sun Newspaper* (rev. edn: 2013), p. 155.  **32.** *The Times*, 13 July 1981; *Guardian*, 16 April 1981; Kogan and Kogan, *Battle for the Labour Party*, p. 130.  **33.** Hansard, 2 June 1981; *Evening Standard*, 20 July 1981; *Sun*, 15 July 1981; *News of the World*, 12 July 1981; *Daily Mail*, 30 July 1981; and see James Curran, 'Goodbye to the Clowns', in Curran, Gabler and Petley (eds.), *Culture Wars*, pp. 27–30.  **34.** Carvel, *Citizen Ken*, pp. 162–3; Hosken, *Ken*, p. 164.  **35.** *The Times*, 23 July 1981; *Daily Telegraph*, 22 July 1981; *Daily Express*, 22 August 1981; Carvel, *Citizen Ken*, pp. 88–9.  **36.** *Sun*, 23 July 1981; Carvel, *Citizen Ken*, p. 89; Hosken, *Ken*, p. 104; Hansard, 23 July 1981; *Daily Mail*, 24 July 1981; the *Standard* is quoted in Carvel.  **37.** *Daily Express*, 29 July 1981; Carvel, *Citizen Ken*, p. 90; *Daily Express*, 19 August 1981; *Sun*, 19 August 1981; *Daily Mail*, 20 August 1981, 12 August 1981; Hosken, *Ken*, p. 106; Curran, 'Goodbye to the Clowns', pp. 32, 34, 36.  **38.** Carvel, *Citizen Ken*, p. 93; *Daily Express*, 22 August 1981; *Daily Mirror*, 22 August 1981; *The Times*, 22 August 1981; Hosken, *Ken*, p. 104.  **39.** *Daily Telegraph*, 24 August 1981; Carvel, *Citizen Ken*, pp. 93–4; *Observer*, 30 August 1981; *Daily Express*, 31 August 1981.  **40.** *The Times*, 14 October 1981.  **41.** *Guardian*, 14 October 1981; *The Times*, 14 October 1981; *Evening Standard*, 13 October 1981; *Daily Mail*, 12 October 1981, 14 October 1981; and see Carvel, *Citizen Ken*, pp. 96–7; Hosken, *Ken*, p. 158; Curran, 'Goodbye to the Clowns', p. 31.  **42.** *Sun*, 13 October 1981; Hosken, *Ken*, pp. 158–9; Livingstone, *You Can't Say That*, pp. 188–90.  **43.** Ibid., p. 189; Carvel, *Citizen Ken*, pp. 124–6  **44.** Ibid., pp. 84, 114–16.  **45.** James Curran, 'The Boomerang Effect: The Press and the Battle for London', in James Curran, Anthony Smith and Pauline Wingate (eds.), *Impacts and Influences: Essays on Media Power in the Twentieth Century* (1987), p. 121; *Guardian*, 3 October 1981, 10 October 1981; *Observer*, 4 October 1981; *Daily Express*, 8 October 1981; Hosken, *Ken*, p. 116; Carvel, *Citizen Ken*, p. 117.  **46.** Ibid., pp. 128–39, 146; Hosken, *Ken*, pp. 117–21.  **47.** *Guardian*, 22 March 1982, 23 March 1982.  **48.** Curran, 'Boomerang Effect', pp. 121–2; Curran, 'Goodbye to the Clowns', p. 36; *The Times*, 14 February 1983; Carvel, *Citizen Ken*, p. 107; see also Julian Barnes in the *Observer*, 23 October 1983.  **49.** Carvel, *Citizen Ken*, pp. 101–2, 107, 231–2; Julian Critchley, *Some of Us: People Who Did Well under Thatcher* (1992), p. 74; *The Times*, 29 June 1983; Russell Davies (ed.), *The Kenneth Williams Diaries* (1993), p. 653; Trewin (ed.), *Hugo Young Papers*, p. 188.  **50.** *The Times*, 14 May 1981; Carvel, *Citizen Ken*, pp. 207–8.  **51.** Hosken, *Ken*, pp. 148, 146; *The Times*, 17 June 1981; Livingstone, *You Can't Say That*, pp. 210–11; *Guardian*, 17 February 1982.  **52.** Ibid., 22 July 1982; Hosken, *Ken*, p. 113; Livingstone, *You Can't Say That*, p. 157. See also Andy Beckett, *Promised You a Miracle: UK80–82* (2015), p. 349.  **53.** Hosken, *Ken*, pp. 143–4; Stephen Brooke, 'Space, Emotions and the Everyday: The Affective Ecology of 1980s London', *Twentieth Century British History*, 28:1 (March 2017), p. 120; *News of the World*, 21 February 1982; *Sun*, 27 July 1984; *Daily Mail*, 19 May 1983; and see Curran, 'Goodbye to the Clowns', pp. 33–4.  **54.** Carvel, *Citizen Ken*, p. 234; White, *London in the Twentieth Century*, pp. 395, 397.  **55.** Hosken, *Ken*, pp. 165–7; Carvel, *Citizen Ken*, pp. 157–8; *Daily Telegraph*, 8 December 1982; *The Times*, 9 December 1982.  **56.** Ibid., 9 December 1982, 10 December 1982, 11 December 1982; *Daily Mirror*, 6 December 1982, 9 December 1982; *Sun*, 8 December 1982; Carvel, *Citizen Ken*, pp. 159–60; Hosken, *Ken*, p. 168; *Guardian*, 27 July 1983.  **57.** *The Times*, 23 February 1983, 29 August 1983; *Guardian*, 27 August 1983, 29 August 1983; *Daily Express*, 29 August 1983. On the Troops Out grant, see also Hosken, *Ken*, p. 169.

# Chapter 25. Attack of the Sloanes

1. *Observer*, 17 May 1981; *The Times*, 18 May 1981, 29 July 1981; *Daily Express*, 19 May 1981.  2. Ben Pimlott, *The Queen: A Biography of Elizabeth II* (1996), pp. 475–6; *Daily*

*Mirror*, 19 November 1980.   3. *The Times*, 28 July 1981, 29 July 1981; *Guardian*, 27 July 1981; *Daily Mirror*, 29 July 1981.   4. *The Times*, 27 July 1981, 28 July 1981, 29 July 1981, 31 July 1981; *Guardian*, 29 July 1981.   5. *Daily Express*, 29 July 1981; *The Times*, 29 July 1981.   6. Tony Benn, *The End of an Era: Diaries, 1980–90* (1992), pp. 141–2; *The Times*, 30 July 1981; *Guardian*, 30 July 1981. On Clay Cross, see also *The Times*, 17 June 1981. 7. *Guardian*, 28 July 1981, 30 July 1981; *The Times*, 29 July 1981, 30 July 1981.   8. Ibid., 27 July 1981, 29 July 1981, 30 July 1981; *Guardian*, 30 July 1981.   9. MO C108, Special – Royal Wedding 1981; MO N403, Special – Royal Wedding 1981.   10. MO W633, Special – Royal Wedding 1981.   11. MO S496, Special – Royal Wedding 1981. For the Newton Abbot programme, see MO Misc., Special – Royal Wedding 1981.   12. Russell Davies (ed.), *The Kenneth Williams Diaries* (1993), p. 639; Sue Townsend, *The Secret Diary of Adrian Mole Aged 13¾* (1982: 2002), pp. 137–9.   13. *The Times*, 30 July 1981; *Guardian*, 30 July 1981; *Daily Express*, 31 July 1981.   14. Ibid., 30 July 1981; *Daily Mirror*, 31 July 1981, 30 July 1981.   15. *The Times*, 31 July 1981, 22 August 1981; *Daily Express*, 5 November 1981; *Daily Mirror*, 5 November 1981.   16. *Daily Express*, 29 July 1981.   17. Jonathan Dimbleby, *The Prince of Wales: A Biography* (1994), pp. 263–5; Pimlott, *The Queen*, p. 473; *The Times*, 25 February 1981; *Daily Mirror*, 25 February 1981.   18. *Sun*, 8 August 1980; *Daily Mirror*, 18 September 1980, 19 September 1980; Roy Greenslade, *Press Gang: How Newspapers Make Profits from Propaganda* (rev. edn: 2004), pp. 353–4.   19. Ibid., pp. 354–7; *Sunday Mirror*, 16 November 1980; *The Times*, 2 December 1980.   20. *Daily Mirror*, 27 July 1981; *Daily Express*, 27 July 1981; *Sun*, 28 July 1981; Piers Brendon and Phillip Whitehead, *The Windsors: A Dynasty Revealed, 1917–2000* (2000), p. 201.   21. Pimlott, *The Queen*, p. 476; Ann Barr and Peter York, *The Official Sloane Ranger Handbook: The First Guide to What Really Matters in Life* (1982), pp. 20–21.   22. *The Times*, 30 May 1980, 29 October 1982, 9 March 1981. On York, see *Guardian*, 29 January 1983.   23. Barr and York, *Official Sloane Ranger Handbook*, pp. 7, 36, 12–13, 59, 114, 117. On knickerbockers for men, see Peter York, *Modern Times* (1984), p. 65. For this section, I carried out some gruelling fieldwork among the people of north Oxfordshire.   24. York, *Modern Times*, pp. 21–2; 'Speech to the Institute of SocioEconomic Studies', 15 September 1975, TFW; *Observer Music Monthly*, 4 October 2009.   25. *Guardian*, 25 September 2015; the original article is reprinted in Jack, *Before the Oil Ran Out: Britain in the Brutal Years* (rev. edn: 1997), pp. 93–100. For Soames's pay in 2012, see *Scotsman*, 10 April 2013.   26. Barr and York, *Official Sloane Ranger Handbook*, p. 20; *The Times*, 31 March 1981, 7 April 1981; *The Face*, January 1981; and see Jon Savage, *Time Travel: Pop, Media and Sexuality, 1976–96* (1996), p. 119.   27. *Tatler*, May 1981; *Daily Express*, 18 June 1981. On *Tatler* in general, see Andy Beckett, *Promised You a Miracle: UK80–82* (2015), pp. 199–201.   28. *Guardian*, 25 September 2015; Jack, *Before the Oil Ran Out*, pp. 95–6. 29. *The Times*, 23 September 1981; and see Charles Sturridge, *The Making of Brideshead: A Note from the Director*, which accompanies the Acorn DVD release of *Brideshead Revisited* (2002).   30. *The Times*, 23 September 1981, 9 October 1981, 15 October 1981, 17 October 1981; *Guardian*, 25 November 1981, 24 December 1981; *Daily Express*, 22 December 1981.   31. *Guardian*, 25 November 1981, 13 October 1981, 24 December 1981; *The Times*, 13 October 1981; *Daily Express*, 22 December 1981.   32. *Fodor's 1982 Guide to Great Britain* (New York, 1982), p. 59; David Cannadine, *In Churchill's Shadow: Confronting the Past in Modern Britain* (2002), p. 240; *Daily Express*, 9 February 1979, 11 July 1977; Raphael Samuel, *Theatres of Memory: Past and Present in Contemporary Culture* (rev. edn: 2012), pp. 51–135, 261; David Cannadine, 'Brideshead Revered', *London Review of Books*, 5:5 (17 March 1983).   33. *Guardian*, 24 December 1981, 11 February 1982.   34. *Daily Express*, 5 December 1981; *The Times*, 10 November 1981.   35. *Guardian*, 26 July 1982, 16 September 1983; *The Times*, 6 September 1983.   36. Jack, *Before the Oil Ran Out*, pp. 181–3.

# Chapter 26. The British Are Coming!

1. Alexander Walker, *National Heroes: British Cinema in the Seventies and Eighties* (1985), pp. 173–5; James Chapman, *Past and Present: National Identity and the British Historical*

*Film* (2005), pp. 271–3; *Daily Mail*, 14 July 2012. **2.** Chapman, *Past and Present*, pp. 276, 279–80, 288–9; *The Times*, 3 April 1981; *Evening Standard*, 2 April 1981; *Financial Times*, 3 April 1981; Walker, *National Heroes*, p. 179; George Orwell, 'Boys' Weeklies', *Horizon*, March 1940, http://theorwellprize.co.uk/george-orwell/by-orwell/essays-and-other-works/boys-weeklies/. **3.** Chapman, *Past and Present*, pp. 274–5, 287–8, 294; *Guardian*, 9 July 2012. **4.** Hugo Young, *One of Us: A Biography of Margaret Thatcher* (rev. edn: 1990), pp. 422–3; Walker, *National Heroes*, p. 179. For Mrs Thatcher and the Jews, see 'Speech to Board of Deputies of British Jews', 15 December 1981, TFW. For a thoughtful reading of the politics of *Chariots of Fire*, see Chapman, *Past and Present*, pp. 294–5, though he arguably underestimates how much the film's patriotic nostalgia would have appealed to Mrs Thatcher, as well as the extent to which she was already invoking 'the rhetoric of national greatness' well before the Falklands War. **5.** Chapman, too, draws attention to this scene: see his *Past and Present*, pp. 291–3. **6.** Ibid., pp. 281–3; Walker, *National Heroes*, p. 180; *Time*, 21 September 1981. **7.** *The Times*, 31 March 1982, 27 January 1982; Walker, *National Heroes*, p. 181. **8.** Chapman, *Past and Present*, pp. 284–6; and see Jeffrey Richards, *Films and British National Identity: From Dickens to Dad's Army* (Manchester, 1997), pp. 168–9. **9.** Garry Whannel, *Fields in Vision: Television Sport and Cultural Transformation* (1992), pp. 143–4; Pat Butcher, *The Perfect Distance: Ovett and Coe: The Record-Breaking Rivalry* (2004), pp. 5, 88–9. **10.** *Daily Express*, 2 July 1980; Butcher, *Perfect Distance*, p. 4. **11.** Ibid., pp. 294–5, 8–9, 27, 35, 150, 169; *The Times*, 11 August 1984. **12.** Butcher, *Perfect Distance*, pp. 24–5, 30–31, 34, 46, 171; *The Times*, 28 August 1981. **13.** Ibid., 20 August 1981, 27 August 1981, 2 January 1980; *Daily Express*, 29 August 1981, 2 September 1981; *Daily Mirror*, 29 August 1981. On the rivalry in general, see also Simon Burnton's thoughtful article in the *Guardian*, 18 April 2012. **14.** *Daily Express*, 29 August 1981, 3 September 1981; Butcher, *Perfect Distance*, pp. 94, 220–21, 223, 159; *Observer*, 8 August 1982. **15.** *Daily Express*, 3 November 1979; Skip Rozin, *Daley Thompson: The Subject Is Winning* (1983: 1984), pp. 7–8. **16.** Ibid., pp. 27, 79. **17.** Ibid., pp. 80, 17, 29–32, 78; *The Times*, 26 July 1984; *Independent*, 26 July 2008. **18.** *The Times*, 26 July 1984; *Guardian*, 8 May 1980; Rozin, *Daley Thompson*, pp. 117, 105. **19.** Ibid., pp. 152–3, 105, 128, 160, 7; *Guardian*, 7 August 1984. **20.** Ibid., 25 July 1980, 6 October 1982; Rozin, *Daley Thompson*, pp. 150, 125, 195; *The Times*, 26 July 1984. **21.** Rozin, *Daley Thompson*, pp. 48–9. **22.** *Guardian*, 7 August 1984; Rozin, *Daley Thompson*, p. 129. See also the interview in the *Independent*, 26 July 2008. **23.** *The Times*, 15 August 1983, 28 July 1980, 26 July 1984; Rozin, *Daley Thompson*, pp. 7, 141; *Guardian*, 12 May 1983, 7 August 1984. **24.** Rozin, *Daley Thompson*, pp. 17, 181; *The Times*, 28 July 1980, 26 July 1984. **25.** Rozin, *Daley Thompson*, pp. 16, 6, 8. **26.** Simon Wilde, *Ian Botham: The Power and the Glory* (2011), pp. 7–8, 31–3. **27.** Ibid., pp. 11, 34–5; *Daily Mirror*, 15 April 1980. The TV interview, recorded for BBC2's *Open to Question* (20 October 1986), is online at https://www.youtube.com/watch?time_continue=682&v=rGH6x98lEjc. **28.** Wilde, *Ian Botham*, pp. 14, 40, 106, 38, 195, 54, 71. **29.** Ibid., pp. 17–18, 21, 69–70; *The Times*, 27 August 1981. **30.** Wilde, *Ian Botham*, pp. 109, 113, 130; *Daily Express*, 20 June 1978; *Daily Mirror*, 3 August 1979, 15 April 1980. **31.** *Daily Express*, 30 June 1978; *Observer*, 26 September 1982; Wilde, *Ian Botham*, pp. 99, 118. **32.** Ibid., pp. 35–6; *Daily Mirror*, 15 April 1980; *Observer*, 26 September 1982. **33.** Wilde, *Ian Botham*, pp. 110–11. **34.** Ibid., pp. 136, 139–40; *The Times*, 19 April 1980; *Observer*, 27 April 1980; *Daily Express*, 19 May 1980. **35.** *The Times*, 13 August 1980, 18 April 1981; Wilde, *Ian Botham*, pp. 158–9, 161–2; *Sunday People*, 26 April 1981. **36.** *The Times*, 4 December 1980, 15 January 1981, 17 September 1980; *Daily Express*, 3 January 1981; Wilde, *Ian Botham*, pp. 150–52. **37.** *Daily Mirror*, 9 June 1981; *The Times*, 18 April 1981; Wilde, *Ian Botham*, pp. 162, 165; *Daily Express*, 9 June 1981, 17 June 1981. **38.** *Daily Mirror*, 22 June 1981; *Daily Express*, 22 June 1981; Wilde, *Ian Botham*, pp. 165–6; Martin Williamson, 'So Nearly Botham's Annus Horribilis', 11 July 2009, http://www.espncricinfo.com/story/_/id/22787118/so-nearly-botham-annus-horribilis; *Guardian*, 2 July 1981. **39.** *Daily Mirror*, 8 July 1981; *Daily Express*, 8 July 1981; Williamson, 'So Nearly Botham's Annus Horribilis'; Wilde, *Ian Botham*, pp. 171–4; *The Times*, 8 July 1981. **40.** *Daily Express*, 8 July 1981; *Daily Mirror*,

8 July 1981.   **41.** Williamson, 'So Nearly Botham's Annus Horribilis'; Wilde, *Ian Botham*, pp. 178–9; *Guardian*, 2 July 2011; *The Times*, 22 July 1981; *Observer*, 19 July 1981. The *Sun* is quoted in Andy Beckett, *Promised You a Miracle: UK 80–82* (2015), p. 26.   **42.** Wilde, *Ian Botham*, p. 179; *Guardian*, 2 July 2011, 6 June 2013; Andrew Miller, '"Pure Village-Green Slogging"', 30 January 2007, http://www.espncricinfo.com/story/_/id/22972796/pure-village-green-slogging.   **43.** *The Times*, 22 July 1981; Wilde, *Ian Botham*, pp. 181–2. See also Crispin Andrews, '"I Don't Think Odds of 500–1 Have Appeared Since"', 15 July 2016, http://www.espncricinfo.com/story/_/id/17081963/bob-willis-1981-headingley-test-england-ashes-win; as well as the features in the *Guardian*, 2 July 2011, 6 June 2013. For footage from the final day, see, for example, https://www.youtube.com/watch?v=HtPw_Ztlm_Q.   **44.** *The Times*, 22 July 1981; *Daily Express*, 21 July 1981, 22 July 1981. **45.** Wilde, *Ian Botham*, pp. 183–5; *Guardian*, 2 July 2011; *Observer*, 29 September 1982; Martin Williamson, 'Beefy's 28-Ball Ashes Broadside', 8 August 2015, http://www.espncricinfo.com/story/_/id/20598515/ian-botham-28-ball-ashes-broadside.   **46.** *The Times*, 17 August 1981; Wilde, *Ian Botham*, pp. 185–6.   **47.** *Daily Mirror*, 3 August 1981, 18 August 1981; *Daily Express*, 3 August 1981, 18 August 1981; Wilde, *Ian Botham*, pp. 175–6.   **48.** *Observer*, 26 September 1982.   **49.** Wilde, *Ian Botham*, pp. 197, 225, 191, 189, 203, 221; Simon Barnes, 'A Genuinely Great Cricketer: An Assessment of Graham Gooch', originally in Graeme Wright (ed.), *Wisden Cricketers' Almanack, 1991* (1991), http://www.espncricinfo.com/wisdenalmanack/content/story/237057.html.   **50.** Wilde, *Ian Botham*, pp. 322–3; *Observer*, 30 September 2007; *Sunday Times*, 25 July 1993; *Independent*, 19 July 1993.   **51.** *The Times*, 4 August 1981.   **52.** *Daily Express*, 13 August 1981, 7 August 1981.

## Chapter 27. She Came, She Saw, She Clobbered

**1.** For an analysis of this scene in context, see James Chapman, *Licence to Thrill: A Cultural History of the James Bond Films* (1999), pp. 207–8.   **2.** *Guardian*, 4 July 1979.   **3.** Anthony King and Robert J. Wybrow (eds.), *British Political Opinion, 1937–2000: The Gallup Polls* (2001), pp. 192, 30; Robert J. Wybrow, *Britain Speaks Out, 1937–87: A Social History as Seen through the Gallup Data* (Basingstoke, 1989), p. 125.   **4.** Alan Clark, *Diaries: Into Politics, 1972–1982* (2000), p. 246; John Hoskyns, *Just in Time: Inside the Thatcher Revolution* (2000), p. 301.   **5.** *The Times*, 27 June 1981, 23 June 1981, 16 June 1981; Charles Moore, *Margaret Thatcher: The Authorized Biography*, vol. 1: *Not for Turning* (2013), pp. 632–4; *Daily Mirror*, 18 June 1981.   **6.** *The Times*, 10 July 1981.   **7.** Clark, *Diaries: Into Politics*, p. 242.   **8.** TNA PREM 19/424, Ingham to Pym, 'Presentation', 8 July 1981; Hoskyns, *Just in Time*, pp. 315–17; Hoskyns to Thatcher, 'PPB', 7 July 1981, TFW.   **9.** Hoskyns to Thatcher, 'Strategy Meeting, Chequers', 24 July 1981, TFW; Hoskyns, Wolfson and Millar to Thatcher, 'Your Political Survival', 20 August 1981, TFW; Moore, *Not for Turning*, pp. 641–3; Hoskyns, *Just in Time*, pp. 326–8.   **10.** *The Times*, 17 July 1981, 6 August 1981; Hansard, 21 July 1981.   **11.** Howe to Thatcher, 'Tax and Public Expenditure: Cabinet on 23 July', 15 July 1981, TFW; Margaret Thatcher, *The Downing Street Years* (1993), p. 148; 'Most Confidential Record', CC (81) 29, 23 July 1981, TFW.   **12.** The two most complete accounts of the meeting are in Hugo Young, *One of Us: A Biography of Margaret Thatcher* (rev. edn: 1990), pp. 218–19; Moore, *Not for Turning*, pp. 637–8; see also Thatcher, *Downing Street Years*, pp. 148–9. For the minutes, which are a bit bland, see CC (81) 29, 23 July 1981, TFW.   **13.** Thatcher, *Downing Street Years*, pp. 149–50; Geoffrey Howe, *Conflict of Loyalty* (1994), p. 223.   **14.** 'Speech to 1922 Committee', 23 July 1981, TFW; Clark, *Diaries: Into Politics*, p. 250; Gow to Thatcher, '1922 Executive', 30 July 1981, TFW.   **15.** Richard V. Allen to Reagan, 'Britain Drifts' (NSC Country File Box 91326, Ronald Reagan Library), 31 July 1981, TFW.   **16.** Nicholas Henderson, *Mandarin: The Diaries of Nicholas Henderson* (1994: 2000), p. 406.   **17.** Howe to Thatcher, 'Fox and Goose', 16 July 1981, TFW; Clark, *Diaries: Into Politics*, p. 249; Moore, *Not for Turning*, pp. 639–40; Thatcher, *Downing Street Years*, p. 150. Charles Douglas-Home's letter is quoted in Christopher Collins's guide to Mrs Thatcher's private files for 1981, at https://

www.margaretthatcher.org/archive/1981cac2.asp.   18. *The Times*, 14 September 1981, 15
September 1981; Ian Gilmour, *Dancing with Dogma: Britain under Thatcherism* (1992), pp.
47–8; Thatcher, *Downing Street Years*, p. 151.   19. *Observer*, 13 September 1981; Jim Prior,
*A Balance of Power* (1986), pp. 171–2; for a slightly different take, see Walters diary, 14
September 1981, TFW.   20. Young, *One of Us*, pp. 220–21; John Campbell, *Margaret
Thatcher*, vol. 2: *The Iron Lady* (2003), p. 120; Thatcher, *Downing Street Years*, p. 151.
21. Nigel Lawson, *The View from No. 11: Memoirs of a Tory Radical* (1992: 1993), p. 140.
22. *Observer*, 20 September 1981; Norman Tebbit, *Upwardly Mobile: An Autobiography*
(1988), pp. 192, 194–5; Hansard, 2 March 1978; Julian Critchley, *Some of Us: People Who Did
Well under Thatcher* (1992), pp. 31–3, 35.   23. Ibid., pp. 40–41; *Sunday Times*, 16 October
1983; Young, *One of Us*, p. 315.   24. Critchley, *Some of Us*, p. 41; Mark Garnett and Ian
Aitken, *Splendid! Splendid! The Authorized Biography of Willie Whitelaw* (2002), p. 274.
25. *Daily Mirror*, 15 September 1981; Moore, *Not for Turning*, pp. 645, 652; Howe, *Conflict of
Loyalty*, p. 250.   26. *The Times*, 14 September 1981, 22 July 1981, 26 August 1981, 23 Sep-
tember 1981.   27. Ibid., 5 November 1981, 4 November 1981, 2 November 1981.   28. Howe,
*Conflict of Loyalty*, pp. 226–7; Keith Britto to Derek Howe, 'Public Opinion Background
Note 83', 1 October 1981, TFW; *The Times*, 23 September 1981, 5 October 1981.   29. Ibid.,
7 October 1981; John Campbell, *Edward Heath: A Biography* (1993), pp. 729–30.
30. Walters to Thatcher, 'Notes on the Heath Speech', 6 October 1981, TFW; Howe to
Thatcher, 6 October 1981, TFW.   31. 'Speech at Monash University', 6 October 1981, TFW;
*The Times*, 7 October 1981; *Guardian*, 8 October 1981; *Daily Express*, 9 October 1981.
32. *Guardian*, 7 October 1981, 8 October 1981; *Observer*, 11 October 1981; *Daily Mirror*, 9
October 1981. The *Panorama* edition 'The Other Ruling Class' was broadcast on BBC1 on
12 October 1981.   33. *Sun*, 14 October 1981, quoted in Alwyn W. Turner, *Rejoice! Rejoice!
Britain in the 1980s* (2010), p. 23; *The Times*, 9 October 1981.   34. Hoskyns, *Just in Time*,
p. 340; *The Times*, 13 October 1981; *Daily Express*, 13 October 1981. For Mrs Thatcher's
appointment with Ken Dodd, see her engagement diary for 12 October, on the Thatcher
Foundation website. For the conference atmosphere, see the *Thames News* clip from 14
October 1981 at https://www.youtube.com/watch?v=Goxp7ERtsJM.   35. *The Times*, 14
October 1981.   36. Ibid., 15 October 1981; *Guardian*, 15 October 1981.   37. *The Times*,
15 October 1981, 16 October 1981; *Observer*, 20 September 1981; *Guardian*, 17 October
1981; and see Tebbit, *Upwardly Mobile*, p. 187; Moore, *Not for Turning*, p. 647.   38. *Guard-
ian*, 17 October 1981; Hoskyns, *Just in Time*, pp. 338–9; *The Times*, 17 October 1981;
'Speech at Conservative Party Conference', 16 October 1981, TFW.   39. Keith Britto to
Derek Howe, 'Public Opinion Background Note 86', 20 October 1981, TFW; *Guardian*, 5
October 1981; Ivor Crewe and Anthony King, *SDP: The Birth, Life and Death of the Social
Democratic Party* (Oxford, 1995), pp. 140–41; *The Times*, 5 October 1981.   40. Crewe and
King, *SDP*, p. 142; *The Times*, 23 October 1981.   41. Ibid., 24 October 1981; *Guardian*,
24 October 1981.   42. *The Times*, 24 October 1981; Crewe and King, *SDP*, pp. 142–3; Bill
Rodgers, *Fourth among Equals* (2000), p. 217; *Guardian*, 7 October 1981.   43. Hugh
Stephenson, *Claret and Chips: The Rise of the SDP* (1982), p. 113; Shirley Williams, *Climb-
ing the Bookshelves* (2009), pp. 292–3; *The Times*, 24 November 1981; *Daily Express*, 28
November 1981.   44. Clark, *Diaries: Into Politics*, p. 272; *The Times*, 27 November 1981;
*Guardian*, 27 November 1981; *Daily Express*, 27 November 1981; *Daily Mirror*, 28 Novem-
ber 1981.   45. *The Times*, 27 November 1981; *Daily Express*, 27 November 1981; *Daily
Mirror*, 28 November 1981.   46. *The Times*, 28 November 1981; *Daily Mirror*, 28 November
1981; *Daily Express*, 27 November 1981.   47. *The Times*, 28 November 1981; Clark, *Diar-
ies: Into Politics*, p. 276; Richard Ingrams and John Wells, *One for the Road* (1982), letter
dated 4 December 1981.   48. Gow to Thatcher, 'Your Meeting with Cecil Parkinson', 26
November 1981, TFW; *The Times*, 28 November 1981; *Guardian*, 28 November 1981;
Campbell, *Edward Heath*, p. 726.   49. Roy Jenkins, *A Life at the Centre* (1991), p. 554;
Campbell, *Edward Heath*, pp. 726–7; *The Times*, 28 November 1981.   50. 'Gang of 25' to
Michael Jopling, 25 November 1981, TFW; Jopling to Thatcher, 4 December 1981, TFW;
and see Young, *One of Us*, p. 241.   51. Keith Britto, 'Public Opinion Background Note 95',
20 December 1981, TFW; the Conservative Research Department paper is quoted in

Christopher Collins's guide to Mrs Thatcher's private files for 1981, at https://www.mar garetthatcher.org/archive/1981cac3.asp.   52. Campbell, *Iron Lady*, p. 122; John Junor, *Memoirs: Listening for a Midnight Tram* (1990), pp. 261–3.

## Chapter 28. The Shadow of the Past

1. See Janet and Allan Ahlberg, *Peepo!* (1981).   2. George Orwell, *The Road to Wigan Pier* (1937: 2001), p. 108; Robert Colls, *George Orwell: English Rebel* (Oxford, 2013), pp. 70–71. The first reviews of *Peepo!* were absurdly joyless: see *Guardian*, 2 October 1981, *New States-man*, 4 December 1981.   3. *Guardian*, 24 June 2006; *Daily Telegraph*, 1 April 2007, 31 May 2008; *Independent*, 15 May 2008.   4. David Duff, *Victoria Travels: Journeys of Queen Victoria between 1830 and 1900, with Extracts from Her Journal* (1970), p. 26; Charles Dickens, *The Old Curiosity Shop* (1840–41: Oxford, 1997), pp. 348–9; J. R. R. Tolkien, *The Lord of the Rings* (1955: 2012), p. 1013; *Guardian*, 27 February 2010, 20 May 2010; and see the BBC Four documentary *Heavy Metal Britannia* (5 March 2010).   5. *The Times*, 4 July 1980, 3 March 1982; *Guardian*, 17 February 1981.   6. *Sunday Times*, 14 February 1982, 15 May 1983.   7. *Guardian*, 20 November 1982; *The Times*, 15 April 2013; and see the Black Country Living Museum, 'The Museum's Story', https://www.bclm.co.uk/about/the-museums-story/1. htm.   8. *New Society*, 25 September 1980; *The Times*, 12 May 1981; Beryl Bainbridge, *English Journey, or, The Road to Milton Keynes* (1984), pp. 70, 68.   9. *New Society*, 23 August 1979; Jonathan Raban, *Coasting* (1986), pp. 224–5.   10. Jeremy Seabrook, *Unemployment* (1982: 1983), p. 167; *Guardian*, 25 February 1982.   11. Ian Jack, *Before the Oil Ran Out: Britain in the Brutal Years* (rev. edn: 1997), pp. 2–3, 6, 36–7.   12. Margaret Drabble, *The Middle Ground* (1980), p. 111; Alan Bleasdale, *Boys from the Blackstuff* (1982: 1985), pp. 251–2, 253. 13. *Guardian*, 24 January 1981; *New Society*, 20 March 1980.   14. Jeremy Seabrook, *City Close-Up* (1971: 1973), pp. 11–12; Jeremy Seabrook, *What Went Wrong? Working People and the Ideals of the Labour Movement* (1978), pp. 12–13, 27–8, 31, 115, 135.   15. Ibid., p. 9; Seabrook, *Unemployment*, pp. 7, 34, 150   16. Orwell, *Road to Wigan Pier*, p. 108; *Guardian*, 4 January 1982.   17. *The Times*, 30 March 1981, 30 June 1981, 18 May 1981, 30 September 1980; *Guardian*, 29 May 1981.   18. Ibid., 26 April 1982.   19. Bainbridge, *English Journey*, p. 154.   20. *The Times*, 29 October 1984; *Guardian*, 27 March 1981; and see Mark Clapson, *A Social History of Milton Keynes: Middle England/Edge City* (2004).   21. *Sunday Times*, 19 October 1980; *Guardian*, 27 March 1981; *The Times*, 20 August 1980, 29 October 1984.   22. Ibid., 21 May 1980; *Guardian*, 20 November 1980.   23. Ibid., 20 November 1980, 26 January 1981.   24. Ibid., 26 January 1981, 28 April 1982; *The Times*, 21 May 1980, 9 November 1983.   25. *Guardian*, 20 November 1980, 26 January 1981.   26. David Smith, *North and South: Britain's Economic, Social and Political Divide* (1989), pp. 115, 32–3, 36, 39, 40; Bainbridge, *English Journey*, p. 8.   27. Smith, *North and South*, p. 19; Raphael Samuel, *Theatres of Memory*, vol. 2: *Island Stories, Unravelling Britain* (1998), p. 165; and see Dave Russell, *Looking North: Northern England and the National Imagination* (Manchester, 2004), pp. 28, 60, 90, 184.   28. Smith, *North and South*, p. 3; *Guardian*, 19 February 1981, 19 January 1983.   29. Paul Theroux, *The Kingdom by the Sea: A Journey around the Coast of Great Britain* (1983), pp. 208–9; Jack, *Before the Oil Ran Out*, pp. 131, 142–3.   30. Ibid., pp. 131–2, 139, 128–9, 133.   31. Ibid., pp. 80, 82–4.   32. Ibid., p. 178.

## Chapter 29. The Land of Make Believe

1. *Daily Mirror*, 11 December 1981, 14 December 1981, 17 December 1981, 21 December 1981, 22 December 1981; *Daily Express*, 12 December 1981, 14 December 1981, 22 December 1981.   2. Russell Davies (ed.), *The Kenneth Williams Diaries* (1993), pp. 645–6; *Daily Mirror*, 14 December 1981.   3. *Daily Express*, 23 December 1981; *Guardian*, 24 December 1981.   4. *Radio Times*, 16–22 January 1982.   5. *Daily Mirror*, 24 December 1981; *Guardian*, 24 December 1981.   6. *Daily Express*, 17 December 1981, 21 December 1981; *Daily*

*Mirror*, 17 December 1981, 14 December 1981; *Guardian*, 17 December 1981. *Guardian*, 24 December 1981, 18 December 1981; *The Times*, 10 November 1981.   7. Ibid., 10 November 1981, 15 December 1981; *Daily Express*, 24 December 1981.   8. MO W633, Autumn Directive 1981; *Guardian*, 22 January 1980; *The Times*, 12 November 1980; Mary Abbott, *Family Affairs: A History of the Family in Twentieth-Century England* (2003), p. 154; MO H260, Spring Directive 1982.   9. *Daily Express*, 28 December 1981, 2 January 1982; *Daily Mirror*, 29 December 1981.   10. MO R470, Autumn Directive 1981; MO W633, Autumn Directive 1981.   11. *Daily Mirror*, 29 December 1981; *The Times*, 26 March 1982.   12. 'Speech to Conservative Trade Unionists', 1 November 1980, TFW; John Campbell, *Margaret Thatcher*, vol. 2: *The Iron Lady* (2003), p. 249.   13. MO H260, Spring Directive 1982; MO G226, Summer Directive 1984.   14. George Orwell, *The Road to Wigan Pier* (1937: 2001), p. 83.   15. Louis Heren, *Alas, Alas for England: What Went Wrong with Britain* (1981), p. 150; *Guardian*, 3 October 1983; Ian Jack, *Before the Oil Ran Out: Britain in the Brutal Years* (rev edn: 1997), p. xvii.   16. *Guardian*, 1 September 1981.   17. Nicklaus Thomas-Symonds, *Nye: The Political Life of Aneurin Bevan* (2015), p. 10; *Guardian*, 20 July 1981, 31 October 1981; and see Jeremy Seabrook, *Unemployment* (1982: 1983), pp. 7–9, 206–7. On consumerism and its critics, see Frank Trentmann, *Empire of Things: How We Became a World of Consumers, from the Fifteenth Century to the Twenty-first* (2016), esp. pp. 342–4.   18. 'Speech Opening Central Milton Keynes Shopping Centre', 25 September 1979, TFW; Beryl Bainbridge, *English Journey, or, The Road to Milton Keynes* (1984), pp. 155–6.   19. *Guardian*, 8 August 1979; *The Times*, 29 October 1984; *Sunday Times*, 19 October 1980.   20. *Guardian*, 19 November 1983; *Wakefield Express*, 21 October 2008; *Yorkshire Post*, 17 October 2013; 'Ridings Shopping Centre: The Heart of Shopping in Wakefield', https://truenorthbooks.com/wp-content/uploads/2016/01/Ridings-Shopping-Centre.pdf.   21. Lincoln Allison, *Condition of England: Essays and Impressions* (1981), p. 39; *The Times*, 30 March 1981.   22. *Guardian*, 9 February 1982, 16 February 1982; *The Times*, 8 May 1982, 8 November 1983.   23. Ibid., 30 March 1981; MO C108, Spring 1981; *Guardian*, 14 April 1982.   24. MO D156, Spring Directive 1982; MO C108, Spring Directive 1982; *Daily Mirror*, 11 January 1982.   25. Ingham to Thatcher, 'BBC Radio 4 – *World This Weekend*', 2 January 1982, TFW; *The Times*, 2 January 1982.   26. Hansard, 26 January 1982, 27 January 1982; *The Times*, 27 January 1982, 21 July 1982; *Daily Mirror*, 27 January 1982.   27. *The Times*, 29 January 1982, 17 February 1982.   28. Walker to Thatcher, 'Memorandum on a Conservative Strategy for the Next Two Years', 16 February 1982, TFW; Sherman to Thatcher, 'How We React to the SD-Alliance', 11 February 1982, TFW.   29. Ferdinand Mount, *Cold Cream: My Early Life and Other Mistakes* (2008), pp. 305–7.   30. Keith Britto, 'Public Opinion Background Note 96', 19 January 1982, TFW; Keith Britto, 'Public Opinion Background Note 101', 21 February 1982, TFW. See also David Sanders, Hugh Ward, David Marsh and Tony Fletcher, 'Government Popularity and the Falklands War: A Reassessment', *British Journal of Political Science*, 17:3 (1987), pp. 281–313; Ivor Crewe and Anthony King, *SDP: The Birth, Life and Death of the Social Democratic Party* (Oxford, 1995), pp. 146–7.   31. *Sunday Express*, 6 March 1982; Geoffrey Howe, *Conflict of Loyalty* (1994), pp. 239–40; *Financial Times*, 1 March 1982; and see Charles Moore, *Margaret Thatcher: The Authorized Biography*, vol. 1: *Not for Turning* (2013), pp. 651, 654.   32. Hansard, 9 March 1982; *Daily Mirror*, 10 March 1982; Keith Britto, 'Public Opinion Background Note 104', 14 March 1982, TFW.   33. 'Note of Liaison Committee Meeting', 10 March 1982, TFW; Keith Britto, 'Public Opinion Background Note 104', 14 March 1982, TFW; *Sunday Express*, 14 March 1982.   34. Keith Britto, 'Public Opinion Background Note 104', 14 March 1982, TFW; *Guardian*, 19 March 1982, 16 March 1982, 4 March 1982; *Observer*, 7 March 1982.

# Chapter 30. Tomorrow's World

1. Tom Lean, *Electronic Dreams: How 1980s Britain Learned to Love the Computer* (2016), p. 107; Magnus Anderson and Rebecca Levene, *Grand Thieves and Tomb Raiders: How*

*British Video Games Conquered the World* (2012), pp. 43–4; Francis Spufford, *Backroom Boys: The Secret Return of the British Boffin* (2003), p. 75. For comparable prices, see, for example, the Currys and Co-op adverts in the *Daily Mirror* on 4 March 1982 and 7 May 1982.   2. Dan Whitehead, *Speccy Nation: A Tribute to the Golden Age of British Gaming* (2012), pp. 7–8; Anderson and Levene, *Grand Thieves*, p. 43; *Guardian*, 9 July 1982, 29 April 1983; *Observer*, 27 March 1983; *The Times*, 16 August 1983; Janan Ganesh, *George Osborne: The Austerity Chancellor* (2012), p. 17.   3. *Guardian*, 11 September 1982, 17 March 1983; *The Times*, 29 January 1973, 7 January 1976, 24 November 1976, 17 January 1977; 'Sinclair: A Corporate History', http://www.nvg.ntnu.no/sinclair/sinclair/corphist. htm; 'Clive Sinclair', *Practical Computing*, 5:7 (1982), http://www.worldofspectrum.org/ CliveSinclairInterview1982/.   4. George Davies, *What Next?* (rev. edn: 1991), p. 153; *Observer*, 16 January 1983; *Guardian*, 17 May 1983, 11 September 1982; 'Clive Sinclair', *Practical Computing*, 5:7 (1982), http://www.worldofspectrum.org/CliveSinclairInterview1982/.   5. Anderson and Levene, *Grand Thieves*, p. 20; *Guardian*, 11 September 1982, 17 March 1983; *Observer*, 16 January 1983; *Daily Mirror*, 2 August 1984, 14 April 1984.   6. Ibid., 24 June 1955, 27 June 1955; Lean, *Electronic Dreams*, pp. 20–23, 27–8; *Observer*, 10 September 1978.   7. 'Now the Chips Are Down' (*Horizon*, BBC2, 31 March 1978) is online at http:// www.bbc.co.uk/iplayer/episode/p01z4rrj/horizon-19771978-now-the-chips-are-down; see also the discussions in Anderson and Levene, *Grand Thieves*, p. 18; Lean, *Electronic Dreams*, pp. 29–30.   8. All six episodes of *The Mighty Micro* (ITV, 29 October–3 December 1979) are online at https://archive.org; the quotation is from the fourth episode. See also Christopher Evans, *The Mighty Micro: The Impact of the Computer Revolution* (1979); *New Scientist*, 6 September 1979, 8 November 1979; Lean, *Electronic Dreams*, pp. 31–3. On Evans and Ballard, see J. G. Ballard, *Miracles of Life: Shanghai to Shepperton: An Autobiography* (2008), pp. 211–15.   9. Lean, *Electronic Dreams*, pp. 41–2; *Observer*, 10 September 1978; *Guardian*, 15 November 1979.   10. Anderson and Levene, *Grand Thieves*, p. 26; Lean, *Electronic Dreams*, pp. 64–5; *Guardian*, 30 January 1980; *The Times*, 30 January 1980.   11. Ibid., 30 January 1980, 11 February 1980, 22 September 1980; *Daily Express*, 3 November 1980; *Cambridge Evening News*, 29 January 1980, http://www.computinghistory.org.uk/ det/5445/Sinclair-ZX80-Launched/; Lean, *Electronic Dreams*, pp. 61, 63–4; *Guardian*, 6 March 1981, 17 March 1983.   12. Ibid., 29 March 1978, 26 May 1978; Maureen McNeil, 'The Old and New Worlds of Information Technology in Britain', in John Corner and Sylvia Harvey (eds.), *Enterprise and Heritage: Crosscurrents of National Culture* (1991), pp. 116– 17; Lean, *Electronic Dreams*, p. 30; 'Election: Who Will Win?', *BBC News* (BBC1, 2 May 1979), http://www.bbc.co.uk/archive/thatcher/6332.shtml; *Observer*, 4 February 1979. I am grateful to Alistair Quarterman for bringing the McNeil essay to my attention.   13. Sir Keith Joseph, 'Micro-Electronics', 8 June 1979, TFW.   14. John Hoskyns, *Just in Time: Inside the Thatcher Revolution* (2000), pp. 115–16; John Biffen, 'Micro-Electronics', 2 July 1979, TFW.   15. 'Interview for *Sunday Times*', 3 May 1981, TFW; McNeil, 'Old and New Worlds', p. 120; Lean, *Electronic Dreams*, p. 92; 'Speech to Welsh CBI Council', 11 December 1980, TFW.   16. *The Times*, 6 January 1981; *Guardian*, 20 August 1981; *New Scientist*, 5 November 1981, 8 April 1982.   17. 'Speech on Microcomputers in Schools', 6 April 1981, TFW; *Guardian*, 7 April 1981, 20 August 1981, 9 July 1982; *New Scientist*, 14 July 1983; McNeil, 'Old and New Worlds', pp. 122–4; and see Richard Fothergill, 'The Microelectronics Education Programme Strategy', April 1981, http://www.naec.org.uk/organisations/ the-microelectronics-education-programme/the-microelectronics-education-programme-strategy.   18. John Radcliffe and Robert Salkeld, 'Towards Computer Literacy: The BBC Computer Literacy Project, 1979–1983' (1983), pp. 3, 5, 10–11, 18–20; Tilly Blyth, *The Legacy of the BBC Micro: Effecting Change in the UK's Cultures of Computing* (2012), pp. 9, 15–16, http://www.nesta.org.uk/publications/legacy-bbc-micro; Anderson and Levene, *Grand Thieves*, pp. 33–5; Lean, *Electronic Dreams*, pp. 94–5. The internal report by Radcliffe and Salkeld can be found at http://www.naec.org.uk/organisations/bbc-computer-literacy-project/towards-computer-literacy-the-bbc-computer-literacy-project-1979-1983, and I am very grateful to the BBC's Alistair Quarterman, once again, for sending me a hard copy.   19. Radcliffe and Salkeld, 'Towards Computer Literacy', pp. 14–15; *Guardian*, 23

February 1981; *The Times*, 4 March 1981; Anderson and Levene, *Grand Thieves*, pp. 35–6, 38; Lean, *Electronic Dreams*, pp. 99–100.   **20.** Blyth, *Legacy of the BBC Micro*, pp. 12–13; Anderson and Levene, *Grand Thieves*, pp. 38, 40; Lean, *Electronic Dreams*, pp. 107.   **21.** *The Times*, 4 July 1975, 29 June 1984, 12 April 1983; *Guardian*, 16 June 1981; Lean, *Electronic Dreams*, pp. 126–7, 50–53; Anderson and Levene, *Grand Thieves*, pp. 21–5, 31.   **22.** Blyth, *Legacy of the BBC Micro*, pp. 12–13; *Guardian*, 16 June 1981; Anderson and Levene, *Grand Thieves*, pp. 38–40.   **23.** *Guardian*, 6 March 1981; 'Clive Sinclair', *Practical Computing*, 5:7 (1982), http://www.worldofspectrum.org/CliveSinclairInterview1982/; Anderson and Levene, *Grand Thieves*, pp. 45, 41–2.   **24.** *The Times*, 15 December 1981; Lean, *Electronic Dreams*, p. 105; *Guardian*, 16 June 1981, 24 November 1981.   **25.** Ibid., 12 January 1982; Radcliffe and Salkeld, 'Towards Computer Literacy', pp. 26–9, 31–2, 44. The ten episodes of *The Computer Programme* (BBC2, 11 January–15 March 1982) are online at https://archive.org/details/computer-programme.   **26.** Radcliffe and Salkeld, 'Towards Computer Literacy', pp. 35–6; *Guardian*, 14 April 1982, 4 November 1982.   **27.** *The Times*, 29 November 1982; Lean, *Electronic Dreams*, pp. 108–9; McNeil, 'Old and New Worlds', pp. 122–4.   **28.** *The Times*, 10 July 1984, 20 March 1984.   **29.** Speech at Anglo-Portuguese Chamber of Trade Lunch', 18 April 1984, TFW; for Mrs Thatcher in Japan in September 1982, see the news clips at https://www.youtube.com/watch?v=bVWnjHFHrzE.   **30.** 'Speech to Conservative Central Council', 26 March 1983, TFW; 'Interview for *Observer*', 11 April 1983, TFW; 'Speech Opening Conference on Information Technology', 8 December 1982, TFW.   **31.** McNeil, 'Old and New Worlds', pp. 121–2; Hansard, 27 November 1981, 29 July 1982; *Guardian*, 26 November 1984; *The Times*, 8 May 1984.   **32.** 'Speech Opening Conference on Information Technology', 8 December 1982, TFW; *Guardian*, 20 August 1981, 8 September 1982; and see Blyth, *Legacy of the BBC Micro*, pp. 29–30.   **33.** Spufford, *Backroom Boys*, p. 75; Lean, *Electronic Dreams*, p. 132; David Linsley, 'A Slayed Beast: History of the Dragon Computer', http://www.binarydinosaurs.co.uk/Museum/Dragon/dragon-history.php.   **34.** *The Times*, 28 September 1982, 1 November 1983.   **35.** *Observer*, 27 March 1983; *Guardian*, 21 March 1984; *New Scientist*, 4 September 1986.   **36.** *Guardian*, 11 January 1983; *The Times*, 14 December 1982; and see McNeil, 'Old and New Worlds', p. 121.   **37.** *Guardian*, 6 March 1981, 16 June 1981, 17 March 1983; Lean, *Electronic Dreams*, pp. 65, 67, 69; Anderson and Levene, *Grand Thieves*, p. 49; *The Times*, 7 September 1982.   **38.** *Guardian*, 10 September 1981. For interesting and amusing thoughts about the potential uses for home computers, see Anderson and Levene, *Grand Thieves*, pp. 48–9, 52–3; Lean, *Electronic Dreams*, pp. 53, 74–9.   **39.** Anderson and Levene, *Grand Thieves*, pp. 48, 53; Lean, *Electronic Dreams*, p. 113.   **40.** *The Times*, 7 September 1982, 22 February 1983; *Observer*, 27 March 1983; *Guardian*, 11 January 1983, 17 March 1983; 'Conservative General Election Manifesto 1983', 18 May 1983, TFW. On Britain's record computer ownership rate, see also Lean, *Electronic Dreams*, p. 117.   **41.** *Guardian*, 29 April 1983, 16 August 1983, 13 January 1983; *The Times*, 15 June 1983, 12 April 1983, 17 April 1983, 18 June 1983, 4 February 1984; *Observer*, 16 January 1983.   **42.** *The Times*, 17 April 1983, 18 June 1983; *Guardian*, 24 April 1984.

# Chapter 31. Strangers in the Night

**1.** Simon Winchester, *Prison Diary, Argentina* (1983), pp. 13–14, 19, 21–22.   **2.** Samuel Johnson, *Thoughts on the Late Transactions Respecting Falkland's Islands* (1771), http://www.samueljohnson.com/falklands.html; Charles Darwin, *Narrative of the Surveying Voyages of His Majesty's Ships Adventure and Beagle*, vol. 3: *Journal and Remarks, 1832–1836* (1839), p. 245; Carol Thatcher, *Below the Parapet: The Biography of Denis Thatcher* (1996), p. 201; Alasdair Pinkerton, '"Strangers in the Night": The Falklands Conflict as a Radio War', *Twentieth Century British History*, 19:3 (2008), p. 346.   **3.** See Sir Lawrence Freedman, *The Official History of the Falklands Campaign*, vol. 1: *The Origins of the Falklands War* (2005), pp. 1–16.   **4.** Jimmy Burns, *The Land That Lost Its Heroes: How Argentina Lost the Falklands War* (rev. edn: 2012), pp. 6–7; J. C. J. Metford, 'Falklands or Malvinas?

The Background to the Dispute', *International Affairs*, 44:3 (1968), p. 463. **5.** Burns, *Land That Lost Its Heroes*, pp. 41–3, 52, 54, 58; Freedman, *Origins of the Falklands War*, pp. 24–7; *Sunday Times Magazine*, 13 August 1978. **6.** Burns, *The Land That Lost Its Heroes*, pp. 109–112; Freedman, *Origins of the Falklands War*, pp. 76–88; Tony Benn, *Conflicts of Interest: Diaries, 1977–80* (1990), pp. 184–5, 248–9. **7.** Lord Carrington, 'Falkland Islands', OD 79 (31), 12 October 1979, TFW; 'FCO Letter to No. 10: Falkland Islands', 12 October 1979, TFW. **8.** Lord Carrington, 'Falkland Islands', OD 80 (46), 27 June 1980, TFW; Lord Carrington, 'Falkland Islands', OD 80 (66), 4 November 1980, TFW; Charles Moore, *Margaret Thatcher: The Authorized Biography*, vol. 1: *Not for Turning* (2013), p. 659; and see Freedman, *Origins of the Falklands War*, pp. 103–23. **9.** *The Times*, 26 November 1980, 27 November 1980; Freedman, *Origins of the Falklands War*, pp. 124–7; Burns, *Land That Lost Its Heroes*, p. 120. On Ridley, see the amusing portrait in Julian Critchley, *Some of Us: People Who Did Well under Thatcher* (1992), pp. 47–56. **10.** Hansard, 2 December 1980; *The Times*, 3 December 1980; Burns, *Land That Lost Its Heroes*, pp. 120–23; and see Freedman, *Origins of the Falklands War*, pp. 129–30, 134–42. **11.** Hugo Young, *One of Us: A Biography of Margaret Thatcher* (rev. edn: 1990), p. 270; Andrew Dorman, 'John Nott and the Royal Navy: The 1981 Defence Review Revisited', *Contemporary British History*, 15:2 (2001), pp. 98–9, 106; 'No. 10 Record of Conversation (MT, Nott, Carrington)', 10 February 1981, TFW; John Nott, 'The Defence Programme', OD 81 (29), 3 June 1981, TFW; TNA PREM 19/416, Clive Whitmore to Brian Norbury, 'The Defence Programme', 8 June 1981; Henry Leach, *Endure No Makeshifts: Some Naval Recollections* (1993), pp. 198–9. **12.** Freedman, *Origins of the Falklands War*, pp. 59–61, 144–7; Dorman, 'John Nott and the Royal Navy', p. 108; TNA PREM 19/416, Carrington to Nott, 'Defence Programme', 5 June 1981; Margaret Thatcher, *The Downing Street Years* (1993), p. 177. **13.** 'Falkland Islands Review (The Franks Report)', 18 January 1983, TFW; Christopher Lee, *Carrington: An Honourable Man* (2018), pp. 418–19; Carrington to Thatcher, 'Falkland Islands', 15 September 1981, TFW. **14.** Young, *One of Us*, pp. 258–62; John Campbell, *Margaret Thatcher*, vol. 2: *The Iron Lady* (2003), pp. 126, 130; 'Defence Secretariat Paper for the Chiefs of Staff: Defence Implications of Argentine Action Against the Falkland Islands', 14 September 1981, TFW. **15.** 'Speech at Kensington Town Hall', 19 January 1976, TFW. **16.** *The Times*, 21 April 1976, 9 July 1981. **17.** Burns, *Land That Lost Its Heroes*, pp. 102–3, 127–9, 130; Martin Middlebrook, *The Argentine Fight for the Falklands* (Barnsley, 2009), pp. 1–2. **18.** Burns, *Land That Lost Its Heroes*, pp, 131, 135–6, 139, 143–4; Middlebrook, *Argentine Fight for the Falklands*, pp. 2–6. **19.** Burns, *Land That Lost Its Heroes*, pp. 147, 164; *Guardian*, 25 February 1982; Freedman, *Origins of the Falklands War*, pp. 154, 159, 162; 'UK Embassy Buenos Aires to FCO: Falklands Talks – Argentine Press Comment', 3 March 1982, TFW. See also 'US Embassy Buenos Aires to State Department: Overview of Argentina', 3 March 1982, TFW; *The Times*, 5 March 1982. **20.** Middlebrook, *Argentine Fight for the Falklands*, pp. 2, 6. On Menéndez, see Burns, *Land That Lost Its Heroes*, pp. 147–8. On the timing, see Freedman, *Origins of the Falklands War*, pp. 220–21. **21.** Rex Hunt, *My Falkland Days* (Newton Abbot, 1992), pp. 177–8, 182, 185–7; Burns, *Land That Lost Its Heroes*, pp. 151–68; Freedman, *Origins of the Falklands War*, pp. 168–74. **22.** On the two parallel operations, see Burns, *Land That Lost Its Heroes*, pp. 154–5, 158, 172; Freedman, *Origins of the Falklands War*, pp. 171–2. Middlebrook, *Argentine Fight for the Falklands*, pp. 7–12, gives a very different account of the affair and does not mention Operation Alpha at all. **23.** Hunt, *My Falkland Days*, pp. 187–8; Burns, *Land That Lost Its Heroes*, pp. 168–9, 173; Moore, *Not for Turning*, p. 661; Hansard, 23 March 1982. **24.** Alan Clark, *Diaries: Into Politics, 1972–1982* (2000), p. 305. **25.** Hansard, 23 March 1982; Clark, *Diaries: Into Politics*, p. 306. **26.** Freedman, *Origins of the Falklands War*, pp. 182–3; Middlebrook, *Argentine Fight for the Falklands*, pp. 13–14; Burns, *Land That Lost Its Heroes*, pp. 174, 176–7. **27.** Middlebrook, *Argentine Fight for the Falklands*, p. 20. **28.** Carrington to Thatcher, 'Falkland Islands', 24 March 1982, TFW; TNA CAB 128/73, CC (82) 12, 25 March 1982; Moore, *Not for Turning*, p. 663; 'Franks Enquiry Evidence Transcript', 25 October 1982, TFW. **29.** Moore, *Not for Turning*, p. 664; *The Times*, 29 March 1982. **30.** Burns, *Land That Lost Its Heroes*, p. 285; Middlebrook, *Argentine Fight for the*

*Falklands*, p. 21; Hansard, 30 March 1982; Moore, *Not for Turning*, p. 664.   **31**. Thatcher, *Downing Street Years*, p. 179; Moore, *Not for Turning*, pp. 665–6.   **32**. Leach, *Endure No Makeshifts*, pp. 209–11 (and see also ch. 1); John Nott, *Here Today, Gone Tomorrow: Recollections of an Errant Politician* (2002), pp. 258–9; Moore, *Not for Turning*, pp. 666–7; Lee, Carrington, pp. 427–8; Thatcher, *Downing Street Years*, p. 179. There are several different accounts of Leach's words: even his own recollections were not always identical, as is only natural. My version has a bit of all of them.   **33**. Burns, *Land That Lost Its Heroes*, p. 290; Hunt, *My Falkland Days*, p. 200.   **34**. For Hunt, see ibid., p. 14 and *passim*, as well the obituaries in the *Guardian*, 12 November 2012, and *Daily Telegraph*, 12 November 2012.   **35**. Hunt, *My Falkland Days*, pp. 200, 202.   **36**. Ibid., pp. 202–3, 206–7, 211–13; and see Pinkerton, '"Strangers in the Night"', p. 350.   **37**. Hunt, *My Falkland Days*, pp. 215–17.   **38**. Ibid., pp. 219–22.   **39**. Ibid., pp. 226–7.   **40**. Ibid., pp. 232–4.   **41**. Ibid., pp. 235–6; Pinkerton, '"Strangers in the Night"', pp. 358–60; John Smith, *74 Days: An Islander's Diary of the Falklands Occupation* (1984), p. 25. I have transcribed the radio exchanges from the long extracts on YouTube.   **42**. Hunt, *My Falkland Days*, pp. 239–40.   **43**. Ibid., pp. 252–3, 256; *The Times*, 5 April 1982; Winchester, *Prison Diary*, p. 29.   **44**. Moore, *Not for Turning*, p. 669; TNA CAB 128/73, CC (82) 14, 2 April 1982.   **45**. Hansard, 2 April 1982; 'FCO Note: Falklands', 2 April 1982, TFW.   **46**. Smith, *74 Days*, p. 28; Pinkerton, '"Strangers in the Night"', pp. 362, 354; *Daily Express*, 3 April 1982; *Guardian*, 3 April 1982.   **47**. Moore, *Not for Turning*, pp. 670–71; Thatcher, *Downing Street Years*, p. 181.   **48**. Moore, *Not for Turning*, p. 670; and see TNA CAB 128/73, CC (82) 15, 2 April 1982.   **49**. *The Times*, 5 April 1982, 3 April 1982; *Daily Express*, 3 May 1982; *Guardian*, 3 April 1982; *Sun*, 3 May 1982.   **50**. Clark, *Diaries: Into Politics*, p. 312; David Owen, *Time to Declare* (1991), p. 547; Hansard, 3 April 1982.   **51**. Ibid.; Tony Benn, *The End of an Era: Diaries, 1980–90* (1992), p. 204; Clark, *Diaries: Into Politics*, p. 312; Kenneth O. Morgan, *Michael Foot: A Life* (2007), p. 412.   **52**. Hansard, 3 April 1982; Benn, *End of an Era*, p. 204; *Guardian*, 29 December 1982; Jonathan Raban, *Coasting* (1986), p. 107.   **53**. Clark, *Diaries: Into Politics*, pp. 313, 333; Moore, *Not for Turning*, p. 673; Hansard, 3 April 1982.   **54**. Max Hastings and Simon Jenkins, *The Battle for the Falklands* (1983), pp. 90, 96, 109–14; Sir Lawrence Freedman, *The Official History of the Falklands Campaign*, vol. 2: *War and Diplomacy* (2005), pp. 48–55; *The Times*, 3 April 1982; *Daily Express*, 5 April 1982; *Daily Mirror*, 5 April 1982.   **55**. Smith, *74 Days*, p. 28; Pinkerton, '"Strangers in the Night"', p. 361; *The Times*, 3 April 1982, 5 April 1982; *Guardian*, 5 April 1982; Middlebrook, *Argentine Fight for the Falklands*, p. 44; Hunt, *My Falkland Days*, p. 250.   **56**. Burns, *Land That Lost Its Heroes*, pp. xii, 316–18, 322; Pinkerton, '"Strangers in the Night"', p. 357. See also *Sun*, 6 April 1982; *Daily Express*, 5 April 1982; Smith, *74 Days*, and Middlebrook, *Argentine Fight for the Falklands*, *passim*.   **57**. *The Times*, 5 April 1982; Anthony Barnett, *Iron Britannia* (1982), p. 48; Roy Greenslade, *Press Gang: How Newspapers Make Profits from Propaganda* (rev. edn: 2004), p. 442.   **58**. *The Times*, 5 April 1982; *Daily Mail*, 5 April 1982; *Daily Express*, 5 April 1982; *Sun*, 6 April 1982; Moore, *Not for Turning*, pp. 674–5; Lee, *Carrington*, pp. 430–32. On the press treatment of the Foreign Office, see Robert Harris, *Gotcha! The Media, the Government and the Falklands Crisis* (1983), pp. 39–40.   **59**. Thatcher to Carrington, 4 May 1982, TFW; Young, *One of Us*, pp. 266–7; Moore, *Not for Turning*, pp. 675–6.   **60**. Nott, *Here Today, Gone Tomorrow*, pp. 278–9; 'Memoir of the Falklands War', *c*. Easter 1983, TFW; Michael Pattison to Clive Whitmore, 5 April 1982, TFW; 'No. 10 Press Release', 5 April 1982, TFW; Clark, *Diaries: Into Politics*, p. 316; MO R470, Falklands Special, 1982.   **61**. Clark, *Diaries: Into Politics*, p. 316; *Guardian*, 6 April 1982.   **62**. 'TV Interview for ITN', 5 April 1982, TFW; *The Times*, 7 April 1982; Gow to Thatcher, 8 April 1982, TFW.

# Chapter 32. We'll Show 'Em We're British

**1**. *Daily Express*, 6 April 1982; *Daily Mirror*, 6 April 1982; Jonathan Raban, *Coasting* (1986), pp. 114–15.   **2**. *Daily Express*, 6 April 1982; *Daily Mirror*, 6 April 1982; Max Hastings and

Simon Jenkins, *The Battle for the Falklands* (1983), pp. 112–13, 117; *Daily Mail*, 6 April 1982.  **3.** Hastings and Jenkins, *Battle for the Falklands*, pp. 109, 118. See also Max Hastings, *Going to the Wars* (2000), p. 274.  **4.** Ken Lukowiak, *A Soldier's Song* (1993: 1999), pp. 7, 9; Vincent Bramley, *Excursion to Hell: Mount Longdon, a Universal Story of Battle* (1991), pp. 4, 6–7.  **5.** Keith Britto, 'Public Opinion Background Note 109', 19 April 1982, TFW; Keith Britto, 'Public Opinion Background Note 108', 12 April 1982, TFW; *Daily Mail*, 6 April 1982; *The Economist*, 17 April 1982.  **6.** Helen Parr, *Our Boys: The Story of a Paratrooper* (2018), pp. 4–5  **7.** Sue Townsend, *The Secret Diary of Adrian Mole Aged 13¾* (1982: 2002), p. 257; MO S496, Falklands Special, 1982; Bramley, *Excursion to Hell*, p. 4; Lukowiak, *Soldier's Song*, p. 6.  **8.** Rex Hunt, *My Falkland Days* (Newton Abbot, 1992), p. 281; Raban, *Coasting*, p. 97.  **9.** *Newsweek*, 10 April 1982; Stephen Howe, 'Decolonisation and Imperial Aftershocks: The Thatcher Years', in Ben Jackson and Robert Saunders (eds.), *Making Thatcher's Britain* (Cambridge, 2012), pp. 242, 237–8; Robert J. Wybrow, *Britain Speaks Out, 1937–87: A Social History as Seen through the Gallup Data* (Basingstoke, 1989), pp. 124, 132.  **10.** Raban, *Coasting*, pp. 101–2, 113; *Sunday Telegraph*, 23 May 1982; Hansard, 3 April 1982.  **11.** *Guardian*, 21 April 1982.  **12.** MO D156, Falklands Special, 1982; MO G218, Falklands Special, 1982; MO S496, Falklands Special, 1982.  **13.** MO C108, Falklands Special, 1982; MO W633, Falklands Special, 1982; MO G226, Falklands Special, 1982.  **14.** MO R470, Falklands Special, 1982.  **15.** *Sunday Times*, 2 May 1982; Jean Seaton, *'Pinkoes and Traitors': The BBC and the Nation, 1974–1987* (rev. edn: 2017), p. 170; Raban, *Coasting*, p. 219; Matthew Parris, *Chance Witness: An Outsider's Life in Politics* (2002: 2013), pp. 305–6.  **16.** Ibid., pp. 306–7  **17.** John Hoskyns, *Just in Time: Inside the Thatcher Revolution* (2000), pp. 376–7; Ferdinand Mount, *Cold Cream: My Early Life and Other Mistakes* (2008), p. 293; Geoffrey Howe, *Conflict of Loyalty* (1994), pp. 452–3.  **18.** Michael Jopling to Francis Pym, 6 April 1982, TFW.  **19.** Alan Clark, *Diaries: Into Politics, 1972–1982* (2000), pp. 317–18.  **20.** Mervyn Jones, *Michael Foot* (1994), pp. 485, 488–9; Tony Benn, *The End of an Era: Diaries, 1980–90* (1992), p. 207.  **21.** *Labour Herald*, 7 May 1982, quoted in John Carvel, *Citizen Ken* (1984), p. 156; *Mail on Sunday*, 30 August 2015; Benn, *End of an Era*, pp. 212, 202, 205, 213, 219, 221; *The Times*, 29 April 1982.  **22.** Ivor Crewe and Anthony King, *SDP: The Birth, Life and Death of the Social Democratic Party* (Oxford, 1995), pp. 158, 161, 165; *The Times*, 21 April 1982; David Owen, *Time to Declare* (1991), p. 514; Bill Rodgers, *Fourth among Equals* (2000), p. 232; John Campbell, *Roy Jenkins: A Well-Rounded Life* (2014), pp. 598, 600; Roy Jenkins, *A Life at the Centre* (1991), p. 566.  **23.** *Guardian*, 29 December 1982; Michael Frayn, 'Festival', in Michael Sissons and Philip French (eds.), *Age of Austerity, 1945–1951* (Harmondsworth, 1964), p. 320.  **24.** Cecil Woolf and Jean Moorcroft Wilson (eds.), *Authors Take Sides on the Falklands* (1982), pp. 10, 15–16, 16–17, 23, 30, 40, 58, 60–61.  **25.** Ibid., pp. 25, 32, 92, 105, 96–7.  **26.** Ibid., pp. 111–12, 26, 65, 79, 102, 94, 26. For a suitably amused review, see Blake Morrison in the *Observer*, 15 August 1982.  **27.** Roy Greenslade, *Press Gang: How Newspapers Make Profits from Propaganda* (rev. edn: 2004), p. 442.  **28.** Robert Harris, *Gotcha!: The Media, the Government and the Falklands Crisis* (1983), pp. 40–41; Greenslade, *Press Gang*, pp. 339, 322–3; *Sun*, 3 May 1979; *Guardian*, 27 April 1981; *The Times*, 16 May 1981.  **29.** Harris, *Gotcha!*, pp. 41–2; Greenslade, *Press Gang*, pp. 419–21.  **30.** *Sun*, 6 April 1982, 7 April 1982, 8 April 1982. Harris, *Gotcha!*, pp. 43–5, is very good on all this.  **31.** Ibid., pp. 40, 45–8; Greenslade, *Press Gang*, p. 444; *Sun*, 19 April 1982, 7 April 1982, 20 April 1982, 10 April 1982, 16 April 1982.  **32.** Harris, *Gotcha!*, p. 54; Greenslade, *Press Gang*, pp. 447, 450; Benn, *End of an Era*, p. 212; *Guardian*, 10 May 1982.  **33.** Raban, *Coasting*, p. 200; *Guardian*, 6 May 1982, 10 May 1982; Owen, *Time to Declare*, p. 550; Sandy Woodward, with Patrick Robinson, *One Hundred Days: The Memoirs of the Falklands Battle Group Commander* (rev. edn: 2012), p. 229.  **34.** Sir Lawrence Freedman, *The Official History of the Falklands Campaign*, vol. 2: *War and Diplomacy* (2005), pp. 201–2, 69; and see 'Memoir of the Falklands War', c. Easter 1983, TFW.  **35.** Freedman, *War and Diplomacy*, pp. 75, 206, 56, 79, 207; Hastings and Jenkins, *Battle for the Falklands*, p. 147; 'CIA Directorate of Intelligence Memorandum: Falklands Islands Situation Report No. 2', 3 April 1982, TFW.  **36.** John Campbell, *Margaret Thatcher*, vol. 2: *The Iron Lady* (2003), pp. 133–4, 139; Charles Moore, *Margaret Thatcher: The Authorized Biography*, vol. 1: *Not for Turning* (2013), p. 682. **37.** Campbell, *Iron Lady*, pp. 135–6, 140; Moore, *Not for Turning*, pp. 680–81; Hugo Young, *One of Us: A Biography of Margaret Thatcher* (rev. edn: 1990), pp. 274, 276; Parr, *Our Boys*, p. 267; Walters diary, 29 April 1982, TFW. **38.** Margaret Thatcher, *The Downing Street Years* (1993), pp. 182–3, 190–91; Freedman, *War and Diplomacy*, pp. 39–47; Moore, *Not for Turning*, pp. 678–9; Jimmy Burns, *The Land That Lost Its Heroes: How Argentina Lost the Falklands War* (rev. edn: 2012), pp. xi–xii, 188–9. **39.** Ibid., pp. 193–4; Freedman, *War and Diplomacy*, pp. 390–99; 'Thatcher Stands by Pinochet', 26 March 1999, http://news.bbc.co.uk/1/hi/304516.stm. **40.** 'No. 10 Record of Telephone Conversation (MT-Mitterrand)', 3 April 1982, TFW; Freedman, *War and Diplomacy*, pp. 519–20; Moore, *Not for Turning*, p. 745; John Nott, *Here Today, Gone Tomorrow: Recollections of an Errant Politician* (2002), p. 305; Thatcher, *Downing Street Years*, p. 182. **41.** Moore, *Not for Turning*, pp. 683–4, 694; *New York Times*, 15 April 1982. **42.** Moore, *Not for Turning*, pp. 685–7; Rentschler diary, 8 April 1982, TFW. **43.** Moore, *Not for Turning*, p. 687; Rentschler diary, 8 April 1982, TFW; and see US Embassy London to State Department, 'Secretary's Meeting with Prime Minister Thatcher April 8: Falkland Islands Crisis', 8 April 1982, TFW. **44.** Haig to Reagan, 9 April 1982, quoted in Rentschler diary, 12 April 1982, TFW. On Haig and Pym, see Moore, *Not for Turning*, p. 688. **45.** Ibid., pp. 693, 688; Rentschler diary, 12 April 1982, TFW. **46.** Moore, *Not for Turning*, pp. 691, 695; TNA CAB 128/73, CC (82) 17, 'Most Confidential Record', 14 April 1982. **47.** Haig to Reagan, 6 April 1982, TFW; Rentschler diary, 16 April 1982, 17 April 1982, TFW; and see Freedman, *War and Diplomacy*, pp. 161–2; Moore, *Not for Turning*, pp. 695–6, 698. **48.** Hastings, *Going to the Wars*, pp. 284–5. **49.** Bramley, *Excursion to Hell*, p. 10; Parr, *Our Boys*, p. 114. For the most evocative description of life on the *Canberra*, see Hastings, *Going to the Wars*, pp. 275–81. **50.** 'Memoir of the Falklands War', c. Easter 1983, TFW; Moore, *Not for Turning*, p. 699; Freedman, *War and Diplomacy*, pp. 221–3, 229–30; Nott, *Here Today, Gone Tomorrow*, p. 297; TNA CAB 148/211, OD (SA) (82) 10, 19 April 1982. **51.** Hastings and Jenkins, *Battle for the Falklands*, pp. 151–2; Freedman, *War and Diplomacy*, pp. 238–9. **52.** Nott, *Here Today, Gone Tomorrow*, p. 302; Moore, *Not for Turning*, p. 703; 'Memoir of the Falklands War', c. Easter 1983, TFW. **53.** 'Pym Memorandum to OD (SA) Committee', 24 April 1982, TFW; 'Memoir of the Falklands War', c. Easter 1983, TFW; TNA CAB 148/211, OD (SA) (82) 15, 24 April 1982; and see Moore, *Not for Turning*, pp. 700–702. **54.** Ibid., pp. 702–3. See also Christopher Collins's thoughts at https://www.margaretthatcher.org/archive/1982retpap2.asp. **55.** Hastings and Jenkins, *Battle for the Falklands*, pp. 153–4; Burns, *Land That Lost Its Heroes*, pp. 339–40; Freedman, *War and Diplomacy*, pp. 244–9. **56.** 'Memoir of the Falklands War', c. Easter 1983, TFW; 'Remarks on the Recapture of South Georgia', 25 April 1982, TFW.

## Chapter 33. The Day of Reckoning

**1.** *Daily Express*, 26 April 1982; *Sun*, 26 April 1982; Max Hastings and Simon Jenkins, *The Battle for the Falklands* (1983), p. 155. **2.** Keith Britto, 'Public Opinion Background Note 111', 4 May 1982, TFW. **3.** *The Times*, 29 April 1982; *The Economist*, 1 May 1982, 8 May 1982; Keith Britto, 'Public Opinion Background Note 112', 10 May 1982, TFW. **4.** *Daily Express*, 30 April 1982; Hansard, 29 April 1982; Tony Benn, *The End of an Era: Diaries, 1980–90* (1992), pp. 217–18. **5.** 'National Security Council Minutes: NSC 0048, South Atlantic Crisis', 30 April 1982, TFW; Reagan to Thatcher, 29 April 1982, TFW; 'Haig off the Record Briefing to Congressmen', 29 April 1982, TFW; 'Haig off the Record Briefing for Press', 30 April 1982, TFW; Sir Lawrence Freedman, *The Official History of the Falklands Campaign*, vol. 2: *War and Diplomacy* (2005), pp. 176–8; Charles Moore, *Margaret Thatcher: The Authorized Biography*, vol. 1: *Not for Turning* (2013), pp. 707–8; *Sun*, 1 May 1982. **6.** 'Speech to Mid-Bedfordshire Conservatives', 30 April 1982, TFW. **7.** 'Memoir of the Falklands War', c. Easter 1983, TFW; Moore, *Not for Turning*, p. 711; Thatcher to Hastings, 8 May 1982, TFW; Hastings and Jenkins, *Battle for the Falklands*, pp.

169–71. 8. 'MT Engagement Diary', 2 May 1982, TFW; 'Memoir of the Falklands War', c. Easter 1983, TFW; Moore, *Not for Turning*, pp. 712–13; Freedman, *War and Diplomacy*, pp. 287–8. 9. Ibid., pp. 256–68. 10. Martin Middlebrook, *The Argentine Fight for the Falklands* (Barnsley, 2009), pp. 96–108; Jimmy Burns, *The Land That Lost Its Heroes: How Argentina Lost the Falklands War* (rev. edn: 2012), pp. 211–12; Freedman, *War and Diplomacy*, p. 285; 'No. 10 Record of Conversation: Falklands: Military Decisions', 2 May 1982, TFW; Moore, *Not for Turning*, pp. 712–13. 11. Freedman, *War and Diplomacy*, p. 292; Middlebrook, *Argentine Fight for the Falklands*, pp. 108–9. 12. Burns, *Land That Lost Its Heroes*, pp. 356, 227; Middlebrook, *Argentine Fight for the Falklands*, pp. 110–16. 13. Freedman, *War and Diplomacy*, pp. 284–93, 315, 736–46; Moore, *Not for Turning*, pp. 714–15. 14. Burns, *Land That Lost Its Heroes*, pp. 211–12; *The Times*, 11 August 1994; Middlebrook, *Argentine Fight for the Falklands*, pp. 115–16; *La Nación* (Buenos Aires), 2 May 2005. 15. Paul Theroux, *The Kingdom by the Sea: A Journey around the Coast of Great Britain* (1983), pp. 36–7; MO D156, Falklands Special, 1982; MO S496, Falklands Special, 1982; Ken Lukowiak, *A Soldier's Song* (1993: 1999), p. 12; Vincent Bramley, *Excursion to Hell: Mount Longdon, a Universal Story of Battle* (1991), p. 24. 16. *Sun*, 4 May 1982; Robert Harris, *Gotcha! The Media, the Government and the Falklands Crisis* (1983), p. 13; Roy Greenslade, *Press Gang: How Newspapers Make Profits from Propaganda* (rev. edn: 2004), pp. 445–6; Lukowiak, *Soldier's Song*, p. 127. 17. Hastings and Jenkins, *Battle for the Falklands*, pp. 179–82; Freedman, *War and Diplomacy*, pp. 290–300; Bramley, *Excursion to Hell*, pp. 25–6. 18. Harris, *Gotcha!*, pp. 66–7; Theroux, *Kingdom by the Sea*, p. 51. 19. Moore, *Not for Turning*, p. 716; 'Telephone Call between the Prime Minister and Sir Anthony Parsons', 8 May 1982, TFW; John Campbell, *Margaret Thatcher*, vol. 2: *The Iron Lady* (2003), p. 140. 20. 'Clipping of MT Interview with *Woman's Own*', 3 August 1982, TFW. 21. Rentschler diary, 4 May 1982, TFW; Freedman, *War and Diplomacy*, pp. 321–2; Campbell, *Iron Lady*, pp. 145–6. 22. Reagan to Thatcher, 5 May 1982, TFW; Freedman, *War and Diplomacy*, pp. 315–26; and see, for example, the discussion of the plan in UK Embassy Washington to Foreign Office, 'Falklands', 5 May 1982, TFW. 23. TNA CAB 128/73, CC (82) 23, 5 May 1982; Moore, *Not for Turning*, pp. 718–19. 24. Ibid., pp. 719–22; 'MT Draft Letter to Reagan', 5 May 1982, TFW; Thatcher to Reagan, 5 May 1982, TFW; and see the excellent commentary by Christopher Collins at https://www.margaretthatcher.org/archive/1982retpap2.asp. 25. Freedman, *War and Diplomacy*, pp. 329–31. 26. Henry Leach, *Endure No Makeshifts: Some Naval Recollections* (1993), p. 217; Harris, *Gotcha!*, p. 72; *Sun*, 5 May 1982; *Daily Mirror*, 5 May 1982; *New Statesman*, 7 May 1982. 27. MO S496, Falklands Special, 1982; MO W633, Falklands Special, 1982. 28. *Daily Express*, 8 June 1982; and see Harris, *Gotcha!*, pp. 17, 22–3, 130–34; Max Hastings, *Going to the Wars* (2000), e.g. pp. 295, 330. 29. Harris, *Gotcha!*, pp. 56–7, 70–71, 95, 103–4; *Daily Telegraph*, 24 March 2002. 30. Theroux, *Kingdom by the Sea*, pp. 135–6, 74; MO S496, Falklands Special, 1982. 31. Hugh Tinker (ed.), *A Message from the Falklands: The Life and Gallant Death of David Tinker, Lieut. R.N., from His Letters and Poems* (1982), quoted in Burns, *Land That Lost Its Heroes*, pp. 358, 363. 32. Theroux, *Kingdom by the Sea*, pp. 127, 153, 213. For the polls, see the various examples in Keith Britto, 'Public Opinion Background Note 112', 19 May 1982, TFW; Keith Britto, 'Public Opinion Background Note 113', 17 May 1982, TFW. 33. Jean Seaton, *'Pinkoes and Traitors': The BBC and the Nation, 1974–1987* (rev. edn: 2017), p. 181. 34. Harris, *Gotcha!*, p. 72; Michael Cockerell, *Live from Number 10: The Inside Story of Prime Ministers and Television* (1987: 1988), pp. 270–71. 35. Harris, *Gotcha!*, p. 72; Richard Ingrams and John Wells, *My Round!* (1983), p. 9; Carol Thatcher, *Below the Parapet: The Biography of Denis Thatcher* (1996), p. 196. 36. Hansard, 6 May 1982; Harris, *Gotcha!*, p. 75; *Sun*, 7 May 1982. 37. *Daily Mirror*, 8 May 1982; Harris, *Gotcha!*, pp. 51–2; Greenslade, *Press Gang*, p. 446. 38. Harris, *Gotcha!*, pp. 77–8; Seaton, *'Pinkoes and Traitors'*, pp. 183–4. 39. Harris, *Gotcha!*, pp. 79–80; Seaton, *'Pinkoes and Traitors'*, p. 184; *Sun*, 11 May 1982. 40. Hansard, 11 May 1982; *The Times*, 12 May 1982; Anthony Meyer, *Stand up and Be Counted* (1990), p. 95. 41. Harris, *Gotcha!*, p. 82; *Evening Standard*, 11 May 1982; *Daily Express*, 12 May 1982, 30 May 1982. 42. *The Times*, 14 May 1982, 15 May 1982; Seaton, *'Pinkoes and*

Traitors', p. 185; Thatcher to Sally Oppenheim, 17 May 1982, TFW; Harris, *Gotcha!*, pp. 88–9. **43.** Campbell, *Iron Lady*, pp. 138–9; 'Speech to the Scottish Conservative Party Conference', 14 May 1982, TFW; *Guardian*, 25 May 1982; and see Christopher Collins's discussion of the speech at https://www.margaretthatcher.org/archive/1982cac3.asp. **44.** Nicholas Henderson, *Mandarin: The Diaries of Nicholas Henderson* (1994: 2000), pp. 462–3; Freedman, *War and Diplomacy*, pp. 364–5, 370–71; Moore, *Not for Turning*, pp. 726–7. **45.** Freedman, *War and Diplomacy*, pp. 445–7, 452–4; TNA CAB 148/211, OD (SA) (82) 37, 18 May 1982. **46.** 'MT Engagement Diary', 19 May 1982, TFW; Moore, *Not for Turning*, pp. 729–31; and see TNA CAB 128/73, CC (82) 28, 20 May 1982. **47.** Hansard, 20 May 1982; *The Times*, 21 May 1982. See also Benn, *End of an Era*, p. 224. **48.** 'Press Statement by Peter J. Clark, Consultant Astrologer', 19 May 1982, TFW. **49.** Bramley, *Excursion to Hell*, pp. 26, 29–30; and see Hastings, *Going to the Wars*, pp. 292–5, which is excellent on the atmosphere in the days before landing. **50.** Bramley, *Excursion to Hell*, pp. 34, 36–8. See also the accounts in Lukowiak, *Soldier's Song*, p. 15; Hastings, *Going to the Wars*, pp. 297–301. **51.** Ibid., pp. 303–4; *Guardian*, 21 May 2007. **52.** 'News Wire Report: Fleet to Begin Landings', 21 May 1982, TFW; Campbell, *Iron Lady*, pp. 150–51; 'Speech in Finchley', 21 May 1982, TFW; 'Memoir of the Falklands War', *c.* Easter 1983, TFW; 'MOD Sitrep at 1645', 21 May 1982, TFW. **53.** 'MOD Sitrep at 2100', 21 May 1982, TFW; Campbell, *Iron Lady*, p. 151; 'Memoir of the Falklands War', *c.* Easter 1983, TFW; 'Statement by Secretary of State for Defence', 21 May 1982, TFW; 'Remarks Returning to No. 10', 21 May 1982, TFW; *The Times*, 22 May 1982. **54.** Sandy Woodward with Patrick Robinson, *One Hundred Days: The Memoirs of the Falklands Battle Group Commander* (rev. edn: 2012), pp. 374, 377–8. **55.** *Daily Mail*, 22 May 1982; *Sun*, 22 May 1982; Hastings and Jenkins, *Battle for the Falklands*, pp. 258–60; David Hart Dyke, *Four Weeks in May: A Captain's Story of War at Sea* (2007), pp. 111, 150–51, 162–5. **56.** Moore, *Not for Turning*, pp. 734–5; 'Memoir of the Falklands War', *c.* Easter 1983, TFW. **57.** Freedman, *War and Diplomacy*, pp. 482–3; Leach, *Endure No Makeshifts*, pp. 217–18; Hastings and Jenkins, *Battle for the Falklands*, p. 250. **58.** Nick Vaux, *March to the South Atlantic: 42 Commando, Royal Marines, in the Falklands War* (1986), pp. 119, 183; Bramley, *Excursion to Hell*, pp. 49–51, 59, 67, 53, 61. **59.** Freedman, *War and Diplomacy*, pp. 554–6; Moore, *Not for Turning*, pp. 740–42; Helen Parr, *Our Boys: The Story of a Paratrooper* (2018), pp. 125–6; Hastings and Jenkins, *Battle for the Falklands*, p. 266; *Guardian*, 4 May 2007; Julian Thompson, *No Picnic: 3 Commando Brigade in the Falklands, 1982* (rev. edn: 1992), p. 71. **60.** Parr, *Our Boys*, pp. 51–2, 132–47; Hastings and Jenkins, *Battle for the Falklands*, pp. 276–87; Freedman, *War and Diplomacy*, pp. 565–75. **61.** *Daily Mirror*, 29 May 1982; *Sun*, 29 May 1982, 31 May 1982; Alan Clark, *Diaries: Into Politics, 1972–1982* (2000), p. 328. **62.** 'White House Record of Telephone Conversation', 31 May 1982, TFW. **63.** Middlebrook, *Argentine Fight for the Falklands*, pp. 230–31, 216–23; Burns, *Land That Lost Its Heroes*, pp. 380–81, 376, 379, 347–9, 354, 382–3. **64.** Hastings and Jenkins, *Battle for the Falklands*, pp. 317–18; Freedman, *War and Diplomacy*, pp. 604–7; *Daily Express*, 6 October 1982; *The Times*, 5 October 2003; and see Simon Weston, *Walking Tall: An Autobiography* (1989). **65.** Freedman, *War and Diplomacy*, p. 607; Lukowiak, *Soldier's Song*, p. 117; *Sunday Telegraph*, 30 April 1989; 'Memoir of the Falklands War', *c.* Easter 1983, TFW; Moore, *Not for Turning*, p. 747; *Daily Mirror*, 10 June 1982, 11 June 1982; *Sun*, 10 June 1982. **66.** Hastings and Jenkins, *Battle for the Falklands*, pp. 331–2; Freedman, *War and Diplomacy*, p. 617. **67.** Parr, *Our Boys*, pp. 158–9, 207, 169–70, 172–3, 178–9, 186–7; Bramley, *Excursion to Hell*, pp. 84–5, 89, 102, 109, 117, 120, 130, 135, 144–5, 148, 177. The final anecdote is from James O'Connell, *Three Days in June* (2013), quoted in *Our Boys*, p. 169. **68.** Lukowiak, *Soldier's Song*, p. 37, 99–100; Bramley, *Excursion to Hell*, pp. 119, 121, 125, 144, 177–8. For more such stories, see, for example, Christian Jennings and Adrian Weale, *Green-Eyed Boys: 3 Para and the Battle for Mount Longdon* (1996). **69.** Lucy Robinson, 'Soldiers' Stories of the Falklands War: Recomposing Trauma in Memoir', *Contemporary British History*, 25:4 (2011), p. 581; *Independent on Sunday*, 16 August 1992; Lukowiak, *Soldier's Song*, p. 101; Parr, *Our Boys*, pp. 222, 228. **70.** 'Memoir of the Falklands War', *c.* Easter 1983, TFW. **71.** Burns, *Land That Lost Its Heroes*, pp. 390, 392; Middlebrook, *Argentine Fight for the Falklands*, p. 270.   **72.** *Evening Standard*, 15 June 1982; Hastings, *Going to the Wars*, pp. 370–76.

## Chapter 34. We Are Ourselves Again

**1.** 'MT Notes of Telephone Conversation', 14 June 1982, TFW; Margaret Thatcher, *The Downing Street Years* (1993), p. 235; Alan Clark, *Diaries: Into Politics, 1972–1982* (2000), p. 332; *The Times*, 15 June 1982; Hansard, 14 June 1982. For an audio clip, which is, as always, slightly different from the Hansard transcript, go to https://www.margaretthatcher. org/document/110952.   **2.** Clark, *Diaries: Into Politics*, p. 333; Charles Moore, *Margaret Thatcher*, vol. 1: *Not for Turning* (2013), p. 750.   **3.** 'Remarks Returning to No. 10', 15 June 1982, TFW; 'Memoir of the Falklands War', *c.* Easter 1983, TFW; Thatcher to R. H. Stuart, 17 June 1982, TFW.   **4.** 'Major General Moore Message', 15 June 1982, TFW; Moore, *Not for Turning*, p. 750; Hansard, 15 June 1982, 17 June 1982; *The Times*, 16 June 1982; Gow to Powell, 22 December 1982, TFW.   **5.** Reagan to Thatcher, 18 June 1982, TFW; Trudeau to Thatcher, 27 June 1982, TFW; George Price to Thatcher, 28 June 1982, TFW; Lee Kuan Yew to Thatcher, 2 August 1982, TFW; Revolutionary Democratic Front of El Salvador to Thatcher, 1 August 1982, TFW.   **6.** *Daily Mail*, 15 June 1982; *Sun*, 15 June 1982; *Daily Express*, 15 June 1982.   **7.** Alan Bennett, *Writing Home* (rev. edn: 2014), p. 168; MO G226, Falklands Special, 1982. On 'V-F Day', see, for example, *Daily Express*, 16 June 1982. **8.** *Guardian*, 18 June 1982, 15 June 1982; *The Times*, 17 June 1982; Tony Benn, *The End of an Era: Diaries, 1980–90* (1992), pp. 228–9.   **9.** Max Hastings and Simon Jenkins, *The Battle for the Falklands* (1983), pp. 354–5; Sir Lawrence Freedman, *The Official History of the Falklands Campaign*, vol. 2: *War and Diplomacy* (2005), pp. 655–6; Rex Hunt, *My Falkland Days* (Newton Abbot, 1992), pp. 298–300.   **10.** See Jimmy Burns, *The Land That Lost Its Heroes: How Argentina Lost the Falklands War* (rev. edn: 2012), pp. 298, 347–7, 354.   **11.** Sandy Woodward, with Patrick Robinson, *One Hundred Days: The Memoirs of the Falklands Battle Group Commander* (rev. edn: 2012), pp. xvii–xx; *The Times*, 21 June 1982.   **12.** Freedman, *War and Diplomacy* (2005), pp. 672–3; Helen Parr, *Our Boys: The Story of a Paratrooper* (2018), pp. 4–5, 273–6, 282; *Daily Mirror*, 9 July 1982; *Daily Express*, 9 July 1982.   **13.** Ken Lukowiak, *A Soldier's Song* (1993: 1999), p. 180; Vincent Bramley, *Excursion to Hell: Mount Longdon, a Universal Story of Battle* (1991), pp. 200, 156, 187   **14.** Parr, *Our Boys*, pp. 270, 321–3, 328–9; Freedman, *War and Diplomacy*, pp. 731–2. For the suicide rate and MoD study, see the government press release, 14 May 2013, https:// www.gov.uk/government/news/falklands-official-statistics-released, and the BBC News report, 'Fewer Falklands War Suicides than Feared, Study Suggests', 14 May 2013, at https:// www.bbc.co.uk/news/uk-22523317.   **15.** The programme was 'Back to the Falklands: Brothers in Arms' (*Panorama*, BBC One, 5 June 2017). For the accompanying BBC News story, see 'Falklands War Veterans Return to Face Their Demons', 5 June 2017, https://www.bbc. co.uk/news/uk-40131987.   **16.** *Western Mail*, 8 June 2007; *Daily Express*, 6 October 1982; *The Times*, 5 October 2003; *Guardian*, 11 October 1982; Simon Weston, 'To See Ourselves as Others See Us', 21 May 2003, https://web.archive.org/web/20040527120059/http://www. adsw.org.uk/documents/conference/Simon%20Weston%202003%20Conference.doc; and see Simon Weston, *Walking Tall: An Autobiography* (1989).   **17.** *Guardian*, 11 October 1982; *Daily Express*, 6 October 1982; *The Times*, 5 October 2003. On Weston and the Argentine pilot, see the interview at https://www.newsandstar.co.uk/news/16702195.theman-who-tried-to-kill-me-is-kind-and-compassionate/.   **18.** Burns, *Land That Lost Its Heroes*, p. 1; John Campbell, *Margaret Thatcher*, vol. 2: *The Iron Lady* (2003), p. 157; Simon Winchester, *Prison Diary, Argentina* (1983), p. 215; *La Nación* (Buenos Aires), 23 August 1999; Raymond Briggs, *The Tin-Pot Foreign General and the Old Iron Woman* (1984), n.p.   **19.** Burns, *Land That Lost Its Heroes*, pp. 477–8. See also Hunt, *My Falkland Days*, p. 378.   **20.** Clark, *Diaries: Into Politics*, pp. 366, 370.   **21.** Bramley, *Excursion to Hell*, p. 210; *Daily Express*, 6 October 1982; *Sunday Times*, 20 June 1982; Keith Britto, 'Public Opinion Background Note 118', 20 June 1982, TFW.   **22.** MO D156, Falklands Special,

1982; MO G218, Falklands Special, 1982; MO R470, Falklands Special, 1982.   23. Parr, *Our Boys*, pp. 243, 362–3; *Daily Express*, 15 June 1982, 16 June 1982; Peter York, *Modern Times* (1984), p. 11.   24. Lewin to Thatcher, 1 July 1982, TFW.   25. Moore, *Not for Turning*, pp. 753, 758; Scott to Thatcher, 13 October 1982, TFW; Thompson to Thatcher, 15 October 1982, TFW.   26. Alwyn W. Turner, *Rejoice! Rejoice! Britain in the 1980s* (2010), p. 114; Moore, *Not for Turning*, p. 752; Sir John Coles, 'Appreciation of Margaret Thatcher', c. 14 June 1984, TFW.   27. Campbell, *Iron Lady*, p. 155; Moore, *Not for Turning*, p. 755; *Wall Street Journal*, 20 June 1982; *The Times*, 21 June 1982.   28. *Daily Mirror*, 16 June 1982; *Spectator*, 19 June 1982; Clark, *Diaries: Into Politics*, p. 336; *Guardian*, 16 June 1982.   29. Campbell, *Iron Lady*, p. 215; Keith Britto, 'Public Opinion Background Note 116', 5 June 1982, TFW; Keith Britto, 'Public Opinion Background Note 118', 20 June 1982, TFW; Keith Britto, 'Public Opinion Background Note 123', 25 June 1982; Bernard Ingham to Thatcher, 'Media Relations – Stocktaking and Look Ahead', 3 August 1982, TFW. See also Ivor Crewe, 'How to Win a Landslide without Really Trying: Why the Conservatives Won in 1983', in Austin Ranney (ed.), *Britain at the Polls, 1983: A Study of the General Election* (Durham, NC, 1985), p. 159.   30. *The Times*, 7 May 1982; and see the Britto poll data cited above, chapter 33, n. 32.   31. David Sanders, Hugh Ward, David Marsh and Tony Fletcher, 'Government Popularity and the Falklands War: A Reassessment', *British Journal of Political Science*, 17:3 (1987), pp. 281–313.   32. *The Economist*, 19 June 1982; Coles, 'Appreciation of Margaret Thatcher', c. 14 June 1984, TFW; Hugh Thomas to Thatcher, 16 June 1982, TFW; *The Times*, 31 March 1983.   33. 'Clipping of MT Interview with *Woman's Own* Magazine', 3 August 1982, TFW; 'No. 10 Record of Conversation (MT-Alexander Solzhenitsyn)', 11 May 1983, TFW.   34. *Guardian*, 16 June 1982; *Daily Mail*, 16 June 1982; Benn, *End of an Era*, p. 239; *The Economist*, 26 June 1982; *Daily Express*, 22 June 1982.   35. Campbell, *Iron Lady*, p. 159; Coles, 'Appreciation of Margaret Thatcher', c. 14 June 1984, TFW; Andy Beckett, *Promised You a Miracle: UK80–82* (2015), p. 269.   36. *Evening Standard*, 15 June 1982; Robert Harris, *Gotcha! The Media, the Government and the Falklands Crisis* (1983), p. 145; Bramley, *Excursion to Hell*, pp. 210–11.   37. Julian Critchley, *Some of Us: People Who Did Well under Thatcher* (1992), pp. 141–2. On the idea of the war as a turning point, see, for example, Graham Stewart, *Bang! A History of Britain in the 1980s* (2013), pp. 130–31; Moore, *Not for Turning*, p. 754; Parr, *Our Boys*, pp. 243–4; and especially Anthony Barnett, *Iron Britannia: Time to Take the Great out of Britain* (1982). On the nostalgic feel of the war, see *Spectator*, 19 June 1982; Burns, *Land That Lost Its Heroes*, pp. x–xi; Parr, *Our Boys*, pp. xv, 267.   38. *Daily Express*, 22 June 1982.   39. 'Speech to Conservative Rally at Cheltenham', 3 July 1982, TFW. On the background to the speech, see Christopher Collins's analysis at https://www.margaretthatcher.org/archive/1982cac4.asp, as well as Moore, *Not for Turning*, pp. 753–4.   40. *The Times*, 19 July 1982; *Daily Express*, 19 July 1982.   41. Clark, *Diaries: Into Politics*, pp. 340–41.   42. *Daily Mirror*, 12 July 1982.   43. Russell Davies (ed.), *The Kenneth Williams Diaries* (1993), p. 648.   44. John Coles to Clive Whitmore, 'Service of Thanksgiving', 2 July 1982, TFW; John Coles to Clive Whitmore, 'Service of Thanksgiving', 5 July 1982, TFW. John Coles to Thatcher, 9 July 1982, TFW; Freedman, *War and Diplomacy*, pp. 663–4; Eliza Filby, *God and Mrs Thatcher: The Battle for Britain's Soul* (2015), pp. 157–9; Moore, *Not for Turning*, pp. 755–7.   45. *The Times*, 27 July 1982, 28 July 1982; *Daily Express*, 27 July 1982; Mark Garnett, *From Anger to Apathy: The British Experience since 1975* (2007), pp. 186–7.   46. Moore, *Not for Turning*, p. 757; Willie Whitelaw, in David L. Edwards (ed.), *Robert Runcie: A Portrait by His Friends* (1990), p. 260; Clark, *Diaries: Into Politics*, pp. 347–8.   47. MO S496, Falklands Special, 1982.

# Index

Page numbers in *italic* indicate cartoons.

*British Steel* (Judas Priest)
673
Brittan, Leon 89, 393
Brixton 509–11, 521,
524–5, 604–5
riots xxiii, 511–14, 524,
588, 649
'Brixton Nick' (housing
project) 249–50
Broadwater Farm,
Tottenham 246, 249
Brocklebank-Fowler,
Christopher 419
Bromley Council 594
Brooking, Trevor 207
*Brookside* 239, 475
Brown, Craig 281
Brown, George 114, 151,
415
Brown, George Mackay
489
Brown, Janet 648
Brown, Ronald 418
Brown, Tina 613, 615
Brownjohn, Alan 771
Bruce-Gardyne, Jock 274,
697
Brummer, Alex 698
Brunner, Karl 263–4, 265
Bruno, Frank 631
Brussels 357–9
Bucks Fizz 702
Budgen, Nicholas 742
budget deficits 197, 270,
439–42, 448, 455
Budgets
1979 99–104
1980 194–5
1981 438–43, 447–52,
454–6, 459–60
1982 706–7
Buford, Bill 217–22
Buggles 300
building societies 240–41
Bullock, Alan, Baron 415
Burger King 133
Burgess, Anthony 616
Burke, Edmund 343
Burn, Gordon 486, 487,
489, 493, 494, 496
Burns, Jimmy 793
Burns, Terry 42, 265
Bury 403
bus fares 584, 593–5
Bush, Kate 398
Bushell, Garry 220, 525
business studies 333
Büsser, Carlos 740, 743–4,
749

Butcher, Pat 625, 626
Butcher, Roland 503
Butler, R. A. 759
Butler, Robin 39, 40
Butlin's 164
Butt, Ronald 200, 346,
521
*Butterflies* 74, 686
Byatt, A. S. 489
by-elections 419, 429–32,
565, 664–8, 769, 834

Cabinet appointments
1979 86–8
1981 (January) 435
1981 (September) 655–9
Cabinet revolt (July 1981)
652–5
Cadogan, Peter 771
Caernarvon Castle 604
Cairncross, Sir Alec 452
Callaghan, James
activist opposition to
344, 352–3
Argentina 734, 742
as a blancmange 355
British Steel 146
computer pioneer 714,
716
EEC 172, 176
exchange controls 108
Falklands War 788, 808
general election of 1979
347–9
filmed swimming by Benn
354
harangued by lunatics
341, 349, 352–3, 366
incomes policies 193
Keynesianism 95
Labour Party
Bishop's Stortford
meeting 1980 354,
355
conference 1979 350
conference 1980 369,
370
leadership 351, 372
manifesto commitments
341–2
North Sea oil money
257–8
nuclear weapons 389,
390, 395
patriotism xxvi
popularity 54
such a nice man 372
unemployment 201, 476
Winter of Discontent 8–9

Callan, Paul 841
Calman, Mel, cartoon 202
Camber Sands 164–5
Cambridge 451–2, 719
*Cambridge Evening News*
714
Cameron, James 767, 826
Campaign for the Feminine
Woman 58–9
Campaign for Labour Party
Democracy *see* CLPD
Campaign for Nuclear
Disarmament *see*
CND
Campbell, Beatrix 69, 71,
72, 79, 118, 123, 157,
464, 469, 472, 482
Campbell, John 83, 167,
178, 425, 738, 830,
837
Canada 778
*Canberra* 762, 841–2
Cannadine, David 617
'Can't Pay, Won't Pay'
campaign 595
Capstick, Sheila 497–8
car industry 303–9,
311–12, 313–28, 674
Carbery, Ethna 565
*The Card* (Bennett) 595
Carrington, Peter (6th
Baron Carrington)
Budget of 1981 448
claims Sir Denis Follows
is made of cement 181
decline of UK 14
EEC 176–7, 178
Falklands 734–5, 737,
744, 751–2, 757–8
as Foreign Secretary 87,
171
funeral for R. A. Butler
759
loyalty 191
Moscow Olympics 181
as 'old school' 88
Reagan, Ronald 444,
447
reception at Number
10 81
resignation 757–8
spending cuts 649, 652
trade unions 143
Trident 389
Carlisle, Mark 655
Carlos, Wendy 281
Carr, Jean (Mass
Observation Project)
119, 121, 605

ALLEN LANE
*an imprint of*
PENGUIN BOOKS

# Also Published

Martyn Rady, *The Habsburgs: The Rise and Fall of a World Power*

John Gooch, *Mussolini's War: Fascist Italy from Triumph to Collapse, 1935-1943*

Roger Scruton, *Wagner's Parsifal: The Music of Redemption*

Roberto Calasso, *The Celestial Hunter*

Benjamin R. Teitelbaum, *War for Eternity: The Return of Traditionalism and the Rise of the Populist Right*

Laurence C. Smith, *Rivers of Power: How a Natural Force Raised Kingdoms, Destroyed Civilizations, and Shapes Our World*

Sharon Moalem, *The Better Half: On the Genetic Superiority of Women*

Augustine Sedgwick, *Coffeeland: A History*

Daniel Todman, *Britain's War: A New World, 1942-1947*

Anatol Lieven, *Climate Change and the Nation State: The Realist Case*

Blake Gopnik, *Warhol: A Life as Art*

Malena and Beata Ernman, Svante and Greta Thunberg, *Our House is on Fire: Scenes of a Family and a Planet in Crisis*

Paolo Zellini, *The Mathematics of the Gods and the Algorithms of Men: A Cultural History*

Bari Weiss, *How to Fight Anti-Semitism*

Lucy Jones, *Losing Eden: Why Our Minds Need the Wild*

Brian Greene, *Until the End of Time: Mind, Matter, and Our Search for Meaning in an Evolving Universe*

Anastasia Nesvetailova and Ronen Palan, *Sabotage: The Business of Finance*

Albert Costa, *The Bilingual Brain: And What It Tells Us about the Science of Language*

Stanislas Dehaene, *How We Learn: The New Science of Education and the Brain*

Daniel Susskind, *A World Without Work: Technology, Automation and How We Should Respond*

John Tierney and Roy F. Baumeister, *The Power of Bad: And How to Overcome It*

Greta Thunberg, *No One Is Too Small to Make a Difference: Illustrated Edition*

Glenn Simpson and Peter Fritsch, *Crime in Progress: The Secret History of the Trump-Russia Investigation*

Abhijit V. Banerjee and Esther Duflo, *Good Economics for Hard Times: Better Answers to Our Biggest Problems*

Gaia Vince, *Transcendence: How Humans Evolved through Fire, Language, Beauty and Time*

Roderick Floud, *An Economic History of the English Garden*

Rana Foroohar, *Don't Be Evil: The Case Against Big Tech*

Ivan Krastev and Stephen Holmes, *The Light that Failed: A Reckoning*

Andrew Roberts, *Leadership in War: Lessons from Those Who Made History*

Alexander Watson, *The Fortress: The Great Siege of Przemysl*

Stuart Russell, *Human Compatible: AI and the Problem of Control*

Serhii Plokhy, *Forgotten Bastards of the Eastern Front: An Untold Story of World War II*

Dominic Sandbrook, *Who Dares Wins: Britain, 1979-1982*

Charles Moore, *Margaret Thatcher: The Authorized Biography, Volume Three: Herself Alone*

Thomas Penn, *The Brothers York: An English Tragedy*

David Abulafia, *The Boundless Sea: A Human History of the Oceans*

Anthony Aguirre, *Cosmological Koans: A Journey to the Heart of Physics*

Orlando Figes, *The Europeans: Three Lives and the Making of a Cosmopolitan Culture*

Naomi Klein, *On Fire: The Burning Case for a Green New Deal*

Anne Boyer, *The Undying: A Meditation on Modern Illness*

Benjamin Moser, *Sontag: Her Life*

Daniel Markovits, *The Meritocracy Trap*

Malcolm Gladwell, *Talking to Strangers: What We Should Know about the People We Don't Know*

Peter Hennessy, *Winds of Change: Britain in the Early Sixties*

John Sellars, *Lessons in Stoicism: What Ancient Philosophers Teach Us about How to Live*

Brendan Simms, *Hitler: Only the World Was Enough*

Hassan Damluji, *The Responsible Globalist: What Citizens of the World Can Learn from Nationalism*

Peter Gatrell, *The Unsettling of Europe: The Great Migration, 1945 to the Present*

Justin Marozzi, *Islamic Empires: Fifteen Cities that Define a Civilization*

Bruce Hood, *Possessed: Why We Want More Than We Need*

Susan Neiman, *Learning from the Germans: Confronting Race and the Memory of Evil*

Donald D. Hoffman, *The Case Against Reality: How Evolution Hid the Truth from Our Eyes*

Frank Close, *Trinity: The Treachery and Pursuit of the Most Dangerous Spy in History*

Richard M. Eaton, *India in the Persianate Age: 1000-1765*

Janet L. Nelson, *King and Emperor: A New Life of Charlemagne*

Philip Mansel, *King of the World: The Life of Louis XIV*

Donald Sassoon, *The Anxious Triumph: A Global History of Capitalism, 1860-1914*

Elliot Ackerman, *Places and Names: On War, Revolution and Returning*

Jonathan Aldred, *Licence to be Bad: How Economics Corrupted Us*

Johny Pitts, *Afropean: Notes from Black Europe*

Walt Odets, *Out of the Shadows: Reimagining Gay Men's Lives*

James Lovelock, *Novacene: The Coming Age of Hyperintelligence*

Mark B. Smith, *The Russia Anxiety: And How History Can Resolve It*